Social Development

**Ross D. Parke and
Alison Clarke-Stewart**

John Wiley & Sons, Inc.

VICE PRESIDENT AND EXECUTIVE PUBLISHER	Jay O'Callaghan
ACQUISITIONS EDITOR	Robert Johnston
EXECUTIVE EDITOR	Christopher T. Johnson
EDITORIAL ASSISTANT	Mariah Maguire-Fong
PRODUCTION SERVICES MANAGER	Dorothy Sinclair
PRODUCTION EDITOR	Janet Foxman
MARKETING MANAGER	Danielle Torio
CREATIVE DIRECTOR	Harry Nolan
DESIGNER	Kevin Murphy
SENIOR PHOTO EDITOR	Lisa Gee
ILLUSTRATION EDITOR	Anna Melhorn
MEDIA EDITOR	Lynn Pearlman
PRODUCTION SERVICES	Bruce Hobart/Laserwords
COVER IMAGE	© Masterfile
COVER DESIGN	M77 Design

This book was set in 10/12 Bembo by Laserwords and printed and bound by RRD/Jefferson City. The cover was printed by RRD/Jefferson City.

This book is printed on acid-free paper. ∞

Library of Congress Cataloging-in-Publication Data:
Parke, Ross D.
   Social development / Ross Parke & Alison Clarke-Stewart.
      p. cm.
   ISBN 978-0-470-59905-1
   1. Child psychology. 2. Child development. 3. Developmental psychology. I. Clarke-Stewart, Alison, 1943- II. Title.
   BF721.P285 2010
   305.231—dc22

                                                                    2010009566

Printed in the United States of America

10 9 8 7 6 5 4 3 2 1

Brief Contents

Contents

Chapter 3   Biological Foundations: Genes, Temperament, and More   73

Chapter 6 Self and Other: Getting to Know Me, Getting to Know You   175

Chapter 9 Schools and Media: Children in an Electronic Age **289**

Chapter 10   Sex and Gender: Vive La Différence?   323

Chapter 11   Morality: Knowing Right, Doing Good   357

Chapter 12   Aggression: Insult and Injury

Chapter 13   Policy: Improving Children's Lives 427

Chapter 14   Overarching Themes: Integrating Social Development 461

Our goal in *Social Development* is to give students and their instructors a comprehensive, scholarly, engaging, and up-to-date treatment of theoretical insights and empirical findings in the field of social development. In writing the book, we have tried to convey the excitement of recent advances along with the accumulated knowledge that forms the basis of the field. We have made the book undergraduate-friendly and hope to arouse students' interest by using lively examples and illustrations. We recognize that the way instructors organize the material covered in a course on social development varies and want to assure them that they can rearrange the sequence in which chapters are read and assign separate sections of chapters to meet their teaching goals.

Theoretical Orientation

Although we cover the traditional theories, our presentation reflects modern thinking that emphasizes systems and ecological approaches and clearly recognizes that social phenomena are multifaceted, multiply determined, and dynamically related to one another. This focus on multiple levels of explanation is the reason we have included cultural-contextual and biological foundations of development and have discussed their interplay across levels.

Emphasis on Cultural Diversity

We have integrated information from cross-cultural research and studies that focus on ethnic and racial diversity within cultures into our discussions of social development. In each chapter, we illustrate these cultural variations both in the text and in features that provide a more detailed examination of a particular culture or cultural issue.

Emphasis on Biological Underpinnings

In the last decade, recognition that we must probe the biological underpinnings of social development has increased. We devote a separate chapter to biological influences on social development, and we introduce biological factors in our discussions of specific aspects of social development in other chapters. We highlight new advances in molecular and behavior genetics, neurological assessments (e.g., fMRI), and the hormonal basis of social development and emphasize the interaction between environmental conditions and the expression of biological predispositions to provide a forward-looking view that we hope will intrigue students and instructors.

Concern with Social Policy

Every year governments spend millions of dollars on programs for children. We review some of these policies and programs that have as their goal improving the lives of children, underscoring the interchange between basic research and social policy. We devote a separate chapter to this discussion—a unique feature of this book—so that readers can more fully understand the policy-making process as well as specific policies aimed at children. Our goal is to make the work in this area relevant to students as citizens, informed consumers of scientific literature, and beginning professionals.

Age Scope of Coverage

Our focus in the book is social development in infancy, childhood, and adolescence. However, we recognize that social development does not stop then, so we have included a special feature—*Into Adulthood*—in each chapter to illustrate how social behaviors change in adulthood, how adult social behavior is influenced by earlier events in childhood and adolescence, or how adolescents manage the transition to adulthood. In addition, in Chapter 7, "Family," we discuss how children's social development is affected by adult development, specifically their parents' development, and how circumstances in parents' lives alter their behavior and, in turn, modify their children's social outcomes.

Chapter Elements

Each chapter begins with examples of hypothetical children of different ages exhibiting the types of social behaviors we discuss in the chapter. At the end of the chapter, bulleted summaries review the chapter's key concepts and main ideas. Key terms, which are indicated in bold text, are defined in chapter margins, listed at the end of each chapter as a reminder to students of their significance, and combined in a Glossary at the end of the book.

Chapter Features

Each chapter contains the following features that address interesting issues in social development. These are designed to underscore and amplify the main themes of the chapter and are intended to be read along with the regular text material. Our goal is to increase students' interest and understanding about topics that are important for achieving each chapter's overall goals.

Research up Close

In these highlighted sections, we examine a single study or set of studies in more detail to provide students a fuller appreciation of the methodological complexities of research on social development. For example, one section describes studies of children raised in orphanages who have problems forming close relationships because of deficits in oxytocin, the "love" hormone. In another chapter, the Research up Close feature describes studies of developmental changes in the frequency and nature of children's lies.

Real-World Application

These sections provide examples of ways that basic science is translated into real-world applications—such as new ways to control violence, school programs to improve children's social skills, policies to lessen the effects of maternal incarceration, and consequences of cyberbullying. Our goal is to show how basic research can be applied to understanding and alleviating real-life problems.

Cultural Context

The focus of the Cultural Context feature is to demonstrate how culture shapes the behaviors and beliefs of children and adults. These sections include descriptions of differences and similarities in children's temperaments, attachment relationships, and self-concepts around the globe. They include a discussion of how effects of physical punishment depend on whether or not punishment is normative in the culture and provide illustrations of the differences in parenting in collective and individualistic cultures.

Bet You Thought That . . .

The goal of this feature is to challenge assumptions about how social development works by providing counterintuitive illustrations, for example, that not all infant smiles are the same, that genes alone do not determine social potential, that babies can "read minds," and that parenting is a brain booster rather than a brain drain.

Into Adulthood

In an era of increasing emphasis on life span development, appreciating that developmental trajectories do not stop at age 21 is important. For this reason, each chapter has a feature that describes some aspect of development beyond adolescence. Examples include a description of how children who begin their aggressive behavior in early childhood are at risk for violent offenses in adulthood, a discussion of how early attachment patterns foreshadow the quality of later romantic ties, and a summary of how the lives of adults differ depending on whether they were shy or bold children.

Insights from Extremes

In these sections, we discuss extreme cases that have led to insights about social development. These cases include children reared in institutions, a child who was isolated from social contact until she was 13 years old, children who are forced to be soldiers, children suffering from autism, and transgender children.

Learning from Living Leaders

Who are the current leaders in social development? How did they become interested in this field? What questions have they tried to answer? What do they think are the most pressing issues in their area? What message do they have for undergraduates? A variety of experts answered these questions, and the Learning from Living Leaders feature summarizes their responses. We hope that these profiles will put a face on researchers in the field and introduce students to some of the paths that lead to becoming a research leader, perhaps inspiring them to consider a career in this field.

At the Movies

Finally, to connect text material with students' interests, we have included a feature describing recent movies that illuminate important themes in each chapter. Examples include *Juno,* an atypical example of teen pregnancy; *Mean Girls,* an illustration of relational aggression in high school; and *Gone Baby Gone,* a demonstration of different levels of moral reasoning.

Uniqueness of This Book

Several components of this text distinguish it from other books devoted to this topic. One is the discussion of the biological underpinnings of social development, both in a separate chapter and within the content of most of the other chapters. The discussion highlights the roles of hormones, such as cortisol and testosterone, in social development. It includes new techniques for probing brain activities and reviews recent work on mirror neurons and the "social brain," which suggest that there are brain-specific correlates of social behaviors, such as empathy, moral decision making, and reactions to televised violence.

This component also includes new work in behavior genetics, which emphasizes the role of environments in controlling the expression of genetic predispositions. Second, the book considers cultural variation both among societies around the world and within our own society. Third, the book has a chapter specifically devoted to social policy that examines in detail the policy process and highlights a number of recent government policy initiatives affecting children's lives. Fourth, the book includes unique features in each chapter, such as Bet You Thought That, Insights from Extremes, and Into Adulthood. Finally, the book presents discussion of research on the cutting edge of the field to capture the excitement of recent advances in this area. To write these discussions, we have not only relied on published sources but also have sought out as-yet-unpublished information from several sources including chapters from the *Wiley-Blackwell Handbook of Childhood Social Development* that is in press, forthcoming articles from experts, and hot topics on the Internet. We believe this book offers students a fresh and unique perspective on social development.

Instructor Resources

Available at www.wiley.com/college/parke

Instructor's Guide

This comprehensive guide provides the following resources: Chapter outlines, chapter summaries, key terms for each chapter (glossary items and additional important terms), and chapter learning objectives. Ideas for lectures, class discussions, demonstrations, student activities (e.g., small research projects that students can conduct), and topics suitable for class debates. A set of handouts that can serve as a review guide for students. Topics and writing guidelines for students' term papers, including suggestions for conducting a literature search, recommendations about the best search engines, suggestions about how to organize a review section by section, and an overview of APA formatting and referencing style. A list of relevant short films generally available from the university or college media resource center and a list of popular films and TV programs to supplement the films listed in the "At the Movies" feature in the textbook. Suggested background readings for each chapter.

Test Bank

Approximately 80 multiple-choice questions, 15 short-answer questions, 10 essay questions, and 20 true/false questions for each chapter. Some of these questions will be available for students to use as a practice quiz.

PowerPoint Slides

PowerPoint slides to serve as a springboard for lectures covering the key points, figures, tables, and key terms in each chapter. These slides can be used as they are or modified to suit the instructor's specific requirements.

Annotated Web Links

A set of web links connecting to relevant written and video materials for each chapter. These can be used to supplement information in the textbook or as a starting point for class assignments.

Student Resources

Available at www.wiley.com/college/parke

Practice Questions

For each chapter, 10-15 practice multiple-choice questions, a set of flashcards for key terms, and 3 sample essay questions that can be turned in to the instructor for evaluation.

Handouts

Handouts that can serve as a review guide for each chapter.

Research Guide

A list of possible term paper topics and guidelines for writing papers, including suggestions for conducting a literature search, recommendations about the best search engines, suggestions about how to organize a review section by section, and an overview of APA formatting and referencing style.

Annotated Web Links

A set of web links connecting to relevant written and video materials for each chapter. These can be used to supplement information in the textbook or as a starting point for class assignments or term papers.

Acknowledgements

In writing this book, we received constructive suggestions from many experts in the field as well as instructors who teach social development. The book is better as a result of their feedback, and we are grateful for their assistance. These reviewers included the following: Joan Grusec, University of Toronto; Scott Miller, University of Florida; John Bates, Indiana University; Susanne Denham, George Mason University; Deborah Laible, Lehigh University; Melanie Killen, University of Maryland; Judith Smetana, University of Rochester; Susan Harter, University of Denver; Jennifer Lansford, Duke University; Steven Asher, Duke University; Gary Ladd, Arizona State University; Patricia Greenfield, University of California, Los Angeles; Rob Crosnoe, University of Texas; Everett Waters, State University of New York at Stony Brook; Philip Rodkin, University of Illinois at Urbana-Champaign; Craig Hart, Brigham Young University; Mark Cummings, University of Notre Dame; Lindsay Chase-Lansdale, Northwestern University; Campbell Leaper, University of California, Santa Cruz; Glenn Roisman, University of Illinois at Urbana-Champaign; Barry Schneider, University of Ottawa; Kenneth Rubin, University of Maryland; Samuel Putnam, Bowdoin College; Julie Dunsmore, Virginia Tech University; Jamie Ostrov, University of Buffalo; Herman Huber, College of Saint Elizabeth; Nancy Furlong, Alfred University; Celina Echols, Southeastern Louisiana University; Robert Marcus, University of Maryland; Cynthia Hall, University of Alabama at Birmingham; Cheryl Goldman, Fitchburg State College; Ashton Trice, James Madison University; Joyce Munsch, California State University, Northridge; Juliana Raskauskas, California State University, Sacramento; Eileen Achorn, University of Texas at San Antonio; and Bonnie Kanner, Worcester State College.

We were able to keep this book as up-to-date as possible by our access to chapters of the forthcoming second edition of the *Wiley-Blackwell Handbook of Childhood Social Development*.

We thank its editors, Peter K. Smith and Craig Hart, for their generosity in sharing the chapters with us.

A special thanks to Chris Cardone, our initial editor at Wiley–Blackwell. She provided invaluable support and guidance in the development and completion of the manuscript. Her commitment to this project and her feedback, encouragement, and enthusiasm along the way are deeply appreciated. Chris Johnson and Robert Johnston, our editors at the Wiley Higher Education division, have done a fine job in seeing this project through the production process and into the hands of users. We are grateful for their support as well as the support of Jay O'Callaghan in the production and launching of the book. Thanks to the many other Wiley staff, including Mariah Maguire-Fong, Janet Foxman, Lisa Gee, Mark Sehestedt, Danielle Torio, Bruce Hobart, and Melissa Kleckner, who contributed to the production and advertising of the book and to the field representatives who continue to work on behalf of this project. We also thank Heather Guzman for her help compiling the reference list.

Learning from Living Authors

Ross D. Parke was Distinguished Professor of Psychology and Director of the Center for Family Studies at the University of California, Riverside. He also taught at the University of Illinois at Urbana-Champaign and at the University of Wisconsin. He is past president of the Society for Research in Child Development from which he received the Distinguished Scientific Contribution to Child Development Award, and of the Developmental Psychology Division of the American Psychological Association, who awarded him the G. Stanley Hall award for his contributions to developmental psychology. He has served as editor of the *Journal of Family Psychology* and *Developmental Psychology* and was associate editor of *Child Development*. He is the author of *Fatherhood*, coauthor of *Throwaway Dads*, and coeditor of *Family-Peer Relationships: In Search of the Linkages; Children in Time and Place; Exploring Family Relationships with Other Social Contexts;* and most recently

Strengthening Couple Relationships for Optimal Child Development. He obtained his Ph.D. from the University of Waterloo, Ontario, Canada, and his work has focused on early social relationships in infancy and childhood, the effects of punishment, aggression, child abuse, fathers' roles in child development, links between family and peer social systems, ethnic variations in families, and the effects of new reproductive technologies on families. He has taught a college course on social development for more than 30 years and is highly regarded as a textbook author with seven editions of *Child Psychology: A Contemporary Viewpoint* to his credit.

Alison Clarke-Stewart is also a leading scholar in social development. She grew up in Canada and completed her undergraduate and master's work at the University of British Columbia before moving to the United States for graduate school. Just before she began her Ph.D. program, she had an epiphany. The violence that erupted that summer culminating in the assassinations of Robert Kennedy and Martin Luther King Jr. led her to decide to study children's social development in the hope that by doing so she might contribute to making the world a better place. After receiving her Ph.D. from Yale University she studied family interactions, child care quality, early childhood education programs, divorce and custody effects, and children's eyewitness testimony—always with the goal of discovering ways people could create more positive experiences for children and enhance their social skills and relationships.

Before her recent retirement, Clarke-Stewart was Professor in the Department of Psychology and Social Behavior and Associate Dean for Research in the School of Social Ecology at the University of California, Irvine. Earlier she taught in the Department of Education and the Committee on Human Development at the University of Chicago. She is a Fellow of the American Psychological Association and the American Psychological Society, a member of the Society for Research in Child Development, a Principal Investigator in the NICHD Study of Early Child Care and Youth Development, and an investigator in the National Children's Study. She was a Fellow at the Center for Advanced Study in the Behavioral Sciences and a Visiting Scholar at Oxford University. She served on the editorial boards of *Social Development* and the *Journal of Applied Developmental Psychology*. She has written four textbooks in child development and is author of *Day Care*, coauthor of *Children at Home and in Day Care*, and co-editor of *The Development of Social Understanding*. Her most recent books include *What We Know about Childcare; Divorce: Causes and Consequences; Divorce Lessons: Real Life Stories and What You Can Learn From Them*; and *Families Count: Effects on Child and Adolescent Development*. She is also coauthor of a leading introductory psychology textbook (*Psychology*) which is now in its 9th edition.

Source: Alan Tobey/iStockphoto.

CHAPTER 1

Introduction: Theories of Social Development

Four-month-old Sydney gazes into her mother's eyes. Her mother returns the gaze and smiles broadly. Sydney smiles back at her mother and coos. This simple social exchange represents the beginnings of social development. Five-year-old James is a bully. He terrorizes the other children in his classroom, takes their toys, hits them, and verbally abuses them. His classmate George is quiet, cooperative, and compliant; he shares his toys and settles disputes peacefully. Not surprisingly, classmates like George better than James. These patterns reflect individual differences in social behavior during early childhood. Twelve-year-old Irma loves to spend time with her best friend Meg. They walk to school together, meet at recess, sit next to each other at lunch, play on the same soccer team, confer about homework, and instant message late into the night. Their close relationship is typical of best friendships in middle childhood. These three hypothetical examples illustrate some of the phenomena of social development in childhood. In this chapter, we discuss the theories that explain these phenomena and the questions that are central to the study of social development.

What is the study of social development? It is many things. It is a description of children's social behavior and how it changes as children get older. It is a description of children's ideas about themselves and other people, their relationships with peers and adults, their emotional expressions and displays, and their ability to function in social groups. It traces continuities and discontinuities in children's social behavior, relationships, and ideas over time. It is also an explanation of the processes that lead to changes in social behavior and to individual differences among children. It includes examination of how other aspects of development—cognitive, perceptual, language, and motor development—underlie children's social behavior. Researchers in the field of social development investigate the influences of parents and peers, schools and the media, and culture and biology on children's social behavior and ideas. For some scholars, unraveling the mysteries of social development is a goal in itself. It allows them to satisfy their curiosity about why some children become juvenile delinquents and others become model teens. It offers insights into the principles and laws that govern social interaction. Other scholars have more practical concerns. They gather information about social development to help people make better decisions about children's lives. They give parents information that will help improve their child-rearing strategies. They give teachers information about how to reorganize their classrooms to support children's social needs. They provide information to guide policymakers' decisions about child-care regulations, school policies, and family welfare. They offer information to help health professionals identify and treat children who are not developing normally. All of these are legitimate goals within the study of social development.

B et You Didn't Know That . . .
Newborns Can Recognize Their Mothers By Smell

Source: iStockphoto.

Each chapter in this book contains a highlighted section describing something about social behavior or social development that may surprise you. Did you know that . . .

• Newborns can recognize their own mothers by smell.

• Even 2-years-olds experience jealousy.

• Aggressive behavior in an 8-year-old can predict criminal behavior at age 30.

• Infants in orphanages have lower levels of the "love" hormone.

• Child abuse can lead to changes in children's brain functioning.

• Having a close friend can make up for being rejected by classmates.

• Adolescent girls who have grown up without a father have a 1 in 3 chance of becoming a teen mother.

You will learn about these and other interesting facts about social development as you read this textbook.

Social Development: A Brief History

The study of children's development is a relatively recent enterprise. In the medieval period, people viewed children as miniature adults and did not even recognize childhood as a distinctive period deserving special attention (Aries, 1962). Children were not valued in the same way or treated with the same care as they are today. Many children died in infancy and early childhood and, if they survived, they were forced to labor in mines and fields. Child labor laws to protect children's health and welfare were not introduced until the 1800s. As people began to recognize children's value and vulnerability, the need to understand their development through scientific study became clear as well.

The scientific study of children's development began with the pioneering work of the evolutionary biologist, Charles Darwin. In his work on the development of emotions in his own and other people's children, Darwin (1872) paved the way for the modern study of emotions—a key element of social development. Following Darwin, psychologist G. Stanley Hall (1904) used questionnaires to document children's activities, feelings, and attitudes. A few years later, John B. Watson (1913) argued that conditioning and learning were the processes by which social and emotional behavior are acquired and modified. His early studies of how infants acquire fear responses through conditioning demonstrated that emotional responses are learnable and that social behavior can be studied scientifically. Around the same time, Sigmund Freud (1905, 1910) offered a more biologically oriented view, claiming that social development was the product of how adults handled children's basic drives, such as the infant's drive to suck. An American psychologist and pediatrician, Arnold Gesell (1928), offered a different view of social development. He argued that social skills, like motor skills, simply unfold over the course of infancy and childhood. Thus, the field began with competing views about social development (Parke & Clarke-Stewart, 2003a). In this chapter, we explore the views reflected in both traditional and modern theories of social development (for a detailed review of the recent history of the study of social development, see Collins, 2010).

Critical Questions about Social Development

As scientists studied children's social development, they confronted and debated a number of critical questions. These questions, which we discuss in this section, have framed the study of development and colored different theories of social development.

1. HOW DO BIOLOGICAL AND ENVIRONMENTAL INFLUENCES AFFECT SOCIAL DEVELOPMENT? In the early history of developmental psychology, scholars took opposing positions on what was known as the nature-nurture issue. Some emphasized the role of nature, that is, heredity and maturation; others emphasized the role of nurture, that is, learning and experience. The former argued that biology is destiny and the course of development is largely predetermined by genetic factors, which guide the natural **maturation** or unfolding of increasingly complex social skills and abilities. Gesell was an early advocate of this view. Opposing this view, scholars such as Watson (1928) placed their emphasis firmly on the environment. They assumed that genetic factors put no restrictions on the ways that environmental events shape the course of children's development and claimed that by properly organizing the environment they could train any infant to become an athlete, an architect, or an attorney.

maturation
A biologically determined process of growth that unfolds over a period of time.

Today no one supports either of these extreme positions. Modern scholars realize that both biological and environmental factors influence social development—although they may disagree about the relative importance of each. The challenge now is to explore how the two sets of factors interact to produce changes and individual differences in children's social abilities. In recent years, researchers have conducted a number of studies to do this. One study, for example, showed that children's aggressiveness is a function of both their testosterone level—biology—and their exposure to aggressive interactions—environment (Moffitt et al., 2006). Another showed that children's sociability with peers is rooted in both their early temperamental characteristics—biology—and their early experiences in the family—environment (Rothbart & Bates, 2006). Today, the question is not which factor, biology or environment, determines development but rather how the expression of an inherited biological characteristic is shaped, modified, and directed by a particular set of environmental circumstances.

Insights from Extremes: Genie—A "Wild Child"

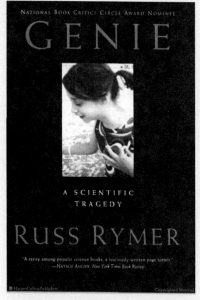

Source: Book cover from Genie by Russ Rymer. Copyright © 1993 by Russ Rymer. A portion of this book appeared in somewhat different form in The New Yorker magazine. Reprinted by permission of HarperCollins Publishers.

Few extreme cases have aroused as much public interest and professional scrutiny as the discovery in November 1970 of a 13-year-old girl who had been living in isolation, locked inside her bedroom, since infancy (Rymer, 1994). The house where "Genie," as she became known, lived was completely dark; all blinds were drawn and there were no toys. Her bedroom, at the back of the house, was furnished only with a wire cage and a potty chair. During the day, Genie was strapped to the potty chair and at night she was locked in bed inside the wire cage. No one in the family was allowed to talk to her, and her food was put out hurriedly without speaking. If her father heard her vocalizing, he beat her and barked

and growled like a dog to keep her quiet. Genie was discovered by authorities when her mother, who was almost blind and also a victim of abuse by Genie's father, ran away from her husband and took Genie with her.

This was not only a human tragedy but also an opportunity to evaluate the impact of extreme environmental input on children's development. When she was rescued, Genie could not stand erect; she walked with a "bunny walk," with her hands up in front, like paws. She was incontinent, unsocialized, malnourished, and unable to chew normally. She was eerily silent. She spoke only a few words and short phrases such as "stop it" and "no more." With therapy and training, Genie eventually learned some words. She also learned to smile. Her demeanor changed, and she became sociable with familiar adults. She was fascinated with classical piano music, and it was speculated that the source of her fascination was that from her isolated bedroom she had been able to hear a neighbor child practicing piano. Genie also learned to express herself through sign language and developed remarkable nonverbal communication skills; she and her caretakers were often approached by strangers who would, without being asked, spontaneously give Genie gifts or possessions. Despite her therapy and experience living with foster parents, Genie was never able to master grammar and had trouble controlling her angry outbursts. She was never able to function independently and, today, in her 50's, she is living in a sheltered home for adults with disabilities, neither speaking nor signing.

This extreme case suggested that there are critical or sensitive periods early in life and development is irreparably impaired if children lack sensory and social stimulation from their environments during these periods. The case stimulated research and popular interest in the role of social stimulation for brain functioning and development of communicative and social skills.

2. WHAT ROLE DO CHILDREN PLAY IN THEIR OWN DEVELOPMENT? A second critical question about social development concerns the extent to which children contribute to their own development. Early scholars tended to believe that children were simply passive organisms who were shaped by external forces. Today, most scholars have moved away from this simple view. Some still insist that children are assertive or shy because of the way their parents rear them or that adolescents become juvenile delinquents because of peer pressure. In general, however, contemporary developmental psychologists believe that children are active agents who, to some extent, shape, control, and direct the course of their own development (Bell, 1968; Kuczynski, 2003). Children, they assert, are curious seekers of information who intentionally try to understand and explore the world about them. They actively seek out particular kinds of information and interactions. In addition, they actively modify the actions of the people whom they encounter. Over the course of development, children participate in reciprocal interchanges with these other people, interchanges that are best described as **transactional** (Sameroff, 2009). For example, children ask their parents for help solving a social problem; their parents offer advice; and, as a result, children's interactions with their parents and peers are modified. Throughout development, children's social behavior is constantly undergoing change as a result of this mutual influence process.

3. WHAT IS THE APPROPRIATE UNIT FOR STUDYING SOCIAL DEVELOPMENT? Psychologists' study of social development has typically focused on the individual child as the unit of analysis. In recent decades, however, psychologists have increasingly recognized that other units also warrant attention. As an outgrowth of the recognition that children have reciprocal interactions with other people, the focus has shifted to **social dyads**. Researchers now study the nature of social interactions and exchanges between pairs of children or between children and their parents and investigate social relationships between these individuals (Collins & Madsen, 2006; Hinde, 1997). Attention is also given to larger units including social triads, such as mother-father-child or a trio of friends (Collins, 2010). In addition, researchers study the social groups that children form or join outside the family. These groups have their own rules and regulations and provide significant contexts for children's social development. Contemporary social development scholars view all of these units—individuals, dyads, triads, and groups—as important for studying social development.

4. IS DEVELOPMENT CONTINUOUS OR DISCONTINUOUS? A fourth question that developmental psychologists have asked is how to characterize the nature of developmental change. Some see development as a continuous process with each change building on earlier experiences in an orderly way. They see development as smooth and gradual, without any abrupt shifts along the path (Figure 1.1a). Others view development as a series of discrete steps and see the organization of behavior as qualitatively different at each new stage or plateau (Figure 1.1b). The concerns of each phase of development and the skills learned in that phase are different from those of every other phase. Jean Piaget and Sigmund Freud both proposed such stage theories of development, suggesting that as children get older, they move through different stages and at each new stage, they learn new strategies for understanding and acquiring knowledge and for managing interpersonal relationships and these new strategies displace earlier ways of dealing with the world. Scientists who endorse a continuous view of development suggest that noticeable changes in behavior are simply part of an ongoing series of smaller shifts.

Recently, some developmental psychologists have suggested that our judgment of continuity or discontinuity depends on the power of the lens we use when we look at changes across ages (Siegler, 2000). If we look from a distance or over a fairly long period of time, marked differences are evident, suggesting that there are distinct developmental stages in social behavior and social relationships. If we look more closely, however, we find that such changes do not happen suddenly. In fact, we find a great deal of variability in social behaviors even at the same point in time: A child may sometimes use a sophisticated and socially appropriate

transactional
Ongoing interchanges between social partners such as a parent and child across time that result in modifications of the social behavior of each.

social dyad
A pair of social partners, such as friends, parent and child, or marital partners.

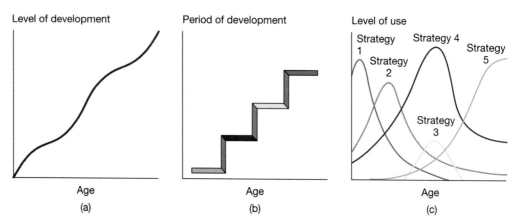

FIGURE 1.1 *Continuity and discontinuity in development. The continuous view (a) looks at development as a gradual series of shifts in skills and behavior with no abrupt changes. The discontinuous view (b) suggests that steplike changes make each stage qualitatively different from the one that preceded it. The third view (c) suggests that different strategies ebb and flow with increasing age and the most successful strategies gradually predominate.*

strategy to interact with a companion and, at other times, rely on a relatively primitive tactic. For example, in the process of learning social skills, a toddler may take turns and ask to play with a peer's toy on one occasion but the next day may grab the toy without asking or waiting. Only after many encounters with peers and toys does the toddler come to use turn taking and requests consistently. When social interactions are examined using a more powerful lens in this way, a very different picture of development appears: one of gradual shifts and changes as children slowly learn new strategies and gradually adopt the best and most advanced ones (Figure 1.1c). Thus, over time, change proceeds in a less linear and a less steplike fashion than continuous or stage theories suggest.

Today, most social development scholars recognize the value of both continuous and discontinuous views; they see development as basically continuous but interspersed with transitional periods in which changes are relatively abrupt. These transitional periods may be the result of physical changes, such as learning to walk, which offers infants new opportunities for interaction, or the onset of puberty, which changes the way children think about themselves (Caspi & Shiner, 2006; Ge et al., 2001). Other transitions may be the result of cultural changes, such as entry into junior high school, which brings children into larger social groups and a more complex social organization. Some view these transitional periods of reorganization as opportunities for intervention or changes in developmental trajectories.

5. IS SOCIAL BEHAVIOR THE RESULT OF THE SITUATION OR THE CHILD? Another critical question about social development is whether children's behavior is the same in different situations—at school, at home, on the playground, and in the street. Do children behave differently in different settings, or do their individual characteristics lead them to behave similarly across situations? Can we describe certain children as honest, dependable, and helpful and expect them to exhibit these qualities at all times? How do these traits manifest themselves in different situations—during a difficult test, in a confrontation with an angry parent, in a competitive game, or with a friend in need? Developmental psychologists differ in the importance they assign to "person factors" versus "situation factors." Many resolve the dilemma by stressing the dual contributions of both personality and situational factors. They point out that children seek out situations in which they can display their personalities. Aggressive children, for example, are more likely to join a gang or enroll in a karate class than to opt for the church choir or a stamp collectors' club (Bullock & Merrill, 1980), but in settings that don't allow or promote aggressive behavior, these same children may be friendly, reasonable, and cooperative. As we discuss in Chapter 3, "Biological Foundations," genetic predispositions lead children to "niche–pick" situations that are compatible with their genetic makeup (Scarr & McCartney, 1983). At the same time, children's selection of these experiences may strengthen their predispositions—for example, their tendency to behave aggressively—as they get older.

6. IS SOCIAL DEVELOPMENT UNIVERSAL ACROSS CULTURES? Children who grow up on a farm in China, in a kibbutz in Israel, in a village in Peru, or in a suburb in the United States have very different experiences. Even within the United States, racial and ethnic groups present children with diverse experiences (Demo et al., 2000; Parke & Buriel, 2006). Another critical question about social development is how much effect these different experiences have on children's social behavior. Psychologists themselves differ as to how much importance they ascribe to culture. Some argue that culture-free laws of development apply to all children in all cultures. For example, children in every culture acquire the basic foundations of social life, such as learning to recognize other people's emotional expressions and to communicate their wishes and desires to others through language. Other psychologists argue that the cultural settings in which children grow up play a major role in their development. In some cultures, for example, older siblings care for children; in other cultures professional caregivers care for them in group settings. It is unlikely that children who grow up in nuclear family arrangements would develop social attitudes and behaviors identical to those of children with these very different child-rearing experiences. Yet other psychologists suggest that *some* aspects of social development are universal and *other* aspects are attributable to culture. For example, although all children develop social understanding, the rates at which social milestones are reached vary across cultures. Today most developmental psychologists take this third position, recognizing universal aspects of development as well as the importance of considering cultural contexts (Gauvain, 2001b; Rogoff, 2003).

 **C**ultural Context:
Parenting Advice Around the Globe

In North America and Western Europe, millions of parenting manuals are sold every year to mothers and fathers eager to learn how to become good parents and raise their children properly. The seven editions of Dr. Benjamin Spock's *Baby and Child Care* have sold more than 50 million copies since the book was first published in 1946; only the Bible has sold more. But would Dr. Spock's book travel well and serve as a useful guide for parents in other cultures? Probably not. Even though Westerners think that their way of caring for infants is obvious, correct, and natural—a simple matter of common sense—it turns out that what people accept as common sense in one society may be considered odd, exotic, or even barbaric in another (DeLoache & Gottlieb, 2000). Different cultures make different assumptions about appropriate or desirable characteristics of children and appropriate or desirable behaviors of parents.

Woman from a Fulani tribe with her child. Source: Alan Tobey/iStockphoto.

The characteristics that our culture values stress the uniqueness and independence of individuals. Based on our belief in free will and our capacity to shape our own destiny, we value autonomy, assertiveness, ambition, and even competitiveness in children. In our culture, parents have the major responsibility for producing children with these desirable characteristics. Although all cultures aim to protect and keep their children safe, members of our culture have invented infant car seats, baby monitors, and nanny cams to protect children. We believe in the power of technology and innovation to make things better—including our children and ourselves. Our parenting advice manuals reflect these beliefs.

Other cultures do not share our assumptions about what child traits are desirable, who should be responsible for child rearing, or even the nature of the threats that children face. In many other cultures, our common sense makes no sense! Instead of a focus on self-confidence and self-aggrandizement, many non-Western cultures value interdependence, modesty, and self-effacement. Among the Fulani (see photo), one of the largest groups in West Africa, who live at the edge of the Sahara desert, the most valued traits include "soemteende"—modesty and reserve, "munyal"—patience and fortitude, and "hakkilo"—care and forethought (Johnson, 2000). Children in Bali, one of the Indonesian islands, are taught not to display positive emotions such as joy when they receive a good grade at school or negative emotions such as anger in public (Diener, 2000).

Many non-Western societies also value shared responsibility for child rearing, and members of the wider community participate in child care. In Beng villages located in the West African Ivory Coast, extended families live together and all family members as well as villagers from other households share in child care. In fact, members of other households are expected to visit a newborn within hours of its birth (Gottlieb, 2000). An extreme example of shared child rearing responsibility is practiced in Ifaluk, a Micronesian island in the North Pacific Ocean. There, more than a third of children are adopted by a second family. These adopted children share the resources of both their biological and their adoptive parents; they sleep in either family's house and receive shelter, protection, and security from both sets of parents. In effect, adopted children have two family networks (Le, 2000). In some cultures, social ties are formed not just with the living but also with the dead. Among the Baganda, an East African group, infants are viewed as reincarnated ancestors, and one of the cultural goals is to maintain ties between the child and the ancestor's spirit. Children's names are selected according to which ancestor's name produces a smile from the baby (DeLoache & Gottlieb, 2000). Protection of children is culturally determined as well, often based on religious beliefs that may include witches or evil spirits that could harm children. Among the Fulani, mothers may ward off evil spirits by rolling their infants in cow dung to make them less desirable and not worth capturing by the evil spirit, or they may place a small knife on the pillow while a baby sleeps to ward off the spirit (Johnson, 2000).

If Western child-rearing experts want to sell their parenting books to mothers in other cultures, they will have to do some serious rewriting. The assumption that our way of raising children is the right way or the only way is clearly wrong. Dr. Spock's advice to parents about raising children would not be very adaptive for children living among the Fulani, the Balinese, the Beng, or the Ifauk. Parents in these cultures need their own parenting manuals written by someone who grew up in their culture and knows the skills that children need to grow into productive and well-adjusted members of their culture. Of course, parents in these cultures don't feel the need for parenting manuals the way Western parents do. They base their practices on tradition and observation, not on reading a book.

7. HOW DOES SOCIAL DEVELOPMENT VARY ACROSS HISTORICAL ERAS? Cultures not only differ from each other but differ themselves over time. Another critical question, therefore, is how these changes affect children's social development. In our own society, dramatic changes in the structure of families and the ways people communicate have occurred over the past decades. Rates of divorce and remarriage have increased, childbearing has been delayed, family sizes have decreased, the likelihood of mothers working outside the home has increased, children's exposure to peers in child care has increased, and computers have increasingly been used to communicate with people we know and people we have never met. The question is whether children develop in the same ways regardless of such shifts in the culture

Even cartoonists appreciate the historical changes that affect childhood.

FIRST DAY OF SCHOOL

1965   2005

Source: *www.CartoonStock.com.*

that surrounds them. Theorists now appreciate that historical changes such as these play a part in shaping children's development (Elder & Shanahan, 2006). The social lives of children and their families are also affected by specific historic events: the Vietnam War in the 1960s, the farm crisis in the American Midwest in the 1980s, the New York terrorist tragedy in 2001, the Hurricane Katrina disaster in 2005, the fall of the Berlin Wall in Germany in 1989, the conflict between Catholics and Protestants in Northern Ireland starting in the late 1960s, the tsunami in Indonesia in 2004, and the global economic recession that began in 2008. Both distinct historical events and more gradual shifts in living arrangements and societal values leave their mark on children's social and emotional development. It is important to keep both types of changes in mind when comparing children's behavior across generations.

Research Up Close:
Children of the Great Depression

Glen Elder (1974, 1998) and his colleagues (Elder & Shanahan, 2006) took advantage of the stock market crash in 1929 and the Great Depression that followed to study how a historical time period can affect children's social development. They found that some participants in a longitudinal research project in California were just entering school when the economy collapsed; others were teenagers. Some of their parents suffered or lost their jobs in the Depression; others remained relatively well off. These natural variations enabled the researchers to compare families who were severely deprived with those who were not and to investigate how family differences affected children at different ages.

In the economically deprived families, dramatic changes in family roles and relationships occurred. The division of labor and power within the family shifted. As fathers' jobs disappeared and income dropped, mothers entered the labor market or took in boarders. As a result,

mothers' power increased and fathers' power, prestige, and emotional significance decreased. The rates of divorce, separation, and desertion rose, especially among couples whose relationship was shaky even before the onset of bad economic times. Parent–child relationships changed in response to economic hardship, too; fathers especially became more punitive and less supportive of their children.

Roles also changed for children. Girls were required to do more household work, and more older boys took outside jobs. Boys tended to move away from the family, becoming more peer oriented. They also frequently became more ill tempered and angry. Both boys and girls were moodier, more easily slighted, and less calm. Because younger children depended more on their parents and thus were exposed to the altered situation at home for longer periods of time, the effects of the Depression were greater for children who were young when catastrophe struck. Many of the effects on children were long lasting. When they became adults, their values, work patterns, and marriages bore the marks of their earlier experiences. Men who were forced to enter the job market as teenagers preferred secure but modest jobs rather than riskier higher-status positions. They were also less satisfied with their work and income. Men and women who had experienced adjustment problems in response to the Depression had less successful marriages. Finally, women who were prone to temper outbursts as children in the Depression became ill-tempered mothers. Thus, the Great Depression affected social roles, emotions, and behaviors across three generations.

8. IS SOCIAL DEVELOPMENT RELATED TO OTHER DEVELOPMENTAL DOMAINS? Another question that is part of the study of social development concerns how changes in children's social behavior are related to changes in other domains of development such as cognition, language, emotion, and motor development. Over a century ago, Darwin (1872) suggested that emotions play a central role in regulating children's social interactions. Today psychologists often examine the role of emotions in children's social development (Denham et al., 2007). They also frequently study the role of cognitive development. Children's cognitive capacity to correctly interpret another person's intentions, for example, is a critical component of social interaction, affecting the child's reactions to the other person's actions (Dodge, Coie, et al., 2006). Development in the language domain plays a key role in social development by providing an essential means of communication (Bloom & Tinker, 2001). Even motor development is important for social development; for example, crawling and walking allow infants to initiate or maintain physical proximity with other people; pointing and gesturing give them a way to engage in social exchanges before they can speak (Saarni et al., 2006). As these examples illustrate, social development is best understood by studying it in the context of other domains of development because advances in other developmental areas facilitate changes in social development. It is also important to recognize the reciprocal nature of this cross-domain influence: Shifts in competence in the social domain affect children's progress in other domains as well as the reverse (Gauvain, 2001a, b).

9. HOW IMPORTANT ARE MOTHERS FOR CHILDREN'S SOCIAL DEVELOPMENT? It was once thought that mothers were the most important influence on children's social development, that they were necessary for children to develop normally, and that no one else mattered much. Commentators and theorists from Sigmund Freud to Dr. Laura championed mothers as the leading players in children's social worlds and some went so far as to suggest that they were the only key players. Although no one today would deny that mothers are important and maybe even the *most* important people for children's early social development, psychologists now appreciate that other people are important too. Fathers, siblings, grandparents, and other relatives are all recognized as influencing children's social development (Dunn, 2002, 2005, 2006; Lamb, 2010). Teachers, child-care providers, coaches, and religious leaders may also contribute (Clarke-Stewart & Allhusen, 2005; Lerner, 2002). We now know that children's social development is embedded in a social matrix in which many individuals guide and support children's progress toward healthy social relationships and social skills.

10. IS THERE A SINGLE PATHWAY OF SOCIAL DEVELOPMENT? Another critical question for social development is whether children all follow the same general path. Early observers of social development, such as Gesell, tended to focus on normative steps that all children take on the road to social maturity. Today most theorists recognize that there are varied routes of development. No single pathway to social success or failure exists. Children may start out at the same place early in development and end up in totally different places later on. Consider this example (Cummings et al., 2000, p. 39):

> *Robin and Staci both had secure relationships with their parents and were functioning well as toddlers. But then Staci's mother and father lost their jobs, and marital problems developed. Her parents became less responsive to Staci's needs and less attentive to her increasingly disruptive behavior. Robin's parents, in contrast, received promotions at work and had a happy and rewarding marriage. They remained warm and responsive and managed family matters constructively. When the children were assessed at age 5, Robin was still secure with both her parents and above average in social competence. Staci was insecure and scored in the clinical range on a measure of adjustment problems.*

multifinality
The divergence of developmental paths in which two individuals start out similarly but end at very different points.

This divergence of developmental paths, in which two individuals start out similarly and end up at very different points, is called **multifinality** (see photo below). It suggests that continuing patterns of transactions between children and their families affect the children's development.

Other children, by contrast, may begin at different places but end up with similar developmental outcomes. Here is an example (Cummings et al., 2000, p. 40):

> *Ann and Amy grew up in very different family circumstances. Ann had an affluent family. Her parents enjoyed an intact marriage and managed child rearing well. Amy lived with her father, who had experienced an acrimonious divorce. At age 6, Ann was well-adjusted; Amy was depressed and withdrawn. However, over the next few years, Amy was able to take advantage of her social and athletic skills to develop good social relations with classmates, and her divorced parents learned ways to interact more amicably. When the children were 10 years old, Ann, whose family circumstances had continued to be supportive and positive, was still a well-adjusted girl, but Amy was also well adjusted and above average in social competence.*

equifinality
The convergence of developmental paths in which children follow very different paths to reach the same developmental end point.

This example illustrates **equifinality**; children followed very different paths to reach the same developmental end point. These two examples make it clear that children do not follow a single path in developing their social skills.

Individual children also respond to their life circumstances in very different ways. Some who experience adverse circumstances suffer permanent developmental disruptions or delays. Others show "sleeper" effects; they seem to cope well initially but exhibit problems later in development. Still others exhibit resilience under the most difficult of circumstances, and some are able not only to cope with risk but actually seem to thrive on it. When they confront new risks later in life, these children are able to adapt to challenges better than children who have experienced little or no risk; they have been "inoculated" by their earlier experiences and learned from them (Luthar & Brown, 2007; Masten & Obradovi, 2006; Rutter, 2006b).

Illustrating the concept of multifinality are sisters Alison and Mariah Carey. After their parents divorced, Alison went to live with her father and became a drug addict, twice arrested for prostitution. Mariah lived with her mother, had little contact with her father, and was named best-selling female pop artist of the millennium at the 2000 World Music Awards. Sources: Splash News and Pictures/NewsCom, © AdMedia/ Photoshot.

11. WHAT INFLUENCES HOW WE JUDGE CHILDREN'S SOCIAL BEHAVIOR? Just as children's social outcomes differ, the ways in which adults judge and label their social behaviors differ. Behaviors such as aggression, affection, and altruism are difficult to define. They are not like height and weight, measurable with a yardstick or on a bathroom scale. So what influences people's judgments of social behaviors? This issue is of interest because how we judge or label someone's behavior affects how we respond to it. For example, labeling a behavior as "aggressive" is more likely to lead to a negative response than labeling it as "assertive."

Three sets of factors—characteristics of the child, the adult, and the context—can subtly influence social judgments and the labeling of social behaviors. We are more likely to judge or label a behavior negatively if it occurs in boys, in children who have been temperamentally difficult as infants, in unattractive children, in children with a history of other forms of deviance, and in children from lower-status families (Cummings et al., 2000; Moeller, 2001; Putnam et al., 2002). We are also more likely to judge a child's behavior negatively if we ourselves are depressed or abusive (Cicchetti & Toth, 2006; Hammen, 2002). Finally, we are more likely to judge a child's behavior negatively if it occurs in a more strict and demanding context (for example, in a classroom rather than a park). Negative labeling not only affects our behavior, it may also lead children to detrimental self-labeling and expose them to additional risks that push them toward more negative behavior.

12. DO DEVELOPMENTAL PSYCHOLOGISTS "OWN" SOCIAL DEVELOPMENT? Developmental psychologists are the scientists who most commonly study children's social development. But does developmental psychology "own" social development? Are developmental psychologists the only ones who study social development? The simple answer is no. Scholars in other fields including pediatrics, psychiatry, anthropology, economics, law, and history, have also contributed to our understanding of children's social development. Pediatricians have advanced our knowledge of the best ways to evaluate and diagnose early social and cognitive capacities of young infants (Brazelton, 1973). Clinical psychologists and psychiatrists have focused attention on abnormal social development, such as autism and conduct disorders (Cicchetti & Toth, 2006; Cummings et al., 2000). Anthropologists have documented cross-cultural variations in children's social lives (Mead, 1928; Weisner, 2008; Whiting & Whiting, 1975). Economists have addressed the effects of poverty on children and families (Duncan & Brooks-Gunn, 1997). Sociologists have provided a better understanding of how social class and social mobility alter children's social outcomes (Featherman et al., 1988; Kohn, 1977). Historians have demonstrated that historical eras shape children's social attitudes, aspirations, and actions (Modell & Elder, 2002). Legal scholars have informed the study of moral behavior. Geneticists have signaled the importance of the interplay between genetics and environment and have identified genes and clusters of genes that control children's social behavior (Gregory et al., 2010; Moffitt et al., 2006; Plomin & Rutter, 1998). In the final analysis, children and their social development are too important to be left in the hands of a single discipline. By combining diverse disciplinary perspectives and encouraging scholars from different disciplines to work together on common problems, we are most likely to figure out the complexities of children's social development (Sameroff, 2009, 2010).

Theoretical Perspectives on Social Development

Theories about how children grow and mature play a central part in the scientific study of children's social development. Theories serve two main functions. First, they help organize and integrate existing information into coherent and interesting accounts of children's development. Second, they lead to testable hypotheses and predictions about children's behavior. Although no theory (yet) accounts for all aspects of social development, some grand theories

psychodynamic theory
Freud's theory that development is determined by innate biologically based drives shaped by encounters with the environment in early childhood.

from the past, such as Freud's psychodynamic theory, Piaget's cognitive structural theory, and Watson's theory of learning, were attempts to explain development in a general way. In contrast, many contemporary theories are focused on a single aspect or domain of development. These theories do not assume that a common set of processes applies across domains; different processes may operate in different areas. Theories vary in their focus and their position on the critical questions we have just discussed. It may be helpful as you read this section to refer to Table 1.1, which provides an overview of how theories are related to some of these critical questions.

Psychodynamic Perspective

Sigmund Freud initiated a revolution in the way we think about development. His views on the critical roles played by instinctual urges and by events in the early years of childhood were radical in the early 1900s and had an enormous influence on psychological and psychiatric thinking. In this section, we discuss both Freudian theory and the developmental theory of Erik Erikson, who accepted many of Freud's basic ideas but expanded them to include the full life span from childhood to old age.

id
In Freud's theory, instinctual drives that operate on the basis of the *pleasure principle*.

ego
In Freud's theory, the rational component of the personality, which tries to satisfy needs through appropriate, socially acceptable behaviors.

superego
In Freud's theory, the personality component that is the repository of the child's internalization of parental or societal values, morals, and roles.

FREUD'S THEORY   According to Freud's **psychodynamic theory** of development, psychological growth is governed by unconscious biologically based drives and instincts, such as sex, aggression, and hunger, and is shaped by encounters with the environment, especially other family members. The developing personality consists of three interrelated parts: the id, the ego, and the superego. The infant is largely under the control of the instinctual **id**, which operates on the *pleasure principle* and tries to maximize pleasure and satisfy needs immediately. As the infant develops, the rational **ego** emerges and attempts to gratify needs through appropriate, socially constructive behavior. The **superego** appears when the child *internalizes*—that is, accepts and absorbs—parental or societal morals, values, and roles and develops a *conscience*, or ability to apply moral values to his or her own acts.

TABLE 1.1   **Theoretical Perspectives' Positions on Some Critical Questions**

Theorist/ Theory	Question 1: Biology (B) versus Environment (E)	Question 4: Continuity (C) versus Discontinuity (D)	Question 5: Situation (S) versus Individual (I)	Question 6: Universal (U) versus Cultural (C)
Freud	B + E	D	I	C + U
Erikson	E	D	I	C + U
Learning	E	C	S	U
Cognitive social learning	E	C	S + I	U
Social information processing	E	C	S + I	U
Piaget	B × E	D	I	U
Vygotsky	E	C	S	C
Ecological	E	C	S	C
Ethological	B + E	D	S	U
Evolutionary	B + E		S	U
Behavior genetics	B × E		I + S	U
Life span	B + E	C	S + I	C

+ Both are important. × Both interact in producing developmental outcomes.

Oedipus complex
Freud's theory that boys become attracted to their mother and jealous of their father.

Electra complex
According to Freud, girls blame their mother for their lack of a penis and focus their sexual feelings on their father.

To Freud, development was a discontinuous process, organized in five discrete stages (see Table 1.2). In the *oral* stage, infants are preoccupied with activities such as eating, sucking, and biting and with objects, such as food, that can be put in the mouth. Freud assumed that infants derive great enjoyment and satisfaction from these oral behaviors. In the second or sometimes third year, priorities change: In this *anal* stage, children are forced to learn to postpone the pleasure of expelling feces, as parents struggle with the task of toilet training. From then until the fifth or sixth year, children are in what Freud called the *phallic* stage: Their sexual curiosity is aroused, and their preoccupation with their own sexual anatomy and the pleasures of genital stimulation alert them to the differences in sexual anatomy of the sexes. During this period, boys become enmeshed in the **Oedipus complex** in which they are attracted to their mother and feel themselves to be jealous rivals of their father but also fear that the father will punish them by cutting off their genitals. The Oedipus complex resolves when boys give up their sexual feelings for their mother and identify with their father. In the **Electra complex** girls blame their mother for their own lack of a penis and focus their sexual feelings on their father,

TABLE **1.2** Freud's and Erikson's Developmental Stages

Age Period (years)	Stage of Development			
	Freud		Erikson	
0–1	**Oral:**	Focus on eating and taking things into the mouth	**Infancy:**	*Task:* To develop *basic trust* in oneself and others *Risk:* *Mistrust* of others and lack of self-confidence
1–3	**Anal:**	Emphasis on toilet training; first experience with discipline and authority	**Early childhood:**	*Task:* To learn self-control and establish *autonomy* *Risk:* *Shame* and *doubt* about one's own capabilities
3–6	**Phallic:**	Increase in sexual urges arouses curiosity and alerts children to gender differences; period critical to formation of gender identity	**Play age:**	*Task:* To develop *initiative* in mastering environment *Risk:* Feelings of *guilt* over aggressiveness and daring
6–12	**Latency:**	Sexual urges repressed; emphasis on education and the beginnings of concern for others	**School age:**	*Task:* To develop *industry* *Risk:* Feelings of *inferiority* over real or imagined failure to master tasks
12–20	**Genital:**	With puberty, sexual desires reemerge and adolescents and adults express these urges in romantic relationships with peers, possibly for reproduction.	**Adolescence:**	*Task:* To achieve a sense of *identity* *Risk:* *Role confusion* over who and what individual wants to be
20–30			**Young adulthood:**	*Task:* To achieve *intimacy* with others *Risk:* Shaky identity may lead to avoidance of others and *isolation*
30–65			**Adulthood:**	*Task:* To express oneself through *generativity* *Risk:* Inability to create children, ideas, or products may lead to *stagnation*
65+			**Mature age:**	*Task:* To achieve a sense of *integrity* *Risk:* Doubts and unfulfilled desires may lead to *despair*

who possesses the penis Freud believed they want. When they finally realize that they cannot possess their father as a mate, girls transfer their feelings to other males. They relinquish their resentment of their mother and instead begin to identify with her.

These dramatic events are followed by the *latency* period, during which, Freud believed, sexual drives are temporarily submerged. In this period, which lasts from about 6 years of age to puberty, children avoid relationships with opposite-sex peers and become intensely involved with peers of the same sex. This turning from the family to the peer group is associated with the acquisition of the social skills necessary to function effectively in the world. In the final stage of Freud's theory, the *genital* period, sexual desires reemerge, but this time they are more appropriately directed toward peers. Once again, biological change—in this case, puberty—plays a significant role in defining the focus of development.

According to Freud, the way in which children negotiate these stages has a profound effect on their later behavior and personality. For example, failure to satisfy needs for oral stimulation in infancy causes adults to be more likely to smoke, chew gum, talk, and kiss a lot. Children who are toilet trained early and strictly are likely to become "anal" adults who are more likely to demand neatness, cleanliness, and orderliness in their rooms and their partners. Research has not provided support for most of Freud's specific theoretical propositions, but the general view that events in infancy and childhood have a formative impact on later development remains a central belief in developmental psychology.

psychosocial theory
Erikson's theory that each stage of development depends on accomplishing a psychological task in interactions with the social environment.

ERIKSON'S THEORY   Erik Erikson accepted many of Freud's general principles, but he gave more emphasis to the effects of the social environment on development. His **psychosocial theory**, like Freud's, was based on the belief that development is discontinuous and proceeds through a series of stages. However, Erikson extended his stages through adulthood (see Table 1.2). For every stage, he specified the personal and social tasks that an individual must accomplish as well as the risks he or she would confront by failing to accomplish the tasks of that particular stage (Erikson, 1950, 1959, 1980).

In Erikson's first stage, the main task is acquiring a sense of basic trust. By learning to trust their parents or caretakers, infants learn to trust their environments and themselves. If they find others untrustworthy, they develop mistrust of both themselves and the world. In the second stage, children in early childhood must learn self-control and develop autonomy; they develop shame and self-doubt if they remain worried about their continuing dependency and their inability to live up to adult expectations. During the third stage, the *play age*, between about 3 and 6 years, children struggle to develop initiative and to master their environment, but at the same time, they often feel guilty if they are too aggressive, too daring. Between 6 and 12 years, during the school age, children try to develop a sense of industry, largely by succeeding at school. This is also a period of constant social comparison in which children evaluate their skills against those of their peers. Real or imagined failure at either academic or social tasks may bring feelings of inferiority.

In the fifth stage, adolescents' main focus is the search for a stable definition of the self—that is, for a self-identity—and the danger is role confusion if they cannot determine who or what they want to be. In the next stage, young adulthood, the task is to achieve intimacy with others and, in particular, a stable intimate and sexual relationship. Problems in earlier stages, such as a shaky sense of identity, may lead to avoidance of relations with others and thus to isolation. The task that confronts the adult in middle age is to create something—children, ideas, or products. If not given expression, this quality of **generativity** can deteriorate into stagnation. In Erikson's last stage, ego integrity is the older adult's goal. When reflection on one's past accomplishments and failures leads to doubt and regret, despair may be the result.

generativity
A concern for people besides oneself, especially a desire to nurture and guide younger people and contribute to the next generation.

PSYCHODYNAMIC PERSPECTIVE: AN EVALUATION   Freud's and Erikson's developmental theories helped shape many of the concerns underlying the modern study of social development including the effect of early experience on later behavior, the influence of the family on social behavior, and the impact of social interaction on development. Freud and

Erikson identified as important many contemporary topics including aggression, morality, gender roles, attachment, and identity.

Many problems plague this theoretical perspective, however. First, the central claims of Freud's theory are difficult to test empirically. Second, his theory was based on information gathered from adults undergoing therapy rather than children behaving socially. Third, Freud's methods of collecting information, such as free association, recollections of childhood experiences, and reports of adult dreams, were potentially biased. Freud may have selectively focused on certain childhood experiences and the patients themselves may have forgotten or distorted their earlier childhood experiences. Finally, the focus on childhood sexuality was both too narrow and too exaggerated to provide a solid base for a theory of development. Although Erikson did study real children, his work suffered from many of the same methodological problems as Freud's. Erikson's observations of children's play, for example, are open to alternative interpretations, and his conclusions are not easily verified. His limited specification of the mechanisms that account for development from one stage to another is another weakness. In spite of these limitations, the psychodynamic perspective casts a long and influential shadow over the field of social development.

Into Adulthood: Fatherhood and Generativity

Erikson argued that the main psychosocial task of middle adulthood is to attain a favorable balance between generativity and self-absorption. By *generativity*, he meant any creative activity that contributes to the positive advancement and encouragement of future generations. It includes efforts as diverse as producing new ideas, new works of art or literature, and new products, nurturing the growth of other individuals, and shepherding the development of a broader community. Adults can express their generativity by becoming parents or mentors. John Snarey (1993) identified three types of generativity in which men can participate: first, biological generativity, when they experience the birth of their biological children; second, parental generativity, when they become involved in rearing their children; third, societal generativity, when they care for younger adults, serving as a mentor, providing leadership, and contributing to generational continuity. Examples of this last type of generativity include serving as a master for an apprentice, coaching an athletic team, founding a neighborhood improvement committee, serving on a board of a community agency, managing employees, and advising or supervising students.

Snarey (1993) examined generativity in 240 men followed from adolescence (age 14) to midlife (age 47). He found that the men who became fathers and thus experienced biological generativity were more societally generative at midlife than the men who remained childless. The men who experienced more parental generativity by being actively involved in nurturing their children's social-emotional development were more likely than less involved fathers to engage in generative activities outside the family. These associations between types of generativity were not due to the men's incomes, educations, or IQs. They were evidence of an underlying attitude. As one son describing his highly involved father's attitude toward the wider community, put it: "My father always takes on other people's problems. He has a big heart."

More generative men also experienced social advantages. Parentally generative fathers had better marriages and experienced more occupational mobility. Perhaps their social-emotional development was promoted by learning to meet the demands of parenting; a father cannot be self-absorbed and preoccupied; he must respond to the needs of his children. This experience would pave the way for the man to share his time and talents to help others in the wider community. In Erikson's terms, the experience of parenting reduces a focus on the self and stimulates generative actions on behalf of others. These generative men followed Erikson's Golden Rule: Do unto others what will advance the growth of others even as it advances your own (Erikson, 1980, p. 36).

Traditional Learning Theory Perspective

Learning theories offer a quite different perspective on development. In this section, we explore several learning theories that have been used to explain social development: classical conditioning, operant conditioning, and drive reduction theory.

CLASSICAL AND OPERANT CONDITIONING   The conditioning approach to development is best exemplified by the work of John Watson, Ivan Pavlov, and B. F. Skinner. According to these theorists, the same principles of learning shape development throughout childhood and, indeed, across the entire life span; development is a continuous process, not occurring in stages; and children play a relatively passive role, directed by events in the environment.

classical conditioning
A type of learning in which a new stimulus is repeatedly presented with a familiar stimulus until an individual learns to respond to the new stimulus in the same way as the familiar stimulus.

A good example of classical conditioning is Pavlov's famous experiment demonstrating that a dog learns to salivate at the sound of a bell if that sound is always associated with the presentation of food (Pavlov, 1927). After repeated pairing of bell and food, the dog salivates at the sound of the bell alone. Watson used classical conditioning to manipulate children's behaviors and emotions. Most famously, he conditioned an 11-month-old infant, Little Albert, to fear furry animals by repeatedly showing the baby, who was easily frightened by loud noises, a white rat and simultaneously making a loud noise. Extrapolating from his work, he boasted, "Give me a dozen healthy infants, well-formed, and my own specific world to bring them up in and I'll guarantee to take any one at random and train him to become any type of specialist I might select—doctor, lawyer, artist, merchant-chief and, yes, even beggar-man and thief, regardless of his talents, penchants, tendencies, abilities, vocations and race of his ancestors" (Watson, 1926, p. 10).

operant conditioning
A type of learning that depends on the consequence of behavior; rewards increase the likelihood that a behavior will recur, but punishment decreases that likelihood.

Operant conditioning occurs when a behavior is systematically followed by a reward or punishment. Following a child's behavior by positive reinforcement in the form of a friendly smile, praise, or a special treat increases the likelihood that the child will exhibit the behavior again. In contrast, punishment in the form of a frown, criticism, or the withdrawal of a privilege such as watching television is likely to decrease the chance that the child will engage in that behavior again. Skinner (1953) explained a wide range of behaviors using operant reinforcement principles, and his followers applied these principles to modify children's social behaviors in classrooms, institutions, and homes, as part of the behavior modification movement of the 1960s and 1970s (Bijou & Baer, 1961, 1978). Skinner also emphasized the importance of reinforcement schedules and showed that if reinforcement is provided on an intermittent schedule rather than continuously (every time the behavior occurs), the reinforced behavior will be more persistent and resistant to extinction.

drive reduction theory
A version of learning theory suggesting that the association of stimulus and response in classical and operant conditioning results in learning only if it is accompanied by reduction of basic primary drives such as hunger and thirst.,

In another version of learning theory, drive reduction theory, Clark Hull (1943) argued that the association of stimulus and response in classical and operant conditioning results in learning only if it is accompanied by drive reduction. Primary drives such as hunger and thirst act as motivators. They create tensions that are reduced when the person eats or drinks, and, as a consequence, the actions of eating or drinking are reinforced and become increasingly strong habits. Through classical conditioning, stimuli associated with the pleasurable feeling resulting from satisfaction of basic drives become rewarding and valued. This theory of drive reduction later became fused with Freud's focus on the feeding situation as a critical context for the development of social relationships. Researchers studying children's early social attachments suggested that nursing at the mother's breast reduces infants' hunger and this is why infants learn to love their mothers. This position was challenged by later theorists.

LEARNING THEORY APPROACHES: AN EVALUATION   Learning theories continue to be useful for explaining some aspects of children's social development. Classical conditioning seems to account for the development of strong emotions in response to certain specific

desensitization
Classical conditioning therapy used to overcome phobias and fears through exposure to increasingly intense versions of the feared stimulus.

objects, and, more important, can be used to reduce such strong emotions through systematic **desensitization** (Gelfand & Drew, 2003). Children can learn to overcome their fear of snakes, dogs, doctors, or the dark by gradual exposure to the feared object or event. For example, a child who is afraid of snakes is asked to imagine a snake, then is shown a snake in a cage at a distance, then is asked to move closer to the snake, and eventually is encouraged to handle the reptile; at each step, the child is taught to relax to counteract the muscular tension associated with fear or anxiety.

Contemporary researchers have also shown the value of operant conditioning for understanding how children's behaviors develop and how they can be modified. Gerald Patterson (1982, 1993, 2002) showed that children's aggressive behavior is often increased by the attention (positive reinforcement) that parents pay to such acts as hitting and teasing. He also showed that punishing these acts by a "time-out"—a brief period of isolation away from other people—can help diminish aggressive behavior. Operant conditioning has been incorporated into many applied programs to help teachers and parents change children's behavior.

Although these approaches can modify children's undesirable behaviors and provide clues about the origins of such behaviors, they are not enough. For one thing, they are not sensitive to developmental changes in children's cognitive, emotional, and social abilities. Their "one-size-fits-all" nature does not differentiate between children at different ages. As children get older and advance in cognitive and verbal abilities, conditioning techniques may be less effective or efficient for modifying behavior. Alternative strategies, such as reasoning and problem solving, which use children's cognitive and verbal skills, become more effective (Gershoff, 2002; Parke, 1974). Conditioning theories also give scant attention to biological differences in children's temperaments and predispositions, which could influence the effectiveness of these approaches for different children (Kochanska & Aksan, 2007). Learning theories offer some general principles of social development but do not provide a complete explanation or account for all individual differences among children.

Cognitive Learning Perspective

cognitive social learning theory
A theory that stresses the importance of observation and imitation in the acquisition of new behaviors, with learning mediated by cognitive processes.

COGNITIVE SOCIAL LEARNING THEORY   According to **cognitive social learning theory**, children learn social behaviors by observing and imitating other people. Albert Bandura was one of the first to demonstrate that children who watched another person behaving aggressively were likely to imitate that person's aggressive actions. They did not need to be rewarded, have a drive satisfied, or have their aggression elicited by a punch. Bandura showed preschool children an adult hitting and kicking a large Bobo doll (a clown doll that pops back up after each hit), either live or on videotape (Bandura et al., 1963). When the children were later given the chance to play with the doll, they were more likely to attack it and play aggressively than were children who had not seen the aggressive model. Moreover, the children reproduced many of the model's behaviors accurately and precisely. Neither the adult model nor the children had received any apparent reinforcement, yet quite clearly the children had learned some specific social behaviors.

As the name *cognitive* social learning theory implies, observational learning goes beyond simple imitation. Children do not imitate automatically; cognition is part of the process. Bandura suggested that four sets of factors determine how well children learn by observing another person's behavior (Bandura, 1989, 1997). First, there are factors that affect whether children pay *attention* to the model's behavior. Children interpret and process the social behaviors they observe on the basis of their past experience, their relationship with the model, the situation in which the observation takes place, and their own personality. They are more likely to pay attention to the model's behavior if they have been rewarded for imitating models in the past, if they have a positive relationship with the model and see him or her as an authority figure, if they are uncertain about how to behave in the situation, and if they have a personality characterized by a high level of attentional focusing. Second, there are factors that affect children's *retention* of the observed behavior. To be able to imitate a behavior, children must be able to remember it, and children who use rehearsal, organization, and other strategies to recall the observed behavior are more effective learners. Third, there are factors that affect children's *reproduction* of the observed behavior. Young children who see an older child or an adult perform a complicated social ritual are not likely to be able to reproduce it, no matter how much attention they paid to the behavior or how often they try to copy it. Finally, in addition to these three sets of cognitive factors, children's *motivation* to reproduce the model's actions affects their learning. They are more likely to imitate the model if they are motivated to do so by extrinsic or intrinsic incentives.

BEYOND MODELING: RECIPROCAL DETERMINATION AND SELF-EFFICACY

In the real world, unlike the psychology laboratory, children not only learn from models' behavior they also influence the model in a process Bandura called *reciprocal determination*. Children's actions produce responses by other people, leading to changes in the social environment and changes in the child, in a kind of social ping-pong game (see Figure 1.2). For example, 3-year-old Alex acts by sharing a toy with a peer; the peer responds positively with a smile; Alex, having been reinforced for his behavior, repeats the action and shares another toy;

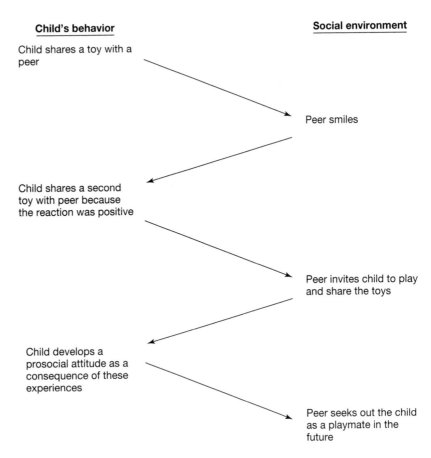

FIGURE 1.2 *Possible route to the development of sharing: Reciprocal determination in action.*

Child's behavior

Child shares a toy with a peer

Child shares a second toy with peer because the reaction was positive

Child develops a prosocial attitude as a consequence of these experiences

Social environment

Peer smiles

Peer invites child to play and share the toys

Peer seeks out the child as a playmate in the future

the peer continues the positive interaction with more shared play; ultimately Alex develops a positive social attitude and the two children form a relationship. In this example, Alex has created a positive play environment for himself through his positive actions. Another child who is suspicious and hostile toward other children is more likely to elicit negative reactions from peers and through continued hostility to create an unfriendly and perhaps lonely environment. Thus, according to cognitive social learning theory, social interactions occur on a two-way street, and children actively contribute to their own social development.

Children also contribute to their own social development by their perception of how competent they are. According to Bandura (1997, 2006), children who perceive themselves to be competent are high in *self-efficacy*; they believe that they can solve social problems and are willing to try. Like *The Little Engine that Could* (Piper, 1930), they say to themselves, "I think I can. I think I can. I think I can." Other children who have low self-efficacy are pessimistic about their ability to deal with a social situation and either avoid trying or put forth only a modest effort when entering a social setting or confronting a social problem. Self-efficacy is especially important for determining whether children—or adults—persist in the face of failure or rejection. Only a person with high self-efficacy would persist when his book manuscript was rejected by 22 publishers (as James Joyce did) or when his singing group failed to get a recording contract because "We don't like their sound" (as happened to the Beatles).

Children develop self-efficacy from a number of sources, according to Bandura. First, self-efficacy comes from direct experience when children have success in previous similar attempts. Second, self-efficacy comes from vicarious experience when children observe other people who are somehow like them succeeding on similar tasks. Third, parents or peers can be sources of self-efficacy; for example, when an adolescent is rejected by his dream date for the high school dance, his peers may convince him that he should try again, raising his sense of social self-efficacy. Fourth, self-efficacy comes from biological and affective reactions to social situations. If a girl is in a state of fear and anxiety every time she contemplates approaching strangers, her self-efficacy about successful social engagement of new people is likely to be low; if she feels calm, her self-efficacy will be high. Finally, self-efficacy can come from a group such as a peer group, a family, a school, or even a neighborhood. The group's shared belief in its ability as a unit to achieve some goal is termed *collective efficacy* (Bandura, 2006).

COGNITIVE SOCIAL LEARNING THEORY: AN EVALUATION The value of the cognitive social learning approach is indisputable (Grusec, 1992), and you will see many examples of insights about social development that have been inspired by this theory in this textbook. Cognitive social learning theory has advanced our understanding of moral behavior, altruism, aggression, gender roles, and the effects of exposure to television. The theory has also been influential in clinical child psychology and has guided the development of therapeutic approaches for helping children overcome fear and phobias. It has been given rigorous experimental testing.

In spite of these strengths, however, the theory has limitations. First, even though it has influenced the study of social development, cognitive social learning theory is not very developmental. Bandura paid little attention to the ways in which observational learning or self-efficacy change with age. Second, although individual differences are recognized in the theory, there is little elaboration of the role of genetic, hormonal, or other biological influences. Third, even though the environment plays an important part in the theory, most of the evidence is based on experimental studies conducted in the laboratory. The degree to which these findings generalize to real-world contexts outside the laboratory is unclear. Finally, the sensitivity of the principles to cultural variations has received relatively little attention.

Learning from Living Leaders:
Joan E. Grusec

Source: Courtesy of Joan E. Grusec.

Joan Grusec is Professor of Psychology at the University of Toronto, where she first learned of social learning theory as an undergraduate. She found it exciting enough to trek off to Stanford University for graduate work with Albert Bandura, abandoning her plans to be a social worker or a historian. Since then, she has been an advocate, chronicler, and modifier of social learning theory. Her early work with Bandura focused

on imitation. Later she studied children's prosocial behavior and parents' discipline processes. She was interested in what makes parents effective in achieving their socialization goals and what makes some parents more effective than others. She found that parents' effectiveness depended on the child's age, the parent's emotional state, and the cultural context. Grusec is a Fellow of the Canadian Psychological Association and the American Psychological Association and has been Associate Editor of the journal *Developmental Psychology*. She believes that developmental psychology is the most exciting area of psychology because it is the only one that brings together under one umbrella a concern with how biology and culture interact over the course of time to make us what we are.

Further Reading

Davidov, M., & Grusec, J. E. (2006). Untangling the links of parental responsiveness to distress and warmth to child outcomes. *Child Development, 77,* 44–58.

Grusec, J. E., & Davidov, M. (2010). Integrating different perspectives on socialization theory and research: A domain-specific approach. *Child Development, 81,* 687–709.

Information-Processing Perspective

Information-processing theories use computer processing as a metaphor for the way people think (Klahr & MacWhinney, 1998; Siegler & Alibali, 2005). A person attends to input information, changes it into a mental representation, stores it in memory, compares it to other memories, generates response possibilities, makes a decision about the most appropriate response, and, finally, takes some action. These operations are analogous to computer processing in which information in the form of symbols is entered into the system, undergoes a series of transformations, and finally provides an answer or output. Information-processing theorists who study development see it as continuous, with the quality of thinking at any age depending on the information the person is able to represent, the ways in which the person can operate on the information, and the amount of information the person can keep in mind at one time (Siegler, 2000).

social information-processing theory
An explanation of a person's social behavior in terms of his or her assessment and evaluation of the social situation as a guide in deciding on a course of social action.

SOCIAL INFORMATION PROCESSING   Social information-processing theory is a version of information-processing theory that provides a powerful analytic tool for understanding social behaviors such as social problem solving and aggression (Dodge, Coie, et al., 2006; Lemerise & Arsenio, 2000). According to this theory, in social situations, children proceed through a series of cognitive processing decisions or steps, such as assessing another child's intention, deciding on possible responses, evaluating the likely outcomes of various courses of action, and finally selecting and acting on their decision (Figure 1.3; for more detail see Chapter 8, "Peers" and Chapter 12, "Aggression").

FIGURE 1.3 *An information-processing model of children's social behavior. Children perceive and interpret a social situation, decide what they want to achieve, review possible responses, choose a behavior they think will accomplish their goal, and act on their decision. The child's "database" consists of memories of other situations and knowledge of social rules and experiences. As the double arrows indicate, the child's thinking and action both draw on the database and contribute to it. Source: Crick & Dodge, 1994.*

SOCIAL INFORMATION PROCESSING: AN EVALUATION   Social information-processing theory has generated many insights about the mental steps children engage in when they deal with a social situation. It underscores the links between cognitive understanding and social behavior and has led to numerous demonstrations of how cognitive processes influence children's social decisions and behavior (Crick & Dodge, 1994; Gifford-Smith & Rabiner, 2004). However, this theory provides little insight into how social-cognitive processing changes with age. The theory has also been criticized for its lack of attention to emotional factors and how they modify cognitive decision-making in social encounters (Lemerise & Arsenio, 2000). It presents a profile of a thoughtful, reflective child who goes through a series of deliberate cognitive processing steps before taking action. It does not account for the fact that much social interaction is routine and automatic and does not require deliberation. It does not account for the impulsive, reactive, even unconscious nature of social responding in familiar situations with familiar people. The value of the social information-processing approach is perhaps most evident in explaining social behavior in novel or unfamiliar social situations or as a description of how modes of social action are initially acquired.

Cognitive Developmental Perspective

To understand children's social development, it is important to understand their cognitive development as well. Two major theorists—Jean Piaget and Lev Vygotsky—have shaped our understanding of cognition in childhood.

assimilation
Applying an existing schema to a new experience.

accommodation
Modifying an existing schema to fit a new experience.

PIAGET'S COGNITIVE DEVELOPMENTAL THEORY   According to Swiss psychologist Piaget, two processes play a major role in increasing children's cognitive understanding (1928). First, children use their current knowledge as a framework for the absorption or **assimilation** of new experiences. Second, children modify their existing knowledge through the process of **accommodation** of their mental structures. As they develop, children increase their understanding through the interplay between these two complementary processes.

TABLE 1.3 **Piaget's Stages of Cognitive Development**

Stage	Age Range	Characteristics and Achievements
Sensorimotor	0–2 years	Differentiates self from objects and other people, seeks interesting sights, develops object permanence and basic understanding of causality, begins to imitate and engage in imaginative play
Preoperational	2–7 years	Begins to use symbols and language; problem solving is intuitive, and thinking is egocentric, irreversible, centered
Concrete operations	7–12 years	Can reason logically about present objects, grasps concept of conservation, can take the perspective of another person, can organize objects into classes and series
Formal operations	>12 years	Thinking is flexible and complex; can think about abstract ideas and hypotheses

According to this viewpoint, children actively interpret and make sense of the information and events they encounter. They are not merely passive receivers of experience who are shaped by the reinforcements and models to which they are exposed; they actively seek experience to increase their knowledge. Because of their continual interpretation and reorganization of experience, children construct their own reality, which may differ from the objective reality perceived by adults. The way children perceive and organize new information depends on their level of cognitive development. Piaget proposed that all children go through a number of stages of cognitive development, each characterized by qualitatively different ways of thinking, organizing knowledge, and solving problems (Figure 1.1b; Table 1.3).

Young children are more bound to sensory and motor information than are adolescents and adults, and they are also less flexible and less able to think symbolically and abstractly. Not until adolescence does the ability to use logic and to engage in deductive reasoning appear. Young children are also more **egocentric**—that is, they are more centered on their own perspective than are older children and are less able to take the viewpoint or understand the feelings and perceptions of others. According to Piaget, we may think of cognitive development as a de-centering process in which the child shifts from a focus on self, immediate sensory experience, and single-component problems to a more complex, multifaceted, and abstract view of the world.

egocentric
Tending to view the world from one's own perspective and to have difficulty seeing things from another's viewpoint.

PIAGET'S THEORY: AN EVALUATION It would be a mistake to underestimate the importance of Piaget's ideas for social development—even though Piaget himself may not have fully appreciated their implications. He was busy investigating children's transactions with inanimate objects and largely ignored the fact that these objects were often in the hands of other people and that children learned about them in the context of social interactions. Piaget's theory was helpful for illuminating how children's cognitive development modifies their social reactions. For example, his concept of **object permanence**—the realization that objects and people do not cease to exist when they are no longer visible—has been used in explaining how children develop emotional attachments to their caregivers. His notion of egocentrism has also been used: When children get older and less egocentric, they are able to switch to different perspectives, and this ability allows them to recognize other people's viewpoints—a critical ingredient in successful social relationships.

object permanence
The realization in infancy that objects and people do not cease to exist when they are no longer visible.

However, Piaget's theory has been criticized for its assertion that development proceeds through a series of universal, invariant, and irreversible stages (Bjorklund, 2000; Flavell, 1997) and its neglect of social, emotional, and cultural influences on development (Gauvain, 2001b). Piaget's methods, especially those involving his interviews of children, have also been criticized for their lack of scientific rigor (Baillargeon, 2002; Dunn, 1988). In spite of these criticisms, Piaget's influence on social development research has been widespread, as you will see in later discussions of social cognition, theory of mind, and moral development.

SOCIAL COGNITIVE DOMAIN THEORY Although Piaget did not invest a lot of energy in trying to explain children's social development, he influenced modern theorists and researchers who did. For example, Lawrence Kohlberg (1969, 1985) and Elliot Turiel (1983) used notions from Piaget's theory to explain how children make social judgments about their world and come to understand social and moral rules. Brian Bigelow (1977) demonstrated how children's conceptions of friendship progress through three stages from relatively concrete expectations that friends help and share to more abstract notions that involve expectations of genuineness, intimacy, and self-disclosure. Perhaps the major advance that the developmental cognitive perspective provided was that it led to the recognition that children categorize social issues into specific *domains* and make different judgments depending on the domain (Smetana, 2006). This notion of **domain specificity** challenged Piaget's theory, which suggested that all domains of knowledge are governed by the same cognitive processes and principles. Social cognitive domain theory focuses on children's understanding of social issues and is less concerned with links between understanding and social behavior or with the processes that underlie children's abilities to make domain-specific judgments.

domain specificity
Processes of development are different for different types of behavior, for example, moral judgments, manners, and peer relationships.

VYGOTSKY'S SOCIOCULTURAL THEORY The developmental theory proposed by Soviet psychologist Lev Vygotsky is unique in its emphasis on the importance of the child's social world (Daniels et al., 2007). Although Vygotsky was a contemporary of Piaget, his **sociocultural theory** of development contrasted markedly. He put forward three principles of cultural influence. First, cultures vary in the settings and practices they provide. Second, these settings and practices facilitate children's development. Third, children learn about their culture from more experienced cultural members. Whereas Piaget generally focused on development achieved by the individual child with little attention to the social context, Vygotsky proposed that development is best understood as a product of social interaction. He suggested that development occurs as children and their more mature social partners—parents, teachers, and older children—work together to solve problems. Thus, his theory focused on dyadic interaction rather than individual behavior. He was also less concerned with children's abilities at a particular point in time than with their potential for growth. To assess this potential and to understand how development occurs, he focused on the **zone of proximal development**, which is the difference between children's level of performance working alone and their level of performance working with a more experienced partner. According to Vygotsky, the assistance provided by other people enables children to reach their full developmental potential and gradually to learn to function on their own. Each child has a set of innate abilities, but input from the child's society in the form of interactions with adults and peers who are more skilled molds these basic abilities into higher-order functions.

sociocultural theory
Vygotsky's theory that development emerges from interactions with more skilled people and the institutions and tools provided by the culture.

zone of proximal development
The difference between children's level of performance while working alone and while working with more experienced partners.

VYGOTSKY'S THEORY: AN EVALUATION Vygotsky offered a fresh perspective from which to view children's development, a new way of measuring children's potential abilities by assessing their zone of proximal development, and new ways of teaching children (Brown & Campione, 1990; Gauvain, 2001a; Rogoff, 1998, 2003). He increased appreciation of the importance of cultural variations and historically based changes. Many view Vygotsky's theory as a corrective to Piaget's neglect of social contextual factors. On the negative side, Vygotsky was not very developmental and provided little description of how social interaction between partners at different levels of competence shifts over the course of development. He did not indicate how changes in physical, cognitive, or socioemotional development determine the types of contexts that society, through parents and others, makes available to the child. Finally, measurement of the zone of proximal development is difficult because we have no simple metric to measure the distance between the child's level of functioning alone and with a partner (Cross & Paris, 1988). In spite of these problems, this theory has stimulated a great deal of research in social and cultural aspects of development (Gauvain, 2001b; Rogoff, 2003).

Learning from Living Leaders: Barbara Rogoff

Source: Courtesy of the Center for Advanced Study in the Behavioral Sciences.

Barbara Rogoff, Professor of Psychology at the University of California, Santa Cruz, has been a major force in bringing attention to the role of culture in children's development. Like many others in the field, she did not plan to be a psychologist. She started out to be a cartoonist and majored in art. Her cultural journey began when as a graduate student at Harvard she became involved in research in a Mayan town in Guatemala. After discovering that how these people thought and acted was closely related to their social experiences, she began a career examining how people learn, how other people help them

learn, and how this varies in different cultural communities. Through her work in different cultures and in a wide array of settings from classrooms to Girl Scouts to school drama groups, she showed how cultural rules govern social development. In her book, *Apprenticeship in Thinking*, she demonstrated the value of Vygotsky's theory as a way to understand how learning takes place in routine everyday social interactions with parents, siblings, and peers. For Rogoff, the pressing issue for the field of social development is how to foster children's development in ways that respect the differences in the values and practices of their cultural communities. Rogoff has received many honors for her work. She is a Fellow of the American Psychological Society, the American Psychological Association, and the American Anthropological Association. She has served as a committee member on the Science of Learning for the U.S. National Academy of Science. She sends this message to students: "You are the generation that can make a real difference in how we understand and foster children's development in the varying communities of the U.S. and the world. I hope you continue to think about these issues long after you finish reading this book."

Further Reading

Rogoff, B. (2003). *The cultural nature of human development.* New York: Oxford University Press.

Rogoff, B., Moore, L., Najafi, B., Dexter, A., Correa-Chávez, M., & Solís, J. (2007). Cultural routines, practices, and repertoires. In J. E. Grusec & P. D. Hastings (Eds.), *Handbook of socialization* (pp. 490–515). New York: Guilford.

Systems Theory Perspective

systems
Developmental contexts made up of interacting parts or components, for example, a family.

For a long time, developmental psychologists have realized that children are affected by a number of different **systems** including the family, the school, the community, and the culture. Taking a systems theory approach means describing how children's development is affected by the interacting components that form one of these systems as well as by single factors within the system. For example, to describe how a child learns to cooperate with others at home, a researcher taking a family systems approach would analyze the interactions the child experiences with individual family members and how these individuals function as a family group to promote the behavior. The description would include the child's interactions with siblings and parents, interactions of the mother–father–child triad, and interactions of the family as a social unit. The aim of systems theory is to discover the levels of organization in social interactions and relationships and how these levels or contexts of social experience are related to each other and, in turn, promote children's social development.

ecological theory
A theory stressing the influences of environmental systems and relations between systems on development.

microsystem
In Bronfenbrenner's ecological theory, the context in which children live and interact with the people and institutions closest to them, such as parents, peers, and school.

mesosystem
In Bronfenbrenner's ecological theory, the interrelations among the components of the microsystem.

exosystem
In Bronfenbrenner's ecological theory, the collection of settings that impinge on a child's development but in which the child does not play a direct role.

BRONFENBRENNER'S ECOLOGICAL THEORY Urie Bronfenbrenner's **ecological theory** is an important application of systems theory (Bronfenbrenner & Morris, 2006). It focuses on the multiple systems in which children are embedded and how they are linked, and it stresses the importance of both the relations between the child and these systems and the relations between the systems themselves. In Bronfenbrenner's view, the child's world is organized as a set of nested systems or contexts, like a set of Russian dolls, ranging from the most immediate (the family or peer group) to the most remote (society's values and laws) (Figure 1.4). The **microsystem** is the system in which a child interacts directly with people and institutions. Over time, the relative importance of these people changes. Parents are most important in infancy and early childhood; peers and teachers become more important in middle childhood and adolescence. The **mesosystem** consists of the interrelations among the components of the microsystem, that is, the relations between parents and teachers, between parents and peers, between family members and a religious institution, and so forth. The **exosystem** is

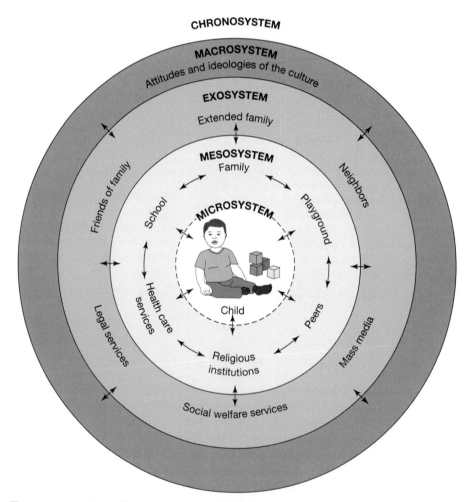

FIGURE 1.4 *Bronfenbrenner's ecological model of development. This model emphasizes the importance of children's interactions with the people and institutions closest to them within the microsystem and mesosystem, as well as the effects of a widening array of social and cultural institutions, attitudes, and beliefs within the exosystem and the macrosystem. The fact that all of these systems change over time is represented by the chronosystem.*
Source: Garbarino, 1982.

macrosystem
In Bronfenbrenner's ecological theory, the system that surrounds the microsystem, mesosystem, and exosystem, representing the values, ideologies, and laws of the society or culture.

chronosystem
The time-based dimension that can alter the operation of all other systems in Bronfenbrenner's model, from microsystem to macrosystem.

composed of settings that impinge on a child's development but with which the child has largely indirect contact. For example, a parent's work may affect the child's life if it requires the parent to travel a great deal or work late into the night. The **macrosystem** represents the ideological and institutional patterns of a particular culture or subculture. Finally, these four systems change over time in what Bronfenbrenner termed the **chronosystem**, as changes occur within the child or in one of the systems. In Bronfenbrenner's theory, development involves the interactions of a changing child and changing ecological systems in all their complexity.

ECOLOGICAL SYSTEMS THEORY: AN EVALUATION   The valuable contribution of the ecological perspective has been to alert us to the broad range of social contexts that affect children's social development. The theory also illustrates the value of the perspectives offered by other disciplines. The inclusion of the neighborhood context, for example, incorporates the work of sociologists and criminologists who have shown links between neighborhood poverty and delinquent activity (Elliott et al., 2006; Sampson & Laub, 1994). The inclusion of the parental work context incorporates the work of economists and organizational scientists (Duncan, 2005). The inclusion of the cultural context incorporates the work of anthropologists (Berry, 2003; Whiting & Whiting, 1975).

This theoretical approach also has limitations. Although it provides a useful descriptive guide to the various contexts or systems that need to be examined, the processes by which each one affects children's development are largely drawn from other theoretical perspectives, such as social learning theory or sociocultural theory. The developmental aspects of the perspective were not articulated in detail, and information about how children's changing capacities alter the effect of exposure to different contexts remains to be collected.

Biological Perspective

A theoretical approach emphasizing the important role of biological factors is increasingly being applied to the study of social development. Three examples of theoretical approaches based on biology are ethological theory, evolutionary theory, and behavior genetics.

ethological theory
A theory that behavior must be viewed in a particular context and as having adaptive or survival value.

ETHOLOGICAL THEORY   The **ethological theory** developed by European zoologists Konrad Lorenz (1952) and Niko Tinbergen (1951) is based on the belief that to understand behavior, scientists must view it as occurring in a particular setting and as having adaptive or survival value and must study it in relation to the organism's biology and the ecosystem in which the organism functions. To learn about children's social behavior, therefore, researchers must consider the children's needs and the nature of the setting in which their behavior takes place, such as a classroom, a playground, or a library.

Ethological researchers have observed human infants and children to find out which behaviors are "species specific" (unique to the human species) and play a functional role in ensuring survival. They have identified behaviors that are common to all children regardless of the culture into which they are born. For example, emotional expressions of joy, sadness, disgust, and anger are similar across a wide range of modern cultures including those of Brazil, Japan, and the United States, as well as nonindustrialized cultures such as the Fore and Dori tribes of New Guinea (Ekman, 1994; Ekman et al., 1987; LaFreniere, 2000). These behaviors appear to have a biological basis and help ensure that caregivers meet children's needs. Although ethologists view the behaviors as biologically based, they also assume that they are modified by experience. For example, with input from parents and peers, children learn to mask their emotions by smiling even when they are unhappy (LaFreniere, 2000; McDowell & Parke, 2005; Saarni et al., 2006). Thus, modern ethologists view children as open to input from the environment, not as captives of their biological roots. One important concept in ethology is the **critical period**, that is, a specific time in an organism's development during which external factors have a unique and irreversible impact.

critical period
A specific time in an organism's development during whch external factors have a unique and irreversible impact.

ETHOLOGICAL THEORY: AN EVALUATION Ethologists have made a number of significant contributions to our understanding of social development. One contribution was the discovery that nonverbal social behaviors—gestures, postures, facial expressions—regulate social exchanges. For example, monkeys often use threat gestures, such as a stare and bared teeth, to ward off attackers or appeasement signs, such as baring the neck or making themselves look smaller, to call a halt to a struggle. Children also make themselves look smaller—kneeling, bowing, lying down—to express appeasement (Ginsburg et al., 1977). A particularly important contribution of ethology to our understanding of social development was its suggestion that infants' signaling behaviors, such as crying and smiling, promote closeness with caregivers. This suggestion became a central component in John Bowlby's theory of the development of attachment (discussed in Chapter 4, "Attachment"). Another contribution from ethology was a better understanding of how children's groups are organized. It turns out that children, like monkeys and chickens, develop specific organizational structures and dominance hierarchies or "pecking orders" (Hawley & Little, 1999). Another contribution was the method of study used in ethology. Ethologists observe children and animals in their natural surroundings and develop detailed descriptions and classifications of behavior that they then try to organize into meaningful patterns. For example, ethologists compute rates of hitting, poking, kicking, and yelling, which are then used to define aggression; ethologists observe a slight lift of the eyebrows, a suggestive smile, and a tilt of the head to define flirtatious behavior. As a result of ethological research, observational approaches to studying children have increased in popularity and detail.

However, there are limits to what is learned from ethology. First, the theory is largely descriptive. Although this is a useful first step, more explanatory principles are needed. Second, the application of the concept of critical periods to human development was criticized because it failed to acknowledge that later environmental experiences can sometimes overcome the effects of early experiences. The concept of a narrowly defined "critical" period has now been replaced with the notion of a "sensitive" period that has more porous boundaries (Bornstein, 1989; Schaffer, 2000). The utility of the critical period concept also has been found to vary across domains of development; some behaviors have a narrow critical or sensitive period; some have a broad window. For example, the window for developing an attachment to a caregiver appears to be the first year of life; the period for learning a second language extends from birth to adolescence.

EVOLUTIONARY DEVELOPMENTAL THEORY Although ethologists and evolutionary psychologists share many basic assumptions, evolutionary psychology focuses on behaviors that ensured survival of the species in the past. Evolutionary psychologists assume that our ancestors developed complex skills to ensure survival by successfully finding a mate for reproduction, rearing children to the age of reproduction, hunting and securing food, and communicating and cooperating with members of the social group. These processes are seen as instrumental to human functioning more broadly and to social development specifically (Bjorklund, 2008; Bugental & Grusec, 2006). After all, one hallmark of evolution is the fact that human beings use their capacities to reason and solve problems in all types of situations—including figuring out how to recognize a familiar group member or escape from a dangerous or threatening enemy. The main questions for developmental evolutionary psychologists are how and when in the course of childhood these adaptive capabilities emerge (Bjorklund & Pelligrini, 2002, 2010).

One of the central principles of evolutionary developmental theory is that we are programmed to reproduce and pass our genes to the next generation. This concept is useful for explaining parents' investment in their children. It also helps explain the higher rates of abuse and homicide in stepfamilies compared with biological families (Daly & Wilson, 1996). According to evolutionary theory, stepparents are less protective and invest fewer resources in stepchildren than biological children because they have no genetic investment in them.

Evolutionary developmental psychologists are also interested in the capabilities children develop that enable them to learn from interactions with other people, for example, the ability to understand other people's intentions. They suggest that this ability appeared relatively late in human evolution and is a feature that distinguishes humans from other primates (Tomasello,

1999, 2008). They are also interested in the adaptive value of immaturity. Childhood play, for example, is a seemingly purposeless activity that may, in fact, be important for children's sense of self-efficacy, for learning and practicing social signaling, and for encouraging curiosity and creativity—regardless of its long-term consequences for adult functioning (Bjorklund, 2008).

EVOLUTIONARY DEVELOPMENTAL THEORY: AN EVALUATION Evolutionary theory illuminates some basic social processes including the capacities that permit social understanding and regulate social behavior. It brings attention to the adaptive functions of some uniquely childish behaviors and has provided insights into the role of biological kin ties. However, critics argue that this approach has limited relevance for addressing issues associated with rapid changes, such as new technological advances or sudden social shifts. Another problem with evolutionary theory is that many of its explanations are post hoc, or after the fact, and rely on the general

According to evolutionary theory, parents give their children attention and resources to ensure the passage of their genes through the next generation. Source: © Media Bakery.

argument that a particular behavior had adaptive value that ensured the survival of the species. Determining the function of a particular behavior is not so easy. As one skeptic observed, "the phylogeny of anatomical structures can be gleaned from fossils but we have no fossils of human behavior" (Miller, 2002, p. 331). Therefore, knowing what function a behavior served many generations ago is difficult. Moreover, behaviors that were adaptive in ancient times may not be adaptive in contemporary society. For example, although understanding others' intentions continues to be a useful skill, physical aggression and a liking of fatty foods appear to be less adaptive. It has also been suggested that evolutionary theory should be integrated with advances in neuroscience because some of the theory's assumptions can be directly evaluated by investigating brain functioning (Panksepp & Panksepp, 2000).

Learning from Living Leaders: David Bjorklund

Source: Courtesy of David Bjorklund.

David Bjorklund is Professor of Psychology at Florida Atlantic University. He has taught there for over 30 years since completing his Ph.D. work at the University of North Carolina. As an undergraduate, Bjorklund wanted to be a clinical child psychologist "saving the world by curing one neurotic child at a time." However, the reality of working with delinquent youth during college made him realize that he was not cut out for a clinical career but was more suited to research. After a lengthy period doing research on children's cognitive development, Bjorklund became an eloquent spokesman for the evolutionary theoretical perspective. His views are described in his book, *The Origins of Human Nature: Evolutionary Developmental Psychology*, which was the first extended treatment of an evolutionary approach to development. Bjorklund believes that our unique intelligence is not technological ability but an ability to negotiate the social environment, to cooperate with others, and to understand their intentions and desires. The central question that concerns him is how human social intelligence evolved. He suggests that many social development issues can be better understood through an evolutionary lens. For example, although child abuse and young males' aggression are no longer adaptive in modern environments, they may have been adaptive in our evolutionary past. Bjorklund hopes that in the future the field will embrace more biological ideas including not only evolution but also the effects of hormones and the central nervous system on social behavior.

He has been widely recognized for his work, receiving the Alexander von Humboldt Research Award and invitations to be a visiting professor in Germany, Spain, and New Zealand. He is editor of the *Journal of Experimental Child Psychology* and served as a contributing editor to *Parents Magazine*. He advises undergraduates to do what works for him, "Write to see what you think."

Further Reading

Bjorklund, D. F. (2008). *Why youth is not wasted on the young: Immaturity in human development*. Oxford: Blackwell.

Bjorklund, D. F., & Pelligrini, A. D. (2002). *The origins of human nature: Evolutionary developmental psychology*. Washington, DC: American Psychological Association.

HUMAN BEHAVIOR GENETICS The field of human behavior genetics began in the 1960s when scientists focused their attention on the relative contributions of heredity and environment to individual differences in human behavior (Plomin et al., 2001). These researchers wondered why some children are outgoing and sociable while others are introverted and shy; why some children—and adults—are chronically aggressive whereas others seek to cooperate and avoid confrontation. Unlike biologists who study heredity, these behavior geneticists conducted their research without directly measuring chromosomes, genes, or DNA. Their primary strategy was to use statistical techniques to estimate the contribution that heredity makes to particular abilities or types of behavior. More recently, advances in genetic science have allowed behavior geneticists to assess genes as well (Gregory et al., 2010; Plomin & Rutter, 1998).

Since the 1960s, behavior geneticists have studied a number of differences in children's social behavior, such as those in sociability, fear, and irritability. These differences appear in the earliest days of life and to some extent persist throughout childhood (Rothbart & Bates, 2006; Sanson et al., 2010; Thomas & Chess, 1986), suggesting that genes influence these behaviors. However, the fact that these behaviors do not always lead to identical outcomes in different children indicates that they are also susceptible to environmental influences (Grigorenko, 2002; Loehlin et al., 1988). Behavior geneticists have shown that both heredity and environment contribute to individual differences in emotionality, activity level, and sociability (Goldsmith, 1983; Kochanska, 1993; Kochanska & Thompson, 1997; Plomin, 1995). This information is of great value in our effort to understand and predict social development.

HUMAN BEHAVIOR GENETICS: AN EVALUATION   The behavior genetics perspective has provided an important corrective to psychologists' long-held emphasis on environmental causes of behavior. Many social behaviors are clearly influenced by genetic factors, although the particular genes or clusters of genes that account for biological predispositions to behave aggressively or altruistically are still not totally known. Although in their early days behavior geneticists were criticized for being reductionist and assuming that genetic factors were more important than environmental factors, modern behavior geneticists acknowledge that inputs from many sources, from genetics to culture, are important in explaining social development. Despite this acknowledgement, measurement of the environment in many behavior genetics studies is quite general and nonspecific. Therefore, the ways in which genetic expression is modified by particular environments remain to be described.

Life Span Perspective

The life span theory of development, as the name implies, extends the frame of development beyond childhood and through adulthood, because people are open to change across their entire lives (Baltes et al., 2006; Elder & Conger, 2000; Elder & Shanahan, 2006). According to this perspective, change over time can be traced to three sets of causes. First, there are *normative events*, which most people encounter at roughly the same age. Some of these events, such as the onset of menstruation in adolescent girls, are biological or maturational. Others normative events are programmed by society, for example, entering school at age 5 or 6, beginning college at age 17 or 18, and marrying in the mid 20s or early 30s. A second set of causes of change involves unexpected events that push development in new directions. Life span theorists term these *nonnormative events* because they do not happen to everyone in the normal course of development and they do not follow any preset schedule. Instead, they happen to any child or family at any time and often without warning or anticipation. Divorce, job loss, and residence change are nonnormative events that affect development. *Historical events* constitute the third set of factors that influence development. People who were born in the same year or age period make up **age cohorts** who share the same historical experiences. For example, people born in 1950 were adolescents during the late 1960s, an era of considerable upheaval and social unrest; people born in 1970 were adolescents in 1989 when the Communist monopoly in Europe collapsed and the Cold War ended; people born in 1980 were adolescents in the 1990s when Internet use exploded and changed the way we communicate.

age cohorts
People who were born in the same time period and share historical experiences.

LIFE SPAN PERSPECTIVE: AN EVALUATION   The life span perspective reminds us that development is a life-long process and that both normative and nonnormative events affect developmental trajectories and outcomes. Its focus on age cohorts underscores the fact that historical eras modify development. Another contribution of this perspective is that it highlights changes in adults' lives, which may, in turn, affect children's development. For example, parents who experience nonnormative stressful events, such as losing a job or getting a divorce, provide less optimal rearing for their children, and this affects children differently, depending on their age. In short, the developmental trajectories of parents and children are linked, and both need to be considered to understand children's development. One of the reasons this perspective has not had more impact on the study of children's social development is that much of the theorizing has involved older adults. As a result, social development researchers have used the perspective mainly as a descriptive aid; few of the processes generated by the theory for older age groups have filtered down to explain children's social development.

A Variety of Theoretical Perspectives

Today no single overarching theory adequately addresses all aspects of social development. Instead, development can be approached from a variety of perspectives. The grand theories of Freud and Piaget, which attempted to explain wide swaths of development, have, for the most part, been replaced by modern theories that are more modest in scope. These contemporary theories offer detailed accounts of particular domains or developmental phenomena and, as a result, some offer better and more complete accounts of certain aspects of development than others. Ethological theory is especially helpful in describing the development of emotional expressions and communication and how children's social groups are organized. Cognitive social learning theory and social information-processing theory offer useful perspectives for explaining aggression. Systems theories offer a framework for studying the influence of the family and social institutions on social development. All of these theoretical perspectives have a place in the broad study of social development, and it is often helpful to draw on several to investigate a particular research question.

Chapter Summary

Social Development

- The field of social development includes descriptions of social behaviors, individual differences in social behavior, and changes in social behavior with age as well as explanations for these changes and differences.

Social Development: A Brief History

- The scientific study of social development began with Darwin's work in the 1800s. Subsequently, competing views were expressed in Watson's behaviorally oriented theory, Freud's biologically inspired theory, and Gesell's maturational theory.

Critical Questions about Social Development

- How do biological and environmental influences affect social development? Modern developmental psychologists recognize the importance of both biological and environmental influences and are concerned with discovering the ways in which these factors interact to produce developmental differences.

- What role do children play in their own development? Most developmental psychologists believe that children actively shape, control, and direct the course of their own development.

- What is the appropriate unit for studying social development? Although researchers have typically focused on individual children, they have increasingly recognized that other units such as dyads, triads, and social groups are also important.

- Is development continuous or discontinuous? Some theorists view social development as a continuous process whereby change takes place smoothly and gradually. Others see development as a series of qualitatively different stages or steps. The more closely we examine development, the more we see ebbs and flows in the acquisition of social skills.

- Is social behavior the result of the situation or the child? Most developmental psychologists stress the complementary roles of situational factors and child differences.

- Is social development universal across cultures? Most developmental psychologists agree that cultural contexts should be considered but believe that universal aspects of development such as emotions, language, and communication coexist with cultural variations.

- How does social development vary across historical eras? Both abrupt and gradual changes in society influence social development.

- Is social development related to other developmental domains? Social development influences and is influenced by emotional, cognitive, language, perceptual, and motor development.

- How important are mothers for children's social development? Although mothers are clearly important in children's social development, other people including fathers, siblings, grandparents, peers, teachers, and religious leaders also are important influences.

- Is there a single pathway for social development? Children may start out at a similar place but end up at very different points (multifinality), or they may follow different paths but end up at the same point (equifinality).

- What influences how we label children's social behavior? Three sets of factors—characteristics of the child, the adult, and the context—influence social judgments and, in turn, how social behaviors are labeled.

- Do developmental psychologists own social development? Scholars in a variety of fields including pediatrics, psychiatry, anthropology, economics, law, and history have made valuable contributions to the field of social development.

Theoretical Perspectives On Social Development

- Theories help organize and integrate knowledge into a coherent account of how children develop and foster research by providing testable predictions about behavior. Historically, grand theories reflected attempts to account for all aspects of development. Modern theories tend to be more narrowly focused attempts to explain specific aspects of social development.

Psychodynamic Perspective

- In Freud's psychodynamic theory, basic biological drives motivate the child. Early experiences are essential for determining later behavior.

- Erikson expanded Freud's theory to include social and cultural influences on development. His psychosocial theory is organized around a series of fundamental personal and social tasks that individuals must accomplish at each stage.

- Psychodynamic theories helped shape many concerns of modern social development, including the effects of early experience in the family and the psychological roots and importance of aggression, morality, gender roles, and attachment. However, the central claims of the theories are difficult to test empirically.

Traditional Learning Perspective

- Traditional learning theories emphasize how new behaviors are acquired through a gradual and continuous process of learning. The theories had important applications and have been used in homes, schools, and clinics to reduce children's behavior problems. Their lack of attention to developmental changes is a limitation.

Cognitive Social Learning Theory

- Bandura focused attention on observational learning. The notions of reciprocal determinism and self-efficacy were important additions to this theoretical position. The lack of attention to developmental issues, the limited ecological validity of the findings, and the limited recognition of the roles of biology and culture are shortcomings of the theory.

Social Information-Processing Theory

- This approach focuses on how children take in, use, and remember information to make decisions about social actions. The lack of developmental focus, the limited role allocated to emotion, and the heavy emphasis on deliberate decision making rather than automatic or habitual responding are limitations of this perspective.

Cognitive Developmental Perspective

- In Piaget's theory of development, children actively seek new experiences and from them construct mental structures. They assimilate new information into existing structures and accommodate structures when the information doesn't fit. Piaget's focus on stages has been questioned, and his lack of emphasis on emotions, culture, and social behavior make his theory of limited use in the field of social development.

Social Cognitive Domain Theory

- This perspective focuses on how children learn to make social judgments about their world. According to this approach, children's social judgments are domain specific.

Vygotsky's Sociocultural Theory

- This theory focuses on the contributions of social and cultural factors to children's development. Children grow and change as a function of their own efforts and the guidance of more skilled others. The theory does not describe how interactions change over the course of development.

Systems Perspective

- According to systems theories, other elements or members of the system influence an individual's behaviors.
- Bronfenbrenner's ecological systems theory stresses the importance of relations between the child and environmental systems, such as the family, school, community, and culture. Development involves the interplay between the child and the microsystem, mesosystem, exosystem, macrosystem, and chronosystem. Lack of developmental focus as well as limited information about the processes that govern cross-level linkages are limitations of this theory.

Biological Perspective

- Ethologists observe behaviors in natural settings and study patterns of behaviors across human and infrahuman species and across human societies and cultures. The theory is largely descriptive.
- Evolutionary psychology asserts that social behaviors reflect survival needs and processes of human evolution. It focused attention on parental investment as a way to ensure intergenerational continuity of genes and on the adaptive value of immaturity. The approach has limited relevance for addressing issues associated with rapid changes. Many explanations are post hoc.
- Behavior genetics addresses the relative contributions of heredity and environment to social development and the interdependence between environmental conditions and whether and when genes are expressed in behavior. The particular genes or clusters of genes that account for social outcomes are still poorly understood, and the way in which the environment is measured is often very general.

Life Span Theory

- This theory emphasizes development over the entire life course. Changes can be traced to normative age–graded events including entry into school, nonnormative events such as divorce, and historical or cohort-related events such as the Great Depression or the Vietnam War.
- The impact of this perspective is limited by the fact that much of the theorizing has involved older adults.

Variety of Theoretical Perspectives

- Social development can be approached from a variety of perspectives and it is often helpful to draw on several theories to explain children's development.

Key Terms

age cohort	egocentric	Oedipus complex
accommodation	Electra complex	operant conditioning
assimilation	equifinality	psychodynamic theory
chronosystem	ethological theory	psychosocial theory
classical conditioning	exosystem	social dyad
cognitive social learning theory	generativity	social information-processing theory
critical period	id	sociocultural theory
desensitization	macrosystem	superego
domain specificity	maturation	systems
drive reduction theory	mesosystem	transactional
ecological theory	microsystem	zone of proximal development
ego	multifinality	
	object permanence	

At the Movies

A number of movies and videos illustrate the ideas and theories discussed in this chapter. *Biography—Sigmund Freud: Analysis of a Mind* (2004) uses photographs, interviews with psychoanalysts and Freud's grandchildren, and even a brief recording that Freud himself made to provide a glimpse into the life of this complex man. Freud didn't intend to get into psychiatry. His dream was to be a research scientist, but because of Jewish quotas, he wasn't permitted to enter that field. Instead, he became a doctor specializing in nervous diseases. A number of clips from this film are available on YouTube (http://www.youtube.com/watch?v = C_AXSd4wxgM; http://www.youtube.com/watch?v = IKWZeIrDvaQ; http://www.youtube.com/watch?v = OtuEyMG8l9U; http://www.youtube.com/watch?v = aHcHxjDMMEQ; http://www.youtube.com/watch?v = 0duFTN69l7s; http://www.youtube.com/watch?v = g2ER0prrIGM).

Lost in Translation (2003) is useful for illustrating Erikson's psychosocial stages of development. The movie explores the relationship between a young woman and a middle-aged man stuck in Tokyo. Both characters are experiencing developmental crises. They help each other articulate their dilemmas and begin to take steps forward.

To find out more about learning theory, you can watch a clip of Pavlov and his salivating dogs at http://www.youtube.com/watch?v = hhqumfpxuzI. A commercial movie portraying classical conditioning is Stanley Kubrick's science fiction drama, *A Clockwork Orange* (1971). A violent youth convicted of murder and rape is given an experimental program of "aversion therapy" in which he is conditioned to detest violence. Watson's classical conditioning of Little Albert is presented with and without voiceover in YouTube clips (http://www.youtube.com/watch?v = Xt0ucxOrPQE and http://www.youtube.com/watch?v = aG6A66iV5tk). Skinner's operant conditioning is illustrated in http://www.youtube.com/watch?v = I_ctJqjlrHA; http://www.youtube.com/watch?v = fLoHH03QAAI; and http://www.youtube.com/watch?v = MPHcw2vz9H0. Social learning theory is illustrated in clips of Bandura and his Bobo doll (http://www.youtube.com/watch?v = ZeE_Ymzc1rE; and http://video.google.com/videoplay?docid = -4586465813762682933).

Television programs discussing the work of Piaget include *L'Épistémologie génétique de Jean Piaget* (1977) and http://www.youtube.com/watch?v = ue8y-JVhjS0. The documentary film *The Genius of Charles Darwin* (2008) includes segments on Darwin's life and discoveries and an attempt to convince a group of school children that evolution explains the world better than religion. Darwin's theory of evolution is discussed in YouTube clips http://www.youtube.com/watch?v = xiFXVzlzfI4 and http://www.youtube.com/watch?v = g6e5H-pogF0s. The movie *Creation* (2009) focuses on Darwin's personal life during the time he was writing *On the Origin of Species* and reveals the struggles he went through balancing his religious faith with his science. Finally, ethological theory is illustrated in the short documentary *Konrad Lorenz: Science of Animal Behavior* (1975). Lorenz's work is also the basis for the movie *Fly Away Home* (1996) in which a young girl becomes the "mother" to a flock of geese and has to teach them how to migrate south for the winter.

In addition to these films focused on psychological theories and theorists are movies that highlight the "critical questions" these theories address. The question of the extent to which social development is influenced by environmental factors is front and center in *NOVA: Secret of the Wild Child* (1997), a documentary about Genie, the 13-year-old girl who was rescued from her home by social workers after a decade with virtually no human contact. For a humorous take on this question, watch *Human Nature* (2001), which follows the ups and downs of a scientist, a naturalist, and a man born and raised in the wild. The scientist trains the wild man in the ways of the world, starting with table manners; the naturalist fights to preserve the man's simian past. On a more serious note, *Where Do the Children Play?* (2002) shows how children's experiences depend on where and when they are born and provides an answer to the question of how social development varies across historical eras. The film opens by examining differences between growing up today and childhood as it was lived 50 years ago and examines how restrictive patterns of sprawl, congestion, and suburban development affect children's development.

The question of whether social development is universal across cultures is addressed implicitly in numerous films showing children's experiences in different cultures. A few of these films are *Families of the World* (1997–2000), a documentary series illustrating cultural differences and similarities among children from Mexico, Japan, India, Egypt, China, Russia, France, the United States, and several other nations. Each film records two children performing their daily activities. Other movies portraying children's experiences in cultures other than our own include *Xiang ri kui* (2005), a dramatic tale about the life of a boy in an urban Chinese family, his conflicts with his father, and how both are affected by society; *La Quinceañera* (2007), a portrait of a Mexican family's love and devotion to each other; *Persepolis* (2007), a portrayal of events through the eyes of a girl experiencing the Iranian Revolution of 1979 and the new Iran ruled by Islamic fundamentalists; and *Slumdog Millionaire* (2008), which offers a glimpse of life in the slums of Mumbai, India. *Babies* (2010) is a visually stunning film that chronicles the lives of four infants—in Mongolia, Namibia, San Francisco, and Tokyo—from first breath to first steps.

CHAPTER 2 Research Methods: Tools for Discovery

Source: Steve Cole/iStockphoto.

Researcher Angela Gonzales wants to know whether boys and girls differ in their use of the Internet for social interactions. She conducts a national survey of U.S. 10-year-olds to find out. Toni Smithson wonders what makes some children more popular than others. To investigate this question, she asks second-grade children to rate their classmates' likability, and then she examines behavior differences between the best and least liked children. Another researcher, James Burks, is interested in whether watching a character on TV behave prosocially encourages children to be more helpful. He carries out a laboratory experiment in which some children are shown an episode of *Sesame Street* in which Big Bird is helpful and cooperative and other children are shown a video of dolphins at Sea World. He then assesses whether the two groups of children differ in their willingness to help the experimenter pick up some dropped papers. These three hypothetical examples illustrate the range of strategies that can be used to study children's social behavior. They differ in their research questions, samples, methods, and data-gathering techniques. In this chapter, we explore the various methods used to study children's social behavior and development.

A theory can provide insights, hunches, and ideas, but to be useful, it must produce predictions that can be tested with empirical research. In this chapter, we describe some of the research methods that psychologists have used to study children's social behaviors and how those behaviors change with age. Like all scientists, these psychologists follow the scientific method. They formulate a hypothesis on the basis of theory and use replicable techniques to collect, study, and analyze data in an effort to test the theory's usefulness. Or they pose a research question and use scientific techniques to gather data from a representative sample so they can answer their query. The decisions that must be made by researchers taking a scientific approach to studying social development include choosing a research method, picking a research design, finding a research sample, and devising a data-collection strategy so that hypotheses can be tested and questions answered in an effective and ethical way.

Getting Started: Formulating Hypotheses, Asking Questions

Doing research is about pursuing ideas that will help chart the course of social development and identify the causes of developmental advances. Thus, research starts with ideas. These ideas can be derived from theory, from previous research, from observations of behavior, or even from old wives' tales. But they should be sensible, innovative, and important. As one expert on research methods in this field wisely observed, "It is important to remember that all the technical skill in the world will not save a study if the ideas behind it are not any good" (Miller, 2007, p. 3). One example of a good idea, which we discuss in this chapter, was the idea that children's social behavior might be affected by their exposure to violence on television.

Between having a good idea and conducting a good study are a number of critical steps. One step is to translate the general idea into clear research hypotheses or questions. If the researcher's goal is to test specific theoretical premises, this step involves proposing testable hypotheses, for example, if children watch violent television, their own aggression will increase because they will imitate the TV models' behavior. If the researcher's goal is descriptive, the challenge will be to find a question or questions that can be answered with empirical data, for example, how often do children watch violent television programs? Before empirical data can be collected, finding out about past work on the topic is important for the researcher; brilliant ideas will not contribute to scientific knowledge if the answers to the researcher's questions are already known! Reviewing past literature is a key step to make sure the study is not merely plowing old ground. Search engines such as PsycINFO are helpful (perhaps **operationalization** essential) to find out about previous studies in the area. Another step in the research process is **operationalization** of the ideas or **constructs** to be studied by translating them into empirically assessable forms, for example, operationalizing "violent television" as television programs showing at least three instances of an adult hitting, kicking, or shooting another person. The researcher must be familiar with the tasks and procedures that other investigators have used in pursuit of the same topic, in this case, how previous researchers have assessed children's aggression. After researchers have formulated their hypotheses or questions and operationalized their research constructs, they make decisions about research designs, methods, samples, and analyses.

operationalization
Defining a concept so that it is observable and measurable.

construct
An idea or concept, especially a complex one such as aggression or love.

Research Methods: Establishing Patterns and Causes

The most common research methods for studying social development are the correlational method, the experimental method, and the case study. Each of these methods can be used to test hypotheses or answer questions about the effects of viewing violent television programs on children's social behavior.

The Correlational Method

The correlational research method involves looking for statistical associations between two variables, that is, determining whether two things are related to each other in a regular and systematic way and finding out how strongly they are related. An illustration of the correlational method applied to the question of whether viewing television is related to aggression in preschool children is found in a study by Jerome and Dorothy Singer (1981). They asked 141 parents about the TV viewing habits of their sons and daughters, including how much time they spent in front of the television set and the types of programs they watched. Then observers (who didn't know what the parents had said) rated how aggressive the children were with classmates in preschool. Their ratings showed that children who were more aggressive at preschool watched more action and adventure shows at home according to their parents. These shows contain a relatively high level of violence. This correlation between aggressive behavior and television viewing did not *prove* that watching violent programs was the reason children displayed more aggression. A correlation between two variables does not mean that one variable necessarily *causes* the increase or decrease in the other; it simply tells us that the two variables are related to each other and indicates the strength or magnitude of their association. Any number of factors other than watching violent television could have contributed to the children's aggressiveness. For example, children who watch violent action and adventure programs might already be aggressive and simply choose to watch these programs. A correlational study does not resolve this issue.

The correlation coefficient is the statistic that provides a numerical estimate of how closely two variables are related to each other and indicates the direction in which they are related. Correlation coefficients range along a continuum from −1.0, the lowest possible negative correlation, to +1.0, the highest possible positive correlation. If two variables are correlated −1.0, this means that for every increase in one variable there is a systematic decrease in the other; if they are correlated +1.0, for every increase in one variable, there is a comparable increase in the other. The coefficient of 0.0 means that the variables are completely unrelated to each other. In studies of social development, researchers generally find correlation coefficients that range from +/− 0.2 to +/− 0.5. These coefficients may be statistically significant; that is, large enough that they have not occurred by chance, but they are considered modest to moderate in size. This suggests that factors other than those included in the research are also associated with children's social behavior.

If correlational research doesn't allow us to determine whether a factor is actually causing children's social behavior, why do we use it? One reason is that we cannot always design a suitable experiment to study our question. The effect of television viewing—if there is one—is likely to be spread out over a long period of time, beginning when children are very young. It is not uncommon for children to be exposed to television even when they are infants (Wartella et al., 2005). Conducting an experiment that provides or manipulates such long-term exposure would be difficult. Likewise, implementing experiments to study the effects of residential mobility, divorce, or child abuse is virtually impossible because these events do not lend themselves to experimental manipulation. Ethical concerns would prohibit using experiments to study these factors, and even without ethical restrictions, parents would likely decline to participate if they were to be randomly assigned to move to a new neighborhood, get divorced, or hit their children. Another reason to use the correlational method is that understanding causal processes is not the only goal of research. Many investigators are simply interested in describing patterns and paths of development as they naturally occur, and the correlational method is an excellent way to examine these patterns; for example, looking for links between increasing cognitive abilities and decreasing displays of aggression.

Laboratory Experiments

The primary way researchers investigate causal connections between environmental events and children's social behavior is by using experiments. In an experiment carried out in a laboratory, researchers hold constant, or equate, every possible factor except the one they have hypothesized will influence the behavior they want to study. They then assign each participant to a group. Participants in the *experimental group* are exposed to the proposed causal factor; participants in the *control group* do not receive this experience. Researchers put people in these groups by using random assignment, which rules out the possibility that the people in the groups differ from one another in some systematic way that could distort the results of the experiment.

In a laboratory experiment on the effects of watching violent television, Robert Liebert and Robert Baron (1972) randomly assigned 136 boys and girls ranging in age from 5 to 9 years to experimental and control groups. The children in the experimental group saw 3 minutes of a crime show containing a chase, two fistfights, two shootings, and a knifing. The children in the control group watched a highly active but nonviolent sports sequence of the same length. Whether the children saw the violent television clip or not was the **independent variable**. The researchers hypothesized that children in the experimental group would behave more aggressively than children in the control group. If they found support for this hypothesis, they could then reasonably conclude that exposure to TV violence was the cause of the increased aggression.

In the second phase of this study, the experimenters told the children that they were to play a game with another child in an adjoining room. The researchers then seated children before a panel that had two buttons labeled "Hurt" and "Help" and told them that the buttons were connected to a panel that the child in the other room was looking at. The experimenter explained that the other child was playing a game that required turning a handle and if children wanted to make it easier for the other child to turn the handle, they could press the Help button, but if they wanted to hinder the other child, pressing the Hurt button would make the handle burning hot. This entire scenario was a deception—the other child was purely imaginary and nothing a child did hurt anyone. (This issue of deception raises ethical questions, which we discuss later in this chapter.) The amount of aggressive behavior the children displayed, operationalized as how long and how often they depressed the Hurt button, was the **dependent variable**. Results of the study indicated that children who had seen the violent TV segment were significantly more likely to "hurt" the other child than were children who had watched the fast-paced but nonviolent sports program. This finding supported the researchers' hypothesis that exposure to TV violence would increase aggression.

Although this study was carefully designed, like many laboratory experiments it had limitations that reduced generalization from its results to the real world. For example, Liebert and Baron had edited their violent TV program to include more acts of violence in 3 minutes than would normally occur on television, even in a violent show. One way to overcome some of the problems of artificiality in the laboratory and increase the real-life applicability or **ecological validity** of a study is to conduct a **laboratory analogue experiment**. In this kind of experiment, researchers try to duplicate in the laboratory features or events that occur naturally in everyday life. For example, they might show children real TV shows over the course of several weeks in a room that resembled a living room and then assess the children's aggression toward real peers in a room that resembled a playroom.

independent variable
The factor that researchers deliberately manipulate in an experiment.

dependent variable
The factor that researchers expect to change as a function of change in the independent variable.

ecological validity
The degree to which a research study accurately represents events or processes that occur in the real world.

laboratory analogue experiment
Researchers try to duplicate in the laboratory features or events that occur naturally in everyday life in order to increase the ecological validity of the results.

In this laboratory experiment, an infant was video recorded reacting to the mother as she behaved in ways specified by the researcher. The independent variable was whether the mother was smiling or not; the dependent variable was whether the baby smiled in response. Source: Courtesy of Maria Legerstee, Infants' Sense of People: Precursors to a Theory of Mind *(2005). New York: Cambridge University Press, Figure 10.1.*

The exact duplication of natural circumstances is not the aim of all experiments, however. Researchers can gain important insights about people's socioemotional tendencies and capacities using laboratory experiments because they can precisely control the critical features of social stimuli and events. For some questions, the laboratory is an ideal place for study. Clearly, research strategies must be matched to the questions researchers are asking.

Field Experiments, Interventions, and Natural Experiments

When researchers want to avoid artificiality and other problems associated with laboratory or even laboratory analogue experiments, they sometimes conduct experiments in people's natural environments. In field experiments and interventions, they deliberately introduce changes in the normal environment; in natural experiments, they take advantage of naturally occurring changes in the everyday world.

field experiment
An experiment in which researchers deliberately create a change in a real-world setting and then measure the outcome of their manipulation.

FIELD EXPERIMENTS In a **field experiment**, investigators deliberately introduce changes into a person's natural environment. In one field experiment, researchers studied the effect of viewing television violence on children's aggressive behavior (Friedrich & Stein, 1973). Preschoolers enrolled in a summer program were the participants. During the first 3 weeks of the study, the researchers simply observed the children during their usual play sessions to achieve a baseline measure of the aggressive behavior each child displayed under normal circumstances. Then, for the next 4 weeks, they showed the children, who were randomly assigned to one of three groups, a 30-minute TV program each day. Some children always saw programs depicting aggression, such as *Batman* and *Superman* cartoons; others saw programs with a message of caring and kindness, such as *Mister Rogers' Neighborhood*; and children in the third group watched neutral shows, such as nature programs or circus movies. The researchers took care to minimize **observer bias** by having the researchers who assessed the children's behavior after the television viewings be unaware of the types of programs the children had seen.

observer bias
An observer's tendency to be influenced by knowledge about the research design or hypothesis.

Results of the study showed that children who had been high in aggressive behavior before the experiment behaved even more aggressively after repeated exposure to aggressive cartoons but not after exposure to the other two kinds of shows. Children who were rated as less aggressive during the initial assessment period and children who watched neutral shows did not increase in aggression. The researchers concluded that exposure to TV violence can increase children's aggressiveness but only if the children were already headed in that direction.

One advantage of field experiments over laboratory experiments is that the results can be more easily generalized to real life. In the study just described, the researchers had not edited the TV programs; they were programs that many of the children watched at home. Moreover, the children's aggressive behavior was measured in an everyday setting, the preschool. Thus, the field experiment offers researchers control over the independent variable (in this case, television viewing), random assignment of participants to groups, and some degree of ecological validity. These researchers could be reasonably confident that they had demonstrated a causal connection between exposure to television violence and increased aggressiveness in aggressive children.

INTERVENTIONS   Sometimes the field experiment is broader in its focus as when an entire program, or **intervention**, is introduced rather than just a few sessions of television viewing. In an effort to minimize the harmful effects of violent TV, a year-long intervention, consisting of 31 brief classroom lessons, was undertaken with 130 children in grades 1–3; the control group consisted of 47 children in classes that did not receive the lessons (Rosenkoetter et al., 2004). Lessons using music, rap, puppets, role play, stories, and film clips emphasized the many ways in which television distorts violence. The intervention resulted in a reduction in girls' viewing of violent TV and girls' identification with violent TV characters. Boys who were initially high viewers of violent TV were judged by their classmates to have reduced their aggression following the intervention. Unlike children in the intervention group, children in the control group did not become less aggressive, watch less violent TV, or identify less with violent characters. Thus, this intervention study suggested that children can be taught to reduce their consumption of violent TV and their aggressive behavior.

intervention
A program provided to improve a situation or relieve psychological illness or distress.

NATURAL EXPERIMENTS   For ethical or practical reasons, researchers may not be able to introduce changes into the natural environment. In these instances, they may be able to take advantage of a **natural experiment** in which they measure the effects of events or changes that occur without their intervention. This approach is often called a *quasi-experiment* because it is not a true experiment in that the research participants are not randomly assigned to experimental conditions. Instead, researchers select children who are naturally exposed to one set of conditions and compare them with children who are not exposed to these conditions. A natural experiment on children's television viewing was conducted by monitoring what happened before and after television was introduced into a small town in Canada (MacBeth, 1996; Williams, 1986). The investigators were able to show that aggressive behavior in children's play increased after TV came to town. Because the researchers did not arrange for the introduction of television to the town, their findings may have more ecological validity than those of laboratory studies or even field experiments. However, the independent variable, TV viewing, was very broadly defined; children watched all kinds of programs, and the researchers did not attempt to examine or control the shows they chose. As a result, we cannot say precisely what aspect of television caused the increase in aggressive play. Moreover, the researchers did not divide participants into randomly assigned experimental and control groups, so they could not rule out the possibility that personal characteristics might have influenced who bought and watched TV.

natural experiment
An experiment in which researchers measure the results of events that occur naturally in the real world.

Insights from Extremes: Lost and Found Children

Source: Patrick Zachmann/Magnum Photos, Inc.

In 1966, communist dictator Nicolai Ceausescu banned birth control and abortion and created financial incentives for women to have more children to increase Romania's population and workforce. The birth rate soared. So did child abandonment. When Ceausescu fell from power in 1989, more than 170,000 children were found languishing in orphanages like this one under appalling conditions. The children's physical needs were attended to, but they had few interactions in which adults held them, talked to them, sang or played with them. Many of the children were cross-eyed, perhaps from a lack of visual stimulation as they lay in their cribs. They were small for their age, and their development was severely delayed. Their IQs were almost 40 points lower than normal, they had profound communication problems, and they suffered from emotional disorders. These orphanages provided a natural experiment whereby researchers could evaluate the impact of sensory, perceptual, and social deprivation on children's development. They also provided an opportunity to carry out interventions by providing these "lost and found" children with new environments. In the Bucharest Early Intervention Project, researchers removed 66 children, ages 6 months to 2½ years, from a Romanian orphanage and placed them in high-quality foster care. For 5 years, they tracked the progress of these children and compared it with the development of children who remained in the orphanage and children who grew up in their own families. Children who were placed in foster care when they were under 1 year of age increased an average of 10 IQ points and had less depression and anxiety than the children who stayed in orphanages (Nelson et al., 2007). These findings illustrate the insights researchers have gained from examining children in extreme circumstances and show the value of both natural experiments and interventions as alternatives to laboratory methods of research (Rutter, Pickles, et al., 2001).

Combining Different Methods

No research strategy is without its strengths and limitations; each can play a role in helping investigators understand human behavior. Often researchers start in an unexplored area by using the correlational method simply to establish some possible relations. The correlational approach is a relatively simple research method that avoids some of the pitfalls of experimental methods such as the ethics of manipulating people and events, but it exerts minimal control over variables and reveals little about cause and effect. The researchers may then use experimental approaches to determine whether the associations they observed with the correlational method are causal.

Among laboratory, field, and natural experiments, there is often a trade-off between control of variables and the generalizability of findings: Variables can be controlled more in the lab, but generalizability is better if data are collected in the field. One way to deal with this trade-off is to combine field and laboratory approaches in a single study. As Figure 2.1 shows, there are two ways to do this; the independent variable can be introduced in the laboratory and the dependent variable measured in the field (cell C), or the independent variable can be introduced in the field and the effect measured in the lab (cell B). (Cell A in the figure represents the traditional lab experiment; cell D represents the usual field experiment.) An example of the first type of combined lab-and-field experiment is to bring youngsters into the lab and show them violent films and then measure changes in their social behavior with peers in the

	Manipulation of independent variable	
	Lab	Field
Assessment of dependent variable — Lab	A	B
Assessment of dependent variable — Field	C	D

FIGURE 2.1 *Manipulation and assessment of variables in field, lab, and combined field-and-lab designs.*

classroom. An example of the second kind of combined lab-and-field experiment is to control children's TV viewing in their own homes by having some parents allow their children to watch violent programs and other parents to allow their children to watch only nonviolent programs and then to conduct an assessment of changes in the children's aggressiveness in the laboratory. The first approach offers more precise control over the independent variable and allows the dependent variable to be measured in a natural way; the second allows greater ecological validity in the independent variable and exerts tighter control over measurement of the dependent variable. Both approaches help researchers increase the generalizability of their findings.

The Case Study Approach

case study
A form of research in which investigators study an individual person or group intensely.

The focus of a **case study** is a single individual or a small group of individuals. Case studies allow investigators to explore phenomena that they do not often encounter, such as an unusual talent, a rare developmental disorder, or a model classroom. Case studies facilitate more intensive investigation because the researchers' efforts are not spread across a large number of participants. They provide rich details about processes under study. They may be useful as precursors or follow-ups to studies using other methods. The chief limitation of the single case approach is the impossibility of generalizing from one individual to other children in other settings.

Real-World Application: Treating an Aggressive Child

Source: Refat Mamutov/iStockphoto.

child, his teachers rushed over to stop him, often lingering to explain why he shouldn't hit other people. But Adrian kept right on hitting. The school psychologist, who thought that Adrian hit other children in part to gain the teachers' attention, told the teachers to ignore Adrian whenever he was aggressive and to tell the other children just to walk away. At first, Adrian reacted to this change in teachers' and children's behavior with an increase in aggressive attacks. However, after a few days of the "silent treatment," his rate of hitting began to drop. To determine whether Adrian's behavior was changing in response to the new strategy, the psychologist asked the teachers to resume paying attention to Adrian when he hit other children. Sure enough, Adrian's rate of hitting increased, suggesting that his need for attention was indeed controlling his aggressive behavior. The teachers were then instructed once again to ignore Adrian's hitting, and once more his rate of hitting dropped.

Sometimes researchers use a case study experiment to try to bring about a change in a particular behavior in one child. For example, a new treatment for child conduct problems could be used with a particular child to see exactly how the treatment works before using it with other children. Consider the case of 4-year-old Adrian. During every play period at school, Adrian hit other children. At first, every time he hit another

This is an example of an ABAB experiment. A is the normal condition that existed before the experiment began; B is the experimental condition. Thus Adrian's initial hitting behavior is represented by the first A, and the experimental treatment—ignoring his behavior and walking away from him—by the first B. The second A reflects the psychologist's instruction that everyone return to the original state of affairs, and the second B reflects the reinstatement of the experimental treatment. If the reinstatement of the experimental treatment again diminishes the undesirable behavior—as it did—we can be pretty sure that the treatment works. As this case study illustrates, we can learn about promising approaches to helping children overcome their problems by careful analysis of the efficacy of a treatment of a single child. Adrian's treatment might or might not work with other children; nothing in the study of a single individual guarantees future success. But it's a first step in the long process of developing scientifically based treatments to curb children's aggression.

Studying Change Over Time

An essential decision for researchers in the field of social development is to determine how they will study changes in social behavior as children get older. Three main designs are available for investigating changes over time: cross-sectional, longitudinal, and sequential.

cross-sectional design
A research design in which researchers compare groups of individuals of different age levels at approximately the same point in time.

THE CROSS-SECTIONAL DESIGN   The most common way to investigate age-related differences is to use a **cross-sectional design**, comparing individuals of different ages. By comparing the social behaviors of groups of children at different ages researchers hope to determine how changes occur over the course of development. In one cross-sectional study, Harriet Rheingold and Carol Eckerman (1970) investigated the development of independence in young children. They recruited six different children at each 6-month age interval between 12 and 60 months. They then placed each child in a naturalistic setting, on a large lawn, and recorded how far the child moved away from his or her mother's side. They found that the older children traveled farther. Rheingold and Eckerman concluded that children's independence increases with age. But perhaps there were other reasons for their finding. The cross-sectional design yields no information about the causes behind age-related changes because we do not know what children in the study were like at younger ages. A longitudinal design is better suited to addressing the issue of individual change over time. In addition, perhaps the older children traveled farther because their mothers had taken them to the park more often than the younger children's mothers who were working full time as a result of a shift in maternal employment patterns. The cross-sectional approach does not establish that differences between groups are strictly related to participants' ages rather than other confounding factors, such as historical changes. To avoid this problem, researchers should repeat their cross-sectional comparisons with other samples of children at a later date.

longitudinal design
A study in which investigators follow the same people over a period of time, observing them repeatedly

THE LONGITUDINAL DESIGN   In a study using a **longitudinal design**, researchers follow a single group of children as they grow. Longitudinal studies vary in the ages at which they begin and the length of time they continue. For example, a study may start when the children are infants and follow them to toddlerhood; it may start at birth and continue to adulthood. No matter how long they last, longitudinal designs have a number of advantages. First, they allow researchers to follow children's development over time and to determine, for example, whether the distance children travel from their mother or the amount of time they spend watching television increases as they get older. Second, longitudinal designs allow researchers to study whether children's behavior patterns are stable, that is, whether toddlers who travel a long distance from their mother's side are more independent of mother later on or whether

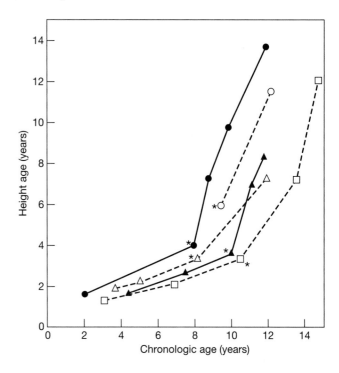

FIGURE 2.2 *Growth curves of five children in a longitudinal study showing that when the children were removed from an abusive home environment (★), they immediately gained in height. This study provides clear evidence that abuse inhibits growth.* Source: Sirotnak, 2008. Image reprinted with permission from eMedicine.com, 2010. Available at: http://emedicine.medscape.com/article/913843-overview.

children who throw more temper tantrums at age 2 are more likely to hit other children at age 4 and get into fights with their peers at age 14. Third, longitudinal designs allow researchers to explore possible causes of changes in behavior over time (see Figure 2.2). They can analyze links between early events (such as watching TV) and later behaviors (such as hitting class-mates) while statistically controlling for earlier behaviors (such as hitting siblings). By examining changes in children's aggressive behavior between one age and another as a function of TV viewing, they are on firmer ground in inferring that TV violence causes aggression.

But the longitudinal design also has disadvantages. It may take years to collect longitudinal data, and researchers often want information more quickly. In addition, there is the problem of losing participants. As time passes, people move, become ill, or simply lose interest, and results may be skewed by a shrinking sample. Moreover, even the sample of individuals who initially agreed to participate in a longitudinal project may not be representative of the general population. Not everyone wants to have their children or themselves observed, measured, and questioned for many years. Another problem with a longitudinal design is that it is not very flexible. It is difficult for researchers to incorporate new insights and methods into a study that is already under way. If a new test or technique is designed 10 years after the study has begun, what can investigators do? They can start over with a new sample and the new test, or they can begin to give the new test to their participants who are already 10 years old. But then they lose the possibility of comparing the children's earlier performance with later performance because the test instruments are not comparable. The best solution is to give children already in the study both the old test and the new test; however, this imposes a greater burden on participants and may require additional funds for the study. Another problem with a longitudinal design is practice effects, that is, the effects of repeatedly testing participants over many years. A way to avoid some of these problems is to conduct a short-term longitudinal study lasting only a few months or a few years. This has the advantages of reducing participant attrition and providing findings that can be used to design subsequent investigations incorporating newer research methods. A final drawback to lengthy longitudinal studies is that findings may be descriptive of only a particular age cohort and lose relevance as times change.

Into Adulthood:
Behavior in Childhood Predicts Adult Outcomes

The longest-running example of a longitudinal study linking childhood and adulthood began 90 years ago when Stanford psychologist Lewis Terman selected 1,528 California 11-year-olds of high intelligence, gave them extensive personality tests, and gathered details about their lives. His original goal was to track these children and assess whether they turned out to be psychologically normal or neurotic, introverted, or sickly eggheads. (It turned out they were neither sickly nor neurotic.) The "Termites," as they're fondly nicknamed because of their participation in the Terman study, have been tracked for decades now, through nearly all the milestones of life; more than half have died. They have provided a unique database from which researchers can determine whether personality types and early experience predict later health and well-being and with which they can investigate links between childhood characteristics, lifestyle choices, and adult success, health, and longevity. The database provides a rich demonstration of the value of a longitudinal design for understanding social development across the course of life.

At the onset of the study, parents rated their children's personality characteristics, including conscientiousness, cheerfulness, and optimism. Then, when they were 30 years old, the participants completed self-reports assessing these characteristics. The characteristic that was most predictive of longevity was conscientiousness, which was expressed in traits such as organization, thoroughness, reliability, and dutifulness (Friedman et al., 1995; Kern & Friedman, 2008). On average, Termites in the top quartile for conscientiousness lived 2 to 4 years longer than those in the bottom quartile. They lived longer because they were less likely to smoke and drink to excess, maintained more optimal weight, and lived more stable and less stressful lives (Friedman, 2008; Friedman et al., 1995; Hampson et al., 2006; Kern & Friedman, 2008). Other childhood traits were not so helpful. Cheerfulness predicted a shorter life (L. R. Martin et al., 2002) in part because cheerful individuals used more alcohol and cigarettes and engaged in more partying and riskier hobbies, such as aviation and hunting (Friedman, 2008). This study clearly illustrates how longitudinal investigations can help us understand the long-term consequences of childhood characteristics. It also showed that fate is not sealed in childhood. People who entered good jobs or good marriages sometimes became more conscientious as a result (Kern & Friedman, 2008).

Learning from Living Leaders:
L. Rowell Huesmann

Source: Courtesy of L. Rowell Huesmann.

Rowell Huesmann is Professor of Psychology and Communication Studies and Director of the Research Center for Groups Dynamics at the University of Michigan (where he was once an undergraduate). He intended to become a computer scientist and study artificial intelligence, but after receiving his Ph.D. from Carnegie-Mellon University, he became intrigued by the issue of how the environment shapes aggressive behavior in children. For the past 40 years, his work has been guided by one question: "What makes one child more aggressive than another?" Huesmann was particularly interested in two possible causes of aggression: the type of discipline parents use and how much and what type of television programs children watch. In a longitudinal study with his colleague, Len Eron, he followed a group of more than 700 American children who were first evaluated for their aggressiveness when they were 5 years of age, to determine whether punitive discipline or violent television was related to later aggression. They found that children who received harsh punishment and watched violent TV programs were more aggressive in childhood and that children who were highly aggressive, especially boys, were more likely as adults to have aggression-related problems, such as criminal convictions, moving traffic violations, drunk driving arrests, and incidents of domestic violence. Huesmann suggests that the next step is to develop a better understanding of the processes that operate during the viewing of media violence at both psychological and neurophysiological levels. Huesmann is editor of the international journal *Aggressive Behavior* and a recipient of the American Psychological Association's award for Distinguished Lifetime Contributions to Media Psychology.

Further Reading

Huesmann, L. R., & Taylor, L. D. (2006). The role of media violence in violent behavior. *Annual Review of Public Health, 27,* 393–415.

Lefkowitz, M. M., Eron, L. D., Walder, L. O., & Huesmann, L. R. (1977). *Growing up to be violent: A longitudinal study of the development of aggression.* New York: Pergamon Press.

THE SEQUENTIAL DESIGN A creative way around the problem of separating age-related changes from changes caused by the unique experiences of a particular age cohort is to use the **sequential design,** which combines features of both cross-sectional and longitudinal studies. In this design, researchers begin as they would in a cross-sectional study by selecting children of different ages, but then they follow the children longitudinally. For example, they might begin by recruiting and testing a sample of 2-year-olds, 4-year-olds, and 6-year-olds, and then every 2 years, they would test these children and add a new sample of 2-year-olds to the study. The study would stop when the oldest children in the initial cohort were 12. Figure 2.3 displays the design of this study.

sequential design
A way of studying change over time that combines features of both cross-sectional and longitudinal designs.

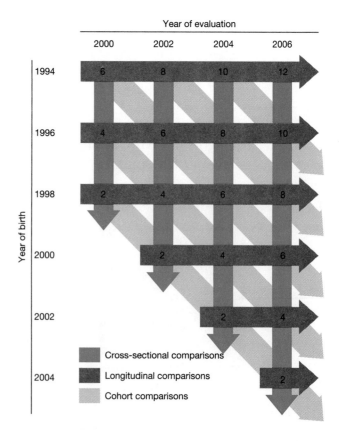

FIGURE 2.3 *Design for a sequential study. This combination of cross-sectional and longitudinal designs allows researchers to examine age-related changes and compare age cohorts at different points in time. The numbers within the arrows are the ages of the groups of children to be studied.*

TABLE 2.1 **Comparison of Methods of Studying Developmental Change over Time**

	Cross-Sectional	Longitudinal	Sequential
Time required for study is relatively	Short	Long	Moderate
Cost of study is likely to be	Low	High	Moderate
Participant attrition during study is most likely	Low	High	Moderate
Risk of staff turnover is	Low	High	Moderate
Possibility of using newest measures is	High	Low	Moderate
Likelihood of practice effect is	None	High	Low or moderate
Ability to assess links between early events and later behavior is	None	High	High for short-term
Ability to assess stability vs. instability of behavior patterns is	None	High	High for short-term
Ability to assess developmental paths of individuals is	None	High	High for short-term
Threat of a cohort effect tends to be	Unknown	High	Moderate

The sequential method offers several advantages. First, researchers can examine age-related changes in children's behavior and look at the stability of individual differences because they test the same children repeatedly. Second, researchers can examine practice effects because although some children are assessed four times, other children are assessed less often. Third, in following different age cohorts, researchers can explore generational effects, or effects of the particular time period in which children were born. For example, they can assess the effect of changes if the school curriculum is modified to emphasize reducing children's aggression. Finally, the sequential design saves time; 6 years after the start of this study, researchers have data spanning a period of 10 years—a 4-year saving over a traditional longitudinal study.

See Table 2.1 for a summary of some of the advantages and disadvantages of the three research designs—cross-sectional, longitudinal, and sequential. Researchers can avoid the problems of each method by combining their components in creative ways.

Selecting a Sample

If researchers wanted to study the typical social behaviors of preschool children, how would they go about it? How many preschool children would they have to study? They couldn't possibly study all of them; they would have to select a group of manageable size made up of children who are representative of the entire population of preschoolers. One of the important decisions in studying social development is how to select the study sample. Also important is the task of recruiting participants. Novice researchers are often surprised to find that getting participants is more time consuming (and frustrating) than running them through the research procedure. It's relatively easy if the researcher can use rats or college students, but otherwise, it's not a matter of simply putting up a sign-up sheet on the office door and hoping that a sample of 9-month-old infants or 14-year-olds will magically appear. Considerable effort must be spent negotiating with hospitals, doctors, child-care centers, school systems, churches, or community centers to convince them of the value of the research and gain access to their patients or attendees.

representative sample
A research sample in which participants are drawn from strata or categories (e.g., social classes or ethnic groups) in the same proportions as they are found in the larger population.

REPRESENTATIVENESS OF THE SAMPLE   If research conclusions are to be generalizable, it is critical that they be based on study of a **representative sample**, that is, a group of participants that possess the same characteristics as the larger population of interest to the researcher. Suppose a team of researchers who want to study the development of aggressive behavior in children selects a sample of children who have been referred to a psychological clinic because of behavior problems at home. The sample has 30 boys and 5 girls, and they all come from a poor neighborhood in a large urban area. The researchers evaluate various aspects of the children's behavior by watching them play with other children and asking them how they would resolve a dispute with a peer. They also assess how each child's parents get along and how much television the children watch. Ultimately, the researchers conclude that boys are more aggressive than girls and that aggression in children is related to watching television. Are they entitled to draw these conclusions? They are not. Children who are brought to a clinic because they have behavior problems at home are different from children whose families do not or cannot seek this kind of help. For this reason, the sample is biased toward children with more affluent or more conscientious parents. The sample is also skewed toward boys. Although it is possible that boys are more aggressive than girls, the sample of girls in this study is disproportionately small. In fact, it is too small to use as the basis for a gender comparison. Given the lack of representativeness in this sample, no basis exists for connecting television viewing with aggressiveness. To draw such a conclusion, the researchers would be better off testing relatively equal numbers of girls and boys (at least as many as 30 of each) who come from similar socioeconomic backgrounds and include both children who are and children who are not attending a clinic for behavior problems. Great care must be taken in generalizing from a restricted sample, for example, a sample that includes only one race, gender, social class, or geographical region. Increasingly, investigators are finding the selection of several samples helpful when each is made up of individuals who vary in race and social class and include both genders. By selecting multiple samples, researchers can be more certain that their conclusions do, in fact, apply to a broad range of people. This strategy can be used by investigators in different regions studying the same issues as well. If researchers in Vancouver, Helsinki, Berkeley, and Athens all produce similar findings, a particular place or sample clearly is not responsible for the results. When researchers use multiple samples and several researchers draw similar conclusions, they can have more confidence in their findings.

THE NATIONAL SURVEY APPROACH In a national survey, researchers select a large, nationally representative group of participants. A stratified sampling strategy is often used to ensure that boys and girls or individuals from different socioeconomic groups are represented in the same proportions as they exist in the general population. The National Longitudinal Survey of Youth (NLSY) is one example of a national survey. The study began in 1979 with a sample of nearly 12,000 participants ranging in age from 14 to 24 years and drawn from 235 geographic areas across the United States. An even larger survey is the National Children's Study, which began in 2009 and eventually will include more than 100,000 U.S. children who will be assessed from before birth to 21 years. Other nations also have national surveys. For example, the National Longitudinal Survey of Children and Youth (NLSCY) in Canada includes more than 30,000 children whose social and emotional development is being followed from birth to early adulthood. Sampling in these surveys must ensure representativeness of age, gender, socioeconomic status, marital status, ethnicity, and race—but some of these groups are more difficult to locate and recruit. Unless researchers make a special effort to include minority groups such as single mothers, Latinos, African Americans, French Canadians, or aboriginals, they will not learn about development in these groups. Therefore, they use a strategy of "oversampling" to recruit participants from these groups at higher rates than their proportions in the population (Miller, 2007).

Although national surveys allow researchers to draw conclusions that apply to entire populations and subpopulations, a major disadvantage is their cost in terms of time and labor. Another disadvantage is that these surveys are not well suited to answering questions about the psychological processes underlying social development. To study psychological processes in 20,000 children takes more time and money than most investigators have at their disposal. For this reason, a more intensive examination of a smaller subsample is sometimes used in combination with a national survey. A sample of 100 or 200 children might be selected from the large national sample and studied in depth to achieve a better understanding of developmental processes. Although this multistage sampling strategy is also expensive and time consuming, it gives researchers the best of both worlds: generalizability of their results to a large population and detailed investigation of social processes.

meta-analysis
A statistical technique that allows the researcher to summarize the results of many studies on a particular topic and to draw conclusions about the size and replicability of observed differences or associations.

effect size
An estimate of the magnitude of the difference between groups or the strength of the association between the factors, averaged across studies in a meta-analysis.

META-ANALYSIS: COMBINING RESULTS ACROSS STUDIES   Meta-analysis is a statistical technique that allows researchers to sum up the results of many studies on a particular topic, for example, the effects of television violence on children's aggressiveness (Cooper, 2009). The technique yields an overall estimate of the magnitude of the difference between experimental and control groups or the strength of associations between factors in correlational studies. This estimate is called the **effect size** (Rosenthal & DiMatteo, 2001). Conducting a meta-analysis permits researchers to draw conclusions about the size and reliability of observed differences rather than simply listing the results of different studies and looking to see whether they are consistent. In one meta-analysis of 217 studies investigating the links between exposure to television violence and child and adolescent antisocial behavior, researchers found a clear association between TV violence and antisocial behavior (Paik & Comstock, 1994). The effect size was 0.30. A more recent meta-analysis produced a similar finding (Bushman & Anderson, 2001). This effect size indicates that the association between watching violent TV programs and behaving aggressively is moderately strong.

Meta-analysis is an invaluable tool. However, a word of caution is needed. Although meta-analysis can provide an estimate of the reliability and strength of differences or associations across studies, the accuracy of that estimate is limited by the samples in the individual studies. If all of the studies in the meta-analysis included only white children from middle-class families, the conclusions would not necessarily apply to children of other classes, races, or ethnicities.

STUDYING DEVELOPMENT CROSS-CULTURALLY   In recent years, researchers have realized that selecting samples from different cultures can be a valuable research strategy. Finding that a behavior pattern is similar across cultures suggests that it is universal, whereas finding that behavior patterns differ markedly across cultures suggests that specific environmental variables play a significant role. Although cross-cultural research can be very informative, it is often difficult and expensive to conduct. Language differences and lack of familiarity with the underlying meanings of different customs and practices can lead researchers to erroneous conclusions. Successful cross-cultural studies benefit from the participation of cultural informants (Fung, 2010; Greenfield, Suzuki, et al., 2006; Rogoff, 2003). These are usually local people who serve as translators and interpreters and help researchers gain the trust of officials and other people with whom they need to collaborate. They also often assist in interpreting research findings. As awareness of cultural contributions to development increases, cross-cultural research is becoming more frequent.

Cultural Context:
Challenges for Researchers

Studying different cultural groups is full of challenges. Here are six suggestions that can help researchers conduct useful cross-cultural investigations:

Treat culture as a set of variables. Originally, cross-cultural researchers simply compared children from different cultures as if culture were a single independent variable. However, cultures are more complex than this.

They consist of many factors, such as beliefs and customs, religious orientations, and political systems. It is important for researchers to identify and disentangle these factors (Harkness & Super, 2002).

Choose representative cultural samples. Because variation within cultures can be as great as between cultures, it is important for researchers to obtain samples that reflect the diversity of the culture and to look at differences within cultures as well as between.

Study cultures that differ in meaningful ways. The era of cataloging differences between cultures just to satisfy our curiosity is over. Purely descriptive inquiries are best left to National Geographic and the Discovery Channel. The goal of contemporary cross-cultural research is to take advantage of naturally occurring variations to test meaningful theoretical hypotheses.

Avoid ethnocentrism. All researchers belong to a culture, and they use that culture as a frame of reference for viewing the customs and beliefs of other cultures. This can lead to characterizations of other cultures as inferior or deficient. The goal for researchers is to shed their own cultural clothing so they can focus on understanding the practices in other cultures (Kurtz-Costes et al., 1997).

Establish cultural equivalence of research instruments. Some researchers simply re-use an experimental paradigm developed in their home culture when they go into the field to do cross-cultural research. Unfortunately, this may lead to things getting "lost in translation." This is literally true when researchers simply translate an interview or questionnaire into another language (Pena, 2007). Although it is common to use a two-step process whereby a bilingual person translates the interview into the other language and then another person translates it back ("back translation"), problems may still exist. The exact equivalent of a verbal expression may not exist in the second language or it may carry a slightly different meaning.

Interpret findings in a culturally appropriate way. Researchers need to be sure that their interpretations of the actions and statements they observe in another culture are consistent with the interpretations that native members of the culture would make. Investigators should talk to informants from the culture before they collect data, include members of the culture in their data collection teams, and discuss the interpretation of the findings with informants after the data are collected and analyzed (Cooper et al., 2005).

Cross-cultural research can yield valuable insights, but these challenges, combined with the logistical problems of making contacts with people in other countries, establishing cooperation with them, and gaining their trust, make this a method for the persistent, patient, and committed.

Gathering Data

After researchers have decided what group or groups of individuals they want to study, they must decide exactly how they will study them. Essentially, they can use three methods of gathering data: asking children about themselves, asking other people who are close to the children about them, and observing children directly. Each approach has its advantages and limitations, and researchers' choices depend on the types of questions they are trying to answer.

Children's Self-Reports

self-report
Information that people provide about themselves either in a direct interview or in some written form, such as a questionnaire.

A **self-report** is information a person provides about himself or herself, typically by answering a set of questions the researcher has compiled. Soliciting such information from children presents special problems. Compared with adults, children are less attentive, slower to respond, and have more trouble understanding the questions that researchers ask. Despite these limitations, some types of information are difficult to obtain any other way (Cummings et al., 2000). As one researcher put it, "The child is the best authority on his own feelings, even if he has some trouble verbalizing those feelings … and … there are aspects of a child's daily life that his parents or teacher know little or nothing about" (Zill, 1986, pp. 23–24). In this researcher's study of a sample of 2,279 children between 7 and 11 years of age, parents' and children's responses to interview questions were judged to be equally truthful. Children's reports may be more limited than those of adults, but they are no less honest. Children were especially truthful when their parents were not present. Thus, interviewing children can provide unique and trustworthy information about children's daily lives and feelings. Special methods such as the "puppet interview" or the "story completion" technique are used to probe the thoughts and feelings of young children in a more indirect and fun way.

Research up Close:
The Puppet Interview Method

Source: Courtesy of Jennifer Ablow and Jeffrey Measelle, University of Oregon.

Assessing the perceptions and feelings of a young child can be a real challenge. Traditional questionnaires and interviews are not suitable for young children because of the children's short attention spans and limited cognitive and language abilities. One solution has come from clinical psychologists who for many years have used puppets to help diagnose and treat young children. Together, the therapist and child make up a story about some problematic aspect of the child's life, using puppets as props to help the child (Irwin, 1985; Woltman, 1972). This approach has been adapted by researchers as a tool for investigating the social experiences and characteristics of young children (see photo). Here is how it works: The interviewer poses a question to two puppets, for example, "What kind of child are you—a nice one or a not-so-nice one?" The puppets then volunteer opposing views about themselves, and the interviewer asks the child to say which puppet he or she agrees with or is most like. Jude Cassidy (1988) is one researcher who has used puppet interviews. She presented 5- and 6-year-olds with two puppets who made either positive

statements about themselves ("I'm a really nice kid a lot of the time") or negative statements ("I'm not a nice kid a lot of the time"). She found that children were able to describe the kind of child they thought they were simply by agreeing with one puppet or the other. Using this method, Cassidy showed that children with different types of early relationships with their mothers developed different self-concepts; those with high-quality relationships were less likely to agree with the puppet who said, "I'm a bad person" than children who had poor-quality relationships. Other researchers have used puppets to assess children's perceptions of their parents' relationships. In one study, 4- to 7-year-old children were presented with two puppets; one puppet said, "My parents fight a lot"; the other puppet said, "My parents don't fight a lot." One puppet said, "After my parents fight, they say they are sorry to each other"; the other puppet said, "After my parents fight, they don't say they are sorry to each other." Children's responses to the puppets were found to be related to reports from their fathers, mothers, and outside observers who watched the couple solve a problem—an indication that the children's responses were reliable assessments of the quality of their parents' marriage (Ablow et al., 2009). Moreover, the children's responses were related to their own aggressive behavior at school; the more conflict the children indicated they saw at home between their parents, the more aggressive and depressed the children were at school (Ablow, 2005). The puppet interview method is clearly a useful and age-appropriate alternative to traditional interviews and questionnaires for probing the views and perceptions of young children.

experience sampling method (ESM)
A data collection strategy by which participants are signaled at random times throughout the day and record answers to researchers' questions, such as: Where are you? Who are you with? What are you doing? Also called the *beeper* method.

Asking children to provide narrative descriptions of their activities over the recent past is another way to get self-reports. Children are asked to describe recent social events, such as a conflict with a peer, a teacher, or a parent. Robert Cairns and his colleagues (Cairns & Cairns, 1994; Xie et al., 2005) asked children, "Has anyone bothered you recently or caused you any trouble or made you mad?" The interviewer then followed up with questions such as, "Who was it? How did it start? What happened? What did you do? How did it end?" This interview protocol provided information about whether conflicts had occurred and how the children handled them. Similar interview protocols have been used to find out about children's positive social exchanges. However, coding narratives is very time consuming, and the reported events often do not represent all of the child's interpersonal exchanges.

To provide a more representative sample of children's experiences, researchers can use the **experience sampling method (ESM)** or "beeper" method. They give children wrist beepers, pagers, Palm Pilots, or smart phones that are programmed to "beep" at random times

Time signaled: ___4:05___   Time filled out:___4:06___

1. Where were you?

in the cafeteria at school

2. Were you at the **after-school program**? (Yes) No

21st Century

3. What was the **main** thing you were doing?

homework

4. What else were you doing?

eating snack

5. Who was **doing** this activity with you? Circle all that apply.

No one	Other adults I know
Mom/stepmom	1 friend
Dad/stepdad	(2 or more friends)
Brother/sister Age_____	Other kids
Adult relative	Boyfriend/girlfriend
Child relative Age_____	Anyone else? Who?
(Teacher(s))	_____
Program staff	

6. Who else was around but doing something else?

No one	Other adults I know
Mom/stepmom	1 friend
Dad/stepdad	2 or more friends
Brother/sister Age_____	(Other kids)
Adult relative	Boyfriend/girlfriend
Child relative Age_____	Adults I don't know
Teacher(s)	Anyone else? Who?
(Program staff)	_____

7. Circle an answer for **each** question about what you were doing.

	Not at all	Some- what	Pretty much	Very much
a. How much choice did you have about this activity?	1	(2)	3	4
b. How important was this activity to you?	1	2	(3)	4
c. Was it interesting?	1	2	3	(4)
d. Was it challenging?	1	2	(3)	4
e. Did you enjoy what you were doing?	1	2	3	4 9
f. How hard were you concentrating?	1	2	(3)	4
g. Were you using your skills?	1	2	(3)	4
h. Did you wish you were doing someting else?	1	2	(3)	4

8. How were you feeling when you were signaled? Circle an answer for **each** feeling.

	Not at all	A little	Some- what	Very much
Lonely	(1)	2	3	4
Happy	1	2	(3)	4
Angry	(1)	2	3	4
Stressed	1	(2)	3	4
Excited	(1)	2	3	4
Bored	1	(2)	3	4
Scared	(1)	2	3	4
Sad	(1)	2	3	4
Relaxed	1	(2)	(3)	4 3
Proud	1	(2)	3	4
Worried	1	(2)	3	4

FIGURE 2.4 *A sample answer sheet completed by a child using the experience sampling method. The child completed these questions when "beeped" throughout the day. Source: Vandell, Shernoff, et al., 2005.*

throughout the day. When the signal sounds, the child records (in a notebook or on the device) answers to the researchers' questions, such as: "Where are you? Who are you with? What are you doing? What is your mood?" This method of data collection allows children to report on their behaviors and feelings in a structured way that samples the settings in which the child's activities take place. Beeper studies have provided a great deal of information about how children spend their time, who they spend their time with, and how their moods are related to their activities (Larson, 2000). This method is particularly helpful for documenting changes in children's feelings over the course of a week, a month, or a year. Figure 2.4 provides an example of a beeper record of a child's activities and moods.

Learning from Living Leaders: Reed Larson

Source: Courtesy of Reed Larson.

Reed Larson knew he wanted to be a psychologist even before he finished high school. He attended his local university, the University of Minnesota, as an undergraduate and then completed his Ph.D. at the University of Chicago. Today he is Professor in Human and Community Development and Psychology and Educational Psychology at the University of Illinois. While in graduate school, Larson became interested in how people spend their time. He and his mentor developed a new method to study this issue, the experience sampling method (ESM). Like most innovative methods that turn out to be popular, the method was relatively simple and easy to use. Sometimes called the beeper method, the ESM tracked people's activities by asking them to wear a beeper set to sound at predetermined times. When the beeper went off, research participants indicated in a diary where they were, who they were with, what they were doing, and how they were feeling. Using this method, Larson gathered

detailed information about how children and adolescents in many countries around the world spend their time, the nature of their social lives, and how their moods and activities change with development. The ESM approach is now used by researchers in a wide variety of fields from geography to anthropology, and it has enriched our understanding of children's daily lives across a variety of settings from home to school to playground. Larson has found his work with the ESM to be rewarding because it led him into a variety of research topics including family and peer relationships, mental health, emotional development, and cross-cultural comparisons. His most recent work has focused on youth development programs such as 4H clubs, extracurricular activities, and structured after-school programs. The work has practical applications that he hopes will help sustain and improve these programs. Larson is currently President of the Society for Research on Adolescence. For him, the most pressing issue in developmental psychology is to understand the changing nature and challenges of the transition from adolescence to adulthood in nations around the world. He believes that we need to focus more on the positive aspects of development in adolescence rather than just on the problems. Consistent with this view, he has a positive message for students: "We need good people to enter the field and your insight and creativity could make a valuable contribution."

Further Reading

Brown, B., Larson R., & Saravathi, T. S. (Eds.) (2002). *The world's youth: Adolescence in eight regions of the globe*. New York: Cambridge University Press.

Larson, R., & Sheeber, L. (2008). The daily emotional experience of adolescents. In N. Allen & L. Sheeber (Eds.), *Adolescent emotional development and the emergence of depressive disorders* (pp. 11–32). New York: Cambridge University Press.

One of the newest approaches to the collection of self-report data is the result of another modern technological advance—the Internet (Fraley, 2004). Instead of asking children or adolescents to complete a paper-and-pencil questionnaire or conducting a phone interview, researchers can contact subjects and present their questions to them online. Most children in Westernized countries have access to a computer and the Internet (Patriarca et al., 2009; Pew Research Center, 2006). Until children of all income levels and ethnic groups have equal access, however, care must be taken to avoid recruiting biased and unrepresentative samples. Despite this problem, this approach to data collection has many advantages. Most obvious, Internet assessments are more convenient for both researchers and respondents. Children do not have to be physically present at a specific time—and neither do the researchers. Moreover, the Internet provides a way of increasing sample sizes and broadening research participation. It even offers an inexpensive and feasible way to include children from other countries. In addition, data collection by means of Internet surveys may be especially valuable for inquiries about sensitive topics that children may feel uncomfortable or embarrassed about answering in a face-to-face interview. Topics such as adolescent drinking, smoking, or sexuality may be more accurately assessed in the relative privacy of an Internet survey. This privacy has its own problems, though; because there is no researcher to supervise, children may not finish the survey or, worse, have someone else finish it for them. Careful follow-up reminders and incentives for completion can help limit these problems. As children become increasingly sophisticated Internet users at younger and younger ages, it is likely that the Internet will become even more valuable for studying social development.

Reports by Family Members, Teachers, and Peers

A second way of collecting data on children's social development is to solicit information from the people who know the children well. Most commonly, researchers seek this information from family members, teachers, peers, or friends.

FAMILY MEMBERS   One advantage of interviewing parents is that their reports are generally based on many observations made over time in a variety of situations. Another advantage is that, even if they are not totally accurate, parents' perceptions, expectations, beliefs, and interpretations of events and behavior may be just as important as objective reality (Bugental & Grusec, 2006; Collins & Repinski, 2001; Okagaki & Bingham, 2005). Children's behavior may be more influenced by their parents' perceptions of them than by their actual behavior.

Because family reports about children's social development are not always reliable, however, investigators have devised various strategies to increase their accuracy. They ask parents to report only very recent events to ensure more reliable memories; they may even phone in the evening to ask which specific behaviors (such as crying or disobeying) children have exhibited during the past 2 hours (Patterson, 1996; Patterson & Bank, 1989). They ask parents to keep a structured diary in which to record the child's behaviors at regular intervals, such as every hour (Hetherington, 1991). Social development researchers have even asked parents to carry the same kinds of beepers they have given child participants and had them record their activities and feelings and those of their children (Larson & Richards, 1994).

Another way that researchers have collected useful data from family members is by asking them to share their "family stories," accounts of personal experiences that have meaning to the family as a whole (Pratt & Fiese, 2004). We all recall stories we were told about our parents' or grandparents' experiences: "When I was your age, I used to walk three miles in the snow to get to school" or "When I was a little girl, I had to feed the chickens and the pigs every day." These stories reflect the values parents are instilling in their children. Family stories can also reveal cross-cultural variation (Wang, 2004a). Chinese and North American families, for example, emphasize different themes in their stories. Chinese families emphasize group loyalty and moral correctness; North American families focus on autonomy and self-assertiveness. Collecting family stories is an alternative to administering questionnaires and interviews and may provide unique information about families' lives.

B et You Thought That . . .
Parents Can Accurately Report Their Children's Early Years

Source: Steve Cole/iStockphoto.

Who knows a child better than his or her parents? Who knows more about the child's rearing than the parents? It would not be surprising if you thought that parents could provide the most accurate reports of their child's early years. Some researchers have thought so too. To find out about children and child rearing they have relied on mothers' reports. However, it turns out that these reports are often unreliable, inaccurate, and systematically distorted. Parents' reports of their early child-rearing practices and details of the timing of their children's developmental milestones are seldom consistent with independent assessments (Holden, 2002, 2009).

In one study, researchers collected mothers' reports of their infant-rearing practices when their children were 3 years old and compared them with reports collected when the children were infants (Robbins, 1963). This was possible because mothers had described their child-rearing practices during regular well-baby check-ups, and the researchers were able to compare these records kept by the pediatricians with mothers' later recollections. They discovered that many mothers had forgotten their earlier practices, and distortions in the mothers' recall tended to line up with the opinions of the child-rearing experts of the day. For example, in the edition of the book *Baby and Child Care* that was

widely used when the mothers were interviewed retrospectively, pediatrician Dr. Benjamin Spock made it clear that he disapproved of allowing children to suck their thumbs and approved of giving them pacifiers. All of the mothers who gave inaccurate reports about their children's thumb sucking denied that the children had ever sucked their thumbs and said that they had given them pacifiers—even though the actual records showed that the babies had sucked their thumbs, not pacifiers.

Why are parents so inaccurate? The simplest reason is that memory is fallible. Distortions fit with idealized expectations, cultural stereotypes, and expert advice. People are motivated to remember themselves in the best possible light. Therefore, parents remember themselves as more consistent, patient, and even-tempered than more objective assessments reveal (Holden, 2002). Parents are also mistaken in their recall of their children's behavior. Because they see their children as extensions of themselves, they are unlikely to report their children's problems. Few parents report that their children's development was slow; instead, they recall that their children were more capable than they really were. They report that their children walked earlier than they actually did and had more friends in preschool than was the case. Parents also gloss over aspects of their children's behavior that others outside the family view negatively. For example, a father might describe his son as a rough-and-tumble "real boy," full of good-natured mischief rather than the scourge of the neighborhood and the bane of his teacher's existence. Parents with more than one child are particularly likely to be confused. When asked to describe Jon, they may produce a composite profile that includes some of Jon and a lot of his brother, Jason. Just as parents sometimes call their children by their siblings' names, they confuse which child did what, when, and to whom.

TEACHERS AND PEERS   To find out about children's behavior in school and other settings when parents aren't present, researchers ask teachers and schoolmates. They may ask teachers to rate children on dimensions such as attentiveness, aggressiveness, and sociability, which the teachers have observed in the classroom or on the playground. They may ask children's classmates to rate how well children are accepted. For example, they might ask all youngsters in a class to rate each of the other children in terms of "How much I like to play with him" or "How much I like to work with her." The researchers then combine the ratings to get a picture of each child's social status in the classroom (Ladd, 2005; Rubin, Bukowski, et al., 2006).

Focus Groups

Another approach to studying social development is to use **focus groups**. Focus groups are commonly used in disciplines such as sociology and anthropology as well as by advertising agencies to help decide how to market soap, shampoo, salad dressing, and Saabs, but recently psychologists have begun to use them too. Usually six to ten adults or children participate. An interviewer poses a set of questions that the members of the group answer. These groups provide a unique opportunity for parents and children to talk about their concerns, values, and goals in a context that is less constrained and more relaxed than the more formal interview format.

This technique is particularly valuable in the early stages of a study when researchers are identifying salient issues for the participants they propose to study. For example, using focus groups has proven useful for identifying the roles of nonfamily mentors such as *compadres* (god-parents) in Latino families when simply asking questions based on European American families would have missed this important aspect of Latino children's socialization. Focus groups can increase the validity of a study by making sure that researchers ask the right questions and include all relevant factors. Focus groups can help researchers construct questionnaires by identifying culturally appropriate and inappropriate items (Silverstein, 2002). Finally, focus groups can help researchers understand cultural preferences in interviewing styles and alert them to topics they should avoid when talking to families of particular ethnic backgrounds.

The value of focus groups is not limited to the early stages of a research project. They are also useful at the end of a study after the data have been collected when researchers are trying to make sense of their findings. Talking to members of a focus group improves "interpretive validity" (Maxwell, 1992) by ensuring that researchers' interpretations of people's behaviors and narrative reports are consistent with the people's own understandings. For example, if researchers have videotaped African American parents and their children discussing common family problems such as curfews, homework, and time spent watching television, they can determine whether their interpretations of the interchanges are accurate by using a focus group of African American families. This approach helps avoid misinterpretations observed in earlier studies when European American researchers saw more conflict and restrictiveness in African American parent–child interactions than African Americans did (Gonzales et al., 1996). Clearly, it is critical to be sure researchers understand the meanings of children's and parents' behaviors and expressions in cultural groups that differ from their own.

Direct Observation

Despite the usefulness of children's self-reports, parents', teachers', and classmates' interviews and questionnaires, and family focus groups, there is often no substitute for **direct observation** of children's behavior. Students of social development make observations in *naturalistic* settings, such as children's homes, school playgrounds, lunchrooms, and after-school clubs and in *structured* settings, such as laboratories or playrooms where they give children and sometimes their parents tasks to perform.

NATURALISTIC OBSERVATION   Data collected in the child's natural settings can provide critical information about how children act in these settings. By using a **naturalistic observation**, researchers can find out how much time children spend interacting with other people and whether their interactions tend to be positive or negative. The problem with observations, though, is that the data are valid only if the presence of an observer has not distorted the participants' behavior. Parents and children often behave differently when they know an outside observer is watching them; for example, they are likely to inhibit their negative behavior (Graue & Walsh, 1998; Russell et al., 1991).

Attempts to minimize distortions in naturalistic observations include conducting repeated observations and using less obtrusive observational methods, such as an inconspicuous camera or an observer who pretends to be reading a notebook. In one study, for example, an observer came to the family's home each evening at dinner time for a period of several weeks (Feiring & Lewis, 1987). Families reported that they gradually become almost unaware of being observed. In another study, researchers observed increases in less acceptable behaviors, such as quarreling, criticizing, punishing, and using obscene language, as the number of observations increased (Boyum & Parke, 1995). Children and parents can become accustomed to being observed and display their real feelings and customary actions as long as researchers fade into the background.

One way for researchers to fade into the background is to observe children's behavior from a distance (Asher et al., 2001). In one study of aggression and bullying, for example, Debra Pepler and her colleagues set up a video camera overlooking a school playground and outfitted each child in the study with a small remote microphone and pocket-sized transmitter (Pepler et al., 1998). The remote mike allowed the researchers to eavesdrop on children's conversations with their peers during lunch and recess. These "eavesdropping" techniques picked up not only children's socially desirable behaviors but also their antisocial behavior and gossiping.

reactivity
The change in a person's behavior due to the fact that he or she is being observed.

The advantage of naturalistic observation is, of course, that researchers can observe children's and adults' behavior in the settings in which they typically occur so generalizability and validity are high. However, there are drawbacks. Problems of **reactivity** can occur, and if the assessments are too brief, the social behaviors of interest may not be observed (Hartmann & Pelzel, 2005). For example, a researcher interested in how parents respond to children's conflicts or cooperation could go home with a blank notebook after a long afternoon of observation if the siblings did not hit or share while she was there. This type of data collection is expensive and time consuming. It takes many more hours to collect samples of specific kinds of social behavior in a naturalistic observation than it does using questionnaires.

observer bias
An observer's tendency to be influenced by knowledge about the research design or hypothesis.

A further problem in naturalistic observation is **observer bias**. Observers' expectations may lead them to distort or misinterpret observed behaviors (Rosenthal, 2002). Researchers may reduce this problem by carefully training observers, clearly defining target behaviors, keeping observers "blind" or unaware of the hypotheses that guide the study, and frequently assessing the reliability or the extent to which two independent observers agree on their observed scores (Miller, 2007).

structured observation
A form of observation in which researchers create a situation so that behaviors they wish to study are more likely to occur.

STRUCTURED OBSERVATION   Researchers also use **structured observation** in a laboratory to elicit specific social behaviors and overcome some of the problems of naturalistic observation. To avoid the problem of infrequently occurring behavior, researchers arrange situations in which the behaviors are likely to occur. For example, they instruct parents to ask the child to obey certain rules or do certain tasks, such as cleaning up and putting away toys at the end of a play session. This structured observation permits an evaluation of the parents'

Research with very young children, like this 6-month-old infant, is becoming increasingly common as psychologists seek to expand knowledge about early social development. A video or digital recording will permit closer study of this child's behavior after the observation session is over. Source: Richard T. Nowitz/Photo Researchers.

disciplinary strategies and the child's compliance. In another structured observation, researchers set up opportunities for children to exercise self-control by not eating a candy or resisting the temptation to touch a wrapped present (Kochanska & Aksan, 2006). In a relatively short time, researchers can collect a variety of measures in a standard set of tasks that permits comparisons across children of different ages and family backgrounds.

Although this approach solves some of the problems of naturalistic observation, there are concerns about whether the observed behaviors are similar to those observed in everyday situations. In fact, children and parents often behave differently in a structured observation. They tend to express less negative emotion and exhibit more socially desirable behavior when observations are conducted in unfamiliar settings, such as a laboratory playroom, a doctor's office, or a hospital setting compared with their own homes (Hartmann & Pelzel, 2005; Johnson & Bolstad, 1973; Lamb et al., 1979).

To increase the ecological validity of structured observations, researchers try to make laboratories feel more like home. They hide an observer behind a one-way window or use a video camera camouflaged in a bookcase. They bring in couches, easy chairs, and magazines. One ingenious solution is to create a "laboratory apartment." Many decades ago, Arnold Gesell (1928) designed a laboratory "hotel" in which mothers and infants could come and stay for a few days under the watchful eyes of an observer who recorded their behaviors as the family went about daily routines of cooking, eating, napping, diaper changing, and playing. More recently, researchers have resurrected the concept of the laboratory apartment as a setting for observing parents and children under more naturalistic conditions (Radke-Yarrow & Klimes-Dorgan, 2002; Zahn-Waxler & Radke-Yarrow, 1982). The "apartment" is fully equipped with all of the comforts of home including sofa and armchairs, toys, kitchen, bathroom, books, and television. Families are videotaped (with hidden cameras) over the course of a day or across several days according to a schedule of events, such as breakfast, television viewing, nap time, toy play and cleanup so that all families are observed under similar structured conditions. Researchers who study marital relationships have used a similar strategy in which couples spend a weekend in a laboratory apartment and researchers watch how they resolve disputes and disagreements (Gottman, 1999; Gottman & Gottman, 2008). This strategy permits more valid generalizability than brief laboratory visits and at the same time increases the likelihood that phenomena of interest, such as parental discipline and marital conflicts, occur so that they can be observed and analyzed. But few researchers have the resources to set up laboratory apartments.

Ways of Recording and Coding Observations

When researchers observe children and their families directly, they must decide what behaviors to record, either live or on video, and how to code them.

specimen record
Researchers record everything a person does within a given period of time.

event sampling
Investigators record participants' behavior only when an event of particular interest occurs.

time sampling
Researchers record any of a set of predetermined behaviors that occur within a specified period of time.

BEHAVIOR OBSERVATIONS If researchers are interested in a broad range of behaviors, they may use a **specimen record** to describe everything the child or parent does during a specified period of time, say an hour or an afternoon. If they are interested in a particular type of behavior, such as the way a child responds to the parents' directions, they may use **event sampling** to capture only those incidents in which a specific event occurs, in this case, when a parent gives the child an order or request. With **time sampling**, the researcher records a set of predetermined behaviors that occur during a specific—relatively brief—time period. For example, if researchers want to observe a family for an hour, they might divide the hour into 120 30-second units, prepare a grid showing behaviors and time blocks, and then put a check beside each behavior that occurred in each block of time. This approach would provide a measure of the frequency of different kinds of behaviors during the hour. If the researcher wanted to examine a continuous stream of behavior, a better strategy would be to record events sequentially across the entire observation period (Bakeman & Gottman, 1997; Hartmann & Pelzel, 2005). This would allow the researcher to discover which behaviors came first and which responses followed; for example, the baby threw her cereal bowl to the floor; her mother scolded her; the baby cried; the mother picked up the baby and comforted her.

This stream of behavior provides a picture of mother–child interaction and enables researchers to answer questions such as, when the baby misbehaves, what is the mother's most common response? Observational methods are central to the study of social development. However, using multiple methods in the same study, such as combining observations with parent surveys or interviews, is also valuable. If findings from a variety of methods converge, researchers can more reasonably conclude that they have operationalized and measured their constructs adequately and their results are valid.

ethnography
Use of intensive observations and interviews to gather data about the beliefs, practices, and behaviors of individuals in a particular context or culture.

participant observation
Research strategy used to gain familiarity with a group of individuals by means of involvement in their activities, usually over an extended period of time.

ETHNOGRAPHIC APPROACHES **Ethnography** is a qualitative approach to research used in a variety of disciplines, especially anthropology; it involves using intensive observations and interviews to gather data about the beliefs, practices, and behaviors of individuals in a particular context or culture. For example, Margaret Mead (1928) gathered detailed accounts of daily life and routines in Samoa by living as a member of the community, interviewing key adults and adolescents, and recording her **participant observations**. More recently, Linda Burton and her colleagues have used the ethnographic approach to study children in neighborhoods, collecting a rich lode of data from field observations, focus groups, participant observations, and life history interviews with children and their families (Burton, 1997, 2007; Burton & Graham, 1998; Burton & Price-Spratlen, 1999).

Ethnographic techniques have some drawbacks, however. They offer somewhat subjective views of the community, context, or culture when community members try to put their group in the most favorable light. The usual routines of the group can be disrupted by the presence and participation of an outside observer. The researcher's field notes may be selective and biased. Analyzing the wealth of information provided by these techniques can be overwhelming. Limited generalizability is another obstacle for ethnography because the focus is usually on a single community or group and it is difficult to determine how much the in-depth portrait is unique to that group or context. Despite these drawbacks, the ethnographic approach is valuable for studying social development, most so when it is used in combination with other more objective approaches. For example, in the study of neighborhoods, researchers can use census tract data, objective descriptions of the physical characteristics of neighborhood conditions, and tallies of neighborhood resources (stores, schools, social services) to complement data gathered using ethnographic observations (Leventhal & Brooks-Gunn, 2000).

Learning from Living Leaders: Linda M. Burton

Source: Courtesy of Linda M. Burton.

Linda Burton is Professor of Sociology at Duke University, but you may have seen her as a game contestant on *The Price is Right, Joker's Wild,* or *Dream Home.* She was born, raised, and educated in California, and taught at Pennsylvania State University where she was the director of the Center for Human Development and Family Research in Diverse Contexts before she went to Duke. Her work focuses on the impact of poverty on families. As an ethnographer, she recognizes that close observation of children and families in their everyday settings such as homes and neighborhoods is a valuable approach to research because it provides richer descriptions of children's lives than other methods. She uses frequent visits and in-depth interviews with participants to better understand family dynamics. She also attends weddings, baby showers, and Sunday outings to observe families in different contexts. Studying poverty from a distance, she believes, gives an unrealistic, biased perspective. The strength of fieldwork is that it allows her to look at the nuanced behaviors people engage in. She also uses surveys, psychological studies, and geographic computer mapping systems to generate insights into the deeper issues of poverty. She is currently involved in a multisite collaborative study of the impact of welfare reform on families and children and an ethnographic study of rural poverty. Burton's interest in poor families began when she was growing up in Compton, a city in California known for its gang violence and a community where many girls are mothers by age 16. She took it as her responsibility to investigate ways to help families in poverty. If she gets on *Deal or No Deal,* she says, she will use her winnings

to help the families she's worked with over the years. But even if she is not a game show winner, Burton has already made a difference in the lives of many poor children and families through her close look at real world poverty.

Further Reading

Burton, L. M. (2007). Childhood adultification in economically disadvantaged families: An ethnographic perspective. *Family Relations, 56,* 329–345.

Roy, K., & Burton, L. M. (2007). Mothering through recruitment: Kinscription of non-residential fathers and father figures in low-income families. *Family Relations, 56,* 24–39.

NONVERBAL MEASURES To assess social development in babies and young children, researchers can observe their nonverbal responses. Even newborn infants make motor responses to social stimuli. Researchers can measure how much they move when a person approaches or talks. They can also record infants' sucking patterns, which change in intensity and duration as they encounter different social stimuli, including faces and voices (Saffran et al., 2006). Other useful nonverbal responses are smiling and vocalizing: 3-month-old babies smile more at their mother's face than at a stranger's, for instance (Camras et al., 1991). Crying is a response researchers can use to tap into babies' internal states because infants use different cries to communicate hunger, pain, and anger (Barr et al., 2000). Another informative nonverbal response is gazing. Researchers use this response in the "visual preference method." They show infants pairs of stimuli, such as two faces (one smiling and one neutral) or a picture of a face and a picture of a target, and measure the amount of time the infant spends looking at each. If infants look longer at one image than the other, it indicates that they are more interested in it.

habituation
An individual reacts with less and less intensity to a repeatedly presented stimulus until he or she responds only faintly or not at all.

Another response that is present in infancy is **habituation**. Babies, like the rest of us, get bored after seeing or hearing the same thing over and over again, and they habituate to a stimulus that is presented repeatedly or for a long time. The intensity of their reaction to the stimulus gradually decreases with each presentation until they respond only faintly or not at all. Babies habituate to sights, smells, tastes, and tactile sensations, and, therefore, these responses can be used to explore infants' social capabilities. Finally, researchers use infants' directed movements to study early social development. Young children use directed movements such as reaching, pointing, crawling, or toddling to express their interest in particular people. All of these nonverbal behaviors can be used as windows into infants' and young children's social responses and development.

psychophysiological
Physiological bases of psychological processes measured by brain activity, brain waves, and heart rate.

INTERNAL RESPONSES In recent years, researchers have begun to use **psychophysiological** techniques to examine internal processes that occur when children encounter social stimuli. Some of these psychophysiological techniques probe the autonomic nervous system (ANS), which controls such functions as heart rate and breathing (Bornstein & Arterberry, 1999). Researchers measure changes in a baby's respiration following changes in the pitch or volume of the mother's voice, for example. The usefulness of techniques probing the ANS is not limited to infants, however; they can provide information about social responses at any age. Changes in heart rate, for example, can be used to assess children's emotional reactions to different stressful events or to assess children's empathic reactions to other children's distress (Eisenberg et al., 2006; Gottman et al., 1997).

Researchers also use psychophysiological techniques to probe what's going on inside children's brains during social experiences and events. Table 2.2 outlines some of these techniques. Although researchers have long been able to measure children's brain waves by using

TABLE 2.2 **Techniques for Studying Human Brain Function and Structure**

EEG (electroencephalography)

What It Is

Recording of the brain's spontaneous electrical activity over a short period of time by means of multiple electrodes placed on the scalp.

Advantage

Detects very rapid changes in electrical activity allowing analysis of stages of cognitive processing

Disadvantage

Provides poor spatial resolution of the source of electrical activity

PET (positron-emission tomography) and SPECT (single-photon emission tomography)

What It Is

A visual image of an injected radioactive substance showing blood flow or glucose use reflecting changes in neuronal activity

Advantage

Provides spatial resolution better than EEG but less than MRI

Disadvantage

Cannot follow rapid changes (faster than 30 seconds); requires exposure to low levels of radioactivity

MRI (magnetic resonance imaging) and fMRI (functional magnetic resonance imaging)

What It Is

MRI is used to provide high spatial resolution of brain anatomy; fMRI is used to provide images of changes in blood flow that indicate specific anatomical details and changes in neural activity

Advantage

Provides high temporal resolution; requires no exposure to radioactivity

Disadvantage

High cost to operate

TMS (transcranial magnetic stimulation)

What It Is

Shows which brain regions are necessary for given tasks by changes after TMS is applied to a location

Advantage

Temporarily disrupts a specific region of brain by exposing it to intense magnetic energy

Disadvantage

Long-term safety not well established

Source: Bernstein et al., 2008.

well-placed electrodes to create an electroencephalograph (EEG), more recent techniques, such as positive-emission tomography (PET) and functional magnetic resonance imaging (fMRI), permit a look at changes in the brain when specific events or experiences occur. (To see a video record of some of these techniques, click on http://videos.howstuffworks.com/hsw/18677-understanding-the-amazing-brain-part-2-video.htm.) These techniques are more easily used with older children and adults, but researchers have modified them for use with infants and young children as well (Figure 2.5). These brain-imaging techniques show differences in brain activity related to what adults or children are thinking or feeling (Figure 2.6). They also reveal differences in the brain structures of children who have grown up in different circumstances, for example, in normal environments or under conditions of social deprivation or abuse (Fox et al., 2010; Nelson et al., 2006).

FIGURE 2.5 *Brain imaging of infants. Infant about to be given a brain scan.* Source: *Alexander Tsiaras/Photo Researchers.*

hormone
Powerful and highly specialized chemical substance produced by the cells of certain body organs, which has a regulatory effect on the activity of certain other organs.

cortisol
A hormone secreted by the adrenal glands in response to physical or psychological stress.

A third kind of psychophysiological technique used to study social development is measurement of **hormone** levels in the body. **Cortisol** is a hormone secreted by the adrenal glands in response to any kind of physical or psychological stress, a natural steroid that increases the activity of the part of the brain involved in vigilance and the control of arousal. Researchers use cortisol to assess children's emotional reactions to stress. In one laboratory, Megan Gunnar and her colleagues ask preschool children to play the "Tasting Game" (Gunnar et al., 2003). They offer the children a taste of sweet tart crystals and then ask them to hold a cotton roll or Q-tip in their mouths to absorb saliva; analysis of cortisol in the children's saliva reveals how well they manage stress. These researchers have found that children who have poorer relationships with other children at school have higher levels of cortisol when they are assessed in their classrooms than children who get along well with their classmates and that children in child care exhibit increased levels of cortisol as the day wears on (Watamura et al., 2003). They and other researchers have also found that infants raised in stressful environments, such as physically abusive homes or violent, crime-ridden neighborhoods, have higher levels of cortisol (Cicchetti et al., 2010; Gunnar, 1994; Nachmias et al., 1996).

FIGURE 2.6 *Here are four fMRI scans. In scan 1, the person was asked to remember a face. Areas at the rear of the brain that process visual information and an area in the frontal lobe were activated. In scan 2, the person was asked to "think about this face." The hippocampus was activated, showing that this part of the brain responds when we are remembering new information. In scans 3 and 4, the person was asked to compare another face to the remembered face. Some of the same visual areas were activated as during the initial memory task, but other areas, such as part of the frontal lobe, were also involved in making a decision about the memory.* Source: *Mark D'Esposito and Charan Ranganath, Department of Psychology & Helen Wills Neuroscience Institute, University of California, Berkeley, 2000.*

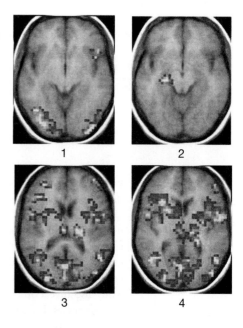

Learning from Living Leaders: Megan Gunnar

Source: Courtesy of Megan Gunnar.

variety of stressful events in children's lives, ranging from separation in child care to severe deprivation in Romanian orphanages. Although biologically minded, she recognizes the importance of environmental factors in determining stress reactions. Her proudest accomplishment–demonstrating that a secure attachment to the mother regulates the neurobiology of stress in infants and young children—illustrates the interplay between biology and environment. Her work identifying contexts that increase children's stress led to efforts to improve adverse early environments such as child care and orphanages. She has been recognized for her work with awards from the American Psychological Association and the Society for Research in Child Development. She hopes that in the future, the increased integration of genetics and neurological development will lead to more effective interventions for children in high stress situations. Her advice for undergraduates is to "Follow the duck, not the theory of the duck. Observe carefully and ponder." She has taken this advice as her guide, and the field has reaped the benefits.

Megan Gunnar is Professor in the Institute of Child Development at the University of Minnesota. She is a pioneer in studying children's stress reactions and has championed the measurement of stress through the collection of saliva, which contains the stress hormone cortisol. She did not set out to become the "queen of cortisol." In college, she thought she would be a music therapist. However, her experience as a Stanford University graduate student working with Eleanor Maccoby set the stage for her career-long pursuit of stress and development. The burning question that guided her work was, "What are the neurobiological and behavioral processes that shape the development of risk and resilience to adverse life circumstances?" To answer this question, she studied a

Further Reading

Gunnar, M. R. (2006). Social regulation of stress in early child development. In K. McCartney & D. Phillips (Eds.), *Blackwell handbook of early child development* (pp. 106–125). Blackwell Press.

Gunnar, M. R., & Talge, N. M. (2007). Neuroendocrine measures in developmental research. In L. A. Schmidt & S. J. Segalowitz (Eds.), *Developmental psychophysiology: Theory, systems, and methods* (pp. 343–366). Cambridge:Cambridge University Press.

Analyzing Data

qualitative study
Research using nonstatistical analysis of materials gathered from a relatively small number of participants to gain an in-depth understanding of behavior and contexts.

After researchers have completed their data collection, the final step in the research process is to analyze the information that has been accumulated. For researchers conducting a **qualitative study**, this requires searching for meaningful themes in the notes and transcripts they have collected during open-ended interviews, participant observations, focus groups, ethnographic observations, and individual cases. This approach is appropriate when the researcher's goal is not to confirm or falsify a hypothesis but to explore the characteristics of a specific individual, group of individuals, or context. For some researchers taking this approach, a series of subjective summaries describing these individuals or contexts represents the final step in the research process. Other researchers use qualitative insights to guide an additional phase in the research process: developing quantitative measures that reflect the qualitative themes and designing a study to investigate them in a larger sample. In this case, the qualitative phase functions as a pilot study that helps ensure that the quantitative inquiry includes relevant aspects of the issue.

quantitative study
Research involving statistical analysis of numerical data.

In a **quantitative study**, analyses involve turning observations, interviews, and test results into numbers and making sense of them. The first step is to summarize the numbers using descriptive statistics, such as the average (mean) score for children in a particular group. For example, the researcher could calculate average aggression scores for children who are high, medium, and low viewers of violent TV programs. The next step is to determine whether these differences are statistically significant or merely due to chance. An analysis of variance (ANOVA) or a *t* test is a statistical technique to determine whether mean differences between groups are reliable and significant. If the researcher's data came from an experiment in which children were exposed to violent TV and then were observed pummeling and punching their peers, the analysis of differences would be used to compare aggressive behavior exhibited by children in the experimental and control groups. Based on the outcome of this statistical test, the researcher can make a first estimate of whether there is support for the hypothesis that watchers of violent TV are more aggressive than nonwatchers. Alternatively, the researcher could investigate whether a significant correlation exists between the amount of violent TV watched and the amount of aggressive behavior displayed.

In most studies, researchers go beyond these simple analyses and investigate the effects of multiple variables. In a study of children's aggressive behavior, for example, they might analyze variables such as the child's ethnicity, IQ, temperament, and gender as well as TV viewing. They can statistically control the contributions of these other variables or compute the relative contributions of each to the child's aggressive behavior. Either way, they would use a multiple-regression analysis. This is an extension of the correlation approach that analyzes associations among a number of variables simultaneously or sequentially. A particular kind of regression analysis, path analysis (Figure 2.7), can be used to investigate whether variables are linked by direct or indirect pathways. For example, the researcher might investigate whether the association between TV viewing and aggressive behavior is simple and direct—children who watch more violent TV are more aggressive—or is mediated by parental punishment—children who watch more violent TV programs are spanked more, leading to more frequent aggression (for more about mediational analyses, see MacKinnon et al., 2007). Multiple-regression analyses can also be used to determine whether one variable moderates the effect of another. For example, is the effect of TV viewing on aggression moderated by the child's temperament so that children with difficult temperaments are more affected by watching violent shows than are children with easy temperaments? In that case, the researcher might conclude that having an easy-going temperament provides a buffer against the effect of violent TV.

Structural equation modeling (SEM) is a powerful type of multivariate analysis that creates "latent" variables representing higher-level psychological constructs—for example, a latent variable representing "aggressiveness" might be derived from the frequency with which a child hits and insults classmates during an observation at school recess, the number of violent tactics

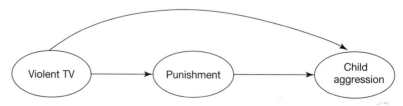

Figure 2.7 *Path analysis showing direct link between violent television watching and child aggression (top line) and indirect link mediated by parental punishment (bottom lines).*

the child endorses in a questionnaire, and the child's preference for sword fighting over playing Scrabble. The researcher then analyzes associations among latent variables to test hypothesized causal relations (for more about SEM see Schumacker & Lomax, 2004).

Statistical techniques are also available to analyze changes in children's social behavior over time. These techniques identify trajectories or growth curves in social behaviors and indicate whether individual differences in these trajectories are related to predictor variables; for example, is watching TV violence related to an increase in aggressive behavior as children get older?

In studies of changes in children's social behavior over time, researchers often face the problem of participant attrition. This can bias the sample because parents with less education and motivation are more likely to drop out. It also reduces sample size and thereby researchers' ability to evaluate their hypotheses. In recent years, strategies have been developed for estimating the scores of the missing participants and using these substitute scores to restore the sample size to an adequate level for statistical analyses (MacKinnon & Dwyer, 2003). This is just one improved statistical technique now available to researchers. Every year, statistical advances allow for more complex analyses. You should remember, though, that the simplest techniques can often provide meaningful results and the most complex techniques cannot salvage a poorly conceptualized study.

Ethics of Research with Children

In recent decades, awareness of the ethical issues involved in doing research with children has been growing. Government boards and professional organizations have suggested guidelines to protect children from dangerous and harmful procedures (see Table 2.3). In addition, all legitimate research projects involving children are scrutinized and approved by an institutional review board (IRB) where the research is conducted. This scrutiny ensures that researchers follow ethical guidelines.

informed consent
Agreement to participate in a study based on a full understanding of its purposes and procedures.

All research with human subjects requires that researchers obtain informed consent from participants before they are enrolled in the study. **Informed consent** is an agreement to participate based on a clear understanding of the purposes of the study and the procedures that will be followed. When participants are children, their parents or legal guardians must provide informed consent on their behalf because the children do not have the capacity to fully understand the goals, risks, and benefits of the research (Institute of Medicine, 2004). If children are recruited through a school or other institution, teachers and administrators provide another layer of consent that is particularly important when parents don't pay close attention to school activities, or when, for some reason, they neglect their children's interests (Fisher, 2008; Thompson, 1990). When children reach an age at which they begin to understand what they are going to be asked to do in a study, usually around age 8, they are also asked to give their assent before the study begins. Using the Internet for data collection is a new approach to research and raises new ethical issues about gaining informed consent (Fraley, 2004). The challenge is to ensure that the participants are old enough to give consent, and if they are not, to obtain parental consent.

Ethical guidelines include the protection of participants from harm—not only physical harm but also psychological and emotional harm. Children have the right not to be made to feel uncomfortable or to act in ways that lessen their own view of themselves or the way other people view them. Review boards examine research protocols carefully to be sure that the procedures will not make children feel embarrassed, rejected, unhappy, or tricked.

Although it is easy to agree in principle that research participants, especially children, should not be harmed, determining what is harmful is not always easy. For example, in an experimental procedure called the "Strange Situation," which is used to assess children's social

TABLE 2.3 **Children's Rights in Social Development Research**

1. *The right to be fully informed.* Every child has the right to full and truthful information about the purposes and procedures of a study in which he or she is to participate.

2. *The right to give informed and voluntary consent.* Every child has the right to agree, orally or in writing, to participate in a research project. If a child is too young to understand the study and make an informed decision, researchers must obtain the informed consent of the child's parents or those who act *in loco parentis* such as teachers or camp counselors who are temporarily responsible for the child.

3. *The right not to be harmed in any way.* Every child has the right not to experience physical or psychological harm as a result of the research procedures.

4. *The right to withdraw voluntarily from research.* Every child has the right to withdraw from participation in the study at any time.

5. *The right to be informed of the results of research.* Every child has the right to information about the results of the research. If the child is too young to fully understand, the information must be provided to the child's parents.

6. *The right to confidentiality.* Every child has the right to know that personal information gathered as part of the research will remain private and confidential and will not be shared with any other individuals or agencies.

7. *The right to full compensation.* Every child has the right to be compensated for time and effort as a research participant even if he or she withdraws from the study. Incentives must be fair and not exceed the range children normally receive; this precaution ensures that incentives are not used to coerce the child to participate.

8. *The right to beneficial treatments.* Every child has the right to profit from any beneficial treatments provided to other participants in the research. When experimental treatments are deemed beneficial, for example, participants in control groups have the right to the same beneficial treatment after the project is completed.

Sources: Based on reports from the American Psychological Association (2002) and the Society for Research on Child Development, Committee on Ethical Conduct in Child Development Research (2007).

relationships with their caregivers, infants are left alone for several minutes, and often they fuss or cry, indicating that they are distressed. This procedure has yielded important information about early social-emotional development, but is the infants' distress justified? The general rule is that if children's level of discomfort or embarrassment does not exceed what they are likely to experience during their regular daily life, it is permitted. Because babies are often left alone briefly, this procedure is considered ethical.

What about deceiving children? In Liebert and Baron's (1972) experiment showing children violent TV programs, was it ethical to let the children believe they were causing another child actual physical harm when they pushed the "hurt" button? How might the children have viewed themselves—or the experimenters—after the study? It is important to debrief children after the experiment is over, but is this enough? Laboratory research involving deception is becoming less common as IRBs demand more careful scrutiny of ethical issues. Another ethical issue is whether providing participants with full disclosure before the study begins is necessary. Even if there is no outright deception, details can sometimes be omitted. What if revealing this information could encourage the parents or children to act in ways that turned the hypotheses into self-fulfilling prophecies? In the final analysis, the guiding principle involves a careful cost-benefit analysis. What effects, if any, might participation in the research project have on the children to be studied, and how do these effects weigh against the possible gains from whatever information may be obtained from the research?

Social developmental research is a tool for increasing our knowledge about children, and it is hoped that children will benefit from the knowledge. Although some investigators and child advocates have called for more stringent criteria regulating the participation of children in psychological research, others worry that too many additional restrictions will seriously impede psychologists' ability to learn more about issues that may ultimately lead to benefits for children. The ethics of research in social development will continue to be a topic of debate for the foreseeable future.

Chapter Summary

Scientific Method, Hypotheses, and Questions

- Following the scientific method, social development researchers use reliable and replicable techniques to collect and analyze data to answer their questions or test their theory-based hypotheses.

Research Methods: Correlations and Experiments

- The correlational method involves computing associations between pairs of variables, varying from −1.0 to + 1.0. Correlated variables are related to each other, but one does not necessarily cause the other.

- A laboratory experiment permits a researcher to establish a causal association by manipulating the independent variable and assessing the effect on the dependent variable in a controlled setting. Researchers randomly assign participants to experimental and control groups.

- One way to increase ecological validity is to conduct a laboratory analogue experiment, trying to duplicate in the laboratory features or events from everyday life.

- Another way to increase ecological validity is to conduct a field experiment, deliberately producing a change in a real-life setting and measuring the outcome.

- In a natural experiment, the investigator measures the effect of a naturally occurring change. Interpreting the results is often difficult because the researcher lacks control over the independent variable and other factors that could affect behavior.

- Lab and field designs can be combined to permit the introduction of the independent variable in the field and measurement of the dependent variable in the lab, or the independent variable can be introduced in the lab and the dependent outcome is measured in the field.

- The case study method takes an in-depth look at a single child or a small group of children who often have some uncommon feature that makes them of special interest.

Study of Change over Time

- In the cross-sectional method, researchers compare groups of children of different ages. This approach is economical, but it yields no information about change or causes of change. The longitudinal method overcomes these two drawbacks because the researcher examines the same children at different times in their lives. Longitudinal research has disadvantages that include high cost, loss of subjects, untested age cohort effects, and limited flexibility to incorporate new measures.

- The sequential method combines features of cross-sectional and longitudinal studies and enables researchers to compare groups of children of different ages, track individual children as they get older, and compare age cohorts.

Sample Selection

- Samples should be representative of the population of interest to the researcher. Stratified sampling can be used to ensure that subgroups of boys and girls or individuals from different ethnic or social class groups are represented in the same proportions as they exist in the population.

Data Collection and Analysis

- Self-reports provide information about children's thoughts, attitudes, and feelings. In the experience sampling method, a "beeper" signals children to record their activities, thoughts, and emotions at random times.

- The accuracy of reports from parents, siblings, teachers, or peers can be improved by focusing on recent events and using structured procedures such as daily diaries, phone calls, or beeper methods.

- A focus group allows children or adults to share their views about different aspects of children's social experience. This strategy is especially useful in the early stages of a research project or with a new cultural group.

- Observations can occur in natural settings, such as a child's home, or in a laboratory. One limitation is that when children and parents know they are being watched, they act in more socially acceptable ways. To minimize such distortions, researchers try to observe unobtrusively for relatively long periods. A structured observation allows researchers to observe children performing in specific situations that occur infrequently in normal everyday life.

- Researchers can record everything the participant does (a specimen record), record only particular events (event sampling), identify which behaviors of a predetermined set occurred during a particular time period (time sampling) or record events in order of occurrence (sequential observation).

- Ethnographic data collection involves becoming a participant observer by spending time with community members and recording information about their activities and the setting.

- To study infants, who cannot express their thoughts and preferences verbally, researchers use nonverbal responses such as visual preferences, habituation to stimuli, physical movement, and sucking patterns.

- Psychophysiological assessments of heart rate, respiration rate, brain activity, and hormone levels are useful for obtaining information about children's responses to social situations and stress.

- In qualitative studies, researchers search for meaningful themes in transcripts of interviews or participant observations. In quantitative studies, statistical analyses are performed to determine differences between groups of children or associations between variables. Multiple-regression analyses are used to examine associations among a number of variables.

Ethics

- Ethical issues are a major consideration in research on children. Guidelines for ethical treatment include the right to informed consent and the right not to be harmed. To determine whether research procedures are ethical, costs to participants are carefully weighed against the potential benefits to the participants or society.

Key Terms

case study	focus group	operationalization
construct	habituation	participant observation
cortisol	hormone	psychophysiological
cross-sectional design	independent variable	qualitative study
dependent variable	informed consent	quantitative study
direct observation	intervention	reactivity
ecological validity	laboratory analogue	representative sample
effect size	experiment	self-report
ethnography	longitudinal design	sequential design
event sampling	meta-analysis	specimen record
experience sampling	natural experiment	structured observation
method (ESM)	naturalistic observation	time sampling
field experiment	observer bias	

At the Movies

A number of movies illustrate the methods researchers use to study social development. One of the best is *The Up Series (Seven Up; 7 Plus Seven; 21 Up; 28 Up; 35 Up; 42 Up; and 49 Up)*. These documentary films demonstrate how a longitudinal design gives unique and invaluable information about development over many years. The series started in 1964 when the filmmaker interviewed 14 children from diverse backgrounds from all over England, asking them about their lives and their dreams for the future. Then, every 7 years, he went back to talk to them, examining the progression of their lives. The series provides an astonishing look at life in the 20th century and demonstrates how children's life paths could and could not be predicted from an early age. Now *The Up Series* has been taken to South Africa where a group of children was filmed starting in 1992 at the age of 7.

A DVD containing films from the 1940s, *1940's Child Psychology & Sociology Tests on Film: History of Child Development & Human Behavior*, shows some classic psychological studies: *Growth Study of Johnny and Jimmy* is a case study intervention in which the researcher gave one infant extra stimulation and documented his physical and psychological development and compared it with an infant given no additional stimulation. *Experimental Studies in the Social Climates of Groups* portrays an experiment in which three groups of children interacted with an adult leader who demonstrated three different styles of management (authoritarian, laissez faire, democratic).

Structured observations are illustrated in *ABC News Primetime Ethical Dilemmas: What Would You Do?* (2007). The producers used a hidden camera to see what people would do when confronted with an ethical dilemma, such as bullies ganging up on an innocent child. This parallels experimental procedures a researcher might follow, but *Primetime* probably didn't get IRB approval. A movie demonstrating a field experiment is *Trust Me: Shalom, Salaam, Peace* (2002). Christian, Jewish, and Muslim boys were sent to a mixed-religion summer camp. The film follows their progress as they engage in camp activities and forge friendships.

A number of films illustrate natural experiments. Films about children living in extreme conditions include *Children Underground* (2001), a documentary following five homeless children in Romania after the collapse of communism led to a life on the street, and *Kids of the Majestic* (2008), a film about orphans living beneath the railway station in Bangalore City. *Soldier Child* (2005) shows the army of brainwashed children in Northern Uganda who were forced to commit unspeakable crimes against their own families. On a more positive note—not all natural experiments have to be negative—*Commune* (2006) shows what happened when artists and activists moved to a remote California wilderness to create a new world in the early 1970s armed only with the slogan "Free Land for Free People." The documentary offers a candid look into the joys and difficulties of free love, nude farming, survival in the wilderness, multiple-parent child rearing, and other aspects of communal living.

CHAPTER 3

Biological Foundations: Genes, Temperament, and More

Source: Kirill Zdorov/iStockphoto.

Baby Kendra stares at her mother's face while she is nursing. Baby Benjamin watches as his father leans over the side of his bassinette. From the first minutes of life, babies gaze, wiggle, and cry. They are adept attention seekers and able to communicate their needs with remarkable effectiveness. Next door, baby Rehema is crying as usual. She is irritable and difficult to soothe. Her parent can't get over how different she is from her older brother—or from other babies in the Mommy and Me playgroup. Down the street, 4-year-old twins Cassie and Sassie dress alike, talk alike, and both want Zhu Zhu pets for Christmas. Underlying the behaviors of all these children are biological foundations of social development, which are the topic of this chapter.

Biology provides a foundation for social development in many ways. Hormones and brain-waves, DNA and physical appearance, as well as reflexes and unconditioned responses are all aspects of biology that underlie social behavior. We have selected four specific aspects of biology that contribute to children's social development to discuss in this chapter. The first is the biological "preparedness" that gives babies a head start in their developmental journey. Visual, auditory, olfactory, and tactile capacities present at birth make infants ready for social interaction and ensure their survival. The second biological foundation we discuss is neurological. We explore brain regions and brain growth and how they are related to social behavior and advances in social development. The third biological foundation is genetics. Genes make each person unique; they shape children's characteristics and affect the ways in which the social world responds to them as well. We examine what genes are and how they are transmitted from generation to generation, how they guide development, and how they interact with environmental factors. Finally, we examine a fourth biological foundation—differences in temperament. From the moment they're born, babies differ from one another in how much and how intensely they gaze, smile, and cry. One baby may sleep most of the time, while another is scanning his surroundings; one baby may be irritable and cry a lot, while another lies quietly. These differences reflect the infants' temperaments.

Biological Preparedness for Social Interaction

Infant are well equipped to respond to their social environments. Their sensory and perceptual systems are biologically prepared to be sensitive to social stimuli such as human voices, faces, and smells, and their capacity to notice and respond to social stimuli propels them into social interactions. Such preparation is clearly adaptive because babies' responsiveness to other human beings increases their caregivers' interest and attention and ensures the infants' well-being.

How Are Babies Prepared?

FROM BIOLOGICAL RHYTHMS TO SOCIAL RHYTHMS   One way in which babies are biologically prepared for social interaction is that their behavior follows biological rhythms, which they soon learn to control and regulate. Babies who acquire biological regulatory skills over the first 3 months of life are able to interact with their mothers in a synchronous way (Feldman, 2006). By "synchrony," we mean that the mother and infant show a predictable degree of responsiveness to each other's signals during a brief interaction. When infants are born 6 to 10 weeks prematurely, biological rhythms, such as the sleep-wake cycle, have not fully developed; this, plus later deficiencies in arousal regulation, are linked to poorer social interaction synchrony with the mother at 3 months. This evidence suggests that, under normal developmental conditions, babies develop biological rhythms that help them deal with the time-based nature of social interaction.

VISUAL PREPARATION FOR SOCIAL INTERACTION   A second way in which infants are biologically prepared for social interaction is that they are attracted to visual social stimuli. They stare longest at objects that have large visible elements, movement, clear contours, and a lot of contrast—all qualities that exist in the human face (Farroni et al., 2005). Faces are appealing because they have boundaries, such as hairlines and chins, and contrasts, such as dark lips and light skin, and are often moving and bobbing. People are also likely to exaggerate their facial expressions when they are interacting with a baby, taking a longer time to make a face and prolonging the expression (Schaffer, 1996). Young infants scan these faces looking at the features they can see best—eyes, mouth, and hair (Figure 3.1; Haith et al., 1977; Maurer & Salapatek, 1976). They are particularly interested in eyes, as their preference for faces that

FIGURE 3.1 *How infants scan the human face. (a) A 1-month-old baby focuses on the outer perimeter of the face, although also showing some interest in the eyes. (b) A 2-month-old scans more broadly and focuses on the features of the face, paying attention to the eyes and mouth, which suggests that some pattern detection may be occurring.* Source: Maurer & Salapatek, 1976.

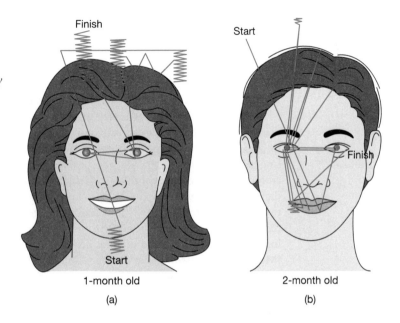

1-month old

(a)

2-month old

(b)

are looking directly at them indicates (Farroni et al., 2002). In fact, studies have shown that when men are given a nasal spray of oxytocin, a neurotransmitter hormone that is released in large quantities in women during labor and childbirth and passed on to their infants through the placenta, they—like infants—pay more attention to the eye areas of the face (Guastella et al., 2008). By 3 months of age, infants identify a face as a unique whole (Dannemiller & Stephens, 1988). They look longer and show more brain activity in response to faces than objects (Johnson, 2000), and they prefer their mother's face to the face of a stranger (Walton et al., 1992). Over the first year of life, infants become increasingly skilled and speedy at processing human faces (Rose et al., 2002; Turati, 2004). Being able to extract information quickly and reliably is critical for developing social abilities. Functional magnetic resonance imaging (fMRI) studies suggest that a cortical region is specifically devoted to face recognition (Tsao et al., 2006; Kanwisher & Yovel, 2006). Whether brain cells in this region are specialized in human infants at birth or need experience to fully activate the "specialty" cells is not yet clear. What is clear is that babies are biologically designed and prepared to respond to faces through their brain architecture.

AUDITORY PREPAREDNESS FOR SOCIAL INTERACTION Babies' auditory system is well developed even before birth. When researchers have monitored changes in fetuses' body movements and heart rates, they have found that they can hear complex sounds outside the mother's body (Kisilevsky & Muir, 1991). Babies can even remember a story they have heard before they were born. In one study, researchers asked pregnant women to read aloud Dr. Seuss's *The Cat in the Hat* twice a day for the last 6½ weeks of their pregnancies. After birth, their infants preferred to listen to *The Cat in the Hat* rather than an unfamiliar book, *The King, the Mice and the Cheese* (DeCasper & Spence, 1986). Apparently, fetuses can distinguish sounds and rhythms. They may even be biologically programmed to respond to the sound of human voices (Aslin, 1987; Saffran et al., 2006). Babies open their eyes wider and look for the speaker when they hear voices. By 4 months of age, they can discriminate differences among almost all of the more than 50 phonetic contrasts in adult languages (Hespos & Spelke, 2004).

Babies especially like a voice that is high in pitch with exaggerated pitch contours (Fernald, 1992; Saffran et al., 2006). In fact, very young babies are able to hear a high-pitched sound better than a low-pitched one (Aslin et al., 1998; Saffran et al., 2006). Adults may be aware of this because they usually speak to infants using a high-pitched and melodic voice (Fernald & Mazzie, 1991). Mothers and fathers are likely to exaggerate their speech. They talk louder and slower and use longer vowels with their infants than when they speak to anyone else. A mother might say, "Hi-swee-eet-ee, Hiii, Hi-i-ya, watcha looking at? Hu-u-uh? O-o-o-o-o-o, yeah, it's mommy ye-e-a-ah" (Stern, 1974, p. 192). Adults also speak to infants and young children in shorter sentences, more slowly, often ending sentences with a rising intonation (Fernald & Morikawa, 1993). Infants prefer to listen to this kind of "baby talk" and enjoy it more than speech directed to an adult (Cooper & Aslin, 1990; Werker et al., 1994) whether the speaker is a man or a woman (Pegg et al., 1992) and even if the speech is not in their native language (Werker et al., 1994). Soon babies develop a preference for the language they hear around them (Kinzler et al., 2007; Mehler et al., 1988), however, and by 9 months of age, they "tune out" words and sounds from other languages (Jusczyk et al., 1993). The familiar tones and speech patterns they hear lead to a pattern of interaction between infants and parents that facilitates early social bonds. Infants also respond to speakers' emotional tones, responding positively to warm and inviting utterances and negatively to angry and prohibitory ones (Mumme et al., 1996). Early auditory skills and preferences thus have functional significance for social development.

SMELL, TASTE, AND TOUCH Infants' senses of smell, taste, and touch provide other avenues for social development. Newborns can discriminate among different odors and tastes and prefer those that adults find pleasant (Rosenstein & Oster, 1988; Steiner, 1979). They cry less, open their eyes, and try to suck when they smell their mother's breast, and they prefer the odor of their mother's milk to that of another mother (Doucet et al., 2007; Porter et al., 1992). Mothers, too, recognize the scent of their babies after only 1 or 2 days (Mennella & Beauchamp, 1996). Clearly, infants' sense of smell provides an early guide to the people in their world, and the ability of babies and their mothers to recognize each other by smell may play a role in the development of their relationship (Porter & Winberg, 1999). Infants also develop preferences for the food flavors consumed by their mothers (Mennella & Beauchamp, 1996). Perhaps one benefit of breast-feeding is that it provides an opportunity for the infant to become familiar with the flavors of the foods favored by the mother, her family, and her culture.

The sense of touch is one of the first senses to develop. The skin is the largest sense organ in the body and from the beginning of fetal life, babies' skin is surrounded and caressed by warm fluid and tissues. After birth, infants are clearly responsive to different types of touch, from gentle stroking to the pain of a blood draw. They smile and vocalize more and cry and fuss less when they are patted, stroked, and rubbed (Peláez-Nogueras et al., 1996; Field, 2001b). In one study, researchers gave premature infants three 15-minute massages daily for 10 days; another group of premies received no massage. The infants given the extra tactile contact averaged 47 percent greater weight gain, were awake and active more of the time, showed more mature behaviors, and spent 6 fewer days in the hospital than the other infants (Field, 1990, 2001a). Infants are also able to discriminate among objects using only their sense of touch (Streri & Pecheux, 1986; Streri et al., 2000). It is likely that infants come to recognize their mothers and fathers by their skin textures and touches as well as the appearance of their facial features.

BEYOND FACES AND VOICES: PRIMED TO BE A SOCIAL PARTNER Infants are attracted to people not simply because of their faces, voices, smells, and touches. They also like their behaviors. By 2 to 3 months of age, infants are enjoying face-to-face play with their parents. They show more positive facial expressions, vocalize more, and exhibit less distress in these interactions than when they play with toys (Legerstee, 1997). In these face-to-face interactions, parents respond contingently and predictably to the infant's gestures and emotional displays. They model positive emotional expressions and encourage the infant to do the same.

They take turns with the infant, inserting their behaviors into pauses in the baby's repeated vocalizations or sucking patterns. Infants contribute to these interactions by gazing, smiling, vocalizing, and reaching. They regulate the interactions largely with their gaze: When the amount of stimulation gets to be too much or the play goes on too long, infants turn away, cry, or distract themselves with something else. Mothers do their best to keep the infants interested with exaggerated facial displays or rhythmic and repetitive vocalizations (for example, see http://www.youtube.com/watch?v=_wEic3Oo9j4&feature=related). When babies look away, however, good mothers respect the child's need for time-out by reducing their stimulation and waiting for the infant to resume the next cycle of activity (Schaffer 1996).

Often, despite the parents' best efforts, things do not go smoothly; missteps occur because either the parent or the baby misreads a social cue or responds too late to the other person's smile or gesture. According to one estimate, only about 30 percent of face-to-face interactions between mothers and infants are smooth and well coordinated (Tronick & Cohn, 1989). Some mothers and children have special problems with their interactions. Infants who are exposed prenatally to cocaine have difficulty managing face-to-face interactions; they are more passive and withdrawn and express more negative affect (Tronick et al., 2005). Mothers who are depressed also have difficulty. Their interactive behaviors are often poorly timed or intrusive; their affective displays are often negative (Campbell et al., 1995). The result is more negative affect and self-directed regulatory behavior by the infant. Researchers have asked mothers to act as if they are depressed so they can investigate this process. Mothers are instructed to be unresponsive, silent, and present a placid unmoving face while they are face-to-face with their infants. As early as 2 to 3 months of age, infants react negatively and become upset at the mother's "still face" (Tronick, 1989). Those who have a history of successful interchanges with the mother try especially hard to solicit the mother's normal behavior by leaning forward, vocalizing, smiling, and reaching out. After attempts to rouse the mother fail, they turn away, drool, lose postural control, and try to calm themselves by sucking their thumbs and rocking.

These focused face-to-face interactions contribute to the infants' growth of social skills and social expectations (Thompson, 2006). Infants learn that adults are responsive to their overtures and that through their actions they can control these other people's behavior. The infants learn that they can alter the course of interaction by their behavior and their emotional expressions (Malatesta et al., 1989). They learn about turn taking. Over time, infants improve their ability to shift attention from one vantage point or person to another (Nelson et al., 2006). They are able to sustain attention for longer periods of time (Kellman & Aterberry, 2006). They learn some rules of social exchanges and begin to realize that their role is to be both an initiator and a responder. Parents learn important lessons as well. They learn to more sensitively and accurately read the baby's signals and to adjust their behavior to maintain the baby's attention and interest. From these early dialogues, parents become increasingly attuned to their infants and, in turn, infants become more attentive to their parents.

Why Are Babies Prepared?

Infants are prepared by evolution to "expect" certain types of environments and to process some types of information more readily and efficiently than others (Bjorklund & Pellegrini, 2002). According to evolutionary theorists, this preparedness is adaptive and useful for ensuring the survival of the human infant and more generally, the species. Because infants depend on the support and nurture of parents and other caregivers for an extended period of time, they are biologically "programmed" to be responsive to social partners and have a set of social responses that ensures that their needs are met. Imagine infants not being equipped with these social propensities that make them attractive social partners and able to elicit care from adults! The conditions that originally led to this set of adaptive behaviors developed in the far distant past when the threat of predators made such behaviors necessary for protection and survival. But even though their original purpose may have disappeared, these capacities have remained to keep parents involved and invested. The evolutionary perspective does not suggest that there is no further learning and refining of early social response and signaling systems; modern evolutionary theorists assume that development depends on being born into and reared in a species–typical environment that supports adaptive behaviors such as the ability to send, receive, and understand social messages (Geary & Bjorklund, 2000; Bjorklund, 2008).

The Neurological Basis of Social Development

The brain provides a second biological foundation of social development. Here we review the basics of brain development and the links between brain development and social progress. (To find out more about the brain, go to http://videos.howstuffworks.com/hsw/20124-understanding-the-amazing-brain-video.htm.)

cerebrum
The two connected hemispheres of the brain.

cerebral cortex
The covering layer of the cerebrum, which contains the cells that control specific functions such as seeing, hearing, moving, and thinking.

THE BRAIN   The largest part of the human brain consists of the two connected hemispheres that make up the **cerebrum**. This mass of tissue is what allows us to have the attributes that make us human, such as speech and self-awareness, and those that we share with other vertebrate animals, such as sensory perception, motor abilities, and memory. The covering layer of the cerebrum, the **cerebral cortex**, is a highly convoluted surface containing about 90 percent of the brain's cell bodies. Although we do not yet know how these cells control complicated traits, we do know that specific functions, such as seeing, hearing, moving, feeling, thinking, and speaking, can be traced to specific regions of the cerebral cortex (see Figure 3.2). For example the frontal cortex is associated with the processing of emotional information (Davidson, 1993; LeDoux, 2000). The limbic system, the set of brain structures that forms the inner border of the cortex, plays a major role in the regulation of emotion and social behavior. The amygdala, one of the structures in the limbic system, plays a major role in the recognition of fear and surprise expressions (Akirav & Maroun, 2007; Kim et al., 2003).

FIGURE 3.2 *The brain's cortex. The cortex is divided into four lobes—frontal, temporal, occipital, and parietal—and specific areas within the lobes tend to specialize in particular functions.* Source: *Postlethwait & Hopson, 1995.*

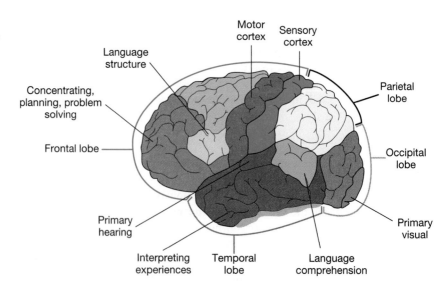

BRAIN GROWTH AND DEVELOPMENT   In the prenatal period, the brain grows very rapidly, and it continues to grow at an amazing pace after birth. The newborn infant's brain weighs only about one fourth as much as a mature brain, but by the time the baby is about 6 months old, the brain weighs half that of an adult brain, and the brain of the 2-year-old weighs three fourths of an adult brain (Shonkoff & Phillips, 2000). Brain development has an orderly sequence during this time, but development is not evenly paced. As well as some gradual continuous growth, periods of relatively rapid development, which are linked to advances in socioemotional development, occur (Fischer & Bidell, 2006). Using a variety of brain recording techniques, researchers have identified several brain growth spurts in infancy and childhood.

First, the motor cortex has growth spurts. As the baby moves from mostly reflexive behavior in the early months of life to voluntary control over movements, the motor area of the brain develops rapidly. When the infant is about 2 months old, the frontal motor cortex undergoes a period of rapid change, and, at the same time, motor reflexes such as rooting (automatically turning the face toward a stimulus and make sucking motions when the cheek or lip is touched) and the startle response disappear and the ability to reach for objects improves. This shift in motor skills also changes the nature of social interaction because the infant is able to initiate social overtures and gain others' attention by reaching. At 8 months of age, another brain spurt occurs; it is associated with the infant's abilities to crawl and to search for hidden objects and people. A brain spurt at 12 months is associated with walking, which, as any parent can tell you, changes infants' relationships with others dramatically. Babies who can walk can explore their environments more fully and initiate contact with others more easily. Their newly found independence also changes the ways in which caregivers respond; parents begin to set limits and restrictions and engage in more "testing of wills" (Biringen et al., 1995).

Changes also occur in the visual cortex. Again, this development occurs in spurts. A growth spurt when the baby is 3 months old, for example, is associated with looking longer at facelike stimuli than nonface stimuli (Dannemiller & Stephens, 1988; Mondloch et al., 1999; Nelson et al., 2006). A growth spurt in the auditory cortex allows the infant to be more sensitive to human voices and language input from caregivers (Nelson, 1999; Nelson et al., 2006). Growth between 18 and 24 months is associated with rapid advances in language development (Goldman-Rakic, 1997).

Another major growth spurt in the cortex occurs in the 5- to 7-year age period. This involves the development of the prefrontal cortex and is associated with the appearance of executive processes, which give children the abilities to think flexibly, act appropriately in challenging situations, plan and organize, control impulses, and allocate attention (Diamond, 2002). These skills are important for social development. For example, the child's ability to regulate attention is linked to higher levels of social skills with peers (NICHD Early Child Care Research Network, 2009).

Finally, brain changes in adolescence are associated with social behavior (Steinberg, 2007). When puberty begins, abrupt changes occur in the interior limbic and paralimbic areas of the brain, regions including the amygdala and the medial prefrontal cortex. These changes are associated with social and emotional processing. Another brain area involving the lateral prefrontal region does not show a growth spurt or reorganization at puberty but continues its gradual development until late adolescence and early adulthood (Chambers et al., 2003; Drevets & Raichle, 1998; Keil, 2006; Kuhn, 2006); this area is associated with executive functioning. The fact that socioemotional processing improves suddenly in early adolescence whereas impulse control develops more gradually may account for adolescents' emotional lability and risk taking. By early adulthood, the gradual maturing of the lateral prefrontal region results in a better balance between the two systems and hence less risk taking (Steinberg, 2007). As this discussion illustrates, brain development is an important contributor to social development.

"Young man, go to your room and stay there until your cerebral cortex matures."

Source: © Barbara Smaller/CondeNast Publications/www.cartoonbank.com.

cerebral hemispheres
The two halves of the brain's cerebrum, left and right.

corpus callosum
The band of nerve fibers that connects the two hemispheres of the brain.

lateralization
The process by which each half of the brain becomes specialized for certain functions—for example, the control of speech and language by the left hemisphere and of visual-spatial processing by the right.

HEMISPHERIC SPECIALIZATION   One of the most important organizing features of the brain is its division into two halves, the **cerebral hemispheres.** The left and right hemispheres, connected by a set of nerve fibers called the **corpus callosum,** are anatomically different and, in general, control different functions (Kandel et al., 2000). However, because of a great deal of cross-wiring between them, the separation is by no means complete. Not only do both hemispheres play some role in most functions but also when one side of the brain suffers damage, the other half may take over some of its functions (see http://videos.howstuffworks.com/hsw/20124-understanding-the-amazing-brain-video.htm; http://videos.howstuffworks.com/hsw/18677-understanding-the-amazing-brain-part-2-video.htm). Hemispheric **lateralization** is the word used to indicate the specialization of each hemisphere for specific tasks.

The right hemisphere controls the body's left side. It processes visual-spatial information, nonspeech sounds such as music, and the perception of faces (Nelson & Bosquet, 2000; Nelson et al., 2006). When damage occurs to the right side of the brain, people often have trouble completing a task requiring visual-spatial perception, their drawing skills deteriorate, they have trouble following a map or recognizing friends, and they become spatially disoriented (Carter et al., 1995). The right hemisphere is also involved in processing emotional information, as the fact that people with right-brain damage have difficulty interpreting facial expressions indicates (Dawson, 1994; Nelson et al., 2006). At the same time, right-hemisphere damage can sometimes make people indifferent to or even cheerful about things that would normally upset them because the right hemisphere is activated in the emotions that make people turn away or withdraw, such as distress, disgust, and fear (Davidson, 1994; Fox, 1991).

The left hemisphere controls simple movement in the right side of the body. It is activated in "approach" emotions such as joy, interest, and anger. It is also associated with language processing. Brain-imaging studies show that speech stimuli produce more activity in the left hemisphere than the right hemisphere even in 3-month-old infants (Dehaene et al., 2002). People with left-hemisphere damage can recognize a familiar song and tell a stranger's face from an old friend's, but they are likely to have trouble understanding what is being said to them or speaking clearly (Springer & Deutsch, 1993). The degree to which people's brains are lateralized, or specialized, has a genetic component: Parents and children usually have similar levels of language lateralization (Anneken et al., 2004).

neuron
A cell in the body's nervous system, consisting of a cell body, a long projection called an *axon,* and several shorter projections called *dendrites;* neurons send and receive neural impulses, or messages, throughout the brain and nervous system.

neuron proliferation
The rapid formation of neurons in the developing organism's brain.

glial cell
A cell that supports, protects, and repairs neurons.

myelination
The process by which glial cells encase neurons in sheaths of the fatty substance myelin.

neural migration
The movement of neurons within the brain that ensures that all brain areas have a sufficient number of neural connections.

synapse
A specialized site of intercellular communication that exchanges information between nerve cells, usually by means of a chemical neurotransmitter.

synaptogenesis
The forming of synapses.

programmed neuronal death
The naturally occurring death of immature nerve cells during early development of the nervous system.

synaptic pruning
The brain's disposal of the axons and dendrites of a neuron that is not often stimulated.

Lateralization begins early in life (Stephan et al., 2003). However, if children experience a brain injury, they often recover functioning because their brain is not fully developed and hemispheric specialization is not yet complete (Fox et al., 1994; Stiles, 2000). For instance, when the left hemisphere is damaged in early infancy, a child can still develop almost normal language ability (Bates & Roe, 2001). In people who are deaf and use sign language to communicate—a language that involves motor movements of the hands—the right side of the brain can take over language functions (Neville & Bruer, 2001; Sanders et al., 2007). Even adults still have a great deal of modifiability, and lost function can often be partially recovered through treatment and practice (Black et al., 1998; Briones et al., 2004). The adult brain has the capacity to regenerate nerve cells (Gould et al., 1999; Rosenzweig et al., 1996).

NEURONS AND SYNAPSES   At birth, a baby's brain has most of its **neurons**, or nerve cells—100 to 200 billion of them (LeDoux, 2002; Nash, 1997; see also http://video.google .com/videosearch?q=brain+parts+and+functions&www_google_domain=www.google.com &emb=0&aq=0&oq=brain+parts#q=the+human+brain&view=2&emb=0). In fact, most neurons are present in the brain by the seventh month after conception (Rakic, 1995). Neurons multiply at a very rapid pace during the embryonic period in a process called **neuron proliferation**; about 250,000 new neurons are added every minute (Kolb et al., 2003). After birth, the brain increases in size because existing neurons grow and the connections between them increase. **Glial cells**, which surround and protect the neurons, also grow. These cells provide structural support to the neurons, regulate their nutrients, and repair neural tissue. Some glial cells are responsible for **myelination**, which covers parts of neurons with layers of a fatty, membranous wrapping called *myelin*. This insulation makes neurons more efficient in transmitting information (Johnson, 1998; Nelson et al., 2006). Most myelination occurs during the first 2 years, although some continues into adulthood (Sampaio & Truwit, 2001). Neurons are always "on the move" as they migrate to their final locations in the brain guided by neurochemical processes (Rosenzweig et al., 1996). This **neural migration** ensures that a sufficient number of neurons serves all parts of the brain. The absence of a sufficient number of neurons in their proper locations is associated with various forms of mental disability and with disorders such as dyslexia and schizophrenia (Johnson, 1998; Kolb et al., 2003; Nelson et al., 2006).

The connections between neurons, known as **synapses**, are as essential as the neurons themselves. Synapses form at the junctions between neurons when the extended axon of one neuron transmits a message to the projected dendrite of another neuron, usually by means of chemicals that cross the small space between them. **Synaptogenesis** begins early in prenatal life, as soon as neurons appear, and soon there are many more synapses than neurons. For example, at birth, an infant has 2,500 synapses for every neuron in the brain's visual cortex. A child of about 2 years old has about 15,000 synapses for every neuron (Huttenlocher, 1994; Huttenlocher & Dabholkar, 1997). In the visual cortex, the number of synapses per neuron is multiplied six times within the first 2 years of life. As a result, infants' visual capacities are greatly enhanced; for example, they become more skilled at focusing on objects and people at different distances (Nelson, 1999; Nelson et al., 2006).

Are all these neurons and synapses necessary? Do they continue to function throughout life? The answer to both these questions is no. The brain is programmed to create more neurons and connections than it needs. With development, two processes reduce the number of neurons and connections (Sowell et al., 2003). **Programmed neuronal death** eliminates immature neurons surrounding new synapses (Kandel et al., 2000). This provides more space at these crucial loci of information transmission. **Synaptic pruning** disposes of understimulated neurons' axons and dendrites (Abitz et al., 2007). This frees space for new synaptic connections. The goals of both neuronal death and synaptic pruning are to increase the speed, efficiency, and complexity of transmissions between neurons and to allow room for new connections that develop as children encounter new experiences (Huttenlocher, 1994; Kolb et al., 2003). By adulthood, each of the brain's approximately 1 trillion neurons makes 100 to 1,000 connections with other neurons. That adds up to about 1 quadrillion synapses in the adult human brain (Huttenlocher & Dabholkar, 1997).

BRAIN DEVELOPMENT AND EXPERIENCE   Two types of processes influence the brain's development (Greenough & Black, 1999). **Experience-expectant processes** depend on experiences that are expected in people's normal environments, such as touch, patterned visual input, sounds of language, affectionate expressions from caregivers, and nutrition. These processes trigger synaptic development and pruning and are critical for normal brain development. When children lack these experiences, their basic abilities are impaired. For example, when children have congenital cataracts, their visual system is deprived of stimulation and fails to develop properly so that, even when the cataracts are later removed, the children are functionally blind. **Experience-dependent processes** depend on experiences that are unique to individuals, that is, experiences encountered in particular families, communities, and cultures. The brain responds to these specific experiences by developing synaptic connections encoding unique experiences. For example, in Mozambique, children's motor cortexes reflect skills associated with hunting and fishing whereas in the United States, children's brains are more developed in the area that reflects the fine motor and eye-hand coordination needed for success at video games.

Studies of humans and other animals have demonstrated how experience can modify brain size, structure, and biochemistry (Black et al., 1998; Rosenzweig, 2003). Lack of stimulation or exposure to traumatic events can damage the brain and cause it to malfunction. In abused children, for example, both the cortex and the limbic system, which are involved in emotions and social relationships, are 20 to 30 percent smaller and have fewer synapses than in nonabused children (Perry, 1997). Children in unstimulating orphanages also have reduced brain activity and less connectivity between regions of the brain (see Figure 3.3; Eluvathingal et al., 2006; Nelson, 2007; Pollak et al., 2010). This may account for the difficulties they have recognizing social signals and forming relationships with other people (Pollak & Sinha, 2002).

experience-expectant processes
Brain processes that are universal, experienced by all human beings across evolution.

experience-dependent processes
Brain processes that are unique to the individual and responsive to particular cultural, community, and family experiences.

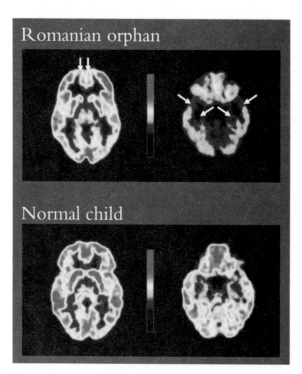

FIGURE 3.3 *How early deprivation affects brain activity. In the brain of a normal child, positron-emission tomography (PET) reveals many regions of high activity whereas the brain of an institutionalized Romanian orphan who suffered extreme deprivation from birth has fewer active regions. The arrows point to the temporal lobes, the most affected part of the brain.*
Source: Courtesy Harry Chugani, from Chugani et al., 2001.

MIRROR NEURONS AND THE SOCIAL BRAIN   When we watch a movie, we often share the experience of the actors. Our hearts beat faster when we see an actor slip from the roof of a tall building. We hold our breath as we watch a predator stalking a victim. Why? Specific neurons and regions of the brain transform what we see into what we would have done or felt in the same situation. As a result, understanding other people does not require lengthy and deliberate thought but rather an intuitive sharing of emotions, sensations, and actions. Our brain attunes itself to the state of the person we are watching or with whom we are interacting and adjusts our own feelings and actions to get into sync with those of the other person (Winkielman & Harmon-Jones, 2006).

mirror neuron
A nerve cell that fires both when a person acts and when a person observes the same action performed by someone else, as if the observer himself or herself were acting.

Mirror neurons are key to this sharing. These are neurons that fire both when a person acts and when a person observes the same action performed by someone else (see http://www. pbs.org/wgbh/nova/sciencenow/3204/01.html). These neurons have been directly observed in monkeys, and activity consistent with mirror neurons has been found in a number of specific brain areas in humans including the motor cortex (Fadiga et al., 1995), the somatosensory cortex (Gazzola & Keysers, 2009), and the inferior frontal gyrus (Kilner et al., 2009). For example, researchers using fMRI recordings have found that when a person observes another person's physical action, activation of the motor cortex occurs (Fadiga et al., 1995). These brain regions have been defined as the *human mirror neuron system* (Iacoboni et al., 2005).

The human mirror neuron system has clear links to social behavior. Mirror neurons are important for learning new skills by imitation (Dinstein et al., 2008; Iacoboni et al., 1999), and they appear to be important for understanding other people's actions and intentions. In one study, researchers used monkeys to illustrate the link between mirror neurons and social understanding. The monkeys watched an experimenter either grasp an apple and bring it to his mouth or grasp an object and place it in a cup. When the monkey observed the "grasp-to-eat" motion, 15 mirror neurons fired, but the mirror neurons registered no activity when the monkey saw the experimenter simply grasp the object and put it in the cup (Fogassi et al., 2005). Clearly, the activity of the neurons reflected the monkey's knowledge of the experimenter's intention to eat the apple. Data from studies of human infants, similarly, suggest that the mirror neuron system helps them understand other people's actions (Falck-Ytter et al., 2006).

The mirror neuron system has also been linked to language acquisition (Théoret & Pascual-Leone, 2002), development of theory-of-mind skills (i.e., understanding other people's mental states, which we discuss in Chapter 6, "Self and Other"; Keysers & Gazzola, 2006), and feelings of empathy (Decety & Jackson, 2004). Researchers have found that people who report that they are more empathic have stronger activation of the mirror neuron system (Jabbi et al., 2007). It has also been suggested that problems with the mirror neuron system may underlie cognitive disorders, and, in particular, that people with autism have deficiencies in social skills, imitation, empathy, and theory of mind because they lack mirror neurons (Dapretto, 2006; Hadjikhani et al., 2006; Oberman et al., 2005).

One area in which the human mirror neuron system is found is what has been labeled *the social brain*—a network of brain regions involved in understanding other people. This part of the brain has increased in size in recent evolution. Its regions include the medial prefrontal cortex (mPFC), inferior frontal gyrus (IFG), temporoparietal junction (TPJ), superior temporal sulcus (STS), interparietal sulcus (IPS), anterior cingulate cortex (ACC), anterior insula (AI), and amygdala (see Figure 3.4). These brain regions are involved in social functions that range from recognizing faces and bodily gestures to evaluating what other people are thinking or feeling, predicting what they are about to do next, and communicating with them (Blakemore, 2008). Brain-imaging studies show that these brain regions are activated when people experience empathy, understand another person's emotion, or interact with other people.

The medial prefrontal cortex seems to have a special role in understanding our own and others' communicative intentions (Kruegera et al., 2009; D'Argembeau et al., 2007). It enables us to encode social event knowledge so we can plan and monitor our own behavior and understand and predict the behavior of others. In one study, for example, when mothers looked at their infant's smiling face their mPFC was activated but when the infant had a neutral face it was not; similarly when infants looked at their mother's smile it activated the baby's prefrontal cortex (Minagawa-Kawai et al., 2009).

The amygdala and the superior temporal sulcus are regions of the social brain that are involved in processing emotional facial expressions (Adolphs & Tranel, 2004; Morris et al., 1998; Narumoto et al., 2001). In one fMRI study demonstrating these connections, college students viewed animated male characters approaching them in a hallway and making either a

FIGURE 3.4 *Regions in the "social brain." Regions include the medial prefrontal cortex (mPFC), the temporoparietal junction (TPJ), the posterior superior temporal sulcus (pSTS), the inferior frontal gyrus (IFG), the interparietal sulcus (IPS), the anterior cingulate cortex (ACC), the anterior insula (AI), the amydala, and the frontal insula (FI).* Source: *Reprinted by permission from Macmillan Publishers Ltd. Blakemore, S.-J. The social brain in adolescence. Nature Reviews Neuroscience, 9, 267–277. (fig 1, p. 269) ©2008.*

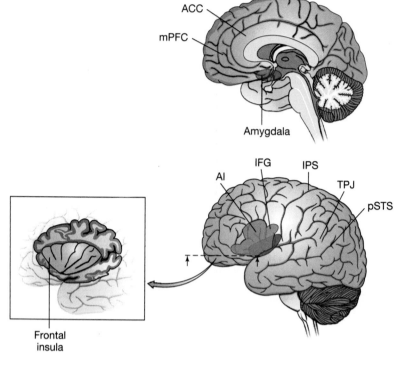

happy face or an angry face (Carter & Pelphrey, 2008). When they saw the angry facial expression, the students experienced increased activation in their amygdala and STS.

Another region of the social brain that is particularly active when people experience emotions is the frontal insula (FI). This area seems to play a role in generating social emotions such as empathy, trust, guilt, embarrassment, and love (Chen, 2009). It also becomes active when a mother hears a crying baby or when someone scrutinizes a face to determine the other person's feelings. The FI provides a link between the person's own emotions and those of other people, making it possible to understand others' feelings. Unusually large "von Economo" neurons expedite communication between the FI and the rest of the brain and enable people to adjust quickly to changing social contexts. In the ancient past, this neural wiring may have given our ancestors a survival edge by enabling them to make accurate, split-second judgments about whom they could trust.

Researchers are beginning to learn how the social brain develops from birth to adulthood. They have found that all regions in the adult social brain show partial responses in infancy. Even at 3 months of age, for example, prefrontal regions are activated when babies process faces (Johnson et al., 2005). However, not until 1 year of age is a mature response seen. At this age, infants, like adults, discriminate between upright and upside-down human faces but don't discriminate between upright and upside-down monkey faces. These results are consistent with the idea that infants' cortical processing of faces is initially relatively broad and poorly tuned and only later in development becomes more specific to the upright human face. Studies of this and other precursors of the social brain network in infancy, including studies of infants' abilities to perceive human emotions and actions, suggest that the brain is adapted to develop within a social context and that this context contributes to specializations in the adult cortex (Grossmann & Johnson, 2007).

With development, cortical tissues supporting social processing become increasingly specialized. Activation in the mPFC decreases in late childhood and adolescence and is replaced by activation of specialized subregions of the mPFC in adults (Blakemore, 2008). In one fMRI study demonstrating this developmental shift, researchers had participants think about potentially embarrassing social situations, such as "Your dad started doing rock 'n' roll dances in the supermarket" (Burnett et al., 2009). Thinking about these situations activated the social brain in both adolescents and adults. However, the mPFC was more active in adolescents than in adults, and the temporal pole was more active in adults than in adolescents. Thus, the relative roles of different areas changed with age, and activity moved from anterior regions (the mPFC) to posterior (temporal) regions, such as STS.

In addition to becoming more specialized, the different cortical regions of the social brain become orchestrated into networks as development proceeds (Johnson et al., 2009). Researchers are now shifting their emphasis from trying to localize particular functions in specific cortical regions to understanding patterns of functional connectivity among regions of the social brain.

Genetics and Social Development

Genetic transmission is a third important biological foundation for social development. (For more information about genes and genetics, see http://videos.howstuffworks.com/hsw/24988-genetics-the-basics-of-genes-video.htm.) Genetic transmission starts with the threadlike structures called *chromosomes* located in each cell nucleus. On these chromosomes are genes, portions of the DNA molecule containing the genetic code. **Genes** are located at particular sites on the chromosome where they code for the production of certain types of protein. When a gene is activated, a copy of it travels from the cell nucleus to the body of the cell where it serves as a template for building a protein molecule. Each of the many different kinds of proteins in the human body serves a different function. All of them working together are what makes a living organism. Genetic variability is the result of three phenomena: the huge number of chromosome combinations that are possible during the formation of sperm and egg cells; the union of ovum with sperm, as 23 chromosomes from the woman unite with 23 chromosomes from the man to form the zygote; and crossing over, which occurs during cell division in the fertilized egg and involves the exchange of genes on homologous chromosomes.

gene
A portion of DNA located at a particular site on a chromosome and coding for the production of a specific type of protein.

Genes contribute to shared characteristics of the human species, such as infants' biological preparedness for social interaction, and to differences among people, such as the outgoing and sociable nature of some individuals and the introverted shyness of others. For years, psychologists interested in social development were curious about the origins of these differences in human behavior, and beginning in the 1960s, with the formation of the field of **human behavior genetics**, focused attention on estimating genetic contributions to the array of individual differences in social behavior (Plomin et al., 2001; Rutter, 2006a).

human behavior genetics
The study of the relative influences of heredity and environment on individual differences in traits and abilities.

At first, behavior geneticists conducted their research without ever directly measuring chromosomes, genes, or DNA. Instead, using sophisticated statistical techniques, they calculated what are called **heritability factors**, or percentage estimates of the contribution that heredity makes to a particular ability or type of behavior. These percentage contributions of heredity depend on environmental influences too. When children experience virtually the same environments, individual differences in social behavior are likely to be the result of heredity factors; when environments are dissimilar, differences in children's social behavior may be the result of environmental factors, and sometimes this obscures the effect of genetic influences. Behavior geneticists try to assess the interactions between genes and environments and to estimate the extent to which each contributes to a trait or behavior.

heritability factor
A statistical estimate of the contribution heredity makes to a particular trait or ability.

The concepts of **genotype** and **phenotype** provide a framework for understanding the interactions of genes and environment. A genotype is the particular set of genes that a person inherits from his or her parents and that determine such characteristics as height and eye color. During the course of development, the genotype interacts with the environment to produce the phenotype, which is the observable and measurable genetic expression of the individual's physical and behavioral characteristics.

genotype
The particular set of genes a person inherits from his or her parents.

phenotype
The visible expression of the person's particular physical and behavioral characteristics; created by the interaction of a person's genotype with the environment.

et You Thought That . . . Genes Determine Your Potential

Many myths and misconceptions exist about genetics. You might share some of them.

If you thought that *genes determine potential*, you're wrong. Genetic factors do affect a person's potential, but so do environmental factors. Change the environment, and potential changes, too. A dramatic illustration of this fact occurs when one identical twin transfuses blood to the other twin through their common placenta during prenatal development. In this rare disorder, known as twin-to-twin transfusion syndrome, the donor twin is born severely underweight and at risk, which creates gross differences in the babies' potential for optimal development, despite their having exactly the same genotype (see http://www.dailymail.co.uk/health/article-452163/The-amazing-little-large-identical-twins.html).

If you thought that *nature and nurture operate separately*, you're wrong again. Both genes and environment are

necessary for development: "No genes, no organism; no environment, no organism" (Scarr & Weinberg, 1983).

Another myth about genetics is that *strong genetic effects = unimportant environmental effects*. Even a trait that is strongly linked to a gene can be increased or decreased by changing the environment. The gene causes variability among individuals; the environment may cause an overall increase in the trait for a whole population.

You may also think that *genetic influence diminishes with age*. But not so—the relation between genes and age is complex. Some characteristics are most strongly related to heredity in early stages of development; others are controlled by genetic factors in later life.

Finally, some people think that *genes regulate only static characteristics*. They are mistaken. Genes affect the dynamics of development as well. The age at which particular characteristics emerge and the sequence in which they appear are determined primarily by genetic makeup.
Source: Rutter, 1992, 2006a.

Methods of Studying Genetic Contributions to Development

The method behavior geneticists use most often to investigate the contributions of heredity and environment to individual differences is the study of family members whose degrees of biological relatedness are known. Studies of this type generally compare adopted children with their biological and adoptive parents, examine similarities and differences between fraternal and identical twins, or explore the effects of similar and different environments on twins and siblings (Plomin et al., 2001; Rutter, 2006a; Rutter, Kreppner, et al., 2001).

BEHAVIOR GENETICS: ADOPTION AND TWIN STUDIES In adoption studies, researchers compare characteristics of adopted children with those of their adoptive parents and their biological parents (Moffitt & Caspi, 2007; Plomin et al., 2001; Rutter, 2006a). They assume that no genetic connection exists between the adoptive parents and children, so any similarity between them is due to environmental influences. The opposite is true for adopted children and their biological parents; their connection is solely hereditary, and any similarity must be the result of similar genetic makeup. (These studies include only adopted children who have no contact with their biological parents.) Researchers in adoption studies also sometimes study the similarities between biological siblings and adopted children who live in the same homes.

In twin studies, researchers compare similarities between identical twins and fraternal twins. Identical, or **monozygotic**, twins are created when a single zygote splits in half and each half becomes a distinct embryo with exactly the same genes; both embryos come from one zygote (*mono* means "one"). Fraternal, or **dizygotic**, twins develop from two different eggs that have been fertilized by two different sperm, producing two different zygotes (*di* means "two").

monozygotic
Identical twins created when a single zygote splits in half and each half becomes a distinct embryo with exactly the same genes; both embryos come from one zygote.

dizygotic
Fraternal twins from two different eggs fertilized by two different sperm, producing two different zygotes.

Fraternal twins are no more similar genetically than any other pair of siblings; on average, they have half their genes in common. Researchers assume that if identical twins show more resemblance on a particular trait than fraternal twins do, the resemblance is strongly influenced by genes. (Take a look at these videos to see some of the similarities between identical twins separated at birth and raised in different households: http://videos.howstuffworks.com/hsw/18564-genetics-the-genetics-of-twins-video.htm; http://videos.howstuffworks.com/hsw/19136-the-mystery-of-twins-happiness-and-genes-video.htm;http://videos.howstuffworks.com/hsw/19132-the-mystery-of-twins-separated-at-birth-video.htm.) However, if on a given trait the two types of twins resemble each other almost equally, the researchers assume that the resemblance is strongly influenced by the environment. This research design has limitations (Gregory et al., 2010). For example, it is possible that being a twin in itself has an effect on social development, so results from twin studies may not be applicable to nontwin populations. In addition, identical twins are more likely than fraternal twins to experience birth defects, which can also contribute to differences between them. Despite these limitations, the twin design remains a useful strategy for assessing genetic influences on social behavior.

A variation of the twin design is to study children whose mothers are identical twins. Because this design is based on the twin status of the parents rather than the children, it is possible to divide variation in parenting into aspects that are attributable to genetic sources and to environmental sources and to estimate the separate consequences of each for child outcomes (Lynch et al., 2006; Neiderhiser et al., 2004). To illustrate, if one twin mother uses harsh punishment and the other does not, a comparison of their children provides a strong test of the causal link between parental punitiveness and child outcomes because, in this type of discordant-twin comparison, most genetic and shared environmental variables are controlled.

SHARED AND NONSHARED ENVIRONMENTS In interpreting the results of studies of child twins, behavior genetics researchers usually assume that twins in the same family experience basically the same environment. But is this a fair assumption? Some investigators have questioned whether twins experience the same environmental conditions. They argue that because of their identical genes and inherited predispositions, identical twins are treated more similarly by their parents, evoke more similar responses from people outside the family, and select more similar settings, companions, and activities than do fraternal twins (Scarr, 1996; Scarr & McCartney, 1983). Thus, identical twins have more **shared environments** than fraternal twins (Rutter, 2006a). However, even fraternal twins have shared environments that include being poor or well off, living in a good or a bad neighborhood, and having parents who are employed or unemployed, in good health or mentally ill (Reiss et al., 2000; Towers et al., 2003). Fraternal twins and other sibling pairs also have more **nonshared environments**, or separate experiences and activities, than identical twins (Dunn & Plomin, 1991; Feinberg & Hetherington, 2001). These nonshared environments include separate activities chosen by each child and different treatments of each child based on gender, temperament, physical abilities, and cognitive skills. Studies show that siblings, including fraternal twins, have many nonshared environments that affect their development (Pike et al., 2001; Plomin, 1995; Plomin & Daniels, 1987). Even small differences in nonshared experiences may cause differences in how the children develop. In fact, even siblings' *perceptions* that their experiences are different—for example, that their parents treat them differently—can affect their behavior, whether or not their perceptions are accurate (Reiss et al., 2000). Some psychologists argue that nonshared influences are more important for understanding development than shared influences, and to evaluate the influence of nonshared environments versus shared environments, they are designing studies in which the sample consists of siblings from the same families rather than children from different families (McGuire, 2001; Plomin et al., 2001; Rutter, 2006a). Clearly, researchers can no longer assume a homogeneous home environment for all siblings and must recognize that both nonshared and shared environmental experiences contribute to development.

shared environment
A set of conditions or activities experienced by children raised in the same family.

nonshared environment
A set of conditions or activities experienced by one child in a family but not shared with another child in the same family.

Learning from Living Leaders: Sir Michael Rutter

Source: Courtesy of Sir Michael Rutter.

Sir Michael Rutter, who was knighted by Queen Elizabeth II in 1992, has been described as the "father of child psychiatry." He is Professor of Developmental Psychopathology at the Institute of Psychiatry, King's College London. His childhood experience of being separated from his family during wartime, as well as his observation of how children cope with serious illness and hospital admission, led him to a career focused on children's social development. Few scholars have had as wide an influence on this field. His research includes studies of behavior genetics, epidemiology, autism, early social deprivation and stress, and continuities and discontinuities in normal and abnormal development.

Rutter also led a research team following Romanian orphans adopted by British families and made a number of significant discoveries about how early experience affects social development. As both an active researcher and a practicing child psychiatrist, Rutter has always stressed the importance of the two-way interplay between research and clinical work. His work clearly illustrates this dual commitment and has resulted in changes in both clinical practice and social policy. He is recognized for helping establish child psychiatry as a medical specialty with a solid scientific base—an accomplishment that he rates as one of his proudest achievements. Rutter is an honorary member of the British Academy and an elected Fellow of the Royal Society and has honorary degrees from a number of European and U.S. universities. His hope for the future is that we will see the effective integration of biological and social approaches in a developmental context, a better joining together of disciplinary perspectives, and a better link between science and practice. He challenges students to "be an iconoclast and not afraid of challenging your seniors. Be self-critical in what you are doing but never lose enthusiasm for new ideas and new discoveries."

Further Reading

Rutter, M. (2006). *Genes and behavior: Nature-nurture interplay explained.* Oxford: Blackwell.

Moffitt, T. E., Caspi, A., & Rutter, M. (2006). Measured gene-environment interactions in psychopathology: Concepts, research strategies, and implications for research, intervention, and public understanding of genetics. *Perspectives on Psychological Science, 1,* 5–27.

MOLECULAR GENETICS: THE HUMAN GENOME PROJECT   The Human Genome Project (HGP) is an international cooperative scientific endeavor, the primary aim of which was to locate and describe all the genes in the human genome (see http://videos.howstuffworks.com/hsw/20131-the-human-genome-mapping-humanity-video.htm). Scientists completed this task in 2003, mapping and sequencing about 20,000 protein-coding genes. Having identified these genes didn't mean that the scientists knew everything about genetic influence, however. Some geneticists compare the segments of genes in the human genome to books on a library shelf: The books are now shelved in the correct order, but scientists still haven't deciphered the meanings of most phrases (genes) and letters (nucleotide sequences) within the volumes. In addition to their work on the human genome, scientists have also studied animal genomes to place the human genome in its evolutionary context (U.S. Department of Energy, 2002; National Institutes of Health, 2002). Researchers have found that more than 1,000 genes appear in the human genome that are not in the rodent genome—including, for example, two families of genes that encode proteins involved in the extended period of pregnancy unique to humans. Other genes have died or stopped functioning, such as those involved in olfactory reception, which may account for humans having a poorer sense of smell than rats.

Although the HGP provides information about the basic workings of the human body, most illnesses, such as cancer or heart disease, and most social behaviors, such as aggression or helpfulness, are determined by multiple genes. Figuring out the gene "packages" that cause these diseases and behaviors is a truly daunting task (Benson, 2004; Plomin et al., 2002). This task is possible only because new technology allows researchers to perform DNA microarrays and genotype a million DNA markers simultaneously. Studies using this technology have shifted research toward studies of genome-wide associations with the ultimate goal of sequencing each individual's entire genome (Plomin & Davis, 2009). So far, results of genome-wide studies indicate that for most complex social traits, genetic effects are much smaller than previously thought, suggesting that hundreds of genes are responsible for the heritability of social behavior in childhood.

Researchers are already using the results of the HGP to advance investigation of social development. Avshalom Caspi and his colleagues have studied one gene identified through the HGP that affects the breakdown and uptake of neurotransmitters in the brain (Caspi et al., 2002; Moffitt & Caspi, 2007). They have found that this gene increases children's antisocial behavior—but only if the children also experienced abuse. As scientists have learned more and more about how genes influence human development, they have discovered that genes never work in isolation but always in combination with environmental influences (Rutter, 2006a; Turkheimer, 2000). In fact, a gene's coded message cannot even be "read" unless it is embedded in an environment that signals when and how it should respond.

Learning from Living Leaders: Avshalom Caspi

Source: Courtesy of Avshalom Caspi.

Avshalom Caspi, Professor of Psychology and Neuroscience, Psychiatry and Behavioral Sciences at Duke University, is a pioneer in the study of behavior genetics. His work addresses three broad questions: How do genetic differences shape the ways people respond to their environments, particularly stressful environments? What are the best ways to measure personality differences between people? How do these differences shape health, wealth, and relationships? In trying to answer these questions, Caspi has employed many methods: psychiatric interviews, epidemiological surveys, molecular genetic assessments, behavior observations, and laboratory assessments. He has probed data from longitudinal studies done in Berkeley, California, in the 1930s; in Dunedin, New Zealand, beginning in the 1970s; and still ongoing in

London, England. Caspi was born in Israel, raised in Brazil, and educated in the United States at Cornell University. He taught at Harvard, the University of Wisconsin, and King's College London before settling at Duke with his wife, collaborator, and faculty colleague, Terrie Moffitt. Caspi has received many honors for his work including the Early Career Contribution award from the American Psychological Association, the Slacker prize for Distinguished Achievement in Developmental Psychobiology, and the Lapouse award for Excellence in Psychiatric Epidemiology. If the challenge for the field of social development is to unravel how genes and environments mutually shape the course of development, Caspi has made a fine start and given us a valuable roadmap for guiding this scientific quest.

Further Reading

Caspi, A., & Moffitt, T. E. (2006). Gene-environment interactions in psychiatry: Joining forces with neuroscience? *Nature Reviews Neuroscience, 7*, 583–590.

Arseneault, L., Milne, B., Taylor, A., Adams, F., Delgado, K., Caspi, A., & Moffitt, T. E. (2008). Evidence that bullying victimization is an environmentally-mediated contributing factor to children's internalizing problems: A study of twins discordant for victimization. *Archives of Pediatrics and Adolescent Medicine, 162*, 145–150.

Models of Genetic Influence

Because the topic of genetic transmission is so complex, scientists have offered a number of increasingly detailed models to help us understand this process. In this section, we discuss some of these models.

THE TRANSMISSION OF TRAITS: A BASIC MODEL   The simplest model of genetic transmission applies to characteristics determined by single genes. Two basic concepts are important in this model. First, because people have pairs of chromosomes, they can have more than one form of each gene. These alternate forms are called **alleles**. One allele comes from the mother, the other from the father. Second, if the alleles from both parents are the same, the person is **homozygous** for that particular gene or for the trait associated with it; if the two alleles are different, the person is **heterozygous** for the characteristic. A person who is homozygous exhibits the trait carried by both alleles. For example, a person with two identical alleles for dark skin has dark skin; a person with two identical alleles for light skin has light skin. Heterozygosity can be expressed in several ways. First, a heterozygous trait may be a blend of the two alleles: A person who is heterozygous for light and dark skin color may have intermediate skin color. Second, a heterozygous trait may be a combination of the two alleles: A person who is heterozygous for blood type may have AB blood because the alleles for blood types A and B combine but do not blend. Third, a heterozygous trait may reflect the dominant allele: A person who is heterozygous for curly and straight hair has curly hair because the allele for curly hair is dominant over the weaker, recessive allele for straight hair. Fortunately, many deleterious alleles that result in serious disorders are recessive, which greatly reduces the incidence of expressed genetic abnormalities in the population. One of the reasons that societies prohibit marriage between close blood relatives is that a harmful recessive allele possessed by one relative is more apt to occur in another relative as well, thus increasing the chance that their children will be homozygous for the harmful trait.

INTERACTIONS AMONG GENES   A more complex model of genetic influence is based on the interaction of multiple genes. Single pairs of alleles do not determine most characteristics of social development, such as sociability, social problem solving, and style of emotional expression. These attributes involve multiple pairs of genes acting together. This may help explain why some traits influenced by genes do not run in families. Socially outgoing extraverts, for example, are sometimes born to parents who are quite shy and go on to have other children who are themselves relatively shy. Development of traits such as shyness and extraversion depends on a certain configuration of many genes, and that particular configuration is not likely to be passed on from parent to child (Turkheimer, 2000). Adding further to the complexity of genetic influences on development, a single pair of alleles may influence more than one trait, and if they are **modifier genes**, may do so not directly but indirectly by affecting how other genes are expressed.

ENVIRONMENT INFLUENCES GENE EXPRESSION   Adding another layer of complexity to genetic transmission is a model that incorporates environmental effects on genetic expression. In this model, heredity does not rigidly fix behavior but establishes a range of possible developmental outcomes that occur in different environments (Gottesman, 1963; Plomin, 1995). This model, stressing the interplay between genes and environment, is more useful for explaining the complexity of social development than the two previous models. See Figure 3.5 for an example of the model. Each of three children (A, B, and C) has a different range of possible scores on a measure of sociability. If all three children experience the same environmental conditions, Child C will always outscore Child A and Child B. However, Child B could achieve a higher score than Child C if he or she experienced a more socially enriched

allele
An alternate form of a gene; typically, a gene has two alleles, one inherited from the individual's mother and one from the father.

homozygous
Alleles for a particular trait from each parent are the same.

heterozygous
Alleles for a particular trait from each parent are different.

modifier genes
Genes that exert their influence indirectly by affecting the expression of other genes.

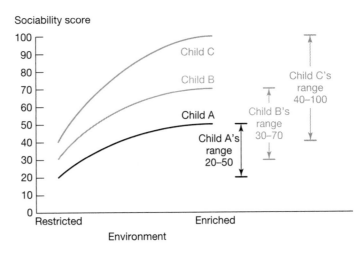

FIGURE 3.5 *Interaction between environment and genotype. Providing a child with an enriched social environment can improve the child's performance on a measure of sociability. However, the child's genotype determines the limits within which his or her performance may vary.* Source: Gottesman, 1963.

reaction range
The range of possible developmental outcomes established by a person's genotype in reaction to the environment in which development takes place.

environment. Child C has the widest **reaction range**: That is, the difference between Child C's performance in a restricted environment and in an enriched environment is larger than the analogous difference for Child B and Child A. Child A has the lowest and the most limited reaction range. This child, whether raised in a stimulating or unstimulating situation, not only scores below average but also is less able to respond to environmental enrichment.

When a reaction range for a trait is extremely narrow, it is said to be highly *canalized* (Waddington, 1962, 1966). The degree to which a trait is canalized affects how much it is influenced by the environment. The development of a highly canalized trait is restricted to just a few pathways, and more intense environmental stimulation is required to alter its course of development. We know that a baby's tendency to babble is strongly canalized, for example, because babbling occurs even in babies who are born deaf and have never heard a human voice; sociability and intelligence are less canalized and can be modified by a variety of social and educational experiences.

The likelihood that a genetically based trait or characteristic will be influenced by environmental forces is also affected by the stage of development at which the environmental events occur. Exposure of a fetus to a virus or a toxic substance prenatally will have a greater effect than the same environmental assault later. For example, exposure to German measles will damage a fetus's hearing but will result in only a mild illness when the child is older.

GENETIC MAKEUP HELPS SHAPE THE ENVIRONMENT   Not only do environments influence the expression of genes but genes also can influence the environment in several ways (Moffitt & Caspi, 2007; Scarr 1996; Scarr & McCartney, 1983; Rutter, 2006a). One way is that parents with certain genetic predispositions create a home environment that suits those predispositions and also suits and encourages these inherited predispositions in their children. Socially competent and outgoing parents are more likely to provide a home with lots of visitors and stimulating conversation, enhancing their children's inherited tendency to be social and encouraging them to enjoy and develop social relationships. Parents who are irritable and unhappy, in contrast, are more likely to provide a negative environment without much social stimulation, encouraging their children, who have similar genetic predispositions, to become antisocial or depressed. This is referred to as a **passive gene-environment association**.

Evidence for passive gene-environment associations comes from two sources (Reiss, 2005). First, studies using twins who are parents have demonstrated genetic influences on parenting. In one study, for example, twin mothers' reports of their own warmth, hostility, and monitoring of their children were more highly correlated if the mothers were identical twins than

passive gene-environment association
The environment created by parents with particular genetic characteristics encourages the expression of these tendencies in their children.

if they were fraternal twins (Neiderhiser et al., 2004). Second, adoption studies have demonstrated genetic links between parenting and children's behavior. The passive genetic effect, whereby parents' genes influence their parental behavior and, in turn, their children's behavior, would be present only in families in which the parents were raising their own biological children, not when children were being reared by unrelated adoptive parents. As expected, researchers in one study found that correlations between adolescent behavior problems and ratings of the quality of family relationships were higher in biological families than in adoptive families (McGue et al., 1996). Findings from these two sources thus suggest that genotypic differences among parents influence parenting and are transmitted to children, who manifest them in their own behavior.

evocative gene-environment association
People's inherited tendencies elicit certain environmental responses.

Genes also influence the environment through people's inherited tendencies to evoke certain responses from others in their social world. This is referred to as an **evocative gene-environment association**. For example, babies with a genetic tendency to smile tend to elicit more positive responses from others than do sober, unresponsive infants (LaFreniere, 2000; Plomin, 1995). In one study of this gene → environment connection, researchers using a sample of more than 1,000 five-year-old twins found that parents' physical punishment was strongly influenced by the children's genetic predispositions to be antisocial and defiant: Links between parents' punishment and children's antisocial tendencies were higher in pairs of children who were identical twins than in pairs of fraternal twins (Jaffee et al., 2004). In a second study, researchers found a high correlation (r = + 0.62) between mothers' negativity directed toward one identical twin adolescent and antisocial behavior shown by the other identical twin adolescent; the correlation was much lower for fraternal twins (r = + 0.27) and approached zero (r = + 0.06) for genetically unrelated stepsiblings (Reiss et al., 2000; Reiss, 2005). These studies provide strong evidence that the same set of genetic influences causes children's antisocial behavior and provokes their parents' negative behavior, leading to increased antisocial behavior in the adolescent.

active gene-environment association
People's genes encourage them to seek out experiences compatible with their inherited tendencies.

The third way in which genes influence environments is that people's genetic predispositions encourage them to seek out experiences compatible with their inherited tendencies (Scarr, 1996; Scarr & McCartney, 1983). They search for, select, or build environments or "niches" compatible with their traits. Thus, people who are genetically predisposed to be gregarious actively seek the company of other people and become involved in a range of social activities; individuals who are aggressive sign up for martial arts classes rather than the chess club (Bullock & Merrill, 1980). This is referred to as an **active gene-environment association**. The importance of this "**niche picking**" likely increases as children get older and have more freedom to choose their activities and companions.

niche picking
Seeking out or creating environments compatible with one's genetically based predispositions.

GENE–ENVIRONMENT INTERACTIONS (G × E)   In the next model of genetic transmission, an active role is identified for both genes and environment, and their contributions are taken beyond additive influences. In this **gene-environment interaction (G × E) model**, genes are expressed in overt behavior only under certain environmental conditions, and, conversely, specific environments affect only individuals with particular genetic predispositions. In other words, an interaction exists between genes and environments so that specific behavioral outcomes emerge only with the right match between the two. This G × E model is especially important for understanding complex traits and behaviors that are common in social development, such as empathy, aggression, and sociability (Leve et al., 2010; Meaney, 2010; Rutter, 2007). It is now possible to identify some specific genes that are related to particular social behaviors and to ask whether children who are at risk of having these genes are more sensitive to specific environmental risks (Plomin & Rutter, 1998). When researchers in one study assessed genes, environment, and behavior in a sample of 1,000 young adults, they found that a genetic predisposition for depression resulted in depressive symptoms only when the person had experienced numerous life stressors during the previous few years and had been abused in childhood (Caspi, Sugden, et al., 2003). That is, a significant interaction occurred between a genotype for depression and a stressful environment (see Figure 3.6). Studies of nonhuman

gene-environment interaction (G × E) model
People in the same environment are affected differently depending on their genetic makeup.

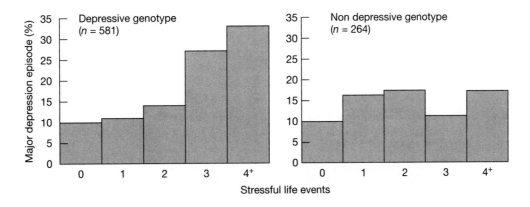

FIGURE 3.6 *Gene-environment interaction (G × E) model. Percentage of individuals meeting diagnostic criteria for depression at age 26, as a function of depressive genotype and number of stressful life events between ages 21 and 26.* Source: *From Caspi, A., Sugden, K., Moffitt, T. E., Taylor, A., Craig, I. W., Harrington, H., . . . Poulton, R. (2003). Influence of life stress on depression: Moderation by a polymorphism in the 5-HTT gene.* Science, 301, *386–389. Reprinted with permission from AAAS.*

primates told a similar story; for example, rhesus monkeys with the depressive gene showed more stress in response to harsh rearing conditions than monkeys without the gene (Barr et al., 2004). Brain-imaging studies of humans also showed more neural activity in the amygdala in response to fearful stimuli for people who had the depressive gene (Heinz et al., 2005).

GENE–ENVIRONMENT FEEDBACK LOOPS An even more complex model of genetic transmission suggests that genes and environments shape development together as genes influence environments, which in turn influence genes, in complex feedback loops (Meaney, 2010; Rutter, 2006a). See Figure 3.7 for an illustration of these feedback loops (Gottlieb, 1991, 1992; Gottlieb & Lickliter, 2004). As the figure indicates, influences are bidirectional, directed from bottom to top and from top to bottom. In addition, although each level generally influences the level directly above or below it, interactions across nonadjacent levels are also possible. The most important point of the feedback loop model is that genes are part of an overall system and their expression is affected by events at other levels of the system including the environment. The message of this model is clear: Genes and environments are inextricably linked and operate in a mutually dependent fashion; it is impossible to treat them as truly separable.

FIGURE 3.7
A multi-level model of gene-environment interactions. Source: *Gottlieb & Lickliter, 2004.*

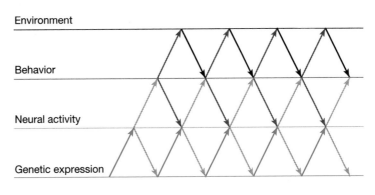

Research up Close: A Genetic Risk for Drug Use

Source: Yvan Dubé/iStockphoto.

Genetic studies have identified one gene, 5-HTT, that helps regulate transmission of serotonin, a chemical messenger in the brain. This gene appears to be linked to increased risk of depression, lack of self-control, and drug use. Most people have two copies of a long version of the gene, but about 40 percent inherit either one or two copies of a short version. Having a short version of the gene reduces serotonin transmission and is the apparent culprit that increases the risk for drug problems. However, whether or not this gene is expressed and results in actual drug use depends on the environment in which the child grows up. This gene × environment (G × E) interaction is well illustrated in a study conducted by Gene Brody and his colleagues (2009). These researchers followed 253 African American children from the time they were 11 years old. The participants in the study were interviewed about their use of cigarettes, alcohol, and marijuana at the beginning of the study and again each year until they were 14. To assess the children's environments, the researchers had their mothers report on their parenting practices. To assess the children's genes, the researchers analyzed DNA obtained from samples of the children's saliva. About 43 percent of the children had either one or two copies of the short version of the 5-HTT gene and, therefore, were genetically susceptible to substance abuse. These children did have a significantly higher rate of substance use and increased their drug use between ages 11 and 14 at a faster rate than children without the genetic risk. However, their parents' behavior also made a difference. When the parents were highly involved and supportive of the children, drug use rose only 7 percent between ages 11 and 14; when the parents were not involved or supportive, the increase was 21 percent. Further support for this G × E interaction comes from a study showing that youth with a genetic predisposition to smoke reduced their smoking if their parents monitored their activities more closely (Dick et al., 2007).

Several explanations have been offered for these findings. One explanation is that a genetic predisposition for substance use is linked to poorer self-control and greater impulsivity, which leads to more substance abuse. Another explanation is that individuals with this genetic predisposition are more sensitive to environmental influences and so are more attuned to, and thus benefit from, involved and protective parenting. Although these studies do not fully prove these explanations, the findings provide clear support for a G × E interaction and underscore the fact that gene expression varies in different social environments. The studies are notable for their integration of molecular genetic data (DNA) and environmental data (assessments of parenting) to forecast substance use and clearly demonstrate the importance of both genes and parenting.

Genetic Anomalies

Children born with genetic abnormalities also demonstrate the connection between biology and social behavior. Chromosomes provide one source of genetic abnormalities. In normal individuals, females have two large X chromosomes; males have one large X and a smaller Y chromosome. Females with only one X chromosome, so called *Turner syndrome*, exhibit unusual social behavior patterns. They tend to be docile, pleasant, and not easily upset, but they have problems in social relationships because their internal reproductive organs and secondary sex characteristics do not develop normally and they are immature, lack assertiveness, and have difficulty processing and interpreting emotional cues (Kesler, 2007). People with a pinched or narrowed X chromosome, *fragile X syndrome*, also have psychological and social problems including anxiety, depression, hyperactivity, attention deficits, and abnormal communication patterns (Garrett et al., 2004; Reiss & Hall, 2007). Children who lack the long arm of chromosome 7 have *Williams syndrome*. Although they have limited intelligence and visual-spatial ability deficits, they are unusually sociable, empathic, and prosocial (Mervis & Klein-Tasman, 2000; Semel & Rosner, 2003).

attention deficit/ hyperactivity disorder (ADHD)
A disorder characterized by a persistent pattern of inattention and hyperactivity or impulsivity.

More common than these chromosomal abnormalities are disorders linked to specific genes or groups of genes. **Attention deficit/hyperactivity disorder (ADHD)** is a persistent pattern of behavior that leads to difficulties at home, in the classroom, and with peers (American Psychiatric Association, 2000; Barkley, 2000). (See http://www.youtube.com/watch?v=mjnFGaCjRfg.) Children with ADHD have trouble sustaining their attention, run into conflict with adults, and often think of themselves as being "no good" (Campbell, 2000). In structured situations such as the classroom, they fidget, tap their feet, poke their neighbors, and talk out of turn. This behavior disturbs peers and disrupts the class, which may help account for the fact that their peers reject 50 to 60 percent of children with ADHD (Henker & Whalen, 1999). They often seem to act before they think, and they find it difficult to follow rules such as, "When your little brother takes one of your toys, don't hit him, or you will be sent to your room," because they have problems tracking contingencies (Barkley, 1998). We know that there is a biological basis for this disorder because brain-imaging techniques reveal abnormalities in several areas (Casey, 2001) and because children with high levels of ADHD tend to have specific variants of a large number of genes, including the dopamine receptor gene DRD4 (Kebir et al., 2009). Evidence also suggests that ADHD behavior is more similar in identical twins than fraternal twins (Plomin, 1990). Genetic anomalies like this one clearly and dramatically demonstrate the strong link between biology and social behavior.

autism
Disorder that begins in childhood, lasts a lifetime and disrupts social and communication skills.

Insights from Extremes: Autism

Teacher helping an autistic boy learn facial features. Source: Ellen B. Senisi.

In 1943, Leo Kanner, the first child psychiatrist, used the word **autism** to describe the withdrawn behavior of 11 children he had seen at Johns Hopkins University Hospital (Kanner, 1943). Case 1, Donald T., was first seen when he was 5 years old. Donald's parents had noticed that their son was happiest when alone. As an infant, he almost never cried to go with his mother, did not seem to notice his father's homecomings, and was indifferent to visiting relatives. He expressed no affection when petted. "He seemed almost to draw into his shell and live within himself." When Donald was 4 years old, his parents brought a boy home to spend the summer with them, but Donald never asked the boy a question or answered a question or romped with him in play. Donald was placed in a tuberculosis preventorium to provide "a change of environment," and while there, he also exhibited a "disinclination to play with children."

When clinicians at Johns Hopkins Hospital observed him, he wandered about smiling, making stereotyped movements with his fingers, crossing them about in the air. He shook his head from side to side, whispering or humming the same three-note tune. Most of his actions were repetitious; his verbalizations were ritualistic. His mother was the only person with whom he had any contact, and she spent all of her time developing ways of keeping him engaged.

Today, autism, or *autism spectrum disorder (ASD)*, the umbrella term for a family of similar disorders, is known to be a troubling condition that begins in childhood, lasts a lifetime, and disrupts a person's social and communication skills. Autistic children lack interest in other people; sometimes they even seem to be averse to human contact. They tend to avoid eye contact and fail to modulate social interactions. They do not develop normal social attachments or express empathy in social relations. Most fail to develop friendships and become social isolates (American Psychiatric Association, 2000; Baron-Cohen, 2003). Signs of autism—including lack of gesturing, vocalizing, and eye contact to initiate communication and inability to pick up cues from watching facial expressions—are evident in the first year of life. Current estimated rates of ASD range from 3 to 7 per 1000 children (Centers for Disease Control and Prevention, 2007; National Institute of Mental Health, 2007). It is three to five times more common for boys than for girls to be diagnosed with ASD (American Psychiatric Association).

Kanner described autism as an innate disorder and foresaw the need for research into the genetics of autism at about the same time that DNA was first identified as the bearer of genetic information. It took courage to offer that hypothesis in 1943 when the prevailing view, based on Freudian psychology, was that this pattern of behavior was due to poor parenting with much of the blame placed on "frigid" or "refrigerator" mothers who rejected their children. Today, although the exact cause of autism is still unknown, it is almost universally accepted that the disorder is biologically based. Chromosomal abnormalities have been found in some children with autism (Drew et al., 1996), and studies of twins have made it clear that genetics is a powerful contributor (Nigg & Goldsmith, 1994; Rutter, 2007). In one study, for example, the concordance rate for autism in identical twins was 60 percent, compared with only 5 percent in fraternal twins (Bailey et al., 1995). It is now estimated that heritability explains more than 90 percent of the risk of autism, assuming a shared environment and

no other genetic or medical conditions (Freitag, 2007; Gupta & State, 2007). But it is also clear that autism is not inherited in a simple fashion. Many genes, perhaps as many as 50, may be involved, each one adding to the risk of autism (Abrahams & Geschwind, 2008). Evidence for changes in DNA sequence, structural rearrangements of DNA including mutations, and epigenetic modifications of DNA, which do not change DNA but are heritable and influence gene expression, have all been reported (Volkmar et al., 2009). Identification of genetic factors and how they interact with environmental factors such as heavy metals and pesticides and biological contributors such as advanced parental age and low birth weight will be important steps in understanding the causes of autism.

Research also indicates a biological basis for autism in the brain (Dawson & Sterling, 2008). Neuroanatomical studies suggest that autism alters brain development soon after conception and affects many parts of the brain (Arndt et al., 2005). Children with ASD show less activity than normal children in areas of the social brain, such as the anterior cingulate cortex and the right anterior insula, when they are processing social information (Di Martino et al., 2009). They also have less activity in mirror neuron regions of the brain when they imitate other people (Oberman et al., 2005; Dapretto, 2006). Moreover, these cortical areas are thinner in adults with ASD than in nonautistic adults (Hadjikhani et al., 2006). Autistic individuals also have poorer connectivity between structures in the social brain (Pelphrey & Carter, 2008; Wicker et al., 2008). The underconnectivity theory of autism hypothesizes that autism is marked by underfunctioning high-level neural connections and synchronization along with an excess of low-level processes (Just et al., 2007). Abnormal brain overgrowth occurs in autistic children during the first 2 to 4 years of life and is followed by abnormally slow growth, especially in the structures that underlie higher-order cognitive, social, emotional, and language functions (Courchesne, 2004).

As the search for the biological bases of autism continues, it is worth noting that Kanner's descriptions of extreme patterns of behavior in a handful of children was the inspiration for much research being conducted today and still provides clues about the neural bases of this disorder. To find out more about ASD, see the following Web sites: http://videos.howstuffworks.com/discovery-health/32569-discovery-health-cme-autism-video.htm; http://www.autismspeaks.org/video/index.php.

Real-World Application: Genetic Counseling, Genetic Selection

Advances in biology and genetics have opened new opportunities for parents to be forewarned about problems in their children's development. For some time now, it has been possible to sample cells from a developing fetus to determine whether the fetus carries genes for certain disorders. With a prenatal sample of cells from amniocentesis or chorionic villi sampling, it is possible to examine the fetus's chromosomes and genes for any signs of chromosome disorder. The critical abnormalities (e.g., missing or extra chromosomes) are clearly visible under a high-powered microscope. In addition, scientists have identified particular pieces of DNA, called *genetic markers*, that can indicate many disorders caused by one or more defective genes. With this knowledge, parents may choose to abort the pregnancy or to prepare for the arrival of a child who will need special care. For most people, this is a very difficult choice and raises the ethical dilemma of deciding when an abnormality is severe enough to warrant termination. If a fetus has a lethal genetic disorder that will lead to a painful death in a few months or years, the choice may be easier than if the disorder is less devastating. What should a parent do about a fetus with Turner syndrome (XO) or Klinefelter syndrome (XXY)? Although these children have both physical abnormalities and cognitive impairments, they are capable of leading productive lives. Confronting prospective parents with such difficult ethical choices is one result of developing the new technology to analyze chromosomes and genes (Murray, 1996). More recent advances in the study of genes and their influence have made it possible to offer "preventive" genetic counseling. Couples wanting to have a child can themselves be tested for defective genes. If they find that they carry defective alleles, they may elect to adopt a child or to conceive a child through an *assisted reproductive technique* in which a donor's egg or sperm is substituted for one of their own. Some day we may be able to replace defective genes in a fetus through gene therapy, thus preventing a genetically determined disorder before it happens. Gene therapy involves inserting normal alleles into patients' cells to compensate for defective alleles. The most effective current technique uses modified viruses (viruses from which harmful properties have been removed) to carry the new genes

into the patient's cells. Scientists have adopted this strategy because viruses are by nature adapted to penetrate another organism's cells. Most often, target cells are first removed from the patient's body, infused with the new gene by way of the virus, and then returned to the body. With federal approval, this procedure was first used in 1990 to treat a 4-year-old girl who had a deadly genetic disorder that shut down her immune system, leaving her defenseless against infections. Doctors inserted the gene needed to produce a critical enzyme that her immune system lacked into some of the child's blood. Ten years later, the girl continued to do well with some additional medication (Thompson, 2000). French scientists have also had some success with gene therapy for immune deficiencies (Fischer et al., 2001). Not all of the news about gene therapy has been good, however. Few effective treatments have been found despite more than 400 clinical trials.

As science enters this new age of genetic screening, selection, and engineering, parents will confront more and more ethical issues (Kass, 2002; Murray, 1996). In the near future, prospective parents may be able to pick and choose the traits they want in their yet-to-be conceived children. Clinics all over the United States already provide would-be parents with in-depth profiles of potential sperm and egg donors. The Xytex Corporation in Atlanta, for example, offers a long list of genetically coded physical attributes, including length of eyelashes, presence of freckles, and whether ear lobes are detached. Experts believe that parents may soon be signing up for "preimplantation genetic diagnosis" of embryos to check for genetic defects and for desirable traits as well. Prospective mothers are already using chat rooms and bulletin boards to specify what kind of child they want: "I want to go shopping with her, play Barbie Dolls, and paint her toenails pink." The leap from genetic selection to genetic engineering may be even more problematic. It is one thing to replace a defective allele in a person who is seriously ill, but what about using gene therapy to improve performance or appearance (Kiuru & Crystal, 2008)? Gene therapy alters genes in a diseased organ to affect a cure, but in the not-so-distant future, "germ-line therapy" could alter the blueprint itself, the human genome, and thus be passed on to offspring. Researchers are, in fact, on the brink of developing low-cost machines that will provide personal DNA profiles "on demand." Just as in the movie *Gattaca*, genetic selection is appealing because it can prevent enormous suffering. Vastly fewer babies hardwired with painful, incurable diseases would be born. It's inevitable that genetic selection will be widespread because—ultimately—parents are the ones who decide. Parents generally do whatever they can to bring into the world children who will be healthy, well-adjusted, and successful. An increase in "above average" genetically selected children will put additional pressure on parents to use the technology so their own kids will have a chance to cope in a society dominated by brainy supermodels. You might give some thought to the ethical considerations that should guide their decisions.

Temperament: Causes and Consequences

The final biological foundation for social development that we discuss in this chapter is infant temperament.

Defining and Measuring Temperament

temperament
An individual's typical mode of response including activity level, emotional intensity, and attention span; used particularly to describe infants' and children's behavior.

Even in their earliest hours, infants' typical responses to the environment are markedly different. One baby cries easily even during moderately stimulating play and is readily distracted; another baby enjoys arousing play and has a good attention span. These behavior patterns reflect the baby's **temperament**, defined as an individual's typical mode of responding to the environment. Considerable evidence suggests that temperament is biologically based and linked to genetics (Posner et al., 2007).

Alexander Thomas and Stella Chess identified a number of temperament dimensions in infants based on interviews with their mothers (Chess & Thomas, 1986; Thomas & Chess, 1986; Thomas et al., 1968). These dimensions included activity level, mood, distractibility, and the tendency to approach or withdraw. Using these dimensions, Thomas and Chess classified infants as "difficult," "easy," or "slow-to-warm-up." Difficult infants (about 10% of the babies) slept and ate irregularly, became easily upset by new situations, and experienced extremes of fussiness and crying (Chess & Thomas, 1986, p. 31):

> *Nothing was easy with Chris. . . . It would take me an hour and a half to get part of a bottle into him and he'd be hungry two hours later. I can't remember once in the first two years when he didn't go to bed crying. I'd try to rock him to sleep but as soon as I'd tiptoe over to put him in his crib his head would lurch up and he'd start bellowing again. He didn't like any kind of changes in his routine. New people and places upset him so it was hard to take him anywhere.*

Easy babies (about 40%) were friendly, happy, and adaptable (Chess & Thomas, 1986, p. 28):

> *John was my touchy feely baby. From the first day in the hospital he cuddled and seemed so contented to be held I could hardly bear to put him down. He didn't cry unless something was wrong—he was wet, or hungry, or tired. We took him everywhere because he seemed to enjoy new things. You could always sit him in a corner and he'd entertain himself. Sometimes I'd forget he was there until he'd start laughing or prattling.*

Slow-to-warm-up babies were low in activity level and tended to respond negatively to new stimuli at first but slowly adapted to new objects and novel experiences after repeated contact with them. Essentially, these children fell somewhere between difficult and easy children; on first exposure to something strange, they might look like difficult children, but they gradually showed quiet interest, like easy children.

Since the early work of Thomas and Chess, Mary Rothbart and her colleagues have developed measures of temperament that include three broad dimensions, similar to those found in nonhuman animals (Putnam et al, 2002; Rothbart, 1981, 2007). These dimensions are more discrete and can be more precisely measured than Thomas and Chess's global temperament types. The three temperament dimensions are (a) effortful control—attentional focusing, inhibitory control, perceptual sensitivity, and low intensity pleasure; (b) negative affectivity—fear, frustration, sadness, and discomfort; and (c) extraversion-surgency—positive anticipation, impulsivity, high activity level, and sensation seeking (see Table 3.1). Of course, temperament is expressed in different ways as children grow older. For example, in infancy, attentional focusing may be indicated by the length of time a baby looks at an object whereas in childhood this component might be measured by the length of time a child continues to work on a puzzle or problem. Despite these changes in specific behaviors, temperament qualities do tend to extend from infancy to adulthood.

TABLE 3.1 **Definitions of Temperament in the Children's Behavior Questionnaire and the Early Adolescent Temperament Questionnaire**

Broad dimensions	Scale definitions
Effortful control	
Attention focus	The capacity to focus attention as well as to shift attention when desired
Inhibitory control	The capacity to plan future action and to suppress inappropriate responses
Perceptual sensitivity	Detection or perceptual awareness of slight, low-intensity stimulation in the environment
Low-intensity pleasure	Pleasure derived from activities or stimuli involving low intensity, rate, complexity, novelty, and incongruity
Negative affectivity	
Frustration	Negative affect related to interruption of ongoing tasks or goal blocking
Fear	Negative affect related to anticipation of distress
Discomfort	Negative affect related to sensory qualities of stimulation, including intensity, rate, or complexity of light, movement, sound, or texture
Sadness	Negative affect and lowered mood and energy related to exposure to suffering, disappointment, and object loss
Soothability	Rate of recovery from peak distress, excitement, or general arousal
Extraversion-surgency	
Activity	Level of gross motor activity including rate and extent of locomotion
Shyness (low)	Behavioral inhibition to novelty and challenge, especially social
High-intensity pleasure	Pleasure derived from activities involving high intensity or novelty
Smiling & laughter	Positive affect in response to changes in stimulus intensity, rate, complexity, and incongruity
Impulsivity	Speed of response initiation
Positive anticipation	Positive excitement and anticipation for expected pleasurable activities
Affiliation	Desire for warmth and closeness with others, independent of shyness or extraversion (in Adolescent Questionnaire only)

Source: Rothbart, 2007.

Cultural Context:
Are Temperaments the Same Around the World?

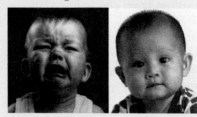

Sources: Kirill Zdorov/iStockphoto, iStockphoto.

Researchers have compiled evidence about whether different cultures have differences in temperament. Their evidence shows that the broad dimensions of temperament described in Table 3.1 are found in different cultures. However, significant differences between cultures exist as well. Perhaps the most consistent difference is between the temperaments of Asian and Caucasian babies. As the photos illustrate, compared with Caucasian babies, Chinese babies are calmer, easier to console, more able to quiet themselves after crying, and faster to adapt to external stimulation or changes (Freedman, 1974; Kagan, 1994). Japanese infants, similarly, are less reactive than Caucasian babies during well-baby examinations and less likely to display intense distress when they are inoculated (Lewis et al., 1993). Chinese preschoolers are

better than Causasians at controlling their impulses—for example, waiting their turn when helping someone build a block tower (Sabbagh et al., 2006). A genetic pattern associated with the impulse problems of ADHD is found in nearly half (48%) of children in the United States; in China, ADHD is virtually unknown, and the genetic pattern occurs in almost no children (2% according to Chang et al., 1996). Links among dimensions of temperament also vary in the two different cultures. Chinese children who are high in effortful control are also less extraverted; U.S. children who are high in effortful control are, instead, less negative (Ahadi et al., 1993). The reason for these differences may stem from the different kinds of behavior valued in the two cultures. In China, parents value shyness and reticence in their children; in the United States, parents like their children not to cry. In China, parents expect their children to control their impulses by age 2; in the United States, parents do not expect impulse control in their children until later in the preschool years. Biological processes of temperament may be shared across cultures, but outcomes apparently vary depending on cultural values (Rothbart, 2007). Cultural beliefs shape temperament, just as temperament shapes behavior (Kerr, 2001; Rothbart & Bates, 2006; Sameroff, 1994, 2009).

The Biological Basis of Temperament

GENETIC FACTORS   Scientists believe that temperament is at least in part genetically determined and that genetic influences become increasingly prominent through early childhood (Dunn & Plomin, 1991; Wachs & Kohnstamm, 2001). They have found that heredity contributes to individual differences in temperament dimensions, such as emotionality, fearfulness, anxiety, activity level, attention span, persistence, and sociability (Kagan & Fox, 2006; Kochanska, 1995; Plomin, 1995). Recently some progress has been made in identifying genes or clusters of genes that are associated with variations in temperament. For example, specific genes are related to the intensity of 1-year-olds' reactions to a stranger (Lakatos et al., 2003) and 3-year-olds' reactions to novel events (Deluca et al., 2003). Even so, the environment plays a moderating role in how these genetic influences are expressed. Infant temperament is affected by the prenatal environment and environmental factors at birth (Riese, 1990). Childhood temperament is affected by interactions with family members (Grigorenk, 2002; Rutter, 2006a). In adulthood, temperament becomes less closely linked to genetic factors, and life experiences become more significant (Plomin et al., 1988). Most psychologists today consider temperament to be the result of both heredity and environment.

NEUROLOGICAL CORRELATES   Researchers have discovered some of the neurochemical and neurological underpinnings of temperament. Neurochemical molecules, such as epinephrine, dopamine, vasopressin, and oxytocin, seem to play a role (Irizarry & Galbraith, 2004). For example, extraversion has been linked to the availability of dopamine (Rothbart & Posner, 2006). Neurologically, individual differences in effortful control, impulsivity, and proneness to frustration have been linked to activity in the anterior and lateral prefrontal areas of the brain (Posner & Rothbart, 2007). Jerome Kagan and his colleagues found that infants and children who were highly reactive to unfamiliar events—timid children—showed more activation in the amygdala region of the brain in novel situations than did children who were low in reactivity—bold children (Kagan & Snidman, 2004; Kagan et al., 2007). As these new lines of research continue, researchers will find out more about the neurochemical and neurological underpinnings of temperament.

Early Evidence of Temperament

Temperamental characteristics appear early—even prenatally. Pregnant women often comment on how active their babies are and in subsequent pregnancies, note differences in their fetuses' squirming and kicking. After birth newborn infants exhibit differences in distress and avoidance, and a few months later, differences in how much they smile at and approach social stimuli. By 2 to 3 months of age, babies differ in their expression of negative emotions such as anger and frustration, and by 7 to 10 months, in their level of fearfulness. Over the next year or so they become able to control and regulate their expression of these emotions through another dimension of temperament, effortful control (Rothbart, 2007). Effortful control allows children to inhibit an emotion or an action (not eat dessert), facilitate an action (eat meat), make plans for future actions (eat more vegetables), and detect errors in actions (don't eat fruit that has turned brown). This regulatory ability has been measured in the laboratory using a variety of tasks in which children must control their behavior. These tasks include delay of gratification (having the child wait before eating a candy that can be seen under a transparent cover); controlled motor behavior (having the child draw a line very, very slowly); controlled stopping and starting (having the child play a go-go-stop game such as Simon Says); controlled attention (having the child pick out small shapes hidden in a large shape); and controlled vocal output (having the child lower the volume of his or her voice) (Kochanska et al., 2000). By the time they are 30 months old, children perform in a consistent manner across these different tasks, and, by 45 months of age, effortful control appears to be a stable characteristic of individual children (Kochanska & Knaack, 2003; Rothbart et al., 2008). By age 7, children are functioning as well as adults on attention tasks reflecting effortful control (Posner & Rothbart, 2007).

Learning from Living Leaders:
Mary K. Rothbart

Source: Courtesy of Mary K. Rothbart.

Mary Rothbart is Distinguished Professor Emerita at the University of Oregon. She is regarded as one of the leading experts on child temperament, and her scale for measuring temperament is widely used by researchers in this country and abroad. She was not always a temperament guru, however, and for several years after completing her Ph.D. at Stanford University, she studied children's humor. Her work on humor revealed a wide range of individual differences in children's smiling and laughter, and this, combined with her observation that differences between her two sons reflected differences between their parents, led her to study children's early temperament. She characterized temperament as biologically based individual differences in reactivity and self-regulation. With her colleague Michael Posner, she studied these differences and wrote the book *Educating the Human Brain*, which describes the early development of attention and self-regulation and explains where, when, and how these characteristics promote social competence, school readiness, and expertise. Her research is valuable for clinical practitioners, alerting them to the importance of individual temperament differences among children. She was honored by the "Birth to Three" organization in Eugene, Oregon, as a "Champion of Children"—her proudest achievement, and she received an award for distinguished contributions to child development from the Society for Research in Child Development and the Gold Medal Award for Life Achievement in the Science of Psychology from the American Psychological Foundation. Rothbart believes that the most pressing issue in developmental psychology is rearing children to be open, loving,

and caring members of society. She suggests to students that "you cannot do anything more important than taking this course in social development because it will benefit you as a parent and citizen and help you understand yourself and others."

Further Reading

Rothbart, M. K., & Sheese, B. (2007). Temperament and emotion regulation. In J. J. Gross (Ed.), *Handbook of emotion regulation* (pp. 331–350). New York: Guilford Press.

Rothbart, M. K., Sheese, B. E., & Posner, M. I. (2008). Executive attention and effortful control: Linking temperament, brain networks, and genes. *Child Development Perspectives, 1,* 2–7.

Consequences and Correlates of Temperament

Temperamental characteristics have consequences for children's social development. Children who are irritable, difficult, impulsive, and emotional experience a higher rate of problems in later life (Goldsmith et al., 2001; Halverson & Deal, 2001; Rothbart & Bates, 2006). Fearful and shy children, whose temperaments are characterized by low levels of extraversion-surgency, are more likely to have **internalizing problems**, such as fear, sadness, and withdrawn behavior, anxiety symptoms and anxiety disorders, guilt and low empathy (Lindhout et al., 2009s; Muris et al., 2009; Ormel et al., 2005; Rothbart, 2007). Children with poor effortful control exhibit more **externalizing problems**, including disruptive, aggressive, and hyperactive behavior (Ormel et al; Valiente et al., 2003). Children with high negative emotionality may have both kinds of problems.

Several factors may contribute to these relations between temperament and later problems. First, children with difficult temperaments may find it more difficult to adapt to environmental demands and may be more affected by stress and the toll it takes on emotional well-being. This is a simple direct continuation of temperamental vulnerability. Second, children with difficult temperaments may elicit more adverse reactions from other people and thus suffer the psychological damage caused by harsh parenting and social rejection (Reiss et al., 2000). Researchers have found that children with difficult temperaments often serve as targets for parental irritability. In this case, the effect of temperament is indirect: Behavioral outcomes are the result of the differential experiences of children with different temperaments.

Third, temperament may interact with conditions in the environment, in a Temperament × Environment interaction comparable to the Gene × Environment interaction we discussed earlier. If parents are under stress, have marital conflicts, are hostile themselves, and lack a supportive family or friendship network, children's difficult temperaments are more likely to develop into externalizing problems than if the family is positive and peaceful (Crockenberg, 1981; Morris et al., 2002; Tschann et al., 1996). Children who suffer the "double whammy" of having a difficult temperament and a harsh or insensitive mother are more likely to develop aggression and acting out problems (Miner & Clarke-Stewart, 2008), anxiety and depression problems (Paulussen-Hoogeboom et al., 2008), and academic and social problems (Stright et al., 2008) compared with children who have only one of these disadvantages. Temperamentally fearful children whose parents use harsh discipline are more likely to develop elevated levels of depression (Colder et al., 1997), poor emotion regulation (Schwartz & Bugental, 2004), and low levels of conscience (Kochanska, 1997), compared with children who either are not fearful or have parents who are not harsh. Children with timid temperaments whose mothers are unsupportive, negative, or depressed are more likely to continue to be fearful (Gilissen et al., 2008) and socially withdrawn (Hane et al., 2008); they have more negative moods and develop more maladaptive ways of regulating their negative

internalizing problems
A type of childhood behavior problem in which the behavior is directed at the self rather than others, including fear, anxiety, depression, loneliness, and withdrawal.

externalizing problems
A type of childhood behavior problem in which the behavior is directed at others, including hitting, stealing, vandalizing, and lying.

emotions (Feng et al., 2008). However, if parents are calm and supportive, difficult children are less likely to suffer long-term negative effects (Calkins, 2002; Rothbart & Bates, 2006). Similarly, fearful children can be led to develop more self-control if their parents use gentle rather than harsh discipline (Kagan & Snidman, 2004; Kochanska, 1997). These findings clearly show that the consequences of temperamental predispositions to some extent depend on how well parents and others are able to accept and adapt to the child's particular characteristics. Thomas and Chess (1986) termed this match between the child's temperament and the child-rearing environment "goodness of fit" and suggested that development progresses more smoothly when parents and children have a good fit and parents are naturally in tune with their infant or adjust their approach to suit their child's temperament.

Finally, associations between temperament and later problems depend on the temperament "package" the child comes with. Temperament traits exhibit Temperament × Temperament interactions in which one temperamental trait, such as fearfulness or high effortful control, protects children from the negative effects of another temperamental trait, such as impulsivity or negative affectivity. Researchers have found that impulsivity is less likely to lead to externalizing behavior problems if children are also high in attentional control (Eisenberg et al., 2004). These children are able to offset the negative effect of their impulsive temperaments by being focused and planful.

Temperament is often viewed as the core of personality. Personality traits have clear links to temperament variables, both concurrently and longitudinally. Both are characterized by positive and negative emotions, and both have clear genetic correlates and are affected by experience. Temperament traits tend to be defined as narrower lower-level traits that are substrates of the Big Five personality factors—extraversion (being gregarious, cheerful, energetic), neuroticism (being afraid, touchy, tearful), conscientiousness (being diligent, planful, focused), agreeableness (being considerate, trusting), and openness (being curious, perceptive). These Big Five factors appear in children as well as adults, according to parent and teacher reports, and are strongly correlated with similar temperament traits ($rs = +0.5$ to $+0.7$). Personality extraversion is correlated with temperamental extraversion-surgency, neuroticism with negative affectivity, conscientiousness with effortful control, agreeableness with affiliativeness (a temperament trait that appears in adolescence), and openness with orienting sensitivity (Caspi & Shiner, 2006; Evans & Rothbart, 2007, 2009). Personality, however, includes a wider range of individual differences in feeling, thinking, and behaving than temperament, including attitudes, beliefs, goals, values, motives, coping styles, and higher-level cognitive functioning. When researchers have combined measures of both temperament and personality characteristics, prediction of children's behavior problems is even stronger than using either one alone (De Pauw et al., 2009).

Into Adulthood:
Shy Children Thirty Years Later

Source: Sheryl Griffin / iStockphoto.

What happens when shy children grow up? Are they still bashful, or do they become the life of the party? Are they socially disadvantaged, or do they make up for their early reticence? To find out, researchers have followed shy children from childhood into adulthood. In one study, children whose behavior was rated by examiners as shy, fearful, and inhibited when they were 3 years old were shy and cautious as young adults (Caspi & Silva, 1995; Caspi, Harrington, et al., 2003). They preferred safe activities over dangerous ones, were cautious rather than impulsive, enjoyed submissive rather than leadership roles, and had little desire to influence others. In another study, children were rated by their elementary school teachers on a scale that ranged from very shy (acutely uncomfortable, feeling panic in social situations) to outgoing (enjoy meeting new people) (Caspi et al., 1988). The very shy children were so emotionally inhibited that other people reported feeling strained and awkward in their company. They were less friendly, less sociable, more reserved, and more withdrawn than other children. Their teachers viewed them as followers rather than leaders. When the researchers tracked down the children and interviewed them 20 to 30 years later, the boys who had been rated as shy in childhood had delayed marrying, having children, and establishing stable careers. They held less prestigious jobs than their more outgoing peers. These men did indeed appear to have been disadvantaged by their shyness. Shy girls had followed a traditional pattern of marriage, childbearing, and homemaking. More than half (56%) had not been employed outside the home or had left the labor force when they married or had a child, compared with a third (36%) of the outgoing girls. The shy girls also typically married men who had a higher occupational status at midlife than the outgoing girls' husbands. At the time these children were growing up, shyness in women was considered a positive feminine attribute, suited to the wife-mother-homemaker role.

This was good news for these girls, but the situation may be different today when we expect outgoing behavior from both women and men.

Several factors probably account for the continuity in shyness observed in these studies. Genetic factors play a part (Rothbart & Bates, 2006). Identical twins are more similar in shyness than fraternal twins (Bartels et al., 2004), and clusters of specific genes and hormones have been related to differences in shyness across individuals and continuities in shyness over time (Hartl & Jones, 2005; Kagan & Fox, 2006). Variation in neurological activity, for example, in the amygdala, also contributes (Kagan et al., 2007). Of course, environmental factors can increase or decrease the stability of shyness across time. Shy 2-year-olds are likely to become more sociable as they grow older if their mothers are less protective and discourage their shy behavior (Rubin et al., 2002) or if they are enrolled in child care before their second birthday (Fox et al., 2001).

Probably no shy child has ever thought that shyness is a good thing. Fortunately, now there are programs to help shy children gain poise and self-confidence. Children can often overcome their shyness through coaching, modeling, and instruction (Bierman & Powers, 2009; Rubin et al., 2009).

Chapter Summary

Biological Preparedness

- Babies are biologically prepared for social interactions at birth because of their biological rhythms and their abilities to regulate them. Infants with better regulation of biological rhythms have more synchronous social interactions with their mothers.
- Newborns are attracted to the properties of human faces—boundaries, hairlines, chins—as well as the movement of faces. By 3 months, infants identify faces as unique patterns. The brain has specialized cells devoted to recognition of faces.
- At birth, babies are attracted to high-pitched sounds, which parents typically use when they talk to them.
- Newborns can distinguish their mother's smell from that of other women. They can also discriminate different tastes and come to prefer tastes they were exposed to during breast-feeding.
- Newborns are responsive to and soothed by touch.
- Babies are attracted by their mothers' responsiveness and expressiveness in face-to-face play. They interact in synchrony by 3 months.

- Preparedness for social interaction has an evolutionary basis; it is adaptive and ensures the survival of the infant.

The Neurological Basis of Social Development

- The cerebral cortex is divided into regions in which cells control specific functions, such as speech, motor abilities, and memory. The cortex and the limbic system play major roles in regulating emotion and social behavior.
- There is an orderly sequence to brain development during infancy with both gradual continuous changes and periods of relatively rapid development. Changes are linked to advances in auditory, visual, motor, and socioemotional development.
- In the 5- to 7-year period, development of the prefrontal cortex is associated with the development of executive processes such as attention, inhibitory control, and planning. Maturation of the cortex continues into adolescence.
- The right cerebral hemisphere controls the left side of the body and is involved in processing visual-spatial information, face recognition, and emotional expressions. The left hemisphere controls the right side of the body and is important for understanding and using language. Hemispheric specialization and lateralization are evident early in infancy and are well developed by age 3.
- Although most of the brain's neurons are present at birth, changes take place in their size, number of connections, or synapses, and production of the surrounding, supportive glial cells. Myelination increases the speed, efficiency, and complexity of transmissions between neurons.
- Neural migration distributes neurons throughout brain regions. The abundance of neurons and synapses is trimmed over time through neuronal death and synaptic pruning.
- The environment plays a critical role in brain development. Enriched environments are related to increases in brain size, connections among neurons, and activities of key brain chemicals. Additional experience can also help reduce damage or defects in one area or hemisphere of the brain.
- Two types of processes influence the development of the child's brain. Experience-expectant processes are universal, that is, shared by all human beings across evolution. Experience-dependent processes are related to experiences in a particular family or culture.

Genetics and Social Development

- Genetic transmission is another important biological foundation for social development and accounts for individual differences between people, such as the outgoing and sociable tendencies versus introversion and shyness.
- Genetic transmission starts with chromosomes, on which are genes—portions of the DNA molecule containing the genetic code.
- Genetic variability is the result of the huge number of possible chromosome combinations, crossing over during cell division in the fertilized egg, and sexual reproduction as 23 chromosomes from a woman unite with 23 chromosomes from a man.
- The genotype is the particular set of genes that a person inherits. It interacts with the environment to produce the phenotype, which is the observable expression of physical and behavioral characteristics.

- The method that behavior geneticists use most often to investigate the contributions of heredity and environment to individual differences is the study of family members whose degrees of biological relatedness are known.

- Children raised in the same family have both shared and nonshared environments.

- The simplest model of genetic transmission applies to characteristics determined by single genes. A more complex model is based on the interaction of multiple genes. Most characteristics of social development involve multiple genes acting together. A third model stresses the interplay between genes and environment.

- Environments influence genes, and genes influence environments. In a passive gene-environment association, parents create an environment that suits their genetic predispositions and may also encourage these inherited predispositions in their children. In an evocative gene-environment association, people's inherited tendencies evoke certain responses from others. In an active gene-environment association, each person's genetic makeup encourages him or her to seek out experiences compatible with inherited tendencies (also known as *niche picking*).

- In the gene × environment (G × E) model of genetic transmission, an active role is given to both genes and environment, and their contributions are taken beyond additive influences.

Temperament: Causes and Consequences

- Temperament is defined as an individual's typical mode of responding to the environment. Temperamental characteristics appear in early infancy.

- Three common temperament dimensions are effortful control, negative affectivity, and extraversion-surgency.

- Heredity contributes to differences in temperament, especially differences in emotionality, activity level, and sociability.

- Temperament has neurological and neurochemical underpinnings.

- Children with less optimal temperament profiles experience a higher rate of problems in later life.

- To some extent, the likelihood of problems depends on the environment in which the child is reared and how well it suits the child's temperamental qualities.

Key Terms

active gene-environment association	**cerebral hemispheres**	**experience-dependent process**
allele	**cerebral cortex**	
attention deficit/ hyperactivity disorder (ADHD)	**cerebrum**	**experience-expectant process**
	corpus callosum	**externalizing problems**
	dizygotic	
autism	**evocative geneenviron- ment association**	**gene**

gene-environment
   interaction (G × E)
   model
genotype
glial cell
heritability factor
heterozygous
homozygous
human behavior
   genetics
internalizing problems
lateralization

mirror neuron
modifier genes
monozygotic
myelination
neural migration
neuron proliferation
neuron
niche picking
nonshared environment
passive gene-
   environment
   association

phenotype
programmed neuronal
   death
reaction range
shared environment
synapse
synaptic pruning
synaptogenesis
temperament

At the Movies

Gattaca (1997) is a thoughtful science fiction drama in which children are selected through pre-implantation genetic diagnosis to ensure they possess the best hereditary traits. Having a child is like shopping on Amazon.com. ("Honey, let's have a blonde rocket scientist with great teeth and a voice like Beyoncé!") Characters battle to find their place and discover who they are destined to be according to their genes. *The Human Genome Project* (2005) is a documentary that explains how automated gene sequencing works, how genes are isolated and fragmented, and how their DNA bases are determined. It also addresses ethical issues. Movies about individuals with genetic anomalies include poignant accounts of people with autism. In *Molly* (1999), loosely based on a true story, a man's autistic sister is released from an institution into his care. She verbalizes little and is obsessed with lining up her shoes in neat rows. When her brother allows her to undergo an experimental medical treatment in which healthy brain cells are harvested from a donor and implanted into her brain, Molly makes a miraculous "recovery," but it is short lived. *Recovered: Journeys Through the Autism Spectrum and Back* (2008) is a documentary about autism, which suggests that there are more effective techniques for recovery, including

one-on-one behavioral therapy. Another documentary, *Messages of Hope from the Autistic Spectrum* (2009), traces a doctor's journey through the spectrum of Autism after his son was diagnosed. *On the Spectrum: Coping with Asperger's & Autism* (2008) shows autistic adults and children overcoming challenges and having success in life. Other documentary films explore the consequences for children's social behavior of other genetic problems, including *ABC News Nightline Fragile X Syndrome* (2007) and *Understanding Hemophilia* (2008).

The value of investigating genetic contributions to social development by studying identical twins is illustrated in video clips of separated twins reunited in adulthood. For example, http://www.youtube.com/watch?v = REhKa3_oHL8 and http://www.youtube.com/watch?v = 0yTCShemS_0. *The Brain* (2008) shows how the brain works, takes the viewer inside the mind of a soldier under fire, examines an autistic person's remarkable skills, and takes on the age-old question of what makes one person good and another evil. *Charlie Rose, The Brain Series, Episode 4, The Social Brain,* provides a description and discussion of this important aspect of brain functioning (http://www.charlierose.com/view/interview/10820?sponsor_id = 1). Two fictionalized accounts of how a person's social and emotional behaviors change after a brain injury are *Regarding Henry* (1991) and *Recovery* (2007). In *Regarding Henry*, a ruthless trial lawyer's life is turned upside down when he is shot in the head during a robbery. He survives the injury with significant brain damage and must relearn how to speak, walk, and function. To the surprise of his wife and daughter, he becomes a loving and affectionate man. In *Recovery*, Alan steps out in front of a passing car and the resulting accident leaves him in a deep coma. His wife is delighted when he comes to, only to discover that the man she loved has disappeared and his behavior now veers from angry to childlike.

CHAPTER 4

Attachment: Learning to Love

At 3 months of age, Jamie watched his mother leave the room, but he did not protest. Instead, he occupied himself by watching the brightly colored mobile above his crib. At 9 months, Jamie frowned, cried, and stood up in his crib to protest his mother's departure. At 15 months, he followed his mother around the house as she did her daily chores and stood at the door calling for her when she went to the mailbox. Jamie had clearly developed a special relationship with his mother. Exploring and explaining this remarkable developmental milestone—the development of a specific attachment—and what comes after is the goal of this chapter.

The development of attachment relationships is a major achievement in the infant's early social life. In the first days, weeks, and months of life, infants come to discriminate between familiar people and strangers, and by the end of the first year or so, they develop a loving attachment to one or two of the special people who are regular participants in their lives: mother, father, an older sibling, perhaps a grandparent. Visible signs of attachment can be seen in the warm greetings children give these people, smiling broadly and stretching out their arms as they approach, and then initiating physical contact by touching and snuggling close. Children also make efforts to stay near these people in unfamiliar situations, crawling or running after them and grabbing on to an arm or a leg. They are often distressed when these special people leave them temporarily. They have formed a deep, affectionate, close, and enduring **attachment** to these important figures.

attachment
A strong emotional bond that forms between infant and caregiver in the second half of the child's first year.

Attachment is of interest to researchers because it is intense and dramatic and because it offers a window into children's social development and emotional well-being. In this chapter, we trace the remarkable journey by which children develop these first love relationships. We present several theories that psychologists have proposed to explain the development of attachment relationships. We then describe the changes in infants' behavior as attachments form, explore the factors that influence the development of attachment relationships, and examine qualitative differences in attachment relationships. We also examine the consequences of attachment for other aspects of children's development and how attachment is transferred from one generation to the next.

Theories of Attachment

A number of theories have been offered to explain the development of attachment including psychoanalytic theory, learning theory, cognitive theory, and ethological theory. Each theory has its own definition of the nature of the child's tie to primary caregivers. Different theories also emphasize different mechanisms underlying the development of attachment relationships and make different assumptions about the factors that are important for attachment development.

Psychoanalytic Theory

According to Freud, infants become attached to their mother because they associate her with gratification of their instinctual drive to obtain pleasure through sucking and oral stimulation. The mother who breast-feeds her baby is a particularly important attachment figure. The baby becomes attached first to the mother's breast and then to the mother herself during Freud's oral stage of development. Although this psychoanalytic explanation turns out to be incorrect—infants form attachments to people who never feed them and for reasons other than enjoyment of sucking—the proffered explanation was important because it drew attention to the notion of attachment in the first place and pointed to the importance of early contact between mother and infant.

Learning Theories

Some learning theorists also associated mother-infant attachment with mother-infant feeding. Drive-reduction learning theorists suggested that the mother becomes an attachment object because she reduces the baby's primary drive of hunger. Wanting the mother's presence becomes a secondary or learned drive because she is paired with the relief of hunger and tension (Sears et al., 1957). Research findings challenged this view that feeding is critical for the development of attachment, however. Harry Harlow separated infant monkeys from their real mothers and raised them in the company of two "surrogate mothers." One "mother" was made of stiff wire and had a feeding bottle attached to it, so it provided food but no physical comfort; the other "mother" was made of soft terrycloth, but it lacked a bottle, so it offered

Source: Photo Researchers.

comfort but no milk (Harlow & Zimmerman, 1959). Counter to the drive-reduction learning theory prediction, baby monkeys preferred to cling to the cloth "mother"—especially in moments of stress—even though it dispensed no food (see photo). Research on human infants told a similar story. Infants reared by a mother who provided food but displayed little affection and a father who spent more time stimulating and playing with the baby were likely to form their first attachment to the father rather than the mother (Schaffer & Emerson, 1964).

Operant-conditioning learning theorists then suggested that the basis for the development of attachment is not feeding, per se, but the visual, auditory, and tactile stimulation that infants receive from their caregivers (Gewirtz, 1969). According to this view, babies are initially attracted to their caregivers because they are the most important and reliable sources of this type of stimulation. As interactions with these caregivers continue over weeks and months, infants learn to depend on and value these special adults, becoming attached to them. The central point of this learning theory explanation is that attachment is not automatic; it develops over time as a result of satisfying interactions with responsive adults. This explanation turns out to be correct but incomplete. One problem is that it cannot explain why children form attachments to an abusive parent if that person is the only caregiver available. A similar phenomenon has been observed in animal studies showing that babies who are treated violently by their mothers continue to seek physical contact with them (Seay et al., 1964).

Cognitive Developmental Theory

The cognitive developmental theory points to other important components of the development of infants' attachment. One component is the infants' ability to differentiate between familiar and unfamiliar people; another is the infants' awareness that people continue to exist even when they cannot be seen. Infants must have the ability to remember what people look like and the knowledge Piaget called *object permanence:* understanding that objects, including people, have a continuous existence apart from the baby's own interactions with them. Some evidence indicates that children as young as 3½ months have some beginning awareness of object permanence (Baillargeon, 2002), although Piaget believed that this awareness did not begin to appear until 7 to 8 months of age.

Infants' cognitive development also helps account for the gradual shift in the ways attachment is expressed. As infants grow older, physical proximity to the attachment figure becomes less important. Children are increasingly able to maintain contact with a parent through words, smiles, and looks. In addition, because they are also able to understand that parental absences are sometimes necessary and usually temporary, they are less upset by separations. Parents can reduce their children's distress over separations further by explaining the reasons for their departures. In one study, for instance, 2-year-olds handled separations from their mothers much better when the mothers gave them clear information ("I'm going out now for just a minute, but I'll be right back") than when the mother left without a word (Weinraub & Lewis, 1977). Thus, cognitive developmental theory offers another important partial explanation of attachment development.

Ethological Theory

The most complete explanation of attachment, and the one used by most attachment researchers today, was proposed by psychiatrist John Bowlby (1958, 1969, 1973). Bowlby was born into an upper-middle-class family in London in 1907. He was raised by a nanny and saw his mother only for a brief period every day because she thought that giving children attention and affection would spoil them. When Bowlby was about 4 years old, his beloved nanny left the family, and when he was 7, he was sent off to boarding school. Not surprisingly, having experienced separations that he later described as tragic and terrible, Bowlby was drawn to investigating the development of early attachments. Later, he had the opportunity to observe children who had been orphaned in World War II. These children's depression and other emotional scars led him to develop a theory about the importance of developing a strong attachment to a primary caregiver, a tie that normally keeps infants close to their caregivers and, therefore, safe.

Although he had been trained in psychoanalysis, Bowlby looked to fields such as evolutionary biology, ethology, developmental psychology, and cognitive science to formulate the innovative proposition that the mechanisms underlying infants' attachment emerged as a result of evolutionary pressure. One set of studies that influenced Bowlby was Lorenz's (1952) demonstration of imprinting in ducklings. Lorenz observed that newborn birds developed an attachment to the first object they saw during a brief, critical period after birth, in a process called **imprinting**. Some of the young ducklings Lorenz studied even became attached to Lorenz himself and followed him around.

imprinting
Birds and other infrahuman animals develop a preference for the person or object to which they are first exposed during a brief, critical period after birth.

Bowlby suggested that attachment has its roots in a similar (though not identical) set of instinctual responses that are important for the protection and survival of the species. The infant's responses of crying, smiling, vocalizing, sucking, clinging, and following (visually at first and later physically) elicit the care and protection that the baby needs and promote contact between infant and parent. As we discussed in Chapter 3, "Biological Foundations," the infant is biologically prepared to respond to the sights, sounds, and nurturance provided by parents. At the same time, parents are biologically prepared to respond to the baby's eliciting behaviors, such as crying, smiling, and vocalizing. As a result of these biologically programmed responses, parent and infant develop a mutual attachment. Evolutionary biases in the infant's learning abilities also interact with the parents' support, making it likely that the infant will use the parent as a **secure base**, a starting point from which the infant can venture forth to explore the world and a haven of safety to which he or she can return in times of danger or stress. According to Bowlby, attachment is linked to exploration. To learn about the environment, the child must explore; but exploration can be tiring and even dangerous, so it is desirable to

secure base
A safety zone that the infant can retreat to for comfort and reassurance when stressed or frightened while exploring the environment.

have a protector nearby. The exploration system functions optimally only when an attachment figure is available and responsive.

One unique value of Bowlby's theory lay in its emphasis on the active role played by the infant's early social signaling systems, such as smiling and crying. Another important feature was the theory's stress on the development of mutual attachments, whereby parent and child form attachments to one another (Cassidy, 2008; Thompson, 2006). A third important feature was that an attachment is a relationship, not simply a behavior of either the infant or the parent (Sroufe, 2002). More controversial was Bowlby's suggestion that infants' early behaviors are biologically programmed. As we have seen, considerable evidence suggests that some attachment behaviors, such as smiling, have social as well as biological origins. Another controversy involved whether mothers were the only ones who could provide the kind of care and support that would foster infants' attachment development. Bowlby did assume that mothers are the best caregivers. But remember, he was formulating his theory in an era when children were cared for exclusively by their mothers—or nannies—and he had missed out on the supportive contact with his own mother that he claimed promoted attachment. Subsequent research has not supported the notion that mothers are necessary for attachment development.

maternal bond
Feeling of attachment by a mother to her infant, perhaps influenced by early postnatal contact.

Insights from Extremes: Maternal Bonding

Source: Martin Lladó / iStockphoto.

In 1976, two pediatricians, Marshall Klaus and John Kennell, published the landmark book *Maternal-Infant Bonding*. Based on their work in a newborn intensive care unit, they had noticed that when babies and mothers were separated immediately after birth, usually because the mother or infant was ill or because the infant was premature, the mothers were more likely to neglect or abuse their infants. They were less comfortable and less certain that the infant was really theirs: "Are you mine? Are you really mine? Are you alive? Are you really alive?" (Klaus & Kennell, 1976, p. 10). Even mothers who had successfully raised other children seemed to have special difficulties with infants who had spent time in the intensive care nursery. According to one mother who missed out on early contact, "I did not see my baby for 11 hours. . . . My sense of loss was as deep as if someone close to me had just died. . . . Hours later when I was brought the child, I knew immediately that I did not want to hold him" (Sutherland, 1983, p. 17). Kennell and Klaus surmised that the separation immediately after birth interrupted some fundamental process between the mother and the new baby. "There is a sensitive period in the first minutes or hours of life during which it is necessary that the mother have close contact with the neonate for later development to be optimal" (Klaus & Kennell, 1976, p. 14). Studies of animal species, such as sheep and goats, supported their hypothesis, showing that when these mothers were not permitted contact with their newborns, they later rejected them. Klaus and Kennell advocated that to develop a deep emotional **maternal bond** with their infants, human mothers should be given skin-to-skin contact with their baby immediately after birth when the infant was in a state of quiet alertness and the mother was particularly receptive to the baby's cues because of her elevated level of the hormone oxytocin.

Klaus and Kennell experimented with giving mothers extra contact with their infants, including skin-to-skin contact, in the hospital immediately after birth and over the next few days. They found that these mothers seemed to develop better rapport with their infants, to hold them more comfortably, and to smile and talk to them more.

They kept their infants closer and kissed and caressed them more often (Hales et al., 1977; Kennell et al., 1974). Other researchers conducted studies with similar results, demonstrating that mothers who experienced early contact with their infants were more likely to breast-feed, continued breast-feeding longer, and behaved and spoke more sensitively to their children (de Chateau, 1980).

The importance of maternal bonding was touted in the medical community and the popular press. In one popular book for mothers, the author wrote of the "avenue of discovery" of mutual feeling of mother and child during the first hour after birth (Kitzinger, 1979, p. 49). Another author claimed that "the separation of mother and baby for a period as short as one to four hours may result in disturbed mothering patterns" (Elkins, 1978, p. 204). Unequivocal acceptance of Klaus and Kennell's bonding theory led to much anxiety and guilt among mothers who had not experienced early contact with their infants. Poor developmental outcomes—eating disorders, religious cult membership, psychological maladjustment, personality disorders, and substance abuse— were all attributed to failures to bond (Conrad et al., 1992; Crouch & Manderson, 1995; Davis, 1990).

These dire predictions turned out to be largely unwarranted because they were based on atypical high-risk samples (Lamb & Hwang, 1982; Meyers, 1984). However, positive practical changes did result from Klaus and Kennell's suggestion that maternal bonding and contact were important. When *Maternal-Infant Bonding* was published, newborn infants were routinely removed from their mothers immediately after birth and kept in hospital nurseries except for feeding. This changed after expectant parents and hospital personnel learned about bonding. Fathers and family members were allowed to remain with the mother during labor and delivery. Mothers were allowed to hold their infants immediately after birth, and in many cases, babies remained in their mother's room throughout their hospital stay. Attention to bonding also led to increased awareness of the natural capabilities of the infant at birth and so encouraged mothers to deliver their babies without anesthesia (which depresses mothers' and infants' responsiveness).

Subsequent research has shown that contact between mother and baby immediately after birth is not necessary for the mother to form a close bond with the infant. Human mothers are more flexible than sheep and goats, and even if they miss the early sensitive period, they can still form close ties with their offspring. Mothers can form a strong bond if they have given birth by a cesarean section or have adopted the child. Fathers can also form bonds with their babies without the benefits of oxytocin or skin-to-skin contact. Early contact may start the process, but later and continuing contact is just as important for developing a bond that is deep and enduring. The development of a parent-infant bond is not momentary magic but an ongoing social process.

How Attachment Develops

Inspired by theories of infant attachment, researchers have investigated infants' early social-emotional development. They have found that infants' attachment does not develop suddenly but emerges gradually.

Formation and Early Development of Attachment

The early development of attachment can be divided into four phases (see Table 4.1). In the first phase, which lasts only a month or two, the baby's social responses are relatively indiscriminate: It doesn't matter whether it's Mom or a door-to-door salesman who holds and smiles at the baby. In the second phase, infants learn to distinguish between familiar people and strangers. They differentiate between their mother's face, voice, and smell and those of other women. However, although they can make these discriminations and prefer a familiar caregiver to a stranger, they do not protest when the familiar caregiver departs; they are not yet truly attached to this particular person. In the third phase, which begins when the baby is about 7 months old, specific attachments develop. Now infants actively seek contact with certain regular caregivers, such as the mother, greeting that person happily and often crying when he or she departs. The baby does not show these behaviors to just anyone—only to

TABLE 4.1 Phases in the Early Development of Attachment

1 Preattachment	0–2 months of age	Indiscriminate social responsiveness
2 Attachment in the making	2–7 months of age	Recognition of familiar people
3 Clear-cut attachment	7–24 months of age	Separation protest; wariness of strangers; intentional communication
4 Goal-corrected partnership	24 months on	Relationships more two sided; children understand parents' needs

Source: Schaffer, 1996.

specific attachment figures. When the child passes the 2-year mark, the attachment relationship moves into the phase Bowlby called the *goal-corrected partnership*. At this point, as the result of advances in cognitive development, children become aware of other people's feelings, goals, and plans and begin to consider these things in formulating their own actions. They become partners in planning how the parent-child dyad will handle a separation.

What It Means to Be Attached

separation distress or protest
An infant's distress reaction to being separated from the attachment object, usually the mother, which typically peaks at about 15 months of age.

Unless children are reared without a regular caregiver—in an institution or in rotating foster care—by the time they are 1 year old, they have formed an attachment to one special person. They prefer this person to others. They actively seek contact and proximity with her more than with anyone else. They follow her around, cuddle, and snuggle. They play with her happily. They may move a short distance away from her side to play, but they return periodically, using her as a secure base. They go to her for comfort if they are tired or ill, hungry or afraid, injured or upset. They often fuss or cry when she leaves them for a brief time, expressing **separation distress** or **separation protest**. They greet her happily when she reappears. If she is gone for a long time (more than a week), the children express grief and mourning.

Learning from Living Leaders:
Michael E. Lamb

Source: *Courtesy of Michael E. Lamb.*

Michael Lamb is Professor of Psychology in the Social Sciences at the University of Cambridge, England. A native of Zambia, Lamb moved to the United States after his undergraduate work in South Africa. Although he aspired to become a leader of a free South Africa, the reality of apartheid forced him to rethink his plans and pursue a psychology career instead. He was particularly excited by John Bowlby's integration of psychoanalytic thought, ethological theory, and control systems theory and was able to follow this interest in his graduate work with Mary Ainsworth. The topic of his dissertation at Yale University—infant-mother and infant-father attachment—set his career path and for many years Lamb was "the father guy" championing the father's role as an attachment figure and a forgotten contributor to child development. In an influential series of books, including *The Role of the Father in Child Development*, now in its fifth edition, Lamb put the father back into the family as a major parenting partner. Lamb credits his childhood experience in another culture where infants interacted with dozens of people for his goal to broaden the cast of characters that are important in children's lives to include fathers. In fact, Lamb saw the father as only one of a number of social influences on children's development, and he went on to study siblings, peers, and nonparental child care providers as well. He also studied how social relationships vary across cultures from Sweden and Israel to African hunter-gatherers. His proudest accomplishment is that his work has made a difference in children's lives. It has been used by courts making decisions about child custody and as a basis for shaping child care policies. The American Psychological Association honored Lamb with a Young Scientist Award early in his career and later the Association for Psychological Science

recognized him with an award for Lifetime Achievement. He offers this positive message to students, "These are exciting times: We have many more investigative tools at our disposal than ever before, and there are so many interesting questions still unanswered. Look carefully at how we've tried to answer them in the past, and note how we've often had to change the question subtly to make it more answerable. How would you like to address the REAL questions?"

Further Reading

Lamb, M. E. (2008). The many faces of fatherhood: Some thoughts about fatherhood and immigration. In S. S. Chuang & R. P. Moreno (Eds.), *On new shores: Understanding immigrant fathers in North America* (pp. 7–24). Lanham, MD: Lexington Books.

Attachment to Whom?

Although infants are capable of forming attachments to any familiar individual, the mother is usually the first object of their affection. In an early study of attachment development, researchers observed 60 infants in Scotland, most from working class families living with both parents, and recorded the infants' separation protest in seven everyday situations including being left alone in a room, being left with other people, and being left in bed at night (Schaffer & Emerson, 1964). In the first year of life, 93 percent of the infants showed that they had formed a specific attachment to their mother by protesting more often and intensely when she left them; only 7 percent had formed a primary attachment to someone other than the mother. Other researchers subsequently reported similar preferences for the mother (Ban & Lewis, 1974; Lamb, 1976; Lytton, 1980).

However, although infants are likely to develop their initial attachment to the mother, they also form attachments to other familiar people with whom they interact frequently and fondly. In the Scottish study, when the infants were 18 months old, only 5 percent were attached *only* to their mother; the others were also attached to their father (75%), a grandparent (45%), or a sibling (24%). These attachments can be very important from an evolutionary perspective because infants' capacity to form relationships with a range of caregivers ensures their survival if the principal caregiver becomes unavailable.

It is not surprising that infants typically form their first attachment to their mother, because mothers are the primary caregivers for most infants during the first year of life (Pleck & Masciadrelli, 2004; Roopnarine et al., 2005). Even in hunter-gatherer societies, where the search for food and other necessities requires the efforts of both men and women, mothers are usually the primary caregivers (Griffin & Griffin, 1992; Morelli & Tronick, 1992). Although fathers do hold, touch, talk to, and kiss their infants as much as mothers when they are given the chance by a researcher (Parke, 1996, 2002; Parke & O'Leary, 1976), at home, they are more likely to participate in caregiving when the mother supports their involvement and views them as competent (Beitel & Parke, 1998) or when the mother is unavailable, for example, if she is recovering from a cesarean section delivery (Pedersen et al., 1980) or is employed outside the home (Coltrane, 1996).

Rather than being the primary caregiver, the father may play a special role in his infant's life by being a playmate. In general, fathers spend four to five times more time playing with their infants than caring for them (Lamb, 1987; Pleck & Masciadrelli, 2004), and compared with mothers, they engage in more physically arousing and unusual games—especially with their sons (Parke, 1996, 2002). Thus, fathers enrich infants' social development by providing unique types of social experiences, and because infants can form multiple attachments, fathers, too, often become attachment objects. Grandparents and siblings, similarly, can become objects of attachment (Howes & Spieker, 2008; Smith & Drew, 2002). However, the number of attachments a child can form is limited. Developing an attachment requires frequent, close, one-to-one interaction, and it would be challenging and exhausting for a baby to engage in such intense interactions with many partners.

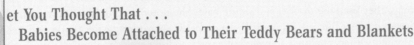

Bet You Thought That . . .
Babies Become Attached to Their Teddy Bears and Blankets

Source: Vyacheslav Oshokin/iStockphoto.

You've probably seen young children holding a scraggly bit of blanket or a well-loved teddy bear, maybe sucking on a corner or an ear. They definitely want that scruff or fluff when they take a nap, and their parents may have to sneak it away to wash when the child is asleep. The term *security blanket* was popularized by Charles Shultz's cartoon strip *Peanuts,* in which Linus dragged around his blanket as a constant companion. Bowlby, too, recognized that these objects can provide comfort and security for the infant. In fact, more than 60 percent of children in the United States have a "security object" or "comfort toy" at some time in their lives (Hobara, 2003; Passman, 1998), and having this object allows them to cope better with new and stressful situations such as separation from their mother (Passman, 1998). Children are more likely to have a security object if their mothers do not breast-feed them, hold them while they go to sleep, or sleep with them in the same bed (Green et al., 2004; Hobara, 2003). Pets such as cats and dogs can also serve as security objects and provide comfort and emotional support for children (Melson, 2003; Serpell, 1996; Triebenbacher, 1998). But are children really "attached" to these objects? In a technical sense, no. Attachment is not just about reducing children's distress. Attachment figures also respond to children's other needs and support their interactions with the world. They give the children an expectation of availability and responsiveness and a sense that they are stronger and wiser than the child. This goes beyond the capacities of the softest blanket, the most loyal dog, the cuddliest kitten. These objects do not offer the extraordinary scaffolding and contingent responsiveness that parents do. Moreover, they are no substitute for "real" attachment relationships. Even with a pet or a blankie, children still need love and attention from their caregivers.

The Nature and Quality of Attachment

secure attachment Babies are able to explore novel environments, are minimally disturbed by brief separations from their mother, and are quickly comforted by her when she returns.

Early attachments are not all the same; they differ in quality from one relationship to another and from one child to the next. The majority of children form attachments to their parents that are secure. A **secure attachment** means that the infant is confident about the parent's availability, responsiveness, and reliability to serve as a secure base. These infants believe that the parent will provide support for their exploration of the world and a safety net if circumstances turn threatening (Waters et al., 2002). Both exploration away from the parent and contact after returning to the parent are important parts of the attachment system, and securely attached infants exhibit a balance between venturing out into the world and staying close to the parent in times of stress and uncertainty. Not all children develop attachments to their parents that are secure and dependable, however. One of the first researchers to study variations in the security of children's attachments to their parents was a student of Bowlby's, Mary Ainsworth.

Different Types of Attachment Relationships

Strange Situation A research scenario in which parent and child are separated and reunited so that investigators can assess the nature and quality of the parent–infant attachment relationship.

Ainsworth (1969) studied infants in Uganda and Baltimore and observed how, in everyday settings, they used the mother as a secure base. She noted considerable variation in their behavior. Some babies achieved a smooth balance between exploring the world and keeping close to mother. Others explored actively but expressed little concern about the mother's whereabouts and showed little proximity seeking to her. Still other babies were passive in proximity-seeking behavior, in exploration, or in both. Because assessing attachment behavior in naturalistic observations was so time consuming, Ainsworth devised a simple and less time-intensive laboratory-based scenario to assess variation in infants' ability to use their mother as a secure base. In the scenario, known as the **Strange Situation (SS)**, the mother leaves the baby in an unfamiliar room, first with a stranger and then alone (see Table 4.2). The infant's behavior when the mother returns to the room is coded to reflect the nature of their relationship (see Table 4.3).

AINSWORTH'S CLASSIFICATION OF ATTACHMENT TYPES Of the white, middle-class Baltimore infants Ainsworth studied, 60 to 65 percent displayed a secure attachment to their mothers: They readily sought contact with her after the stress of her departure in the unfamiliar setting and were quickly comforted by her, even if they were initially quite upset.

TABLE 4.2 **The Strange Situation**

1	Mother, baby, and observer	30 seconds	Observer introduces mother and baby to experimental room and then leaves. (Room contains appealing toys scattered about.)
2	Mother and baby	3 minutes	Mother sits quietly while baby explores; if necessary, play is stimulated after 2 minutes.
3	Stranger, mother, and baby	3 minutes	An unfamiliar woman enters. First minute: stranger is silent. Second minute: stranger talks to mother. Third minute: stranger approaches baby. After 3 minutes, mother leaves unobtrusively.
4	Stranger and baby	3 minutes or less	First separation episode. Stranger is responsive to baby.
5	Mother and baby	3 minutes or more	First reunion episode. Mother returns to room and greets and/ or comforts baby and then tries to settle the baby again in play. Mother then leaves, saying "bye-bye."
6	Baby alone	3 minutes or less	Second separation episode.
7	Stranger and baby	3 minutes or less	Continuation of second separation. Stranger enters and responds to baby's behavior.
8	Mother and baby	3 minutes	Second reunion episode. Mother enters, greets, and then picks up baby. Meanwhile, stranger leaves unobtrusively.

These infants also were secure enough to explore the novel environment when the mother was present. They did not whine and cling to her but actively investigated their surroundings as if the mother's presence gave them confidence. In a familiar situation at home, these children were minimally disturbed by minor separations from the mother and greeted her happily when she returned. In Ainsworth's coding scheme, these infants were classified as having a secure attachment (Type B).

The remaining children were classified as having an insecure attachment—either an insecure-avoidant attachment (Type A) or an **insecure-ambivalent attachment** (Type C). Insecure-avoidant children showed little distress over the mother's absence in the Strange Situation at least on her first departure, and then they actively avoided her on her return. They turned away from their mother, increased their distance from her, and paid her no attention. After the mother's second departure, during which time these infants were sometimes visibly upset, they again avoided the mother. About 20 percent of the children studied by Ainsworth and other researchers in the United States were insecure avoidant. Insecure-ambivalent children might become extremely upset when the mother left them in the Strange Situation but were oddly ambivalent toward her when she returned; they were likely to seek contact with her and then angrily push her away. About 10 to 15 percent of children in the United States display this pattern of attachment.

BEYOND AINSWORTH'S A-B-C CLASSIFICATION

Later researchers identified another type of insecure attachment: **insecure-disorganized attachment** (Type D) (Solomon & George, 2008). When insecure-disorganized infants are reunited with their mothers in the Strange Situation, they act disorganized and disoriented. They look dazed, freeze in the middle of their movements, or engage in repetitive behaviors, such as rocking. These children seem to be apprehensive and fearful of their attachment figure and are unable to cope with distress in a consistent and organized way even though their mother is available. These four attachment types (A, B, C, and D) can be identified in the Strange Situation when children are about a year old. Similar attachment patterns have been observed in older children, ages 3 through 6, if mother-child separations in the Strange Situation are lengthened to reflect changes in children's maturity (Cassidy & Marvin, 1992; Main & Cassidy, 1988; Solomon & George, 2008). Children's physical proximity and affect continue to be assessed in these Modified Strange Situations as in the original Strange Situation, but conversation and dialogue between child and parent play a more central role in these assessments of older children (see Table 4.3).

OTHER STRATEGIES FOR ASSESSING ATTACHMENT

Other methods for assessing attachment have also been developed. One method involves coding children's behavior in the Strange Situation along specific scales rather than classifying children into attachment types (Fraley & Spieker, 2003). Researchers have coded children's behavior in the two reunion episodes on four scales: *proximity and contact seeking*, *contact maintenance*, *avoidance*, and *resistance* (pouting, fussiness, angry distress). They have then reduced these scales to two dimensions using factor analysis. One dimension is proximity-seeking versus avoidance, which reflects the degree to which children's attachment systems are organized around the goal of proximity maintenance, ranging from using the caregiver as a secure haven to minimizing contact with the caregiver. The second dimension is anger and resistance, which represents the amount of overt conflict and anger expressed toward the caregiver. Compared with the traditional taxonomy of three attachment types (secure, avoidant, ambivalent), these continuous measures offer several statistical advantages. They indicate greater stability in individual differences in attachment behavior over long spans of time, they have greater statistical power to explain variance in attachment behavior, and they provide stronger associations with theoretically relevant variables such as maternal responsiveness.

insecure-avoidant attachment
Babies seem not to be bothered by their mother's brief absences but specifically avoid her when she returns, sometimes becoming visibly upset.

insecure-ambivalent attachment
Babies tend to become very upset at the departure of their mother and exhibit inconsistent behavior on the mother's return, sometimes seeking contact, sometimes pushing their mother away. (This is sometimes referred to as *insecure-resistant* or *anxious-ambivalent attachment*.)

insecure-disorganized attachment
Babies seem disorganized and disoriented when reunited with their mother after separation.

TABLE 4.3   **Attachment Classification**

1 Year Old	6 Year Old
Secure attachment	
On reunion after brief separation from parent, child seeks physical contact, proximity, interaction; often tries to maintain physical contact. Readily soothed by parent and returns to exploration and play.	On reunion, child initiates conversation and pleasant interaction with parent or is highly responsive to parent's overtures. May subtly move close to or into physical contact with parent, usually with rationale such as seeking a toy. Remains calm throughout.
Insecure-avoidant attachment	
Child actively avoids and ignores parent on reunion, looking away and remaining occupied with toys. May move away from parent and ignore parent's efforts to communicate.	Child minimizes and restricts opportunities for interaction with parent on reunion, looking and speaking only as necessary and remaining occupied with toys or activities. May subtly move away with rationale such as retrieving a toy.
Insecure-ambivalent attachment	
Although infant seems to want closeness and contact, parent is not able to effectively alleviate the child's distress after brief separation. Child may show subtle or overt signs of anger, seeking proximity and then resisting it.	In movement, posture, and tone of voice, child seems to try to exaggerate both intimacy and dependency on parent. May seek closeness but appears uncomfortable, for example, lying in parent's lap but wriggling and squirming. Shows subtle signs of hostility.
Insecure-disorganized attachment	
Child shows signs of disorganization (e.g., crying for parent at door and then running quickly away when door opens; approaching parent with head down) or disorientation (e.g., seeming to "freeze" for a few seconds).	Child seems almost to adopt parental role with parent, trying to control and direct parent's behavior either by embarrassing or humiliating parent or by showing extreme enthusiasm for reunion or overly solicitous behavior toward parent.

Sources: Ainsworth et al., 1978; Kerns, 2008; Main & Cassidy, 1988; Main & Hesse, 1990; Solomon & George, 2008.

The Attachment Q-Set (AQS; Waters, 1995) is based on a lengthy observation of the child at home or on the judgment of the parent or other caregiver who knows the child well. The mother, other caregiver, or observer sorts a set of 90 cards containing phrases that describe a child's behavior into sets ranging from those that are most descriptive of the child to those that are least descriptive (see Table 4.4 for sample items). This method, which is useful for children between the ages of 1 and 5, provides a score that reflects how much children resemble a hypothetical securely attached child, but it does not classify the type of attachment insecurity. A meta-analysis of studies in which children were assessed with the AQS revealed that its scores were moderately related to security in the Strange Situation and that the AQS distinguished between normal children and children with clinical problems (van IJzendoorn et al., 2004). AQS ratings provided by objective observers were more highly related and therefore more valid than ratings provided by mothers.

The California attachment procedure (CAP) focuses on how children use the mother as a secure base when they experience stressful events such as a loud noise or a scary robot

TABLE 4.4 Items from the Attachment Q-Set Illustrating the Behavior at Home of a Child Who is Securely Attached or Insecurely Attached to the Mother

Secure Attachment	Insecure Attachment
Child readily shares with mother or lets her hold things if she asks to.	Child refuses to share with mother.
Child is happy or affectionate when returning to mother between or after play times.	When child returns to mother after playing, he is sometimes fussy for no clear reason.
When child is upset or injured, mother is the only one he allows to comfort him.	When he is upset or injured, child will accept comforting from adults other than mother.
Child often hugs or cuddles against mother, without her asking or inviting him to do so.	Child doesn't hug or cuddle much unless mother hugs him first or asks him to give her a hug.
When child finds something new to play with, he carries it to mother or shows it to her from across the room.	Child plays with new object quietly or goes where he won't be interrupted.
Child keeps track of mother's location when he plays around the house.	Child doesn't keep track of mother's location.
Child enjoys relaxing in mother's lap.	Child prefers to relax on the floor or on furniture.
Child actively goes after mother if he is upset or crying.	When child is upset about mother leaving him, he sits right where he is and cries. Doesn't go after her.
Child clearly shows a pattern of using mother as a base from which to explore. Moves out to play; returns or plays near her; moves out to play again, etc.	Child is always away from mother or always stays near her.

Source: Waters, 1987, Attachment Q-set, Version 3; http://www.psychology.sunysb.edu/attachment/measures/content/aqs_items.pdf

instead of being separated from her and then reunited (Clarke-Stewart et al., 2001). Like the Strange Situation, this assessment is coded into Ainsworth's attachment types. However, it has been found to provide a more valid measure of attachment than the Strange Situation for children such those involved in child care who are accustomed to routine separations from their mothers.

Learning from Living Leaders: Everett Waters

Source: Courtesy of Everett Waters.

Everett Waters is Professor of Psychology at the State University of New York at Stony Brook and a graduate of the University of Minnesota. He received the Boyd R. McCandless Early Career Award from the American Psychological Association and the 2009 Bowlby-Ainsworth Award for contributions to attachment theory and research. Like many other developmental psychologists, he started out on a different career path. He planned to be a chemist, but the novelty of ions and compounds soon wore off and life changed when he took a volunteer position with Mary Ainsworth. This experience with one of the pioneers of attachment theory led to his life-long interest in attachment and social development. In his research, Waters has tried to discover how infant-parent and adult-adult attachment relationships play out in real life and how early attachment experiences are represented in memory and influence later parenting and adult-adult attachment behavior. His work has documented the stability of attachment patterns from infancy to early adulthood while showing that attachment remains open to revision in light of experience. Waters made an important methodological contribution by devising the Attachment Q-Set, which permits assessment of attachment in the home and other naturalistic settings. He is also interested in the practical implications of attachment theory. He hopes that educators and clinicians will adopt Bowlby's ideas for parenting and therapy, but he believes in taking things slowly because "people can get hurt when we jump too directly from discovery to practice." He sees the practical payoffs coming in the next generation of attachment work. According to Waters, the most pressing issue for the field of social development today is to "observe more, think more about cognition, self, and emotion and their roles in attachment relationships,

and think more carefully in general—perhaps though the use of computer modeling." In the future, he predicts that attachment will find its place in a broader theory of the many sources of human security and will be better understood in terms of basic cognitive processes. His advice to undergraduates is to read widely, especially people who write well, such as Stephen J. Gould and Jared Diamond, learn to think clearly and critically, and take time to do careful real-world observations before designing studies or measures. On a personal note, Waters reminds us that "good relationships and good kids do happen, but they don't just happen."

Further Reading

Waters, H., & Waters, E. (2007). The attachment working model concept. *Attachment and Human Development, 8,* 185–197.

www.johnbowlby.com

ultural Context:
Assessing Attachment in Different Cultures

Source: Kwaku Alston//Getty Images, Inc.

Many researchers have wanted to know whether Ainsworth's Strange Situation is valid in cultures other than the United States, so they have tried it in different countries around the world. Their results suggest that children with different caregiving experiences behave differently in this assessment of attachment (van IJzendoorn & Sagi-Schwartz, 2008). The Strange Situation depends on creating a situation in which an infant is somewhat stressed and therefore displays proximity-seeking behavior to the attachment figure;

but infants differ in how familiar they are with key components of the scenario—being left by the mother and interacting with an unfamiliar woman—and this affects how stressful they find it.

In the United States, most parents encourage their infants to play with toys, exercise their motor skills, and nap alone. They stress active, exploratory behavior. Few bring their babies into bed with them. Gusii infants in Kenya, in contrast, are accustomed to being held by their mothers for a large part of the day until they are 1 year old. Puerto Rican mothers also stress close contact with their infants (Harwood et al., 1995). Japanese infants are in close contact with their mothers from the time they are born; mothers rarely leave their babies alone, they hold and carry them and give them little floor freedom, and they usually sleep in the same bed (Colin, 1996; Rothbaum, Weisz et al., 2000; van IJzendoorn & Sagi-Schwartz, 2008). Infants in Uganda are unaccustomed to brief separations from their mothers; they experience only lengthy separations while their mothers work (Colin, 1996). Compared with U.S. babies, infants in all these cultures find Strange Situation separations more strange and stressful; they show more distress and find accepting the mother's comfort more difficult. They are more likely to be ambivalent and less likely to be avoidant than U.S. infants. In the photo, a Japanese toddler clings tightly to her mother's legs, preventing her from leaving. In Germany, Sweden, and Great Britain, parents stress infants' early independence even more than U.S. parents; not surprisingly then, German, Swedish, and British infants are more likely to be avoidant in the Strange Situation than are American infants (Colin, 1996; Schaffer, 1996).

In view of these findings, we may ask whether the Strange Situation is the best instrument for assessing attachment relationships in other cultures. In cultures where babies are treated very differently from how they are in the United States, it is a good idea to make sure the Strange Situation is a good predictor of their behavior at home, perhaps by using the Attachment Q-Set. If the two measures don't agree, it is probably better to use the direct observations of attachment behavior at home. Although some items in the AQS are somewhat culture bound, researchers have found considerable overall cross-cultural consistency in mothers' Q-sorts in China, Colombia, Germany, Israel, Japan, Norway, and the United States (Posada et al., 1995).

ATTACHMENT TYPES AND THE BRAIN Geraldine Dawson and her colleagues examined EEG activity in the prefrontal cortex of 1-year-old infants during a series of episodes that were similar to a Strange Situation (SS): Mother plays with infant; stranger enters; familiar experimenter plays with infant; mother leaves (Dawson et al., 2001). They found that infants whose behavior in this abbreviated SS indicated that they were insecurely attached to their mothers compared with infants who were securely attached showed relatively less activity on the left side of the prefrontal cortex and relatively more activity on the right side. Because other researchers have found that the left prefrontal cortex is specialized for the expression of positive approach emotions such as joy and interest, whereas the right prefrontal cortex is specialized for the expression of negative withdrawal emotions such as distress, disgust, and fear (Coan et al., 2006; Dawson, 1994), a clear and logical correspondence between attachment and brain activity was suggested. Securely attached infants, who are happy and interested in interacting with their mothers in the SS, show more brain activity on the positive (left) side of their prefrontal cortex during this kind of activity; insecurely attached infants, who withdraw from their mothers or express anger toward them in the SS, show more activity on the negative (right) side in these situations. Other researchers have found neurological correlates of attachment in adulthood as well. In one fMRI study, for example, women who said they had an avoidant attachment relationship with their husband showed increased activation in the negative (right) side of the prefrontal cortex under threat of mild electric shock when holding their spouse's hand but less activation on that side when holding the hand of a stranger (Coan et al., 2005). Although findings from these studies are preliminary, they suggest that attachment security is reflected in neurological activity measured in attachment-evoking contexts. In the future, researchers will likely increase their efforts to use brain-imaging techniques to study attachment (Coan, 2008). Biological tools offer an important perspective on the mechanisms through which early attachment experiences come to be reflected in behavior.

Parents' Role in Infants' Attachment Development

Attachment, it should be clear, is a *relationship*, developing out of interactions between two people. The infant's attachment to the parent is not an infant trait like weight or intelligence. It is a product of both the infant's and the parent's predispositions and behavior. In this section, we discuss the parents' input into infants' attachment development.

BIOLOGICAL PREPARATION Even before a baby is born, parents are getting ready to provide the type of care that is necessary for their infant's attachment development. Mothers undergo hormonal changes during pregnancy and childbirth that make them sensitive to infant cries and primed for the tasks of motherhood (Corter & Fleming, 2002). Fathers also undergo hormonal changes (Storey et al., 2000). For many men, testosterone levels drop after the baby's birth when they first interact with their infant. These men with lower testosterone levels are more responsive to infant cues such as crying and are likely to hold a baby doll longer than men whose testosterone levels do not decrease (Fleming et al., 2002). Hormonal shifts are especially marked for men who are closely involved with their wives during pregnancy, which suggests that intimate ties between partners during pregnancy can stimulate hormonal changes. Fathers who have more than one child and therefore more experience with babies have even lower testosterone levels than first-time fathers (Corter & Fleming, 2002) or childless men (Gray et al., 2006). In brief, hormones prepare mothers and fathers to begin parenting their infant.

LINK BETWEEN CAREGIVING AND ATTACHMENT   After the baby is born, the development of a secure attachment depends on close contact between infant and parent. A study conducted in Israel demonstrates this clearly. In that country, some families live in *kibbutzim,* or communal villages, and their children spend the day together in a group care center. In some of these kibbutzim, infants also stay in the center at night; in other kibbutzim, they spend the night with their families. Avi Sagi-Schwartz and his colleagues studied the effects of these different arrangements on the children's attachment relationships (Sagi et al., 1994). Infants who spent the night at home with their families were more likely to develop secure attachments than infants who stayed in the center (60% vs. 26%). Presumably, this was because their parents had more opportunities for close interactions with them; the researchers had equated the two groups for other factors, including early life events, the quality of mother–infant play, and the quality of the care centers.

Developing a secure attachment also depends on specific aspects of the parent's behavior. Ainsworth identified four features of mothers' behavior that were associated with the quality of their infants' attachments (Ainsworth et al., 1978). First, mothers of securely attached infants were sensitive to their baby's signals, interpreted them accurately, and responded to them promptly and appropriately. Second, mothers of secure infants geared their behavior to the baby's state, mood, and interests and did not interrupt or interfere with the baby's activity. Third, secure infants' mothers were accepting of their baby, and their acceptance overrode any frustrations, irritations, or limitations they felt, so they were never rejecting of the baby. Fourth, mothers of secure infants were physically and psychologically available; they were aware of the baby, alert to the baby's signals, and actively acknowledged and responded to them; they did not ignore the baby. More recent studies have supported Ainsworth's early findings (Belsky & Fearon, 2008; Braungart-Rieker et al., 2001; Tarabulsy et al., 2005). It is understandable that an infant who experiences this kind of sensitive and accepting care would have positive expectations of the mother's availability and responsiveness and develop a secure attachment relationship with her.

Even more convincing evidence of a link between the quality of maternal behavior and the quality of infant attachment came from an experimental study (Anisfield et al., 1990). Lower-income inner-city mothers of newborns were divided into two groups: one group received soft baby carriers, the other group was given rigid "car seat" type carriers. The researchers predicted that the soft infant carriers would increase physical contact between infants and mothers and facilitate the development of maternal responsiveness. In fact, the mothers given the soft carriers were more sensitive and responsive to their infants' vocalizations at 3 months, and 83 percent of their babies were securely attached to their mothers at 13 months compared with only 39 percent of the infants whose mothers were given car seat carriers. Across a variety of studies, researchers have consistently found that a sensitive and responsive style of caregiving is associated with the development of secure attachments (see meta-analyses of correlational studies by Atkinson et al., 2000; De Wolff & van IJzendoorn, 1997; van IJzendoorn et al., 2004; meta-analysis of intervention studies by Bakermans-Kranenburg et al., 2003; and recent studies by Chaimongkol & Flick, 2006; Fearon et al., 2006; Mills-Koonce et al., 2007;

Tarabulsy et al., 2008). The link between sensitive parenting and attachment security is not limited to mothers, moreover. Fathers' sensitivity is also related to infants' development of a secure attachment to them (van IJzendoorn & De Wolff, 1997). Nor is the link limited to North American families. It has also been found in studies of mothers and infants in Australia (Harrison & Ungerer, 2002), Brazil (Posada et al., 2002), and South Africa (Tomlinson et al., 2005)—to name a few.

The link between parent and infant appears in the earliest months of life as parents continuously adjust their behavior to the baby's so that the pair is engaged in a smooth-flowing "dance." This dance has been described as "interactive synchrony" (Van Egeren et al., 2001). When mother-infant pairs achieve interactive synchrony in the first few months, infants are more likely to develop a secure attachment to the mother in the second half year of life. In one longitudinal study, infants were observed in their homes with their mothers at 1, 3, and 9 months of age, and at 12 months the infant's attachment to the mother was assessed in the Strange Situation (Belsky & Fearon, 2008; Isabella, 1993). Securely attached infants had more synchronous patterns of interaction with their mother (even at 1 and 3 months of age) than did insecurely attached babies; the interactions of the insecurely attached children were more one sided.

The development of a secure attachment also depends on the parents' insightfulness. Parents who are more insightful appreciate their infant's feelings, make accurate and empathic interpretations of the baby's signals, and adjust their responses to suit the baby's needs. Insightfulness prevents them from focusing too much attention on the child's behavior and gives them the flexibility to consider the child's particular motives and intentions rather than following some preset notion of what an infant should need or want. To assess mothers' insightfulness, researchers have shown them videotapes of their own interactions with their babies (playing, diapering, being distracted) and asked them: "What do you think was going through your child's head? What did she/he think, feel?" (Koren-Karie et al., 2002). Mothers who provided more insightful answers to these questions were more sensitive to their infants, and their infants were more securely attached.

These parenting characteristics continue to be important as children get older. When the mother is supportive and attuned to the child's needs in adolescence and the two are able to maintain their relationship in spite of disagreements, their attachment relationship is more likely to be secure (J. P. Allen et al., 2003). A similar pattern is evident for fathers; when the father is not harsh during conflicts with the child and the two can maintain a positive relationship in the midst of disagreements, the adolescent-father attachment is more likely to be secure (Allen et al., 2007).

In contrast to the secure attachments formed to these supportive, sensitive, synchronous, and insightful parents are attachments to parents who are intrusive, inconsistent, or unaffectionate. Children are likely to develop insecure-avoidant attachments to parents who are intrusive or rejecting—who fail to respond to the infant's signals, rarely have close bodily contact, and often act angry and irritable when they are together (Belsky & Fearon, 2008; Cassidy & Berlin, 1994). It is reasonable that these infants would keep their attention directed to toys and avoid seeking contact with their parent in the Strange Situation if this is the behavior they have come to expect. Children are more likely to develop insecure-ambivalent attachments to parents who are unaffectionate and inconsistent—who sometimes respond and other times ignore their baby's needs (Belsky & Fearon, 2008; Isabella, 1993). These infants are preoccupied with the parent's availability in the Strange Situation because they don't know whether to expect a kind word or a cold glance, and this preoccupation prevents them from leaving the parent's side to explore the room.

Infants who form insecure-disorganized attachments to their parents are likely to have experienced the worst caregiving. Their parents often neglect them or abuse them physically. In one study, researchers found that 82 percent of abused infants developed insecure-disorganized attachments to their parents compared with only 19 percent of infants who were

TABLE 4.5 Distribution of Attachment Types in Institutionalized Children

Strange Situation Classification	Institution Group (N = 95) (%)	Home Reared Group (N = 50) (%)
Secure	19%	74%
Avoidant	3	4
Ambivalent	0	0
Disorganized	65	22
Unclassifiable	13	0

Source: Zeanah et al., 2005.

not mistreated (Carlson et al., 1989). The disorganized approach-avoidance behavior these maltreated infants display in the Strange Situation may actually be an adaptive response because these babies do not know what to expect but realize that it could be very bad (Solomon & George, 2008). Babies of depressed mothers also exhibit approach-avoidance behavior and sadness during reunions in the Strange Situation and are classified as having insecure-disorganized attachments. When depressed mothers are observed with their babies, they display little eye contact and minimal responsiveness; instead, they tend to avert their gaze (Field, 1990; Greenberg, 1999). Mothers who are frightened or frightening are also likely to have infants with insecure-disorganized attachments (Lyons-Ruth & Jacobvitz, 2008; True et al., 2001). These mothers are a source of both comfort and fear, which leads to the infant's disorganized behavior. Finally, being reared in an institution without a consistent caregiver is likely to lead to insecure-disorganized attachment. In one study of 1- to 2½-year-olds in an orphanage in Bucharest, researchers found that caregivers' interactions with the children were characterized by lack of eye contact, mechanical interaction patterns, little talking, slow responsiveness to distress, and ineffective soothing (Zeanah et al., 2005). As you see in Table 4.5, only 19 percent of the children had formed a secure attachment to a caregiver; 65 percent were classified as disorganized. Some of the children from the orphanage were randomly selected and placed in foster care (Smyke et al., 2010). When attachment was assessed at age 3½, 49 percent of these children had formed a secure attachment to their foster mother; only 18 percent of the children who were still in the orphanage had a secure attachment to a caregiver.

Research up Close:
Early Experience, Hormones, and Attachment

Underlying the development of insecure attachments in institutionalized infants are hormonal deficiencies. Two hormones are necessary for the development of healthy secure attachments in animals and humans (Carter, 2005). One hormone is oxytocin, known as the "cuddle hormone" or "love hormone." Levels of this hormone increase when an infant experiences warm physical contact with a familiar person. The second hormone is vasopressin. Higher levels of this hormone are related to the infant's recognition of familiar people. Animal studies have shown that treatment with oxytocin increases infants' social behaviors

and the development of specific attachments (Carter & Keverne, 2002). Even in adulthood exposure to oxytocin via a nasal spray increases a person's trust of other players in a game (Kosfeld et al., 2005). But does early social deprivation in institutions alter the levels of these social hormones? To find out, researchers measured these hormones in 4-year-olds who had lived in Russian or Romanian orphanages before being adopted by U.S. families (Wismer Fries et al., 2005). Despite the fact that these children had been living in stable, caring families for 3 years, they showed deficits in both social behaviors and social hormones when compared with U.S. children raised by their biological parents. The adopted children from the orphanages were less socially responsive and more likely to have insecure-disorganized attachments to their adoptive parents, and when they interacted physically with their adoptive mothers (playing, touching, whispering, tickling), their level of oxytocin did not increase as it did for the children reared by their biological parents. The hormone that did increase was the stress-related hormone cortisol, indicating that these children continued to experience interactions with their adoptive mothers as stressful and were unable to control their emotional arousal (Wismer Fries et al., 2008). The previously institutionalized children also had lower levels of vasopressin than the home-reared children when they interacted with a stranger, and, related to this deficiency, they were poorer at identifying facial expressions of emotion and matching facial expressions to happy, sad, and fearful scenarios (Camras, Perlman, et al., 2006; Wismer Fries & Pollak, 2004). Whether or not these children will be able to develop healthy relationships in later life and overcome the effects of their early deprivation is unclear. What is clear is that early experience can alter hormones that affect the brain, that this affects infants' capacity for social interaction, and that this, in turn, is likely to lead to less than optimal attachment patterns.

ATTACHMENT IN FAMILY AND COMMUNITY CONTEXTS Attachment relationships between infants and parents do not develop in a vacuum. They are embedded in family and community contexts, which can influence attachment development. One context that affects the child's attachment to parents is the relationship between the mother and father. A secure attachment is more likely when parents have a happy marriage (Belsky & Fearon, 2008; Thompson, 2008).

Socioeconomic status is another contextual factor that influences the quality of children's attachments. In low-income families, attachment relationships are more likely to be insecure. Economic and emotional risks associated with poverty—including not having enough food, living in a rough neighborhood, experiencing domestic violence, and using alcohol and drugs—reduce maternal sensitivity, and, in turn, increase the likelihood that infants will develop insecure attachments (Raikes & Thompson, 2005). The more risks there are, the more likely this outcome. For example, researchers have found that in very poor families, when mothers were less sensitive toward their children and the children were undernourished as well, 93 percent of the children developed insecure attachments compared with only 50 percent of adequately nourished children from low-income families (Valenzuela, 1997).

These links between poverty and insecure attachment are not inevitable, however; social support in the community can alleviate problems in the family. Secure infant-mother attachments are more likely in very poor families that have a social safety net composed of supportive and helpful neighbors and kin. This allows the mother to develop and maintain a sensitive and responsive pattern of interaction with her infant, which in turn promotes a secure infant-mother attachment. Researchers have documented a relatively high likelihood of secure attachments in poor communities in South Africa, for example, where infants and young children are considered to belong to the community and the responsibility for their safety and well-being is a collective one (Tomlinson et al., 2005). Finding links between children's attachments and community characteristics is consistent with Bronfenbrenner's ecological-systems theory (Bronfenbrenner & Morris, 2006) and reminds us that attachment is not simply a dyadic issue but is influenced by family circumstances and community support as well.

internal working model
A person's mental representation of himself or herself as a child, his or her parents, and the nature of his or her interaction with the parents as he or she reconstructs and interprets that interaction.

CONTINUITY IN ATTACHMENT FROM PARENT TO CHILD The type of care that the parents received when they were young children provides another context for children's attachment development (Bretherton & Munholland, 2008). Children form what Bowlby referred to as **internal working models** or "attachment representations" that reflect their parents' styles of interaction with them. These working models are modified as children grow into adulthood and reconstruct and reinterpret their early experiences. When they become parents, mothers and fathers tend to re-create relationships with their children that replicate their working models of their own relationships in childhood.

A number of techniques have been used to measure internal working models of attachment in children. In the narrative story method, children are given dolls representing family members and the interviewer begins a story about an attachment-related event, such as "Your mother is late coming to pick you up one day . . ." (Emde et al., 2003). The interviewer then encourages the child to complete the story. The story the child tells is assumed to reflect the child's internal working model of his or her attachment relationship with the mother. Other assessments rely on children's abilities to understand and describe their experiences with their parents. Researchers have found that securely attached 3-year-olds describe positive social events with their parents more accurately than do insecurely attached children, a finding that is consistent with the view that working models are mental schemas that organize and guide the types of social information children notice and remember (Belsky et al., 1996; Waters & Waters, 2007).

Researchers have also developed techniques to measure internal working models of attachment in adults. One technique they use is the Adult Attachment Interview (AAI) developed by Mary Main and her colleagues (Hesse, 2008; Main et al., 1985). In this interview, adults are questioned about their childhood relationships with their parents, and based on the coherence of their narratives, are classified into one of three groups (see Table 4.6). *Autonomous* adults reveal in their interviews that although they value close relationships with their parents and others, they are objective about these relationships. They tend not to idealize their own parents but have a clear understanding of their relationships with them and are able to describe both their positive and their negative traits. *Dismissing* adults dismiss and devalue attachment and frequently claim that they cannot recall incidents from their childhoods. When they do remember anything, it is often a recollection of an idealized parent: "I had the world's greatest mom!" Adults in the third group are *preoccupied* with earlier family attachments. They recall many conflict-ridden incidents from their childhoods and cannot organize them into a coherent pattern.

Researchers using the AAI have found strong support for Bowlby's prediction that parents' recollections of their childhoods would be related to their children's attachments to them. In Main's research, infants of autonomous mothers were likely to have secure attachments to them; infants with dismissing mothers were likely to have avoidant attachments; and infants of preoccupied mothers were often insecure ambivalent (Main et al., 1985). Further evidence of intergenerational continuity in attachment from parent to child comes from a study in which researchers interviewed pregnant women about their attachment histories and then measured their infants' attachments at 1 year of age (Fonagy et al., 1991). This research design enabled

TABLE 4.6 Relations between Mothers' and Children's Attachment Types

	Attachment Category	
Child	**Mother**	
Secure	Autonomous	Mother is not dealing with unresolved concerns about her own experience and thus is able to be sensitive to her child's communications.
Insecure-avoidant	Dismissing	Mother is reluctant to acknowledge her own attachment needs and thus is insensitive and unresponsive to her child's needs.
Insecure-ambivalent	Preoccupied	Mother is confused about her attachment history and thus is inconsistent in her interactions with her child.

Source: Main et al., 1985.

the investigators to rule out the possibility that the mothers' experiences with their babies had tainted their memories of their own childhoods. Like Main, these researchers also found significant links between mothers' recollections of their childhood relationships and children's attachment relationships with them. Other researchers using prospective designs have found similar results (Hesse, 2008). A meta-analysis of 18 samples involving 854 infant-mother pairs from six different countries revealed that 82 percent of autonomous mothers had secure infants and 64 percent of dismissing mothers had insecure-avoidant infants (van IJzendoorn, 1995). Studies with fathers yielded similar results (Crowell & Treboux, 1995; Grossmann et al., 2008; Grossmann & Fremmer-Bombik, 1994; van IJzendoorn, 1995). Likewise, studies in foster families showed a high level of concordance between foster mothers' recollections of their childhood relationships with parents and their foster children's attachment quality (Dozier et al., 2001). This suggests that the intergenerational transmission of attachment is the result of parents' attachment-fostering behaviors, not a genetic link between parent and child.

A fourth group of adults has been identified since Main developed her AAI classification scheme. These individuals were able to overcome their early insecure attachments and develop secure relationships with their romantic partners, spouses, and offspring. They may have been helped by a therapist; they may have experienced a positive loving relationship with a peer; they may simply have been resilient. These individuals are referred to as *earned secure*. Researchers followed the progress of earned-secure women in a longitudinal study extending from birth to age 23 (Roisman et al., 2002). Even though these women had insecure attachment relationships with their mothers in childhood, by their early 20s, they had developed high-quality romantic relationships and formed secure internal working models of attachment relationships. Their romantic ties were comparable to those of individuals who were continuously secure. Early relationships clearly affect later relationships, but the die is not cast irrevocably and forever in childhood.

ATTACHMENT OF CHILDREN IN CHILD CARE   Psychologists have been concerned about attachment development in children who are in child care and separated from their mothers every day. These children do form close relationships with their parents (Clarke-Stewart & Allhusen, 2002, 2005; Lamb & Ahnert, 2006), but are their attachments as secure as those formed by infants who spend their time at home with their mothers?

Researchers first examined this question by comparing infants' behavior in the Strange Situation. On average, infants in full-time child care were somewhat more likely to be classified as insecurely attached compared with infants not in full-time care (36% versus 29%; Clarke-Stewart, 1989). These results appeared to suggest that child care could hinder the development of a secure attachment. However, perhaps factors other than child care explained the difference. One factor might be the Strange Situation. Infants are judged insecure in the SS if they do not run to their mothers after a brief separation. But infants who experience daily separations from their mothers might be less disturbed by the separations in the Strange Situation and therefore seek less proximity. A second factor might be the mother: Perhaps mothers who value independence in themselves and their children are more likely to be employed whereas mothers who emphasize closeness with their children are more likely to stay home. A third factor might be the stress of handling both a baby and a job, which could interfere with the mother's ability to provide the sensitive and supportive care that fosters development of a secure attachment. Finding that insecure attachment was more common for infants in child care did not, by itself, prove that child care was harmful.

To find a definitive answer to the question of whether child care interfered with infants' attachment development, the U.S. government funded the NICHD Study of Early Child Care and Youth Development, a large study in 10 sites around the country. More than 1,300 infants were randomly selected from hospitals at birth and tracked through age 15. Their development was assessed repeatedly. The results showed that when factors such as parents' education, income, and attitudes were statistically controlled, infants in child care were no more likely to be insecurely attached to their mothers than infants not in care. However, when they were placed in poor-quality child care in which the caregivers were not very sensitive and responsive to their needs and their mothers were not very sensitive to their needs at home, infants were less likely to develop secure attachments than if they were in good-quality care and their mothers were sensitive and responsive (Belsky et al., 2007; NICHD Early Child Care Research Network, 1997b, 2005, 2006). Apparently poor-quality care worsens a risky situation at home and increases the likelihood that infants will have problems forming secure attachments to their parents.

Research also shows that good-quality child care can compensate for poor care at home by giving children an opportunity to form secure attachments outside the family. Children with an insecure attachment to their mother but a secure attachment to a child care provider are more socially competent than insecurely attached children who have not formed a positive relationship outside the family (Howes & Spieker, 2008; van IJzendoorn & Sagi-Schwartz, 2008). Having a child care provider who stays with the child over a period of time is particularly important. Children more frequently seek caregivers who have been on the child care staff longer, and these caregivers are able to soothe the children more effectively than caregivers with unstable employment records (Barnas & Cummings, 1994). Clearly, minimizing staff turnover in child care can help children's attachment development (Lamb & Ahnert, 2006). Staff training to improve caregivers' sensitivity is also important (Galinsky et al., 1995). The more training that child care staff members have, the more likely it is that children will develop secure attachment relationships with them (Clarke-Stewart & Allhusen, 2002).

Real-World Application: Attachment When Mother Goes to Prison

In the United States, more than 1.3 million children have mothers who are in prison (Mumola, 2000). These children are likely to have attachment problems. Some of them are not even allowed to form an attachment to their mother. Some women (6% of those in prison) are pregnant at the time of their arrest, but few prisons permit them to keep their infants with them (Gabel & Girard, 1995). In most cases, they are permitted only a few days of contact before they must relinquish the infant and return to their cells. As a result, the mother has little opportunity to bond with her baby or for the baby to form an attachment to the mother. In France, in contrast, children can stay with their mothers in prison up to the age of 18 months. This allows them time to form a mutual attachment.

Even if an attachment has already developed before the mother goes to prison, incarceration is likely to adversely affect its quality. In one study, researchers examined attachment representations in 54 children whose mothers were in prison (Poehlmann, 2005). The children were read four story stems: (a) a child spills juice at dinner, (b) a parent comforts a child who falls off a rock and hurts his or her knee, (c) a child thinks he or she has seen a monster and calls the parent, and (d) a child is separated from a parent leaving on a trip. Nearly two thirds of the children told narratives that included intense ambivalence, disorganization, violence, or detachment.

An insecure attachment to the incarcerated mother can lead to adverse outcomes for the children. About 70 percent of young children with incarcerated mothers have internalizing problems, such as anxiety, depression, shame, and guilt (Bloom & Steinhart, 1993; Dressel et al., 1992), and many exhibit externalizing behaviors, such as anger, aggression, and hostility (Johnston, 1995; Parke & Clarke-Stewart, 2003b). Children adjust to their mother's incarceration better if their grandmother takes over their care rather than if they are placed in foster care (Bloom & Steinhart, 1993; Mumola, 2000). A grandmother can provide more continuity and familiarity and facilitate more frequent and consistent contact with the incarcerated mother. Children who experience more regular contact with their incarcerated mother adjust better. However, correctional policies make it difficult for mothers and children to stay in touch.

Prisons are typically located in remote areas, often long distances from where the children live, making visitation extremely difficult for families with limited resources (Kaplan & Sasser, 1996). This problem is more acute for women than for men because there are fewer prisons for them. According to one estimate, incarcerated women are, on average, 160 miles farther from their families than are incarcerated men (Coughenour, 1995). Visits to mothers are also rare because children are not always eligible to visit, few visitors are allowed at one time, visits allow no privacy, visiting rooms are not child friendly, and children are anxious about making visits (Bloom & Steinhart, 1993; Simon & Landis, 1991). About half of incarcerated parents do not receive any visits from their children (Snell, 1994), and even when children do visit,

it is not often. A U.S. Department of Justice study found that only 8 percent of incarcerated mothers saw their children as often as once a week (Mumola, 2000).

After the mother's prison term is over, she must begin the task of reestablishing her relationship with her child. This is difficult because children are likely to have established new relationships while the incarcerated mother was absent, for example, with a grandmother or foster care parent. Moreover, the experiences that the incarcerated mother has suffered in prison affect her ability to reintegrate into the family and provide supportive care for her child (Solomon, 1988). To lessen the negative effects of parental incarceration, prison policies should minimize the length of separation, minimize disruption in the children's lives, and allow parents and children to maintain contact.

Effects of Infant Characteristics on Attachment

As we discussed in Chapter 3, "Biological Foundations," some babies are more difficult to care for than others. Could this affect the quality of their attachment? Some researchers have found a link between infants' temperament characteristics and attachment relationships. Irritable newborns who have trouble orienting to people have been found in some studies to be more likely to develop insecure attachments (Spangler & Grossmann, 1993; Susman-Stillman et al., 1996). However, not all studies document a link (Vaughn et al., 2008). It seems that if infant temperament does affect attachment development, other factors moderate its influence. A difficult infant isn't necessarily destined to have a poor relationship with the mother. If parents receive help and support from other family members and friends, they can usually cope with a difficult baby, and when adequate social support is available, irritable infants are no more likely than easy ones to become insecurely attached (Crockenberg, 1981). Professional intervention can also help. In a study in the Netherlands, irritable infants whose mothers were taught how to behave more sensitively and responsively developed better attachment relationships than did irritable infants in a control group (van den Boom, 1994). Of the infants whose mothers received training, 68 percent were classified as securely attached at 1 year whereas only 28 percent of the infants in the control group were securely attached. However, if the mother is socially isolated or has poor relationships with other adults, she is more likely to have problems fostering a secure attachment with a difficult infant (Levitt et al., 1986). Thus, the effects of temperament on attachment cannot be separated from the influence of the total social context in which the baby is developing (Sroufe, 1996; Vaughn et al., 2008).

Stability and Consequences of Attachment

Does a secure attachment to Mom or Dad continue through childhood? Does a child who has a secure relationship with parents develop secure relationships with other adults later on or form closer relationships with peers? In this section, we discuss the stability and consequences of attachment for children's development.

Stability and Change in Attachment Over Time

A number of longitudinal studies have been conducted to track children's attachments over time. In one study, 68 percent of children seen at 3 to 4 years of age showed similar attachment classifications when retested in the Strange Situation 2 years later (Moss et al., 2005). In a study in Germany, attachment classifications at age 1 predicted 90 percent of secure attachments and 75 percent of insecure classifications at age 6 (Wartner et al., 1994). Even across longer intervals, stability of attachment has been observed. Waters and his colleagues (2000) found that 72 percent of the children in their sample who were classified as secure in infancy were secure 20 years later—an impressive level of stability across a long period. A meta-analysis of attachment stability from infancy to adulthood yielded a moderately high association equivalent to a correlation of about + 0.40 (Fraley, 2002). This stability does not mean that attachment security in infancy acts as a protective inoculation against later problems. It more likely means that parents who understand what it is to be a good secure base and provide their child with sensitive and responsive care make a point of providing this kind of support throughout childhood and adolescence as well as when the child is a baby.

But general stability in the quality of parent-child relationships doesn't mean that change is impossible (Waters et al., 2000). Substantial numbers of children with insecure attachments as infants do manage to develop better relationships with their parents by school age. In one study, 42 percent of the children who were insecure at 1 year became secure by 5 years (Lounds et al., 2005); in another study, 57 percent of infants with disorganized attachments at 1 year were secure at 4 years (Fish, 2004). Change can go either way, but it is more common for insecure children to become secure. Perhaps this is because mothers who are not entirely successful with infants find that as their children become older, they can read their signals more easily. Perhaps it is because family circumstances change. A change from insecure to secure attachment is particularly likely if the child comes from an upwardly mobile low-income family. As the family gains financial resources, the parents begin to experience less stress in their lives; they become more available to the child and interact in ways that are more responsive to the child's needs (Thompson et al., 1982). Although it is more unusual, secure attachment relationships may become insecure if the family's life circumstances deteriorate as a result of job loss, illness, death, or divorce. In the photo below, a girl's face reflects the pain experienced by children whose parents

Source: © *Media Bakery.*

divorce. As her world turns upside down, her secure attachments to her parents may well be undermined. In one study, researchers found that when the quality of mother-child communication declined and hostility and conflict or exposure to a traumatic family event such as death of the child's grandparent increased, preschool children shifted from secure to insecure attachments (Moss et al., 2005). Clearly, attachment relationships are responsive to changes in parents' behavior and circumstances (Thompson, 2006; Waters et al., 2000).

Attachments in Older Children

Attachment relationships with parents continue to develop through childhood and adolescence as children mature and their social worlds expand (Brockmeyer & Waters, in press). In the later preschool years, opportunities to explore outside the home create a major shift in how children use their parents as a secure base and how their parents supervise and support the children's exploration.

To maintain a secure relationship, children and parents must develop clearer and more elaborate expectations about each other's behavior and goals, and parents must support and facilitate the children's exploration while continuing to provide a sense of protection and security. As children get older, they and their parents communicate over longer distances. Although the specific forms of communication change as a result of this increased distance, parent-child relationships continue to involve exploration and approach on the child's side and secure-base support from the parents. When children reach middle childhood, they can also develop attachment relationships with close friends and, in adolescence, with romantic partners (Furman et al., 2002). These relationships coexist with the attachments already formed to parents; they do not replace them (Allen, 2008; Allen et al., 2007). The children's goal is to achieve a balance between maintaining close ties with family while gaining autonomy to expand their social network to include close attachment ties with peers.

Consequences of Attachment

As children develop, the quality of their attachments to their parents has consequences for other relationships and cognitive, social, and emotional skills.

ASSOCIATIONS WITH EXPLORATION AND COGNITIVE DEVELOPMENT
Compared with infants who have insecure attachments to their parents, infants with secure attachments exhibit more complex exploratory behavior (Main, 1973). When they are given a problem to solve, they are more interested, persistent, and effective than insecurely attached children (Matas et al., 1978). They display less frustration and less crying and whining. They also engage in more symbolic and pretend play—for example, transforming a block of wood into an imaginary car or a stick into a witch's broom. They do better on IQ tests, too. In research in the Netherlands and Israel, for example, the security of children's attachments to their mothers, fathers, and other caregivers predicted intelligence scores at age 5 (van IJzendoorn & Sagi-Schwartz, 2008; van IJzendoorn et al., 1992). Attachment security in adopted children also was related to more advanced cognitive abilities at age 7 in another study in the Netherlands (Stams et al., 2002). In a third study, children in Reykjavik, Iceland, who were securely attached to their parents at age 7 were more attentive in the classroom and had higher grades at ages 9, 12, and 15 than children whose attachment representations were avoidant, ambivalent, or disorganized (Jacobsen & Hofmann, 1997). Even at older ages, adolescents whose attachment representations in the AAI before they entered college were classified as autonomous became better students at college because they prepared more for exams and had more effective work habits than students whose attachment representations were dismissing or preoccupied (Larose et al., 2005). Children with secure attachment relationships are likely to succeed in situations that require cognitive ability and effort both because their emotional security facilitates exploration and mastery of the physical environment and because their parents' sensitive and responsive care promotes cognitive development as well as attachment security.

IMPLICATIONS FOR SOCIAL DEVELOPMENT   Secure attachment relationships may also facilitate children's later social development. The most dramatic evidence of this comes from studies of socially isolated primates. When Harlow isolated monkeys from all social contact for their first year, they were seriously disturbed. When they were visited by normal monkeys, they withdrew to a corner, huddling or rocking. As adults, they were unable to have normal sexual relations. When some of the females did have babies through artificial insemination, they ignored them, and when the infants became distressed, they physically abused and sometimes even killed them (Harlow, 1964; Harlow & Suomi, 1971; Suomi, 2008).

Of course, we cannot duplicate this experiment with human infants. However, many studies suggest that the quality of an infant's attachment to parents is relevant for later social development (Thompson, 2006). A particularly important longitudinal study by Alan Sroufe and his colleagues in Minnesota in which children were followed from infancy to young adulthood illustrates the importance of early attachments for later social behavior (Carlson et al., 2004; Sroufe et al., 2005). Securely and insecurely attached infants had very different social trajectories. When they were 4 to 5 years of age, children who had been securely attached to their mothers in infancy were rated by their teachers as more emotionally positive, more empathic, and more socially competent than children who had been insecurely attached. They whined less, were less aggressive, and displayed fewer negative reactions when other children approached them. They had more friends and their classmates considered them more popular. The securely attached children continued to be rated as more socially competent when they 8 and 12 years old (Simpson et al., 2007; Sroufe et al., 2005). Moreover, they were more likely to develop close friendships with peers and to form friendships with other securely attached children. They construed their friendships as closer, more emotionally connected, and more skilled in conflict resolution than children who had been insecurely attached in infancy. At age 19, adolescents with a history of secure attachment were more likely to have close family relationships, long-term friendships, high self-confidence, and determination regarding personal goals.

Similar findings were reported in the NICHD Study of Early Child Care and Youth Development. Compared with those who were insecurely attached to their mothers in infancy, children who were securely attached were rated as being more socially competent and having fewer externalizing and internalizing behavior problems in preschool and first grade (NICHD Early Child Care Research Network, 1997b), and those who were securely attached to their mothers at age 2 or 3 had better social problem-solving skills, were less lonely, and had better quality friendships between ages 4 and 10 (Lucas-Thompson & Clarke-Stewart, 2007; McElwain et al., 2008; Raikes & Thompson, 2008). Other researchers have found similar links between the quality of early attachment and later school-age peer competence and friendship patterns (Contreras et al., 2000; Schneider et al., 2001). They have also found that security of attachment as assessed with the AAI is related to better relationships with peers and fewer internalizing and externalizing problems in adolescence (Allen, 2008; Allen et al., 2007). A meta-analysis of 69 samples (5,947 children) confirmed the link between insecure attachment and later externalizing problems especially for boys ($d = .31$; Fearon et al., 2010). Children with disorganized attachments were at the highest risk for developing these problems.

Just as Bowlby argued, the links between early attachment and social outcomes are mediated by children's internal working models. Sroufe and his colleagues in the Minnesota study (2005) assessed children's internal working models of relationships at various times throughout childhood. For example, in the preschool years, they evaluated children's relationship expectations, attitudes, and feelings. Securely attached children's relationship models were characterized by expectations of empathy between partners, a high expectation of sharing during play, and constructive approaches to conflict resolution (e.g., taking turns, seeking adult assistance, or getting another toy). The investigators found that children's working models and social behavior mutually influenced each other over time. Working models of relationships in the preschool period predicted social behavior in middle childhood; working models of relationships in middle childhood predicted social behavior at 12 and 19 years; social behavior in middle childhood predicted working models of relationships in early adolescence. You can see this pattern of cross-time relations between working models and social behavior in Figure 4.1.

Emotions also create a bridge between attachment and social behavior. The security of attachment affects the way children process emotional information and understand and regulate emotions. Preschoolers who are securely attached to their mothers are better than insecurely attached children at understanding emotions (Laible & Thompson, 1998; Ontai & Thompson, 2002). This difference in emotional understanding is, in part, due to the elaboration of emotion themes in mother-child conversations in families of securely attached children (Raikes & Thompson, 2008). At older ages, securely attached children are also better at regulating their emotions in challenging situations (Conteras et al., 2000; Kobak & Cole, 1994). This probably contributes to the high quality of their peer relationships in childhood and adolescence.

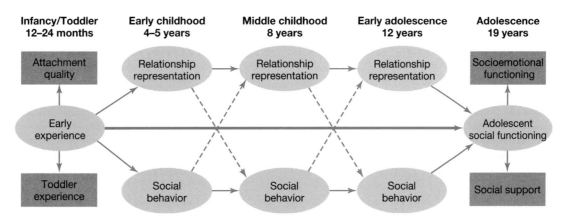

| Infancy/Toddler 12–24 months | Early childhood 4–5 years | Middle childhood 8 years | Early adolescence 12 years | Adolescence 19 years |

FIGURE 4.1 *A model of cross-time relations between working models of relationships and social behavior. Working models were inferred from the child's representations of relationships with peers and family based on an interview in early childhood, drawings in middle childhood, and narratives in early adolescence; social behavior was inferred from teacher ratings of the child's peer competence and emotional health at all three ages.* Source: Carlson, E. A., Sroufe, L. A., & Egeland, B. (2004). *The construction of experience: A longitudinal study of representation and behavior.* Child Development, 75, 66–83.

In summary, secure attachments to parents facilitate children's mastery of the social world. They increase the child's trust in other social relationships and facilitate the development of mature affectional relationships with peers. Longitudinal studies aimed at defining the links between early parent–infant interaction and later relationships in adolescence and adulthood demonstrate the long-term stability of the social effects of early attachment (Thompson, 2008). The long-term consequences of attachment security are evident not just in biologically related families but also in families of adopted children (Stams et al., 2002).

Learning from Living Leaders: L. Alan Sroufe

Source: Courtesy of L. Alan Sroufe.

Alan Sroufe is Professor of Child Development at the Institute of Child Development, University of Minnesota. He knew that he wanted to be a psychologist when he was in high school, so he pursued (and received) a Ph.D. in clinical psychology from the University of Wisconsin. In spite of the fact that his relatives wondered why he was in school so long, his parents were supportive of his education, which clearly paid off. While he was in graduate school, Sroufe became interested in early development as a way to understand pathology, and he found his way to Bowlby's and Ainsworth's work on attachment. From that time on, he has been guided by three questions: Do early experiences have special significance? How are their effects carried forward? What accounts for continuity and change in development? To answer these questions, Sroufe and his colleague, Byron Egeland, launched the Minnesota Longitudinal Study of Risk and Adaptation in the mid 1970s. They assessed attachment patterns in infancy and then followed the course of attachment and social development over the next 30 years. Results of the study were published in the book *The Development of the Person*. This book sums up Sroufe's view that development is a hierarchical construction, in which early experience has a special place because it frames subsequent encounters with the world yet is reinterpreted in light of these encounters. Sroufe has contributed ideas and data to attachment theory and has also drawn out practical applications from the theory. Early intervention projects around the world are based on his Steps toward Enjoyable, Effective Parenting (STEEP) model. Sroufe received the Distinguished Teacher Award from the University of Minnesota, the Distinguished Scientific Contribution to Child Development Award from the Society for Research in Child Development, and an Honorary Doctorate from the University of Leiden. His message for undergraduates: "The questions that are of most interest to you, for example, how you became the person you are, are

scientific questions and can be addressed using the models in our field. They don't have simple answers (like 'your genes made you who you are') but they are answerable."

Further Reading

Sroufe, L. A. (2002). Attachment and development: A prospective longitudinal study from birth to adulthood. *Attachment and Human Development, 7*, 349–367.

CONSEQUENCES FOR SELF-ESTEEM Children's attachment security is also related to self-esteem (Thompson, 2006). In one study, researchers assessed the attachments and self-concepts of 6-year-old children (Cassidy, 1988). Children who were securely attached viewed themselves more positively, although they were able to acknowledge their less-than-perfect qualities. Insecure-avoidant children tended to view themselves as perfect. Insecure-ambivalent children showed no clear pattern. A group of children classified as insecure-controlling (similar to the insecure-disorganized classification) had negative self-concepts. Later studies confirmed the link between attachment and self-esteem: Securely attached preschoolers viewed themselves more positively and their self-concepts were more stable over time than insecure children's (Goodvin et al., 2008). In brief, research suggests that the quality of early attachment is related to the degree to which children view themselves positively and realistically—both important capacities for social development.

ATTACHMENTS TO BOTH MOTHER AND FATHER ARE RELATED TO LATER DEVELOPMENT Children may develop different kinds of attachment relationships with their mothers and fathers. In one study, researchers classified 1-year-old infants according to whether they were securely attached to both parents, securely attached to their mother but not their father, securely attached to their father but not their mother, or securely attached to neither parent (Main & Weston, 1981). They then observed the infants' reactions to a friendly clown. The infants who were securely attached to both parents were more responsive to the clown than those who were securely attached to only one parent, and the infants who were securely attached to neither parent were the least responsive of all. These results suggest that if you want to know about an infant's emotional security, it is important to view the child as part of a family system and assess attachment relationships with both parents (Mikulincer et al., 2002; Parke & Buriel, 2006). If other adults—grandparents, nannies, child care providers—are also a significant part of the child's world, they should be included in assessments of attachment in order to get the most complete and accurate prediction of children's development (Howes & Spieker, 2008; van IJzendoorn & Sagi-Schwartz, 2008; van IJzendoorn et al., 1992).

ATTACHMENT OR PARENTING: WHICH IS CRITICAL FOR LATER DEVELOPMENT? It is clear that attachment quality is an important predictor and precursor of later cognitive, social, and emotional development. However, are the effects on later development due to the attachment relationship itself or to the care and family circumstances that support it? A number of explanations for the link between attachment quality and later development have been offered (Lewis, 1999; Lewis et al., 2000). First, an "extreme early effects" explanation suggests that early attachment protects children from later traumas and experiences. Second, a "mediating experiences" explanation suggests that continuity across time is due to the stability of parents' behavior and environmental conditions rather than the nature of earlier attachment patterns. Children who are securely attached at 12 months are likely to be receiving sensitive, responsive mothering at that age and to continue to receive this kind of mothering as they mature. Their mothers are likely to respect their autonomy and support their efforts to cope independently with new experiences while standing ready to give direct help when needed. Therefore, the well-adjusted social behavior of these children at later ages may reflect the current healthy state of their relationship with their parents rather than being an outcome of the relationship that existed years earlier. As stated previously, when children's environments change, their attachments are likely to change as well. Improvements in life circumstances increase security; increased family adversity decreases security (Thompson, 2006). According to this explanation, it is not the child's early attachment pattern that accounts for later social behavior but the continuity or discontinuity of the child's experiences and relationships with parents. A third explanation suggests that attachment is a "dynamic interaction process." In this view, children's attachment histories modify how they perceive and react to changes in their family environment. Securely attached children may be able to weather declines in parental responsiveness better than insecurely attached children.

To test these three possible explanations, researchers in the NICHD Study of Early Child Care and Youth Development examined relations between early attachment to mother and social competence during preschool and early elementary school under conditions of declining, stable, or improving maternal care (NICHD Early Child Care Research Network, 1997b). They found that links between attachment and later outcomes were mediated by the quality of parenting, supporting the "mediating experiences" explanation. When parenting quality improved over time, children's outcomes were better; when parenting quality declined, children had poorer outcomes. The researchers also found support for the "dynamic interactive process" explanation: Children who had insecure attachments in infancy did better (had fewer externalizing problems) when parenting quality improved over time and did worse (had more externalizing problems) when parenting quality declined. However, securely attached children were protected from changes in parenting quality: Their social outcomes were not altered by declines or improvements in parenting. Changes in family relationships and experiences clearly mattered for some children in this study, but the nature of children's prior attachments was an important modifier of how they reacted to fluctuations in their social worlds. The message is clear: Both early attachment history and contemporary social conditions must be considered to understand the long-term consequences of attachment security.

nto Adulthood:
From Early Attachment to Later Romantic Relationships

Many researchers have been curious about whether there are links between early attachment relationships and intimate relationships in adulthood. Cindy Hazan and Phillip Shaver (1987, 1990) looked at this issue by translating Ainsworth's three attachment types into a questionnaire to assess how adults approach intimate relationships. According to the questionnaire, adults with *secure* intimate relationships enjoyed closeness and found intimacy easy to establish. They agreed with the following statements: "I find it relatively easy to get close to other people. I am comfortable depending on other people and having them depend on me. I don't usually worry about being abandoned or about having someone get too close to me." Adults with *avoidant* relationships were uncomfortable with closeness and found it difficult to trust their partners. They agreed with the statements: "I am somewhat uncomfortable being close to others. I feel nervous when people start to get too close. Often, I feel like people want me to be more intimate than I feel comfortable being. I find it difficult to allow myself to depend on other people. I find it difficult to

trust people completely." Adults with *ambivalent* relationships worried constantly about being abandoned. They agreed with the statements: "I find that other people are reluctant to get as close as I would like. I often worry that someone I am close to doesn't really love me or won't want to stay with me. I want to merge completely with another person and this sometimes scares people away." Hazan and Shaver found that the percentages of these three types in adult samples were similar to those found in studies of infants. Just over 50 percent of the adults endorsed the secure attachment type, just under 33 percent were avoidant, and the rest were ambivalent. Hazan and Shaver also found that these attachment types were related to the adults' memories of their relationships with their parents in childhood and to the adults' work activities, which the researchers suggested were functionally equivalent to exploratory activities in childhood. Securely attached adults had work and love in balance. They had higher overall satisfaction and confidence in their work than the other adults, but they also placed a higher value on relationships than on work and said that, if forced, they would choose relationship success over work success. Adults with ambivalent attachments emphasized love over work. They felt insecure about their jobs and were most likely to claim that love concerns interfered with their work. They had difficulty focusing on work tasks except when they perceived them as an opportunity to gain love and respect. They reported the lowest average income of the three groups, presumably because their insecure attachments actually interfered with their job performance and productivity. Avoidant adults emphasized the importance of work over love. They preferred to work alone, used work to avoid having friends or a social life, and did not take enjoyable vacations from work. Hazan and Shaver's research demonstrated parallels between attachment types in infancy and adulthood. But it did not establish whether there are longitudinal continuities from attachment in infancy to relationships in adulthood.

Researchers in the Minnesota longitudinal study found that attachments to parents in infancy were linked to romantic relationships in adulthood. Young adults who experienced a secure relationship with their mother as assessed in the Strange Situation in infancy were more likely to produce coherent discourse describing their romantic relationship and to experience better relations with their romantic partner in conflict and collaboration tasks (Roisman et al., 2005). Similarly, in a longitudinal study in Germany, researchers found significant links between attachment security to the mother (assessed in infancy and at age 6) and more secure romantic relationships at age 22 (Grossmann et al., 2002, 2008). There is no direct leap from mother's lap to love and romance. It's more complicated than that. As we have noted, changes in family circumstances can affect children's internal working models and disrupt the influence of early relationships (Berlin et al., 2008). But if children start out with secure attachments to their parents—or if they work through their childhood issues in therapy and "earn" relationship security—they have a better chance of ending up happy in love.

Chapter Summary

- During the second half of the first year, infants form attachments to the important people in their lives.

Theories of Attachment

- According to the psychoanalytic view, the basis for the infant's attachment to mother is oral gratification.

- According to the learning view, the mother becomes a valued attachment object because she is associated with hunger reduction.

- According to the cognitive developmental view, before they develop an attachment, infants must be able to differentiate between mother and a stranger and must be aware that the mother continues to exist even when they cannot see her.

- Bowlby's ethological theory of attachment stresses the role of instinctual infant responses that elicit the parent's care and protection and focuses on the way the parent acts as a secure base.

- The maternal bonding theory suggests that the attachment the mother feels to her infant is affected by early mother-newborn contact.

How Attachment Develops

- The first step in the development of attachment is learning to discriminate between familiar and unfamiliar people. In the second step, babies develop attachments to specific people. These attachments are revealed in the infants' protests when attachment figures depart and their joyous greetings when they are reunited.

- Most infants develop their first attachment to their mother and rely on her for comfort. Later, infants develop attachments to their fathers and possibly with their grandparents and siblings.

- As children mature, they develop new attachment relationships with peers and romantic partners. Adolescent attachment relationships coexist with the attachments already formed to parents and siblings.

The Nature and Quality of Attachment

- Early attachments are different in quality from one relationship to another and from one child to the next.

- The quality of an infant's attachment can be assessed using observations of mother and infant at home. Ainsworth developed a laboratory assessment called the Strange Situation in which the child's interactions with the mother are observed after the two have been briefly separated and reunited.

- Typically, 60 to 65 percent of infants are classified as securely attached to their mothers in the Strange Situation: They seek contact with her after the stress of her departure and are quickly comforted even if they were initially quite upset.

- Securely attached infants are confident in their mother's availability and responsiveness. They use the mother as a secure base, venturing away to explore the unfamiliar environment and returning to her as a haven of safety from time to time.

- Insecure-avoidant infants show little distress over the mother's absence in the Strange Situation and actively avoid her on her return. Insecure-ambivalent children may become extremely upset when the mother leaves them in the Strange Situation but are ambivalent to her when she returns; they seek contact with her and then angrily push her away.

- Insecure-disorganized infants act disorganized and disoriented when they are reunited with their mothers in the Strange Situation; they are unable to cope with distress in a consistent and organized way even though their mother is available.

- When parents are available, sensitive, and responsive to their infant's needs and the two interact in a synchronous way, the child is more likely to develop a secure attachment. Contextual factors in the family and community are also related to attachment.

- Infants reared in socially impoverished environments may have hormonal deficits that alter their social responsiveness and lead to attachment problems.

- A baby's temperament may play a role in the quality of the infant-parent attachment but only in combination with the caregiver's behavior.

Stability and Consequences of Attachment

- The quality of attachment is relatively stable across time but may change if the environment improves or deteriorates.

- Early attachments shape a child's later attitudes and behaviors. Children who were securely attached as infants are more likely to be intellectually curious and eager to explore, have good relationships with peers and others, and view themselves positively.

- Children's internal working models provide a mediating mechanism that serves as a link between attachment and later outcomes.

- Parents' internal working models of experience with their parents are likely to influence their parenting behavior and their infant's attachment. Mothers and fathers classified as autonomous, dismissing, and preoccupied according to the Adult Attachment Interview (AAI) are likely to have infants who are secure, avoidant, and ambivalent, respectively.

- Insecurely attached infants are more likely to become secure than the reverse.

- Support has been found for two explanations of attachment stability: The "mediating experiences" view suggests that continuity across time may be due to the stability of parents' behavior and environmental conditions rather than the nature of earlier attachment patterns. The "dynamic interaction process" view suggests that children's attachment histories modify how they perceive and react to changes in their family environment.

Key Terms

attachment	**insecure-disorganized**	**secure base**
imprinting	**attachment**	**separation distress or**
insecure-ambivalent	**internal working model**	**separation protest**
attachment	**maternal bond**	**Strange Situation**
insecure-avoidant	**secure attachment**	
attachment		

At the Movies

Many movies focus on attachment relationships between children and parents. *Rabbit-Proof Fence* (2001) is one that depicts how attachment bonds buffer children from adversity and are maintained even under difficult circumstances. As the result of an Australian government policy that required aboriginal children to be "resocialized," three children were separated from their families but escaped and endured an arduous journey to be reunited with their parents. *I Am Sam* (2001) is a movie illustrating a child's unshaking attachment to her father despite his mental problems. Sean Penn plays a mentally challenged man raising his daughter by himself and eventually winning custody of her with help from a caring network of friends and neighbors. As the movie vividly demonstrates, the bond between Sam and his daughter is stronger than any disability. The strength of attachment bonds between children and parents is also illustrated in the movie *Losing Isaiah* (1995). A young, crack-addicted mother (Halle Berry) tries to regain custody of her infant son 3 years after he was adopted by a middle-class white family. The attachment between Isaiah and his adopted mother demonstrates how attachments form even in the absence of biological ties and poignantly illustrates the conflict between claims of biological and adoptive parents. *Autumn's Eyes* (2005) looks at a family in poverty from the perspective of an observant 3-year-old girl who longs to reunite with her incarcerated mother.

Attachment between siblings is the theme of *Where's Molly* (2006). At age 6, Jeff lost his 3-year-old sister, Molly, when she was placed in an institution because of her mental disability. One day she was there as Jeff's constant companion; the next day, she was gone forever. Just before Molly's 50th birthday, Jeff and his wife were able to locate and reconnect with her. Jeff's quest to reestablish contact with his sister illustrates the strength of sibling bonds.

Another theme of movies involves the psychological problems that result from growing up without a secure attachment. In *Good Will Hunting* (1997), Matt Damon plays a young man who grew up in abusive foster homes and never formed such an attachment. With the help of a psychologist (Robin Williams), he overcomes his distrust of others. This film illustrates not only the early antecedents of attachment-related problems but also the possibilities for recovery. *Martian Child* (2008) traces the story of a boy who was abandoned and placed in foster care. He claims to be on a mission from Mars, stays in a large box all day, fears sunlight, and wears a belt of flashlight batteries so he won't float away. He is befriended and ultimately adopted by a widower (John Cusack), who with patience and understanding helps the boy develop an attachment bond and adjust to the real world.

If you are curious about the founders of attachment theory, you can check out two documentary films. *Mary Ainsworth and the Growth of Love* outlines the development of attachment in infancy and illustrates the twists and turns of Ainsworth's life, including her meetings with Bowlby and her design of the Strange Situation. The companion film, *John Bowlby: Attachment Theory across Generations,* focuses on the impact of attachment relationships on adult behavior and the transmission of attachment patterns to the next generation. Bowlby's children and colleagues speak about his legacy, and a 20-year study of a British boy documents the impact of attachment on later development. Bowlby's ethological theory of attachment is the emotional lynchpin in *The Story of the Weeping Camel* (2003), a film in which a newborn camel chooses its birth mother as its primary target for food, comfort, and protection, and through body movement, vocalizations, and eye contact, does everything possible to persuade its mother to accept it.

CHAPTER 5

Emotions: Thoughts About Feelings

Source: Kathy McLaughlin/The Image Works.

At 6 months of age, Claire smiled widely whenever her mother smiled and reached down to pick her up from her crib. At 9 months, Claire frowned and turned away from her Aunt Susie, whom she had not seen since she was 2 months old. When she was 1 year old, Claire laughed and giggled as she and her dad played peekaboo. When she was 2, Claire looked sad when her mother cried. These changes in emotions and emotional expressions and their consequences for social development are the topics covered in this chapter.

Children display a wide range of emotional expressions from the time they are infants. They communicate their feelings, needs, and desires by means of these expressions and, thereby, influence other people's behavior. When the baby smiles, the mother is almost sure to smile back; when the baby screams, a stranger will stop approaching and back away. In this chapter, we describe why emotions are important and present several theories that help explain emotional development. We explore children's earliest emotional expressions—smiling, laughing, frowning, crying—and examine other emotions such as pride, shame, guilt, and jealousy that develop later. We also discuss how infants and children learn to recognize emotions in others, regulate their own emotions, and think about emotions. We describe how parents, siblings, teachers, and peers socialize children's expressions and regulation of emotion. Finally we examine problems in emotional development, with a focus on childhood depression.

What Are Emotions?

primary emotions
Fear, joy, disgust, surprise, sadness, and interest, which emerge early in life and do not require introspection or self-reflection.

secondary or self-conscious emotions
Pride, shame, guilt, jealousy, embarrassment, and empathy, which emerge in the second year of life and depend on a sense of self and the awareness of other people's reactions.

Emotions are complex: They involve a subjective reaction to something in the environment, are generally accompanied by some form of physiological arousal, and are often communicated to others by some expression or action. They are usually experienced as either pleasant or unpleasant. Infants may react to the taste of a new infant formula with disgust, experiencing it as unpleasant and responding with an accelerated heart rate. Because they have not yet learned to hide their emotions, they let their parents know in no uncertain terms of their displeasure—wrinkling up their faces, spitting up, perhaps even crying. As children progress through childhood and adolescence, their expressions and awareness of emotions become more refined and complex, influenced by a growing emotion "lexicon" and an ability to regulate emotional arousal, manage emotional expressiveness, and process the emotional expressions of others (Saarni, 2007). It is useful to distinguish between early primary emotions and later secondary emotions. **Primary emotions** include fear, joy, disgust, surprise, sadness, and interest; they emerge early in life and do not require introspection or self-reflection. **Secondary** or **self-conscious emotions** include pride, shame, guilt, jealousy, embarrassment, and empathy; they emerge later and depend on a sense of self and an awareness of other people's reactions (Lewis, 1998; Saarni et al., 2006).

Why Are Emotions Important?

Emotions have a variety of functions in children's lives. First, they are a way that children let other people know how they feel: They are a window into children's likes and dislikes and communicate their general views of the world. Second, emotions are linked to children's social success. Being able to express and interpret emotions is as important as being able to solve an intellectual problem. As Daniel Goleman's popular book, *Emotional Intelligence* (1995), illustrated, navigating successfully in the world of emotions is a critical ingredient of social success. Third, emotions are linked to children's mental and physical health. Children who are excessively sad and despondent are likely to develop problems such as poor concentration and to withdraw from social interaction. In extreme cases, these children's self-esteem may deteriorate. Physical health suffers too when emotional development goes awry. Children reared in environments in which positive emotions are rarely experienced often have problems managing stress and anxiety. The difficulty these children have modulating their reactions to stress is reflected in heightened levels of cortisol (a biological marker of stress response), and this, in turn, may lead to physical problems (Gunnar, 2000; Rutter, 2002a). Children may also suffer impaired physical health when they are exposed to emotional hostility between their parents (Gottman et al., 1996). Clearly, emotions play a number of critical roles in children's development.

Perspectives on Emotional Development

What leads children to develop healthy emotions and emotional intelligence? Emotional development is influenced by both nature and nurture, by both biology and environment. In this section, we examine three theoretical perspectives that are useful in explaining aspects of children's emotional development.

Biological Perspective

The biological perspective is useful for explaining the expression of basic emotions. According to the structural view of emotions, first suggested by Charles Darwin (1872), emotional expressions are innate and universal, rooted in human evolution, and based on anatomical structures. Research showing that facial expressions of basic emotions such as happiness, sadness, surprise, fear, anger, and disgust are the same in different cultures confirmed the claim that emotional expressions are universal (Ekman, 1972). Studies of emotional expressions in infants supported the claim that emotional expressions are innate: whether they were born prematurely or at the normal age of 40 weeks after conception, all infants began to smile at 46 weeks postconception—regardless of how long they had been exposed to smiling faces (Dittrichova, 1969). Research showing that each emotion is expressed by a distinct group of facial muscles supported the claim that emotional expressions are based on anatomical structures (Ekman, 2003). In addition, studies of the brain showed that the left cerebral hemisphere controls the expression of the emotion of joy; the right hemisphere, the expression of fear (Davidson, 1994; Fox, 1991). A biological basis for basic emotions was also evident in genetic studies showing that identical twins are more similar than fraternal twins in the age at which they first smile, the amount they smile, the onset of their fear reactions to strangers, and their general degree of emotional inhibition (Plomin et al., 2001; Robinson et al., 1992; Rutter, 2006a). Thus, across a variety of research investigations, evidence consistently demonstrates that biology contributes to the expression of emotions and that children's basic emotions are based on and constrained by biological features and processes including anatomy, brain organization, and genes.

Learning Perspective

The learning perspective is useful for explaining individual differences in emotional expression. The frequency with which children smile and laugh is related to their caregivers' behavior (Denham et al., 2007). When parents respond with enthusiasm to their infant's smiles it encourages the infant to smile more; this has been verified in studies showing that when adults respond to a baby's smiles with positive stimulation, the baby's rate of smiling increases (Rovee-Collier, 1987). Learning experiences can also reinforce children's fear responses (Denham et al., 2007). Children may become classically conditioned to fear the doctor who gives a painful shot during their first office visit. They may also acquire fear through operant conditioning, for example, when an adverse consequence, such as a painful fall, follows climbing up a high ladder. Children learn still other fears simply by observing other people's reactions (Bandura, 1989), for example, if they see their mother jump and scream when she spies a spider. In all of these cases, the frequency and circumstances of children's expressions of positive and negative emotions have been modified by the environment. In addition, parents can help their children learn to manage their emotional expressions by rewarding certain emotional displays, or they can interfere with their children's emotional development by being punitive and dismissing the children's emotional expressions (Gottman et al., 1996).

Functional Perspective

According to the functional (or functionalist) perspective (Saarni et al., 2006), the purpose of emotions is to help people achieve their social and survival goals, such as making a new friend or staying out of danger. These goals arouse emotions: Joy and hope arise in the anticipation of forming a new friendship; fear arises when circumstances are threatening. In both instances, the emotions help the person reach the goal. The emotion of hope leads children to initiate interaction with the would-be friend; the emotion of fear leads them to flee the dangerous situation. Thus, one way emotions function is that they impel children toward their goals.

A second way emotions function is that emotional signals provide feedback that guides other people's behavior. The way the potential friend reacts when the child makes a social overture is a critical determinant of how the child feels and acts. If the would-be friend responds positively, the child feels happy and pursues the interaction; if the would-be friend frowns, the child withdraws and perhaps tries to make friends with someone else. Similarly, if the child smiles at a caregiver, that person is more likely to come close and begin a conversation. In adulthood, too, emotional expressions affect other people's behavior. Researchers have found, for example, that if people display positive emotions during a contract negotiation, they are more successful in getting the contract signed and the deal closed (Kopelman et al., 2006), and if restaurant servers express positive emotions by smiling, telling a joke, giving a compliment, forecasting good weather, or drawing a smiley face on the bill, they get higher tips (Guéguen 2002; Lynn 2004; Seiter, 2007).

A third way emotions function is that memories of past emotions shape how people respond to new situations. Children who have been routinely rebuffed by potential friends become more wary; children who have been successful in their social overtures become more confident. In both instances, emotional memories affect children's behavior and help them adapt to their environments. Thus, emotions help children achieve their goals, establish and maintain social relationships, and adapt to their environments (Saarni et al., 2006).

No single theoretical perspective explains all aspects of emotional development. Each of these three perspectives—biological, learning, and functional—is useful for answering specific questions about how emotional development progresses.

Development of Emotions

Most parents watching their baby smile, frown, laugh, and cry will agree that infants are able to express a wide range of emotions at a very early age. In one study, 99 percent of mothers reported that their 1-month-old infant clearly displayed interest; 95 percent observed joy; 85 percent, anger; 74 percent, surprise; 58 percent, fear; and 34 percent, sadness (Johnson et al., 1982). These women based their judgments not only on their babies' facial expressions, vocalizations, and body movements but also on the situations in which these behaviors occurred. For example, a mother who watched her baby staring intently at the mobile above her crib was likely to label the infant's emotion "interest" and to label the emotion expressed by gurgling and smiling when the mobile bounced up and down "joy."

But relying on mothers' judgments may not be the best way to find out about infants' emotions. Researchers distinguish among infants' expressions of emotions by means of detailed coding systems that document changes in facial expressions and movements. These systems assign finely differentiated scores to different parts of the face (e.g., lips, eyelids, forehead) and to specific infant movement patterns. Researchers then use these scores to judge whether an infant has displayed a particular emotion. One elaborate coding system for infant emotional expressions is the Maximally Discriminative Facial Movement, or Max (Izard et al., 1983); see Figure 5.1. This coding scheme has been used to code expressions of emotions of interest, joy, surprise, sadness, anger, fear and, disgust in infants from birth to 2 years and is used by many researchers studying infant emotions.

FIGURE 5.1 *Maximally Discriminative Facial Movement (Max) Coding System. To identify facial expressions of emotion, observers code movement in three regions of the face: (A) brows, (B) eyes, nose, and cheeks, (C) mouth, lips, and chin. This example shows an infant's expression of anger. In drawing A, brows are lowered and drawn together (Max code 25). In drawing B, eyes are narrowed or squinted (Max code 33). In drawing C, the mouth is angular or squarish (Max code 54). In drawing D, we see the full expression of anger (Max code 25/33/54).* Source: Izard, C. E., & Dougherty, L. M. (1982). Two complementary systems for measuring facial expressions in infants and children. In C. E. Izard (Ed.), Measuring emotions in infants and children (pp. 97–126). New York: Cambridge University Press. With permission from Cambridge University Press.

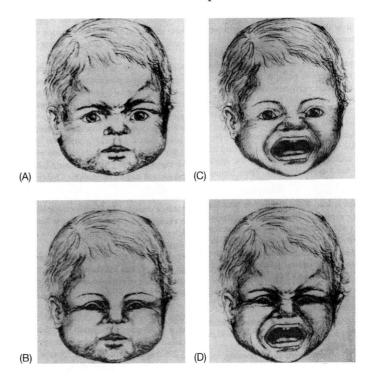

See Table 5.1 for a brief chronology of the milestones of emotional development in a typical child. With this general overview of early emotional development as a guide, in the next section we discuss the development of specific important emotions.

Primary Emotions

Beginning at an early age, babies experience the primary emotions of joy, fear, distress, anger, surprise, sadness, interest, and disgust. These emotions are directly related to the events that caused them. Fear is a direct response to a visible threat; distress is a direct result of pain; and joy often results from interacting with a primary caregiver.

JOY Joy is reflected in infants' smiling and laughter. If you watch closely, you can see smiles even in newborn infants. These **reflex smiles** are usually spontaneous and appear to depend on the infant's internal state (Fogel et al., 2006; Wolff, 1987). Most caregivers interpret them as signs of pleasure, however, and this gives the caregivers pleasure and encourages them to cuddle and talk to the baby. In this sense, these smiles have adaptive value for the infant by ensuring caregiver attention and stimulation. Smiling helps keep caregivers nearby and thus becomes a means of communication and an aid to survival (Saarni et al., 2006).

Between 3 and 8 weeks of age, infants begin to smile in response to external stimuli including faces, voices, light touches, and gentle bouncing, as well as to internal states (Sroufe, 1996). They are particularly interested in people, and a high-pitched human voice or a combination of voice and face reliably elicits **social smiles** in babies between 2 and 6 months. By the time they are about 3 months old, babies smile more at familiar faces than unfamiliar ones (Camras et al., 1991; Saarni et al., 2006). This suggests that smiling has begun to signal pleasure, not just emotional arousal. Additional research evidence shows that 3-month-olds smile more when their mothers reinforce their smiles with reciprocal smiles and vocalizations than when equally responsive women who are strangers reinforce their smiles (Wahler, 1967). These findings are consistent with the learning and functional views of emotional development and suggest that infant smiling becomes more discriminating as babies mature. A baby's pleasure at watching

reflex smile
A upturned mouth seen in the newborn that is usually spontaneous and appears to depend on some internal stimulus rather than on something external such as another person's behavior.

social smile
An upturned mouth in response to a human face or voice, which first occurs when the infant is about 2 months old.

TABLE 5.1 **Emotional Expressions and Understanding in Infancy and Early Childhood**

< 1 month	Shows distress by crying
1 month	Exhibits generalized distress; may be irritable by late afternoon
2 months	Shows pleasure; mildly aroused by sight of a toy; makes a social smile
3 months	Displays excitement and boredom; smiles broadly and often; cries when bored; may show wariness and frustration
4 months	Laughs, especially at certain sounds; cries less; gurgles with pleasure; shows beginnings of anger; begins to recognize positive emotions in others such as joy
5 months	Is usually gleeful and pleased but sometimes frustrated; turns head from disliked food; smiles at own image in mirror; may begin to show wariness of strangers
6 months	Matches emotions to others, e.g., smiles and laughs when mother does; may show fear and anger
7 months	Expresses fear and anger, defiance, affection, shyness
8 months	Displays more individuality in emotional expression
9 months	Shows negative emotions when restrained; frowns when annoyed; actively seeks others' comfort when tired; nighttime crying may reappear; most display real fear of strangers
10 months	Exhibits intense positive and negative emotions; occasionally irritable
11 months	Has more variability in emotions; individual temperament is more evident
12 months	Becomes distressed when others are distressed; cries when something is not to liking; may show early signs of jealousy; laughs often at own cleverness; struts/preens when walking
15 months	Shows more mood swings; is more caring to age mates; is annoyed by dirty hands; strongly prefers certain clothing; may fret or cry often but usually briefly
18 months	Can be restless and stubborn; may sometimes have tantrums; sometimes shy; uses objects such as a blanket or a favorite stuffed animal to soothe self; is jealous of siblings
21 months	Makes some efforts to control negative emotions; can be finicky and exacting; makes more efforts to control situations
2 years	Can be contrary but also appropriately contrite; responds to others' moods; can be very intense; may be overwhelmed by changes; can be upset by dreams; begins to understand emotional display rules; shows nonverbal signs of guilt
2½ years	Shows shame, embarrassment, and clearer expressions of guilt; can label emotional expressions
3 years	Shows wide range of secondary emotions such as pride, shame, embarrassment, jealousy; recognizes primary emotions such as happiness, sadness, fear, and anger on the basis of facial expressions
4 years	Shows increased understanding and use of emotional display rules
5 years	Identifies external causes of emotions
6 years	Begins to understand how two or more emotions can occur simultaneously
7 years	Understands the influence of beliefs on emotions
9 years	Understands that a person can have multiple, mixed, or even contradictory and ambivalent emotions

Note: This developmental timetable represents overall trends identified in research. Individual children vary in the ages at which they exhibit these behaviors. Sources: LaFreniere, 2000; Kopp, 1994; Pons et al., 2004; Saarni et al., 2006; Sroufe, 1996.

Duchenne smile
A smile reflecting genuine pleasure, shown in crinkles around the eyes as well as an upturned mouth.

a familiar face is revealed in other ways as well. For instance, researchers have found that 10-month-old infants generally reserve a special kind of smile for their mothers, rarely offering it to strangers (Fox & Davidson, 1988). These special smiles, called **Duchenne smiles**, involve not just an upturned mouth but wrinkles around the eyes as well, making the whole face seem to light up with pleasure (Ekman, 2003; Ekman et al., 1990).

Of course, not all babies smile equally often. Consistent with the learning perspective, how much infants smile depends on the social responsiveness of their environment. This was demonstrated in an Israeli study showing that infants who were reared in family environments where they received a lot of attention smiled more than infants who were raised either in a communal living arrangement in a kibbutz or in an institution where the level of social responsiveness was low (Gewirtz, 1967). Differences in smiling are also related to the infant's gender. From the time they are born, girls smile more than boys (Korner, 1974), and this difference continues into adulthood (LaFrance et al., 2003). It has been suggested, consistent with the biological perspective, that this difference is genetic. However, separating genetic factors from environmental influences is difficult because parents expect and elicit more smiles from girls than from boys. The interplay of environmental and biological factors is also demonstrated in research comparing the frequency of smiling in different countries and ethnic groups. This research shows that European American males and females differ more in their smiling rates than African American males and females, consistent with the finding that African American parents treat their sons and daughters more alike than do European American parents (LaFrance et al., 2003).

Infants express their joy in giggles and gales of laughter as well as by smiling, and these expressions of emotion also change with age. Researchers have studied what makes babies of different ages laugh by showing them various stimuli or engaging them in different activities. Alan Sroufe and his colleagues exposed 4- to 12-month-old infants to auditory stimuli, such as lip-popping, whispering, or whinnying sounds; tactile stimuli including bouncing the baby; visual stimuli including a human mask; and social stimuli, such as playing peekaboo (Sroufe & Wunsch, 1972). Auditory stimuli elicited few laughs at any age. Tactile stimuli elicited a substantial amount of laughter, but only at 7 to 9 months. Visual and social stimuli elicited more laughter overall and the likelihood of this laughter increased with age. When the researchers studied 12- to 24-month-olds, they found that the babies particularly enjoyed activities in which they could participate, such as covering and uncovering the mother's face with a cloth or playing tug-of-war with a blanket (Sroufe, 1996). Other research showed that laughing continued to increase in frequency and become more social as children matured (LaFreniere, 2000; Saarni et al., 2006).

et You Thought That . . .
A Smile Is a Smile Is a Smile

Many people think that children's smiles are all the same. But even infants use different smiles to express different positive emotions. Some smiles are coy, others gleeful, and others riotous (Messinger & Fogel, 2007). Figure 5.2 illustrates several different types of infant smiles.

Over a century ago a French physician, Guillaume Duchenne (1862), discovered that not all smiles are equal. He noted that smiles involving not just an upturned mouth but wrinkles around the eyes as well are qualitatively different from smiles with an upturned mouth but no eye constriction. What we now call *Duchenne smiles* are those with the crinkly eyes. In adults, these smiles are genuine expressions of joy, whereas smiles that do not involve the eyes are merely efforts to be polite or courteous (Ekman et al., 1990). Martin Seligman, author of *Authentic Happiness* (2002), labeled these inauthentic smiles *Pan American smiles* because they are the expressions that Pan American stewardesses plastered on their faces in television ads and often used when they were providing in-flight service. Waiters and store clerks, as well as airline attendants, often dispense polite

Simple smile

Duchenne smile
(eye constriction)

Play smile
(mouth opening)

Duplay smile
(eye constriction &
mouth opening)

FIGURE 5.2 *Examples of different types of infant smiles. Simple smiles are elicited by internal states and by social and nonsocial stimuli. Duchenne smiles reflect genuine pleasure. Play smiles signal playful excitement and arousal. Duplay smiles signal a shared excited positive engagement with a partner. Source: Messinger, D. S., & Fogel, A. (2007). The interactive development of social smiling. In R. V. Kail (Ed.), Advances in child development and behavior (Vol. 35, pp. 327–366). San Diego, CA: Elsevier Academic Press. Copyright Elsevier, (2007).*

but inauthentic smiles because genuine Duchenne smiles are difficult to fake. The facial muscles involved in the Duchenne smile are difficult to voluntarily control. If you don't feel it, you can't easily produce a "real" smile.

Even babies display these "real" and "fake" smiles (Dawson et al., 1997; Messinger & Fogel, 2007). In one study, 10-month-olds produced Duchenne smiles when their smiling mothers approached them but were more likely to produce smiles without eye constriction when they were approached by an impassive stranger (Fox & Davidson, 1988). In other studies, even younger babies displayed genuine smiles more when they were interacting with smiling caregivers than when they were alone, and these Duchenne smiles lasted longer than non-Duchenne smiles (Messinger et al., 1999, 2001). During Duchenne smiles, infants also babble more than when they are smiling without eye constriction, suggesting that they are experiencing genuine pleasure and engagement with their partners (Hsu et al., 2001). Duchenne smiling is a way to express shared joy (Messinger & Fogel, 2007). Different parts of the brain are involved in real and fake smiles as well. EEG recordings revealed that the 10-month-olds' Duchenne smiles were associated with relatively more activation of the left frontal cerebral hemisphere. Similar patterns of brain activation are found in adults (Ekman et al., 1990; Murphy et al., 2003).

The frequency of Duchenne smiling varies among individuals, and this difference is related to overall emotional well-being. In one study, researchers found that in college yearbook photographs about half of the students displayed Duchenne smiles and the other half, Pan Am smiles (Harker & Keltner, 2001). When they were contacted at ages 27, 43, and 57, the Duchenne smilers were more likely to be married and satisfied with their lives than the merely polite yearbook smilers. Of course, this does not mean that smiling leads to social success, but it

does indicate that genuine smiling and social well-being are related.

Babies show a third kind of smile when they play, a combination of the Duchenne smile and a wide-open mouth. This *play smile* is associated with rapid breathing, vocalization, and laughter. It signals excitement and arousal (Bolzani-Dinehart et al., 2003, 2005) and is seen when excitement has built up in later phases of tickle games and peekaboo (Fogel et al., 2006). A relaxed open-mouth display in nonhuman primates is similar to this open-mouth smiling in human infants and is thought to be evolutionarily linked to human laughter (Waller & Dunbar, 2005). It is seen most often when two animals are playing together, and their play bouts tend to last longer, indicating that the interaction is mutually enjoyable.

A fourth type of smile seen in infants is a combination of a Duchenne smile and a play smile. This *Duplay smile* involves both eye constriction and mouth opening. It is seen in young infants at the beginning of a face-to-face play bout with a caregiver, especially a smiling mother (Adamson & Frick, 2003; Delgado et al., 2002; Messinger et al., 2001). When the mother is unresponsive and displays a still face, the smile disappears (Acosta et al., 2004; Weinberg & Tronick, 1994). Among 6- to 12-month-old infants, Duplay smiles occur during physical play with parents and at the climax of a tickle game (Dickson et al., 1997). This type of smile apparently signals a shared excited positive engagement with a partner (Messinger & Fogel, 2007).

As children grow older, they acquire even more smiles. According to emotions expert Paul Ekman (Ekman, 2004; Ekman & Friesen, 1982), at least 17 types of smiles are exhibited in adulthood. Each smile serves a different social function, involves different facial muscles, and may even activate different parts of the brain. In short, a smile is not just a smile; smiling has many faces.

FEAR A second primary emotion that appears in infancy is fear. Researchers have identified two phases in the emergence of this emotion (Sroufe, 1996). In the first phase, from 3 to 7 months of age, infants develop wariness, which they exhibit when they encounter events they do not understand. At first, in this phase, infants are not afraid when they are confronted by an unfamiliar person. In fact, they are quite interested. Often, they look longer at the stranger than at a familiar person, and if the mother is present when the stranger appears, they may look back and forth between her face and the stranger's, as if comparing them. At about 5 months of age, interest starts to be replaced with a sober stare. By 6 months, infants react to strangers with a sober expression and perhaps a little distress. This is clear evidence of wariness. Over the next month or so, infants' distress increases and by 7 to 9 months, the second phase of fear development begins: Infants show true fear. They have an immediate negative

FIGURE **5.3** *Onset of stranger distress. At 8 months of age, half of the 14 children in this longitudinal study showed distress at the appearance of a stranger in a laboratory, and within a month or so, this distress reaction was clearly dominant. Source: Emde et al., 1976.*

reaction to an event or person they don't recognize and don't like. When they see a stranger standing nearby and watching them, they are likely to stare, whimper, turn away, and begin to cry. Figure 5.3 shows a summary of the progression over the first year of life from interest in strangers (compares faces) to stranger wariness (looks sober) to **stranger distress** or **fear of strangers** (Emde et al., 1976).

Fear of strangers was once believed to be a developmental milestone that was both inevitable and universal. Researchers now know it is neither (LaFreniere, 2000; Saarni et al., 2006). Stranger distress does emerge in a majority of infants between 7 and 9 months in European American and some other cultures including Hopi Indians (Dennis, 1940) and in Uganda (Ainsworth, 1963). However, in cultures that emphasize shared caregiving among relatives, such as the Efe in Africa, babies show little fear of strangers (Tronick et al., 1992). In contrast, in cultures in the Middle East where parents are wary of strangers because of their history of terrorism, infants react to strangers with intense fear (Sagi et al., 1985). Moreover, even within the European American culture, babies do not all react to strangers with the same level of fear. For some infants, greeting and smiling continue to be the most frequent reactions (Rheingold & Eckerman, 1973). Whether a baby is fearful of a stranger depends on a host of variables including who the stranger is, how he or she behaves, the setting in which the encounter occurs, and the child's experiences with strangers in the past (Table 5.2; Mangelsdorf et al., 1991; Saarni et al., 2006).

When babies meet strangers in their own homes, they are less afraid than when they meet them in an unfamiliar setting, such as a research laboratory (Sroufe et al., 1974). Similarly, if the infants are sitting on their mother's or father's lap—a familiar and comforting context—when the stranger approaches, they rarely show fear (Bohlin & Hagekull, 1993; Morgan & Ricciuti, 1969).

A baby's reaction also depends on how the parent reacts to the stranger. When infants see their mother interacting positively with the stranger, they are likely to smile, approach the stranger, and offer toys (Feinman & Lewis, 1983). Conversely, when the mother looks worried, the baby is apt to cry more and smile less at the stranger (Boccia & Campos, 1989; Mumme et al., 1996). Infants use the parent as a social reference point when they find themselves in unfamiliar or uncertain situations. They use the mother's emotional cues to guide their own reactions (Saarni et al., 2006). This **social referencing** undergoes clear changes as infants develop. Younger infants are likely to act first and look later; older infants are more likely to check with the parent before they act. Between 6 and 9 months of age, infants look at the mother but do not study her face; by 14 months, they stare intently at her face, apparently aware that this is the best source of emotional information (Walden, 1991).

stranger distress or fear of strangers
A negative emotional reaction to unfamiliar people, which typically emerges in infants around the age of 9 months.

social referencing
The process of "reading" emotional cues in others to help determine how to act in an uncertain situation.

TABLE 5.2 Factors Influencing Infants' Fear of Strangers

Factor	More Fear	Less Fear
Setting	Unfamiliar setting (e.g., lab)	Familiar setting (e.g., home)
Parent's availability	Distant from parent	Close to parent
Parent's behavior	Parent reacts to stranger in sober or negative way	Parent reacts to stranger in positive or encouraging way
Characteristics of stranger	Adult size and features	Child size and features
Behavior of stranger	Passive, sober, threatening	Active, smiling, friendly
Predictability of event	Unpredictable	Predictable
Infant's control over event	Low control	High control
Cultural norms about strangers	Cultural wariness of strangers	Cultural acceptance of strangers
Infant's experience with strangers	Negative experiences (e.g., doctor gives inoculation)	Positive experiences (e.g., visitors bring gifts)

Another contextual factor that affects infants' responses to strangers is the degree to which the situation allows the infant some control over the stranger's behavior (Mangelsdorf et al., 1991). Babies are less fearful if they can control the stranger's approach, for example, so that the stranger stops coming when the infant frowns, frets, or turns away. The characteristics and behavior of the stranger matter, too. Infants are less afraid of child strangers than adult strangers—because they are smaller and have more childish features. They are less afraid of active, friendly strangers who talk, gesture, smile, imitate the baby, and offer toys than of passive, silent, sober strangers (Mumme et al., 1996; Saarni et al., 2006).

separation anxiety
Fear of being apart from a familiar caregiver (usually the mother or father) which typically peaks at about 15 months of age.

Other fears may be more universal across cultures and contexts. One common fear in infancy is associated with being separated from mother or other familiar caregiver, as we discussed in Chapter 4, "Attachment." This fear, referred to as **separation anxiety** and reflected in separation distress or separation protest, tends to peak at about 15 months in U.S. and Canadian babies and displays a similar timetable in such diverse cultures as Guatemala and Botswana (Figure 5.4). Fear of heights is common as well and serves a clear evolutionary function by protecting infants from serious falls down steep inclines. An apparatus known as the *visual cliff* has

Perhaps if Mom hadn't backed away to take a picture, this 1-year-old wouldn't have felt so threatened by Santa Claus. Source: Kathy McLaughlin/The Image Works.

been used to study infants' fear of heights (see photo). The apparatus consists of a glass surface placed over a checkerboard base that is close to the glass on one side, the so-called shallow side, and some distance below it on the deep side. The infant is placed on the shallow side and encouraged to crawl across the deep side to reach the mother. At about 6 months of age, infants begin to refuse to crawl from the shallow side to the deep side—indicating that they see and fear the drop (Gibson & Walk, 1960). Experience walking and perhaps falling contributes to the onset of this fear (Campos et al., 1992, 2000).

All fear reactions change as children's understanding increases (Lagattuta, 2007). In general, fears become less about physical events and are more influenced by cognitive interpretations (Sayfan & Lagattuta, 2009). With age, children become less fearful of separations and strangers and more fearful of social evaluation, rejection, and failure (see Table 5.3). Children also explain fears more in terms of cognitive interpretations as they become older (Muris et al., 2008). Children at 3 to 5 years old

Source: Elizabeth Crews / The Image Works.

explain people's fears in terms of their physical attributes (the baby is afraid because she is tiny) or the physical characteristics of the feared stimulus (the boy is afraid because the bee can sting him). Older children (and adults) explain fears in terms of mental states (the baby is afraid because she is too young to realize what the bee is) or in terms of the feared stimulus and the person simultaneously (the boy is not afraid because he knows that if he stands still the bee won't sting him). Thus, with age, children learn that it is not a stimulus per se that induces fear but that fear reactions are mediated by the person's thoughts, beliefs, and knowledge. Children's ability to understand the difference between real and imaginary events, which also increases with age, helps them manage their fears: 7-year-olds are able to reduce their fears better than 4-year-olds by reminding themselves that ghosts, witches, and monsters are just imaginary (Sayfan & Lagattuta, 2009).

FIGURE 5.4 *Separation protest. Although children from four different cultures varied as to the intenseness with which they protested their mothers' departures, they all tended to reach a peak of distress at about the same age, between 13 and 15 months.* Source: Reproduced with permission of Kagan J. Kearsley and of the publisher from Infancy: Its Place in Human Development *by Jerome Kagan, R. B. Kearsley, and P. R. Zelazo, p. 107, Cambridge, Mass: Harvard University Press, Copyright © 1978 by the President and Fellows of Harvard College.*

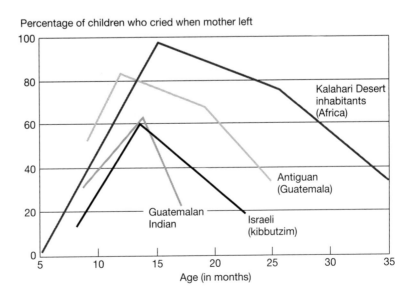

TABLE 5.3 Children's Fears

Age	Stimuli Causing Fear
0–1 year	Loss of support; loud noises; unexpected, looming objects; strangers; heights
1–2 years	Separation from parent; injury; strangers; baths (down the drain with the water)
2–3 years	Separation from parent; animals, especially large dogs; insects; darkness
3–6 years	Separation from parent; animals; darkness; strangers; bodily harm; imaginary beings such as monsters and ghosts; nightmares
6–10 years	Snakes; injury; darkness; being alone; burglars; new situations such as starting school
10–12 years	Negative evaluations by peers; school failure; thunderstorms; ridicule and embarrassment; injury; burglars; death
Adolescence	Peer rejection; school failure; breaking up; family issues such as divorce; war and other disasters; the future

Sources: Gelfand & Drew, 2003; Goetz & Myers-Walls, 2006.

ANGER Anger is another primary emotion. According to Carroll Izard, a pioneer in the study of infant emotions, newborns' first negative expressions are not anger, per se, but express startle (e.g., in response to a loud noise), disgust (e.g., in response to a bitter taste), and distress (e.g., in response to pain). Not until they are 2 to 3 months old do infants reliably display facial expressions of anger (Izard 1994; Izard et al., 1995). In one study, when researchers gently restrained their arms, few 1-month-old babies showed angry expressions, but half of the 4- to 7-month-olds did (Stenberg & Campos, 1989). Not unlike adults, infants usually display anger in response to particular external events (Saarni et al., 2006; Sroufe, 1996). For example, at 6 months of age, babies responded to being inoculated by a physician with an expression of anger (Izard et al., 1987); at 7 months, they expressed anger when researchers offered them a teething biscuit and then took it away just before they could chomp down on it (Stenberg et al., 1983). It seems that babies respond to emotional provocations in predictable ways and anger is elicited by pain and frustration (Denham et al., 2007).

SADNESS Sadness, too, is a reaction to pain and frustration, but in infancy it occurs less often than anger. Young infants become sad when parent-infant communication breaks down, for example, when a usually responsive caregiver stops responding to the baby's social overtures (Tronick et al., 2005; Weinberg & Tronick, 1998). In older infants, separation from the mother or other familiar caregiver for some period of time can lead to sadness. However, sadness is not simply a reaction to events such as these; it also is a signal children can use to control their social partners. In one study, researchers recorded 2-year-olds' expressions of anger, fear, and sadness in threatening and frustrating situations—when approached by a stranger or having a toy taken away (Buss & Kiel, 2004). They found that when the children were looking at their mother they expressed sadness more frequently than fear or anger—an indication that they were using this emotional display to elicit the mother's support. Sadness is an effective emotional signal for eliciting care and comfort from adults and therefore serves an important evolutionary function by promoting infants' survival.

Secondary Emotions

In the second year of life, babies begin to experience more complex secondary emotions including pride, shame, jealousy, guilt, and empathy. These social or self-conscious emotions depend on children's abilities to be aware of, talk about, and think about themselves in relation to others (Barrett, 1995; Lewis, 2000, 2001, 2007; Tracy et al., 2007). Such emotions play important roles in social development: Pride and shame help define children's feelings about themselves and others; jealousy is expressed when children assess other children who seem to have an advantage; guilt motivates children to apologize; empathy leads children to perform prosocial acts.

PRIDE AND SHAME   When children are pleased with their accomplishments, they are likely to show pride; when they perceive that someone finds them wanting or deficient, they are likely to express shame. Children express the latter by hanging their head, lowering their eyes, covering their face, and hiding. To feel shame, they must be able to assess their own behavior and judge whether it is acceptable in the eyes of others. Michael Lewis and his colleagues found that by the time children were 3 years old, solving a problem that was not particularly difficult elicited joy, but succeeding on a difficult task produced pride (Lewis, 1992; Lewis et al., 1992). Failing a difficult task caused sadness, but failing an easy task led to shame. When researchers told older children stories about people achieving something either by their own efforts or by chance or luck, they found that 7-year-olds used the word *proud* to reflect good outcomes regardless of whether the characters had succeeded through their own efforts, but 10-year-olds realized that feeling proud could occur only when the good outcomes were the result of a person's own efforts (Thompson, 1989).

Learning from Living Leaders: Michael Lewis

Source: Robert Wood Johnson, School of Medicine.

Michael Lewis is Professor of Pediatrics and Psychology and Director of the Institute for the Study of Child Development at the Robert Wood Johnson Medical School, Rutgers University. After excursions into engineering, sociology, and market research, Lewis received a Ph.D. in experimental and clinical psychology from the University of Pennsylvania. An early interest in how the lack of social contact alters children's social needs led to a life-long career studying children's social development. During this career, Lewis has tried to understand the nature of children's social relationships with family members, peers, and friends. His proudest accomplishments include his work on secondary emotions such as pride, embarrassment, shame, and guilt. His book *Shame, the Exposed Self* was an influential effort to broaden the range of emotions that developmental psychologists study. Lewis hopes that the field of social development will expand understanding of the links between emotions, social cognition, and the self, and will use advances in research on clinical problems, such as autism, to provide insights into social and emotional development. Lewis is a Fellow of the New York Academy of Sciences, the American Association for the Advancement of Science, and the Japan Society for the Promotion of Science. In 2008, he received the Urie Bronfenbrenner award for lifetime contributions to developmental psychology from the American Psychological Association. He advises undergraduates to remember that development is affected by accidents, chance encounters, effort, and luck. There is always hope for the future!

Further Reading

Lewis, M. (2007). *The rise of consciousness and the development of emotional life.* New York: Guilford Press.

JEALOUSY Jealousy is a common emotion, which is experienced from early childhood, when a sibling gets more of a parent's attention, to adolescence, when a friend flirts with a teen's new romantic partner (Lewis, 2007; Lewis & Ramsay, 2002). Indeed, jealousy can occur as early as 1 year of age. Researchers have found that children express jealousy when their mother directs attention away from them toward another child, a newborn infant, or even a doll (Case et al., 1988; Hart et al., 1998). Brenda Volling and her colleagues (2002) explored jealousy in pairs of siblings—16-month-olds and their preschool-age brothers or sisters. When mothers or fathers played with one child and encouraged the sibling to play alone, both younger and older children expressed jealousy of the sibling who received the parent's attention. However, the way the children expressed their jealousy depended on their age. The younger children showed their jealousy with expressions of distress, the older children with anger and sadness. Children who reacted with more jealousy could not focus on their play activities as well as children who were not so jealous. Jealous children also had a poorer understanding of emotions. Jealousy between siblings was less prevalent when their relationships with their parents were secure and trusting and their parents had a happy marriage. These close and positive relationships apparently served as a protective factor buffering children from sibling jealousy.

GUILT Children also begin to experience feelings of guilt when they are quite young. Grazyna Kochanska and her colleagues tested children at 22, 33, 45, and 56 months of age (Kochanska et al., 2002). They presented each child with an object that belonged to the experimenter, for example, a favorite stuffed animal that the experimenter had kept from her childhood or a toy she had assembled herself, and asked the child to be very careful with it. However, the objects had been "rigged" and fell apart as soon as the children began to handle them. According to the researchers, at 22 months, children "looked guilty" when the mishap occurred—they frowned, froze, or fretted. At 33 to 56 months, children expressed fewer overt negative emotions, but guilt "leaked out" in more subtle ways, such as squirming and hanging their heads. More development is necessary before children can talk about guilt intelligently. In another study, researchers asked 6- and 9-year-old children to describe situations in which they had felt guilty (Graham et al., 1984). Only the 9-year-olds understood the emotion and its relation to personal responsibility. The 6-year-olds described themselves as feeling guilty even when they had little control over the outcome of a situation: "I felt guilty when I accidentally hit my brother too hard and his nose bled." The 9-year-olds realized that to feel guilty, it was necessary to be responsible for the outcome: "I felt guilty when I didn't turn in my homework because I was too lazy to do it." Other researchers have also found that younger children focus on simple outcomes and older children understand that unless they themselves caused the outcome, they do not need to feel guilty (Saarni et al., 2006).

empathy
A shared emotional response that parallels another person's feelings.

EMPATHY **Empathy** is an emotional response to another person's emotion, most often distress. It involves sharing and understanding the other person's feelings. Often it is described as putting oneself into another's (emotional) shoes. Evidence of empathic responding can be seen in functional magnetic resonance imaging of the brain. In one study, for example, researchers scanned the brains of 7- to 12-year-old children while they were watching short animated films depicting people in painful and nonpainful situations (Decety et al., 2008). When the children saw the people who were in pain, it activated the same neural circuits as are activated when children experience pain firsthand.

The earliest precursor of empathic responding to distress is newborns' crying in response to hearing other infants cry (Dondi et al., 1999; Hoffman, 1981, 2000). Martin Hoffman

(2000) termed this response "rudimentary empathic responding." Near the end of the first year, infants begin to exhibit a second kind of response, which Hoffman labeled "egocentric empathic distress." By this age, infants have begun to develop a sense of themselves as separate from others and, as a result, seek comfort for themselves in response to another's distress. They typically become agitated or cry in response to another child's distress, but they make little effort to help the other child. In the second year, toddlers begin to experience empathic concern for others; they try to comfort or console them, not just themselves. At 13 or 14 months old, they often approach and comfort another child in distress. This comforting, though, is quite general. When children are about 18 months old, they not only approach a distressed person but offer specific kinds of help. For example, they may offer a toy to a child with a broken toy or a Band-Aid to an adult with a cut finger. Hoffman labeled this level "quasi-egocentric empathic distress" because these children are still unable to distinguish between their own feelings and those of other people. Later in the second year, children are capable of understanding that other people's feelings and perspectives are different from their own and are increasingly aware of the others' feelings. In this stage of "true empathic distress," children make more appropriate responses to another person's distress rather than egocentric responses. Researchers have found a developmental increase in young children's empathic responding to their mothers' distress (van der Mark et al., 2002) and to their peers' distress (Lamb & Zakhireh, 1997). Younger children experience empathy only when the distressed person is present. As they grow older, they also respond to stories of other people's distress. By mid- to late childhood, they can respond with empathy to another person's general condition, such as being handicapped or poor. Adolescents are able to respond to difficulties experienced by groups of people, such as those who are politically oppressed, disease ridden, or undernourished. Cognitive advances allow older children and adolescents to understand the plight of less fortunate groups and to respond with empathy (Eisenberg et al., 2003).

Individual Differences in Emotional Expressiveness

Clear individual differences exist in children's emotional expressiveness beginning in early infancy. Some babies smile more readily and laugh more heartily; others react more fearfully to novel people and events or are more easily angered (LaFreniere, 2000). These differences in emotional reactions are related to the differences in temperament that we discussed in Chapter 3, "Biological Foundations." They are reflected in one of Thomas and Chess's (1986) temperament dimensions—mood—and all three of Rothbart's (1981, 2007) temperament dimensions—negative affectivity (which includes fear and sadness), effortful control (which includes pleasure from low-intensity activities), and extraversion-surgency (which includes pleasure from high-intensity experiences). They are also related to the behaviorally inhibited temperament that characterizes children who are shy, fearful, anxious, and upset by mildly stressful situations (Kagan, 1998; Kagan & Snidman, 2004). These associations with temperament suggest that biological factors play a central role in how intensely children react to emotionally arousing situations and how well they regulate their reactions. Individual differences in positive and negative emotionality are also related to children's overall adjustment. Children whose emotions are more negative experience a higher rate of developmental problems; children who are emotionally more positive have higher self-esteem, more social competence, and better adjustment (Goldsmith et al., 2001; Halverson & Deal, 2001; Lengua, 2002; Rothbart & Bates, 2006).

Learning from Living Leaders: Carolyn Saarni

Source: Courtesy of Carolyn Saarni.

Carolyn Saarni obtained a Ph.D. from the University of California at Berkeley with a specialty in developmental psychology and then received postdoctoral training in clinical psychology. Since 1980, she has been a Professor in the Graduate Department of Counseling at Sonoma State University, where she trains prospective marriage and family therapists and school counselors. Saarni was one of the first researchers to examine the development of emotional display rules, which she did by studying children's reactions when they were given a "disappointing gift." She has coedited a number of publications including *Lying and Deception in Everyday Life* and *Children's Understanding of Emotion*. She also wrote *The Development of Emotional Competence*, which describes specific skills that make up emotional competence. Saarni has given talks in many countries including Germany, Japan, and China. Most recently, she was a visiting scholar in the Languages of Emotion Cluster at the Free University of Berlin. In recognition of her excellent teaching, she was awarded the Outstanding Professor Award from Sonoma State University.

Further Reading

Saarni, C. (2007). The development of emotional competence: Pathways to helping children become emotionally intelligent. In R. Bar-On, J. G. Maree, & M. J. Elias (Eds.), *Educating people to be emotionally intelligent* (pp. 15–36). New York: Praeger.

Development of Emotional Understanding

To be emotionally competent, it is not enough to simply be able to express emotions. It is important to understand emotions as well. Children must acquire knowledge about emotions and be able to recognize them in themselves and in others. They also need to learn the causes and consequences of emotions, the situations in which it is appropriate to display certain ones, and how to modify them in themselves and others. Milestones in the development of emotional knowledge are included in Table 5.1.

Recognizing Emotions in Others

It has been estimated that between the ages of 3 and 6 months, babies are exposed to parents' and other caregivers' facial expressions of emotion 32,000 times (Malatesta, 1982). During this peak period of face-to-face interaction, parents' facial expressions represent an effective way to communicate their feelings and wishes to infants who cannot yet understand language. Learning to interpret the adults' expressions is a formidable task for the babies, but during these interactions, infants do learn to recognize some emotions. They recognize positive emotions more often and earlier than negative ones (Denham et al., 2007; Izard et al., 1995).

Consistent with the functionalist perspective, infants' recognition of joy before anger has functional value. Recognition of joy provides rewarding experiences for the infant. It strengthens the mother-infant bond and facilitates mutually rewarding experiences, particularly if the baby's recognition of joy leads to expression of joy. Anger recognition is not adaptive in the first half year of life. Threatening situations call for coping responses that are beyond the capacity of the 6-month-old (La Barbera et al., 1976). The joy-anger recognition sequence parallels the course of the infant's own emotional displays, in which smiling and laughter appear before frowning (LaFreniere, 2000).

Consistent with the learning perspective, early experience affects children's abilities to recognize emotions. Most infants recognize their mother's emotional expressions earlier than they recognize those of their father or a stranger because they have spent more time with her. Moreover, babies who spend more time interacting with their mother are more successful at recognizing her expressions than babies who spend less time with their mother (Montague & Walker-Andrews, 2002).

The quality of older children's interactions with their parents also makes a difference in their ability to recognize emotions. Abused children who experience high levels of threat and hostility are able to identify anger expressions better than nonabused children, but they are less capable of detecting expressions of sadness (Pollak & Sinha, 2002). Abused children also interpret positive, negative, and equivocal events as equally plausible causes of sadness and anger—presumably because of their inconsistent emotional experiences (Perlman, Kalish, et al., 2008). Children who are neglected rather than abused also show deficits in emotional understanding (Sullivan et al., 2008) as do children reared in group institutions such as understaffed orphanages (Fries & Pollak, 2004). The environment clearly affects children's ability to recognize emotions.

By the time they are 3 or 4 years old, children who have not been abused, neglected, or institutionalized can recognize and correctly label other people's expressions of happiness, sadness, anger, and fear (Denham et al., 2010; Stifter & Fox, 1987). Children from different cultures follow a similar developmental timetable for recognizing basic emotions. For example, U.S. and Japanese preschool children are able to verbally label emotions at about the same age (Bassett et al., 2008; Fujioka, 2008). Abilities to recognize emotions continue to improve as children grow up. School-age children increase their understanding that different events elicit different emotions and that enduring patterns of personality affect individuals' emotional reactions. They develop a better grasp of the causes of emotions and of the ways to modify their own and others' emotional states (Denham et al., 2010). They also learn to discriminate among subtle facial expressions. By age 9, children can quite reliably discriminate between Duchenne smiles and non-Duchenne smiles, which they could not do at age 6 (Gosselin et al., 2002). This discrimination ability continues to improve during middle childhood and adolescence (Del Giudice & Colle, 2007), probably contributing to children's increased abilities to participate successfully in peer group activities and to sustain social interactions (Denham et al., 2007; Saarni et al., 2006).

Cultural Context:
Expressing and Understanding Emotions in Different Cultures

Studies of emotions in different cultures have revealed that the facial expressions used to convey basic emotions such as fear, anger, joy, sadness, and disgust are similar worldwide (Ekman,1992; Elfenbein & Ambady, 2002). Moreover, the course of development is similar across cultures. As children grow, they improve in understanding a range of emotions, read nonverbal expressions more accurately, appreciate that a person's displayed emotion may be different from underlying feelings, and learn to regulate their own emotions (Tenenbaum et al., 2004). However, culture does influence some aspects of emotional expression and development.

Parents in different cultures vary in the extent to which they encourage their children's emotional expressions. In individualistic cultures, such as that of the United States, emotional expressions are considered spontaneous manifestations of inner feelings, and so parents encourage them (Matsumoto et al., 2008). In contrast, in collectivist societies, individual feelings are inseparable from feelings of the group, and control or suppression of emotions is valued and encouraged for the sake of group harmony (Masuda et al., 2008). Thus, it is not surprising that U.S. and Canadian parents encourage emotional expressiveness more than Asian parents (including those in China, Japan, India, and Nepal), who prefer emotional reserve, serenity, and contentment above gleeful, angry, or depressed outpourings (Cole et al., 2002; Raval et al., 2007; Shek, 2001). Asian parents react positively to children's suppression of emotion (Zahn-Waxler et al., 1996). They try to anticipate and prevent their children's displays of negative emotion, whereas U.S. parents respond to negative displays and help their children cope with their feelings (Rothbaum et al., 2002). Parents themselves also express different emotions in these different cultures: U.S. mothers express more positive emotions than Asian mothers (Camras et al., 2008). Moreover, parents talk about emotions in culturally scripted ways. To encourage children's emotional reserve and concern for others, Asian parents talk more about other people's emotions and less about the child's emotions (Wang, 2001). Their focus is on "teaching the child a lesson" and instilling social norms rather than discussing how the child feels (Wang & Fivush, 2005).

Variations in the ways parents socialize their children's emotions are not lost on the children. In Asian cultures, which focus on awareness of others' feelings, children are better at reading other people's facial expressions than are U.S. children (Markham & Wang, 1996), but they are less knowledgeable about emotion terms, presumably because they have discussed their own emotions less (Wang, 2003). Children in different cultures also differ in their displays of emotions. Girls in the United States display more smiles and overall expressivity than Chinese girls, just as their mothers do (Camras, Bakeman, et al., 2006). In Asian cultures in which parents teach careful control of emotions, endorse interpersonal harmony, and see anger as interfering with inner peace and social harmony, children restrain their emotional expressions. In one study, researchers compared the emotional reactions of elementary school children in Asia and the United States (Cole et al., 2002). They interviewed the children about how they would react to a difficult interpersonal situation, such

as someone spilling a drink on their homework or accusing them falsely of stealing, and asked how they would feel and whether they would want others to know their feelings. The U.S. children were more likely to feel angry and thought that expressing anger in a socially acceptable way was justified. The Asian children said that they might feel shame but they would not reveal shame or anger in response to the emotionally upsetting problem. Learning to follow the emotional display rules of the culture is an important developmental accomplishment because competence in implementing these rules is linked to good social relationships with peers (Parke et al., 2006; Valiente & Eisenberg, 2006).

Recently, kindergarten and early primary teachers in several Chinese cities have begun to implement a program in their schools to increase children's knowledge of emotions and emotional expressions (Partnership for Children News, 2006, 2008). In the 6-month program, children listen to stories about Zippy—a stick insect—and his friends, confront and solve problems together, cope with the death of the fragile insect, and, at the end of the program, look forward to new beginnings. "Zippy's Friends" trains children to express their feelings. "Before, the children could only use basic words such as 'happy' and 'unhappy'; now, they are able to tell you whether they are 'worried,' 'lonely,' or 'jealous,'" reported one teacher. Parents observed differences at home, too: "My 5-year-old son used to have an explosive temper; now, when he gets angry, he takes a deep breath and meditates on happy thoughts."

emotional display rule
An implicit understanding in a culture of how and when an emotion should be expressed.

Beyond Recognition: Thinking About Emotions

As they grow, children go beyond merely recognizing emotions to thinking more deeply about them. They think about the emotions they would feel if they went to a birthday party, had a favorite pet die, or heard a loud, unexpected bang. They think about whether people can feel more than one emotion at the same time.

MATCHING EMOTIONS TO SITUATIONS: EMOTIONAL SCRIPTS   As they mature, children develop a more complete understanding of the meanings of emotion terms and the situations that evoke different types of feelings. This understanding is based on a collection of emotional scripts that enable children to identify and predict emotional reactions to specific events (Saarni et al., 2006). Children begin to create these emotional scripts at a young age. In one study, a researcher told 3- and 4-year-old children simple stories about events such as getting lost in the woods, having a fight, or going to a party and then asked the children to tell her the emotions they thought the characters in the stories would be likely to feel (Borke, 1971). The children easily identified situations that would lead to happiness, and they were reasonably good at picking out stories in which children would feel sadness or anger. Other research showed that 3- and 4-year-old children could also describe situations that evoked the emotions of excitement, surprise, and fear (Cole & Tan, 2007; Levine, 1995). Clearly, young children know which emotions go with

emotional script
A scheme that enables a child to identify the emotional reaction likely to accompany a particular event.

which situations. With further development, they acquire more complex emotional scripts. By age 5, they generally understand situations that lead to emotions with recognizable facial displays (e.g., anger displayed in frowning) or that lead to a particular kind of behavior (e.g., sadness displayed in crying or moping). By age 7, they can describe situations that elicit emotions with no obvious facial or behavioral expressions, such as pride, jealousy, worry, and guilt. By age 10, children can describe situations that elicit relief or disappointment (Harris et al., 1987).

This developmental sequence has been observed in a number of countries including Great Britain, the United States, the Netherlands, and Nepal (Harris, 1989, 1995). But there are differences in specific emotional scripts in these different countries. For example, in the United States, children typically react to a parent's request to stop playing and go to bed with anger because it interrupts their play, but children in Nepal are happy because they know they will be sleeping with their parents, not all alone (Cole & Tamang, 1998).

MULTIPLE EMOTIONS, MULTIPLE CAUSES   Another aspect of emotional understanding is the awareness that a person can have more than one feeling at a time and can even experience conflicting feelings. Although infants show signs of experiencing conflicting feelings, such as being fascinated by a toy robot but wary or even frightened at the same time, the capacity to understand and describe mixed emotions develops slowly. As one young child responded when asked if a person could feel mixed emotions, "You'd have to be two different people to have two feelings at the same time" (Harter & Buddin, 1987, p. 398). In a study of children between the ages of 4 and 12 years, Susan Harter asked children to describe situations that would make them feel two same-valence emotions, such as happy and excited, or two opposite-valence emotions, such as happy and sad. Most 6- and 7-year-olds could describe situations that would elicit two emotions of the same valence, but only older children were able to describe situations that would make them feel two opposite-valence mixed emotions. Not until they were 10 to 12 years old were children able to conceive of opposite feelings existing simultaneously. Table 5.4 summarizes the developmental progression in children's ability to understand multiple and conflicting feelings (Harter, 2006; Harter & Buddin, 1987).

In another study of children's ability to understand mixed emotions, researchers showed 5- to 12-year-olds an excerpt from the animated film *The Little Mermaid,* culminating with King Triton and daughter Ariel's bittersweet separation and farewell (Larsen et al., 2007). When the children were interviewed about what they had seen, the older ones (8 years or older) were more likely than the younger ones to report that King Triton experienced mixed emotions in the emotionally complex situation—and that they too had experienced mixed emotions as they watched the film clip.

In a study of children 3 to 11 years of age, researcher Paul Harris and his associates identified three periods in children's thinking about emotions (Pons et al., 2004). In the first period

TABLE 5.4 **Children's Understanding of Multiple and Conflicting Emotions**

Approximate Age	Children's Understanding
4 to 6 years	Conceive of only one emotion at a time: "You can't have two feelings at the same time."
6 to 8 years	Conceive of two emotions of the same type occurring simultaneously: "I was both happy and proud that I hit a home run." "I was upset and I was mad when my sister messed up my things."
8 to 9 years	Conceive of two distinct emotions in response to different situations at the same time: "I was bored because there was nothing to do and mad because my mom punished me."
10 years	Conceive of two opposing feelings when the events are different or there are different aspects of the same situation: "I was sitting in school worrying about the next soccer game but happy that I got an A in math." "I was mad at my brother for hitting me but glad my dad let me hit him back."
11 to 12 years	Conceive of the same event causing opposing feelings: "I was happy that I got a present but disappointed that it wasn't what I wanted."

Sources: Harter, 2006; Harter & Buddin, 1987.

children began to understand important *external* aspects of emotions. In this period, the majority of 3-year-olds were able to recognize primary emotions such as happiness, sadness, fear, and anger on the basis of external (facial) expressions, and the majority of 5-year-olds were able to identify external causes of emotions. Children of this age could anticipate the sadness a child feels at the loss of a favorite toy or the happiness when receiving a gift, and they understood that two characters in the same situation could feel different emotions because they had different desires. In the second period children began to understand the *psychological* nature of emotions. From age 7 on, the majority of children understood that emotional expressions are produced by inner states, not solely by situations, that beliefs determine a person's emotional reaction to a situation, and that a discrepancy can exist between the outward expression of emotion and the actual emotion the person feels. In the third period in the development of thinking about emotions children understood that a person can *reflect* on a given situation from various perspectives and therefore experience different feelings, either concurrently or successively. From age 9 on, the majority of children understood that a character could have multiple, mixed, and even contradictory and ambivalent emotions. These three periods were hierarchically organized, with earlier understanding being a necessary condition for the emergence of later understanding.

Emotion Regulation

emotion regulation
The managing, monitoring, evaluating, and modifying of emotional reactions to reduce the intensity and duration of emotional arousal.

Another important aspect of emotional development is **emotion regulation** (Cole et al., 2004; Morris et al., 2007; Thompson & Meyer, 2007). As anyone who has sat next to a child on a lengthy airplane flight would surely agree, it is essential that children learn to manage their emotions. Children need to monitor and modify their emotional reactions and reduce the intensity and duration of their emotional arousal and negative outbursts (Brenner & Salovey, 1997; Thompson & Meyer, 2007). One reason this is important is that being able to regulate emotions makes children feel better. A second reason is that emotion regulation increases the likelihood that other people (including the ones sitting next to them on the airplane) will respond to the children positively. Changes in emotional regulation abilities are associated with maturation of the brain's prefrontal cortex (Thompson & Meyer, 2007).

The origins of emotional regulation appear even before birth when fetuses sooth themselves by putting their thumbs in their mouths. Young infants use very simple tactics for regulating their emotions; for example, when they confront a stranger, they fuss or look away (Mangelsdorf et al., 1995). As they grow older, they learn to turn away, cover their face, soothe themselves, or distract themselves with play when they encounter something frightening (Bridges & Grolnick, 1995; Mangelsdorf et al., 1995).

Preschoolers use emotion-regulation tactics that include self-distraction, orientation of attention toward or away from a stimulus, and approach or retreat from a situation (Denham et al., 2010). They begin to see connections between their regulation efforts and changes in their feelings, and they become more flexible in choosing contextually optimal means of coping. Behavioral disorganization resulting from strong emotion decreases dramatically in this age period. By the end of preschool, children can control their reactions to frustration by pouting and complaining rather than crying and screaming or throwing themselves or their toys on the floor. They have also learned emotional display rules that dictate what emotions to show under what circumstances, and they begin to be able to separate their feelings from their expression of emotions (Lewis & Michaelson, 1985). Children acquire knowledge about display rules before they are proficient regulators of their own displays, however (Saarni, 1999). In their earliest attempts to follow display rules, young preschoolers typically simply exaggerate or minimize their emotional displays. By the time they are 8 to 10 years old, children have learned display rules so they can smile even when they feel unhappy, feign distress that is not really felt, and mask amusement when they know they shouldn't laugh (Garner & Power, 1996; Saarni et al., 2006; von Salisch, 2008).

Over the elementary school years, children become more aware of the range of possible regulatory strategies and their efficacy in different situations, and they increasingly use cognitive and behavioral coping strategies to regulate their emotions (Denham et al., 2010; von Salisch, 2008). For example, when they are away at camp, they control the misery of homesickness by seeking out someone to talk to and help them feel better rather than crying, withdrawing, or suffering a headache or stomach ache (Thurber & Weisz, 1997). To some extent, culture shapes the form of emotional regulation that children use. Western societies socialize children to use active problem-focused regulatory strategies; Asian societies promote endurance as a way to regulate negative emotions, "save face," and maintain social harmony (Chin, 2007; Lee & Yang, 1998).

Although all children learn to regulate their emotions, some children do it better than others. Those who do it best start with biological advantages. As we indicated in our discussion of temperament in Chapter 3, infants and children vary in both their emotional reactivity and their capacity to modify the intensity and duration of their emotions by engaging in such strategies as gaze aversion, thumb sucking, and proximity seeking to a caregiver (Rothbart & Bates, 2006; Rothbart & Derryberry, 1981). Children who are both temperamentally reactive and poor at controlling their attention (unable to focus on a comforting object or thought) are poor emotion regulators (Denham et al., 2007; Valiente & Eisenberg, 2006). They are stuck in a double bind that taxes their ability to "unhook" from an intense emotional experience. This double bind is reflected in biological measures: children who exhibit poor emotion regulation in response to a frustrating task (waiting for a prize) have higher levels of negative affectivity and lower cardiac vagal tone—a physiological index of heart rate that measures the ability to recover from emotional challenge (Santucci et al., 2008).

Emotion regulation abilities are important predictors of children's later adjustment (Fox & Calkins, 2003). Children who are better at regulating their anger in preschool by shifting attention away from the frustrating situation are less aggressive and disruptive when they enter school (Gilliom et al., 2002). Children who are more knowledgeable about display rules and better at using them are also more socially competent and better liked by their peers (McDowell & Parke, 2000, 2005; Parke et al., 2006). Controlling emotional arousal and displays is not only good for children's well-being but is also good for children's interactions with the world. Being able to regulate their emotional displays helps children get the attention and approval they seek (Tronick et al., 2005). Adults respond more positively when children smile or look sad rather than crying or throwing things (Howes, 2000).

Into Adulthood:
Controlling Negative Emotions in Adulthood

Source: © Media Bakery.

Childhood is not the only time people can improve their strategies for dealing with negative emotions. They can also do it in adulthood. One effective coping strategy that older adults use is to direct their attention to positive thoughts (Charles et al., 2003; Mather et al., 2004). When participants in one study were asked to look at pictures of faces portraying sadness, anger, fear, and happiness, college students stared longest at fearful faces, but older adults spent the most time looking at happy faces (Isaacowitz et al., 2006). They had apparently taken to heart the lyricists' suggestions to "accentuate the positive, eliminate the negative, latch on to the affirmative," and "always look on the bright side of life." The older couple in the photo are clearly enjoying looking through their photo album and remembering good times.

According to socioemotional selectivity theory, as they age, people increasingly perceive time as finite, and so they place more effort on regulating their emotions to enhance positive experiences and diminish negative ones (Charles & Carstensen, 2007). One way they do this is to engage in processes to promote disengagement from negative situations. For example, they get less angry in response to interpersonal conflicts than younger adults do (Charles & Carstensen, 2008). They also enjoy social interactions more than younger people do because they are more selective about their social partners and restrict their social network to loved ones (Carstensen et al., 1997). Older adults also have more positive memories than younger adults, because they distort them to be more emotionally gratifying (Mather & Carstensen, 2005). They remember positive faces better than negative faces whereas younger adults do not exhibit this bias (Mather & Carstensen, 2003). Even in their initial attention to stimuli, older adults focus on the positive, and when they look at positive images, it activates their ventromedial prefrontal cortex—the region of the brain associated with emotion regulation—more than looking at negative images; for young adults, the opposite is true (Leclerc & Kensinger, 2008).

Older adults report that they are better at regulating their emotions than they were when they were younger (Lawton, 2001), that they experience fewer negative emotions (Gross et al., 1997; Lawton et al., 1993), and that their negative emotional episodes are less enduring (Carstensen et al., 2000). When they are asked to describe everyday problem situations, older adults say that they regulate their anger by redirecting their thoughts and behaviors away from the situation and attempting not to feel or show an emotional reaction; they do not confront the emotion, ruminate about it, or express anger to the person seen as the cause of the problem (Blanchard-Fields & Coats, 2008; Coats & Blanchard-Fields, 2008). When experimenters deliberately induce negative emotions, older adults are more effective at repairing their mood than younger adults are (Kliegel et al., 2007). Compared with younger adults, older adults express anger outwardly less often and report more inner control of anger using calming strategies (Phillips et al., 2006). Older adults have generally better emotional well-being than younger adults, and improved management of their negative emotions is an important reason.

Socialization of Emotion

Children can learn about emotions by watching how people respond to them emotionally and by observing how people respond to each other. Watching Mom and Dad argue, siblings squabble, and Grandma smile at a sister are all ways of learning about the world of emotions. Susanne Denham (1998) has identified three ways in which people socialize children's emotions (Figure 5.5). First, they provide models of emotional expressiveness. Second, they react to children's emotions in ways that encourage or discourage them. Third, they act as emotional coaches by talking about their own and other people's emotional responses.

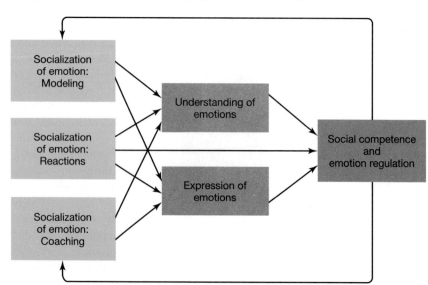

FIGURE 5.5 *A model of emotional socialization. Socialization practices lead to changes in understanding and expression of emotions, which, in turn, lead to changes in social competence and the ability to regulate emotions.* Source: Emotional Development in Young Children (Paper) *by Susanne A. Denham. Copyright 1998 by Guilford Publications, Inc. Reproduced with permission of Guilford Publications, Inc. in the format textbook via Copyright Clearance Center.*

Learning from Living Leaders:
Susanne A. Denham

Source: Courtesy of George Mason University.

Susanne Denham is Professor at George Mason University and an expert on children's early emotional development. Although she set out to be a pediatrician, she became a developmental psychologist instead after changing her major and completing graduate work at the University of Maryland. She traces her interest in understanding and helping young children to an early age when she was fascinated by infant toys,

often worked as a babysitter, and suffered through her mother's struggle with depression. Her work has focused on three questions: How do parents teach their children to express, regulate, and understand their emotions? How does knowing how to deal with feelings promote children's competence with their peers? How can we create and improve measures of children's social-emotional competence? Researchers and students all over the world have used her puppet-based Affect Knowledge Test. Her work has had applied value too: She has designed a program to improve preschoolers' emotional competence and created an assessment of emotional competence that teachers can use. Looking to the future, she sees more integration of emotional development work with brain science and psychophysiological measurement, more applications that are based on developmental science, and a move toward findings being taken seriously by policy makers. She will be pursuing her new interest in the development of forgiveness in children. Her advice to students: "Listen and watch kids! Follow your passion for understanding children. Let it condense into a focus and don't be afraid to continue your studies."

Further Reading

Denham, S., & Burton, R. (2003). *Social and emotional prevention and intervention programming for preschoolers*. Amsterdam: Kluwer-Plenum.

Socialization by Parents

Children learn a great deal about expressing emotions by watching their parents. Some parents are subdued and restrained in their emotional reactions; others are demonstrative and intense. Many studies have shown that children's emotions reflect those of their parents; they are similar in levels of emotional expressiveness and the types of emotions they display. Children who grow up with parents who exude positive emotions are more likely to express positive emotions; children whose parents respond sensitively to distress are more empathic; children with parents who often display hostility and conflict show more negative emotions (Ayoub et al., 2006; Denham et al., 2007; Eisenberg, Gershoff, et al., 2001; Halberstadt et al., 2001). These links between parents' and children's emotions do not end in childhood; reciprocal patterns of emotional exchanges are observed between adolescents and their parents as well (Kim et al., 2001).

   Children also learn emotion regulation from their parents. If parents are positive when they interact with their children and provide comfort when the children are angry or distressed, the children develop more constructive reactions to anger, regulate their emotions better, and know how emotions should be displayed (Eisenberg & Fabes, 1994; McDowell & Parke, 2005). When parents scold or punish their children for expressing emotions, especially negative ones, children have difficulty regulating their emotions (McDowell & Parke, 2000; Parke et al., 2006; Valiente & Eisenberg, 2006). Abused children are especially poor at emotional regulation (Edwards et al., 2005; Pollak & Sinha, 2002; Shipman et al., 2007). Parents who belittle their children's emotions—"There's no reason for you to be sad"—or show little interest in how the child is feeling—"Don't worry about it; go watch TV"—are not teaching children how to regulate their emotions either. Parents who fight in front of their children are also failing to provide help with emotion regulation. Children exposed to high levels of domestic violence have more trouble regulating their emotions (Katz et al., 2007); however, if parents can constructively settle their disputes, children are less likely to have emotion regulation problems (Cummings & Davies, 2010).

Parents can actively coach their children and give them "lessons" that help them understand and regulate their emotions. According to psychologist John Gottman, even concerned, warm, and involved parents sometimes have attitudes toward their own and their children's emotions that get in the way of their being able to talk to their children. These parents need to channel their caring into basic coaching skills. In his book, *The Heart of Parenting: Raising an Emotionally Intelligent Child*, Gottman identified five aspects of parenting that constitute "emotion coaching" (Gottman & DeClaire, 1997):

1. *Being aware of the child's emotions.* For example, the parent says, "I see that you are feeling sad because you are sick and can't attend the party today."

2. *Recognizing emotional expression as an opportunity for intimacy and teaching.* For example, one mother took advantage of what happened when her daughter couldn't decide whether to get in or out of the new wading pool. When the girl finally had a meltdown, her mother told her she couldn't act like that. She let the girl cry for a while and then consoled her and talked about what had happened. The daughter learned that some emotional expressions are not acceptable and that talking about rather than venting feelings can have a positive outcome because everyone went back to the pool and had a good time (Denham, 1998).

3. *Listening empathically and validating the child's feelings.* For example, one mother, looking at a book with her preschooler, interpreted the emotionally arousing pictures: "They were frightened," she said, "They grabbed the dog and brought it to safety. See the worried looks?" "They look so scared," said her daughter (Colwell & Hart, 2006).

4. *Labeling emotions in words children can understand.* For example, one mother said, "The boy was surprised and a little scared when the jack-in-the box popped up," rather than saying the boy was "discombobulated"—a word the child would not understand.

5. *Helping children come up with an appropriate way to solve a problem or deal with an upsetting situation.* For example, one parent said, "I know you are frustrated that you can't play with your sister's new toy right now, so let's look for a toy that you can play with until it is your turn to try the new toy."

Gottman found that children of parents who used these emotion-coaching techniques were more emotionally competent than children who were not coached by their parents. Children whose parents give them lessons such as these are better able to manage emotional upset on their own by soothing themselves when they are upset; they are better at understanding people, have better friendships with other children, and are more accepted by their peers (Gottman et al., 1996; Gottman & DeClaire, 1997). They are better at taking the viewpoint of another person and at understanding their own and others' emotions. In related research, Judy Dunn and her colleagues found that 3-year-old children's conversations with their mothers about feeling states predicted the children's abilities to understand other people's emotions at age 6 (Dunn, 2004; Dunn & Hughes, 1998; Dunn et al., 1995). Another way that parents help their children learn about emotions is by reminiscing with them about shared emotional experiences in the past. Children whose mothers engage in such reminiscing are able to tell more coherent and emotionally expressive autobiographical narratives and are better at regulating their emotions (Fivush, 2007). In general, children whose mothers discuss feelings more are better able to recognize others' emotions and have better emotional regulation (Garner, 2006). Of course, these are all correlational findings, and perhaps mothers who are good emotion socializers have children whose temperaments facilitate their emotional understanding. However, experimental work in which researchers use story vignettes to explain to children the causes of emotional reactions also improve children's emotional understanding—suggesting that parents do, in fact, play a causal role in shaping children's emotional competence (Tenenbaum et al., 2008).

Mothers who are good at regulating their own emotions are especially good emotion socializers for their children, offering more lessons and a better balance between positive and negative emotions (Perlman, Camras, et al., 2008). Their children know more about facial expressions and emotion situations. Similarly, mothers with more positive emotions are better emotion socializers; they are sensitive to their children's emotional states, share positive emotions with them, and contribute to their sense of pride and efficacy (Hoffman et al., 2006). Fortunately, having one parent who is a good supporter of the child's emotional learning can compensate for having a second parent who is not (McElwain et al., 2007).

Socialization by Other Children

Peers and siblings also socialize children's emotions. When a child displays anger, other children are apt to respond with anger, rejection, or disapproval (Denham et al., 2007; Fabes et al., 1996); when a child acts happy, peers are likely to approve (Sorber, 2001). These peer reactions teach children the consequences of expressing negative and positive emotions. Peers can help children improve their emotional understanding and knowledge as well. In one study, kindergarten children who had good relationships with their peers increased in emotional knowledge over the year more than children who were socially isolated—presumably because they had more opportunities to learn about the nuances of emotions in their interactions with their peers (Dunsmore & Karn, 2004). Engaging in pretend play with siblings and friends also helps children understand other people's feelings (Dunn & Hughes, 2001). Similarly, children learn about emotions when their siblings make positive or negative responses or alert their parents to the child's angry outburst (Denham et al., 2007; Dunn, 1988, 2004). Programs such as More Fun with Brothers and Sisters teach children how to identify, monitor, evaluate, and modify their emotional reactions to their siblings. These programs improve children's emotion regulation skills and lead to more positive relationships between siblings (Kennedy & Kramer, 2008).

Research up Close:
Emotional Development in a High School Theater Program

Most work on emotional socialization focuses on young children. However, emotional socialization continues in adolescence. Reed Larson and Jane Brown (2007) investigated how new emotional skills were learned during adolescence in the process of putting on a high school production of *Les Miserables*. Using detailed qualitative interviews and observations over the period from casting to production, they identified the emotions the adolescents experienced and explored how participation in the theater production altered adolescents' emotional development.

Disappointment was a common early emotion because many students didn't receive their hoped-for role. But this disappointment dissipated within a week or two as the students talked their disappointment through with their friends and became engaged in the roles they were given. As they became involved in rehearsals and began to master their roles, the students reported frequent experiences of excitement, satisfaction, elation, and "adrenaline rush." Often the elation spread through the group. As Marina described it, "Energy is very contagious when you're on stage so, like if I sing loud and I get excited about it, it usually just kind of spreads and other people catch on." As time progressed and demands mounted, feelings of anger and interpersonal stress were reported. These negative emotions, too, were contagious. Nearly all of the students described frustration with peers who were egotistical or obstructionist. Toward the end of the period, several students suffered from bouts of anxiety as they anticipated performing in front of an audience; again group support helped settle frayed nerves and keep the nervous actors on track. The emotional climax was the elation they all felt when they successfully performed *Les Miserables*. In the interviews following the performance, several youth reported sadness that the play was over.

This theater experience offered these youth a distinct set of emotional experiences including disappointment, elation, frustration, and anxiety. From these experiences, several types of emotional learning occurred. First, the students reported gaining abstract knowledge about emotions, especially links between emotions and personalities. They learned that some of their fellow actors were more volatile and emotional than others and that differences in emotionality could be authentic or a matter of display. They increased their awareness of their own emotional patterns as well. Several reported learning through the imaginative process of creating their characters as they stepped into someone else's shoes and experienced someone else's emotions. In addition, the students reported gaining knowledge about the factors that influence emotions, such as fatigue, stress, criticism, and success. They also described becoming sensitive to how emotions influenced the group. When the group was happy, their work went "a lot smoother." Another major advance was learning how to manage anger and interpersonal stress.

The students reported developing strategies for dealing with the disappointment of not getting a desired role, managing anxiety, and reducing the stress created by the demands the production put on their time. Their most frequent theme was learning to manage the interpersonal stress they experienced during the production. Their anger, particularly toward peers, created a challenge but also appeared to be a stimulus for learning.

Two years later, when the students were re-interviewed, several reported that learning to restrain their negative reactions to others was one of the most important lessons they learned from their theater experience. They learned to keep their own anger in check, "chill out," and "calm down." They also learned to compensate for factors that increased their anger. When one student, Jack, observed how tiredness made him more emotional, he said: "You kind of have to learn to recognize that and go 'Okay, I've had a long day and I need to be gentler than usual' because I know I'm going to have a short fuse and it's going to be hard for me to deal with some things." Another thing the students learned about emotion was to use positive emotion to enhance their work. Sara described learning to use comedy to lighten the mood of the group and smooth tense situations. The students almost always described the process they had gone through as one in which they and their peers were collaborators in active learning, helping each other understand emotional episodes and talking through how to handle them. They credited the adult leaders with facilitating the process, not by trying to "teach" them about emotions in the abstract, but by creating conditions in which they learned from the emotions that occurred in their work.

Socialization by Teachers

Teachers also facilitate children's emotional development. Especially in the preschool years, teachers play a significant role in the development of the emotional skills that are so important to children's social success. Teachers use physical comfort and distraction to help toddlers regulate their negative emotions. With preschoolers, they use verbal mediation and explanations to help the children understand the causes of their anger, frustration, or sadness and teach them constructive ways of expressing negative emotions (Ahn, 2003). Although there is pressure to push academic learning in preschool to prepare kids for elementary school, several investigators have recognized that emotional learning is an important component of school readiness and have trained teachers to help preschoolers improve their emotional competence (Denham & Burton, 2003; Izard et al., 2008).

Real-World Application:
Teachers as Promoters of Emotional Competence

Let's be honest. Four-year-olds are lovable, but they are also self-centered, impulsive, and prone to meltdowns. Teaching them to understand other children's emotional signals and regulate their own emotions can help them avoid a conflict or a meltdown. The Preschool Promoting Alternative Thinking Strategies (PATHS) curriculum was designed to help teachers create an environment to promote children's learning of social-emotional skills. It contains 30 lessons that Head Start teachers deliver once a week during "circle time" (Domitrovich et al., 2007). The primary objectives of the curriculum were (1) to develop children's awareness and communication regarding their own and others' emotions, (2) to teach self-control of arousal and behavior, (3) to promote positive self-concept and peer relations, (4) to develop children's problem-solving skills by fostering integration of self-control, affect recognition, and communication skills, and (5) to create a positive classroom atmosphere that supports social-emotional learning. In addition to the lessons, teachers promoted the concepts through activities such as group games, art projects, and book reading.

Children who participated in the PATHS program had a larger emotion vocabulary at the end of the program. They were able to correctly label emotional expressions and were more accurate in identifying feelings and facial expressions than children who were not exposed to the curriculum. PATHS children also gained in their ability to correctly identify situations that elicit different basic emotions. In addition, exposure to PATHS significantly reduced children's anger attribution bias: PATHS participants were less likely to misidentify emotional expressions as angry compared with children without the PATHS experience. Increasing children's emotion knowledge and reducing their anger bias increased the likelihood that PATHS children would be successful in social situations with peers. In fact, teachers in the PATHS classrooms described their students as significantly more cooperative, emotionally aware, and interpersonally skilled than teachers in the control classrooms.

Another preschool curriculum addressed both reading words and reading emotions—a sensible approach because children's academic and socioemotional skills are intertwined. Karen Bierman and her colleagues divided 44 Head Start classrooms into two groups: half followed a traditional Head Start curriculum; the other half followed a program called REDI (Research Based Developmentally Informed) Head Start (Bierman et al., 2008). This program included teaching children specific emotional management and social problem-solving skills as well as reading readiness. One of the stars of the program was Twiggle the Turtle, who followed the counsel of a wise old turtle. According to the old turtle, when Twiggle got upset, he should go inside his shell, take a deep calming breath, and say what bothered him and how it made him feel: "Cross your arms to be like Twiggle in his shell," the teachers would tell the preschoolers. "Practice what James should say if Suzie takes the toy he wants, or if Billy says something mean to Tommy." Instead of the vague "Use your words" advice that preschool teachers often offer, "Be like Twiggle" became the thing to say. As Bierman observed, "You'd see children over in the blocks center, and someone stands up and does the turtle and talks, and someone else does the turtle and talks, and then they sit down and play again" (*Minneapolis Star Tribune*, 2008). By year's end, preschoolers in the REDI program scored higher than children in

Here a teacher demonstrates the Twiggle the Turtle conflict-resolution lesson to 4-year-olds at The Bennett Family Child Care Center in University Park, Pennsylvania. Source: © AP/Wide World Photos.

the regular Head Start program on tests of school readiness—both social and academic. They had better skills for recognizing emotions in others and responding appropriately to situations involving a conflict. Among the REDI children, 70 percent showed little or no disruptive behavior compared with 56 percent in the regular classes. Moreover, parents of children in the REDI group reported fewer instances of impulsivity, aggression, and attention problems at home than did parents of children in the traditional program.

When Emotional Development Goes Wrong

In spite of their individual differences, most children develop emotional patterns that serve them well in dealing with normal social and emotional challenges. However some children have emotional problems including excessive anger, fear, anxiety, or depression that can impair their social functioning. Excessive anger may lead to aggression and violence, as we discuss in Chapter 12, "Aggression." Excessive fears may cause considerable discomfort for children and their families. Fortunately, most of these fears disappear within a few years (Gelfand & Drew, 2003). A small number of fears and phobias are more long lasting, persisting across the life span including acrophobia (fear of heights) and fear of physical illness. Anxiety disorders characterized by a general apprehensiveness and low self-confidence also can last into the adult years (Ollendick & King, 1998).

childhood depression
A mood disorder often manifested in despondent mood and loss of interest in familiar activities but possibly expressed as irritability and crankiness and difficulty concentrating or focusing on tasks.

The most common emotional problem in childhood is **childhood depression**. It is diagnosed when a child has seemed depressed or has lost interest or pleasure in nearly all activities for at least two weeks. The dominant mood may be irritability and crankiness rather than sadness and dejection. Family members often notice that these children are withdrawn or have stopped the activities they formerly enjoyed—for example, a child who had enjoyed playing soccer may begin to make excuses not to practice. Depression often interferes with appetite and eating, and parents may note the child's failure to make normal or expected weight gains. Another common effect of depression is an impaired ability to think, concentrate, or focus on a task. A precipitous drop in grades may signal depressive problems in a child or adolescent. Somatic complaints (e.g., headache, stomach pain) are not uncommon in depressed children. Nearly twice as many girls as boys experience childhood depression (Goodman & Gotlib, 2002; Hammen, 2005).

Although depression in childhood is low in frequency (2%), in part because of the difficulty of reliably diagnosing it, it is relatively stable and similar to depression in adults (Cole et al., 2008). It is diagnosed in a considerable number of young people beginning at about age 15. One unfortunate consequence of depression is an increase in suicide. Researchers in the Centers for Disease Control and Prevention (CDC) found that about 17 percent of high school students seriously considered suicide and 13 percent made specific suicide plans (CDC, 2007). Suicide is the third leading killer of adolescents, following car accidents and homicide (Berman et al., 2005; CDC, 2007). It is the second leading cause of death among college students. About 3 percent of older adolescent girls and 1 percent of boys make at least one serious suicide attempt (CDC, 2009). Females are much more likely to attempt but to fail at suicide than are males. One reason is that they are more likely to use methods such as overdosing with drugs or poisons or suffocation, whereas males tend to use methods that have faster and surer results, such as shooting or explosives.

Culture also plays a role in suicide. Suicide rates are high in countries such as Japan, which has a long history of viewing suicide as an honorable tradition. In Muslim and Catholic countries, where suicide is viewed as a violation of religious teachings, rates are low. In North America, Native American and aboriginal youth have high rates of suicide; one study found their suicide rate to be five times higher than that of youth in the general population (Chandler et al., 2003). Many factors including poverty, loss of traditional culture, limited educational and job opportunities, and alcohol and drug use contribute to these elevated rates. Among inner-city African American and Latino gangs, suicide rates are rising (Rotherman-Borus et al., 2000).

Although depression and suicide are often linked, this is not always the case (Jellinek & Snyder, 1998). In one large study, 42 percent of the adolescents who attempted suicide did not have a history of depression (Andrews & Lewinsohn, 1992). Suicide is related to a general sense of overwhelming hopelessness, although it also may result from the accumulation of adverse life events, such as family conflicts, loss of a family member due to illness, death, or divorce, breakups or problems in romantic relationships or friendships, school failure, being apprehended in a forbidden or embarrassing act or situation, or real or imagined mental or physical illness (Jellinek & Snyder, 1998). Many adolescents who attempt suicide feel that they have no source of emotional support. They may be alienated from their families and may have had disruptions or losses in intimate relations and relations with peers that give them a sense of isolation and helplessness.

Insights from Extremes: When Children Commit Suicide

When Dan Kidney was 11 years old, his parents found him hanging with a belt around his neck from a chin-up bar in the doorway between his bedroom and bathroom. He was a popular kid, good-looking, and growing up with all the advantages of a well-educated family. Yet Dan's father and mother had suspected their son was troubled in ways he wouldn't admit. He never threatened to harm himself, but he seemed depressed and sometimes agitated in the months leading up to his suicide. We do not expect children as young as Daniel to commit suicide, but this unfortunately is not a unique case. An 11-year-old British boy was bullied so badly at school and on the bus that he took his own life. His father found him with his shoelaces tied around his neck and to the sides of his bunk. A 10-year-old boy in the United States was found lifeless by his brother after he had overdosed on medication, cut himself, and finally hanged himself from his bunk bed. He left a picture that he had drawn of himself hanging and a note saying, "Children are not meant to be ignored." An 11-year-old girl in Shanghai jumped to her death from a sixth-floor window at her school on the first day back from vacation. Her teacher reported that the girl was unhappy with her mother and the two had been in conflict over the winter break.

These tragedies provide three clear insights. One is that children are not immune to the pressures and disappointments that lead adolescents and adults to end their lives. In fact, 25 percent of preadolescents have considered suicide at least once (American Association of Suicidology, 2006) although the actual rate of successful suicides among children is low. Among children under 12 years of age, only 4 of 500,000 commit suicide in any given year. More alarming is the fact that in the United States, this figure has doubled since 1979 (CDC, 2009). The second insight is that children are as capable of planning and carrying out suicide as are adolescents and adults. Children from 6 to 12 years old have committed suicide by jumping from heights, running in front of trains or cars, drowning, stabbing, scalding, burning, and hanging. The most common methods used by 10- to 14-year-olds are shooting (50%), hanging (33%), and poisoning (12%). The third insight to be drawn from these tragedies is that children experience profound emotions and act on them, just as older people do. These tragic cases have led to efforts to prevent childhood suicide by making parents and teachers more aware of early warning signs, such as mood changes, withdrawal, and despondency. The National Academy of Sciences has called on the U.S. government to make children's mental health a national priority.

Causes of Childhood Depression

Like many human disorders, depression is caused by multiple factors. Just as normal emotional development is multiply determined, so is atypical emotional development.

BIOLOGICAL CAUSES Several lines of research suggest that there are biological causes of children's depression. Behavior genetics research shows that childhood depression is more likely in children of clinically depressed parents and the association is stronger for biological children and between identical twins (Cicchetti & Toth, 2006; Goodman & Gotlib, 2002). Brain research shows that depression is associated with brain functions. For example, the amygdala region of the brain has been found to have elevated activation when children of depressed mothers are shown fearful faces (Monk et al., 2008). However, children whose mothers have recovered from depression exhibit normal brain activity, which suggests that the mother's behavior also plays a role in children's early depression (Embry & Dawson, 2002). How much family interactions versus genetic influences contribute to childhood depression remains an open question (Gotlib et al., 2006; Hops, 1996; Silberg et al., 2001).

SOCIAL CAUSES Studies supporting social explanations of childhood depression show that the experiences of children with depressed mothers differ from those with nondepressed mothers. Depressed mothers are more tense, disorganized, resentful, and ambivalent and less sensitive, communicative, and affectionate with their children (Cummings et al., 2000; NICHD Early Child Care Research Network, 1999). Furthermore, depressed mothers are more likely to perceive their children's behavior negatively (Hammen, 2005, 2009). Impaired relationships with depressed parents probably undermine children's emotional development, leading to poorer understanding of their own emotional states and perhaps most critically poorer ability to regulate their emotions, especially negative ones (Hoffman et al., 2006; Maughan et al., 2007). This, in turn, can contribute to the development of depression (Cole et al., 2008; Kovacs et al., 2008). Peers can also play a role in children's mental health. Elementary school children who were shy and socially anxious and who were also excluded by their peers were at higher risk for depression than nonanxious and better accepted classmates (Gazelle & Ladd, 2003). Life stressors have also been found to contribute to childhood depression (Hammen, 2005).

learned helplessness
A feeling that results from the belief that one cannot control the events in one's world.

COGNITIVE CAUSES Another explanation of depression invokes the concept of **learned helplessness**, which results from the belief that one is helpless to control the events in one's world (Seligman, 1974). The learned helplessness theory of depression suggests that depressed children not only experience feelings of helplessness but also attribute their failures in controlling the world to enduring personal shortcomings. Essentially, this cognitive theory asserts that children become depressed when they perceive themselves as having failed to achieve desired outcomes in their lives (Garber & Martin, 2002).

Treating Childhood Depression

Depressed children and adolescents can benefit from a wide range of interventions. Antidepressant drugs such as fluoxetine (Prozac) and sertraline (Zoloft) are widely prescribed and somewhat effective. In one study, 56 percent of children with major depression improved with Prozac compared with only 33 percent of a placebo group (Emslie et al., 1997). Unfortunately, antidepressant drugs are dangerous, and an overdose can be lethal (Gelfand & Drew, 2003). In 2004, the U.S. government began to require warning labels to accompany these antidepressant drugs in light of the increased risk of suicide associated with their use in a small percentage of adolescents. However, the rates of suicide showed a sharp increase at the same time that the use of antidepressants among adolescents declined, which suggests that parents need to be aware of warning signs of suicide whether their teens are on antidepressant drugs or not (CDC, 2007).

cognitive behavior therapy
A therapy technique useful for treating depression in adolescents that teaches strategies for dealing with depressive moods and acquiring a more positive outlook.

Cognitive behavior therapy is one of the most effective approaches for treating depression in adolescents (Hammen, 2005; Hollon & Dimidjian, 2009). This type of therapy is typically conducted in small groups of adolescents over a number of weeks. The goals are to reduce the teenagers' self-consciousness and feelings of being different and to provide them with relaxation techniques and self-control tactics to help them control their dark moods. The therapy also emphasizes positive strategies such as improving peer relations, setting realistic goals, and learning how to get more fun out of activities. In one series of studies, between 54 and 67 percent of treated adolescents no longer met the criteria for depression after therapy (Clarke et al., 1992; Lewinsohn & Rohde, 1993). Among teenagers with similar depressive problems who were on a waiting list for therapy and served as controls, only 5 to 48 percent no longer met the criteria. Unfortunately, nearly one third of adolescents treated with cognitive behavior therapy experienced a recurrence of depression within two years (Birmaher et al., 2000). Prevention programs have been effective in reducing mild depression. In one study, children at risk for depression were given training in cognitive and problem-solving skills (Gillham et al., 1995). Two years later, when researchers evaluated these children, they found fewer depressive symptoms than in a control group.

Chapter Summary

Why Are Emotions Important?

- Children communicate their feelings, needs, and wishes to others and regulate other people's behavior through emotional expressions.

Primary and Secondary Emotions

- Biological, learning, and functional theories explain different aspects of emotional development.
- Babies begin expressing primary emotions of anger, joy, fear, and sadness early in life.
- Smiling begins with the newborn's reflex smile, which depends on the baby's internal state. Social smiles appear between 3 and 8 weeks. By 12 weeks, infants smile selectively at familiar faces and voices, depending on the situation. By 4 months, infants begin to laugh. Both laughter and smiling express joy and play a critical role in maintaining the proximity of the caregiver to the baby.
- Fear emerges gradually in the first year. Babies tend to be less fearful in a familiar setting and when they feel as if they have some control over the situation. Social referencing helps them know how to behave in unfamiliar situations.
- In the second year, children develop secondary or self-conscious emotions such as pride, shame, guilt, jealousy, and empathy. These emotions rely on the development of self-awareness.

Individual Differences in Emotional Expressiveness

- Differences in emotional expressiveness are rooted in biology and have important implications for children's later adjustment.

Development of Emotional Understanding

- In the first 6 months of life, infants begin to recognize emotional expressions in other people. They typically recognize positive emotions before negative ones, which has functional value because it strengthens the infants' bond with caregivers.
- As children mature, they develop an understanding of emotion terms. Emotional scripts help them identify the feelings that typically accompany particular situations. They learn that people can experience more than one emotion at a time and two emotions may conflict.

Emotion Regulation

- A major challenge for children is to learn how to modify, control, and regulate emotions so they are less frequent and less intense.
- By the preschool years, children begin to follow emotional display rules that dictate which emotions to show under what circumstances. Culture affects these rules, and the display of such emotions as anger and shame may be sanctioned in one culture but disapproved of in another.

Socialization of Emotion

- Parents influence children's emotional expressions, understanding, and regulation. They serve as models for emotional displays, and by reacting to the child's emotional expressions encourage or discourage such displays. Children whose parents serve as coaches in helping them understand and manage their emotions are better able to handle emotional upset on their own and are more accepted by their peers. Belittling or dismissing children's emotions or punishing children for their expression may prevent children from learning how to manage their own feelings and understand other people's emotions.
- Peers and teachers also play a role in the socialization of children's emotions.

When Emotional Development Goes Wrong

- Children sometimes experience extreme anger, fear, phobias, anxiety, or depression.
- The prevalence of depression increases in adolescence and is higher in girls than boys. In extreme cases, suicide sometimes occurs, especially among some minority groups.
- Biological, social, and cognitive factors are all potential contributors to the development of depression. Medications, cognitive therapy, and prevention programs are ways of treating child and adolescent depression.

Key Terms

childhood depression

cognitive behavior
   therapy

Duchenne smile

emotion regulation

emotional display rule

emotional script

empathy

learned helplessness

primary emotions

reflex smile

secondary or
   self-conscious
   emotions

separation anxiety

social referencing

social smile

stranger distress or fear
   of strangers

At the Movies

Most movies about children's emotions accentuate the negative. For example, *12 and Holding* (2005) portrays the raw, unguarded emotions of pain, longing, rage, and revenge in troubled children entering adolescence and conveys how these lonely, insecure children became so consumed by their feelings that they lost sight of ordinary social boundaries. A child's emotions are also at the heart of the film *Atonement* (2007), so named because a girl's false accusation of her older sister, consequent feelings of guilt, and attempts to atone for her actions are central to the plot. Poignant portrayals of negative emotions in childhood are often found in movies about divorce. For example, in *Shoot the Moon* (1982), the oldest daughter is mature enough to see what is happening when her parents split up but too immature to handle the aftermath. She doesn't know whether to love or hate her father for leaving the family and angrily refuses to forgive him.

Some movies provide an opportunity for teaching children how to deal with negative emotions. These include blockbusters such as *The Incredible Hulk* (2008), which graphically illustrates what happens when a man (who happens to have been exposed to gamma rays) is under emotional stress and fills with rage—he turns into a destructive, murderous, giant green monster. The movie also shows how the Hulk learned to control his emotions through meditation and love. In addition to popular movies like *The Incredible Hulk*, numerous educational films focus on children's emotions, such as *Larryboy—The Angry Eyebrows* (2002), in which the lesson of letting go of anger is conveyed by the superhero alter ego of Larry the Cucumber from VeggieTales; *Live & Learn—Dealing with Anger* (2008), in which children learn different approaches to handling their anger when their expectations aren't met; *Dragon Tales—Whenever I'm Afraid* (2004), in which stories about overcoming fear offer help for anxious children; and *Trevor Romain—Taking the "Duh" Out of Divorce* (2008), in which an animated character is helped to work through anger, fear, and sadness when her parents announce their divorce. *The Transporters* (2007) teaches autistic children how to recognize emotions such as anger and sadness through the exploits of vehicles including a train, a ferry, and a cable car. This film is the brainchild of Simon Baron-Cohen, director of the Autism Research Centre at Cambridge University. He and his colleagues have shown that when autistic children between the ages of 4 and 7 years watch the video for at least 15 minutes a day for 1 month, they catch up with normal children in their ability to identify emotions.

CHAPTER 6

Self and Other: Getting to Know Me, Getting to Know You

Source: iStockphoto.

I'm 3 years old and I live in a big house with my mother and father and my brother Jason and my sister Lisa. I have blue eyes and a kitty that is orange and a television in my own room. I know all my ABCs. Listen. A, B, C, D, F, G, I, K. I am really strong. I can lift this chair.

I am 6 and in first grade. I can do lots of stuff real good. Lots! I can run fast, climb high, and I'm good at schoolwork. If you are good at things you can't be bad at things at least not at the same time. I know some kids who are bad at things but not me.

I'm 9 years old and in fourth grade and I'm pretty popular, at least with girls. That's because I'm nice to people and helpful and can keep secrets. Mostly I am nice to my friends although if I get into a bad mood I sometimes say something that can be a little mean. At school I feel pretty smart in certain subjects like language arts and social studies. But I feel pretty dumb in math and science. Even though I'm not doing well in these subjects, I still like myself as a person because math and science aren't as important to me as how I look and how popular I am.

I just turned 13 and I'm talkative, pretty rowdy, and funny with my friends. I like myself a lot when I am around my friends. With my parents I'm more likely to be depressed. I feel sad, mad, and hopeless about ever pleasing them. What they think about me is still really important, so when they are on my case it makes me dislike myself as a person. At school I get better grades than most but I don't brag about it because that's not cool. I'm shy, uncomfortable, and nervous around people I don't know well.

I'm 15 and what am I like as a person? I'm complicated! With my really close friends, I am very tolerant, understanding, and caring. With a group of friends, I'm rowdier but usually friendly and cheerful, but I can be pretty obnoxious if I don't like how they are acting. At school I'm serious, even studious but a goof-off too, because if you're too studious, you're not popular. So, I go back and forth which means my grades aren't great. But that causes problems at home, where I am pretty anxious around my parents. I don't understand how I can switch so fast from being cheerful with my friends then coming home and feeling anxious and getting frustrated and sarcastic with my parents. I think a lot about who is the real me, but I can't resolve it. There are days when I wish I could just become immune to myself.

I am 18 and a high-school senior and I am a pretty conscientious person particularly when it comes to homework. I want to go to law school even though my parents would rather I go into teaching. Every now and then I get a little lackadaisical, but that's normal. You can't be a total "grind." I've become more religious as I have gotten older but I'm not a saint or anything. Religion gives me a sense of purpose and a guide to what kind of adult I'd like to be. I'm not as popular as a lot of other kids, but I don't care what other kids think anymore. I try to believe that what I think is what counts. I'm looking forward to leaving home and going to college, where I can be more independent, although I'm a little ambivalent. I'll always be a little dependent on my parents, but I'm looking forward to being on my own.

These children's responses to the question "What are you like as a person?" illustrate one of the main topics of this chapter, how the notion of the "self" changes with age. (Harter, 2006, pp. 513, 521, 526, 531, 540, 545–46).

The *sense of self*, or the awareness of the self as differentiated from other people, is crucial for children's development (Harter, 2006). In this chapter, we examine how children develop their sense of self. We also discuss how children feel about themselves—their self-esteem—and think about themselves—their identity. As their knowledge about self increases, children acquire knowledge about other people. They also learn to communicate with these other people. These three areas of development—(1) understanding self, (2) understanding others, and (3) communicating with others—have major implications for children's social adjustment and their ability to successfully navigate in the social world.

The Sense of Self

individual self
Aspects of the self that make a person unique and separate from others.

relational self
Aspects of the self that involve connections to other people and develop out of interactions with others.

collective self
A person's concept of self within a group, such as a group based on race or gender.

The **individual self** refers to aspects of the self that make a person unique. For example, a person may see himself or herself as hard working, physically fit, and confident—all characteristics of the individual. Other types of selves are also possible (Brewer, 1991; Sedikides & Brewer, 2001). The **relational self** refers to aspects of the self that involve connections to other people and develops out of social interactions (S. Chen et al., 2006). The internal working model of attachment that we discussed in Chapter 4 is an example of a relational self. It represents the child in relation to other people, such as parents or siblings, and involves a conception of the self as a social partner. The **collective self** refers to the person's concept of self within a group, such as a group based on race, ethnicity, or gender. In a discussion about race, for example, the collective self of an African American student might be salient. We discuss the collective self later in this chapter when we explore the issue of racial and ethnic identity.

As technology advances, new ways of expressing the self are broadening the scope of possible selves. The *online self* is one relatively recent form of self-representation. In the electronic universe of Internet forums and multiplayer games, participants assume online identities or selves, which may or may not map onto their real-life self in terms of gender, race, occupation, and education. These selves act as a means of impression management or an opportunity to try out new identities (Greenfield, Gross, et al., 2006). Another opportunity for a new self comes from the technology of personal genomics. It is now possible to purchase an individualized profile of your *genomic self*, which contains information about your biological and psychological traits (Pinker, 2009). Whether this technology yields information that is reliable or helpful remains to be seen.

Developmental Origins of Self-Concept

Research on children's awareness of their individual selves has focused on a process that has its roots in early infancy. Babies as young as 18 weeks of age happily gaze at their reflections in a mirror—but they do not realize that they are looking at themselves. To study the development of children's self-recognition, researchers have shown children their reflections, turned them away from the mirror and put a red spot on their nose or a sticker on their forehead, and then turned them back to the mirror to see how they react (Brooks-Gunn & Lewis, 1984; Bullock & Lutkenhaus, 1990; Lewis, 1991). The researchers assume that if children know they are looking at their own reflection, they will touch their face to see what is on it. Using this simple method, investigators have found that children under 1 year of age act as if some other child is behind the mirror; they stare at the mirror and don't touch their own face (Brooks-Gunn & Lewis, 1984). Some time during the second year of life, children begin to recognize their own image, and by the time they are 2, almost all children giggle, show embarrassment, or act silly at the sight of their own red nose or stickered forehead. They are clearly exhibiting self-recognition. At this age, however, the sense of self-recognition is restricted to the "here and now." When researchers delay the time between putting a sticker on the child's face and showing the child a videotape of the sticker being put on his or her face, 2- and 3-year-olds do not demonstrate self-recognition by reaching up and touching or removing the sticker, and they may describe the sticker in the videotape as being on "his" or "her" face rather than saying it is on "my" face (Miyazaki & Hiraki, 2006; Povinelli et al., 1996). Children have trouble representing and remembering past self-images until they are about 4 years old.

Children's views–and descriptions—of themselves become more detailed, specific, and psychological as they grow up (Damon & Hart, 1986; Garcia et al., 1997; Harter, 2006; Sakuma et al., 2000). Susan Harter (1999) identified three stages in the development of self-descriptions in childhood and another three in adolescence. The opener to this chapter illustrates these six stages by quoting self-descriptions given by children at six different ages.

This baby may think she's found a friend in the mirror. It will be a few more months before she realizes that the "friend" is herself. Source: iStockphoto.

When they are 3 or 4 years old, children describe themselves in terms of observable physical features ("I have blue eyes"), preferences ("I like pizza," "I like to swim," "I watch TV"), possessions ("I have an orange kitty"), and social characteristics ("I have a brother, Jason"). Particular skills are touted ("I can count," "I run fast"), even though their self-assessments are often inaccurate—they may not be able to count past 3 or run faster than their peers. There is a disjointed lack of coherence in their self-descriptions because children of this age cannot integrate their compartmentalized representations.

When they are 5 to 7 years old, children describe themselves in terms of their competencies, "I am good at running, jumping, and school work." They are beginning to coordinate compartmentalized concepts but not concepts that are opposites such as good and bad, smart and dumb. They are still very positive in their self-descriptions and overestimate their abilities.

By age 8 to 10, children are more aware of their private selves and their unique feelings and thoughts, and they begin to describe themselves in more complex terms. They use labels that focus on abilities ("I am smart") and interpersonal attributes ("I am popular, nice, and helpful"). They integrate success in different areas ("I am smart in language and social studies but dumb in math and science"). In addition, their self-constructs become increasingly aligned with the values, roles, and preferences of their cultural community.

In early adolescence, beginning at age 11, children describe themselves in terms of social relationships, personality traits, and other general, stable psychological characteristics. Their self-descriptions focus on interpersonal attributes and social skills ("I am good-looking, friendly, and talkative") competencies ("I am intelligent"), and emotions ("I am cheerful," or "I am depressed"). Children recognize that they have different selves in different social contexts, with their father, their mother, their friends, their teachers, and their teammates. They begin to describe themselves in abstract terms, such as intelligence, but their abstractions are still compartmentalized.

In middle adolescence, young people are introspective and preoccupied with what others think of them. What were formerly unquestioned self-truths become problematic self-hypotheses. Multiple "me's" crowd the self-landscape as the adolescent acquires new roles. The growing ability to think in the abstract allows the adolescent to create a more integrated view of the self. For example, an adolescent might conceive of herself or himself as intelligent by combining the qualities of being smart and creative but at the same time think of herself or himself as an "airhead" or "misfit" because she or he feels socially out of sync with others. At this age, adolescents have trouble integrating self-representations to resolve apparent contradictions. They don't understand how they can be different in different roles, and they experience conflict over opposing self-attributes.

In late adolescence, self-descriptions emphasize personal beliefs, values, and moral standards. Adolescents think about future and possible selves. They integrate potentially contradictory attributes and develop a coherent theory of the self. For example, the older adolescent may reconceptualize the opposing notions of "cheerful" and "depressed" as "moody," thus resolving apparent contradictions in his or her sense of self (Harter, 2006).

Cultural Context: How Culture Shapes Self-Representations

To appreciate how culture shapes children's self-descriptions, consider these two 6-year-olds describing themselves:

I am a wonderful and very smart person. A funny and hilarious person. A kind and caring person. A good-grades person.

I'm a human being. I'm a child. I'm my mom and dad's child, my grandma and grandpa's grandson. I'm a hard-working child.

It should not surprise you to find out that the first child is European American and the second is Chinese. These self-descriptions echo the values of Western and Asian cultures. Westerners emphasize an autonomous self that can be described in terms of unique personal traits; Asians emphasize an interdependent self that can be described in terms of social roles and responsibilities in a network of relationships. Qi Wang (2001, 2004b) explored self-representations in the United States and China by asking adults and children to describe themselves so that the researchers "could write a story about them." European American children's descriptions were more "personal"—referring to personal attributes ("I'm cute"), preferences ("I love playing piano"), possessions ("I have a teddy bear"), and behaviors unrelated to other people ("I'm happy"). Chinese children's descriptions were more "social"—referring to group memberships ("I'm a girl"), and interpersonal relations ("I love my Mommy," "My cousins and I do lots of things together").

Culture leaves its imprint on other dimensions of the self-concept, as well, such as the level of positivity and pride expressed in self-descriptions. Western cultures encourage children to embrace positive self-views; Asian cultures value self-criticism and humility because they facilitate group solidarity and harmony. Not surprisingly, in Wang's research, European American children were more likely to describe themselves in positive terms ("I am beautiful, "I am smart"), whereas Chinese children used nonevaluative descriptors ("I play games," "I go to school").

How do children learn these cultural ways of representing themselves? Wang observed Chinese and American mothers sharing memories about their family with their 3-year-olds (Wang & Ross, 2007). American mothers focused attention on the child and what the child had accomplished, acknowledged the child's expressions of individuality, and socialized the child to remember personal experiences highlighting individual uniqueness and autonomy.

Mother: *Do you remember when we were at Nana's on vacation, and we went down to the dock at Grandmommy's? You went swimming?*

Child: *Um-hum.*

Mother: *What did you do that was really neat?*

Child: *Jump off the dock.*

Mother: *Yeah. That was the first time you've ever done that.*

Child: That was like a diving board.

Mother: You're right, it was. And where did Mommy have to stand?

Child: In the sandy spot.

Mother: In the sandy spot, right. Mommy said, "Wait, wait, wait! Don't jump 'til I get into my sandy spot!"

Child: Why?

Mother: 'Cause you remember how I told you all the leaves pile up on the bottom of the lake? And it makes it a little mushy. And so, you jumped off the dock and then what did you do?

Child: Swim.

Mother: To . . .

Child: Nana.

Mother: Yeah. All by yourself.

In contrast, Chinese mothers focused on group actions with the mother playing a leading role and posing pointed questions. They used the story telling opportunity to remind the child of his or her place in the social hierarchy and the need to follow the rules to maintain social connectedness and harmony. There was little discussion of the child's individual or unique qualities.

Mother: That day, Mom took you to take a big bus and go skiing in the park. What did you play at the place of skiing? What did you play?

Child: Played . . . played the . . .

Mother: Sat on the ice ship, right?

Child: Yes. Then . . .

Mother: We two rowed together, right?

Child: Then . . . then . . .

Mother: Then we rowed and rowed, rowed round a couple of times, right?

Child: Um.

Mother: We rowed around a couple of times. Then you said, "Stop rowing. Let's go. Go home." Right?

Child: Um.

Mother: Then we took a bus to go home, right?

Child: Um.

This research suggests that sharing family memories is one way children learn how to think about their present and past selves in a way that fits their culture.

Difficulty Developing a Sense of Self: Autistic Children

Autism affects children's ability to develop a sense of self. Some children with autism seem not to recognize themselves as independent social beings (Dawson et al., 1998). They exhibit delays or deficits in self-recognition. When researchers in one study showed autistic children (ages 3 to 13) their reflections in a mirror, 31 percent failed to demonstrate recognition of their mirror image (Spiker & Ricks, 1984). More recent studies have confirmed that children with autism spectrum disorder (ASD) show delays in self-recognition (Nielsen et al., 2006). Moreover, even when autistic children do recognize themselves in the mirror, they demonstrate little emotional response. This is consistent with the suggestion that autistic children are less proficient in understanding emotions than are normally functioning children (Baron-Cohen, 2001; Losh & Capps, 2006; Rump et al., 2009). Researchers have found that autistic children—unlike normal children—show similar neurological responses to their own face, a familiar face, and an unfamiliar face—a further indication that they do not distinguish between self and other (Gunji et al., 2009).

Self-Perceptions

self-esteem
The evaluative component of self that taps how positively or negatively people view themselves in relation to others.

Global Self-Esteem

The development of self has an evaluative component that taps how positively or negatively children view themselves in relation to others. Are they as good as their friends, better than their classmates, worse than their neighbors? Few topics have captured the attention of parents, teachers, and children themselves as much as this concept of **self-esteem**—a global evaluation of one's worth as a person (Harter, 1999). The numerous school programs, popular articles, and Web sites offering ways to increase children's self-esteem illustrate this preoccupation (e.g., http://www.childrens-self-esteem.com/self-esteem-children.html; http://www.superheroselfesteem.com).

The preoccupation with elevating children's self-esteem is based on evidence that children who have high self-esteem view themselves as competent and capable and are pleased with who they are, whereas children who have low self-esteem view themselves as inadequate and inferior to others (Harter, 1999, 2006). Individuals with high self-esteem also are happier than those with low self-esteem (Baumeister et al., 2003). In addition, high self-esteem in childhood is linked to a variety of positive adjustment outcomes including school success, good relationships with parents and peers, and lack of anxiety and depression (Harter, 1999, 2006). However, the direction of cause and effect in these links is not always clear. Good performance is as likely to lead to high self-esteem as the reverse, and when variables such as the child's competence are controlled, links between self-esteem and positive social outcomes tend to be reduced (Baumeister et al., 2003). Self-esteem can have a dark side, too. High self-esteem does not prevent children from smoking, drinking, taking drugs, or engaging in early sex. If anything, it fosters experimentation that can increase early sexual activity and drinking (Baumeister et al., 2003). High self-esteem can also be related to prejudice and antisocial behavior. In one study, aggressive adolescents with high self-esteem were more likely than those with low self-esteem to justify their antisocial behavior and belittling of victims (Menon et al., 2007). This finding raises a warning flag: Promoting self-esteem for all children may have pitfalls. In any event, researchers have not found that boosting children's self-esteem—by therapeutic interventions or school programs—leads to better social outcomes (Baumeister et al., 2003).

Domain-Specific Perceptions

In addition to developing an overall global sense of self-worth, children develop domain-specific self-perceptions in areas such as scholastics, athletics, and appearance. A child may have a high self-perception of competence in schoolwork but a poor self-perception of competence on the athletic field. Harter (1982, 1999) developed a measure for assessing both global self-esteem and specific self-perceptions. With her assessment instrument, children rate themselves on global self-worth ("I am a worthwhile person") and in five domains: scholastic ability, athletic competence, physical appearance, behavioral conduct, and social acceptance (Table 6.1). Using this measure, researchers have found meaningful distinctions between global self-esteem and self-perceptions in specific areas and have constructed individual profiles of self-evaluation across the five domains.

TABLE 6.1 **Sample Items from the Harter Self-Perception Profile for Children**

Really True for Me	Sort of True for Me	Really True for Me
Scholastic competence		
Some kids feel like they are just as smart as other kids their age	BUT	Some kids aren't so sure if they are as smart
Athletic competence		
Some kids are very good at sports	BUT	Some kids are not very good at sports
Global self-worth		
Some kids are often unhappy with themselves	BUT	Other kids are pretty pleased with themselves

Source: Harter, 1982, 1999.

Learning Self-Appraisal

How do children develop their self-perceptions? In early childhood, self-appraisals are not very accurate or realistic. Most children under 8 years rate themselves positively—too positively. Even children who always strike out when they are at bat may say they are "good at athletics," and even the class troublemaker may claim to be "well behaved." For children of this age, self-perceptions may reflect what they "want to be" rather than who they are. However, although discrepancies between self-ratings and reality do exist, children's self-assessments relate moderately well to their teachers' assessments, which suggests that children's views of their own competencies have at least some reality (Harter, 2006).

With development and a history of feedback from others, children become more realistic in their self-appraisals. The "strike-out kid" no longer has a view of himself or herself as a baseball star and the class troublemaker has had enough detentions and trips to the principal's office to realize that he or she is not a good candidate for a "well-behaved child" poster (Harter, 2006). Children who are rejected by their peers accept this judgment and view themselves as low in social competence (Rubin, Bukowski, et al., 2006). Children also distinguish among different kinds of competence and view themselves as better in some domains than others. They attach more importance to the domains they excel in. The "strike-out" child turns out to be a "math whiz" and places higher value on scholastic achievement than athletic skills. The "class troublemaker" turns out to be popular with peers and makes having friends an important part of his or her self-appraisal.

How children evaluate themselves in different domains affects their overall sense of self-esteem, depending on the importance they place on each domain. A student comes to college having been a star on the football field in high school but finds that the college does not value athletics and does not even have a football team. Athletic prowess can no longer serve as the basis for the student's high global self-esteem. Scholastic success is what is valued at the college, but this is not his strongest area. His overall sense of worth as a person suffers. However, if he joins the drama club, finds out that he is good at singing and dancing, rates himself high on artistic competence, and regards this domain as important, he can regain a high level of global self-esteem (Harter, 2006).

Over time, a reciprocal relation develops between children's self-perceptions in a domain and the interest, motivation, and effort they devote to activities in that domain. For example, when children perceive that they are socially competent, they are likely to approach social situations with a lot of self-confidence, which increases their success in social interactions; success, in turn, bolsters their confidence and their social self-perception. Support for this reciprocal link between self-appraisals and real-life experience has been found in several domains, including academics, athletics, and social acceptance (Harter, 2006; Marsh et al., 2007; Valentine et al., 2004).

Learning from Living Leaders:
Susan Harter

Source: Courtesy of Susan Harter.

Susan Harter is Professor of Psychology and Head of the Developmental Psychology Program and the Center for the Study of Self and Others at the University of Denver. Following the completion of her Ph.D. at Yale University, she served as the first female faculty member in that psychology department. Her interest in psychology had an early beginning. She performed her first science experiment in fourth grade—pairing a hen with a duck egg. After hatching, the duck "imprinted" on the hen, and Harter was hooked on a career in science. Her interest in social development was gradual: First, she was fascinated by animals on the farm she grew up on, then by children through her teacher/mother, and finally she developed an interest in adolescents. Her focus since then has been the influence of socialization on the development of self-esteem, and she is best known for her well-used instrument for assessing dimensions of self-esteem. Harter has also examined the construction of multiple selves as individuals move into adolescence and "false-self" behavior in which adolescents don a false self for peers and parents as a strategy for gaining more social support. Her work has clear practical applications and has been a major impetus behind the national focus on fostering children's self-esteem. She has developed social interventions for enhancing "realistic" self-esteem in children and adolescents. Instead of the global approach many schools use, she recommends a focus on raising self-perceptions in areas of greatest value to individual students. Her hope is that future developmental psychologists will use a variety of approaches from social to neurological and will make research relevant and accessible to the real world. Her advice for undergraduates: "Don't put the methodological cart before the conceptual horse! Instead find a burning question that intrigues you and then select or develop measures, not the other way around."

Further Reading

Harter, S. (1999). *The construction of the self: Developmental perspectives*. New York: Guilford.

Gender Variations in Global Self-Esteem

Researchers studying self-esteem have asked whether differences in children's levels of self-esteem might be related to their gender. They have found that girls have lower global self-esteem than boys beginning in middle childhood and that this difference is particularly evident in adolescence (Kling et al., 1999; Mellanby et al., 2000; Van Houtte, 2005). One might think that societal shifts toward increased gender equality would have lessened this difference between the sexes. However, the discrepancy in global self-esteem has not changed over the past 30 years.

Why does a gender difference in self-esteem occur? Several explanations have been offered. First, boys are more dominant and assertive than girls, especially in mixed-gender groups; this may contribute to a feeling of greater power and influence on the part of boys. Opportunities to participate in athletics also may be a factor. In spite of Title IX, a program to promote more opportunities for girls to participate in sports, status and resources still favor boys, who are still perceived as having more athletic ability than girls. Moreover, girls don't elect to participate in athletics as much as boys do; some even see it as a threat to their femininity. Among both boys and girls, self-esteem is higher for those who participate in sports than for their nonathletic peers (Harter, 2006). Nor is this gender difference restricted to North American samples. Girls in England, Australia, Ireland, Switzerland, Italy, Holland, China, and Korea also see themselves as less competent than boys in athletics (Harter, 2006).

Physical appearance contributes to the gender difference in self-esteem as well. A clear link exists between children's ratings of their appearance and their overall self-esteem (Harter, 1999, 2006). Unfortunately, few girls can live up to the ideals of beauty in the popular media. Movies, magazines, and TV all focus on the importance of looks that are impossible to achieve—in part because many of them are the result of air-brushing, digital retouching, and combining body parts from different models. The images showcase thinness, tallness, and large breasts. Perhaps in the future, more ads showing girls and women of all shapes and sizes will start a trend toward more realistic images on TV and will have a positive effect on girls' self-esteem (see the film produced by the Dove Self-Esteem Fund: http://www.youtube.com/watch?v = 4ytjTNX9cg0).

Social Determinants of Self-Esteem

Factors in their social environments at home and at school influence children's global self-esteem.

FAMILY INFLUENCES Stanley Coopersmith (1967) found that when parents were accepting, affectionate, and involved with their children, set clear and consistent rules, used noncoercive disciplinary tactics, and considered the child's views in family decisions, their children had higher self-esteem in middle childhood and adolescence than children whose parents lacked these virtues. In more recent research, as well, investigators have found that adolescent girls whose mothers were more affectionate had higher self-esteem and adolescent boys whose mothers were more psychologically controlling, intrusive, and manipulative had lower self-esteem (Ojanen & Perry, 2007). Similarly adolescents whose parents were authoritative—affectionate but firm—had higher self-esteem than adolescents whose parents were authoritarian—controlling and punitive (Lamborn et al., 1991). Children with abusive parents also have lower self-esteem than children with nonabusive parents (Cicchetti & Toth, 2006). Parents' approval seems to be particularly important for fostering self-perceptions in the domains of scholastic competence and good conduct (Harter, 1999).

INFLUENCE OF PEERS AND MENTORS   Children's self-esteem becomes increasingly influenced by their peers' opinions as the children grow older. Peers are especially important for promoting adolescents' self-perceptions in the domains of physical appearance, popularity, and athletic competence (Harter, 1999). Interestingly, support from peers in the "public domain"—that is, in classes, clubs, teams, and work settings—is more important than support from close friends in the "private domain" (Harter, 1999). Perhaps this is because public support is viewed as more objective and credible than support from caring but biased friends. Even feedback from anonymous peer strangers can affect children's self-esteem. In one experiment, preadolescents were asked to complete a personal profile describing their intelligence, agreeableness, trustworthiness, sense of humor, and so on (Thomaes et al., 2010). They were told that their personal profile and picture would be posted on the *Survivor Game* Web page to be evaluated by peer judges. Children who received negative feedback from the alleged peer judges reported declines in their self-esteem; children who received positive feedback reported a boost in self-esteem. This study demonstrated a short-term effect of peer opinion on children's self-esteem. Of course, in real life, the sustained evaluation by peers is what matters.

Mentors such as coaches, teachers, and family friends are also influential sources of support for self-esteem. In one study, for example, 6th- to 8th-graders who thought they had received more support from their teachers increased in self-esteem (Reddy et al., 2003; Rhodes & Frederikson, 2004). Experimental studies of mentoring programs such as Big Bothers Big Sisters have also shown positive effects on children's self-esteem (Rhodes et al., 2000). About 3 million youth in the United States are currently in these programs (Rhodes & DuBois, 2006), which apparently work by increasing children's scholastic confidence and improving their relationships with their parents. However, the impact of the programs is often modest and depends on the consistency, quality, and duration of the mentoring (DuBois & Rhodes, 2006).

PRAISING CHILDREN AND BOOSTING SELF-ESTEEM   When parents lavish supposed self-esteem boosters on their children—"You're so smart!" "You're the best soccer player on your team!" "Your coloring is genius!"—does this, in fact, promote their self-esteem? A growing body of research suggests that praising children for their talent and intelligence doesn't help them achieve success; it sets them up for disappointment. These children are likely to stumble at school when faced with challenges that don't immediately reinforce the accolades they hear at home. They're also more likely to avoid tasks at which they may fail than children who are praised instead for their hard work. Carol Dweck (2008) compared two groups of 5th graders who took an IQ test involving relatively easy puzzles. One group was praised as being intelligent and the other for making a good effort. In subsequent testing, the children who had been praised for being "smart" backed away from a difficult assignment when an easier one was offered. They took their failure at another very difficult test as a sign they weren't smart at all. In a final IQ test, which was exactly the same as the first one, the children who were tagged as intelligent did about 20 percent worse than they had the first time. The children praised for their effort improved their scores by 30 percent. By labeling a child smart or talented, parents are, in effect, "outsourcing" the child's self-esteem. The more children are praised, the more

Learning from Living Leaders: Carol S. Dweck

Source: Courtesy of Carol S. Dweck.

Carol Dweck is Professor of Psychology at Stanford University. Since receiving her Ph.D. from Yale University, she has taught at the University of Illinois, Columbia, and Harvard. Her work examines the self-conceptions people use to guide their behavior. She is a strong believer in the concept of "mind-set" and thinks that with the right one, you can have a more successful social and intellectual life. This is the message of her book *Mindset* based

on more than three decades of research in which she has been figuring out why some people achieve their potential and others, equally talented, don't. The key isn't ability; it's whether the person looks at ability as something inherent or something that can be developed. She started her career studying animal motivation, focusing on the "learned helplessness" that occurs when animals don't do what they are capable of because they have given up after repeated failures. She wondered how humans cope with failure and found that people who attributed failure to lack of ability became discouraged whereas people who thought that they simply hadn't tried hard enough were inspired by setbacks. Dweck's work has clear practical value, and she has designed a computer-based training module, Brainology, to help children develop a mind-set based on the belief that they can succeed if they make an effort. She has taken her own work to heart, too. She began playing the piano in adulthood and learned to speak Italian in her 50s, even though these are things that adults are not supposed to be good at learning. There is clearly hope for all of us, from students to late life learners, if we take Dweck seriously and develop the right mind-set.

Further Reading

Dweck, C. S. (2006). *Mindset: The new psychology of success*. New York: Random House.

they look over their shoulder, wondering: "Am I going to get praise? Do people think this is good?" It is better to foster in children a "growth mind-set" that they can develop their abilities through effort. To do this, parents should focus on children's efforts and how they tackle tasks. They should praise children's strategies and progress rather than their intelligence. They should praise socially desirable behaviors and self-improvement rather than abilities. Praise needs to be specific and sincere, not exaggerated and unwarranted. Stepping out of the way and letting children solve problems on their own will also help them build true self-esteem (Baumeister et al., 2003; Dweck, 2008; Young-Eisendrath, 2008).

Identity Formation

identity
The definition of oneself as a discrete, separate entity.

Forming a sense of **identity** involves defining oneself as a discrete, separate entity and addressing the questions "Who am I?" and "What will I become?" in terms of religious views, political values, gender preference, and occupational aspirations. This process is a major challenge in adolescence (Moshman, 2005; Schwartz, 2001). Erik Erikson was one of the first psychologists to study adolescents' identity development. His fifth developmental stage focused on the search for a stable self-identity. Failure to achieve a stable identity, Erikson claimed, results in identity confusion—a state he illustrated with a line from Arthur Miller's play *Death of a Salesman*, when Biff says, "I just can't take hold, Mom. I can't take hold of some kind of life." Although empirical support for Erikson's theory has been limited in part because of the difficulty of testing his ideas, his work has been an important catalyst for research and theorizing.

Following Erikson's lead, James Marcia (1966, 1993) described a period during which adolescents experience a crisis of decision making when alternative identities are explored, options tried, and new ways of being are imagined. For example, an adolescent boy thinks about pursuing various occupations, such as becoming a chef, a doctor, or a jazz musician. He buys cookbooks and watches *Top Chef*, becomes a fan of medical dramas on TV, and practices the saxophone every night. He also visits several religious groups to experience different religious beliefs and customs. As he goes through this examination of possible selves, four types of identity outcome are possible (Table 6.2). The goal for every young person is to achieve a stable and satisfying identity, but as this table indicates, not everyone achieves the desired state of commitment to an identity. The fortunate ones actively engage in identity exploration and, in the end, commit themselves to a satisfactory and acceptable identity.

Identity achievement—the most developmentally advanced identity outcome—is associated with several positive outcomes, including high self-esteem, cognitive flexibility, mature moral reasoning, clear goal setting, and better goal achievement (Kroger, 2004; Moshman, 2005; Snarey & Bell, 2003). Adolescents who have achieved a sense of identity are able to develop close intimate relationships with others more readily than youth who have still not achieved a stable and mature sense of self (Stein & Newcomb, 1999).

Some adolescents—the *foreclosed* group—remain committed to their childhood values and beliefs and do not use adolescence as a period to explore other potential identities. Compared with other adolescents, they are more authoritarian and inflexible and more susceptible to extreme ideologies and movements, such as cults or radical political movements (Saroglou & Galand, 2004).

Another group of adolescents actively explore but fail to reach any resolution about who they are and what they believe and value. Marcia (1966, 1993) describes them as being in *moratorium;* they have reached a plateau and are still in the process of identity formation. These adolescents tend to be anxious and intense, and they often have strained or ambivalent relationships with their parents and other authority figures (Kroger, 2004). However, they are better adjusted than those with a foreclosed or a diffused identity status (Berzonksy & Kuk, 2000).

Adolescents with a *diffused* identity neither engage in exploration nor are concerned about committing themselves to a particular identity; they "take life as it happens." These individuals are viewed as the least mature in their identity development. Some are delinquents and abuse drugs; others are lonely or depressed; still others are angry and rebellious (Kroger, 2004). Their "lack of caring" attitude is often linked with academic problems and a sense of hopelessness (Snarey & Bell, 2003; Berzonsky & Kuk, 2000).

Marcia (1993) viewed these four identity outcomes not as stages but as different levels in the identity process. Individuals can shift from one to another even over the course of adolescence. For example, an adolescent in a state of moratorium may settle on and achieve an identity only to shift back to a moratorium state some time later. These shifts are especially likely when the adolescent achieves identity early in development. For adolescents in the foreclosure and diffusion groups, cycling between states of identity is less common because they never developed a

TABLE 6.2 Four Identity Outcomes

Identity diffusion	Person has experienced neither identity crisis nor identity commitment.
Identity foreclosure	Person has made a commitment without attempting identity exploration.
Identity moratorium	Person is actively involved in exploring different identities, but has not made a commitment.
Identity achievement	Person has gone through exploration of different identities and made a commitment to one.

Source: Marcia, 1966.

sense of self-identity in the first place. In a recent longitudinal study of identity in early to late adolescence, researchers found evidence of these back-and-forth shifts (Meeus et al., 2010). However, in general, over this age period the number of adolescents who had diffused identities or were in moratorium decreased and the number who were committed to a foreclosed identity or an achieved identity increased. Not all adolescents underwent identity shifts; about 60 percent remained in the same identity level from early to late adolescence.

Identity formation is clearly not over in adolescence and according to one meta-analysis identity change may be more prevalent in young adulthood (Roberts et al., 2006). Many young adults continue to struggle with identity issues, especially now that education is an extended commitment and dependency on parents for financial support lasts longer than in the past (Arnett, 2000, 2006). In fact, the largest shifts toward a stable identity take place during the college years (Waterman, 1999).

A number of factors influence adolescents' identity development. For one, biological changes contribute to the self-identity process. Puberty signals a clear break from childhood and reminds the adolescent that adulthood is approaching. An awareness of self as a sexual being emerges as well, which stimulates exploration of sexual identity and sexual relationships. Changes in cognitive functioning also affect adolescents' abilities to achieve an identity. Advances in cognitive development during adolescence permit more abstract reasoning, which, in turn, allows adolescents to think more deeply about themselves. As a result, they not only appreciate discrepancies between their "ideal" and actual selves but also recognize that they present different selves in different contexts. As one adolescent expressed it: "I am an extravert with my friends. I'm more likely to be depressed with my parents. I can be a real introvert around people I don't know well." Clearly, this adolescent is aware of multiple identities that appear in different social contexts.

Into Adulthood:
Identity Formation Continues

Emerging adulthood—the age period between the late teens and the mid-20s—is a period of unprecedented freedom to explore identity options. "Shall I become a doctor? Is this really what I want?" "Should I be a writer?" This freedom in a time of high hopes and big dreams is exciting. However, it is also a time of anxiety and uncertainty as establishing an identity becomes increasingly important. College students are more likely to have achieved an identity if their parents are supportive, respect their wishes and needs, and avoid intrusive and manipulative strategies (Luyckx et al., 2007). If parents are not sensitive and attuned, college students are more likely to have a fragmented sense of identity.

Identity formation continues after emerging adulthood if it has not yet been achieved. When researchers in Finland studied a sample of adults at ages 27, 36, and 42, they found that development along a sequence from identity diffusion to identity achievement was the most frequent trajectory and that identity achievement was related to having a prolonged education, making a later transition to adult working life, and starting a family "on time"—not too early, not too late (Fadjukoff et al., 2005, 2007). A U.S. study following adults from age 30 to 60 also showed that identity development continues during adulthood (Cramer, 2004). The greatest change occurred during the period from early to middle adulthood when the likelihood of having an achieved identity increased and the likelihood of having identity diffusion decreased. Having an achieved identity was associated with being more intelligent, experiencing success in work, having positive marital and family relationships, and participating in community and political activities. Adults with a foreclosed identity were likely to have strong positive relationships with their parents and relatives, participate in lodge activities, and become more politically conservative. Adults experiencing identity moratorium were likely to have weak relationships with their parents, participate in community and political activities, and become more liberal.

TABLE 6.3 **Faces of Ethnic Identity**

Ethnic knowledge	Children know that their ethnic group has distinguishing characteristics including behaviors, traits, customs, styles, and language.
Ethnic self-identification	Children categorize themselves as a member of a particular ethnic group.
Ethnic constancy	Children understand that the distinctive features of their ethnic group are stable across time and situation and that membership in the group does not change.
Ethnic behaviors	Children enact and endorse behavior patterns that distinguish their ethnic group.
Ethnic preferences	Children feel positive about belonging to their ethnic group and prefer their ethnic group's behavior patterns.

Source: Bernal et al., 1993.

Ethnic Identity

As our society has become more heterogeneous, interest has increased in how children learn to identify themselves in terms of their race and ethnicity. For children who are part of the majority race or ethnic group, the issue is not a salient one, but children and youth who are members of minority groups face the challenge of how to balance their sense of distinctive identity while still functioning in the broader culture (Phinney, 2000). **Ethnic identity** refers to the sense of belonging to a certain race or ethnic group. It has several components (see Table 6.3).

ethnic identity
Recognition of being a member of a particular race or ethnic group.

DEVELOPMENT OF ETHNIC IDENTITY Ethnic identity emerges gradually over childhood and adolescence. In infancy, babies look longer at faces of their own race than faces of other races (Kelly et al., 2005). Preschool children continue to show that they are aware of cues to race and ethnicity, such as skin color, and they prefer to play with children from their own group. Minority-group children reach this awareness and preference earlier than other children (Milner, 1983). However, preschool children have only a global understanding of their culture and use ethnic labels in a rote fashion. "I'm Chinese American because my family told me so." Not until early elementary school do they understand what ethnic labels mean (Bernal et al., 1993). At this point, they recognize that the ethnic term Chinese American means that their parents or grandparents were born in China and later migrated to the United States. Preschool children also have limited understanding of ethnic group constancy. They do not recognize that their ethnicity is not changeable but remains one of their permanent characteristics. In early elementary school, children become aware that they are Chinese American, African American, Mexican American, and so on and that this identity does not change over time or context (Ocampo et al., 1997).

Preschool children participate in many activities that are culture or subculture specific. They hit a piñata at their birthday party and enjoy tamales if they are of Mexican heritage. But they may not recognize that these experiences are unique to their culture. Only as they develop cognitively in the early school years do they begin to recognize which behaviors are part of the majority culture and which are unique to their own ethnic group. Positive feelings and preferences for ethnic-group activities also begin to develop during this period. Younger children prefer activities because they are what they do with their family; in elementary school, children realize that these activities are distinctive expressions of their ethnic background.

Although progress in ethnic awareness is made in middle childhood, the most active period of ethnic-identity development is adolescence when the general process of self-definition begins (Quintana, 2008, 2010). One researcher discovered, for example, that active exploration of identity issues in African American children was being pursued by one third of 8th graders, one half of 10th graders, and increasing numbers through college (Phinney, 1989, 1992). Other researchers have also found that African American and Latino American children explored their ethnic identities more and became more proud of their ethnic group during adolescence (Pahl & Way, 2006, S. French et al., 2006).

How quickly and completely adolescents achieve a clear sense of their ethnic identity varies for individuals. In one study, researchers found that a substantial number of minority students had achieved an ethnic identity in 11th grade (26% of Latino students, 39% of Asian American students, and 55% of African American students; Umana-Taylor et al., 2004). Other students had a foreclosed identity (34% of Latinos, 13% of Asians; 24% of African Americans); they had settled on and adopted an ethnic identity at an early age without much question. A third group of students had devoted little energy and thought to ethnic identity issues and were characterized as adopting an unexamined or diffuse ethnic identity (23% of Latinos and Asian Americans, 8% of African Americans). The smallest number of students were in a state of moratorium (9% of Latinos, 13% of Asian Americans, 8% of African Americans).

Having achieved a clear, positive ethnic identity is related to high self–esteem, more optimism, and more social competence, as well as more positive feelings toward the ethnic group (Chavous et al., 2003; Wong et al., 2003; Yip & Fuligni, 2002). This is especially true for adolescents who do not experience much ethnic discrimination, for example, if they are in classes where the majority of students are members of their own ethnic group (Greene et al., 2006). Youth run a risk if they don't identify with their ethnic group. If they identify too strongly with the dominant culture, they are often criticized and ostracized by their ethnic group peers for being "too white." Labels such as "Oreo," "banana," and "apple"—colored on the outside but white on the inside—are pejorative terms directed at minority African Americans, Asian Americans, and Native Americans who identify with the values, styles, and aspirations of the majority culture. These adolescents may experience rejection by their ethnic peers and develop strategies such as hiding their grades or pretending that they don't care about "White success" (Ogbu, 2003). In a study of African American adolescents aged 11 to 16, Margaret Spencer found that the ones who identified with the majority culture exhibited lower achievement and less self-esteem than the ones with a clear African American identity (Spencer et al., 2001, 2003). Students with anti-White attitudes also performed poorly. It appears that minority students benefit from embracing their ethnicity and forming a positive ethnic identity without disparaging the majority culture. Minority adolescents with a strong positive ethnic identity are also less likely to become delinquents (Bruce & Waelde, 2008), do better in school (Adelabu, 2008), experience less depression (Mandara et al., 2009), and have more positive attitudes toward other ethnic groups (Phinney et al., 2007).

This young adolescent, lighting Kwanzaa candles with his father, is exploring his ethnic identity.
Source: © Media Bakery.

BIRACIAL AND BICULTURAL CHILDREN AND YOUTH   Children who are biracial, that is, are adopted into a family from a different race or have parents from two different races, face unique challenges in forging an ethnic identity (Umana-Taylor et al., 2004). With a White American mother and a Black African father, U.S. President Barack Obama struggled with identity issues for many years. As he describes in his book, *Dreams from My Father*, he finally settled on a Black identity but only after a childhood and adolescence in which he was unsure of his place in the wider society. Was he Black? Was he White? Black children raised in White families often suffer as well. In their study of Black children adopted by White parents, Sandra Scarr and her colleagues found that nearly half of the sample at age 17 exhibited symptoms of social maladjustment (DeBerry et al., 1996). The adolescents who had formed an identity as either Black or White were better adjusted than those with no clear ethnic identity.

But what about children whose parents come from two cultures or are immigrants from a different culture? Do they, too, have to pick one or the other? Or can they develop a *bi*cultural identity—adopting both the norms and attitudes of the majority or new culture and the valued and cherished traditions from the minority culture? Bicultural identity involves simultaneous adoption of the languages and practices of two cultures (Ramirez, 1983). Developing such an identity would permit children and adolescents to meet the dual expectations they encounter every day as they move between minority and majority settings. As one adolescent from an immigrant family put it, "Being invited to someone's house, I have to change my ways from how I act at home, because of cultural differences. . . . I am used to it now, switching off between the two. It's not that difficult" (Phinney & Rosenthal, 1992, p. 160).

The four identities that a Mexican American adolescent can form are illustrated in Figure 6.1: a bicultural identity, in which the adolescent identifies as belonging to both the European American majority and the Mexican American minority; a Mexican identity, in which the adolescent identifies solely with the Mexican ethnic group; a European American identity, in which the adolescent identifies solely with the majority culture; and a marginal identity, in which the adolescent is not strongly identified with either majority or minority. Adolescents who adopt a marginal identity are "decultured"; they have rejected their ancestral culture and are alienated from the majority culture (Berry, 2008). They are likely to have social and psychological problems. In today's multiethnic world, adolescents with a bicultural identity have the best physical and psychological health (Chun et al, 2003; Buriel & Saenz, 1980). Their ability to operate in two social worlds helps them develop interpersonal skills and high self-esteem (Buriel et al., 1998, 2006).

FACTORS THAT PROMOTE ETHNIC IDENTITY　Parents play a major role in the development of children's ethnic identity by imparting knowledge about cultural traditions, instilling pride in their ethnic heritage, and preparing children for the hardships that can accompany minority status, such as prejudice and discrimination (Sanders Thompson, 1994; Spencer,

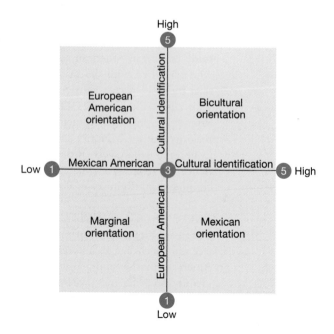

FIGURE 6.1　*Types of ethnic identity. When Mexican American adolescents rate themselves on two 5-point scales—level of European American cultural identification and level of Mexican American cultural identification—their scores can be used to place them in the four ethnic identity groups shown here.* Source: Parke & Buriel, 2006.

2006). This socialization process serves a protective function and makes children more resilient in the face of prejudice (Miller, 1999). In one study, 8th grade African American children who said that they had received frequent messages about race pride and a moderate amount of preparation for bias from their parents had higher self-esteem when faced with discrimination than children whose parents did not provide these forms of support (Harris-Britt et al., 2007). In another study, a higher level of racial socialization in African American families was associated with less aggression and acting out in adolescence (Bannon et al., 2004). Most minority group parents do socialize their children regarding ethnic issues and prejudice (Stevenson, 1994), especially older children (Hughes & Chen, 1997, 1999). Parents who do not socialize their children leave them vulnerable and unprepared for discrimination (Spencer, 2006).

As children enter adolescence, their peers become another socializing force and shaper of ethnic identity. In high school, most students hang out with members of their own ethnic group. They tend not to know classmates in other ethnic groups well because they see these students more as members of those groups than as individuals (Steinberg et al., 1992). Adolescents who have more contact and friendships with others in their own ethnic group have more stable ethnic identities than adolescents with few same-race friends (Yip et al., 2010). However, there are positive effects of across-group contact as well. Adolescents who have more extensive contact with members of other ethnic groups in school tend to develop more mature ethnic identities and more favorable attitudes toward people of other ethnicities (Phinney et al., 1997).

Real-World Application: Sexual Orientation and Identity

It has been estimated that about 5 percent of adolescents identify themselves as gay, lesbian, or bisexual (Rotherman-Borus & Langabeer, 2001). The recognition that they prefer a member of their own sex as a sexual partner is usually a gradual process. Many gay and lesbian adults recall that even as children, they had feelings that were different from their peers' (Bailey & Zucker, 1995). As early as 4th grade, some expressed doubts about their heterosexuality (Egan & Perry, 2001; Carver et al., 2004). They responded more negatively to such questions as "Some boys definitely think they'll get married one day" or "Some girls definitely think that they will be a mother one day." They expressed less interest in activities stereotypically linked to their own gender, such as babysitting for girls and playing baseball for boys, and they were more likely to express dissatisfaction with their own gender. Compared with children who were confident of their heterosexuality, they were more likely to report an impaired self-concept.

This questioning phase was typically followed by a "test and exploration" phase in adolescence during which time homosexual and bisexual teens were ambivalent about their same-sex preference and began to explore these feelings (Savin-Williams, 1998; Savin-Williams & Cohen, 2004). During the "identity acceptance" phase, they began to accept their same-sex orientation. "Identity integration" was the final phase in this identity process, as gay, lesbian, and bisexual individuals accepted their orientation and acknowledged their identity to others. Today, about 55 percent of homosexual and bisexual college students disclose their sexual identity to their parents; a decade ago only 45 percent did (Savin-Williams & Ream, 2003). They also disclose this information at a younger age than they did 10 years ago, on average, at age 17 rather than in their mid-20s (D'Augelli, 2006).

The adolescent's declaration of a homosexual identity is received with more or less acceptance by different people in the community. Fathers are less accepting of their son's or daughter's homosexual orientation than are mothers, and members of conservative religious groups are also less accepting (D'Augelli, 2006). Asian Americans and Latino Americans are less tolerant than European Americans (Dube et al., 2001). Many homosexual individuals (20% to 40%) experience discrimination, rejection, and outright hostility (D'Augelli, 2006).

Development of Knowledge about Others

Learning about oneself is only half of the social-development picture; children must also learn to understand the social cues, signals, intentions, and actions of others.

Early Understanding of Intentions and Norms

By the time they are a year old, infants begin to understand that people's actions are intentional and goal directed (Thompson, 2006b). For example, they recognize that when people look at, reach for, or point to an object, they are interested in that object (Woodward, 2003; Woodward & Guajardo, 2002). After the first year, infants create joint-attentional states with adults by looking at the same object or using their own actions of pointing and reaching to bring the adult's attention to the object (Tomasello & Rakoczy, 2003). By 18 months of age, toddlers also begin to recognize simple social norms. They recognize that a broken object is a violation of how things ought to be and that rouge on your nose is not how people should look (Lewis, 2000). By the end of their second year, they can describe norms, or scripts, for social routines such as bedtime rituals, family mealtimes, and what happens when children are dropped off at child care (Bauer, 2002; Nelson, 1993). Knowledge of these scripts provides the foundation for understanding a broad range of social events, including greeting a friend, lining up for school lunches, and following rules for games such as Monopoly or soccer. Knowing scripts conserves children's social energy, ensures social predictability, and helps smooth out peer interactions.

script
A mental representation of an event or situation of daily life including the order in which things are expected to happen and how one should behave in that event or situation.

Later Understanding of Mental States: Theory of Mind

As they grow older, children also come to understand other people's mental states—thoughts, beliefs, desires—and how they affect behavior (Harris, 2006; Tager-Flusberg, 2007). This understanding has important implications for social development because it allows children to move beyond observable actions and appearances and respond to unseen states. Researchers studying children's development of a theory of mind have used stories to find out whether children realize how characters' actions are based on their mental states (Wimmer & Perner, 1983). For example, they tell a story about a young boy named Maxi who puts his candy in a cupboard in the kitchen and goes into another room to play. While Maxi is off playing, his mother moves his candy from the cupboard to a drawer. After a while, Maxi returns and wants his candy. The researcher then asks the child where Maxi will look for his candy. Older preschoolers (4 to 5 years old) typically say that Maxi will search in the cupboard because they know that Maxi will look where he believes the candy to be, not where they themselves know the candy is. Their answer indicates that they know that Maxi's behavior is based on his mental state and are able to separate what Maxi believes to be true from what they know to be true. Younger children (3 years old) fail the test. They ignore Maxi's mental state and say that he will look for the candy in the drawer. Studies using this "false-belief" story-telling technique suggest that children's understanding of mental states develops during early childhood (Wellman et al., 2001).

theory of mind
Children's understanding that people have mental states such as thoughts, beliefs, and desires that affect their behavior. It allows children to get beyond people's observable actions and appearances and respond to their unseen states.

This intellectual capability exists in almost all people and to some extent in primates as well (Tomasello et al., 2005). Children with autism, however, show delays or in some cases serious deficits in developing a theory of mind because they do not understand that mental states can cause behavior or that other people's mental states may be different from their own (Baron-Cohen, 2000; Lillard, 2006). Therefore, they are unable to evaluate other people's behavior on the basis of their mental states. In one study of children with autism, researchers found that only 20 percent succeeded in a false-belief task compared with about 80 percent of normal children (Baron-Cohen et al., 1985). The inability of children with autism to develop a complete theory of mind may, in part, account for their poor communicative and social skills (Baron-Cohen, 2003). Among normal children, developing a theory of mind is a critical step in the movement toward social competence (Carpendale & Lewis, 2006; Tomasello et al., 2005). Without it, social exchanges would often be misunderstood and lead to brief and ineffective social interactions. In fact, individual differences in false-belief understanding and other aspects of theory of mind predict children's current and later social competence with peers and friends (Cutting & Dunn, 2002).

Research up Close:
The Brain Beneath Theory of Mind

Researchers have used event–related brain potentials (ERP) and brain-imaging techniques such as fMRI to investigate whether theory of mind has a neurological basis (Baron Cohen et al., 1999; Castelli et al., 2002). They have focused on the prefrontal cortex area of the brain because it is a likely location for processing the tasks used to assess theory of mind and because it undergoes rapid growth in the late preschool period. In one study, researchers examined activity in the prefrontal cortex when children were given false-belief tasks (Liu et al., 2009). Children 4 to 6 years old were shown a cartoon story and asked to make judgments about the character's mental states (beliefs) and reality. The structure of all trials was the same. They began with a cartoon character, such as Garfield the Cat, standing next to two boxes and two animals. Then the cartoon character put one animal in one box and the other animal in the other box and walked in front of the boxes so that he could not see into either one. Next, one of the animals in the boxes jumped out of the box and either moved to the other box or went back into the same box. Children were asked to make a "reality judgment" ("*Really*, where is the animal?") and a "think judgment" ("Where does Garfield *think* it is?") while the researchers continuously recorded their brain activity using a network of 128 electrodes embedded in an elastic "helmet." Children who gave correct answers to questions about the cartoon characters' beliefs showed the same neural pattern as adults in the prefrontal cortex region. Children who failed the task did not show this neural pattern (Figure 6.2).

This study confirmed that the prefrontal cortex plays a role in the development of theory of mind. Because this area of the brain continues to develop in childhood,

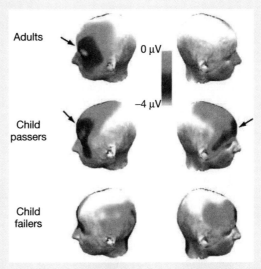

FIGURE 6.2 *Patterns of brain activity for adults, children who passed the false-belief task, and children who failed it. Maps of scalp electrical activity for each group showing mean amplitude difference for "reality" responses subtracted from "think" responses.* Source: Liu et al., 2009. Neural correlates of children's theory of mind. Child Development, 80, 318–326. Society for Research in Child Development. Reprinted with permission of Wiley-Blackwell.

most children who fail the task can catch up. Children with autism may not be so fortunate. They are not neurologically equipped to pass these tasks. However, if they are given interventions aimed at improving their social perspective-taking ability they do develop neural response patterns that more closely resemble typical children (Wang et al., 2006). Clearly, understanding other people's states of mind has a neurological basis, but it is important to remember that the brain is modifiable by experience.

et You Thought That . . . Babies Are Not Mind Readers

Source: University of Illinois at Urbana-Champaign News Bureau.

The ability to make sense of other people's actions requires an understanding of their mental states. This sounds like a pretty advanced idea. You probably think that infants would be incapable of such "mind reading." In fact, until recently, scientists agreed that infants cannot understand other people's mental states. Recent research suggests otherwise, however. Renee Baillargeon (seen in this photo) devised a method to assess infants' knowledge of mental states by observing their looking behavior. Specifically, she showed infants different events and measured the amount of time they spent looking at each of them. Babies tend to look longer at events they find surprising. Baillargeon used this method to study 15-month-old infants' ability to predict a woman's behavior on the basis of her belief about a toy's hiding place in either a green box or a yellow box (Onishi & Baillargeon, 2005). The first step in the study was to familiarize the infants with the study materials and procedures (familiarization trials). The infants saw a woman play with a toy watermelon slice for a few seconds, then hide it inside a box, and then reach inside the box. The second step was to show the infants a scenario in which the woman formed a true belief or a false belief about where the toy was hidden (belief induction trial). To create a false belief that the toy was hidden in the yellow box, the woman watched the toy move from the green box to the yellow box, and then she left the scene; in her absence, the toy was returned to the green box. To create a true belief that the toy was hidden in the yellow box, the woman watched the toy put in the yellow box and stay there. Finally, in the third step of the study (the test trial), the woman reached into either the green box or the yellow box. Baillargeon predicted that if the infants expected the woman to search for the toy on the basis of her belief about its location rather than on the basis of the infant's knowledge of its actual location, they should look reliably longer when that expectation was violated. For example, if the woman had a false belief that the toy was hidden in the yellow box and she looked for it in the green box, the infants would stare longer. Baillargeon found that infants did look reliably longer when the woman looked for the toy in the box that was not consistent with her belief about where it was hidden. These results supported the view that even infants know that other people have beliefs that can be false and differ from the child's own beliefs and that these beliefs affect the other person's behavior. Baillargeon had shown that infants have some rudimentary ability to "read minds" and the beginnings of a theory of mind even if they are not capable of answering verbal questions about other people's false beliefs.

Understanding Psychological Trait Labels

When and how children come to think of other people as psychological beings is another important aspect of social understanding. In the preschool years, children describe others in terms of their physical characteristics ("She is big, has red hair, and lives on my street"), just as they describe themselves. Gradually, they begin to use psychological descriptions ("She is helpful and nice") and show signs that they understand trait labels. Four-year-olds can use trait labels to infer how a person would react to an event such as encountering a crowd of people (Heyman & Gelman, 1999). They say that a "shy" person would not be happy to see lots of people but a "not shy" person might be pleased. However, children's understanding of trait labels is incomplete at this age and they may rely on their own or normative responses such as "Everyone is happy when there are lots of people at the mall."

When they are 5 to 7 years of age, children begin to recognize that people have psychological or personality attributes that distinguish them from each other and that these qualities are stable enough to predict how people will act at different times and in different situations. A "mean" peer can be counted on to steal the candy from your school lunch, distract you in the middle of a video game, and push you down in the park. If the "meanie" did these things last month, last week, or today, you can sadly assume that he or she will do them, or something equally unpleasant, tomorrow (Flavell et al., 2002). Children of this age use trait labels in evaluative ways, judging the "goodness" or "badness" of the other person's actions.

By age 9 or 10, children describe another person's actions less in terms of good or bad and more in terms of stable psychological traits such as being selfless, generous, stingy, or selfish (Alvarez et al., 2001). They generalize across situations to use trait terms such as "smart" to describe a boy who is good at math, science, and social studies and "friendly" to describe a girl who initiates conversations with other children, talks to adults who visit her classroom, and invites newcomers to play at her house after school. They replace generic terms with more specific labels, for example "mean" becomes "annoying," "hurtful," or "inconsiderate" (Livesley & Bromley, 1973; Yuill & Pearson, 1998). They view traits as stable (Lockhart et al., 2002). Over the middle school age period, children also become aware that appearance and reality sometimes conflict, and this leads to skepticism of other people's claims about themselves (Heyman, 2008). In one study, researchers asked children whether self-reports are reliable sources of information about personal traits (Heyman & Legare, 2005). When they were asked about nonevaluative traits, such as shyness or nervousness, both 6-year-olds and 10-year-olds accepted self-reports without question. However, when they were asked about the trustworthiness of self-reports for evaluative traits, such as intelligence or social skill, older children were more skeptical than younger ones. They recognized that people sometimes distort the truth about their own traits in order to make a good impression. Skepticism is an important part of interpersonal relations and provides protection against being manipulated or duped.

Adolescence heralds a more complete understanding of other people's traits. Adolescents realize that people are full of complexities and contradictions and have public and private faces. They appreciate that traits persist over long spans of time but behaviors vary depending on situations and internal states (Flavell et al., 2002; Harter, 2006). For example, a 16-year-old describes his younger brother: "He loves to be with people. . . . Most of the time he's good-natured and a lot of fun . . . but when we play soccer . . . he gets mad when he loses the ball. . . . Later I've found him crying in his room" (Livesley & Bromley, 1973).

This developmental progression in understanding people's psychological traits can be framed in terms of the psychological theories embraced by children at different ages (Flavell et al., 2002). Before age 7 or 8, children's descriptions resemble those of a demographer or a behaviorist; they focus on observable characteristics and behaviors and environmental circumstances. In middle childhood, children become trait theorists who believe that psychological characteristics are fixed and stable across time and situation. By adolescence, children have accepted an interactionist perspective, recognizing that personal traits interact with situational influences in determining behavior.

Stages in Perspective Taking

Robert Selman and his colleagues identified five stages in understanding the thoughts and perspectives of other people (Selman, 1980, 2003; Selman & Byrne, 1974; Selman & Jacquette, 1978). These stages begin with children's egocentric view and proceed toward more complex social understanding and social consideration, as children learn to differentiate between their own perspectives and those of others and to understand others' views and the relations between these views and their own (see Table 6.4).

Table 6.4 **Developing the Ability to Take Different Perspectives**

Stage 0: Egocentric perspective	Children neither distinguish their own perspectives from those of others nor recognize that other people may interpret experiences differently.
Stage 1: Differentiated perspective	Children realize that they may have either the same or a different perspective from another person. They cannot judge accurately what the other person's perspective may be.
Stage 2: Reciprocal perspective	Because children can see themselves from another's perspective and know the other person can do the same thing, they can anticipate and consider another's thoughts and feelings.
Stage 3: Mutual perspective	Children can view their own perspective, a peer's perspective, and their shared or mutual perspective, from the viewpoint of a third person.
Stage 4: Societal or in-depth perspective	Children can see networks of perspectives, such as the societal, Republican, or African American point of view.

Source: Selman & Jacquette, 1978.

Learning from Living Leaders: Robert L. Selman

Source: Courtesy of Robert L. Selman.

Robert Selman is Professor of Education and Human Development at the Harvard Graduate School of Education and Professor of Psychology in the Department of Psychiatry at the Harvard Medical School. After he received a Ph.D. from Boston University, Selman did clinical work with children who had problems with social relationships. This led him to conduct research on the antecedents of children's capacity to form and maintain social relationships. He studied children's abilities to coordinate points of view and use negotiation strategies. He also investigated the social awareness of children and adolescents in contexts in which they interact with others from different ethnic and cultural backgrounds. He currently is studying the relation between children's social awareness and academic skills and has written a guide for improving both. Selman has always worked on both basic and practical issues. His hope for the future is a better integration of social, ethical, and civic development in public schools. His wise advice for you is to make sure your research questions are both important for society and personally meaningful.

Further Reading

Selman, R. L. (2003). *The promotion of social awareness.* New York: Russell Sage Foundation.

Advancing Social Understanding

Not all children are equally adept in understanding other people's intentions, mental states, traits, and perspectives. What predicts these differences in social understanding?

CHILD ABILITIES   Social understanding is embedded in children's social tendencies and intellectual abilities. Children who have higher levels of social understanding also do better on standard intelligence tests and exhibit more frequent prosocial behavior, such as helping and sharing, on the playground and in the classroom (Eisenberg et al., 2006).

PARENTAL INFLUENCES   Conversations with parents also play a role in the development of children's social understanding. Researchers in a number of studies have demonstrated that children in families who frequently talk about mental states are more likely to succeed on theory-of-mind tasks than children whose parents do not provide such scaffolding (Dunn, 1988; Dunn, Brown, & Beardsall, 1991; Dunn, Brown, Slomkowski, et al., 1991; Brophy & Dunn, 2002; Ruffman et al., 2002; Taumoepeau & Ruffman, 2006, 2008). Even early in infancy, mothers' tendency to talk to their infants as separate psychological entities predicts their later theory-of-mind performance (Meins et al., 2002). It is particularly helpful when parents' conversations with their children include explanations of the causes and effects of mental states, using words such as "because," "how," and "why"—"How did she feel when the lamp broke?" "She was mad because she thought he did it on purpose" (Dunn, Brown, & Beardsall, 1991; Dunn, Brown, Slomkowski et al., 1991; LaBounty et al., 2008). The reciprocal nature of the conversation is important as well. Researchers have found that when 2- to 4-year-old children and their mothers had more connected conversations, the children's social understanding was advanced (Ensor & Hughes, 2008). Being tuned into each others' talk is apparently important for understanding another person's point of view; ignoring a partner's statement or switching to a new topic is less helpful.

SIBLINGS AND FRIENDS   Interactions with siblings and friends also provide opportunities for children to learn about people's thoughts and traits. Two types of interaction may be particularly helpful: pretend play and dispute resolution. These two activities involve perspective-taking and role-playing, which are likely to increase children's social understanding (Howe et al, 2002; Foote & Holmes-Lonergan, 2003). Interactions with siblings and friends may also be important because they involve discussions about shared concerns, interests, and goals. Children do not often have these discussions with adults; with adults, they generally talk about their own goals, not the adult's. In interactions with siblings and friends, children frequently confront discrepancies between their own desires and the desires of the other children, and exposure to such discrepancies predicts increased understanding of false beliefs (Brown et al., 1996). In fact, children who have siblings perform better on false-belief tasks than children without siblings (Perner et al., 1994)—unless their sibling is their twin (Cassidy et al., 2005). Twins may be too similar to boost each other's social understanding. Having parents who mediate siblings' disagreements and guide them in resolving their disputes also helps. Researchers have trained parents in mediation techniques, such as helping children establish ground rules, identifying points of contention and common ground, and encouraging children to discuss their feelings and goals and generate solutions to their problems. When parents implement these techniques, their children's social understanding increases, and conflicts between siblings decrease; the children become more knowledgeable about their sibling's perspective and understand that the sibling can legitimately interpret disputes differently from how they view the situation (Smith & Ross, 2007). This experimental work provides compelling evidence that learning constructive conflict resolution, not just being exposed to conflicts, improves children's understanding of other people.

EXPERIENCES OUTSIDE THE FAMILY   Experiences outside the family can also promote children's social understanding. One example comes from studies of child "brokers"—children in immigrant families who translate for their non-English-speaking parents as they negotiate with doctors, employers, and government officials. Children who serve in this brokering role have higher scores on theory-of-mind tests than children who do not (Love & Buriel, 2007).

This cultural brokering experience may increase children's awareness of others' mental states and the links between mental states and social behavior. Teachers can also instruct children in perspective-taking skills at school. Robert Selman (2003) developed a school-based program that uses social dilemmas faced by a character in a novel to teach children to solve social disputes by taking the perspective of the other person. Other effective school programs have increased children's understanding of other people's perspectives, points of view, and feelings as part of a curriculum aimed at improving children's social relationships (Kress & Elias, 2006).

CULTURAL INFLUENCES   Researchers have asked whether changes in children's social understanding are universal and occur in all cultures at the same ages. In one study, they interviewed children from the Baka community of hunter-gatherers in central Africa about people's beliefs and desires (Avis & Harris, 1991). By 5 years of age, most children were able to predict correctly what an adult would find in a container that had been left for a moment and emptied. These results were consistent with studies showing that 5-year-old children in other cultures also succeed on theory-of-mind tasks (Harris, 2006). However, some cultural variations in children's social understanding have been observed (Harris, 2006; Lillard, 1998). One variation is that children's use of trait terms to describe other people becomes aligned with the values of their cultural community. Between the ages of 8 and 15 years, U.S. children increasingly use trait terms to describe someone's helpful actions; children in India increasingly use social context terms (i.e., need for assistance and obligation to help) to describe helpful acts (Miller, 1987). Another difference is that Chinese children are more skeptical than U.S. children about the reliability of other people's self-reports of evaluative traits such as honesty, in part because Chinese culture discourages disclosure of thoughts and feelings and encourages modesty (Heyman et al., 2007). Thus, although all normal children acquire a theory of mind at roughly the same age, the ways in which they learn to describe, evaluate, and explain others' behavior is shaped by cultural norms and belief systems.

Stereotyping and Prejudice

In multiethnic and multiracial societies such as the United States, Canada, Europe, Australia, and the Middle East, children routinely encounter others who differ from them in language, skin color, and cultural and religious customs. Two aspects of how children deal with this diversity are particularly important: *stereotyping*—how children categorize or label individuals in the other groups—and *prejudice*—whether they express negative attitudes toward these individuals.

stereotype
A general label applied to individuals based solely on their membership in a racial, ethnic, or religious group, without appreciation that individuals within the group vary.

stereotype consciousness
The knowledge that other people have beliefs based on ethnic stereotypes.

STEREOTYPING   A **stereotype** is a label applied to members of a racial, ethnic, or religious group without appreciation that individuals within the group are different from each other (Killen et al., 2006). By age 5, children already exhibit some ethnic and racial stereotypes. In one study, children aged 5, 7, and 9 years were shown a picture story about two children, a Black child and a White child, and asked to remember what each child in the story did (Davis et al., 2007). At all three ages, children had better recall for stereotyped activities that the Black child performed (specifically, running fast, dancing well, and being aggressive and loud) than nonstereotyped activities performed by the Black child (specifically, working hard, liking family, and being smelly and greedy). By age 10, almost all children in another study exhibited **stereotype consciousness**, meaning that they knew that people hold racial and ethnic stereotypes. They exhibited this knowledge by agreeing with statements such as "White people think Black people are not smart" (McKown & Weinstein, 2003). Children were more aware of these broadly held stereotypes if they themselves were from stigmatized groups—probably because of the increased salience of stereotypes in these children's daily lives. Children with stereotype consciousness used this knowledge to interpret social exchanges and were likely to explain negative interracial interactions as reflecting discrimination (McKown & Strambler,

2009). By 8–9 years old, children are aware of the difference between a personal belief and a stereotype and can separate their personal views about members of a group from the group stereotype (Augoustinos & Rosewarne, 2001).

prejudice
A set of attitudes by which an individual defines all members of a group negatively.

PREJUDICE   Children who think about other people in terms of stereotypes are more likely to have a **prejudice** against those people; people who are prejudiced define all members of a group not just as similar but also as bad (Aboud, 2008). Ethnic prejudice, like ethnic stereotyping, is evident by the time children are 5 years old. In one study in Australia, White children endorsed more negative adjectives (such as "dirty," "bad," and "mean") in describing drawings of Black people than White people and used more positive adjectives (such as "clean," "good," and "nice") in describing White people than Black people (Augoustinos & Rosewarne, 2001). Similarly, English Canadian children exhibited prejudice toward French Canadian children (Powlishta et al., 1994), and Jewish Israeli children exhibited prejudice toward Arabs (Teichman, 2001). Between 5 and 9 years, as cognitive understanding increases, children begin to appreciate the ways in which different groups are similar, to infer that people have internal similarities despite superficial differences in appearance, and to realize that not all individuals within a group are the same—and their prejudice decreases (Aboud, 2008). During late childhood and adolescence, however, prejudice increases again in part because of the focus on personal and ethnic identity in this age period (Aboud, 2005; Teichman, 2001).

The ways in which prejudice is expressed also change as children get older. In early childhood, prejudice is expressed by avoidance and social exclusion; in late childhood and adolescence, it is expressed in conflict and hostility (Aboud, 2005). However, by this age, some young people have learned the social costs of overt expressions of prejudice, and so they hide their true feelings. Instead of displaying public prejudice, their prejudice is "implicit"— that is, unconscious or automatic. The Implicit Association Test (IAT) measures the speed with which children classify a series of faces as either Black or White and a series of words as either good— "joy," "love," "peace," "pleasure"—or bad—"terrible," "horrible," "nasty," "awful" (Baron & Banaji, 2006). Implicit prejudice for White children is measured by comparing how fast they respond to stereotyped pairings (White faces/good words; Black faces/bad words) and nonstereotyped pairings (White faces/bad words; Black faces/good words). Prejudice is inferred when response times to the stereotyped pairings are shorter than response times to nonstereotyped pairings. Using this test, researchers have found that White children in 4th and 5th grades express implicit prejudice against African Americans, and their implicit prejudice is not related to their explicit prejudice assessed with a questionnaire (Sinclair et al., 2005). Implicit prejudice is important because it is related to children's behavior toward members of other ethnic

In late childhood, ethnic prejudice may be implicit; minority children may be excluded from activities, but ethnicity is not given as the reason. Source: © Media Bakery.

groups. In one study, for example, German 8th graders who scored high on implicit prejudice toward Turks, an immigrant group in Germany, were less likely to include a Turkish player in a computer game than were players who scored lower on implicit prejudice (Degner et al., 2009). Clearly, implicit prejudice affects children's behavior even though they are unaware of it. (If you are interested in determining your own level of implicit prejudice, go to buster.cs.yale.edu/implicit/index.html.)

DETERMINANTS OF STEREOTYPING AND PREJUDICE Researchers have found that when adults are shown faces from a different race it activates neural activity in the amygdala—a region of the brain associated with fear, anger, and sadness (Cunningham et al., 2004). Being primed to react with negative emotions when encountering persons of a different race may be adaptive from an evolutionary perspective and may suggest that prejudice has a biological basis (Hirschfeld, 1996, 2008). However, prejudice occurs as the result of many social factors as well, including prejudiced messages from parents, peers, schools, and media. For young children parents are the most important factor in promoting prejudice, and their influence begins early. Researchers in one study found that parents' racial socialization began by the time their children were only 18 months old and predicted the children's racial attitudes at ages 3 and 4 years (Katz, 2003). Parents are especially influential if their children closely identify with them and see them as appropriate models for their own behavior (Sinclair et al., 2005). However, children may develop prejudices even if their parents do not express them (Aboud & Doyle, 1996; Ritchey & Fishbein, 2001). In fact, parents are sometime shocked to discover how prejudiced their children are. Media depictions of minorities in negative and stereotyped ways contribute to children's prejudices (Comstock & Scharrer, 2006), and in adolescence, peers provide the norms that govern contact with and attitudes toward members of other ethnic groups.

PROMOTING STEREOTYPES AND PREJUDICE Researchers Rebecca Bigler and Lynn Liben (2006, 2007) conducted a series of studies to investigate how children develop prejudices. They arranged for elementary school children to wear either yellow or blue tee shirts to school for several weeks, creating two perceptually distinct groups of children similar to groups based on racial characteristics. Sociological research has shown that prejudice is more likely when the groups are distinct (Bigler et al., 1997); this is why societies sometimes increase a group's perceptual distinctiveness, for example, by requiring Jews to wear yellow stars in Nazi Germany. Teachers in the studies were instructed either to segregate or to integrate the children wearing the yellow shirts and the blue shirts for classroom activities and to label the children by their shirt color or not. Stereotyping increased when teachers labeled the children as the Yellows and the Blues and when the yellow and blue groups were of unequal sizes (i.e., majority and minority). Prejudice increased when classroom activities were segregated. It is clear that stereotypes and prejudice can be created. Can they be reduced?

CAN STEREOTYPES AND PREJUDICE BE REDUCED? One approach to reducing prejudice is to increase contact between members of groups who are prejudiced toward each other. In several studies, researchers have found that contact with members of another group in a positive and nonthreatening context can reduce prejudice (Pettigrew & Tropp, 2006; Schofield & Eurich-Fulcer, 2001). In a classic study, the Robbers Cave Experiment, two groups of 11-year-old boys at a summer camp, whose prejudice against each other had been fostered by team competitions such as a tug-of-war and a scavenger hunt, were brought together to solve a common problem, fixing a broken water main at the camp (Sherif, 1966). After the cooperative experience of repairing the water problem, the campers' attitudes toward members of the other group improved. Contemporary researchers have also found that reducing competiveness is an important way to decrease prejudice (Abrams & Rutland, 2008).

A second way to reduce children's prejudice is to have adults point out the individual characteristics of members of the other group. When teachers were asked to encourage students in their classes to pay attention to individual characteristics of their classmates rather than racial qualities, for example, prejudice in students decreased (Aboud & Fenwick, 1999).

Third, minimizing stereotypes of racial and ethnic groups in media such as books, television, and movies is another strategy for reducing children's stereotyping and prejudice (Comstock & Scharrer, 2006). In one study, researchers modified storybooks used in shared book-reading sessions to feature a friendship between a majority child and a minority child (Cameron et al., 2006). The British 5- to 11-year-olds who heard the stories became more positive toward minority children than did the children who had not heard the stories, especially when the individual attributes of the story characters were emphasized.

Insights from Extremes:
The Most Extreme Prejudice—Genocide

Throughout history, people have sometimes expressed the most extreme form of prejudice—genocide. This term refers to the mass killing or serious harming of a national, ethnic, racial, or religious group. It also includes other methods of eliminating the group, such as preventing births or forcibly transferring children from one group to another (Article 2 of the United Nations Convention on the Prevention and Punishment of the Crime of Genocide). If large differences exist between groups, the majority group may consider the minority to be less than human (Chalk & Jonassohn, 1990). It is a small step for them then to believe that eliminating the other group is necessary to protect their own group. One well-known example of genocide was the Holocaust in Nazi Germany in WWII in which 6 million Jews were killed. A second example of genocide was the mass murder of Tutsis in Rwanda in 1994. Over a period of 100 days, an estimated 800,000 Tutsis were killed by Hutus after the Rwandan president's plane was shot down, sparking a campaign of violence. The Hutu radio station broadcast inflammatory propaganda urging the Hutus to "kill the cockroaches." Tutsis fled their homes in panic and were snared and butchered at checkpoints. Women and younger men were especially targeted because they represented the future of the Tutsi minority. More recently, in Darfur, Sudan, President Omar al-Bashir's forces drove about 2.5 million Sudanese, including substantial numbers of the Fur, Massalit, and Zaghawa ethnic groups, into camps of displaced persons. They then inflicted severe sexual assaults on them. A common tactic was for the Janjaweed militia and Sudan's armed forces to gang-rape women and girls who came out of the camps to collect firewood, grass, or water. "Janjaweed babies" born of the rapes were then abandoned or killed by the mother's ethnic group. In 2008, prosecutors at the International Criminal Court filed three charges of genocide against President al-Bashir, who had "masterminded and implemented a plan to destroy in substantial part three tribal groups because of their ethnicity." The genocide in Darfur has claimed 400,000 lives since 2003, and more than 100 people continue to die each day.

These assaults on humanity demonstrate the negative consequences of prejudice and show how ordinary people can commit extraordinarily terrible crimes in their efforts to preserve their own group. They alert us to the vulnerability we all share that may lead us to carry out atrocities on behalf of our ethnic, racial, or political group. Since 1991, teaching students about the Holocaust has been a required part of the national curriculum in U.S. schools. Yet, teachers often find that students in these classes believe that genocide could not happen today. Some teachers counter this belief by teaching their students about the genocides in Rwanda and Darfur.

Communication Between Me and You: The Role of Language

Understanding other people requires the ability to communicate with them, primarily by using language. Speech is, by its very nature, a social phenomenon. It is critical for understanding other people, interacting with them, communicating information to them, and controlling their actions; it is also important for expressing one's own feelings, desires, and opinions. Children begin to acquire this essential tool when they are still infants, but progress depends on the social support provided by others in the context of social interactions (Hoff, 2006).

Components of Language

phonemes
The smallest sound units that affect meaning in a language.

semantics
The meanings of words and word combinations.

syntax
The part of grammar that prescribes how words combine into phrases, clauses, and sentences.

pragmatics
A set of rules that specify appropriate language for particular social contexts.

To communicate effectively, children need to master four aspects of language. They need to know about the sounds of language—about **phonemes**, the language's basic units of sound, and about how phonemes are put together to form words, phrases, and sentences. They need to know about the meanings of language—about **semantics**, the meanings of specific words, and about how words are used and combined in phrases, clauses, and sentences. Third, children need to know **syntax**, the grammar that specifies how words are combined into sentences. Fourth, they need to know **pragmatics**, that is, the rules for using language in particular contexts, such as the playground or the classroom (Bates, 1999).

Steps Toward Language Fluency

PREVERBAL COMMUNICATION Infants' earliest communications take place during interactions with caregivers (Fogel, 1993; Lock, 2004). Parents and infants often engage in a kind of dialogue of sounds, movements, and facial expressions. Smiles, in particular, seem important for helping infants learn how to coordinate vocalizations and translate expressions into effective communication (Yale et al., 2003). Although these early exchanges may seem at first to be "conversations," a closer look suggests that they are really "pseudo-conversations" because the parents are responsible for maintaining their flow (Jaffe et al., 2001). Parents insert their behavior into the infant's cycles of responsiveness and unresponsiveness, building what seems to be conversation out of the baby's burps and sneezes. For instance, a baby gurgles and the mother replies by vocalizing. She waits for the baby's response, but if none is forthcoming, she prompts the baby by changing her expression, speaking again, or gently touching. These interactions help the infant become a communicative partner by the end of the first year (Golinkoff, 1983). In some cultures, such as the Mayans of Mexico (Brown, 2001), the Walpiri of Australia (Bavin, 1992), and some groups of African Americans in the southern United States (Heath, 1983), parents do not regard infants as conversational partners (Hoff, 2006), and so they do not directly address them; however, they hold the babies so they can see the adults talking and what they are talking about (Lieven, 1994).

Infants also learn to use gestures to communicate (Fogel, 1993; Lock, 2004). By the time they are 6 months old, they respond with gestures when they are offered or shown things, and they begin to use pointing gestures to guide others' attention to particular objects. By pointing, they learn the names for objects that interest them (Golinkoff & Hirsh-Pasek, 1999), and they also learn that a social partner—usually the parent—is a valuable source of information and assistance. Infants use gestures to get their parents to do something for them; for example, they point to a teddy bear on a high shelf to have the parent get it down. Older preverbal children use this form of communication very effectively, often checking to make sure the listener is looking in the right direction and is able to respond to their request (Bates et al., 1989). With age, children reduce their use of gestures and rely increasingly on verbal skills to communicate their needs and wishes (Adamson, 1995).

cooing
A very young infant's production of vowel-like sounds.

babbling
An infant's production of strings of consonant-vowel combinations.

BABBLING AND OTHER EARLY SOUNDS   **Cooing** is the first kind of vocalization infants produce—vowel-like sounds that often consist of "oo" sounds that resemble the cooing sounds pigeons make. It starts at the end of the first month, often during social exchanges between infant and caregiver. **Babbling**—producing strings of consonant-vowel combinations—begins in the middle of the first year. Early babbling is the same, no matter what language the baby hears (Thevenin et al., 1985). Even the early babbling of deaf babies sounds like the babbling of hearing babies (Crystal, 2007; Lenneberg et al., 1965). Differences in babbling begin to emerge in the middle of the second half-year. French and Japanese babies' babbling contains more nasal sounds than that of Swedish and English babies, just as French and Japanese words contain more nasal sounds than Swedish and English words (De Boysson-Bardies et al., 1992). Babies are starting to "tune in" to the language they hear spoken around them. By the end of the first year, they can utter strings of sounds made up of phonemes in their native language that sound very much like real speech but are not. This "pseudospeech" attracts the attention of family members and in combination with nonverbal signals such as pointing and gesturing is a way for infants to share their discoveries and desires with the rest of the world.

Semantic Development: The Power of Words

Between 10 and 15 months of age, children usually utter their first real words (Fenson et al., 1994). By the age of 2, on average, they can say approximately 900 root words, and by the age of 6, their vocabularies have increased to 8,000 words. The number of words children can understand far exceeds the number of words they can produce (Huttenlocher, 1974); for example, when they can produce only 10 words, they already understand about 100.

HOW AND WHY CHILDREN ACQUIRE WORDS   Although learning words is difficult, infants apparently come to the task with certain constraints or principles that help them get word learning "off the ground" (Hollich et al., 2000). The first thing they seem to know is that words stand for people, objects, actions, and events. Later, they come to understand the principle that a novel word refers to a novel person, object, action, or event rather than a familiar one. Children's acquisition of words is also aided by the social-communicative context in which words occur. Words are learned in the course of everyday social exchanges with more competent language users, and children's vocabularies reflect the words used by their parents and in their culture (Bornstein & Cote, 2006; Crain-Thoreson & Dale, 1992; Hoff & Naigles, 2002; Huttenlocher et al., 1991; Tamis–LeMonda et al., 2006). The words children learn first generally represent people they know—"Daddy," "Mommy," "Auntie" (Bornstein & Cote, 2006), objects they can act on—"shoes," "socks," "toys" (Clark, 1983), and actions they can perform—"walk," "run" (Huttenlocher et al., 1987). They use these first words for social communication: A girl says "book" while looking at her mother and pointing to a book she wants her mother to read to her; a boy says "jump" as he is about to leap off the couch and wants his father to catch him.

holophrase
A single word that appears to represent a complete thought.

telegraphic speech
Two-word or three-word utterances that include only the words essential to convey the speaker's intent.

The Acquisition of Grammar: From Words to Sentences

At first, children use these single words, often accompanied by gestures, to express ideas that would be expressed in sentences by an adult (Dale, 1976). For example, they say "Teddy," meaning "Give me my teddy bear" or "My teddy bear is under the table." These single words representing complete thoughts are known as **holophrases**. By the time they are 2, children are beginning to put words together in what is called **telegraphic speech**. Their utterances of two or three words include only the crucial words needed to convey their message—for example, "Give Teddy," not "Give me my teddy bear." These utterances are called *telegraphic* because, like telegrams, they exclude unimportant words. In the third year of life, simple sentences become more complex as children begin to understand the rules of adult grammar and can include auxiliary verbs, tenses other than the present, and pronouns and articles (Valian, 1986). Children's efforts to figure out the rules of grammar are aided by their parents (Tomasello, 2006), who provide models of sentences in the correct word order ("Yay! You kicked the ball!"), extend the children's simple sentences (child says "Kick ball"; mother replies, "Yes, you kick the ball"), and recast the children's incorrect sentences (child says "I kick it"; mother replies, "Yes, you kicked it"). Most fundamental forms of grammar are acquired by children by the time they are 5 years old. All of these grammatical advances improve social communication, allowing children to indicate their wants and wishes with greater precision and clarity and respond more appropriately to their partners' wants and wishes as well.

Learning the Social Uses of Language

After children have acquired words and rules of grammar, what becomes important is deciding which words and phrases to use in different social situations and with different people.

THE RULES OF PRAGMATICS   To be effective communicators, children must learn the rules of pragmatics. First, they must learn that they should engage the attention of their listener before speaking. Second, they must learn to be sensitive to their listener's feedback. If children don't know when listeners can't understand them, they will not be successful communicators. Third, children must learn to adjust their speech to be appropriate for different listeners. For example, when they speak to younger children, they should speak in simpler sentences; when they are talking to older adults, they should use polite words, not slang. Fourth, children must learn to adjust their speech to the situation. It's acceptable to speak loudly or rudely on the playground or street but not in a church, a classroom, or at the dinner table. It's more likely to be effective to say politely, "May I have one of your crayons?" or "Please pass the jam" rather than demanding, "Gimme a crayon (or jam)!" Fifth, children must learn that to participate in a conversation, they must be not only effective speakers but also skilled listeners. They must take turns speaking and remain silent while others speak. Finally, children must learn to evaluate their own and others' messages for clarity and usefulness. They must correct their own messages when necessary and let another speaker know when they do not understand (Glucksberg et al., 1975; Hoff, 2006).

LEARNING TO ADJUST SPEECH TO AUDIENCE   By 2 years of age, children are remarkably adept at engaging the attention of a listener and responding to listener feedback. Researchers in one study videotaped the communicative interactions of 2-year-olds in a preschool class (Wellman & Lempers, 1977). The results clearly demonstrated the children's

Preschool children use language and gestures to communicate about their ongoing activities and express their wishes and desires. They adjust their speech to the situation and audience, here, telling a secret. Source: Ekaterina Monakhova/iStockphoto.

communicative competence. If the children intended to point out a particular object to another child, they almost always addressed their listener when they were playing together (82%) or when the listener was at least not involved with someone else (88%). They directed communications to other children when they could see each other (97%) and when they were physically close (91%). They made sure that when they spoke, they were close to the object they were talking about (92%) and that the listener was also close to the object (84%). They were very effective in engaging their listeners, and most of their messages (79%) met with adequate responses. The children also adjusted their communication to the situation: They communicated more in difficult situations, for example, when an obstacle was between the listener and the object. Finally, the children responded to feedback from their listeners. More than half the time, when the speakers received no response, they repeated their message in some form, but they hardly ever repeated messages when they received an adequate response (only 3%). Other researchers have found that children as young as 1½ are usually successful (77%) when they repeat or revise a response to a failed message (Golinkoff, 1986). They have also found that children as young as 2 adjust their speech when talking to other children of different ages. For example, they use more repetitions and attention-eliciting words ("hey," "hello," and "look") when talking to their baby brothers and sisters than when addressing their mothers (Dunn, 1988; Dunn & Kendrick, 1982). Preschool children also adjust their speech when speaking to peers of different status: They use more deferential speech with a higher-status peer and more assertive speech with a lower-status peer (Kyratzis & Marx, 2001). Preschool children's communicative competence does have some limitations, of course. Preschoolers are more effective in conversations that are one-to-one, face-to-face, and about single, familiar objects in their immediate environment than in conversations in groups, on the phone, or about absent objects or their own feelings, thoughts, or relationships (Cameron & Lee, 1997; Dunn, 1988; Ervin-Tripp, 1979; Shatz, 1994).

LEARNING TO LISTEN CRITICALLY Children are not always aware that they do not understand a message. If the message is very simple and the lack of clarity is very obvious, even 3-year-olds can act in appropriate ways to resolve the communication gap. This was demonstrated when researchers gave 3- and 4-year-olds requests that were ambiguous ("Give me the cup," when there were four cups on the table) or impossible ("Bring me the refrigerator"), and the children recognized that the requests were problematic and requested more information (Revelle et al., 1985). However, when the task requires more thought and the lack of clarity is less obvious, even school-age children may not realize that they do not understand a message. In one experiment, researchers gave 1st- and 3rd-graders game instructions that left out essential information (Markman, 1977). First-graders were generally unaware that information was missing and had to be urged to try to play the game before they realized they didn't know enough to do so. Children can be taught to be more effective listeners and ask for clarifications (Cosgrove & Patterson, 1977; Patterson & Kister, 1981). Listening skills continue to be a critical ingredient of successful social exchanges and sustained social relationships throughout childhood, adolescence, and adulthood (Gottman et al., 2007).

Chapter Summary

The Sense of Self

- By the end of the first 6 months of life, infants can distinguish between themselves and others, and by the end of the first year, attain rudimentary self-recognition.
- By 4 years of age children can distinguish between past and present selves.
- At first, children use concrete terms to describe themselves (physical attributes, possessions, preferred activities). Later they include psychological traits. Adolescents' view of self is more integrated and includes the possibility of contradictory traits.

- Children with autism exhibit delays or deficits in self-recognition.
- Gender, culture, and family influence the development of self.

Self-Perceptions

- *Self-esteem* refers to a sense of global self-worth and is distinct from evaluations of competence in specific areas such as scholastic ability, athletic skill, physical appearance, behavioral conduct, and social acceptance.
- High self-esteem is linked to positive adjustment including school success, good relationships with parents and peers, and less risk taking, anxiety, and depression.
- High self-esteem fosters experimentation, which may increase early sexual activity and drinking.
- Girls have lower global self-esteem than boys beginning in middle childhood.
- The quality of the parent-child relationship affects self-esteem. Parents who are authoritative (firm, clear, and affectionate) have adolescents with higher self-esteem.
- Peers and mentors are also influential sources of support for self-esteem
- As children develop, their positive and often unrealistic views of their abilities gradually come into line with objective evaluations.

Identity Formation

- A major task of adolescence or young adulthood is to develop a stable identity, including a sexual and ethnic identity. *Ethnic identity* refers to the sense of belonging to a certain ethnic or racial group.
- Influences on adolescents' identity development include social, biological, and cognitive factors.
- Achievement of a stable identity is associated with good adjustment.
- Biracial and bicultural adolescents face challenges in achieving a clear identity.

Development of Social Knowledge about Others

- Children improve their abilities to understand others' social actions, intentions, motives, and goals as well as learning about the norms and social scripts that guide social interactions.
- Work on theory of mind is uncovering when and how children come to understand other people's mental states—thoughts, beliefs, desires—and how they affect behavior.
- Children who are autistic show delays or in some cases deficits in developing a theory of mind.
- Social interactions with family members and friends as well as cultural routines and practices are important to the development of social understanding.
- Children's descriptions of others' attributes and traits undergo developmental shifts from concrete, physical, and simple to abstract, psychological, and differentiated.

Stereotyping and Prejudice

- *Stereotypes* are general labels applied to individuals based solely on their membership in a racial, ethnic, or religious group without appreciating that individuals within the group vary. By age 8–9, children can separate stereotypes from personal views.

- Prejudiced individuals define members of a group not just as similar but also as bad. Between 5 and 9 years, children come to understand that not all individuals in a group are the same, and their prejudice decreases.
- In late childhood and adolescence, as identification with an ethnic group increases, so does prejudice.
- The many causes of prejudice include prejudiced messages from parents, peers, schools, and media.
- Approaches to reducing prejudice include increasing contact between members of different groups, having adults point out the individual characteristics of members of other groups, and minimizing stereotypes of racial and ethnic groups in books, television, and movies.

The Role of Language

- Language helps children to interact, to communicate information, to express feelings, wishes, and views, to control actions, and to modify emotions.
- Before they are able to speak, babies produce sounds such as cooing and babbling.
- The social communicative context in which words occur aids children's acquisition of language.
- The rules for language usage, known as *pragmatics,* determine whether speech is appropriate for the audience and situation.

Key Terms

babbling

collective self

cooing

ethnic identity

holophrase

identity

individual self

phoneme

pragmatics

prejudice

relational self

script

self-esteem

semantics

stereotype

stereotype consciousness

syntax

telegraphic speech

theory of mind

At the Movies

Relevant movies for this chapter include those focused on self-esteem, identity, stereotyping, and prejudice. One film that shows a child raising her self-esteem is *Whale Rider* (2002), a story about an 11-year-old girl in a patriarchal New Zealand tribe who believes she is destined to be the new chief and fights her grandfather and a thousand years of tradition to fulfill her destiny. In *Akeelah and the Bee* (2006), another 11-year-old girl overcomes her personal insecurities and low self-esteem, her economically disadvantaged background, and pervasive cultural stereotypes to achieve success in spelling bees.

Movies about identity development include *Real Women Have Curves* (2002), the story of a first-generation Mexican-American teenager who is torn between her mainstream ambitions and her cultural heritage. *Towelhead* (2008) presents a collision of racism, acculturation, and cultural identity set against the backdrop of the American family. The film *Just Black?* (1991) consists of interviews with young men and women of mixed racial heritage who discuss their struggle to establish a racial identity and question whether there is room in the United States for multiracial identity. Movies exploring young gay men's search for their sexual identity include *Redefining Normal* (2008), *The Art of Being Straight* (2008), and *Lonely Child* (2005).

The award-winning film *Eye Was Blind* (2005) explores religious and interracial issues and forces viewers to examine the fact that they may have their own stereotypical ways of judging people based on their physical appearance, culture, and race. Racial prejudice is vividly portrayed in *4 Little Girls* (1997), which recounts the events leading up to the bombing of the 16th Street Church in Birmingham, Alabama, at the height of the Civil Rights Movement. In *Mozlym* (2008), a young African American fights his way out of the ghetto and into college but discovers his own prejudices while he is making a film on Muslims and violence.

Hotel Rwanda (2004) is one of a number of excellent movies on the horrors of genocide. It focuses on the efforts a Rwandan man made to save the lives of his family and more than a thousand other refugees by granting them shelter in his besieged hotel. The film was nominated for several Academy Awards and is listed by the American Film Institute as one of the 100 most inspirational movies of all time. It has been called an African *Schindler's List*. *Schindler's List* (1993) is another Academy Award-winning movie in which a man saved lives from a genocide, in this case, more than a thousand Jews from the Holocaust.

CHAPTER 7

Family: Early and Enduring Influences

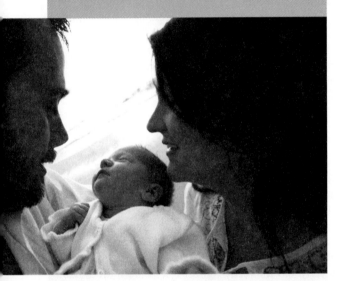

Source: © Media Bakery.

Alice lives with her mother and father and grandmother and nine brothers and sisters. Her parents are strict about rules and make sure that all the children are in bed with lights out before 10 every night. Aletha has never met her father; she lives alone with her mother next door to her aunt and cousins. Sometimes she stays overnight with her cousins; her mother doesn't mind. Allan has two fathers who were married in San Francisco and are looking forward to adopting another child soon. All of these children live in families—but their families are dramatically different. In this chapter, we describe some of these differences and discuss the strong and enduring effects families have on children's social development.

What is a family? It is a social unit in which adult spouses or partners and their children share economic, social, and emotional rights and responsibilities and a sense of commitment and identification with each other. Families vary in their structure—one parent or two, a single child or several—but all families have common functions. For one thing, they are children's earliest and most sustained source of social contact. They also offer the most intense and enduring of all interpersonal bonds. In addition, families share memories of the past and expectations for the future, and this continuity over time makes family relationships qualitatively different from shorter-lived relationships with playmates, friends, teachers, neighbors, and coworkers. Because they are first, most intense, and most enduring, family relationships are the standard against which other relationships are judged.

socialization
The process by which parents and others teach children the standards of behavior, attitudes, skills, and motives deemed appropriate for their society.

Families are also systems for **socialization**, which means that family members channel children's impulses into socially accepted outlets and teach children the skills and rules they need to function in society. When children are very young, parents begin the process of socialization to ensure that the children's standards of behavior conform to those regarded as desirable and appropriate by the parents and society. From the moment of birth, whether the child is wrapped in a pink or blue blanket, placed in a sling or nestled in a bassinet, indulged by a parent or left to cry it out, socialization has begun.

family system
A group of people composed of interdependent members and subsystems; changes in the behavior of one member of the family affect the functioning of the other members.

The **family system** is composed of a number of "subsystems"—including those of mother and father; mother and child; father and child; mother, father, and child; and subsystems involving siblings. Socialization takes place within each of these subsystems, which we discuss in this chapter. We also discuss how differences in family socialization are related to social class, culture, and history, and we explore some of the major changes in the structure and functioning of the family in recent decades.

The Family System

The family is a complex system made up of interdependent members and subsystems, and this had implications for the ways families function. Most simply, changes in the behavior of one member of the family affect the functioning of the other members (Bronfenbrenner & Morris, 2006; Kuczynski & Parkin, 2007; Sturge-Apple et al., 2010). For example, if the father's role in the family shifts, changes also occur in the mother's role and the children's experiences. Family members influence each other both directly and indirectly. Direct effects are more obvious: spouses affect each other by praising or criticizing; parents affect their children by hugging or spanking; children affect their parents by clinging or talking back. Indirect effects involve a two-step process: fathers affect their children indirectly by modifying their relationship with their mother, which then affects the child's development; mothers affect their children indirectly by modifying the quantity and quality of father-child interaction, which in turn affects the child's behavior; children influence the relationship between their mother and father indirectly by altering the behavior of either parent.

In a well-functioning family system, parents have a good relationship with each other, they are caring and supportive of their children, and the children are cooperative and responsible and care for their parents. In a dysfunctional family system, parents have an unhappy marriage, they are irritable with their children, and the children exhibit antisocial behavior, which intensifies problems in the parents' relationship. It is difficult to reverse the negative quality of these family interactions because systems in general resist change. This is why, for example, negative patterns of interaction intensify and solidify in families with an aggressive child (Dishion & Bullock, 2002; Katz & Gottman, 1997). If family members make no effort to communicate rationally, to defuse anger, or to solve problems, they are likely to become locked into a pattern of interaction that promotes or sustains maladaptive behavior in family members. The key to good family functioning is adaptability.

The Couple System

The "founding" subsystem within the family system joins the two partners. Developmental psychologists have sometimes overlooked the significance of this subsystem, but the nature of this relationship unquestionably has important effects on children's development. Directly or indirectly, the quality of the couple's union facilitates—or hampers—the quality of parenting, sibling relationships, and children's development.

HOW DOES THE COUPLE'S RELATIONSHIP AFFECT CHILDREN?   When partners offer each other emotional and physical support and comfort, the likelihood that they will provide this type of support and caring to their children is high. Research has shown that when partners are mutually supportive, they are more involved with their children, their child-rearing practices are more competent, and their relationships with their children are more affectionate and responsive (Cowan & Cowan, 2002; Katz & Gottman, 1997). In turn, children whose parents are mutually supportive and affectionate are well adjusted and positive (Goeke-Morey et al., 2003).

Parents who are in conflict and lash out at each other with hostility, belligerence, and contempt inflict problems on their children (Cummings & Merrilees, 2010; Grych & Fincham, 2001). When the conflict occurs in the child's early years, the children are unlikely to develop emotionally secure attachments to their parents (Frosch et al., 2000). When the conflict occurs in later years, the children are likely to become aggressive or depressed (Katz & Gottman, 1993, 1996).

Children are directly affected by their parents' conflict when they witness their arguments and fights. Mark Cummings and his colleagues showed children live or videotaped interactions between adult actors behaving like two conflicted parents in a home setting. The actors

disagreed about issues such as which movie to see or argued about who would wash the dishes. The more frequent and violent their conflicts and the more often the arguments were about something a child had done or said, the more likely children were to be upset and to blame themselves for the incident (Cummings et al., 2002). Moreover, when the actors failed to settle their disputes, the children were more angry and distressed than when the adults resolved their conflicts (Cummings et al., 1993).

Cummings and his associates also conducted research in which children observed conflicts between their parents rather than actors. These studies also demonstrated that the children's level of distress increased as the intensity and destructiveness of their parents' fights increased (Davies et al., 2006). Children who observed intense and destructive conflicts between their parents suffered from emotional insecurity, depression, anxiety, behavior problems, relationship difficulties, and poor emotion regulation, even years later (Cummings et al., 2006; Cummings & Davies, 2010; Cummings & Merrilees, 2010). In some cases, children's biological capacity to manage stress was impaired (Davies et al., 2007). However, if parents handled their disagreements constructively, showing respect for each other's opinions, expressing mutual warmth and support, and modeling effective conflict negotiation strategies, this lessened the harmful effects on children. Exposure to constructive conflict could even teach children how to negotiate conflict and resolve disagreements with others outside the family. Children were most likely to have problems if their parents expressed anger frequently, intensely, physically, and without resolution (Cummings & Merrilees, 2010).

The indirect effect of parental conflict occurs when marital difficulties affect parents' child-rearing practices and child-rearing practices affect children's development. Parents in conflicted marriages are likely to have parenting styles that are angry and intrusive, and their children, in turn, display a good deal of anger when they interact with their parents (Katz & Gottman, 1997) or with other children (Cowan et al., 1994; Perry-Jenkins et al., 2000; Kahen et al., 1994; McCloskey & Stuewig, 2001; Stocker & Youngblade, 1999).

Several different theoretical explanations have been offered to account for the effects of parental conflict on children's social development. Each has received empirical support. Social learning theory suggests that children learn how to interact with people and resolve conflicts by watching their parents; if parents fight, children learn aggressive interaction strategies (Crockenberg & Langrock, 2001). A second explanation, based on attachment theory, suggests that as a result of exposure to conflict between their parents, children experience emotional arousal and distress and develop a sense of emotional insecurity, which leads to later problems in social interactions (Cummings & Davies, 2010). In support of this viewpoint, researchers have found that children's insecure representations of their parents' relationship were a significant intervening mechanism in the association between parents' conflict and children's emotional difficulties in early elementary school (Sturge-Apple et al., 2008). According to a third theory, which emphasizes children's cognitive processes, the impact of parental conflict depends on how children understand it. If they perceive the conflict as threatening, they become anxious, depressed, and withdrawn; if they perceive the conflict as being their fault, they are more likely to act out; if the parents resolve the conflict, the children are less likely to have these problems because they expect that they, too, will be able to resolve conflicts (Grych & Cardoza-Fernandes, 2001; Grych & Fincham, 1990). A fourth theory suggests that poor parental mental health accounts for the effects of parental conflict on children's functioning. In one study supporting this viewpoint, Cummings and his colleagues found that parental depression mediated the impact of marital distress on adolescents' depressive symptoms (Cummings et al., 2005). A fifth explanation is that the effect of parental conflict on children's social behavior is, in part, genetic. Researchers have found a stronger link between marital conflict and adolescent conduct problems in families in which the mothers or fathers are identical twins than in families in which the mothers or fathers are fraternal twins (Harden et al., 2007).

Regardless of the theoretical explanation—all of which have merit—it is valuable to view the links between parental conflict and child adjustment as reciprocal and transactional, not a one-way effect from parents to children. When Cummings and his colleagues examined the relations between parental discord and child outcomes across three time points, they found that parental discord at the first time predicted children's negative emotional reactivity at the second time. Children's negative reactivity was related to dysregulated behavior (children did more yelling and causing trouble) and agentic behavior (children made more efforts to intervene in their parents' conflicts). Children's agentic behavior then predicted decreased parental discord at the third time point (Schermerhorn et al., 2007). This suggests that as a result of their children's efforts, parents may have become more aware of the negative effects of their marital discord and, as a consequence, reduced their overt conflict. Children's dysregulated behavior predicted increases in marital discord and elevations in children's adjustment problems.

Researchers have implemented programs to help parents improve their relationship and thereby help their children. Cummings and his colleagues (2008) devised a program for couples with 4- to 8-year-old children in which they were taught about the effects of constructive and destructive marital conflict. Compared with parents in a control group who merely read the same information, couples who participated in the program increased their knowledge about marital conflict, engaged in more constructive and less destructive conflict, and their children were better adjusted than those of the control group. These effects were still evident a year later. In another program, parents of 4-year-olds participated in professionally led group discussions on parenting or marital issues (Cowan et al., 2005). Their children exhibited less aggressive acting out, suffered from fewer internalizing problems, experienced fewer problems with their peers, and even 10 years later were still doing better socially and had fewer behavior problems than children whose parents were in a control group (Cowan & Cowan, 2010).

Learning from Living Leaders: E. Mark Cummings

Source: Courtesy of E. Mark Cummings.

Mark Cummings, Professor of Psychology at Notre Dame, has devoted his career to studying marital relationships, parenting, and child adjustment. He did not start out to become a psychologist; he wanted to be a physicist and then a physician. But an undergraduate course in social development and his own recollections of loss, separation, and conflict in childhood hooked him on trying to understand children and families. After graduate work at UCLA, he worked at the National Institute of Mental Health, developing a model of family influences on children's socioemotional development. He used this model as the framework for a series of empirical studies. Many of his studies involve laboratory analogue experiments, simulations of events that happen in families, for example, exposing children to an argument between two adults. His major discovery was that seeing adults arguing can have profound effects on children's social and emotional well-being. This finding has made people more aware of how families function as a breeding ground for psychopathology. Cummings is now developing a program to teach parents how to handle their everyday differences—for their children's sakes.

Further Reading

Cummings, E. M., & Merrilees, C. E. (2010). Identifying the dynamic processes underlying links between marital conflict and child adjustment. In M. S. Schulz, M. K. Pruett, P. Kerig, & R. Parke (Eds.), *Strengthening couple relationships for optimal child development* (pp. 27–40). Washington, DC: American Psychological Association.

AND BABY MAKES THREE: THE IMPACT OF A NEW BABY ON THE COUPLE SYSTEM Just as the couple's relationship affects the children, children affect the couple's relationship. The most immediate effect occurs after the birth of the couple's first child. This significant life change brings with it a shift toward a more traditional division of labor (Cowan & Cowan, 2000, 2010) and less marital satisfaction as well (Twenge et al., 2003). Satisfaction declines more markedly in women (Cowan & Cowan, 2000, 2010), perhaps because the shift toward a traditional division of labor often means that they give up their jobs and stay home with the baby. Fathers' satisfaction also decreases but more slowly; it may be only gradually that men become aware of the restrictions a baby imposes on their lives.

The effect of children on the couple's relationship is especially marked if either the child or the couple has problems. A child with a difficult temperament or physical handicap heightens family stress and may increase parental conflict. If couples are already in conflict, the birth of a child can stress them to the breaking point. Couples who are satisfied with their relationship before the child's birth usually weather the pressures of this life transition reasonably well and are less likely to find their relationship in shreds than couples who were experiencing problems before the child's arrival. Thus, although the birth of a child rarely destroys a good relationship between the mother and father, the presence of a difficult child may be enough to undermine a fragile relationship (Hogan & Msall, 2002).

Into Adulthood: Transition to Parenthood

Source: © Media Bakery.

Although bringing a child into a family is generally heralded as a happy event, becoming parents poses risks. To make the transition less stressful, psychologists have designed programs to strengthen couple relationships and reduce the adverse consequences of the transition to parenthood. In the *Becoming a Family* project, Philip and Carolyn Cowan (2000, 2010) studied 72 couples who were expecting their first baby and 24 couples who had not yet decided whether to become parents. They selected one third of the expectant couples to participate in a 6-month group intervention that concluded 3 months after the birth of their baby. In weekly sessions, a clinically trained married couple encouraged these parents-to-be to raise any issues they were grappling with. Both wives and husbands described their dreams of creating an ideal family and talked about the impending

birth. Interestingly, everyone had trouble imagining what would happen after the baby was born. After the birth, the couples confronted changes, problems, and conflicts. Who would give up what? Who would take responsibility for what? How could they keep the marital relationship fulfilling while dealing with the child's incessant demands? The researchers assessed family functioning, the quality of the marital relationship, parenting effectiveness, and parents' adjustment in late pregnancy and when the children were 6 months, 18 months, 3 years, and 5 years old. At the 18-month assessment, the effects of the intervention were encouraging. Fathers in the intervention group were more involved and satisfied with their parenting and reported less negative change in their marital satisfaction, sexual relations, and social support. Mothers in the intervention group were more satisfied with the division of labor and with their marriages overall; they were happier with their sexual relations, and they seemed better able to balance life stresses and social supports. Fewer of the intervention couples were separated or divorced. By the time the children were in kindergarten, though, some of the positive effects of the early intervention had worn off. Although higher couple satisfaction continued in the intervention group, there were few differences in parenting styles or children's behavior. The researchers concluded that to sustain good family functioning, giving "booster shots" from time to time over the family life cycle would be helpful (Schulz et al., 2006).

The Parent-Child System

Most parents have some beliefs about the qualities they would like to see their children develop and the child-rearing methods that should encourage them. How parents go about this process of rearing their children and how successful they are is the topic of this section.

HOW PARENTS SOCIALIZE CHILDREN   Although socialization begins when the infant is born, it becomes more deliberate as children achieve greater mobility and begin to use language. When children reach this point, their parents cuddle and pet them and praise them for all sorts of achievements that they and society regard as desirable. They no longer accept behavior just because it's "cute." They stop children from climbing out of their cribs, banging on pots and pans, and hitting the kitty. Some parents stay relatively relaxed and permissive as their children engage in these activities. For other children practicing newfound motor skills and exploring the world becomes a real trial because parents restrain them with playpen bars and a barrage of "No's!" Parents' efforts to socialize their children increase as children go through the preschool years and are maintained until parents are satisfied with the result or give up in frustration.

Most parents try to socialize their children to behave politely, get along with others, value honesty and hard work, and achieve a myriad of other goals that vary somewhat from family to family. For example, among aboriginal parents in Canada, socialization goals include respecting cultural traditions and being proud of their heritage (Cheah & Chirkov, 2008). Regardless of their specific goals, though, parents use learning principles to teach their children social rules and roles. They use reinforcement when they explain acceptable standards of behavior and then praise or punish the children according to whether they conform to or violate these rules. They use modeling when they demonstrate behaviors they want the children to adopt. They also inadvertently use modeling when they act in ways they don't intend the child to imitate. If parents lie to their friends, ridicule their coworkers, and bully their children, these negative behaviors are as likely to be adopted by the children as are the parents' positive behaviors and more likely to be emulated than the behaviors parents preach about.

DIFFERENCES IN SOCIALIZATION APPROACHES   In addition to having somewhat different socialization goals, parents differ in the ways they go about the job of socialization. One difference is related to their emotional involvement: Some parents are warm and responsive in their approach to socialization; others are cold and rejecting. When parents are warm and loving, socialization is more effective. Children whose parents are responsive, warm, and engaging are more socially competent (Grimes et al., 2004) and popular (Henggeler et al., 1991; Isley et al., 1996, 1999) than children with rejecting parents. A second difference is related to the parents' level of control: Some parents are permissive and undemanding, pretty much allowing children to do as they wish; others are demanding and restrictive. The ideal seems to be a happy medium. If parents use the minimum amount of pressure necessary to bring the children's behavior into line with the parents' goals, children are more likely to cooperate and to internalize their parents' standards (Crockenberg & Litman, 1990; Holden, 2009). If parents exert too little control, their children are more likely to have externalizing behavior problems (Barber & Harmon, 2002). If they exert too much control, they may influence the children's immediate behavior, but in the long run the children may come to view themselves as helpless and unworthy and may avoid contact with the parents—which gives the parents less opportunity to socialize them.

A key aspect of strict control is physical punishment—spanking, slapping, shaking, beating. According to one meta-analysis, physical punishment is linked to a variety of negative outcomes, especially increases in children's aggression (Gershoff, 2002). This is a controversial topic, however, and not everyone agrees that spanking is bad (Baumrind et al., 2002). In a more recent meta-analysis, researchers compared different types of physical punishment, including (1) conditional spanking, which was used to back up milder disciplinary tactics such as reasoning and time-outs; (2) physical punishment as the predominant disciplinary tactic; and (3) severe punishment, including shaking and spanking that was anger driven and out of control (Larzelere & Kuhn, 2005). Only the latter two types of physical punishment were associated with negative child outcomes, including antisocial behavior and poor conscience development. In fact, conditional spanking was associated with reductions in noncompliance and antisocial behavior even more than nonphysical disciplinary tactics such as ignoring, time-outs, and loss of privileges. These findings suggest that mild, judicious physical punishment can be an effective disciplinary strategy. This view is consistent with experimental studies demonstrating that the negative effects of punishment can be avoided by making punishment contingencies clear and reinforcing appropriate behaviors (Matson & Taras, 1989; Walters & Grusec, 1977).

authoritarian parenting
Child-rearing style that is harsh, unresponsive, and rigid and tends to use power-assertive methods of control.

permissive parenting
Child-rearing style that is lax and inconsistent and encourages children to express their impulses freely.

authoritative parenting
Child-rearing style that is warm, responsive, and involved and sets reasonable limits and expects appropriately mature behavior from children.

uninvolved parenting
Child-rearing style in which parents are indifferent and neglectful and focus on their own needs rather than those of their children.

PARENTING STYLES   Putting together the emotional and control dimensions of parenting led researchers to identify four parenting styles (see Figure 7.1). **Authoritarian parenting** is emotionally rejecting and highly controlling. **Permissive parenting** is emotionally positive and low in control. **Authoritative parenting** is emotionally positive and firmly controlling. **Uninvolved parenting** is emotionally negative and low in control.

Diana Baumrind was the first psychologist to link authoritarian, authoritative, and permissive socialization styles with child outcomes (Baumrind, 1967). Observing preschool children in their daily activities for 14 weeks, she identified three groups of children who had widely varying patterns of behavior: Children in one group were energetic and friendly; children in a second group were conflicted and irritable; and children in the third group were impulsive and aggressive. Baumrind then interviewed the children's parents and observed them interacting with the children at home and in the laboratory. Later she followed the parents and children through adolescence (Baumrind, 1991). What she found was that children in the energetic-friendly group, who were more socially competent in every way, were likely to have authoritative parents. They permitted the children considerable freedom and were not intrusive. However, they imposed restrictions in areas in which they had more knowledge or insight, and they were firm in resisting children's efforts to get them to acquiesce to demands. They expected appropriately mature behavior from the children, setting reasonable limits but also being responsive and attentive to the children's needs. The children developed high levels of self-esteem, adaptability, competence, and internalized control; they were popular with their peers and seldom behaved in antisocial ways. Positive outcomes were still evident in adolescence, especially for sons.

In contrast, conflicted-irritable children, who tended to be fearful and moody, were likely to have authoritarian parents. These parents were rigid, power-assertive, harsh, and unresponsive to the children's needs. The children had little control over their environments and received little gratification. Baumrind suggested that these children often felt trapped and angry but also fearful of asserting themselves in a hostile environment. In childhood and adolescence, these children, especially the boys, were lacking in self-confidence, less socially competent, more unfriendly, and less likely to be leaders of their peers.

Children in the impulsive-aggressive group were likely to have permissive parents. These parents had affectionate relationships with

FIGURE 7.1 *Parenting styles. Combining the dimensions of control and emotion produces four different parenting styles. Source: Maccoby & Martin, 1983.*

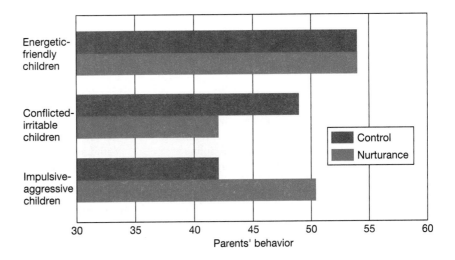

FIGURE 7.2 *Dimensions of parental behavior and children's characteristics. Parents of energetic-friendly children had higher scores on both dimensions: control and positive emotion (nurturance).* Source: Baumrind, 1967.

their children, but because of their excessively lax and inconsistent discipline and their encouragement of the children's free expression of impulses, they did not diminish the children's uncontrolled, noncompliant, and aggressive behavior. (Baumrind's findings are summarized graphically in Figure 7.2.)

Later researchers identified the fourth parenting style, uninvolved (Maccoby & Martin, 1983) or disengaged (Sturge-Apple et al., 2010). This type of parenting reflects the behavior of parents who are indifferent to their children. They do whatever is necessary to minimize the costs of having children—giving them as little time and effort as possible. They focus on their own needs before those of the children. Particularly when children are older, these parents frequently fail to monitor their activities. When asked the classic question, "It's 10 o'clock—do you know where your children are?" these parents often have to admit they do not. Children with uninvolved parents are likely to be impulsive, aggressive, noncompliant, and moody (Sturge-Apple et al., 2010; Thompson, 2006b). As adolescents, they may be delinquents (Dishion & Bullock, 2002). When parents increase their involvement, children's problem behaviors decrease and social skills improve (El Nokali et al., 2010).

The characteristics of parents who display each of the four parenting styles and the typical behaviors of their children are summarized in Table 7.1.

TABLE 7.1 **Relations between Parenting Style and Children's Characteristics**

Parenting Style	Child Characteristics
Authoritative parent	*Energetic-friendly child*
Is warm, involved, responsive	Is cheerful
Shows pleasure and support of child's constructive behavior	Is self-controlled and self-reliant
Considers child's wishes and solicits opinions; offers alternatives	Is interested and curious in new situations
Sets standards, communicates them clearly, and enforces them firmly	Has high energy level
Does not yield to child's coercion	Maintains friendly relations with peers
Shows displeasure at bad behavior; confronts disobedient child	Cooperates with adults
Expects mature, independent, age-appropriate behavior	Copes well with stress
Plans cultural events and joint activities	

(continued)

TABLE 7.1 *Continued*

Parenting Style	Child Characteristics
Authoritarian parent	*Conflicted-irritable child*
Shows little warmth or positive involvement	Is moody, unhappy, aimless
Does not solicit or consider child's desires or opinions	Is fearful, apprehensive, easily annoyed
Enforces rules rigidly but doesn't explain them clearly	Is passively hostile and deceitful
Shows anger and displeasure; confronts child regarding bad behavior and uses harsh, punitive discipline	Alternates between aggressive behavior and sulky withdrawal
Views child as dominated by antisocial impulses	Is vulnerable to stress
Permissive parent	*Impulsive-aggressive child*
Is moderately warm	Is aggressive, domineering, resistant, noncompliant
Glorifies free expression of impulses and desire	Is quick to anger but fast to recover cheerful mood
Does not communicate rules clearly or enforce them	Lacks self-control and displays little self-reliance
Ignores or accepts bad behavior; disciplines inconsistently	Is impulsive
Yields to coercion and whining; hides impatience, anger	Is aimless; has few goal-directed activities
Makes few demands for mature, independent behavior	
Uninvolved parent	*Impulsive-aggressive-noncompliant-moody child*
Is self-centered, neglectful, unresponsive	Is moody, insecurely attached, impulsive, aggressive, noncompliant, irresponsible
Pursues self-gratification at expense of child's welfare	Has low self-esteem and is immature, alienated from family
Tries to minimize costs (time, effort) of interaction with child	Lacks skills for social pursuits
Fails to monitor child's activity, whereabouts, companions	Is truant, associates with troubled peers, may be delinquent, is sexually precocious
May be depressive, anxious, emotionally needy	

Sources: Baumrind, 1967, 1991; Hetherington & Clingempeel, 1992; Maccoby & Martin, 1983; Sturge-Apple et al., 2010.

Learning from Living Leaders: Diana Baumrind

Source: Courtesy of Diana Baumrind.

Diana Baumrind is a Research Scientist at the Institute of Human Development at the University of California, Berkeley, the same institution from which she received her Ph.D. in clinical, developmental, and social psychology. The underlying theme of her work is the reciprocal rights and responsibilities of individuals in relationships of unequal power. This has led her to study relationships between parents and children and between research investigators and participants. She is the leading authority on how contrasting patterns of parental authority affect the development of character and competence in children and adolescents. As a consequence of her work, authoritative parenting is generally recognized as the best way to promote children's socioemotional adjustment. Baumrind has always been committed to applying her findings to socially significant policy issues and has contributed to policy debates on physical punishment, child maltreatment, drug abuse, and human rights. Although she is a respected leader in the field, she has never held a tenured (secure) position at a university.

Instead, she has relied on government and foundation grant support. This is often a difficult path, but Baumrind found that it allowed her to coordinate her professional objectives with her family responsibilities and to do things "her way," by which she means "doing the best job possible without regard to fads or fashions in psychology or funding priorities." In recognition of her contributions to developmental psychology, Baumrind was given the esteemed G. Stanley Hall Award from the American Psychological Association. Her credo for the next generation of students is to follow her lead and "Do good well."

Further Reading

Baumrind, D. (2005). Patterns of parental authority and adolescent autonomy. In J. Smetana (Ed.), *New directions for child development: Changes in parental authority during adolescence* (pp. 61–69). San Francisco: Jossey-Bass.

WHY PARENTS HAVE DIFFERENT PARENTING STYLES   Where do these differences in parents' styles of socializing their children come from? There are many sources. One is the quality of the parents' relationship with each other. Parents in good marriages are more likely to be authoritative (Cowan & Cowan, 2002; Katz & Gottman, 1997). A second source of differences in parenting styles is parents' personalities (Belsky & Barends, 2002). Parents with less agreeable personalities (measured outside the child-rearing context) are more authoritarian—less responsive, more rejecting, and more power assertive (Clark et al., 2000; Koenig et al., in press). Parents' abilities also affect their parenting styles: Parents who are poor at taking another person's perspective are more authoritarian (Gerris et al. 1997); parents who are good at adapting to changing or stressful circumstances are more authoritative (van Bakel & Riksen-Walraven, 2000). Parents' mental health affects their behavior as well: Neurotic parents—that is, parents who are depressed, anxious, and obsessive—are more negative and rejecting with their children (Belsky et al., 1995). An uninvolved style of parenting is often found in parents who are depressed (Goodman & Gotlib, 2002; Hammen, 2009) or stressed by marital discord or divorce (Hetherington & Kelly, 2002). Their own anxiety and emotional neediness drives these parents to pursue self-gratification at the expense and neglect of their children's welfare (Patterson & Capaldi, 1991). Another factor that affects parenting styles is how much education parents have: Parents with less education use more authoritarian discipline (Carpenter, 1999; Kelley et al., 1992). Another source of parenting styles is the parent's family of origin. Whether they know it or not, parents are affected by the experiences they had with their own parents when they were young (Murphy-Cowan & Stringer, 1999; Smith & Drew 2002; Wakschlag et al., 1996). To some extent, parenting styles are transmitted from one generation to the next.

The circumstances in which families live also have an influence on parents' behavior. Parents who live in dangerous neighborhoods are more likely to be authoritarian (Leventhal & Brooks-Gunn, 2000) and place more restrictions on their children's activities (O'Neil et al., 2001). Their style of strict control may be adaptive because living in a dangerous neighborhood brings with it a higher risk that children will be harmed or become involved in antisocial activities (Dodge et al., 2005). When parents move to more affluent and less dangerous neighborhoods, they use less harsh discipline than parents who remain in poor neighborhoods (Leventhal & Brooks-Gunn, 2003). The parents' culture is another important source of ideas about how to socialize children (which we discuss later in this chapter).

Finally, children's behavior affects parenting styles (Kochanska, 1997; Koenig et al., in press). It is not uncommon for people—especially people who have never had children—to think that the main direction of effects in the family is from parents to children. In fact, socialization is a two-way street, a process of mutual shaping by which parents modify children's behavior and children influence the behavior of their parents (Bronfenbrenner & Morris, 2006; Kuczynski & Parkin, 2007). Children with difficult temperaments or behavior problems provoke increasingly coercive socialization strategies from their parents (Dodge & Pettit, 2003; Laird, Pettit, Bates, et al., 2003; Reid et al., 2002). Children with fearful temperaments are more accepted by their parents (Lengua & Kovacs, 2005) and respond to more subtle parental socialization strategies (Kochanska et al., 2007). These child effects have been observed not only in correlational studies but in experiments. In one experiment, researchers paired conduct-disordered boys with mothers of normal boys and asked them to play freely for 5 minutes, to clean up the materials they were using, and to solve some math problems (Anderson et al., 1986). The mothers were more negative and controlling with the conduct-disordered boys than with normal boys—whether they were their own sons or other boys. Child effects on parenting styles have also been demonstrated in behavior genetics studies. In one study, children who were at risk for antisocial behavior because their biological mothers acted in antisocial ways in high school (ran away from home, got into fights, ditched school) were more likely to elicit harsh and hostile treatment from their adoptive parents than were children without this risk (O'Connor et al., 1998). Clearly, children's characteristics affect parenting.

Research up Close:
Transmission of Hostile Parenting across Generations

Laura Scaramella and Rand Conger (2003) used a prospective study across three generations to examine the degree to which hostile parenting in the first generation was passed on to parents in the second generation (Figure 7.3, Path a). They also looked at whether hostile parenting in the second generation was related to children's behavior problems in the third generation (Path b).

Their study offered the methodological advantage of having independent raters assess parent behavior and child behavior at each time point. It also included assessments of an important child characteristic, negative emotional reactivity. This was an important component

of the study because children who react to environmental restrictions with negative emotionality may provoke their parents' hostility, and their negative temperaments may cause them to be more prone to developing problems in response to hostile parenting. In technical jargon, children's temperaments may moderate both continuities in parenting across generations and effects of parenting on children's emotional development (Paths c and d).

The researchers observed 75 ninth graders in the laboratory as they and their parents tried to resolve common family problems (curfew disagreements, homework disputes). They recorded the degree of hostile parenting (angry and coercive disciplinary tactics). Five to 8 years later, when the 9th graders had entered adulthood and become parents themselves, they were observed with their 18-month-old toddlers in a toy cleanup task. The researchers were thus able to assess the amount of hostile parenting used by these young parents with their own children. The toddlers were evaluated for negative emotional reactivity (anger, distress, struggle) when the researchers restrained their arms.

As expected, the young parents who had been treated by their own parents in a hostile and angry fashion when they were in 9th grade were more likely to be hostile toward their own children a decade later. Moreover, the more hostile the young parents were, the more disobedient, aggressive, sullen, and withdrawn their toddlers were. Children's temperaments mattered too: Continuity of parenting was evident only when children were above the median on negative emotional reactivity. In families in which children had more positive temperaments, hostile parenting in the first generation

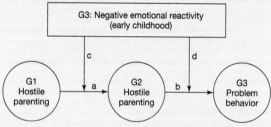

FIGURE 7.3 *Continuities in hostile behavior across generations. G1 = first generation; G2 = second generation; G3 = third generation. Source: Scaramella, L. V, & Conger, R. D. (2003). Intergenerational continuity of hostile parenting and its consequences: The moderating influence of children's negative emotional reactivity. Social Development, 12, 420–439. Reprinted with permission of Wiley-Blackwell.*

did not predict hostile parenting in the second. One interpretation of these findings is that children's negative emotional reactivity stresses parents, and stressed parents react to their children's behavior with well-learned behaviors from their own childhoods.

Taken together, these results begin to address the questions of why not all people who were raised by hostile parents become hostile and why not all children with hostile parents develop behavior problems. Highly reactive children may not be at risk for problems if their parents' own childhood experiences were not hostile, and hostile parenting may not lead to later conduct problems if children are not emotionally reactive. However, the combination of earlier hostile child rearing by parents and later negative emotionality in offspring is likely to ignite a sequence of events that intensifies problems over time.

Intergenerational studies such as this one have a number of limitations. One limitation is that because they require contact with a sample over an extended period of time, they are complicated and expensive and often suffer from participant attrition. In addition, these researchers were not able to fully explore the influence of fathers. First generation father data were not available for one quarter of the sample because the parents had divorced. Researchers in the future can contribute more information about the important issue of cross-generational parenting continuity by using larger and more complete samples.

SOCIALIZATION: FROM BIDIRECTIONAL TO TRANSACTIONAL   Today, child development researchers recognize that socialization is bidirectional—that parents' behavior affects children's and children's behavior affects parents'. But looking at socialization over time suggests that the process is even more complex. Children and their parents change each other over time in a transactional process (Sameroff, 2009, 2010). To demonstrate the transactional nature of socialization, researchers have documented across-time links between parents' and children's behaviors. In one study, they showed that children's ability to regulate their impulsive behavior at age 7 predicted fewer punitive maternal reactions when the children were 9, which in turn predicted better regulation of impulses by the children when they were 11 (Eisenberg et al., 1999). In another study, researchers showed that parents' warmth toward their children predicted the children's empathy 2 years later and children's externalizing behavior problems predicted less warm and responsive parenting over the same period (Zhou et al., 2002). In a third study, researchers found that parents' inconsistent discipline predicted higher levels of irritability in their 8- to 11-year-old children, and children's positive emotionality predicted higher levels of maternal acceptance a year later (Lengua & Kovacs, 2005).

MOTHERS' AND FATHERS' PARENTING   Over the past decades, there has been a significant shift in how much fathers participate in children's lives. In the 1970s, fathers were only about one third as engaged with their children as mothers were; today it's closer to three quarters (Pleck, 2010; Pleck & Masciadrelli, 2004). Nevertheless, even today, fathers typically spend less time with their children than mothers do (Pleck, 2010; Pleck & Masciadrelli, 2004) and are less likely to supervise the children's play with peers (Bhavnagri & Parke, 1991; Ladd & Pettit, 2002). This difference appears not only in the United States but also in other countries including Great Britain, Australia, France, Belgium, and Japan (Zuzanek, 2000). But despite the fact that fathers spend a limited amount of time with their children, they have an important influence on the children's development. Studies show that fathers make a significant contribution to their children's social behavior, independent of the mother's contribution (Boyum & Parke, 1995; Carson & Parke, 1996; Hart et al., 1998; Isley et al., 1996; McDowell et al., 2002). If fathers are more positive and prosocial in their interactions with their children, the children are more competent with peers; if fathers are confrontational and angry in their interactions, their children are less competent.

Fathers are more likely to be involved in play activities with their children than mothers are (Yeung et al., 2001). The quality of their play differs, too. Fathers' play is more physically arousing; mothers play conventional games, interact with toys, and talk more (Parke, 1996, 2002). Even with adolescents, fathers are more playful than mothers—joking and teasing (Shulman &

Klein, 1993). Fathers may use their distinctively arousing style as a way to increase the salience of their interactions despite their more limited time with the child. Or men may just be more physical than women: Human males of all ages are more boisterous than females (Maccoby, 1998). However, physical play is not such a central part of the father-infant relationship in all cultures (Roopnarine, 2004). Fathers are not more likely than mothers to play with their children in Sweden or on Israeli kibbutzim (Hwang, 1987), and in China, Malaysia, Italy, and India, neither mothers nor fathers engage in physical play with their children (Hewlett, 2004; New & Benigni, 1987; Roopnarine, 2004). These cross-cultural data suggest that cultural and environmental contexts as well as biological factors shape parents' play patterns.

et You Thought That...
Parenting Is a Brain Drain, Not a Brain Booster

Source: Tetra Images / Stockphotopro, Inc.

Parenting is hard work. It involves multitasking, loss of sleep, frayed nerves, and weakened social relationships. You may think that that this parenting burden would lead to a brain drain as parents strain to keep up with child-rearing demands. If you think so, you are wrong. It turns out that parenting is good for your brain. According to Craig Kinsley and Kelly Lambert (2006), research indicates that the dramatic hormonal fluctuations that occur during pregnancy, birth, and lactation may remodel the female brain, increasing the size of neurons in some regions and producing structural changes in others. Estrogen and progesterone apparently enlarge the cell bodies of neurons in the area of the hypothalamus, which regulates basic maternal responses, and increase the surface area of neuronal branches in the hippocampus, which governs memory and learning. When researchers studied the brains of lactating mother rats using functional magnetic resonance imaging (fMRI), they found that activity in the mother's brain that is integral to reinforcement and reward increased significantly when mothers nursed their pups (Ferris et al., 2005). In pregnant rats, neurons in the hypothalamus increased as the pregnancy progressed (Kinsley et al., 2006). In essence, the hormones of pregnancy "rev up" these neurons in anticipation of birth and the demands of motherhood. After birth, these neurons direct the mother's attention and motivation to her offspring, enabling her to provide care, protection, and nurture.

Mothers' reproductive experience also enhances spatial learning and memory. Researchers have found that young female rats that had experienced one or two pregnancies were better than virgin rats at remembering the location of a food reward in mazes, and mother rats were faster than virgins at capturing prey (crickets) (Kinsley & Lambert, 2008). Pregnant and lactating rats also suffered less fear and anxiety (as measured by levels of stress hormones in their blood) than virgin rats when confronted with challenges such as forced swimming or exploring a novel environment (Wartella et al., 2003) because of reduced neuronal activity in the brain regions of the hippocampus that regulate stress and emotion (Love et al., 2005). Oxytocin, the hormone that triggers birth contractions and milk release, also appears to have effects on the hippocampus that improve learning and long-term memory. In addition, motherhood is associated with an increase in the number and complexity of glial cells, the connective tissue of the central nervous system that enhances learning and spatial memory (Tomizawa et al., 2003). Finally, rat mothers are good at multitasking; they nearly always beat virgins in competitions that involve simultaneously monitoring sights, sounds, odors, and other animals (Higgins et al., 2007; Lambert & Kinsley, 2009). These benefits last, too. Mother rats up to 2 years old—equivalent to human females older than age 60—learn spatial tasks significantly faster and remember them longer than virgin rats (Gatewood et al., 2005). Examination of their brains reveals fewer deposits of amyloid precursor proteins, which seem to play a role in the deterioration of the aging brain (Love et al., 2005).

But what about human mothers? Researchers have also used fMRI to examine the brains of human moms as they listen to their babies cry (Lorberbaum et al., 1999). The patterns observed were similar to those of the rodent mothers. Other researchers have found that the brain areas that regulate reward become activated when human mothers merely gaze at their children (Bartels & Zeki, 2004). Human brains also undergo changes in sensory regulatory systems that parallel the alterations in other animals. Human mothers are capable of recognizing their infants' odors and sounds, possibly because of enhanced sensory abilities (Corter & Fleming, 2002). Mothers with high postbirth levels of the hormone cortisol are also more attracted to and motivated by their babies' scents and are better able to recognize their infants' cries (Everette et al., 2007). A possible long-term effect of motherhood is suggested by the finding that women who had been pregnant at or after the age of 40 were four times more likely to survive to age 100 than women who had been pregnant only earlier in life (Perls & Fretts, 2001). Perhaps pregnancy and motherhood enhance women's brains at a crucial period when the menopause-induced decline in reproductive hormones is starting.

Males gain mental benefits from being parents, too. When researchers tested mother and father marmosets, a small Brazilian monkey, on a "foraging tree" where they had to learn which containers held the most food, both mothers and fathers outperformed nonparents (Lambert & Kinsley, 2009). Similarly, in a mouse species in which the male contributes significantly to parental care, researchers found that fathers were quicker than nondads to investigate novel stimuli, such as Lego blocks (Kinsley & Lambert, 2008). In brief, reproductive and child-rearing experience promotes changes in the brain that alter skills and behavior, particularly among mothers, but possibly among fathers as well. Being a parent is apparently good for the brain, not a brain drain.

The Coparenting System

coparenting
How parents work together as a team; can be cooperative, hostile, or unbalanced.

Although mothers and fathers often act separately when they deal with their children, their actions are related, and this creates another subsystem within the family—the **coparenting** system. Researchers studying this system have identified three different coparenting patterns (McHale, 2010; McHale et al., 2002). In some families, coparenting is cooperative, cohesive, and child centered; these families are likely to have a high degree of family harmony. In other families, coparenting is hostile; these parents actively compete against each other for their children's attention and loyalty. In the third type of coparenting, spouses invest different amounts of time and energy in parenting, leading to an imbalance in their involvement with the child. This discrepancy can result from "gatekeeping," when one parent limits or controls the other parent's level of participation. For example, if a mother assumes that women are more fit for parenting than men, she may set up subtle barriers that limit the father's involvement (Beitel & Parke, 1998).

Researchers have found that these three coparenting patterns are related to children's social development—even after they control for other factors, such as the mother's well-being, the overall quality of the parents' marriage, and the mother's and father's warmth when interacting with the child individually (Cox & Paley, 2003). Children exposed to hostile-competitive coparenting in their first year are likely to exhibit high levels of aggressive behavior in early childhood; children who are exposed to large discrepancies between the parents are likely to develop anxiety (Fivaz-Depeursinge & Corboz-Warnery, 1999; McHale, 2010; McHale et al., 2002). Cooperative coparenting, in contrast, has positive effects on children's social-emotional development (McHale, 2010) and can even reduce the negative effects of a problematic temperament (Schoppe-Sullivan et al., 2009).

The Sibling System

More than 80 percent of families in the United States and Canada have more than one child, and the number, spacing, and relations among these children affect the functioning of the entire family. Most children spend more time interacting with their siblings than with their parents or anyone else (Dunn, 2002; Larson & Verma, 1999). Interactions between siblings provide plenty of opportunities for children to learn positive and negative ways of interacting and may be more emotionally intense than exchanges with other family members and friends (Katz et al., 1992). As one 9-year-old put it, "My sister knows more about me so I'm kind of closer to her than to my friends" (Hadfield et al., 2006).

Insights from Extremes: When Is a Family Too Large?

Family size in the United States has decreased steadily over the past century. Your great grandmother may have had 8, 9, or even 10 children because this was an economic necessity to help maintain the family farm or business. Extended families often shared a household and everyone—aunts, uncles, cousins, grandparents—helped care for the children. But now, when both parents are likely to work outside the home and relatives tend to live far away, large families are more difficult to manage. The average number of children in a family today is only 1.8 (Bellamy, 2000). The challenges of caring for a large family were brought to national attention in January 2009, when Nadya Suleman, a single mother who already had six young children, gave birth to octuplets. How could she possibly cope with the task of caring for 14 children? Guidelines for child care facilities suggest that at least one caregiver is needed for every four infants to ensure that the babies receive proper care. This means that at least four caregivers would be needed to care for Suleman's children. If she had been living in an earlier era when extended family members were available to share the burden of raising large broods of babies, or if

she had lived in another culture where all members of the community share the child care load, the challenge would not be so daunting. But in our culture today, Suleman is facing an enormously difficult task. This extreme case illustrates the difficulties involved in parenting a large family, being a single mother, and having limited financial and personal resources for child care. Many experts are worried about the consequences for these children's development. The "octomom" case also raises questions about the use of alternative reproductive technologies. Suleman conceived the octuplets, as well as her six older children, by in vitro fertilization (IVF). Although it is normal to have only two or three embryos implanted by IVF, in this case, as Suleman requested, the doctor implanted at least six embryos. This extreme case not only underscores the challenges of caring for a large number of children but also suggests that as a society, we need to examine the ethics and wisdom of unregulated use of in vitro fertilization. Sometimes too many is just too much. By the time the octuplets were just 6 months old, Suleman told a reporter she regretted having had more than two or three embryos implanted (*Us Magazine*, August 20, 2009).

HOW ARE SIBLINGS AFFECTED BY BIRTH ORDER?   Position in the family—that is, whether a child is born first, second, or later—creates distinct experiences for children. Firstborn children experience a period during which they reign supreme in the eyes of their parents only to be displaced by the birth of a younger sibling with whom they must share their parents' affection. "Only" children enjoy the parents' exclusive attention forever. The lives of later-born children are filled with the doings and demands of other children from the day they are born. Not surprisingly, researchers have discovered differences among children depending on their birth order. Firstborn children are generally more adult oriented, helpful, and self-controlled than their siblings, and they tend to be more studious and conscientious (Herrera et al., 2003; Zajonc & Mullally, 1997). Indeed, firstborns are overrepresented in *Who's Who* and among Rhodes scholars. Firstborn sons tend to be conservative and like to maintain the status quo, perhaps because of the expectations and demands their parents place on them; second-born sons are more likely to support change and innovation (Sulloway, 1995). Later-born children also tend to be less fearful and anxious than their firstborn siblings; they experience less guilt, have less difficulty coping with stressful situations, are less likely to be treated for psychological problems, and have more self-confidence and social poise (Dunn, 2002; Teti, 2002). Like firstborns, only children are likely to be high achievers, but sustained by their close relationship with their parents, they are less anxious and show more personal control, maturity, and leadership (Falbo & Polit, 1986). In social relations both inside and outside the family, only children seem to make more positive adjustments than children who are involved in sibling rivalry.

These differences in children based on birth order are not large, and we have been careful to use words such as *tendency* and *likely* to describe them because of their modest magnitude. The behaviors and personalities of first born children, later-born children, and only children overlap a great deal, and similarities between siblings are likely to outweigh differences. Nevertheless, birth order is an interesting aspect of a child's social experience and an important component of the family context.

BIRTH ORDER AND PARENT-CHILD INTERACTIONS   It is the parents, to a large extent, who determine whether firstborn children find the changes precipitated by the arrival of a sibling seriously distressing (Teti, 2002). When the new baby is born, parents typically have less interaction with their older children, and mothers become more coercive and engage in fewer playful interactions with them (Dunn, 1993; Teti, 2002), particularly if the new addition to the family is either unwanted or unplanned (Barber & East, 2009). As a result, firstborn boys especially are likely to have emotional and behavioral problems (Dunn, 1993). If mothers continue to be responsive to the needs of their older children and help them understand the feelings of their younger sibling, intense sibling rivalry is less likely (Howe & Ross, 1990). If fathers become more involved with their firstborn children after the new sibling arrives, this, too, can counter the children's feelings of displacement and jealousy. In fact, one positive effect of the birth of a second child may be that fathers get more involved in child care (Kramer & Ramsburg, 2002; Parke, 2002). Friends, too, can serve as buffers in this potentially stressful situation. In one study, researchers found that preschool children who had good friends were less upset when their lives were disrupted by the birth of a new baby than children who did not get along well with their peers (Kramer & Gottman, 1992). Moreover, the preschoolers with good friends were more accepting and behaved more positively toward their new sibling. In a 13-year follow-up of the children in this study, the researchers found that the children who had experienced rewarding friendships before the birth of their sibling had better relationships with the sibling in adolescence (Kramer & Kowal, 2005). Even having contact with other children outside the family, such as in day care, may serve as a buffer when a sibling is born. Sometimes, though, after the arrival of a second child, mothers reduce their work hours and remove their older children from child care (Baydar et al., 1997). This is a good example of Bronfenbrenner's ecological theory in practice. A change that takes place inside the family—in the family "mesosystem"—when a new sibling is born results in a change in contact with the outside world—the "exosystem"—when the older sibling stops participating in day care (Volling, 2005).

Even though brothers and sisters grow up in the same household with the same parents, they may be treated differently or at least perceive themselves to be treated differently by their parents. These differences create nonshared environments within the family that lead to different developmental consequences for the siblings. If children perceive themselves to be treated worse than their sibling, adverse effects such as heightened sibling rivalry and increased stress are common (Teti, 2002). In one study, children who perceived themselves to be less favored by their parents were more likely to experience an increase in externalizing problems (Richmond et al., 2005). In another study, the more adolescents perceived their treatment by their parents to be unfavorable compared with treatment of their siblings, the less positive they felt about themselves (Barrett Singer & Weinstein, 2000). Fortunately, most children see their parents' differential treatment as reasonable. In one study of 11- to 13-year-olds, only one quarter viewed their parents' behavior as unfair or capricious (Kowal & Kramer, 1997). The majority accepted it and understood that siblings' different ages, needs, and personal attributes accounted for the parents' behavior. Only when children didn't understand or tolerate parents' differential treatment did they view their relationships with their siblings negatively.

BIRTH ORDER AND SIBLING INTERACTIONS   Position in the family also affects how children interact with their siblings. Older sisters often act as caregivers; a firstborn girl in a large family may warm bottles, change diapers, and soothe a squalling infant with the efficiency and skill of a young mother (Edwards & Whiting, 1993). Older siblings can also serve as resources for their younger siblings in times of stress, particularly if the children do not have a supportive adult or helpful friend (Conger & Elder, 1994; Hetherington & Kelly, 2002; Teti, 2002). Sisters especially are protective in a family crisis such as a divorce (Hetherington & Clingempeel, 1992).

Older siblings also serve as teachers for their younger siblings (Watson-Gegeo & Gegeo, 1986, p. 37):

Older sister:	*Then when you're full, you just speak like this, "I don't want any more now."*
Younger brother:	*(Whining) What?*
Older sister:	*I don't want to eat any more now.*
Younger brother:	*I don't want?*
Older sister:	*Then you just speak as I said, like this, "I don't want any more now."*
Younger brother:	*I don't want.*
Older sister:	*I'm full now.*
Younger brother:	*Full now.*
Older sister:	*I'm full. I don't want to eat any more now.*
Younger brother:	*Don't want to eat any more now.*

Whereas older siblings look to parents as their main source of social learning; younger siblings use both parents and older siblings (Dunn, 1993; Pepler et al., 1982). In one study, 70 percent of younger siblings reported getting social advice from siblings, especially from older sisters (Zukow-Goldring, 2002). The style of teaching that siblings use depends on the children's ages. Preschool-age older siblings are likely to use demonstrations as they try to teach their younger sibs how to do things. School-age older siblings are more likely to use detailed verbal instruction and scaffolding (i.e., hints and explanations), especially when the younger sibling is quite young (Howe et al., 2006; Recchia et al., 2009). The children's culture affects sibling teaching. Researchers have found, for example, that school-age Mayan children teaching their younger siblings to make tortillas used demonstration and scaffolding but less verbal instruction than is common in Western cultures where formal schooling is more prevalent (Maynard, 2004). Older siblings also act as managers, supervisors, and gatekeepers who extend or limit younger siblings' opportunities to interact with other children outside the family (Edwards & Whiting, 1993; Parke et al., 2003). In these contexts, older siblings may act protective and helpful—"My older brother and sister stick up for me around the house and in the street"—or they may act dominating—"My older brother is always bossing me around and messing with my stuff" (Hadfield et al., 2006). Typically, older siblings do both. They show more nurturing behavior and more antagonistic behavior, such as hitting, kicking, and biting, toward their younger siblings compared with the younger siblings' behavior toward them (Campione-Barr & Smetana, 2010; Dunn, 1993; Teti, 2002).

But older siblings are not always a positive influence; they also can serve as deviant role models, encouraging early sexual activity, drug use, and delinquency in their younger brothers and sisters (East, 1996; East & Khoo, 2005; Garcia et al., 2000). In one study of African American youth, older siblings' willingness to use drugs when they were 12 years old predicted their younger siblings' drug use two years later (Pomery et al., 2005). This effect was especially evident when the families lived in high-risk neighborhoods where opportunities and pressures to use illicit substances were high.

Having good relationships with siblings can compensate for poor relationships with peers. In two studies, researchers found that children with poor peer relationships were buffered from adjustment problems if they had a positive relationship with a sibling (East & Rook, 1992 McElwain & Volling, 2005). The reverse was also true: Children with poor relationships with their siblings were buffered from adverse effects if they had high-quality friendships (McElwain & Volling, 2005). Only when relationships with both siblings and friends were poor did children in this study show high levels of aggressiveness and disruptive behavior (Figure 7.4).

Sibling relationships change as children grow older. When siblings reach adolescence, they become more alike, share more interests, and are less concerned about grabbing their parents' attention than when they were younger (Dunn, 2002). Sibling rivalry and ambivalence

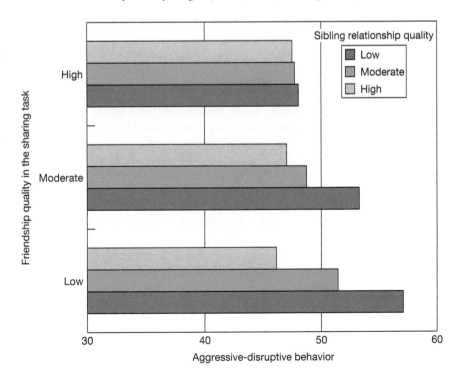

FIGURE 7.4 *Association between friendship quality and parent-reported aggressive-disruptive behavior as a function of sibling relationship quality in a sharing task.* Source: Copyright © 2010 by the American Psychological Association. Reproduced with permission. McElwain, N. L., & Volling, B. L. (2005). Preschool children's interactions with friends and older siblings: Relationship specificity and joint contributions to problem behavior. Journal of Family Psychology, 19, 486–496. *The use of APA information does not imply endorsement by APA.*

are likely to diminish and intimacy between siblings typically increases. Sibling relationships become even closer if parents are positive and accepting (Kim et al., 2007). In adolescence, siblings communicate more openly with each other about their appearance, peer relationships, social problems, and sexuality than they do with peers or parents. The quality of adolescents' sibling relationships may have long-term consequences. Men who had poor-quality relationships with their siblings in their youth were more likely to experience major depression and use more mood-altering drugs by the time they were 50 (Waldinger et al., 2007). This association may suggest that better sibling ties serve a protective function that helps children develop better mental functioning or that sibling relationships continue to be important positive resources across the life span.

The Family Unit: Stories, Rituals, and Routines

In addition to the family subsystems we have discussed, the family unit itself is an agent of socialization. Families develop distinct *climates*, which provide different socialization contexts for children (Fiese & Schwartz, 2008; McHale 2010). Storytelling, routines, and rituals are powerful methods parents and children use to create their family climate.

Stories help transmit family values and reinforce the uniqueness of the family as a unit. They teach children about their identity and often encapsulate a message about the family (Sherman, 1990). Families retell stories because this enables them all to get involved and creates a sense of familiarity (Norrick, 1997). One source of family stories is family history. Family members recount stories about their own early experiences, and these stories are handed down across generations, shaping interactions and expectations among family members. Using stories, parents can teach their children about the kinds of behavior that the family values. The following is an example of a family story told by a mother to her 4-year-old child, which underlines the grandparents' importance and kindness (Fiese & Bickham, 2004, p. 268):

> When I was a little girl I lived with my grandfather and grandmother. Grandpa had a big, comfy chair, and I would crawl up on his lap, and he would tell me stories. And one of my favorite things was to comb Grandpa's hair. One day I decided to comb his hair, but he didn't know that I had some little ponytail holders and some pins, and I put little curls all on the top of his head, and he fell asleep. And when he woke up he had the prettiest curls you ever saw all over his head, and he didn't even mind. Wasn't that nice?

Mothers who tell stories like these about their own childhoods, emphasizing themes of closeness, nurturance, and play, have been found to engage in more turn-taking and reciprocal interactions with their children; mothers who tell stories that emphasize either achievement or rejection by family members are less engaged and, when they interact with their children, are more intrusive and directive (Fiese, 1990). When parents and children jointly retell family stories, those who identify themselves as "storytelling families" and those whose stories focus on hard work and accomplishment are more satisfied and better functioning than families who are not storytellers or who tell stories focused on chaos and fear (Kellas, 2005).

routines
Day-to-day activities such as making dinner or washing the dishes.

rituals
Family activities involving formal religious observances and family celebrations.

Family routines and rituals are other important elements of socialization (Fiese, 2006; Pratt & Fiese, 2004). **Routines** are day-to-day activities that keep the family functioning such as making dinner or washing the dishes. **Rituals** involve formal religious observances, family celebrations, and rites of passage. They have a symbolic value and tend to explain "this is who we are as a family." They also provide continuity across generations. Both routines and rituals have benefits for children. Household routines are linked to better adjustment for children who live in single-parent, divorced, or remarried households (Fiese et al., 2002; Cicchetti & Toth, 2006; Luthar et al., 2000). Bedtime routines are related to better sleep habits for children (Fiese, 2006). Mealtime routines predict that children and adolescents will have higher self-esteem and fewer emotional problems and will be less likely to use drugs and alcohol (Center on Addiction and Substance Abuse (CASA), 2007; Eisenberg et al., 2004, 2008; Fiese et al., 2006; Hofferth & Sandberg, 2001).

An important question is whether family stories, routines, and rituals truly contribute to better outcomes for children or are just proxies for other aspects of good family relationships. In one study, researchers found that associations between mealtime routines and adolescents' substance use remained significant even after adjusting for family connectedness, suggesting that they do have value above and beyond family relationships (Eisenberg et al., 2008). Nevertheless, intervention studies are needed to determine whether a change in family routines would, by itself, lead to improved outcomes in children and adolescents.

Real-World Application: "Let's Have Dinner"

When you were growing up, did your family eat dinner together? This activity may be more important than you thought. Social critics bemoan the loss of family dinners in our fast-food society, and parenting experts suggest that "the family that eats together stays together" (Grant, 2001). They are preaching to the choir. More than 80 percent of parents in one study viewed family dinners as important, and 79 percent of teens considered eating family meals to be among their top-rated family activities (Zollo, 1999). Survey research suggests that a majority of children and adolescents regularly eat dinner with their families (Child Trends, 2005; Videon & Manning, 2003). However, family meals are brief, lasting, on average, only 18 to 20 minutes (Center on Addiction and Substance Abuse, 2007). Can these brief encounters benefit children? They obviously provide opportunities for family members to connect and briefly catch up on the day's events (Fiese, 2006). But what is the best way to involve children in the family dinner? How can parents make mealtimes meaningful and pleasant when children would rather be playing, watching TV, or texting? Based on extensive qualitative observations of mealtime routines and rituals, Barbara Fiese came up with some helpful guidelines to facilitate family dinners for children of different ages (Table 7.2; Fiese & Schwartz, 2008).

TABLE 7.2 The ABC's (Activities, Behaviors, Communication) of Family Mealtimes across Developmental Periods

Age (years)	Activities	Behaviors	Communication
0–1	Introduce solid foods slowly—one at a time	Have short meals of 10 to 15 minutes.	Imitate sounds that child makes. Introduce names of foods.
2–5	Turn off the television during mealtimes. In early years, introduce finger foods. In later years, have children prepare food with adult supervision.	Set a regular mealtime. Expect good manners—say please and thank you. Have mealtimes last around 15–20 minutes.	Talk about what happened in neighborhood. Talk about what happened when siblings were in school.
6–11	Turn off the television. Have child assist in preparing at least one meal per week.	Strive for five regular meals together as a family. Assign a role for each child (setting the table, clearing the table, washing dishes).	Talk about what happened in school. Tell family stories. Plan for the weekend.
12–16	Turn off the television and cell phone. Have children assist in meal planning for the week.	Set aside one meal per week when everyone is expected to be home.	Talk about current events. Explore different careers. Talk about different countries. Talk about family history.

Source: Fiese & Schwartz. Reclaiming the family table: Mealtimes and child health and well being. *Social Policy Report Volume XXII, Number IV*, © 2008. Reproduced with permission of the Society for Research in Child Development.

Family Variation: Social Class and Culture

Every family is embedded in a larger social system— termed the *macrosystem* in Bronfenbrenner's ecological theory (Bronfenbrenner & Morris, 2006). In this section, we discuss how two aspects of the macrosystem—social class and culture—affect what happens in the family.

Differences in Family Values and Practices Related to Socioeconomic Status

There is a long history of research relating parents' beliefs and practices to their social class or socioeconomic status (SES), a construct that comprises three related demographic characteristics: education, income, and occupational status. Differences in parents' use of language are especially notable (Hart & Risley, 1995; Hoff et al., 2002). Lower SES mothers talk to their children less and are not as tuned in to the children's speech as higher SES mothers are (Hoff-Ginsberg & Tardif, 1995). Mothers with lower SES tend to be more authoritarian and punitive (Hart & Risley, 1995; Kelley et al., 1993; Straus & Stewart, 1999). They are more likely to issue brusque orders and less likely to give lengthy explanations. Higher SES parents reason with their children and present choices and then subtly influence the decisions the children make (Lareau, 2003). SES differences in parents' responsiveness and use of punitive discipline have been observed in cultures throughout the world—in Europe and Israel that have high standards of living and in regions of Africa that have low standards of living (Bradley & Corwyn, 2005).

earning from Living Leaders: Vonnie C. McLoyd

Source: Courtesy of Vonnie C. McLoyd, University of Michigan.

Vonnie McLoyd is Professor of Psychology at the University of North Carolina. She received her Ph.D. from the University of Michigan and taught there for many years. She is now at the University of North Carolina–Chapel Hill. Her goal is to understand the processes that contribute to emotional and social resilience in economically disadvantaged children and adolescents. She is known for her work on the effects of

poverty on family life and child development and recently completed a project examining the behavior of children whose low-income single mothers were welfare recipients or welfare leavers. Her book, *African American Family Life,* made a major contribution to understanding of the links among economic conditions, race, and child adjustment and led to renewed debate about the effects of physical punishment on minority children and adolescents. McLoyd is committed to examining the implications of her research for both practice and policy. She served as Director of the Children in Poverty Program at the Center for Human Growth and Development at the University of Michigan, is Past President of the Society for Research on Adolescence, Associate Editor of the *American Psychologist,* a member of the MacArthur Network on the Transition to Adulthood and has received an award from the Society for Research in Child Development for her Distinguished Scientific Contributions to Child Development.

Further Reading

McLoyd, V. C., Aikens, N. L., & Burton, L. M. (2006). Childhood poverty, policy, and practice. In W. Damon & R. Lerner (Series Eds.), K. A. Renninger & I. E. Sigel (Vol. Eds.), *Handbook of child psychology: Vol. 4. Child psychology in practice* (6th ed., pp. 750–775). Hoboken, NJ: Wiley.

Cultural Patterns in Child Rearing

The culture in which the family is embedded also influences parents' socialization practices. Parents in traditional cultures are less responsive and affectionate than parents in modern, technologically advanced cultures (Bradley & Corwyn, 2005). High rates of spanking and harsh punishment are common. Yoruba parents in Nigeria, for example, believe that children's comments are not worth paying attention to; children should simply heed their wiser and more knowledgeable elders; physical punishment is imposed for what we in North America consider mere childish indiscretions. Parents in Indonesia punish their children for not showing respect to adults; in one study, only 42 percent of Indonesian parents allowed their children to express negative emotions toward adults compared with 86 percent of U.S. parents (Zevalkink, 1997).

Socialization practices also differ in individualistic and collectivistic cultures. Predominantly individualist cultures, such as the United States, Canada, and Europe, value individual autonomy and emphasize competition, self-actualization, dominance, and open expression of emotion. Collectivist cultures value interrelatedness and connectedness with the group and emphasize social harmony, cooperation, empathy, accommodation to the needs of others, and sometimes deference to authority. Although both individualistic and collectivist values are found in all societies, meta-analysis of more than 50 studies of people (mostly college students) in different cultures revealed that people in the United States and Canada are more individualistic than people in India, Hong Kong, Japan, Korea, Singapore, and Taiwan and less collectivistic than people in India, Hong Kong, Taiwan, Israel, Nigeria, Mexico, China, and Brazil (Oyserman et al., 2002).

nuclear family
Parents and their children living together.

extended family
A unit of people that includes relatives such as grandparents, aunts, uncles, nieces, and nephews as well as members of the nuclear family.

These differences are reflected in family structures and parenting styles. The spirit of collectivism in Latino culture is evident in child-rearing practices that encourage children to develop an identity embedded firmly in the context of their *familia* (Buriel et al., 2006; Parke & Buriel, 2006; Sarkisian et al., 2007). For many Latinos, the word *familia* includes not only the **nuclear family** but also the **extended family**—including grandparents, aunts, uncles, nieces, and nephews—and even goes beyond blood relatives to include fictive kin such as godparents. Because of the value of familism and respect based on age and gender, in Latino culture grandmothers are often the symbolic heads of extended families and are sought after for advice and support in child rearing (Ramos-McKay et al., 1988). It is important for Latinos to be *bien educado or* "well educated," not only in the sense of a good formal

Both nuclear and extended families are important in most Latino cultures, which emphasize sharing and cooperation in good times and bad. Source: Blend Images/ Stockphotopro, Inc.

education but also having the ability to function successfully in any interpersonal situation without being disrespectful. Children are expected to be *bien educados* in their relations with adults (Valdes, 1996). Befitting this goal, Latino parents are more authoritarian and less authoritative than European American parents (Dornbusch et al., 1987; Schumm et al., 1988; Steinberg et al., 1991).

In Asian families, parenting reflects collectivism and Confucian principles such as family unity and respect for elders. Children are taught to place family needs before their own individual desires and to show obedience and loyalty to their parents. Asian parents emphasize family cooperation and obligation. In general, they are more authoritarian, restrictive, and directive than European American parents (Chao & Tseng, 2002).

Reflecting West African traditions of spirituality, harmony, and communalism, African American families are more interdependent than European American families (Boykin & Toms, 1985; McLoyd & Ceballo, 1998; McLoyd et al., 2000). They are more likely to live near their extended kin, to interact with them frequently, and to have a strong sense of family and familial obligation; household boundaries are fluid, and there is willingness to absorb relatives (Harrison et al., 1990; Hatchett & Jackson, 1993). The extended family is particularly important because of the large number of female-headed households. Grandparents are involved in about one in three of these families (Pearson et al., 1990). Having the grandmother present increases the moral-religious emphasis in the household (Tolson & Wilson, 1990). Whether they live together or not, when the grandmother is emotionally close to the mother, child rearing goes more smoothly (Wakschlag et al., 1996). Regardless of the grandmother's role, African American parents are more authoritarian, more likely to stress obedience to adults, and more likely to impose physical discipline than European American parents are (Dodge et al., 2005; Portes et al., 1986; Steinberg et al., 1991).

Learning from Living Leaders: Raymond Buriel

Source: Courtesy of Raymond Buriel.

Raymond Buriel, Professor of Psychology and Chicano/a Studies at Pomona College, is a pioneer in the study of Latino families in the United States. Although the topic of cultural diversity is now widely recognized as important, Buriel decided that this was a worthwhile topic for study more than 30 years ago. As the son of Mexican immigrants growing up in a barrio in Southern California, he noticed differences in the family patterns of native-born and immigrant children. Children from immigrant families were more involved with their families, showed more *respeto* (respect) for their parents, and had a stronger sense of family obligation. His career has been focused on understanding how differences like these in immigrant and native-born Mexican American families affect children's development. He discovered that "biculturalism" is an adaptive strategy for immigrant families and that "deculturation" across successive generations is deleterious. As children become more acculturated to American ways and leave behind their traditions, their social lives deteriorate. Buriel's recent work has focused on cultural "brokering," in which children serve as linguistic and cultural interpreters for their immigrant parents. This is a burdensome task for children, who already face challenges of their own. Buriel's work in this area has had practical consequences. Now in California, health providers are required by law to provide professional interpreters and to translate documents for patients rather than imposing this task on their children. Buriel has won many teaching awards and is a founding member of the Latino/a Caucus of the Society for Research in Child Development. He hopes that students will write the next chapters in psychology by critically examining their own culturally related impressions of life.

Further Reading

Buriel R., Love, J. A., & De Ment, T. L. (2006). The relation of language brokering to depression and parent–child bonding among Latino adolescents. In M. H. Bornstein & L. R. Cote (Eds.), *Acculturation and parent–child relationships: Measurement and development* (pp. 249–270). Mahwah, NJ: Erlbaum.

Cultural Context:
How Effects of Parenting Vary across Cultures

At a basic level, effects of parenting are similar across cultures. Responsive and affectionate parenting is related to positive child outcomes, and hostile, rejecting parenting is related to negative outcomes (Bradley & Corwyn, 2005; Hill et al., 2003). However, significant differences occur in one area, physical punishment. Children who are physically disciplined in countries where it is common and culturally accepted are not as anxious or aggressive as children who are physically disciplined in countries where it is rare. For example, in Kenya, India, and Italy, physical punishment is the norm, and children who receive more of it do not become as aggressive or anxious as children

who are punished more in China, Thailand, and the Philippines, where physical punishment is less common (Gershoff et al., 2010; Lansford et al., 2005; Figure 7.5). Apparently, if children perceive that physical punishment is widely accepted within their cultural group, being spanked does not signify rejection or unfair treatment by their parents (Rohner et al., 1996). But if they are the only ones in their neighborhood being hit, they are more likely to act out or withdraw.

Ethnic differences in the United States parallel these differences between cultures. Harsh control—including physical punishment—is linked to higher rates of externalizing behavior problems in European American families but is unrelated to child outcomes in African

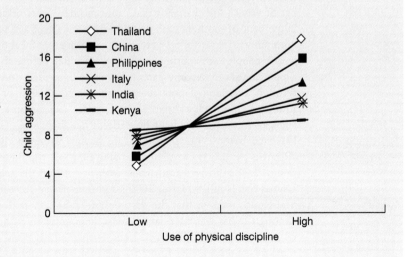

FIGURE 7.5 *Links between physical discipline and child aggression in countries where use of physical punishment is normative (Kenya, India, and Italy) or non-normative (China, Thailand, Philippines).* Source: Lansford, J. E., Chang, L., Dodge, K. A., Malone, P. S., Oburu, P. Palmerus, K., . . . Quinn, N. (2005). *Cultural normativeness as a moderator of the link between physical discipline and children's adjustment: A comparison of China, India, Italy, Kenya, Philippines, and Thailand.* Child Development, 76, 1234–1246. Reprinted with permission of Wiley-Blackwell.

American families, in which punishment is more common (Deater-Deckard et al., 1996; Slade & Wissow, 2004). It is more weakly related to child outcomes in Asian American families, in which discipline is more restrictive (Chao & Tseng, 2002).

A word of caution: Advocates of physical punishment sometimes use these findings to argue that making physical punishment more normative would reduce or eliminate its harmful effects. This argument neglects the question of whether the societal rate of physical punishment affects the societal level of violent behavior. Jennifer Lansford and Kenneth Dodge (2008) addressed this issue in a study of 186 cultures distributed across the six major regions of the world. More harsh and frequent use of physical punishment, they found, was related to more warfare, interpersonal violence, and inculcation of aggression in children. Thus, although the link between children's individual experience of punishment and aggressive behavior is weaker in cultural groups where physical punishment is normative, those groups that use more physical punishment also exhibit higher levels of violence. By making physical

punishment normative, the overall impact could be an increase in societal aggression and hostility as children internalize cultural norms and generalize them to using physical force to solve problems (Deater-Deckard et al., 2003). The net result would be higher levels of violence in cultural groups in which physical punishment of children is the norm.

Many international agencies deem the practice of physical punishment a violation of human rights and have urged nations to institute domestic bans on it (Gershoff & Bitensky, 2007). Since the beginning of 2007, Chile, Costa Rica, the Netherlands, New Zealand, Portugal, Spain, Uruguay, and Venezuela have adopted legal bans on corporal (physical) punishment of children by parents, teachers, and other caregivers, bringing the number of countries with such bans to 23 (Global Initiative to End All Corporal Punishment of Children, 2009). An additional 91 of the world's 231 countries and principalities have banned corporal punishment of children by teachers and school administrators. The United States has yet to join the nations that have banned corporal punishment.

The Changing American Family

Just as differences exist between families in different cultures, differences also exist across different historical eras. According to Bronfenbrenner's ecological theory, children and families are embedded in a "chronosystem," meaning that they are affected by changing times. U.S. families today are different from those in earlier days—even a decade or two ago—in a number of ways. One change is that more mothers are working outside the home. In 1968, only 20 percent of mothers with a child under 1 year of age were in the labor force; in 2008, this number was close to 60 percent (U.S. Bureau of Labor Statistics, 2009). Another change is that couples are waiting until they are older before they marry and have their first child. Opportunities to become parents have also expanded. Infertile couples can now have children through a variety of new reproductive technologies, or they can follow the old-fashioned route, adoption. Homosexual couples, too, can become parents, and the number of lesbian and gay parents as heads of households has increased. The number of single-parent families has risen because more women are having babies without marrying. In 1960 there were 22 births per 1,000 unmarried females; in 2002, the figure was 44 births (Children's Defense Fund, 2004). Births to unmarried women account for nearly 40 percent of babies born in the United States (CBS News, 2006). Another reason for the increased number of single-parent households today is that the divorce rate is higher. It doubled between 1960 and 1980, and although it has not risen since then, demographers estimate that 40 to 50 percent of marriages today will end in divorce and 60 percent of these divorces will involve children. One third of children in the United States will also experience the remarriage of one or both of their parents, and 62 percent of remarriages end in divorce. Thus, more parents and children are undergoing multiple marital transitions and rearrangements in family relationships. In the following sections, we look at how these changes in the family have affected parenting and child development. Although the changes have presented new opportunities, 73 percent of mothers believe that, compared to when they were children, being a mother is more difficult today (CBS News Poll, 2009).

Parental Employment and Child Development

As mothers spend more time on the job and less time in the home, family roles and patterns of functioning have changed. These changes and the stress that working mothers experience on the job influence parenting practices and children's behavior.

WORKING MOTHERS   Both working mothers and their children complain that they have too little time to spend together (Booth et al., 2002; Perry-Jenkins et al., 2000). However, there is actually little difference in how much time working mothers and nonworking mothers spend with their children or the types of activities they engage in (Gottfried et al., 2002). What mothers have done as a result of taking on employment is to reallocate their time and priorities, delegate some household work to others, increase the enrollment of their children in preschool or after-school programs, and redefine their parenting role. Fathers in families with employed mothers have also increased their parenting involvement (Pleck, 2010).

Public concern about the effects of maternal employment is decreasing. In 2003, according to the U.S. Bureau of Labor Statistics (2009), 61 percent of U.S. citizens believed that children are better off if their mother stays home; however, in 2009, only 50 percent held this view. Researchers have found that the role model provided by a working mother has a positive effect on children's perceptions of men and women. Children of working mothers have more egalitarian views of gender roles, and, in middle-class families, higher educational and occupational goals (Hoffman, 2000; Hoffman & Youngblade, 1999). These differences are likely due to the fact that working mothers model achievement of occupational goals and encourage their children to be self-sufficient and independent at earlier ages than full-time homemaker mothers do (Hoffman, 2000). Compared with homemakers' children, working mothers' daughters are more likely to see women's roles as involving freedom of choice, satisfaction, and competence; are more career oriented, independent, and assertive; and have higher self-esteem (Hoffman, 2000). Sons of working mothers not only perceive women to be more competent but also view men as warmer and more expressive. Part of the reason for this difference in perceptions of men may be that men in dual-career families participate more in family and child-rearing tasks than men with stay-at-home wives (Pleck, 2004). Note, however, that even in dual-career families, women still perform most of the child care and housework: two thirds compared with men's one third (Coltrane & Adams, 2008).

Research has not provided unequivocal answers to the question of how maternal employment affects other aspects of children' social development. Some researchers have found negative associations between maternal employment when children are very young and children's later social-emotional well-being (Han et al., 2001). However, other researchers have found no negative effects on children's attachment security (Huston & Rosenkrantz Aronson, 2005), behavior problems, or self-esteem (Harvey, 1999). In a longitudinal study from infancy to age 12, one team of researchers found no association between maternal employment and children's socioemotional development (Gottfried et al., 2002, 2006). Some researchers have even found that, for children in low-income families, maternal employment is related to fewer behavior problems (Dunifon et al., 2003). Children may be at increased risk when they reach adolescence because mothers who work encourage their children's autonomy (Zaslow et al., 2005). If thoughtfully coordinated with the children's abilities, this encouragement may facilitate independence at a developmentally appropriate time. If not, working mothers' encouragement of autonomy and lack of supervision and monitoring may press independence on adolescents too early, creating problems. Boys especially are likely to respond negatively to premature pressure for autonomy.

In general, individual differences among children and mothers appear to be more important than simply whether the mother is an employee or a homemaker. Both homemaker mothers who derive a sense of satisfaction and self-efficacy from their homemaking role and working mothers who enjoy their employment report that they have more positive relations with children than unhappy homemakers who would like to be employed (Hoffman, 2000). In evaluating the effects of maternal employment, therefore, it is important to consider all relevant factors, including the mother's reasons for working, how satisfied she is with her job, how many demands her employment places on her and her family, how positive her family is about her employment, and whether she can find good substitute care and supervision for her children while she is at work.

WORK STRESS AND CHILDREN'S ADJUSTMENT   In recent years, many workers—men and women—have experienced an increase in work hours, a decrease in job stability, a rise in temporary jobs, and, especially among low-wage workers, a decrease in relative income (Mischel et al., 1999). These factors all play into the work-family equation and increase the likelihood that parents and children will suffer. Stress at work takes a toll on children, parents, and marriages (Crouter & Bumpus, 2001). Fathers who experience work stress are less sensitive and engaged with their children and their wives (Goldberg et al., 2002; Repetti, 1989, 1996). After a particularly stressful or heavy workday, mothers, too, are likely to withdraw from their children (Repetti & Wood, 1997), and if they have negative experiences at work, are angrier and more withdrawn from their husbands (Schulz et al., 2004; Story & Repetti, 2006). The parent's work schedule can also be stressful and have negative effects on children. In one study, researchers found that children's language development was impaired if their mothers worked nonstandard schedules, including night shifts or rotating shifts (Han, 2005). In contrast, positive work experiences can enhance the quality of parents' behavior. Parents whose jobs were more satisfying and complex and offered them more independence and problem-solving opportunities were warmer, less strict, and more supportive of their children's autonomy (Greenberger et al., 1994; Grimm-Thomas & Perry-Jenkins, 1994; Grossman et al., 1988), and their children had fewer behavior problems (Cooksey et al., 1997). As Bronfenbrenner's ecological systems theory suggests, work and family contexts are inextricably linked.

Parenting after Thirty

Couples today are marrying later than they did previously (3 to 4 years later than in the 1950s) and becoming parents at older ages as well (Martin et al., 2005). Reasons for these delays include improved employment and career opportunities for women and increased flexibility in gender roles for both men and women. Couples now often want to have completed their educations and become established in their careers before they take on the responsibilities of parenthood. Birth control and social norms make it possible and popular to postpone forming a family.

Perhaps because they waited longer (and sometimes tried harder), older mothers feel more responsible about parenting, enjoy it more, and express more positive affect with their infants than younger mothers do (Ragozin et al., 1982). They spend more social time with their infants and are more successful in eliciting vocal and imitative responses from them, perhaps because, as a result of their own maturity, they have gained more social and cognitive skills. The increase in parenting competence extends only to age 30, however (Bornstein & Putnick, 2007). Perhaps by this age, women's cognitive and emotional development have reached maturity, making further shifts in parenting quality unlikely. Moreover, waiting too long increases risks of birth defects as well as increasing maternal fatigue (Mirowsky, 2002).

Older fathers have more flexibility and freedom to balance the demands of work and family than younger fathers, and they are three times more likely to have regular responsibility for some part of their children's daily care (Daniels & Weingarten, 1988). They are more involved in the parental role and experience more positive affect associated with child rearing (Cooney et al., 1993; NICHD Early Child Care Research Network, 2000). When they interact with their children, these older fathers engage in less strenuous physical play and more stimulation with talk and toys than younger fathers. This may reflect a lessening of physical energy with age, or it may be that older parents have less stereotyped views of men's "proper" role (Neville & Parke, 1997; Parke & Neville, 1995). Waiting too long to become a parent has a down side for fathers as well as mothers, though. As men age, they produce lower quality sperm that increase the risk of birth defects (Wyrobek et al., 2006). Men as well as women have ticking biological clocks.

New Reproductive Technologies

Modern reproductive technologies offer hope for couples who cannot conceive a child. Intracytoplasmic sperm injection (ICSI) was developed to circumvent problems when the man has a low sperm count, low sperm motility, or abnormally shaped sperm (Schultz & Williams, 2002). In vitro fertilization (IVF) was developed to circumvent problems when the woman's fallopian tubes are blocked. It can be used with a male donor's sperm if the man's supply of sperm is inadequate or with a female donor's egg if the woman cannot produce an egg. Alternatively, a zygote can be implanted in the uterus of a surrogate mother who then carries the baby to term. More than 50 million couples worldwide have turned to assisted reproductive technologies to overcome their infertility, and more than 1 million children have been conceived as a result (Schultz & Williams 2002). Today, more than 1 percent of births involve these new reproductive procedures (Schieve et al., 2005).

The risk of birth defects in infants conceived through ICSI or IVF is about 30 to 40 percent higher than in spontaneously conceived infants (Hansen et al., 2005). However, if they survive, these children do as well as children conceived in the usual manner in terms of their relationships with their mothers, their self-esteem, and the likelihood they will have behavioral or emotional problems (Gibson et al., 2000; Golombok, 2006; Golombok et al., 2001, 2002; Hahn & DiPietro, 2001; Patterson, 2002). In part, these children do well because of the eagerness and commitment of their parents, who made such extraordinary efforts to have them (Golombok, 2006; Golombok et al., 2004). Researchers have found that these parents tend to feel warmer and more protective toward their infants and toddlers than parents who have their children the usual way (Gibson et al., 2000; Golombok, 2006; Hahn & DiPietro, 2001).

Adoption: Another Route to Parenthood

Not every couple takes advantage of new reproductive technologies. Some couples adopt a child. They choose adoption for a variety of reasons: because they are infertile, are older and at risk for chromosomal abnormalities, want to avoid a family-related genetic disorder, or want to give an at-risk infant or a foster child a good home. In the United States, 2 to 4 percent of children are adopted (Stolley, 1993).

In general, adopted children have a higher risk of psychological problems than nonadopted children (Brodzinsky & Pinderhughes, 2002). But if adoption removes them from adverse conditions, such as long-term foster care or an institutional environment, it is better than staying in these dire circumstances (Rutter, 2002a, b). The benefits of adoption in these cases depend on the age at which the child is adopted. Children whose adoption takes them out of adverse circumstances when they are infants do better than those who remain in adversity for a longer period. Michael Rutter and his colleagues (Rutter, Kreppner, et al., 2001) found that infants from orphanages in Romania who were adopted before they were 6 months old were just as socially and emotionally well adjusted as adoptees who had not suffered early deprivation. Children who were exposed to a longer period of deprivation or experienced adverse events such as prenatal exposure to drugs, multiple placements in foster care, or physical or sexual abuse, however, could not completely rise above their early disadvantages even if they were placed in good adoptive families.

Since the 1970s, adoptive procedures have become more open and it is now quite common for birth parents, adoptive parents, and adoptees to know each other or at least know each others' identities. In spite of concerns that open adoptions would undermine adoptive families and lead to confusion and adjustment problems for adopted children, few problems have been found (Grotevant, 2007; Grotevant & McRoy, 1998). Children, birth parents, and adoptive parents all benefit from open placements. The children have fewer behavior problems; the adoptive parents have more secure relationships with the children; and the birth parents feel less depressed, guilty, and regretful (Brodzinsky & Pinderhughes, 2002; Grotevant, 2007).

Gay and Lesbian Parents

Homosexual families are created in two ways: (1) when a gay or lesbian parent leaves a heterosexual partner who is the child's biological parent and then initiates a new homosexual relationship in which the two partners together care for the child, or (2) when a gay or lesbian couple who do not have children from a previous relationship choose to become parents through adoption or donor insemination.

Research suggests that lesbian mothers who have divorced their heterosexual partners differ little from heterosexual mothers in terms of self-concept, general happiness, and overall adjustment (Patterson, 2006). We know less about divorced gay fathers because only a small minority of these men are granted custody of their children or live with them (Patterson, 2004). Most of our knowledge about gay and lesbian parenting comes from studies of homosexual couples who choose to become parents. Research comparing these families with heterosexual families finds that gay and lesbian parents tend to share household duties more equally than do heterosexual couples (Solomon et al., 2004). Nevertheless, in lesbian families, the biological mother tends to be more involved in child care and the nonbiological mother spends longer hours in paid employment. As in heterosexual families, when both partners share in the child care tasks, they are more satisfied and their children are better adjusted (Patterson, 1995).

In general, children in lesbian families develop normally. There is no evidence that they are any more likely than children in heterosexual families to have emotional or social problems, nor is there any appreciable evidence of altered gender roles (Golombok, 2006; Rivers et al., 2008; Wainright & Patterson, 2008). A large majority of children with gay fathers also grow up to be heterosexual adults. No evidence indicates that they are at a disadvantage compared with children of heterosexual fathers. Moreover, although gay fathers undoubtedly face prejudice and discrimination, their children describe their relationships with their fathers as warm and supportive (Patterson, 2004). Available evidence suggests that increased acceptance of gay and lesbian parents would benefit children reared in these households. Warm and loving parents who feel confident and comfortable about their place in society are more likely to have children who are secure, feel good about themselves, and return their parents' affection.

Parenting Alone

As we have noted, another major change in families is that more mothers are going it alone. They are having babies without a husband or they are finding themselves alone after a divorce. What are the effects of growing up in these single-mother families? In general, the children do worse on developmental measures than children in two-parent families. In a national study in Canada, Ellen Lipman and her colleagues (2002) found that 6- to 11-year-old children from single-mother families had more social and psychological problems than children from two-parent families. In a national study in the United States, researchers similarly found that preschool children in single-mother families were less securely attached to their mothers and behaved more negatively with them than children in two-parent families (Clarke-Stewart et al., 2000). But there were differences depending on the type of single-mother family. Children whose mothers had never married were less sociable and socially skilled and displayed fewer positive behaviors with their mothers than children whose mothers were single because they were separated or divorced. In a national study in Finland, differential consequences of single parenthood were also apparent even when the children were grown up: boys whose mothers who were unmarried until their sons were at least 14 years old were eight times more likely to be repeat violent offenders compared with boys who grew up in two-parent households, but if mothers became single as the result of divorce, their sons were only twice as likely to be violent offenders as boys who grew up in two-parent families (Koskinen et al., 2001). One reason for the differences among single-parent families in the United States is that the median family income of never-married mothers is only half that of divorced mothers (Bianchi, 1995; Clarke-Stewart et al., 2000). These mothers are also younger and less educated than divorced mothers and more likely to be African American. They may have more psychological problems. Stress, financial hardship, and lack of social support all contribute to poorer child outcomes in single-mother families just as they do in two-parent families (Golombok, 2000; Lipman et al., 2002).

Divorce and Remarriage

One hundred years ago, the annual divorce rate in the United States was only about one divorce for every thousand people. By 1980, the rate had climbed to just over five divorces for every thousand people. This increase was associated with a reduction in the legal and moral restrictions against divorce and a shift in the focus of family life from economic dependence to emotional fulfillment. Since 1980, the tide has turned again, and divorces have declined. Today the rate is just under four divorces per thousand people—the lowest it has been in more than 30 years. However, despite this decline, the divorce rate in the United States remains the highest of any country in the Western world.

Divorce has no single cause, but its probability rises when husbands and wives come from different ethnic backgrounds, lack the religious conviction that divorce is wrong, abuse alcohol or other substances, and have poor communication skills or mental health problems (Clarke-Stewart & Brentano, 2006). Couples are especially likely to divorce if they experience high levels of stress from having limited education, facing economic hardship, getting married at a young age, and being overwhelmed with the responsibility of having children, especially children with problems or children born before the marriage.

Divorce is not a single event. It involves a series of steps that start long before the couple separates, continue through the pain of separation and the difficulty of setting up two separate households, and reverberate through often lengthy legal proceedings. Although a divorce may eventually prove to be a positive solution to a destructive family situation, for most family members the period following the separation is very stressful. During the first year after the divorce, parents' feelings of distress and unhappiness increase, relationships between parents and children become more troubled, and children's social and emotional well-being usually worsens (Hetherington & Stanley-Hagen, 2002). In the second year, when families are adapting to their new status, many parents experience an improvement in their sense of personal well-being, interpersonal functioning, and family relations. In the long run, children in stable, well-functioning single-parent households are better off than children in conflict-ridden intact two-parent families. This does not mean that the path is easy or that divorce is beneficial for all children, however.

EFFECTS OF DIVORCE ON CHILDREN   Researchers have found that on average children from divorced families have more behavioral and emotional problems than children from two-parent families. They are more aggressive, noncompliant, and antisocial, less prosocial, have lower self-esteem, and experience more problems in their peer relationships (Amato,

2001; Clarke-Stewart & Brentano, 2006; Hetherington, 2006; Hetherington et al., 1998). In addition, children in divorced families have less positive relationships with their fathers, especially when divorce occurs in early childhood and especially when the child is a girl (Amato, 2006). After divorce, fathers are less likely to maintain contact with their daughters than their sons (Manning & Smock, 2006).

These differences between children in divorced and intact families are not large. A meta-analysis of studies comparing children in divorced and intact families showed that for psychological adjustment (depression and anxiety), the effect size was .31 and for conduct problems (aggression and misbehavior), it was .33 (Amato, 2001). This means that, on average, children with divorced parents scored about one third of a standard deviation lower than children with continuously married parents on assessments of psychological well-being and good behavior. Researchers have also found that compared with children from intact families, children from divorced families are about twice as likely to skip school or be suspended, to get into trouble with the police, to become pregnant as teenagers, to be unemployed in their late teens and early twenties, and to experience clinical levels of distress and depression (Clarke-Stewart & Brentano, 2006; Zill et al., 1993; Hanson, 1999). About one third of the children in divorced families have behavior problems or unwanted teen pregnancies and about one fourth have adjustment problems or poor social relationships, compared with only one tenth to one seventh of children from intact families (Hetherington & Kelly, 2002; McLanahan, 1999; Wolchik et al., 2002). Although divorce effects are not large, they have a stronger effect on children's problem behavior and psychological stress than do race, birth order, illness, death of a family member, or parents' low education. In fact, the link is larger than the link between smoking and cancer. The effects can be long lasting, too: The Terman longitudinal study in California showed that adults who experienced their parents' divorce died at younger ages than adults whose parents stayed married (Friedman et al., 1995).

Learning from Living Leaders: E. Mavis Hetherington

Source: University of Virginia.

Mavis Hetherington, Professor Emerita of Psychology at the University of Virginia, really wanted to write fiction. She took psychology courses only to help her with characterization. Lucky for the field of social development she did! Over the course of her career as a scientist and teacher she has produced important contributions to social development, earning her numerous awards from the American Psychological Association, the Association for Psychological Science, and the Society for Research in Child Development. Her major goal was to understand how families affect children's functioning. In pursuing this goal, she was influenced by an article exploring the bidirectionality of influences between parent and child, an idea that became a central theme in her research. During her 50-year career, she investigated reciprocal family influences, the effects of father absence on children's development, and the effects of divorce and remarriage on adults' and children's lives. In her popular book *For Better or for Worse*, she shared the results of her research with a broad audience and offered advice on how to ease the pain of divorce. Although Hetherington is primarily known for her work on divorce, remarriage and stepparenting, she has also been a major contributor to the integration of genetics into developmental psychology, helping to document the interplay between genetic factors and family environments in shaping parenting and children's social outcomes. Following her own example, she advises the next generation of students to "pick a topic that you are passionate about and remember that research is not just hard work but fun too."

Further Reading

Hetherington, E. M., & Kelly, J. (2002). *For better or for worse.* New York: Norton.

WHO IS AFFECTED MOST?   Not everyone is affected equally by parents' divorce. The age of the child when the parents separate makes a difference. It is often assumed that if parents separate when their children are either very young or all grown up, the effect of the divorce will be minor. Effects may indeed be less severe for these two age groups, but researchers have found that divorce can affect children at all ages. Infants from divorced families are more likely than those in intact families to be insecure and disorganized in their attachments to their mothers and fathers (Solomon & George, 1999) and less positive and engaged in play with their parents (Clarke-Stewart et al., 2000). Children who are a few years older when their parents divorce are likely to be confused, fearful, and anxious and may regress to more immature forms of behavior (Clarke-Stewart & Brentano, 2006). As one college student recalls (Clarke-Stewart & Brentano, 2005, p. 111):

> *I was four years old when my parents divorced, and I felt confused and bewildered. I started sucking my thumb and withdrew from activities with other children. I was very fearful about being abandoned by my mother, and I did not understand why I was being forced to see my father. I felt I did not know him and was angry at him without understanding the reason. I remember only feeling really "safe" in my mother's presence. She was the only person I could trust.*

School-age children understand the concepts of "divorce" and "separation" better than younger children, but they, too, are usually shocked, worried, and sad when they find out that their parents are separating. Six- to 8-year-olds are particularly upset about the loss of their father and they experience anxiety and depression. At 8 to 10, children are more likely to get angry—about the divorce, about moving away from their friends, about their parents' suffering, and about custody problems, such as living in two homes. Many children of this age ruminate about the divorce: One study found that 40 percent of these children spent time thinking about the divorce at least once a day—even a year afterward (Weyer & Sandler, 1998). Many children at this age suffer psychosomatic stress symptoms—headaches, vomiting, dizziness, sleep problems, and inability to concentrate (Bergman et al., 1987). As one college student who was in fifth grade when her parents split up recalled (Clarke-Stewart & Brentano, 2005, p. 115):

> *My parents' separation was the most devastating event in my life. I remember getting sick after I was informed of my parents' plans. I was sick for a week; all I did was sleep and vomit.*

With adolescence comes increased awareness and understanding of the parents' problems, but adolescents still tend to see things from their own perspective: "How could you do this *to me?*" They are more likely than their peers in intact families to engage in risky behaviors involving sex, drugs, and alcohol, and, in turn, to get into trouble at school or with the law (Kirby, 2002). They may feel abandoned, anxious, and depressed. They may contemplate suicide (Simons et al., 1999).

A number of studies have suggested that divorce is worse for boys than for girls. In a study by Hetherington (1989), for example, preschool boys from divorced families were more likely than preschool girls to behave aggressively and immaturely. Boys might have more problems than girls for a number of reasons: boys are physiologically more vulnerable to stress than girls; parents and teachers are stricter with boys' outbursts; boys in divorced families usually lose their male role model because they live with their mother; and boys get less emotional support from their overstressed parents, who find that their noisy, physical, and oppositional behavior makes them more exhausting and difficult to parent. Gender differences are not always observed, however. Meta-analyses reveal that boys are not more adversely affected in terms of psychological adjustment (Amato, 2001). However, boys from divorced families have significantly poorer social adjustment compared with girls from divorced families: They have more problems with popularity, loneliness, cooperativeness, and parent-child relations. Several large-scale studies have found that boys from divorced families also have more behavior problems than girls including shoplifting, damaging property, being picked up by police, and going to court (Morrison & Cherlin, 1995; Mott et al., 1997; Simons et al., 1996).

It has been suggested that boys and girls are both affected by divorce but they express it in different ways: Boys are more likely to externalize their distress and girls to internalize it. There is some support for this idea. In letters written to their parents by children in divorce-adjustment groups, boys' themes were more angry; girls' were more anxious (Bonkowski et al., 1985). Boys also are more likely than girls to have fights with their divorced mothers (Brach et al., 2000), and in adulthood, young women from divorced families have more long-term anxiety, depression and relationship difficulties (Dixon et al., 1998; Feng et al., 1999; McCabe, 1997; Rodgers et al., 1997). Another suggestion that has some support is that girls suffer more before the divorce and boys after it. In one study, adolescent girls showed negative effects prior to separation whereas boys showed them after the divorce (Doherty & Needle, 1991), and in a simulation of parents fighting, boys were more likely to exhibit aggression after the fight; girls were more likely to be distressed during it (Cummings et al., 1985). A third suggestion is that the reaction to parental divorce is stronger for boys at younger ages and for girls in adolescence. Supporting this suggestion, researchers have found that adolescent daughters of divorced parents show increases in antisocial behavior, emotional disturbances, and conflicts with their mothers; they may be sexually active, get pregnant, and get married (Hetherington, 1998; 2006). In later years, they are more likely than women whose parents did not divorce to have relationship problems and to find themselves, like their parents before them, in divorce court (Amato, 2006; Hetherington, 2006). Boys do not show these effects in adolescence and adulthood.

Perhaps more important than gender, however, are individual qualities that help children adjust to their parents' divorce. Children who are psychologically healthy, happy, and confident adapt to the new challenges and stressful experiences brought on by the divorce more easily than children with psychological problems before the divorce (Tschann et al., 1990). In fact, they may even gain from the experience and become better at social problem solving (Hetherington, 1989, 1991). High intelligence helps buffer children from the negative effects of divorce (Hetherington, 1989; Katz & Gottman, 1997). Having an easy temperament also helps children recover from their parents' divorce. Children adjust better to divorce if they have a more optimistic, constructive, and realistic outlook. These children have fewer psychological problems in childhood (Guidubaldi et al., 1987; Mazur et al., 1999), and, as young adults, are more secure in their romantic relationships (Walker & Ehrenberg, 1998).

DIVORCE AND THE SINGLE-PARENT HOUSEHOLD How do we account for these effects of divorce on children? Of the many explanations, one of the most important is that children of divorce are growing up in single-parent households, which are at increased risk for multiple stresses that make child rearing difficult. In fact, a period of diminished parenting often follows divorce (Hetherington & Stanley-Hagan, 2002). Mothers themselves are suffering from the divorce and therefore are likely to be self-involved, erratic, and inconsistent in dealing with their children. They often fail to control and monitor their children's behavior adequately. Children reciprocate in the immediate aftermath of divorce by becoming

Divorced mothers often have difficulty managing their sons without the backup of the father's discipline. Source: Stockbyte/Getty Images, Inc.

more demanding, noncompliant, and aggressive or by whining and being overly dependent. Divorced mothers and sons are particularly likely to engage in escalating, mutually coercive exchanges.

Children also suffer because they have lost the home and lifestyle to which they were accustomed. Their family income has dropped, and their mothers often have trouble making ends meet. Some children are forced to take on more household responsibilities after the divorce, which leads to resentment and rebellion. Children find the adjustment to divorce easier if they experience fewer stressors, such as burdensome household chores, responsibility for younger siblings, moving to a new town, and repeated trips to court (Clarke-Stewart & Brentano, 2006).

Although parenting improves markedly in the second year after divorce, problematic parenting is more likely to be sustained with sons—especially temperamentally difficult sons. Divorced mothers and daughters are likely eventually to form close relationships, although mothers may have to weather their daughters' acting out in adolescence (Hetherington & Clingempeel, 1992; Hetherington & Kelly, 2002). When divorced mothers manage to be warm and consistent in their discipline, their children—of both genders—have fewer adjustment problems (Wolchik et al., 2000). Authoritative parenting is associated with more positive adjustment of children in divorced families, just as it is in intact families. If divorce reduces stress and conflict and leads to better functioning of parents, children tend to benefit in the long run.

Another key to the well-being of children in divorced families is the children's relationship with their nonresidential parent, most often their father. As long as the two divorced parents can agree on child-rearing methods and maintain a cordial relationship, frequent visits with the nonresidential parent are linked to more positive adjustment in children (Dunn et al., 2004; Fabricius et al., 2010). These visits are particularly helpful for sons. They are especially important if they allow the nonresidential parent to maintain a parental role by supervising homework, making meals, celebrating holidays, and so on rather than just becoming a casual adult pal. When conflict between parents continues, however, especially if it makes the child feel caught in the middle, frequent contact with the nonresidential parent is associated with problematic behavior by the child (Buchanan et al., 1992; Buchanan & Heiges, 2001). Frequent contact is also bad if the father has a history of antisocial acts such as stealing and fighting (DeGarmo, 2010). Clearly, what benefits children is having positive contact with the nonresidential parent in the absence of conflict, stress, and antisocial behavior.

sole custody
A form of postdivorce child custody in which the child is exclusively with either the mother or the father.

joint physical custody
A form of postdivorce child custody in which parents make decisions together regarding their child's life and also share physical custody so that the child lives with each parent for about half the time.

joint legal custody
A form of postdivorce child custody in which both parents retain and share responsibility for decisions regarding the child's life, although the child usually resides with one parent.

DOES CUSTODY MATTER? Does it matter whether children are in sole custody with their mother or their father or in joint custody with both parents? Most children today are placed in sole custody with their mother. Mothers obtain primary physical custody in close to 80 percent of cases and fathers in about 10 percent; joint physical custody is awarded in only about 4 percent of divorces (Argys et al., 2006; Logan et al., 2003). But is mother custody always the best arrangement? Researchers have found that father custody is advantageous for children's self-esteem, anxiety, depression, and behavior problems (Clarke-Stewart & Hayward, 1996). Custodial fathers have higher incomes than custodial mothers and are more likely to have emotional support from family and friends. Moreover, when children are in father custody, mothers are more likely to stay involved with them than fathers are when children are in mother custody. Thus, children in father custody have the advantage of continued close ties with both parents. In a national study of 1400 adolescents ages 12 to 16 years only one third in mother custody maintained a positive relationship with their father, whereas more than half of those in father custody maintained a close relationship with their mother (Peterson & Zill, 1986). This does not mean that courts should automatically place all children with their fathers, however. Fathers who *seek* custody are more emotionally invested in their children and more effective parents than fathers who do not seek custody. Moreover, in one study, even though children in father custody were found to do better than children in mother custody *on average*, they were not better adjusted than children in mother custody who also had high levels of contact with their fathers (Clarke-Stewart & Hayward, 1996).

If contact with both parents is important for children's adjustment after divorce, is the solution, then, joint custody? In a joint legal custody arrangement, both mother and father share the responsibility for decisions concerning their children's lives, but the children may reside with only one of the parents. In a joint physical custody arrangement the children live with each parent for close to half the time and have physical access to both mother and father on a regular basis. This arrangement may give children a sense of security and lessen their sense of abandonment by one parent. According to a meta-analysis of 33 studies, children in joint physical or legal custody were better adjusted than children in sole custody; they showed fewer behavior problems and emotional difficulties and had higher self-esteem and better family relationships (Bauserman, 2002). However, many factors can undermine the success of joint custody. If parents have dramatically different lifestyles, contradictory values, or poor communication skills, if they cannot set aside their conflicts, or if they want to move to different areas, joint custody is challenging and tends to be unstable. If children are very young, if parents use them as pawns in their battles, or if joint custody is court ordered against the parents' will, the results for children are likely to be negative (Clarke-Stewart & Brentano, 2006). Joint custody works best when the conflict between parents is minimal and children don't feel caught in the middle. Even with cooperating parents, children can feel torn by joint custody. Here is one student's experience of being shuttled back and forth between Dad's house and Mom's house every day (Clarke-Stewart & Brentano, 2005, p. 203):

> It was 4:30 a.m. when Daddy cracked open the door and picked me up from my warm bed to carry me to the cold van. Then it was my sister's turn. He would lay each of us down in the bed he had made for us in the back of the van. Then he would make one last trip into the house to get our overnight bags full of clothes, homework, and, once a month, a child support check for Mom. At 5:00 a.m. we would arrive at Mom's house. Then Daddy would once again put each of us over his shoulder and carry us in. My sister and I would try to go back to sleep until 6:30 a.m., when it was

time to get up for school. Mom packed our lunches and drove us to school. Then Daddy would be back to pick us up when he got off work at 3:30. We would have dinner with him, finish our homework, pack our bags, go to bed, and then the routine would be repeated. This happened five days a week, from the time I was six until I was fourteen. On the weekend, we would spend one and a half days with Mom and one and a half days with Dad.... The only positive thing about this custody arrangement was that I knew I had two parents who really cared about me. Otherwise, everything was extra difficult because it had to be divided—where we went for holidays, who we sat beside at school banquets, where we had our birthday parties.... The stress was terrible because I was always thinking about how I was going to divide myself.

Joint custody is clearly not a panacea for divorced families, and there are many ways to make it unworkable. In the long run, its advantage may be its symbolic value to parents and children. It offers a sign to fathers that they retain their rights and obligations as parents and conveys to children the message that both their parents love them and that their fathers are still important.

REMARRIAGE   About three quarters of divorced people remarry (Kreider & Fields, 2001). For divorced women, remarriage is the surest route out of poverty, and a new partner can provide emotional support and help in child rearing. However, remarriage is not a guarantee of happiness or a fix for children's problems. Children in stepfamilies have more emotional problems than children in intact families or even divorced families (Clarke-Stewart & Brentano, 2006; Cherlin & Furstenberg, 1994; Hetherington et al., 1998; Pryor, 2008). More antagonistic relationships among siblings, especially brothers, are also found in stepfamilies compared with intact families (Conger & Conger, 1996; Dunn & Davies, 2000; Hetherington et al., 1998). These differences are not permanent, however (Amato, 1994). Although the majority of stepchildren exhibit problems during the transition period immediately following remarriage, most show considerable resilience, and three quarters have no long-term problems (Hetherington & Jodl, 1994). Younger children adjust more easily; teens have a difficult time accepting their parent's remarriage and are at greater risk for externalizing problems such as using alcohol, becoming delinquent, and having early sexual intercourse. They also report more conflict with their stepparents than adolescents in intact families have with their parents (Hetherington, 1991; Hetherington & Stanley-Hagen, 2002). This is not surprising because stepparents are less nurturing and affectionate with their stepchildren than biological parents are with theirs (Clarke-Stewart & Brentano, 2006; Pryor, 2008).

Chapter Summary

- Families are social units in which adult spouses or partners and their children share economic, social, and emotional rights and responsibilities as well as a sense of commitment and identification with each other. Families are also systems for socialization, which means that family members channel children's impulses into socially accepted outlets and teach children the skills and rules they need to function in society.

The Family System

- The family is a complex system involving interdependent members and subsystems whose functioning may be altered by changes in the behavior or relationships of other members. The functioning of the couple system, parent-child system, and sibling system are interrelated and influence children's social well-being.

- The couple subsystem is often regarded as the basis of good family functioning. Increased parent-child involvement and positive parent-child relationships have been found when spouses are mutually supportive.

- Conflict between the parents, which can affect children directly or indirectly, is associated with negative feelings and behaviors directed toward the children and with problems in children's social development. Particularly when conflicts are unresolved, children are likely to react with negative emotions. The effects of conflict are reciprocal, with children and parents influencing each other over time.

- Children have an impact on the couple relationship. The birth of the first child is associated with a shift toward more traditional masculine and feminine roles. Both mothers and fathers report declines in marital satisfaction following the birth, but fathers are slower to express the decline. Temperamentally difficult or handicapped children may be enough to destroy an already fragile marriage.

- Although socialization begins when an infant is born, it becomes more deliberate as children develop. Parents teach social rules directly and serve as models whom the child may imitate.

- Parents' relationships with their children can be categorized along the dimensions of emotion and control.

- Authoritative parenting, involving warmth and consistency and firm control, leads to the most positive social and emotional development in children. Authoritarian parenting (low warmth and high control) leads to conflicted and irritable children.

- Many factors influence the use of these parenting styles including the couple's relationship, the parents' mental health, and the children's temperaments and behavior.

- During socialization, children and parents influence each other in mutually interlocking interactions that are best described as transactional.

- Fathers and mothers make unique contributions to their children's development by their distinctive interactive styles: Mothers are more verbal, fathers more physical.

- A cooperative coparenting system can contribute to positive social development; competitive or imbalanced coparenting can lead to poor social outcomes.

- The number, gender, and spacing of the children affect a family's functioning. As family size increases, parents and children have less opportunity for extensive contact, but siblings experience more contact with each other.

- Firstborn children often show emotional and behavioral problems after the birth of a sibling, but the mother's reaction, efforts to include the firstborn, and the father's involvement moderate this. Firstborns are more adult oriented, helpful, self-controlled, conforming, and anxious than later-born siblings.

- Families share stories, routines, and rituals that transmit values, teach family roles, and reinforce the family's uniqueness.

Family Variation: Social Class and Culture

- Each family is embedded in a larger social system termed the *macrosystem* in Bronfenbrenner's ecological theory.

- Parents with lower SES tend to be more authoritarian; those with higher SES reason with their children and present more choices.

- Parents' socialization practices are influenced by their culture, their workplace experiences, and their neighborhood.

The Changing American Family

- Effects of maternal employment depend on the mother's reason for working, her satisfaction with her role, the attitudes of and demands placed on other family members, and the quality of substitute care provided for the children. Work-related stress for working parents can negatively affect couples and children.
- People are becoming parents later today than in the past. Later parenthood has some positive aspects, for example, parents may be better established in careers and be more flexible about family roles.
- New reproductive technologies offer hope for couples who cannot conceive a child. Although the risk of birth defects in infants conceived through these methods is higher than natural conception, the children do not have abnormal levels of psychological problems.
- Adoption can protect infants and children by removing them from adverse rearing environments. Adopted children are at risk for psychological problems, but age, gender, and prior living conditions determine the level of risk.
- Gay and lesbian parents are becoming increasingly common. Evidence suggests that children in these families develop normally.
- Parenting alone is also becoming more common. In general, children do more poorly if their single mothers are younger, poorer, and never married.
- In the first year following divorce, children tend to be disturbed, but in the long run, most are able to adapt to their parents' divorce. Family interactions immediately following divorce are characterized by inept parenting and distressed, demanding, noncompliant children.
- Children of different ages vary in their understanding of divorce and reactions to it. Effects are more negative for preadolescent sons and adolescent daughters. Children who have an easy temperament and other psychological resources adapt to divorce more easily than children with psychological problems before the divorce.
- Most children reside with the mother after divorce, although contact with both parents is valuable for children's adjustment. Joint custody works best when conflict between parents is minimal and children don't feel caught in the middle.
- Children's responses to remarriage vary depending on their previous family experience and their age when the remarriage occurs. It is particularly difficult for adolescents.

Key Terms

authoritarian parenting	**joint legal custody**	**routines**
authoritative parenting	**joint physical custody**	**socialization**
coparenting	**nuclear family**	**sole custody**
extended family	**permissive parenting**	**uninvolved parenting**
family system	**rituals**	

At the Movies

Every cinema multiplex every weekend shows movies that offer insights into family life. Moviemakers often produce films based on their own family experiences, and viewing these movies can be educational, nostalgic, or even therapeutic. Among movies illustrating positive and supportive family relationships, *Crooklyn* (1994), Spike Lee's semiautobiographical labor of love about his African American family, depicts how parents committed to their children stand by them and care what happens to them even though they sometimes become frustrated and angry. *Grace Is Gone* (2007) investigates a father's sensitivity and love as he struggles to tell his daughters the devastating news that their mother has died on the battlefield in Iraq. A film providing an excellent illustration of ethnic differences in family practices is *What's Cooking?* (2000), which portrays how Thanksgiving is celebrated in four households—Vietnamese, Jewish, African American, and Mexican American. The film illuminates the particular tensions experienced in families from different ethnic groups. Movies about children going through divorce also address family tensions. *Children of Love* (2002) portrays three children of divorced parents dealing with issues of loyalty and love. This is a touching story about the emotional experiences of broken families. *The Squid and the Whale* (2005) presents an emotionally honest story of two teenage boys dealing with their parents' divorce. Based on the screenwriter's childhood experiences, the movie captures the pain and confusion that lurk beneath the boys' anger and bluster, provides a clear picture of the pros and cons of family transitions, and illustrates how well-intentioned parents affect their adolescents in profound ways. *Kramer vs. Kramer* (1979) depicts a husband who learns how to be a nurturing father after his wife walks out on him. This movie marked the beginning of a social movement in the 1980s that led to reform of child custody laws so that gender-specific preferences for custodial parents were replaced with the standard of selecting the "best psychological parent." A humorous take on the issue of how postdivorce visitation limitations can interfere with relations between children and their noncustodial parents is *Mrs. Doubtfire* (1993). Working mothers provide another popular movie theme. In the fictional movie *The 24-Hour Woman* (1999), Grace slowly goes crazy trying to be both superproducer and a supermom. In the more sober documentary *Double Burden: Three Generations of Working Mothers* (1992), three single working mothers struggle to put clothing on their children's backs and food on the table. A number of movies about gay and lesbian families are also available and enlightening; an example is *Making Grace* (2004), which shows how two women create a family and confront the challenges and joys of motherhood including those unique to lesbians.

CHAPTER 8

Peers: The Wider World of Social Development

Source: Jani Bryson/iStockphoto.

When Sarah was 1 year old, she got 2-year-old Anna's attention by tugging on her arm and vocalizing at her loudly. When Sarah was 3, she asked Anna to play and imitated her behavior, following her around and copying whatever she did. When Sarah was 8, Anna was more interested in hanging out with the other girls in her class at school, and Sarah was inconsolable as her repeated attempts to play with Anna were rejected. When they were in middle school, both girls found themselves acting in the school play, and they became best friends forever. The difference in their ages no longer mattered, and they felt close because they shared a history of play dates, church activities, and neighborhood events, and a strong interest in musical theatre and books about vampires. These examples illustrate some of the ways children interact with each other and develop friendships as they grow up. These interactions and relationships are the focus of this chapter.

Children's relationships with peers differ from their relationships with adults. Peer relationships are briefer, freer, and more equal. They are more likely to involve shared positive emotions and conflicts (Gerrits et al., 2005). They offer children opportunities for new types of interpersonal exploration, facilitate the growth of social competence, and open the way for children to form associations outside the family. They offer children a cultural community of their own in which they share behavioral patterns and practices (Howes & Lee, 2006). In this chapter, we describe children's interactions with peers and how these interactions change as children grow. We examine the special roles peers play in children's socialization. We also consider the many factors that affect children's acceptance by peers and explore the effects of peer rejection. We look at the ways adults can promote children's acceptance by peers, discuss the ways children develop friendships, and describe children's behavior in peer groups.

Definitions and Distinctions

Several definitions and distinctions are important to understand the research on children's peer interactions and relationships. First is the distinction between a peer and a friend. A *peer* is another child of roughly the same age; a *friend* is a peer with whom the child has a special relationship. Peers are part of the child's social world. They populate the school classroom, the neighborhood, and after-school clubs. They interact with the child during the course of daily routines, sharing information about tasks, engaging in conversations, and playing together on the playground. These interactions with peers are often short, do not involve strong commitments, and are limited to a specific context such as the classroom or the playground. They may be one sided because they do not necessarily involve reciprocal liking or mutual respect. From these interactions, children develop close relationships with a small number of peers. These are their friends. Friends interact on a regular and sustained basis, develop expectations about future interactions, and engage in reciprocal actions such as sharing stories and secrets and supporting one another. Dyadic relationships with friends are characterized by reciprocal liking and, thus, differ from relationships with other peers.

A second distinction in peer research is between dyads and groups of children. The interactions between peers and friends that we have described relate to *dyads,* or pairs of children. Children also form groups of peers with defined boundaries and social organization. These groups include cliques, teams, and crowds. Groups develop their own norms, rules, and hierarchies, which regulate the activities of the group members. Interactions with peers, friendships with peers, and groups of peers all represent different forms of peer ties and serve different functions in children's social development.

Developmental Patterns of Peer Interaction

For many years, psychologists ignored or denied the possibility that very young children are capable of having social interactions with each other. Data collected over the last three decades, however, clearly prove that children are active social partners from a very early age. Table 8.1 summarizes changes in peer interactions and relationships with age.

First Encounters in Infancy

In the first 6 months of life, babies touch and look at each other and are responsive to each other's behaviors. But these early behaviors can't be considered truly social in the sense that an infant seeks and expects a response from another baby. It is not until the second half of the first year that infants begin to recognize a peer as a social partner (Brownell, 1990; Howes, 1987). Between 6 and 12 months infants start trying to interact with other infants by vocalizing, waving, and

TABLE 8.1   The Child's Development of Peer Interactions and Friendships

0–6 months	Touches and looks at another infant and cries in response to the other's crying
6–12 months	Tries to influence another baby by looking, touching, vocalizing, or waving
	Interacts with other infants in a generally friendly way but may sometimes hit or push
1–2 years	Begins to adopt complementary behavior such as taking turns, exchanging roles
	Engages in more social play throughout the period
	Begins to engage in imaginative play
2–3 years	In play and other social interaction, begins to communicate meaning; for example, invites another child to play or signals that it's time to switch roles
	Begins to prefer peers to adult companions
	Begins to engage in complex cooperative and dramatic play
	Starts to prefer same gender playmates
4–5 years	Shares more with peers
	Has goal to maximize excitement and enjoyment through play
	Begins to sustain longer play sequences
	Is more willing to accept roles other than protagonist
6–7 years	Reaches a peak in imaginative play
	Shows stable preference for same-gender playmates
	Main friendship goal is coordinated and successful play
7–9 years	Expects friends to share activities, offer help, be physically available
	Seeks to be included by peers and avoid rejection
9–11 years	Expects to be accepted and admired by friends
	Expects friend to be loyal and committed to the relationship
	Is likely to build friendships on the basis of earlier interactions
	Main friendship goal is to be accepted by same-gender peers
11–13 years	Expects genuineness, intimacy, self-disclosure, common interests, and similar attitudes and values in friends
13–17 years	Important friendship goal is understanding of the self
	Begins to have romantic relationships
17 years	Expects friends to provide emotional support
	Romantic relationships provide both intimacy and support

These are age approximations; individual children vary greatly in the ages at which developmental changes occur. Sources: Collins et al., 2009; Hartup, 1996; Rubin, Bukowski, et al., 2006.

touching. Although they sometimes hit and push each other, often these babies' social behavior is friendly (Hay et al., 2000; Rubin, Bukowski, et al., 2006). Here is an example of two babies interacting (Mueller & Lucas, 1975, p. 241):

> Larry sits on the floor and Bernie turns and looks toward him.
> Bernie waves his hand and says "da," still looking at Larry.
> Bernie repeats the vocalization three more times before Larry laughs.
> Bernie vocalizes again and Larry laughs again.
> The same sequence of Bernie saying "da" and Larry laughing is repeated twelve more times before Bernie turns away and walks off.

Social exchanges between infants are noticeably different from those with adults (Rubin, Bukowski, et al., 2006). They are shorter and less sustained because infants are less reliably responsive than adults. They are also more equal because adults usually take the lead in maintaining interactions with infants.

Social Exchanges between Toddlers

Between the ages of 1 and 2, children make gains in locomotion and language, and this increases the complexity of their social exchanges (Dunn, 2005; Rubin, Bukowski, et al., 2006). They develop the ability to engage in complementary social interactions (Howes,

These babies have a clear interest in each other and can interact in simple ways.
Source: Jani Bryson/iStockphoto.

1987). That is, they can take turns and reverse roles in their play, alternating between "hider" and "seeker," for example. They also begin to imitate each other and show awareness that they're being imitated (Eckerman, 1993). When they have positive social interactions, they're more likely to smile or laugh than they did when they were infants (Mueller & Brenner, 1977). Their interactions also last longer (Ross & Conant, 1992). As they grow older, children increasingly prefer to interact with peers rather than adults (Eckerman et al., 1975).

But can infants interact with more than one other child at a time? Children of this age often spend time in groups—in Mommy-and-Me playgroups or in child care centers. So how do they interact when more than one other child is present? Researchers studying 2-year-olds in groups of three children discovered that although sometimes play consisted of two children playing while the third just watched, more than half of the time all three children participated actively and directed vocalizations, gestures, and movements toward each of the other two children in quite complex social exchanges (Ishikawa & Hay, 2006).

pretend play
Make-believe activity in which objects are used symbolically.

In the late toddler period (2 to 3 years), children's main social achievement is sharing meaning with a partner (Mueller, 1989). Children suggest a particular activity by looking at their partner and then running to a tricycle or a set of Legos. They give a signal to switch roles by saying "My turn!" and tugging on a doll. They communicate that they both share knowledge by smiling at each other as the doll changes hands. This sharing of meaning makes it possible for children to play a wider range of games and engage in **pretend play** together (Howes, 1987).

associative play
Interaction in which young children share toys, materials, and sometimes conversation, but are not engaged in a joint project.

Peer Play in Early Childhood

cooperative play
Interaction in which children share goals and work together to achieve them.

Eighty years ago Mildred Parten (1932) described the ways children play together in early childhood and the categories she identified are still used today. Table 8.2 summarizes the types of peer play Parten observed among 3- to 5-year-olds. Children of this age may engage in any of these different types of play, depending on the circumstances, but as they get older, they are increasingly likely to play together in the more complex and social ways reflected in **associative play** and **cooperative play** and decreasingly likely to simply watch or play alongside each other in **parallel play**. Negative exchanges and conflicts also increase over the preschool years (Rubin, Bukowski, et al., 2006). In fact, social play and conflicts seem to go together. Young children who frequently initiate conflicts with peers are also the most sociable and the most likely to initiate peer interactions (Brown & Brownell, 1990).

parallel play
Interaction in which very young children are doing the same thing, often side by side, but are not engaged with each other.

TABLE 8.2 **Types of Play in Preschool-age Children**

Onlooker behavior

Children watch or converse with other children engaged in play activities. About half of 2-year-olds engage in this type of play.

Parallel play

Children play in similar activities, often side by side, but do not engage one another. This type of play is common in 2-year-olds but diminishes by the time a child is 3 or 4.

Associative play

Children play with other children but do not necessarily share the same goals. They share toys and materials and may even react to or comment on another child's ongoing activities (e.g., sharing paints or remarking on another child's art work). However, they are still not fully engaged with each other in a joint project. This type of play is commonly seen in 3- and 4-year-olds, less often in 2-year-olds.

Cooperative play

At ages 3 to 4, children begin to engage in play in which they cooperate, reciprocate, and share common goals. Some examples of cooperative play are building a sand castle, drawing a picture together, and playing a fantasy game in which characters interact with each other.

Source: Parten, 1932.

Pretend play seems to be particularly important in the development of social competence in early childhood. It permits children to experience the roles and feelings of others in a playful context, and it teaches them to function as part of a social group and coordinate their activities with other children. Pretend play first appears about halfway through the second year, usually with mother or an older sibling, but as children develop social skills and have more opportunities to meet other children, peers become the most common pretend-play partners (Dunn, 1988; Haight & Miller, 1993). By age 3, children's pretend play is quite complex, cooperative, and dramatic. By this age, children can share symbolic meanings in their pretend play (Fein, 1989), and this ability increases as they grow (Goncu, 1993). As a result, 4-year-olds have longer play sequences and can negotiate roles, rules, and themes of pretend play more easily than 3-year-olds. When they are 3, all children want to be Batman, but as 4-year-olds, they are willing to accept the lesser role of Robin, recognizing that their turn as Batman will come later. The pretend play of 5-year-olds includes slow-motion fistfights and gun battles and prolonged, staggering death scenes with broad and exaggerated gestures. It includes dressing up and acting out complex rituals such as getting married or being rescued by a prince. Pretend play peaks when children are about 6 years old. By this time, it involves highly coordinated fantasies, rapid transitions between multiple roles, and unique transformations of objects and situations (MacDonald, 1993; Power, 2000). Although pretend play is common in Westernized countries (Smetana, 2002), in many collectivist, group-oriented cultures, such as Kenya, Mexico, and India, and among Bedouin Arabs, children rarely engage in this kind of play (Ariel & Sever, 1980; Edwards, 2000).

Peer Society in the School Years

After children start school, they continue to increase their social interactions with other children and decrease their social interactions with adults. In one study, researchers found that from 1 to 12 years of age, children spent progressively more time with child companions and fewer hours with adults (Ellis et al., 1981; see Figure 8.1). The nature of peer interactions shifts during this period as well. Physical aggression toward peers decreases and generosity and helpfulness increase (Eisenberg et al., 2006). The hallmark of the school years is concern about being accepted by peers and fitting in with classmates.

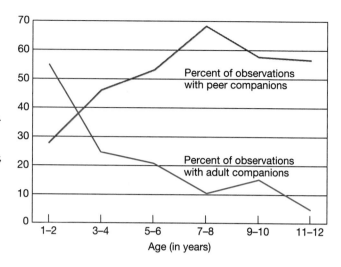

FIGURE 8.1 *At about the age of 2½, children begin to spend more social time with other children as companions and less social time with adult companions.* Source: Copyright © 2010 by the American Psychological Association. Reproduced with permission. Ellis, S., Rogoff, B., & Cromer, C., *Age segregation in children's social interactions.* Developmental Psychology, 17, 399–407. The use of APA information does not imply endorsement by APA.

THE IMPORTANCE OF THE PEER'S AGE The type of peers children choose to spend time with also changes over the school years. The age of the peer becomes a more important factor, and companionship with same-age peers increases. Children's preference for age mates serves a special role in social development because these peers share interests and abilities (Maccoby, 1998). In Western societies, age segregation in classrooms and on sports teams facilitates this trend. In many other cultures, however, older children play with younger ones as well as caring for and teaching them (Zukow-Goldring, 2002).

THE IMPORTANCE OF THE PEER'S GENDER Gender also matters in children's choice of play companions. Up to age 3 or 4, children are equally likely to choose same-gender or other-gender companions for play. Up to age 7, they are willing to play with a peer of the opposite sex. But over the course of elementary school, both boys and girls increasingly choose playmates of the same gender and exclude children of the other gender (Maccoby, 1998). The gender-exclusivity rule has exceptions, of course, but they often operate underground. For example, a girl and boy may spend time together at church or in the neighborhood, but they keep their friendship a secret from their classmates (Gottman, 1986; Thorne, 1986). They don't want to be teased or taunted at school.

Gender segregation is obvious at school as boys and girls play different games and use different equipment (Blatchford et al., 2003; Leaper, 1994, p. 29):

Jake and Danny are playing on the big swing, and Laura runs up, calling excitedly, "Can I get on?" "No!" says Jake emphatically, "We don't want you on here. We only want boys on here. . . . We like to have boys."

Children segregate themselves into gender-specific groups because of their different interests and play styles even in first grade (Silvern, 1995, p. 3):

"Girls like to talk about girl things" says Katrina . . . [while] Mike and his crowd are readying their plastic spoons to flip raisins, and David is concentrating on blowing enough bubbles to move his chocolate milk from the carton onto the table.

Researchers have documented the differences in boys' and girls' play styles. Girls tend to play quiet games, in small groups, near school buildings, and close to adult supervision (Thorne, 1986). They are inclined to prefer play involving artistic endeavors, books, or dolls. They like unstructured activities, such as talking and walking (Savin-Williams, 1987). They are more intimate and exchange more information than boys (Fabes et al., 2003; Lansford & Parker, 1999; Zarbatany et al., 2000). Boys tend to play high-energy, run-and-chase games in large groups that take up nearly 10 times as much space as girls' play (Thorne, 1986). Noise and boisterousness often characterize boys' play. Boys are more competitive in their play than girls are, and, as they become older, boys tend to prefer organized games controlled by rules (DiPietro, 1981; Eisenberg et al., 1982; Maccoby, 1998). Even the nature of pretend play differs: Boys are more likely to enact superhero roles whereas girls portray mommies and princesses (Haight & Miller, 1993). It's no surprise, then, that children want to play with children of their own gender—play may not go so well when Superman swoops in to save an unwilling damsel in distress or boys race through a quiet circle of girls playing with Barbie dolls.

Both boys and girls are more competitive in groups than in dyads, but the difference is more marked for boys (Benenson et al., 2001). Boys are particularly active and forceful when the group includes only boys. In a mixed-gender group, boys become less boisterous and girls more so because children adjust their behavior to fit the style of play that is preferred by their other-sex playmates (Fabes et al., 2003). It is important not to exaggerate gender differences in play styles, however. Both boys and girls participate in both cooperative and competitive activities, and the play behaviors of boys and girls have many similarities (Underwood, 2004).

Peer Interactions in Adolescence

High school students spend nearly 30 percent of their waking hours with peers during a typical week not including the time they spend together in class. This is twice as much as they spend with parents and other adults (13%). This pattern of involvement with peers is particularly salient in Western cultures (Brown, 2004). Researchers have found that, on average, 12th graders in the United States spend 2½ hours each day talking with a peer—more than twice as much as students in Korea and Japan (Larson & Verma, 1999). Moreover, in contrast to younger ages, peer interaction in adolescence is under relatively limited adult guidance and scrutiny.

When they are with their peers, adolescents are usually engaged in recreation and conversation (Larson & Richards, 1994; Larson & Verma, 1999), and in these activities they pick up ideas about how they should act. Peers offer the perspective of equals who share abilities, goals, and problems. They are experts in what's cool and happening, and they influence teens' styles of interpersonal behavior, selection of friends, and choice of fashion and entertainment. Peers have a stronger influence on whether teens use alcohol, tobacco, and illegal drugs, especially marijuana, than parents do (M. Allen et al., 2003). Peer influence is especially significant if adolescents lack parental support. Adolescents whose parents are warm, supportive, and authoritative are less susceptible to peer pressure than adolescents whose parents do not have these qualities (Steinberg, 1986). It also helps if the parents of adolescents' *friends* are authoritative. In one study, adolescents whose friends described their parents as authoritative were less likely to use drugs and run afoul of the law than adolescents whose friends described their parents as authoritarian (Fletcher et al., 1995). This association was significant even when researchers statistically controlled for the influence of the adolescents' own parents.

In adolescence, gender segregation in peer activities breaks down a bit as dating begins (Brown & Klute, 2006; Richards et al., 1998), and peer groups with shared interests in sports, school, and other activities are used as a means of exploring and enhancing self-identities (Brown & Klute, 2006). We explore adolescents' romantic relationships and peer groups later in this chapter.

Peers as Socializers

In childhood and adolescence, peers are important socializers who influence children's values and behaviors just as parents do.

MODELING BEHAVIOR   Peers influence each other by acting as social models. Children learn a great deal about how to behave simply by observing the actions of their peers. Even 2-year-olds imitate each other and so are able to sustain an interaction and learn more sophisticated forms of play, such as tossing a ball back and forth (Eckerman, 1993). Older children learn about social rules by watching their peers. On the first day at a new school, for instance, a child might learn that students stand when the teacher enters the room, that it is risky to shoot spitballs, and that the big redheaded kid should be avoided because he's a bully. By imitating their peers, especially the ones who don't get in trouble, children learn class rules and develop social skills that help them get along with their new classmates. In adolescence, young people copy peer models as they decide what to wear, how much to eat, when to start smoking, whether to join a gang, and if they should skip school (Dishion et al., 2001). Peers' influence can be positive or negative. Given a choice, children are most likely to imitate peers who are older, more powerful, and more prestigious (Bandura, 1989).

REINFORCING AND PUNISHING BEHAVIOR Peers also influence each other in more deliberate ways. As the term *peer pressure* implies, peers not only model behaviors but also actively try to convince other children to engage in them. They tell children how to behave and reinforce them with praise and positive reactions for behaviors they approve of or punish them with criticism and negative reactions for behaviors they dislike. Peers are increasingly likely to reinforce each other as they get older (Charlesworth & Hartup, 1967).

Researchers have documented how peers' positive reinforcement in the form of approval affects children's social behavior. In one case study, they examined the effects of peer praise on the social involvement of three socially withdrawn girls (Moroz & Jones, 2002). Teachers rewarded the girls' classmates for publicly praising the girls' social behavior during brief, daily sessions, and the effects of the peers' praise were observed during recess. After the experimental manipulation, all three girls behaved more sociably; they participated more in group activities and were more engaged with peers. Researchers have also observed effects of peers' negative actions on other children's behavior. For example, they have seen that children play less with toys regarded as being for the opposite gender after they have been criticized by their peers for doing so (Lamb et al., 1980). Similarly, when adolescents are greeted with peers' jeers for their choice of clothing or their taste in friends, they are likely to adjust their dress code or change their companions. Perhaps most obvious and most often documented by researchers is the effect of peer pressure to engage in antisocial behaviors (Sullivan, 2006). Peer pressure in this case includes modeling the antisocial behavior, encouraging friends to do it too, reinforcing them by hanging out together when they engage in the antisocial behavior, and criticizing or dropping peers who don't get with the program.

social comparison
The process by which people evaluate their own abilities, values, and other qualities by comparing themselves with others, usually their peers.

SOCIAL COMPARISON A third way that peers influence each other is by providing standards against which children measure themselves. Children have few objective ways to rate their own characteristics, abilities, and actions, and so they turn to other people, particularly peers. Through a process of **social comparison**, they watch and evaluate their peers and then use what they've learned to evaluate themselves. Social comparison helps children define who they are and determine how well they think they "stack up" against their peers. Such comparison plays a major role in determining self-esteem (Harter, 2006). If children think that they are as good as their peers, their self-esteem is high, but if they see themselves as falling short, their self-esteem suffers. Comparing themselves with their peers is adaptive. If a boy wants to know how good a fighter he is, it's better if he thinks about how well he's done in neighborhood scuffles and how tough his peers think he is rather than comparing himself with professional boxers. If a girl wants to evaluate her reading ability, she is better off comparing herself with other children in her class rather than judging herself by how well her older sister reads. As a basis for self-definition, the peer group is unequaled. Children use social comparison with their peers as a way to evaluate themselves with increasing frequency in the early years of elementary school (Harter, 2006), and, once begun, this process never really stops.

Cultural Context:
Peer Roles and Relationships in Different Cultures

Peers' roles vary in different cultures. Compared with U.S. youths, adolescents in Japan spend less time with peers, and their parents' values play a more prominent role (Rothbaum, Pott, et al., 2000). Latino children, similarly, are more family oriented and less influenced by peers (DeRosier & Kupersmidt, 1991). Their parents often directly discourage peer interactions (Ladd, 2005; Schneider, 2000). Even styles of relating to peers vary across cultures. Italian children are more likely than Canadian children to embrace debates and disputes with their friends, and, perhaps as a result of their tolerance for conflict, their friendships are more stable (Casiglia et al., 1998). Children in China, India, and Korea are more cooperative and compliant with their peers than are children in Canada and the United States (Farver et al., 1995). In one study, for example, researchers found that 85 percent of Chinese 5-year-olds' interactions with peers were cooperative and considerate, whereas 78 percent of Canadian children's interactions involved conflicts from simple disagreements to aggressive attacks (Orlick et al., 1990). Differences between ethnic groups in the United States parallel these differences between cultures. Korean American preschoolers use more polite requests and statements of agreement and less frequently tell their peer partners what to do or refuse their peer's suggestions than do European American children (Farver et al., 1995; Farver & Shin, 1997). This difference is related to the different ways that Asian and American cultures view the relative importance of individuals and groups (Chen & French, 2008). In individual-oriented societies, a person's identity is determined largely by personal accomplishments, whereas in group-oriented collectivistic societies, identity is related to membership in a larger group (Schneider, 2000; Schneider et al., 1997). Children's peer relationships reflect these cultural orientations.

Another difference reflected in peer relationships is the particular types of social behavior that the culture values. In traditional Chinese culture shyness and sensitivity are valued in children and are believed to reflect accomplishment, maturity, and understanding (X. Chen et al., 2006; Chen, Chen et al., 2009). Not surprisingly, then, Chinese children accept peers who have these characteristics, whereas Canadian children tend to reject them (Chen & Tse, 2008; Chen et al., 1992). Among older children and adolescents, even in China, shy and sensitive peers tend to be rejected (Chen & Rubin, 1994; Chen et al., 2005), in part because of the expectation that as children grow up, they must become more assertive. Historical shifts in China are changing children's social values, however. Although Chinese children of elementary school age accepted peers' shyness in 1990, they did not do so in 2002 (Chen et al., 2005). Perhaps the shift toward a market-oriented economy in China with its focus on assertiveness and self-direction is responsible for this change. In rural areas of China, shyness is still associated with better social and psychological adjustment in children (Chen & Wang, 2006; Chen, Wang et al., 2009). This will likely change as economic transformation expands to these areas. Clearly, in our efforts to understand peer relationships, we need to consider both cultural and historical contexts.

Peer Status

sociometric technique
A procedure for determining a child's status within her or his peer group; each child in the group either nominates others whom she or he likes best and least or rates each child in the group for desirability as a companion.

Peers are important because they give children a sense of acceptance or status in the world outside the family. In this section, we discuss psychologists' studies of children's peer status. We examine the ways their peers' views of them affect children, and we consider how we can promote children's acceptance by peers.

Studying Peer Status: Acceptance and Rejection

The most common way to study children's peer status is with sociometric techniques. These techniques measure peer acceptance and rejection by assessing how much children like or dislike each another (Hymel et al., 2010). In the "nominations" sociometric technique,

popular children
Youngsters who are liked by many peers and disliked by very few.

average children
Youngsters who have some friends but who are not as well liked as popular children.

neglected children
Youngsters who are often socially isolated and, although they are not necessarily disliked, have few friends.

controversial children
Youngsters who are liked by many peers but also disliked by many.

rejected children
Youngsters who are disliked by many peers and liked by very few.

perceived popularity
Ratings of how well a child is liked by his or her peers, made by teachers, parents, and children.

researchers ask each child to name a number of peers (usually three) whom they like most in their class and the same number of peers whom they like least (Coie et al., 1982). The researcher then sums the scores of most-liked and least-liked nominations for each child. **Popular children** are those who receive the largest number of most-liked nominations and the fewest least-liked ones. **Average children** receive some of both types of nomination but not as many most-liked nominations as popular children. **Neglected children** receive few most-liked and few least-liked votes; they are not necessarily disliked by their classmates; they are isolated and friendless. **Controversial children** receive a large number of most-liked nominations and a large number of least-liked nominations. **Rejected children** receive many least-liked nominations and few most-liked nominations. Because children are asked to name peers whom they don't like, ethical concerns have been raised that using this technique will cause further social problems for disliked children. However, evidence suggests that, if administered carefully, with efforts to prevent negative consequences, the nominations technique does not pose significant risks (Hymel et al., 2002; Mayeux et al., 2007).

The nominations approach has the advantage of being quick and easy to administer. However, by limiting the number of choices, researchers miss information about how children feel toward most of their classmates. An alternative approach is to use a "roster-and-rating" sociometric procedure (Parker & Asher, 1993). Children are given a list of all their classmates and asked to rate on 5-point scales how much they like to play with each of them, work with them, and so on. Each child's level of acceptance is then determined from his or her average rating. Both of these sociometric approaches are useful. Nominations are helpful for questions concerning children's most extreme likes and dislikes; rating-scale assessments are better for finding out how each child feels about everyone else in the group. Rating-scale measures of acceptance are also better for detecting changes in acceptance when interventions are carried out to help children with peer relations problems (Asher et al., 1996).

This prom king and queen exemplify popularity as both preference and prominence, having been elected to their positions by their classmates and recognized as school leaders.
Source: © Media Bakery.

A third method for assessing peer status is gathering information about children's **perceived popularity**. Teachers, parents, peers, and children themselves can be asked to rate individual children's level of popularity. In childhood, perceived popularity is quite strongly related to popularity assessed with sociometric techniques; in adolescence, these associations are weak because for youth, popularity is a construct that involves social prominence—visibility and recognition—rather than simple preference—liking or disliking (Closson, 2009).

Factors That Affect Peer Acceptance

Children's status as popular, rejected, or neglected depends on their behavior and their cognitive and social skills. It also depends on superficial factors, such as the child's name and physical appearance.

BEHAVIORS THAT MAKE A DIFFERENCE
Researchers have investigated how children's peer status is related to their behavior. Two types of popular children have been identified. The majority of popular children are friendly toward their peers and well liked by them. They are assertive but not disruptive or aggressive. When they join a play group, they do

it smoothly so that the ongoing action continues without interruption (Black & Hazen, 1990; Newcomb et al., 1993). They are good at communication, help set the rules for the group, and engage in more prosocial behavior than less popular children. A small number of children and adolescents who are perceived to be popular, however, display a mix of positive and negative behaviors (Closson, 2009; Hawley, 2003a; LaFontana & Cillessen, 2009). These *popular-aggressive* kids are athletic, arrogant, and aggressive but at the same time are viewed as "cool" and attractive. They wield high levels of social influence even though their actions are often manipulative rather than prosocial (Cillessen & Mayeux, 2004; Cillessen & Rose, 2005; Rodkin et al., 2000). Their classmates imitate their styles of dress and taste in music and want to be friends with them so that they can be part of the in-group. Even school bullies may enjoy this kind of popularity, although their peers may avoid them for fear of becoming their next victim (Juvonen et al., 2003). The popular-aggressive phenomenon illustrates the adaptive value of aggression; for these individuals, aggression provides a route to power and influence (Hawley et al., 2007). However, it is also a risk. Adolescents who are high in perceived popularity—typically popular-aggressive kids—show increased alcohol use and sexual activity over the years of high school (Mayeux et al., 2008).

aggressive-rejected children
Youngsters who are not accepted by their peers because of their low level of self-control and high level of aggression.

nonaggressive-rejected children
Excluded youngsters who tend to be anxious, withdrawn, and socially unskilled.

There are also two types of rejected children. **Aggressive-rejected children** have poor self-control and exhibit frequent aggression and behavior problems (French, 1990; Parkhurst & Asher, 1992). **Nonaggressive-rejected children** are anxious, withdrawn, and socially unskilled (Crick & Ladd, 1993; Gazelle & Ladd, 2003; Oh et al., 2008). Social withdrawal is one of the strongest correlates of peer rejection in middle childhood and adolescence (Deater-Deckard, 2001; Newcomb et al., 1993) and appears in other cultures, such as India, as well (Prakash & Coplan, 2007).

Neglected children, whose peers ignore them but do not necessarily reject them, are shy, quiet, and less aggressive than other children (Ladd, 2005). Two types of children are neglected. *Socially reticent* children watch others from afar, remain unoccupied in social company, and hover near but do not engage in interaction. *Unsociable* or *socially uninterested* children are not anxious or fearful but simply refrain from social interaction because they prefer to play alone (Rubin et al., 2009).

BIOLOGICAL PREDISPOSITIONS Underlying these behaviors that affect peer status are biological predispositions evident in children's temperaments. Children who are likely to be rejected by their peers because they are disruptive, aggressive, and hyperactive are temperamentally active, outgoing, impulsive, and unfocused: that is, their temperaments are characterized by high extraversion-surgency (Berdan et al., 2008) and poor effortful control (Ormel et al., 2005; Valiente et al., 2003). Children who are likely to be rejected or neglected by their peers because they are withdrawn are temperamentally unsociable: they are less likely to smile and gaze during interactions with their mothers in early infancy (Gerhold et al., 2002) and have low extraversion-surgency in early childhood (Ormel et al., 2005). Children who are likely to be popular because their interactions with peers are frequent and competent have temperaments that are neither inhibited nor impulsive (Corapci, 2008).

As in other areas of development, temperament interacts with experience to predict peer status. Children are more likely to be rejected by their peers if they are exposed to high levels of conflict between their parents *and* have a temperament that is low in effortful control (David & Murphy, 2007). They are more likely to become socially withdrawn if their mothers are negative *and* they have a shy temperament (Hane et al., 2008). Evidence that peer status has biological underpinnings has also been shown in studies of children's hormone levels (lower levels of trait cortisol are associated with poor-quality peer relationships; Booth et al., 2008) and heart rate (better regulation of heart rate is related to higher peer status; Graziano et al., 2007).

SOCIAL-COGNITIVE SKILLS Children are more likely to be accepted by their peers if they have the social knowledge and skill to ask new acquaintances for information ("Where do you live?"), offer information ("My favorite sport is basketball"), or invite other children to join them in an activity ("Wanna help me build this fort?") (Putallaz & Gottman, 1981). These children are comfortable in new social situations and want to interact with other children, feel confident that they have something useful to contribute, and act interested in learning what others in the group are like. Children who have a better understanding of other people's mental states and more awareness of their emotions and motives are less likely to be anxious and withdrawn or aggressive and disruptive than children who lack this knowledge (Hoglund et al., 2008). Children who lack social skills and hover silently on the outskirts of the group or make aggressive or inappropriate remarks are behind from the beginning.

Approaching a new social situation is similar to solving a cognitive problem. Children approaching a group of peers need to understand the others' communications clearly, interpret their behavior accurately, formulate their own goals and strategies based on these interpretations, make useful decisions about how to act, communicate clearly to others, and try out and then evaluate their own social strategies. This is quite a tall order, especially for a young child, and some children are better at it than others. To examine the interplay of these skills, Kenneth Dodge devised a model of social information processing, which we presented in Chapter 1, Figure 1.3 (Crick & Dodge, 1994; Dodge, 1986). This model stresses the cognitive steps in evaluating social situations. As children progress through the steps in the model, they make decisions or take actions that are accurate or inaccurate, helpful or unhelpful. Here are two hypothetical examples of what might happen when a child encounters a social situation:

> Joni, 7 years old and quite socially competent, sees two girls playing a board game. She notices that one of the girls smiles at her in a friendly way (step 1, encodes cues). She thinks that the girl would like her to play (step 2, interprets cues), and decides that she, too, wants to play with the two girls (step 3, clarifies goals). She reviews possible actions to accomplish her goal—smile back, ask to join in, just stand there—and considers how the girls might react to each possible choice (step 4, reviews actions/responses). Joni decides to make a friendly comment about the girls' game (step 5, decides). Just then the smiling girl looks up again, and Joni smiles back and says, "Looks like fun" (step 6, acts). The girls invite her to play the next game.

> Jamie, a 6-year-old boy who is less socially competent, sees two boys playing, but because he's looking at their sneakers he misses the friendly look one boy gives him (step 1, fails to encode the social cue). Jamie decides that the boys are unfriendly (step 2, incorrectly interprets cues) and wonders what he might do. He thinks of some things he could say—ask the boys why they don't ask him to play, call them mean and ugly—and fails to consider how they might react (step 3, fails to clarify goal; step 4, fails to review possible acts and responses). Jamie decides on the latter approach (step 5, decides) and blurts out, "You two are really selfish not to let me play!" (step 6, acts). It's no great surprise that the boys ignore him, and eventually he moves off.

Using this model, Dodge compared 5- to 7-year-old children who were rated as being either socially competent or socially incompetent by their teachers and peers (Dodge, 1986). The children were shown a videotape of situations similar to the ones Joni and Jamie encountered in which a child is trying to join the play of two other children, and asked what they would do in each of five of the steps in the model (step 3 was omitted in this study). The researchers found that socially incompetent children were less likely to notice and interpret the cues correctly, generated fewer competent responses, and chose less appropriate responses. The researchers then asked the children to participate in an actual peer-group entry situation with two children from their class. Children who understood what to do when they viewed the videotape were better at the real task of gaining entry into the peer group. In a related study conducted by these researchers, 8- to 10-year-olds were asked how they would respond to a peer's provocation (e.g., knocking over a block tower in an ambiguous way so the child couldn't tell if it was accidental or not). Children who were rated by their teachers or peers as being particularly aggressive showed more deficits at each step of the social information-processing model and responded in less competent ways when another child actually provoked them. These studies provide clear evidence that cognitive skills used to process social information are involved in children's interactions with peers.

Deficits in social understanding can lead to maladaptive behavior, poor interactions, and reduced peer acceptance. However, the opposite is also true: Peer rejection can lead to deficits in social information processing (Gifford-Smith & Rabiner, 2004). Dodge and his colleagues (2003) found that children who were rejected by their peers in kindergarten became less competent in social information processing by grades 2 and 3. The relations between information processing and peer interactions are reciprocal.

ARE CHILDREN ALWAYS REFLECTIVE?   Although the social information-processing model has clear strengths, it does not explain all social interactions with peers. Children do not always respond reflectively and thoughtfully; sometimes their behavior is impulsive or automatic. They make many social decisions outside conscious awareness. They may think that they are aware of their decisions, but, in fact, assessment of brain activity suggests that the decision-making sequence has already been completed while the child is still thinking about what to do (Klaczynski, 2005). As children are exposed to social situations, they develop a set of "social habits" that they employ when they encounter similar situations. This automaticity of social behavior has its advantages. It permits a quick response, saves time and cognitive energy that would otherwise be used deliberating among alternatives, and makes for a more efficient social life. At the same time, it can lead to problems, especially if assumptions about the new situation are not correct—for example, if a boy responds aggressively to a perceived slight by a peer because he assumes the peer is a bully, even though the peer did not intend to cause harm. In such situations, children assume that negative or ambiguous behaviors directed toward them are intentionally hostile and respond without deliberation (Cates et al., 1996; Fite et al., 2008; Gifford-Smith & Rabiner, 2004); their responses have become so scripted and routinized that conscious reflection plays little part in their behavior.

The step-by-step social information-processing approach may be a better model for encounters in new or ambiguous situations than in familiar situations or with well-known peers. Researchers have found that when children respond quickly, they are more likely to rely on habitual behaviors than when they are given plenty of time to consider their responses (Rabiner et al., 1990). The social information-processing model may also be more suitable for explaining the reactions of children who are by temperament more reflective, rational, and deliberative and less useful for impulsive children (Dodge & Pettit, 2003). Because children's cognitive assessments and behavioral responses in social situations are influenced by their feelings as well as their thoughts, emotions should also be incorporated into the social information-processing model (Burks et al., 1999; Lemerise & Arsenio, 2000).

CHILDREN'S GOALS IN SOCIAL INTERACTIONS   Children's goals affect their strategies in social situations, and this, too, is related to their peer status (Asher et al., 2008). Children who want to create or maintain social relationships are likely to use prosocial strategies and to be accepted by their peers; children whose goal is to dominate others may choose coercive strategies and be rejected. Researchers have asked children how they would respond in hypothetical social situations, such as, "Your family has moved to a new town and this is your first day at a new school. Recess starts, and the children go out to play. *What would you like to do?*" High-status, popular children offer positive goals and strategies. For example, they say they would like to make friends with the children in the schoolyard and they would ask the children to play. They describe outgoing and sociable behaviors to achieve this goal. In contrast, low-status, rejected children are more likely to describe hostile goals and strategies and to say that they would try to avoid the situation—for instance, "I'd probably just go play outside by myself." Socially withdrawn children pursue low-cost social goals and use indirect strategies to initiate social interactions, for example, asking "Could you look at this?" rather than coming out and saying "Can I play with you?"

Learning from Living Leaders: Steven R. Asher

Source: Courtesy of Steven R. Asher.

Steven Asher is Professor of Psychology and Neuroscience at Duke University (http://fds.duke.edu/db/aas/pn/faculty/asher). He went to college at Rutgers University thinking he would major in history and become a lawyer, but he became a psychology major after he was inspired by his introductory psychology class. When a faculty member suggested that he go to graduate school, his reaction was, "What's that?" He knew about law schools but nothing about Ph.D. programs. Soon, though, he found out, and went to the University of Wisconsin where he received his degree under the mentorship of Ross Parke, the coauthor of this textbook. After graduation, Asher established himself as an expert on children's peer relationships. He developed a number of innovative methods for assessing children's loneliness, friendship quality, and sociometric standing, and he

showed that children with low sociometric status and few peer friendships suffer serious social-emotional consequences. He also advocated and designed social skills training programs to help improve the lives of rejected and neglected children. He realized how special friends are even in young children's lives when he overheard his son Matt, then 4 years old, talking to his best friend Jessica (a year older): "Jessica, if you and I had been born the same day we could play together every day until we die." Matt spoke these words with great tenderness and a sense of regret that their different ages had deprived them of a full year of time together! According to Asher, anyone who watches children closely will be struck by the emotional power of their friendships. He believes that the most pressing issue today is to find out what skills children need to be successful in friendships. Asher is co-editor of *The Development of Children's Friendships* and *Peer Rejection in Childhood* and has written many articles about children's peer relations. He is a Fellow of the American Psychological Association, the Association for Psychological Science, and the American Educational Research Association and has served on the Governing Council of the Society for Research in Child Development. He has this message for students: "There aren't many courses that have the potential to enrich your life as a parent, a friend, a mentor, and a caring and scientifically minded citizen. This is one of those courses. So dig in, have fun with the course, and ask the tough questions that will help you, your classmates, and your teacher to grow."

Further Reading

Asher, S. R., & Paquette, J. A. (2003). Loneliness and peer relations in childhood. *Current Directions in Psychological Science, 12,* 75–78.

PHYSICAL APPEARANCE   Another factor that influences children's peer status is how they look. When adults meet for the first time at a party or a bar, they base their initial appraisals on superficial physical characteristics. Children do this too. Even newborns, when they are shown photos of unfamiliar faces that have been judged by adults to be "attractive" or "unattractive," look more at the attractive ones (Langlois et al., 2000; Slater et al., 2000). Three-year olds show the same preference, choosing attractive faces over unattractive ones (Langlois, 1986).

Adults also tend to attribute positive qualities to individuals who are physically attractive, and children do this as well (Langlois & Stephan, 1981; Langlois et al., 2000). Children expect to find characteristics such as friendliness, fearlessness, and willingness to share in good-looking peers and expect unattractive children to be aggressive, antisocial, and mean. Have these expectations any basis in reality? Judith Langlois and her colleagues (2000) reported research that indeed confirms these expectations and even suggests that attractiveness may be more important than we thought. In a number of studies, even people who knew them well judged attractive children more positively than unattractive children. They were rated higher on social appeal, interpersonal competence, and psychological adjustment. Objective observers also found them to be better adjusted. The attractive children were also more popular (Langlois et al., 2000). This link between attractiveness and popularity has been confirmed in other studies as well. When African American children in grades 4 and 7 were asked what makes a boy or girl popular, physical appearance was one of the characteristics they mentioned most often (Xie et al., 2006). In another study, children and adolescents described obese peers as less attractive and rated them as less liked (Zeller et al., 2008).

BLENDING IN   Another factor that affects peer status is children's ability to blend in. Children who look or act "odd" are unlikely to be popular; children with disruptive or hyperactive behavior are likely to be rejected (Mrug et al., 2009; Pedersen et al., 2007). Some researchers argue that the reason peers reject socially withdrawn children is that they don't fit in; their demeanor runs contrary to age-specific norms and expectations for social interaction (Rubin, Bukowski, et al., 2006, Rubin et al., 2009). Atypical behavior becomes more salient to the peer group as children get older, which may explain why the association between social withdrawal and peer rejection increases with age (Ladd, 2006).

Even unusual names sometimes mean being "odd person out." Children learn very quickly which names are popular and thus "acceptable" or "desirable." As a result, they're more likely to be friendly to a peer with a name that's familiar, such as Michelle or Michael, Jennifer or Jason, than to a child with a name that's currently out of favor, such as Horace or Myrtle (Rubin, Bukowski, et al., 2006). They like children with gender-typical names rather than names that are usually given to the opposite sex; pity the boys named Ashley, Alexis, Courtney, and Shelby (Figlio, 2007). They also prefer peers who play in what other children consider acceptable ways. When children violate gender-role patterns, they are not so popular. Classmates criticized preschool boys who played with dolls rather than trucks, for example, five to six times more often than children who conformed (Fagot, 1985a). High school students who were nonconventional in their appearance and mannerisms were less accepted by their peers than those who conformed to social conventions (Horn, 2007).

Wearing the "right" clothes also makes a difference. In one study, 8- to 12-year-olds in Britain said that children who wore name-brand athletic shoes would be more popular and able to fit in with their peers better than children wearing generic athletic shoes (Elliott & Leonard, 2004). They also claimed that they would prefer to talk to these children.

Children from a majority ethnic group are more popular too; they blend in because they are similar to most of their classmates. In a study of 7th graders in Indonesia, for example, boys in the two majority ethnic groups (Sundanese and Javanese) were less lonely than boys in minority groups (Eisenberg et al., 2009). In a study of U.S. children in child care, similarly, children who lacked peers with a shared ethnic heritage struggled with peer interactions (Howes et al., 2008).

Consequences of Peer Rejection

Children have many unpleasant ways of expressing their dislike of their peers. "Dork!" "Fag!" "Fatty!" In one study of children in grades 3 through 6, children were creative and cruel in the ways they rejected disliked peers (Asher et al., 2001). They shunned them ("Let's go to my house so we can get away from Frankie."), controlled them ("Get away from me, Josh!"), said mean things about them ("I really can't stand Janie. She gives me the creeps."), denied them access to others ("You aren't in the club—we don't need you."), and attacked them directly by hitting or saying things such as "You know what you got in your brain? A load of bricks." When children are rejected by their peers, effects can be dismal. We discuss some of these effects in this section.

WHAT DETERMINES HOW CHILDREN REACT TO REJECTION?   Children respond to being rejected by their peers in different ways, depending on their characteristics (Asher et al., 2001; see Table 8.3). They are more likely to interpret ambiguous comments as rejection and

TABLE 8.3 **What Determines How Children React to Rejection?**

Rejection Characteristic	Response
Clarity of the rejecting child's communication	If the rejecting child's intention is unclear—for example, in a noisy cafeteria, where it is difficult to tell whether the rejecting child is ignoring or simply didn't hear the rejected child—more sensitive children will react as if they have been rejected.
Identity of the rejecting child	When the rejecting child is a close friend or family member, the rejected child is likely to be more distressed than if the rejecting child is a casual acquaintance.
Personality of the rejected child	A rejected child who broods over slights attributes negative events to his or her own inadequacies rather than to external causes, believes that his or her abilities or characteristics can't be changed, or approaches social situations as a test of his or her own "okayness" rather than as an opportunity to meet new people and learn new things is more likely to be distressed by perceived rejection.
Behavior of the rejected child	The rejected child's response to rejection may influence the intensity and duration of the rejecting behavior; for example, responding vengefully or failing to stand up for oneself can make a situation worse. Children who respond with humor may turn the rejection into something funny and thus gain the rejecting child's acceptance.
Social support of the rejected child	A rejected child who has friends and other sources of support can cope with rejection more easily.
Consistency of the rejection	A rejected child who experiences rejection frequently and consistently is more likely to expect and even anticipate it.

Source: Adapted from Asher et al., 2001.

respond with distress if they are sensitive to rejection and frequently receive negative feedback. They are less likely to interpret ambiguous comments as rejection if they are self-confident and approach social situations in a positive way rather than dreading that they won't measure up. Children who maintain a sense of humor and respond in a joking or playful way to a peer's rebuff can often turn the situation around and gain the acceptance they seem at first to be denied whereas children who react aggressively or shrink back and fail to stand up for themselves are likely to find themselves rejected again and again. Children's reactions to rejection depend on who is doing the rejecting as well. Rejection is more hurtful if it comes from a peer the child is close to or admires.

Bet You Thought That . . .
Names Would Never Hurt You

Remember your mother telling you "sticks and stones may break your bones but names will never hurt you"? Bet you thought she was right. If you did, you (and your mom) were wrong. Being called names or rejected in other ways by peers is undeniably painful. More than 2000 years ago, Aristotle wrote that "without friends no one would choose to live," and in the centuries since then, writers, musicians, playwrights, and poets have all described the profound human pain that results from the loss or lack of social bonds. In some countries, social isolation is used as an extreme form of legal punishment, even interchangeable with the death penalty. Our everyday language emphasizes the pain of broken social bonds and rejection by peers when we speak of "broken hearts" and "hurt feelings." Now researchers using neuroimaging have documented the fact that social rejection hurts and have shown that physical pain and social pain have similar neurological bases (Eisenberger & Lieberman, 2004).

In one study, young adults played a ball-tossing game on the computer (Eisenberger et al., 2003). They were told that they were playing "Cyberball" against two other players on the Internet. When these other "players" excluded the study participants from the game, the participants' fMRI records showed increased activity in the anterior cingulate cortex—a brain area that is linked to the uncomfortable feeling of physical pain. The more

the participants reported that they felt rejected and distressed in the Cyberball game, the higher was their neural response in this area. The Cyberball participants also showed increased activity in the right ventral prefrontal cortex—a region of the brain associated with regulating feelings of pain (Figure 8.2). When there was more activity in this neural region the excluded participants reported feeling less stress. Apparently, this area of the brain is involved in reducing the distress of rejection just as it helps people manage the discomfort of physical pain. Further investigation by these researchers showed that reactions to being rejected during a Cyberball game in the virtual world were similar to reactions to social rejection in the real world (Eisenberger et al., 2007).

FIGURE 8.2 *Right ventral prefrontal cortex (RVPFC) activation associated with social pain regulation and physical pain regulation.* Source: *Reprinted from* Trends in Cognitive Sciences, 8, *Eisenberger, N. I., & Lieberman, M. D., Why rejection hurts: A common neural alarm system for physical and social pain.* Trends in Cognitive Sciences, 8, *294–300, with permission from Elsevier.*

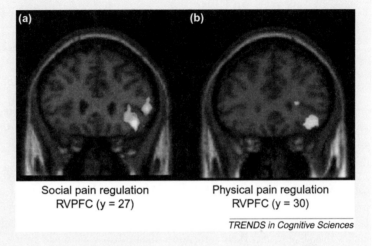

Social pain regulation
RVPFC (y = 27)

Physical pain regulation
RVPFC (y = 30)

TRENDS in Cognitive Sciences

SHORT- AND LONG-TERM CONSEQUENCES OF REJECTION   Being rejected can lead to both short-term and long-term problems. Loneliness is one of the immediate problems. Rejected children often report feeling lonely; they are more likely to feel socially isolated and alienated than children of any other peer status. Here are some examples of how rejected and lonely children feel (the first two examples are from Hayden et al., 1988; the third example is from a Web site where people describe things they believed when they were children, http:// iusedtobelieve.com/):

Today everybody's going to Mary Ann's party. I'm the one that gets left behind. I'm not invited to the party so I won't do anything on the weekend. Anywhere the whole group goes, I don't. I'm just the person that gets left back. Maybe they don't realize that I get left, that I'm there, but it happens all the time.

It was a Sunday. All the stores were closed. Jason, a friend, had to go to his aunt's. I decided to call on Jamie, but no one was home. I went to turn on the TV and only church stuff was on. I went upstairs to play, but it was so boring. The dog was behind the couch so I didn't want to bother him. Mom was sleeping. My sister was babysitting. It wasn't my day. There was no one to talk to or play with, nothing to listen to.

I was very lonely when I was little, so I used to make-believe myself a lot of friends. I used to stare up into the sun or lightbulbs to get the colorful splotches in my eyes. I thought this was them. When they faded away, I was sad.

Even in kindergarten, rejected children are lonely (Kochenderfer & Ladd, 1996). Nonaggressive-rejected children typically feel lonelier than aggressive-rejected children (Parkhurst & Asher, 1992). It helps to have at least one friend. Rejected children who have a stable friendship with even one other child are likely to feel less lonely than totally friendless children (Parker & Asher, 1993; Sanderson & Siegal, 1991). As well as feeling lonely, children whose peers reject them tend to have difficulties in school; they have poorer quality relationships with their teachers and more trouble with their grades (Parker & Asher, 1987; Rubin et al., 2009). They are less active and cooperative in the classroom (Ladd et al., 2008) and more likely to drop out of school entirely and to develop patterns of criminal activity (Nelson & Dishion, 2004). They are likely to develop behavioral and emotional problems, including anxiety, depressive symptoms, and low self-esteem (Hoglund et al., 2008; Klima & Repetti, 2008; Nesdale & Lambert, 2008; Pedersen et al., 2007). They may even develop physical health problems (Brendgen & Vitaro, 2008).

mutual antipathy
A relationship of mutual dislike between two people.

Research up Close:
When "Love Thine Enemy" Fails

Mutual antipathy is the feeling people have when they dislike or even hate each other. This kind of mutual dislike can be the result of many factors including perceived insults, slights, conflicts, unresolved disputes, and relationships that have gone sour and ended badly (Hartup & Abecassis, 2002). In one study of U.S. 3rd graders, 65 percent reported having at least one same-gender relationship characterized by mutual antipathy, and some children reported as many as three (Hembree & Vandell, 2000). In a study of 5,000 children in the Netherlands, 5th and 8th graders nominated the classmates they liked least. Boys were more likely than girls to have mutual dislikes with same-gender peers; children with same-gender antipathies were likely to be antisocial, to fight and bully, or to be victimized (Abecassis et al., 2002). Not surprisingly, rejected and controversial children are more likely to be involved in these kinds of relationships than popular and average children (Rodkin & Hodges, 2003). Children with mutual antipathies expect the worst from their disliked peers: 10-year-olds in a study in Estonia, for example, attributed more hostility and expected more hostile responses when their partner was an enemy rather than a neutral peer (Peets et al., 2007). Mutual antipathies can also have negative effects on children's development: The more numerous the child's antipathies, the poorer the child's socioemotional adjustment and academic performance (Hembree & Vandell, 2000). Having enemies in preadolescence foreshadows later problems in adolescence: Boys who had same-gender mutual antipathies at age 10 were more likely to have problems with substance addiction and delinquency in adolescence; for girls, same-gender antipathies predicted lower achievement (Abecassis et al., 2002). Just as having friends is a protective factor for development, having enemies puts children at risk.

Occasionally peer rejection can have short-term negative consequences and long-term positive consequences. In middle school, George Clooney developed Bell's palsy, a debilitating condition that partially paralyzes the face. His left eye closed and he was unable to eat or drink properly, earning the nickname Frankenstein. "That was the worst time of my life," he says. "You know how cruel kids can be. I was mocked and taunted, but the experience made me stronger." Source: Splash News and Pictures/NewsCom.

Insights from Extremes: From Rejection to Revenge?

On April 20, 1999, at Columbine High School in Littleton, Colorado, two high school seniors, Eric Harris and Dylan Klebold, carried out one of the worst massacres in U.S. history. Using home-made bombs, sawed-off shotguns, a semiautomatic rifle, and a 9 millimeter semiautomatic pistol, they killed 12 students and a teacher and wounded 23 others before committing suicide. Their plan was to plant bombs in the cafeteria and shoot survivors of the blast as they escaped. This plot was planned for more than a year. Why did these boys plot, plan, and execute this attack? According to some observers, Eric and Dylan were isolated, excluded from school cliques, and bullied (Kass, 2000). When one Columbine student, an athlete, was asked how the school treated the two shooters, his reply pointed to peer rejection, "Sure, we teased them. But what do you expect if you come to school with weird hairdos? It's not just jocks; the whole school was disgusted with them. They're a bunch of homos, grabbing each other's private parts. If you want to get rid of someone, usually you tease 'em. So the whole school would call them homos, and when they did something sick, we'd tell them, 'You're sick and that's wrong'" (Gibbs & Roche, 1999).

But the Columbine massacre was not simply the result of peer rejection leading to revenge. Brooks Brown, one of the survivors of the massacre, suggests that there was a "perfect storm" of factors at the school leading to the attack, including students who were bullies, teachers who were bullies, teachers who allowed bullies, and a school administration that did nothing about it (Simon, 1999). In addition, Eric and Dylan had access to guns and bomb-making components and spent many hours playing violent video games, such as *Doom*, and watching violent films, such as *Natural Born Killers* (Block, 2007). Most significantly, the boys also suffered from mental health problems. A journalist's examination of the boys' diaries (Cullen, 2009) characterized Dylan as an angry, erratic depressive and Eric as a sadistic psychopath who dehumanized their peers as "robots," "zombies," and "sheep" and designed their massacre to demonstrate their own innate superiority.

A number of insights have been gained from this tragedy and other mass shootings on high school campuses. School administrators and teachers have learned that they need to pay more attention to students' interactions, and more school programs have been developed to reduce and prevent bullying (Juvonen et al., 2003). Schools have instituted "zero tolerance" policies against weapons on school grounds. Parents have learned that they should look for warning signs in their children's activities and behavior. Advocates have pleaded for stricter gun control laws and increased control over violent media fare. Researchers have conducted studies on the destructive role of peer rejection, the results of which inform this chapter.

CAN PEER STATUS CHANGE?   In general, children's peer status is quite stable over time. Popular children do sometimes lose their high status, and neglected children occasionally gain some social acceptance, but rejected children are unlikely to change their social status (Coie & Dodge, 1983). In part, this stability is the result of **reputational bias**, the tendency of children to interpret peers' behavior on the basis of past encounters and impressions (Hymel et al., 1990). When children are asked to judge peers' negative behavior, they are likely to excuse a child whom they earlier liked, giving that child the benefit of the doubt, but they do not excuse a peer whom they didn't like. Reputation colors children's interpretations of peers' actions and helps account for the stability of children's status across time (Denham & Holt, 1993; Hymel, 1986). However, reputation is not the only contributor to peer status stability. The behavior and characteristics of the children themselves also contribute. Proving this point, when researchers brought boys together and assigned them to new social groups, the boys tended to attain the same peer status as they'd had before—even though the boys in

reputational bias
Tendency to interpret peers' behavior on the basis of past encounters with and feelings about them.

their new groups had no knowledge of their earlier reputations (Coie et al., 1990). Boys who had been widely accepted before were popular again; boys who'd been rejected continued their depressing isolation.

Promoters of Peer Acceptance

Clearly, it would be a good idea if psychologists could figure out a way to help children with low social status improve their social skills and gain acceptance among their peers. It would also be good to figure out how to encourage popular children to be more inclusive of socially inept peers. Some people believe that early training in social skills can help children find ways to celebrate each other's strengths and offer support for each other's weaknesses. Parents, teachers, and peers are possible sources of such training.

Parents as Promoters of Peer Acceptance

Parents can help their children develop better peer relationships in a variety of ways (McDowell & Parke, 2009; Parke & O'Neil, 2000). They can be teachers, coaches, and social arrangers for their children's peer interactions. They can also interact with their children in ways that demonstrate and promote positive social behaviors.

PARENTS AS POSITIVE PARTNERS Researchers have documented strong links between children's relationships with their parents and their relationships with peers, suggesting that when mothers and fathers are trusted partners, children are more likely to acquire social interaction skills (Isley et al., 1996; McDowell & Parke, 2009; Parke et al., 2004). When relationships with parents are full of mutual warmth, acceptance, and agreeableness, children are more prosocial and empathic with their peers and—as a consequence—are better liked; when relationships with parents are negative and control- ling, children are less liked by their peers and have lower peer status (Clark & Ladd, 2000; Grimes et al., 2004; Harrist et al., 1994; Putallaz, 1987; Putallaz & Heflin, 1990). Children who have emotionally secure attachments to their parents are more socially competent and develop better friendships with peers (Lindsey et al., 2009; Lucas-Thompson & Clarke- Stewart, 2007; McElwain et al., 2008; Simpson et al., 2007). They are less lonely and have better social problem-solving skills (Raikes & Thompson, 2008). In one study, children who were securely attached when they were 1 year old were more socially competent with peers in elementary school; this forecast more secure relationships with close friends at age 16, which, in turn, predicted less negative affect in conflict resolution and collaborative tasks with romantic partners in adulthood (Simpson et al., 2007). Withdrawn children's parents are often overprotective, overcontrolling, and intrusive (Coplan et al., 2004; Lieb et al., 2000; Parke et al., 2004; Rubin et al., 2001). These parenting behaviors are thought to reinforce children's feelings of insecurity, resulting in a transactional cycle of hopelessness and helplessness in the children and overcontrol and protection from the parents (Rapee, 1997; Wood et al., 2003). A similar transactional process would account for reciprocal rela- tions between aggressive–rejected children and their parents (Dodge, Coie, et al., 2006; Rubin, Bukowski, et al., 2006).

The specific social skills that children learn through interactions with their parents include encoding and decoding emotions, regulating emotions, making accurate judgments about people's intentions and behavior, and solving social problems (Eisenberg, 2000; Eisenberg & Fabes, 1994; Ladd, 2005; McDowell & Parke, 2005; Parke et al., 2006). The ability to encode and decode emotional signals is acquired to some extent in the context of parent-child play, especially arousing physical play (Parke et al., 2004). Through physically playful interaction with their parents, especially fathers, children learn how to decode social and emotional signals and how to use emotional signals to regulate other people's behavior. This ability to decode and encode emotional expressions is related to children's social competence with peers (Halberstadt et al., 2001). Children's ability to regulate their own emotional arousal is also related to their social competence with peers (Eisenberg, 2000; Parke et al., 2006). Attentional abilities, which are critical for noticing and tracking interactive partners' social cues, constitute a third set of skills acquired in the family. Children of socially responsive and warm parents have better attentional abilities and, in turn, higher peer competence in 1st and 3rd grades (NICHD Early Child Care Research Network, 2009).

Children also learn how to interact with their peers by observing their parents' interactions. Children whose parents have a more loving, intimate spousal relationship express these qualities in their own best friendships (Lucas-Thompson & Clarke-Stewart, 2007). Adolescents whose parents are frequently in conflict are less likely to be accepted by their peers, have fewer friends, and express negative qualities in their best friendships (Vairami & Vorria, 2007). They also express more hostility in their romantic relationships (Stocker & Richmond, 2007).

How do children transfer the strategies they acquire in the family to their interactions with peers? Some psychologists have suggested that they develop internal mental representations that guide their behavior—referred to as working models (Bretherton & Munholland, 2008), scripts, or cognitive maps (Grusec & Ungerer, 2003). In one study, researchers found that children with more affectionate, responsive parents had more positive mental models (consisting of positive goals, constructive problem-solving strategies, and nonhostile attributions in response to dilemmas about their parents and peers), and these children were better liked than children with less positive mental models (Rah & Parke, 2008).

PARENTS AS COACHES AND TEACHERS   No one is more eager for children to learn social skills than their parents. Thus, it is not surprising that parents also promote their children's social abilities and peer acceptance by direct instruction. Parents can prepare their children for successful and satisfying social relationships through specific coaching and teaching (Bhavnagri & Parke, 1991; Ladd & Pettit, 2002; Lollis et al., 1992; Pettit & Mize, 1993). They can reinforce children's social behavior by praising and rewarding their best attempts and suggesting alternative approaches when their efforts fail. They can teach children a general concept or strategy, give examples of successful behaviors, and then guide the child through multiple rehearsals of a particular action. They can review the child's rehearsals and show the child how to evaluate his or her own behavior. In this way, parents can advise their children about helpful approaches for interacting with peers, direct them to the most useful social strategies, and support them as they try out new ideas.

Of course, this kind of coaching works only when parents themselves are socially skilled or are following a prepared script. In an Australian study, researchers found clear differences between the coaching methods used by mothers of children with high peer status and mothers of children with low peer status (Finnie & Russell, 1988; Russell & Finnie, 1990). Mothers of high-status children generally suggested positive social strategies, for example, that children propose alternative actions when they couldn't agree with another child. These mothers also suggested more rule-oriented strategies, for example, that children propose turn-taking instead of fighting over toys. In contrast, mothers of low-status children tended to suggest avoidance strategies, for example, that children ignore peers' unfriendly behavior, or they suggested nonspecific tactics, such as just "getting to know" the other child or "staying out of trouble." When they actually joined in the children's activities, the two groups of mothers showed different levels of social skill. The mothers of high-status children encouraged communication among the children generally and actively helped their own child join in conversation. The mothers of low-status children often took control of a game, disrupted the children's play, or simply avoided supervising the group.

Equally important for promoting children's social abilities and peer acceptance are the behaviors parents model when they interact with other adults and children. Children observe everything their parents do and say, and they pick up on their parents' social ways. They watch as their parents demonstrate polite requests and ask interested questions or make rude interjections and egocentric demands. It's easy for parents to forget this; they have to be "on" all of the time if they expect their children to imitate their positive social behaviors, not their negative "mistakes."

PARENTS AS SOCIAL ARRANGERS AND MONITORS   Another way parents can promote their children's relations with peers is by giving them opportunities for peer interaction (Ladd, 2005). The first step may be selecting housing in a neighborhood where children can find suitable playmates and there are good facilities for children's play. This does not necessarily mean the richest neighborhood in town. In one study, researchers discovered that children's peer relations were not as easy or abundant in an affluent neighborhood as they were in a low-income neighborhood (Berg & Medrich, 1980; Medrich, 1981). In the well-to-do community, children lived so far apart that their parents had to chauffeur them around to preplanned social events, and many children had only one or two friends. In the low-income urban neighborhood, peers were plentiful and lived nearby, play tended to be more spontaneous and frequent, and each child typically had four or five close friends. In violent communities, however, children are deficient in their emotion regulation skills and more likely to be rejected by their peers (Kelly et al., 2008). If children live in unsafe neighborhoods, parents need to act as social arrangers by monitoring their children's activities and choice of playmates (Brody et al., 2001; O'Neil et al., 2001).

Being good social arrangers is particularly important for parents of very young children. It's up to them to schedule play dates, enroll their children in organized activities, and send them to child care. This effort pays off. Comparing the social activities of children whose parents were good arrangers with those of children whose parents did not facilitate peer contacts, Gary Ladd and his colleagues found that the boys whose parents initiated peer contacts for their sons had a clear advantage: They had a larger range of playmates, more frequent play companions outside school, and were better liked by their peers than boys whose parents did not make these efforts (Ladd & Golter, 1988; Ladd & Pettit, 2002; Ladd et al., 1992). Continued efforts by parents to arrange social opportunities for their children may also be valuable. Involvement in religious institutions is one way parents can provide their older children with opportunities to gain valuable experiences with peers. In one study, adolescents who were involved in church in the 8th grade had better peer relationships in the 12th grade (Elder & Conger, 2000).

Each of the three parental strategies we have discussed—having positive parent-child interactions, giving good advice, and arranging social events—is important and all three strategies taken together provide the strongest prediction of children's social competence and social acceptance (McDowell & Parke, 2009).

One final way that parents can promote their children's positive peer relations is by monitoring their activities. Researchers have found that school-age children whose parents monitored their social activities became less rejected by their peers (Sandstrom & Coie, 1999), and if their parents were well informed about the children's peer relationships and activities, the children had closer and more stable peer relationships (Krappmann, 1986). In adolescence, parents' monitoring shifts from direct involvement to more remote checking in, but it continues to be important. Adolescents whose parents fail to monitor their activities with peers are more likely to engage in delinquent behavior and have poorer mental health (Hair et al., 2008). They are more likely to associate with deviant peers (Knoester et al., 2006). Monitoring children's activities is not just the parents' job, though; it is a shared responsibility (Kerr & Stattin, 2000;

Laird et al., 2003b). Parents' ability to monitor their children relies on the extent to which the children are willing to share information about their activities and companions (Mounts, 2000). In one study of high-risk adolescents, researchers found that these young people often actively thwarted their parents' monitoring attempts (Schell, 1996). For example, they misled their parents about where they were going, making it difficult for the parents to track their activities. Parents are more likely to know about their children's activities if the children are sociable and expressive (Crouter et al., 1999). For parental monitoring to be successful, parents must be realistic about their children's abilities to take responsibility and regulate their impulses, and children must see the parents' supervision as fair.

WHEN PARENTS FAIL: PEER REJECTION OF ABUSED CHILDREN   Parental abuse of children is likely to interfere with their development of good peer relationships. Researchers have found that chronically abused children are more likely to be rejected by their peers, and the more extensive the abuse, the greater the rejection; (see Figure 8.3; Bolger & Patterson, 2001). Abused children have difficulty forming and maintaining friendships, especially if the abuse occurred in the preschool years. Children who are physically abused are likely to be rejected because they are aggressive. Abused children are also often unable to regulate their emotions, and this too leads to peer rejection (Shields et al., 2001). Being abused increases the likelihood that peers will victimize children, especially boys, just as their parents have (Schwartz et al., 1997). Children who are neglected by their parents are also more likely to be neglected by their peers (Bolger et al., 1998; Garbarino & Kostelny, 2002).

Researchers As Promoters of Peer Acceptance

Researchers can help children who are lonely, socially awkward, or withdrawn improve their social skills and increase their acceptance among their peers (Bierman & Powers, 2009). In one study, Ladd and his colleagues taught preschoolers and 3rd-graders to use three methods of communication with their peers: asking questions in a positive tone, offering useful suggestions, and making supportive statements (Ladd, 1981, 2005; Mize & Ladd, 1990). Over a 3-week period, children participated in eight sessions, each about an hour long, in which the adult coach offered instruction and guidance, let the children practice on their own, and then reviewed the practice sessions with them. Immediately after these sessions and 4 weeks later, the children's classroom behavior had improved and their popularity increased.

FIGURE 8.3 *Abused children are often rejected, and the longer the abuse continues, the more likely and lengthy is the rejection.* Source: Bolger, K. E., & Patterson, C. J. (2001). *Developmental pathways from child maltreatment to peer rejection.* Child Development, 72, *549–568. Reprinted with permission of the Society for Research in Child Development and Wiley-Blackwell.*

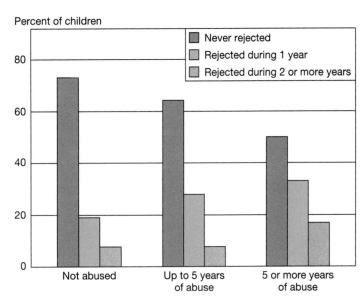

Another way researchers have helped children improve their social skills is by increasing their self-efficacy. When researchers asked children to explain "what happened" after their efforts to begin a new relationship with a peer were rebuffed, some children said there had been a misunderstanding or they simply hadn't tried hard enough and expressed confidence that they could succeed the next time (Dweck, 2006; Goetz & Dweck, 1980). Other children said it was just hard for them to make friends. The first group of children saw the problem as temporary and fixable; the second group thought it reflected their lack of ability. To prevent this defeatist thinking, the researchers focused children's attention on trying out new things rather than viewing failure as a measure of their inability to perform (Erdley et al., 1997). They divided the children into two groups—a learning-goal group and a performance-goal group—and told them they were trying out for membership in a pen pal club. The researchers then told the learning-goal group that the important thing was that the task would help them "practice and improve" their ways of making friends. "Think of it as a chance to work on your skills, and maybe learn some new ones." The researchers told the second group that they were interested in "how good" children were at striking up new friendships: "Think of it as a chance for you to see how good you are at making friends." The children given the learning goal were more persistent and ultimately more successful than the children given the performance goal. This is consistent with Bandura's social self-efficacy theory, which we discussed in Chapter 1, and with other research showing that children who have higher social self-efficacy are more likely to persist even when they face initial rejection and failure (Ladd, 2005).

Researchers also can teach children who are not accepted by their peers how to cooperate, be responsive communicators, support or validate other children's ideas and actions, and play games and sports (Asher & Hopmeyer, 2001). Rejected children need to be taught specific social skills because they are not likely to know how to interact with others or to try very hard to do so. They are generally not very prosocial, helpful, or cooperative in their peer interactions and tend to be negative, withdrawn, and unresponsive. Anxiety and fear of rejection may prevent them from risking friendly overtures. Games and sports offer useful contexts for teaching children these skills and a chance to develop and display the kinds of competence that can gain them social acceptance. Here is an example of a research "coach" teaching a child about cooperation in a game (Oden & Asher, 1977, p. 500):

Coach:	*Okay, I have some ideas about what makes a game fun to play with another person. There are a couple things that are important to do. You should cooperate with the other person. Do you know what cooperation is? Can you tell me in your own words?*
Child:	*Ahh . . . sharing.*
Coach:	*Yes, sharing. Okay, let's say you and I are playing the game you played last time. What was it again?*
Child:	*Drawing a picture.*
Coach:	*Okay, tell me then, what would be an example of sharing when playing the picture-drawing game?*
Child:	*I'd let you use some pens, too.*
Coach:	*Right. You would share the pens with me. That's an example of cooperation. Now let's say you and I are doing the picture-drawing game. Can you also give me an example of what would not be cooperating?*
Child:	*Taking all the pens.*
Coach:	*Would taking all the pens make the game fun to play?*
Child:	*No.*

Coach: *So you wouldn't take all the pens. Instead, you'd cooperate by sharing them with me. Can you think of some more examples of cooperation? [The coach waited for a response.] Okay, how about taking turns. . . . Let's say you and I [the coach gives examples]. Okay, I'd like you to try out some of these ideas when you play [a particular new game] with [another child]. Let's go and get [the other child], and after you play, I'll talk to you again for a minute or so and you can tell me if these things seem to be good ideas for having fun at a game with someone.*

Researchers trying to improve children's social acceptance can increase their effectiveness by following a multifaceted approach, including assistance with children's poor attentional and self-regulatory skills and academic difficulties because these problems often accompany peer rejection (Bierman & Powers, 2009).

Learning from Living Leaders: Gary W. Ladd

Source: Courtesy of Gary W. Ladd.

Gary Ladd is Professor of Family and Human Development and Associate Director of the School of Social and Family Dynamics at Arizona State University (https://sec.was.asu.edu/directory/person/323736). His interest in peer relationships began in an earlier career as a school psychologist when he found that children's social problems in classrooms, on playgrounds, and on the school bus were more challenging than their academic problems. This realization led him to study strategies that could be used to help neglected and rejected children improve their relationships with classmates. He found that a combination of coaching and modeling was effective, and his work led to changes in classroom practices and educational policies. Ladd also studied the effects of experiences in the family on children's peer relationships. He discovered that when parents provided opportunities for their children to interact with peers this was an important way to help children form social ties. In the Pathways Project, Ladd followed children from before they entered school until they were in high school. He found that children's early behavioral dispositions in combination with their social experiences, such as peer rejection or acceptance, predicted later developmental outcomes and mental health. Ladd is editor of the *Merrill Palmer Quarterly*, a journal devoted to understanding children's development. He has been a Fellow at the Center for Advanced Study in the Behavioral Sciences at Stanford University, a Spencer Foundation Fellow, and a recipient of awards for excellence in teaching. For him, the most pressing issue in social development is how to provide children access to safe, socially supportive, and academically challenging school environments—regardless of their gender, race, ethnicity, or national origin. He encourages research that will increase understanding of peer relations in different cultures and document the effects of ethnic and political violence on children.

Further Reading

Ladd, G. W. (2005). *Children's peer relationships and social competence: A century of progress.* New Haven, CT: Yale University Press.

Peers Can Help Too

Peers also can help children improve their social skills and experience increased peer acceptance. Unpopular children are likely to find it easier to gain acceptance when they interact with younger, less threatening children. Harlow first observed this phenomenon; he found that the negative effects of being isolated from other monkeys early in life could be reversed by sustained contact with younger monkeys (Suomi & Harlow, 1972). This finding led researchers to examine the effect that contact with younger peers had on withdrawn 4- and 5-year-old children (Furman et al., 1979). As the primate research predicted, the withdrawn children became more sociable.

Interacting with children of both sexes is another way peers can help. Cross-gender and same-gender play can introduce boys and girls to a broader range of behavioral styles and activities (Rubin, 1980). It can expand unpopular children's pool of potential friends and promote a better understanding of qualities that both sexes share. In one study, researchers demonstrated that 3rd- and 4th-graders who had both cross-gender and same-gender friendships were more socially skilled and accepted than children whose only friendships were with peers of the other gender (Kovacs et al., 1996). Similarly, children may gain peer acceptance when they make the transition to middle school because it offers them the opportunity to interact with a larger number and variety of peers (Rubin et al., 2009).

When Peers Become Friends

Our discussion so far has focused on how well children are accepted by their peers, typically their classmates. Another important aspect of peer relations is the particular friendships children form with a few peers. These two kinds of peer relations are somewhat independent. A child can be rejected or neglected by his or her classmates but still have at least one friend; another child can be widely accepted by classmates but lack a close friend (Parker & Asher, 1993).

Age Changes in Friendship

In this section, we discuss how children's friendships and concepts of friendship change with age (see Table 8.1 for a overview of developmental changes in friendships).

EARLIEST FRIENDSHIPS   Even 1- and 2-year-old children form rudimentary friendships. They have preferences for particular playmates, which they express in their positive and negative give-and-take exchanges (Ross et al., 1992). A clear sign of early friendship formation is that not just any other child will do to hold the doll or pound the plastic peg. These young children know who their friends are and seek interactions with these specific peers. Moreover, their preferences are not fleeting: 50 to 70 percent of early friendships last more than a year (Howes, 1996), and in some cases several years (Dunn, 2005).

During the preschool years, children form friendships based on similarities of age and gender and become friends with peers who show behavior tendencies similar to their own. Highly active children seek each other out, and quieter children pal around. This tendency to associate with similar others is called **homophily**, which means "love of the same" (Ryan, 2001). Even at this young age, children behave differently with friends and nonfriends: They direct more social overtures to friends, cooperate more with them, and show more positive behaviors toward them (Dunn, 2005; Dunn et al., 2002). Their friendships are marked by support and exclusivity (Sebanc, 2003). Older preschoolers are more likely than younger preschoolers to participate in reciprocated friendships. However, as many as one quarter of children do not form friendships in the preschool period (Dunn, 1993). Children who are more successful in forming friendships have more advanced social-cognitive abilities, including perspective-taking ability, understanding of other people's social intentions, ability to read other peoples' emotions, and regulation of their own emotional states. Although relationships in the preschool

homophily
The tendency of individuals to associate and bond with others who are similar.

period do not carry the same psychological meaning as later friendships do, they may lay the groundwork for friendships throughout childhood (Dunn, 2005; Ladd, 2005).

CHANGING FRIENDSHIP GOALS   As children grow up, the goals and processes involved in forming friendships change (see Table 8.4; Parker & Gottman, 1989). For children ages 3 to 7, the goal is coordinated play, and all of the children's social processes are organized to promote successful and fun playful interactions. For children ages 8 to 12, the goal changes to concern about being accepted by same-gender peers. Children want to know the norms of the group so they can figure out which actions will lead to acceptance and inclusion and which to rejection and exclusion. The most salient social process is **negative gossip**, which involves sharing negative information about another child. When this works well, the partner responds with interest, more negative gossip, and a feeling of solidarity. For example, here are two girls, Erica and Mikaila, gossiping about another girl, Katie (Gottman & Mettetal, 1986, p. 204).

negative gossip
Adverse or detrimental information shared about another child with a peer.

Erica:	*Katie does lots of weird things. Like, every time she makes a mistake, she says, "Well, sorry." (Sarcastic tone)*
Mikaila:	*I know.*
Erica:	*And stuff like that.*
Mikaila:	*She's mean. She beat me up once. (Laughs) I could hardly breathe she hit me in the stomach so hard.*
Erica:	*She acts like . . .*
Mikaila:	*She's the boss.*

self-disclosure
The honest sharing of information of a very personal nature, often with a focus on problem solving; a central means by which adolescents and others develop friendships.

Often gossip is used as a way to establish the norms for the group, and as this example shows, it is important not to be too aggressive or bossy. In adolescence, the focus of friendship shifts to self-understanding. Self-exploration and **self-disclosure** are the principal social processes, and intense honesty and problem solving accompany them. Adolescents begin to grapple with understanding the meaning of emotions in relationships, especially as dating and romantic relationships become more common.

CHANGING FRIENDSHIP EXPECTATIONS   Children's expectations about relationships with friends also change as they get older (see Table 8.5; Berndt, 2002; Bigelow, 1977; Bigelow & LaGaipa, 1975; Schneider, 2000; Smollar & Youniss, 1982; Youniss, 1980). When

TABLE 8.4   Developmental Changes in Friendship Concerns

	Primary concerns	Main processes and purposes of communication	Emotional development
Early childhood (3–7 years)	To maximize excitement, entertainment, and enjoyment through play	To coordinate play, escalate and de-escalate play activity, talk about activities, and resolve conflicts	To learn to manage arousal during interaction
Middle childhood (8–12 years)	To be included by peers, avoid rejection, and present oneself to others in a positive way	To share negative gossip with others	To acquire rules for showing feelings
Adolescence (13–17 years)	To explore, know, and define oneself	To disclose oneself to others and to solve problems	To integrate logic and emotion and understand the implications of emotions for relationships

Source: Gottman & Mettetal, 1986.

TABLE 8.5 Developmental Changes in Expectations of Friends

Reward-cost stage (grades 2–3)

Children expect friends to offer help, share common activities, provide stimulating ideas, be able to join in organized play, offer judgments, be physically nearby, and be demographically similar to them.

Normative stage (grades 4–5)

Children expect friends to accept and admire them, bring loyalty and commitment to the friendship, and express similar values and attitudes toward rules and sanctions.

Empathic stage (grades 6–7)

Children begin to expect genuineness and the potential for intimacy in their friends; they expect friends to understand them and be willing to engage in self-disclosure; they want friends to accept their help, share common interests, and hold similar attitudes and values across a range of topics.

Source: Bigelow, 1977.

children are about 7 or 8, they expect friends to be demographically like them, to provide stimulating ideas, offer help, give judgments, share common activities, and be able to join them in organized play. When they are 9 or 10, children think friends should be nice to each another and help each other. They expect loyalty and trust. They expect that friends will accept and admire them, will be committed to the friendship, and will express values and attitudes toward rules that are like their own. They continue to expect friends to offer judgments and share common activities. At age 11 or 12, children still expect friends to accept and admire them, enhance their sense of self-worth, and be loyal and committed, but they also begin to expect genuineness and the potential for intimacy. They expect friends to understand them and to be willing to self-disclose; they want friends to accept their help, share common interests, and hold attitudes and values like theirs across a range of topics, not just rules. Beyond age 12, adolescents continue to expect genuineness, the potential for intimacy, and common interests in their friends, but they also think that it is important for friends to provide emotional support.

Children in other cultures differ somewhat in their friendship expectations. The role of friendship in promoting self-worth is less salient in many non-Western cultures where the development of the self is not considered a major developmental task. Children seldom report the enhancement of self-worth as an important function of friendship in China (Chen et al., 2004), Indonesia (French et al., 2005), or if they have an Arab or Caribbean background (Dayan et al. 2001). Another cultural difference is that emotional intimacy may be a more common aspect of friendship expectations in affluent Western cultures; in cultures with subsistence economies, expectations of instrumental support are more common (Beer, 2001; Keller, 2004).

Interactions with Friends

To find out how children actually interact with their friends, John Gottman and his colleagues conducted studies of children ranging in age from 3 to 7 years (Gottman, 1983; Gottman & Parker, 1986; Parker & Gottman, 1989). They set up tape recorders in children's homes and listened while children played with their best friends or with unfamiliar children on three different days. Friends had more positive exchanges, communicated more clearly, established common ground more easily, exchanged more information, disclosed more about themselves, and were able to resolve conflicts more effectively than strangers. Other studies confirmed these findings. Children express more positive affect in their interactions with friends than with nonfriends (Hartup, 1996; Ladd, 2005; Schneider, 2000). They share more with friends

(Berndt, 2004), although when friends are tough competitors, sharing decreases (Berndt, 1986, 2004). Being friends does not mean that children never disagree (Hartup, 1996; Laursen et al., 1996). In fact, friends disagree more than nonfriends, but their conflicts are less heated, and the children are more likely to stay in contact after an argument (Hartup et al., 1988). Friends are more likely to resolve conflicts in an equitable way and ensure that the resolution preserves their friendship (Hartup, 1996; Laursen et al., 1996). They are more self-disclosing than acquaintances (Berndt, 2004; Berndt & Perry, 1990; Simpkins & Parke, 2001) and more knowledgeable about each other: They know each other's strengths and secrets, wishes and weaknesses (Ladd & Emerson, 1984; Schneider, 2000).

The specific ways in which friendship is expressed vary somewhat in individualistic and collectivist cultures. Although mutual assistance is a common aspect of friendship (French et al., 2005), for children in individualistic Western cultures, assistance usually consists of giving advice and cognitive support; in collectivist cultures, instrumental and material support is more important (Chen et al., 2004; DeRosier & Kupersmidt, 1991; D. C. French et al., 2005, 2006; Gonzalez et al., 2004). Intimacy also varies across cultures; in a number of collectivistic cultures, including South Korea, Cuba, and Israeli kibbutzim, friendships are more intimate than in individualistic cultures such as the United States and Canada (D. C. French et al., 2006; Gonzalez et al., 2004; Sharabany, 2006).

Insights from Extremes:
When Children Love and Protect Each Other

During World War II, many young Jewish children were spirited out of Nazi Germany and its occupied territories and brought to Great Britain for safety. From December 1938 to September 1939, about 10,000 children traveled by train and ferry in the "Kindertransport." Anna Freud observed six of these children who had been rescued when they were 4 years old and taken to Bulldog Banks, a small English country home that had been transformed into a nursery (Freud & Dann, 1951). The children had been torn from their families and kept in concentration camps from the time they were infants. When they got to Bulldog Banks, the children ignored or were actively hostile to their adult caretakers, biting, spitting, or swearing at them, calling them *bloder ochs* ("stupid fools"). With each other, however, they formed intense, protective relationships and resisted being separated even for special treats like pony rides. When one child was ill, the others wanted to remain with her. They showed little envy, jealousy, rivalry, or competition. Their level of sharing and helping was remarkable. On one occasion, the children were eating cake, and John began to cry because there was no cake left for a second helping. Ruth and Miriam, who had not yet finished their cake, gave him theirs. On another occasion, one of the children lost his gloves, and another child loaned him gloves without complaining about the cold. In scary situations, the children were able to overcome their fears and help or comfort each other. Once, when a dog approached, the children were terrified. In spite of her fear, Ruth walked bravely over to Peter, who was screaming, and gave him her toy rabbit for comfort. Later, on the beach, Ruth was throwing pebbles into the water. When he saw a big wave coming, Peter, overcame his fear, rushed over to Ruth, calling out: "Water coming, water coming," as he dragged her back to safety. These children's circumstances were clearly unusual. Being at Bulldog Banks was the first time they had lived in an environment where all adults were kind. It was not surprising, therefore, that they initially reacted to the adults with suspicion and negativity. What is more surprising is the extent to which they formed close bonds with each other. Their behavior demonstrates the intensity of relationships that can develop between young children and the ways such relationships can contribute to children's emotional survival. Although most childhood friendships are not this intense, this extreme example provides a useful lesson about how children's friendships can provide comfort and care as well as fun and games.

Learning from Living Leaders: Willard W. Hartup

Source: Courtesy of Willard W. Hartup.

Willard (Bill) Hartup is Professor Emeritus at the Institute of Child Development, University of Minnesota. As a young man, a friend urged him to read Freud, and this led him to study psychology. When he became a graduate student at Harvard, he worked with two of the leading scholars in social development, Robert Sears and Eleanor Maccoby, and became hooked on a lifelong mission to understand children's social behavior. Hartup realized that peers were a neglected but potentially important part of social development. This insight arose, in part, from overhearing conversations between his son and a friend on the way to nursery school as they were

plotting how to inflict mayhem on another peer. Another incident involved an exchange with a student who asked Hartup what we know about peers and child development. After answering "not much," he organized a seminar that led him to a career studying this issue. Over the next 40 years, he conducted both experimental and observational research on friendships and more recently on enemies. He has shown that peers can be both rewarding and annoying, helpful and hurtful. Hartup has received much deserved recognition for his work, including awards for Distinguished Scientific Contributions from the *International Society for Behavioral Development* and the *Society for Research in Child Development* and the G. Stanley Hall Award from the Developmental Psychology Division of the American Psychological Association. He believes that one of the most pressing issues in social development research is to discover the long-term effects of peer relations on later development. In the future, he sees the possibility of developing a workable model of gene-environment interaction that will do a better job of predicting developmental outcomes. His advice for undergraduates is to "write, write, and write some more. Take a wide variety of courses in the arts and sciences, including biology, and be prepared: The psychology of the future is unlikely to be the same as the psychology of the past."

Further Reading

Hartup, W. W. (2006). Relationships in early and middle childhood. In D. Perlman & A. Vangelisi (Eds.), *Handbook of personal relationships* (pp. 177–190). Cambridge, UK: Cambridge University Press.

Friendship Patterns

Friendships are not always smooth. Fights occur, friends hurt each other, and friendships sometimes end. Children lose and replace friendships, sometimes within days or weeks, sometimes over a span of years. To examine children's friendship patterns, researchers in one study observed 8- to 15-year-olds at a summer camp (Parker & Seal, 1996). They identified five different friendship patterns. In the *rotation* group, children readily formed new relationships but their social ties showed little stability. These children were playful teasers. They were always up on the latest interesting gossip, but they were also aggressive, bossy, and untrustworthy. The *growth* group consisted of children who added new relationships and kept the existing ones. These children were neither bossy nor easily pushed around. In the *decline* group were children whose friendships broke up and were not replaced. These children were caring, shared with others, and, like those in the rotation group, engaged in playful teasing; they were often judged to be "show-offs." Children in the *static* group maintained a stable pool of friendships and added no new ones. They were less apt to tease others, but they were also less caring; the girls in this group were known for their honesty. Finally, children in the *friendless* group made no friends at all throughout the summer. Others perceived these children as timid, shy, and preferring to play alone. They couldn't deal with teasing and were easily angered. In addition, they were rated as less caring, sharing, and honest than their peers. As would be expected, these children were the loneliest. Clearly, children's friendship patterns demonstrate wide variation.

Another examination of friendship patterns revealed gender to be a factor in the stability of children's peer relationships. In a study of 10- to 15-year-olds, researchers found that girls' closest same-gender friendships were more fragile than those of boys (Benenson & Christakos, 2003). The researchers suggested that girls' tendency to form close friendships in isolation from the larger group might jeopardize their relationships. Boys' same-gender friendships are more often embedded in a larger group of relationships, which provides a safety net and access to third-party mediators, allies, and alternative partners.

Another reason girls' friendships may be more fragile is the intimacy expressed in them (Rose, 2002). Girls are more likely than boys to worry that a friendship might end or feel that they've done something to damage a friendship. In girls' friendships, there is more "co-rumination"—conversation in which friends talk together about their personal problems and negative feelings. Although this leads to more positive friendships over time, it also increases girls' depression and anxiety (Rose et al., 2007). In addition, when things go wrong, girls may intensify the problem by divulging intimate secrets about their friend to others, and this betrayal may hasten the demise of the friendship. Boys, in contrast, are less intimate with each other, less likely to divulge personal information about their friend, and, when problems arise, more likely to confront the friend directly (Rose & Rudolph, 2006).

The Pros and Cons of Friendship

For most children, having a friend is a positive experience. Friends provide support, intimacy, and guidance. Children with friends are less lonely and depressed (Berndt, 2004; Hartup, 1996). Even rejected-aggressive and withdrawn children often develop friendships in spite of their difficulties gaining or maintaining acceptance by the wider peer group (Pedersen et al., 2007; Rubin et al., 2009), and friends can buffer these children from loneliness and sadness (Laursen et al., 2007; Parker & Asher, 1993; Sanderson & Siegal, 1991). Children with lots of friends can deal with getting low grades without becoming depressed (Schwartz et al., 2008). Long-term outcomes are better, too. In one study, researchers found that 5th graders who had a reciprocated best friendship were better adjusted when they reached adulthood (Bagwell et al., 1998). Compared with young adults who had been friendless in 5th grade, they were less depressed, less likely to be involved in delinquent activities, and had better relationships with both their families and their peers.

But not all friendships are supportive and beneficial. Some pose risks rather than offering protection (Bagwell, 2004). Withdrawn children's friends are likely to be withdrawn and victimized themselves (Rubin, Bukowski, et al., 2006, Rubin, Wojslawowicz, et al., 2006, Rubin et al., 2009), and these friendships provide less fun, help, and guidance than other friendships (Rubin, Bukowski, et al., 2006). Similarly, rejected children's friendships are likely to be with other rejected children and to be characterized by conflict rather than intimacy (Poulin et al., 1999); these children often encourage each other's deviant behaviors, such as cheating, fighting, and using drugs (Bagwell, 2004; Dishion & Dodge, 2006). It is important to consider the nature and quality of the relationship when weighing the value of friendship. When children have poor-quality friendships, they are more depressed (La Greca & Harrison, 2005) and more likely to be victimized, especially if they have been rejected by their larger peer group (Malcolm et al., 2006).

Romantic Relationships

Adolescence is the time when romantic relationships first develop (Collins et al., 2009). However, many people, including parents and teachers, underestimate the significance of these relationships. In this section we discuss three of the most commonly held myths about adolescent romance.

TEENAGE LOVE AFFAIRS REALLY DO MATTER

Myth 1: *Adolescent romantic relationships are rare and brief.*

Reality: Adolescent romantic relationships are neither uncommon nor transitory. By middle adolescence, most youth have been involved in at least one romantic relationship. In one study, 36 percent of 13-year-olds, 53 percent of 15-year-olds, and 70 percent of 17-year-olds reported having a specific romantic relationship within the preceding year and a half, and 60 percent of the 17–18-year-olds said that their romantic relationships had lasted 11 months or more (Carver et al., 2003). High school students have more frequent interactions with romantic partners than with parents, siblings, or friends (Laursen & Williams 1997).

Myth 2: *Adolescent romantic relationships are unimportant.*

Reality: Adolescent romances are significant for adolescent functioning. On the negative side, adolescents in romantic relationships report more conflicts, have more mood swings, and, when the relationship breaks up, experience more symptoms of depression than adolescents who do not have romantic relationships (Harper et al. 2006; Harper & Welsh, 2007; Joyner & Udry, 2000). Depression also accompanies a romantic relationship with negative qualities (Harper & Welsh, 2007; La Greca & Harrison, 2005; Zimmer-Gembeck et al., 2001, 2004), a promiscuous dating pattern (Zimmer-Gembeck et al., 2001), or negative romantic experiences (Ayduk et al., 2001; Davila et al., 2004; Grello et al., 2003; Harper & Welsh, 2007). On the positive side, adolescents in romantic relationships have higher self-worth, experience less social anxiety, and feel more part of their peer group than adolescents without romantic partners (Harter, 1999; La Greca & Harrison, 2005; La Greca & Prinstein, 1999; Pearce et al., 2002; Zimmer-Gembeck et al., 2001).

Adolescent romantic relationships may have long-term consequences as well. Researchers in a German study found that adolescents with positive, intimate romantic relationships formed more committed relationships in young adulthood than adolescents who lacked romantic relationships (Seiffge-Krenke & Lang, 2002). In another study researchers found that adolescents who dated few partners steadily were better off in their early adulthood relationships than adolescents who dated a large number of different partners casually (Collins, 2003; Collins & van Dulmen, 2006). Long-term consequences of adolescent romantic ties have not always been found (Roisman et al., 2004), however, so although the short-term significance of adolescent romance is quite clear, the verdict on long-term consequences is not.

Myth 3: *Romantic relationships simply mirror other social relationships.*

Reality: It is true that adolescents' romantic relationships are related to their other relationships. Adolescents who have close relationships with their parents tend to have closer romantic relationships (Conger et al., 2000). If they can successfully resolve conflicts with their parents, they can do so with their romantic partners (Cui & Conger, 2008; Donnellan et al., 2005); if their parents are harsh, they are likely to behave aggressively with their romantic partners (Capaldi & Clark, 1998; Kim et al., 2001). Adolescents' relationships with romantic partners are also related to their relationships with friends. Friendships serve as models and sources of social support for romantic relationships (Connolly & Goldberg, 1999; Connolly et al., 2004). Children with higher quality friendships or representations of friendships develop closer romantic ties in adolescence (Collins & Sroufe, 1999; Furman & Shomaker, 2008; Furman et al., 2002). Adolescents who have hostile relationships with peers express more hostility in their romantic relationships (Leadbeater et al., 2008; Stocker & Richmond, 2007). However, despite these associations, relationships with parents and peers are clearly different from relationships with romantic partners and satisfy different needs for adolescents. Parents are valued for their educational and career advice, friends for style tips and gossip, and romantic partners for emotional intimacy and sharing future plans (Furman et al., 2002). In addition, adolescents have more conflicts when they are observed interacting with a romantic partner than with a close friend (Furman & Shomaker, 2008).

CHANGES IN ROMANTIC DYNAMICS OVER TIME   Romantic relationships change quite dramatically between early and late adolescence (Collins et al., 2009). The frequency of romantic involvement increases and so does the length of time in a relationship (Carver et al., 2003). The peer group plays a major role in partner choice in early adolescence. **Peer group networks** and romantic relationships, in fact, probably support each other: Peer group networks support early romantic pairings, and romantic pairings facilitate connections between peers in the network (Connolly et al., 2000; Furman, 2002). Young adolescents date partners that their peer group network approves of or views as "cool." Appearance, clothes, status, and other superficial features guide young adolescents' choices. Older adolescents focus more on characteristics that underlie intimacy and compatibility, such as personality, values, and particular interests (Zani, 1993). They have more interdependence with their romantic partner (Laursen & Jensen-Campbell, 1999) and are more likely than younger adolescents to compromise with their partner as a way of solving problems.

peer group network
The cluster of peer acquaintances who are familiar with and interact with one another at different times for common play or task-oriented purposes.

Interaction in Groups

Children and adolescents form hierarchical groups with common goals and rules.

Dominance Hierarchies

dominance hierarchy
An ordering of individuals in a group from most to least dominant; a "pecking order."

Even in preschool, children in a group form a **dominance hierarchy**, or "pecking order" (Hawley, 1999; Rubin, Bukowski et al., 2006). In fact, evidence of a hierarchy has been observed in children as young as 1½ to 3 (Hawley & Little, 1999). At this age, dominant children are likely to be strong, cognitively mature, and persistent, and girls often dominate boys. After age 3, boys more often take the dominant roles. For the next few years, dominance is based on children's ability to direct the behavior of others in the group, lead them in play, and physically coerce them. In middle childhood and early adolescence, dominance becomes based on leadership skills, attractive appearance, academic performance, athletic prowess, and pubertal development.

Preschool children's dominance hierarchies are simpler and more loosely differentiated than older children's, and they tend to perceive their own positions in the pecking order as a bit higher than they really are; as children mature, they become increasingly accurate at judging their position (Hawley, 2007). Regardless of age, dominance hierarchies emerge quickly. In one study, researchers found that unacquainted primary school boys began to develop a coherently organized social structure within the first 45 minutes of contact (Pettit et al., 1990).

Group hierarchies serve a number of important functions. One is to reduce levels of aggression among group members. In fact, aggression is rarely seen in a group with a well-established hierarchy. All it takes is for a high-ranking member to use a threatening gesture to keep lower ranking group members in line. A second function is to divide the tasks of the group, with lower-status members taking worker roles and director roles going to the more dominant members. Third, dominance hierarchies determine the allocation of resources (Hawley, 2002). In a study of adolescents at summer camp, researchers found that the dominant teens frequently ate the biggest pieces of cake, sat where they wanted to, and slept in the preferred sleeping sites (Savin-Williams, 1987). Clearly, rank has its privileges for individuals of all ages.

"WITH JESSE CALDWELL'S FAMILY MOVING OUT OF TOWN, I'VE BEEN PROMOTED IN THE PLAYGROUND PECKING ORDER."

Source: www.CartoonStock.com

Cliques, Crowds, and Gangs

clique
A peer group formed on the basis of friendship.

In middle childhood, children may form a **clique**, a group based on friendship and shared interests (Brown & Klute, 2006; Schneider, 2000; Kindermann et al., 1995; Chen et al., 2003). Cliques range in size from three to nine children, and members usually are of the same gender and race. By the time children are about 11 years old, most of their interaction with peers occurs in the context of the clique. Membership in a clique enhances children's psychological well-being and ability to cope with stress. Cliques are evident in adolescence as well, but across the high school years, they decline in importance as a result of *degrouping* or loosening clique ties.

crowd
A collection of people whom others have stereotyped on the basis of their perceived shared attitudes or activities— for example, populars or nerds.

The clique is replaced by the **crowd**—a collection of people who share attitudes or activities that define a particular stereotype: *jocks, brains, populars, nerds, skaters, gangstas, stoners, freaks, goths* (Shrum & Cheek, 1987). They may or may not spend much time together (Brown, 1990; Brown & Huang, 1995; Brown & Klute, 2006), but crowd members say that the crowd provides support, fosters friendships, and facilitates social interaction (Brown et al., 1986). Identifying with a crowd in the first year of high school predicted better adjustment in the third year of high school in one study (Heaven et al., 2008), and in another study adolescents who affiliated with a peer crowd were less likely to have feelings of social anxiety (La Greca & Harrison, 2005). Of course, the particular crowd also makes a difference: Adolescents were better adjusted if they were affiliated with a high-status peer crowd such as jocks, brains, or populars (Heaven et al., 2008; La Greca & Harrison, 2005). In the late adolescent years, crowds tend to disband, and the importance of crowd affiliation declines (Brown et al., 1986) as adolescents focus instead on close dyadic friendships and romantic relationships.

Into Adulthood:
What Happens When Jocks, Brains, and Princesses Grow Up

You probably remember from your high school days the athletic *jocks* who dominated the sports teams, the *brains* who were preoccupied with good grades, and the *princesses* who ran the pep squad and almost everything else. Maybe you referred to them by different names, but chances are your high school had its versions. What happens when these adolescents grow up? To find out, researchers Bonnie Barber, Jacquelynne Eccles, and Margaret Stone (2001) followed 900 adolescents from 10th grade into adulthood. When the study began, the coming-of-age movie, *The Breakfast Club*, which depicted students in different high school crowds, was popular, and the students were asked to pick which type of crowd fit them best: jocks, brains, criminals, princesses, or basket cases. The researchers described criminals as tough, rebellious, and hated by their peers and adults; princesses were well liked, influential, and had high social status; brains were into good grades even at the expense of popularity; jocks were the sports team players; basket cases were loners who isolated themselves from the rest of their peers. Of the students in the study, 28 percent identified themselves as jocks, 40 percent as princesses, 12 percent as brains, 11 percent as basket cases, and 9 percent as criminals.

When they were 24 years old, former jocks and brains exhibited the most success and criminals and basket cases, the least. Criminals and basket cases were the most depressed and worried and reported the lowest levels of self-esteem; 25 percent of the basket cases had been treated by a psychologist compared with only 6 percent of the jocks. Jocks had their problems, though; they and the criminals drank the most and were most likely to be in alcohol recovery programs. Criminals, especially men, used marijuana most and were least likely to have graduated from college (only 17% compared with about 30% of the basket cases, jocks, and princesses and 50% of the brains). Jocks, particularly the women, were earning more money than any other group.

Why did crowd identity in 10th grade have such lasting predictive effects? The most likely reason is that adolescents identified with crowds that fit their preferred behavioral patterns and personalities (Brown, 1989, 1990), and these patterns of behavior carried forward into adulthood. As young adults, jocks joined athletic clubs, where they made successful business contacts and then went out for drinks; brains pursued their interest in education and volunteer work (Raymore et al., 1999); criminals and basket cases continued to have mental health problems. The links across age reflect both self-selection into crowds and participation in activities associated with crowds that help consolidate the person's identity and provide opportunities for acquiring new skills and expanding social contacts with other like-minded peers (Barber et al., 2001).

gang
A group of adolescents or adults who form an allegiance for a common purpose.

A **gang** is a group of adolescents or adults who form an allegiance for a common purpose. The gang may be a loose-knit group or a formal organization with a leader or ruling council, gang colors, gang identifiers, and a gang name. Formal gangs are often involved in criminal activity. Being in a gang thus may lead to delinquency and other negative activities. Being part of a gang may also restrict adolescents' social contacts. Belonging to a gang makes it difficult for adolescents to change their lifestyles or explore new identities because they are "channeled" into social ties with individuals who share their values and identities (Brown & Klute, 2006). Gangs also encourage stereotyping; adolescents are biased in their use of reputational or stereotypic information about members of other gangs, especially in ambiguous situations (Horn, 2003).

Real-World Application: Youth Gangs

Gangs have been around for hundreds of years. Pirates operated as gangs. In the 19th century gangs of immigrants—Irish, Italian, Polish—protected their neighborhoods in cities such as New York. Youth gangs began in Los Angeles (L.A.) in 1969 with the formation of a Black street gang called the "Cribs," a term that referred to their youthfulness. The initial intent of this gang was to continue the revolutionary ideology of the 1960s and act as community leaders and protectors of their local neighborhoods, but the revolutionary rhetoric did not last. The Cribs began to commit robberies and assaults. They were renamed the "Crips" after they were described by the victims of one assault as young cripples carrying canes. Crip gangs soon multiplied in L.A., and other gangs formed. Today the Crips and their most notorious rivals, the Bloods, have "franchise" gangs operating in cities across the country. It is estimated that the United States has about 25,000 youth gangs (Snyder & Sickmund, 2006).

In general, youth gangs consist of a loosely organized group of individuals who engage in criminal activity to provide funding for their activities and to further the gang's reputation on the street (Snyder & Sickmund, 2006). Gangs identify themselves with a common name or sign. They dress similarly or wear the gang's colors—the Crips, blue, the Bloods, red. They mark their turf with graffiti in their colors, displaying their gang symbols. Many gangs also adopt certain types of hairstyles and communicate through the use of hand signals. When new members join a gang, they must usually go through an initiation. The most common initiation involves "jumping in" in which the young person is given a beating by all of the gang members. Most gang members (94%) are male (Snyder & Sickmund, 2006), but gangs that accept female members sometimes rape them as their initiation. Getting a tattoo with gang symbols may be another part of the initiation (Deschesnes et al., 2006). Sometimes the new gang member must also participate in a mission. This can be anything from stealing a car to engaging in a firefight with a rival gang. Some gangs don't consider anyone a full member until that person has shot or killed someone.

Young people join gangs for a variety of reasons. Boredom is one; if young people have nothing else to occupy their time, they sometimes turn to mischief to entertain themselves. But this is not the most important reason. Many young people gravitate to gangs out of a need to belong to something (Rizzo, 2003). A gang gives them an identity and offers them love from a new "family." The need for attention and the desire for material goods are also reasons to join a gang. Many gangs exist mainly as moneymaking enterprises, committing thefts and dealing drugs. Another reason young people join gangs is for the power and protection it provides from other gangs and threats. Gangs also give young people instant recognition and reputation ("rep"), respect from their gang "homeboys," and power to retaliate if "gangbangers" from a rival gang disrespect ("dis") them. Adolescents join gangs because they are recruited but also because they are at an age when they are particularly susceptible to peer pressure. If they live in a gang-dominated area or go to a school with a strong gang presence, they are likely to find that many of their friends are joining gangs and they also join. Not surprisingly, researchers have found that gang members are more likely to come from poor and dysfunctional families, to have neglectful parents, and to live in communities where they are surrounded by poverty, drugs, and gangs. They see no chance of getting a decent job, leaving their poor neighborhood, or getting an education, so joining a gang seems like the road to riches. Members also usually have problems long before they join the gang; in elementary school, their peers reject them and they fail in their class work and act in antisocial ways (Dishion et al., 2005). Their teachers and peers rate them as more aggressive than nongang members (Craig et al., 2002).

The consequences of being in a gang are dire. Gang membership facilitates delinquent behavior, violence, and drug use (Gatti et al., 2005; Snyder & Sickmund, 2006) and promotes continued serious offending in young adulthood (Stouthamer-Loeber et al., 2004). It increases the likelihood that gang members will be victims of violence (Taylor et al., 2007) and suffer psychological distress (Li et al., 2002). Gangs may harm members in more subtle ways as well, cutting them off from people and opportunities that could help them with the transition to adulthood and disrupting their lives even after they have moved beyond the gang. Young adults who have been in gangs are more likely to end their education prematurely, have children early, and fail to establish stable work lives—all of which are associated with an increased likelihood of being arrested as adults (Snyder & Sickmund, 2006).

One gangbanger who is in prison for shooting a member of a rival gang has this to say to would-be gang members (http://www.gangsandkids.com/):

> I must tell you there's nothing good that comes from being a gang member! True, you have some good times but in the end you wind up going to a lot of funerals or visiting a lot of prisons! Now if that's your idea of a life then the gang scene is for you—drugs, murder, mayhem, prison, and death! Oh yeah, while you're hanging out with your homies and home girls drinking, getting high, fighting rival members, or just committing any kind of crime, it's all cool! But when it turns into a life or death situation then you want to take time to reflect and question your present position in life! Ask yourself, do you really want to spend your life in prison under the control of someone else 24-7? Or how about dodging bullets every time you walk to the store? Maybe you would like to bury someone every other week? It's up to you! But the gang life is for people who don't care about life. Open your eyes and reflect before it's too late. What exposed me to the fact that gangbangin' (what some call a second family) is B.S. and that my misguided loyalty to my gang family was a waste of time was the fact that over the last 24 years, not one of my homeboys or homegirls has wrote me a letter, sent me a care package, or even came to pay me a visit! But you know who was there for me "standing tall through it all"?—my mother! The moral to my story is simple: love and respect yourself and know yourself! Then you'll recognize that a real friendship starts with yourself. Also respect your parents because when all the smoke clears, they'll be the only ones still on your side and by your side.

Chapter Summary

Peer Interactions

- Children's interactions with peers are briefer, freer, and more equal than interactions with adults. These interactions facilitate interpersonal exploration and growth in social competence.

Developmental Patterns of Peer Interaction

- Infants interact with peers by vocalizing and touching.
- Toddlers exchange turns and roles during interactions with peers; major achievements include sharing meaning with a peer and engaging in mutual pretend play.
- Children increase their preference for interacting with peers rather than adults as they grow.
- Companionship with peers of the same age increases over the school years.
- Children are likely to choose same-gender play partners.
- In adolescence, gender segregation lessens as dating begins. Peer relationships are used to explore and enhance identities.

Peers as Socializers

- Peers act as models of social behavior, reinforce and punish each another, serve as standards against which children evaluate themselves, and provide opportunities for developing a sense of belonging.
- Peers have a stronger influence than parents on adolescents' lifestyle choices.
- Patterns of peer interaction and influence are different in different cultures.

Peer Status

- Peer status is assessed with sociometric techniques by having children identify peers they like and don't like; peer acceptance is assessed with ratings of how much children like or dislike each classmate. Children are classified as popular, rejected, neglected, controversial, or average.

- Peer status depends on children's abilities to initiate interaction, communicate effectively, respond to others' interests and behaviors, and cooperate in activities.

- Popular children engage in prosocial behavior and help set the norms for the group. Nonaggressive-rejected children tend to be withdrawn and lack social skills. Aggressive-rejected children have low self-control and exhibit problem behaviors. Neglected children are less talkative and more shy and anxious. Controversial children are liked by many peers and disliked by many others.

- According to social-cognitive information-processing theory, children attend to the cues in a social situation, interpret other children's behavior, decide what their own goals are and how to achieve them, decide to take certain actions, and act on their decisions.

- Children may not always respond to social situations in a reflective and thoughtful way; sometimes their behavior is impulsive or automatic.

- In comparison to unpopular and socially unsuccessful children, those who are popular and socially successful have more positive goals and strategies, more self-confidence and persistence, can try a new approach when another has been unsuccessful, are more attractive, and blend in with other children.

- Being unpopular can lead to short-term problems such as loneliness and low self-esteem and long-term problems such as depression. Having at least one friend can reduce loneliness.

- Social status tends to remain stable across time and situations, especially for rejected children.

Promoters of Peer Acceptance

- Parents serve as partners from whom children acquire social skills, act as social coaches, and provide opportunities for children to have peer interactions.

- Researchers can help children improve their social skills by coaching.

- Peers themselves can help rejected children improve their social skills and experience more peer acceptance.

When Peers Become Friends

- Children develop close friendships with only a few peers.
- The goals and expectations of friendship change with age.
- Friends communicate more clearly and positively, disclose more about themselves, exchange more information, establish more common ground, and are able to resolve conflicts more effectively than nonfriends.
- Boys' same-gender friendships are less fragile than those of girls because they are often embedded in a larger group of relationships.
- Friends provide support, intimacy, and guidance. However, some friendships encourage deviant behavior, such as cheating, fighting, and using drugs.
- Withdrawn and aggressive children have friends with characteristics similar to their own.
- Romantic relationships in adolescence are an important and distinctive form of social relationship.

Interaction in Groups

- Children form hierarchically organized groups with common goals and rules of conduct.
- In middle childhood, children form cliques, which enhance their well-being and ability to cope with stress.
- In high school, children may be thought of by their peers as belonging to a specific crowd.
- A gang is a group of adolescents or adults who form an allegiance for a common purpose. The gang may be a loose-knit group or a formal organization; organized gangs are often involved in criminal activity.

Key Terms

aggressive-rejected
    children
associative play
average children
clique
controversial children
cooperative play
crowd
dominance hierarchy

gang
homophily
mutual antipathy
negative gossip
neglected children
nonaggressive-rejected
    children
parallel play
peer group network

perceived popularity
popular children
pretend play
rejected children
reputational bias
self-disclosure
social comparison
sociometric technique

At the Movies

Friendship themes are common in movies. In *The Kite Runner* (2007), two boys, Amir and Hassan, form a deep friendship, playing and kiting on the streets of Kabul, Afghanistan, in the 1970s. Hassan defends Amir from a violent older boy, demonstrating his loyalty. But when Amir witnesses Hassan being beaten and raped by the older boy and does not help him, the friendship comes to an end. This film offers a moving illustration of the persistent guilt and regret that can result from a violated friendship. In *Son of Rambow* (2007), two British 11-year-olds who seem to have nothing in common meet in the hallway at school. One boy is there because he comes from a strict religious family and is not allowed to watch a movie; the other boy is there because he has been causing trouble again. Both boys are isolated at home and at school, and despite their superficial differences, they have much in common and form a deep friendship. This movie takes you inside the world of childhood, reminds you what it's like to be a child, and convinces you of the importance of lasting friendship. *The Mighty* (1998) offers a moving portrayal of a childhood friendship between two seriously handicapped boys. Kevin's medical condition has twisted his body and stunted his growth; Max has a large body but his mind is slow. Through their friendship, the boys overcome their complementary mental and physical limitations, stand up to bullies, and defend the vulnerable. This movie provides a clear demonstration of the benefits of a close friendship. *Welcome to the Dollhouse* (1996) is a dark comedy about an awkward 7th-grader who is taunted and put down by her peers because of her physical appearance. Her parents offer no support or helpful coaching, and her little sister makes deprecating comments. This movie has no happy ending, but it will help you empathize with young teens who suffer from peer rejection and pass on their anger and frustration to other children who are even less popular.

Other movies offer insights into additional aspects of peer relations discussed in this chapter. *Clueless* (1995) is a movie about high school cliques, friendships, and romances; it focuses on three self-absorbed, fashion-obsessed teens who are almost pulled apart by jealousy over boys but find that friendship wins out in the end. Scores of movies have been made about teen romances, but two that portray the intensity and poignancy of young love are *Romeo and Juliet* (1968) and *David and Lisa* (1962). In the latter, David is an obsessive who cannot bear to be touched, and Lisa is a schizophrenic who speaks only in rhymes. Affection and kindness are not cures for mental illness in real life as they appear to be in this movie, but the film's portrayal of young love is strikingly tender. *Crips and Bloods: Made in America* (2009) is a documentary that tells the story of the two most infamous African American gangs in South Los Angeles and chronicles the decades-long cycle of destruction and despair that defines modern gang culture.

CHAPTER 9

Schools and Media: Children in an Electronic Age

Source: Ranald Mackechnie/Getty Images, Inc.

Owen, who is 3, loves to watch *Barney and Friends* on TV. He sings along as the 6-foot purple dinosaur leads songs and games about respect, courtesy, and manners. Lainie, age 4, can't get enough of *Thomas [the Tank Engine] & Friends*. She watches intently as the train engines learn what it is to be a Really Useful Engine, and as she watches, she is exposed to lessons about responsibility, helping, the value of encouragement, and the importance of treating others with kindness. For Ethan, who is 5, *Sesame Street* is a favorite. It combines entertainment with education and not only teaches him about the alphabet but also imparts prosocial lessons about sharing and honesty. These three television shows are among the most popular programs for preschool children today—but do they influence children's social development? The answer is revealed in this chapter, which focuses on input from schools and electronic media.

In this chapter, we discuss how children are influenced by sources of socialization in addition to the family and peers, specifically, schools and the electronic media, including television, video games, and the Internet. Television is part of children's lives from an early age, and by the time they are 4 or 5 years old, many children also spend substantial amounts of time playing video and computer games. They have often started school by this age, too, and as the years go by, school activities fill more and more of their time. Even during after-school hours, schooling affects children's daily routines through homework assignments and participation in sports, clubs, and other extracurricular activities. Together, schools and the electronic media fill much of children's waking time, and it would not be surprising to find that, as a result, they affect children's social development.

The Role of the School in Social Development

Children today spend more time in school than ever before—more hours each day and more days each year. U.S. children now go to school an average of five hours a day, 180 days a year. In 1880, children in the United States attended school only about 80 days a year. Not only are children spending more hours and days in school, but also they are beginning school at younger ages and staying until older ages.

Although the primary purpose of schools is to instruct children in academic subjects, schools are much more than places to learn to write, solve math problems, and locate Zimbabwe on a map. Schools have another, informal, agenda as well: teaching the rules, norms, and values children need to get along in society and helping them develop the skills they need to interact with their peers. On their way to learning math and English, children learn about social expectations, emotional self-regulation, and standards and codes of conduct (Epstein, 2001; Greenfield, Suzuki, et al., 2006). Thus, schools are important contexts for socialization. They are also venues in which children interact with peers in settings from classrooms to cafeterias and playgrounds to practice fields. During these interactions, children develop social skills and advance their social understanding. Some schools do a better job of promoting children's social development than others. In this section, we discuss features of the school environment that affect how well schools foster social development.

"My objective is to have each student become more insightful, compassionate, introspective, and empathetic. In your case I will settle for quiet."

Source: www.CartoonStock.

Schools as Social Communities

Schools are not merely classrooms, or buildings, or playgrounds. Children develop a sense of community in their schools when they, their teachers, and the school staff share goals and values, support each others' efforts, and believe that everyone makes an important contribution to school life (McDevitt & Ormrod, 2007; Osterman, 2000). Children do better socially in schools in which they have a strong sense of community; they have more positive attitudes toward school, exhibit more prosocial behavior, have lower rates of disruptive behavior, are less emotionally distressed, and have lower rates of violence and drug use; they are also less likely to ditch or drop out of school (Osterman, 2000).

The mechanism through which these positive effects of a sense of community are achieved is probably "collective efficacy," which, as we defined in Chapter 1, refers to people's shared beliefs in their collective power to achieve a goal or produce a desired result (Bandura, 2000, 2006). When a sense of community exists, teachers, students, and administrators are more likely to share goals and believe that they can achieve these goals through collective and cooperative action. In a study of collective efficacy at 79 elementary schools, researchers found that student achievement was better when teachers believed in their collective efficacy to motivate and educate students (Bandura, 1993). Collective efficacy was also a significant positive predictor of students' academic performance in high school (Goddard et al., 2004). Although researchers have not yet linked collective efficacy directly to children's social behavior, they have shown that children who do better academically are likely to exhibit better social behavior (Reid et al., 2002). Moreover, they have found that the emotional climate in elementary school classrooms is more positive when teachers report having more influence on school policy and feelings of efficacy (Pianta et al., 2007). Therefore, promoting collective efficacy is likely to improve both student achievement and classroom climate and perhaps social behavior as well.

School Size and Organization

From an outsider's point of view, a large school may seem to have more going for it with its substantial exterior dimensions, its specialized classrooms, and its crowd of students. The small school with its less imposing edifice, smaller number of rooms, and fewer students may seem less impressive. But appearances can be deceiving.

BIG SCHOOL; SMALL SCHOOL   Much of the school's influence on children's social development comes through extracurricular activities such as clubs and sports, car washes and bake sales. You may think that large schools offer students a wider variety of these extracurricular activities: band *and* orchestra, football *and* soccer, French Club *and* Japanese Club, Painting Club *and* Digital Arts Club, Students against Land Mines *and* Young Democrats for Social Justice. However, in one study of school size, researchers found that large and small schools did not differ much in the variety of activities they offered, and more importantly, students' participation rates in extracurricular activities were actually higher in the smaller schools (Barker & Gump, 1964). In smaller schools, students had more opportunities to join teams and clubs because there were more positions than students to fill them. Students also felt a greater obligation to play an active role in the school and developed a stronger sense of belonging. Large schools had too many students for the limited number of positions available so many students were reduced to spectator roles. Other researchers have also found that larger school size is associated with less extracurricular participation and less student attachment to the school and teachers (Crosnoe et al., 2004). The reduced sense of identification and involvement of students in larger schools may be part of the reason that dropout rates tend to be higher in large schools than small schools (Lee & Burkam, 2003).

Participation in extracurricular activities is linked to a number of positive outcomes. Students who participate in these activities have higher self-esteem, better school attendance, higher achievement motivation, and lower likelihood of drinking or using drugs than students who do not participate in extracurricular activities (Child Trends, 2008). They are less likely to get involved in delinquent behavior, become pregnant, experience depression, or commit suicide (Dusek, 1991; Mahoney, 2000).

A study of youth participation in high school sports illustrates the value of these activities (Simpkins et al., 2006). Students who participated in organized sports 10 hours a week or more in comparison with those who did not participate were less depressed, had higher self-esteem, were more likely to be part of a positive peer group (one that valued school and adhered to parents' rules), and felt a stronger sense of belonging to the school. In contrast to the view that extracurricular activities are unimportant—a view often held by budget-minded school officials—these findings suggest that clubs and sports actually help children and adolescents navigate their school years successfully.

Despite the advantages of extracurricular participation in small schools, the size of the average U.S. school rose from 127 students to 653 students between 1940 and 1990 (Mitchell, 2000). Educators have suggested that although changing the size of already existing schools is difficult, smaller units within the school could be designed to achieve a closer match with the needs of students. These "schools within schools" could provide more behavior settings in which students could develop a sense of identity and belonging that might prevent them from dropping out of school and enhance the likelihood of positive socioemotional outcomes (Linney & Seidman, 1989; Seidman & French, 1997).

AGE GROUPINGS IN SCHOOLS   The way that different grades are organized also affects children's development (Roeser et al., 2000; Wigfield et al., 2006). Traditionally, school was separated into two age-based segments: the first 8 years and the next 4 years. Today, a different organizational scheme is popular. In this arrangement, the first six grades of elementary school are grouped together, followed by 3 years of junior high or middle school (grades 7 to 9), followed by 3 years of high school (grades 10 to 12). Research suggests that this organizational change was not a positive one for children. Most notably, students who go to middle school and enter a new school for 7th grade are likely to experience more social and academic problems than children who stay in their familiar elementary school setting. Their self-esteem drops, they tend to be less involved in activities and clubs, and they perceive themselves as less integrated into their school and peer group than children who do not make the shift to a secondary school for 7th grade (Eccles & Roeser, 2003; Roeser et al., 2000).

What is the reason for these negative consequences? Compared with elementary schools, middle schools are larger, causing students to feel more alienated and anonymous. Students are less likely to become involved in school activities, and this reduces their sense of belonging and their sense of social competence. Instruction patterns change, too, from a single classroom with one teacher in elementary school to a variety of teachers and classes for different subjects in middle school. Students are less likely to form close supportive relationships with middle school teachers than elementary school teachers. In middle school, children's friendship networks are disrupted as a result of attending classes with children from different elementary schools, and competition among peers is fiercer because of this change and more stringent grading policies. Together, these changes make the transition to middle school a challenge for younger students, and, not surprisingly, may undermine their social competence and lead to an increased likelihood of dropping out (Wigfield et al., 2006).

Shifting to a middle school is also likely to have a negative effect because preadolescents are undergoing other transitions as well, including the onset of puberty and the beginning of dating (Eccles, 2007; Wigfield et al., 2006). The shift to a new school at this age does not provide a good **stage-environment fit**. Researchers have found that children—especially girls—who experience three or more transitions in this age period have less self-esteem, participate in fewer extracurricular activities, and have lower grades than children who do not undergo so many transitions at once (Mendle et al., 2007; Simmons et al., 1987). The implications seem clear: If change comes too suddenly, is too early, or occurs in too many areas at once, children are likely to suffer. They do better in terms of self-esteem and behavioral coping if they have some "arena of comfort" in their lives.

Although most attention has been given to the transition from elementary school to middle school, the shift from middle school to high school can also be a challenge. For many students, entry into high school exposes them to a fully compartmentalized curriculum, more academic tracking, and an even more impersonal social climate, in part, simply because of school size. These students may experience a drop in their grades and an increase in social isolation; girls are particularly likely to have adjustment problems such as loneliness and anxiety when they make the

stage-environment fit
The degree to which the environment supports a child's developmental needs.

transition to high school (Barber & Olsen, 2004). The ethnic balance of the high school affects how well minority youth manage the transition. Latino and African American youth are more negatively affected when their high school has fewer students from their ethnic group than when the school offers the same ethnic balance as their middle school (Benner & Graham, 2009).

No single age-grouping system for schools is ideal for all children, however. Individual differences influence how well children negotiate transitions between schools. Children who perceive that they have diminished control or importance are likely to experience more stress and depression than children with more positive perceptions (Rudolph et al., 2001). Several educational organizations, such as the Carnegie Foundation and the National Middle Schools Association, have proposed ways to reform secondary schools to reduce the negative impact of school transitions. They have suggested turning large schools into sets of smaller learning communities, increasing teacher awareness of the special needs of young adolescents, and providing advising and counseling for all students. Adolescents in schools that have implemented these reforms have higher self-esteem, fewer behavior problems, and less fear about bad things happening to them at school than students whose schools continue to offer them business as usual (Felner et al., 1997; MacIver et al., 2002).

COEDUCATIONAL VERSUS SAME-GENDER SCHOOLS   The question of whether single-gender schools for girls and boys or coeducational schools with both boys and girls attending are better for children's development has long been debated. In 1972, a law was passed in the United States making coeducation in public schools obligatory. After that, many studies were conducted showing that boys and girls learn differently and that girls, especially, often fail to reach their potential in coeducational schools. As a result, in 2002, the law mandating coeducation was revoked and single-gender schools became a legal option. Over the next seven years, the number of public schools offering same-gender classes increased from 11 to 518.

Does it matter? Most evidence has shown that achievement and career aspirations are higher, especially for girls, in single-gender schools (American Association of University Women, 1998; Lee & Bryk, 1986; Perry, 1996; Sax, 2005; Watson et al., 2002; Van de Gaer et al., 2004). Moreover, girls in all-girls schools are more likely to enroll in traditionally "masculine" classes such as the physical sciences, computer science, and engineering (Koppe et al., 2003), and boys in all-boys schools are more likely to enroll in traditionally "feminine" classes, such as art, drama, music, and foreign languages (Sax, 2005). Although these outcomes are in academic areas, the reasons for the advantage of same-gender schools may be social. Children in same-gender schools are less distracted by opposite-sex classmates, participate more actively in class discussions, and develop more self-confidence and self-esteem (Baker, 2002; Cairns, 1990). However, because same-gender schools are often private rather than public, the quality of the instruction and the motivation of both students and teachers may be higher in these school contexts than in public schools (Datnow, 2002). We cannot attribute the observed advantages solely to the same-gender school environment. This topic needs further research. It is too early to close the debate or close coed schools in favor of single-gender ones.

Class Size and Organization

Not only are children's social experiences and development affected by differences in school size and organization; they are even more strongly influenced by variations in class size and organization.

ADVANTAGES OF SMALL CLASSES   Being in a small class, like being in a small school, is beneficial for children's social development, particularly in the early grades. Research in the United States, the United Kingdom, and Israel has demonstrated that in small classes teacher-child contacts are more frequent and personalized and children are better behaved, interact more with their peers, and are less likely to be victimized (Blatchford, 2003; Finn & Pannozzo, 2004; Khoury-Kassabri et al., 2004). Students in small classes contribute more to class activities, pay more attention in class, are less likely to "fool around" and be disruptive, and exhibit less antisocial behavior and more prosocial behavior (Finn et al., 2003). Small class size is also associated with a more positive emotional climate in elementary school classes (Pianta et al., 2007). Smaller classes appear to promote an atmosphere in which students are more supportive and caring about each other. Not surprisingly, teachers in smaller classes are more satisfied as well (Blatchford, 2005).

BENEFITS OF OPEN CLASSROOMS   Teachers can organize their classrooms and class activities in different ways. They can stand in front of the class and lecture, or they can have students move around, work in small groups, help each other with projects, and participate in decision making. Teachers implement this **open classroom** organization because they believe children learn best by being involved and participating actively in their own learning rather than passively listening to the teacher spout knowledge. Researchers have not always found that children learn better in open classrooms, but these classrooms do offer social benefits (Minuchin & Shapiro, 1983). Elementary school children in open classrooms have more varied social contacts, develop more positive attitudes toward school, and show more self-reliant and cooperative behavior in learning situations. High school students in open classrooms participate more in school activities, have more varied social relationships, and create fewer disciplinary problems.

open classroom
A relatively unstructured organization in which different areas of the room are devoted to particular activities and children work either alone or in small groups under the teacher's supervision.

COOPERATIVE LEARNING   **Cooperative learning** involves small groups of students working together (see photo). Often the group is heterogeneous with children of different abilities and backgrounds trying to solve problems. No child is singled out to be the leader; the goal is to maximize the learning of all students and create relationships among diverse children. Most studies of cooperative learning show that this classroom technique has a positive effect on children's self-esteem and increases their concern about peers and their willingness to help each other (Minuchin & Shapiro, 1983; Slavin, 2005; Slavin & Cooper, 1999). Children in cooperative groups also interact more with children of other ethnic groups and, as a result, exhibit less ethnic conflict (Renninger, 1998). The benefits of cooperative learning are especially pronounced for Latino and native Hawai'ian children, in part because this type of learning is more compatible with the learning style practiced in families with a collectivist cultural orientation (Aronson & Gonzalez, 1988; Aronson & Patnoe, 1997; Tharp & Gallimore, 1988). Unfortunately, in the real world, elementary school students in the United States spend almost all of their class time (more than 90%) in their seats listening to a teacher or working alone and very little time (less than 5%) working in small groups (Pianta et al., 2007).

cooperative learning
A teaching technique in which small groups of students work together.

Students in a cooperative learning situation work together, here to solve math problems.
Source: Ellen B. Senisi.

peer tutoring
A method of instruction in which an older, more experienced student tutors a younger, less experienced child.

PEER TUTORS   Teachers sometimes arrange for **peer tutoring** in which an older, more experienced student tutors a younger or less able child (Slavin, 1996). Peer tutors can teach children social skills as well as improving their math and reading abilities. For example, in one study, 9- to 13-year-olds improved the social skills of special education students by implementing a social skills curriculum (Blake et al., 2000). Although both tutors and tutees can benefit in a variety of ways, tutors usually gain more; they increase in self-esteem and status and derive satisfaction from helping others (Dansereau, 1987). Many students including low achievers of all ethnic backgrounds and children with psychological disabilities can benefit from peer tutoring both socially and academically (Cochran et al., 1993).

et You Thought That . . .
Homeschooled Children Were Socially Disadvantaged

Educating children at home is an increasingly popular alternative to formal schooling. In the United States, more than 1 million children are homeschooled. Parents select this option for many reasons: religion (33%), a better learning environment (30%), objections to what schools teach (14%), or a belief that their children are not being challenged (11%) (Princiotta & Bielick, 2006). Research supports the parents' choice. Homeschooled students perform better on standardized tests than children who attend schools (Basham, 2001; Klicka, 2001; Lines, 2000a, b). However, as we have pointed out, school involves more than academic learning; it provides valuable opportunities for children to associate with peers and learn social skills. A major criticism of homeschooling is that it deprives children of experience with peers, especially those of different ethnic and religious backgrounds, and this may result in feelings of social isolation and loneliness or social problems such as the inability to get along with peers. As one mother put it, "It seemed to me that several of my friends in high school who had been homeschooled had a very hard time developing socially."

Was this parent right to worry? If you think so, think again. Research suggests that concern about homeschooled children's social development is unwarranted (Shaw, 2008). When trained counselors watched videotapes of mixed groups of homeschooled and schooled children playing, they observed that the homeschooled children exhibited fewer behavior problems, not more (Shyers, 1992). In another study, researchers found that homeschooled children were better adjusted, happier, and more sociable than traditionally schooled peers

(Moore, 1986). Homeschooled children in a third study had higher self-perceptions in the areas of academic achievement and socialization than schooled children (Taylor, 1986). The long-term effects of homeschooling seem to be positive as well. In one study, 71 percent of adults who had been homeschooled participated in community services such as coaching or volunteering compared with 37 percent of traditionally educated adults (Ray, 2003). They were also more involved in civic affairs, voted more than twice as often, and claimed to be happier.

Why do homeschooled children thrive socially? For one thing, they are not socially isolated. Homeschooling parents often take advantage of social opportunities for their children at museums, community centers, athletic clubs, after-school programs, churches, science preserves, and parks. Groups of homeschooling families also sometimes join together to create homeschool co-ops that meet regularly so the children can interact with peers and form friendships. Some states even have laws permitting homeschooling families to take advantage of public school resources so the children can participate in sports teams or school band and take art classes with other children. In addition, homeschooled children are likely to have siblings.

There is one important caveat to the research on homeschooling, however. Researchers have not randomly assigned children to be homeschooled, and parents who choose this option tend to be better educated and more motivated to promote their children's academic and social success than parents who simply put their children on the school bus every morning (Klicka, 2001). Caveat aside, available evidence suggests that homeschooling does not produce social isolates or misfits.

The Teachers' Impact

Teachers play several roles in the classroom: instructor, social model, evaluator, and disciplinarian, to name a few. How teachers manage each role can affect children in a variety of ways.

TEACHER-STUDENT RELATIONSHIPS   The quality of the relationships that children form with their teachers is an important contributor to the children's social and academic success (Hughes & Kwok, 2006). Children whose relationship with the teacher is full of conflict don't like school much and are not very cooperative in the classroom; they become less helpful and cooperative and more aggressive and depressed over time (Birch & Ladd, 1997, 1998; Jia et al., 2009; Pianta et al., 1995). Children who have an overly dependent relationship with the teacher also have problems; they are less engaged in school activities and more aggressive or socially withdrawn with their peers (Birch & Ladd, 1997; Howes et al., 1994; Pianta, 1999). Children whose relationship with the teacher is close and warm, however, have a higher level of school adjustment, higher self-esteem, and are more likely to be accepted by their peers (Hughes & Kwok, 2006; Jia et al., 2009). These associations have been observed in both younger and older children and in other countries as well (Jia et al., 2009; Lee & Burkam, 2003; Yang, 2001).

The teacher-student relationship may be especially important for the social adjustment of minority children. In one study, aggressive African American and Latino children who formed positive relationships with their 2nd- or 3rd-grade teachers were observed to be less aggressive 1 year later; however, the association was not as strong among European American children (Meehan et al., 2003). One reason that European American children were less affected may be that teachers are generally more supportive of them anyway so when they are more positive it has less impact than for minority children. Teachers do tend to use more positive and less negative speech with European American children than with African American and Latino children (Tenenbaum & Ruck, 2007). They are also more positive in their interpretations of European American children's misbehavior (Hill & Bromell, 2008). They see this misbehavior as indicating that the children are bored and they should give them more interesting materials. However, when teachers see African American children misbehaving, they interpret it as indicating that the children are simply not engaged in learning. Another reason that the quality of the teacher-student relationship matters more for minority children may be that immigrant parents from a collectivist cultural orientation value personal relationships between teachers and students more than do parents from the individualistic majority (Greenfield, Suzuki, et al., 2006). Regardless of the specific reason, a positive relationship with a teacher can be a protective factor for children at risk for later adjustment problems in school.

KEEPING CONTROL: CLASSROOM DISCIPLINE AND MANAGEMENT   Teachers spend a good deal of their time trying to manage their class and disciplining unruly children. The techniques they use can have significant effects on children's social behavior. Some teachers use poker chips or candies to encourage children to behave and to learn their school work. Others use verbal approval, systematically praising children's appropriate behavior. Teachers' attempts to apply operant reinforcement principles to classroom control have been quite successful. Numerous studies have demonstrated the effectiveness of systematic reinforcement for controlling children's behavior (Cashwell et al., 2001; Chang, 2003; Kazdin, 2000). Today it is common for teachers to set up the classroom so that children accumulate points, tokens, or gold stars that they can then exchange for material rewards such as candy or toys. In addition, children may pool their rewards for special treats such as parties or field trips.

Using operant conditioning principles is clearly better for children than having teachers shout at them or let the class go wild. Using these tangible rewards has a down side, however. Under some circumstances, material rewards may undermine the teacher's agenda and children's progress. Activities that are intrinsically interesting to children may lose their appeal if the children are rewarded for doing them (Lepper & Henderlong, 2000). For example, rewarding children for helping other students has been shown to undermine the children's internalized sense of moral obligation (Kohn 1993; McLean, 2003). Token programs have a place in the classroom, but teachers need to exercise care in choosing the target activities and in applying the reward system.

Classroom management also involves the ways that class tasks are assigned and completed. To the extent that these decisions reflect an understanding of the students' cultural backgrounds, classroom management is easier. When teachers of Latino children appreciate that collectivistic cultures value helpfulness and adjust their classroom practices accordingly, discipline problems decrease (Rothstein-Fisch & Trumbull, 2008). Without this awareness, teachers often assign individual children to classroom roles, such as chalkboard cleaner and attendance monitor. When friends help each other, these teachers admonish them, saying, "That's Marco's job. You have your own job to do!" They construe the students' helping not only as off task and unproductive but also, worse, as cheating. When teachers appoint two children to each task or allow children to help one another, however, cleanup time becomes pleasant. This type of management in which teachers support children for being helpful instead of punishing them for interfering with a classmate's responsibility increases efficiency, task completion, and classroom harmony.

TEACHER EXPECTATIONS AND CHILDREN'S SUCCESS   Although most teachers would deny it, early in the school year they form impressions about how well new students will do. These impressions affect the children's classroom performance. In a classic study, Robert Rosenthal and Lenore Jacobson (1968) planted expectations about certain children in the minds of some elementary school teachers. They told the teachers that these students—whom the researchers had chosen randomly—were "bloomers" who would show unusual gains during the school year. Eight months later, the bloomers showed a significantly larger increase in IQ scores than other students. These results—dubbed the **Pygmalion effect** after the Greek myth of Pygmalion, a sculptor whose statue of a woman came to life—were an impressive demonstration of a **self-fulfilling prophecy**. Believing that certain students were exceptionally bright, the teachers treated them differently—they gave them more chances to participate in class and more time to answer questions; they praised them more often for correct answers and criticized them less frequently for wrong ones. By giving the children special treatment, the teachers reinforced the expected patterns of behavior (Brophy, 1998). Subsequent research suggested that Pygmalion effects were also due to changes in children's expectations; when teachers thought children would do well, the children adopted a similar set of elevated expectations, which, in turn, resulted in increased achievement (Kuklinski & Weinstein, 2001). These variations in teacher expectations may contribute to the differential success rates of minority and majority students. Teachers hold the highest expectations for Asian American students, the lowest expectations for Latino and African American students (Tenenbaum & Ruck, 2007)—and the students' performance mirrors these expectations. Research has demonstrated self-fulfilling prophecies at work in Head Start classes, in programs for children who are mentally retarded, and in institutions for adolescents, as well as in regular classrooms (Kuklinski & Weinstein, 2001). A meta-analysis of 479 studies indicated that Pygmalion effects are nontrivial in size (mean $r = .30$; Rosenthal, 2006). Although most of these studies focused on children's academic success, some suggested that teachers' expectations of children's social behavior affect their social success.

Pygmalion effect
A phenomenon in which teachers' expectations that students will do well are realized.

self-fulfilling prophecy
Positive or negative expectations that affect a person's behavior in a manner that he or she (unknowingly) creates situations in which those expectations are fulfilled.

School-Family Links

Schools and classrooms are important contexts for promoting children's self-esteem and social skills. But how effective they are depends on the support they are given by parents. In this section we discuss some of the links between schools and families.

SCHOOL CULTURE; HOME CULTURE   Children from lower social socioeconomic levels and minority ethnic groups generally have a more difficult time in school than White middle-class children because the former face a different set of cultural values and norms at school from those they are familiar with at home (Hill, 2010). School is a middle-class institution based on middle-class values and staffed by middle-class teachers, and, in the United States, strongly influenced by the individualistic orientation of European Americans (Greenfield, Suzuki, et al., 2006; Hill, 2010). These differences between poor and minority children and middle-class teachers can lead to misunderstandings. In one study, European American and Latino children, their parents, and their teachers, were asked to reflect on several common school scenarios. For example (Raeff et al., 2000, p. 66):

> *It is the end of the school day, and the class is cleaning up. Denise is not feeling well, and she asks Jasmine to help her with her job for the day, which is cleaning the blackboard. Jasmine isn't sure she will have time to do both her own job and Denise's. What do you think the teacher should do?*

Teachers responded to this scenario in an individualistic fashion, suggesting that the teacher should find another child to clean the blackboard and not endanger Jasmine's ability to complete her task. However, children and parents gave responses that depended on their cultural backgrounds. European American children and their parents echoed the teachers' responses. Immigrant Latino children and especially their parents were likely to endorse a collectivistic response and suggest that Jasmine should help her sick classmate with her job. For these children, there was a clear discontinuity between the orientation of the school and the orientation of the family. Research on parent-teacher conferences with Latino parents provides further illustration of this culture gap. When teachers praised a child's individual achievement, Latino parents were uncomfortable because the focus was on the individual rather than the group (Greenfield et al., 2000).

These findings do not mean that lower-class and minority-group parents believe their children's education is unimportant (Fuligni & Tseng, 1999; Hill & Sprague, 1999; Portes & Rumbaut, 2001). African American and Latino mothers placed a higher value on their children's education than European American mothers in one study of elementary school children (Steinberg et al., 1992), and in a study of nearly 8,000 San Francisco Bay area adolescents and their parents, African American parents were clearly concerned about their children's education (Steinberg et al., 1991). In a third study, Latino parents, especially immigrants, such as Mexican Americans, were also concerned about their children's education, although they were less directly involved than European American parents, perhaps because of language barriers and their own limited formal education (Greenfield, Suzuki, et al., 2006). Thus, parents and teachers share a concern about children's education although they do not see eye-to-eye on children's behavior in the classroom (Hill, 2010). It is clear that any program aimed at improving the school experience of poor and minority children requires that teachers be exposed to multicultural values and ideas so they have a better understanding of the cultural background of their students.

Learning from Living Leaders: Nancy E. Hill

Source: Courtesy of Nancy E. Hill.

Nancy Hill, an expert on family–school relations, is Professor of Education at Harvard University. After her graduate work at Michigan State University and postdoctoral study at Arizona State University, she taught at Duke University before going to Harvard. Her primary research interests include understanding family socialization in diverse contexts. Specifically, she studies how socialization varies across ethnic and socioeconomic groups and is influenced by neighborhood processes and other contexts such as schools. She also studies demographic variations in the relations between family dynamics and children's development. Her recent research includes Project PASS (Promoting Academic Success for Students), a longitudinal study that examines family predictors of children's school performance from kindergarten through 4th grade. Another study, ACTION/ACCIONES, is a multiethnic, longitudinal study of parental involvement in education at the transition between elementary and middle school. She collaborates with the Study Group on Race, Culture, and Ethnicity, an interdisciplinary group of nationally known scholars who are developing theories and methods to define and understand the cultural contexts of diverse families. She hopes her work will be used to promote better relations between families and schools, thereby improving the lives of minority children who are often at a disadvantage in school.

Further Reading

Hill, N. E., & Torres, K. A. (2010). Negotiating the American dream: The paradox of aspirations and achievement among Latino students and engagement between their families and schools. *Journal of Social Issues, 66,* 95–112.

Cultural Context:
Matching Classroom Organization to Cultural Values and Practices

School is a cultural setting, and children's success there depends to a great extent on the match between the classroom's social organization and the child's expectations. Awareness of students' cultural backgrounds is critical when teachers plan their classroom activities. In the typical class in the United States, teachers instruct each child, either individually or as part of the class, or students work alone at their desks. For most European American students this arrangement works well. But it may not work as well for students from other cultures. Researchers have found that children from Native American communities, for example, experience a clash between the social rules of the classroom and the social rules and routines at home (Phillips, 2001). At home, they have a high degree of autonomy in deciding when and whether they will talk, and they often interact in groups. At school, they are less willing to speak in front of the class or to respond when called on by the teacher than are European American children.

Researchers in Hawai'i have tried to reduce the home-school mismatch for their students (Tharp, 1989; Tharp & Gallimore, 1988). In the traditional classroom arrangement, Hawai'ian children tend to pay little attention to the teacher and instead look for attention from their classmates, which fits with their cultural emphasis on cooperation and collaboration. The Kamehameha Early Education Program (KEEP) for kindergarten and primary school children encouraged children's collaboration and cooperation. Among the features of the program were (1) peer-learning centers in the classroom, (2) small-group classroom organization so that children worked in independent groups of four to five students with the teacher moving from group to group to offer intensive instruction, and (3) encouragement of children's cooperative responses, for example, by having them co-narrate stories. Hawai'ian children did much better in this type of classroom organization than in traditional classes. Not only were their academic scores higher but also their social behavior was better; there was less disruption in the class, more cooperation, and more positive relationships with classmates and the teacher.

PARENTS' INVOLVEMENT IN SCHOOLS According to one recent estimate, about 70 percent of U.S. school children have parents who attend at least one school or class event during the school year (Herrold & O'Donnell, 2008). However, many parents never participate in school activities, especially when their children are in the higher grades (Epstein & Sanders, 2002; Herrold, & O'Donnell, 2008). When parents are involved in school activities and attend parent-teacher conferences, join the PTA, or volunteer in the classroom, their children tend to do better both academically and socially, according to a meta-analysis of 50 studies (Hill

& Tyson, 2009). However, not all forms of involvement are equally effective. Relegating parents to the playground committee rather than having them participate in school decision making is less beneficial for children (Pena, 2000). Parental involvement is more effective if it allows parents to communicate their expectations to teachers and show their children that they value education (Hill & Tyson, 2009). Kindergarten children whose parents were involved in these ways were more cooperative, prosocial, and self-controlled than children whose parents were not involved (McWayne et al., 2004).

What determines how much parents are involved in their children's school activities? Parents are usually less involved if they are busy, stressed, or marginalized, for example, if they are single, poor, or from a minority group (Adler, 2004; Epstein & Sanders, 2002; Xu & Corno, 1998). School practices also influence parents' involvement. When schools welcome *all* parents and provide information about how they can become involved, parents respond with increased participation (Sanders et al., 1999). Recent immigrants and even members of more established ethnic minority groups such as African Americans often feel unwelcome at school because of language barriers or cultural differences (Adler, 2004; Garcia Coll et al., 2002). In a qualitative study of family-school interactions, researchers found that Latino parents with lower education levels had interactions with school personnel that left them feeling inferior, embarrassed, helpless, and ashamed (Auerbach, 2002). These parents are often less knowledgeable about schools and how they work, which in turn leads them to participate less in school activities (Greenfield, Suzuki, et al., 2006; Vega et al., 2005).

Several programs to increase the involvement of minority parents in children's schooling have proven successful. In these programs, teachers communicate how parents can help their children in school, and parents communicate their goals, values, beliefs, and practices. In a project in Los Angeles to increase teachers' cultural understanding, researchers found that teacher-parent as well as teacher-child relationships improved (Trumbull et al., 2003). Teachers grew closer to minority families because they were able to understand their cultural perspective. As one teacher said, "I understand them better and am less judgmental and more sympathetic . . . [about] why the children are absent—'We had to go to Tijuana because grandmother is sick'—or why they come to class with the whole family. I was open [before], but now I understand why [they do these things]" (Trumbull et al., 2003, p. 57). Teachers also adopted a more personal and informal style of interacting with the families. They designed new classroom activities that demonstrated their understanding of families' cultural values and increased the number of parent volunteers in the classroom. They changed parent-teacher conference schedules to accommodate parents' needs and initiated group parent conferences, which Latino parents found more comfortable than one-on-one meetings. They provided the parents with a better appreciation of school goals and values. Finally, they functioned as more effective advocates for students and families within the school system. As a result of these changes, communication improved and respect increased on the part of both parents and teachers. In the final analysis, children benefit when the culture gap between their family and their school is reduced (Collignon et al., 2001; Duran et al., 2001).

SCHOOL AS A BUFFER FOR CHILDREN   When children are exposed to deficiencies at home, the school environment can buffer them against failure. Buffering occurs even in preschool when children with an insecure attachment to their mother are better adjusted if they develop a secure attachment to a preschool caregiver (Howes & Spieker, 2008). In school, too, a supportive classroom environment can buffer children from the negative effects of an unsupportive family. Gene Brody and his colleagues (2002) explored this issue in a sample of African American mothers and their 7- to 15-year-old children. Children whose mothers were not involved in their activities and provided minimal monitoring did better if their teachers provided clear rules, their classrooms were well organized, and their classmates participated extensively in class activities. These children had more ability to regulate their emotions and were less aggressive, depressed, and delinquent than children whose mothers and schools were both unsupportive. Clearly, being in a good school environment can give children from deficient families a protective edge and allow them to succeed even though their home context is not supportive.

AFTER-SCHOOL PROGRAMS Because both parents often work full time, children may need somewhere to go after school. Approximately 20 percent of 6- to 12-year-olds in the United States are latchkey children, who let themselves into their homes after school and look after themselves until their parents get home (Urban Institute, 2000). Not surprisingly, self-care increases as children get older, and most adolescents are in self-care at least some of the time. On the positive side, self-care places demands on children for responsibility and maturity (Belle, 1999). But it has a downside as well. These children are at higher risk for problems such as antisocial behavior, poor grades, heightened stress, and substance abuse (Belle, 1999; Lord & Mahoney, 2007)—because children are most likely to become victims or participate in antisocial behavior during after-school hours (see Figure 9.1). The risks of leaving children alone are not lost on parents. As one mother fretted, "It puts more pressure on me worrying about what she's doing in the afternoon. From 3 p.m. on I can't be totally relaxed. I'm thinking about whether she's home doing her homework" (Belle, 1999, p. 87). Parents can reduce the risks associated with self-care by distal monitoring, in which they check in by phone, and by establishing clear rules and expectations about permitted activities, friends, and places to go (Belle, 1999).

After-school programs provide an alternative to self-care. They offer activities that help children learn new skills—for example, computer, academic, and art skills. High-quality after-school programs are characterized by physical and psychological safety, supportive relationships with adults and peers, opportunities to belong to a group, and positive social norms (Eccles & Gootman, 2002). Elementary school children enrolled in such programs benefit in many ways. They have better emotional adjustment, better peer relationships, and better conflict-resolution skills than other children; they also have better grades and are less likely to use drugs or engage in delinquent behavior (NICHD Early Child Care Research Network, 2004a; Mahoney et al., 2007; Vandell, Pierce, et al., 2005; Vandell, Shumow, et al., 2005). Parents whose children are in high-quality after-school programs feel better, too: "Justin's after-school program relieves me of the fear of him being caught on the streets unattended. He's playing with a selected group of kids. He's not strapped to the TV. I feel so comfortable with the program and teachers" (Belle, 1999, p. 88). Poorly supervised and disorganized after-school programs, however, can be detrimental to children's development (Mahoney et al., 2009). Parents need to be careful to choose quality after-school care.

latchkey children
Youngsters who must let themselves into their homes after school because their parents are working outside the home.

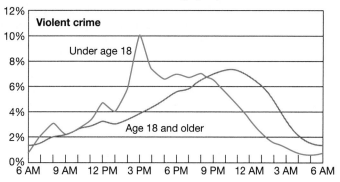

FIGURE 9.1 *Children under age 18 experience a spike in violent victimization right after the end of the school day.* Source: *Office of Juvenile Justice and Delinquency Prevention, 1999.*

Learning from Living Leaders: Deborah Lowe Vandell

Source: Michelle Kim/UCI.

Deborah Vandell is Chair of the Department of Education at the University of California, Irvine. After completing graduate work at Harvard and Boston University, she taught at the University of Texas at Dallas and then at the University of Wisconsin, Madison, in Educational Psychology, Human Development and Family Studies, and Psychology. Her

research has focused on three issues: (a) the effects of early child care and education on children's development, (b) the effects of after-school programs and activities on children and youth, particularly low-income children of color, and (b) children's relationships with peers, parents, siblings, teachers, and mentors. Her research methods include observations, interviews, and surveys and her work spans ages from infancy to adolescence. Her findings have clear practical implications and have been used as the basis for improving the quality of child care and after-school programs for children. Vandell has served on advisory boards and panels for the National Academy of Science, the National Institutes of Health, the U.S. Department of Education, and the National Institute for Early Education Research as well as several foundations, and she has provided testimony before the U.S. Congress and other federal, state, and local governmental bodies.

Further Reading

Vandell, D. L., Pierce, K. M., & Dadisman, K. (2005). Out-of-school settings as a developmental context for children and youth. In R.V. Kail (Ed.), *Advances in child development and behavior, Vol. 33* (pp. 43–77). New York: Academic.

School Integration

Few topics have generated as much controversy in the United States as racial segregation of schools. In 1954, the Supreme Court mandated an end to segregated education, asserting that separate educational facilities are inherently unequal (*Brown v. Board of Education*, 1954). Desegregation was expected to improve African American students' self-esteem and achievement levels; it was also expected to lead both African American and European American students to view each other more positively and to prepare them to live in an increasingly multiethnic society.

If the criterion for judging the success of this grand national experiment is improved self-esteem and achievement for African American students, the results are mixed. Although some studies have reported increased self-esteem and academic achievement among African American children in integrated schools, not all studies have documented these advantages (Wells, 1995). However, if the criteria are increased opportunities for African American students and more positive interracial attitudes, studies are more consistently positive (Pettigrew, 2004). Compared with those from segregated schools, African American children from integrated schools are more likely to attend and graduate from predominantly European American colleges, more likely to work with European American coworkers, and more likely to have good jobs. They are more likely to live in interracial neighborhoods, have European American friends, and express more positive attitudes toward European Americans. European Americans from integrated schools also have more positive attitudes toward African Americans than do European Americans from segregated schools. A meta-analysis showed that 94 percent of 515 studies supported the hypothesis that intergroup contact in integrated schools would reduce racial prejudice, especially when the school gave groups equal status and fostered cooperation and discouraged competition between them (Pettigrew & Tropp, 2006).

Racial integration in the classroom is also associated with feelings of safety and social satisfaction. In a study of 6th-grade classrooms, researchers found that African American and Latino students felt safer and less lonely in school, were less harassed by their peers, and had higher self-worth when they were in ethnically diverse classrooms rather than classrooms with a single ethnic group (Juvonen et al., 2006). A similar pattern was observed at the school level; in more ethnically diverse schools, students felt safer and less lonely and victimized. Many efforts have been made to improve cross-group relationships among students in integrated schools. In one project, for example, 830 first- and second-graders were given a series of sessions over 4 weeks to help them widen their acquaintances to include children from other groups. The program led children to be more inclusive in selecting their most preferred playmate (Houlette et al., 2004).

Unfortunately, residential segregation and, therefore, school segregation have increased in the United States over the past few decades (Orfield & Gordon, 2001). In many cities, school desegregation programs have ended because there are not enough European American children living in the city to integrate the schools, because parents don't want to have their children bused to integrated schools, and because courts no longer mandate integration. Even in schools that are integrated, class enrollments can create de facto segregation. In many such schools, African American and Latino students are enrolled in lower level classes than European American students, and there are few opportunities for them to interact. American parents of all races do still support school integration, however (Pettigrew, 2004), so perhaps, in the future, integration policies along with new and creative ways to implement them will be reinvigorated.

Electronic Media and Children's Social Lives

Electronic media have totally changed children's lives over the past few decades. Today television, electronic games, Internet access, and cell phones are unquestionably important in most children's lives from a very early age. By the time they are 16, most U.S. children have spent more time watching TV than attending school or sleeping. Nearly 99 percent of households in the United States have a TV set, and video game consoles such as Xbox 360, Playstation 3, and the Wii are found in 83 percent of homes with children. In fact, according to a nationally representative survey of more than 2,000 eight- to 18-year-olds, the typical child lives in a home with an average of four TVs, three VCR/DVD players, two video game consoles, and two computers (Rideout et al., 2005). Surveys indicate that 50 percent of children and 97 percent of youth in the United States are connected to the Internet (Roberts & Foehr, 2004; Ybarra, 2004) and that 65 percent of children and 80 percent of teens have a mobile phone—15 percent of them, a smart phone (CTIA, 2009; Pew Internet, 2009; Statistics and Cell Phones, 2008).

Watching Television and Playing Video Games

Television can be a positive influence on children, showing them examples of tolerance and kindness. However, negative consequences, largely due to the portrayal of aggression and violence, have concerned parents around the world. In 2001, the American Academy of Pediatrics recommended that children under 2 years of age not be allowed to watch TV and older children not have television sets in their bedrooms (American Academy of Pediatrics, Committee on Education, 2001). In this section, we ask and answer important questions about children's television viewing and video game playing and their effects on children's social development.

Over the course of a week, children in the United States spend an average of 4 hours watching TV and more than 1 hour playing video and computer games (Comstock & Scharrer, 2006). Source: Ranald Mackechnie/Getty Images, Inc.

HOURS OF INVOLVEMENT   Television viewing starts in infancy. In one study 40 percent of infants under 3 months of age looked at a turned-on TV set for at least an hour a day (Zimmerman et al., 2007). In another study, children under 2 years of age averaged about 2 hours daily (Wartella et al., 2005). One in four of these children had a TV in his or her bedroom. Children do not generally become steady TV viewers until they're older, however. Between ages 2 and 9, the average amount of time children spend watching television daily is about 3 hours; viewing time peaks in preadolescence (ages 10–13) when children watch about 4 hours a day; for teenagers (age 13–17), viewing time is about 2½ hours per day (Figure 9.2; Comstock & Scharrer, 2006; Roberts & Foehr, 2004). This pattern of TV viewing is widespread; similar trends have been found across Europe, Canada, and Australia (Larson & Verma, 1999). Video game playing also peaks in middle childhood: At 8 to 10 years of age, 73 percent of boys play video games for an average of 1½ hours a day; by the time they are 16 or 17, they play for only ½ hour a day (Rideout et al., 2005). By multitasking, children are able to spend time playing video games and watching TV simultaneously.

How much television children watch and how much time they spend playing video games is related to their family characteristics. Children watch more TV if they are from poor, African

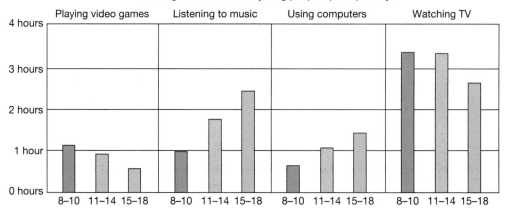

FIGURE 9.2   *Children's use of media. As children get older, they watch less TV and spend less time playing video games; they spend more time listening to music and using the computer.* Source: Rideout et al., 2005. Report Generation M2: "Media in the Lives of 8 to 18 Year Olds," (#8010) The Henry J. Kaiser Family Foundation, January 2010. This information was reprinted with permission from the Henry J. Kaiser Family Foundation. The Kaiser Family Foundation is a non-profit private operating foundation, based in Menlo Park, California, dedicated to producing and communicating the best possible analysis and information on health issues.

American, or single-parent families (Comstock & Scharrer, 2006). They watch more TV if their parents watch more, if there are more TV sets in the house, and if there is a TV set in their bedroom (Rideout et al., 2005; Woodard, 2000). Video game playing is unrelated to family income, but boys play more than twice as much as girls (Rideout et al., 2005). In part, this is because most games are male oriented rather than designed with girls' interests and tastes in mind (Subrahmanyam & Greenfield, 1999). Young people who grow up with video game consoles in their bedrooms spend more time playing than those without—a difference that remains even when age, gender, race, and socioeconomic status are held constant (Rideout et al., 2005). Children who spend the most time watching TV are also the most avid users of computers and video games.

CONTENT OF TELEVISION SHOWS AND VIDEO GAMES   Children watch a variety of programs on TV including cartoons, situation comedies, family-oriented programs, and educational shows such as *Sesame Street*. Boys watch more action-adventure and sports programs; girls prefer social dramas and soap operas (Valkenburg, 2004). As they get older, children watch fewer children's programs and more general audience fare (Wright, Huston, Vandewater, et al., 2001). Unfortunately, these programs contain a great deal of violence; on average, 91 percent of prime-time network programs from 1973 through 1993 contained violence (Gerbner, Morgan, et al., 1994). More disturbing, 70 percent of Saturday morning programs, whose viewers are primarily children, contained violence. Weekend cartoons were particularly violent; 95 percent contained violence, and violent acts were presented at a rate of 21 per hour. These rates have remained stable or increased from the 1960s to the present. Depictions of violence during the 8 p.m. hour were 41 percent more frequent, and, during the 9 p.m. hour, 134 percent more frequent in 2002 than in 1998 (Schulenburg, 2006). Movie DVDs and video games also exhibit a steady stream of violence. An analysis of the content of top-grossing PG-13 films showed that violence permeated nearly 90 percent of the films and nearly half of the violent actions were lethal (Webb et al., 2007). More than 85 percent of video games have violent content (Subrahmanyam et al., 2001). According to a national survey, 77 percent of 8- to 10-year-old boys have played Grand Theft Auto (Rideout et al., 2005), a game famous for its extreme violence. Despite the best efforts of children's television advocacy groups, the amount of violence shown in the electronic media has not decreased since studies were first conducted in the late 1960s (Bushman & Anderson, 2001).

At the same time, the amount of "offensive content," that is, vulgar language and sexually explicit content, in television programs and video games has increased (Comstock & Scharrer, 2006). Young people see nearly 14,000 sexual images or messages on TV in a year (Strasburger & Wilson, 2002). Sexual content is a standard feature of situation comedies, soap operas, and prime-time programs aimed at older children and adolescents as well as adults. In a survey of 900 television programs airing between 7 a.m. and 11 p.m., researchers found that 66 percent contained sexual messages, with a rate of four sexual references per hour (Kunkel et al., 2001). This exposure to sexual images on TV is often inadvertent rather than deliberate; it is simply part of the program territory (Cantor et al., 2003). Women are also often portrayed as passive sexual objects in music videos (Jhally, 1995). Most of these sexual depictions in TV programs, games, and music videos are devoid of any indication of the risks and responsibilities of sexual intimacy (Comstock & Scharrer, 2006); only a few media programs are directly aimed at raising public awareness of issues such as rape, AIDS, and contraception (Agha, 2003).

Do Children Understand What They See?

magic window thinking
The tendency of very young children to believe that television images are as real as real-life people and objects.

To understand what they see on television and in video games, children need to be able to distinguish between fantasy and reality. Displaying what has been called magic window thinking, very young children are likely to believe that TV images are as real as the people and objects around them (Bushman & Huesmann, 2001). Three-year-olds walk to the TV screen to wave at their favorite characters or try to touch them (Valkenburg, 2004). They think that

Big Bird and Bugs Bunny are real (Howard, 1998), that *Sesame Street* is a place where people actually live, that TV characters can see and hear them when they are watching them, and that everything on the screen actually exists inside the TV set (Nikken & Peeters, 1988; see Table 9.1). (Maybe they'll have more trouble thinking this with flat screen TVs—there's a research project for you!) Children react similarly to video games. According to one young game player, "I used to think that all video game characters, like Mario and Sonic, were real and they would come and visit me so I could be friends with them" (http://iusedtobelieve .com). As children get older and their cognitive skills increase, their ability to distinguish fantasy from reality improves. Four-year-olds understand that the characters and objects they see on TV are not actually inside the television set (Flavell et al., 1990). Older children understand that most shows are made up, scripted, and rehearsed (Wright et al., 1994).

Children's developing cognitive skills also help them understand cause-and-effect relations in television shows. The ability to connect an action with its consequence may protect children from some of the negative effects of viewing TV violence. A number of researchers have found that if a character in a TV show is punished for aggressive acts, children are less likely to imitate those acts (Bushman & Huesmann, 2001). Unfortunately, however, only 20 percent of violent acts on TV are punished or criticized (Center for Media and Public Affairs, 1999). Moreover, because the complex plots of television programs often separate a character's aggressive action from the consequence of that action, young viewers have difficulty linking the crime with the punishment. In one study, a researcher showed 3rd-, 6th-, and 10th-grade children an aggressive TV sequence (Collins, 1983). One group of children saw a sequence in which the characters were punished immediately; a second group had to wait through a commercial before they saw the punishment. Although the commercial break didn't affect the older children who have longer memory spans, 3rd-graders who saw the delayed punishment sequence were more likely to indicate that they would behave aggressively than were 3rd-graders who saw the immediate punishment.

The inability of young children to link actions and outcomes in regular TV programming may contribute to the heightened effect of TV aggression on younger viewers (Bushman & Huesmann, 2001). However, even young children can be taught to draw a distinction between what they see on television and what is acceptable in the real world. In one study, children participated in small-group discussions over a 2-year span in which they were taught that TV is an unrealistic portrayal of the real world, aggressive behaviors are not as common in real life as they are on TV, and it is inappropriate to behave like aggressive TV characters (Huesmann et al., 1984). Compared with

TABLE 9.1 What Young Children Believe About TV

I was watching Sesame Street once when Mr. Snuffalupagus was walking right behind Gordon and I shouted out "he's right behind you!!!" Gordon turned to the camera (me) and replied, "Did you say 'he's right behind me?'" From that day forward I never sat in front of the TV in my underwear again.

I used to believe television was just another window in our house and sesame street characters were my neighbors.

I used to think that the people on TV can hear you talking at home, so whenever my parents started talking about something else i felt bad for the newsreaders, coz i thought that they knew they were being ignored.

I used to believe that before color television was invented the world was actually black and white.

I used to believe that in films, when the scene changed, the people who were in the previous scene would freeze until it was their time to talk again.

I thought if you turned the TV off while a person was on screen, they would die! I used to wait for ages for a scene without people in to turn it off.

When I was a little girl I believed that movies were recorded from cameras in the sky, so I would go around playing like I was in a movie.

When I was little, my family was sitting in the living room watching the news. Operation Christmas Child was on the report, and when I heard that the kids didn't get presents, I took one of my presents from under our Christmas tree and tried to give it to one of the kids on the tv.

Source: http://iusedtobelieve.com/

children who did not participate, children in the discussion groups were less aggressive at the end of the 2-year period. Helping children understand that what they see on TV is not reality (even in reality shows) can help reduce the harmful effects of viewing TV violence.

Television's Positive Effects

Educational TV programs have been shown to have positive effects on children's cognitive and language development (Comstock & Scharrer, 2006). But does television have a positive effect on children's social development? Researchers have assessed the impact of watching *Mister Rogers' Neighborhood* on young children's prosocial behavior. This program focuses on understanding feelings, expressing sympathy, and helping others. The children who watched *Mister Rogers* not only learned the specific prosocial content shown in the program but were able to apply that learning to other situations involving their peers (Anderson et al., 2001; Comstock & Scharrer, 2006; Huston & Wright, 1998; Singer & Singer, 2001). Similarly, shows such as *Sesame Street* and *Barney*, which also encourage prosocial behaviors such as sharing and cooperating, increase prosocial actions in young viewers (Mares & Woodard, 2001). This is especially true among young children from middle- and upper-class families whose parents watch the programs with them and encourage their altruistic behavior. Positive effects of prosocial television programs have been found in many different cultures. Watching *Rechov Sumsum* or *Shara'a Simsim*, which are *Sesame Street* programs designed to promote respect and understanding among children in Israel and in the West Bank and Gaza, was linked to Israeli and Palestinian preschoolers' increased use of prosocial justifications for resolving conflicts and increased use of positive attributes in describing members of the other group (Cole et al., 2003). A meta-analysis of 34 studies revealed that watching prosocial television content was consistently related to children's having higher levels of social interaction and altruism and lower levels of aggression and stereotyping (Mares & Woodard, 2005). These effects endure through adolescence (Lee & Huston, 2003). In addition, watching TV programs and playing video games can strengthen group identity. It has been suggested that adolescents' media preferences serve as a badge of identity that young people use to define themselves (Huntemann & Morgan, 2001).

Learning from Living Leaders:
Aletha C. Huston

Source: Courtesy of Aletha C. Huston, University of Texas.

Aletha Huston is Professor of Child Development at the University of Texas at Austin (http://www.he.utexas.edu/ hdfs/ahuston.php). Although she started out as a chemistry major, she became interested in social development as a result of working with Albert Bandura, the social-learning theorist, at Stanford University. The goal of her work has been to describe the processes by which observation of social behavior (primarily on TV) influences children's learning and behavior. In addition, she has studied the effects of poverty and child care on children's development. Her proudest accomplishment is that she was the first researcher to go beyond studying violent television programs to study prosocial television programs. This began a long program of research in which she investigated the potential of television for teaching children social and cognitive skills and contributed to a movement to improve children's television rather than simply criticizing it. The Federal Communications Commission frequently cites her work in decisions about children's television, and she has been widely recognized for her work. The most pressing issue today, according to Huston, is how to introduce knowledge about children's development into the policy process. She sees multidisciplinary work, combining developmental sciences, sociology, policy analysis, and economics, as an exciting trend that will lead to better understanding of complex problems. As an undergraduate, she was frightened by the idea of doing original research because she thought it required a new theory or something remarkably creative, but her message to students today is, "Don't be intimidated. You can start small, working with good mentors, and grow into doing good work."

Further Reading

Huston, A. C., Bickham, D. S., Lee, J. H., & Wright, J. C. (2007). From attention to comprehension: How children watch and learn from television. In N. Pecora, J. Murray, & E. A. Wartella (Eds.), *Children and television: Fifty years of research* (pp. 41–64). Mahwah, NJ: Erlbaum.

Negative Effects of Television and Video Games

The negative consequences of watching violent or sexual television programs and playing violent or sexual video games are numerous and widespread. We discuss some of the most significant of these negative effects in this section.

TELEVISION BIASES PERCEPTIONS   Television is an important source of knowledge about other people, and the more time children (and adults) spend "living" in the world of television, the more likely they are to report perceptions of social reality that reflect what they see on television (Gerbner et al., 1980). Unfortunately, television's representations of life and society are often inaccurate. As a result, people who view TV extensively tend to overestimate the degree of danger and crime in the world and underestimate the trustworthiness and helpfulness of other people (Gerbner, Gross, et al., 1994). This has a clear negative effect on children's social development. The biasing effect of video games has not been studied, but it is likely to be similar.

TELEVISION AND VIDEO GAMES DISPLACE OTHER ACTIVITIES   TV and video games can also have a negative effect on children's social development because they displace other activities, such as sports, clubs, and conversations. In a study in Canada, researchers compared children's social activities in three towns: one town had no TV reception, one town got only one channel, and one town received four channels (MacBeth, 1996; Williams & Handford, 1986). The results were clear: Children were most involved in community activities in the town without TV and least involved in the town with four channels. After television became available in the town without TV, children's attendance at dances, parties, and sports declined. Similar results were found in a South African study: People who viewed TV extensively were less likely to participate in organized sports and other activities outside the home and spent less time with friends (Mutz et al., 1993). Even when children are with their friends, they are likely to be watching TV or playing video games rather than having meaningful conversations and social interactions (Huesmann & Taylor, 2006; Larson & Verma, 1999; Subrahmanyam et al., 2001). Even if TV is only playing in the background, it can be a disruptive and distracting influence (Schmidt et al., 2008). "Background television" also interferes with children's interactions with their parents: When TV is playing both the frequency and quality of parent–child social exchanges decline (Kirkorian et al., 2009).

TELEVISION STEREOTYPES MINORITY GROUPS   Television also biases children's attitudes toward ethnic groups (Berry, 2000, 2003; Greenberg & Mastro, 2008; Signorielli & Morgan, 2001). Television characters are overwhelmingly likely to be European American; in 2002, 73 percent were European American, followed far behind by African Americans (16%), Latinos (4%), Asian/Pacific Islanders (3%), and Native Americans (<1%), (Diversity on Television, 2002). From 1998 to 2003, Latinos were four times more likely than non-Latino White actors to play domestic workers and almost three times as likely to play criminals, and both Latinos and Middle Easterners were more likely to be criminals than to have professional jobs such as doctor or judge (Children Now, 2004). In fact, nearly half of Middle Eastern characters were criminals. The 8 p.m. hour—when children are most likely to be watching—and situation comedies—the most popular genre for children—were least likely to show ethnic diversity and racially mixed casts. Children of all ethnic groups associate European American characters on TV with being rich, intelligent, and well educated and ethnic minority characters with breaking the law, being economically stressed, and acting lazy or goofy (Children Now, 1998).

Studies of the effects of TV viewing on racial attitudes suggest that children's prior notions have a considerable impact on the way TV depictions affect their views (Huston & Wright, 1998). Rather than producing bigotry, television may be strengthening existing negative attitudes. Either way, there is still plenty of reason for concern. In the 2008 TV season, the networks continued to underrepresent ethnic minorities (Armstrong & Watson, 2008), although the good news was that children's television—Disney Channel and Nickelodeon in particular—had increased diversity (Wyatt, 2008). Nevertheless, there is still room for increased inclusion and better roles for minority actors.

TELEVISION AND VIDEO GAME VIOLENCE LEADS TO AGGRESSION   One of the most serious negative effects of television on children's social development is the increased aggression children exhibit after watching violence on TV or in video games (Anderson et al., 2007; Dubow et al., 2007). Heavy doses of TV violence can affect children's attitudes and behavior, leading them to view violence as an acceptable and effective way to solve interpersonal conflict (Bushman & Huesmann, 2001). This effect of TV violence has been documented not only in the United States but also in other countries including Australia, Finland, Britain, Israel, Poland, the Netherlands, and Poland. The effect of television viewing on children's aggression is discussed in more detail in Chapter 12, "Aggression."

desensitization
The process by which people show diminished emotional reaction to a repeated stimulus or event.

TELEVISION AND VIDEO GAME VIOLENCE LEADS TO DESENSITIZATION   Another negative outcome of watching TV and video game violence is **desensitization**. Frequent viewers and players tend to become desensitized to violence; they show less emotional reaction when viewing televised aggression (Cantor, 2000) and less physiological reaction (e.g., a changed heart rate) to real-world aggression after playing a violent video game (Carnagey et al., 2007). Children who watch televised violence may also become less emotionally aroused by violent scenes and more tolerant of real-life violence (Drabman & Thomas, 1976).

TELEVISION AND SEXUALITY   It is not only television's violent content that is of concern. The abundance of sexual images and unrealistic, stereotypic, and potentially unhealthy sexual messages on TV may also affect children (Ward, 2003; Ward & Friedman, 2006). Television emphasizes a "recreational" orientation to sex, often outside a committed relationship, with little reference to contraception, pregnancy prevention, or sexually transmitted infections (Kunkel et al., 2003). In one study, researchers found that high school students who were more frequent viewers of sex-laden prime-time programming supported recreational sex and sexual stereotypes (Ward & Friedman, 2006). This could have been because they already had formed attitudes about sex and chose to watch TV shows that validated them rather than having attitudes created by TV. The researchers, therefore, conducted an experiment in which they showed the students clips from popular dramas and sitcoms, such as *Seinfeld* and *Friends* showing sex as recreation, women as sex objects, and men as sex driven. Adolescents in the control group saw clips of nonsexual scenes from the same programs. The adolescents who saw the sexual clips were more likely to agree that women are sex objects and expressed more stereotyped attitudes than adolescents in the control condition, suggesting that sex-stereotyped TV can promote sex-stereotyped attitudes. Adolescents who said that they watched TV for companionship were more likely than those who said they watched TV for fun to endorse the sexual stereotypes. Perhaps adolescents who rely on TV rather than peers for companionship are more accepting of TV messages and use them to define social norms and values. In fact, other researchers have found that TV viewing has a stronger effect on adolescents who lack friends (Morgan & Rothschild, 1983).

Heavy TV viewing is also related to altered perceptions of peers' sexual behavior. The more adolescents watch TV, with its titillating shows such as *Gossip Girl* and *90210*, the more they assume that their peers are sexually active (Eggermont, 2005). Moreover, teens who watched television shows with heavy sexual content were twice as likely to engage in sexual intercourse over the next year as teens who watched TV without this content (Collins et al., 2004), and more viewing of sexual content was also linked to a higher likelihood of pregnancy (Chandra et al., 2008).

Television does have the potential to be a positive influence on sexuality. A depiction of date rape followed by a rape-crisis hotline number in the popular teen program *Felicity* resulted in an increased number of calls after the episode (Folb, 2000), and heightened exposure to contraception advertisements was associated with increased awareness of safe sex practices (Agha, 2003). In general, though, TV's role in the development of young people's sexual attitudes and behavior is more likely to be negative than positive.

Real-World Application: Advertising Influences Children's Choices

On average, children are exposed to nearly 40,000 TV commercials every year, and at least 10,000 of them advertise products in which they might take an interest (Kunkel, 2001). Sugary cereals, fast-food snacks, and expensive and sometimes silly or even dangerous toys are frequently the subjects of advertising directed at children (Byrd-Bredbenner, 2002; Matthews, 2008). Parents and developmental psychologists are understandably concerned because so many ads advocate items that are not good for children.

But do children pay attention to these ads? Probably not as much as advertisers wish. Children's attention wanes when commercials appear, and this tendency increases with age. In one study, even 4- and 5-year-olds could distinguish between a commercial and the program itself, but only 1 percent of them realized that the goal of the ad was "to try to make you buy things" (Gaines & Esserman, 1981). From about 8 years of age, children begin to become more skeptical and critical of advertising—a trend that peaks by age 12 (Bousch, 2001).

Despite children's limited understanding of the purpose of TV commercials, ads can influence both younger and older children's preferences. In one study, researchers exposed 5- to 8-year-olds to several different commercials (Gorn & Goldberg, 1982). Some children saw sweet snack commercials; others saw ads for fruit or fruit juice or a public service message emphasizing a balanced diet. Children who watched just one sweet snack commercial were more likely to choose sweet snacks over healthy alternatives—juice or fruit. In other studies, too, children from ages 4 to 12 have been found to prefer brands of drinks, snacks, cereals, and sugary foods that they saw advertised on television (Buijzen et al., 2008; Pine & Nash, 2003). Children who watched more commercial TV had more positive attitudes toward junk food and consumed more of it; however, when researchers showed them ads for nutritious foods it promoted healthy attitudes and beliefs (Dixon et al., 2007).

The influence of television advertising is also seen in children's choice of toys. Researchers have found that when young children write to Santa, the ones who watch more TV, especially if they watch alone, ask for more toys in their stockings (Pine & Nash, 2002) and are more likely to ask specifically for the toys advertised on TV (Pine et al., 2007). Advertising is also related to older children's requests for toys, CDs, clothes, computer games, and sports equipment as well as to their level of materialism, increasing their belief that it is important to have a lot of money and own a lot of things (Buijzen & Valkenburg, 2003).

When children are exposed to commercials on TV, they try to influence their parents to buy what they've seen advertised. In one study, 85 percent of children asked their parents to buy them something they had seen in a TV ad (Greenberg et al., 1986). Children's requests and pleadings for advertised products increase parent-child conflicts (Valkenburg, 2004). Thus, commercials create not only an economic drain on the family but an emotional strain as well. Advertising leads to purchase requests, and purchase requests lead to parent-child conflict and child disappointment if the request is denied, and disappointment leads to increased dissatisfaction with life (see Figure 9.3; Buijzen & Valkenburg, 2003). Parents can reduce these undesired effects of television advertising by explaining to their children that the purpose of advertising is to sell products and that advertising does not always tell the truth; attempts to restrict children's exposure to commercial television content are not effective (Buijzen & Valkenburg, 2005).

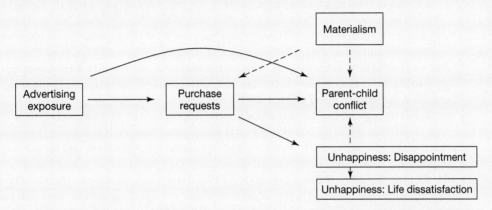

FIGURE 9.3 *Observed unintended effects of advertising. Being exposed to advertising is related to children's making more purchase requests and having more materialistic attitudes; making more purchase requests leads to more conflicts with parents and more disappointments.* Source: *Buijzen, M., & Valkenburg, P. M. The unintended effects of television advertising: A parent-child survey.* Communication Research, 30, *pp. 483–503, copyright ©2010. Sage Publications. Reprinted by Permission of Sage Publications.*

How Can Parents and Siblings Modify TV's Negative Effects?

According to a national survey of more than 30,000 U.S. 6- to 11-year-olds, children are particularly likely to have behavior problems if they are frequent television viewers and their parents are not actively involved in their lives (Mbwana & Moore, 2008). Children who watched more than 3 hours of television a day, who did not communicate very well with their parents, and whose parents knew few or none of their friends had the highest levels of externalizing problems (acting out) and internalizing problems (depression and anxiety).

Parents can help diminish the negative impact of TV on their children in a number of ways. One is to watch television programs with the children. This message seems to be getting across to parents: The proportion of time children reported watching TV with their parents increased from 5 percent in 1999 to 32 percent in 2004 (Rideout et al., 2005). "Co-viewing" television programs is especially helpful for general audience fare. Watching TV with Mom or Dad can help children cope with fear aroused when the programs are scary. In fact, children say that their most common strategy when they are afraid of what they are watching on TV is to "sit by Mom or Dad" (Huston & Wright, 1998). Children often watch TV with their siblings as well (Roberts et al., 1999), and preschoolers who watched a scary show with an older sibling were less upset than preschoolers who watched the show alone (Wilson & Weiss, 1993).

A second strategy to diminish the negative impact of TV is for parents to be active mediators and help children understand and interpret the programs they are watching (Huston & Wright, 1998; Valkenburg, 2004; Wright, Huston, Murphy et al., 2001). Parents can help younger children make connections between actions and their consequences. When adults help children make these connections, in fact, younger children's understanding of TV plots is just as good as that of older children (Collins et al., 1981). Moreover, children whose parents explain events and clarify information tend to be more imaginative, less aggressive, and less hyperactive (Singer et al., 1988).

A third strategy to diminish the negative impact of TV is for parents to express their disapproval of what they see on TV (Anderson et al., 2003). In one study, researchers had an assistant watch television with a child and either approve of the violent actions they saw—"Boy, he really landed a good one." "Terrific!"—or disapprove—"That's awful." "He's really hurting him" (Grusec, 1973). Children who heard the disapproving remarks were less likely to behave aggressively after the TV show than children who watched with an assistant who responded approvingly.

A fourth strategy to counteract the negative effects of TV is for parents to encourage children to empathize with victims and take their perspective. In one study, 6th-grade boys who watched an aggressive Woody Woodpecker cartoon were subsequently less aggressive if the adult experimenter asked them to think about the victim of Woody's behavior (Nathanson & Cantor, 2000). Boys who watched without the empathic commentary were more aggressive. Unfortunately, parents rarely explain content, discuss values, or interpret the meaning of TV programs for their children (Hogan, 2001).

A fifth strategy parents can use to reduce the negative effects of television on their children is to restrict the children's TV exposure and video game choices. It is not clear how common this practice is (Hogan, 2001). Parents' ability to regulate their children's media use is decreasing as more television sets, electronic games, and computers have migrated to kids' rooms (Rideout et al., 2005; Valkenburg, 2004). Only about half of the 8- to 18-year-olds in one national study said that their families had rules about TV watching and only one fifth had rules about which games they could play (Rideout et al., 2005).

To facilitate parents' ability to restrict their children's exposure to violent TV, the 1996 Telecommunications Act required TV manufacturers to incorporate a "V-chip" so parents could block "V-rated" (violent) programs. More than 50 million TVs now have V-chips, but researchers have found that only about 7 percent of all parents actually use them although most are concerned about the effect of violence on their children (Kaiser Family Foundation, 2001). One problem is that TV ratings are confusing and inconsistent (Comstock & Scharrer, 2006; Kunkel et al., 2001). In fact, one study found that ratings of TV programs for violence and sexual content were more often inaccurate than accurate: 65 percent of programs containing violence were not labeled with a V, and 80 percent of sexually explicit programs were not labeled with an S (Kunkel et al., 2001). In addition, blocking out programs using a V-chip may make them all the more attractive to children (Brown & Cantor, 2000). Recording programs on a digital video recorder (DVR) also allows parents to control what their children view. But children can figure out how to control the recorder themselves. Direct parental control is still probably the simplest and most effective solution to the problem of regulating children's TV program choices.

Into Adulthood:
Still Playing Games?

Young adults today are the first generation to have grown up playing video games. From Atari to Nintendo to the Xbox, gaming has been part of their lives. But what happens when they reach adulthood? Do they give up games for a job, a marriage, a mortgage, and children? Apparently not. According to a report by Entertainment Software Association (2009), the typical gamer today is 35 years old.

So what are the consequences when gamers grow up? Some journalists blame video games for the underachievement of modern "child-men." They compare young men in the 1960s—who were holding down solid jobs, striving to be good husbands and fathers, and laying property plans for the future of their families—with today's young men "languishing in a playground of drinking, hooking up, and playing Halo 3" (Hymowitz in Smith, 2008). This view has prompted a passionate response from adult gamers who claim that gaming is a hobby—nothing more—even though they confess that they sometimes get up to play between 4 and 7 a.m. (Smith, 2008). According to a survey of 802 adults, those who are gamers live a well-rounded life; 93 percent read books or daily newspapers; 94 percent follow news and current events; 61 percent engage in religious activities; 50 percent spend time painting, writing, or playing an instrument; and on average, they spend three times more time each week in these and other "recreational" activities than they do playing video and computer games (Fahey, 2005).

Adult game players differ from adolescent players. In a survey of players of Everquest, the most popular massively multiplayer online role-playing game (MMORPG), researchers found that the number of hours played peaked at age 20–22 (average 29 hours per week) and declined thereafter (to 23 hours per week by age 30) (Griffiths et al., 2004). Adult gamers were significantly more likely than adolescents to be female (20% versus 7%). They were less likely to sacrifice their education or work to play the game (7% versus 23%) and more likely

to sacrifice a hobby (28% versus 19%) or social time with friends and family (21% versus 12%). They were less likely to say that violence was their favorite aspect of the game. Clearly adult players are more "mature" in their gaming activity.

Parents are a growing segment of the adult gaming population. For them, time is the biggest challenge. When their children are young and making demands, parents need games they can save at the drop of a diaper (Struck, 2007). As children grow, parents want games they can play with them or at least in front of them. A study released by the Entertainment Software Association (2009) found that 35 percent of U.S. parents play videogames regularly and 80 percent of these "gamer parents" play with their children. These parents believe that playing has brought their families closer together, and they appreciate that as parents they should be involved with whatever their kids are doing, whether it's baseball or video games.

From what we know now, it appears that game playing continues into adulthood and becomes integrated into family life as parents share their gaming interest with their children. The long-term effects this will have on the next generation will no doubt be influenced by how video games themselves evolve and mature. In the end, they may turn out to be a more positive context for social development than Little League. So stay tuned!

Internet and Cell Phone Connectivity

Move over, television and Nintendo! Children today are not only watching TV and playing video games but also are spending hours online—on computers and smart phones. The Internet is a complex virtual world that children actively participate in rather than something they merely watch—like TV—or use—like a computer program (Yan & Greenfield, 2006). It is a new social context in which young people co-construct their own environments through e-mail, instant messaging, blogs, chat rooms, bulletin boards, Facebook, MySpace, YouTube, and Twitter. Adolescents use these forums to explore social issues such as identity, self-worth, and sexuality. The Internet opens up a myriad of possibilities to communicate and interact with a diverse array of other users with similar interests and values (Bargh & McKenna, 2004). The scope of Internet communications can be small and intimate—when school friends message each other—or grandly global—when participants from India, Australia, and Finland interact through cyberspace. The most worrisome thing about the Internet is that it exposes children to invasion of privacy, explicit pornography, online harassment, and cyber bullying. Although communication from pedophiles and predators is also a concern, the frequency of this kind of threat is relatively low (Berkman Center for Internet and Society, 2008).

Internet Access and Use

Children value the Internet a great deal. When asked which medium—phone, TV, radio, or computer—they would choose to bring with them to a desert island, more children and adolescents chose a computer with Internet access than any other medium (Rideout et al., 1999).

Contrary to popular conceptions, there are few gender differences in Internet use in terms of time or preferred activities (Gross, 2004). Both boys and girls use the Internet for visiting Web sites, downloading music, instant messaging, and e-mailing. There are two exceptions to this gender-balanced pattern. First, as we have already mentioned, boys are the heavy users of games including online gaming. This probably accounts for the misconception that boys are more intense Internet users than girls. However, heavy users make up a small minority—only 5 percent—of Internet users (Gross, 2004). Second, boys are more likely than girls to be consumers of sexually explicit images on the Internet; about 25 percent of boys say they look at this type of material at least once a week whereas only 5 percent of girls do (Peter & Valkenburg, 2006).

Effects of Internet Involvement

What are the effects of extended Internet involvement? We know that being glued to the keyboard has physical risks—increased risk of obesity, seizures, and hand injuries, for example (Subrahmanyam et al., 2001). But are there social risks as well?

INTERNET IDENTITY   Exploring and expressing one's identity is a strong motivator for using the Internet. Adolescents who feel that important aspects of their identity—for example, their sexual orientation—cannot be expressed in real life search for chat rooms in which they can express these characteristics (Long & Chen, 2007). They explore different identities in multiplayer online role-playing games and social networking sites such as Facebook and MySpace, actively trying to manage social feedback before they present themselves to others in real-life, face-to-face situations. Adolescents also use personal homepages to express and explore their evolving identities (Schmitt et al., 2008). The effects of online identities on children's psychological adjustment or development of a real-life self are just beginning to be explored. However, one study found that lonely adolescents who used the Internet to experiment with their identities became more socially competent (Valkenburg & Peter, 2008).

EFFECTS ON SOCIAL RELATIONSHIPS   Although there was initially some suggestion that extended Internet use led to increased loneliness and decreased real-life social involvement, more up-to-date evidence has not supported this finding. In the original study, researchers followed a sample of families who, in the mid-1990s, did not yet have computers (Kraut et al., 1998). The researchers gave each family a computer and Internet access. Two years later, the families reported a small but reliable increase in depression and loneliness as a function of the amount of time they used the Internet. A follow-up study of the sample three years later, however, revealed that these negative effects had disappeared (Kraut et al. 2002). Moreover, in a new sample of families, the researchers found that Internet use was associated with positive psychological and social outcomes across nearly all measures of individual adjustment and involvement with family, friends, and community. For example, the more time people spent on the Internet, the more time they spent face-to-face with family and friends. Some differences were identified, however, depending on the user's characteristics. Using the Internet generally predicted better outcomes for extraverts and those with more social support but worse outcomes for introverts and those with less support.

Other researchers have shown that children use the Internet as a way to make new friends. In one survey of 1500 U.S. children and adolescents aged 10 to 17 years, researchers found that 17 percent had developed a close friendship with a person they had met online (Wolak et al., 2002). In another survey of 12- to 17-year-olds, 32 percent indicated that the Internet helped them make new friends (Lenhart et al., 2001). In the majority of cases (69%), adolescents who form online friendships have contact with these people outside the Internet through phone or snail mail, but face-to-face meetings are less common (Mitchell et al., 2001). Most new online relationships are less intense and less supportive than face-to-face relationships with friends and relatives (Subrahmanyam et al., 2001). Multiuser domains (MUDs) and massively multiplayer online role-playing games (MMORPGs) are two sources of online social relationships. Nearly all adolescents in one study made at least one personal relationship when participating in MUD games, and most made four or five contacts, including close friendships (44%), friendships (26%), and romantic relationships (26%) (Parks & Roberts, 1998). In sum, the Internet is a venue for maintaining social ties and forming new, albeit weaker, ties. The Internet is also a way of widening social contacts. In one study, for example, European American adolescents reported that interaction with people from other ethnic groups was a salient and influential aspect of their online experience (Tynes et al., 2008).

Researchers have conducted laboratory experiments to study the formation of Internet relationships. In these studies, pairs of previously unacquainted adolescents meet each other for the first time either in an Internet chat room or face to face. Those who meet first on the Internet report that they like each other more than those who meet first face to face—even when, unbeknown to them, it is the same partner both times (McKenna et al., 2002). With their online friends, adolescents found it easier to express their "true" selves, those aspects of themselves they felt were important but private (Bargh et al., 2002). The relative anonymity of the Internet contributes to close relationship formation by reducing the risks inherent in self-disclosure.

Internet communication can also support friendships made off-line. One study found that 48 percent of 12- to 17-year-olds said that the Internet improved their relationships with existing friends; only 10 percent said that the Internet led them to spend less time with off-line friends (Lenhart et al., 2001). Although most social relationships originate outside the Internet it is used to keep in touch as children rush home from school to instant message (IM) friends to whom they've said goodbye half an hour earlier. Adolescents in a study in China, in fact, reported that they used IM to improve their interpersonal relationships in real life (Lee & Sun, 2009). In the United States, adolescent girls use IM as a form of communication to demonstrate their popularity, include and exclude others from friendship groups, share gossip, fight with others, negotiate social interactions, and talk about boys (Stern, 2007).

Teens also have romantic relationships via the Internet. They use the Internet to "pair off" (exit from a chat room to engage in private messaging) after providing age, sex, location (a/s/l) information (Subrahmanyam et al., 2004). Pairing off in this way allows them to socialize in a relatively anonymous and gender-equal medium. Cyber dating provides a safe place to "practice" new types of relationships. The benefits are reduced, of course, but so are the risks that come with face-to-face interaction. Rejection in an online setting probably stings less than rejection by someone you know well and see every day.

Research up Close:
Role-Playing Games and Social Life

MMORPGs, such as Asheron's Call, Everquest, and World of Warcraft, offer a place where players can experience teamwork, encouragement, and fun and where players can express themselves in ways they may not feel comfortable doing in real life because of their appearance, gender, sexual orientation, or age. To find out how these online role-playing games affect people's social lives, Helena Cole and Mark Griffiths (2007) surveyed nearly 1,000 players from 45 countries. The players reported that MMORPGs were highly interactive environments providing many opportunities to form friendships and emotional relationships. In fact, the opportunity for

Source: Permission courtesy of Blizzard Entertainment.

social interaction was a major contributor to the players' enjoyment, and a high percentage of them claimed that they had made life-long friends. However, it is difficult to draw conclusions from a correlational study such as this one in which participants selected themselves to be part of the project. Perhaps outgoing and gregarious individuals were more likely to choose such gaming opportunities, and their social predispositions created the highly social atmosphere of MMORPGs.

Joshua Smyth (2007) solved this problem by conducting an experimental study of the effects of MMORPGs on players' social well-being. One hundred 18- to 20-year-olds (73% male; 68% Caucasian) were randomly assigned to play arcade games, console games, solo computer games, or MMORPGs for 1 month. The researcher then examined the effects of being assigned to play these different types of game on participants' game usage, health, well-being, sleep, socializing, and academic activities. MMORPG players differed significantly from the other three groups. They said that they had spent more hours playing the game, had experienced more enjoyment while playing, had more interest in continuing to play, and had acquired more new friendships. That was the good news. They also reported that they had experienced worse health and sleep quality and more interference with their real-life socializing and academic work. These studies suggest that MMORPGs do provide social opportunities but at a cost. The challenge is to find ways to successfully blend new social opportunities in the world of cyberspace with social relationships in your own real-life community.

EFFECTS OF INTERNET SEX   The Internet also presents sexual risks. Adolescents are exposed to pornography and other adult sexual material—whether they are looking for it or not—and they express their sexuality in chat rooms—with strangers, often in degrading and unsolicited ways that have nothing to do with relationships (Greenfield, 2004; Subrahmanyam et al., 2004; Subrahmanyam & Greenfield, 2008). Analyzing a large sample of online conversations, researchers found that in teen chat rooms, adolescents were, on average, exposed to one sexual comment every minute and an obscenity every two minutes (Subrahmanyam et al., 2006).

Exposure to pornography on the Internet can cause children anxiety and upset. In fact, among 10- to 17-year-olds in one study, 25 percent said that they had unintentionally encountered sexual material, and a significant number were upset or embarrassed by this type of content (Mitchell et al., 2003). Exposure to sexual images and sexual chat is not always accidental, however; adolescents actively participate in online discussions about sexual issues and concerns, and, as already noted, some adolescents, especially boys, seek out sexually explicit images (Peter & Valkenburg, 2006). Internet chat rooms offer teens the opportunity to explore sexual issues, such as birth control, abortion, rape, premarital sex, and even adoption, with the anonymity, affordability, and accessibility of cyberspace (Subrahmanyam & Greenfield, 2008). Males and females differ in their styles of communication about sexual issues in teen chat rooms (Subrahmanyam et al., 2006). Chatters identified as female produce more implicit sexual communication (e.g., "Eminem is hot, cause he is really hot"); chatters identified as male produce more explicit sexual communication (e.g., "what up horny girls IM me"). Teens clearly turn to the Internet to explore their sexual feelings and share information with peers. Online chat rooms may be suitable for adolescent sexual exploration, but youth who participate in chat rooms are also at more risk for unwanted sexual solicitation (Mitchell et al., 2001). According to a study of nearly 700 students in the Czech Republic, 16 percent of those who used the Internet had tried cybersex, including talking about sex, exploring sexuality, undressing, and masturbating, and both boys and girls were equally likely to be cybersex participants (Vybíral et al., 2004). Whether cybersex or simply online chat about sexuality affects real-life intimate relationships remains unclear and is a topic for future research.

Learning from Living Leaders: Patricia M. Greenfield

Source: Courtesy of Patricia M. Greenfield.

Patricia Greenfield is Professor of Psychology and Director of the Children's Digital Media Center at the University of California, Los Angeles (www.cdmc.ucla.edu). As a graduate student at Harvard University, she was introduced to cross-cultural research and began a career studying how different cultures deal with technological advances and the development of formal education. Over the course of her career, she showed how the introduction of new media transforms the ways we communicate with each other, form social relationships, and learn new social roles. She began studying media effects on children in the United States when she received a phone call from a local radio station about a new program for children that the station had started to develop. This led to her 11-year-old daughter's job as a radio advice columnist for kids and to Greenfield's interest in studying the effects of radio and television on children. Her interest in computers and video games followed from her son's fascination with them and his ability to learn to program much faster than she could. Electronic media became a family focal point, and the intergenerational process of cultural transmission went in both directions as both her son and her daughter went into media-related careers. Greenfield's history offers an example of how social scientists' choice of problems is often influenced by their children's interests. It illustrates the point that children influence their parents as well as the reverse. Greenfield has received numerous awards for teaching and research, including an award for outstanding behavioral science research from the American Association for the Advancement of Science and the Urie Bronfenbrenner Award for Lifetime Contribution to Developmental Psychology in the Service of Science and Society. She frequently talks to reporters about children and the new media.

Further Reading

Subrahmanyam, K., & Greenfield, P. M. (2008). Media technology and adolescence: Identity, interpersonal connection and well-being. *Future of Children, 18,* 119–146.

EFFECTS ON MENTAL HEALTH The Internet may also lead to mental health problems. Although it has been heralded as a venue for breaking down barriers and connecting people who might otherwise be marginalized (McKenna & Bargh, 2000), the anonymity of Internet communications may lead to inappropriate online behavior (Postmes & Spears, 1998; Postmes et al., 1998). The Internet may be conducive to aggressive behavior from children and adolescents who feel freer to express their negative opinions when they cannot be seen and do not have to witness the impact of their words on other people. In one study of online conversations about race and ethnicity in teen chat rooms, researchers found that when the chat room was monitored by an adult, participants had only a 19 percent chance of being exposed to a racial or ethnic slur, but when the chat room was unmonitored, the chance of slurs was 59 percent (Tynes et al., 2004).

Researchers have documented "flaming wars" when Internet users hurl insults and threats at each other and Internet harassment when users make rude or nasty comments or intentionally embarrass other users in retaliation for a perceived wrong. Internet harassment is a significant psychological issue for young people. A national survey indicated that about 7 percent of U.S. youth between the ages of 10 and 17 who used the Internet had been harassed in the past year; most of them (72%) were harassed by someone they met online (Finkelhor et al., 2000; Ybarra, 2004; Ybarra & Mitchell, 2004a, b). One third of the harassed youth reported feeling very or extremely upset; one third experienced at least one symptom of stress following the incident. Boys who were harassed were more than three times as likely to report a major depression as boys who were not harassed. The consequences of negative online onslaughts have even included suicide. In future studies, researchers should investigate whether young people report depressive symptoms in response to negative Internet experiences or whether depression increases the risk of negative online incidents.

Another way in which the Internet can increase children's and adolescents' mental health problems is by fostering communication between individuals with problems. Researchers have found that adolescents solicit and share information about their problems—for example, self-injurious behavior—via online message boards, (Whitlock et al., 2006). These researchers identified more than 400 self-injury message boards, most populated by females who described themselves as between 12 and 20 years of age. Findings indicated that online interactions clearly provided social support for otherwise isolated adolescents but also suggested that online interchanges normalized and encouraged self-injurious behavior and added potentially lethal behaviors to self-injurers' repertoires.

Cell Phone Connections

Cell phones provide instant access to people 24/7, creating a major shift in the social experiences of both children and adolescents. In one recent U.S. survey, about half the teens polled said that their cell phone had improved the quality of their lives, improved their communication with friends by making it a richer experience, and improved their social lives (CTIA, 2009). Almost all said that their cell phone was the way they stayed in touch with peers, one third had used the cell phone to help a peer in need, and about 80 percent said the phone made them feel safer. Teenagers in Australia, similarly, said that their mobile phones provided numerous benefits and were an intrinsic part of their lives; some of these young people were so attached to their phones that the researchers considered it an addiction (Walsh et al., 2008). In Japan, too, researchers are concerned about cell phone addiction. Researchers in one study in Tokyo found that more than half of junior high school students used their phones to exchange e-mails with schoolmates more than 10 times a day (Kamibeppu & Sugiura, 2005). These young adolescents thought that their phone was useful for their friendships, but they also experienced insecurity and stayed up late at night engaged in e-mail exchanges; they believed that they could not live without their cell phone.

Cell phones foster social connections with peers across time and space. They allow young people to exchange moment-by-moment experiences in their daily lives with special partners and thus to have a more continuous sense of connection with friends. Cell phones also can diminish social tolerance because they reduce children's interactions with others who are different from them (Kobayashi & Ikeda, 2007). In addition to connecting peers, cell phones connect children and parents. Researchers studying teenagers in Israel concluded that, in that hazardous environment, mobile phones were "security objects" in parent-teen relationships—important because they provided the possibility of contact and communication at all times (Ribak, 2009).

Insights from Extremes: The Risks of Sexting

On July 3, 2008, Jessica Logan, a teenager from Cincinnati, Ohio, committed suicide after her nude photo, meant for her boyfriend, was forwarded to other girls at her school (Celizic, 2009). She was the subject of jokes, taunts, and ridicule for several months after the incident and "just could not live it down," according to her father. This tragic loss of life was the final outcome of "sexting"—sending sexually explicit messages or photos electronically, usually between cell phones but also over the Internet. Sexting is a growing trend in the United States and other countries including

Britain, Australia, Canada, and New Zealand. According to a 2009 survey, one in five teenagers has sent explicit photos to another person (Harsha, 2009). Although these exchanges are intended to be private, the material can be distributed to others. Some "sexts" have even ended up on forums used by child sex offenders.

This distribution of private images not only damages the victim but also the person who shares the image may face serious legal consequences for violating the victim's privacy. In several cases, teenagers who have either sent nude pictures of themselves or forwarded revealing pictures of others have been prosecuted for child pornography. For example, Phillip Alpert, an 18-year-old boy in Orlando, Florida, who sent a copy of a naked picture of his 16-year-old ex-girl friend to dozens of her friends, received 5 years probation and was placed on the sex-offender registry, a label he will carry with him until he is 43 (Feyerick & Steffen, 2009). He was also kicked out of college, lost many of his friends, and had trouble finding a job because of his status as a convicted felon. Most teens, at one time or another, make stupid decisions, engage in risky behavior, and test their limits. This is how they learn and grow. But with instant gratification just a click away, simple teen thoughtlessness is catapulted onto a new stage. Modern technology enables teens to make instantaneous errors without reflecting on the long-term consequences for themselves or others.

The publicity surrounding tragic outcomes of sexting, such as the suicide of Jessica Logan or the sentencing of Phillip Alpert, has raised the awareness of parents, teachers, and teens about the perils of this practice. Schools have initiated educational programs to inform students, and organizations are developing guidelines to help parents and teens understand the risks associated with this new social trend (National Campaign to Prevent Teenage and Unplanned Pregnancy, 2009; Web Wise Kids, 2009). Following their recommendations may reduce the practice of sexting and may save the lives of future Jessicas and prevent the legal consequences for others like Phillip.

Chapter Summary

Role of Schools in Social Development

- Schools have an informal agenda of socializing children by teaching them the rules, norms, and values they need to make their way in society and helping them develop the skills to interact successfully with their peers.

- Schools are communities of teachers, students, and staff. Children who develop a sense of community in school do better socially and have lower rates of violence and drug use; they are also less likely to drop out of school.

- In small schools, children are more likely to participate in extracurricular activities and less likely to drop out than in large schools.

- Making the transition from elementary school to middle school or from middle school to high school can affect children's self-esteem negatively.

- Children in single-gender schools do better academically and perhaps socially than children in coeducational schools, perhaps because of differences in the characteristics of the schools and the parents who select them.

- In small classes, teacher-child contacts are more frequent and personalized and children are better behaved, interact more with their peers, and are less likely to be victimized.

- Elementary school children in open classrooms have more varied social contacts, develop more positive attitudes toward school, and show more self-reliance and cooperation in learning situations. High school students in open classrooms participate more in school activities, have more varied social relationships, and create fewer disciplinary problems.

- Cooperative learning involves small groups of students working together. This classroom technique has a positive effect on children's self-esteem, concerned feelings about peers, willingness to help, and enjoyment of school.

- Peer tutoring in which an older, more experienced student tutors a younger child has benefits for both the tutor and the pupil, but tutors usually gain more. They benefit in self-esteem and status, and they derive satisfaction from helping others.
- Children whose relationship with the teacher is close and warm have high levels of school adjustment and are likely to be accepted by their peers. Minority children are especially likely to benefit from close teacher-child ties.
- Children are likely to succeed academically and socially when teachers expect them to do so, demonstrating a self-fulfilling prophecy or "Pygmalion effect."
- Teachers have less positive expectations for poor and minority children.
- When parents are involved in their children's school, the children tend to do better, especially if the parents' involvement includes communicating expectations to teachers and communicating the value of education to children.
- Children in high-quality after-school programs have better emotional adjustment, better peer relationships, better conflict resolution skills, and less delinquency than latchkey children.
- Children from integrated schools feel safer and more satisfied and develop more positive interracial attitudes than children from segregated schools.

Television and Video Games

- Television viewing is a major influence on children's social behavior. Viewing begins early in life and increases until adolescence.
- Children watch a variety of programs, including cartoons, situation comedies, family-oriented programs, and educational shows. Boys watch more action-adventure and sports programs; girls prefer social dramas and soap operas.
- Very young children display magic window thinking in which they do not distinguish between TV or video game fantasy and reality.
- Programs that teach children about social rules and expectations, such as *Sesame Street* and *Mister Rogers' Neighborhood,* have positive effects on children's prosocial behavior.
- Negative effects of television and video games include biasing children's perceptions; children who are extensive TV viewers tend to overestimate the degree of danger and crime in the world and underestimate people's trustworthiness and helpfulness.
- TV and perhaps video games curtail children's social interactions and activities such as sports and clubs.
- TV portrayals of minority groups often support ethnic stereotypes.
- Exposure to violent TV and video games leads to desensitization and increased aggression.
- Exposure to sexually suggestive media fare leads to more acceptance of sexuality, earlier sexual activity, and higher rates of pregnancy.
- TV advertising influences children's consumer choices, especially preferences for food and toys that may be either unhealthy or dangerous.
- Parents can modify the effects of media viewing by serving as interpreters of media messages and as managers of access to programs and games.

Internet and Cell Phones

- Boys are more likely to be heavy gamers and access more sexual material than girls.
- The Internet is a new venue for maintaining social ties and forming new, albeit weaker, ties as well as for exploring identities.

- Children are exposed to pornography and other adult sexual material—often inadvertently—which can cause anxiety and upset. Internet chat rooms offer teens the opportunity to explore sexual issues and feelings.

- The Internet can affect children's and adolescents' mental health, especially by online harassment. It can also foster exchange of information between individuals with problems, such as self-injurious behavior.

- Cell phones foster social connections with peers across time and space; they may become "addictive"—if children think they can't live without them—or dangerous—if children use them for sexting.

Key Terms

cooperative learning	**magic window thinking**	**Pygmalion effect**
desensitization	**open classroom**	**self-fulfilling prophecy**
latchkey children	**peer tutoring**	**stage-environment fit**

At the Movies

Schools and electronic media are not just textbook topics but also popular subjects for movies. This selection of films and television programs might make you think more deeply about the issues discussed in this chapter.

Teachers in Film. *The Ron Clark Story* (2006) dramatizes the true story of a teacher who moved to Harlem and was given the "opportunity" to educate an unruly 6th-grade class. He has a hard time trying to reach the tough kids, but he perseveres, asserting his "we-are-family" creed and enforcing his multiple classroom rules. Gradually, the class warms up to him, and the story ends happily. The ending is not so happy in *The Class* (2008). This French movie focuses on the clash between naive students and flawed teachers. One teacher's class is populated by teenagers from diverse backgrounds. He works to gain their trust and teach them, but his own frustrations sabotage his progress. These films illustrate the challenges teachers have in connecting with students on their developmental and emotional levels.

School Integration. One of a number of films exploring the effects of school desegregation is the HBO Documentary, *Little Rock Central High: 50 Years Later* (2007). In 1957, after the Supreme Court ordered desegregation in its *Brown vs. the Board of Education* decision, nine African American students were prevented from entering Little Rock Central High School by an angry mob of Whites. This film follows present-day Central High students and faculty as well as one of the original "Little Rock Nine" who reflects on how much and

how little has changed since she courageously crossed the school's steps nearly half a century ago. In a second television documentary, *I Sit Where I Want: The Legacy of Brown v. Board of Education* (2004), students at a racially mixed magnet school in Buffalo try to get their fellow students to do more racial mingling in the lunchroom and spend more time in each other's homes. *Remember the Titans* (2000) depicts school integration in 1971 in suburban Virginia when federal mandate closed an African American school and a White school and sent the students from both to T.C. Williams High School. Tensions arose when players of different races were forced together on the same football team, but the boys and the coaches learned to depend on and trust each other.

Movies about the "Small Screen." The effects of television are exaggerated in two thought-provoking satirical comedies: In *Being There* (1979), a simple-minded gardener is put out on the street after his millionaire benefactor dies. He has no knowledge of the world except what he has learned from television, but his empty-headed pronouncements and generalizations are taken to be profoundly intelligent and insightful. In *The Truman Show* (1998) Jim Carrey is an insurance agent who lives with his chronically nice wife in the largest TV set ever built where everyone except him is an actor. The message of these movies, that television will overrun lives and saturate brains, should provide insights about children glued to the tube.

Media Stereotypes. The documentary *Reel Bad Arabs: How Hollywood Vilifies a People* (2006) explores a long line of degrading images of Arabs in the movies—from

Bedouin bandits to sinister sheikhs and gun-wielding terrorists. It offers devastating insights into the origin of these stereotypic images, their development at key points in U.S. history, and why they matter so much today.

Video Gaming and Internet Issues. *Avatars Offline* (2002) examines the multibillion-dollar gaming industry and explores how MMORPGs such as Everquest and Star Wars Galaxies are part of mainstream U.S. culture and changing the lives of those who play them. The PBS documentary *Frontline: Growing Up Online* (2008) looks inside the world of cyber-savvy teenagers who are on MySpace, YouTube, Facebook, or Friendster every day, socializing with friends and strangers, trying on identities, and building virtual profiles of themselves. The program shows how teens often find themselves on the opposite side of a digital divide from their parents, grappling with issues their parents never had to confront from instant Internet fame to online sexual predators. The issue of Internet deception is a popular movie topic. In one movie, *Internet Dating* (2008), a man who describes himself as a 7-foot tall Lakers basketball player turns out to be a 5-foot burger flipper. Deception is a particular concern when it hides a sexual predator as in the short film *First Date* (2006) in which an ex-con arranges an encounter with an underage boy he has met online. In the feature film *Hard Candy* (2005), predatory Internet hook-ups are turned on their head. After three weeks of online chat, a 14-year-old girl meets the 32-year-old man she has been communicating with and proposes they go to his house. Once there, she gets the man drunk, ties him up, and accuses him of pedophilia. For the rest of the movie, she engages in a torturous game of mouse and cat—quite the reverse of what usually happens when a pedophile lures a child to a meeting.

All of these movies are more than a diversion with popcorn; they provide new insights into serious issues of social development in an electronic age.

CHAPTER 10

Sex and Gender: Vive La Différence?

Source: © Media Bakery.

Gail likes to pretend her doll is a baby. She sympathizes when her friend falls and skins her knee, and she comes quickly when Mother calls. Gary prefers to play with trucks and trains. He ignores it when his playmate falls, and he keeps on playing after his mother calls him. How much does the behavior of these two hypothetical children reflect differences between girls and boys? Are girls generally more sociable and sympathetic than boys? And, if so, why? This chapter answers these questions.

In all societies, girls and boys behave differently in some ways, are viewed and treated somewhat differently, and have different roles when they grow up. At the same time, males and females behave similarly in many ways, receive equivalent treatment, and have comparable roles. The challenge for psychologists is to determine which behaviors fall into which category and how these differences and similarities originate: Are they the result of innate differences that are fixed for all time, or are they the result of multiple influences such as biology, cognition, and socialization? In this chapter, we discuss research that addresses these questions.

Getting Started: Defining Sex and Gender

gender typing
The process by which children acquire the values, motives, and behaviors considered appropriate for their gender in their particular culture.

gender-based belief
An idea that differentiates males and females.

gender identity
The perception of oneself as either male or female.

Traditionally, the word *sex* was used to refer to a person's biological identity as male or female, and *gender* was used to refer to the person's socially constructed identity. Today, the terms are often used interchangeably. The process by which children acquire social behaviors viewed as appropriate for their sex (or gender) is referred to as **gender typing** (Ruble et al., 2006). This is a multidimensional concept: Children begin by developing **gender-based beliefs** that include awareness of their own gender, understanding of gender labels applied to them and to others, and knowledge of gender stereotypes. Early in life, children also develop a **gender identity**, a perception of themselves as either male or female and as having the characteristics and interests that are appropriate for their gender. After developing a gender identity, children develop **gender-role preferences**, or desires to possess certain gender-typed characteristics. Children's choices of toys and play partners reflect these preferences. Children also acquire the concepts of **gender stability**, the belief that males remain male and females remain female, and **gender constancy**, the belief that superficial changes in appearance or behavior do not alter one's gender. **Gender stereotypes** are beliefs that members of a culture hold about acceptable or appropriate attitudes, activities, traits, occupations, and physical appearance for each gender. **Gender roles** are the general patterns of appearance and behavior associated with being a male or a female in a particular culture.

Gender Stereotypes

gender-role preference
Desire to possess certain gender-typed characteristics.

gender stability
The fact that males remain male and females remain female.

gender constancy
The awareness that superficial alterations in appearance or activity do not alter gender.

Our culture has consistent stereotypes of male and female roles. The stereotyped male role involves controlling and manipulating the environment. Men are expected to be independent and self-reliant, strong willed and assertive, dominant and competitive, decisive, direct, active, adventurous, worldly, and strong. They are expected to control their emotions, even under stress, and to be able to easily separate feelings from ideas. The stereotyped female role involves supporting husband and family. Women are expected to be pretty, sociable, loving, sensitive, considerate, gentle, sympathetic, sentimental, and compassionate. In general, people regard the expression of warmth in personal relationships, the display of anxiety under pressure, and the suppression of overt aggression and sexuality as more appropriate for women than for men (Prentice & Carranza, 2002; Seem & Clark, 2006). Gender stereotypes also apply to children: Girls are supposed to be sweet, gentle, pretty, wear dresses and jewelry, play with dolls and toy kitchens, and be concerned with their appearance whereas boys are expected to be rough, tough, and brave; like sports and video games; and play with toy cars, guns, construction toys, and action figures (De Caroli & Sagone, 2007; Miller et al., 2009).

Children are aware of these adult and child gender stereotypes from an early age. In one study, 2-year-olds looked longer—indicating they were surprised—when they saw pictures of a man doing stereotypical female things, such as putting on make-up, than when they saw a woman doing these things (Serbin et al., 2002). Children's knowledge of stereotypes increases rapidly between ages 3 and 5 and is well developed by the time they enter school (Signorella et al., 1993). From this age until they are 7 or 8, children are quite inflexible about gender stereotyping (Ruble et al., 2006). By age 8 or 9, they begin to be more flexible about what's

gender stereotype
Belief that members of a culture hold about acceptable and appropriate attitudes, interests, activities, psychological traits, social relationships, occupations, and physical appearance for males and females.

gender role
Composite of the behaviors actually exhibited by a typical male or female in a given culture; the reflection of a *gender stereotype* in everyday life.

acceptable for members of each sex to do—although most still say they wouldn't be friends with a boy who wore lipstick or a girl who played football (Levy et al., 1995). Development of stereotype knowledge continues through 5th grade and is evident in children's descriptions of what men, women, girls, and boys are like (Miller et al., 2009). Girls are more knowledgeable about stereotypes than boys are, and by middle childhood, they are also more flexible about them (Ruble et al., 2006).

Despite the concern with gender equality that began with the Women's Movement in the 1960s, gender stereotypes have remained remarkably stable (Bergen & Williams, 1991; Hosoda & Stone, 2000; Twenge, 1997). Attitudes may be changing, but the process is glacial. In studies documenting some slight shifts, researchers have found that men now are less likely to say they are tough and aggressive than they did in the 1970s (Spence & Buckner, 2000), and students in counseling psychology define a mentally healthy woman as not only nice and nurturing—the stereotypic view of femininity—but also independent and up for a challenge—stereotypic masculine traits (Seem & Clark, 2006). For the most part, though, gender stereotypes about occupations remain the same (Liben & Bigler, 2002). Both children and adults still think of doctors, dentists, mechanics, pilots, plumbers, truck drivers, firefighters, electricians, architects, police officers, and engineers as male, and librarians, nurses, teachers, secretaries, dancers, hair dressers, and decorators as female (Kee et al., 2005; Oakhill et al., 2005). These gender differences in occupations illustrate how gender-role development is embedded in a societal context and reflects differences in males' and females' status and power (Wood & Eagly, 2002). Cross-cultural studies show that these stereotypes are widespread, not only in North America but also in a range of societies in South America, Europe, Africa, and Asia (De Caroli & Sagone, 2007; Whiting & Edwards, 1988; Williams & Best, 1990).

Some variation in how strongly people subscribe to gender stereotypes exists, however. Women who have a college education are less likely to have a stereotyped view of the feminine role than less educated women, and women's views are less stereotyped than men's (Basow, 1992; de Pillis et al., 2008; Pasterski et al., 2010; Seem & Clark, 2006)—even in countries outside North America (e.g., in China; Wang & Liu, 2007). In spite of these variations, almost everyone views aggression as more characteristic of males and interpersonal sensitivity as more characteristic of females (Dodge, Coie, et al., 2006).

Cultural Context:
Cultural Differences in Gender Stereotypes

Gender stereotypes appear in every culture, and similarities across cultures greatly outweigh differences (Best, 2004). However, gender stereotypes do seem to be more pronounced in traditional cultures where male-female differences in social status are larger (Wood & Eagly, 2002). Clear gender stereotypes in China were demonstrated at the opening ceremony of the 2008 Olympics, when a cute, girly Chinese 9-year-old was asked to lip-synch over the singing voice of another girl because the singer was considered not pretty enough to perform. Thalma Lobel and her colleagues (2001) studied gender stereotypes held by Chinese children in Taiwan—a traditional,

collectivistic, hierarchical culture that emphasizes adherence to social roles, interdependence among individuals, and fitting in with the social context—and children in Israel—a modern, individualistic, egalitarian culture that emphasizes independence, self-expression, and the pursuit of personal goals and interests. They predicted that Chinese children would be less flexible and less accepting of violations in gender stereotypes than Israeli children. To test the prediction, they read 3rd- and 5th-grade children stories about a boy or a girl who had either stereotyped masculine or stereotyped feminine interests. Each child heard one story. In the masculine-boy story, children heard that "Sing Ming (or Ron) is a boy your age who lives around here. He likes to play with boys and to play baseball (or football). He often plays War Game (or plays with model airplanes)." The feminine-girl story paralleled the masculine-boy story but included stereotyped feminine choices such as playing with dolls. In the counter-stereotyped stories, the child in the story violated gender stereotypes. In the masculine-girl story, Siou May (or Ruthi) liked to play baseball (football) and War Game (model airplanes) with boys. In the feminine-boy story, the boy played with girls and dolls. To assess the children's attitudes toward the four story characters, researchers asked them to rate each character on stereotypic masculine traits (aggressive, strong, and brave) and stereotypic feminine traits (gentle, cries easily, and likes to dress up).

Children in both cultures distinguished between boy characters who behaved in masculine and feminine ways, but the difference was much more marked in the traditional Chinese culture than in the modern Israeli culture. Children were also asked to rate how popular the story characters were with their peers. Chinese children said that boys who behaved in stereotypic masculine ways would be more popular than boys who behaved in feminine ways; the difference was much less for children in Israel. Finally, children were asked how much they liked the boy or girl in the story, how much they would want to be friends with the child, and how willing they would be to engage in various activities with each child. As in the other assessments, Chinese children indicated that they liked masculine boys better than feminine boys relatively more than did children in Israel.

These findings provide clear evidence that children in a more traditional, collectivistic culture are less tolerant when boys violate gender stereotypes. Traditional cultures stress adherence to social norms and judge any transgressions harshly; collectivistic cultures stress the significance of social norms and the importance of conformity. Moreover, in hierarchical cultures, individuals tend to abide by their roles and to be aware of others' roles. All of these characteristics increase concerns with gender consistency and intensify the saliency of gender transgressions.

However, the findings in Lobel's study provided less evidence of a cultural difference when girls violated gender stereotypes. Both Chinese and Israeli children thought that girls who played with dolls were more feminine and girls who played War Game were more masculine, and they liked the feminine girl more than the masculine girl. But they did not think that the feminine girl would be more popular with peers. Other studies conducted in Western cultures have also shown that a girl exhibiting masculine behavior is not judged as harshly as a boy exhibiting feminine behavior, and that a girl who behaves in a masculine manner is not perceived as less popular than a girl who behaves in a feminine manner (Ruble et al., 2006). Lobel's study found this latitude toward counter-stereotypic behavior by girls in Taiwan as well. It seems that the Westernization of Taiwan has resulted in girls being positively reinforced for exhibiting stereotypic masculine behaviors. As global communications and technological advances permit more cross-cultural sharing of attitudes and information, cultural differences in gender stereotypes for boys may also lessen.

Gender Differences in Behavior, Interests, and Activities

How accurately do gender stereotypes reflect differences in the actual behaviors of males and females? Consistent male-female differences in some behaviors and characteristics are evident in childhood, and others develop as men and women are influenced by work, power, status, child-bearing, and homemaking experiences (Eagly, 1996; Halpern et al., 2007; Hyde, 2005; Leaper & Friedman, 2007; Ruble et al., 2006; Underwood, 2004). For the most part, these differences parallel gender stereotypes. It is essential to keep in mind, however, that the characteristics of males and females overlap (Figure 10.1). Some males are more compliant and verbal than some females; some women are stronger than the average man and are successful in traditionally male sports such as boxing, basketball, soccer, and hockey. Women may become architects, mathematicians, engineers, and scientists as well as nurses and librarians. Although differences between males and females do indeed exist, it is important not to exaggerate them. Most differences are quite small (Hyde, 2005). It's not that men are from Mars and women are from Venus, as you may have heard; it's more as if men are from Montana and women are from Virginia. Moreover, gender differences in social relationships and emotional well-being are particularly small (Meadows et al., 2005).

Behavior Differences in Childhood

On average, girls are physically and neurologically more advanced at birth, learn to walk earlier, and reach puberty at younger ages than boys. As infants, they prefer to look at faces rather than objects (Connellan et al., 2000), and by 4 months of age, the average duration of mutual gazing between infant girls and women is four times longer than that between infant boys and women (Leeb & Rejskind, 2004). Girls maintain more eye contact than boys during social interactions (Dunham et al., 1991) and are better at recognizing and processing facial expressions (McClure, 2000). They tend to have better verbal skills—talking more, learning words more quickly, reading better, and displaying more verbal creativity—than boys. Girls are generally more compliant than boys with the demands of parents and

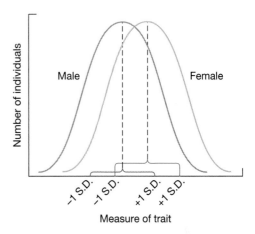

FIGURE 10.1 *Overlapping bell-shaped curves. These distributions show the values for a trait in which females, on average, score higher than males. In this example, the difference between the means (the vertical lines) is about 80 percent of 1 standard deviation (S.D.), giving an effect size, d, of about 0.8.*

other adults, more nurturing toward younger children, and more fearful at older ages. Girls are able to read emotional signals at younger ages and by school age they are likely to be more sensitive, kind, considerate, and empathic than boys. Girls are more likely than boys to ask for help as well as offering it (Benenson & Koulnazarian, 2008), to be more emotionally responsive with their mothers (Bornstein et al., 2008), and to control their emotions better (Else-Quest et al., 2006). Girls are likely to engage in more social conversation and self-disclosure with their friends and also care more about their friendships; they usually play in smaller groups (Rose & Rudolph, 2006).

Boys have advantages in muscular development and lung and heart size compared with girls, and they usually do better at activities involving strength and motor skills. The majority of boys have visual-spatial abilities that allow them to read maps, aim at targets, and manipulate objects in space easily; girls are less likely to have these abilities (Newhouse et al., 2007). As newborns, boys prefer to look at objects such as mechanical mobiles more than moving faces (Connellan et al., 2000). In general, boys are more physically active than girls; they tend to play in larger groups and larger spaces and enjoy noisier, more strenuous physical games. From the age of 2, boys engage in riskier behaviors and are injured at a rate that is two to four times that of girls (Morrongiello & Hogg, 2004). On the playground, boys are usually the overtly aggressive ones; they push and punch each other more than girls do (Baillargeon et al., 2007; Card et al., 2008; Ostrov, 2006). They are often concerned with dominance rather than friendship (Rose & Rudolph, 2006), and they are more competitive than girls (Fabes et al., 2003).

Interests and Activities in Childhood

Children also exhibit gender-typed interests from an early age (Beal, 1994; Ruble et al., 2006). Even before they can talk or reach for a toy, infants express preferences by where and how long they stare. Using techniques to measure these visual preferences, Lisa Serbin and her colleagues (2001) found that boys and girls differed in their attraction to dolls and cars. By the time they were 1 year old, girls looked at dolls more than boys did, and this difference was even stronger by the time they were 1½ (see Figure 10.2). Boys preferred looking at vehicles such as cars and trucks when they were 1½ a preference that increased by age 2. Another study

FIGURE 10.2 *By 18 months, boys and girls prefer to look at gender-typed toys. Boys prefer looking at vehicles, and girls prefer to look at dolls.* Source: Serbin, L. A., Poulin-Dubois, K. A., Colburne, K. A., Sen, M. G., & Eichstedt, J. A. (2001). Gender stereotyping in infancy: Visual preferences for and knowledge of gender-stereotyped toys in the second year. International Journal of Behavioral Development, 25, 7–15, copyright © 2010 Sage Publications Ltd. Reproduced by permission of Sage Publications Ltd.

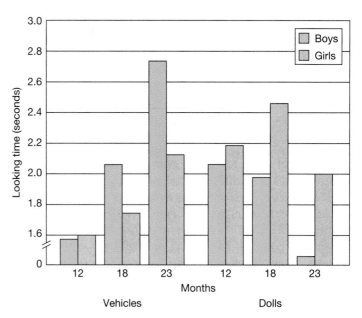

found that boys and girls demonstrated clear preferences for playing with gender-appropriate toys in a child care center when they were 1½ to 3 years old (O'Brien et al., 1983). These preferences persist as children grow up. In a study of 5- to 13-year-olds, girls preferred dolls and stuffed animals and boys preferred manipulative toys, vehicles, and action figures (Cherney & London, 2006). Girls ask their parents for more clothing, jewelry, dolls, and domestic items than boys do; boys request more sports equipment, vehicles, military toys, and action figures (Etaugh & Liss, 1992). Toys that girls like tend to be associated with appearance—dolls, costumes, jewelry—and those for boys are associated with action, aggression, and violence—trucks, cars, planes, action figures, and weapons (Blakemore & Centers, 2005).

Some signs indicate that children's toy choices may be broadening a bit. In their letters to Santa, boys and girls make plenty of gender-stereotyped requests, but girls are as likely as boys to ask for bikes, sports equipment, and male dolls, and boys are as likely as girls to request clothing, educational items, and art toys (Marcon & Freeman, 1996). Moreover, some toys considered in 1975 to be masculine (e.g., science toys, Legos, larger vehicles) or feminine (e.g., toy vacuum cleaners) were considered neutral in 2005 (Blakemore & Centers, 2005). However, the fact that researchers studying nonhuman primates have found toy choices paralleling those observed in human children—specifically, young female animals prefer playing with dolls and young males prefer playing with a toy car (Alexander & Hines, 2002; Williams & Pleil, 2008)—suggests that some of these differences in child preferences are unlikely to disappear.

Girls dressed up and played with dolls 100 years ago just as they do today. Source: © NMPFTKodak Collection/SSPL/The Image Works.

In addition to choosing gender-typed toys, boys and girls develop gender-typed interests. In a survey of more than 2,000 children between the ages of 7 and 11, researchers found that boys liked shooting, boxing, wrestling, doing martial arts, playing on a team, and fixing and making things more than girls did whereas girls enjoyed sewing, cooking, dancing, and looking after younger children more than boys did (Zill, 1986). In middle childhood and adolescence, girls spend more time in feminine leisure activities such as dancing, writing, making crafts, and creating art than in masculine activities such as hunting, fishing, building, or playing competitive sports (McHale et al., 2004). Boys and girls even choose different types of books. Girls prefer romantic tales and boys are more likely to opt for horror stories and violent adventures (Collins-Standley et al., 1996). This parallels their preferences for different TV shows—girls preferring soaps and social dramas and boys, action-adventure and sports (Valkenburg, 2004). Finally, girls and boys engage in different gender-typed chores around the house. Girls are more likely to make beds, prepare meals, wash dishes, clean, and do laundry; boys are more likely to repair things, take out the garbage, and mow the lawn (Coltrane & Adams, 2008).

Changes in Adolescence and Adulthood

Although gender-typed preferences and interests are evident in childhood, many boys and girls participate in activities for both genders. In adolescence, however, *gender intensification* is observed. With the onset of puberty, young people shift toward more typical gender-typed patterns of behavior (Larson & Richards, 1994; McHale et al., 2004). In one study, tomboyish girls reported that at about age 12 they began to adopt more traditionally feminine interests and behaviors owing to pressures from their parents and peers and to their own increasing interest in romantic relationships (Burn et al., 1996). Other researchers observed that, during adolescence, consistent with gender stereotypes, girls became more emotionally expressive and boys more emotionally restricted (Polce-Lynch et al., 2001), and girls became more involved in caring for others and boys less so (Aubé et al., 2000). Recently researchers have found less evidence of gender intensification, suggesting that adolescents today may feel less constrained by gender stereotypes than they did in earlier decades (Priess et al., 2009).

Gender roles are likely to intensify when adults become parents. Even among couples who are committed to equally sharing household tasks, the onset of parenthood generally heralds the emergence of traditional gender roles (Cowan & Cowan, 2000; Parke, 2002). These roles emphasize women's **expressive characteristics**—nurturance, sympathy, concern with feelings, orientation toward children—and men's **instrumental characteristics**—task and occupation orientations. Women tend to become more autonomous as they and their children grow older but return to a more feminine orientation in their later years, perhaps because they have a greater need for help (Hyde et al., 1991; Maccoby, 1998). Older men tend to become more expressive and nurturant. Altogether, then, gender typing is a dynamic process that, to some extent, continues across the life span.

expressive characteristics Those aspects of a person involving nurturance and concern with feelings. They are more typical of females.

instrumental characteristics Those aspects of a person involving task and occupation orientation. They are more typical of males.

Stability of Gender Typing

In spite of these overall shifts in gender typing during childhood, adolescence, and adulthood, individuals who are strongly masculine or feminine at one age tend to continue to be strongly masculine or feminine as they age. Researchers studying a representative sample of 5,500 boys and girls in England found that children whose behavior was most gender typed in the preschool years were still most gender typed at age 8 (Golombok et al., 2008). Even adult behavior may be predicted from gender-typed interests in childhood. In a longitudinal study in the United States that began in the 1930s, boys who were interested in competitive games and activities that required gross motor skills and girls who were interested in noncompetitive games, cooking, sewing, and reading were involved in similar gender-typed activities in adulthood (Kagan & Moss, 1962). Stability was especially strong when children's characteristics were congruent with gender stereotypes. Whether gender typed stability from childhood to adulthood is as strong today, when adults' activity choices are so much more varied and flexible, is an open question.

Into Adulthood:
Occupations for Men and Women

THE WORK THAT WOMEN DO—BARRED FROM ONLY TWO OCCUPATIONS" read the headline of a *New York Times* article in 1895. Data from the 11th U.S. census had been compiled, showing "the number of persons ten years of age and over engaged in gainful occupation." The only two occupations from which women were barred were officers of the U.S. Army and Navy and soldiers, sailors, and marines. Most occupations had only a small handful of women working in them, however, including one pilot, one well-borer, a wheelwright, and a few white-washers, roofers, distillers, tinsmiths, woodchoppers, coal miners, and brewers. Women were most likely to be servants; more than one quarter of working women were servants, and 84 percent of servants were female. Women also made up the majority of nurses, midwives, housekeepers, teachers, musicians, and workers in occupations related to female clothing—making dresses, gloves, corsets, hats, hosiery, lace, embroidery, and buttons, and doing laundry. Men were the majority in all other occupations including actors and authors, bakers and bartenders, physicians and surgeons.

Times have changed since 1895. Women have entered male-dominated occupations and given up work as servants and corset makers. Between 1960 and 1980, the number of women managers increased 800 percent, and women professionals increased 300 percent (Beller, 1985). Since then, women have continued to enter occupations dominated by men (Longley, 2005). The biggest shift has been in auto body repair, in which the proportion of workers who were women increased 400 percent. Other traditionally male jobs in which the proportion of female workers increased markedly were police detectives, engineers, mechanics, firefighters, and pilots. But an increase in the proportion of women in an occupation does not mean a huge increase in absolute numbers. For example, there are still only 5,000 women in the United States working in auto body repair. The disproportionate representation of men and women in different occupations continues: Men are the majority of clergy, physicians, and surgeons; women are the majority of housekeepers, nurses, and teachers.

As a result of this occupational segregation, men and women experience an earnings gap. Although the overall labor force participation of females has increased from about 20 percent when the *New York Times* article was published in 1895 to about 60 percent today, women's economic standing has increased only modestly. On average, today women are paid 22 percent less than men (Blau & Kahn, 2006). Occupational choice is an important factor in this gender wage gap because jobs dominated by women are generally lower paying than those dominated by men. Women often choose occupations that pay less because they need time off to have children and flexible hours to care for their families (Coogan & Chen, 2007). They are also less likely to be hired in high-paying occupations because employers don't want workers who may leave for a period of time or indefinitely. Women with children are less likely to be hired than are male applicants, and if they are hired, they are offered lower salaries (Correll & Benard, 2005). Half of the gender gap in earning is a result of employers paying women less even when they do the same job as a man (Bayard et al., 2003). Gender discrimination is demonstrated in research showing that male-to-female transsexuals earn, on average, 32 percent less after their transition whereas female-to-male transsexuals earn 2 percent more (Schilt & Wiswall, 2008). Women are also discriminated against if they ask for higher salaries whereas men are not (Babcock, 2007). Many efforts have been made to eliminate labor market discrimination. Woman's wages increased as a result of the Equal Pay Act of 1963, Title VII in 1964, and the Equal Employment Opportunity Commission in 1972. It is noteworthy, however, that the first bill President Obama signed after taking office in 2009 was the Lilly Ledbetter Wage Discrimination Act named for a woman who discovered that she had been paid less than her male colleagues after working for 19 years at a Goodyear plant in Alabama.

The occupations adults choose are to some extent influenced by their gender-role orientation. Men with more traditional gender-role attitudes are likely to enter male-dominated fields such as mechanical engineering rather than nontraditional occupations such as elementary school counseling (Dodson & Borders, 2006). Choosing an occupation consistent with a traditional gender role has advantages. When men enter a female-dominated field such as nursing, they report higher rates of sickness, absence, and work-related problems; women in a male-dominated occupation such as accounting are likely to have high anxiety scores and work-related problems (Evans & Steptoe, 2002). In addition, men with a more traditional gender-role orientation earn more than men with less traditional beliefs (Judge & Livingston, 2008). The reverse is true for women. Of course money isn't supposed to be as important for women: Undergraduate women rank goals related to happiness and fulfillment higher than career goals more often than men do (Abowitz & Knox, 2003), and women express stronger interest in jobs that will allow them to help others, whereas men express stronger interest in jobs that make money (Weisgram et al., 2010).

Sex Differences in Gender Typing

Just as men are more bound by gender stereotypes than women are, boys are more gender typed in their play and toy choices than girls are (O'Brien et al., 1983). Boys' preference for gender-stereotyped toys remains constant as they age, whereas girls' interest in gender-stereotyped activities decreases (Cherney & London, 2006). In addition, boys are more likely than girls to develop "extremely intense interests" in objects and activities, and these passionate interests are often gender stereotyped, for example, collecting trains, building models, and competing in go-cart races (DeLoache et al., 2007).

For what reason are boys less likely to cuddle a doll than girls are to play with a truck? For one thing, adult Western culture is basically male oriented: Men are given more esteem, privileges, and status than women, and all are encouraged to do things that are regarded as higher status. The male role is also more clearly defined than the female role, and the pressure for boys to conform to the masculine gender stereotype is higher than for girls. Boys shy away from "girly" things because if they don't, they'll receive derision from other boys and criticism from their parents. Both parents and peers condemn boys for crying, for retreating in the face of aggression, for wearing girls' clothes, and for playing with dolls. In contrast, parents and peers tend to accept a girl's occasional temper tantrums, rough-and-tumble play, blue jean apparel, and play with trucks. In fact, one survey found that more than half of women and girls described themselves as being tomboys, participating in sports and playing with boys' toys at some point during childhood (Morgan, 1998). Although sissy boys are rejected, tomboy girls are tolerated.

Bet You Thought That. . .
Gender Identity was Determined by Biological Sex

Josie Romero, a transgender child who was born a boy named Joey, is the subject of a television documentary, "Age 8 and Wanting a Sex Change." Source: *Bancroft/Fame.*

For most people, gender identity is congruous with biological sex. However, for transgender individuals, gender identity does not match their assigned biological sex. These people experience an incongruity that is severe, disturbing, and long lasting. They usually suffer gender dysphoria—a deep unhappiness because their gender identity reflects one sex but their genitals another. Often they experience depression, anxiety, fear, anger, self-mutilation, low self-esteem, or suicidal ideation. This incongruity was once considered a psychological disorder. However, over the past few decades, discomfort with pathologizing individuals for gender variance has increased (Hill et al., 2007).

Gender identity issues usually begin in early childhood (Mallon & DeCrescenzo, 2006). Transgender children prefer dressing like the opposite sex (cross-dressing). They participate in the games and activities of the other sex and avoid those of their own sex: Transgender boys play house, draw pictures of princesses, play with dolls, dress up, and have girls as playmates; transgender girls play Batman and Superman, baseball, hockey, and other competitive contact sports, preferably with boys. Transgender children insist that they are or want to be of the other sex. They also have negative feelings toward their genitals. A girl may insist she will grow a penis and stand to urinate. A boy may fantasize about being a girl, sit to urinate, and wish to be rid of his penis. When Joey (the child in the photo) was 4, he started telling people he was a girl. He liked to wear orange clothing because it was closest to pink. At age 5 he refused to have his hair cut and was often mistaken for a girl. Another transgender boy, Brandon, would search the house for something to drape over his head—a towel, a doily, a bandanna—when he was just a toddler (Rosin, 2008). His mother finally figured out that he wanted something that felt like long hair. He spoke his first full sentence when the family was out at a restaurant: "I like your high heels," he told a woman in a fancy red dress. At home, he would rip off his clothes as soon as his mother put them on him and try on something from her closet—a purple undershirt, lingerie, shoes. At the toy store, he headed straight for the aisle with the Barbies and the pink and purple dollhouses. One afternoon he climbed out of the bathtub and began dancing in front of the mirror with his penis tucked between his legs. "Look, Mom, I'm a girl," he told her happily. "Brandon, God made you a boy for a special reason," she told him. "God made a mistake," Brandon replied without hesitation.

Signs that a child has transgender preferences may occur as early as 2 or 3 years of age, and transgender individuals commonly report having had feelings of confusion and discomfort with their assigned gender as early as age 4 (Vitale, 2001). However, most transgender people do not form or reveal a transgender gender identity until adolescence or adulthood (Hines, 2006). Most transyouth try to keep their gender issues secret until they

cannot hold them back any longer (Mallon & DeCrescenzo, 2006). A transyouth's revelation usually takes parents by surprise, which is often followed by shock, denial, anger, grief, guilt, shame, and concern about the youth's safety, health, surgery, employment, and future relationships. These young people have few social supports from their friends and relatives. "Get that boy into sports!" "Don't let that girl be a tomboy" are among the kinder things they may hear. Fathers especially have difficulty accepting their child's gender variance (Wren, 2002). As one dad said, "I can accept that my child is transsexual but if I ever see him in a dress I'll hit him." Mothers are more likely to find ways to convey compassion and care and to see their child's atypical gender identity development as legitimate. Parents who are most tolerant believe that the child's condition was caused by nature (biology), not nurture (problems in the family), and, in fact, some evidence suggests that sex differentiation of the brain may be responsible for gender variance (Blackless et al., 2006).

Gender-variant young people have sometimes been confused with gay and lesbian youth. Indeed, most gender-variant children cease to desire to be the other sex by adolescence and instead grow up to identify as homosexual. Because it is impossible to determine whether a child will become transsexual or homosexual as an adult, gender-variant children cannot be treated with hormones of the other sex as gender-variant adults are. Recently, doctors have begun to treat children with drugs that suppress puberty and create a state of suspended development so that the children can postpone a decision about their future until later in adolescence (Cohen-Kettenis et al., 2008). Joey began taking testosterone blockers at age 8 and will begin female hormones at age 12. As we find out more about gender variance, we are likely to see substantial changes in the way parents, doctors, and society treat it.

Insights from Extremes: The First American Transsexual

Christine Jorgensen, born George William Jorgensen, Jr., May 30, 1926, in New York City, is famous for having been the first well-known individual to have male-to-female sex-reassignment surgery (Meyerowitz, 2002). As a child, Jorgensen was a frail, introverted little boy who ran from fistfights and rough-and-tumble games. In 1945, he was drafted into the army, and when he returned home, he became increasingly concerned over his lack of male physical development. He began taking the female hormone estradiol. He intended to go to Sweden where he had found that doctors were performing sex-reassignment surgery, but at a stopover in Copenhagen, he met Dr. Christian Hamburger, a Danish endocrinologist. He ended up staying in Denmark, and under Dr. Hamburger's direction, began hormone replacement therapy and a series of surgeries to remove his testicles and penis and construct a vagina. On December 1, 1952, a media sensation erupted when the *New York Daily News* carried a front-page story under the headline "Ex-GI Becomes Blonde Beauty," announcing that Jorgensen had become the recipient of the first "sex change." This claim was not actually true: This type of surgery had been performed by German doctors in the late 1920s and early 1930s. But what was different in Jorgensen's case was the addition of hormone therapy. When Jorgensen returned to New York in February, 1953, she became an instant celebrity. She used her fame to become a spokesperson for transsexual and transgender people, and during the 1970s, she toured university campuses to speak about her experiences. She was known for her directness and wit, and once demanded an apology from Spiro Agnew, the U.S. vice president, when he called another politician "the Christine Jorgensen of the Republican Party." Jorgensen worked as an actress and nightclub entertainer, singing songs that included, most poignantly, "I Enjoy Being a Girl." She continued her act until 1982. In 1989, the year of her death, Jorgensen said that she had given the sexual revolution "a good swift kick in the pants." She also gave gender researchers a kick by demonstrating that a person's gender identity is not always consistent with his or her gender chromosomes and that these individuals can make a successful psychological transition from one gender to another. Her courageous behavior opened the door for others to express transgender urges, for society to begin to accept gender diversity, and for researchers to study gender complexities.

Biological Factors in Gender Differences

What is behind the differences in the behaviors and characteristics of boys and girls, men and women? Biology is one important contributor. Biological factors affecting gender typing include evolution, hormonal functions, genetic factors, and the brain.

Evolutionary Theory and Gender Development

The evolutionary theory stresses the principles of natural selection and adaptation. These principles can be applied to gender development to explain gender-typed behaviors that increase the likelihood that a person's genes will be passed on to the next generation. To be able to pass genes from one generation to the next, individuals need to have mating strategies that enhance their reproductive success. Males need aggressive and competitive skills to compete successfully with other males in attracting mates. Females need strategies for attracting and keeping mates who are able to provide resources and protection for their offspring; they also need skills and interests that commit them to child rearing (Buss, 1994, 2000; Geary, 1998, 2006). According to evolutionary theory, these two sets of complementary strategies have led to the evolution of gender differences in behavior in both animals and humans—including males' expression of strength, power, and aggression and females' concern with physical appearance and caregiving skills.

However, the evolutionary explanation has limitations (Ruble et al., 2006; Wood & Eagly, 2002). First, testing it is difficult. Second, it applies to females and males as groups but does not explain individual differences among males and females. Third, it does not account for recent rapid changes in gender roles due to technology that has lessened the importance of male-female differences in size and strength. Fourth, cross-cultural research showing considerable variability in gender roles across cultures has challenged its assumptions (Wood & Eagly, 2002). Finally, evolutionary theory has been criticized as being too strongly linked to genetic determinism rather than offering a fully interactive position that embraces the role of the environment (Lickliter & Honeycutt, 2003).

Hormones and Social Behavior

Hormones are also biological contributors to gender differences and gender typing. Hormones associated with sexual characteristics and reproductive functions are present in differing concentrations in males and females beginning in infancy. Testosterone is the principal and most potent male hormone, or androgen. Estrogen and progesterone are the principal female hormones. Each sex has a great deal of its own hormones and a small amount of the other sex's hormones; that is, males have a high level of testosterone and a low level of estrogen and progesterone, and females have a high level of estrogen and progesterone and a low level of testosterone.

These hormones organize the fetus's biological and psychological predispositions to be masculine or feminine, and a hormone surge in puberty activates these early predispositions (Hines, 2004). The contributions hormones make to the social behaviors of males and females have been clearly demonstrated in animal studies. When researchers injected pregnant monkeys with testosterone during the second quarter of pregnancy, for example, the monkeys' female offspring exhibited social behavior patterns characteristic of male monkeys, such as threatening gestures, mounting behavior, and rough-and-tumble play (Young et al., 1967). When researchers injected male hormones into normal female monkeys after birth, these females also become more assertive, sometimes even attaining prime dominance status in their monkey troop (Zehr et al., 1998).

Human studies also demonstrate effects of hormone levels. John Money and his colleagues studied what happened when female fetuses had unusually high levels of androgens (Money, 1987; Money & Ehrhardt, 1972). These girls exhibited traditionally masculine behaviors and interests. They enjoyed vigorous athletic activities such as ball games and showed little interest in playing with dolls, babysitting, or caring for younger children. They preferred simple clothing and showed little concern with cosmetics, jewelry, or hairstyles. Not only were their interests more like those of boys but also their assertiveness and attitudes toward sexuality and achievement resembled males'. Additional studies of fetally androgenized girls indicated that they preferred boys as playmates, chose toys usually preferred by boys, and exhibited behaviors more common in males such as rough and tumble play (Berenbaum & Snyder, 1995; Hines, 2006, 2009; Reiner & Gearhart, 2004). The higher their exposure to prenatal androgens, the stronger were these girls' preferences for masculine play and activities (Berenbaum, 2001; Servin et al., 2003). Their masculine preferences persisted in spite of their parents' efforts to encourage their feminine play (Pasterski et al., 2005). In other studies, genetic males who were born without a penis and raised as girls exhibited typical male behavior, presumably because of their high levels of testosterone (Reiner & Gearhart, 2004). In fact, for both girls and boys, a high level of fetal testosterone predicts more male-typical play (Auyeung et al., 2009) and less empathy (Chapman et al., 2006). Aggression, too, has been linked to testosterone levels. In one study, researchers asked mothers to rate their 3- to 10-year-old daughters' aggressiveness (Pasterski et al., 2007). Girls with congenital adrenal hyperplasia, a genetic condition that produces excessive androgens, were rated as more aggressive and had more fights than their sisters without the condition. Clearly, all this research proves that hormones play an important role in gender-role development (Berenbaum, 2006).

Gender and the Brain

Everyone knows that men and women think and act differently—women are willing to ask for directions and say "I love you"; men would rather ask for beer and pretzels and watch wrestling. But joking aside, male and female brains are somewhat different in structure and function (see Figure 10.3; Cahill, 2006; Yamasue et al., 2009). It has even been suggested that there is a "female brain"—which is organized to be socially adept, empathic, friendly, and

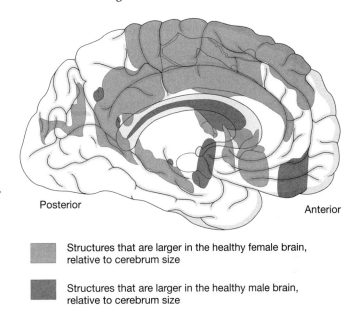

FIGURE 10.3 *Sex differences in the structure of the brain.* Source: Cahill, 2006, adapted from Goldstein, J. M., Seidman, L. J., Horton, N. J., Makris, N., Kennedy, D. N., Caviness, V. S., Faraone, S. V., & Tsuang, M. T. (2001). Normal sexual dimorphism of the adult human brain assessed by in vivo magnetic resonance imaging. Cerebral Cortex, 11, 490–497.

Posterior

Anterior

Structures that are larger in the healthy female brain, relative to cerebrum size

Structures that are larger in the healthy male brain, relative to cerebrum size

sensitive to social and emotional signals—and a "male brain"—which is oriented to objects and organized to systematize information (Baron-Cohen, 2002). Supporting this suggestion, researchers have found that in females' brains, on average, the ratio of gray matter to white matter is relatively larger than in males' brains (J. S. Allen et al., 2003), particularly in the social brain regions (Yamasue et al., 2009; see Figure 3.4 in Chapter 3, "Biological Foundations"). Brain-imaging studies reveal that females show more activation in these social regions of the brain than males do, for example, in the left prefrontal cortex when they look at humorous cartoons (Azim et al., 2005) and in the medial frontal cortex when they empathically react to an opponent's loss in a gambling game (Fukushima & Hiraki, 2006). Studies using structural MRI have demonstrated that these regions are likely to be smaller in individuals with autism spectrum disorder, who, it has been suggested, have extreme "male brains" (Baron-Cohen, 2002; Yamasue et al., 2009).

Another sex difference in the brain involves the amygdala, a brain structure that plays a major role in processing emotions (Goldstein et al., 2001; Hamann, 2005; Nopoulos et al., 2000). Although men have a larger amygdala than women (adjusted for total brain size), women have a relatively larger orbital-frontal region (Gur et al., 2002), which is responsible for modulating input to the amygdala (LeDoux, 2000). This means that females have relatively more cortex available for modulating emotional input, which could result in more efficient processing of emotions and better consolidation of emotional memories. Studies have also documented a gender difference in the human mirror neuron system with females exhibiting stronger empathic responses than males (Cheng et al., 2006; Schulte-Rüther et al., 2008; Yang et al., 2009).

The extent to which brain functioning is organized across the two cerebral hemispheres is another difference between males' and females' brains. As we discussed in Chapter 3, the right hemisphere in most people is involved in processing visual and social-emotional information, such as faces and emotional expressions, and the left hemisphere is responsible for processing verbal information. It has been suggested that men's brains are more lateralized than women's, that is, more specialized for processing language in the left hemisphere and visual information in the right. Although not all studies show a sex difference in lateralization (Sommer et al., 2004, 2008), support for this suggestion has been found in brain imaging studies of phonological processing (Cohen-Bendahan et al., 2004; Lindell & Lumb, 2008; Shaywitz et al., 1995; Sommer et al., 2008) and visual processing (Bourne, 2008; Hiscock et al., 1995). Even infants show this sex difference in lateralization in a word comprehension task (Hines, 2004). In addition, men whose left hemisphere is damaged are more likely to experience verbal deficits than women with left-hemisphere damage, and men whose right hemisphere is damaged show more spatial deficits than women with right-hemisphere damage (Halpern, 2000). The end of the corpus callosum, a bundle of fibers connecting the left and right hemispheres, which facilitates transfer of information between the two hemispheres, is larger in females than males (Driesen & Raz, 1995), which may account for the reduced lateralization in females. Together, these studies provide support for the view that male and female brains are distinctive and may help explain the social and emotional advantage of females.

Genetics of Gender

In 2008, a team of Swedish researchers released the results of a large study of genetic differences in the human brain (Reinius et al., 2008). They found 1,349 genes that are expressed differently in the brains of men compared with of the brains of women, providing the strongest evidence to date that sex differences in the brain are genetically programmed. In the 1970s and 1980s, gender was believed to be primarily a social construct. Children learned how to "do gender"— boys learned that they should play with trucks and girls learned that they should play with dolls. Until quite recently, even scientists assumed that sex differences in the expression of genes would be confined to genes on the X and Y chromosomes. However, we now know that genes scattered across all 46 chromosomes are expressed differently in male and female brains. We also know that the extent to which individuals' behavior is gender typed relates to genetic factors. Studying a sample of nearly 4,000 three-year-olds, behavior genetics researchers found higher correlations between monozygotic twins than dizygotic twins in gender-typed behavior—for example, liking guns, playing soldier, and enjoying rough-and-tumble play versus liking jewelry and dolls, playing house, dressing up, and liking pretty things (Iervolino et al., 2005). A moderate genetic influence was found, especially for girls, as was a strong environmental influence, especially for boys. Perhaps the reason boys were more influenced by the environment is that parents and peers provide stronger feedback and are more likely to criticize boys for gender-inappropriate behavior (Ruble et al., 2006). Boys are also more likely than girls to believe that other people think of cross-gender typed play as "bad" and to be influenced by this belief (Banerjee & Lintern, 2000; Raag, 1999; Raag & Rackliff, 1998).

Biology and Cultural Expectations

Investigators have found that by the age of 4 or 5, girls interact more often and more actively with babies than boys do. For example, when asked to care for a baby, boys are inclined to watch the baby passively, whereas girls are likely to engage in taking care of the baby (Berman, 1987; Blakemore, 1990). This difference is consistent with biological explanations of gender differences. It fits with the evolutionary perspective, which argues that females are more committed to parental activities than males. The difference is also consistent with the suggestion that physical and hormonal factors allowing women to bear and breast-feed children program females to be responsive to the sights and signals of infants and children. These behavioral tendencies, however, could also be due to cultural expectations and training (Parke, 2002). In adolescents and adults, gender-based differences are less apparent under conditions of privacy than in situations in which people know that they are being observed (Berman, 1987). When experimenters have used subtle measures of adults' responsiveness to infants' crying, such as changes in blood pressure, electrical skin conductance, or responses of the autonomic nervous system, they have not detected differences between mothers and fathers (Frodi et al., 1978; Lamb, 2004). It seems likely that gender-linked responses to babies are affected both by biological and evolutionary programming and by cultural conditioning.

Cognitive Factors in Gender Typing

Gender typing also has a cognitive basis. Children's own understanding of gender, gender roles, and gender rules contributes to gender typing. In one of the earliest attempts to explain the cognitive basis of gender typing, Sigmund Freud (1905) proposed that children form their gender identity at around age 5 or 6 when they become curious about their own sexual anatomy and are alerted to differences in the sexual anatomy of males and females. After forming a gender identity, Freud suggested, children acquire either feminine or masculine traits and behaviors through a process of **identification** with the same-sex parent. More recently, explanations of gender typing have been proposed in the two major theoretical approaches to cognitive development. According to cognitive developmental theory children categorize themselves as female or male on the basis of physical and behavioral clues and then behave in ways they understand to be gender appropriate, making stable gender-typed choices by the time they are 6 or 7 years old. According to information-processing gender-schema theory children begin to develop their own naive theories about gender differences and form schemas of gender-appropriate behaviors when they are about 2 or 3 years old. Both of these theories share the assumption that children take an active role in perceiving and interpreting information from the environment and creating environments that support their theories. They differ in their ideas about when children acquire different types of gender information and how knowledge modifies gender-role activities and behavior. We discuss these two cognitive theories in the next section.

identification
The Freudian concept that children think of themselves as being the same as their same-sex parent.

Cognitive Developmental Theory

cognitive developmental theory of gender typing
Kohlberg's theory that children use physical and behavioral clues to differentiate gender roles and to gender type themselves very early in life.

In his **cognitive developmental theory of gender typing**, Lawrence Kohlberg (1966) proposed that from an early age, children begin to differentiate between male and female roles and perceive themselves as more like same-sex than opposite-sex models. These processes begin before Freud's proposed process of identification and without deliberate teaching. Using physical and behavioral clues, such as hairstyle and clothing, children categorize themselves as male or female. They then find it rewarding to behave in gender-appropriate ways and to imitate same-gender models. For example, a girl thinks, "I am a girl because I am more like my mother and other girls than I am like my father or boys; therefore I want to dress like a girl, play girl games, and feel and think like a girl." Consonance between children's actual gender—the way they see themselves—and their behaviors and values is critical for their self-esteem.

According to Kohlberg all children go through three phases in understanding gender. First, between the ages of 2 and 3, they acquire basic gender identity, recognizing that they are either a girl or a boy. Second, by the age of 4 or 5, they acquire the concept of gender stability, recognizing that males remain male and females remain female. The little boy no longer thinks he might grow up to be a mommy, and the little girl gives up her hopes of becoming a superhero. Third, by about 6 or 7 years, children acquire the notion of gender constancy, recognizing that superficial changes in appearance or activities do not alter gender. Even when a girl wears jeans and plays football and a boy has long hair and a burning interest in needlepoint, they recognize—and their peers recognize too—that gender remains constant. This achievement is important, Kohlberg argued, because gender constancy influences gender-typed choices.

Researchers who have tested Kohlberg's theory have confirmed that both boys and girls acquire gender identity first, an understanding of gender stability next, and finally an appreciation of gender constancy (Martin & Little, 1990; Slaby & Frey, 1975). Children in cultures other than those of North America show a similar progression in their understanding of gender (Munroe et al., 1984), although those in nonindustrialized cultures and lower-income families generally reach milestones about a year later than middle-class children in the United States and Canada (Frey & Ruble, 1992).

Children begin to recognize males and females as distinct categories when they are still infants and cannot understand labels and language. In one study, 75 percent of 12-month-olds were able to recognize male and female faces as belonging to distinct categories (Leinbach & Fagot, 1992). This is not the same thing as recognizing that they themselves belong to one of these categories, but it suggests that the process of understanding gender begins earlier than Kohlberg proposed. The ability to understand gender labels such as *boy* and *girl* is not far behind. In a study using parental diaries of children's speech, researchers found that 25 percent of children used gender labels—*girl, boy, woman, man, lady, guy*—by 17 months and 68 percent by 21 months (Zosuls et al., 2009). Children who knew and used gender labels were more likely to show increases in gender-typed play between these two ages. However, 2-year-old children still have a very limited understanding of gender identity (Fagot & Leinbach, 1992). Although they recognize that some activities and objects are associated with each gender—for example, that men wear neckties and women wear skirts—it's not until they're about 3 years old that children grasp the concept that they themselves, along with other children, belong to a gender class or group. Even then confusions may remain. Consider the following exchange between two 4-year-old boys. Leo accused Jeremy, who wore a barrette to preschool, of being a girl because "only girls wear barrettes." When Jeremy pulled down his pants to show that he really was a boy, his young classmate retorted, "Everyone has a penis; only girls wear barrettes" (Bem, 1983, p. 607).

Genital knowledge is an important determinant of understanding gender constancy. Sandra Bem (1989, 1993) showed preschool children anatomically correct photos of a nude boy and a nude girl and then showed them pictures of the same children dressed in clothing appropriate to their gender or appropriate for the other gender. Even when boys wore dresses or girls wore pants, nearly 40 percent of the children correctly identified the gender of the child. When Bem then tested the preschoolers' understanding of genital differences between the sexes, she found that nearly 60 percent of the children who possessed genital knowledge but only 10 percent of those who lacked it had displayed gender constancy. Children apply gender constancy to themselves slightly earlier than they apply it to others. Preschoolers achieved gender constancy for themselves by age 4½ but did not understand that the concept applied to other children until they were 5½ (C. L. Martin et al., 2002).

Gender-Schema Theory: An Information-Processing Approach

gender-schema theory
The view that children develop schemas, or naive theories, that help them organize and structure their experience related to gender differences and gender roles

According to **gender-schema theory**, children develop *schemas* that help them organize and structure experience related to gender differences and gender roles (Bem, 1993, 1998; Martin & Halverson, 1983; Martin & Ruble, 2004; C. L. Martin et al., 2002). These generalizations about which toys and activities are "appropriate" for boys versus girls and what jobs are "meant" for men versus women tell children what types of information to look for in the environment and how to interpret this information.

Children develop schemas based on their own perceptions and the information that parents, peers, and cultural stereotypes provide. Children use these gender schemas to evaluate and explain behavior. For instance, when they were told about a child who spilled some milk, children evaluated the behavior more negatively if the child was a boy because of the stereotype that boys are bad (Giles & Heyman, 2004; Heyman & Giles, 2006). They appraised the risk of injury as higher for girls than for boys because of the stereotype that girls are fragile—even though boys actually incur more injuries than girls do (Morrongiello et al., 2000). The links between gender schemas and the child's own behavior are presumed to occur through selective attention to and memory for own-sex relevant information and through motivation to be like same-sex others.

To determine how gender-role schemas affect the way children see things, researchers showed 5- and 6-year-olds pictures of males and females involved in activities that were either gender-consistent (e.g., a boy playing with a train) or gender-inconsistent (e.g., a girl sawing wood) (Martin & Halverson, 1983). A week later, they asked the children to recall the pictures. When the children described the gender-inconsistent pictures, they tended to distort information by changing the gender of the actor. When they recalled gender-consistent pictures, they were more accurate and more confident of their memories. Other studies have reported similar findings. In addition, girls recall feminine toys, peers, and activities more easily than boys do; boys are better at remembering masculine toys, peers, and activities (Martin, 1993; Signorella et al., 1993). In effect, children become "sexist self-socializers" as they work at remembering and developing the masculine and feminine attributes they view as consistent with their self-image as male or female.

Individual children vary in the extent to which they have well-formed gender schemas (Signorella et al., 1993). Some children are "gender schematic" and highly sensitive to gender information whereas other children are "gender aschematic" and focus more on other aspects of information. Not surprisingly, gender-schematic children displayed better memories for gender-consistent information and were more likely to distort gender-inconsistent information than gender-aschematic children (Levy, 1994). Part of the reason they remembered gender-consistent information may be that they paid more attention to same-gender information. In a naturalistic study of TV viewing, researchers found that boys who had a better grasp of gender constancy watched male characters and programs that featured male characters more than boys who had not yet fully achieved gender constancy did (Luecke-Aleksa et al., 1995). Gender-constant girls also watched same-gender characters more than girls without gender constancy did. Gender-role schemas clearly alter the ways in which children process social information and either recall it accurately or distort it to suit their prior concepts.

Comparison of Cognitive Developmental and Gender-Schema Theories

These two theories make different predictions about how gender-typed knowledge influences gender-role activities and behavior. The cognitive developmental theory predicts that achievement of gender constancy will influence children's gender-typed choices and, therefore, prior to the 5- to 7-year age period, the children should have little preference for gender-appropriate activities. Gender-schema theory suggests that children need only basic information about gender, such as identification of the sexes, to begin forming and following rules about it. On this issue, gender-schema theorists appear to be correct. Gender labeling is sufficient to affect children's gender-typed activity preferences (Martin, 1993; Martin & Little, 1990). Even just telling children in one study that an attractive novel toy was something that children of the other sex really liked resulted in the toy being dropped like a hot potato (Martin et al., 1995). Gender-typed play, such as choosing trucks or dolls as appropriate toys, apparently does not depend on children's understanding of gender stability or gender constancy.

Learning from Living Leaders: Carol Lynn Martin

Source: Courtesy of Carol Martin.

Carol Martin is one of the originators of gender-schema theory. After completing her graduate work at the University of Georgia, she took her current position as Professor of Human Development in the School of Social and Family Dynamics at Arizona State University. As an undergraduate, she was interested in anthropology, genetics, and psychology, but psychology became her passion. She started graduate school in experimental psychology with classes in memory and perception but switched to developmental psychology, which she enjoyed. Eventually she found what she loved doing most: studying children's social development. Her major goal has been to understand gender development: how children develop a sense of their own gender identity, how they develop stereotypes about males and females, how stereotypes and identity influence their behavior and thinking, and how gender-normative behavior is linked to adjustment. She traces her interest in gender development not so much to her own childhood experiences of gender bias—although she does recall a male cousin who didn't have to help with the dishes—but to a provocative professor who challenged her views about gender. She became aware of how gendered children's thinking is when she heard a boy saying, "I'm a boy and I'm proud, proud, proud" and saw how boys are the "kings" on the playground. Today she is particularly interested in the influence of sex segregation on children's gender development and later success. She is collaborating with a team of researchers on the Sanford Curriculum Project, a large-scale research and curriculum

development project focused on improving gender relationships in children and adolescents by changing styles of interaction and communication between females and males. She is a member of the Society for Research in Child Development, the National Council on Family Relations, and the American Psychological Association.

Further Reading

Martin, C. L., & Ruble, D. N. (2003). Children's search for gender cues: Cognitive perspectives on gender development. *Current Directions in Psychological Science, 13*, 67–70.

Martin, C. L., & Ruble, D. N. (2010). Gender-role development. *Annual Review of Psychology, 61*, 353–381.

Social Influences on Gender Typing

Family, peers, teachers, and television all influence children's development of gender-typed behavior. They are models and shapers, encouragers and enforcers.

Theories of Social Influence

social cognitive theory of gender development
An explanation of gender role development that uses cognitive social learning principles such as observational learning, positive and negative feedback, and the concept of self-efficacy.

The most influential theoretical account of social influences on gender typing is the **social cognitive theory of gender development**, which Bussey and Bandura (1999) developed by applying the principles of Bandura's social cognitive learning theory to gender development. According to this theory, one way that children learn about gender issues is through observational learning. By watching other children and adults of both sexes, children learn which behaviors are appropriate for their own sex and actively construct notions of appropriate appearance, occupations, and behaviors for both sexes. They use this knowledge to develop concepts of gender-appropriate behavior. Children also learn about gender by responding to positive and negative feedback provided by others when their behavior is gender appropriate or inappropriate. Peers, parents, and teachers are enforcers of acceptable gender-appropriate behavior. Although external influences at first regulate this behavior, over time children develop internalized expectancies that gender-appropriate choices are likely to lead to positive outcomes and gender violations to lead to penalties and punishments. Sometime between 3 and 4 years of age, children shift from external regulation to self-regulation, using self-praise and self-sanctions to maintain their adherence to personal standards of gender-appropriate behavior (Bussey & Bandura, 1992). Children's desire to have a sense of self-efficacy and perceive that they are skilled and competent in the realm of gender motivates, guides, and regulates their choices of gender-role appropriate actions and opportunities, which, in turn, strengthens their gender-linked interests and beliefs. In brief, personal conceptions about gender, activity patterns linked to gender, and environmental influences that promote or discourage gender-related behavior all contribute to children's gender development.

This theory of gender development has some similarities with the cognitive developmental and gender-schema theories, including its emphasis on the importance of cognition and the active role of the child in developing an understanding of gender. However, the social cognitive theory places more emphasis on the roles of motivational, affective, and environmental influences on gender development than do the other two theories. It also recognizes the embeddedness of gender development in a matrix of societal institutions. The **social structural theory of gender roles** focuses specifically on factors such as institutionalized constraints on male and female opportunities in educational, occupational, and political spheres as determinants of gender roles (Wood & Eagly, 2000). It shares with feminist perspectives the view that the distribution of power and status between men and women in the home, the work force, and political arenas strongly influences gender development (Miller & Scholnick, 2000). Both the social cognitive and the social structural theories emphasize the importance of tracking changes in societal influences across historical eras and stress the significance of societal and institutional constraints in accounting for children's and adults' gender-linked expectations and behaviors.

social structural theory of gender roles
An explanation of gender roles that focuses on factors such as institutionalized constraints on male and female opportunities.

Parents' Influence on Children's Gender-Typed Choices

Parents have the strongest influence on children's early gender typing (McHale et al., 2003). They're the first people children observe closely, and they're also the first ones who try to teach children and shape their behavior. When children are still infants, their parents are already sending them messages about gender roles and stereotypes. The process starts at birth when parents give the baby a name—boyish Brad or feminine Angelina—and bring him or her home to a nursery decorated in blue or pink with a sports theme or flowers. Parents announce the gender of their babies to the world by the ways they dress them. A group of researchers watching 1- to 10-month-olds in a shopping center found that baby boys were dressed in simple blue or red clothes while baby girls were dressed in pink garments with ruffles and lace and had bows, barrettes, and ribbons in their hair (Shakin et al., 1985). Gender-typed clothing announces the child's gender and ensures that even strangers will respond to the child in a gender-appropriate way (Fagot & Leinbach, 1987). When the boys and girls are older, parents dress them in either pants or dresses, style their hair in buzz cut or curls, select toys and activities that they deem gender appropriate, promote the children's association with same-sex playmates, and often react with dismay or criticism when the children behave in ways they consider gender inappropriate. They fill boys' rooms with action-oriented toys—vehicles, machines, army equipment, soldiers, and sports equipment—and girls' rooms with family-focused toys and feminine decor—dolls, dollhouses, and floral-patterned and ruffled furnishings (Pomerleau et al., 1990). Thus, well before children make lists of toys they'd like to receive for birthdays or holidays, parents are actively shaping their youngsters' tastes and preferences. Parents also provide opportunities for boys and girls to learn gender-typed behaviors by enrolling them in different types of gender-typed activities, clubs, and sports—for example, boys on baseball teams and girls in ballet classes (Leaper & Friedman, 2007). Parents are significantly more gender stereotyped about children's engagement in extracurricular activities than are nonparental adults (Killen et al., 2005).

Parents' Behavior toward Girls and Boys

The influence of parents on children's gender typing goes beyond choosing bats and balls or dolls and tutus. Parents also behave differently toward their sons and daughters from the moment they first meet.

BEHAVIOR WITH INFANTS AND TODDLERS Parents perceive boys and girls as different as soon as they are born. Consistent with evolutionary theory, which emphasizes strength and competitiveness in males and nurturance in females (Geary, 1998), parents describe their newborn daughters as smaller, softer, cuter, more delicate, and more finely featured than they describe their sons. They emphasize their sons' size, strength, coordination, and alertness and their daughters' fragility and beauty (Rubin et al., 1974; Stern & Karraker, 1989). In view of these differences in parents' perceptions, it is not surprising that they also treat their sons and daughters differently. They tend to be more verbally responsive with daughters than with sons; they talk more to girls in infancy and at older ages and use more supportive and directive speech (Clearfield & Nelson, 2006; Kitamura & Burnham, 2003; Leaper & Friedman, 2007; Leaper et al., 1998). They are harsher with boys (McKee et al., 2007).

This differential perception and treatment of infant boys and girls is even more marked for fathers than for mothers (Stern & Karraker, 1989). From the time they hear they are going to have a baby, fathers-to-be show a preference for sons, and after the baby is born, fathers are more likely to play and talk with their sons than with their daughters, especially when the baby is a firstborn (Parke, 2002; Schoppe-Sullivan et al., 2006). When the children are toddlers, fathers spend more time watching, touching, and playing with sons than daughters. They indulge in rough-and-tumble antics and talk to their sons in a kind of macho way, saying things such as "Hey, Tiger!" (Parke, 2002). With daughters, they are likely to cuddle gently rather than engaging in active play. In contrast, mothers tend to treat baby girls and baby boys much the same way (Leaper, 2002; Lytton & Romney, 1991). This pattern of differences in mothers' and fathers' interactions with sons and daughters suggests that the social forces involved in gender typing begin at birth and that fathers, through their markedly different treatment of boys and girls, may contribute to the gender-typing process more than mothers.

BEHAVIOR WITH OLDER CHILDREN   As children grow, parents actively encourage and reinforce their gender-typed behavior. One area in which this has been observed is play. In one study, researchers watched how mothers and fathers reacted to their 3- and 5-year-old sons' and daughters' play, purposely manipulating the children's choices of toys (Langlois & Downs, 1980). Both masculine toys, such as soldiers and a gas station, and feminine toys, such as a dollhouse and kitchen utensils, were available, but the researchers specifically told the children to play with toys that were either gender appropriate or gender inappropriate. They then recorded parents' reactions to the children's toy choices. Fathers exerted pressure on their children—both sons and daughters—to play with gender-typed toys. They rewarded them for playing with gender-appropriate toys and punished them for playing with cross-gender toys. Mothers took the same approach with their daughters but were less consistent with their sons; sometimes they punished them and sometimes rewarded them for playing with cross-gender toys. In other studies as well, researchers have found that fathers are more likely than mothers to disapprove of their children's engagement in activities that are considered appropriate for the other gender (Leve & Fagot, 1997). Men are also more likely than women to purchase gender-typed toys, especially for boys (Fisher-Thompson, 1990; Fisher-Thompson et al., 1995).

A second area in which parents encourage different behaviors in their sons and daughters is dependence and independence. Parents encourage boys to be independent, to explore, and to assume personal responsibility; they encourage girls to be dependent, obedient, and maintain close family ties (Leaper & Friedman, 2007; Ruble et al., 2006). They are more protective of daughters' physical well-being. Although they are likely to encourage both sons' and daughters' independence and maturity in safe activities such as tidying up their rooms, putting away their toys and clothes, and getting dressed, they treat boys and girls differently in riskier areas. When asked to imagine that their child had been injured, parents reacted with concern to less severe injuries of their daughters (Morrongiello & Hogg, 2004). They were more likely to stop children fighting when their daughter was involved as either a perpetrator or a victim (Martin & Ross, 2005). Parents think that boys should be able to engage in venturesome activities at earlier ages than girls, for example playing away from home without telling the parents where they are, running errands in the neighborhood, crossing the street alone, and using sharp scissors (Pomerantz & Ruble, 1998). Parents are more likely to pick up and supervise girls after school and to set restrictions and curfews (Parke & Buriel, 2006; Ruble et al., 2006). Many psychologists are concerned that restricting girls' freedom may lead them to feel less adequate and discourage them from exploring the world and taking risks (Ruble et al., 2006).

A third area in which parents encourage differences between their sons and daughters is achievement. Parents encourage their boys to achieve and compete more than they encourage their girls (Ruble et al., 2006). During the school years, differential treatment of boys and girls is particularly marked in the areas of math and science achievement (DeLisi & McGillicuddy-DeLisi, 2002). Parents are more likely to encourage their sons to work on math and science activities (Eccles et al., 2000). When visiting a science museum, parents in one study were more likely to explain the interactive exhibits to their sons than their daughters (Crowley et al., 2001). In another study, although 6th-grade girls and boys expressed equal interest in science and earned the same grades, their parents underestimated their daughters' interest, believed that science was more difficult for them, and were less likely to give the girls scientific explanations when working on a physics-related task (Tenenbaum & Leaper, 2003). Fathers are more likely to stress the importance of achievement, a career, and occupational success for sons than for daughters; they are more concerned about their daughters' interpersonal interactions (Block, 1983). Even when parents are reading bedtime stories, mothers teach their sons more than their daughters. They supply their sons with unfamiliar names ("Look, here's a giraffe. Can you say *giraffe*?"), but with their daughters they emphasize the pleasure of the interaction (Weitzman et al., 1985) and they focus on feelings and emotions rather than information and learning (Cervantes & Callanan, 1998). These differences in parents' behavior are not lost on their children. When parents have strongly stereotyped beliefs about boys' and girls' abilities, their children have matching views—regardless of their own ability levels (Eccles et al., 1993, 1998). Girls achieve more when their parents have more gender-egalitarian attitudes and are more balanced in their treatment of boys and girls (Leaper & Friedman, 2007; Updegraff et al., 1996).

The degree to which parents encourage gender differences in their children varies some-what across ethnic groups. African American parents value early independence for both sons and daughters and make fewer gender distinctions in deciding who is to carry out which family roles and tasks than European American parents do (Gibbs, 1989). African American parents also encourage girls to be aggressive and assertive and boys to express emotion and nurturance more than European American parents (Allen & Majidi-Abi, 1989; Basow, 1992). Mexican American parents, in contrast, have more strictly differentiated gender-role socialization standards than European American parents (Coltrane & Adams, 2008). The behavior of children reflects their parents' socialization (Ruble et al., 2006). For example, compared with European American girls, Mexican American girls place less emphasis on educational achievement, consistent with their socialization into the traditional role of wife and mother, and Mexican American boys are more assertive than European American boys in keeping with the traditional emphasis on male "machismo" (Adams et al., 2007).

Modeling Parents' Characteristics

Beyond providing gender-appropriate toys, parents influence the gender-role development of their children by modeling gender-typed behavior. Mothers' and fathers' attitudes, actions, and lifestyles provide models their children can follow in working out their gender roles. One study found a link between parents' and children's gender beliefs: Parents who were highly traditional in their own gender roles had children who knew more about gender stereotypes

(Turner & Gervai, 1995). In another study, researchers observed a link between parents' and children's behavior styles: Boys with strong, "masculine" fathers and weak, "feminine" mothers were more likely to exhibit masculine characteristics and less likely to exhibit feminine characteristics than boys with weak fathers and powerful mothers (Hetherington, 1965). The ways in which mothers and fathers divide household tasks is another source of parental modeling that may influence children's gender typing. Researchers have found that when parents are traditional in their division of tasks, their children are more knowledgeable about gender distinctions (Serbin et al., 1993; Turner & Gervai, 1995). See Table 10.1 for highlights of children's gender-role development and gender-role socialization by parents.

Children clearly imitate the gender-typed behaviors of their same-sex parent. Source: © Media Bakery.

TABLE 10.1 Development of Gender Typing and Gender Roles

Infancy	Parents dress baby and decorate nursery in pink or blue.
	They describe a boy as "strong" and "active" and a girl as "sweet."
	Fathers greet a boy with expressions such as, "Hey, Tiger," and girls with expressions such as "Hello, little darling."
1–3 years	Parents select gender-appropriate toys, promote contact with same-gender playmates, disapprove when a child displays behavior that is "inappropriate" for her or his gender.
	Fathers are more likely to gender type children than are mothers.
	Children recognize male and female faces as belonging to two distinct categories.
	Children can correctly label own gender but have limited understanding of gender identity and its wider implications.
	As they approach 3 years of age, children begin to grasp concept of gender identity.
3–5 years	Children understand that they themselves and some other children belong to a gender *class*.
	Children have developed clear preferences for gender-appropriate toys.
	Girls interact more with babies and in a more active way than boys do.
	Children are more gender stereotyped than adults.
	Children begin to understand the concept of gender stability.
5–7 years	Boys are more likely than girls to play in same-gender groups.
	Children spend much more time with same-gender playmates than with other-gender children.
	Children understand gender stability and gender constancy (by age 7).
7–11 years	Children develop patterns of interest in activities that are consistent with cultural gender stereotypes.
	Most children display knowledge of gender-typed traits.

Note: Developmental events represent overall trends identified in research studies. Individual children vary greatly in the ages at which they exhibit these developmental changes. Sources: Beal, 1994; Leaper & Friedman, 2007; Maccoby, 1998; Pasterski et al., 2010; Ruble et al., 2006.

esearch up Close:
Gender Roles in Counterculture Families

Researchers in the Family Lifestyles Project followed more than 200 families in southern California, beginning in the 1970s, and investigated relations between lifestyles and children's gender development (Eiduson et al., 1988). Some of the families were traditionally married couples and others had unconventional family configurations—single parents, common-law couples, and couples in communes or other group arrangements. Among these nonconventional families were a sizable number (78) who had a high commitment to gender-egalitarian beliefs and values. The parents in these *avant garde* and *countercultural* families were likely to be active in progressive political activities, such as antiwar demonstrations and environmental activism. They were committed to feminism and attempted to practice it in their everyday lives. They shared domestic, financial, and child care tasks or reported that the fathers performed them exclusively.

When the children in these families were about 6 years old, the researchers brought each child and his or her parents to a university center for a one-day visit (Weisner & Wilson-Mitchell, 1990). They interviewed the parents about how they put their gender values into practice raising their children, and they assessed the children's gender typing in several areas: appearance, activities and interests, social relationships, and personal-social attributes (e.g., *adventurous, considerate, outgoing, calm*). In comparison with children reared by traditional married couples, children in the avant garde and countercultural families were less gender typed in their chosen activities and interests and less gender stereotyped in their assumptions that girls could be engineers and firefighters and boys could be librarians and nursery school teachers. More than 70 percent of the children in the avant garde and countercultural families

gave nonstereotyped answers to questions about appropriate occupations for boys and girls in comparison with only 40 percent of the children in traditional families. The avant garde and countercultural children were very much like the traditional family children in other ways, though, such as their play preferences and their basic knowledge of the ways in which familiar play objects (e.g., dishes, trucks, dolls, racing cars) are culturally gender typed. Children from avant garde and countercultural families had acquired the normal cultural schemas for gender typing, regardless of their family's unconventional lifestyle. They were not counter-stereotyped; instead, they tended to be **multischematic**; that is, they displayed either conventional or egalitarian gender-typing schemas depending on the situation. They had multiple schemas available, and they had developed selective criteria for when to use each one. This capacity to be flexible and multischematic was part of a more general pattern that characterized these children's families. Their parents regularly engaged in negotiations and discussions about all kinds of cultural standards, debating and questioning the standards, and including the children in their discussions. This process encouraged the children to think about and question beliefs and behavior rather than always adopting either conventional or countercultural standards. Some family styles observed in the study, however, made children even more rigidly gender stereotyped. Children who were reared in devotional communes that strongly emphasized culturally conventional gender roles were even less likely to be open minded about gender than children in conventional married families. This study, thus, provided a clear demonstration of how parents can modify their children's gender roles toward more gender-differentiated roles or more gender-egalitarian roles.

When Father Is Absent

multischematic
Possessing multiple ideas about appropriate behaviors that can be displayed depending on the particular situation.

As we have said, fathers are more likely than mothers to treat sons and daughters differently. For this reason, we might expect that children from families in which fathers are absent or away for long periods would be less gender typed. The absence of a male model and the lack of opportunities for children to interact with a man might also lead to difficulties developing a gender identity and a gender role. Researchers have found that when fathers are permanently away because of divorce or death, are temporarily unavailable because of occupational demands or military service, or simply show little interest in their children, young boys sometimes have problems in their gender-role development and behave more like girls (Ruble et al., 2006; Stevenson & Black, 1988). Problems are most severe when the father's unavailability occurs before the boy is 5 years old. As children grow up and have wider social contacts, other male models from among the child's peers, siblings, teachers, and sports heroes can compensate for the father's absence.

The effects of father's absence on gender typing in girls are minimal—or at least delayed until adolescence when they show up in the girls' behavior with the opposite sex. Researchers following girls in the United States and New Zealand from age 5 to age 18 found that father's absence was associated with an elevated risk of early sexual activity and pregnancy, and the earlier the father left, the greater the risk (see Figure 10.4; Ellis et al., 2003). These links were still evident even after the researchers controlled for family conditions such as poverty, exposure to violence, inadequate parental guidance, and lack of supervision. These findings can be explained by psychological theories: learning theories suggest that the father-absent girls had not developed the social skills and confidence they needed for normal heterosexual relationships because they had missed out on interactions with a man who rewarded and enjoyed their femininity and modeled ways to behave with the opposite sex. Evolutionary theory suggests that girls in homes without a father viewed male parental investment in families as unreliable and unimportant and as a result were more likely to form casual sexual liaisons (Bjorklund & Shackelford, 1999; Geary, 1998).

Studies of children who grow up in lesbian households have challenged the importance of the father's contribution to gender typing, however. Children reared in lesbian families do not differ in gender-role behavior from children reared in heterosexual households. Boys and girls with lesbian parents choose traditionally gender-oriented toys, activities, and friends, and as young adults, do not report precocious sexual activity (Patterson & Hastings, 2007). These studies suggest that children can learn gender roles in a variety of family arrangements.

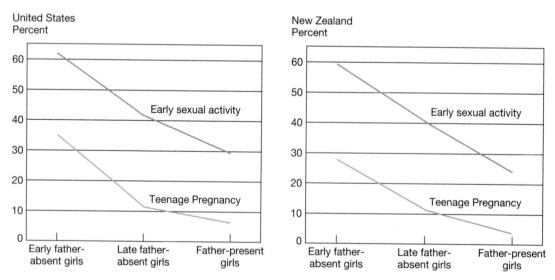

FIGURE 10.4 *The effects of father absence on girls' early sexual activity and pregnancy. Teenage girls in the United States and New Zealand were far more likely to engage in early sexual activity when they lost their fathers, especially if the father's absence occurred before they were 5 years old. Source: Ellis, B. J., Bates, J. E., Dodge, K. A., Fergusson, D. M., Horwood, L. J., Pettit, G. S., and Woodward, L. (2003). Does father absence place daughters at special risk for early sexual activity and teenage pregnancy?* Child Development, 74, 801–821. *Reprinted with permission of the Society for Research in Child Development and Wiley-Blackwell.*

Learning from Living Leaders: Charlotte J. Patterson

Source: Courtesy of Charlotte Patterson, University of Virginia.

Charlotte Patterson is Professor of Psychology at the University of Virginia where she teaches child development and psychology of sexual orientation. Since receiving a B.A. from Pomona College and a Ph.D. in psychology from Stanford University, she has pursued research in developmental psychology, focusing especially on development in families with lesbian and gay parents. Her interest in these families was inspired by her recognition that mainstream psychology generally ignored them even though their numbers were increasing and by her experience raising two daughters with a lesbian partner. Her goal was to document the effects of growing up in this type of family on children's psychosocial adjustment, gender typing, gender identity, and gender preferences. Her work has shown that these children are well adjusted and very similar to children in two-parent heterosexual families. Results from Patterson's research have frequently been used in judicial proceedings related to child custody and adoption in lesbian and gay families. Patterson has also testified as an expert witness in several high-profile cases including *Bottoms v. Bottoms,* in which a lesbian mother was sued by her own mother for custody of her child, and *Baehr v. Miike,* in which two lesbian couples and a gay couple challenged the ban on same-sex marriages in Hawai'i. She has been recognized for her pioneering work in this area by the Society for Psychological Study of Lesbian and Gay Issues (a Division of the American Psychological Association), which presented her its annual award for Distinguished Scientific Contributions. She also received an Outstanding Achievement Award from the APA Committee on Lesbian, Gay and Bisexual Concerns and the Carolyn Attneave Diversity Award from Division 43 of the American Psychological Association (Family Psychology) for contributions that advance the understanding and integration of diversity into family psychology.

Further Reading

Patterson, C. J. (2006). Children of lesbian and gay parents. *Current Directions in Psychological Science, 15,* 207–268.

Siblings as Gender Socialization Agents

Siblings also influence children's gender choices, attitudes, and behaviors. In one longitudinal study, researchers investigated whether the gender-role attitudes, activities, and attributes of firstborn children predicted the same qualities in their second-born siblings (McHale et al., 2001). The study found that the younger siblings' gender typing was indeed related to their older siblings' attributes—even more strongly than to their parents'. Other researchers have found that the sex of the siblings matters too. Children with sisters tend to develop more feminine qualities; children with brothers, more masculine qualities (Rust et al., 2000). Brother-brother pairs engage in more boyish play, throwing balls, making vehicles go "vroom," and shooting toy weapons; sister-sister and older sister-younger brother pairs engage in more feminine pursuits, doing art activities, playing with dolls, and playing house (Stoneman et al., 1986). Firstborn boys with brothers have the most stereotyped gender attitudes; children with an older sibling of the opposite sex have less stereotypical gender-role concepts (Crouter et al., 2007). Even parents are affected by siblings' gender: When they decorate their children's rooms, they choose the most boyish items for sons with older brothers (Rheingold & Cook, 1975).

Influence of Books and Television

As children grow, influences outside the family become increasingly important for gender-role development. The books children read generally portray male and female roles in gender-stereotyped ways. Although educators have advocated for a more egalitarian presentation, children's literature still contains many gender stereotypes. A comparative study of elementary school children's reading textbooks over a period of 15 years offered some hopeful signs. Girls appeared in a wider range of activities in the later books than in the earlier ones (Purcell & Stewart, 1990). Nevertheless, books still often show females as more passive, dependent, and engaged in a narrower range of occupations than men and show males as more assertive and action oriented (Turner-Bowker, 1996). This gender stereotyping is evident even in books labeled "nonsexist" (Diekman & Murnen, 2004).

Television programs are also sources of gender stereotyping. Males on television are more likely than females to be aggressive, decisive, professionally competent, rational, stable, powerful, and tolerant; females are portrayed as warmer, happier, and more sociable and emotional. When women on television are aggressive, with a few notable exceptions, such as *Xena, Warrior Princess*, they are usually inept or unsuccessful and are more likely to be shown as victims than initiators of violence. Females are less likely than males to be leading characters and more likely to play comedy roles, to be married or engaged, and to be young and attractive (Comstock & Scharrer, 2006; Huston & Wright, 1998). A trend toward showing women in a wider range of occupational roles has been noted (Coltrane & Adams, 2008; Douglas, 2003). In fact, in one survey, only 4 percent of female TV characters were portrayed as homemakers (Heintz-Knowles, 2001). However, even in television commercials, males more often portray authorities and make voice-over comments about products' merits, whereas women play the role of consumer, displaying interest in the products (Coltrane, 1998). When women are shown as experts, they are likely to be discussing food products, laundry soap, or beauty aids.

These stereotyped presentations are of particular concern because children tend to watch actors of their own gender on TV. In both North America and Asia, researchers have found that boys prefer male characters and girls prefer females and that children prefer gender-consistent content; that is, boys like violent fare and girls prefer peaceful content (Knobloch et al., 2005). Their gender schemas guide the specific programs children watch, and what they view shapes their gender beliefs—creating an endless cycle of gender typing and stereotyping (Leaper & Friedman, 2007).

The influence of stereotyped presentations of male and female roles is demonstrated by research showing that children who view TV extensively are more likely to have stereotyped notions of gender and to conform to culturally accepted gender typing (Berry, 2000; Ward & Friedman, 2006). In the study of what happened when television was introduced in a small town in Canada, which we discussed in Chapter 9, "Schools and Media," researchers found significant increases in children's stereotyped gender attitudes 2 years later (Kimball, 1986; MacBeth, 1996). Television can also be used to reduce children's gender-role stereotypes. In one study, 5- and 6-year-old children who were shown a cartoon in which the characters played nontraditional roles (e.g., girls helped build a clubhouse) developed less stereotyped gender-role attitudes (Davidson et al., 1979). *Freestyle,* a television series that attempted to counteract children's gender stereotypes, was moderately successful in increasing acceptance of boys and girls who exhibited nongender-typed behaviors. For example, 9- to 12-year-old viewers were more accepting of girls who participated in athletics and mechanical activities and of boys who engaged in nurturant activities (Johnston & Ettema, 1982). However, the effects of most TV-based interventions have been relatively modest, short lived, and effective only with young children (Comstock & Scharrer, 2006). More substantial and pervasive changes in books and television must be made to reduce children's development of gender-role stereotypes.

Real-World Application: Do Computers Widen the Gender Gap?

Computers are commonplace in classrooms and homes, after-school clubs and summer camps, but do they provide boys and girls an "even playing field" genderwise? When computers first became available, computer use by girls and boys differed widely (Lepper, 1985; Lepper & Gurtner, 1989). As many as ten boys were enrolled in basic computer classes for every one girl, and the ratio was higher in more advanced classes. Boys also played more computer games than girls did and believed that these games were more acceptable for them (Funk & Buchman, 1996). They even claimed that girls who spend a lot of time playing games are unpopular and that if they want to be popular, they should not play games, especially "the fighting games." (Girls, by the way, did not agree.)

Many factors can explain this gender discrepancy in computer use. One is that the computer field was dominated by males and had fewer female role models to attract girls. Another reason is that computer labs tended to be competitive and noisy, which boys found more comfortable than girls. Third, schools typically presented computers as mathematical tools in spite of the fact that they had many other uses. Computer labs were usually found in the math department, and credits for computer courses often counted toward math requirements. Because girls often believe that they have less math ability than boys, this arrangement kept them away from computers

and sometimes from careers in math and science (Shea et al., 2001). A fourth reason for the gender discrepancy in computer use was that most computer programs seemed to have been written for boys (Subrahmanyam et al., 2001). Even specifically educational games could turn girls off with their macho titles: Alien Addition, Demolition Division, Spelling Baseball. Finally, another reason that boys originally spent more time and were better than girls at computer games was that their peers encouraged and rewarded them for doing so more than they did girls (Funk & Buchman, 1996; Lawry et al., 1995).

According to recent reports, the gender gap in computer use is closing, partly because of the expanding range of available applications, including e-mail, chat rooms, and educational pursuits, not just computer programming and games. Recent data suggest that girls and boys are spending equal amounts of time on the computer and are equally confident about their computer skills. But the computer activities they favor still differ; girls use computers for social contact whereas boys use them for games (see photos). Girls and boys both embrace computers when they offer functions that fit their interests (Subrahmanyam et al., 2001). Thus, computers themselves do not widen the gender gap, but until there are computer programs and opportunities that appeal equally to both boys and girls, they will not eliminate it.

Peers, Gender Roles, and Gender Segregation

Peers serve as models and enforcers of society's gender-role standards and are the strongest influence on children's gender-typed behavior by the time they are in school (Leaper & Friedman, 2007; Rose & Rudolph, 2006). To investigate the effect of peers as models, researchers exposed

3rd- and 4th-graders to peer models who displayed preferences for a variety of objects (Bussey & Perry, 1982). Children were more likely to play with a gender-neutral toy or even a cross-gender toy after observing a same-gender model do so. To investigate the effect of peers as enforcers, researchers watched 200 preschoolers at play over several months' time (Fagot, 1985a). They found that peers reacted strongly when children violated appropriate gender-role behavior patterns. Boys who played with dolls rather than trucks had a particularly tough time; they were criticized five to six times more often than boys who conformed to stereotype. Peers were less harsh in their treatment of girls who played firefighters rather than nurses; they tended to ignore rather than criticize them. When peers rewarded appropriate gender-role behavior, children persisted longer in the rewarded type of activity, especially if the reward came from a same-sex peer.

gender segregation
A child's choice to spend time with same-gender peers.

This pattern of peer interaction is related to children's **gender segregation** into same-sex playgroups. Look at any school playground, and you will see that children are playing with others of the same sex. Although parental influence may play a role in setting the process in motion, by the time they are in preschool, children spontaneously choose same-gender play partners without adult encouragement, guidance, or pressure (Maccoby, 1998; Pellegrini et al., 2007). In one study of preschool children, both boys and girls had more than twice as many interactions with same-sex peers as with other-sex peers, were faster to return to them after their play had been interrupted, and started playing with them more quickly (Martin & Ruble, 2010). These patterns were apparent even after only a few weeks of preschool. Other research indicated that, by the end of preschool, children spent nearly 3 times as much time with same-sex play partners as with children of the other sex, and by age 6, they spent 11 times as much time with same-sex partners (Maccoby,1998). Boys were even more likely than girls to congregate in same-sex groups (Benenson et al., 1997). This trend continues in elementary school; children like same-sex peers better than other-sex peers and are less likely to behave negatively toward them (Underwood, Schockner, et al., 2001). Gender segregation is evident across many cultures, including the United States, India, and some African countries. Thus, children live in segregated worlds, which, in turn, encourage separate styles of interaction that are distinctly male and female. With their same-sex peers, girls play house and boys act out adventures. These activities provide opportunities for practicing gender-typed behaviors. Girls' play offers practice in nurturant, affiliative, and collaborative behavior; boys' play offers practice in assertive and competitive behavior. This is another way in which children learn and maintain gender roles.

To investigate gender segregation in more detail, Carol Martin and Richard Fabes (2001) followed preschoolers over the course of one school year. They found that gender segregation increased during the year and that boys' and girls' activities were clearly different when they played in same-sex groups. The more time boys spent together, the higher was their activity level. Boys who spent more time with other boys engaged in increasing amounts of rough-and-tumble play and overt aggression, spent less time with or near adults, and expressed more positive emotion (i.e., had more fun). In contrast, the activity and aggression of girls who spent more time with other girls decreased and they spent more time with or near adults. Thus, same-gender segregation provided distinctive socializing experiences for boys and girls (Maccoby,1998). Consistent with these findings, researchers in another study found that preschool boys chose friends who had high activity levels but preschool girls chose friends with low activity levels; in short, children chose friends whose activity level fit their comfort zone (Gleason et al., 2005).

Eleanor Maccoby (1990, 1998) suggested several reasons for children's gender segregation. First, girls view boys' rough-and-tumble play style and competition-dominance orientation as aversive, so they avoid interacting with boys. This emotional reaction to opposite-sex interactions is particularly strong for highly gender-typed children (Martin & Ruble, 2010). Second, boys and girls prefer different activities: boys like sports and games and girls enjoy socializing and watching TV (Cherney & London, 2006; Mathur & Berndt, 2006). Third, girls find managing boys difficult. They interact with other girls easily using their preferred tactic of making polite suggestions, but this tactic is not very effective with boys, who use and respond to direct demands. So, girls begin to avoid boys. These preferences for playing with children

Learning from Living Leaders:
Eleanor E. Maccoby

Source: Courtesy of Eleanor E. Maccoby.

Few scholars have contributed as much to our understanding of sex differences and gender roles in childhood as Eleanor Maccoby, Professor Emerita at Stanford University. Maccoby received her undergraduate education at Reed College and the University of Washington and completed her doctoral work in experimental psychology at the University of Michigan in 1950. Her interest in gender differences stemmed in part from her own experience balancing the roles of mother and scholar. After adopting her second child, she worked part-time and virtually stopped doing research until her children were grown. When she returned to academia full time, she

gave up sleep so she could be both mother and researcher. Juggling these roles was an even greater challenge for professional women when Maccoby was doing it than it is today when maternal employment is so widely accepted. In the 1950s, Maccoby began teaching child psychology at Harvard and researching patterns of child rearing, contributing to a major study of how parents socialize their children. In the late 1960s, she began exploring sex differences in development, and in 1974, she published *The Psychology of Sex Differences* (with Carol Jacklin), a comprehensive synthesis of research on gender. In the political climate of the 1970s with the Women's Movement promoting the argument that women were capable of tasks previously restricted to men, this book inspired much debate. In her 1998 book, *The Two Sexes: Growing Up Apart, Coming Together,* Maccoby spelled out her theory of gender segregation and documented how relationships with the other sex differ across the life cycle. Maccoby has received many awards in recognition of her groundbreaking work including the American Psychological Foundation's Gold Medal Award for Lifetime Achievement and election to the National Academy of Sciences.

Further Reading

Maccoby, E. E.(1998). *The two sexes: Growing up apart, coming together.* Cambridge MA: Harvard University Press.

of the same sex may lead not only to gender segregation but also to differences in children's abilities. For example, boys' preference to spend most of their time with a group of boys limits the types of social skills they develop. Because they are interacting in a group, they develop competitive and assertive skills; because they are interacting only with boys, they do not learn how to disclose personal information or express their emotions—or, in the vernacular, "get in touch with their feminine side" (Leaper & Friedman, 2007).

Schools and Teachers

Schools provide the final influence on children's gender typing that we discuss. Teachers and schools deliver gender-related messages to children just as parents, peers, and the media do (Leaper & Friedman, 2007; Ruble et al., 2006).

THE SCHOOL CULTURE   In most school systems, although men hold the positions of power, such as principal and superintendent, women, as teachers, create the school culture, which at least in the beginning favors girls. In elementary school, female teachers tend to frown on the independent, assertive, competitive, and boisterous qualities that have been encouraged in boys since infancy. They like girls, who are more verbally oriented, well behaved, and willing to follow rules, better. Girls also tend to like school better than boys do and perform better in class. For many boys, school is not a happy place. They have difficulty adjusting to school routines and create problems for teachers; girls find school consistent with their gender preferences (McCall et al., 2000; Ruble et al., 2006).

Girls' advantage in the early grades is brief, however. Their achievement levels decline as they get older, and by college, the proportion of female underachievers exceeds the proportion of male underachievers (Eccles et al., 1993; Wigfield et al., 2006). The conforming and dependent behaviors that elementary school teachers encourage in girls may be detrimental in the long run. Dependency is negatively related to intellectual achievement. Independence, assertiveness, and nonconformity are much more likely to lead to creative thinking and problem solving and to high levels of achievement by both girls and boys (Dweck, 2001, 2006).

Psychologists have found that achievement in competitive activities often threatens girls and women. Some cope with their conflict about achievement by concealing their ability, particularly from boys (Ruble et al., 2006). For example, a girl may tell a boy that she received a lower grade than she actually did in a course they are both taking. Or she may intentionally perform below her capabilities. Even women who are highly successful professionals sometimes seek to disguise their achievement by appearing superfeminine: They try to be not only super women in their careers but also superwives, supermothers, and supervolunteers.

TEACHER ATTITUDES AND BEHAVIORS Teachers often react to boys and girls in gender-typed ways. They are more responsive to girls' social initiatives such as talking and gesturing and to boys' assertive behavior such as pushing and shoving (Hendrick & Stange, 1991). Not surprisingly, by the end of preschool, girls talk to the teacher more and boys are more assertive (Fagot, 1985a). This is good for the girls, but not necessarily for the boys. Teachers also criticize boys more than girls for cross-gender behaviors such as dressing up or playing with dolls (Fagot, 1985a). Although educators once believed that increasing the number of male teachers would counteract female teachers' treatment of boys and girls, both male and female teachers react more positively to children involved in "feminine" activities, such as art, writing, and helping others, no matter what the child's gender is (Fagot, 1985b).

Boys and girls have traditionally differed in their performance on verbal and quantitative tasks, girls doing better in language and boys in mathematics (Eccles et al., 1998; Shea et al., 2001). However, girls are actually better than boys at math computation and have as much knowledge of mathematics and algebra. Why, then, do enrollments in school courses, selection of college majors, and adult career choices reflect the idea that boys are better at math? One reason is that teachers continue to encourage boys more than girls in mathematical pursuits (Wigfield et al., 2006). Of course this is not the only reason. Boys perceive themselves as more competent in math and girls view mathematics as a male domain. Even in later elementary school when girls outperform boys in language arts, math, science, and social studies, girls think of themselves as good only in language because that's what they are supposed to be good at (Pomerantz et al., 2002). Jacquelynne Eccles (2007) found that U.S. children in 5th through 12th grades thought that boys were better at math than girls despite the fact that their actual mathematics performance showed no gender differences. European researchers, similarly, have found that among 4th- and 5th-grade Italian children, boys were more confident than girls about their math abilities despite comparable competence (Muzzatti & Agnoli, 2007). In the future, teachers can try to shift children's perceptions of gender differences in mathematics to be more accurate by encouraging and praising both girls and boys equally.

Androgyny

Many psychologists believe that traditional ideas of gender roles are too narrow. To speak and act as if each person is either "masculine" or "feminine" in his or her interests, attitudes, and behavior makes little sense because, in reality, most people possess a combination of characteristics that can be described as masculine or feminine. Any person, male or female, can be tender and nurturant with children, assertive at work, fiercely competitive on the tennis

androgynous
Possessing both feminine and masculine psychological characteristics.

court, and an excellent cook. People who possess both masculine and feminine characteristics are termed *androgynous* (Bem, 1981, 1998; Spence, & Buckner, 2000). Children as well as adults can be androgynous; these children are less likely to make gender-typed choices of toys and play activities (Harter, 2006). They are better adjusted and more creative (Norlander et al., 2000). Children who are either masculine or androgynous have higher self-esteem than those with only feminine characteristics (Boldizar, 1991; Ruble et al., 2006). Children who both accept themselves as a typical member of their own gender and believe that it is okay to cross gender boundaries are better adjusted than those who are not secure in their gender role (Carver et al., 2004; Egan & Perry, 2001).

Facilitating children's development of the desirable characteristics of both genders—social sensitivity, nurturance, open expression of positive feelings, assertiveness, and independence—would, therefore, be constructive. But can children be taught to be more androgynous? As the following exchange between a psychologist's 4-year-old son and his young friend illustrates, the task may not be easy:

Son: *My mother helps people. She's a doctor.*

Friend: *You mean a nurse.*

Son: *No. She's not that kind of doctor. She's a psychologist. She's a doctor of psychology.*

Friend: *I see. She's a nurse of psychology.*

With effort, children can be taught to use fewer stereotypes. Researchers lessened children's stereotyping of work roles using ten occupations that children typically view as masculine (e.g., dentist, farmer, construction worker) or feminine (e.g., beautician, flight attendant, librarian) (Bigler & Liben, 1990, 1992). They first taught the children that gender is irrelevant. Then they focused the children's attention on two other ways of looking at job appropriateness: liking a job and having the skills needed for it. For example, construction workers must like to build things and must have the skill to drive big machines. The researchers then gave one group of children practice problems in which they had to specify why each job was a good match for the person. If the children based their answers on gender rather than interest or skills, they received corrective feedback. Children in a control group participated in a group discussion about the roles of specific occupations within the community with no emphasis on gender typing. When they were tested later, children in the experimental group gave more non-gender-stereotyped answers, not only for the occupations involved in the lessons and the practice questions but also for a range of other occupations. For instance, when they were asked who could do activities such as police work and nursing, they more often replied, "both men and women." Children in the control group still argued that "girls can't be firefighters." Consistent with gender-schema theory, children in the experimental group also had better recall of counter-stereotypic information in a later memory test than children in the control group. Although children in both groups remembered stories about Frank the firefighter and Betty the beautician, children in the experimental group also remembered stories about Larry the librarian and Ann the astronaut.

In preschools where teachers consciously attempt to minimize gender stereotyping, children spend more time in mixed-gender groups and less time in conventional gender-typed activities than children in traditional preschools; both boys and girls play house and gas up their toy trucks (Bianchi & Bakeman, 1983). Clearly, children's gender roles and attitudes are modifiable. In some countries, such as Sweden, citizens have made an explicit commitment to gender equality, and opportunities to observe males and females engaging in nongender-stereotyped jobs and activities have resulted in increases in androgynous attitudes among children (Coltrane & Adams, 2008; Tenenbaum & Leaper, 2002). In the United States, attitudes toward gender roles are changing slowly and will likely continue to change as more people broaden their behavioral repertoires to cross gender lines.

Chapter Summary

Gender Definitions

- The process by which children acquire values and behaviors viewed as appropriate for males and females within a culture is called *gender typing*. Children develop gender-based beliefs, including gender stereotypes, which are reflected in gender roles. Children form a gender identity and begin to develop gender-role preferences early in life.

Gender-Role Stereotypes

- Within our culture, males are expected to be independent, assertive, and competitive; females are expected to be passive, sensitive, and supportive. These beliefs have changed little over the years despite the efforts of feminists and other advocates of gender equality.

Gender Differences in Development

- On average, girls are more physically and neurologically advanced at birth, excel early in verbal skills, and are more nurturant toward younger children. Boys have more mature muscular development and are more aggressive.
- Although differences exist, the overlap between the two sexes is more than the differences between them.
- Children exhibit gender-typed preferences as early as 1 year of age.
- Girls tend to conform less strictly to gender-role stereotypes than do boys, possibly because parents and teachers exert greater pressure on boys to adhere to the masculine role. Girls may also imitate the male role because it has higher status and privilege. Although some boys and girls receive support for cross-gender behavior, most are encouraged to behave according to traditional stereotypes.
- Adult behavior can be predicted from gender-typed interests in elementary school. Greater stability occurs when personal characteristics are consistent with gender stereotypes.
- Gender roles may intensify in adolescence and when adults become parents.

Biological Factors in Gender Differences

- Males and females use different strategies to achieve reproductive success and, according to evolutionary theory, these strategies have led to gender differences such as females' emphasis on physical appearance, sensitivity, and caregiving skills and males' emphasis on strength, power, and aggression.
- Hormones organize biological predispositions to be masculine or feminine during the prenatal period, and the increase in hormones during puberty may activate these predispositions.
- Male and female brains are somewhat different in structure and function. Female brains are more active in social regions and tend to be less lateralized than the male brain. This may explain the female tendency to be more flexible about gender-related behavior than males.
- More than 1,000 genes are expressed differently in male and female brains, and the extent to which individuals' behavior is gender typed is related to genetic factors.

Cognitive Factors in Gender Typing

- Children's understanding of gender and gender stereotypes may contribute to their acquisition of gender roles.
- Kohlberg's cognitive developmental theory suggests that children first categorize themselves as male or female and then feel rewarded by behaving in gender-consistent ways. Gender-typed behavior should not appear until children understand gender constancy.
- Gender-schema theory suggests that children need only basic information about gender to develop mental schemas that help them organize their experiences and form rules concerning gender. Research supports gender-schema theory rather than Kohlberg's theory; it indicates that gender labeling is enough to affect gender-typed toy and activity preferences.
- Some children are more "gender-schematic" than others; some are multischematic.

Social Influences on Gender Typing

- The social cognitive theory of gender development applies the principles of Bandura's social cognitive learning theory to gender development. Social structural theories of gender focus on institutionalized constraints on male and female opportunities in educational, occupational and political spheres.
- Parents initiate children's gender typing by organizing boys' and girls' environments differently, dressing them in different clothes, and giving them different toys to play with. Parents also treat them differently. They see boys as stronger, even at birth, and play with them more roughly and actively. As children grow, parents protect girls more and allow them less autonomy than boys.
- Parents also influence children's gender typing through role modeling.
- Fathers are stricter about their children's gender typing than are mothers.
- Older siblings affect younger siblings' gender role development.
- Children's gender roles may be impaired if their fathers are absent or uninvolved, but no evidence indicates any impairment in the gender roles of boys and girls raised in lesbian families.
- Male and female characters in children's books and on television are typically portrayed in gender-stereotypic ways. Children who view TV extensively have more gender-stereotyped views. Attempts to use television programs to reduce gender stereotypes have been successful, but their effects have been modest and short-lived.
- Peers also serve as an important source of gender-role socialization. They act as models and enforcers of gender-typed behavior and choices. They react negatively when other children violate gender standards, and this typically results in behavior changes. Gender segregation and play with peers also provides opportunities to learn gender-typical roles.
- Teachers often react to children in gender-stereotypic ways and tend to criticize boys more than girls.

Androgyny

- Most people are not strictly feminine or masculine but androgynous, possessing both masculine and feminine characteristics.
- Children who are more androgynous make less stereotyped play and activity choices and are likely to have higher self-esteem than those who have traditionally feminine characteristics.

Key Terms

androgynous

cognitive developmental
    theory of gender
        typing

expressive characteristics

gender-based belief

gender constancy

gender identity

gender role

gender-role preference

gender-schema theory

gender segregation

gender stability

gender stereotype

gender typing

identification

instrumental
    characteristics

multischematic

social cognitive theory of
    gender development

social structural theory
    of gender roles

At the Movies

Many movies explore gender issues. *Memoirs of a Geisha* (2005) tells the story of one young woman being trained in the Japanese geisha tradition and illustrates the transmission of the feminine ideal through social learning and self-identification. Some movies focus on children who don't conform to their assigned gender role. *Billy Elliot* (2000) is an 11-year-old boy who doesn't like the brutal boxing lessons at his school. He stumbles out of the boxing ring and onto the ballet floor and confronts disapproval for his nonconforming behavior. In *Dress Code* (1999), 8-year-old Bruno likes to wear dresses—which causes him plenty of problems. This movie raises more questions than it answers, but it does illustrate the difficulty children face when they do not conform to gender-role expectations. In a third movie, *Night Fliers* (2008), a boyish looking girl experiences difficulty in adjusting to a new school where she is bullied and harassed.

Other movies focus on the challenges that transgender individuals face. In *Ma Vie en Rose (My Life in Pink)* (1997), Ludovic is a 7-year-old boy who is sure that he was meant to be a girl—and he waits for a miracle to "correct" this mistake. He cross-dresses, generally acts like a girl, and can't wait to grow up to be a woman. As a result, his schoolmates ostracize him, his family misunderstands him, and bigoted neighbors eventually run him out of town. This movie addresses the complex issues of gender identity through a child's eyes. *Boys Don't Cry*

(1999) portrays the problems of a transgender individual in young adulthood. When Brandon moves to a tiny Nebraska town, he hangs out with the guys, drinking and cussing, and charms young women, who've never met a more sensitive and considerate young man. But Brandon has forgotten to mention that he was actually born a girl. When his friends find out, his life is ripped apart. This wrenching movie, based on actual events, won a Best Actress Academy Award for Hillary Swank. A transgender male-to-female teen is the focus of the movie *Trained in the Ways of Men* (2007). This emotional documentary describes the life and death of Gwen Araujo and the subsequent trials of her killers. It presents information about what transgender means and provides some surprising, thought-provoking answers to questions such as "What gender are you?" and "How do you know?"

A number of films, such as *13 Genders* (2004) and *Gender Rebel* (2006), explore gender variation by interviewing people who identify themselves as neither male nor female. Other films deal with alternative gender roles in other cultures; one example is *Blossoms of Fire* (2000), about the Isthmus Zapotecs of southern Oaxaca, Mexico; another example is *Two-Spirit People* (1992), about the berdache tradition in Native American culture. Finally, some movies highlight the benefits of androgyny. In *It's a Boy Girl Thing* (2006), a studious, sensitive girl and a dumb jock experience a magical swap of bodies and find themselves adopting the positive behaviors of the other gender.

CHAPTER 11 Morality: Knowing Right, Doing Good

Source: © AP/Wide World Photos.

It's exam time in the 7th grade. Ray sits with his brow furrowed in focused attention, trying to solve the math problem in front of him. He should have spent more time studying last night, he thinks. Becca, sitting behind him, should have spent more time studying, too. But she isn't trying to solve the problem; she is trying to see what answer Ray comes up with so she can copy it. She peeks surreptitiously over Ray's shoulder hoping the teacher won't notice. The behavior of these two children illustrates clear differences in moral behavior. Why do the two behave so differently? Is it age, gender, upbringing, or the situation? In this chapter, we discuss the course of moral development and how these and other factors affect it.

Anyone who spends time watching children in the classroom can spot differences in their moral behavior. Some children clearly obey the rules while others whisper or pass notes, furtively glance at the textbook they have hidden under their desk, or look for answers on another student's paper. Differences are also evident on the playground. Some children help and comfort classmates who have lost their books or scraped their knees; they share their lunch with a child who has misplaced hers. Other children ignore these opportunities and go on playing, chatting, and eating. What contributes to these variations in children's behavior? How do moral values develop in young children? How do children become capable of generosity and compassion?

In this chapter, we provide some answers to these questions as we discuss the moral development of children. Moral development can be divided into several components. One is a *cognitive* aspect. Children develop knowledge about ethical rules and make judgments about the "goodness" or "badness" of certain acts. Another component is the *behavior* that moral development involves: Children behave in "good" or "bad" ways in situations that require ethical decisions. Third, moral development involves *emotions*; children have feelings about their "good" and "bad" behaviors. We discuss each of these components and also the development of positive moral behavior, that is, "prosocial" behavior. We examine how these judgments, emotions, and behaviors change with age and how parents, peers, and the broader culture influence them.

Moral Judgment

Jean Piaget and Lawrence Kohlberg offered explanations for the development of moral standards and judgments based on the principles and processes of cognitive growth. In their theories, moral development was simply part of cognitive development.

Piaget's Cognitive Theory of Moral Judgment

Piaget investigated children's moral development in two ways: by studying how children's attitudes toward rules in games changed as the children got older and by examining the way children's judgments of the seriousness of transgressions changed with age. Based on his observations, Piaget proposed that children's moral concepts develop in an unvarying sequence through three stages.

premoral stage
Piaget's first phase of moral development in which children show little concern for rules.

moral realism
Piaget's second stage of moral development in which children show great respect for rules and apply them quite inflexibly.

moral absolutism
Rigid application of rules to all individuals regardless of their culture or circumstance.

immanent justice
The notion that any deviation from rules will inevitably result in punishment or retribution.

STAGES OF MORAL REASONING   In the **premoral stage**, young children show little concern for or awareness of rules. When playing games such as marbles, they don't try to play systematically with the intention of winning. They just play for the satisfaction of manipulating the marbles and finding out how they can be used in different ways. When children are about 5 years old, they move into the stage Piaget called **moral realism** in which they are concerned about rules that come from some authority, usually their parents, and they see rules as unchanging and not to be questioned. They settle disputes with firmly stated conviction that they are right "because my daddy (or mommy) says so." In this stage, **moral absolutism** prevails. If asked whether kids in other countries could play marbles with different rules, children are sure they could not. They also subscribe to the notion of **immanent justice**: They see any deviation from the rules as inevitably resulting in punishment. Someone or something is going to punish you, one way or another. The punishment might take the form of an accident or a mishap controlled by inanimate objects or by God. A child who has lied to her mother may later fall off her bike, skin her knees, and think, "That's what I get for lying to Mom." In this stage, children also evaluate the seriousness of an immoral act solely in terms of its consequences; they don't consider the perpetrator's intentions.

moral reciprocity
Piaget's third stage of moral development in which children recognize that rules may be questioned and altered, consider the feelings and views of others, and believe in equal justice for all.

Piaget's stage of **moral reciprocity** begins when children are about 11 years old. At this stage, judgments are characterized by the recognition that social rules are arbitrary agreements that can be questioned and changed. Children realize that obedience to authority is neither necessary nor always desirable and that violations of rules are not always wrong or inevitably punished. In judging another's behavior, children at this stage can consider the other person's feelings and viewpoint. They believe that if behavior is to be punished, the punishment should be related to both the wrongdoer's intentions and the nature of the transgression. The punishment should also be of such a nature that it somehow makes up for the harm done or helps teach the wrongdoer to behave better in the future. Children at this stage also believe in "equalitarianism"; that is, they believe that there should be equal justice for all. According to Piaget, mature morality includes an understanding and acceptance of social rules as well as a concern for equality and reciprocity in human relationships.

In one set of experiments, Piaget read children pairs of stories and then asked if the children in each story were equally guilty or if one child was naughtier and why (Piaget, 1932, p. 122):

Story I. A little boy who is called John is in his room. He is called to dinner. He goes into the dining room. But behind the door there is a chair, and on the chair there is a tray with 15 cups on it. John couldn't have known that there was all this behind the door. He goes in, the door knocks against the tray, "bang" to the 15 cups and they all get broken!

Story II. Once there was a little boy whose name was Henry. One day when his mother was out he tried to get some jam out of the cupboard. He climbed up on a chair and stretched out his arm. But the jam was too high up and he couldn't reach it. But while he was trying to get it, he knocked over a cup. The cup fell down and broke.

Clearly, Henry tried to deceive his mother and therefore should be considered less moral. But the child in the stage of moral realism is likely to say that John is naughtier because he broke more cups even though his act was unintentional. A child who has reached the stage of moral reciprocity is likely to say that Henry is naughtier, and when asked if it makes any difference that the other child broke more cups replies, "No, because the boy who broke 15 cups didn't do it on purpose."

EVALUATION OF PIAGET'S THEORY Piaget's theory of moral development has been the subject of many studies since 1932. In those conducted in industrialized Western countries such as the United States, Britain, France, and Switzerland, across a wide range of populations and social classes, investigators have found regular age trends for both boys and girls in the development of moral judgment from moral realism to moral reciprocity as Piaget's theory predicted. However, the findings in other cultures have been less consistent. For example, researchers have found that among the people of ten Native American tribes, the belief in immanent justice increased rather than decreased with age, and only two of the ten groups showed the shift toward increased flexibility in the conception of rules (Havighurst & Neugarten, 1955).

It also appears that Piaget underestimated children's capacities. Even 6-year-old children are able to consider an actor's intentions when the situation is presented in a way they can understand. For example, when researchers presented stories acted out and videotaped rather than read, 6-year-old children responded to the actors' intentions as well as older children did (Chandler et al., 1973). Viewing the scenarios provided additional information about the actors' emotional states, which helped the children infer the actors' intentions. One reason Piaget underestimated children's abilities was that he gave them only the bare bones of the stories.

Another reason that Piaget underestimated children's abilities was that he mixed actors' intentions with action outcomes. He invariably required children to judge whether someone who caused a small amount of damage in the service of a bad intention was "worse" than someone who caused a large amount of damage but had good intentions. When researchers present stories in which good and bad intentions and good and bad outcomes can be evaluated separately, even elementary school children use intentions as a basis for judgment (Bussey, 1992; Helwig et al., 2001; Zelazo et al., 1996). For example, if the story of the broken cups is retold with a focus on intentions (the child breaks the cups either trying to sneak a cookie or trying to help his mother) but the outcome is the same for all stories (the child breaks 6 cups), children have no trouble understanding the role of intention. By creating variations on Piaget's basic stories, researchers have been able to isolate factors that affect children's moral judgment. They have found that judgments about rightness and wrongness depend on both whether the consequences of actions are positive or negative and whether the consequences are intended or accidental.

Kohlberg's Cognitive Theory of Moral Judgment

Kohlberg (1969, 1985) based his theory of moral development on Piaget's, but he refined and expanded the stages. Like Piaget, Kohlberg believed that children's cognitive capabilities determine their level of moral reasoning and that moral development builds on concepts grasped in the preceding stage.

LEVELS AND STAGES OF MORAL JUDGMENT Kohlberg studied moral development by presenting a series of moral dilemma stories in which people had to choose either to obey rules and authority or to respond to the needs and welfare of others. The participants in the studies were asked to say what they thought the person in the dilemma should do and why. Here is one sample story (Colby et al., 1983, p. 77):

> *Heinz needs a particular expensive drug to help his dying wife. The pharmacist who discovered and controls the supply of the drug has refused Heinz's offer to give him all the money he has, which would be about half the necessary sum, and to pay the rest later. Heinz must decide whether or not to steal the drug to save his wife; that is, whether to obey the rules and laws of society or to violate them to respond to the needs of his wife. What should Heinz do, and why?*

preconventional level
Kohlberg's first phase of moral development in which justification for behavior is based on the desire to avoid punishment and gain rewards.

Based on his interviews, Kohlberg formulated three broad levels of moral development, each subdivided into two stages. The levels and stages were based not only on whether the interviewees said that the person in the story should obey the rules or should respond to the needs of others but also on the reasons they gave and on the ways their choices were justified.

At Level I, the **preconventional level**, moral judgment was based on the desire to avoid punishment (Stage 1) or to gain rewards (Stage 2). Kohlberg called this level *preconventional* because reasoning at this level was not yet based on the conventions—rules and norms—that guide social interactions in society. At Level II, the **conventional level**, moral judgment is based on the motive to conform: in Stage 3, a person conforms to get approval from others; in Stage 4, the person conforms with society's rules, laws, and conventions such as duty to family, marriage vows, or the country. Only at Level III, the **postconventional level**, is moral judgment based on an internalized ethical code that is relatively independent of others' approval or disapproval. In Stage 5, morality is based on society's consensus about human rights; in Stage 6, it is based on abstract principles of justice and equality. People who have reached this level view rules and laws as arbitrary but respect them because they protect human welfare. They believe that individual rights can sometimes justify violating these laws if the laws are destructive. (For more detail on the stages of moral reasoning, see Table 11.1.)

conventional level
Kohlberg's second phase of moral development in which moral judgment is based on the motive to conform, either to get approval from others or to follow society's rules and conventions.

postconventional level
Kohlberg's third phase of moral development in which judgments are controlled by an internalized ethical code that is relatively independent of the approval or disapproval of others.

According to Kohlberg, this sequence of six stages is fixed; that is, all people pass through the stages in the same order and once attaining a level, a person will not go back to an earlier stage. The stages may occur in different people at different ages, and not all individuals reach the highest level. Research conducted by Kohlberg and his associates supported the general sequence of stages the theory set out (Colby et al., 1983; Colby & Kohlberg, 1987; Kohlberg, 1985). Participants in the research were asked to make judgments about moral dilemmas over a 20-year period. All but two moved from lower to higher stages, and no one skipped a stage.

TABLE 11.1 **Kohlberg's Theory of Moral Development**

Level I—Preconventional Morality

Stage 1

Obedience and punishment orientation	To avoid punishment, children defer to prestigious or powerful people, usually their parents. The morality of an act is defined by its physical consequences.

Stage 2

Naive hedonistic and instrumental orientation	Children conform to gain rewards. They understand reciprocity and sharing, but this reciprocity is manipulative and self-serving rather than based on a true sense of justice, generosity, sympathy, or compassion. It is a kind of bartering: "I'll lend you my bike if I can play with your wagon"; "I'll do my homework now if I can watch the late-night movie."

Level II—Conventional Morality: Conventional Rules and Conformity

Stage 3

Good boy/girl morality	Children's good behavior is designed to maintain approval and good relations with others. Although children still base judgments of right and wrong on others' responses, they are concerned with others' approval and disapproval rather than their physical power. They conform to their family's and friends' standards to maintain goodwill. However, they are starting to accept others' social regulations and to judge the goodness or badness of behavior in terms of a person's intent to violate these rules.

Stage 4

Authority and morality that maintain social order	People blindly accept social conventions and rules and believe that rules accepted by society should be maintained to avoid censure. They conform not only to other individuals' standards but also to the social order. This is the epitome of "law-and-order" morality that unquestioningly accepts social regulations. People judge behavior as good according to whether it conforms to a rigid set of rules. Many people never go beyond this conventional level of morality.

Level III—Postconventional Morality: Self-Accepted Moral Principles

Stage 5

Morality of contract, individual rights, and democratically accepted law	People's moral beliefs have a flexibility they lacked in earlier stages. Morality is based on an agreement among individuals to conform to norms that appear necessary to maintain the social order and the rights of others. However, because this is a social contract, people within a society can modify it when they rationally discuss alternatives that might be more advantageous to more members of the society.

Stage 6

Morality of individual principles and conscience	People conform to both social standards and internalized ideals. Their intent is to avoid self-condemnation rather than others' criticism. People base their decisions on abstract principles involving justice, compassion, and equality. This morality is based on a respect for others. People who have attained this level of development have highly individualistic moral beliefs that may at times conflict with rules accepted by the majority of society.

Source: Kohlberg, 1969.

Younger children gave more preconventional (Level I) responses; older children provided more conventional (Level II) responses. Most participants stopped at this level of reasoning (Stage 4). A few (10%) continued to develop moral reasoning in their 20s, reaching Stage 5 in young adulthood. None, however, reached Stage 6 (Figure 11.1).

The sequence of six stages is not only fixed, according to Kohlberg, but also universal; that is, the development of individuals in countries around the world follows the same set of stages (although the ultimate level of moral reasoning attained might vary across cultures as it does across individuals within the same culture).

FIGURE 11.1 *How does moral reasoning develop? In Kohlberg's study, about 20 percent of the boys at age 10 used Stage 1 reasoning, but it had disappeared by age 16. Stage 2 reasoning was used by 60 percent of the boys at age 10, but by fewer than 10 percent at age 24. Stage 4 reasoning was most common at age 36, but about a third of these individuals still used Stage 3 reasoning.* Source: *Colby, A., Kohlberg, L., Gibbs, J., & Lieberman, M. (1983). A longitudinal study of moral judgment.* Monographs of the Society for Research in Child Development, 48 *(Serial No. 200). Fig 1, p. 46. Reprinted with permission of Wiley-Blackwell.*

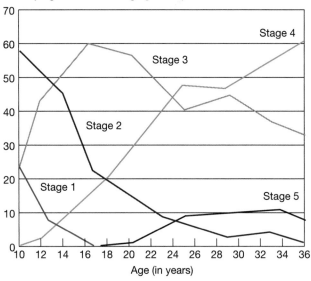

Insights from Extremes: Moral Heroes

Among the many influences on children's moral development are parents, peers, coaches, and clergy. However, throughout history, generations of children and adults have been inspired to reach higher levels of moral thought and action by moral heroes: individuals who go beyond the call of duty and challenge us do the right thing even at a cost. Three of these heroes served as models for Kohlberg's highest stages of moral development. Abraham Lincoln succeeded in ending slavery in the United States by means of his extraordinary courage and perseverance, clear sense of moral purpose, and firm commitment to the view that "skin color makes no difference because all people are equal." A continent away and nearly a century later, Mahatma Gandhi worked to increase the rights of people in India. Using nonviolent civil disobedience as a strategy, he succeeded in bringing about social change including the reduction of poverty, expansion of women's rights, and improvement of relations between religious and ethnic factions.

Although he was jailed, beaten, and suffered through hunger strikes, Gandhi persisted in working for moral causes on behalf of the Indian people. After a 30-year struggle, his efforts were responsible for freeing India from British colonial rule. His birthday, October 2nd, is commemorated worldwide as the International Day of Nonviolence. Gandhi was an inspiration for Martin Luther King, Jr., the leader of the U.S. Civil Rights Movement. In the 1950s and 1960s, King adopted Gandhi's tactics of nonviolent disobedience as he led the Montgomery Bus Boycott, the Montgomery voter protest, the Selma march, and the famous march on Washington, D.C., where he delivered his "I Have a Dream" speech. King raised public consciousness of the Civil Rights Movement and established himself as one of the greatest moral leaders in U.S. history. These moral heroes share several key characteristics including self-sacrifice for the purpose of a greater good, a clear sense of moral duty and obligation, and an unwavering sense of what is right. Their lives provide insights into the highest level of moral development.

LIMITATIONS OF KOHLBERG'S THEORY   Empirical research since Kohlberg's death in 1987 has provided support for some key aspects of his theory. The notion that people proceed through the stages of moral judgment in an invariant fashion has received support through Stages 3 and 4 (Turiel, 2006; Walker et al., 2001). Stages 5 and 6 have less clear support in part because of the small number of people who reach these lofty moral heights. Empirical findings have also been consistent with Kohlberg's view that progress is toward higher rather than lower stages. When researchers have tested whether children, adolescents, and adults can be induced to shift their moral reasoning to another level by using role-playing scenarios or peer modeling, for example, they have generally found that people prefer more advanced reasoning and that shifting a person's moral judgment to a higher stage is easier than shifting it to a lower one (Turiel, 2002, 2005, 2006).

Empirical research has been less supportive of other aspects of Kohlberg's theory. Although studies conducted in different cultures from Alaska to Zambia show that individuals go through the stages of moral reasoning in the same order and few skip a stage or go back to a lower one, supporting Kohlberg's claim that the stages are universal, cultural differences have been found (Gibbs et al., 2007). People in collectivist cultures—Papua New Guinea, Taiwan, and Israeli kibbutzim, for example—explain their answers to moral dilemmas by pointing to the importance of the community rather than personal standards. People in India include in their moral reasoning the importance of acting in accordance with gender and caste and with maintaining personal purity (Shweder et al., 1997). Kohlberg's focus on individual rights and obligations underestimated moral development in some other cultures and excluded some culturally unique domains of morality (Shweder et al., 1997; Snarey & Hooker, 2006; Wainryb, 2006).

Researchers have also found that history shapes people's views of morality. Events such as the Civil Rights Movement and the 9-11 attack on the World Trade Center in New York sensitize people to issues of fairness and justice (Turiel, 2002, 2006; Wainryb & Pasupathi, 2008). People who grow up in different eras tend to have different understandings of moral issues. Those who suffer severe economic loss may be more sensitive to the plight of the poor and thus may endorse more liberal attitudes. In short, the times in which people live can affect their moral judgments (Rest et al., 2000; Turiel, 2002, 2006). Psychologists now suggest that morality is a social construction that evolves from the experiences, institutions, and deliberations of a community that is bound by both culture and historical epoch.

Another limitation of Kohlberg's theory is that it was based on only one type of data: verbal responses to interviews about moral dilemmas. Kohlberg required his respondents to be able explain their moral judgments; they had to be verbally articulate and able to reason aloud. It has been suggested that this may be one reason Kohlberg found so little evidence of judgments at Stage 5 and Stage 6. Researchers have found that people are more likely to endorse postconventional reasoning if they are asked to respond to multiple-choice questions rather than an open-ended interview (Rest et al., 2000).

Kohlberg's theory is also limited because its hypothetical moral dilemmas differ from real-life dilemmas. Kohlberg assumed that when people make moral decisions, they imaginatively take the perspective of another person in an impartial way. In real life, moral decision makers usually know the people who are the objects of their moral judgment, have feelings for them, have a history of past interactions, and expect repercussions in the future (Krebs et al., 1997). These moral decision makers are usually involved in the moral conflict, which often evokes strong emotions, and have a vested interest in the outcome (Frank, 2001; Greene et al., 2001; Haidt, 2001; Krebs et al., 1997; Nesse, 2001). People tend to make Stage 3 or 4 moral judgments in response to impersonal philosophical dilemmas but lower-stage judgments in response to more personal real-life dilemmas (Wark & Krebs, 1996).

In spite of these limitations, Kohlberg's pioneering work revolutionized the way people think about moral development. Because of his influence, cognitive judgment remains a central aspect of explanations of morality. Since Kohlberg's time, psychologists have modified his theory and extended his investigations. They have enlarged the domain of ethical issues studied and softened Kohlberg's notion of developmental stages, suggesting that instead of being a stepwise staircase, development consists of shifting distributions of frequencies as children give increasingly complex reasons for their moral judgments. They have also extended Kohlberg's research to include more concrete examples of moral reasoning.

NEW ASPECTS OF MORAL DEVELOPMENT   Some of the limitations of Kohlberg's theory have led to productive revisions and expansions of the study of moral development. Carol Gilligan (1982) expanded the moral domain to address gender issues and the dimension of caring. Because Kohlberg's research participants included only boys and men, she questioned whether girls and women would show the same pattern of moral reasoning. She suggested that females might take a more caring approach to moral dilemmas than males, who tend to emphasize individual rights and principles of justice. When Gilligan asked boys and girls whether Heinz should steal the drug to save his wife's life, she found evidence of such gender differences. Boys' responses were more likely to emphasize logic and the balance between life and property rights; girls' responses often had an interpersonal focus, considering the impact the theft might have on Heinz, his wife, his wife's condition, and their relationship. Since Gilligan conducted her exploration of girls' and boys' moral reasoning, researchers have found some support for her claim of gender-linked moral orientations when men and women are asked to talk about real-life moral issues (Jaffee & Hyde, 2000). However, when they are asked about hypothetical moral dilemmas, the ways males and females reason are not substantially different (Jaffee & Hyde, 2000; Raaijmakers et al., 2005; Walker, 2006). Moreover, evidence from neural imaging studies suggests that different parts of the brain are involved in decision making about issues of justice and issues of caring—regardless of gender (Robertson et al., 2007). Gilligan (1993) now argues that the scope of morality should be broadened to include the caring perspective for all people, male and female.

A second revision of Kohlberg's theory was the recognition that people's moral reasoning may vary in different situations. Kohlberg assumed that a person applies the same level of moral reasoning to all moral issues (Colby & Kohlberg, 1987). Critics argued, however, that different contexts pull for different forms of moral judgment (Krebs & Denton, 2005). The business world is guided by a Stage 2 moral order based on instrumental exchange, marriage is guided by a Stage 3 moral order based on mutuality, and the legal system is guided by a Stage 4 moral order based on maintaining society. Critics suggested that with development, people expand their range of moral reasoning and the way they process moral information depends on both their mental structures and the types of moral dilemmas they confront. People move in and out of moral *orders,* not *stages* of moral development. With the exception of describing young children who consistently make Stage 1 moral judgments because they have not acquired other structures of moral reasoning, saying that people are *in* a stage of moral development on the basis of their moral judgments made in response to Kohlberg's moral dilemmas is misguided.

A third revision of Kohlberg's theory was an expansion to include the area of civil rights and liberties, such as freedom of speech and freedom of religion (Helwig & Turiel, 2010). Researchers who have begun to study this neglected aspect of moral reasoning have found that as children mature, their appreciation of the freedoms we take for granted increases. In one study in Canada, for example, freedom of speech was endorsed as a right by 62 percent of 6-year-olds, 92 percent of 8-year-olds, and 100 percent of 10-year-olds (Helwig, 1998). The majority of children at all ages viewed freedom of speech as a "natural right" that is independent of authority or laws. However, the rationales the children used to justify civil rights changed with age. The youngest children supported civil liberties based on the need for personal choice and expression. By age 8, they were beginning to become aware that civil rights are linked to social and political issues as well as personal ones. They defended these rights as necessary for fostering communication among individuals and promoting the correction of social injustice through petitions and protests. The 10-year-olds recognized that freedom of speech was a central aspect of democracy because it "gave people a say." In adulthood, people's support for civil rights relates to their moral reasoning and their political attitudes. In one study in the United States, adults who scored high on postconventional moral reasoning and identified themselves as liberal were less likely to support restrictions on the civil liberties of U.S. citizens, foreign nationals, and terrorist suspects and sympathizers than were those identifying themselves as conservative (Crowson & DeBacker, 2008). Judgments about civil rights change when competing moral issues are involved. For example, when children were simply asked whether they endorsed freedom of speech and religion, nearly all said they did (Helwig, 2003, 2006). However, when these freedoms conflicted with freedom from physical and psychological harm, far fewer endorsed freedom of speech.

Children's judgments about forms of government also change as they age. When asked to compare different government systems, children as young as 1st grade viewed democratic forms of government as fairer than nondemocratic forms such as a meritocracy or an oligarchy of the wealthy, and they increasingly preferred democratic forms as they got older (Helwig, 2006). They also became better able to weigh conflicting issues such as restrictions on freedom of speech in different government systems. By 5th grade, children were more likely to judge restrictions of freedom of speech as acceptable if the limitations stemmed from democratic rather than nondemocratic systems. Surprisingly, even children in nondemocratic countries espouse democratic ideas. For example, children have been found to endorse freedom of speech in the Druze, a traditional, hierarchically organized Muslim society in Israel (Turiel & Wainryb, 1998), and in China, which has a communist political system (Helwig et al., 2003). These children prefer democratic forms of government to nondemocratic ones because they are based on principles of representation and majority rule (Helwig et al., 2007). The concept of civil rights appears to be a universal aspect of children's developmental understanding.

Cultural Context:
Justice versus Interpersonal Obligations in India and the United States

The significance of a caring and interpersonal perspective on moral reasoning may have broader implications than Gilligan realized when she attributed this perspective to females. Cross-cultural research has revealed that more than 80 percent of Hindu children and adults in India endorse interpersonal considerations in judging moral dilemmas, whereas only about one third of children and adults in the United States do. Joan Miller and her colleagues asked 3rd- and 7th-grade children and college-age adults in New Haven, Connecticut, and Mysore, India, to rate the undesirability of incidents in which people were described as breaching either justice or interpersonal obligations (Baron & Miller, 2000; Miller & Bersoff, 1992). In this phase of the study, the researchers tried to adjust their examples so that participants considered all incidents to have the same or nearly the same importance. In the second phase of the study, they gave participants conflict situation stories in which actors could fulfill one kind of behavioral obligation (justice or interpersonal) only by violating the other. Here is one of the

Hindu children in India are taught that all life is sacred and caring for others is a moral duty. Source: *Christoper Pillitz/ The Image Bank/Getty Images, Inc.*

conflict situation stories presented to U.S. participants (Miller & Bershoff, 1992, p. 545):

Ben was in Los Angeles on business. When his meetings were over, Ben planned to travel to San Francisco to attend his best friend's wedding. He needed to catch the very next train if he was to be on time for the ceremony and to deliver the wedding rings. However, Ben's wallet was stolen in the train station. He lost all his money and his ticket to San Francisco. Ben approached several officials and passengers and asked them to loan him money to buy a new ticket. But no one was willing to lend him the money. While Ben was sitting on a bench trying to decide what to do next, a well-dressed man sitting next to him walked away for a minute. Ben noticed that the man had left his coat unattended. Sticking out of the man's coat pocket was a train ticket to San Francisco. Ben knew that he could take the ticket and use it to travel to San Francisco on the next train. He also saw that the man had more than enough money in his coat pocket to buy another train ticket.

Participants were asked to decide which of the following two alternative actions Ben should choose:

1. *Ben should not take the ticket from the man's coat pocket*—even though it means not getting to San Francisco in time to deliver the wedding rings to his best friend. This is a justice-based response.

2. *Ben should go to San Francisco to deliver the wedding rings to his best friend*—even though it means taking the train ticket from the other man's coat pocket. This is an interpersonal response.

Indian participants were more than twice as likely as Americans to choose interpersonal responses. The more serious the violation, the more likely they were to switch to a justice response, but even then they clearly preferred interpersonal responses. Indian participants also tended to describe interpersonal responses as moral imperatives whereas Americans described them as personal choices unless the situation was life threatening. Because the Hindu religion holds that all life is sacred and Hindu culture emphasizes social duties as the starting point of society, Indians view helping others in moral terms no matter how minor the issue. This view is not so different from the one Gilligan referred to as a feminine perspective. However, it seems that caring and interpersonal moral reasoning is not feminine per se but simply a view of morality that is not strictly or solely based on the concepts of justice and individual rights.

Turiel's Social Domain Theory

Since Kohlberg's time, the study of moral development has been most extensively expanded by Elliot Turiel's social domain theory (Helwig & Turiel, 2010; Smetana, 2006; Turiel, 1983, 2006). According to this theory, morality is one of several strands or domains of children's social knowledge, which also include knowledge about social norms and conventions and concerns about privacy and personal choices. Investigations inspired by social domain theory have focused on children's understanding of rules in these other domains—for example, rules about eating, dressing, talking, and expressing differences—and how they differ from moral rules against cheating, lying, and stealing. At first, researchers emphasized children's ability to distinguish between the different domains; more recently, they have examined children's reasoning in situations that involve multiple domains and explored how children and adolescents use social reasoning to evaluate important and complex issues in their everyday lives.

social conventional domain
An area of social judgment focused on social expectations, norms, and regularities that help facilitate smooth and efficient functioning in society.

SOCIAL CONVENTIONAL DOMAIN   The **social conventional domain** involves the social expectations and regularities that help facilitate smooth and efficient functioning of a social system, for example, norms for table manners, modes of greeting, and other forms of etiquette; bathing practices; respect for positions in a social hierarchy; and reciprocity in social exchanges (Smetana, 2006). To study whether children distinguish between these social conventions and moral rules, researchers have asked them how wrong they think it would be to hit someone, to lie, or to steal—moral violations—and how wrong it would be for a student to address a teacher by his or her first name, for a boy to enter a girl's bathroom or vice versa, or for someone to eat lunch with fingers rather than utensils—social-conventional violations. Children of all ages consistently view moral violations as worse than violations of social conventions (Bersoff & Miller, 1993; Turiel, 2002, 2006; Turiel & Wainryb, 2000). Even children as young as 3 years old can distinguish between moral and social-conventional rules (Smetana & Braeges, 1990). However, preschool children generally make this distinction only with respect to familiar situations. Not until they are 9 or 10 years old do they apply the distinction to both familiar and unfamiliar situations (Smetana, 1995; Turiel, 2006).

Children view moral violations as worse than transgressions of social conventions because the former result in harm to another person and violate norms of justice and fairness. As they mature, children expand their notions of what harm is (Smetana, 2006). In early childhood, it is concrete and physical; in middle childhood, harm results from unfairness defined in terms of inequality between persons; in preadolescence, harm happens from failure to consider individual differences in needs and status; in adolescence, the concept of harm becomes more comprehensive and is applied more consistently across different moral issues. Both children and adolescents believe that moral rules are obligatory, absolute, universally applicable, invariant, and normatively binding (Smetana, 2006). When asked if it would be acceptable to steal in a country that has no laws against stealing, for example, children as young as 6 years old say it would be wrong. In contrast, children believe that social conventions are arbitrary, relative, alterable, consensually agreed on, and vary across communities and cultures. They recognize that deviations from social conventions are merely impolite or disruptive violations of social rules and traditions. They know that conventional rules, unlike moral rules, depend on social expectations, social norms, and the power of authorities such as parents and teachers (Helwig 2006; Turiel, 2002, 2006; Wainryb, 2006). Regardless of religious background, children view stealing and harming another person as morally wrong but regard variations in religious conventions, such as day of religious observance, dietary rules, and dress codes, as acceptable (Nucci, 2002; Nucci & Turiel, 1993).

psychological domain
An area of social judgment focused on beliefs and knowledge of self and others.

PSYCHOLOGICAL DOMAIN Another domain of social knowledge, which is separate from the moral and social-conventional domains, is the **psychological domain**. It reflects an understanding of self and others as psychological systems and includes a number of different types of issues: *Personal* issues that affect only the self, such as preferences and choices about one's body, privacy, choice of friends, and recreational activities; *prudential* issues that have immediate physical consequences for the self, such as safety, comfort, and health; and *psychological* issues that involve beliefs and knowledge of self and others and choices about revealing aspects of the self to others.

In these areas, unlike the moral domain, individual choices are acceptable. Having spiked hair, getting a tattoo, and watching violent movies are personal issues, not moral ones; smoking, drinking, and taking drugs are prudential concerns, not moral ones. Prudential transgressions are not as bad as moral transgressions, because they harm only the self, not someone else (Smetana, 1988). In one study of children's understanding of moral and prudential issues, children judged a scenario in which a person pushed someone off a swing and he or she got hurt—a moral violation—as more serious than a scenario in which a person deliberately jumped off the swing and was hurt—a prudential act (Tisak & Turiel, 1984). They were more concerned about the type of harm—moral (affecting another person) or prudential (affecting oneself)—than its severity.

Children also understand that different people have different psychological beliefs. For example, some people believe that the way to be a good friend is not to tell the other person how they really feel whereas other people believe that sharing their intimate feelings is an important aspect of friendship. Children realize that the beliefs of these people are different but think that neither is necessarily wrong. Children are also tolerant of people's different religious beliefs; for example, they think that it is all right if someone believes that there are 38 gods or that only people who die on Tuesday become angels even if this conflicts with their own religious beliefs (Wainryb et al., 2001).

Children are particularly open minded about personal issues, such as friendship preferences, hairstyle choices, and clothing decisions (Nucci, 1996). These personal choices are an important part of defining themselves as different from others (Nucci, 2002). Therefore, it is not surprising that as children move into adolescence, they increasingly appeal to personal choice when they have a conflict with their parents (Smetana, 1989; Yau & Smetana, 2003). Even in cultures with a relatively collectivist orientation, such as China, children distinguish between personal choices and moral rules and do so increasingly as they mature (Nucci et al., 1996; Yau & Smetana, 2003).

Learning from Living Leaders: Elliot Turiel

Source: Courtesy of Eliot Turiel.

Elliot Turiel is Professor of Education at the University of California, Berkeley. After deciding to be a psychologist in his junior year of college, his career path was set during graduate school at Yale when he discovered Lawrence Kohlberg's influential work on children's moral reasoning. His goal since then has been to discover how human beings develop understandings of right and wrong and how morality can be distinguished from other types of norms and preferences. He is widely recognized for his pioneering insight that morality is distinguished

early in childhood from social conventions and customs and for his discovery of the different types of social experiences that contribute to different domains of judgment. His formulation of social domain theory, a framework that recognizes the different domains of social development, is his proudest accomplishment. His recent work concerns how people deal with institutionalized injustices that go against their moral judgments. His interest in morality and justice was inspired by his own early childhood experiences in Greece during World War II when he benefited from the actions of individuals who were willing to resist the social system and combat persons in power and authority who were engaging in serious injustices. Turiel is esteemed around the globe for his work; he is past president of the Jean Piaget society and an honorary member of the Italian Society for Research in Child Development. His hope for the future is that researchers will take more seriously the capacity of humans for reasoning and making moral choices.

Further Reading

Turiel, E. (2006). The development of morality. In W. Damon & R. Lerner (Series Eds.), & N. Eisenberg (Vol. Ed.), *Handbook of child psychology*, *Vol. 3: Social, emotional, and personality development* (6th ed., pp. 789–857). Hoboken, NJ: Wiley.

JUDGMENTS ABOUT COMPLEX ISSUES Most of the research on social domains has examined how children evaluate moral, social-conventional, and personal issues separately. In real life, though, people often confront situations that combine these multiple domains. For the most part, moral considerations take priority over social-conventional and personal ones (Smetana, 2006). However, a conflict between rules in different domains may lead to ambiguities and uncertainties that cause people to subordinate morality to other concerns. Stanley Milgram's (1974) experiments on obedience provide a well-known example of a situation in which individuals subordinated moral judgment to social-conventional judgment. Participants in these studies complied with the norm of obeying an authority figure (a social convention) when the experimenter asked them to administer electric shocks to people in another room (a moral violation). A real-life situation in which people may subordinate moral judgment to judgment in the psychological domain is making a decision about abortion. This decision depends on the person's views about whether killing a fetus is murder (a moral issue), whether women have the right to control their own reproductive health (a personal issue), and whether it is physically risky to have the surgery (a prudential issue). Women who classify the decision as a personal issue rather than a moral one are more likely to approve of abortion (Smetana, 1981, 2006).

An example of a multidomain issue that is salient in children's lives is the exclusion of other children from a social group. Melanie Killen and her colleagues found that elementary school children used moral, social-conventional, and personal reasons to explain why exclusion is either right or wrong (Killen & Stangor, 2001; Killen et al., 2002; Killen et al., 2006). When asked whether it was okay to exclude children from a group solely on the basis of their race or gender, the children often condemned exclusion, saying that it violates the principles of fairness and equality (a moral reason). The children were more likely to view exclusion as acceptable, however, if they themselves did not have friends from other races; they claimed that exclusion was acceptable because "it's what's always been done" (a conventional reason). The children were also more accepting of exclusion when asked whether it was right to exclude children (a) based on their low level of expertise in the activity as well as their race and gender (using a social-conventional argument such as the need to maintain the goals of the group) or (b) based on their relationship to other children in the group as well as race and gender (using a personal argument such as that it was better to exclude a classmate than a sibling). Young adolescents provided multiple reasons to justify or condemn exclusion: They said, for example, that gender-based exclusion was wrong because it unfairly denied boys and girls equal opportunity (a moral reason), was okay because sometimes girls and boys are in separate groups to make the groups work better (a social-conventional reason), or was okay because it was up to the child to decide (a personal reason).

In brief, when faced with complex issues, children apply a range of reasons drawn from different domains and make decisions based on their age and experience. When they are young, they are able to make judgments about single-domain issues more easily and consistently than judgments about complex issues (Crane & Tisak, 1995; Killen, 1990). As they mature, their ability to understand the subtleties of complex issues increases.

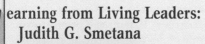

Learning from Living Leaders: Judith G. Smetana

Source: Courtesy of Judith G. Smetana.

Judith Smetana, Professor of Psychology at the University of Rochester, earned a bachelor's degree from the University of California at Berkeley and master's and doctoral degrees from the University of California at Santa Cruz. The overall purpose of her research is to determine how people form ideas about right and wrong and make moral choices. In the 1970s and 1980s, she published widely on women's decision making about abortion. Since then, she has written about preschoolers' understanding of right and wrong and how they distinguish between moral imperatives (stealing is wrong) and social conventions (boys don't wear dresses). She is conducting studies

of disclosure and secrecy in adolescent-parent relationships including a daily-diary study of Latino, African American, and European American high school students. She is also interested in selfishness and selflessness and how spirituality, religiosity, compassionate love, and concepts of social justice are related to adolescents' civic involvement and service on behalf of others. Experience with her own children shaped some of her research on selfishness: "It was striking to me how my kids were cited in their high school as the kind of kids who go out of their way to help other people, and yet at home they didn't always act that way with me." Her work has practical implications because it helps parents understand why they have conflicts with their adolescent children and how they can best handle these disputes. Smetana hopes that in the future researchers will integrate the study of cultural and ethnic variations in development with the study of basic developmental processes. She received an early career award from the Foundation for Child Development and recently completed a term as secretary of the Society for Research in Child Development.

Further Reading

Smetana, J. G. (2006). Social domain theory: Consistencies and variations in children's moral and social judgments. In M. Killen & J. G. Smetana (Eds.),) *Handbook of moral development* (pp. 119–154). Mahwah, NJ: Erlbaum.

How Children Learn the Rules and Distinguish between Social Domains

According to social domain theory, children construct different forms of social knowledge based on different types of experiences with other people. In this section, we discuss the influences of experiences with parents, teachers, siblings, and peers.

PARENTS' AND TEACHERS' ROLES IN MORAL AND SOCIAL CONVENTIONAL REASONING   Judy Dunn and her colleagues spent many hours observing toddlers' interactions with their mothers at home to identify experiences that might teach the children about moral issues and social rules (Dunn, 2006, 1989; Dunn et al., 1987). They found that the children began to understand right and wrong as early as 16 months of age and rapid increases in understanding occurred between the ages of 2 and 3 years. The mothers, meanwhile, were engaging their young children in "moral dialogues" about rules, and the children were nodding or shaking their heads or providing verbal answers to their mothers' inquiries. In the following example, Ella, age 21 months, commented on her own responsibility for a transgression (Dunn, 1988, p. 30):

Ella:	*[At table, throws toy to floor, a previously forbidden act. Looks at mother.]*
Mother:	*No! What's Ella?*
Ella:	*Bad bad baba.*
Mother:	*A bad bad baba.*

By the time they were 3 years old, children were justifying their actions or mothers were justifying their rules in most disputes. These justifications might invoke the child's own wants, needs, or feelings ("But, I need that"), a social rule ("That doesn't belong to you"), the feelings of another ("Rachel will be cross if you do that"), or the consequences of the actions ("You'll break it if you do that"). As these examples clearly show, moral and social-conventional reasoning appears early and is practiced in family interactions.

When children are a little older, their moral judgments are most effectively advanced if their parents initiate discussions about other people's feelings, use disciplinary techniques that involve reasoning and explanation, and promote democratic family discussions (Hoffman, 1984, 2000; Parke, 1977; Walker et al., 2000). These parenting strategies promote children's moral development by stimulating them to think about their actions and the implications of their actions for the welfare of others. Parents' reasoning is most effective when it is clearly linked with the child's violation of a moral rule and when it highlights the consequences of the act for the other person's moral rights. A general reprimand such as "You shouldn't do that to other people" (invoking a social rule) is less effective than a specific explanation such as "You should not hit people because it hurts them and makes them sad" (providing a moral explanation)

Children also learn during their family interactions that breaking moral rules and breaking social-conventional rules lead to very different consequences. At a very early age, they find out that the consequences of eating spaghetti with their hands, spilling their milk, or wearing their sweater inside out are less serious than the consequences of taking their sibling's toy or pulling their sibling's hair. Mothers tend to allow children much more choice and freedom regarding personal and social-conventional issues than moral ones (Nucci & Weber, 1995). Parents' reasoning is most effective if it is domain-appropriate. Domain-appropriate responses to moral transgressions focus on the harm or injury they cause; domain-appropriate responses to conventional transgressions focus on the disorder they create (Nucci, 1984). Observational studies of parents' responses to children's transgressions indicate that mothers naturally coordinate their explanations with the nature of the misdeed (Smetana, 1995, 1997). Parents rarely focus on the consequences of the act for another person (a moral concern) when a child breaks a conventional rule, nor do they reason about social order (a conventional concern) in response to a child's moral transgression. In one study, mothers of 2-year-olds responded to social-convention violations with rules that focused on disorder: "Don't throw your coat on the floor. Look at the mess you made!" However, they responded to moral transgressions by focusing on the consequences of the acts for the other person's rights and welfare: "You hurt her. Think how you would feel if somebody hit you!" (Smetana, 1995, 2006). By varying their explanations to suit the domain, parents help their children understand which issues are moral and absolute and which are social conventions or personal choices and more flexible. Children also learn about the different types of rules from caregivers and teachers as well as their parents. These adults respond differently to children's moral and social convention transgressions just as parents do (Smetana, 1984, 1997, 2006). However, children view teachers' authority as limited to rules at school (Smetana, 2002; Weber, 1999). Children evaluate all adults' messages in terms of their domain appropriateness and reject messages that are domain inappropriate (Killen & Sueyoshi, 1995; Killen et al., 1994; Nucci, 1984).

Parents' and teachers' effectiveness also depends on how well the message fits the child's developmental level. Giving a moral explanation to a 1-year-old isn't very effective and is likely to elicit only a blank stare. As children's cognitive capacities increase in the second year, adults can shift from controlling behavior with physical interventions such as distracting or removing the children from the situation to using verbal strategies such as brief explanations to deal with transgressions (Dunn, 2006; Dunn & Munn, 1987). When children are 3 years old, adults can use concrete rationales to guide their behavior, for example, telling them that a toy might break. This will be more effective than invoking an abstract rule about ownership (Parke, 1974; Walker & Taylor, 1991). Adults' explanations that are slightly more sophisticated than the children's current level of understanding expose children to more mature thinking, challenge them, and are likely to advance their moral understanding (Turiel, 2006).

Parents' influence on children's moral development does not stop at the end of childhood. Adolescents also understand that their parents may legitimately regulate their moral behavior (Padilla-Walker & Carlo, 2006; Smetana 1995, 2006). Adolescents even accept some parental regulation of social-conventional and prudential matters, such as smoking and using drugs and alcohol (Hasebe et al., 2004). However, they are less likely to accept it when their parents try to regulate personal matters, such as their appearance, friendship choices, or spending decisions. Conflicts between teenagers and parents most often arise in this area of personal issues and occur with increasing frequency as adolescents mature (Smetana, 2006). Conflicts that mix social-conventional and personal issues—for example, when parents demand that adolescents clean up their rooms or take a shower—are particularly intense. Parents' refusal to give adolescents reasonable control over their personal issues may be bad for the young people's psychological adjustment. In one study, Japanese and U.S. teens who viewed their parents as overcontrolling about personal issues, such as hair style or choice of music, reported more anxiety and depression (Hasebe et al., 2004). In another study African American adolescents were better adjusted if their parents exerted some control over their personal issues in early adolescence but had lower self-esteem and more depression when parental control extended to mid- or late adolescence (Smetana et al., 2004). Gaining control over personal issues apparently becomes more important as adolescents get older.

Authoritative parents are most likely to establish clear and legitimate boundaries between moral, conventional, and personal issues for their adolescents (Smetana, 2006). Authoritarian parents treat their adolescents' conventional transgressions, such as cursing and putting their elbows on the table, as if they were moral transgressions, and they treat personal issues, such as choice of clothes and hairstyle, as if they were social-conventional issues. Permissive parents are likely to treat all issues as personal.

SIBLING AND PEER INFLUENCES ON MORAL AND CONVENTIONAL JUDGMENTS Siblings and peers as well as adults play a part in helping children learn moral and social-conventional rules. Turn-taking difficulties, disputes over possessions, social exclusion, teasing, taunting, and hurting each another are all opportunities for learning these rules and are more likely to occur in interactions with other children than with adults (Ross & Conant, 1992). Researchers have found that 2- and 3-year-olds who experienced significant sibling rivalry had more knowledge about how to hurt and upset other people when they were 5 or 6 years old than did children whose relationship with their sibling was close and affectionate; the latter children had a more mature moral orientation (Dunn et al., 1995). Similarly, 4-year-olds with close, intimate friendships gave more mature justifications when discussing hypothetical moral transgressions than children who lacked close friendships (Dunn et al., 2000). For example, these 4-year-olds talked about excluding a friend from play in terms of the friend's feelings and the implications of the exclusion for the relationship with the friend. They also had a better understanding of inner states and emotions, which may in part have contributed to their moral development. Children frequently talk with each other about moral transgressions, which helps them learn about moral rules and concepts (Dunn, 1988), and their experiences of friendship loyalty and betrayal provide highly emotional forums for moral learning (Singer & Doornenbal, 2006). Other children react to children's moral and social-conventional transgressions differently, just as adults do, and this facilitates children's development as well. In one study, 2- and 3-year-olds in a child care center were observed to react more emotionally and to retaliate more often when another child committed a moral transgression than a social convention transgression (Smetana, 1984, 2006). The 3-year-olds could articulate the moral and social rules, distinguish between them, and use them to manipulate and manage their peers' behavior.

THE ROLE OF CULTURE Social domain researchers have shown that children all over the world distinguish among the three domains—moral, social-conventional, and psychological. This has been demonstrated for children living in a wide variety of places: shanty towns and middle-class neighborhoods in Colombia (Ardila-Rey & Killen, 2001; Ardila-Rey et al., 2009), middle- and lower-class neighborhoods in Northeastern Brazil (Nucci et al., 1996), rural and urban areas of China (Helwig, 2006), ancient Druze culture and urban Tel Aviv in Israel (Turiel & Wainryb, 1998), rural Nigeria (Hollos et al., 1986), India (Neff, 2001), Korea (Song et al., 1987), and Japan (Killen & Sueyoshi, 1995). However, the content of social conventions varies dramatically across cultures. In India, a social-conventional issue for girls and women is wearing traditional apparel (a sari) and having a face marking (a bindi). For girls in Mennonite and Amish communities in Canada and the United States, social conventions include wearing long dresses and bonnets. Women in the Middle East follow the Islamic dress code, covering their hair, their bodies, and sometimes their faces; see http://www.youtube.com/watch?v=HgXgpngHf60. These social-conventional rules are meant to maintain social order in these traditional cultures. The content of personal issues, similarly, varies across cultures. However, despite these culture-based differences in the content of social conventions and personal issues, children still judge violations in the moral domain as more serious than infractions in the social-conventional and psychological domains.

Moral Behavior

The second component of moral development is moral behavior. Morality involves not only knowing the rules but also following them; it involves not only knowing what is right but also doing it. Children's lives are full of temptations that pull them away from the morally correct action. They must learn to resist these temptations and exert control over their behavior. The development of self-control is considered to be an essential process in the development of moral behavior.

et You Thought That . . .
Moral Judgment Leads to Moral Action

It would not be surprising if you thought that moral knowledge leads to better behavior. Otherwise, why would parents and teachers put so much effort into teaching children moral rules? Kohlberg believed that moral judgment and moral behavior are related. He thought that people first figure out what is right and then decide whether they are responsible for implementing the moral course of action, and finally, if they are responsible, they attempt to perform the moral action (Kohlberg & Candee, 1984). But moral behavior is not simply a consequence of moral knowledge, and moral judgment stages are only weakly related to behavior (Krebs & Denton, 2005). Researchers have found that the maturity of children's moral judgment does not necessarily predict how they actually behave. Especially in young children, moral judgment and moral behavior are often unrelated (Blasi, 1983; Straughan, 1986). Children's behavior is frequently impulsive and not guided by rational and deliberate thought (Burton, 1984; Walker, 2004). A boy may have reached Kohlberg's Stage 3 of "good-boy" morality. He may be able to tell a researcher that it is wrong to hit young children because they do not really know what they're doing (Batson & Thompson, 2001). However, when his younger brother breaks his favorite toy, this boy may kick his sibling. Thought does not always guide action.

Moral judgments and moral behavior in older children and adults are more likely to be related (Kochanska et al., 2002). People who have reached Kohlberg's Stage 5 are less likely to cheat or inflict pain on others and are more likely to endorse free speech and oppose capital punishment than people at lower levels in Kohlberg's framework (Gibbs, 2010; Gibbs et al., 1995; Judy & Nelson, 2000; Kohlberg & Candee, 1984; Pizarro & Bloom, 2003). In a meta-analysis of research on moral development and behavior, researchers found that developmentally delayed moral judgment was strongly associated with juvenile delinquency even after they had controlled for study participants' age, gender, intelligence, socioeconomic status, and cultural background (Stams et al., 2006).

Researchers who consider whether a person classifies an issue as moral, social conventional, or personal find stronger associations between moral judgment and behavior. For example, women are more likely to decide against having an abortion if they see it as a moral issue rather than a personal issue (Smetana, 1983). Children are more likely not to grab another child's toy if they think this would be a moral transgression rather than a personal issue, and adolescents who think that hitting and hurting another person is a moral matter are less aggressive than teens who view these actions as personal (Guerra et al., 1994). In brief, whether a link exists between moral judgment and moral action requires consideration of a person's stage of moral judgment *and* his or her classification of the issue as a moral one.

Self-Regulation of Behavior

self-regulation
The ability to use strategies and plans to control one's behavior in the absence of external surveillance, including inhibiting inappropriate behavior and delaying gratification.

delay of gratification
Putting off until a later time possessing or doing something that gives one immediate pleasure.

The ability of children to inhibit impulses and behave in accordance with social and moral rules in the absence of external control is called **self-regulation**; it is an important aspect of moral development. According to Claire Kopp (1982, 1991, 2002; Kaler & Kopp, 1990), development of self-regulation proceeds through three phases. In the *control phase*, children depend on adults for demands and reminders about acceptable behavior. In the *self-control phase*, children comply with adults' expectations even if the adults are at that moment not making demands and watching to see whether the children comply. In the *self-regulation phase*, children are able to use strategies and plans to direct their own behavior and help them resist temptation, and they exhibit **delay of gratification**. In one study demonstrating children's increasing ability to control their own behavior, Kopp and her colleagues showed 18-, 24-, and 30-month-old children attractive objects, such as a toy telephone, and then told them not to touch the objects right away (Vaughn et al., 1984). The 18-month-olds had minimal self-control: They were able to wait only 20 seconds before they touched the objects. The 2-year-olds had limited self-control: the 24-month-olds waited 70 seconds and the 30-month-olds waited nearly 100 seconds before touching the objects. During the remaining preschool period, children continued to develop self-control and self-regulation (Kochanska et al., 2001; Kopp, 2002). In the late preschool period, children's move to more mature self-regulation is accompanied by advances in the development of the frontal cortex (Shonkoff & Phillips, 2000).

INDIVIDUAL DIFFERENCES IN SELF-REGULATION Although all children progress from control by others to self-control and then to self-regulation, some children progress through these phases more rapidly and achieve higher levels of self-regulation than others. Some children reach the self-regulation phase by age 4 or 5; others continue to rely on adult control in order to comply with rules. Children who are early self-regulators have a stronger sense of "moral self"; they endorse and **internalize** parental values and rules, and they make conscious efforts to control their behavior even when it requires giving up or postponing pleasurable outcomes (Kochanska, 2002; Kochanska et al., 2001).

Actions of parents and other caregivers facilitate children's development of self-regulation. A cooperative, affectionate, and mutually responsive relationship with parents helps children develop a strong **conscience** or internal guide to moral standards of behavior. They internalize their parents' values and standards at a younger age and can use these internalized rules and values to guide their actions even when they are not under the watchful eye of an adult (Kochanska et al., 2008; Kochanska & Murray, 2000). Children are eager to comply with internalized rules because they want to maintain positive ties with their parents.

Individual differences in self-regulation are also related to children's temperaments. According to Grazyna Kochanska (1993, 1995), the process through which children develop self-regulation involves two aspects of temperament: passive inhibition and active inhibition. Fear and anxiety lead to passive inhibition, which often operates without awareness; effortful control leads to active inhibition, which is conscious and deliberate (Kochanska et al., 2001; Rothbart et al., 2000). Researchers have assessed preschool children's active inhibition by measuring how well they can slow their motor activity, make a clear effort to pay attention, and suppress or initiate activity in response to a specific signal such as in a Simon Says game. Children who are able to deliberately inhibit their actions in these ways become better self-regulators. They show more internalization of rules of conduct and comply more with the rules in the absence of adult surveillance (Kochanska et al., 1997, 2001; Kochanska & Thompson, 1997). Children who exhibit more active inhibition at age 5 are less likely to cheat in a game at age 7 than children without this temperamental quality (Asendorpf & Nunner-Winkler, 1992). Passive inhibition is related to the development of self-regulation through an interaction with parental discipline. Gentle maternal discipline promotes conscience development in children who have a fearful inhibited temperament but does not work for children who are not fearful. For these children, discipline focused on positive motivation is more likely to promote self-regulation (Kochanska, 1995, 1997).

internalize
The process by which children acquire the rules and standards of behavior laid down by others in their culture and adopt them as their own.

conscience
Internalized values and standards of moral behavior.

nto Adulthood:
The Love of Money Is the Root of All Evil

Moral challenges do not end in childhood. Adults also face moral dilemmas in their daily lives. Many of these dilemmas seem to follow from the Biblical wisdom that "the love of money is the root of all evil" (1 Timothy 6:10). In the economic meltdown of 2008–2009, many people were shocked to discover the extent to which they were surrounded by others behaving badly to increase their wealth—manipulating the stock market, offering subprime mortgages, taking companies into debt while accepting bonuses, and cheating on their income taxes. Bernie Madoff was convicted of operating a Ponzi scheme described as the largest investor fraud ever committed by a single person. Federal prosecutors estimated his clients' losses at almost $65 billion. Madoff was sentenced to 150 years in prison, the maximum allowed. His moral transgression may be particularly egregious, but many other

Swindler Bernie Madoff (left) exits the Federal Courthouse in Manhattan, New York, January 14, 2009. Source: Marc H. Miller/Sipa Press/NewsCom.

people take advantage of the system to avoid spending money—shoplifting or pirating music and DVDs—or to get more money than they deserve—playing solitaire at work or turning in inflated business expenses. Adult life has many opportunities to cheat, and people who lack a moral "backbone" may fall prey to temptation. They may violate moral rules knowingly, or they may reframe moral issues as personal, prudential, or social conventional.

Consider the collapse of the Enron Corporation in 2001 or the stock market in 2009. Were these disasters the result of greed-motivated immoral behavior or of unfortunate but well-intentioned capitalistic decisions? Most people at Enron, on Wall Street, or in the banks giving out "liar loans" (in which borrowers' stated incomes were inflated) would argue that they were following company rules and working to maintain the organization and protect the welfare of their clients or coworkers. Their decisions, they would say, were in the social-conventional domain, not the moral domain. The people who lost money as a result of these decisions view the situation from a different perspective. For them and for many observers, these decisions were based on

failed self-regulation by people who placed a higher priority on profit than prudence: "a product of the culture of greed, dishonesty, ethical blindness and wishful thinking that has characterized much of corporate America" is how newscaster Ted Koppel (2002) put it. According to behaviorally oriented economists, emotions such as greed contribute significantly to economic decision making and often override moral decision making. People may know the right thing to do, but the emotions of the moment in combination with the ability to reframe the issue to suit short-term goals often result in immoral actions that harm others' long-term welfare.

Another example of questionable moral behavior that may come closer to home for you is pirating music or movies from the Web. Most Americans see downloading movies without paying for them as tantamount to a "minor parking violation" (Robertson, 2007). They justify this behavior by saying that the pirated material is only for personal use (it's a personal issue, not a moral one) and the large corporations and celebrities who would receive the royalties are already too rich. Playing solitaire on the office computer during regular working hours also can be viewed as a moral issue or an issue of personal discretion. Perhaps the player feels underpaid for the hard work performed and sees this as a way to correct an unfair situation. As one supporter of solitaire rights said, "I would never work at a company that wouldn't allow me to use company resources to enjoy myself at the cost of productivity. That is just inhuman." Or is it *immoral?* One final economic issue adults face—every year—is filing their income tax returns. In 2001, the IRS reported a $197 billion "tax gap" from underreported income. About 14 percent of Americans consider this a personal issue and merely a way to "keep what belongs to them" (Pew Research Center, 2006).

The take-home message is clear. Adhering to moral principles is a life-long challenge, and the ways adults respond differ. Although some people consistently take the moral high road, others reframe moral issues as social conventional or personal to avoid doing the right thing. Still others recognize an issue as moral but have a low level of moral reasoning. For example, they may be in Kohlberg's "law and order" stage and behave as President Obama described the actions of executives who accepted huge bonuses at one company (AIG) after it had been bailed out with billions of taxpayer dollars: "It was legal, but not moral" (*The Tonight Show*, March 19, 2009).

Consistency of Moral Behavior across Situations and Time

The fact that self-regulation is related to temperament might lead one to expect that children would be relatively consistent in their moral behavior—and they are. In one extensive investigation of 11,000 school-age children, researchers provided opportunities for cheating, stealing, and lying in a variety of situations: athletics, social events, at school, at home, alone, and with peers (Burton, 1963). They discovered that children had a general tendency to behave either morally or immorally, although their behavior was also affected by situational and motivational factors such as fear of detection, peer support for deviant behavior, and the importance of the outcome for the child.

Children are also relatively consistent in their moral behavior at different ages. Researchers found that children who complied with moral rules at 22 months of age tended to show a similar pattern at 45 months (Aksan & Kochanska, 2005). Children who displayed good self-control in the preschool period were better self-regulators in adolescence and young adulthood: Their parents rated them as more likely to plan, to be attentive, and to be able to deal with frustration when they were 14 (Mischel et al., 1988; Shoda et al., 1990), and, at age 27, men who had delayed gratification in preschool were less likely to use crack or cocaine (Mischel & Ayduk, 2004; Peake et al., 2001). Other research indicates that having a deficient conscience in childhood—marked by callousness, impaired moral emotions, and limited internalization of rules of behavior—can launch a trajectory leading to immoral behavior in adolescence and adulthood (Frick et al., 2003; Frick & Ellis, 1999; Lykken, 1995; Shaw & Winslow, 1997).

Research up Close:
Children Telling Lies

One of the most common breaches of moral behavior is lying, and researchers have explored when and why children lie. In one study, Anne Wilson and her colleagues observed 2- and 4-year-olds at home during everyday routines (Wilson et al., 2003). Two years later they observed the children again. At each time point, they recorded six 90-minute observations. The audiotaped records were later transcribed and incidents of lying were coded. Nearly all the children (96%) lied at some point during the observations, and the rate of lying increased with age: 2-year-olds lied about once every 5 hours, 4-year-olds, once every 2 hours, and 6-year-olds, every hour and a half. Children told lies to avoid responsibility for transgressions, to accuse siblings, or to gain control over another person's behavior. Boys lied more than girls—even after adjusting for the fact that boys had more to cover up. When parents realized that their children were lying, they rarely addressed the act of lying itself but often challenged the veracity of the lie or addressed the underlying transgression. Older siblings lied more often than younger ones, and parents who allowed older siblings to lie at Time 1 had children who lied more at Time 2. Older children also told more complex lies than younger ones. They offered deceptive elaborations about their motives and actions—"I didn't mean to hit him"—whereas younger children used simple explanations, such as blaming the sibling for their misbehavior—"Jonelle broke the car." This study provides valuable descriptive data about young children's lying. A second study supplemented this information with evidence that between 7 and 11 years of age children increasingly tell "little white lies" to be polite (Xu et al., 2010).

In a third study of lying, Genyue Fu and his colleagues (2007) compared children's attitudes toward lying in two different cultures, Canada and China. Children ages 7, 9, and 11 were read stories about characters facing moral dilemmas and asked to decide whether they should lie or tell the truth to help the collective group but harm themselves or vice versa. For example, here is one story (Fu et al., 2007, p. 293):

Here is Susan. Susan's teacher was looking for volunteers to represent the class in a spelling competition at their school. Susan could not spell very well but thought the competition would be a good chance to improve her spelling skills. Susan thought to herself, "If I volunteer, our class will not do well at the spelling competition, but if I don't volunteer, I will miss out on the chance to improve my spelling skills."

Children were asked, "If you were Susan, what would you do? Would you give yourself a good chance to improve your spelling skills and tell your teacher you are a good speller, or would you help your class and tell your teacher you are not a good speller?" Chinese children were more likely to lie to help the collective group and harm themselves; Canadian children did the opposite (see Figure 11.2). This study clearly demonstrates that children's moral judgments about lying reflect cultural values.

From these three studies we learn that children lie often and increasingly—to get out of trouble, to get control of or help other people, to be polite. Lying is apparently affected by children's culture and family experiences. Boys, firstborns, and children with permissive parents are particularly likely to lie.

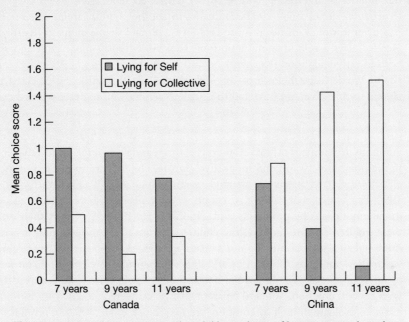

FIGURE 11.2 *Chinese and Canadian children's choices of lying to protect themselves or the collective group. Source: Copyright © 2010 by the American Psychological Association. Reproduced with permission. Fu, G., Xu, F., Cameron, C. A., Heyman, G., & Lee, K. Cross-cultural differences in children's choices, categorizations, and evaluations of truths and lies. Developmental Psychology, 43, 278–293. The use of APA information does not imply endorsement by APA.*

Moral Emotions

The third component of moral development involves emotions. We have all experienced "feeling bad" when we break a rule or sometimes even when we think of breaking a rule. We feel remorse, shame, or guilt. These emotions play a role in regulating moral actions and thoughts and help us negotiate the struggle between wishes and rules.

Development of Moral Emotions

As we discussed in Chapter 5, "Emotions," children experience the moral emotion of guilt as early as 2 years of age. When Kochanska and her colleagues gave children a toy that was rigged to fall apart and told them to be very careful when they handled it, the 22-month-olds looked guilty when the toy fell apart—they frowned, froze, or fretted; 33-month-olds squirmed and hung their heads (Kochanska et al., 2002). If these children had merely been surprised when the toy broke, their reactions would not likely have involved these signs of negative affect and tension. The children seemed to realize that they had done something wrong, and they felt bad as a result. Researchers now suggest that the period between 2 and 3 years is normal for the emergence of guilt and the beginning of conscience (Emde & Buchsbaum, 1990; Groenendyk & Volling, 2007; Kochanska, 1993).

MORAL EMOTIONS AND CHILD CHARACTERISTICS Not all children feel equally guilty when they violate a moral rule, however. Children with more fearful temperaments experience more guilt after violating a rule. In Kochanska's research, for example, children who were more fearful in scary situations, such as climbing a ladder, falling backward on a trampoline, or interacting with a clown, displayed more guilt when they "broke" the toy (Kochanska et al., 1994, 2002). Similarly, in another study, parents rated their children who had been fearful as infants as more prone to guilt and shame at age 6 (Rothbart et al., 1994). Gender plays a role in moral emotions, too. Girls display more guilt and shame than boys both in early childhood (Kochanska et al., 2002; Stipek et al., 1992) and in middle childhood (Zahn-Waxler, 2000). Perhaps this reflects the fact that girls are expected to adhere more closely to rules than are boys and thus may experience more upset when they violate them.

MORAL EMOTIONS AND PARENTS' BEHAVIOR Parents influence children's moral emotions in a number of ways. One way is by creating a positive or negative emotional climate in the home. In a warm and supportive climate, children are motivated to listen to their parents' messages and internalize affective reactions such as guilt and shame (Grusec & Goodnow, 1994; Kochanska et al., 2008). A second way parents contribute to children's development of moral emotions is by providing explanations. If parents simply assert their power and punish their children for wrongdoing, the children are less likely to feel guilt; if parents explain the rules and provide reasons for not violating them, children exhibit more guilt and remorse when they transgress (Forman et al., 2004). When the parent says, "You know better than to hit your sister—you should be *ashamed* of yourself," the child connects the transgression with a moral emotion. When the parent says, "You were a *bad* boy for hitting her," the child learns to evaluate himself in emotional terms (Stipek et al., 1992). Through these exchanges, children learn to react with guilt or shame after a rule violation, and they use memories of these emotions as deterrents to future misdeeds.

A third way parents contribute to children's development of moral emotions is by forcefully expressing their own emotions. When mothers respond to their children's moral transgressions with intense negative affect, their children are more likely to make reparations than when the mother's message is affectively neutral (Grusec et al., 1982; Zahn-Waxler et al., 1979). When parents dramatize their distress and express their anger, children's attention focuses on the harm or injustice they have caused (Arsenio & Lemerise, 2004; Lemerise & Arsenio, 2000). This does not mean that parents should throw screaming fits. Too much parental anger is negatively arousing for children and is likely to inhibit their focus on feelings. Too much emotional arousal leads children to self-oriented, aversive emotional reactions, such as fear or sadness, rather than other-oriented reactions, such as **sympathy** (Eisenberg et al., 1988, 2006).

sympathy
The feeling of sorrow or concern for a distressed or needy person.

Finally, parents contribute to children's development of moral emotions by responding to the children's emotional expressions. If parents respond positively when their children express remorse, shame, or guilt, the children learn that expressing these emotions is a way of mitigating parental reprimands and restoring or repairing their relationship with the parent (Parke, 1974; Thompson et al., 2006).

Parents' behavior is particularly important for children who do not have a temperament that predisposes them to develop moral emotions. Researchers have found that children with inhibited temperaments are generally likely to develop feelings of guilt, and their parents' behavior doesn't make a significant difference. But children with uninhibited temperaments develop feelings of guilt only if their parents provide consistent discipline (see Figure 11.3; Cornell & Frick, 2007).

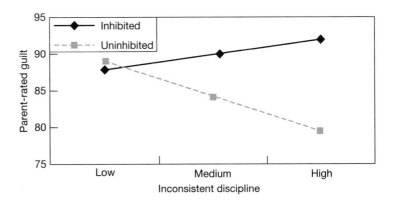

FIGURE 11.3 *Interaction between temperament and discipline in the prediction of parent-rated guilt. Source: Cornell, A. H., & Frick, P. J. (2007). The moderating effects of parenting styles in the association between behavioral inhibition and parent-reported guilt and empathy in preschool children.* Journal of Clinical Child & Adolescent Psychology, 36, *305–318. Taylor & Francis, reprinted by permission of the publisher, Taylor & Francis Group, http://www.informaworld.com.*

Do Moral Emotions Affect Moral Behavior?

Does feeling guilty after a moral transgression predict that the child will not repeat it? In research on children's guilt, Kochanska and her colleagues assessed children's moral behaviors: that is, whether they obeyed their mother's prohibition not to touch a set of attractive toys after she left the room, whether they obeyed her request to put away the toys after she left the room, and whether they obeyed a rule set by the experimenter, such as not cheating on a guessing game (Aksan & Kochanska, 2005). They found that these behaviors were not related to moral emotions until

"What do I think is an appropriate punishment? I think an appropriate punishment would be to make me live with my guilt."

Source: © Barbara Smaller/The New Yorker Collection/www.cartoonbank.com.

the children were almost 4 years old. When children were tested at age 4½, those who had displayed more guilty reactions at earlier ages continued to be less likely to play with forbidden toys (Kochanska et al., 2002). Their anticipation of guilt apparently served as a deterrent to subsequent misbehavior and rule violations. Children who showed early signs of guilt also developed stronger moral selves; they described themselves as more concerned about rules, more committed to rule-compatible behavior, and generally more morally concerned at 4½ (Kochanska, 2002). Although the moral emotions of guilt, shame, and remorse make children uncomfortable, they clearly serve a positive function in their moral development.

This link between moral emotions and moral behavior has also been observed in older children and adolescents. Children prone to guilt in the 5th grade were less likely to be arrested, convicted, and incarcerated in adolescence even when researchers controlled for their family income and mother's education (Tangney & Dearing, 2002). Guilt-prone college students were less likely to abuse drugs and alcohol (Dearing et al., 2005). Adolescents who said that they experienced more intense moral emotions when they were just *imagining* that they had committed moral transgressions reported less delinquent behavior (Krettenauer & Eichler, 2006). Shame does not appear to serve the same inhibitory functions as guilt and may even be a detrimental factor (Dearing et al., 2005; Stuewig & McCloskey, 2005; Tangney et al.,

1996). Shame-proneness was correlated with more externalizing symptoms in childhood (Ferguson et al., 1999) and more intentions toward illegal behavior in adolescence (Tibbetts, 1997). Shame-proneness in 5th grade predicted later risky driving, earlier initiation of drug and alcohol use, and a lower likelihood of practicing safe sex (Tangney & Dearing, 2002). Guilt, not shame, is most effective in motivating people to choose the moral path (Tangney et al., 2007). Whether feeling too much guilt is detrimental to children's development remains to be determined. But it has been suggested that children who are excessively guilt prone may become self-berating, depressed, and anxious (Zahn-Waxler & Kochanska, 1990).

Real-World Application: Adolescents' Competence to Stand Trial as Adults

Source: © AP/Wide World Photos.

In this photo, a teenage boy sits by his lawyer, waiting to hear his sentence. He was convicted of murder for dropping stones onto passing cars from a highway overpass, killing two women and injuring four other motorists (CBS News, 2000). In spite of evidence that children's moral judgment improves with age, it is not clear whether adolescents are as morally capable or culpable as adults and, therefore, how they should be treated by the legal system. Laurence Steinberg and his colleagues have tried to determine whether young people meet the criteria for adult blameworthiness and should be tried in adult courts and have concluded that they should not be (Steinberg & Cauffman, 2001; Steinberg & Scott, 2003; Steinberg et al., 2003).

Several factors are necessary to determine guilt. First, to be guilty of a crime, a person must commit the act voluntarily, knowingly, and with some ability to form a reasonable expectation of the potential consequences of the action. Cognitive abilities, such as the competency to make logical decisions and to foresee the implications of those decisions, are necessary. These cognitive abilities are unlikely to have developed before age 15. Emotional capacities are also important. Adolescents are more likely than adults to indicate that they would engage in illegal behaviors, such as shoplifting, smoking marijuana, or joy riding in a stolen car. They also score lower on measures of psychosocial maturity, including responsibility (the capacity to make an independent decision), perspective (the capacity to place a decision within a broad temporal and interpersonal context), and temperance (the capacity to exercise self-restraint and impulse control). Individuals who score lower on these measures of psychosocial maturity are less likely to make socially responsible decisions in hypothetical situations. In short, because they are less psychosocially mature, adolescents make poorer decisions and are more likely to say that they would engage in illegal activities than adults. The implication of these findings is not that adolescents should not be held responsible for their crimes but that their diminished ability to make prudent decisions can be a mitigating factor that should be recognized in their legal treatment.

Second, people who have committed a crime must possess the cognitive, social, and emotional competence to stand trial. They must have the ability to consult a lawyer with a reasonable degree of understanding and the ability to make decisions about waiving their rights, entering pleas, and other procedural matters. Going to court is a complex matter that requires sophisticated understanding and reasoning skills to assist counsel in mounting a defense: logical decision-making skills, reliable memory to provide accurate information about the offense, future-oriented thinking to understand the consequences of different pleas, social perspective taking to understand the roles and motives of lawyers and judges, and awareness of their own motives and psychological states. Adolescents under age 15 are unlikely to have these skills. More than one third cannot define the word *rights,* and most do not understand court proceedings well enough to protect themselves in adversarial legal settings. They do not fully appreciate the implications of the right to remain silent, to accept a plea bargain, or to testify as a defendant. A significant number do not understand the roles of different court personnel and a defendant's rights at trial. Adolescents are more likely to confess rather than remain silent in response to interrogation by an authority figure, and they are more likely to accept a plea bargain rather than go to trial even though doing so may not be in their best interest. They think fewer risks are involved in various decision options, are less likely to believe that the risks will actually happen, and minimize the seriousness of the risks if they do occur. Together, these findings suggest that trying an adolescent in an adult court without careful evaluation of his or her competence is likely to place a young offender at serious risk for unfair legal treatment. Because the rules of juvenile court are more flexible and permit judges more leeway in sentencing, they provide a more appropriate venue than adult courts for providing justice for juvenile offenders.

The Whole Moral Child

We have examined cognitive, behavioral, and emotional components of moral development separately. However, in real life, these components occur together, interact, and sometimes even conflict, and one of the tasks of development is to integrate them. The separate components begin to come together to guide children's decision making and action in the late preschool period. From 3 to 4 years of age, children show increasing coherence across the components of moral conduct and emotion. Children who are able to follow moral rules in the absence of external surveillance (moral behavior) are more likely to experience guilt in anticipation of or after committing a transgression (moral emotion). Cognitive aspects (understanding moral rules and social conventions) are integrated next. By the time they enter school, most children have connected the moral dots and developed a coherent moral self or conscience (Kochanska & Aksan, 2006). They can refrain from prohibited acts, follow rules in games, and feel guilty when they transgress; they have a cognitive appreciation of rules and standards of conduct and are able to cognitively represent consequences of violations of those standards for themselves and others.

The process of integrating these components and developing a conscience continues through childhood. About half of the 6-year-olds in one study still expected that people who violated a moral rule, for example by stealing, would feel happy because they had satisfied their own desire rather than experiencing the moral emotions of remorse or guilt (Nunner-Winkler, 2007). They were also not likely to behave morally by resisting a real-life temptation to cheat. As they matured, the children were increasingly likely to understand that moral transgressions lead to remorse and were less likely to violate moral rules by stealing or cheating (the percentage who recognized that rule violation would lead to remorse or guilt was 65% at age 8, 75% at age 17, and 80% at age 22).

Children's integration of moral components is also reflected in the fact that their knowledge of social domains is related to their moral behavior and moral emotions. Whether children define a real-life dilemma as personal, conventional, or moral influences how they act and how they feel (Smetana, 2006; Killen et al., 2006). For example, if children think that excluding a child from their social group is a social-conventional issue because it demonstrates group loyalty and maintains group solidarity, they are likely to actually exclude the other child and are unlikely to feel remorse, shame, or guilt. If they see exclusion as a moral issue because it violates the other child's rights, they are deterred by their anticipation of feeling a negative emotion such as guilt or shame and are less likely to exclude the child.

Not all children are successful in integrating the components of morality and developing a strong moral self. Some have limited cognitive understanding, don't anticipate how their actions will harm others, and experience little remorse or guilt when they commit a moral misdeed. In the extreme, these children may grow up to become psychopaths (Frick & Morris, 2004; Lykken, 1995). They illustrate what happens when children fail to integrate the cognitive, affective, and behavioral aspects of the moral system that serves as a regulatory guide for most socialized individuals.

Learning from Living Leaders: Grazyna Kochanska

Source: Courtesy of Grazyna Kochanska.

Grazyna Kochanska is Professor of Developmental Psychology at the University of Iowa. Her proudest accomplishment is that she overcame the disadvantages and difficulties of arriving in the United States from Poland and was able to achieve success. With her Ph.D. from the University of Warsaw she obtained a position at the National Institutes of Health in Washington, D.C., where she pursued an interest in social development, particularly moral behavior. Her focus was on how children develop a conscience—an inner sense of right and wrong that

becomes an effective guide for conduct—and why some children become callous, disruptive, and antisocial while others become rule abiding, responsible, prosocial, and regulated. In a series of longitudinal studies, she showed how family interaction patterns and children's temperaments contribute to the development of conscience. She believes that in the future research in social-emotional development will involve a richer integration of constructs measured at multiple levels—from biological to ecological—and an in-depth understanding of developmental mechanisms and processes over time. Her message for undergraduate students suggests that a research career is not for everyone: "It is not a leisurely lifestyle. You should ask yourself: Do you believe you can work very hard all day, every day? Are you willing to face constant challenges and setbacks and strive hard to overcome them? Do you enjoy working toward distant, self-imposed goals with little or no immediate gratification? Do you see research activity as a path of personal commitment rather than 'work'? If you answered 'yes' to these questions—go for it! If they gave you pause—choose another career."

Further Reading

Aksan, N., & Kochanska, G. (2005). Conscience in childhood: Old questions, new answers. *Developmental Psychology, 41,* 506–516.

Prosocial and Altruistic Behavior

prosocial behavior
Conduct designed to help or benefit other people.

altruistic behavior
Intrinsically motivated conduct intended to help others without expectation of acknowledgment or reward.

Being able to resist the temptation to violate moral rules is only part of the story of moral development; the other part is behaving in a positive way. Moral development is more than "knowing right"; it is also "doing good." **Prosocial behavior** is voluntary behavior intended to benefit another person. It includes sharing, caring, comforting, cooperating, helping, sympathizing, and performing "random acts of kindness." Prosocial behavior can also include actions designed to help groups of people, societies, nations, even the world. **Altruistic behavior** is prosocial behavior that is performed without thought for one's own immediate welfare, without expectation of reciprocity or acknowledgment (often anonymously), and sometimes even at the sacrifice of one's own long-term needs and wishes. The beginnings of prosocial behavior appear in quite young children; truly altruistic behavior occurs only at later ages (Eisenberg et al., 2006).

How Prosocial Behavior and Reasoning Develop

In this section, we discuss how children's prosocial behavior and reasoning about prosocial actions vary with age and gender and how stable their prosocial behavior is over time.

AGE CHANGES IN PROSOCIAL BEHAVIOR   Infants exhibit early signs of sharing by pointing to interesting sights and objects and by the time they are 1 year old they are showing and giving toys to mothers and fathers and even strangers (Hay, 1994; Rheingold et al., 1976). Children engage in these early sharing activities without prompting or direction and without being reinforced by praise or gifts. By the time they are 2 years old, they display a wide range of prosocial actions, such as giving verbal advice ("Be careful"), indirectly helping (getting an adult to retrieve another child's toy), sharing (giving food to their sister), providing distraction (closing a book that has made their mother sad), and protecting or defending (trying to prevent another person from being injured, distressed, or attacked) (Garner et al., 1994; Rheingold, 1982). Children become increasingly likely to engage in prosocial behavior as they grow older and become more cognitively mature (Eisenberg et al., 2006; Zahn-Waxler et al., 2001). Increasing emotional knowledge helps them detect other people's subtle emotional cues and realize when they need help (Denham, 1998; Eisenberg et al., 2006; Garner et al., 1994). See Table 11.2 for more details about age changes in prosocial and altruistic behavior.

STABILITY IN STYLES OF PROSOCIAL BEHAVIOR   Individual differences in prosocial behavior appear early in childhood and are quite stable as children develop. In one study, researchers observed 2-year-old children's different styles of dealing with their mother's distress; when the children were 7 years old, about two thirds exhibited the same style as they had earlier (Radke-Yarrow & Zahn-Waxler, 1983). In another study, researchers found that children's nurturant and sympathetic behavior toward peers was moderately stable from preschool through elementary school (Baumrind, 1971). Children's willingness to donate to needy children, assist an adult (e.g., by helping pick up paper clips), and offer help to others were consistent across elementary school

---

TABLE 11.2 **Prosocial and Altruistic Behaviors**

Birth–6 months

- Reacts emotionally to others' distress (crying or general upset)

6–12 months

- Exhibits sharing behavior
- Displays affection to familiar persons

1–2 years

- Plays cooperative games
- Comforts people in distress
- Helps parents with household tasks
- Shows and gives toys to adults

2–3 years

- Shares
- Exhibits increasingly planned caregiving and helping
- Verbally expresses intention to help
- Gives helpful verbal advice
- Tries to protect others

3–10 years

- Is hedonistically motivated to perform prosocial acts
- Recognizes others' needs even when they conflict with own
- Justifies prosocial behavior by reference to notions of good and bad and consideration of approval and acceptance from others

10–17 years

- Justifies helping according to internalized values and concern with rights and dignity of others
- May believe in individual and social obligations and the equality of all individuals
- May base self-respect on living up to own values and accepted norms

Note: These data represent overall trends identified in research studies. Children vary in the exact ages at which they exhibit these behaviors.
Sources: Eisenberg et al., 2006; Hay & Rheingold, 1983.

prosocial reasoning
Thinking and making judgments about prosocial issues.

hedonistic reasoning
Making a decision to perform a prosocial act on the basis of expected material reward.

needs-oriented reasoning
Prosocial judgments in which children express concern for others' needs although their own needs may conflict with them.

empathic reasoning
An advanced type of prosocial reasoning involving sympathetic responding, self-reflective role taking, concern with the other's humanness, and guilt or positive affect related to the consequences of one's actions.

(Eisenberg et al., 2006). Prosocial behavior toward peers also was relatively stable in adolescence (Wentzel et al., 2004) as was valuing the concern for others in young adulthood (Pratt et al., 2004). Prosocial behavior seems fairly consistent across time: children who start out being generous, helpful, and kind are likely to continue to exhibit these prosocial qualities as they mature.

PROSOCIAL REASONING   Nancy Eisenberg and her colleagues formulated a model of the development of **prosocial reasoning** that parallels Kohlberg's model of moral reasoning (see Table 11.3; Eisenberg et al., 1999, 2006, Eisenberg, Zhou, et al., 2001). To test the model, they devised a number of hypothetical scenarios about prosocial dilemmas. Here is an example (Eisenberg-Berg & Hand, 1979, p. 358):

> *One day a girl named Mary was going to a friend's birthday party. On her way she saw a girl who had fallen down and hurt her leg. The girl asked Mary to go to her house and tell her parents so they could come and take her to the doctor. But if Mary did run and get the child's parents, she would be late to the birthday party and miss the ice cream, cake, and all the games. What should Mary do? Why?*

Eisenberg and her colleagues interviewed children using these scenarios. The youngest children (age 4) used **hedonistic reasoning** to justify prosocial actions; they said that people should behave prosocially because they would get material rewards. This type of reasoning decreased with age. The second type of reasoning children used was **needs-oriented reasoning**, in which they expressed concern about the needs of others even if these needs conflicted with their own. This reasoning type peaked in middle childhood and then leveled off. The most advanced types of prosocial reasoning were **empathic reasoning** (involving sympathetic responding) and **internalized reasoning** (justifying prosocial behavior based on internalized values to maintain societal obligations or to treat all people as equal). These types of prosocial reasoning, like Kohlberg's Stage 5 moral reasoning, did not occur until adolescence or later. Other researchers using Eisenberg's model found that adolescents' prosocial reasoning was related to their prosocial behavior: hedonistic reasoning was related to less sharing and empathy; needs-oriented reasoning was related to more prosocial behavior; internalized prosocial

TABLE 11.3   Development of Prosocial Reasoning

Level	Orientation	Mode of Prosocial Reasoning
1	Hedonistic	Concerned with self-oriented consequences. Decision to help or not help another is based on consideration of direct gain to self, future reciprocity, and concern for people to whom the person is bound by affectional ties.
2	Needs-oriented	Expresses concern for physical, material, and psychological needs of others even if they conflict with own needs. Concern is expressed in the simplest terms without verbal expressions of sympathy, evidence of self-reflective role taking, or reference to internalized affect such as guilt.
3	Approval-seeking	Uses stereotyped images of good and bad persons and behaviors and consideration of others' approval and acceptance in justifying prosocial or nonhelping behaviors.
4	Empathic	Judgments include evidence of sympathetic responding, self-reflective role taking, concern with the other's humanness, and guilt or positive affect related to the consequences of actions.
	Transitional	Justifications for helping or not involve internalized values, norms, duties, or responsibilities, and may refer to the necessity of protecting the rights and dignity of other persons. These ideas, however, are not clearly stated.
5	Internalized	Justifications for helping or not are based on internalized values, norms, or responsibilities, the desire to maintain individual and societal contractual obligations, and the belief in the dignity, rights, and equality of all individuals.

Source: Eisenberg et al., 1983.

internalized reasoning
The most advanced type of prosocial reasoning in which justifications for helping are based on the importance of maintaining societal obligations or treating all people as equal.

reasoning was related to prosocial behavior requiring some cognitive reflection beyond simple acts such as helping someone pick up dropped books (Carlo et al., 2003).

ARE GIRLS MORE PROSOCIAL THAN BOYS? Some people have suggested that girls are more prosocial than boys, but gender differences in prosocial behavior depend on the particular action (Eisenberg et al., 2006; Fabes & Eisenberg, 1996). Differences are most noticeable for acts of kindness and consideration; girls consistently display more of these types of prosocial behavior than boys do. Girls are also more empathic than boys; they have more capacity to experience the emotions that others feel (Zahn-Waxler et al., 2001), especially as they get older (Eisenberg et al., 2006). Girls are somewhat more likely than boys to engage in instrumental helping, comforting, sharing, and donating, but gender differences in these behaviors are smaller. No gender differences have been observed in situations in which prosocial actions are anonymous (Carlo et al., 2003). Men have even been observed to behave more prosocially than women in extreme circumstances, such as making life-risking rescues from floods or mountaintops (Becker & Eagly, 2004). In less risky situations, such as donating an organ or volunteering for the Peace Corps, men and women are similar.

Gender differences are more pronounced when data come from self-reports and reports by family members and peers rather than in data gathered by objective observers (Hastings, Rubin, et al., 2005). This suggests that some gender differences reflect people's conceptions of what boys and girls are supposed to be like rather than how they actually behave (Eisenberg et al., 2006; Hastings et al., 2007). Parents stress the importance of politeness and prosocial behavior more for daughters than for sons (Maccoby, 1998). Moreover, when girls behave prosocially, parents attribute these behaviors to inborn tendencies, whereas they attribute boys' prosocial behaviors to the influences of socialization. These findings do not mean that gender differences are only in the eye of the self or the beholder, but apparently they are affected by gender stereotypes and the belief that girls are made of "everything nice" (Grusec et al., 2010; Hastings et al., 2007). Gender differences in prosocial behavior also increase with age, presumably because children become more aware of gender stereotypes and internalize these in their self-image (Eisenberg et al., 2006).

Learning from Living Leaders: Nancy Eisenberg

Source: Courtesy of Nancy Eisenberg.

Nancy Eisenberg is Regents Professor of Psychology at Arizona State University, where she has been engaged in

trying to understand the development of prosocial behavior in children for several decades. Her graduate studies at the University of California at Berkeley and her early book, *The Roots of Prosocial Behavior in Children*, made her one of the world's leading figures in this area. Her specific goal is to understand the factors that account for individual differences in children's altruism, empathy, and sympathy. She uses multiple methods and designs including psychophysiology, naturalistic observations, lab-based experiments, and cross-cultural comparisons. Her work has taken her to China, Indonesia, France, and Brazil in search of commonalities and differences in prosocial understanding and behavior. One of her proudest achievements was her invitation to share her insights about the origins of altruism and compassion with the Buddhist spiritual leader, the Dalai Lama, in India. A selection of dialogues from this conference appears in *Visions of Compassion: Western*

386 Chapter 11 Morality: Knowing Right, Doing Good

Scientists and Tibetan Buddhists Examine Human Nature. She is the founding editor of *Child Development Perspectives,* a journal devoted to summaries of new and emerging topics, and is the recipient of several awards for her scholarly work including the 2007 Ernest R. Hilgard Award for Career Contribution to General Psychology from the American Psychological Association.

Further Reading

Eisenberg, N., Fabes, R. A., & Spinrad, T. L. (2006). Prosocial behavior. In W. Damon & R. M. Lerner (Series Eds.) & N. Eisenberg (Vol. Ed.), *Handbook of child psychology: Vol. 3. Social, emotional, and personality development* (6th ed., pp. 646–718). Hoboken, NJ: Wiley.

Determinants of Prosocial Development

Prosocial behavior and development are rooted in biology, environmental factors, culture, empathy, and perspective taking. We discuss each of these types of influence in this section.

BIOLOGICAL INFLUENCES   Prosocial behavior is linked to biology in a number of ways: It is foreshadowed in infancy, rooted in evolution, affected by genes, evident in brain activity, and associated with temperament. As we discussed in Chapter 5, "Emotions," newborn babies are distressed when they hear another baby cry. They also show signs of sharing in their first year, as we noted earlier in this chapter. These behaviors are precursors of prosocial emotions and actions. Because they appear so early in life, their existence suggests that human beings are biologically prepared to respond empathically and to engage in prosocial activities.

The fact that behaviors such as helping, sharing, and consoling are seen even among nonhuman animals suggests evolutionary roots of prosocial behavior (Preston & de Waal, 2002; Sober & Wilson, 1998). Evolutionists explain these prosocial behaviors with the notion of "kin selection." Animals' cooperation and, if necessary, sacrifice of their own interests for those of others increase the probability that their kin will survive and reproduce. Thus, even if they die, their surviving relatives will pass their genes to the next generation. It follows that individuals should direct more prosocial behavior to closely related relatives than to distant relatives or unrelated individuals (Hastings, Zahn-Waxler, et al., 2005). In fact, research shows this to be the case: People are more willing to help others who are genetically related to them than to help nonrelatives, and the closer the relationship, the more willing they are to help (Eisenberg et al., 2006).

Evidence that genes influence prosocial behavior comes from studies showing that identical twins are more alike in their prosocial behavior and empathic concern than fraternal twins (Davis et al., 1994; Deater-Deckard et al., 2001; Zahn-Waxler et al., 1998). It also comes from studies showing that extremes of prosocial behavior are exhibited by children with certain genetic abnormalities. For example, children who have Williams syndrome (marked by loss of the long arm of chromosome 7) are more empathic and prosocial than normal children (Mervis & Klein-Tasman, 2000; Semel & Rosner, 2003). According to genetic studies, the contribution of genetic factors to prosocial behavior is not terribly strong in childhood (Knafo & Plomin, 2006; Vierikko et al., 2006), but by adolescence, genetic factors account for at least 30 percent of the variability in individuals' prosocial behavior, and in adulthood the contribution is even more pronounced (Rushton et al., 1986). The search for specific genes underlying prosocial behavior is just beginning. Some single genes, such as the dopamine D4 receptor gene (Bachner-Melman et al., 2005) and variants of the arginine vasopressin 1a receptor gene (Knafo et al., 2008), have been linked to adults' prosocial behavior. However, the search is complicated. So far, more than 25 genes have been associated with one single prosocial behavior, self-reported cooperativeness (Comings et al., 2000). Because multiple genes are associated with prosocial behavior, the search for specific genetic factors will undoubtedly continue for some time. Moreover, the fact that genetic factors contribute to prosocial behavior in adolescents and adults more than in children suggests that some of the contributing genes become active only with maturation (Knafo & Plomin, 2006), and this complicates the search even further.

Various types of brain studies have demonstrated the neurological basis of prosocial behavior. Studies of people with brain lesions show that these individuals often have deficits in empathy (Eslinger, 1998). Brain-imaging studies reveal that specific brain regions are activated when people hear sad stories (Decety & Chaminade, 2003), feel empathy (Amodio & Frith, 2006; Singer et al., 2004) and compassion (King et al., 2006), take another person's perspective (Ruby & Decity, 2001), donate money to a food bank (Harbaugh et al., 2007), and make moral decisions (De Quervain et al., 2004; Heekeren et al., 2003). The mirror neuron system that we discussed in Chapter 3, "Biological Foundations," could be a neurological mechanism underlying these connections (Iacoboni & Dapretto, 2006). The correlation between the activation of the mirror neuron system and empathic concern in a number of studies supports this view (Decety & Jackson, 2004; Jabbi et al., 2007; Schulte-Rüther et al., 2007).

Temperament also plays a role in children's prosocial behavior. Another person's distress has been found to make children with highly inhibited temperaments more upset than children with less inhibited temperaments (Young et al., 1999). Similarly, children who can regulate their emotions better, as indexed by measures of their heart rate, are more likely to exhibit comforting behavior (Eisenberg et al., 1996).

In sum, various biological factors—innate preparation, evolution, genetics, neurology, and temperament—predispose children to behave prosocially. These biological influences interact with the environment in determining how prosocial children are.

ENVIRONMENTAL INFLUENCES   Environmental inputs from family, peers, teachers, and the mass media contribute to children's prosocial development. Consistent with cognitive social-learning theory (Bandura, 1989, 2002, 2006), children acquire prosocial concepts and behavior by watching and imitating prosocial models. In laboratory experiments, children who see people donate or share with others are likely to do the same (Eisenberg et al., 2006; Hart & Fegley, 1995). Children whose parents model prosocial behavior by being warm, supportive, and positive to them are more prosocial and altruistic (Eisenberg et al., 2006). Parents who act as prosocial models in the community also foster their children's prosocial behavior. For example, when parents are engaged in volunteer service, their children follow by becoming involved in volunteer work of the same kind, such as working in a homeless shelter or for an environmental cause (McLellan & Youniss, 2003).

In addition to providing models of prosocial behavior, when parents focus their children's attention on the consequences of their actions this, too, can promote children's prosocial behavior. Carolyn Zahn-Waxler and her colleagues had mothers tape-record their children's reactions to distress over a 9-month period, beginning when the children were 18 months old (Zahn-Waxler et al., 1979). They also asked the mothers to simulate distress from time to time. For example, the mother might pretend to be sad (sobbing briefly), in pain (bumping her head and saying "ouch"), or suffering respiratory distress (coughing and choking). Overall, the children reacted to distress in a prosocial way about one third of the time. However, there were substantial individual differences among the children; some children responded to most distressing situations (60% to 70% of the time) whereas others never did. Children were more likely to respond helpfully if their mothers had taught them to pay attention to the consequences of their behavior. These mothers might say, for example, "Tom is crying because you pushed him," or, even more strongly and effectively, "When you hurt me, I don't want to be near you." Consistent with these findings, other researchers have found that children whose mothers pointed out a peer's distress in an affectively charged manner tended to react empathically (Denham et al., 1994). In contrast, mothers' use of physical restraint (moving away from the child or moving the child away from the victim), physical punishment ("swatting him a good one"), unexplained prohibitions ("Stop that!"), or angry explanations ("I've told you and told you not to do that. You're not a nice person.") was likely to interfere with the development of prosocial behavior.

Another way parents can encourage their children's prosocial behavior is by responding to emotions in a sensitive way. Children behave more prosocially if their parents tolerate the children's emotional distress rather than punishing them for it (Roberts, 1999; Strayer & Roberts, 2004), if the parents try to find out why their children are feeling anxious or upset (Eisenberg et al., 1993), and if the parents explain their own feelings of sadness to their children (Denham, 1998; Denham et al., 2007).

Finally, parents can promote children's prosocial behavior by giving them opportunities to perform prosocial acts. For example, they can assign the children household tasks. Even 2-year-olds will help adults in tasks such as sweeping, cleaning, and setting the table (Rheingold, 1982). Allowing children to help in these ways is consistent with Vygotsky's sociocultural theory of development in which children learn by being apprentices. Parents can also encourage their children's prosocial behavior by providing them with opportunities to help outside the home. Children who have opportunities to engage in volunteer activities develop more prosocial attitudes and behavior (Johnson et al., 1998; Metz et al., 2003; Pratt et al., 2003).

Peers also influence children's prosocial behavior. In general, like "birds of a feather," children flock together with others who are similar to them. Children who are not very prosocial spend their time with peers who lack a spirit of kindness; highly prosocial children play with peers who are kind and cooperative. As a result of this "prosocial segregation," children who are not particularly generous or helpful have few chances to learn prosocial practices. However, if given the chance, peers can act as models of prosocial behavior. In one study, preschoolers who were exposed to prosocial peers at the beginning of the school year were observed to engage in more prosocial peer interactions later in the year (Fabes et al., 2002). In another study, preschoolers who initiated more prosocial behavior toward their peers received more prosocial behavior from peers a year later (Persson, 2005). In a third study, children with friends who were rated as more prosocial than they were more helpful and considerate 2 years later whereas children with friends who were rated as less prosocial showed diminished prosocial behavior (Wentzel et al., 2004). Finally, in a fourth study, researchers found that adolescents whose close friends were more prosocial increased more in their prosocial goals and behavior over a 1-year period, especially if their relationship was very positive and they interacted frequently (Barry & Wentzel, 2006).

Teachers also can influence children's prosocial behavior. Training elementary school teachers to encourage and reward children's prosocial behavior as part of a schoolwide violence prevention effort (the PeaceBuilders Program) led to increases in students' reports of their own prosocial behavior 1 year later (Embry et al., 1996; Flannery et al., 2003).

Television is another learning medium for prosocial behavior (Comstock & Scharrer, 2006). As we pointed out in Chapter 9, "Schools and Media," when children watch programs focused on understanding the feelings of others, expressing sympathy, and helping, they learn general rules about prosocial behavior and apply that learning to interactions with their peers (Anderson et al., 2001; Comstock & Scharrer, 2006; Huston & Wright, 1998; Singer & Singer, 2001). This is especially true for children whose parents watch the programs with them and encourage their altruistic behavior (Mares & Woodward, 2001).

Finally, pets offer another opportunity for children to learn prosocial behavior. Young children who have a dog or cat at home have been found to have high scores on measures of prosocial behavior (Toeplitz et al., 1995), and if they have a bond with their pet, they exhibit more empathy (Poresky & Hendrix, 1989).

CULTURAL INFLUENCES   In some cultures, children are given a major responsibility for taking care of siblings and performing household tasks (Eisenberg et al., 2006). Cross-cultural studies conducted in Mexico, Japan, India, and Kenya suggest that children who perform more domestic chores and spend more time caring for their infant brothers, sisters, and cousins, are more altruistic (Whiting & Edwards, 1988; Whiting & Whiting, 1975). Similar results have been found in cultures that stress communal values, such as the Aitutaki of Polynesia, the Papago Indian tribe in Arizona, and many Asian cultures (Chen, 2000; Eisenberg et al., 2006; Zaff et al., 2003). Children raised in communal Israeli kibbutzim, which stress prosocial and cooperative values, are more prosocial than their city-reared peers (Aviezer et al., 1994), and Mexican

American children are more prosocial than European American children (Knight et al., 1982) until they grow older and are acculturated to U.S. norms (de Guzman & Carlo, 2004).

EMPATHY AND PERSPECTIVE TAKING   Two final important contributors to prosocial behavior are empathy and perspective taking (Eisenberg et al., 2005; Hoffman, 2000). By the time they are 2 years old, children have the capacity to empathize with another person's emotional state. Another person's expression of distress elicits a similar emotion in a child who is watching. This empathic ability often motivates children to engage in prosocial actions that relieve not only the other person's distress but also the child's own emotional upset. Prosocial acts that result in the other person's having positive feelings can vicariously produce similar positive emotions in the helping child. Researchers have found that children who are particularly empathic are also more prosocial (Eisenberg et al., 1990, 2006). The relation between empathy and prosocial behavior is found in a variety of cultures including Italy, Japan, Turkey, and the United States (Asakawa & Matsuoka, 1987; Bandura et al., 2003; Kumru & Edwards, 2003; Vitaglione & Barnett, 2003).

Perspective taking is the capacity to understand another's point of view. Researchers have found links between prosocial behavior and the capacity for perspective taking (Eisenberg et al., 2006; Strayer & Roberts, 2004). Preschool children who are able to take another person's perspective are more prosocial than those who don't have this ability (Zahn-Waxler et al., 1995). However, perspective-taking ability alone may not be enough to produce prosocial behavior if a child doesn't have the motivation or the social assertiveness necessary to act prosocially. Several researchers have found that children who demonstrated perspective-taking ability and were socially assertive or sympathetic toward others were more prosocial than children who were good at perspective taking alone (Denham, 1998; Denham & Couchoud, 1991). In one study, for example, the children who donated the most money to help a child who was burned in a fire were the ones who had good perspective-taking ability, were sympathetic, and understood the value of money (Knight et. al., 1994). In another study, juvenile delinquent adolescents who were more prosocial were more concerned with, could identify with, and understood a victim's situation, feelings, and perspective (Stams et al., 2008).

Figure 11.4 illustrates a model of how empathy and perspective taking contribute to prosocial behavior. When researchers tested this model with groups of 5-, 9-, and 13-year-old

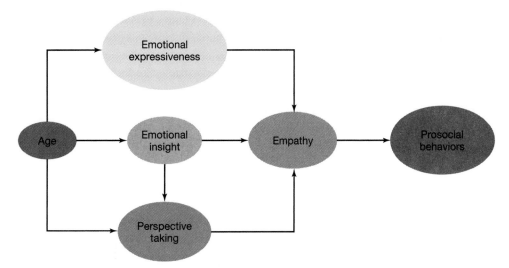

FIGURE 11.4   *Empathy, perspective taking, and prosocial behavior. According to this model, empathy is the principal determinant underlying prosocial behavior. Underlying empathy are emotional expressiveness, emotional insight, and perspective-taking abilities.* Source: Roberts, W., & Strayer, J. (1996). *Empathy, emotional expressiveness and prosocial behavior.* Child Development, 67, 449–470. (fig 1, p. 450). Reprinted with permission of Wiley-Blackwell.

children, they found that perspective taking contributed to empathy and empathy to prosocial behavior (Roberts & Strayer, 1996). Interestingly, empathy predicted boys' prosocial behavior with everyone but only girls' prosocial behavior with friends. Empathy may be a more important predictor of prosocial behavior toward friends for girls than for boys because girls' friendships are closer and more intimate than those of boys.

In the final analysis, prosocial behavior is best viewed as multidetermined (Grusec et al., 2010). A number of biological influences, including neurological and genetic factors as well as environmental influences including family, peers, and culture, all need to be considered to understand variations in children's prosocial behavior.

Chapter Summary

- Three aspects of moral development are cognition, behavior, and emotion.

Moral Judgment

- Piaget and Kohlberg proposed theories of moral development involving stages through which children progress as their cognitive capacities increase.

- In Piaget's premoral stage, young children show little concern for rules. In the moral realism stage, children judge rightness and wrongness based on immanent justice and objective consequences and believe that rules are unchanging and unquestionable. In the moral reciprocity stage, children recognize intentionality and the arbitrariness of social rules.

- Piaget underestimated children's abilities: Young children can distinguish between intentions and consequences if material is presented in a less complex manner than he used.

- In Kohlberg's preconventional level of development, moral judgment is based on the desire to avoid punishment (Stage 1) or gain rewards (Stage 2). At the conventional level, moral judgment is based on conformity to obtain approval (Stage 3) or to comply with society's rules (Stage 4). At the postconventional level, moral judgment is based on society's consensus about human rights (Stage 5) or abstract principles of justice (Stage 6). Moral judgment continues to develop in adulthood, but few individuals reach the postconventional level.

- Kohlberg's theory was criticized because it ignored the effects of cultural and historical circumstances. The theory has been expanded to include interpersonal caring and civil rights.

- Turiel's social domain theory suggested that moral reasoning is one of several domains of social knowledge. Other domains include social conventions (e.g., knowledge about table manners) and the psychological domain (personal preferences, prudential concerns, and knowledge about self and others). Children learn quite early to distinguish among these domains. They judge violations of moral rules as being worse than violations in other domains because the former result in harm to another person and violate norms of justice and fairness.

- Moral reasoning often involves multiple domains. Moral considerations generally take priority over social-conventional and personal issues.

Moral Behavior

- Moral behavior is more likely to be related to moral judgment in older children and when the person views the issue as moral rather than social conventional or personal.

- Self-regulation is the ability to inhibit impulses and behave in accord with social and moral rules in the absence of external control.

- The development of self-regulation is fostered by a positive, responsive mother-child relationship and a temperament characterized by active inhibition and effortful control.
- There is a high degree of consistency in children's moral or immoral behavior across time and situations. However, factors such as fear of detection, peer support for deviant behavior, and the importance of the outcome for the child do influence children's willingness to cheat, lie, or steal.

Moral Emotions

- Emotions such as remorse, shame, and guilt are frequent responses to committed or anticipated moral transgressions.
- Girls and children with fearful temperaments are more likely to experience moral emotions.
- Parents encourage children's development of moral emotions by providing a warm and supportive climate in the home and offering emotion-charged explanations when children violate a rule.
- Moral emotions are related to moral behavior beginning at age 3 or 4.
- Cognitive, behavioral, and emotional aspects of moral development co-occur, interact, and sometimes even conflict. Whether children define a dilemma as personal, conventional, or moral (a cognitive process) influences how they act (behavior) and how they feel (emotion).

Prosocial and Altruistic Behavior

- Helping, sharing, and empathizing appear by the time children are 2. Altruistic behavior appears later in development.
- Individual differences in styles of prosocial behavior are relatively stable over time.
- Children's prosocial reasoning develops through a number of stages before it becomes based on internalized values and norms.
- Girls tend to be kinder and more considerate than boys.
- Evidence of helping and sharing in infrahuman animals suggests that evolution has prepared us for prosocial behavior. Genetic factors influence individual differences in prosocial behavior.
- Parents, peers, television, pets, and culture all influence the likelihood of children's acting prosocially.
- Empathy and perspective taking contribute to children's capacity for prosocial and altruistic behavior.

Key Terms

altruistic behavior	moral absolutism	prosocial behavior
conscience	moral realism	prosocial reasoning
conventional level	moral reciprocity	psychological domain
delay of gratification	needs-oriented	self-regulation
empathic reasoning	reasoning	social conventional
hedonistic reasoning	postconventional level	domain
immanent justice	preconventional level	sympathy
internalize	premoral stage	
internalized reasoning		

At the Movies

Many movies illuminate moral issues. They vividly convey moral—or immoral—acts, portray moral and immoral characters, and provoke the audience to think deeply about morality. Those noted here are just a few of such movies. *Gandhi* (1982) is a biography of Mahatma Gandhi, the man who used nonviolent civil disobedience to end the subjugation of the Indian people. Gandhi was one of the few individuals whom Kohlberg considered to exemplify the abstract principles of justice and equality found in Stage 6 moral reasoning. His leadership and example inspired many people and many governments throughout the world to have higher levels of morality. Other movies focus on the moral behavior of less known individuals. *A Dry White Season* (1989) is the story of a white man in South Africa who is awakened to the brutality and injustice of apartheid. *Hotel Rwanda* (2004) focuses on the hotel manager who protected more than 1200 people from killers' machetes in the Rwandan genocide in 1994. *Sophie Scholl: The Final Days* (2005) follows college student Sophie Scholl's last 6 days from the time she was arrested for distributing anti-Nazi leaflets until she was found guilty of treason and executed. All these true stories challenge you to evaluate your own strength of moral character. Would you risk your life the way these people did?

A movie that contrasts different levels of moral reasoning in the United States is *Gone Baby Gone* (2007). A young child has been kidnapped, and a massive search is conducted to find her. The child's aunt enlists the aid of a private detective. The movie contrasts the absolute moral standard espoused by that detective: "Murder's wrong, plain and simple," with the situational moral standard expressed by some police officers: "Depends on who you're killing." This movie is more than just a crime drama about the unethical methods by which some cops solve crimes; it is a moral tale suggesting the superiority of developing community through empathy, cooperation, and concern about the lives of other people.

Moral issues are not always embedded in stories about life and death, crime, and crisis, however; they are also expressed in fiction and fantasy. *Groundhog Day* (1993) is a hilarious movie with a moral message: Doing good has benefits. *Pay it Forward* (2000) has the same message. The pay-it-forward concept came from the personal experience of the woman who wrote the novel and adapted it for the screen. When her car caught fire at the side of a road, two men put out the fire, but before she could thank them, they disappeared. She later returned the favor by helping a woman stranded at the side of the road, and instead of accepting thanks, she asked the stranger to pay it forward to the next person in need of help. Although this movie is pure Hollywood, the notion of paying it forward reinforces the idea that individuals are responsible for the welfare of the community and encourages an optimistic and prosocial outlook on life. Today, the Pay It Forward Foundation focuses on inspiring and assisting young people to make a positive contribution to society.

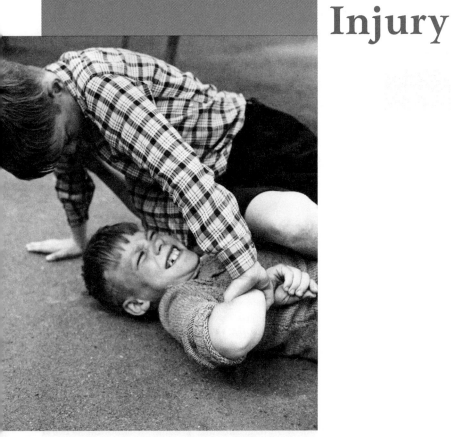

CHAPTER 12 Aggression: Insult and Injury

Source: Erich Auerbach/Hulton Archive/Getty Images, Inc.

Jason wants to get on a swing in the preschool playground, so he pushes Tom off. Cindy spreads a rumor about Hannah, and as a result, Hannah is excluded from the junior high school lunch group. A 14-year-old in Moses Lake, Washington, walks into a math class armed with a high-powered rifle and two handguns, opens fire, and kills the teacher and two students. These three examples illustrate children's aggression. In this chapter, we discuss the types and causes of aggression and how aggression can be controlled.

Aggression comes in many forms: some merely annoying, others injurious or even deadly. What is the common thread that unites such diverse actions? The term *aggression* refers to behavior that is intended to and in fact does harm another person by inflicting pain or injury. The notion of *intention* is crucial: It separates acts of aggression from the actions of doctors and

proactive aggression
Behavior in which a person is hurt or injured by someone who is motivated by a desire to achieve a specific goal.

reactive aggression
A form of hostile behavior in response to an attack, threat, or frustration, usually motivated by anger.

physical aggression
A form of hostile behavior that inflicts physical damage or discomfort.

dentists who must at times cause pain to preserve and protect people's health. Of course, a definition that involves intent is problematic because it is sometimes difficult to determine whether an action was intentional or accidental. An alternative definition focuses simply on the form of the act; for example, biting, kicking, swatting, and punching would be considered aggressive. Ethologists Konrad Lorenz and Nikolaas Tinbergen used the term this way to describe the actions of animals, birds, and fish, but it is more difficult to apply to humans; for us, sometimes a punch on the shoulder is merely a friendly greeting. Another approach is to focus on the action's outcome; if a person is harmed or injured, the behavior would be classified as aggression regardless of the hitter's intention. This definition has problems, too. It includes accidental injuries, which most people would not consider to be the result of aggression, but not behavior intended to cause harm that results in no injury. The best approach is to consider the aggressor, the victim, and the community: An act is aggressive if the aggressor intends it to harm the victim, the victim perceives it to be harmful, and it is considered aggressive according to the norms of the community. People use local standards in applying the term *aggression* just as courts and jurors use local standards to judge guilt in criminal actions (Dodge, Coie, et al., 2006). Understanding the factors that determine whether an act is considered aggressive is important because the way we label actions influences the way we react to them.

Types of Aggression

verbal aggression
Words that inflict pain by yelling, insulting, ridiculing, humiliating, and so on.

social aggression
Making verbal attacks or hurtful nonverbal gestures, such as rolling the eyes or sticking out the tongue.

relational aggression
Behavior that damages or destroys interpersonal relationships by means such as exclusion or gossip.

direct aggression
Physical or verbal hostile behavior that directly targets another person.

indirect aggression
Hostile behavior committed by an unidentified perpetrator that hurts another person by indirect means.

Aggression can be categorized into different types. First, the *function* of aggression may be reactive or proactive. A desire to achieve a specific goal motivates **proactive aggression**. For example, a younger child hits another child to get a toy or pushes the other child off a swing in order to use it; an older child bullies a classmate to achieve the goal of increased social power. This type of aggression is also sometimes referred to as *instrumental aggression* because it is instrumental in achieving a goal. It is often premeditated and calculating. **Reactive aggression** occurs in response to a threat, attack, or frustration. For example, a child hits another child who has just insulted him or her or calls the other child a bad name. This type of aggression is usually motivated by anger or hostility and, for this reason, is sometimes called *hostile aggression*. It is often impulsive.

Second, aggression has different *forms*. **Physical aggression** involves inflicting physical damage or discomfort on another person by hitting, shoving, poking, or shooting. **Verbal aggression** is using words to inflict pain: yelling, insulting, ridiculing, humiliating, name-calling, arguing, teasing. **Social aggression** includes hurtful nonverbal gestures, such as rolling the eyes or sticking out the tongue, as well as verbal attacks (Coyne et al., 2010; Underwood, 2004). **Relational aggression** refers to excluding others from a social group, hurtfully manipulating or sabotaging their social relationships, or damaging their social position (Crick & Gropeter, 1995; Underwood, Galen, et al., 2001). Each of these types of aggression can be expressed either directly or indirectly (Dodge, Coie, et al., 2006). **Direct aggression** means that the attack (with either physical means or words) is made directly on the person. **Indirect aggression** involves inflicting pain by destroying the person's property, getting another person to carry out the attack, or damaging the person's social standing through rumors or lies; the perpetrator's identity is not known (see Table 12.1). Although it is possible to distinguish among these different types of aggression, children who are aggressive tend to use all of them; the correlation between children's frequency of indirect (or relational) aggression and direct aggression in a meta-analysis of 98 studies was an exceptionally high 0.76 (Card et al., 2008).

Aggression can be maladaptive or adaptive. Although it is common to focus on the maladaptive aspects, ethological and evolutionary theories suggest that aggression can have adaptive value because of its role in protection, survival, and even developmental growth (Hawley, 2003b; Hawley et al., 2007). In early childhood, aggressive interchanges can teach young children how to settle conflicts and disputes and promote their social-cognitive growth (Hawley,

A direct physical attack such as this may be what we think of first when we hear the word aggression, *but more subtle forms of mean behavior are also common in childhood.* Source: Erich Auerbach/ Hulton Archive/Getty Images, Inc.

TABLE 12.1 **Examples of Direct and Indirect Physical, Verbal, and Relational Aggression**

Physical aggression	Direct	Pushing, hitting, kicking, punching, or shoving a person
	Indirect	Destroying a person's property, getting someone else to physically hurt the person
Verbal aggression	Direct	Insulting, putting down, name-calling, or teasing a person
	Indirect	Gossiping, saying mean things behind a person's back, urging someone else to verbally abuse the person
Relational aggression	Direct	Excluding, threatening to stop liking a person
	Indirect	Spreading rumors or lies, exposing secrets about a person, ignoring or betraying the person, building an alliance that excludes the person

Sources: Dodge, Coie, et al., 2006; Ostrov & Crick, 2007; Underwood, Galen, et al., 2001.

2003b; Vaughn et al., 2003). In middle childhood, aggression can be used as a way to attract peers and impress them with the aggressor's toughness (Rodkin et al., 2000). In adolescence, demonstration of aggressive prowess may be a key to maintaining membership or rising in the status hierarchy of a gang (Prinstein & Cillessen, 2003; Thornberry et al., 2003). These adaptive advantages may be mixed with maladaptive outcomes, however; gaining status with peers can lead to increases in deviant activities and increased contact with authorities including law enforcement.

In brief, aggression is a multifaceted set of behaviors varying in form, function, and adaptiveness. In this chapter, we discuss the ways in which different forms of aggression change over the course of development, the causes and consequences of aggressive behavior, and strategies for reducing or preventing aggression in children and youth.

Patterns of Aggression

In this section we discuss patterns of aggression related to age, gender, and stability over time.

Developmental Changes in Aggression

Age brings about dramatic differences in the frequency, forms, and functions of aggression (see Table 12.2). Aggression in infancy, which usually begins by the end of the first year, most often involves squabbles over toys and is therefore considered proactive or instrumental (Caplan et al., 1991). Aggression in these earliest disputes is physical and direct—hitting, grabbing, and poking—not verbal or indirect. Over the next year, conflicts over possessions continue and the frequency of physical aggression increases. In one study, 87 percent of peer encounters at 21 months were marked by physical conflict (Hay & Ross, 1982).

During the preschool period, proactive aggression continues to be more frequent than reactive or hostile aggression, but instances of reactive aggression occur as well (Ostrov & Crick, 2007). Verbal aggression begins and becomes more frequent (Caplan et al., 1991). Aggressive outbursts—tantrums, peer conflicts, sibling battles—peak in 2- to 3-year-olds, but, to the relief of parents everywhere, decline thereafter (Dodge, Coie, et al., 2006; Tremblay et al., 2005). Most obvious is the decrease in physical aggression. The NICHD Study of Early Child Care and Youth Development identified a clear decline in physical aggression over the preschool years: Mothers reported that when their children were 2 to 3 years old, 70 percent hit, pushed, or kicked others, but only 20 percent did so when they were 4 to 5 years old (NICHD Early Child Care Research Network, 2004b). Children's increased abilities to regulate and control their actions and to delay gratification are linked to these decreases in aggression. Acquiring strategies such as distracting themselves from an object they want helps children reduce their impulse to take toys or punch peers. Children who are able to shift their attention and ignore frustrating stimuli have better anger control and exhibit less aggression (Gilliom et al., 2002).

The decline in physical aggression continues through elementary school. Only 14 percent of children in the NICHD Study exhibited physical aggression when they were in 1st grade and only 12 percent did so in 3rd grade (NICHD Early Child Care Research Network, 2004b). In this age period, children are able to attain most of their goals without using aggressive tactics. They can set a goal, decide on a plan of action, and monitor progress toward the goal because development of their prefrontal cortex increases their executive-functioning capacity (Barkley et al., 2002; Bjorklund, 2000). For this reason, in this age period aggression changes from predominantly proactive to predominantly reactive. Instead of using aggression to gain or maintain control over toys and territory, children increasingly use it to settle interpersonal scores that arise from perceived threats and personal insults. They realize that their peers may act purposely to hurt them and make them feel bad, and they become increasingly likely to retaliate (Gifford-Smith & Rabiner, 2004). Direct verbal insults and name calling and indirect verbal aggression by gossiping or saying mean things behind someone's back become more common in this period. Relational aggression also becomes more frequent as children threaten not to play with other children or spread rumors and lies about them (Coyne et al., 2010; Underwood, 2003).

During adolescence, physical aggression continues to decline in frequency for most children. Verbal insults and taunts continue and more sophisticated forms of relational aggression such as forming cliques and building coalitions increase (Coyne et al., 2010). For a small minority of adolescents an increase in serious aggressive incidents occurs. In part, this may reflect adolescents' lack of a fully mature prefrontal cortex (Steinberg, 2007). The percentage of individuals who first engage in a serious violent offense, such as aggravated assault and robbery or rape that results in injury and may involve a weapon, increases from almost zero in the preteen years to 5 percent at age 16 (Dodge, Coie, et al., 2006). The overall prevalence rate of violent offenses also increases in adolescence, peaking at age 17 when 19 percent of males and 12 percent of females report having committed at least one serious violent attack. African American and Latino adolescents are particularly likely to be arrested and incarcerated for such offenses (Guerra & Smith, 2006). African American youth make up 15 percent of the adolescent population but 26 percent of juvenile arrests and 44 percent of detainees (Children's Defense Fund, 2004). Latino youth are three times more likely to be incarcerated

TABLE 12.2 **Development of Aggressive Behavior**

Infancy: 0–2 years	• Children express anger and frustration • Some early signs of aggression (pushing, shoving) appear • Differences in irritability predict later aggression
Preschool years: 2–6 years	• Proactive /instrumental aggression occurs • Expressions of verbal aggression increase • Boys are more physically aggressive than girls • Relational aggression (excluding from playgroup, ignoring) begins to appear
Elementary years: 6–10 years	• Reactive /hostile aggression occurs • Proactive aggression decreases • Boys use both physical aggression and relational aggression • Girls' reliance on relational aggression becomes more marked • Relational aggression (gossip, rumors) becomes more sophisticated • Physical aggression declines • Aggressive children may do poorly in school and be rejected by peers • Parental monitoring becomes important to deter delinquency
Adolescence	• Aggressive children select aggressive, deviant peer groups • Relational aggression continues (excluding from clique, alliance building) • Violent aggression increases among some youth, • Rates of violent behavior are much higher for boys than girls • Hormonal changes are associated with increases in reactive aggression in boys • Individual differences in hormone levels are important determinants of levels of aggression

Note: These age approximations are based on trends identified in research studies. The age at which developmental changes occur in individual children varies greatly. Sources: Coie & Dodge, 1998; Dodge, Coie, et al., 2006; Ostrov & Crick, 2007; Underwood, 2004.

than European American adolescents (Children's Defense Fund, 2004; Villarruel et al., 2002). Limited economic opportunities, dangerous neighborhoods, and a color-biased legal system all contribute to these ethnic disparities.

Gender Differences in Aggression

Gender is another important source of differences in aggression. Few differences appear in infancy, but by the time they are toddlers, boys are more likely than girls to instigate and to be involved in direct physical aggressive incidents, such as hitting, pushing, and tripping, as well as overt verbal attacks, such as name-calling, taunting, and threatening (Card et al., 2008; Maccoby, 1998). This difference is evident across all socioeconomic groups in the United States and across a wide variety of other countries, including Britain, Canada, China, Switzerland, Israel, Ethiopia, Kenya, India, Japan, the Philippines, Mexico, New Zealand, and Spain (Archer, 2004; Broidy et al., 2003; Dodge, Coie, et al., 2006; Whiting & Whiting, 1975).

The forms of aggression boys and girls favor also differ in important ways. Even among 3- to 5-year-olds, boys are more physically aggressive than girls (Crick et al., 1997, 2006), and these differences persist. In a six-site cross-national study, researchers found that, on average, boys were more physically aggressive than girls from childhood through adolescence and even the most aggressive girls were not as aggressive as the most aggressive boys (Broidy et al., 2003). In the National Longitudinal Survey of Children and Youth in Canada, about 4 percent of the boys exhibited frequent physical aggression from age 5 to age 11, but for girls only 2 percent exhibited frequent physical aggression at age 5 and by age 11, less than 1 percent did (Lee et al., 2007). Hence, the results showed a decreasing trend in the prevalence of physical aggression for girls but not for boys. In adolescence, approximately five times as many boys as girls were arrested for violent crimes such as aggravated assault and criminal homicide in a longitudinal study of children in New Zealand from age 5 to age 21, and these marked male-female differences in physical aggression continued into adulthood (Moffitt et al., 2001). For comparable rates of self-reported violent crimes in the United States see Figure 12.1 (Coie & Dodge, 1998). In addition, men who were aggressive boys were likely to commit violent offenses including drunk driving, spousal abuse, and criminal traffic violations, whereas women who were aggressive girls were likely to commit nonviolent offenses, such as drug use (Bushman & Huesmann, 2001; Huesmann et al., 1984).

Boys' aggression exceeds girls' in other ways too. Rates of nonphysical antisocial behavior, including lying, cheating, and stealing, were higher for boys than for girls in a study of children in the United States and 12 other countries (Crijnen et al., 1997) and in the longitudinal study in New Zealand (Moffitt et al., 2001). Boys are also about twice as likely as girls to violate the rights of others and break age-appropriate social norms and rules (Dodge, Coie, et al., 2006), and they are more likely than girls to retaliate after being attacked (Darvill & Cheyne, 1981). Although females are sometimes the victims of male aggression in childhood (Rodkin & Berger, 2008) and in later dating and romantic relationships (Archer, 2002), boys are more likely to attack other boys than to attack a girl (Barrett, 1979).

Girls are more likely than boys to disapprove of aggression and to anticipate parental disapproval for acting aggressively (Huesmann & Guerra, 1997; Perry et al., 1989). They are more likely than boys to use strategies such as verbal objection and negotiation to resolve their conflicts, methods that make the escalation of a quarrel into overt verbal or physical aggression less likely (Eisenberg et al., 1994). This does not mean that girls are not aggressive, but they use different tactics to achieve their goals.

In the preschool period, girls use concrete and relatively unsophisticated forms of relational aggression, such as excluding ("You can't come to my birthday party.") or ignoring (covering their ears when a peer is talking), more often than they use direct verbal or physical aggression (Card et al., 2008; Nelson et al., 2005). In the elementary school years, girls increase their use of relational aggression by damaging or destroying interpersonal relationships (Card et al., 2008; Cote et al., 2007; Crick et al., 2004; Underwood, 2003). They may exclude other girls ("You can't sit with us at lunch anymore."), besmirch their reputations, or gossip about their negative qualities ("Did you hear that she really do be stinkin' sometimes?") (Dodge, Coie, et al., 2006). In middle school, girls

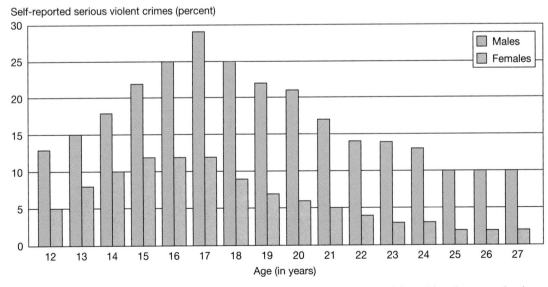

Self-reported serious violent crimes (percent)

FIGURE 12.1 *Self-reported rates of violent crimes among adolescents and young adults. Although more males than females commit violent offenses such as aggravated assault (assault with intent to commit a crime), robbery, and rape, girls' involvement in criminal behavior peaks when they are about 2 years younger than boys. Source: Coie & Dodge, 1998. Reprinted with Permission of John Wiley & Sons, Inc.*

prefer to harm others by indirect means of social ostracism rather than direct confrontation, and as girls enter adolescence, they make increasing use of the aggressive strategy of excluding peers from their social clique (Crick et al., 1999, 2004; Underwood, 2003; Xie et al., 2005). They use relational aggression as a way to solidify their status in the group by undermining someone else's.

Although girls use relational aggression more often than physical or verbal aggression, they do not use it more than boys. Boys use relational aggression just as much as girls, but they use other aggressive tactics even more (Card et al., 2008; Pepler et al., 2005; Underwood, 2003). What are the reasons that girls prefer relational slights whereas boys prefer physical slaps? First, girls are more oriented toward social relationships and value social ties more than boys do (Leaper & Friedman, 2007; Maccoby, 1998). Therefore, a form of aggression that harms social relationships is a more reasonable social strategy for females (Crick et al., 1999; Coyne et al., 2010). Second, reducing other girls' social status may be a way for girls to gain the advantage in attracting boys—an important goal according to evolutionary theory (Artz, 2005; Bjorklund, 2000). Third, relational aggression is a more socially acceptable way for girls to be mean (Crick et al., 1999; Dodge, Coie, et al., 2006). Physical aggression is not viewed as "ladylike." When boys are physically aggressive, they are perceived as "behaving like men."

Relational aggression may not be as blatantly obvious or physically injurious as punching or pummeling, but it is still a problem. Children know that relational aggression hurts. Preschool girls and boys think that relational and physical aggression are equally hurtful and likely to make a person feel sad (Crick et al., 2004). Older girls continue to view relational aggression as just as hurtful as physical aggression, but boys, having been on the receiving end of more punches, think that physical aggression hurts more (Galen & Underwood, 1997; Underwood, 2003). Another problem with relational aggression is that girls and boys who engage in it, like those who use physical aggression, are more likely to be rejected by their peers than children who do not (Crick, 1997; Crick et al., 2004, 2006).

Learning from Living Leaders: Nicki Crick

Source: Courtesy of Nicki Crick.

Nicki Crick is Professor and Director of the Institute of Child Development at the University of Minnesota. Although she originally planned to become a biomedical engineer, she was inspired by Albert Bandura's research on social cognition and decided to pursue a career in developmental and clinical psychology instead. In 1992, she received her Ph.D. in psychology from Vanderbilt University (her advisor was Ken Dodge) and set out to prove that girls as well as boys are aggressive but express it in different ways. Her work focused on relational aggression—its antecedents, correlates, and consequences. She showed that gossip, exclusion, and reputation bashing have serious consequences for victims, just as hitting and tripping do, and she challenged the belief that "sticks and stones will break my bones but names will never hurt me." Crick has used her research to develop intervention programs to help reduce children's relational aggression and bullying in schools. She received the Distinguished Scientific Award for Early Career Contributions from the American Psychological Association for her work. Crick predicts that more long-term longitudinal studies of relational aggression will be conducted over the next two decades, especially ones that investigate biological, emotional, and cognitive factors. Her advice for undergraduates is the same advice that has guided her career: "Discover your passion and follow it!"

Further Reading

Crick, N. R., Ostrov, J. M., & Kawabata, Y. (2007). Relational aggression and gender: An overview. In D. Flannery, I. Waldman, & A. Valsonyi (Eds.), *Cambridge handbook of violent behavior and aggression* (pp. 245–259). New York: Cambridge University Press.

Stability of Individual Differences in Aggression

From an early age, some children display more anger and aggression than others. Do these children end up being more aggressive later on? In other words, how stable are individual differences in aggression? Researchers have found that aggression is stable over time for both boys and girls (Cairns & Cairns, 1994; Dodge, Coie, et al., 2006; Olweus, 1979). A child who is rated as being highly aggressive compared with classmates in 1st grade is likely to be rated as highly aggressive compared with classmates in 12th grade and to have more trouble with the law in adulthood (Bushman & Huesmann, 2001; Huesmann et al., 1984). In fact, aggressiveness is as stable as intelligence. Although both physical and relational aggression are stable, physical aggression is especially so (Vaillancourt, Brendgen, et al., 2003).

However, although aggression is stable, it is not 100 percent so. Only a small percentage of children are very aggressive in early childhood and maintain this high level of aggression for their entire lives. In the NICHD Study of Early Child Care and Youth Development, about 18 percent of children remained consistently high in aggressiveness between toddlerhood and 3rd grade (NICHD Early Child Care Research Network, 2004b). In research in Canada, about 13 percent of highly aggressive 5-year-olds were still highly aggressive in adolescence (Nagin & Tremblay, 1999); more boys (11%) than girls (1%) remained in the stable high physical aggression group between 6 and 12 years (Joussemet et al., 2008).

early starters
Children who start to behave aggressively at a young age and often remain aggressive through childhood and adolescence.

Children who start to behave aggressively early in development and remain aggressive—so-called **early starters**—are at most risk for negative outcomes (Patterson et al., 1989). For example, children who remained aggressive from toddlerhood to 3rd grade in the NICHD study showed the most severe adjustment problems at age 12 compared with children who either remained low in aggression or decreased in aggressiveness (Campbell et al., 2006). Similarly, in the six-site study mentioned earlier, children who displayed high levels of aggression in the early years and consistently high levels of physical aggression throughout childhood were likely to show both violent and nonviolent delinquency in adolescence (Broidy et al., 2003). In contrast, **late starters**, those who began to act aggressively only in adolescence, engaged in delinquent behavior for a limited time during their teen years but tended not to do so in adulthood. The late starters probably avoided the social rejection and school failure that plagued early starters, and this may have protected them. Gender differences are particularly evident for early starters. Researchers in the New Zealand study found that almost all the children who began their aggressive behavior early in life were boys (10% boys versus 1% girls) whereas those who started later were more equal by gender (26% boys versus 18% girls) (Moffitt & Caspi, 2001).

late starters
Children who begin to act aggressively in adolescence and tend not to continue their aggressive behavior in adulthood.

Into Adulthood:
From Childhood Aggression to Road Rage

Aggression in adulthood includes a wide variety of behaviors—from reckless driving to premeditated murder. Violent road rage and abuse of a spouse or a son or daughter are forms of aggression that are unique to adulthood. Fortunately, overall rates of aggression decline in early adulthood. In one large British sample, for example, David Farrington (1993) found that the likelihood that a man would commit a burglary dropped from 11 percent at age 18, to 5 percent at age 21, to 2 percent by age 32. U.S. researchers also found that aggression decreases between the ages of 18 and 25 and violent crimes decline even more after age 35 (Sampson & Laub, 2003). Adults are expected to rely less on physical force and more on nonconfrontational methods for settling their disputes. They continue to use indirect or relational methods to express aggression (Xie et al., 2005), but these methods are preferable to physical attacks and are less likely to lead to criminal prosecution.

Although aggression declines overall, some individuals are more likely than others to continue their aggressive ways. Children who begin their aggressive careers early (early starters) are most likely to persist in using aggression in adulthood (Dodge, Coie, et al., 2006; Farrington, 1995). To illustrate, researchers in one longitudinal study found that children who were highly aggressive at age 8 were more likely than their less aggressive peers to abuse their spouse or child, get a traffic ticket, drive while drunk, and engage in criminal activities in early adulthood (Huesmann et al., 1984). In another study, researchers observed broader consequences of early aggression: Boys who had problems with anger and aggression when they were 8 to 10 years old had erratic work lives, held lower status jobs than their parents, and were more likely to be divorced when they were 40 years old compared with their more even-tempered peers; girls with temper problems married men with low occupational mobility, were less competent and more ill-tempered as mothers, and were more likely to be divorced (Caspi et al., 1987). A third

study found that children in Finland who were more aggressive at age 8 were more likely to suffer from drinking problems and unemployment in adulthood (Kokko & Pulkkinen, 2000).

Not every aggressive child becomes an aggressive adult who batters his or her spouse and speeds on the highway. Researchers have found that two factors can protect against a lifelong pattern of aggression. The first factor is a stable marriage. When an adult who is at risk of becoming a criminal is fortunate enough to find and marry the "right" person—one who is socially positive and not aggressive—he or she is less likely to commit a crime, engage in violence, or divorce (Rutter, 1989; Sampson & Laub, 2003). Adults whose partners are involved in deviant or criminal activity, in contrast, are likely to engage in criminal activity and become more poorly adjusted (Giordano et al., 2003; Ronka et al., 2001). The second factor that disrupts an aggressive trajectory is employment. Having a steady job lowers the likelihood of violent criminal activity in adulthood; it helps to lift people out of poverty, makes it less likely that they will associate with deviant peers, and enhances their self-responsibility (Sampson & Laub, 2003).

Causes of Aggression

What makes some children more aggressive and starts them on an aggressive trajectory? Factors in several domains—biological, environmental, sociocultural, and sociocognitive—influence development in a transactional, interactive process. Figure 12.2 presents a model of aggression that can serve as a guide for understanding these causes.

Biological Origins of Aggressive Behavior

GENETICS AND AGGRESSION   Interest in the genetic roots of aggression is enormous, and researchers discover new facts every year. Researchers in one study found that mothers' ratings of their 18-month-olds' physical aggression were more similar for identical twins than nonidentical twins—suggesting a genetic predisposition is involved (Dionne et al., 2003). Studies of adolescents also produced evidence of genetic involvement. Responding to a questionnaire that contained such items as "Some people think that I have a violent temper," identical twins rated themselves more similarly than did nonidentical twins (Gottesman & Goldsmith, 1994). Researchers in the Netherlands, Sweden, and Britain have obtained similar results (Eley et al., 1999; Van Den Oord et al., 1996). In a Canadian study of twins the heritability for social aggression was about 20 percent; for physical aggression, it was 50 percent (Brendgen et al., 2005). A meta-analysis of 42 twin studies and 10 adoption studies revealed a moderate association (effect size = .41) between genetics and antisocial behavior (Rhee & Waldman, 2002). The antisocial behavior of early starters is more heritable than that of late starters (Moffitt, 2006).

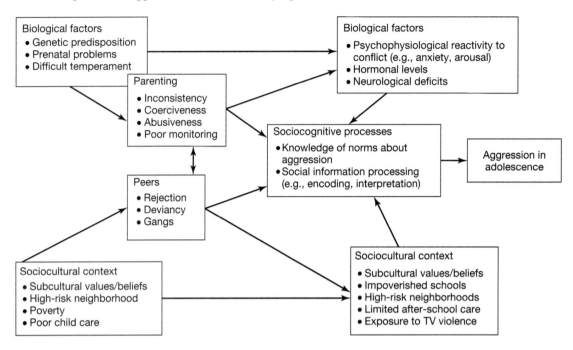

FIGURE 12.2 *A biopsychological model of the transactional development of aggression, starting with the earliest age on the left side of the figure and ending with adolescent aggression on the right side. Source: Copyright © 2010 by the American Psychological Association. Reproduced with permission. Dodge, K. A., & Pettit, G. S. (2003). A biopsychosocial model of the development of chronic conduct problems in adolescence.* Developmental Psychology, 39, *349–371. The use of APA information does not imply endorsement by APA.*

Learning from Living Leaders:
Terrie E. Moffitt

Source: Courtesy of Terrie E. Moffitt.

Terrie Moffitt is a citizen of the United Kingdom and the United States and holds positions in both countries: She is Professor of Social Behavior and Development at King's College London and Professor of Psychology, Psychiatry and Neuroscience at Duke University. When she was in college, she wanted to major in English literature, but she chose psychology because her best grades were in her psych courses. She went on to graduate school in psychology and received her Ph.D. in clinical psychology from the University of Southern California. In graduate school, she learned about the power of the longitudinal research design, and that design led her to an interest in tracking social development (or more accurately, antisocial development) over time. In 1987, she met Avshalom Caspi at a conference, and in 1990, they became partners in research and in life. Two questions have been at the center of their research: What happens to children who have behavior problems when they grow up? How do nature and nurture work together to influence children's behavioral outcomes? Moffitt and Caspi followed a sample of children in New Zealand from birth to adulthood and are following another sample in England. By observing children across time, they have detected differences in patterns of antisocial behavior related to gender and to the age at which the children first exhibit antisocial behavior. Early starters are more likely than late starters to become serious offenders in adulthood. In 2007, Moffitt received the Stockholm Prize in Criminology, and in 2008, the International Society for the Study of Behavioural Development presented her its Distinguished Scientific Contribution Award. Moffitt believes that the most pressing need in this area of research is to prevent psychiatric disorders in adulthood by intervening when children first display problem behavior. In the future, she predicts, more psychologists will use neuroimaging and molecular genetics to study social development because they are the newest tools in the field. Her message for undergraduate students is a very positive one: "The life of a behavioural scientist is a wonderful life, full of questions that are important to everyone, always stimulating, never boring."

Further Reading

Moffitt, T. E., & Caspi, A. (2007). Evidence from behavioral genetics for environmental contributions to antisocial conduct. In J. Grusec & P. Hastings (Eds.), *Handbook of socialization* (pp. 96–123). New York: Guilford Press.

An early temperament characterized by anger and irritability increases the likelihood a child will be aggressive. Source: *Leigh Schindler/ iStockphoto.*

TEMPERAMENT AND AGGRESSION   One way that genes start a child on a path to aggression is evident soon after birth when parents discover that their infant's temperament is irritable, irregular, and difficult. One study found that infants with these temperament traits in the first year of life were more hostile when they were 3 years old (Bates, 1987). According to another study, two thirds of the children who were rated as noncompliant, overactive, and ill tempered at age 3 had externalizing behavior problems, including physical aggression, when they were 9 years old (Campbell, 2000). Impulsivity also predicts aggressiveness (Raine et al., 1998; Tremblay et al., 1994). Another study found that young children who lacked self-control were more likely to become aggressive at an early age and to remain so (Moffitt & Caspi, 2001). Similarly, children with less inhibited temperaments in preschool scored higher on a combined measure of physical and relational aggression in elementary school (Park et al., 2005). Another temperament quality linked to aggression is fearfulness. Fearful toddlers were more likely to persist in aggressiveness through age 8 compared with less fearful toddlers (Shaw et al., 2003). In brief, aggressiveness is more likely if children have difficult, ill-tempered, impulsive, or fearful temperaments.

MY BRAIN MADE ME DO IT: THE NEUROLOGICAL BASIS OF AGGRESSION   Links have been found between aggression and neurotransmitters—chemicals in the body that facilitate or inhibit the transmission of neural impulses within the central nervous system (CNS) (Moeller, 2001). **Serotonin** is one neurotransmitter that is involved in regulating the activity of the endocrine glands. It affects attention and emotional states and may be involved in aggression in both animals and humans (Herbert & Martinez, 2001). Studies with rats and rhesus monkeys have shown that deficits in CNS serotonin are linked to heightened levels of severe aggression (Ferrari et al., 2005; Suomi, 2003). Men and women with poor impulse control and high rates of criminality, explosive aggression, and impulsive violence, also have low CNS serotonin (Linnoila & Virkkunen, 1992; Virkkunen et al., 1994). The monoamine oxidase

serotonin
Neurotransmitter that regulates endocrine glands, alters attention and emotions, and is linked to aggression.

A (*MAOA*) gene, which regulates levels of serotonin, is linked with reduced volume in the prefrontal cortex and the amygdala, brain structures associated with antisocial behavior (Raine, 2008). The link between serotonin and aggression has not been as clear in research with children, but some studies suggest that children with low levels of serotonin have higher levels of physical aggression (Halperin et al., 2006; Kruesi et al., 1992; Mitsis et al., 2000).

BLAME IT ON MY HORMONES   Testosterone is the major hormone that has been linked to aggression in nonhuman animals, and the links are evident, although less dramatic, among human adolescents as well (Book et al., 2001; Moeller, 2001). Researchers in the United States observed that adolescent violent offenders have higher levels of testosterone than nonviolent offenders (Brooks & Reddon, 1996). Researchers in Sweden, similarly, found that 15- to 17-year-old boys whose blood contained higher levels of testosterone were more impatient and irritable and this impatience, in turn, increased the boys' readiness to engage in unprovoked and destructive aggressive behavior (Olweus et al., 1988). This study suggested that testosterone has an *indirect* effect on aggression; it leads to irritability, and irritability increases aggressive behavior. Another study that demonstrated an indirect effect of testosterone on aggression was conducted in Canada. Its researchers found that testosterone was related to larger body mass and this, in turn, was linked to increased physical aggression (Tremblay et al., 1998). Perhaps the most convincing evidence that testosterone is related to aggression comes from an experimental study in which adolescents who were deficient in testosterone received doses of the hormone (Finkelstein et al., 1997). Increases in physical aggression and aggressive impulses resulted. Even when the researchers controlled for such factors as the child's temperament and the parents' child-rearing practices, hormonal effects were evident. Hormones affect aggression in girls as well as boys. In one study, researchers discovered that increases in girls' estradiol (a form of estrogen) during puberty were positively linked with expressions of anger and aggression in interactions with parents (Inoff-Germain et al., 1988), and in a meta-analysis, researchers confirmed that testosterone was linked with aggression in both boys and girls (Book et al., 2001).

The link between testosterone and aggression is not a one-way street, though. Although increasing testosterone levels increases children's aggression, the reverse is also true. Dominance in conflict leads to a rise in testosterone levels. For example, winners of judo or coin-tossing contests have been observed to have elevated levels of testosterone after they win whereas losers show no change in testosterone level (Dodge, Coie, et al., 2006; McCaul et al., 1992).

PRENATAL CONDITIONS   Conditions in the prenatal environment that lead to physical problems in the child can also increase the likelihood of later antisocial behavior. Most notably, smoking by women who are pregnant lowers their babies' birth weight and doubles the risk that the children will later exhibit antisocial, aggressive behavior (Fergusson et al., 1998; Weissman et al., 1999). Children are also more aggressive if they were exposed to cocaine prenatally (Bendersky et al., 2006).

Social Influences on the Development of Aggression

The likelihood that children will develop patterns of aggressive behavior also depends on the environment. In the meta-analysis of 42 twin studies and 10 adoption studies mentioned earlier (Rhee & Waldman, 2002), the researchers found significant associations between antisocial behavior and children's environments as well as their genes. In this section, we explore how family, peers, neighborhoods, culture, and mass media are related to the development of aggression.

PARENTS AS INTERACTIVE PARTNERS   The family provides the first opportunities for children to learn how to act either aggressively or peacefully. These opportunities begin in infancy. Children are less likely to become aggressive if they establish secure relationships with their parents in their first year. If they develop insecure, especially disorganized, attachments, they are more likely to have aggressive behavior problems when they are 5 to 7 years old (Lyons-Ruth, 1996; Lyons-Ruth & Jacobvitz, 2008; Moss et al., 2006). This is especially true if the family has problems, for example, is poor or the mother is a single parent and the level of family stress is high (Dodge, Coie, et al., 2006; Shaw et al., 1995).

After infancy, if the parents are critical and negative or controlling and limiting of the child's autonomy the child is more likely to exhibit physical and relational aggression (Deater-Deckard, 2000; Moffitt et al., 2006; Sandstrom, 2007); if the parents are warm and support-ive children are less likely to be aggressive (Hart et al., 1998; Joussemet et al., 2008; Nelson et al., 2006). A controlling parental style also contributes to a stable aggressive pattern over time (Joussemet et al., 2008). The reason for this connection between parenting style and child aggression may be that aggressive children imitate their parents' negative behavior (Bandura, 1989) or that the parents' negative emotional expression and limits on autonomy interfere with the children's ability to regulate their own emotions, which, in turn, leads to more aggressive behavior (Eisenberg, Gershoff, et al., 2001; Grolnick, 2003).

Parents who are punitive in the way they discipline their children also have negative results (Straus, 2005). In spite of bumper stickers reminding them that "Children are not for hitting," many parents—94 percent of parents of 3- to 4-year-olds, according to one estimate—spank their children (Straus & Stewart, 1999). As we suggested in Chapter 7, "Family," mild or judi-cious spanking is not a problem, but severe and unremitting physical punishment is associated with increases in aggression (Larzelere & Kuhn, 2005). The impact of physical punishment on children's aggressiveness also depends on the quality of the parent-child relationship. Physical punishment is especially likely to lead to aggressive behavior when the parent-child relation-ship lacks warmth (Deater-Deckard & Dodge, 1997) or when the use of this tactic is unusual in the culture (Lansford et al., 2005).

ABUSIVE PARENTING AND AGGRESSION   Abusive parenting increases children's aggression and other antisocial behavior (Dodge, Coie, et al., 2006; Luntz & Widom 1994). Preschool children who are physically maltreated are more aggressive in kindergarten and display more physical violence in late adolescence (Lansford et al., 2002). Even after consid-ering genetic transmission, researchers have found that the link between physical abuse and aggressiveness is significant. In a British study of more than 1,000 pairs of twins, researchers found that although genetic factors accounted for approximately two thirds of the variation in children's antisocial behavior at age 7, the effect of physical maltreatment was still significant after they controlled for this genetic effect (Jaffee et al., 2004). In addition, genetic factors did not account for significant variation in children's experience of physical maltreatment, which reduces the possibility that heritable characteristics of the child provoked the abuse. Some researchers have suggested that abuse interferes with children's development of empathy and perhaps their ability to correctly "read" other people's emotions (Pollak & Tolley-Schell, 2003); these deficits could lead to increased aggression (Main & George, 1985; Manly et al., 1994). It is likely that abuse has both direct and indirect effects on children's aggression.

A COERCION MODEL OF AGGRESSION   Gerald Patterson and his colleagues at the Social Learning Center in Eugene, Oregon, have been studying the effects of family environ-ments on the development of aggression in children since the 1970s. They have found that parents and children inadvertently "train" each other by means of cycles of mutually coercive behavior (Dishion & Patterson, 2006; Patterson, 1982, 2002; Snyder et al., 2003). First, par-ents interfere with children's ongoing activity; they turn off the TV or scold the children for not finishing homework. Second, the children respond by complaining, whining, and pro-testing; they counterattack and defy the parents. Third, the parents give in to the children's complaints and stop scolding and demanding. From the children's viewpoint, this represents a small "victory" because their counteroffensive worked. Therefore, in the fourth turn of the cycle, children stop their defiance and noncompliance. This works the first time around, but later, when parents try to discipline the children again, the children again engage in counter-offensive behavior and with each subsequent "battle" their behavior becomes increasingly aggressive. The children have learned that coercive (and ultimately aggressive) behavior helps them control their parents; the parents have learned that to get their children to do what they want them to do, they have to exert firmer and firmer control.

These coercive cycles expand to include siblings as well. Children learn that the coercive behaviors that help them control their parents' behavior also work with their siblings. When brothers or sisters engage in coercive exchanges, especially if the older sibling is already aggressive, the younger sibling is likely to become aggressive too (Slomkowski et al., 2001). A combination of sibling conflict and rejection by parents is an especially potent recipe for fostering the development of conduct problems (Garcia et al., 2000). These patterns of coercive behavior can continue across generations as children on the receiving end of coercive parenting repeat this style of discipline with their own children and increase the children's aggression (Scaramella & Conger, 2003). Fortunately, cross-generational continuity is not inevitable. When children are less emotionally reactive, no link across generations is observed (Scaramella & Conger, 2003; see Figure 7.3 in Chapter 7, "Family").

PARENTS AS PROVIDERS OF OPPORTUNITIES FOR AGGRESSION   Parents also shape their children's aggressive development through their management of the children's activities. Some parents can accurately report what their children are doing and with whom at all hours of the day and night; other parents don't know if their children are hanging out on a street corner, playing hooky, doing homework, or attending a school dance. The failure of these parents to monitor their children's whereabouts, activities, and social contacts can increase the children's aggressive behavior (Patterson & Stouthamer-Loeber, 1984). By the time they go to middle school, children whose parents are not closely monitoring them are more likely to develop aggressive behavior patterns; they exhibit higher rates of delinquency, engage in more theft and vandalism, and have poorer relations with peers and teachers (Pettit et al., 2001; Snyder et al., 2003).

Parental monitoring is more likely and adolescents' antisocial behavior less likely when parents and adolescents spend time together and have an enjoyable relationship and when the adolescent views monitoring as appropriate (Laird, Pettit, Dodge, et al., 2003). Parents who act as gatekeepers can keep their children away from harmful influences that increase their aggression (O'Neil et al., 2001). In brief, children are more likely to develop aggressive patterns of behavior if their parents are unaware of their activities and make no effort to prevent negative experiences.

THE INFLUENCE OF PEERS   Children can also learn aggressive behavior patterns from their peers. When early-starter aggressive children enter school, two things are likely to happen: Their peers reject them, and they experience academic failure. Both of these disappointments lead children to behave more aggressively (Buhs & Ladd, 2001; Ladd et al., 1999). Peer rejection is a painful and unwelcome experience for children, and those who are rejected become more aggressive over time (Dodge et al., 2003; Snyder et al., 2008). In turn, this aggressiveness leads to more rejection in a vicious cycle of rejection and aggression that continues through childhood.

In adolescence, children learn aggressive behavior patterns from their peers by hanging out with pals who pick on other kids or break the law. If the peer group supports relational **deviancy training** aggression, adolescents become increasingly mean in this way (Werner & Hill, 2010); if the Amplification of peer group supports delinquent activity, adolescents become more delinquent (Coie, 2004). aggression that occurs Aggressive youth seek each other out and amplify each other's deviance. They train each other when adolescents are in antisocial behavior and foster positive attitudes toward delinquency (Dishion et al., 2001). In with and learn from this so-called **deviancy training**, adolescents talk about, rehearse, and plan negative activities, aggressive peers.

usually with lots of positive feedback from each other (Dodge, Dishion, et al., 2006; Snyder et al., 2008). Aggressive peers increase adolescents' antisocial aggressive conduct both by modeling deviant actions and by providing opportunities for disruptive, aggressive behavior. Researchers in one study found that friends who engaged in disruptive behavior, such as disobedience or truancy, were more likely to engage in delinquent behavior, both at the time and a year later (Keenan et al., 1995). Their delinquent behavior included both overt aggression, such as fighting, and covert aggression, such as stealing. The most extreme deviancy training occurs when adolescents are members of a gang. Teenagers in gangs are three times more likely to engage in violent offenses than adolescents who are not gang members (Spergel et al., 1989). Joining a gang increases children's illegal and violent activity; dropping out of the gang reduces the frequency of these activities (Thornberry et al., 2003; Zimring, 1998).

NEIGHBORHOODS AS BREEDING GROUNDS   Children can also pick up aggressive behavior in their neighborhood. Adults living in neighborhoods with high levels of poverty and unemployment tend to be more aggressive (Beyers et al., 2003). They direct this aggression toward each other and toward the children. Mothers in these neighborhoods are likely to use coercive and punitive parenting techniques (Guerra et al., 1995; McLoyd et al., 2006), which, in turn, lead their children to behave more aggressively and become involved in gangs (Tolan et al., 2003).

Exposure to violence in the neighborhood distresses children, especially young children, and increases their aggressive tendencies. Researchers have observed a consistent link between neighborhood violence and children's aggression. Low-income urban African American children who are exposed to more neighborhood violence have more externalizing problems including aggression and, later, violence (Farver et al., 2005; Jones et al., 2005; Kliewer et al., 2004; Osofsky et al., 2004; Ozer, 2005) and are more likely to belong to gangs than children who are exposed to less neighborhood violence (Howell & Egley, 2005). Children from dangerous neighborhoods are also more likely to be bullies than children from safe neighborhoods (Espelage et al., 2000).

In a large-scale study of nearly 1,000 adolescents living in 78 Chicago neighborhoods, researchers found a link between exposure to firearm violence and subsequent aggressive behavior (Bingenheimer et al., 2005). Adolescents who were exposed to firearm violence within the last year—that is, who had been shot at or had seen someone else shot at—were twice as likely to engage in violent activities such as attacking someone with a weapon, shooting someone, or being in a gang fight in which someone was hurt as were adolescents who were not exposed to gun violence. These investigators carefully controlled for other factors that might have contributed to adolescents' aggression including growing up in a single-parent family, spending more time with deviant peers, and living in a dangerous neighborhood, yet they still found a link between aggression and exposure to gun violence. Even more surprising, repeated exposure to gun violence wasn't necessary to have an effect on adolescent aggression; a single exposure was enough. Thus, neighborhoods can be both effective and efficient breeding grounds for violence.

CULTURE AS A DETERMINANT OF AGGRESSION   The frequency of aggression varies around the world; it is common in some societies and virtually nonexistent in others (Bergeron & Schneider, 2005). Rates of death by homicide illustrate this variation, ranging from 1.0 per 100,000 people in Norway to 1.4 in Canada, 7.6 in the United States, and 25.8 in Brazil (World Health Organization, 1999). Anthropologists have identified peaceful and violent cultures: The Semai and Chewong of Malaysia, the Buid of the Philippines, certain Inuit societies in Canada, and some Zapotec communities in Mexico have very low levels of aggression among children and adults (Howell & Willis, 1989; Sponsel & Gregor, 1994). In contrast, among the Waorani and Jivaro of Ecuador and the Mae Enga of the New Guinea highlands, homicide, warfare, blood feuds, physical punishment of children, infanticide, and head-taking raids are common (Robarchek & Robarchek, 1998). In a comparison of 28 different cultures, researchers found that those focused on individualism, ambition, and success, such as the United States, Australia, and Greece, had more child and adolescent aggression than collectivist cultures with their focus on group solidarity, such as Taiwan, Thailand, and Indonesia (Bergeron & Schneider, 2005). Societies that placed a high value on hierarchy, status, and power also had higher levels of aggression than cultures in which members cooperated voluntarily and had a high level of egalitarian commitment. Clearly cultural values and practices play a role in fostering or minimizing aggression.

Insights from Extremes: Child Soldiers

More than 250,000 children around the world are child soldiers, and the number increases every day. Thousands of children are being recruited and trained as armed soldiers in civil wars in countries from Chad and Colombia to Sri Lanka and Somalia (see map). According to the Child Soldiers Global Report 2008 (Coalition to Stop the Use of Child Soldiers, 2008), 21 territories around the globe engaged children in conflicts between 2004 and 2007. Government armed forces in Angola, Burundi, Congo, Rwanda, Sudan, and Uganda recruited children as young as 7 and 8 years of age; in Sierra Leone, rebel forces recruited children as young as 5 years old. Governments and armed groups use children because they are a cheap and plentiful resource and easier to condition into fearless killing and unthinking obedience than adolescents and adults (Amnesty International, 2000). The children's underdeveloped ability to assess danger makes them more willing to take risks that teenagers and adults refuse. They are more impressionable, and their value systems and consciences are not yet fully developed. Many of these children are abducted or kidnapped by the armed groups. Often they are forced to watch the soldiers kill their parents. The young recruits are then forced to march to training camps. Those who can't carry their loads or keep pace with the others are killed. Those who attempt escape are severely punished. Girls are routinely raped. In the training camps, children go through brutal indoctrination to transform them into combat soldiers and cold-blooded killers. They are exposed to violence, torture, mutilation, and rape. New recruits are often forced to kill or perpetrate acts of violence against others, even members of their own village or family. Some groups also practice cannibalism, making young recruits drink the blood or eat the flesh of their victims. The recruits are often told "it will make you stronger," but the real motivation is to

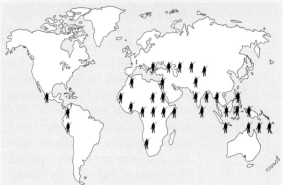

Source: © AP/Wide World Photos.

"force children to quiet their emotional reactions to seeing people killed and demolish their sense of the sanctity of life" (Wessells, 2006). Drugs such as brown-brown (cocaine mixed with gun powder) help disengage the child's actions from any sense of reality. Children who refuse to take the drugs are beaten or killed (Amnesty International, 2000). Revenge is also used as a motivator. Children are told to "visualize the enemy, the rebels who killed your parents, your family, and those who are responsible for everything that has happened to you" (Beah, 2007). Initially most children experience a mixture of disgust, guilt, and self-contempt (Wessells, 2006). But as time goes on, they are likely to rationalize their actions by telling themselves, "I didn't want to do it. I had to follow orders or I would be killed," or they see their acts as surreal, as if in a dream.

By tracing what happens to children who go through this dehumanizing experience we gain a better understanding of the impact of brutality and a keener appreciation of children's resilience and capacity to overcome adversity (Cicchetti & Toth, 2006; Masten, 2006). Several studies have tracked the fate of child soldiers. In one, 39 boys in Mozambique, who had been forced to become soldiers but then had been rescued, were examined to assess their readjustment to normal life (Boothby, 2006). The length of time in the base camp was a major determinant of how well they adapted. Those who spent less than 6 months in the camp tended to define themselves as victims rather than soldiers. Although they were aggressive and distrustful, they showed feelings of remorse and experienced rapid decreases in antisocial behavior after their rescue. In contrast, children who were in the camp for a longer period had crossed some type of identity

threshold; they identified with their captors and viewed themselves as members of the National Resistance Movement. After they were rescued, however, even these boys gradually experienced remorse and control over their aggression and formed positive attachments to their new adult caregivers. Only three boys continued to exhibit hostility and a desire for revenge. For them, the struggle to leave an environment in which killing was encouraged and reenter one in which killing was condemned was too difficult. However, the successful reentry and adjustment of the other child soldiers illustrates the amazing capacity of children to recover—with the social support of caring adults and communities—even after exposure to a life of violence and inhumanity. Our current theories of risk and resilience have been supported by these insights from extremes (Luthar, 2003; Masten, 2006). Today, aid organizations and international governmental organizations such as UNICEF recognize that children who have been soldiers need more than physical help to recover from their experiences. They need healing from emotional difficulties and traumatic experiences, protection from re-recruitment, training in peaceful roles, careful reintroduction into their communities, and opportunities to build trust and practice nonviolent conflict resolution.

VIOLENCE IN THE ELECTRONIC MEDIA   Children are bombarded by violent images as they view movies, watch television, play video games, and surf the Internet. It has been estimated that by the end of elementary school, the average U.S. child has seen more than 8,000 murders and 100,000 other violent acts on network television (Bushman & Anderson, 2001). Nor is media fare limited to physical violence; nearly all Disney movies and 77 percent of television programs contain portrayals of relational aggression (Coyne & Whitehead, 2008; Linder & Gentile, 2009).

There is little doubt that exposure to TV violence increases children's aggressive behavior (Comstock & Scharrer, 2006). Both experimental and correlational studies document this link. In one correlational study in northern New York state, for example, television viewing and aggressive behavior were assessed in a sample of 707 families over a 17-year period (Johnson et al., 2002). Adolescents who spent more time watching television were more aggressive in subsequent years—even after researchers controlled for their earlier aggressive behavior, family disadvantage, and neighborhood violence. Overall, research suggests that television violence accounts for about 10 percent of the variance in children's aggression (Dodge, Coie, et al., 2006)—an effect that is about the same size as cigarette smoking on lung cancer. TV and film violence has a particularly strong effect on children who are already aggressive (Bushman, 1995; Leyens et al., 1975). Just as TV violence is linked to children's physical aggression, exposure to relational aggression on television, especially if it is rewarded, is linked to increased relational aggression (Linder & Gentile, 2009). Childhood viewing of TV violence has long-term effects as well as immediate ones. When children were retested as adults in their early 20s, those who had watched a great many violent television programs in early elementary school were more aggressive than infrequent viewers of violence (Huesmann et al., 2003). They displayed more physical aggression, more verbal aggression, and had more traffic violations and arrests.

Exposure to TV violence affects children more if they believe it portrays real events. Children who were told that a violent film clip was real (a newsreel of an actual riot) later reacted more aggressively than children who believed that the film was a Hollywood production (Atkin, 1983). As children develop and are able to make the fiction-reality distinction, TV violence has less effect on their aggressive behavior (Bushman & Huesmann, 2001).

Video games and computer games offer children images of violence and the opportunity to act aggressively in a virtual world. It has been suggested that these games, too, can increase children's aggressiveness (Anderson et al., 2007). The results of one survey indicated that young adolescents who played violent video games reported more frequent aggressive behavior, such as arguing with their teachers and getting involved in physical fights (Gentile et al., 2004). This was true for both adolescents whose usual level of aggression was high and those who were not usually aggressive. Moreover, these links between violent video games and aggression are evident across time and culture. Children and adolescents in both the United States and Japan who habitually played violent video games were more aggressive 3 to 6 months later, even after controlling for their earlier level of aggression (Anderson et al., 2008). Experimental studies confirm these correlational results: Children who played video games with aggressive themes in an experiment acted more aggressively in free play and when faced with frustration than did children who played games with nonaggressive themes (Irwin & Gross, 1995). In a meta-analysis of studies in this area, researchers found that the link between violent game play and aggressive behavior was small but meaningful; effect size = .19 (Anderson & Bushman, 2001). Although boys reported that they liked violent video games more than girls did, the effect of exposure was similar for both sexes. The Internet is another source of violent images. YouTube, for example, offers provocative and disturbing videos of young people fighting; more than 30,000 videos of "kids fighting" and 75,000 of "girls fighting" are only a click away.

We are just beginning to understand the neurological underpinnings of exposure to media violence. Neuroimaging studies using functional magnetic resonance imaging (fMRI) techniques show that some regions of the brain (such as the prefrontal cortex) are less activated when children are exposed to violent video games (Wang et al., 2009; Weber et al., 2006) and to violent scenes in movies compared with nonviolent scenes (Murray et al., 2006). This brain region is related to lessened activation of neural mechanisms associated with self-control, which may, in part, explain why exposure to violence increases aggression.

Combined Biological and Social Influences on Aggression

To understand the development of aggression, all these factors must be considered together: genetic and other biological predispositions toward anger; disciplinary harshness, coercive interactions, and physical abuse in the family; association with deviant peers; living in a dangerous neighborhood; and exposure to media violence. Any one of these factors can push a child toward aggressive behavior; experiencing a multitude of them almost certainly ensures an aggressive outcome as these factors pile up and pile on the child.

Researchers have investigated the effects of combinations of these factors. They have studied the combined effects of genes and environments. A study of 6,000 Dutch families with adopted children showed the cumulative effect of genes and environment clearly (Mednick & Christiansen, 1977). Of children who had *both* an adoptive parent and a biological parent who were convicted of a criminal offense, 25 percent were themselves convicted of an offense; of children who had only a biological parent who was a convicted criminal, 20 percent were convicted; among children with only an adoptive parent who had a criminal record, 15 percent were convicted; and of children with neither an adoptive parent nor a biological parent who had a criminal record, only 14 percent were convicted. Results of a study in Sweden were similar but even more striking, probably because it included only boys (Cloninger et al., 1982):

If both biological and adoptive parents were criminals, 40 percent of the adopted boys engaged in a criminal act; if only the biological parent was a criminal, only 12 percent did; if only the adoptive parent was a criminal, only 7 percent did; and if neither parent was a criminal, a mere 3 percent of adopted boys engaged in criminal acts. Another way researchers have demonstrated the combined effects of genes and environments is by showing that when children experience adverse events at home, those who are genetically at risk for antisocial behavior are more likely to become aggressive than those who are not genetically at risk (Dodge, Coie, et al., 2006). One study of twins found that physical abuse by parents increased the chance that a child would have a conduct disorder by 24 percent if his or her twin had a conduct disorder but by only by 2 percent if the twin did not (Jaffee et al., 2005). Clearly, when adverse environmental conditions team up with genetic factors, aggressive outcomes are more likely. (To see an illustration of the combined effect of genes and environment in one man's lifestory, go to http://www.zotzine. uci.edu/2010_03/fallon.php.)

Researchers also have studied how adverse environments exacerbate aggressiveness in children who begin life with biological problems linked to aggression. They have found that a difficult, ill-tempered, or impulsive early temperament is more likely to predict later aggression when conditions in the environment support aggressive behavior. For example, impulsive boys who grew up in poor neighborhoods were more likely to become violent offenders than impulsive boys who lived in more affluent neighborhoods (Lyman et al., 2000). They have found that environmental conditions interact with neurotransmitters. For example, in one longitudinal study, children who had both low levels of serotonin and a history of family conflict developed into the most violent offenders by age 21 (Moffitt et al., 1997). Researchers also have found that prenatal biological problems interact with postnatal environmental conditions (Raine, 2002). For example, in a study in Finland, the children of mothers who smoked before they were born (prenatal problem) *and* who grew up without a father (environmental problem) exhibited violent behavior 12 times more than did children without these problems (Rasanen et al., 1999). In a study in Denmark, researchers found that children were twice as likely to have a record of violent offenses at age 19 if they experienced complications before birth *and* maternal rejection after birth (Raine et al., 1994, 1997). A study in Australia indicated that the most aggressive adolescents at age 15 had been exposed to both biological risks—such as maternal illness, low birth weight, or a difficult temperament—*and* environmental risks—for example, poverty, maternal rejection, or harsh discipline (Brennan et al., 2003). Biological and environmental conditions clearly combined to produce antisocial outcomes in this study. This was especially true for physical aggression that started early and continued through adolescence: Two thirds of the early starters had experienced combined biological and environmental adversity.

Researchers have also studied how combinations of different environmental factors operate in concert to increase children's aggressiveness. In one series of studies, researchers found that aggressive adolescents were likely to have experienced punitive discipline in early childhood, negative peer interactions in middle childhood, and association with deviant peers in late childhood (see Figure 12.3; Patterson et al., 1989).

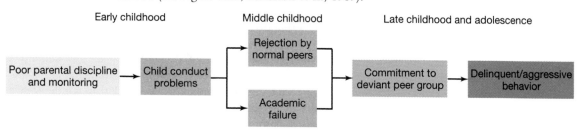

FIGURE 12.3 *Developmental progression of aggressive behavior. Parents and peers both play a part in the development of children's antisocial behavior but at different points in time. Source: Patterson, G. R., DeBarshyshe, B., & Ramsey, R. (1989). A developmental perspective on antisocial behavior.* American Psychologist, 44, *329–335. Copyright © 2010 by the American Psychological Association. Reproduced with permission. The use of APA information does not imply endorsement by APA.*

In another study, researchers found that adolescents who lived in poor neighborhoods and were involved with antisocial peers at age 15 were more likely to be violent at age 18 (Herrenkohl et al., 2003). Researchers have also shown that children who have at least one good thing going for them can be protected from a spiral into aggression. For example, adolescents who lived in poor neighborhoods were less likely to be affected by exposure to community violence if they had positive relationships with their parents (Kliewer et al., 2004; Ozer, 2005). Aggressive children were less likely to be violent at age 18 if their parents monitored their activities and they attended religious services at age 15 (Herrenkohl et al., 2003). Even physically abused children were less likely to be violent if they were involved in a religious community and had parents and peers who disapproved of antisocial behavior (Herrenkohl et al., 2005). The more of these "protective factors" children experienced, the less likely they were to be aggressive (Herrenkohl et al., 2003). In brief, the development of either high or low levels of aggression is best accounted for by multiple influences across a range of domains, not by single factors or single domains.

Research up Close:
Genes, Environmental Triggers, and Aggressive Behavior

Researchers Avshalom Caspi, Terrie Moffitt, and their collaborators have documented how genes and environments work together to increase the likelihood that children will be aggressive (Caspi et al., 2002). Unlike earlier studies using parents' histories of violence as a proxy for children's genetic propensity for aggression, their study involved a specific "candidate gene" thought to be related to aggression—the monoamine oxidase A (*MAOA*) gene. This gene encodes the *MAOA* enzyme, which metabolizes neurotransmitters such as norepinephrine, serotonin, and dopamine, rendering them inactive. Genetic deficiencies in *MAOA* activity have been linked to aggression in both animals and humans. Caspi and Moffitt expected that low *MAOA* activity—insufficient to temper the neurotransmitters associated with aggression—would predispose a person to developing a high level of violent behavior.

Because they knew that genes don't act on their own, Caspi and Moffitt looked for environmental conditions that might lead to expression of this genetic predisposition, and they chose child abuse as a likely trigger. They knew that children who are physically abused are at risk for developing aggressive and antisocial behaviors (Rutter et al., 1998; Keiley et al., 2001) but that only half of them do so (Widom, 1989). Caspi and Moffitt reasoned that being reared under abusive circumstances would be more likely to result in aggressive tendencies if the children were also genetically programmed for aggression. They then tested whether the *MAOA* gene

was a genetic factor that made abused children more prone to exhibit violent behavior.

Using a sample of 442 boys from their longitudinal study in New Zealand, Caspi and Moffitt compared the boys who had been physically abused by a family member with those who had not. They included only boys in the study because the *MAOA* gene is X-linked and therefore its effect would be more evident in boys than girls. To identify boys with violent behavior, the researchers measured four outcomes: conduct disorders assessed according to criteria of the *Diagnostic and Statistical Manual of Mental Disorders* (*DSM-IV*); convictions for violent crimes identified by the police; a personality disposition toward violence measured by a psychological test; and symptoms of antisocial personality disorder identified by people who knew the boys well. Of the boys who had both a history of childhood maltreatment and the gene for low *MAOA*, 85 percent displayed a pattern of aggressive-antisocial behavior in adolescence and early adulthood. Only 20 percent of the boys who had low *MAOA* and did not experience abuse displayed this pattern of antisocial behavior (Figure 12.4). Caspi and Moffitt's finding has been confirmed in several other studies demonstrating the combined effects of the *MAOA* gene and childhood adversity (Foley et al., 2004; Kim-Cohen et al., 2006). Similarly, researchers have found that youth with a gene that increases susceptibility to alcohol dependence are more likely to develop externalizing behavior problems if their parents also fail to monitor their activities (Dick et al., 2009).

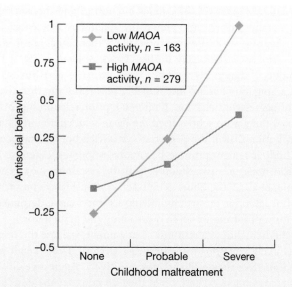

FIGURE 12.4 *Antisocial behavior as a function of genes and environment. Children who were most aggressive had the gene for low MAOA activity and experienced severe maltreatment. Source: From Caspi, A., McClay, J., Moffitt, T. E., Mill, J., Martin, J., Craig, I. W., Taylor, A., & Poulton, R. (2002). Role of genotype in the cycle of violence in maltreated children. Science, 297, 851–854. Reprinted with permission from AAAS.*

Sociocognitive Factors in the Development of Aggression

Genes, hormones, parents, peers, neighborhoods, and media all contribute to the development of aggression, but the final component involves children's cognitive processes. Cognitive encoding, interpretation, and understanding guide children's social behavior and affect decision making in potentially aggressive situations. To illustrate, consider the reactions of two different children to the same encounter in the school lunchroom. A classmate spills milk on Harry's new tennis shoes. Harry realizes it was an accident, accepts his classmate's apology, and jokes about the incident—"Got milk?!" When a classmate spills milk on Jerome's new tennis shoes, in contrast, Jerome jumps to the conclusion that his classmate did it on purpose; he turns around, gives the boy a shove, and knocks the boy's lunch tray on the floor. Clearly, Harry and Jerome see the world through different lenses. Harry views his social environment as friendly and benign where sometimes "stuff happens." Jerome sees the world as a hostile place where other people purposely do mean and hurtful things. These two profiles characterize the cognitive outlooks of nonaggressive and aggressive children.

Social information-processing theory is a useful framework for examining these two different outlooks (see Figure 1.3 in Chapter 1, "Introduction"; Crick & Dodge, 1994; Dodge, 1986; Dodge & Pettit, 2003; Gifford-Smith & Rabiner, 2004). According to this theory, children come to a social situation with a set of neural capabilities that have been honed over time and are represented in memory. When the children are presented with a new set of social cues, for example, someone spilling milk on their shoes, their response depends on how they process these cues.

First, they encode the cues. Aggressive children do not notice the full range of cues because of their poor attentional and encoding skills; they attend selectively to aggressive cues. For example, children who have been physically abused attend more to angry threatening faces than to happy faces (Pollak & Tolley-Schell, 2003). In the case of Harry and Jerome, Harry notices his classmate's stricken face as well as the milk spilled on his shoes whereas Jerome doesn't notice the classmate's expression but focuses his attention solely on his damaged shoes.

Second, children interpret the cues as intentional and threatening or accidental and harmless. In our example, Harry interpreted the spilling as accidental; Jerome, as intentional and threatening. Aggressive children are more likely than nonaggressive children to interpret other people's behavior as intentionally hostile (Crick & Dodge, 1994; Dodge, Coie, et al., 2006; Gifford-Smith & Rabiner, 2004). They have a **hostile attribution bias**; that is, they tend to assume that ambiguous acts are intentionally mean. Interpreting cues in this way increases the likelihood of aggressive behavior. Children's prior relationship history with the perpetrator matters, too. If the person who caused the harm is an enemy, the child is more likely to make a hostile attribution than if the perpetrator is a friend or neutral peer (Peets et al., 2007).

hostile attribution bias
A tendency to interpret neutral or ambiguous social behavior of another person as being hostile.

Third, children review possible behavioral responses. Aggressive children generate fewer responses than nonaggressive children, and the responses they generate are of lower quality (Dodge, Coie, et al., 2006; Shure & Spivack, 1980). Harry considers options such as ignoring the incident, laughing it off, or minimizing its importance. Jerome's options focus on retaliation in the form of hitting or verbally attacking the perpetrator.

Fourth, children choose a response. They might evaluate the response for its moral acceptability or its likely reaction from the other person. They weigh possible consequences and pick the response that they evaluate most positively. Aggressive children are less likely to consider possible consequences, and when they do consider the costs and benefits, their "mental arithmetic" leads them to choose an aggressive action (Dodge, Coie, et al., 2006). Aggressive children view aggressive responses as more legitimate, less morally "bad," and more acceptable than do nonaggressive children (Crick & Werner, 1998; Erdley & Asher, 1998). They expect more positive pay-off for behaving aggressively (Fontaine et al., 2002). Thus, Jerome thinks that hitting his classmate will save face, which is more important than being reprimanded by the lunchroom monitor, whereas Harry decides that the negative consequences (violation of his moral standards or getting a detention) are too great.

Finally, children translate the selected response into action. Even here, aggressive and nonaggressive children differ. Aggressive ones are less competent at enacting and role-playing socially appropriate nonaggressive actions (Burleson, 1982; Dodge, Coie, et al., 2006).

As children go through these steps, they receive feedback from other people's facial expressions and behavioral responses, and the steps recycle. Over time, children develop characteristic styles of processing cues at each step. They develop social information-processing "templates" or "working models" that serve as maps to guide them in their social encounters and exchanges with other children. These cognitive-social processes are the final piece of the larger puzzle that constitutes the causes of aggressive behavior.

Learning from Living Leaders: Kenneth A. Dodge

Source: Courtesy of Kenneth A. Dodge, photo from Duke University, Sanford School of Public Policy.

Ken Dodge is Professor of Public Policy Studies and Psychology at Duke University. He received his Ph.D. in clinical psychology from that university in 1978 and went on to teach at the University of Indiana and Vanderbilt before coming "home." He is best known for his development of the social information-processing model of social behavior. According to this model, children in social situations go through a series of thoughts, interpretations, and evaluations before they decide how to behave. The model has been widely used to explain why some children behave more aggressively than others. It brings together ideas from cognitive science and developmental psychology and was an important corrective to earlier accounts of aggression that simply focused on children's behavior. Dodge has now broadened his original model to include biological factors as well as cognitive and social ones. He and his colleagues have also developed an intervention program aimed at preventing antisocial behavior in young children. The Fast Track program has proven valuable for reducing children's aggression. Dodge's research reflects his dual commitment to scientific theory and the application of scientific theory to problems in society. He is a Fellow of the Academy of Experimental Criminology and a Fellow of the Association for the Advancement of Science. His long-term

goal is to use basic research as a guide for policies that will reduce violence.

Further Reading

Dodge, K. A., Coie, J. D., & Lynam, D. (2006). Aggression and antisocial behavior in youth. In W. Damon & R. L. Lerner (Series Eds.), & N. Eisenberg (Vol. Ed.), *Handbook of child psychology: Vol. 3. Social, emotional, and personality development* (6th ed., pp. 719–788). Hoboken, NJ: Wiley.

Bullies and Victims

bullying
Use of aggression against weaker individuals to gain status or power.

One particular expression of aggression is bullying, a form of aggression that involves repeated abuse of power in a relationship. Researchers have identified some children who regularly act as bullies and others who are consistently victims. In a national survey of nearly 16,000 children in 6th to 10th grades in the United States, 13 percent were identified as bullies and 11 percent as victims (Nansel et al., 2001). A third group of children, 6 percent in the survey, were "bully-victims"; they were victimized by other children but also acted as bullies, often against weaker children. A study of nearly 900 children in Canada reported that 10 percent were consistently high in bullying behavior from early to late adolescence; 13 percent reported moderate levels of bullying in early adolescence that decreased to almost no bullying by the end of high school; and 31 percent maintained moderate levels of bullying (Pepler et al., 2008). The issue of bullying has attracted worldwide attention. In 2007, a group of scholars from Switzerland, South Korea, Italy, Norway, Finland, the Netherlands, Portugal, Austria, Australia, Canada, Spain, the United Kingdom, and the United States met in Switzerland and signed the Kandersteg Declaration Against Bullying in Children and Youth to increase recognition of the problem and develop ways to reduce or prevent it. This declaration states that bullying is a violation of the basic human right to be respected and safe and that it the moral responsibility of adults to ensure that these rights are honored. More than 80 percent of U.S. schools already have written policies prohibiting bullying (Knox, 2006).

BEHAVIOR OF BULLIES AND VICTIMS Bullies use both direct aggression—hitting, pushing, threatening, taunting—and indirect aggression—spreading rumors and breaking lunchboxes. They use both physical aggression and relational aggression. Girl bullies are relatively more likely to use relational tactics; boy bullies to be physical (Crick & Bigbee, 1998). Bullying can be adaptive if it gains status and power over the victim and popularity and admiration from peers (Caravita et al., 2009; Salmivalli et al., 2010; Vaillancourt, Hymel, et al., 2003; Veenstra et al., 2007). Bullies tend to choose their victims carefully to avoid any loss of peer affection by selecting targets who are not likely to be defended by socially significant others (Veenstra et al., 2010). This finding suggests that peers play a role in bullying incidents. In fact, Canadian researchers found that peers were involved in 85 percent of bullying episodes on the playground (Craig & Pepler, 1997; O'Connell et al., 1999). Of these peers, 21 percent actively supported the bullies; another 54 percent watched passively; only 25 percent intervened on behalf of the victims. Furthermore, as they mature, children who witness bullying are increasingly likely to reinforce the bully and decreasingly likely to defend the victim (Pöyhönen & Salmivalli, 2008). This is consistent with findings showing that acceptance of bullying increases with age (Salmivalli & Voeten, 2004) whereas intentions to help the victims decrease, at least up to age 15 (Rigby & Johnson, 2006).

victimization
The process of being threatened or harmed on a consistent basis by a more powerful peer.

Victimization can take several forms. Some children, especially boys, are physically attacked or threatened if they don't obey their peers (Perry et al., 2001). Girls are more likely to be targets of relational victimization than physical attacks (Crick & Bigbee, 1998; Crick et al., 1999). Children who are bullied may be either *passive victims* who are nonaggressive in response to bullying or *provocative victims* who engage in aggressive behavior when they are attacked. Most victims are passive. These children send implicit signals that they will not defend themselves or retaliate against the bully. They may cry easily and often appear anxious or weak (Hodges & Perry, 1999). In fact, victims are weak (Card & Hodges, 2008; Olweus, 1999, 2001); if they were members of the school football squad or wrestling team, bullies would probably leave them alone. They are also anxious and unsure of themselves (Card & Hodges, 2008). In one study, children in 1st grade who had more internalizing symptoms—including crying easily, worrying excessively, being overly fearful, and feeling sad—were targets of bullying in 3rd grade (Leadbeater & Hoglund, 2009). Without realizing it, passive victims encourage their attackers by acting submissive, making a feeble effort to persuade the bully to stop, or giving in to the bully's demands and surrendering their possessions (Crick et al., 1999; Juvonen et al., 2003; Perry et al., 1990). The shy, timid nature of anxious, withdrawn children makes them easy targets. They may evoke victimization precisely because they present themselves as physically and emotionally weak and unlikely to retaliate (Rubin, Bukowski, et al., 2006, Rubin et al., 2009). Researchers have found that these children are at high risk for peer victimization (Grills & Ollendick, 2002; Hanish & Guerra, 2004; Kochenderfer-Ladd, 2003). Because social withdrawal is a strategy often used to cope with victimization (Gazelle & Rudolph, 2004), it has been suggested that these children experience a transactional cycle: They are initially withdrawn and then experience victimization, and this, in turn, increases their withdrawal (Rubin et al., 2009).

Provocative victims are more outgoing in their response to bullying than are the passive victims: They argue, disrupt the bully's actions, and try to return the attack. Even so, they are not very effective. They somehow manage to provoke and irritate other children without convincing them that they'll follow through on their hostile threats. Aggressive children in 1st grade are themselves likely to become victims by 3rd grade despite their continued aggressiveness (Leadbeater & Hoglund, 2009). Simply being aggressive is not enough to avoid being victimized; being *effectively* aggressive is essential for stopping a bully.

CONSEQUENCES OF BULLYING   Bullying can have negative effects on both bullies and victims. Bullies may develop conduct disorders and elevated levels of school disengagement (Juvonen et al., 2003) and suffer from severe depression even in adolescence and young adulthood (Klomek et al., 2008, 2009). They may attempt suicide. Victims are likely to be rejected by other peers and experience problems in school (Boulton & Smith, 1994; Ladd & Troop-Gordon, 2003; Olweus, 2001). They have low social status and low self-esteem, and they, too, experience depression (Juvonen et al., 2003; Ladd, 2005; Leadbeater & Hoglund, 2009; Nangle et al., 2003; Schwartz et al., 2001). They have difficulty forming new friendships (Ellis & Zarbatany, 2007) and suffer in terms of academic achievement (Thijs & Verkuyten, 2008). Even just witnessing other children being bullied can take a toll, especially for children who have poor emotion-regulation skills (Kelly et al., 2008). Children who are regular targets of victimization frequently remain victims through their school years (Khatri et al., 1994; Kochenderfer-Ladd & Wardrop, 2001), and, not surprisingly, the longer they are victims, the more serious are the consequences in terms of increasing depression, anxiety, and social withdrawal (Goldbaum et al., 2003). In extreme cases, victims commit suicide. Even in adulthood, people who were abused by their peers in early adolescence report depression and low self-esteem (Olweus, 1999; Rigby, 2001). Bully-victims are even more likely than either bullies or victims to be avoided by their classmates and to show high rates of conduct problems and school disengagement (Junoven et al., 2003).

cyberbullying
Using threats, embarrassment, or humiliation against a victim with some form of interactive digital medium.

Bullying affects children's hormone levels as well as their psychological well-being. The immediate aftermath of being bullied once or twice is a rise in stress indexed by an increased cortisol level (Carney & Hazler, 2007). However, when children are exposed to bullying on a regular basis, their cortisol levels drop, suggesting that they have become numb or desensitized to the stress of being bullied. Having a lower-than-normal cortisol level may have physical and psychological consequences, including chronic anxiety, mood problems, and fearfulness.

Real-World Application: Cyberfighting and Cyberbullying

Electronic media offer children and adolescents experiences that were never possible before. Today young people can see what it's like to live at the North Pole or in a village in Laos; they can communicate with a stranger on the other side of the world or share shorthand messages with a friend after lights out. New electronic technologies have broken boundaries between people. But these new electronic tools have a dark side as well. They expose children to aggressive models and opportunities to act aggressively. Not only do children engage in aggressive acts against fantasy figures while playing Grand Theft Auto but also they engage in aggression against real people using the Internet as a venue.

This aggression may be a physical assault as when children or adolescents videotape a fight and post it on a site such as YouTube, MySpace, or girlfightsdump.com. These fights include the dangerous "sport" of helmet boxing, in which two children don helmets and gloves and hit each other in the head until one of them gives up or passes out. They also include attacks in which a group of young people gangs up on a classmate and pummels the victim into unconsciousness. Posting the record of the fight on the Internet gives the attackers their 15 minutes of fame, torments the victim by showing his or her defeat and distress to the world, and provokes copycat conflicts in a vicious cycle of "cyberfighting." Another recent form of cyber aggression is a "flash mob"—a crowd of adolescents connected through Facebook and Twitter who descend on a location and attack the people they find there.

The aggression may also be verbal. In **cyberbullying**, a child or adolescent is tormented, threatened, harassed, humiliated, embarrassed, or otherwise targeted by another child or adolescent using the Internet, a mobile phone, or other interactive digital device. Everything from text messaging to e-mail can be used to cyberbully victims. Some people even create Web sites solely dedicated to harassment. Other sites, such as juicycampus.com, become venues for cyberbullying. Methods of cyberbullying include sending mean or vulgar messages or images, posting sensitive, private information about another person, pretending to be someone else to make that person look bad, spreading malicious rumors, intentionally excluding someone from an online group, and even sending death threats.

As use of electronic media increases, so does cyberbullying. Twice as many children and adolescents in 2005 said they were victims of online harassment as had in 2000 (Wolak et al., 2006). In surveys, 42 percent of students in grades 4 to 8 said they had been bullied while online (ABC News, 2006), and 36 percent of 12- to 17-year-olds reported that someone had said threatening or embarrassing things about them through e-mail, instant messages, Web sites, chat rooms, or text messages (Fight Crime: Invest in Kids, 2006).

Cyberbullying differs from in-person bullying in a number of ways: It can occur at any time of the day or night, its messages and images can be distributed quickly to a wide audience, and it is often done anonymously, which makes it difficult (and sometimes impossible) to trace. Cybervictims and cyberbullies spend much of their time online. They have poorer relationships with their parents, are more likely to run away from home, skip school, cheat on tests, and use drugs and alcohol than children and adolescents who are not harassed online (Hinduja & Patchin, 2007, 2009; Ybarra & Mitchell, 2004b). Of particular interest, they engage in more aggressive behavior and are the target of bullying off-line as well as online. Cybervictims are more likely to have social problems and to be victims off-line; cyberbullies are more likely to have problems with rule breaking and aggression off-line (Ybarra & Mitchell, 2004a, 2007). Cyberbullies are also likely to go to schools where most students approve of bullying (Williams & Guerra, 2007).

When children are bullied online, they do not always tell adults what is happening, so it is difficult for parents to intervene and offer guidance or protection. One survey found that only 35 percent of teens and 51 percent of preteens who had been cyberbullied had told their parents (Fight Crime: Invest in Kids, 2006). In fact, it may be difficult for a child to know that he or she is a victim of cyberbullying. In 2006, 13-year-old Megan Meier met a "cute boy" named "Josh Evans" on MySpace. He flattered her and she fell hard. But then "cute boy" turned on Megan, saying he heard she was cruel to her friends, and he posted messages saying things like "Megan Meier is a slut," and eventually, "This world would be a better place without you." The cyber exchange devastated Megan, and she committed suicide. Later, it was discovered that an adult neighbor was behind the online "relationship" and Josh Evans did not exist. After this tragedy, Megan's parents pushed hard for measures to protect children online, and several jurisdictions implemented legislation prohibiting harassment over the Internet. In March 2007, the American Advertising Council in partnership with the National Crime Prevention Council, the U.S. Department of Justice, and Crime Prevention Coalition of America, launched a public service campaign to educate preteens and teens about how to help end cyberbullying. Web sites providing information about how to prevent cyberbullying have proliferated since Megan Meier's suicide (e.g., http://stopbullyingnow.hrsa.gov/adult/index-Adult.asp?Area=cyberbullying), and StopCyberBullying.org has created a pledge in Megan's honor, which it encourages everyone to sign.

The Megan Pledge

By taking this pledge:
- I agree to take a stand against cyberbullying.
- I agree not to use technology as a weapon to hurt others.
- I agree to think before I click.
- I agree to think about the person on the other side.
- I agree not to join in cyberbullying tactics or be used by cyberbullies to hurt others.
- I agree to be part of the solution, not part of the problem.

Cyberbullying is an urgent real-world problem that demands and is receiving attention. The major challenge now is to get adolescents to take the Megan pledge and abide by it.

CONDITIONS LEADING TO BULLYING   Bullies and victims are created by both their own genetic makeup and conditions in the environment. According to a British study of 1,116 families with 10-year-old twins, genetic factors accounted for 61 percent of the variation in bullying and 72 percent of the variation in victimization (Ball et al., 2008). Even before bullying begins, children who will become bullies or victims can be identified. They have trouble regulating their emotions, and provocative victims have poor social skills and low levels of inhibition (Burk et al., 2008). In their early years, victimized children tend to have anxious attachments to their mothers (Perry et al., 2001), and provocative victims are likely to be exposed to physical abuse, harsh discipline, and marital violence (Schwartz et al., 1997). Victimized boys are likely to have overprotective mothers who hinder their development of autonomy or encourage their expressions of fear and anxiety (Curtner-Smith et al., 2010; Finnegan et al., 1998; Georgiou, 2008; Olweus, 1993). Victimized girls are likely to have coercive, rejecting, and unresponsive mothers who make the girls vulnerable to victimization by impeding their ability to form close social ties (Curtner-Smith et al., 2010; Finnegan et al., 1998). Bullies' mothers also tend to be unresponsive (Georgiou, 2008), and bullies who continue their attacks through high school have parents who communicate with them less, have more conflicts with them, and are poorer at monitoring their activities than the parents of children who stop their bullying ways (Pepler et al., 2008).

Children can be protected by having positive relationships with their peers. In one study, the more friends children had, the less likely they were to be victimized (Hodges et al., 1997). But not just any friends will do; friends who were physically strong or aggressive and were not victimized themselves were the ones who served a protective function (Laursen et al., 2007). Having friends not only protected children from victimization but also increased the likelihood that they would have high self-esteem and would not "invite" an attack or submit to it (Hodges et al., 1999). In another study, researchers found that children who lost a best friend and failed to replace him or her by the end of the school year were at increased risk of being victimized (Bowker et al., 2006). Apparently having friends—the right type of friends—can buffer children from victimization.

Control of Aggression

catharsis
Discharging aggressive impulses by engaging in actual or symbolic hostile acts.

So far in this chapter we have discussed the many factors that push children toward aggressiveness. In this final section we focus on ways to reduce or control aggression.

et You Thought That . . .
You Could Reduce Aggressive Feelings by "Letting off Steam"

For many years, psychologists and the general public believed that one way to reduce aggression was to "let off steam" or "let your feelings out." One of the most persistent beliefs about aggression was that if people had ample opportunity to engage in aggressive acts, whether actually or symbolically—a process known as catharsis—they would be less likely to act on hostile aggressive urges. This belief was based on the idea that aggressive urges build up in a person and unless this accumulating reservoir of aggressive energies is drained, a violent outburst might occur. The implications were clear: Provide people with a safe opportunity to behave aggressively—such as hitting a punching bag—and decrease the likelihood of antisocial aggression. Therapists bought punching bags for their offices and Bobo dolls, pounding boards, and toy guns and rubber knives for their playrooms. Advice columnists agreed. For example, Ann Landers (1969) once advised a reader that hostile feelings must be released and went on to recommend that children be taught to vent their anger against furniture rather than against people. A reader responded: "I was shocked at your advice to the mother whose 3-year-old had temper tantrums. My younger brother used to kick the furniture when he got mad. He's 32 years old now and still kicking the furniture. He is also kicking his wife, the cat, the kids, and anything else that gets in his way. Why don't you tell mothers that children must be taught to control their anger? This is what separates civilized human beings from savages."

Despite the popularity of the catharsis notion, research evidence tends to support the view of this sensible Ann Landers reader. Most studies suggest that aggressive experiences promote rather than "drain off" aggressive urges. In one study, researchers allowed 3rd-grade children to shoot a toy gun after being frustrated by a peer who interfered with a task they were working on (Mallick & McCandless, 1966). Another group of children was allowed to work on a nonaggression-related task—arithmetic problems—after the peer upset them. Then all the children were given a chance to express their aggression toward the peer who had upset them. The researchers used a rigged procedure in which the children thought they were delivering a shock to the other child. Results of the study demonstrated that whether the children shot the toy gun or worked on math problems after they were frustrated by the peer made little difference in the delivery of "shocks." Catharsis did not reduce aggression.

COGNITIVE MODIFICATION STRATEGIES   One effective way to reduce children's aggression is to change their thinking about social situations. As noted earlier, aggressive children often process other people's behavior incorrectly and do not know how to solve social problems (Dodge & Pettit, 2003; Gifford-Smith & Rabiner, 2004). Teaching them how to read other people's behavioral cues has led to decreased hostile attribution bias and decreased aggression (Hudley & Graham, 1993). The approach was especially effective with reactively aggressive children, who are particularly poor at reading other people's cues and intentions. A more comprehensive program that taught children to distract themselves and use relaxation methods when they were provoked, take another person's perspective and make accurate attributions about intentions, say "no" to peer pressure, and reach nonviolent solutions to social problems was also successful in reducing boys' aggression (Lochman & Wells, 2004). Making aggressive children stop and think about social problems, consider alternative responses, and contemplate negative consequences of aggression for themselves and others and teaching children to cooperate and take turns are also strategies that can reduce aggression (Guerra et al., 1997; Kazdin, 2003).

PARENTS AS AGENTS FOR AGGRESSION REDUCTION   Another way to reduce children's aggression is to improve their parents' behavior. Many programs based on the model of coercive interaction cycles identified by Patterson and his colleagues (2002) have attempted to do this. Often termed Parent Management Training (PMT), the goal in these programs is to extinguish parents' coercive behavior in favor of contingent, consistent, and clear rules that lead to child compliance. These programs do reduce children's aggression (Dishion & Kavanaugh, 2000) and probably improve the quality of life for parents too. Meta-analyses show that PMT programs are very effective for families with children under 10 years of age (Serketich & Dumas, 1996) and moderately effective for families with 10- to 17-year-olds (Woolfendon et al., 2002).

Other parenting programs have been used to reduce aggressive behavior in preschool children attending Head Start programs (Webster-Stratton, 1998) and to reduce the delinquent behavior of juveniles in the court system (Chamberlain et al., 2007; Eddy et al., 2004). In a third program, parents of 3- to 8-year-old children referred to a clinic because of their antisocial behavior were taught to praise and reward their children, provide clear rules, and give consistent and nonharsh consequences when the children violated the rules (Scott, 2005). A year after the program ended, only half as many children had clinical levels of aggression as before the program started (37% versus 68%). In a fourth program, parents of at-risk middle school students were taught these same skills, and as a result, reduced their critical and negative habits, leading to a decrease in their children's antisocial behavior (Irvine et al., 1999). In yet another program, parents of children with attention deficit hyperactivity disorder (ADHD) were taught to use less punitive disciplinary strategies; their children subsequently exhibited lower levels of aggressive and disruptive behavior—but only if they also received stimulant medication, such as Ritalin (Hinshaw et al., 2000). This study supports the view that although parental discipline affects children's aggressive behavior, biological factors matter as well.

SCHOOLS AS VENUES FOR INTERVENTION   School-based programs have also been used to improve aggressive children's social problem-solving skills and reduce their aggression (Kress & Elias, 2006; Stevahn et al., 2000). An evaluation of children in 15 elementary schools in New York that were participating in the Resolving Conflict Creatively Program indicated that children whose teachers taught them lessons in creative conflict resolution had slower rates of growth in hostile attribution bias, aggressive negotiation strategies, self-reported conduct problems, aggressive fantasies, and teacher-reported aggressive behavior (Aber et al., 2003). In another school-based program, teachers were taught to reduce children's disruptive behavior by using the Good Behavior Game (Ialongo et al., 2001; van Lier et al., 2004), a program that rewarded the whole class—with a pizza party or a day without homework—if any child in the class improved.

However, if a few wiseguys (or gals) disrupted the class, everyone suffered—the teacher canceled recess, increased homework, or gave the class a detention. This program reduced aggression for 1st graders, and the effects lasted until at least the end of elementary school.

In a school-based project specifically targeted at reducing children's bullying, Karin Frey and her colleagues implemented a program for 3rd through 6th graders in three schools (Frey et al., 2005, 2009). The Steps to Respect program had three components: (a) schoolwide antibullying policies and procedures; (b) a classroom-based cognitive-behavioral curriculum to address peer norms about bullying and teach children social-emotional skills for responding to bullying and increasing peer acceptance; and (c) a selective coaching intervention for students involved in bullying. After 3 months in the program, participating children were involved in 25 percent fewer bullying incidents on the playground than children in control-group schools. Children who were bystanders to bullying were also less likely to encourage it. After 2 years in the program, bullying dropped by 31 percent, and bully-supportive bystander behavior decreased 73 percent in comparison with bullying and bully support in control schools. The effects were most pronounced for students who did the most bullying before the program started and for students who received individual coaching.

AGGRESSION PREVENTION: A MULTIPRONGED EFFORT Because many factors determine aggression, taking a multifaceted approach to reducing it may be most effective. An anti-bullying program in Norway exemplifies such an approach. After three boys committed suicide as a result of extreme harassment by classmates in 1982, school officials launched a national campaign against bullying and implemented a prevention program in every school. The program developed by Dan Olweus had four goals: (a) to increase public awareness of the problem, (b) to actively involve teachers and parents, (c) to provide support and protection for victims of aggression, and (d) to develop clear classroom rules to combat aggressive behavior. Teachers were given a booklet that described the nature and scope of aggression in the schools and offered practical suggestions about what they could do to control or prevent aggressive behavior. The booklet encouraged teachers to intervene in bullying situations and give students the clear message that "aggression is not acceptable in our school." Parents also received basic information about bullying and were offered assistance if their child was either a bully or a victim. Children participated in class meetings where they

This poster is part of a schoolwide campaign to reduce bullying. Source: *Courtesy Jaguar Educational www .jaguared.com.*

Bullying isn't tolerated in our school

We have a right to ...

- Feel safe in the classroom
- Not experience peer pressure
- Not be teased or abused
- Be forgiven for our mistakes
- Be respected for who we are
- Be accepted just as we are

discussed bullying and the class rules. Based on data from about 2,500 students in 4th through 7th grades, researchers found that the frequency of bully and victim problems decreased by 50 to 70 percent at both 8 months and 20 months after the program began. Fewer children reported being attacked by others or acting aggressively themselves. In addition, vandalism, theft, and truancy declined significantly, and student satisfaction with school life rose appreciably (Olweus, 1993, 1997, 2004).

The Fast Track Project is a multifaceted effort to combat children's aggressive and antisocial behavior in the United States (Conduct Problems Prevention Research Group, 2004). First-graders from poor families are given lessons to help them with social problem solving, emotional understanding, and communication and to teach them how to regulate their emotions. Children with the most serious problems (10% of the sample) also receive academic tutoring, extra social skills training, and a parent intervention designed to improve parenting skills. Researchers found that by the end of the school year, children in Fast Track were less aggressive, had improved academically, and had developed better social-emotional skills than children in a control group. They got along better and were better liked by their peers. Their parents' skills and involvement in school activities had improved as well. By the end of 3rd grade, 37 percent of the children in Fast Track still had no conduct problems compared with 27 percent of the control group. Positive effects persisted through 5th grade (Foster et al., 2006). These effects were significant but modest in size. Clearly, eliminating childhood aggression in poor children is a difficult challenge.

A third multipronged effort to reduce aggression focused on a group of very high risk adolescent male offenders who had already experienced at least four arrests and 8 weeks of incarceration. In general, recidivism rates for juvenile offenders, even those who receive treatment, exceed 70 percent. But most treatments are either narrow (focusing on a single factor) or extreme (placing the youth in an institution or foster care). Scott Henggeler and his colleagues used Bronfenbrenner's ecological model of development as the basis for a program of multisystemic therapy (MST) to treat these offenders and their multiproblem families. The program focuses on parental discipline, emotional reactions in the family, and the adolescent's school performance and affiliation with peers. To assess the program, researchers randomly assigned 96 juvenile offenders to either an MST treatment group or a typical treatment involving social agencies, curfews, enforced school attendance, and monitoring by a probation officer (Henggeler et al., 2009; Taylor et al., 2004). Five months after the program started and the adolescents had had 33 hours of direct contact with a therapist, the recidivism rate for the MST group was only 42 percent compared with 62 percent in the group who received the typical treatment, and only 20 percent of the MST youth had been incarcerated compared with 68 percent of the typical-treatment group.

In a study comparing the effects of including single or multiple factors in the program, researchers confirmed that only a combination of factors (classroom-based peer intervention and family intervention aimed at enhancing parenting skills and parent-child communication) was effective in reducing children's aggression (Metropolitan Area Child Study Research Group, 2002). The length of the program also mattered. In one study, children were assigned to a program of parent training, teacher training, and cognitive problem solving that lasted from 1st grade through 6th grade or from 5th grade through 6th grade (Hawkins et al., 1999). By age 18, adolescents in the 6-year program were significantly less likely to exhibit delinquency and violence than children who had been in the 2-year program or no program at all. The addition of "booster shots" to reinstate the original treatment after a program ends is also helpful in maintaining lower levels of aggression (Dodge, Coie, et al., 2006, Dodge, Dishion, et al., 2006; Kress & Elias, 2006). Clearly, mounting a multifaceted assault is important for reducing children's antisocial behavior. Although such efforts are expensive, they may be cost effective (Foster et al., 2006). According to Dodge (2008), a chronic violent offender costs society about $2 million, so a prevention program that costs $1,000 per child would be cost effective if only 1 out of 200 children was diverted from a life of violence.

Cultural Context: Preventing Youth Violence

Young people in ethnic and racial minority communities in the United States are at greater risk for high rates of aggression and violence than majority youth, and it has been suggested that prevention and intervention efforts should be tailored to the unique needs of these communities (Guerra & Smith, 2006). Cynthia Hudley and April Taylor (2006) outlined a model to serve as a guide for culturally sensitive programs for minority youth. First, programs should be culturally *effective*: Service providers' knowledge, attitudes, and skills should equip them to function successfully within the community. Second, programs should be culturally *responsive*: Curricular materials and methods should reflect participants' cultural strengths and support their success both within their own culture and in the mainstream; strategies for violence prevention should be presented in ways that support cultural values and practices. Third, programs should be culturally *engaged*: Participants should be taught to understand and embrace their cultural niche. This includes learning about their culture, taking pride in their heritage, and developing a positive sense of themselves.

Here are some examples of culturally sensitive programs that were designed to reflect these principles. One program for 5th and 6th grade children in Hawai'i combines a focus on traditional Hawai'ian values, such as respect for the land (*aina*) and care for the ocean (*malama*) with culture-free elements, such as conflict management and problem-solving techniques. This program has been effective in increasing the children's pride in being Hawai'ian, and the program organizers hope that by increasing children's ethnic pride, they will reduce their violence as well (Takeshita & Takeshita, 2002; Mark et al., 2006).

The Tribal Youth Program was established to empower Native American communities to resolve social problems using spiritual and cultural aspects of their native traditions (Hurst & Laird, 2006). Interventions in the Tribal Youth Program include youth tribal courts that are consistent with cultural traditions for dealing with troubled youth, such as increased community service and immersion in tribal history and traditions, home detention systems that reduce the need to separate youth from their family members, and culturally based assessments such as talking circles, sand tray paintings, and adventure programs. These programs have been found to be effective in reducing youths' antisocial behavior (McKinney, 2003).

Perhaps the most convincing evidence that cultural tailoring can increase program effectiveness comes from a test of two social skills training curricula in which one group of African American youth received only the basic curriculum, including training in cooperation, problem solving, and emotion regulation, and the other group received that curriculum plus a component focused on African American history (e.g., Martin Luther King's "I have a dream" speech) and African American values (e.g., the importance of extended family) (Banks et al., 1996). Only the members of the group who participated in the culturally enhanced program decreased their anger and increased their self-control.

Clearly, adapting violence prevention programs to fit the cultural backgrounds of their participants is important. The cultural appropriateness of the intervention and the relevance of the program for participants' everyday lives increase the effectiveness of these efforts (Dodge, Coie, et al., 2006, Dodge, Dishion, et al., 2006; Kress & Elias, 2006).

Chapter Summary

Definitions of Aggression

- An act is aggressive if the aggressor intends it to harm the victim, the victim perceives it to be harmful, and it is considered aggressive according to the norms of the community.
- Types of aggression include proactive (or instrumental) aggression, which occurs in the service of a goal such as acquiring an object, and reactive (or hostile aggression), which occurs in response to a threat, attack, or frustration.

Developmental Changes in Aggression

- Types of aggression change in frequency with development. Proactive aggression is most common in infancy and early childhood. In middle childhood, reactive aggression becomes more common than proactive aggression. Children also become more verbal and less physical in their aggression. Relational aggression becomes more common and sophisticated. In adolescence, serious violent offenses, such as assault, robbery, and rape, increase.

- Individual differences in aggression are quite stable from childhood to adulthood. A small number of children are physically aggressive at a young age (early starters) and remain highly aggressive; the majority of individuals show a steady decline in aggression after their early years. Individuals who are late starters begin to act aggressive during adolescence and are less likely to show long-term patterns of aggression in adulthood.

Gender Differences in Aggression

- Boys are more physically aggressive than girls. Girls are more likely to use verbal strategies to solve their conflicts. Both boys and girls use relational aggression, but girls use more relational aggression than physical aggression whereas the reverse is true for boys.

Causes of Aggression

- Aggressive children are likely to have aggressive relatives, irritable and impulsive temperaments, lower levels of serotonin, higher levels of testosterone, and prenatal complications.

- Parenting behavior including erratic and severe physical punishment and overly strict control contribute to elevated levels of child aggression.

- Association with deviant peers can increase the possibility that a child will engage in aggressive activities. Poverty and high-crime neighborhoods can also promote aggressive behavior. Individualistic cultures have higher rates of aggression than collectivist societies.

- Violent TV and video games are associated with increases in aggressive behavior.

- Children who have or experience more of these adverse factors are at greatest risk for aggressiveness.

Bullies and Victims

- Bullying is a major issue in schools in many countries. It can be direct (verbal or physical) or indirect. Victims are either passive (do not react aggressively to being bullied) or provocative (respond aggressively to being bullied). Some children are both bullies and victims.

- Being either a chronic bully or a chronic victim has psychological consequences, such as increased anxiety, depression, and social withdrawal.

- Having a best friend, especially a physically strong one, can reduce victimization.

- Cyberfighting and cyberbullying can lead to negative psychological outcomes, including suicide.

Control of Aggression

- Catharsis or "letting off steam" is an ineffective aggression control strategy.

- Aggression can be reduced by teaching children how to read other peoples' behavior more accurately and encouraging them to be more sensitive to the views and feelings of others.

- Multifaceted intervention programs in which children, parents, teachers, and schools participate are effective approaches to reducing aggression.

Key Terms

bullying

catharsis

cyberbullying

deviancy training

direct aggression

early starters

hostile attribution bias

indirect aggression

late starters

physical aggression

proactive aggression

reactive aggression

relational aggression

serotonin

social aggression

verbal aggression

victimization

At the Movies

A number of movies have highlighted relational aggression. In *Mean Girls* (2004), home-schooled Cady enters a public high school and immediately crosses paths with Queen Bee, Regina, the leader of the school's most fashionable clique, The Plastics. When Cady falls for Regina's ex-boyfriend, the Queen Bee is stung and schemes to destroy Cady's social future. The "girl-world" war that ensues has the whole school running for cover. *Mean Girls* was written by *Saturday Night Live's* Tina Fey, based on a nonfiction book, *Queen Bees and Wannabes*. *Odd Girl Out* (2005) also focuses on girls' relational aggression, this time in middle school. It portrays the brutality of the mean girls' jealousy, lies, rumors, name-calling, manipulation, and social exclusion; the girls in the film even create a hate Web site on which they put embarrassing pictures of their victim. In the end, the victim stands up to the bullies. The implication is that this act will eliminate the mean girls' harassment. Happy endings are likely more common in films than in real life. Both these films (and other dramas, such as the television show *Gossip Girl*) underscore the harm and pain that relational aggression can cause and serve as a reminder of the need to educate teens and tweens about the dangers of just being "mean."

Physical aggression and bullying by boys is also a popular topic for movies. In *Ben X* (2007), a boy with Asperger's syndrome is a target for school bullies. He spends his time playing an online game in an attempt to block out reality, but as the bullies' relentless attacks push him over the edge, his online dream girl appears to him and helps him devise a plan to make the bullies pay. This film, based on a true story, blends fantasy and harsh social realism in an original way. A more shocking portrayal of youth violence appears in the movie *Green Street Hooligans* (2005), a gritty film about English gangs of hooligans that encourage their local football teams by throwing violent brawls with their rivals. When a Harvard student moves to London, he finds himself in the middle of one of these gangs. At first, he is afraid and reluctant to fight, but he becomes desensitized to the violence and joins in. This movie illuminates an environment in which violence is a major aspect of life as we see in high-risk neighborhoods where gangs provide power and companionship. *This Is England* (2006) is a story about a boy from a poor neighborhood who is drawn into a British gang of skinheads. The film handles the complexities of violence and race with sensitivity and increases viewers' understanding of the allure of being part of a gang. The award-winning film *Bowling for Columbine* (2002) explores the nature and causes of violence in the United States, focusing on the massacre at Columbine High School. The film shows how culture in the United States often condones violence through its media messages, online games, and easy access to guns.

CHAPTER 13

Policy:
Improving
Children's Lives

Source: © AP/Wide World Photos.

Joanne, age 16, is the single mother of a 6-month-old baby; she lives with her mother, who is also unmarried and living on food stamps. Across town, Jolene and Juan work to support their four children, but their jobs pay minimum wage and they often don't have enough to pay their bills. They are especially worried about what will happen if one of their children gets sick because their jobs do not provide health insurance. Tim and Trish, parents of a third family in a more affluent neighborhood, have a 7-month-old, and it is time for Trish to go back to work. Trying to find child care that is safe and affordable is proving to be a real challenge. Finally, in a fourth family, Sam worries that his temper is getting out of control. He finds himself spanking his children harder and harder. As these examples illustrate, not everyone in the United States lives the American dream—happy, prosperous, and safe. In this chapter, we discuss four major problems affecting American children and their families and some policies seeking to alleviate them.

In the United States, one of the richest countries in the world, many families and children are struggling to make ends meet. To survive and perhaps improve their lives, these families need help. Government policies and programs seek to do just that—to improve the lives of families and children by preventing or reducing their problems. Although private organizations such as businesses and charitable agencies also provide programs, our focus in this chapter is primarily on policies implemented by state and federal governments. **Social policy** refers to a set of planned actions to solve a social problem or attain a social goal; government-based social policy is often referred to as **public policy**.

Social policies have a number of purposes (Zigler & Hall, 2000). First, they provide information. In 1912, the U.S. government established the Children's Bureau to provide statistical information about children. Today, government offices and private organizations, such as the New America Foundation and Child Trends, provide yearly updates on the status and needs of children and families. Second, policies provide funding to achieve goals such as child protection and family support. A third purpose of policy is to provide services to prevent or reduce problems; these include programs such as Head Start for preschoolers and abstinence education for teenagers. A fourth purpose of policy is to provide an infrastructure to support efforts on behalf of children; the House Select Committee on Children and Families and the Senate Children's Caucus address children's policy issues in the U.S. Congress. In this chapter, we examine some important social problems that children and families face in the United States and discuss some social policies that endeavor to reduce these problems and prevent harmful effects on children's social and emotional well-being. When relevant, we also describe contrasting policies that have been implemented in other countries to address the same problems.

social policy
A set of planned actions to solve a social problem or attain a social goal.

public policy
Government-based social policy.

What Determines Public Policy for Children?

What problems should social policies for children address? Although this is a simple question, policy decisions always represent trade-offs and compromises based on societal needs, budgetary limitations, and political agendas. To appreciate the dynamic nature of the policy-making process, consider how child policy priorities have changed in the last 100 years. In the late 1800s, the main concern for U.S. policy makers was working conditions for children; in the middle of the 20th century, preventing moral and sexual transgressions by children (particularly girls) was a major issue (Schlossman & Cairns, 1993). Now policy concerns include poverty, health insurance, child care, teenage parenthood, and child abuse. Clearly, policy concerns reflect the needs and political priorities that are salient during different historical eras.

A second question is how much money should be allocated for child-related policies. Social policies are effective only to the extent to which funds are available to support them. In recent years, the U.S. government has spent nearly half of its discretionary budget on military forces; far less has gone to programs for children, in part because U.S. policy makers assume that families are responsible for the health and well-being of their children (Coltrane & Collins, 2001). Among developed countries, the United States has the highest rate of poverty but spends the least to reduce it.

A third question is who decides how the money should be used. In the United States, the federal government, the states, and local counties or communities often share policy-making authority (Capizzano & Stagner, 2005). Two common forms of federal funding for child and family policies are block grants and matching grants. A *block grant* is a fixed amount of money provided by the federal government to a state to promote a broadly defined area such as maternal employment or school improvement; with a *matching grant,* the federal government and the state share the costs of the program.

A fourth question is what is the research base for the policy. Over the past few decades, governments in the United States and other Western countries have become concerned that

These children and their single mother live in El Centro, California, where the unemployment rate in 2009 was 23 percent, the highest in the United States. They can be helped by public policies offering the mother economic assistance, job training, parenting-skills training, food stamps, health care, and subsidized housing, and policies giving the children high-quality child care, preschool education, and health benefits. Unfortunately, California is experiencing a massive budget crisis that has resulted in deep cuts to programs and services statewide. Source: *David McNew/Getty Images, Inc.*

policies be based on scientific evidence and have used this evidence as a factor in the mix of ideology, interests, and institutional constraints that underlie policies (Huston, 2008). The No Child Left Behind law of 2002, for example, included the phrase "scientifically based research" more than 100 times (National Research Council, 2007).

Types of Public Policy

primary prevention policies
A set of planned actions designed to alter environmental conditions and prevent problems before they develop.

secondary prevention policies
A set of planned actions targeted at children who are already at risk of developing serious problems.

Temporary Assistance for Needy Families (TANF)
Federal legislation that provides block grants to states, introduces time limits on cash assistance to individuals, and imposes work requirements.

Public policies for children come in many sizes and shapes. They differ in whether they focus on preventing or ameliorating problems, whether they focus on children or parents, and whether they provide economic aid, social services, or psychological support.

Primary prevention policies are designed to alter environmental conditions and prevent problems before they develop; examples include regulation to reduce the amount of lead in the environment and provision of safe schools for all children. **Secondary prevention policies** focus on children who are already at risk of developing problems. Head Start is an example of a secondary prevention effort; others are listed in Table 13.1 (Gershoff et al., 2005). These policies all target low-income families and children, but they differ in the types of support they provide.

The goal of one type of policy is *economic improvement* for families. Programs implementing this type of policy–for example, **Temporary Assistance for Needy Families (TANF)**— are based on the assumption that economic security will reduce stress and provide better home environments for children. A second type of policy is *service oriented*. Programs based on this type of policy help families meet their basic needs by providing food stamps, health care, child care, and housing. A third type of policy, *parent-directed intervention*, supports parents psychologically and improves their child-rearing skills with the hope that this will enhance children's development. A fourth type of policy focuses on *intervention with parents and children:* Children are helped through preschool education, child care, and health benefits; parents are assisted through education, job training, and parenting-skills training. Finally, there are policies that *target children directly* by improving the quality of schools in impoverished areas or funding supplementary after-school programs.

Policies that focus on ameliorating or "fixing" problems after they have developed or because they resisted prevention efforts include programs to reduce gang violence by teaching aggressive children how to solve social problems and programs to encourage pregnant teens to stay in school by providing on-site child care for their babies.

TABLE 13.1   **Examples of Policies and Programs for Children**

Type of policy	Target	Goal	Programs	Strategies
Economic support for poor families	Low-income families	To decrease family's dependence on public aid	Temporary Assistance for Needy Families (TANF)	Temporary cash aid Work requirement Child care assistance Marriage support Recovery of child support payments Requirement that single mothers < 18 yrs old must live with adult
Services for poor families	Low-income families	To help families meet basic needs by providing food, health care, child care, and housing	Food Stamp Program National School Lunch Program Special Supplemental Food Program for Women, Infants, and Children (WIC)	Food stamps to buy selected healthy food Free meals at school for eligible children Nutrition education Food supplements Health and social service referrals
Intervention with poor parents	Low-income parents	To reduce risks associated with poor parenting	Promoting Safe and Stable Families Program	Home visiting to teach about developmental milestones, parenting practices, early learning activities Family preservation services, such as crisis intervention, management of home finances, obtaining social services Family support services such as respite care, early developmental screening, tutoring, health education
Interventions for poor parents and children	Low-income parents and children	To provide direct services and support to low-income parents and children through preschool/child care for children and services for parents	Head Start Early Head Start Comprehensive Child Development Program	Preschool education Health care Developmental screening Parent education Job training Parenting skills
Programs for poor children	Children in low-income neighbor-hoods	To assist poor children directly through services provided in schools, child care, and community settings to improve their academic success and reduce social deviance	Title I Improving the Academic Achievement of the Disadvantaged	Funding for schools in poor communities Provision of after-school programs

Source: Gershoff et al., 2005.

Children in Poverty: A Social Policy Challenge

In the United States, about 18 percent of children live in families with incomes below the poverty line (Moore et al., 2009). Many policy makers have focused attention on the adverse life situations of these low-income families.

Economic Hardship and Social Disadvantage

Poverty is not only a lack of monetary resources; it comes with social disadvantages as well. Powerlessness is one disadvantage. The poor have less influence over society than other families and are less likely to be treated well by social organizations. Their lack of power, information, and education restricts their options. They have reduced choices of occupations and housing, have increased vulnerability to job loss and unemployment, and may be subject to impersonal and sometimes unfair bureaucratic decisions in the legal system. They often find themselves in a cycle of disadvantage as economic hardship leads to social, educational, and employment failures, which spiral downward so that they lose even the resources they had. In view of their limited power and lack of resources, it is not surprising that many poor people experience psychological distress, feel helpless, insecure, and controlled by external forces, and are unable to support and nurture their children (McLoyd & Ceballo, 1998; McLoyd et al., 2001).

Effects of Poverty on Children

How do poverty and its associated social disadvantages affect children? Poor children are at risk from the time they are born. Compared with children from more affluent families, they are twice as likely to have low birth weight, twice as likely to spend time in the hospital, and almost twice as likely to die during childhood (Duncan & Brooks-Gunn, 2000). Being poor is also bad for children's emotional health: Poor children are one third more likely to suffer from emotional or behavioral problems, seven times more likely to suffer from child abuse or neglect, more than twice as likely to encounter violent crime, and almost four time as likely to drop out of school (Children's Defense Fund, 2004). Being poor in early childhood is especially detrimental (Duncan & Brooks-Gunn, 2000). Children whose parents made $10,000 more during their first 5 years were nearly three times as likely to finish high school as children without this family income; increased income later in childhood or adolescence was less significant (Duncan et al., 1998).

Poverty affects children through many routes. First, there is the quality of the home environment (Bradley et al., 2001): Children in poor families have fewer books, toys, educational games, and computers than children in more affluent families. Second, poverty is linked to parents' physical and emotional problems, which affects their parenting and impairs their children's emotional and social development. Third, poor families usually live in neighborhoods with high crime and unemployment, little supervision of children, and limited resources; these neighborhoods can adversely affect children's development (Leventhal & Brooks-Gunn, 2000). Fourth, family disruptions, such as moving to a different location or breaking up the family unit, which are more common in poor families, can leave children without the support of friends and familiar teachers, alter their sense of security, and culminate in adjustment problems in adolescence (Adam & Chase-Lansdale, 2002).

Programs to Reverse Effects of Poverty

A number of policies have been implemented to combat the effects of poverty on children's development. Some focus on children directly and others increase parental income or job skills as a way of lifting families out of poverty.

Learning from Living Leaders: Jack P. Shonkoff

Source: Courtesy of Jack P. Shonkoff, photo from Harvard Graduate School of Education.

Jack Shonkoff is a pediatrician who is Professor of Child Health and Development at the Harvard School of Public Health and the Harvard Graduate School of Education and Professor of Pediatrics at Harvard Medical School and Children's Hospital Boston. He chairs the National Scientific Council on the Developing Child and is the founding director of the Center on the Developing Child at Harvard. These organizations foster collaboration among leading scholars in neuroscience, developmental psychology, pediatrics, and economics. Their mission is to bring science to bear on public policy decision making that affects the lives of young children. After he received his M.D. from New York University, Shonkoff started his career as a pediatrician expecting to take care of kids and families, but he soon realized that the answers to children's health needs went far beyond the doctor's office. He became interested in broader policy issues and moved from the medical world into the world of social policy. Since then, his career has been devoted to understanding how research and policy mutually influence each other, especially how research can guide the development of effective early interventions for children. He wants to use science to help policy makers understand how adverse experiences in early childhood disrupt children's brain architecture and how effective interventions can shift the odds toward more favorable outcomes. He also wants developmental science to inform policy discussions about welfare reform, housing, family leaves, and environmental protection. Dr. Shonkoff has received many professional honors including membership in the Institute of Medicine of the National Academy of Sciences and the award for Distinguished Contributions to Public Policy for Children from the Society for Research in Child Development.

Further Reading

Shonkoff, J. (2010). Building an enhanced biodevelopmental framework to guide the future of early childhood policy. *Child Development, 81*, 343–353.

HEAD START Beginning in the 1960s, researchers and policy makers implemented a variety of programs to promote the development of poor children. One of the largest and best known preventive programs was **Head Start**, which was intended to give 3- and 4-year-old children a daily preschool experience. Originally, it included social services, medical care, and health education for parents. However, funding cuts eliminated many of the parent services. Today Head Start Performance Standards require comprehensive services for children (education, health and nutrition, mental health, and social services) and parent involvement. Head Start is the flagship educational program for young children in the United States. The number of children it serves has increased from about 720,000 in 1995 to 908,400 in 2007—but it still reaches fewer than half of all eligible children (Administration for Children and Families, 2007; RESULTS, 2008).

A new phase of Head Start began in 1995 when it was recognized that providing support for children before age 3 might be even better. This new program—Early Head Start—was designed to serve infants and toddlers from poor families. It provides a wide range of services including child care, parenting education, and high-quality comprehensive child development services delivered via home visits. Early Head Start programs vary according to community and family needs, but all programs provide some combination of these elements. The effectiveness of Early Head Start was evaluated in a study of 3,000 families who were randomly assigned to Early Head Start or a control group (Love et al., 2005). After about 20 months in the program, children in Early Head Start performed better than control children. They had

Head Start
A federally funded program that provides preschool experience, social services, and medical and nutritional care to disadvantaged preschool children.

A preschool teacher reads to a Head Start class in Washington, DC. Source: Paul Conklin/PhotoEdit.

advanced language development, displayed more emotional engagement with their parents, and were less aggressive. Their parents were more emotionally supportive, read to the children more, and spanked them less than parents in the control group. Clearly Early Head Start has been successful, at least in the short term.

Evaluations of the Head Start program itself also identified some positive results. In the National Head Start Impact Study, a randomized experimental evaluation of a representative sample of Head Start programs, significant effects were evident after 9 months in the program. Three-year-old children in Head Start had fewer behavior problems, and their parents were more likely to read to them and less likely to spank them than children who were not in Head Start. However, the study found no impact of Head Start on children's aggressive behavior, social withdrawal, or social skills (Puma et al., 2005). Experimental programs that cost more than Head Start, started earlier, lasted longer, were more comprehensive, and were affiliated with university researchers have been more successful (Barnett, 1995, 1996; Masse & Barnett, 2002; McComick et al., 2006; Reynolds & Temple, 1998; Seitz, 1990). Programs such as the Perry Preschool Program in Michigan and the Carolina Abecedarian Project have had positive effects that lasted into adulthood (Ramey et al., 1998; McLaughlin et al., 2007; Schweinhart et al., 2005).

Learning from Living Leaders: Deborah A. Phillips

Source: Courtesy of Deborah A. Phillips, photo from Georgetown University.

Deborah Phillips is Professor of Psychology at Georgetown University and Codirector of the University's Research Center on Children in the United States. Prior to this appointment she was Executive Director of the Board on Children, Youth and Families of the National Research Council. Her main interests are early child development, child poverty, and the intersection of child development and public policy. Her research focuses particularly on the developmental effects of early childhood programs. Her interest in policy stems from her experience as a Congressional Science Fellow in Child Development, a program that places scientists in staff and advisory positions in Congress for a year to forge connections between science and policy, and as a mid-career fellow at Yale University's Bush Center in Child Development and Social Policy. She has been a major contributor to understanding the importance of training child care workers as a way to improve child care quality, and she has shown that the long-term social and economic outcomes of early intervention programs such as Head Start make investment in these programs worthwhile. With Jack Shonkoff, she co-edited the highly influential book, *From Neurons to Neighborhoods: The Science of Early Development*, which called for a truly inter-disciplinary approach to child development and child and family policies. Her goal is not only to help inform policy through research but also to teach the next generation of policy researchers to be fluent in the languages of both scholarship and policy.

Further Reading

Ludwig, J., & Phillips, D. A. (2008). The long-term effects of Head Start on low-income children. *Annals of the New York Academy of Science, 1136*, 257–68.

Personal Responsibility and Work Opportunity Reconciliation Act of 1996 (PRWORA)
Federal legislation designed to reduce single-parent families' long-term reliance on welfare or cash assistance.

WELFARE REFORM POLICIES   In 1996, the U.S. Congress passed the **Personal Responsibility and Work Opportunity Reconciliation Act (PRWORA)** as the culmination of several decades of efforts to reduce single-parent families' long-term reliance on welfare. As part of PRWORA, the government implemented TANF, a policy that provided assistance for single parents through block grants to states. Unlike welfare, this policy introduced time limits on cash assistance and imposed work requirements on recipients. It required recipients to be searching or preparing for a job and then engaging in full-time work within 2 years of receiving their first aid check and limited aid to a maximum of 5 years. Proponents of welfare reform argued that requiring single mothers to leave welfare for work would provide the most reliable pathway out of poverty and that work requirements would promote healthier child development by enhancing mothers' self-esteem and introducing productive daily routines into family life. Opponents argued that children's well-being would worsen as mothers became overwhelmed by the work requirements and time-limited aid and that the new requirements would deepen the poverty of some families, forcing young children into unacceptable child care environments and decreasing parents' abilities to monitor their older children (Chase-Lansdale et al., 2003).

So who was right? What were the effects of TANF? Researchers found that parents benefited from going to work and earning money. Mothers who moved into stable employment and increased their incomes experienced improved psychological well-being and reported less domestic violence (Cheng, 2007; Coley et al., 2007; Gennetian & Miller, 2002). But how did the children fare? In one of the most comprehensive evaluations of this issue, researchers assessed the effects of welfare reform on children's well-being in five states (Connecticut, Florida, Indiana, Iowa, and Minnesota), focusing on children between the ages of 5 and 12 whose families had been randomly assigned to a TANF program or not (Administration for Children and Families, 2004). Their main finding was that although the new welfare policy increased adults' employment and earnings, it did not result in either widespread harm or widespread benefit to children. Overall, effects on children were relatively few in number and small in size. Children did, however, seem to benefit from increases in family income. Pamela Morris and her colleagues synthesized the results of a dozen TANF experiments (Morris 2002; Morris et al., 2005). They found that welfare policies that increased parents' employment but did not affect family income had few effects on children's social behavior or psychological problems. Welfare policies that increased both parents' employment and family income did benefit the children. The effects were small but notable. Findings on adolescents in two studies suggested that the programs might be less beneficial for this age group; increased adolescent problem behavior (drinking, smoking, minor delinquency) were observed when parents moved from welfare to work, presumably because they were not able to provide as much supervision and monitoring.

earning from Living Leaders:
Lindsay Chase-Lansdale

*Source: Courtesy of Lindsay Chase-Lansdale,
photo credit: Kim McElroy.*

Lindsay Chase-Lansdale is Professor of Human Development and Social Policy in the School of Education and Social Policy at Northwestern University. Her intellectual perspective combines the study of societal conditions that harm families with an emphasis on families' strengths and abilities to adapt to adversity. She has studied the effects of economic hardship, welfare reform, marriage, divorce, adolescent parenthood, immigration, and maternal employment on children and youth. To help these children, she has proposed policies that bring together ideas from psychology, psychobiology, demography, sociology, and economics. Her books—*Escape from Poverty: What Makes a Difference for Children?* and *For Better and for Worse: Welfare Reform and the Well-Being of Children and Families*—illustrate her interdisciplinary approach to social problems. She has also worked to promote synergy among scholars from diverse disciplines by launching an innovative research center called *Cells to Society (C2S): Center on Social Disparities and Health* at Northwestern's Institute for Policy Research. The center's mission is to bring together researchers from life sciences, biomedical sciences, and social sciences to study the origins, consequences, and policy solutions for contemporary health inequalities. Chase-Lansdale learned about social policy as a Congressional Science Fellow in Child Development. She is a Fellow of the American Psychological Association and the Association of Psychological Science and a recipient of the Society for Research on Adolescence Social Policy Award. She was a cofounder of the *Social Policy Report*, a publication of the Society for Research in Child Development that provides reviews of current policy issues for practitioners and researchers and *A Resource Guide to Careers in Child and Family Policy*, a valuable tool for students who wish to pursue jobs in the social policy arena. She is convinced that students cannot learn about policy from courses alone; they need to work in policy settings, which will challenge and expand their notions of research, decision making, and political influence.

Further Reading

Chase-Lansdale, P. L., Moffitt, R. A., Lohman, B. J., Cherlin, A. J., Coley, R. L., Pittman, L. D., Roff, J., & Votruba-Drzal, E. (2003). Mothers' transitions from welfare to work and the well-being of preschoolers and adolescents. *Science, 299,* 1548-1552.

INPUT AND OUTCOME: GETTING WHAT YOU PAY FOR   Do effective policies usually cost more than ineffective ones? There is some suggestion that this is true for policies targeting poverty. TANF programs that provided income supplements to families had a more positive impact on children than less-costly programs that just mandated that parents get jobs. Intensive and expensive early childhood intervention programs had a larger impact on children's development than less intensive and expensive programs. Sharon and Craig Ramey (1992) identified a number of qualities that characterize effective programs for poor families. Programs had high success rates if they began early in life and continued over a long period of time, involved parents as well as children, focused on improving both parent-child relationships and families' natural support systems, and involved community resources such as those providing education, job training, and employment services. Programs that had these qualities were relatively expensive. The Carolina Abecaderian Project, for example, cost $40,000 per child a year. Head Start currently costs about $7,000. Although some analysts have concluded that the benefits of Head Start exceed its costs, they also note that increased Head Start funding is related to enhanced effects (Ludwig & Phillips, 2007). Policy decisions are always constrained by budgets, and the reality is that the amount of money governments can invest in children's development is limited. Nevertheless, detrimental effects of poverty can be reduced more if we invest more in effective and expensive programs.

Real-World Application: Early Intervention with Children in Poverty

One of the most successful (and expensive) interventions for poor children is the Carolina Abecedarian Project (Campbell et al., 2001; McLaughlin et al., 2007; Ramey et al., 1998). This project entailed a carefully controlled scientific study of the benefits of early childhood education for poor African American children. Four cohorts of infants born between 1972 and 1977 were randomly assigned to either the educational program (57 children) or a control group (54 children). Children in the program group received full-time, high-quality education in a child care setting from infancy through age 5. The factors responsible for the high quality of education included small classes, well-educated teachers, low staff turnover, and a strong curriculum consisting of individualized activities or "games" that focused on children's social, emotional, and cognitive development. Children in the program attended the center for 5 days a week all year long. Their mothers also received intensive parent education. Children in the control group experienced a variety of child care settings during their infant and preschool years.

By the time the children were 1 year old, their abilities had already begun to diverge, and by the time they were 4 years old, the children in the program scored 13 points higher than the control group on an IQ test (Ramey et al., 1998). The program group did better than the control group in elementary school too, and, at age 21, adults who had been in the program as infants and preschoolers were twice as likely to still be in an educational program as those in the control group (40% versus 20%). They were more likely to be attending or to have graduated from a 4-year college (35% versus 14%). They had also waited longer before having children (19 years versus 17 years) and were more likely to be employed (65% versus 50%). They reported fewer symptoms of depression (26% versus 37% met the criteria for depression). When researchers investigated the effect of the program on the children's mothers, they found that those whose children had been in the program were more likely than control mothers to have graduated from high school and to have received postsecondary training; they were more likely to be self-supporting and less likely to have borne subsequent children (Campbell et al., 1986; Ramey et al., 1983). Analysts who performed a cost-benefit analysis of the Carolina Abecedarian Project found that it generated roughly $4 in benefits for every $1 invested (Masse & Barnett, 2002). These benefits included participants' lifetime earnings (projected to be $143,000 more for those in the program), their mothers' lifetime earnings (projected to be $133,000 more for those in the program), savings to school districts because participants were less likely to require special or remedial education, and health benefits because participants were less likely to smoke. Early intervention is apparently a worthwhile investment.

Child Care: A Problem Lacking a Unified Policy

Another policy issue for state and federal governments is child care for young children. In the mid-1970s, about one quarter of U.S. children under age 6 were cared for by someone other than their mother for significant portions of each week; by 1999, more than half were (Urban Institute, 2002). The primary reason for this dramatic increase was the rise in maternal employment. For single and divorced mothers, work and child care are not a choice; they are an economic necessity. In fact, 70 percent of single mothers with preschool children are in the labor force compared with 53 percent of married mothers. In a tight economy, however, even two-parent families often need more than one paycheck to cover the bills. Women also work because they find their jobs to be a source of social and emotional satisfaction. Another factor that has increased the use of child care is geographic mobility. A century ago, young parents were likely to live near extended family who could look after the children, and nearly half of them had a mother, mother-in-law, sister, or older daughter to help with child care. Today only one fifth of U.S. parents can count on extended family to provide child care. A final reason for the increase in child care is that views about what children need for their social and cognitive development have changed. Regardless of whether mothers work, most parents believe that children benefit from spending time in a setting where they can learn their colors and interact with their peers.

Choosing Child Care: What's a Parent to Do?

In choosing child care, parents balance three things: cost, convenience, and quality. Quality may be most important, but it's the most difficult to define and to find. Parents want child care that is safe and secure with a warm caregiver and opportunities for the child to learn. Features that experts use to define quality, such as a small size group of children, a low child-adult ratio, and a high level of caregiver training, are lower on parents' priority lists. In spite of their concern about quality, moreover, most parents do little comparison shopping. Instead they rely on the recommendations of friends, relatives, and neighbors. A brief visit or a phone call is usually the extent of their background work. In the richest country in the world and one with careful regulations for the quality of everything from carpet fibers to airline operations, it would be comforting to think that good-quality child care was guaranteed. Nothing could be further from reality, and over the past 30 years, quality has deteriorated, not improved (Clarke-Stewart & Allhusen, 2005).

family child care home
A child care arrangement in which an individual cares for three or four children in his or her home.

center care
A licensed and regulated type of child care facility operated by trained professional caregivers and providing educational opportunities, peer contacts, and materials and equipment.

TYPES OF CHILD CARE   Parents can choose from three types of child care: in their own home, in a family child care home, or in a center. A nanny who comes to the family's home offers personalized care for the child and perhaps some housekeeping, but this is usually the most expensive type of care. No licensing requirements apply to nannies and often they are untrained. A **family child care home** is a setting in which an adult, most often a mother, cares for a small group of children, usually of different ages, in her own home. Often these homes are in the parents' neighborhood and therefore are convenient and relatively inexpensive. Although many are licensed by the state, many more are unregulated and operate "under the radar." They typically do not offer organized educational activities.

Center care stands in sharp contrast to these two types of care. Most centers offer educational opportunities, peer contacts, and a variety of materials and equipment. Center care workers are usually trained and have some college education, and the centers are licensed and regulated. Finding a slot at a highly desirable child care center can be a challenge. Many parents sign up at a center as soon as they get a positive pregnancy test. They also need to start saving. Child care is the second largest family expense (after housing). In 2003, the average cost of center care was $5000 a year—higher than the tuition at most public universities. Child care expenses take up 7 percent of the budget for families with incomes above the poverty line and 20 percent for poor families. Although poor families on TANF qualify for federal support to help offset child care costs, only 15 to 20 percent actually receive this help.

Effects of Child Care on Children

QUALITY OF CHILD CARE MATTERS   We know that the quality of child care makes a difference for the children. Children in higher quality care are more sociable, considerate, compliant, controlled, and prosocial; they are better adjusted, less angry and defiant, and have higher self-esteem than children in poorer quality care (Clarke-Stewart & Allhusen, 2005). They also have more positive relationships with the caregivers in their child care arrangement. The NICHD Study of Early Child Care and Youth Development found that children in higher quality care exhibited more positive interactions with other children and were reported by their caregivers to have fewer behavior problems and to be more socially skilled than children who experienced lower quality care (NICHD Early Child Care Research Network, 1998, 2001, 2003b). Even children's physiology is related to the quality of their child care. Several studies have found that children who received more attention, warmth, and stimulation from their caregivers—an index of high-quality care—were less likely to have increased cortisol levels over the course of the day—a physiological reaction to stress (Dettling et al., 2000; Gunnar et al., 2010). Child care quality has a modest long-term effect on children's cognitive and socioemotional development through kindergarten and 1st grade (Peisner-Feinberg et al., 2001), and, according to the NICHD Study, even through age 15 (Belsky et al., 2007; Vandell et al., 2010). Effects of quality are larger for children who had difficult temperaments in infancy (Pluess & Belsky, 2009).

WHAT IS QUALITY CARE? Many components make up high-quality care (Table 13.2). One is the physical environment. When each child's physical space is very limited, children in the setting are more aggressive with their peers and more destructive with their toys; they spend more time doing nothing and less time interacting (Connolly & Smith, 1978; Rohe & Patterson, 1975). Children are also less cooperative and constructive when there are not enough toys and materials to go around (Brown, 1996).

A second component of quality is the number of children in the setting. Those settings that have too many children, especially too many for each caregiver to look after, can have detrimental effects on the children. Studies have shown quite consistently that overall quality of care suffers when child-adult ratios are high; caregivers in these settings are less sensitive, responsive, and positive, and children are less socially competent and less likely to have secure attachment relationships with their caregivers (Clarke-Stewart & Allhusen, 2005).

A third aspect of quality care relates to the activities for the children. An ideal program gives children some structured activities as well as opportunities for free play and free choice. Children in highly structured classes are less happy, less compliant, more stressed, and have lower opinions of their own competence (Stipek et al., 1995, 1998). High-quality programs also offer children a balanced menu of academic and social lessons; programs that focus solely on academic work are unlikely to promote social development (Finkelstein, 1982; Sylva et al., 2003).

The fourth component of child care quality is the caregivers' qualifications. Those who have higher levels of education and more training in child development are more likely to provide high-quality care, and the children in their care are more involved, cooperative, and competent in their play, engage in more complex play with peers, and are more likely to develop secure attachment relationships with their caregivers (Clarke-Stewart & Allhusen, 2005).

Finally, care quality relates to the stability of the staff. The National Staffing Study found that centers with the lowest rates of staff turnover had the highest overall quality (Whitebook et al., 1990). Caregivers who stay in the child care setting longer have more opportunity to get to know the children, read their signals more accurately, and respond to them more appropriately. As they spend more time in a child care setting, caregivers become more engaged with the children, more affectionate and responsive, and form closer relationships (Cummings 1980; Raikes, 1993; Whitebook et al., 1990).

TABLE **13.2** Components of Good Child Care: What to Look For

- *Plenty of materials.* A center with only a few exciting toys that every child wants to play with has more fighting.
- *Ample staff.* There should be at one caregiver for every three or four infants. Some programs claim to have that ratio, but it turns out that the afternoon groups are combined and there are more children per adult.
- *Balance between structure and free time.* Preschoolers in highly structured programs experience higher stress levels.
- *Great caregivers.* Having a degree in child development or early childhood education is associated with better care but equally important is whether the caregivers are caring and responsive.
- *Low staff turnover.* Replacing a third of the staff every year causes the atmosphere to be more chaotic and children to feel less secure and connected. High turnover may also be symptomatic of other poor conditions such as low staff salaries.

TIME IN CHILD CARE Even if they are in high-quality child care, children may exhibit some negative behaviors. Children who spend more time in care—more hours, more months, and more years—are louder, more assertive, more aggressive, and more disobedient than children who spend less time there (NICHD Early Child Care Research Network, 2002, 2003a). One reason for the elevated likelihood of externalizing behaviors is that extended periods in child care can cause stress. When researchers have measured toddlers' salivary cortisol as an index of feeling stressed they have found that cortisol levels rise across the day for children in child care but tend to decrease for children at home (Gunnar et al., 2010; Watamura et al., 2003). Children who are more socially fearful are especially likely to experience high and increasing cortisol levels across the day while in child care. For girls, the increase in cortisol is associated with anxious, vigilant behavior; for boys it is associated with angry, aggressive behavior. The externalizing behaviors displayed by children who spend a great deal of time in child care do not rise to the level at which clinicians are concerned, but they can be a nuisance for teachers when the children are in school (NICHD Early Child Care Research Network, 2005). Peers may not mind, though. Children who spent the most time in child care were more likely than children who spent less time in care to be categorized as popular-aggressive in elementary school (Rodkin & Roisman, 2010).

Learning from Living Leaders: Kathleen McCartney

Source: Courtesy of Kathleen McCartney.

Kathleen McCartney is Professor in Early Childhood Development and Dean of Education at Harvard University. Her research informs theoretical questions on early experience and answers policy questions about child care, early childhood education, and poverty. Since 1989, she has been a principal investigator in the NICHD Study of Early Child Care and Youth Development. This study of 1,350 children from birth through age 15 is one of the most comprehensive studies of the short-term and long-term effects of early child care. The findings have been published in numerous articles and are summarized in a 2005 book, *Child Care and Child Development*. McCartney received her bachelor's degree from Tufts University and her Ph.D. from Yale. While at Yale, she

was a fellow at the Bush Center in Child Development and Social Policy. She served as director of the Child Study and Development Center, a laboratory school for children from birth through kindergarten, when she was on the faculty of the University of New Hampshire. Today she is one of the country's experts on child care. According to McCartney, tests of child care policy provide convincing evidence about whether or not, and how, child care assistance can affect patterns of child care use. McCartney is coeditor of the *Handbook of Early Child Development* and *Best Practices in Quantitative Methods for Developmentalists*. She is a Fellow of the American Psychological Association, the Association of Psychological Science, and the American Educational Research Association, and was the recipient of the award for Distinguished Contributions to Education in Child Development from the Society for Research in Child Development in 2009. Education is a common thread in her family. Three of her four siblings work in the field, she is married to a teacher, and her stepson is a teacher, too. In her view, "Education is the single most important ingredient for a just society."

Further Reading

McCartney, K., & Weiss, H. (2007). Data for a democracy: The evolving role of evaluation in policy and program development. In J. L. Aber, S. J. Bishop-Josef, S. M. Jones, K. T. McLearn, & D. A. Phillips (Eds.), *Child development and social policy: Knowledge for action* (pp. 59–76). Washington, DC: American Psychological Association.

How Can Policy Help?

Child care in the United States lacks unified government policy. At times in our history, the government has been poised to develop a comprehensive plan, but this has not happened, and the United States may never experience the level of federal involvement found in many other countries. The governments in many European countries and Japan, for example, make a substantial contribution to the cost of child care (see Figure 13.1; Organisation for Economic Co-operation and Development [OECD], 2008). In the United States, parents pay for child care costs themselves unless they are poor and receive a welfare supplement or are eligible to participate in a government-subsidized program.

Policies could help U.S. parents in their quest for high-quality care in a number of ways. The first way is by increasing the availability of care. Finding high-quality child care is difficult for parents because it's simply not widely available. One way to increase availability would be to expand the public school system. Expansions might include extended school days in which before- and after-school care is provided in a safe, educational environment. Another expansion would be to extend the public educational system downward to include 4-year-olds. Many states have implemented or are exploring the possibility of universal preschool for 4-year-olds, which is already common in countries throughout Europe. In France and Italy, for example, about 95 percent of all 3- to 5-year-olds are enrolled in state-sponsored preschools.

Even if quality care is available, though, parents may not find it. The second way governments could help parents find high-quality care is by increasing their knowledge about care. Many parents are first-time users with little experience and an urgent need. They may assume that they have few choices and restrict their search. Even if they do search, they are not particularly astute or conscientious observers. In one study, researchers found that parents consistently rated the quality of their children's classes higher than trained observers did (Cryer & Burchinal, 1997). Government policy could increase parents' knowledge by providing written materials, YouTube videos, and public service announcements on TV focused on components of quality care. Government support has already been used to create child care resource and referral services, which are a useful starting point when parents are searching for care.

A third way policy could help parents find quality care is by providing more money to pay for care. Affordability is a major issue for most parents. Because parents with high incomes

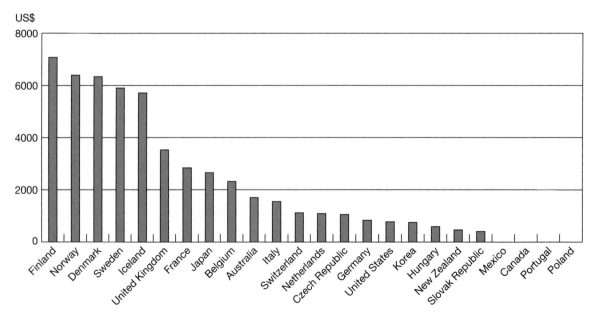

FIGURE 13.1 *Public expenditure on child care per child in 2005 per country converted to U.S. dollars. Source: Organisation for Economic Co-operation and Development (2010), OECD Family database, www.oecd.org/els/social/family/database.*

can afford high-quality care and parents with very low incomes are eligible for government-subsidized care, middle-income families are the ones likely to receive the poorest quality of care (Cost, Quality and Child Outcomes Study Team, 1995; NICHD Early Child Care Research Network, 1997a; Phillips et al., 1994). Public investment in child care has been estimated to be about $600 per child in the United States compared with up to $7000 in European countries, where a combination of subsidies, tax benefits, and employer contributions cover the bulk of child care costs (see Figure 13.1; Gornick & Meyers 2003; OECD, 2008). Research indicates that in the United States, states with more generous child care subsidy policies have child care centers offering higher-quality care (Rigby et al., 2007).

A fourth policy to improve child care quality would be to supplement caregivers' wages. We know that it's better if caregivers stay in a setting for a longer period and provide a stable, predictable child care environment, yet turnover rates in child care are among highest of any profession, hovering around 30 percent per year (U. S. Bureau of Labor Statistics, 1998)—a rate similar to that of workers in fast-food restaurants (Ritzer, 2007). By comparison, only 7 percent of public school teachers leave their jobs each year. Paying caregivers more would likely encourage them to stay longer. In 1996, the average hourly wage of child care workers in the United States was $6.12, far less than that for kindergarten teachers ($19.16). Wages were the primary determinant of staff turnover in the National Staffing Study: Teachers who were paid only $4.00 per hour or less left at twice the rate of those who earned more than $6.00 (Whitebook et al., 1990). An effort to improve child care quality for military families is instructive (Campbell et al., 2000; Zellman & Johansen, 1998). The U.S. armed services oversee a child care system that serves more than 200,000 children every day at more than 300 locations worldwide. In 1989, Congress enacted the Military Child Care Act in response to reports of extremely poor child care conditions. This act made pay for child care workers comparable to that for other jobs on military bases that required similar levels of training, education, and responsibility. As a result, staff turnover dropped from 48 percent to 24 percent.

Fifth, policies could be implemented to regulate quality. In 2009, the National Association of Child Care Resource and Referral Agencies examined state child care regulations in 50 states, the District of Columbia, and the Department of Defense. The average grade was a shocking F. No state earned an A or B, and only Washington, D.C., earned a C. Staff were being hired without background checks. Inspections were infrequent. State licensing offices had unmanageable caseloads. Child-to-staff ratios were not in line with suggested standards. The Department of Defense got the top score, a B. States can solve some of these problems without huge infusions of money. For example, checking employee rolls against sex offender registries requires only a modest budget increase. Other factors such as child-to-staff ratios cannot be addressed unless centers increase their tuition (which many families are already struggling to afford) or find other sources of funding to pay for more staff members. Changes in state and federal laws would be required to set minimum levels of quality and to impose penalties when centers do not comply. When states have more stringent regulations, child care quality is higher (Kisker et al., 1991; Rigby et al., 2007).

Finally, it might be possible for policy to limit the number of hours children spend in care; but it is unlikely that parents would find this policy acceptable.

Research up Close:
The Florida Child Care Quality Improvement Study

In the 1990s, Florida provided a natural laboratory to study two indexes of child care quality: child-adult ratios and caregivers' education (Howes et al., 1995, 1996). In 1992, state legislators mandated a change in child-teacher ratios from 6:1 to 4:1 for infants and from 8:1 to 6:1 for toddlers. In 1995, they imposed an additional requirement: for every 20 children in a child care facility, there should be at least one staff person with a child development associate credential or equivalent education or experience. Researchers seized the opportunity to conduct a study of the effects of these changes in child care regulations. They randomly selected 150 licensed centers in four Florida counties that were representative of child care within the state. Within these centers, they focused on 450 classrooms and examined them before and after the legislation. During the 3 years of data gathering, questionnaires were collected and interviews and observations were conducted. Center directors were asked about their perceptions of the effects of the mandated changes. Teachers were asked about their educational backgrounds. Observations were made in an infant class, a toddler class, and a preschool class in each center to assess child-adult ratios, caregivers' interactions with the children, and overall quality of care. Detailed assessments of two randomly chosen children in each class were made on a sample of 900 children. Teachers also completed ratings of these children's behavior problems.

Researchers found that when child-staff ratios were reduced, overall program quality improved, teachers became more sensitive and responsive and relied less on negative discipline, and children engaged in more complex play with other children, gained more in cognitive development, and were more securely attached to their teachers. When the proportion of staff with specialized training increased (from 26% to 53%), teachers were more responsively involved with the children, and teachers with the most advanced training had the highest scores on classroom quality and sensitivity with the children; children spent more time engaged in learning activities and complex play and were more securely attached to their teachers.

Although this study was not a controlled experiment—it did not have a randomly assigned control group in which child care regulations did not change—it did have an advantage over correlational studies because it demonstrated that changes in child care legislation preceded changes in child care quality and that changes in child care quality preceded changes in children's behavior. The study also revealed some of the problems of policy research. Although it was mandated that centers increase caregivers' training and decrease the number of children per caregiver, not all centers complied. The proportion of trained staff still did not reach the level required by the state, and center directors did not think that the new ratios improved quality—just that they were more expensive. Many directors did not even expect that the new regulations would be enforced. Enacting policy change and conducting policy research is clearly very challenging.

Teenage Pregnancy: Children Having Children

Surveys suggest that almost half of 9th to 12th graders in the United States have had sexual intercourse (Kaiser Family Foundation, 2005), and nearly 18 percent of teenage girls become pregnant (Perper & Manlove, 2009). Teenage pregnancy grabs our attention every time a celebrity adolescent like Jamie Lynn Spears or Sarah Palin's daughter Bristol reveals she is expecting. Of all the industrialized nations, the United States has the highest teen birth rate (see Figure 13.2). U.S. teenagers have almost twice as many babies as do British adolescents, more than four times as many as do teens in France, and more than eight times as many as in Japan (Darroch et al., 2001). Teen pregnancy rates in the United States vary from 8 percent in New Hampshire to 30 percent in Mississippi (Perper & Manlove, 2009). Between 1991 and 2005, the teen pregnancy rate in the United States declined and the rate of births to teen mothers dropped from 4.3 percent to 2.6 percent for white teens, from 10.5 percent to 8.2 percent for Latina teens, and, most dramatically, from 11.8 percent to 6.1 percent for African American teens (Moore, 2009). In 2006, however, the 14-year decline stopped. Between 2005 and 2007, the birth rate for girls aged 15 to 19 increased by 5 percent (Moore, 2009). It is too soon to say whether this is just a blip on the landscape or the harbinger of things to come, but concerns have been raised. In an online survey completed by 10,000 teenage girls in November 2008, 64 percent said they were sexually active; 52 percent had unprotected sex; and 20 percent hoped to become teenage moms (Tyra's Sex Survey Shocks, 2008).

FIGURE 13.2 *Teenage births in global perspective. In 2004, the United States had the highest teenage birth rate of industrialized nations. Source: Courtesy of the World Bank, 2006.*

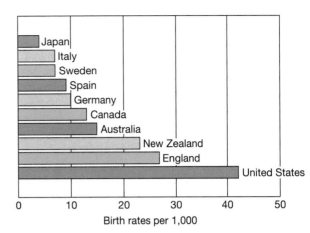

Birth rates per 1,000

B et You Thought That . . .
More Teens Are Having Sex Than Ever Before

You probably have some misconceptions about teenage sexuality in the United States. See if you can pass this true-false quiz.

1. **More teens are having sex today than 15 years ago.** *True or false?*

2. **More than a third of teenagers have sex by age 14.** *True or false?*

3. **Boys are more likely to have sex than girls.** *True or false?*

4. **Most teen girls have sex in a steady relationship.** *True or false?*

5. **Most teens have only one sexual partner.** *True or false?*

6. **Most girls are forced into their first sexual experience.** *True or false?*

7. **Most teens who have sex regret doing so.** *True or false?*

8. **Most teens have sex while using alcohol or drugs.** *True or false?*

9. **Few teens use condoms the first time they have sex.** *True or false?*

ANSWERS

1. *False.* The percentage of teens who had sex declined between 1991 and 2007 (from 54% to 48%).

2. *False.* Only 6 percent of females and 8 percent of males have sex before age 14.

3. *False.* More females than males have sex by age 19 (70% versus 65%).

4. *True.* Most sexually experienced teen girls (78%) are in a steady relationship the first time they have sex.

5. *False.* Almost two thirds of sexually experienced teens aged 15–19 have multiple sexual partners.

6. *False.* Only 10 percent of females who had sex as teenagers report that their first sexual experience was coerced.

7. *True.* Sixty percent of sexually experienced teenagers wish that they had waited longer.

8. *False.* Only a quarter of teens who had sex reported using drugs or drinking alcohol.

9. *False.* Of teenagers who have sex, 66 percent of girls and 71 percent of boys say they used a condom during their first sexual experience.

Source: Holcombe et al., 2009.

Factors Leading to Teen Pregnancy

Teens who are likely to become pregnant are different in a number of ways from teens who do not. First, teens who are sexually active differ from teens who are virgins: They are less conventional and conservative in their values, have more unsupervised time after school (Cohen et al., 2002), are more likely to have a sexually active best friend (Jaccard et al., 2005), and are more likely to have spent their childhood without their father (Ellis et al., 2003). Second, teens who take sexual risks such as having multiple partners and not using condoms differ from teens who practice safe sex: They have poorer self-regulatory skills in childhood (Raffaelli & Crockett, 2003) and their parents are more likely to be economically disadvantaged, not active in a religion, and not warm and responsive toward their children (Manlove et al., 2008; Moore & Brooks-Gunn, 2002). Third, teens who actually become pregnant differ from those who do not: They are more likely to live with a single parent, have problem behaviors and low confidence in themselves and their educational futures, and intend to have children early (Chandra et al., 2008). In addition, their mothers are more likely to have dropped out of school and been teen mothers themselves (Abma et al., 2004). These underlying causes of teen pregnancy—including adolescents' values, goals, social-emotional abilities, and family characteristics and conditions—are complicated and difficult to combat.

An additional factor contributing to teen pregnancy is television. In a national study of about 2,000 teens (12 to 17 years old), those who frequently watched television programs containing sexual content were twice as likely to be involved in a pregnancy over the following 3 years as peers who watched few such shows (Chandra et al., 2008). Television programs seldom highlight the risks of sex, so exposure to sex on television may create the illusion that there is little risk to engaging in sex without using contraceptives. It may also accelerate the initiation of sexual intercourse by showing young people doing it; teens who watch more TV programs with sexual content initiate sex earlier (Collins et al., 2004).

Outcomes of Teen Pregnancies

The factors that increase the risk of a teen pregnancy continue to have negative effects after the baby is born. In this section, we discuss the problems that the mother, the baby, the grandparents, the mother's siblings, and the baby's father face.

PROBLEMS FOR TEENAGE MOTHERS   More than half of the girls who become pregnant decide to keep their babies and become single mothers. If they have already left school, they are unlikely to return; if they have not yet dropped out of school, they are likely to do so and are unlikely to catch up educationally after the baby is born. Without education, these young mothers are limited in the types of jobs they can secure and their earning power is low. They can rarely afford child care, and, unless relatives or others can care for the child, they may have to give up their jobs and go on welfare. They find themselves in a cycle of low educational attainment, few skills, economic dependence, and poverty. Although almost a quarter of teenage mothers are married and another third have a fairly stable relationship with the father of their baby, more than half face personal, economic, and social problems that make supporting and caring for their children very difficult (Moore & Brooks-Gunn, 2002).

PROBLEMS FOR CHILDREN OF TEENAGE MOTHERS   Babies of teenage mothers also have problems. In fact, it has been suggested that the impact of the conditions under which teenage mothers and their children live is worse for the children than for their mothers. This may be because the children have always lived under these conditions whereas some of the mothers grew up in better circumstances. The children of teenage mothers are less likely than babies of older mothers to survive their first year (Phipps et al., 2002). They receive less positive and stimulating care from their parents and are more likely to be abused (Moore & Brooks-Gunn, 2002). They are more likely to develop behavior problems and to do poorly in school (Furstenberg et al., 1989; Moffitt, 2002). They display higher levels of aggression and have less ability to control impulsive behavior. By adolescence, they have higher rates of school failure and delinquency. They also become sexually active at younger ages and are more likely to become pregnant before age 20 (Kiernan, 2001; Kiernan & Smith, 2003). Part of the reason for these poor outcomes is that teen moms are not always competent parents; they have personal problems and lack resources (Leadbeater & Way, 2001; Moore & Brooks-Gunn, 2002). They are likely to be less warm and nurturing than older mothers and have lower educational aspirations for their children. The children do better if they have strong attachments to their fathers and if their mothers are prepared for maternal responsibilities and know about children and parenting before the baby is born (Miller et al., 1996; Whitman et al., 2001).

PROBLEMS FOR OTHER FAMILY MEMBERS Even the younger sisters of teenage mothers can be affected by the arrival of a nephew or niece. Often they must take time away from schoolwork to help care for the baby, and they are at increased risk for drug and alcohol use and for becoming pregnant themselves (East & Jacobsen, 2001). Grandmothers can provide support and guidance and help teen moms become better parents, but they may have to reduce their own activities to do so, and confrontations and conflicts with the teen mom are common (Caldwell et al., 1998; Hess et al., 2002; Oberlander et al., 2007). Teen mothers do better if their mothers are supportive.

PROBLEMS FOR TEENAGE FATHERS Adolescent boys are more likely to become teenage fathers if they are poor and prone to behavior problems (Moore & Florsheim, 2001). Most of these teen dads are unprepared for fatherhood—socially, emotionally, and financially. As one 17-year-old said, "I sure was surprised about my baby. I'd never been around babies much before, and for the longest time I just knew something was wrong with her. She didn't make much noise unless she was crying, and she slept all the time. I'm telling you, it was a real drag!" (Robinson, 1988, p. 39).

Although society tends to fault teenage fathers for their failure to support their babies and their babies' mothers, some do see their children regularly and provide help with caregiving (Coley & Chase-Lansdale, 1998). Two thirds of European American fathers and nearly as many Latino fathers marry their "baby mamas"; only one quarter of African American fathers do (Sullivan, 1993). However, even when they do marry, young fathers are two to three times more likely than older fathers to separate or divorce (Furstenberg et al., 1989; Brooks-Gunn & Moore, 2002). One national study reported that nearly half of teenage dads visited their child at least once a week; only 13 percent never visited (Lerman & Ooms, 1993). But as children grew up, contact was likely to decline; 57 percent of the adolescent fathers visited once a week when the child was 2 years or younger, 40 percent when the child was 2 to 4 years, 27 percent when the child was 5 to 7 years, and 22 percent when the child was older. Nearly one third of the children in the oldest group never saw their fathers at all. These declines continue across childhood and adolescence (Furstenberg and Harris 1993). Unmarried teen fathers contribute little financial support for several reasons (Cherlin, 1996; Kiselica, 2008; Ku et al., 1993). First, most teenage boys lack the earning power to help much; second, the mother's parents may try to exclude the young father, assuming that his support is unlikely anyway; third, some teen fathers simply don't want the responsibility.

HAPPY ENDINGS Happily, many teenage parents develop good lives for themselves and their children. Researchers in two studies have followed African American teen mothers into middle age (Furstenberg et al., 1987; Horowitz et al., 1991). Not all were destined to a life of poverty and welfare. In their early 30s, one third had completed high school and nearly one third had completed some post high school education. About three quarters were working; only one quarter were on welfare. They were most likely to be doing well if they had attended a special school for pregnant teens, had high aspirations at the time the baby was born, and their parents were well educated. Teenage child bearing need not lead to negative life outcomes for the mothers or their children. Just think of King Henry VII of England, whose mother gave birth at age 13, or President Barack Obama, whose mother was 18 when he was born.

Into Adulthood:
When Teen Mothers Grow Up

The stories of three women in the Baltimore Study of Teenage Motherhood illustrate how teen mothers can have entirely different life trajectories (Furstenberg et al., 1987). These stories represent three different patterns of adaptation to early childbearing: failing to achieve domestic or economic security (Doris), struggling to maintain economic independence (Iris), and achieving marital success and economic stability (Helena). Clearly, there is no single pathway for teen mothers into or through adulthood.

Doris fit the stereotype of what happens to a teenage mother. She was unmarried and dropped out of school when she became pregnant at age 16. She went on welfare and continued to receive public assistance for the next 17 years, even when she was—briefly—married. Doris had three children by three different men, none of whom she married. She was employed periodically but never for more than a few years, and the work never gave her enough income to get off welfare. During her late 20s, she had a lengthy relationship with the father of her third child. But he left the household, and in her 30s, Doris was living alone with her three children and her grandchild, the 2-year-old son of Doris's second child.

Iris also became pregnant at 16, but she finished high school and then married the baby's father the year after the child was born. The marriage lasted about 10 years during which time they had a second child. Except for the period right after the children were born, Iris always worked. After her marriage broke up, she went on public assistance for 2 years. She began a new relationship with another man, but it did not last. When it dissolved, Iris moved in with her mother rather than going back on welfare. As soon as she could afford it, she moved out, and in her 30s, she was living with her two children as a single parent. For 5 years, she had been employed as a business administrator for the Baltimore School District. Iris managed to get by with assistance from her family and supportive services from the government; her best financial years were when she was married and working.

When Helena became pregnant, her parents insisted that she delay her marriage to Nelson, the father of her child, until she had completed her schooling and had a secure job. She and Nelson were married around the time she turned 20 and have been married for nearly 14 years. During most of this period, both Helena and Nelson have been steadily employed. They live in a comfortable garden apartment on the outskirts of Baltimore with their two children.

Reducing Teen Pregnancy

As we have pointed out, the United States has a higher rate of teenage pregnancies than other Western nations. Some of this disparity is attributable to demographic differences between the countries, but a large part is the result of different policies to reduce teen pregnancy. This is evident because the rates of sexual activity in the other countries are as high as those in the United States, and teenagers' use of abortion is equally low.

SUPPORT FROM THE MEDIA   One policy that could reduce teen pregnancy involves the media. Restricting sexual content on television and peppering the airwaves with public service announcements about safe sex could be helpful. In a survey of U.S. youth, 72 percent reported that they gained at least some of their knowledge about sex from the media (Kaiser Family Foundation, 2003). Broadcasters could be encouraged to include more realistic depictions of sex and its unintended negative consequences for teens. However, even these portrayals might not reduce teen pregnancy. Researchers have found that youth who lack sexual experience are more likely to say they will participate in an unsafe sexual behavior portrayed on TV (such as a one-night stand)—regardless of the positive or negative outcomes portrayed (Nabi & Clark, 2008). The National Campaign to Prevent Teenage Pregnancy (www.teenpregnancy.org), initiated in 1996, incorporates pregnancy-prevention messages directly into youth-oriented entertainment media by sharing its messages and research with media professionals such as TV writers and movie producers (Donahue et al., 2008; Sawhill, 2002). Although it is difficult to determine the impact of this campaign, it is likely that at least some of the decline in teen pregnancies observed between 1996 and 2006 was due to media-based public awareness.

SEX EDUCATION IN SCHOOLS   The most important policy to reduce teen pregnancy is sex education in the schools. In the United States, however, this is the subject of contentious debate. Many educators argue that comprehensive sex education effectively reduces the number of teenage pregnancies; their opponents argue that comprehensive sex education encourages sexual activity. PRWORA increased funding for one particular form of sex education; it made about $88 million available annually for programs complying with the definition of "abstinence education" (Table 13.3).

Hundreds of balloons were released from the steps of the capitol in Jackson, Mississippi, May 3, 2006, during the Mississippi Department of Human Services annual abstinence rally, where teenagers were warned about the dangers of premarital sex. Source: © AP/ Wide World Photos.

TABLE 13.3 **Definition of Abstinence Education**

Abstinence education should . . .

1. Have as its exclusive purpose teaching the social, psychological, and health gains to be realized by abstaining from sexual activity.
2. Teach abstinence from sexual activity outside marriage as the expected standard for all school-age children.
3. Teach that abstinence from sexual activity is the only certain way to avoid out-of-wedlock pregnancy, sexually transmitted diseases, and other associated health problems.
4. Teach that a mutually faithful, monogamous relationship in the context of marriage is the expected standard of sexual activity.
5. Teach that sexual activity outside the context of marriage is likely to have harmful psychological and physical effects.
6. Teach that bearing children out of wedlock is likely to have harmful consequences for the child, the child's parents, and society.
7. Teach young people how to reject sexual advances and how alcohol and drug use increases vulnerability to sexual advances.
8. Teach the importance of attaining self-sufficiency before engaging in sexual activity.

Source: Title V, Section 510 (b)(2)(A-H) of the Social Security Act (P.L. 104-193.

How effective is abstinence education for reducing teen pregnancy? One team of researchers found that only a small portion (14%) of the decline in teen pregnancy rates since these programs began could be attributed to teens waiting longer to start having sex (Santelli et al., 2007). They concluded that abstinence promotion by itself is insufficient to help adolescents prevent unintended pregnancies. Another team of researchers conducted an experimental study in which more than 2,000 youth were randomly assigned to abstinence education programs or a control group and administered a follow-up survey 4 to 6 years later (Trenholm et al., 2007). Youth in the program group were no more likely than control group youth to have abstained from sex (about half of both groups reported remaining sexually abstinent), and the two groups had initiated sex at the same average age (14.9 years). Among those who reported having had sex, youth in both groups had similar numbers of sexual partners. The abstinence programs did not increase the likelihood of using a condom (23% of both groups reported always using a condom), which is not surprising because these curricula do not provide accurate information about the effectiveness of condoms (Kirby, 2008; Lin & Santelli, 2008). Numerous state evaluations of federally funded sex education programs have yielded similar results. A review of 11 state-based evaluations found that abstinence-only programs showed little evidence of sustained long-term impact on attitudes and intentions (Hauser, 2004). Worse, they showed some negative effects on youth's willingness to use contraception to prevent sexually transmitted diseases.

Virginity pledges (public promises to remain a virgin until marriage) and purity rings are common components of abstinence-only programs. Does this increase their effectiveness? Under certain very limited conditions, pledging may help adolescents delay sexual intercourse. A study of participants in the National Longitudinal Study of Adolescent Health found that the onset of sexual activity was delayed 18 months among pledgers—but only in schools where pledgers were the minority, so their pledging was "special" (Bearman & Brückner, 2001). Moreover, pledgers were one third less likely than nonpledgers to use contraception when they did become sexually active. In a subsequent study of this sample that matched pledgers and nonpledgers on factors such as economic status and attitudes toward sex and religion, researchers found that pledgers and nonpledgers did not differ as to premarital sex or sexually transmitted diseases 5 years after their pledge (Rosenbaum, 2009). Most surprising, 82 percent of the pledgers denied that they had ever pledged.

More effective in preventing teen pregnancy than abstinence programs and promise rings are sex education programs that give teens accurate and complete information about safe sex and the use of contraception. Comprehensive sex education programs, which emphasize both abstinence and the use of protection for those who do have sex, have a relatively positive effect. Using data from the National Survey of Family Growth, researchers found that 86 percent of the decline in teen pregnancy rates between 1995 and 2002 was the result of improved contraceptive use (Santelli et al., 2007). Sexually active teens were more likely to use contraceptives, more likely to use multiple methods of contraception (e.g., the pill with condoms), and more likely to use effective methods of contraception in 2002 than they were in 1995. A decline in teen contraceptive use since 2005 is one likely cause of the recent increase in the teen birth rate (Moore, 2009). A review of 48 studies evaluating the effects of comprehensive sex education programs on adolescents' sexual behavior found that about two thirds of these programs affected young people's sexual behavior in a positive way, both delaying initiation of sex and increasing the use of condoms and other contraceptives (Kirby, 2008).

In other countries, sex education is an accepted component of national policy. In the United Kingdom, the policy includes sex education and contraceptive and advice services for young people and encouragement of their parents to talk to them about sex and relationships. In the Netherlands, sex education includes a curriculum focused on values, attitudes, and communication skills, as well as biological aspects of reproduction; the Dutch media encourage open dialogue; and the health care system guarantees confidentiality and nonjudgmental providers. In Sweden, teenagers are given access to free contraceptives, including emergency contraceptives, and abortion as a backup. To reduce teen pregnancy in the United States, public policy programs could give teenagers accurate information about contraception and sexual behavior, make contraceptive services and supplies available and accessible, and promote the value of responsible behavior including contraceptive use and pregnancy planning.

Learning from Living Leaders: Kristin Anderson Moore

Most of the people we have featured in these Living Leader profiles are professors; Kristin Moore is Senior Research Scholar at Child Trends, an independent research and policy center focused on improving outcomes for children. Child Trends identifies emerging issues, evaluates important programs and policies, and provides evidence-based guidance for policy and practice. It covers a range of areas including child welfare and teen pregnancy and tracks indicators of the well-being of children and youth over time to provide a clear picture of how children and

families in the United States are doing. The center's mission is to improve outcomes for children by providing research data and analyses to the people and institutions whose decisions and actions affect children including policy makers, program providers, foundations, and the media. Moore was Executive Director and then President of Child Trends from 1992 to 2006, when she chose to return to full-time research. Currently, she heads the Youth Development research area at Child Trends. She was a founding member of the Task Force on Effective Programs and Research at the National Campaign to Prevent Teen Pregnancy

Source: Courtesy of Kristin Anderson Moore, photo from Child Trends, Inc.

Child Development's Centennial Award for her achievements on behalf of children and in 2009 she received the William Foote Whyte Award from the Sociological Practice and Public Sociology Section of the American Sociological Association "for her career-long efforts in using sociological research to develop policy, evaluate programs, and further understanding of society. The fact that the beneficiaries of all these efforts are children makes it all the more laudable." Moore's career is a reminder that scholars outside of academia make important contributions to the well-being of children.

Further Reading

Manlove, J., Franzetta, K., & Moore, K. A. (2006). Adolescent sexual relationships, contraceptive consistency, and pregnancy prevention approaches. In A. C. Crouter & A. Booth (Eds.), *Romance and sex in adolescence and emerging adulthood: Risks and opportunities* (pp. 181–212). Mahwah, NJ: Erlbaum.

and served as a member of the bipartisan federal Advisory on Welfare Indicators. In 1999, she was awarded the Foundation for

Support for Teenage Mothers

In addition to providing programs to reduce teen pregnancy, public policies could reduce problems associated with teen pregnancy by providing support for teen parents. One type of support is education and employment assistance. Research suggests that if a teenage mother acquires more education and becomes economically independent she and her child have fewer problems than others without these resources (Kalil & Ziol-Guest, 2005; Moore & Brooks-Gunn, 2002). Another type of support is to instill in teen mothers the belief that they can have a successful future (Moncloa et al., 2003). A third type of support is marriage assistance. Once a teen has become a parent, marriage is one of the best routes out of poverty. Marriage also provides the children a relationship with their father or stepfather, and this has positive social consequences. But marriage is a difficult path when the couple starts off with a baby in tow; the majority of marriages entered into by teenage mothers end in divorce (Cherlin, 1996; Clarke-Stewart & Brentano, 2006). Young people have limited abilities to judge what makes a good life partner and limited maturity to deal with the stresses of marriage and child rearing. Policies that offer teenagers guidance and assistance in developing and maintaining stable marriages could reduce the problems inherent in teen pregnancy.

Child Abuse within the Family

In 2006, more than 3.5 million children in the United States were assessed for evidence of child abuse or neglect. Close to 1.0 million were confirmed as victims: 64 percent suffered neglect, 16 percent were physically abused, 9 percent were sexually abused, and 7 percent experienced emotional maltreatment; more than 1,500 died (Children's Rights, 2008; U.S. Department of Health and Human Services, 2007). Because many instances of child abuse are not reported or are discovered only after the abuse has continued for a long time, these figures underestimate the prevalence of abuse. Children are starved, beaten, burned, cut, chained, isolated, or left to lie in their own excrement. They are sexually molested. They are even murdered. Young children are particularly vulnerable to abuse and neglect. About half of abuse victims are under 7 years of age; about one quarter are under 3. Almost half of the children who die from maltreatment are under 1 year of age; more than three quarters are under 4 (see Figure 13.3). The majority of victims are abused by family members; nearly 80 percent of abusers are parents (Child Trends, 2007; U.S. Department of Health and Human Services, 2008). Boys and girls are about equally likely to be victims.

FIGURE 13.3
*Death as a result
of maltreatment at
different ages. Children
are far more likely to
die as the result of
abuse or neglect when
they are very young.*
Source: U.S. Department
of Health and Human
Services, 2008.

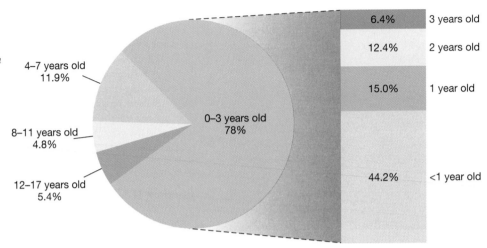

Child Abuse: A Family Affair

What can possibly lead to this inhuman treatment of children? Many students reading this book probably think that no one they know would ever abuse a child or that only someone who is really mentally ill would inflict grievous physical harm on defenseless children. However, child abusers are found in all social classes, religions, and ethnic groups, in mansions and mobile homes, and there is little evidence that severe mental illness characterizes abusive parents.

physical abuse
Physical injury or maltreatment by a responsible person that harms or threatens a child's health or welfare.

Physical abuse is defined as physical injury or maltreatment by a responsible person so that the child's health or welfare is harmed or threatened. It includes beating, biting, burning, hitting, kicking, punching, scalding, shaking, shoving, slapping, and not letting the child eat, drink, or use the bathroom. The adult need not have intended to hurt the child for an act to constitute physical abuse. Shocking as it may seem, mothers are frequently the ones who physically abuse their children because they generally spend more time with them (Azar, 2002; Cicchetti & Toth, 2006). Physical abuse is most likely to occur to young children in large families.

sexual abuse
Inappropriate sexual activity between an adult and a child for the perpetrator's pleasure or benefit.

Sexual abuse is defined as contact or interaction between a child and an adult when the child is being used for sexual stimulation of the adult or another person. It can include actual physical contact, such as fondling or rape, but it also includes making a child watch sexual acts or pornography, using a child in any aspect of the production of pornography, or making a child look at an adult's genitals. Sexual abuse occurs at ages from infancy through adolescence; the median age is 9 years. Girls are four times more likely to be victims of sexual abuse than

Child abuse is a problem that requires stringent preventive and ameliorative policies. Source: nautilus_shell_studios/iStockphoto.

boys (Feerick et al., 2006). About one quarter of child sexual abuse victims are abused by a parent (U.S. Department of Health and Human Services, 2008).

child neglect
Failure of a responsible adult to provide for a child's physical, medical, educational, or emotional needs.

   Child neglect is the failure of a parent or other caregiver to provide for a child's basic needs. The neglect may be physical (failure to provide necessary food or shelter, or lack of appropriate supervision), medical (failure to provide necessary medical or mental health treatment), educational (failure to educate the child or attend to special education needs), or emotional (inattention to the child's emotional needs, failure to provide psychological care, or permitting the child to use alcohol or other drugs).

   Two factors most commonly associated with abusive behavior by parents are a distressed, often sexually unsatisfying couple relationship and a history of abuse in the family (Azar, 2002). This does not mean that parents are destined to repeat their parents' mistakes. Only about one third of parents who were abused when they were young abuse their own children (Cicchetti & Toth, 2006). Mothers who break this intergenerational cycle are more likely to have a close marital relationship and to have received therapy (Egeland et al., 1988). Abusive parents are often socially isolated (Belsky, 1993). They have fewer friends, relatives, or neighbors to whom they can turn in times of stress. Their isolation may contribute to the fact that they frequently do not seem to recognize the seriousness of their behavior, and they may blame the child rather than themselves for the abuse. In addition, abusive parents are likely to have unrealistic expectations for their child's behavior (Azar, 2002; Feerick et al., 2006).

   Children's characteristics also play a role in the abuse drama. Children with birth defects, physical and intellectual disabilities, irritable and negative temperaments, or exasperating behavior problems are more likely to be abused. The combination of a difficult infant and a "helpless" mother who does not believe she has the power to influence her infant's development is a recipe for abuse (Bugental & Happaney, 2004). Physical abuse is usually preceded by an escalating cycle of verbal and physical aggression (Straus & Donnelly, 1994). Abusive mothers give threatening commands, strong criticism, and physical punishment (Cicchetti & Toth, 2006). In addition, their behavior is often unpredictable; they respond the same way whether the child has just succeeded in a task or thrown a tantrum (Mash et al., 1983). The mother's physical reactions reflect this failure to discriminate between desirable and undesirable behaviors. Abusive mothers experience both a smiling baby and a crying baby as physiologically arousing and emotionally aversive (Frodi & Lamb, 1980). This distorted reaction to the child's behavior increases the stress and confusion in an already disturbed parent-child relationship.

The Ecology of Child Abuse

Although abuse occurs in all types of families, there is a cluster of environmental factors that make it more likely. Physical abuse and neglect are more likely to occur in a family that lives in poverty (Duncan & Brooks-Gunn, 2000). Several reasons have been suggested for this association; among them are the stressors associated with being poor, the violence that often pervades poor neighborhoods, and the limited access poor people have to social services. Parents' unemployment is another ecological feature related to abuse. Occurrences of abuse rise after parents, especially fathers, lose their jobs (Steinberg et al., 1981). Stress, frustration, and increased contact between parents and children may all contribute to this link between job loss and child abuse. Third, child abuse rates differ across neighborhoods, even after levels of poverty are statistically controlled. Neighborhoods that offer more social resources—friends, neighbors, relatives, community centers—are protective; they provide advice, guidance, and physical and financial assistance that help parents avoid abusive behavior. Neighborhoods that are less friendly and more run down, dangerous, and transient exacerbate the family's plight and increase levels of abuse (Garbarino & Sherman, 1980; Leventhal & Brooks-Gunn, 2000; Parke et al., 2010).

   Families are also embedded in cultural and societal contexts that contribute to abuse. Changes over the past several decades that may have increased the stress on parents and contributed to an increase in child abuse include a heightened divorce rate, increased geographical mobility, increased demand for child care, and decreased medical coverage. In addition, the media have promoted widespread indifference to violence or even acceptance of it as a solution to social problems, which also may have contributed to child abuse (Straus, 2001; Straus & Donnelly, 1994). Some social scientists suggest that the high incidence of child abuse in the United States is related to tolerance of physical punishment (Donnelly & Straus, 2005; Gershoff, 2002). Child abuse is relatively uncommon in some other cultures, such as China, where adults rarely punish children physically. Our cultural approval of violence may combine with parents' lack of social, economic, and emotional resources and lead to child abuse.

No single factor causes child abuse. Abuse is more common when families have to deal with a pileup of stressful conditions—poverty, single parenthood, substandard housing, limited educational opportunities, poor health, a difficult child—in a culture that tolerates aggression and condones physical punishment. Abuse is less common when only one risk factor is present or stress is buffered by protective factors, such as a supportive marital relationship, a supportive social network, accessible community resources, and strong personal qualities (Azar, 2002; Cicchetti & Toth, 2006).

Consequences of Abuse

The consequences of abuse can be devastating. Abused and neglected children often experience adverse outcomes throughout their lives (Child Welfare Information Gateway, 2006; Cicchetti & Toth, 2006; Goldman et al., 2003). In childhood, sexually abused children, particularly girls, often display bed-wetting problems. Sexually abused boys are more likely than nonabused boys to have somatic complaints, such as stomachaches. Both boys and girls who are sexually abused display inappropriate sexual behavior directed toward themselves and others and engage in play and fantasy with sexual content. They are more likely than nonabused children to be anxious and withdrawn (Trickett & Putnam, 1998). Physically abused children are more likely than nonabused children to be depressed and anxious, suffer from eating disorders, exhibit self-injurious behavior, and experience suicidal thoughts and attempts. They are more likely to suffer from a serious psychological disturbance such as post-traumatic stress disorder. They have lower self-esteem and are more likely to experience fears and nightmares. They are also more likely to have difficulty regulating their emotions (Cicchetti & Toth, 2006; Kim & Cicchetti, 2010). Part of this problem may be physiological. Infants who receive frequent spankings have higher cortisol responses to stress (Bugental et al., 2003). Even as infants, physically abused children have less secure attachments and are more noncompliant with, resistant to, and avoidant of their mothers. As they advance through school, they are less prosocial and empathic, more aggressive and likely to be rejected by their classmates (Bolger & Patterson, 2001; Howe & Parke, 2001; Shields et al., 2001). These behavior problems may continue into adulthood; abused children are more likely to become abusive, violent, criminal adults. The majority of abused children do not become delinquents or violent offenders, however. Problems are exacerbated if abuse begins before age 5 (Keiley et al., 2001). Long-term effects of abuse are most likely if children remain in low-income environments with multiple stresses and few supports (Cicchetti & Toth, 2006).

Cultural Context:
Child Abuse and Children's Rights

Historically, children have had few legal rights. Not until the mid-20th century was children's right to protection from abuse recognized. In 1989, the United Nations passed a bold declaration on the rights of children, the Convention on the Rights of the Child (CRC). With the support of 190 countries, this document is the most widely ratified human rights treaty in history. It sets forth a broad range of provisions including children's right to a positive family environment, basic health and welfare, education, leisure, and cultural activities. Since the CRC was adopted, the world has seen dramatic gains for children. However, violence against children continues. A few examples of continuing child maltreatment include trafficking of children to work on plantations in West Africa, child soldiers fighting in Sudan and Sierra Leone, Chinese girls sold off as young brides, sexual exploitation of children in Sri Lanka and Thailand, and child labor in India (Betencourt et al., 2010; de Silva, 2007; Segal, 2001). Human trafficking is the third most profitable criminal activity, surpassed only by trafficking drugs and weapons. To address these concerns, the United Nations added two protocols to the CRC in 2000: the Sex Trafficking Protocol directed at the sale of children, child prostitution, and child pornography, and the Child Soldiers Protocol designed to ensure the right of children not to be enlisted as soldiers in armed combat. As newspaper and TV reports dramatically illustrate, however, child sex trafficking and rifle toting are still common.

One obstacle to reducing child maltreatment is that cultures differ in what they consider abuse and how they interpret children's rights. Many Western countries (although not the United States or Canada) classify corporal punishment—including hitting, slapping, pinching, shaking, hitting with a belt, paddle, ruler, or stick—as physical abuse. Other countries accept corporal punishment of children. In Sri Lanka, caning a child is still a permitted form of punishment in government schools (de Silva, 2007). Physical punishment is an acceptable way to discipline children in Kenya as well (Onyango & Kattambo, 2001). In Romania, almost everyone (96%) is comfortable with beating a child as a form of discipline and believes that that beating will not have any negative effect on the child's development (Muntean & Roth, 2001). In India, one researcher found that 58 percent of parents engaged in "normal" corporal punishment, 41 percent in "abusive" discipline, and 3 percent in "extreme" discipline (Segal, 1995).

What is considered neglect also varies from country to country. In India, because of extreme poverty, many girls are seen as a financial burden to their families and are forced to marry in exchange for money. In some cases, the girls are sold to brothels instead (Segal, 2001). A distinct type of neglect occurs in Japan. For years, unwanted children were placed in coin-operated lockers and, in many cases, died because they were not found in time. This became a serious social problem in the mid-1970s. Approximately 7 percent of infanticides in Japan during this period were of coin-operated locker babies (Kouno & Johnson, 1995). Since that time, this type of neglect has dropped dramatically thanks to an increase in locker inspections and educational programs on contraception. Neglect in Romania often takes the form of child abandonment by poor, uneducated parents (Muntean & Roth, 2001).

Although abuse is found in all countries, each country's government determines how it is defined, treated, and prevented. If governments could agree on a single definition of abuse this would be a step forward in the effort to protect children's rights. It would also be a step forward if children around the world were made aware of their rights. As a 16-year-old Nigerian boy observed, "Most children in virtually every nook and cranny of the world have very little or no idea of their rights. Even their teachers are ignorant of the fact that these rights exist. How can you protect or defend what you know little or nothing about?" (*Voices of Youth Newsletter*, October 2007, p. 2). Although we have made progress in recognizing children's right to live free from abuse, problems remain around the world.

Policies to Prevent Abuse

The economic cost of locating, evaluating, treating, and providing alternative care for victims of child abuse and neglect in the United States was a staggering $104 billion in 2007 (Wang & Holton, 2007). In contrast, only $742 million was used to strengthen families and *prevent* abuse (Kids Are Waiting, 2008).

PROGRAMS THAT PREVENT ABUSE   One approach aimed at preventing child abuse is to educate parents and increase their understanding of children's behavior and development. In one such program, parents who were at risk of becoming abusive because they were single, uneducated, immigrants, or had a history of abuse were assigned to one of three groups (Bugental et al., 2002). In the program group, the parents were taught a number of basic skills, such as how to set family goals, obtain quality health care, and manage money, as well as how to reframe and solve child-related problems. In the comparison group, parents were taught only the basic skills. In the control group, they were just given information about community services. The results were clear: Mothers in the program group were less harsh and physically abusive with their infants than mothers in the other two groups. Thus, teaching parents how to think more clearly about infant problems and how to solve them is one effective way to reduce child abuse.

A second approach prevents abuse by increasing parents' child-rearing skills. In one such program, the Nurse-Family Partnership®, nurses visit mothers at home from the time they are pregnant until the children are 2 years old. The nurses help the mothers improve their prenatal health before the baby is born and then they help them provide more sensitive, responsive, engaged, and competent care to the child. They also try to enhance the family environment by involving other family members, especially fathers, in the home visits, by linking families with needed health and human services, and by improving parents' economic self-sufficiency, helping them complete their education, find work, and plan future pregnancies. In a controlled experiment to evaluate this program, researchers found that parents who had been in the program had 48 percent fewer substantiated reports of child abuse and neglect than parents in the control group (Olds et al., 1997). Today, this program operates in 28 states and serves over 20,000 families every day (www.nursefamilypartnership.org). In SafeCare, another program focused on parenting skills, home visitors conduct in-depth, structured skill assessments of at-risk and maltreating parents and then teach them parent-infant interaction skills. Families in this program were less likely than comparison families to be reported for child maltreatment or to have their children removed from the home (Edwards & Lutzker, 2008). Not all parenting programs are successful in preventing child maltreatment, but this approach can be effective when well-trained professional home visitors make repeated visits and provide parents with instruction based on sound psychological theory (Astuto & Allen, 2009; Duggan et al., 2004; Holton & Harding, 2007; MacMillan et al., 2009; Olds et al., 2002).

Sometimes even a simple intervention can reduce abuse. When researchers discovered that child abuse was particularly likely to occur after kids' report cards were sent home, school personnel in Baltimore began to enclose messages to parents with each report card (Mandell, 2000). The messages, printed on colorful cards, suggested positive parenting techniques and provided crisis intervention phone numbers. Public service announcements on TV also aired the week the report cards were sent home. One year later, the Maryland State Attorney's Office reported that incidents of known child abuse as a result of a bad report card had decreased from 90 to 2.

This intervention in Baltimore involved providing parents with parenting instruction as well as taking a third approach to abuse prevention: connecting families with a support network. By giving parents phone numbers they could call in a crisis if they needed help or advice, the intervention reduced the families' isolation and increased their access to social support. This has been an effective strategy for preventing abuse in other programs, too (Azar, 2002). A particularly helpful form of support is the "crisis nursery," which provides temporary emergency care at any time, day or night, for children who are at risk of being abused or neglected. Most crisis nurseries offer free child care for a maximum of 30 days a year. They may also include support services such as family counseling and parenting classes. In an evaluation of five crisis nurseries in Illinois, researchers found that 90 percent of the parents who had used them said that their stress levels decreased as a result, 96 percent said that their parenting

In the Nurse-Family Partnership, nurses visit mothers and help them provide sensitive care to their infants. Child abuse is reduced as a result. Source: Courtesy of Nurse-Family Partnership.

skills improved, and 98 percent reported a reduced risk of child maltreatment (Cole et al., 2005). The Childhelp® National Child Abuse Hotline, which can be reached 24-7 at its toll-free number, 1.800.4-A-CHILD®, also offers crisis intervention, information, and referrals to thousands of emergency, social service, and support resources.

A fourth strategy for reducing child abuse is to communicate with the public at large. This was also part of the Baltimore report card intervention through its televised public service announcements. Media campaigns to prevent child sexual abuse have been explored with some success; at least they increase people's knowledge about abuse (Self-Brown et al., 2008) and provide an avenue for children to report maltreatment. They might also be used to try to reduce society's tendency to tolerate violence and physical punishment of children (Donnelly & Straus, 2005).

Finally, programs that address children directly are the fifth approach to preventing child abuse, particularly sexual abuse. Evaluations of these "child-empowerment" programs indicate that children as young as 3 can be taught some self-protection skills, especially if parents are involved and the children are taught to identify and resist inappropriate touching and are reassured that the abuse is not their fault (Finkelhor, 2007; Kenny et al., 2008). There is some suggestion that a national decline in substantiated sexual abuse cases (49% between 1993 and 2004) can be attributed to proliferation of these programs. However, although some programs have been associated with children's disclosure of abuse and one program was linked with a lower rate of victimization, there have been no true experimental studies, and the effectiveness of child-empowerment programs is not conclusively established (Nelson et al., 2001).

Reviews of all these different approaches to preventing child abuse suggest that the most effective programs do the following: (a) target physical abuse and neglect rather than sexual abuse (because sexual abuse is more difficult to prove and to prevent), (b) begin when a child is born and last several years; (c) target multiple risk factors in the family, (d) provide services that are responsive to individual family needs and sensitive to the family's culture, (e) give control to the local community, and (f) employ staff who are well trained and competent (Nelson et al., 2001; Portwood, 2006). A significant limitation of most programs is that they do not alleviate family poverty, which is a major risk factor for child maltreatment. To prevent abuse, families also need to be supported by social policies that promote access to income, employment, education, and housing.

Insights from Extremes: Suggestive Interrogations and Legal Policy

On August 12, 1983, a woman called police to report that her 2-year-old son had been sexually abused by Raymond Buckey at the McMartin Preschool in Manhattan Beach, California. Police detectives interviewed the boy and other parents to determine whether their children, too, had been abused, and based on the parents' concerns, the Los Angeles District Attorney's office asked Children's Institute International (CII), an agency for treating abused and neglected children, to investigate. Between November 1983 and March 1984, CII examiners interviewed nearly 400 children who had attended McMartin Preschool. They diagnosed 369 of these children as having been abused. Allegedly, these children had been forced to participate in satanic rituals and sex games. Buckey and six

other staff members were indicted by a grand jury on 115 counts of child sexual abuse.

After the longest and most costly criminal case in U.S. history, however, charges against the teachers were dropped, and Buckey was set free. The jury had concluded that the interviews, which they watched on videotape, were so suggestive and coercive that it was not possible to determine what had actually happened to the children. Analyses conducted since then indicate that the interviewers sought to have children admit abuse rather than finding out whether any abuse had occurred (Coleman et al., 1999; Schreiber et al., 2006). Children were prodded and charmed, cajoled and tricked, until they finally gave the interviewers what they wanted, some "yucky secrets." When children agreed with the interviewers, they were praised. When they disagreed, the interviewers expressed disbelief or disapproval. Often the interviewers introduced new suggestive information about abuse—"Did Miss Peggy take her clothes off?" "I bet she looked funny didn't she?" They also invited children to pretend or speculate about supposed abusive events—"Do you think Mr. Ray might have done some of that yucky touching? Where do you think he would have touched her?"

Before the McMartin case, children's testimony about abuse was accepted without question as being truthful. Almost everyone believed that children could not lie or be "coached" to make erroneous statements about sexual abuse. The McMartin case opened the door to skepticism and caution. It inspired researchers to conduct studies of children's susceptibility to coercive interviews. These studies revealed that children who are interviewed suggestively can produce false narratives, allegations, and accusations—even about behaviors that could be misinterpreted as abuse (Ceci & Bruck, 1995; Clarke-Stewart et al., 2004; Thompson et al., 1997). These erroneous narratives are often coherent and detailed and cannot be detected as false by professionals. Children are particularly suggestible about sexual abuse if they are young, their memories have faded with time, they are asked suggestive questions, and the interviewer pressures them (Goodman & Melinder, 2007).

As a consequence of the McMartin case and the research it inspired, legal policy and practice have changed substantially. Now many police officers and child protection workers are taught to interview children about possible abuse using simple and direct childlike words, explaining words the child does not understand, using the child's own words for sexual terms, and avoiding suggestive questions. They are trained to follow guidelines developed by professional organizations (Goodman & Melinder, 2007), which suggest that they begin by building rapport ("Tell me what school you go to."), practice free recall ("Tell me about your last birthday party."), provide information about the ground rules for the interview ("It's OK to say 'I don't know.'"), ask open-ended questions about the specific incident ("Tell me why you came to talk to me." "What happened next?"), and then ask more focused questions ("I heard that someone may have done something to you that wasn't right. Tell me everything about that, everything you can remember."). The goals of the interview are to maximize the amount of information provided by the child and to minimize contamination of the information. In an effort to find and prosecute child abusers, using techniques such as these is critical to uncover "the truth, the whole truth, and nothing but the truth." In Canada and many other countries, this type of interview has become the standard in investigations of child sexual abuse. Requiring interviewer training as legal policy would also advance investigations of child abuse in the United States.

FEDERAL AND STATE POLICIES   Social policy for child abuse prevention in the United States has focused on protecting children from abusive parents. It does this, first, by requiring that people report suspected child abuse to authorities and, second, by removing children from an abusive situation (Erickson, 2000; Goldman et al., 2003; U.S. Department of Health and Human Services, 2008). Child abuse and neglect have been considered serious enough problems to warrant federal intervention and regulation since 1974. That was the year Congress passed the Child Abuse Prevention and Treatment Act (CAPTA), the first federal policy that mandated reporting of abuse. CAPTA established minimum standards that defined child maltreatment and required that maltreated children be identified and reported to authorities. Individual states could decide how to implement reporting requirements and how to provide services to maltreated children and their families, but they must comply with the child abuse and neglect guidelines mandated under CAPTA in order to receive federal funds. All states now have systems to respond to reports of suspected child abuse and neglect and trained professionals to make evaluations and determine whether intervention and services are needed. School personnel, medical and mental health professionals, and police and fire investigators are all mandated reporters of abuse.

As a result of CAPTA and the state legislation that followed, U.S. policies moved in the direction of removing children from abusive family environments and placing them in foster care. These policies were based on the belief that parents have a fundamental right, protected by the Constitution, to raise their children as they see fit but the state has the power and authority to take action to protect children from significant harm. At first, children tended to be kept in foster care until their parents were rehabilitated, which often led to many years in care. Therefore, in 1997, President Bill Clinton signed the Adoption and Safe Families Act (ASFA), which favored speedy termination of parental rights and expedited adoption after 15 months in foster care. ASFA was criticized, however, because of research showing that children can maintain multiple attachments including those to their abusive parents. When ASFA was reauthorized in 2002, it was amended to reaffirm the importance of making reasonable efforts to preserve and reunify families. The Keeping Children and Families Safe Act of 2003 required states to engage in efforts to attempt family reunification unless the parents were guilty of torture, abandonment, or sexual abuse or had killed another child. Research suggests that foster care placement leads to benefits for abused children compared with children who remain at home or are reunified with their parents (MacMillan et al., 2009).

Today, family and juvenile courts have the authority to decide what happens to children after a petition alleging abuse or neglect has been filed, usually by Child Protective Services (CPS). The court is responsible for making the final determination about whether children should be removed from their homes, where they should be placed, and whether parental rights should be terminated. In most jurisdictions, child maltreatment is criminally punishable when a parent has committed an act against a child such as assault, abandonment, emotional, physical, or sexual abuse, indecent exposure, or child endangerment.

Although the intended purpose of federal and state child abuse policies is benevolent, they are not without problems. Child protection systems have been the subject of numerous investigations every time a child in the system dies from abuse. These agencies are underfunded and overburdened, often give their workers inadequate training and poor supervision, and fail to focus on children's safety and family's needs for therapeutic services (Krugman & Leventhal, 2005; Vieth, 2006). In addition, most child abuse reports are not investigated. To remedy these problems, as with all the other social policies we have discussed in this chapter, requires increased expenditure of government funds. Progress at preventing child abuse is slow and expensive.

Chapter Summary

Definitions, Aims, and Types of Social Policy

- *Social policy* refers to a set of planned actions whose goal is solving a social problem or attaining a social goal; government-based social policy is referred to as *public policy*.

- Social policies are designed to provide information, funding for programs and services, services to prevent or solve problems, and an infrastructure to support efforts on behalf of children.

- Policy decisions represent compromises based on societal needs, budgetary limitations, and political agendas. Policy makers increasingly use scientific information as one basis for policies.

- Programs may be focused on prevention or intervention. Primary prevention policies alter social and environmental conditions to reduce the likelihood that social problems will develop. Secondary prevention policies provide services for at-risk groups. Policy-based interventions involve treating children and families who have already been identified as having problems.

Poverty

- In the United States, 18 percent of children live in poverty.

- Poor parents generally have limited power, feel helpless and insecure, have little choice of occupation or housing, and are vulnerable to job loss and unemployment.

- Poverty makes child rearing difficult and leads to adverse outcomes for children.

- Poverty affects children through poor-quality home environments, high rates of parental physical and emotional problems and conflicts, neighborhoods characterized by social disorganization and limited resources, and increased family disruptions.

- Among the best-known programs for poor children is Head Start, which has reported modest gains in children's academic and social performance.
- Welfare reform involving supplemental income is linked to improved school engagement and social behavior; younger children benefit more than older children.

Child Care

- More than two thirds of children in the United States are cared for by someone other than their parents partly because of maternal employment and geographic mobility.
- In choosing child care, parents balance cost, convenience, and quality. However, most do little comparison shopping.
- Major care forms are care in the child's own home, care in a family child care home, and care in a center. Centers are most likely to emphasize educational opportunities, peer contacts, and materials and equipment, and to be licensed and regulated.
- Children in high-quality care are more sociable, considerate, compliant, controlled, and prosocial; they are better adjusted, less angry and defiant, have higher self-esteem and better relationships with their child care caregivers than children in poor-quality care.
- Child care in the United States lacks unified government policy. Parents pay for child care costs themselves unless they are poor and receive a welfare supplement or are eligible for a government-subsidized program.
- Possible policies to improve child care include increasing parental knowledge about its effects, providing parents with more money to pay for it, supplementing wages of child care workers as a way to reduce turnover, and regulating quality standards.

Teenage Pregnancy

- Nearly 18 percent of teenage girls in the United States become pregnant—the highest rate of teen pregnancy in industrialized nations.
- Teens who become pregnant are more likely than those who do not to have low self-confidence and limited educational aspirations, to belong to an ethnic minority, to have unsupervised time, to live without their father, to view sexually oriented TV, to engage in sexual activity, and to come from a family in which parents are poor, uneducated, nonreligious, and unresponsive to the teen.
- More than half of pregnant teens decide to keep their babies and become single mothers. Teen mothers are likely to quit school, go on public assistance, and live in poverty.
- Children of teen mothers are likely to have behavior problems and low self-control. Lack of economic resources, less competent parenting, and higher rates of abuse and neglect contribute to these poor child outcomes.
- Adolescent males are more likely to become fathers if they are poor and prone to behavior problems. Lack of responsibility, poor earning power, and family interference all contribute to a decline in father-child contact over time.
- Policies to reduce rates of teen pregnancy involve comprehensive sex education; abstinence-only programs are not effective.
- Education and employment assistance and marriage support for teenage mothers could reduce the negative outcomes for them and their children.

Child Abuse

- In 2006, nearly 1 million cases of child abuse or neglect were substantiated in the United States. Young children are particularly likely to be victims.

- Mothers are frequently the ones who physically abuse their children partly because they spend more time with them than other family members do.

- Sexual abuse occurs at ages from infancy through adolescence. Girls are four times more likely to be victims than boys.

- Ecological factors such as poverty, parental unemployment, divorce, mobility, and cultural values that tolerate aggression and physical punishment all contribute to child abuse.

- Children's characteristics such as birth defects, physical and intellectual disabilities, irritable and negative temperaments, and exasperating behavior problems also increase the likelihood of abuse.

- Abuse occurs in all social classes, religions, racial, and ethnic groups, and there is little evidence that severe mental illness characterizes abusive parents. However, abuse is most likely to occur in the presence of multiple risk factors.

- Abusive parents themselves may have been abused, are socially isolated, and have unrealistic beliefs about young children's abilities.

- Child abuse is preceded by escalating verbal and physical aggression that is often unpredictable and not contingent on the child's actual behaviors

- Consequences of child abuse include insecure attachment in infants, problems with emotional regulation and aggressive behavior in toddlers, poor relations with peers and adults and low self-esteem as children get older, and delinquency in adolescence.

- Programs to educate parents and enhance their parenting skills are effective in reducing child abuse.

- Policies in the United States have focused on protecting children from abusive parents by requiring that people report suspected child abuse to authorities and that authorities remove children from abusive situations and place them in foster care.

Key Terms

center care	physical abuse	sexual abuse
child neglect	primary prevention	social policy
family child care home	policies	Temporary Assistance
Head Start	public policy	for Needy Families
Personal Responsibility	secondary prevention	(TANF)
and Work Opportunity	policies	
Reconciliation Act of		
1996 (PRWORA)		

At the Movies

Many movies touch on the problems we have discussed in this chapter. Among those focused on poverty, *God Bless the Child* (1988) illustrates the trials and tribulations of a single mother trying to cope with her dire situation. This movie will open your eyes to those less fortunate and give you a better understanding of poverty in the United States. *Protection* (2000), a film about a family falling apart, was written and directed by a man with a background in child protection. This docudrama looks at both sides of the child protection issue and presents a harsh, realistic look at social services. *Ladybird, Ladybird* (1994) is the true story of a British woman who fights

Social Services to get custody of her four children who were removed from her care after they were injured in a fire and she was declared an unfit mother.

Movies about child care include *The Nanny Diaries* (2007), the story of a young woman who becomes a nanny for a wealthy family in the elite culture of Manhattan's Upper East Side. It provides an interesting illustration of some of the problems of nanny care. The funniest movie about child care is Eddie Murphy's *Daddy Day Care* (2003). Two fathers lose their jobs and are forced to become stay-at-home dads. With no job possibilities on the horizon, they open their own day care facility. Although the movie is full of laughs, it actually presents some serious issues about the challenges of creating high-quality care.

Perhaps the best known recent movie about teen pregnancy is *Juno* (2007). A 16-year-old high school junior discovers she's pregnant after a one-time experience with a boy who's just a friend. She is pragmatic about her situation and decides to place her baby with an adoptive couple. Her parents are supportive, and in the end, things work out and Juno continues with her life. There has been some worry that teen pregnancy has been made cool by this movie—the so-called "Juno effect." Other movies show less positive and more typical outcomes of teen pregnancy. In *Quinceañera* (2006), Magdalena is anxiously awaiting her 15th birthday when she'll celebrate her quinceañera. Her world starts to crumble when she discovers she is pregnant. She is abandoned by her family and deserted by the baby's father. This film shows the flip side to Juno's upbeat portrayal of teen pregnancy. But Magdalena manages a happy ending. *Riding in Cars with Boys* (2001) provides a more accurate portrayal of teen pregnancy. Beverly finds herself at age 16 a wife and mother. She is determined to finish high school and go to college, but that goal becomes difficult, especially after her marriage begins to fall apart. This film deals with the long-term aftermath of a teen pregnancy that completely derails

the mother's life. *The Pregnancy Pact* (2010) explores the costs of teen pregnancy with a story of a fictional "pregnancy pact" set against the backdrop of actual news reports about teen pregnancy from June 2008.

Movies about child abuse include *Mommie Dearest* (1981), which shows how Joan Crawford, one of the great classic Hollywood actresses, abused her adopted daughter Christina. At first, Joan lavished her daughter with attention and luxuries, but as Christina began to rebel against her mother's stringent demands and standards, Joan became increasingly abusive. This film is perhaps most useful for showing that child abuse can occur even in very wealthy families. Quite a different family is the backdrop for *Indiscretion* (2006). In her Hispanic family, 12-year old Sophia endures a bleak childhood with constant battering from her mother. In a cry for help, she ties a message to a balloon and releases it from her bedroom window, which sets off a series of events that unfold over the course of the movie. *Mystic River* (2003) takes the long view by showing how childhood sexual abuse can persistently haunt its victims. It gives a nuanced portrayal of the ugly reality of child abuse. But at least it's fiction. *An American Crime* (2007) is based on a shocking true story. Sylvia and her sister were left by their parents for an extended stay at the home of single mother, Gertrude, and her six children. Times were tough, and Gertrude slowly self-destructs as the burden of her financial needs and her unstable nature become just too much. This film is a cold, chilling tale of abuse and torture. *Switching Parents* (1992) explores the foster care system in which abused and neglected children are often placed and illustrates how the system sometimes fails them. It exposes problems in the policy of reunifying children with their abusive or neglectful parents. The film is based on the case of Gregory Kingsley, who made legal history in the United States when, at age 12, he went to court and "divorced" his parents so that he could remain with his foster family and not be uprooted again.

CHAPTER 14 Overarching Themes: Integrating Social Development

Source: Photo by John Dominis/Time Life Pictures/Getty Images, Inc.

Throughout this book, we have reviewed the results of hundreds of studies of children's social behavior and development. We have described theories that attempt to explain the detailed and complex information amassed by researchers and have discussed how researchers collect and analyze that information. As is true in any field of science, research-based knowledge is constantly expanding and changing, and we realize that a good deal of the information presented in this book will be reexamined and modified in the future. We recognize that although our understanding of children's social development today is vast, much remains to be discovered. With this in mind, in this final chapter, we identify some broad principles underlying the current state of knowledge about social development and suggest some ideas about how to increase knowledge in the future. Social development is a vibrant and exciting area of study, and further research can contribute to the healthy development of children and the betterment of society.

What We Know: Some Take-Home Principles

Views of the Social Child

THE CHILD IS SOCIALLY COMPETENT FROM AN EARLY AGE Scientists once considered infants to be helpless, passive creatures who, with limited abilities, were simply awaiting the imprint of the adult world. Today we view infants as competent and active beings who possess a wide range of social and emotional capabilities. When they are born, infants can use their sensory, perceptual, and motor capacities to respond to social signals and communicate their needs. In their first year of life, infants can use social referencing to guide their behavior in uncertain situations and can produce social signals to alert others to interesting events. By their second year, infants can infer that other people have thoughts, feelings, and intentions. These social-emotional skills provide a foundation for continued social development.

THE CHILD'S SOCIAL BEHAVIOR IS ORGANIZED Social behaviors such as crying, smiling, and looking are not disorganized reflexes or random reactions; they are organized response patterns that enable even very young infants to interact with others. Based on experiences with their caregivers, infants soon develop working models of their social world, which serve as organizing guides that permit them to react to social partners in orderly and predictable ways. As they grow, children use social information in increasingly organized and strategic ways to evaluate social situations and decide on their next social moves.

THE CHILD'S SOCIAL BEHAVIOR BECOMES INCREASINGLY SOPHISTICATED As children mature, social skills exhibited in rudimentary form at early ages become increasingly sophisticated and occur in increasingly complex contexts. For example, at first, children can use their turn-taking skills with an adult, who is a skilled social partner; later they can take turns with a less socially skilled peer partner. At first, children can communicate their desire for a particular toy when they are face to face with their partner; later they can communicate even when they are not face to face because they have acquired perspective-taking knowledge and can visualize what their partner sees. At first, children engage in moral reasoning in the course of their everyday social exchanges by invoking property ownership rules and pointing out the consequences of another's actions; later they can demonstrate this level of moral reasoning about an abstract, hypothetical moral dilemma. As these examples suggest, as children develop they demonstrate social competence in more mature forms and under more challenging conditions. They learn when to use their social skills and how to execute them in an ever widening range of circumstances. Social development is not only acquiring social skills but also being able to deploy these skills in circumstances involving more abstract tasks and in the face of competing demands.

THE CHILD IS EMBEDDED IN LEVELS OF SOCIAL COMPLEXITY The behavior of the individual child is embedded in a set of social interactions, relationships, and networks (Bronfenbrenner & Morris, 2006; Hinde, 1997). At the simplest level, the child has dyadic *interactions* with another person—a parent, a peer, a sibling, or a stranger. These interactions depend on the characteristics of both people and reflect the sum and product of their behaviors. Somewhat more complex are triadic interactions involving the child and two other people, such as mother and father or two siblings. Even more complex interactions involve more than three players. At the next general level of complexity, children develop longer term *relationships,* which depend on the participants' shared history and expectations about future social interchanges. Dyadic relationships include the child's attachments to mother and father, friendships with peers, and mutual antagonistic relationships with adversaries. Somewhat more complex are triadic relationships among mother, father, and child or among three siblings or three friends. Relationships represent a unique level of social organization and involve characteristics such as commitment, mutual support, and trustworthiness, which cannot be understood by simply observing interactions. The next level of complexity is the *social* *group*—a network of social relationships with its own rules and identity. The groups in which children are embedded include cliques, clubs, and gangs. At an even higher level of complexity are *social networks* of which children are not necessarily members. These networks—such as the extended family, parents and teachers, or parents and their religious institutions—influence children indirectly. Finally, at the highest level of complexity, children are embedded in a *society* or *culture* with its traditions, values, beliefs, and social institutions.

CHILDREN'S INTERACTIONS WITH OTHER PEOPLE ARE RECIPROCAL AND TRANSACTIONAL   From infancy onward, children influence the behavior of other people around them and are influenced by the reactions of these other people in return. Infants play an active role in eliciting and modifying their parents' behaviors by smiling and crying. In turn, their parents' reactions to these social signals modify the pair's behavioral patterns and exchanges. Infants who frequently display fussy and irritable behavior may provoke either highly involved, attentive behavior while parents try to calm them down or weary and withdrawn behavior as parents tune them out. Infants with an easy and engaging style are likely to elicit involved and pleasant reactions from their parents, leading to mutually satisfying patterns of interaction; infants with an irritable and difficult style are more likely to elicit negative reactions leading to less satisfying patterns of interaction. When they are older, children talk to their parents and evoke their help in solving social problems and, as a result of their parents' assistance, modify their social interactions with parents, siblings and peers. Over the course of development, the social behavior of children and adults is constantly undergoing change as a result of this mutual influence process. The resulting pattern of mutual modification over time is best described as *transactional*.

Organization and Explanation of Children's Social Behavior

ASPECTS OF DEVELOPMENT ARE INTERDEPENDENT   Shifts in other domains, including motor skills, language abilities, and cognitive functions, play a role in social development. These diverse domains of development are inseparable, interrelated, and interdependent. Infants' motor abilities to crawl or walk expand their social possibilities: No longer do they depend on crying or vocalizing to get a caregiver's attention and they can initiate social contact by moving closer at will. Children's acquisition of language opens new possibilities for expressing wants, wishes, and desires that previously could only be inferred from gestures or cries. Children's advances in cognitive understanding allow them to appreciate other people's intentions, wishes, and desires, which changes the nature of social exchanges and eventually the quality of children's relationships with others. Understanding other people's feelings also allows children to feel empathy and express sympathy, and this in turn promotes prosocial behavior. In short, social development is a "package deal" that is fueled by advances in other areas.

SOCIAL BEHAVIOR HAS MULTIPLE INTERACTING CAUSES   Social behavior is influenced by a number of interacting causes, including biological factors, such as genetics, brain organization, and hormonal levels, and environmental factors, such as parents' behavior, peer relations, school experiences, and popular culture. All these factors influence each other as well as the child. Neighborhood conditions influence parenting practices. School conditions provide opportunities for peer contact. Genetic factors affect brain functioning. Environmental conditions influence how genes are expressed. Only by recognizing the interdependent nature of different causal factors can we fully understand how social development occurs. *Systems theory approaches* that emphasize the interplay among biological and environmental systems are increasingly recognized as ways to organize the multiple causes of social development coherently.

ALL CAUSES ARE IMPORTANT   No single set of causes is more "real" than another. The tendency to treat some causal factors as fundamental and therefore more important is misleading. Some researchers act as if biological processes are more important, more scientific, and more valid and view brain scans or hormonal assessments as "better" than nonbiological assessments based on observations or reports of behavior. This is a mistake. To understand social development, we should recognize that biological causes are not more important than school experiences; genes are not more important than parents. Both levels of explanation represent different pieces of the puzzle and together enrich our understanding of social behavior and development. It is our task to figure out how different causal factors work together to facilitate or hinder children's social development.

Social Agents and Contexts for Social Development

SOCIAL BEHAVIOR IS INFLUENCED BY SOCIAL AGENTS IN SOCIAL SYSTEMS In the family system, children are affected by mothers, fathers, and siblings and the relationships among parents and siblings. They are affected by the extended family network of aunts, uncles, cousins, and grandparents and by the ties between the nuclear family and the extended family. Larger social systems include schools, communities, media, and society. In these systems, peers, teachers, neighbors, clergy, physicians, actors, sports heroes, and politicians influence children. Our task is to specify how social development is altered as a result of exposure to these multiple social systems and how changes in one social system reverberate through the other social systems. Understanding how the influences of systems change over development is another task.

SOCIAL BEHAVIOR VARIES ACROSS BOTH SITUATIONS AND INDIVIDUALS Human beings have the ability to adapt to the demands of different situations. For this reason, children behave differently in different situations—in the home, the laboratory, the school, the peer playgroup. This does not mean that situations alone determine children's behavior, however. Children's individual characteristics also matter. In an unfamiliar situation in which a stranger confronts a child, for example, all children react with some apprehension. But their temperament constrains their degree of upset and anxiety. Shy and inhibited children are likely to be afraid; extraverted children may be fearless. Our goal is to determine how individual differences among children modify the degree and form of their reactions to different situations.

SOCIAL DEVELOPMENT OCCURS IN A CULTURAL CONTEXT No single description of social development applies to all children in all cultures, social classes, and racial and ethnic groups. In different regions and communities, children have different experiences. They require different social skills to become productive and accepted members of their cultural group. If children live in a multicultural society they may receive conflicting messages from different sources. Observing the socialization of children across a variety of cultures and in different ethnic and social class groups can be a source of insights about social development and a way to increase tolerance of cultural and ethnic diversity.

SOCIAL DEVELOPMENT OCCURS IN A HISTORICAL CONTEXT As social conditions shift over time, children and families are confronted with experiences that differ from those of their predecessors. Their experiences reflect new economic conditions, lifestyle patterns, employment practices, and immigration demographics. Technological advances such as the invention of printing or the introduction of the Internet, which change the ways in which people communicate, have substantial effects on children's social development. Describing the social development of children in different historical eras and determining whether the processes that account for development are similar or different across historical periods is important. It is essential to continue research so we can update our understanding of social development as the social world morphs over time.

SOME ASPECTS OF SOCIAL DEVELOPMENT ARE UNIVERSAL Although historical and cultural influences are important, some aspects of social development are universal: They occur in all cultures and historical epochs. Social development is affected by universally shared achievements such as learning to walk and talk, which occur at approximately the same time and order in all cultures. Children's basic emotional expressions are universal as well, even though the rules that govern when emotions are displayed are culturally sensitive. The biological preparedness of infants for social interaction is evident in all cultures, but the ways that adult caregivers modify infants' early social signals differ across cultures. Determining which aspects of social behavior are universal and which are culturally determined is a continuing challenge.

Progress and Pathways of Social Development

DEVELOPMENT MAY BE GRADUAL AND CONTINUOUS OR RAPID AND DRAMATIC   Against a background of gradual development, of "every day and every way getting better and better," children experience periods of sudden rapid change. Some are biological changes such as growth spurts in infancy and adolescence, rapid advances in prefrontal cortex development around age 5 or 6, and the onset of puberty in adolescence. Others are normative or culturally programmed social changes such as school transitions or beginning to vote, drive, or drink at specific ages. Some changes are unexpected nonnormative events, such as the death of a parent or friend, a natural disaster, or the loss of a parent's employment. Our task is to understand both rapid and gradual changes.

EARLY EXPERIENCE IS IMPORTANT, BUT ITS EFFECTS ARE NOT IRREVERSIBLE For many years, the accepted assumption about early experience was that it had long-lasting and irreversible effects. Evidence has challenged this view, suggesting that even the effects of early adverse experiences can be overcome. These early adverse experiences include mothers' smoking or drinking during pregnancy; nonstimulating rearing in infancy; living with parents who are depressed, abusive, poor, or uneducated; and growing up in a group home or foster care. Examples of resiliency and recovery from these early experiences abound. Children reared in orphanages or institutions can recover or at least improve if they move to stimulating adoptive families. Infants who are adopted after the first year are still capable of forming attachments to their new caregivers. Although many children who are abused early in life suffer long-term consequences, others develop into well-functioning adults who do not repeat this pattern when they become parents themselves, especially if they marry a supportive and nonabused partner. Continuity of problems from childhood to later years is most likely to result from continued adversity throughout childhood, not from early adverse experience alone. The ease with which children can "bounce back" from early experiences varies with the length and intensity of the adversity. The longer and more severe the poor conditions, the more difficult it is to overcome negative effects.

THERE IS NO SINGLE PATHWAY TO NORMAL OR ABNORMAL DEVELOPMENT It is a well-established observation that people reach their goals by different routes. They may follow the conventional path of getting an education and marrying a classmate, or they may achieve success by winning the lottery and getting fixed up by the millionaire matchmaker. Children, too, take different routes through development; no single pathway is always the "best" or the "worst." Children may start life with disadvantages because of a difficult temperament or a depressed mother; they may overcome great risks because they are resilient or become derailed by minor obstacles because they are not. There is clearly more than one pathway through childhood and adulthood. We can learn from people who take the typical path and from people who follow the road not taken. Tracking the development of children with problems such as autism, for example, can teach us about certain aspects of social development, such as reading another person's emotions and developing insight into others' perspectives and beliefs. Similarly, understanding social development in normal children can give us insights into how children with social problems cope and how we can help them.

TRACING BOTH NORMATIVE PATHWAYS AND INDIVIDUAL PATHWAYS IS IMPORTANT   Throughout this book, we have described the age-related norms of social development. These norms are useful guides for knowing what to expect of children at certain ages and when specific social skills are likely to emerge. At the same time, individual children have different trajectories of social development. For example, some children start to act aggressively early in life, but others show this tendency for the first time during their teen years. Some children are shy as infants and remain shy for life, but others start out shy and move into the normal range of social assertiveness. Norms are useful, but recognizing and tracking the variety of individual developmental trajectories is important as well.

DEVELOPMENT IS A LIFELONG PROCESS   Social development in infancy and childhood is important and interesting. But development does not stop at the end of adolescence. Human beings of every age continue to respond to, learn from, and change as a result of new experiences. These experiences include marriage and divorce, financial success and failure, becoming parents and grandparents, losing friends and independence. One of our goals in studying development over the life span is to identify the types of childhood experiences that account for successful or not-so-successful adult development. Another goal is to understand how adult development affects children. The age at which an adult becomes a parent is one factor that illustrates this association. When a woman enters parenthood during her teen years rather than in her 20s or 30s, the social, economic, and even cognitive environment she provides for her infant will be radically different. Her identity and education and occupational roles are unsettled, she is less likely to have achieved financial stability, and she may not know how or be able to devote herself to stimulating her child. If we are to understand children's social development, we must consider the parents' development as well.

Glimpsing the Future: Methodological, Theoretical, and Policy Imperatives

Methodological Imperatives

QUESTIONS TAKE PRIORITY OVER METHODS   Without a sound and sensible question, even great methodological creativity will not advance our understanding of social development. Once a question has been identified, the researcher chooses a method that will answer it. Sometimes this means using a less preferred method, but it may be the only method available. For example, to address a central question of social development, "What aspects of the early social environment are crucial for optimal social adaptation?" researchers are unlikely to conduct experiments by setting up a variety of child-rearing environments and randomly assigning infants to them. Instead, they must pursue the question by taking advantage of natural experiments or carrying out field studies. Although these methods have problems and limitations, pursuing a meaningful question with a less optimal method is better than investigating an unimportant question with a more sound method—unless you're just doing it for course credit!

NO SINGLE METHOD WILL SUFFICE   Many research methods are available to examine the complex and multifaceted domain of social development. Naturalistic observations, clinical interviews, laboratory and field experiments, genetic and neurological assessments, and questionnaires and standardized tests can all provide valuable information about children's social behavior. To provide a complete and definitive answer to any research question, using a variety of methods to collect data is important. Doing so will ensure that results are reliable and valid. When new methods are devised, questions that have already been examined can be revisited. For example, advances in assessing unconscious prejudice (with the Implicit Association Test, which we discussed in Chapter 6) can be used to investigate the question "What is the role of unconscious processes in social interactions?" New statistical techniques for analyzing growth curves can be used to reexamine how parenting practices influence children's social development over time. Using multiple methods to look at facets of social development from different angles will provide broader and deeper understanding.

NO SINGLE REPORTER WILL SUFFICE   Different reporters provide unique perspectives on children's social behavior, which means that children's self-reports, parents' ratings of children, siblings' observations, teachers' assessments, peers' evaluations, and coaches' comments are all valuable sources of information. Teachers know how children function in class and on the playground. Peers know who is popular, who is rejected, and who is a member of a clique. Children themselves are the best source of information about their own attitudes, feelings, dreams, goals, and hopes for the future. Parents know whether children do their chores or fight with their younger siblings. Siblings may be a good source of information about whether children can keep secrets. Groups of children or adults can provide a sense of whether a neighborhood is safe, a school provides a positive climate for children, or a subculture values honesty. To get the full scoop on social development, collecting information from many reporters is necessary.

NO SINGLE SAMPLE WILL SUFFICE   To capture the diversity of children's social lives, studying more than one sample is often necessary. Using a variety of samples will capture the cultural, ethnic, and socioeconomic richness of children's development, both within the United States and throughout the world, and will tell us whether findings are replicable and generalizable. Cross-cultural comparisons can be used as natural experiments to test theories about influences on social development. For example, carefully choosing samples from different regions around the globe and examining the effects of different disciplinary practices on children's cooperative behavior in these different cultures can provide information about whether influences are universal or culture specific. In recent years, the use of nationally representative samples has increased confidence in the generalizability of findings. However, the continued use of small samples of known representativeness is still valuable because it allows researchers to conduct more detailed measurements of theoretically important processes. This in-depth probing of psychological processes may not be possible with large representative samples because of time and money constraints. New strategies that combine representative sampling with detailed examination of processes in a subset of individuals from the large sample offer a promising solution.

Theoretical Imperatives

NO SINGLE THEORY WILL SUFFICE   At present, no single theory provides a full and complete explanation of children's social development—and perhaps never will. Contemporary developmental psychologists believe that the complex nature of social development requires explanations of smaller pieces of the developmental puzzle rather than a theory that is all encompassing. These psychologists prefer theories of specific phenomena—such as gender typing, attachment, aggression, or moral development—rather the grand theories, such as those of Freud and Piaget, which were proposed during the last century. One of the challenges for the future is to integrate the phenomena of social development into a coherent overarching theory illuminating how the "whole child" develops. Systems theories reflect attempts to achieve this goal, but providing a unified approach to social development is still in its early stages.

NO SINGLE DISCIPLINE WILL SUFFICE   A number of scientific disciplines besides psychology contribute in important ways to our understanding of children's social development. Anthropology provides a cross-cultural perspective on child socialization. Sociology offers a societal viewpoint on the systems and institutions in which children are embedded. The field of pediatrics illuminates the role of physical health in children's social development. Clinical psychology and psychiatry offer an understanding of children's deviant and abnormal development. History views children's development through the lens of time. Neuroscience and molecular and behavior genetics provide information about the biological basis of social behavior. Multidisciplinary approaches in which researchers from different disciplines come together to focus on a specific aspect of social development are likely to be productive in the future. It takes a village of disciplines to understand the complexities of social development.

Policy Imperatives

RESEARCH ON SOCIAL DEVELOPMENT CAN INFORM SOCIAL POLICY   Findings from research about how children's social development is influenced by their social experiences can be used to improve social policies, such as those pertaining to parenting education, child care, preschool programs, school transitions, teenage pregnancy, adolescent risk taking, divorce, neighborhood poverty, immigration, and television content. Sharing knowledge of research findings helps policy makers design scientifically based interventions and prevention programs aimed at improving the social lives of children.

SOCIAL POLICY CAN INFORM RESEARCH ON SOCIAL DEVELOPMENT   The dialogue between policy makers and researchers needs to go both ways. Social policy decisions, including shifts in welfare rules, increases in child care opportunities, changes in immigration deportation policies, neighborhood relocation initiatives, and altered routes to parenthood via new reproductive technologies, are natural experiments and provide rich opportunities for researchers to track the consequences of policy changes on the lives of children and families and in the process learn more about social development. These studies can also evaluate the effectiveness of the policy changes and offer feedback to policy makers concerning the value of their decisions for improving children's social lives. In this way, citizens can be more confident that government funds—your tax dollars—are being spent wisely and effectively.

ONE-SIZE-FITS-ALL SOCIAL POLICIES ARE INADEQUATE   Because families and communities are diverse, there is a need to provide social policies and services tailored to meet the needs of different cultural groups. Policy makers who recognize the customs and traditions of these diverse groups are more likely to develop social programs that are effective in achieving their goals of optimizing children's social development. Inexpensive changes that improve cultural appropriateness often can produce dramatic changes in policy effectiveness. For example, inviting Latino parents to teacher conferences in small groups rather than individually has been observed to increase parents' attendance and participation, create stronger family-school partnerships, and improve children's school progress. Clear improvements in policy have been achieved by recognizing the unique needs of particular ethnic groups.

SOCIAL DEVELOPMENT IS EVERYONE'S RESPONSIBILITY   Ensuring children's successful social development is everyone's responsibility. Parents, teachers, coaches, clergy, and, in fact, all citizens have a responsibility to encourage and support social policies in the best interest of children. Being informed about children's development through books, TV, and the Internet and using that knowledge to urge policy makers to promote child-friendly policies is a task we can all share.

At the Wedding

Before you close this book, look back at the wedding photo that opened this chapter. It illustrates many of the social development themes and principles we have discussed. The wide range of ages represented by the wedding participants illustrates the theme that social development is a lifelong process. The presence of the extended family gathered for the wedding provides a clear example of the theme that children are embedded in a social network of relationships. Imagine the number of individuals in this photo who have had a socializing influence on each child. The theme that children's development is affected by *nurture* is reflected in the photo by clear evidence that parents and elders have taught the children to be quiet and attentive when being photographed. The effect of *nature* is implicit in the family resemblances among grandparents, parents, and children in the photo. Visible variations between adults in the photo illustrate the theme that different individuals follow diverse pathways from infancy to adulthood. Yet the very event of a wedding suggests that some aspects of development—such as forming loving relationships culminating in marriage—are universal. The photo reminds us of the themes that social behavior is affected by culture and by historical era. This wedding ceremony is colored by Chinese customs but the white dress and bouquet illustrate the influence of modern Western customs as well. The photo also provides a reminder of the theme that social behaviors vary across situations. While sitting for the wedding photo, the children are quiet, but when they are released by the photographer they will undoubtedly become more celebratory at the wedding reception. It was probably harder for some children than others to sit still for this portrait—reflecting the theme that there are biological differences in individuals' social behavior. Children who are by nature quiet and shy would have an easier time than children who are temperamentally outgoing or hyperactive. Being Chinese gave the children in this photo an advantage in staying calm. Highly active children would be better suited for the post wedding party where there is less structure and more opportunity for boisterous fun. Thus, even a single snapshot can illustrate some of the myriad themes that characterize social development across time, place, and culture.

Glossary

accommodation Modifying an existing schema to fit a new experience.

active gene-environment association People's genes encourage them to seek out experiences compatible with their inherited tendencies.

age cohorts People who were born in the same time period and share historical experiences.

aggressive-rejected children Youngsters who are not accepted by their peers because of their low level of self-control and high level of aggression.

allele An alternate form of a gene; typically, a gene has two alleles, one inherited from the individual's mother and one from the father.

altruistic behavior Intrinsically motivated conduct intended to help others without expectation of acknowledgment or reward.

androgynous Possessing both feminine and masculine psychological characteristics.

assimilation Applying an existing schema to a new experience.

associative play Interaction in which young children share toys, materials, and sometimes conversation, but are not engaged in a joint project.

attachment A strong emotional bond that forms between infant and caregiver in the second half of the child's first year.

attention deficit/hyperactivity disorder (ADHD) A disorder characterized by a persistent pattern of inattention and hyperactivity or impulsivity.

authoritarian parenting Child-rearing style that is harsh, unresponsive, and rigid and tends to use power-assertive methods of control.

authoritative parenting Child-rearing style that is warm, responsive, and involved and sets reasonable limits and expects appropriately mature behavior from children.

Autism Disorder that begins in childhood, lasts a lifetime and disrupts social and communication skills.

average children Youngsters who have some friends but who are not as well liked as popular children.

babbling An infant's production of strings of consonant-vowel combinations.

bullying Use of aggression against weaker individuals to gain status or power.

case study A form of research in which investigators study an individual person or group intensely.

catharsis Discharging aggressive impulses by engaging in actual or symbolic hostile acts.

center care A licensed and regulated type of child care facility operated by trained professional caregivers and providing educational opportunities, peer contacts, and materials and equipment.

cerebral cortex The covering layer of the cerebrum, which contains the cells that control specific functions such as seeing, hearing, moving, and thinking.

cerebral hemispheres The two halves of the brain's cerebrum, left and right.

cerebrum The two connected hemispheres of the brain.

childhood depression A mood disorder often manifested in despondent mood and loss of interest in familiar activities but possibly expressed as irritability and crankiness and difficulty concentrating or focusing on tasks.

child neglect Failure of a responsible adult to provide for a child's physical, medical, educational, or emotional needs.

chronosystem The time-based dimension that can alter the operation of all other systems in Bronfenbrenner's model, from *microsystem* to *macrosystem*.

classical conditioning A type of learning in which a new stimulus is repeatedly presented with a familiar stimulus until an individual learns to respond to the new stimulus in the same way as the familiar stimulus.

clique A peer group formed on the basis of friendship.

cognitive behavior therapy A therapy technique useful for treating depression in adolescents that teaches strategies for dealing with depressive moods and acquiring a more positive outlook.

cognitive developmental theory of gender typing Kohlberg's theory that children use physical and behavioral clues to differentiate gender roles and to gender type themselves very early in life.

cognitive social learning theory A theory that stresses the importance of observation and imitation in the acquisition of new behaviors, with learning mediated by cognitive processes.

collective self A person's concept of self within a group, such as a group based on race or gender.

conscience Internalized values and standards of moral behavior.

construct An idea or concept, especially a complex one such as aggression or love.

controversial children Youngsters who are liked by many peers but also disliked by many.

conventional level Kohlberg's second phase of moral development in which moral judgment is based on the motive to conform, either to get approval from others or to follow society's rules and conventions.

cooing A very young infant's production of vowel-like sounds.

cooperative learning A teaching technique in which small groups of students work together.

cooperative play Interaction in which children share goals and work together to achieve them.

coparenting How parents work together as a team; can be cooperative, hostile, or unbalanced.

corporal punishment The intentional infliction of physical pain as a method of changing behavior.

corpus callosum The band of nerve fibers that connects the two hemispheres of the brain.

cortisol A hormone secreted by the adrenal glands in response to physical or psychological stress.

critical period A specific time in an organism's development during which external factors have a unique and irreversible impact.

cross-sectional design A research design in which researchers compare groups of individuals of different age levels at approximately the same point in time.

crowd A collection of people whom others have stereotyped on the basis of their perceived shared attitudes or activities—for example, populars or nerds.

cyberbullying Making threats or using embarrassment or humiliation directed at a victim with some form of interactive digital medium such as the Internet.

delay of gratification Putting off until a later time possessing or doing something that gives one immediate pleasure.

dependent variable The factor that researchers expect to change as a function of change in the independent variable.

desensitization Classical conditioning therapy used to overcome phobias and fears through exposure to increasingly intense versions of the feared stimulus; the process by which people show diminished emotional reaction to a repeated stimulus or event.

deviancy training Amplification of aggression that occurs when adolescents are with and learn from aggressive peers.

direct aggression Physical or verbal hostile behavior that directly targets another person.

direct observation Researchers go into settings in the real world or bring participants into the laboratory to observe behaviors of interest.

dizygotic Fraternal twins from two different eggs fertilized by two different sperm, producing two different zygotes.

domain specificity Processes of development are different for different types of behavior, for example, moral judgments, manners, and peer relationships.

dominance hierarchy An ordering of individuals in a group from most to least dominant; a "pecking order."

drive reduction theory A version of learning theory suggesting that the association of stimulus and response in classical and operant conditioning results in learning only if it is accompanied by reduction of basic primary drives such as hunger and thirst.

Duchenne smile A smile reflecting genuine pleasure, shown in crinkles around the eyes as well as an upturned mouth.

early starters Children who start to behave aggressively at a young age and often remain aggressive through childhood and adolescence.

ecological theory A theory stressing the influences of environmental systems and relations between systems on development.

ecological validity The degree to which a research study accurately represents events or processes that occur in the real world.

effect size An estimate of the magnitude of the difference between groups or the strength of the association between the factors, averaged across studies in a meta-analysis.

ego In Freud's theory, the rational component of the personality, which tries to satisfy needs through appropriate, socially acceptable behaviors.

egocentric Tending to view the world from one's own perspective and to have difficulty seeing things from another's viewpoint.

Electra complex According to Freud, girls blame their mother for their lack of a penis and focus their sexual feelings on their father.

emotion regulation The managing, monitoring, evaluating, and modifying of emotional reactions to reduce the intensity and duration of emotional arousal.

emotional display rule An implicit understanding in a culture of how and when an emotion should be expressed.

emotional script A scheme that enables a child to identify the emotional reaction likely to accompany a particular event.

empathic reasoning An advanced type of prosocial reasoning involving sympathetic responding, self-reflective role taking, concern with the other's humanness, and guilt or positive affect related to the consequences of one's actions.

empathy A shared emotional response that parallels another person's feelings.

equifinality The convergence of developmental paths in which children follow very different paths to reach the same developmental end point.

ethnic identity Recognition of being a member of a particular race or ethnic group.

ethnography Use of intensive observations and interviews to gather data about the beliefs, practices, and behaviors of individuals in a particular context or culture.

ethological theory A theory that behavior must be viewed in a particular context and as having adaptive or survival value.

event sampling Investigators record participants' behavior only when an event of particular interest occurs.

evocative gene-environment association People's inherited tendencies elicit certain environmental responses.

exosystem In Bronfenbrenner's ecological theory, the collection of settings that impinge on a child's development but in which the child does not play a direct role.

experience sampling method (ESM) A data collection strategy by which participants are signaled at random times throughout the day and record answers to researchers' questions, such as: Where are you? Who are you with? What are you doing? Also called the *beeper* method.

experience-dependent processes Brain processes that are unique to the individual and responsive to particular cultural, community, and family experiences.

experience-expectant processes Brain processes that are universal, experienced by all human beings across evolution.

expressive characteristics Those aspects of a person involving nurturance and concern with feelings. They are more typical of females.

extended family A unit of people that includes relatives such as grandparents, aunts, uncles, nieces, and nephews as well as members of the nuclear family.

externalizing problems A type of childhood behavior problem in which the behavior is directed at others, including hitting, stealing, vandalizing, and lying.

family child care home A child care arrangement in which an individual cares for three or four children in his or her home.

family system A group of related people composed of interdependent members and subsystems; changes in the behavior of one member of the family affect the functioning of the other members.

field experiment An experiment in which researchers deliberately create a change in a real-world setting and then measure the outcome of their manipulation.

focus group Group interview in which an interviewer poses questions that are answered by the participants.

gang A group of adolescents or adults who form an allegiance for a common purpose.

gender constancy The awareness that superficial alterations in appearance or activity do not alter gender.

gender identity The perception of oneself as either male or female.

gender role Composite of the behaviors actually exhibited by a typical male or female in a given culture; the reflection of a *gender stereotype* in everyday life.

gender segregation A child's choice to spend time with same-gender peers.

gender stability The fact that males remain male and females remain female.

gender stereotype Belief that members of a culture hold about acceptable and appropriate attitudes, interests, activities, psychological traits, social relationships, occupations, and physical appearance for males and females.

gender typing The process by which children acquire the values, motives, and behaviors considered appropriate for their gender in their particular culture.

gender-based belief An idea that differentiates males and females.

gender-role preference Desire to possess certain gender-typed characteristics.

gender-schema theory The view that children develop schemas, or naive theories, that help them organize and structure their experience related to gender differences and gender roles.

gene A portion of DNA located at a particular site on a chromosome and coding for the production of a specific type of protein.

gene-environment interaction (G × E) model People in the same environment are affected differently depending on their genetic makeup.

generativity A concern for people besides oneself, especially a desire to nurture and guide younger people and contribute to the next generation.

genotype The particular set of genes a person inherits from his or her parents.

glial cell A cell that supports, protects, and repairs neurons.

habituation Individual reacts with less and less intensity to a repeatedly presented stimulus until he or she responds only faintly or not at all.

Head Start A federally funded program that provides preschool experience, social services, and medical and nutritional care to disadvantaged preschool children.

hedonistic reasoning Making a decision to perform a prosocial act on the basis of expected material reward.

heritability factor A statistical estimate of the contribution heredity makes to a particular trait or ability.

heterozygous Alleles for a particular trait from each parent are different.

holophrase A single word that appears to represent a complete thought.

homophily The tendency of individuals to associate and bond with others who are similar.

homozygous Alleles for a particular trait from each parent are the same.

hormone Powerful and highly specialized chemical substance produced by the cells of certain body organs, which has a regulatory effect on the activity of certain other organs.

hostile attribution bias A tendency to interpret neutral or ambiguous social behavior of another person as being hostile.

human behavior genetics The study of the relative influences of heredity and environment on individual differences in traits and abilities.

id In Freud's theory, instinctual drives that operate on the basis of the *pleasure principle*.

identification The Freudian concept that children think of themselves as being the same as their same-sex parent.

identity The definition of oneself as a discrete, separate entity.

immanent justice The notion that any deviation from rules will inevitably result in punishment or retribution.

imprinting Birds and other infrahuman animals develop a preference for and follow the person or object to which they are first exposed during a brief, critical period after birth.

independent variable The factor that researchers deliberately manipulate in an experiment.

indirect aggression Hostile behavior committed by an unidentified perpetrator that hurts another person by indirect means.

individual self Aspects of the self that make a person unique and separate from others.

informed consent Agreement to participate in a study based on a clear and full understanding of its purposes and procedures.

insecure-ambivalent attachment Babies tend to become very upset at the departure of their mother and exhibit inconsistent behavior on the mother's return, sometimes seeking contact, sometimes pushing their mother away. (This is sometimes referred to as *insecure-resistant* or *anxious-ambivalent attachment*.)

insecure-avoidant attachment Babies seem not to be bothered by their mother's brief absences but specifically avoid her when she returns, sometimes becoming visibly upset.

insecure-disorganized attachment Babies seem disorganized and disoriented when reunited with their mother after a brief separation.

instrumental characteristics Those aspects of a person involving task and occupation orientation. They are more typical of males.

internal working model A person's mental representation of himself or herself as a child, his or her parents, and the nature of his or her interaction with the parents as he or she reconstructs and interprets that interaction.

internalize The process by which children acquire the rules and standards of behavior laid down by others in their culture and adopt them as their own.

internalized reasoning The most advanced type of prosocial reasoning in which justifications for helping are based on the importance of maintaining societal obligations or treating all people as equal.

internalizing problems A type of childhood behavior problem in which the behavior is directed at the self rather than others, including fear, anxiety, depression, loneliness, and withdrawal.

intervention A program provided to improve a situation or relieve psychological illness or distress.

joint legal custody A form of postdivorce child custody in which both parents retain and share responsibility for decisions regarding the child's life, although the child usually resides with one parent.

joint physical custody A form of postdivorce child custody in which parents make decisions together regarding their child's life and also share physical custody so that the child lives with each parent for about half the time.

laboratory analogue experiment Researchers try to duplicate in the laboratory features or events that occur naturally in everyday life in order to increase the ecological validity of the results.

latchkey children Youngsters who must let themselves into their homes after school because their parents are working outside the home.

late starters Children who begin to act aggressively in adolescence and tend not to continue their aggressive behavior in adulthood.

lateralization The process by which each half of the brain becomes specialized for certain functions—for example, the control of speech and language by the left hemisphere and of visual-spatial processing by the right.

learned helplessness A feeling that results from the belief that one cannot control the events in one's world.

longitudinal design A study in which investigators follow the same people over a period of time, observing them repeatedly.

macrosystem In Bronfenbrenner's ecological theory, the system that surrounds the *microsystem*, *mesosystem*, and *exosystem*, representing the values, ideologies, and laws of the society or culture.

magic window thinking The tendency of very young children to believe that television images are as real as real-life people and objects.

maternal bond Feeling of attachment by a mother to her infant, perhaps influenced by early infant contact.

maturation A biologically determined process of growth that unfolds over a period of time.

mesosystem In Bronfenbrenner's ecological theory, the interrelations among the components of the microsystem.

meta-analysis A statistical technique that allows the researcher to summarize the results of many studies on a particular topic and to draw conclusions about the size and replicability of observed differences or associations.

microsystem In Bronfenbrenner's ecological theory, the context in which children live and interact with the people and institutions closest to them, such as parents, peers, and school.

mirror neuron A nerve cell that fires both when a person acts and when a person observes the same action performed by someone else, as if the observer himself or herself were acting.

modifier genes Genes that exert their influence indirectly by affecting the expression of other genes.

monozygotic Identical twins created when a single zygote splits in half and each half becomes a distinct embryo with exactly the same genes; both embryos come from one zygote.

moral absolutism Rigid application of rules to all individuals regardless of their culture or circumstance.

moral realism Piaget's second stage of moral development in which children show great respect for rules and apply them quite inflexibly.

moral reciprocity Piaget's third stage of moral development in which children recognize that rules may be questioned and altered, consider the feelings and views of others, and believe in equal justice for all.

multifinality The divergence of developmental paths in which two individuals start out similarly but end at very different points.

multischematic Possessing multiple ideas about appropriate behaviors that can be displayed depending on the particular situation.

mutual antipathy A relationship of mutual dislike between two people.

myelination The process by which glial cells encase neurons in sheaths of the fatty substance myelin.

natural experiment An experiment in which researchers measure the results of events that occur naturally in the real world.

naturalistic observations Information collected in the child's natural settings, at home, in child care, or in school without interfering with the child's activities.

needs-oriented reasoning Prosocial judgments in which children express concern for others' needs although their own needs may conflict with them.

negative gossip Adverse or detrimental information shared about another child with a peer.

neglected children Youngsters who are often socially isolated and, although they are not necessarily disliked, have few friends.

neural migration The movement of neurons within the brain that ensures that all brain areas have a sufficient number of neural connections.

neuron A cell in the body's nervous system, consisting of a cell body, a long projection called an *axon*, and several shorter projections called *dendrites*; neurons send and receive neural impulses, or messages, throughout the brain and nervous system.

neuron proliferation The rapid formation of neurons in the developing organism's brain.

niche picking Seeking out or creating environments compatible with one's genetically based predispositions.

nonaggressive-rejected children Excluded youngsters who tend to be anxious, withdrawn, and socially unskilled.

nonshared environment A set of conditions or activities experienced by one child in a family but not shared with another child in the same family.

nuclear family Parents and their children living together.

object permanence The realization in infancy that objects and people do not cease to exist when they are no longer visible.

observer bias An observer's tendency to be influenced by knowledge about the research design or hypothesis.

Oedipus complex Freud's theory that boys become attracted to their mother and jealous of their father.

open classroom A relatively unstructured organization in which different areas of the room are devoted to particular activities and children work either alone or in small groups under the teacher's supervision.

operant conditioning A type of learning that depends on the consequence of behavior; rewards increase the likelihood that a behavior will recur, but punishment decreases that likelihood.

operationalization Defining a concept so that it is observable and measurable.

parallel play Interaction in which very young children are doing the same thing, often side by side, but are not engaged with each other.

participant observations Research strategy used to gain familiarity with a group of individuals by means of involvement in their activities, usually over an extended period of time.

passive gene-environment association Environment created by parents with particular genetic characteristics encourages the expression of these tendencies in their children.

peer group network The cluster of peer acquaintances who are familiar with and interact with one another at different times for common play or task-oriented purposes.

peer tutoring A method of instruction in which an older, more experienced student tutors a younger, less experienced child.

perceived popularity Ratings of how well a child is liked by his or her peers, made by teachers, parents, and children.

permissive parenting Child-rearing style that is lax and inconsistent and encourages children to express their impulses freely.

Personal Responsibility and Work Opportunity Reconciliation Act of 1996 (PRWORA) Federal legislation designed to reduce single-parent families' long-term reliance on welfare or cash assistance.

phenotype The visible expression of a person's particular physical and behavioral characteristics created by the interaction of the person's genotype with the environment.

phonemes The smallest sound units that affect meaning in a language.

physical abuse Physical injury or maltreatment by a responsible person that harms or threatens a child's health or welfare.

physical aggression A form of hostile behavior that inflicts physical damage or discomfort.

popular children Youngsters who are liked by many peers and disliked by very few.

postconventional level Kohlberg's third phase of moral development in which judgments are controlled by an internalized ethical code that is relatively independent of the approval or disapproval of others.

pragmatics A set of rules that specify appropriate language for particular social contexts.

preconventional level Kohlberg's first phase of moral development in which justification for behavior is based on the desire to avoid punishment and gain rewards.

prejudice A set of attitudes by which an individual defines all members of a group negatively.

premoral stage Piaget's first phase of moral development in which children show little concern for rules.

pretend play Make-believe activity in which objects are used symbolically.

primary emotions Fear, joy, disgust, surprise, sadness, and interest, which emerge early in life and do not require introspection or self-reflection.

primary prevention policies A set of planned actions designed to alter environmental conditions and prevent problems before they develop.

proactive aggression Behavior in which a person is hurt or injured by someone who is motivated by a desire to achieve a specific goal.

programmed neuronal death The naturally occurring death of immature nerve cells during early development of the nervous system.

prosocial behavior Conduct to help or benefit other people.

prosocial reasoning Thinking and making judgments about prosocial issues.

psychodynamic theory Freud's theory that development is determined by innate biologically based drives shaped by encounters with the environment in early childhood.

psychological domain An area of social judgment focused on beliefs and knowledge of self and others.

psychophysiological Physiological bases of psychological processes measured by brain activity, brain waves, and heart rate.

psychosocial theory Erikson's theory that each stage of development depends on accomplishing a psychological task in interactions with the social environment.

public policy Government-based social policy.

Pygmalion effect A phenomenon in which teachers' expectations that students will do well are realized.

qualitative study Research using nonstatistical analysis of materials gathered from a relatively small number of participants to gain an in-depth understanding of behavior and contexts.

quantitative study Research involving statistical analysis of numerical data.

reaction range The range of possible developmental outcomes established by a person's genotype in reaction to the environment in which development takes place.

reactive aggression A form of hostile behavior in response to an attack, threat, or frustration, usually motivated by anger.

reactivity The change in a person's behavior due to the fact that he or she is being observed.

reflex smile A upturned mouth seen in the newborn that is usually spontaneous and appears to depend on some internal stimulus rather than on something external such as another person's behavior.

rejected children Youngsters who are disliked by many peers and liked by very few.

relational aggression Behavior that damages or destroys interpersonal relationships by means such as exclusion or gossip.

relational self Aspects of the self that involve connections to other people and develop out of interactions with others.

representative sample A research sample in which participants are drawn from strata or categories (e.g., social classes or ethnic groups) in the same proportions as they are found in the larger population.

reputational bias Tendency to interpret peers' behavior on the basis of past encounters with and feelings about them.

rituals Family activities involving formal religious observances and family celebrations.

routines Day-to-day activities such as making dinner or washing the dishes.

script A mental representation of an event or situation of daily life including the order in which things are expected to happen and how one should behave in that event or situation.

secondary or self-conscious emotions Pride, shame, guilt, jealousy, embarrassment, and empathy, which emerge in the second year of life and depend on a sense of self and the awareness of other people's reactions.

secondary prevention policies A set of planned actions targeted at children who are already at risk of developing serious problems.

secure attachment Babies are able to explore novel environments, are minimally disturbed by brief separations from their mother, and are quickly comforted by her when she returns.

secure base A safety zone that the infant can retreat to for comfort and reassurance when stressed or frightened while exploring the environment.

self-disclosure The honest sharing of information of a personal nature, often with a focus on problem solving; a central means by which adolescents and others develop friendships.

self-esteem The evaluative component of self that taps how positively or negatively people view themselves in relation to others.

self-fulfilling prophecy Positive or negative expectations that affect a person's behavior in a manner that he or she (unknowingly) creates situations in which those expectations are fulfilled.

self-regulation The ability to use strategies and plans to control one's behavior in the absence of external surveillance, including inhibiting inappropriate behavior and delaying gratification.

self-report Information that people provide about themselves either in a direct interview or in some written form, such as a questionnaire.

semantics The meanings of words and word combinations.

separation anxiety Fear of being apart from a familiar caregiver (usually the mother or father), which typically peaks at about 15 months of age.

separation distress or protest An infant's distress reaction to being separated from the attachment object, usually the mother, which typically peaks at about 15 months of age.

sequential design A way of studying change over time that combines features of both cross-sectional and longitudinal designs.

serotonin Neurotransmitter that regulates endocrine glands, alters attention and emotions, and is linked to aggression.

sexual abuse Inappropriate sexual activity between an adult and a child for the perpetrator's pleasure or benefit.

shared environment A set of conditions or activities experienced by children raised in the same family.

social aggression Making verbal attacks or hurtful nonverbal gestures, such as rolling the eyes or sticking out the tongue.

social cognitive theory of gender development An explanation of gender role development that uses cognitive social learning principles such as observational learning, positive and negative feedback, and the concept of self-efficacy.

social comparison The process by which people evaluate their own abilities, values, and other qualities by comparing themselves with others, usually their peers.

social conventional domain An area of social judgment focused on social expectations, norms, and regularities that help facilitate smooth and efficient functioning in society.

social dyad A pair of social partners, such as friends, parent and child, or marital partners.

Social information-processing theory An explanation of a person's social behavior in terms of his or her assessment and evaluation of the social situation as a guide in deciding on a course of social action.

social policy A set of planned actions to solve a social problem or attain a social goal.

social referencing The process of "reading" emotional cues in others to help determine how to act in an uncertain situation.

social smile An upturned mouth in response to a human face or voice, which first occurs when the infant is about 2 months old.

social structural theory of gender roles An explanation of gender roles that focuses on factors such as institutionalized constraints on male and female opportunities in educational, occupational, and political spheres.

socialization The process by which parents and others teach children the standards of behavior, attitudes, skills, and motives deemed appropriate for their society.

sociocultural theory Vygotsky's theory that development emerges from interactions with more skilled people and the institutions and tools provided by the culture.

sociometric technique A procedure for determining a child's status within her or his peer group; each child in the group either nominates others whom she or he likes best and least or rates each child in the group for desirability as a companion.

sole custody A form of postdivorce child custody in which the child is exclusively with either the mother or the father.

specimen record Researchers record everything a person does within a given period of time.

stage-environment fit The degree to which the environment supports a child's developmental needs.

stereotype A general label applied to individuals based solely on their membership in a racial, ethnic, or religious group, without appreciation that individuals within the group vary.

stereotype consciousness The knowledge that other people have beliefs based on ethnic stereotypes.

Strange Situation A research procedure in which parent and child are separated and reunited so that investigators can assess the nature and quality of the parent-infant attachment relationship.

stranger distress or fear of strangers A negative emotional reaction to unfamiliar people, which typically emerges in infants around the age of 9 months.

structured observation A form of observation in which researchers create a situation so that behaviors they wish to study are more likely to occur.

superego In Freud's theory, the personality component that is the repository of the child's internalization of parental or societal values, morals, and roles.

sympathy The feeling of sorrow or concern for a distressed or needy person.

synapse A specialized site of intercellular communication that exchanges information between nerve cells, usually by means of a chemical neurotransmitter.

synaptic pruning The brain's disposal of the axons and dendrites of a neuron that is not often stimulated.

synaptogenesis The forming of synapses.

syntax The part of grammar that prescribes how words may combine into phrases, clauses, and sentences.

systems Developmental contexts made up of interacting parts or components, for example, a family.

telegraphic speech Two-word or three-word utterances that include only the words essential to convey the speaker's intent.

temperament An individual's typical mode of response including activity level, emotional intensity, and attention span; used particularly to describe infants' and children's behavior.

Temporary Assistance for Needy Families (TANF) Federal legislation that provides block grants to states, introduces time limits on cash assistance to individuals, and imposes work requirements.

theory of mind Children's understanding that people have mental states such as thoughts, beliefs, and desires that affect their behavior. It allows children to get beyond people's observable actions and appearances and respond to their unseen states.

time sampling Researchers record any of a set of predetermined behaviors that occur within a specified period of time.

transactional Ongoing interchanges between social partners such as a parent and child across time that result in modifications of the social behavior of each.

uninvolved parenting Child-rearing style in which parents are indifferent and neglectful and focus on their own needs rather than those of their children.

verbal aggression Words that inflict pain by yelling, insulting, ridiculing, humiliating, and so on.

victimization The process of being threatened or harmed on a consistent basis by a more powerful peer.

zone of proximal development The difference between children's level of performance while working alone and while working with more experienced partners.

References

ABC News. (2006, September). *I-Safe.Org survey*. Retrieved from: http://en.wikipedia.org/wiki/Cyber-bullying

Abecassis, M., Hartup, W. W., Haselager, G., Scholte, R., & van Lieshout, C. F. M. (2002). Mutual antipathies in middle childhood and adolescence. *Child Development, 73*, 1543–1556.

Aber, J. L., Bishop-Josef, S. J, Jones, S. M., McLearn, K. T., & Phillips, D. A. (Eds.) (2006). *Child development and social policy: Knowledge for action*. Washington, DC: American Psychological Association.

Aber, J. L., Brown, J. L., & Jones, S. M. (2003). Developmental trajectories toward violence in middle childhood: Course, demographic differences and response to school-based interventions. *Developmental Psychology, 39*, 324–348.

Abitz, M., Damgaard-Nielsen, R., Jones, E. G., Laursen, H., Graem, N., & Pakkenberg, B. (2007). Excess of neurons in the human newborn mediodorsal thalamus compared with that of the adult. *Cerebral Cortex, 17*, 2573–2578.

Ablow, J. C. (2005). When parents conflict or disengage: Children's perceptions of parents' marital distress predict school adaptation. In P. A. Cowan, C. P. Cowan, J. C. Ablow, & V. K. Johnson (Eds.), *The family context of parenting in children's adaptation to elementary school* (pp. 189–208). Mahwah, NJ: Erlbaum.

Ablow, J. C., Measelle, J. R., Cowan, P. A., & Cowan, C. P. (2009). Linking marital conflict and children's adjustment: The role of young children's perceptions. *Journal of Family Psychology, 23*, 485–499.

Abma, J. C., Martinez, G. M., Mosher, W. D., & Dawson, B. S. (2004). *Teenagers in the United States: Sexual activity, contraceptive use, and childbearing, 2002, Vital Health Statistics, 23*(24). Hyattsville, MD: National Center for Health Statistics.

Aboud, F. E. (2005). The development of prejudice in childhood and adolescence. In J. F. Dovidio, P. Glick, & L. A. Rudman (Eds.), *On the nature of prejudice: Fifty years after Allport* (pp. 310–326). New York: Blackwell.

Aboud, F. E. (2008). A social-cognitive developmental theory of prejudice. In S. M. Quintana & C. McKown (Eds.), *Handbook of race, racism, and the developing child* (pp. 55–73). Hoboken, NJ: Wiley.

Aboud, F. E., & Doyle, A.-B. (1996). Parental and peer influences on children's racial attitudes. *International Journal of Intercultural Relations, 20*, 371–383.

Aboud, F. E., & Fenwick, V. (1999). Exploring and evaluating school-based interventions to reduce prejudice in preadolescents. *Journal of Social Issues, 55*, 767–785.

Abowitz, D., & Knox, D. (2003). Goals of college students: Some gender differences. *College Student Journal, 37*, 550–556.

Abrahams, B. S., & Geschwind, D. H. (2008). Advances in autism genetics: On the threshold of a new neurobiology. *Nature Reviews Genetics, 9*, 341–355.

Abrams, D., & Rutland, A. (2008). The development of subjective group dynamics. In S. R. Levy & M. Killen (Eds.), *Intergroup attitudes and relations in childhood through adulthood* (pp. 47–65). New York: Oxford University Press.

Acosta, S., Messinger, D., Cassel, T., Bauer, C., Lester, B., & Tronick, E. Z. (2004, July). *How infants smile in the face-to-face/still-face*. Paper presented at the meeting of the International Society for Research on Emotions, New York.

Adam, E. K., & Chase-Lansdale, L. (2002). Home sweet home(s): Parental separations, residential moves and adjustment problems in low-income adolescent girls. *Developmental Psychology, 38*, 792–805.

Adams, M., Coltrane, S., & Parke, R. D. (2007). Cross-ethnic applicability of the Gender-based Attitudes Toward Marriage and Child Rearing Scales. *Sex Roles, 56*, 325–339.

Adamson, L. B. (1995). *Communication development during infancy*. Madison, WI: Brown & Benchmark.

Adamson, L. B., & Frick, J. E. (2003). The still face: A history of a shared experimental paradigm. *Infancy, 4*, 451–473.

Adelabu, D. H. (2008). Future time perspective, hope and ethnic identity among African American adolescents. *Urban Education, 43*, 347–360.

Adler, S. M. (2004). Home-school relations and the construction of racial and ethnic identity of Hmong elementary students. *School Community Journal, 14*, 57–75.

Administration for Children and Families. (2004). *Temporary Assistance for Needy Families (TANF), Sixth Annual Report to Congress XIII. TANF Research and Evaluation*. Washington, DC: U.S. Department of Health and Human Services. Retrieved from: http://www.acf.hhs.gov/programs/ofa/data-reports/annualreport6/ar6index.htm

Administration for Children and Families (2007). *Head Start Program Information Report*. Washington, DC: U.S. Department of Health and Human Services.

Adolphs, R., & Tranel, D. (2004). Impaired judgments of sadness but not happiness following bilateral amygdala damage. *Journal of Cognitive Neuroscience16*, 453–462.

Agha, S. (2003). The impact of a mass media campaign on personal risk perception, perceived self-efficacy and on other behavioral predictors. *AIDS Care, 15*, 749–762.

Ahadi, S. A., Rothbart, M. K., & Ye, R. (1993). Children's temperament in the U.S. and China: Similarities and differences. *European Journal of Personality, 7*, 359–377.

Ahn, H. J. (2003, April). *Teacher's role in the socialization of emotion in three child care centers*. Paper presented at the biennial meeting of the Society for Research in Child Development, Tampa, FL.

Ainsworth, M. D. (1963). The development of infant-mother interaction among the Ganda. In D. M. Foss (Ed.), *Determinants of infant behavior* (Vol. 2, pp. 67–104). New York: Wiley.

Ainsworth, M. D. (1969). Object relations, dependency and attachment: A theoretical review of the infant-mother relationship. *Child Development, 40*, 969–1025.

Ainsworth, M. D., Blehar, M., Waters, E., & Wall, S. (1978). *Patterns of attachment*. Hillsdale, NJ: Erlbaum.

Akirav, I., & Maroun, M. (2007). The role of medial prefrontal cortex-amygdala circuit in stress effects on the extinction of fear. *Neural Plasticity*, 30873.

Aksan, N., & Kochanska, G. (2005). Conscience in childhood: Old questions, new answers. *Developmental Psychology, 41*, 506–516.

Alexander, G. M., & Hines, M. (2002). Sex differences in response to children's toys in nonhuman primates (Cercopithecus aethiops sabaeus). *Evolution & Human Behavior, 23*, 467–479.

Allen, J. P. (2008). The attachment system in adolescence. In J. Cassidy & P. R. Shaver (Eds.), *Handbook of attachment: Theory, research, and clinical applications* (2nd ed., pp. 419–435). New York: Guilford Press.

Allen, J. P., McElhaney, K. B., Land, D. J., Kuperminc, G. P., Moore, C. W., O'Beirne-Kelly, H., & Kilmer, S. L. (2003). A secure base in adolescence: Markers of attachment security in the mother-adolescent relationship. *Child Development, 74*, 292–307.

Allen, J. P., Porter, M., McFarland, C., McElhaney, K. B., & Marsh, P. (2007). The relation of attachment security to adolescents' paternal and peer relationships, depression, and externalizing behavior. *Child Development, 78*, 1222–1239.

Allen, J. S., Damasio, H., Grabowski, T. J., Bruss, J., & Zhang, W. (2003). Sexual dimorphism and asymmetries in the gray-white composition of the human cerebrum. *Neuroimage, 18*, 880–894.

Allen, L., & Majidi-Abi, S. (1989). Black American children. In J. T. Gibbs & L. N. Huang (Eds.), *Children of color* (pp. 148–178). San Francisco: Jossey-Bass.

Allen, M., Donohue, W. A., Griffin, A., Ryan, D., & Turner, M. M. (2003). Comparing the influence of parents and peers on the choice to use drugs: A meta-analytic summary of the literature. *Criminal Justice and Behavior, 30*, 163–186.

Alvarez, J. M., Ruble, D. N., & Bolger, N. (2001). Trait understanding or evaluative reasoning: An analysis of children's behavioral predictions. *Child Development 72*, 1409–1425.

Amato, P. R. (1994). The implications of research findings on children in stepfamilies. In A. Booth & J. Dunn (Eds.), *Stepfamilies: Who benefits? Who does not?* (pp. 81–87). Hillsdale, NJ: Erlbaum.

Amato, P. R. (2001). Children of divorce in the 1990's: An update of the Amato & Keith (1991) meta-analysis. *Journal of Family Psychology, 15*, 355–370.

Amato, P. R. (2006). Marital discord, divorce, and children's well being. In A. Clarke-Stewart & J. Dunn (Eds.), *Families count* (pp. 179–202). New York: Cambridge University Press.

American Academy of Pediatrics, Committee on Education (2001). Children, adolescents and television. *Pediatrics, 107*, 423–426.

American Association of Suicidology. (2006). *Youth suicide fact sheet*. Washington, DC: American Association of Suicidology.

American Association of University Women. (1998). *Single-sex education in grades K–12: What does the research tell us?* Washington, DC: American Association of University Women Educational Foundation.

American Psychiatric Association. (2000). *Diagnostic and Statistical Manual for Mental Disorders* (4th ed.). Washington, DC: American Psychiatric Association.

American Psychological Association. (2002). *The ethical principles of psychologists and code of conduct*. Washington DC: Office of Ethics, American Psychological Association. Retrieved from http://www.apa.org/ethics

Amnesty International. (2000). *Hidden scandal, secret shame: Torture and ill-treatment of children*. London: Amnesty International Publications.

Amodio, D. M., & Frith, C. D. (2006). Meeting of minds: The medial frontal cortex and social cognition. *Nature Reviews Neuroscience, 7*, 268–277.

Anderson, C. A., & Bushman, B. J. (2001). Effects of violent video games on aggressive behavior, aggressive cognition, aggressive affect, physiological arousal and prosocial behavior: A meta-analytic review of the scientific literature. *Psychological Science, 12*, 353–359.

Anderson, C. A., Gentile, D. A., & Buckley, K. E. (2007). *Violent video game effects on children and adolescents: Theory, research, and public policy*. New York: Oxford Press.

Anderson, C. A., Sakamoto, A., Gentile, D. A., Ihori, N., Shibuya, A., Yukawa, S., Naito, M. & Kobayashi, K. (2008). Longitudinal effects of violent video games on aggression in Japan and the United States. *Pediatrics, 122*, 1067–1072.

Anderson, D. R., Huston, A. C., Schmitt, K., Linebarger, D. L., & Wright, J. C. (2001). Early childhood television viewing and adolescent behavior: The Recontact Study. *Monographs of the Society for Research in Child Development, 66* (Serial No. 264).

Anderson, K. E., Lytton, H., & Romney, D. M. (1986). Mothers' interactions with normal and conduct-disordered boys: Who affects whom? *Developmental Psychology, 22*, 604–609.

Anderson, P., Doyle, L. W., & the Victorian Infant Collaborative Study Group (2003). Neurobehavioral outcomes of school-age children born extremely low birth weight or very preterm in the 1990s. *Journal of American Medical Association, 289,* 3264–3272.

Andrews, J. A., & Lewinsohn, P. M. (1992). Suicidal attempts among older adolescents: Prevalence and co-occurrence with psychiatric disorders. *Journal of American Academy of Child and Adolescent Psychiatry, 31,* 655–662.

Anneken, K., Konrad, C., Drager, B., Breitenstein, C., Kennerknecht, L., Ringelstein, E. B., & Knecht, S. (2004). Familial aggregation of strong hemispheric language lateralization. *Neurology, 63,* 2433–2435.

Archer, J. (2002). Sex differences in physically aggressive acts between heterosexual partners: A meta-analytic review. *Aggression & Violent Behavior, 7,* 213–351.

Archer, J. (2004). Sex differences in aggression in real-world settings: A meta-analytic. *Review of General Psychology, 8,* 291–322.

Ardilla-Rey, A., & Killen, M. (2001). Middle class Colombian children's evaluations of personal, moral, and social-conventional interactions in the classroom. *International Journal of Behavioral Development, 25,* 246–255.

Ardilla-Rey, A., Killen, M., & Brenick, A. (2009). Moral reasoning in violent contexts: Displaced and non-displaced Colombian children's evaluations of moral transgressions, retaliation, and reconciliation. *Social Development, 18,* 181–209.

Argys, L. H., Peters, E., Cook, S., Garasky, S., Nepomnyaschy, L., & Sorensen, E. (2006). Measuring contact between children and nonresident fathers. In S. Hofferth & L. Casper (Eds.), *Handbook of measurement issues in family research* (pp. 375–398). Mahwah, NJ: Erlbaum.

Ariel, S., & Sever, I. (1980). Play in the desert and play in the town: On play activities of Bedouin Arab children. In H. B. Schwartzman (Ed.), *Play and culture* (pp. 164–175). West Point, NY: Leisure Press.

Aries, P. (1962). *Centuries of childhood.* New York: Knopf.

Armstrong, J., & Watson, M. (2008). *Diversity in entertainment: Why is TV so white?* Retrieved from: http://www.ew.com/ew/article/0,,20206185,00.html

Arndt, T. L., Stodgell, C. J., & Rodier, P. M. (2005). The teratology of autism. *International Journal of Developmental Neuroscience, 23,* 189–199.

Arnett, J. J. (2000). Emerging adulthood: A theory of development from the late teens through the twenties. *American Psychologist, 55,* 469–480.

Arnett, J. J. (2006). Emerging adulthood: Understanding the new way of coming of age. In J. J. Arnett & J. L. Tanner (Eds.), *Emerging adults in America: Coming of age in the 21st century* (pp. 3–19). Washington, DC: American Psychological Association.

Aronson, E., & Gonzalez, A. (1988). Desegregation, jigsaw, and the Mexican-American experience. In P. A. Katz & D. A. Taylor (Eds.), *Eliminating racism: Profiles in controversy* (pp. 301–314). New York: Plenum.

Aronson, E., & Patnoe, S. (1997). *The jigsaw classroom: Building cooperation in the classroom* (2nd ed.). New York: Addison Wesley Longman.

Arsenio, W. F., & Lemerise, E. A. (2004). Aggression and moral development: Integrating social information processing and moral domain models. *Child Development, 75,* 987–1002.

Artz, S. (2005). The development of aggressive behaviors among girls: Measurement issues, social functions, and differential trajectories. In D. J. Pepler, K. C. Madsen, C. Webster, & K. S. Levene (Eds.), *The development and treatment of girlhood aggression* (pp. 105–136). Mahwah, NJ: Erlbaum.

Asakawa, K., & Matsuoka, S. (1987). A developmental study of empathy in childhood. *Japanese Journal of Educational Psychology, 35,* 231–240.

Asendorpf, J. B., & Nunner-Winkler, G. (1992). Children's moral motive strength and temperamental inhibition reduce their immoral behavior in real moral conflicts. *Child Development, 63,* 1223–1235.

Asher, S., & Hopmeyer, A. (2001). Loneliness in childhood. In G. G. Baer, K. M. Minke, & A. Thomas (Eds.) *Children's needs: Development, problems and alternatives* (pp. 279–292). Silver Spring, MD: National Association of School Psychologists.

Asher, S. R., MacEvoy, J. P., & McDonald, K. L. (2008). Children's peer relations, social competence and school adjustment: A social tasks and social goals perspective. In M. L. Maehr, S. Karabenick, & T. Urdan (Eds.), *Advances in motivation and achievement: Vol. 15. Social psychological perspectives* (pp. 357–390). Bingley, UK: Emerald.

Asher, S. R., Parker, J. G., & Walker, D. L. (1996). Distinguishing friendship from acceptance: Implications for intervention and assessment. In W. M. Bukowski, A. F. Newcomb, & W. W. Hartup (Eds.), *The company they keep: Friendship in childhood and adolescence* (pp. 366–405). New York: Cambridge University Press.

Asher, S. R., Rose, A. J. & Gabriel, S. W. (2001). Peer rejection in everyday life. In M. Leary (Ed.), *Interpersonal rejection* (pp. 105–142). New York: Oxford Press.

Aslin, R. (1987). Visual and auditory development in infancy. In J. Osofsky (Ed.), *Handbook of infant development* (2nd ed., pp. 5–97). New York: Wiley.

Aslin, R. N., Jusczyk, P. W., & Pisoni, D. B. (1998). Speech and auditory processing during infancy: Constraints on and precursors to language. In W. Damon (Series Ed.), D. Kuhn & R. Siegler (Vol. Eds.), *Handbook of child psychology: Vol. 2. Cognition, perception and language,* (5th ed., pp. 147–198). New York: Wiley.

Astuto, J., & Allen, L. (2009). Home visitation and young children: An approach worth investing in? *Society for Research in Child Development Social Policy Report, 23* (4).

Atkin, C. (1983). Effects of realistic TV violence vs. fictional violence on aggression. *Journalism Quarterly, 60,* 615–621.

Atkinson, L., Niccols, A., Paglia, A., Coolbear, J., Parker, K. C. H., Poulton, L., . . . Sitarenios, G. (2000). A meta-analysis of time between maternal sensitivity and attachment assessments: Implications for internal working models in infancy/toddlerhood. *Journal of Social & Personal Relationships, 17,* 791–810.

Aubé, J., Fichman, L., Saltaris, C., & Koestner, R. (2000). Gender differences in adolescent depressive symptomatology: Towards an integrated social-developmental model. *Journal of Social & Clinical Psychology, 19,* 297–313.

Auerbach, S. (2002). 'Why do they give the good classes to some and not to others?' Latino parent narratives of struggle in a college access program. *Teachers College Record, 104,* 1369–1392.

Augoustinos, M., & Rosewarme, D. L. (2001). Stereotype knowledge and prejudice in children. *British Journal of Developmental Psychology, 19,* 143–156.

Auyeung, B., Baron-Cohen, S., Ashwin, E., Knickmeyer, R., Taylor, K., Hackett, G., & Hines, M. (2009). Fetal testosterone predicts sexually differentiated childhood behavior in girls and in boys. *Psychological Science, 20,* 144–148.

Aviezer, O., van IJzendoorn, M. H., Sagi, A., & Schuengel, C. F. (1994). "Children of the dream" revisited: 70 years of collective early child care in Israeli kibbutzim. *Psychological Bulletin, 116,* 99–116.

Avis, J., & Harris, P. L. (1991). Belief-desire reasoning among Baka children: Evidence for a universal conception of mind. *Child Development, 62,* 460–467.

Ayduk, O., Downey, G., Kim, M. (2001). Rejection sensitivity and depressive symptoms in women. *Personality and Social Psychology Bulletin, 27,* 868–877.

Ayoub, C. C., O'Connor, E., Rappolt-Schlichtmann, G., Fischer, K. W., Rogosch, F. A., Toth, S. L., & Cicchetti, D. (2006). Cognitive and emotional differences in young maltreated children: A translational application of dynamic skill theory. *Development and Psychopathology, 18,* 679–706.

Azar, S. T. (2002). Parenting and child maltreatment. In M. H. Bornstein (Ed.), *Handbook of parenting: Vol. 4. Social conditions and applied parenting* (2nd ed., pp. 361–388). Mahwah, NJ: Erlbaum.

Azim, E., Mobbs, D., Jo, B., Menon, V., & Reiss, A. L. (2005). Sex differences in brain activation elicited by humor. *Proceedings of the National Academy of Sciences, 102,* 16496–16501.

Babcock, L. C. (2007, July 30). Cited by Vedantam, S. Salary, gender and the social cost of haggling. *Washington Post.* Retrieved from: http://www.washingtonpost.com/wp dyn/content/article/2007/07/29/AR2007072900827_pf.html

Bachner-Melman, R., Gritsenko, I., Nemanov, L., Zohar, A. H., Dina, C., & Ebstein, R. P. (2005). Dopaminergic polymorphisms associated with self-report measures of human altruism. *Molecular Psychiatry, 10,* 333–335.

Bagwell, C. L. (2004). Friendships, peer networks and antisocial behavior. In J. B. Kupersmidt & K. A. Dodge (Eds.), *Children's peer relations* (pp. 37–57). Washington, DC: American Psychological Association.

Bagwell, C. L., Newcomb, A. F., & Bukowski, W. M. (1998). Preadolescent friendship and peer rejection as predictors of adult adjustment. *Child Development, 69,* 140–153.

Bailey, A., Le Couteur, A., Gottesman, I., Bolton, P., Simonoff, E., Yuzda, F. Y., & Rutter, M. (1995). Autism as a strongly genetic disorder: Evidence from a British twin study. *Psychological Medicine, 25,* 63–77.

Bailey, J. M., & Zucker, K. J. (1995). Childhood sex-typed behavior and sexual orientation: A conceptual analysis. *Developmental Psychology, 31,* 43–55.

Baillargeon, R. (2002). The acquisition of physical knowledge in infancy: A summary in eight lessons. In U. Goswami (Ed.), *Blackwell handbook of childhood cognitive development* (pp. 47–83). Oxford, UK: Blackwell.

Baillargeon, R. H., Zoccolillo, M., Keenan, K., Cote, S., Perusse, D., Wu, H., Boivin, M., & Tremblay, R. E. (2007). Gender differences in physical aggression: A prospective population-based survey of children before and after 2 years of age. *Developmental Psychology, 43,* 13–26.

Bainum, C. K., Lounsbury, K. R., & Pollio, H. R. (1984). The development of laughing and smiling in nursery school children. *Child Development, 55,* 1946–1957.

Bakeman, R., & Gottman, J. (1997). *Observing behavior* (2nd ed.). New York: Cambridge University Press.

Baker, D. (2002). Good intentions: An experiment in middle school single-sex science and mathematics classrooms with high minority enrollment. *Journal of Women and Minorities in Science and Engineering, 8,* 1–23.

Bakermans-Kranenburg, M. J., van IJzendoorn, M. H., & Juffer, F. (2003). Less is more: Meta-analyses of sensitivity and attachment interventions in early childhood. *Psychological Bulletin, 129,* 195–215.

Ball, H. A., Arseneault, L., Taylor, A., Maughan, B., Caspi, A., & Moffitt, T. E. (2008). Genetic and environmental influences on victims, bullies, and bully-victims in childhood. *Journal of Child Psychology and Psychiatry, 49,* 104–112.

Baltes, P. B., Lindenberger, U., & Staudinger, U. M. (2006). Life span theory in developmental psychology. In W. Damon & R. M. Lerner (Series Eds.), & R. M. Lerner (Vol. Ed.), *Handbook of child psychology: Vol. 1. Theoretical models of human development,* (6th ed., pp. 569–664). Hoboken, NJ: Wiley.

Ban, P. L., & Lewis, M. (1974). Mothers and fathers, girls and boys: Attachment behavior in the one-year-old. *Merrill-Palmer Quarterly, 20,* 195–204.

Bandura, A. (1989). Social cognitive theory. In R. Vasta (Ed.), *Annals of child development: Vol. 6. Six theories of child development* (pp. 1–60). Greenwich, CT: JAI Press.

Bandura, A. (1993). Perceived self-efficacy in cognitive development and functioning. *Educational Psychologist, 28,* 117–148.

Bandura, A. (1997). *Self-efficacy*. New York: Freeman.

Bandura, A. (2000). Exercise of human agency through collective efficacy. *Current Directions in Psychological Science, 3,* 75–78.

Bandura, A. (2002). Selective moral disengagement in the exercise of moral agency. *Journal of Moral Education, 31,* 101–119.

Bandura, A. (2006). Toward a psychology of human agency. *Perspectives on Psychological Science, 2,* 164–180.

Bandura, A., Caprara, G. V., Barbaranelli, C., Gerbino, M., & Pastorelli, C. (2003). Role of affective self-regulatory efficacy in diverse spheres of psychosocial functioning. *Child Development, 74,* 769–782.

Bandura, A., Ross, D., & Ross, S. A. (1963). Imitation of film-mediated aggressive models. *Journal of Abnormal and Social Psychology, 66,* 3–11.

Banerjee, R., & Lintern, V. (2000). Boys will be boys: The effect of social evaluation concerns on gender-typing. *Social Development, 9,* 397–408.

Banks, R., Hogue, A., & Timberlake, T. (1996). An Afrocentric approach to group social skills training in inner-city African American adolescents. *Journal of Negro Education, 65,* 414–423.

Bannon, W., Rodriguez, J., McKay, M. M. (2004). Racial socialization and African American youth externalizing behavior. *Abstracts of Academy Health Meeting, 21,* 1149.

Barber, B. K., & Harmon, E. (2002). Parental psychological control of children and adolescents. In B. K. Barber (Ed)., *Intrusive parenting: How psychological control affects children and adolescents* (pp. 15–52). Washington, DC: American Psychological Association.

Barber, B. K., & Olsen, J. A. (2004). Assessing the transition to middle and high school. *Journal of Adolescent Research, 19,* 3–30.

Barber, B. L., Eccles, J. S., & Stone, M. R. (2001). Whatever happened to the jock, the brain, and the princess? *Journal of Adolescent Research, 16,* 429–455.

Barber, J. S., & East, P. L. (2009). Home and parenting resources available to siblings depending on their birth intention status. *Child Development, 80,* 921–939.

Bargh, J. A., & McKenna, K. Y. A. (2004). The Internet and social life. *Annual Review of Psychology, 55,* 573–590.

Bargh, J. A., McKenna, K. Y. A., & Fitzsimons, G. M. (2002). Can you see the real me? Activation and expression of the "true self" on the Internet. *Journal of Social Issues, 58,* 33–48.

Barker, R. G., & Gump, P. V. (1964). *Big school, small school: High school size and student behavior*. Stanford, CA: Stanford University Press.

Barkley, R. A. (1998). *Attention deficit/hyperactivity disorder: A handbook for diagnosis and treatment* (2nd ed.). New York: Guilford Press.

Barkley, R. A. (2000). *Taking charge of ADHD*. New York: Guilford Press.

Barkley, R. A., Shelton, T. L., Crosswait, C., Moorehouse, M., Fletcher, K., Barrett, S., . . . Metevia, L. (2002). Preschool children with disruptive behavior: Three-year outcome as a function of adaptive disability. *Development and Psychopathology, 14,* 45–67.

Barnas, M. V., & Cummings, E. M. (1994). Caregiver stability and toddlers' attachment-related behavior towards caregivers in day care. *Infant Behavior and Development, 17,* 141–147.

Barnett, W. S. (1995). Long-term effects of early childhood programs on cognitive and school outcomes. *The Future of Children, 5,* 25–50.

Barnett, W. S. (1996). *Lives in the balance: Age 27 benefit-cost analysis of the High/Scope Perry Preschool Program*. Ypsilanti, MI: High/Scope Press.

Baron, A. S., & Banaji, M. (2006). The development of implicit attitudes: Evidence of race evaluations from ages 6 and 10 and adulthood. *Psychological Science, 17,* 53–58.

Baron, J., & Miller, J. G. (2000). Limiting the scope of moral obligations to help: A cross-cultural investigation. *Journal of Cross-Cultural Psychology, 31,* 703–725.

Baron-Cohen, S. (2000). Theory of mind and autism: A fifteen year review. In S. Baron-Cohen, H. Tager-Flusberg, & D. J. Cohen (Eds.), *Understanding other minds* (pp. 3–20). New York: Oxford Press.

Baron-Cohen, S. (2001). Theory of mind and autism: A review. *International Review of Research in Mental Retardation, 23,* 169–184.

Baron-Cohen, S. (2002). The extreme male brain theory of autism. *Trends in Cognitive Sciences, 6,* 248–254.

Baron-Cohen, S. (2003). *The essential difference: Male and female brains and the truth about autism*. New York: Basic Books.

Baron-Cohen, S., Leslie, A. M., & Frith, U. (1985). Does the autistic child have a "theory of mind"? *Cognition, 21,* 37–46.

Baron-Cohen, S., Ring, H., Wheelwright, S., Bullmore, E. T., Brammer, M., Simmons, A., & Williams, S. C. R. (1999). Social intelligence in the normal and autistic brain: An fMRI study. *European Journal of Neuroscience, 11,* 1891–1898.

Barr, C. S., Newman, T. K., Shannon, C., Parker, C., Dvoskin, R. L., Becker, M. L., . . . Higley, J. D. (2004). Rearing condition and rh5-HTTLPR interact to influence limbic-hypothalamic-pituitary-adrenal axis response to stress in infant macaques. *Biological Psychiatry, 55,* 733–738.

Barr, R. G., Hopkins, B., & Green, J. A. (Eds.) (2000). *Crying as a sign, a symptom, and a signal*. London: MacKeith Press.

Barret, K. C. (1995). A functionalist approach to shame and guilt. In J. P. Tangney & K. W. Fischer (Eds.), *Self-conscious emotions: The psychology of shame, guilt, embarrassment, and pride* (pp. 25–63). New York: Guilford Press.

Barrett, D. E. (1979). A naturalistic study of sex differences in children's aggression. *Merrill-Palmer Quarterly, 25,* 193–203.

Barrett Singer, A. T., & Weinstein, R. S. (2000). Differential parental treatment predicts achievement and self-perceptions in two cultural contexts. *Journal of Family Psychology, 14,* 491–509.

Barry, C. M., & Wentzel, K. R. (2006). Friend influence on prosocial behavior: The role of motivational factors and friendship characteristics. *Developmental Psychology, 42,* 153–163.

Bartels, A., & Zeki, S. (2004). The neural correlates of maternal and romantic love. *Brain and Cognitive Sciences, 21,* 1155–1166.

Basham, P. (2001). *Homeschooling: From the extreme to the mainstream* (2nd ed.). Vancouver, BC: Fraser Institute.

Basow, S. A. (1992). *Gender stereotypes and roles.* Pacific Grove, CA: Brooks/Cole.

Bassett, H. H., Warren H., Mun S. R., Graling K., & Denham, S. (2008, July). *Roles of preschoolers' demographic characteristics on development of emotion knowledge in a US sample.* Paper presented at the biennial meeting of the International Society for the Study of Behavioral Development, Würzburg, Germany.

Bates, E. (1999). Natura e cultura nel linguaggio [On the nature and nurture of language]. In R. Levi-Montalcini, D. Baltimore, R. Dulbecco, & F. Jacob (Series Eds.), & E. Bizzi, P. Calissano, & V. Vorterra (Vol. Eds.), *Frontiere della biologia [Frontiers of biology]: The brain of Homo sapiens* (pp. 241–265). Rome: Giovanni Trecami.

Bates, E., & Roe, K. (2001). Language development in children with unilateral brain injury. In C. A. Nelson & M. Luciana (Eds.), *Handbook of developmental cognitive neuroscience* (pp. 281–307). Cambridge, MA: MIT Press.

Bates, E., Thal, D., Whitsell, K., Fenson, L., & Oakes, L. (1989). Integrating language and gesture in infancy. *Developmental Psychology, 25,* 1004–1019.

Bates, J. E. (1987). Temperament in infancy. In J. D. Osofsky (Ed.), *Handbook of infant development* (2nd ed., pp. 1101–1149). New York: Wiley.

Batson, C. D., & Thompson, E. R. (2001). Why don't moral people act morally? Motivational considerations. *Current Directions in Psychological Science, 10,* 54–57.

Bauer, P. J. (2002). Long-term recall memory: Behavioral and neuro-developmental changes in the first 2 years of life. *Current Directions in Psychological Science, 11,* 137–141.

Baumeister, R. F., Campbell, J. D., Krueger, J. I., & Vohs, K. D. (2003). Does high self-esteem cause better performance, interpersonal success, happiness, or healthier lifestyles? *Psychological Science in the Public Interest, 4,* 1–44.

Baumrind, D. (1967). Child care practices anteceding three patterns of preschool behavior. *Genetic Psychology Monographs, 75,* 43–88.

Baumrind, D. (1971). Current patterns of parental authority. *Developmental Psychology Monographs, 1,* 1–103.

Baumrind, D. (1991). Effective parenting during the early adolescent transition. In P. A. Cowan & E. M. Hetherington (Eds.), *Family transitions* (pp. 111–164). Hillsdale, NJ: Erlbaum.

Baumrind, D. (2005). Patterns of parental authority. In J. Smetana (Ed.), New directions for child development: *Changes in parental authority during adolescence* (pp. 61–69). San Francisco: Jossey-Bass.

Baumrind, D., Larzelere, R. E., & Cowan, P. A. (2002). Ordinary physical punishment: Is it harmful? Comment on Gershoff (2002). *Psychological Bulletin, 128,* 580–589.

Bauserman, R. (2002). Child adjustment in joint-custody versus sole-custody arrangements: A meta-analytic review. *Journal of Family Psychology, 16,* 91–102.

Bavin, E. L. (1992). The acquisition of Walpiri. In D. I. Slobin (Ed.), *The crosslinguistic study of language acquisition* (Vol. 3, pp. 309–371). Hillsdale, NJ: Erlbaum.

Bayard, K., Hellerstein, J., Neumark, D., & Troske, K. (2003). New evidence on sex segregation and sex differences in wages from matched employee-employer data. *Journal of Labor Economics, 21,* 887–922.

Baydar, N., Greek, A., & Brooks-Gunn, J. (1997). A longitudinal study of the effects of the birth of a sibling during the first 6 years of life. *Journal of Marriage and Family, 59,* 939–956.

Beah, I. (2007). *A long way gone: Memoirs of a boy soldier.* New York: Farrar, Strauss, & Giroux.

Beal, C. R. (1994). *Boys and girls: The development of gender roles.* New York: McGraw-Hill.

Bearman, P. S., & Brückner, H. (2001). Promising the future: Virginity pledges and the transition to first intercourse. *American Journal of Sociology, 106,* 859–912.

Becker, S. W., & Eagly, A. H. (2004). The heroism of women and men. *American Psychologist, 59,* 163–178.

Beer, B. (2001). Anthropology of friendship. In N. J. Smelser & P. B. Baltes (Eds.), *International Encyclopedia of the Social and Behavioral Sciences* (pp. 5805–5808). Kidlington, UK: Elsevier.

Begley, S. (1997, Spring/Summer). How to build a baby's brain. *Newsweek* (Special Issue), 28–32.

Beitel, A. H., & Parke, R. D. (1998). Parental involvement in infancy: The role of maternal and paternal attitudes. *Journal of Family Psychology, 12,* 268–288.

Bell, R. Q. (1968). A reinterpretation of the direction of effects in studies of socialization. *Psychological Review, 75,* 81–95.

Bellamy, C. (2000). *The state of the world's children.* New York: Oxford University Press.

Belle, D. (1999). *The after-school lives of children.* Mahwah, NJ: Erlbaum.

Beller, A. H. (1985). Changes in the sex composition of U.S. occupations, 1960–1981. *Journal of Human Resources, 20,* 235–250.

Belsky, J. (1993). Etiology of child maltreatment: A developmental ecological analysis. *Psychological Bulletin, 114,* 413–434.

Belsky, J., & Barends, N. (2002). Personality and parenthood. In M. H. Bornstein (Ed.), *Handbook of parenting: Vol. 3. Being and becoming a parent* (2nd ed., pp. 415–438). Mahwah, NJ: Erlbaum

Belsky, J., Crnic, K., & Woodworth, S. (1995). Personality and parenting: Exploring the mediating role of transient mood and daily hassles. *Journal of Personality, 63,* 905–929.

Belsky, J., & Fearon, R. M. P. (2008). Precursors of attachment security. In J. Cassidy & P. R. Shaver (Eds.), *Handbook of attachment: Theory, research, and clinical applications* (2nd ed., pp. 295–316). New York: Guilford Press.

Belsky, J., Spritz, B., & Crnic, K. (1996). Infant attachment security and affective cognitive information processing at age 3. *Psychological Science, 7,* 111–114.

Belsky J., Vandell, D. L., Burchinal, M., Clarke-Stewart, K. A., McCartney, K., Owen, M. T., & the NICHD Early Child Care Research Network. (2007). Are there long-term effects of early child care? *Child Development, 78,* 681–701.

Bem, S. L. (1981). Gender schema theory: A cognitive account of sex typing. *Psychological Review, 88,* 354–364.

Bem, S. L. (1983). Gender schema theory and its implications for child development: Raising gender-aschematic children in a gender-schematic society. *Signs: Journal of Women in Culture and Society, 8,* 598–616.

Bem, S. L. (1989). Genital knowledge and gender constancy in preschool children. *Child Development, 60,* 649–662.

Bem, S. L. (1993). *The lenses of gender: Transforming the debate on sexual inequality.* New Haven, CT: Yale University Press.

Bem, S. L. (1998). *An unconventional family.* New Haven, CT: Yale University Press.

Bendersky, M., Bennett, D., & Lewis, M. (2006). Aggression at age 5 as a function of prenatal exposure to cocaine, gender, and environmental risk. *Journal of Pediatric Psychology, 31,* 71–84.

Benenson, J. F., Apostoleris, N. H., & Parnass, J. (1997). Age and sex differences in dyadic and group interaction. *Developmental Psychology, 33,* 538–543.

Benenson, J. F., & Christakos, A. (2003). The greater fragility of females' versus males' closest same-sex friendships. *Child Development, 74,* 1123–1129.

Benenson, J. F., & Koulnazarian, M. (2008). Sex differences in help-seeking appear in early childhood. *British Journal of Developmental Psychology, 26,* 163–169.

Benenson, J. F., Nicholson, C., Waite, C., Roy, R., & Simpson, A. (2001). The influence of group size on children's competitive behavior. *Child Development, 72,* 921–928.

Benner, A.D., & Graham, S. (2009). The transition to high school as a developmental process among multi-ethnic urban youth. *Child Development, 80,* 356–376.

Benson, E. S. (2004). Behavior genetics: Meet molecular biology. *American Psychological Association Monitor, 35,* 42–45.

Berdan, L. E., Keane, S. P., & Calkins, S. D. (2008). Temperament and externalizing behavior: Social preference and perceived acceptance as protective factors. *Developmental Psychology, 44,* 957–968.

Berenbaum, S. A. (2001). Cognitive function in congenital adrenal hyperplasia. *Endocrinological Metabolic Clinics, North America, 30,* 173–92.

Berenbaum, S. A. (2006). Psychological outcome in children with disorders of sex development: Implications for treatment and understanding typical development. *Annual Review of Sex Research, 17,* 1–38.

Berenbaum, S. A., & Snyder, E. (1995). Early hormonal influences on childhood sex-typed activity and playmate preferences: Implications for the development of sexual orientation. *Developmental Psychology, 31,* 31–42.

Berg, M., & Medrich, E. A. (1980). Children in four neighborhoods: The physical environment and its effect on play and play patterns. *Environment and Behavior, 12,* 320–348.

Bergen, D. J., & Williams, J. E. (1991). Sex stereotypes in the United States revisited: 1972–1988. *Sex Roles, 24,* 413–423.

Bergeron, N., & Schneider, B. H. (2005). Explaining cross-national differences in peer-directed aggression: A quantitative synthesis. *Aggressive Behavior, 31,* 116–137.

Bergman, L. R., El-Khouri, B., & Magnusson, D. (1987). Reactions to separation: Separated children's separation at age 13. Individual development and adjustment (Report No. 68, Department of Psychology). Stockholm: University of Stockholm.

Berkman Center for Internet and Society (2008). *Enhancing child safety and online technologies.* [Final Report of the Internet Safety Technical Task Force.] Cambridge, MA: Berkman Center for Internet and Society.

Berlin, L. J., Cassidy, J., & Appleyard, K. (2008). The influence of early attachments on other relationships. In J. Cassidy & P. R. Shaver (Eds.), *Handbook of attachment: Theory, research, and clinical applications* (2nd ed., pp. 333–347). New York: Guilford Press.

Berman, A. L., Jobes, D. A., & Silverman, M. M. (2005). *Adolescent suicide: Assessment and intervention* (2nd ed.). Washington, DC: American Psychological Association.

Berman, P. W. (1987). Children caring for babies: Age and sex differences in response to infant signals and to the social context. In N. Eisenberg (Ed.), *Contemporary topics in developmental psychology* (pp. 25–51). New York: Wiley.

Bernal, M. E., Knight, G. P., Ocampo, K. A., Garza, C. A., & Cota, M. K. (1993). Development of Mexican American identity. In M. E. Bernal & G. P. Knight (Eds.), *Ethnic identity: Formation and transmission among Hispanics and other minorities* (pp. 31–46). Albany: State University of New York Press.

Berndt, T. J. (1986). Sharing between friends: Contexts and consequences. In E. C. Mueller & C. R. Cooper (Eds.), *Process and outcome in peer relationships* (pp. 105–128). New York: Academic Press.

Berndt, T. J. (2002). Friendship quality and social development. *Current Directions in Psychological Science, 11*, 7–10.

Berndt, T. J. (2004). Friendship quality and social development. In M. Gauvain & M. Cole (Eds.), *Readings on the development of children* (4th ed., pp. 250–269). New York: Macmillan.

Berndt, T. J., & Perry, T. B. (1990). Distinctive features and effects of adolescent friendships. In R. Montemeyer, G. R. Adams, & T. P. Gullotta (Eds.), *From childhood to adolescence: A transition period?* (pp. 269–287). Thousand Oaks, CA: Sage.

Bernstein, D., Penner, L., Clarke-Stewart, A., & Roy, E. J. (2008). *Psychology* (8th ed.). Boston: Houghton Mifflin.

Berry, G. (2000). Multicultural media portrayals and the changing demographic landscape: The psychosocial impact of television representations on the adolescent of color. *Journal of Adolescent Health, 275*, 57–60.

Berry, G. L. (2003). Developing children and multicultural attitudes: The systematic psychosocial influences of television portrayals in a multi media society. *Cultural Diversity and Ethnic Minority Psychology, 9*, 360–366.

Berry, J. W. (2008). Family acculturation and change: Recent comparative research. In S. Chuang & R. Moreno (Eds.), *On new shores. Understanding immigrant fathers in North America* (pp. 25–45). Lanham, MD: Lexington Books.

Bersoff, D. M., & Miller, J. G. (1993). Culture, context, and the development of moral accountability judgments. *Developmental Psychology, 29*, 664–676.

Berzonsky, M. D., & Kuk, L. S. (2000). Identity status, identity processing style, and the transition to university. *Journal of Adolescent Research, 15*, 81–98.

Best, D. L. (2004). Gender roles in childhood and adolescence. In U. P. Gielen & J. Roopnarine (Eds.), *Childhood and adolescence: Cross-cultural perspectives and applications. Advances in applied developmental psychology* (pp. 199–228). Westport, CT: Praeger.

Betancourt, T. S., Borisova, I. I., Williams, T. P., Brennan, R. T., Whitfield, T. H., de la Soudiere, M., . . . Gilman, S. E. (2010). Sierra Leone's former child soldiers: A follow-up study of psychosocial adjustment and community reintegration. *Child Development, 81*

Beyers, J. M., Bates, J. E., Pettit, G. S., & Dodge, K. A. (2003). Neighborhood structure, parenting processes, and the development of youths' externalizing behaviors: A multilevel analysis. *American Journal of Community Psychology, 31*, 35–53.

Bhavnagri, N. P., & Parke, R. D. (1991). Parents as direct facilitator of children's peer relationships: Effects of age of child and sex of parent. *Journal of Social and Personal Relationships, 8*, 423–440.

Bianchi, B. D., & Bakeman, R. (1983). Patterns of sex typing in an open school. In M. B. Liss (Ed.), *Social and cognitive skills: Sex roles and children's play* (pp. 219–233). New York: Academic Press.

Bianchi, S. (1995). The changing demographic and socioeconomic characteristics of single parent families. *Marriage and Family Review, 20*, 71–97.

Bierman, K. L., Domitrovich, C. E., Nix, R. L., Gest, S. D., Welsh, J. A., Greenberg, M. T., . . . Gill, S. (2008). Promoting academic and social-emotional school readiness: The Head Start REDI program. *Child Development, 79*, 1802–1817.

Bierman, K. L., & Powers, C. J. (2009). Social skills training to improve peer relationships. In K. H. Rubin, W. M. Bukowski, & B. Laursen (Eds.), *Handbook of peer interactions, relationships, and groups* (pp. 603–621). New York: Guilford Press.

Bigelow, B. J. (1977). Children's friendship expectations: A cognitive-developmental study. *Child Development, 48*, 246–253.

Bigelow, B. J., & LaGaipa, J. J. (1975). Children's written descriptions of friendship: A multidimensional analysis. *Developmental Psychology, 11*, 857–858.

Bigler, R. S., Jones, L. C., & Lobliner, D. B. (1997). Social categorization and the formation of intergroup attitudes in children. *Child Development, 60*, 530–543.

Bigler, R. S., & Liben, L. S. (1990). The role of attitudes and interventions in gender-schematic processing. *Child Development, 61*, 1440–1452.

Bigler, R. S., & Liben, L. S. (1992). Cognitive mechanisms in children's gender stereotyping: Theoretical and educational implications of a cognitive-based intervention. *Child Development, 63*, 1351–1363.

Bigler, R. S., & Liben, L. S. (2006). A developmental intergroup theory of social stereotypes and prejudice. In R. V. Kail (Ed.), *Advances in child development and behavior* (Vol. 34, pp. 39–89). San Diego: Elsevier.

Bigler, R. S., & Liben, L. S. (2007). Developmental Intergroup Theory: Explaining and reducing children's social stereotyping and prejudice. *Current Directions in Psychological Science, 16*, 162–166.

Bijou, S. W., & Baer, D. M. (1961). *Child development: A systematic & empirical theory.* New York: Appleton Century-Crofts.

Bijou, S. W., & Baer, D. M. (1978). *Behavior analysis of child development.* Englewood Cliffs, NJ: Prentice Hall.

Bingenheimer, J. B., Brennan, R. T., & Earls, F. J. (2005). Firearm violence exposure and serious violent behavior. *Science, 308*, 1323–1326.

Birch, S. H., & Ladd, G. W. (1997). The teacher-child relationship and children's early school adjustment. *Journal of School Psychology, 35*, 61–79.

Birch, S. H., & Ladd, G. W. (1998). Children's interpersonal behaviors and the teacher-child relationship. *Developmental Psychology, 34*, 934–946.

Biringen, Z., Emde, R. N., Campos, J. J., & Appelbaum, M. I. (1995). Affective reorganization in the infant, the mother, and the dad: The role of upright locomotion and its timing. *Child Development, 66*, 499–514.

Birmaher, B., Brent, B. A., Kolko, D., Baugher, M., Bridge, J., Holder, D., . . . Ulloa, R. E. (2000). Clinical outcome after short-term psychotherapy for adolescents with major depressive disorder. *Archives of General Psychiatry, 57*, 29–36.

Bjorklund, D. F. (2000). *Children's thinking: Developmental function and individual differences* (3rd ed.). Belmont, CA: Wadsworth.

Bjorklund, D. F (2008). *Why youth is not wasted on the young: Immaturity in human development*. Oxford, UK: Blackwell.

Bjorklund, D. F., & Pellegrini, A. D. (2000). Child development and evolutionary psychology. *Child Development, 71*, 1687–1708.

Bjorklund, D. F., & Pellegrini, A. D. (2002). *The origins of human nature: Evolutionary developmental psychology*. Washington, DC: American Psychological Association.

Bjorklund, D. F., & Pellegrini, A. D. (2010). Evolutionary perspectives on social development. In P. K. Smith & C. H. Hart (Eds.) *Wiley-Blackwell handbook of childhood social development* (2nd ed.). Oxford, UK: Wiley-Blackwell.

Bjorklund, D. F., & Shackelford, T. K. (1999). Differences in parental investment contribute to important differences between men and women. *Current Directions in Psychological Science, 8*, 86–89.

Black, B., & Hazen, N. (1990). Social status and patterns of communication in acquainted and unacquainted preschool children. *Developmental Psychology, 26*, 379–387.

Black, J. E., Jones, T. A., Nelson, C. A., & Greenough, W. T. (1998). Neuronal plasticity and the developing brain. In N. E. Alessi, J. T. Coyle, S. I. Harrison, & E. Eth (Eds.), *Handbook of child and adolescent psychiatry: Vol. 6. Basic psychiatric science and treatment* (pp. 31–53). Hoboken, NJ: Wiley.

Blackless, M., Besser, M., Carr, S., Cohen-Kettenis, P. T., Connolly, P., De Sutter, P., . . . Wylie, K. (2006). Atypical gender development: A review. *International Journal of Transgenderism, 9*, 29–44. Retrieved from: http://www.gires.org.uk/genderdev.php

Blake, C., Wang, W., Cartledge, G., & Gardner, R. (2000). Middle school students with serious emotional disturbances serve as social skills trainers and reinforcers for peers with SED. *Behavioral Disorders, 25*, 280–298.

Blakemore, J. E. O. (1990). Children's nurturant interactions with their infant siblings: An exploration of gender differences and maternal socialization. *Sex Roles, 22*, 43–57.

Blakemore, J. E. O., & Centers, R. E. (2005). Characteristics of boys' and girls' toys. *Sex Roles, 53*, 619–633.

Blakemore, S.-J. (2008). The social brain in adolescence. *Nature Reviews Neuroscience, 9*, 267–277.

Blanchard-Fields, F., & Coats, A. H. (2008). The experience of anger and sadness in everyday problems impacts age differences in emotion regulation. *Developmental Psychology, 44*, 1547–1556.

Blasi, A. (1983). Moral cognition and moral action: A theoretical perspective. *Developmental Review, 3*, 178–210.

Blatchford, P. (2003). A systematic observational study of teachers' and pupils' behavior in large and small classes. *Learning and Instruction, 13*, 569–595.

Blatchford, P. (2005). A multi-method approach to the study of school class size differences. *International Journal of Social Research Methodology: Theory and Practice, 8*, 195–205.

Blatchford, P., Baines, E., & Pellegrini, A. (2003). The social context of school playground games: Sex and ethnic differences, and changes over time after entry to junior school. *British Journal of Developmental Psychology, 21*, 481–505.

Blau, F. D., & Kahn, L. M. (2006). The U.S. gender pay gap in the 1990s: Slowing convergence. *Industrial and Labor Relations Review, 60*, 45–66.

Block, J. H. (1983). Differential premises arising from differential socialization of the sexes: Some conjectures. *Child Development, 54*, 1335–1354.

Block, J. J. (2007). Lessons from Columbine: Virtual and real rage. *American Journal of Forensic Psychiatry, 28*, 5–33.

Bloom, B., & Steinhart, D. (1993). *Why punish the children? A reappraisal of the children of incarcerated mothers in America*. San Francisco: National Institute of Corrections.

Bloom, L., & Tinker, E. (2001). The intentionality model and language acquisition. *Monographs of the Society for Research in Child Development, 66* (Serial No. 267).

Boccia, M., & Campos, J. (1989). Maternal emotional signals, social referencing, and infants' reactions to strangers. *New Directions for Child and Adolescent Development, 44*, 25–49.

Bohlin, G., & Hagekull, B. (1993). Stranger wariness and sociability in the early years. *Infant Behavior and Development, 16*, 53–67.

Boldizar, J. P. (1991). Assessing sex typing and androgyny in children: The Children's Sex Role Inventory. *Developmental Psychology, 27*, 505–515.

Bolger, K. E., & Patterson, C. J. (2001). Developmental pathways from child maltreatment to peer rejection. *Child Development, 72*, 549–568.

Bolger, K. E., Patterson, C., & Kupersmidt, J. B. (1998). Peer relationships and self-esteem among children who have been maltreated. *Child Development, 69*, 1171–1197.

Bolzani-Dinehart, L. H., Messinger, D. S., Acosta, S., Cassel, T., Ambadar, Z., & Cohn, J. (2003, April). *A dimensional approach to infant facial expressions.* Paper presented at the biennial meeting of the Society for Research in Child Development, Tampa, FL.

Bolzani-Dinehart, L. H., Messinger, D. S., Acosta, S. I., Cassel, T., Ambadar, Z., & Cohn, J. (2005). Adult perceptions of positive and negative infant emotional expressions. *Infancy, 8,* 279–303.

Bonkowski, S. E., Boomhower, S. J., & Bequette, S. Q. (1985). What you don't know can hurt you: Unexpressed fears and feelings of children from divorcing families. *Journal of Divorce, 9,* 33–45.

Book, A. S., Starzyk, K. B., & Quinsey, V. L. (2001). The relationship between testosterone and aggression: A meta-analysis. *Aggression and Violent Behavior, 6,* 579–599.

Booth, A., Granger, D. A., & Shirtcliff, E. A. (2008). Gender- and age-related differences in the association between social relationship quality and trait levels of salivary cortisol. *Journal of Research on Adolescence, 18,* 239–260.

Booth, C. A., Clarke-Stewart, K. A., Vandell, D. L., McCartney, K., & Owen, M. T. (2002). Child-care usage and mother-infant "quality time." *Journal of Marriage and Family, 64,* 16–26.

Boothby, N. (2006). What happens when child soldiers grow up? The Mozambique case study. *Intervention, 4,* 244–259. Retrieved from: http://www.interventionjournal.com/downloads/43pdf/boothby.pdf

Borke, H. (1971). Interpersonal perception of young children: Egocentrism or empathy. *Developmental Psychology, 5,* 263–269.

Bornstein, M. H. (1989). Sensitive periods in development: Structural characteristics and causal interpretations. *Psychological Bulletin, 105,* 179–197.

Bornstein, M. H., & Arterberry, M. E. (1999). Perceptual development. In M. H. Bornstein & M. E. Lamb (Eds.), *Developmental psychology: An advanced textbook* (4th ed., pp. 231–274). Mahwah, NJ: Erlbaum.

Bornstein, M. H., & Cote, L. R. (2006). *Acculturation and parent-child relationships: Measurement and development.* Mahwah, NJ: Erlbaum.

Bornstein, M. H., & Putnick, D. L. (2007). Chronological age, cognitions, and practices in European American mothers: A multivariate study of parenting. *Developmental Psychology, 43,* 850–864.

Bornstein, M. H., Putnick, D. L., Heslington, M., Gini, M., Suwalsky, J. T. D., Venuit, P., . . . de Galperin, C. Z. (2008). Mother-child emotional availability in ecological perspective: Three countries, two regions, two genders. *Developmental Psychology, 44,* 666–680.

Boulton, M. J., & Smith, P. K. (1994). Bully/victim problems in middle-school children: Stability, self-perceived competence, peer perceptions and peer acceptance. *British Journal of Developmental Psychology, 12,* 315–329.

Bourne, V. J. (2008). Examining the relationship between degree of handedness and degree of cerebral lateralization for processing facial emotion. *Neuropsychology, 22,* 350–356.

Bousch, D. M. (2001). Mediating advertising effects. In J. Bryant & J. A. Bryant (Eds.), *Television and the American family* (pp. 397–414). Mahwah, NJ: Erlbaum.

Bowker, J. C. W., Rubin, K. H., Burgess, K. H., Booth-LaForce, C., & Rose-Krasnor, L. (2006). Behavioral characteristics associated with stable and fluid best friendship patterns in childhood. *Merrill-Palmer Quarterly, 52,* 671–693.

Bowlby, J. (1958). The nature of the child's tie to his mother. *International Journal of Psychoanalysis, 39,* 350–373.

Bowlby, J. (1969). *Attachment and loss: Vol. 1. Attachment.* New York: Basic Books.

Bowlby, J. (1973). *Separation and loss.* New York: Basic Books.

Boykin, A. W., & Toms, F. D. (1985). Black child socialization: A conceptual framework. In H. P. McAdoo, J. L. McAdoo, & J. Lewis (Eds.), *Black children: Social, educational, and parental environments* (pp. 33–51). Thousand Oaks, CA: Sage.

Boyum, L., & Parke, R. D. (1995). Family emotional expressiveness and children's social competence. *Journal of Marriage and Family, 57,* 593–608.

Brach, E. L., Camara, K. A., & Houser, R. F. (2000). Patterns of interaction in divorced and non-divorced families: Conflict in dinnertime conversation. *Journal of Divorce & Remarriage, 33,* 75–89.

Bradley, R. H., & Corwyn, R. F. (2005). Caring for children around the world: A view from HOME. *International Journal of Behavioral Development, 29,* 468–478.

Bradley, R. H., Corwyn, R. F., McAdoo, H. P., & Coll, C. G. (2001). The home environment of children in the United States Part I: Variations by age, ethnicity, and poverty status. *Child Development, 72,* 1844–1867.

Brain Sex Matters (2009, March). *Research news.* Retrieved from: http://www.brainsexmatters.com/news.php

Braungart-Rieker, J. M., Garwood, M. M., Powers, B. P., & Wang, X. (2001). Parental sensitivity, infant affect and affect regulation: Predictors of later attachment. *Child Development, 72,* 252–270.

Brazelton, T. B. (1973). Neonatal Behavior Assessment Scale. *Clinics in developmental medicine, No. 50.* London: Spastics International Medical Publications.

Brendgen, M., Dionne, G., Girard, A., Boivin, M., Vitaro, F., & Perusse, D. (2005). Examining genetic and environmental effects on social aggression: A study of six-year-old twins. *Child Development, 76,* 930–946.

Brendgen, M., & Vitaro, F. (2008). Peer rejection and physical health problems in early adolescence. *Journal of Developmental & Behavioral Pediatrics, 29,* 183–190.

Brennan, P. A., Hall, J., Bor, W., Najman, J. M., & Williams, G. (2003). Integrating biological and social processes in relation to early-onset persistent aggression in boys and girls. *Developmental Psychology, 32*, 309–323.

Brenner, E. M., & Salovey, P. (1997). Emotion regulation during childhood: Developmental, interpersonal, and individual considerations. In P. Salovey & D. J. Sluyter (Eds.), *Emotional development and emotional intelligence: Educational implications* (pp. 168–195). New York: Basic Books.

Bretherton, I., & Munholland, K. A. (2008). Internal working models in attachment relationships: Elaborating a central construct in attachment theory. In J. Cassidy & P. R. Shaver (Eds.), *Handbook of attachment: Theory, research, and clinical applications* (2nd ed., pp. 102–127). New York: Guilford Press.

Brewer, M. B. (1991). The social self: On being the same and different at the same time. *Personality and Social Psychology Bulletin, 17*, 475–482.

Bridges, L. J., & Grolnick, W. S. (1995). The development of emotional self-regulation in infancy and early childhood. In N. Eisenberg (Ed.), *Social development. Review of personality and social psychology* (pp. 185–211). Thousand Oaks, CA: Sage.

Briones, T. L., Klintsova, A. Y., & Greenough, W. T. (2004). Stability of synaptic plasticity in the adult rat visual cortex induced by complex environment exposure. *Brain Research, 1018*, 130–135.

Brockmeyer, S., & Waters, E. (in press) Secure base use and support from infancy to adulthood: We should measure what develops. In E. Waters (Ed.) *Measuring attachment.* New York: Guilford Press.

Brody, G. H., Beach, S. R. H., Philibert, R. A., Chen, Y.-F., Lei, M.-K., Murry, V. M., & Chen, Y. (2009). Parenting moderates a genetic vulnerability factor on longitudinal increases in youths' substance use. *Journal of Consulting and Clinical Psychology, 77*, 1–11.

Brody, G. H., Dorsey, S., Forehand, R., & Armistead, L. (2002). Unique and protective contributions of parenting and classroom processes to the adjustment of African-American children living in single-parent families. *Child Development, 73*, 274–286.

Brody, G. H., Ge, X., Conger, R., Gibbons, F. X., Murry, V. M., Gerrard, M., & Simons, R. L. (2001). The influence of neighborhood disadvantage, collective socialization and parenting on African American children's affiliation with deviant peers. *Child Development, 72*, 1231–1246.

Brodzinsky, D. M., & Pinderhughes, E. (2002). Parenting and child development in adoptive families. In M. H. Bornstein (Ed.), *Handbook of parenting: Vol. 1. Children and parenting* (2nd ed., pp. 279–311). Mahwah, NJ: Erlbaum.

Broidy, L. M., Nagin, D. S., Tremblay, R. E., Bates, J. E., Brame, B., Dodge, K. A., . . . Pettit, G. S. (2003). Developmental trajectories of childhood discipline behaviors and adolescent delinquency: A six-site, cross-national study. *Developmental Psychology, 39*, 222–245.

Bronfenbrenner, U., & Morris, P. (2006). The ecology of developmental processes. In W. Damon & R. M. Lerner (Series Eds.) & R. M. Lerner (Vol. Ed.), *Handbook of child psychology: Vol. 1. Theoretical models of human development* (6th ed., pp. 793–828). Hoboken, NJ: Wiley.

Brooks, J. H., & Reddon, J. R. (1996). Serum testosterone in violent and non-violent young offenders. *Journal of Clinical Psychology, 52*, 475–483.

Brooks-Gunn, J., & Lewis, M. (1984). The development of early visual self-recognition. *Developmental Review, 4*, 215–239.

Brophy, J. (1998). Classroom management as socializing students into clearly articulated roles. *Journal of Classroom Interaction, 33*, 1–4.

Brophy, M., & Dunn, J. (2002). What did Mummy say? Dyadic interactions between young "hard to manage" children and their mothers. *Journal of Abnormal Child Psychology, 30*, 103–112.

Brown, A. L., & Campione, J. C. (1990). Communities of learning and thinking, or a context by any other name. *Human Development, 21*, 108–126.

Brown, B. B. (1989). The role of peer groups in adolescents' adjustment to secondary school. In T. G. Berndt & G. W. Ladd (Eds.), *Peer relationships in child development* (pp. 188–215). New York: Wiley.

Brown, B. B. (1990). Peer groups and peer cultures. In S. S. Feldman & G. R. Elliot (Eds.), *At the threshold: The developing adolescent* (pp. 171–196). Cambridge, MA: Harvard University Press.

Brown, B. B. (2004). Adolescents' relationships with peers. In R. M. Lerner & L. Steinberg (Eds.), *Handbook of adolescent psychology* (2nd ed., pp. 363–394). New York: Wiley.

Brown, B. B., Eicher, S. A., & Petrie, S. (1986). The importance of peer group ("crowd") affiliation in adolescence. *Journal of Adolescence, 9*, 73–96.

Brown, B. B., & Huang, B. (1995). Examining parenting practices in different peer contexts: Implications for adolescent trajectories. In L. J. Crockett & A. C. Crouter (Eds.), *Pathways through adolescence: Individual development in relation to social contexts* (pp. 151–177). Mahwah, NJ: Erlbaum.

Brown, B. B., & Klute, C. (2006). Friendships, cliques, and crowds. In G. R. Adams & M. D. Berzonsky (Eds.), *Blackwell handbook of adolescence* (pp. 330–348). Malden, MA: Blackwell.

Brown, B. B., Larson, R., & Saravathi, T. S. (Eds.). (2002). *The world's youth: Adolescence in eight regions of the globe.* New York: Cambridge University Press.

Brown, E. (1996). Effects of resource availability on children's behavior and conflict management. *Early Education & Development, 7*, 149–166.

Brown, E., & Brownell, C. A. (1990, March). *Individual differences in toddlers' interaction styles*. Paper presented at the biennial conference of the International Society on Infant Studies, Montreal, Quebec, Canada.

Brown, J. D., & Cantor, J. (2000). An agenda for research on youth and the media. *Journal of Adolescent Health, 27*, 2–7.

Brown, J. R., Donelan-McCall, N., & Dunn, J. (1996). Why talk about mental states? The significance of conversations with friends, siblings, and mothers. *Child Development, 67*, 836–849.

Brown, P. (2001). Learning to talk about motion UP and DOWN in Tzeltal: Is there a language-specific bias for verb learning. In M. Bowerman & S. C. Levinson (Eds.), *Language acquisition and conceptual development* (pp. 512–543). Cambridge, UK: Cambridge University Press.

Brownell, C. A. (1990). Peer social skills in toddlers: Competencies and constraints illustrated by same age and mixed-age interaction. *Child Development, 61*, 838–848.

Brown v. Board of Education.(1954). Retrieved from: http://caselaw.lp.findlaw.com/scripts/getcase.pl?court=US&vol=347&invol=483

Bruce, E., & Waelde, L. C. (2008). Relationships of ethnicity, ethnic identity, and trauma symptoms to delinquency. *Journal of Loss & Trauma, 13*, 395–405.

Buchanan, C. M., & Heiges, K. L. (2001). When conflict continues after the marriage ends: Effects of postdivorce conflict on children. In J. Grych & F. D. Fincham (Eds.), *Interparental conflict and child development* (pp. 337–362). New York: Cambridge University Press.

Buchanan, C. M., Maccoby, E. E., & Dornbusch, S. M. (1992). Adolescents and their families after divorce: Three residential arrangements compared. *Journal of Research on Adolescence, 2*, 261–291.

Bugental, D. B., Ellerson, P. C., Lin, E. K., Rainey, B., Kobotouic, A., & O'Hara, N. (2002). A cognitive approach to child abuse prevention. *Journal of Family Psychology, 16*, 243–258.

Bugental, D., & Grusec, J. (2006). Socialization processes. In W. Damon & R. M. Lerner (Series Eds.), & N. Eisenberg (Vol. Ed.), *Handbook of child psychology: Vol. 3. Social, emotional, and personality development* (6th ed., pp. 366–428). Hoboken, NJ: Wiley.

Bugental, D. B., & Happaney, K. (2004). Predicting infant maltreatment in low income families: The interactive effects of maternal attributions and child status at birth. *Developmental Psychology, 40*, 234–243.

Bugental, D. B., Martorell, G. A., & Barraza, V. (2003). The hormonal costs of subtle forms of infant maltreatment. *Hormones & Behavior, 43*, 237–244.

Buhs, E. S., & Ladd, G. W. (2001). Peer rejection as an antecedent of young children's school adjustment: An examination of mediating processes. *Developmental Psychology, 37*, 550–560.

Buijzen, M., Schuurman, J., & Bomhof, E. (2008). Associations between children's television advertising exposure and their food consumption patterns: A household diary-survey study. *Appetite, 50*, 231–239.

Buijzen, M., & Valkenburg, P. M. (2003). The unintended effects of television advertising: A parent-child survey. *Communication Research, 30*, 483–503.

Buijzen, M., & Valkenburg, P. M. (2005). Parental mediation of undesired advertising effects. *Journal of Broadcasting and Electronic Media, 49*, 153–165.

Bullock, D., & Merrill, L. (1980). The impact of personal preference on consistency through time: The case of childhood aggression. *Child Development, 51*, 808–814.

Bullock, M., & Lutkenshaus, P. (1990). Who am I? Self-understanding in toddlers. *Merrill-Palmer Quarterly, 36*, 217–238.

Buriel R., Love, J. A., & De Ment, T. L. (2006). The relation of language brokering to depression and parent–child bonding among Latino adolescents. In M. H. Bornstein & L. R. Cote (Eds.). *Acculturation and parent–child relationships: Measurement and development* (pp. 249–270). Mahwah, NJ: Erlbaum.

Buriel, R., Perez, W., de Ment, T. L., Chavez, D. V., & Moran, V. R. (1998). The relationship of language brokering to academic performance, biculturalism, and self-efficacy among Latino adolescents. *Hispanic Journal of Behavioral Sciences, 20*, 283–297.

Buriel, R., & Saenz, E. (1980). Psychosocial characteristics of college-bound and noncollege-bound Chicanas. *Journal of Social Psychology, 110*, 245–251.

Burk, L. R., Park, J., Armstrong, J. M., Klein, M. H., Goldsmith, H. H., Zahn-Waxler, C., & Essex, M. J. (2008). Identification of early child and family risk factors for aggressive victim status in first grade. *Journal of Abnormal Child Psychology, 36*, 513–526.

Burks, V., Laird, R., Dodge, K., Pettit, G., & Bates, J. (1999). Knowledge structures, social information processing, and children's aggressive behavior. *Social Development, 8*, 220–236.

Burleson, B. R. (1982). The development of comforting communication skills in childhood and adolescence. *Child Development, 53*, 1578–1588.

Burn, S. M., O'Neil, A. K., & Nederend, S. (1996). Childhood tomboyism and adult androgyny. *Sex Roles, 34*, 419–428.

Burnett, S., Bird, G., Moll, J., Frith, C., & Blakemore, S.-J. (2009). Development during adolescence of the neural processing of social emotion. *Journal of Cognitive Neuroscience, 21*, 1736–1750.

Burton, L. M. (1997). Ethnography and the meaning of adolescence in high-risk neighborhoods. *Ethos, 25*, 208–217.

Burton, L. M. (2007). Childhood adultification in economically disadvantaged families: An ethnographic perspective. *Family Relations, 56*, 329–345.

Burton, L., & Graham, J. (1998). Neighborhood rhythms and the social activities of adolescent mothers. *New Directions for Child and Adolescent Development, 82,* 7–22.

Burton, L. M., & Price-Spratlen, T. (1999). Through the eyes of children: An ethnographic perspective on neighborhoods and child development. In A. S. Masten (Ed.) *Cultural processes in child development* (pp. 72–96). Mahwah, NJ: Erlbaum.

Burton, R. V. (1963). The generality of honesty reconsidered. *Psychological Review, 70,* 481–499.

Burton, R. V. (1984). A paradox in theories and research in moral development. In W. M. Kurtines & J. L. Gewirtz (Eds.), *Morality, moral behavior, and moral development* (pp. 193–207). New York: Wiley.

Bushman, B. J., (1995). Moderating role of trait aggressiveness in the effects of violent media on aggression. *Journal of Personality and Social Psychology, 69,* 950–960.

Bushman, B. J., & Anderson, C. A. (2001). Media violence and the American public: Scientific facts versus media misinformation. *American Psychologist, 56,* 477–489.

Bushman, B. J., & Huesmann, L. R. (2001). Effects of televised violence on aggression. In D. Singer & J. Singer (Eds.), *Handbook of children and the media* (pp. 223–254). Thousand Oaks, CA: Sage.

Buss, D. M. (1994). Individual differences in mating strategies. *Behavioral & Brain Sciences, 17,* 581–582.

Buss, D. M. (2000). Evolutionary psychology. In A. Kazdin (Ed.), *Encyclopedia of psychology* (pp. 277–280). Washington, DC: American Psychological Association and Oxford University Press.

Buss, K. A., & Kiel, E. J. (2004). Comparison of sadness, anger, and fear facial expressions when toddlers look at their mothers. *Child Development, 75,* 1761–1773.

Bussey, K. (1992). Lying and truthfulness: Children's definitions, standards and evaluative reactions. *Child Development, 63,* 129–137.

Bussey, K., & Bandura, A. (1992). Self-regulatory mechanisms governing gender development. *Child Development, 63,* 1236–1250.

Bussey, K., & Bandura, A. (1999). Social cognitive theory of gender development and differentiation. *Psychological Review, 106,* 676–713.

Bussey, K., & Perry, D. G. (1982). Same-sex imitation: The avoidance of cross-sex models or the acceptance of same-sex models? *Sex Roles, 8,* 773–784.

Byrd-Bredbenner, C. (2002). Saturday morning children's television advertising: A longitudinal content analysis. *Family & Consumer Sciences Research Journal, 30,* 382–403.

Cahill, L. (2006). Why sex matters for neuroscience. *Nature Reviews Neuroscience, 7,* 477–484.

Cairns, E. (1990). The relationship between adolescent perceived self-competence and attendance at single-sex secondary school. *British Journal of Educational Psychology, 60,* 207–211.

Cairns, R. B., & Cairns, B. D. (1994). *Lifelines and risks: Pathways of youth in our time.* Cambridge, UK: Cambridge University Press.

Caldwell, C. H., Antonucci, T. C., & Jackson, J. S. (1998). Supportive/conflictual family relations and depressive symptomatology: Teenage mother and grandmother perspectives. *Family Relations, 47,* 395–402.

Calkins, S.D. (2002). Does aversive behavior during toddlerhood matter? The effects of difficult temperament on maternal perceptions and behavior. *Infant Mental Health Journal, 23,* 381–402.

Cameron, C. A., & Lee, K. (1997). The development of children's telephone communication. *First Language, 21,* 387–429.

Cameron, L., Rutland, A., Brown, R., & Douch, R. (2006). Changing children's intergroup attitudes toward refugees: Testing different models of extended contact. *Child Development, 77,* 1208–1219.

Campbell, F. A., Breitmayer, B. J., Ramey, C. T. (1986). Disadvantaged single teenage mothers and their children: Consequences of free educational day care. *Family Relations, 35,* 63–68.

Campbell, F.A., Pungello, E. P., Miller-Johnson, S., Burchinal, M., & Ramey, C. T. (2001). The development of cognitive and academic abilities: Growth curves from an early childhood educational experiment. *Developmental Psychology, 37,* 231–242.

Campbell, N. D., Appelbaum, J. C., Martinson, K., & Martin, E. (2000). *Be all that we can be: Lessons from the military for improving our nation's child care system.* Washington, DC: National Women's Causes Center.

Campbell, S. B. (2000). Developmental perspectives on attention deficit disorder. In A. Sameroff, M. Lewis, & S. Miller (Eds.), *Handbook of child psychopathology* (2nd ed., pp. 383–401). New York: Plenum Press.

Campbell, S. B., Cohn, J., & Meyers, T. (1995). Depression in first-time mothers: Mother-infant interaction and depression chronicity. *Developmental Psychology, 31,* 349–357.

Campbell, S. B., Spieker, S., Burchinal, M., Poe, M. D., & NICHD Early Child Care Research Network. (2006). Trajectories of aggression from toddlerhood to age 9 predict academic and social functioning through age 12. *Journal of Child Psychology and Psychiatry, 47,* 791–800.

Campione-Barr, N., & Smetana, J. (2010). "Who said you could wear my sweater?" Adolescent siblings' conflicts and associations with relationship quality. *Child Development, 81,* 464–471.

Campos, J. J., Anderson, D. I., Barbu-Roth, M. A., Hubbard, E. M., Hertenstein, M. J., & Witherington, D. (2000). Travel broadens the mind. *Infancy, 1,* 149–220.

Campos, J. J., Bertenthal, B., & Kermonian, R. (1992). Early experience and emotional development: The emergence of wariness of heights. *Psychological Science, 3,* 61–64.

Campos, J. J., Hiatt, S., Ramsey, D., Henderson, C., & Svejda, M. (1978). The emergence of fear on the visual cliff. In M. Lewis & L. Rosenblum (Eds.), *The origins of affect* (pp. 149–182). New York: Plenum Press.

Campos, J. J., Langer, A., & Krowitz, A. (1970). Cardiac responses on the visual cliff in prelocomotor human infants. *Science, 170,* 196–197.

Camras, L. A., Bakeman, R., Chen, Y., Norris, K., & Cain, T. R. (2006). Culture, ethnicity, and children's facial expressions: A study of European American, mainland Chinese, Chinese American, and adopted Chinese girls. *Emotion, 6,* 103–114.

Camras, L. A., Kolmodin, K., & Chen, Y. (2008). Mothers' self-reported emotional expression in Mainland Chinese, Chinese American, & European American families. *International Journal of Behavioral Development, 32,* 459–463.

Camras, L. A., Malatesta, C., & Izard, C. (1991). The development of facial expressions in infancy. In R. Feldman & B. Rime (Eds.), *Fundamentals of nonverbal behavior* (pp. 73–105). New York: Cambridge University Press.

Camras, L. A., Perlman, S. B., Fries, A. B. W., & Pollak, S. D. (2006). Post-institutionalized Chinese and Eastern European children: Heterogeneity in the development of emotion understanding. *International Journal of Behavioral Development, 30,* 193–199.

Cantor, J., Mares, M. L., & Hyde, J. S. (2003). Autobiographical memories of exposure to sexual media content. *Media Psychology, 5,* 1–31.

Cantor, N. (2000). Life task-problem solving: Situational affordances and personal needs. In E. T. Higgins, A. W. Kruglanski, & W. Arie (Eds.), *Motivational science: Social and personality perspectives. Key reading in social psychology* (pp. 100–110). New York: Psychology Press.

Capaldi, D., & Clark, S. (1998). Prospective family predictors of aggression toward female partners for at-risk young men. *Developmental Psychology, 34,* 1175–1188.

Capizzano, J., & Stagner, M. (2005). The role of federal and state governments in child and family issues: An analysis of three policy areas. In R. M. Lerner, F. Jacobs, & D. Wertlieb (Eds.), *Applied developmental science* (pp. 249–268). Thousand Oaks, CA: Sage.

Caplan, M., Vespo, J. E., Pederson, J., & Hay, D. F. (1991). Conflict over resources in small groups of 1- and 2-year-olds. *Child Development, 62,* 1513–1524.

Caravita, S., DiBlasio, P., & Salmivalli, C. (2009). Unique and interactive effects of empathy and social status on involvement in bullying. *Social Development, 18,* 140–163.

Card, N. A., & Hodges, E. V. E. (2008). Peer victimization among schoolchildren: Correlations, causes, consequences, and considerations in assessment and intervention. *School Psychology Quarterly, 23,* 451–461.

Card, N. A., Stucky, B. D., Sawalani, G. M., & Little, T. D. (2008). Direct and indirect aggression during childhood and adolescence: A meta-analytic review of gender differences, intercorrelations, and relations to maladjustment. *Child Development, 79,* 1185–1229.

Carlo, G., Hausmann, A., Christiansen, S., & Randall, B. A. (2003). Sociocognitive and behavioral correlates of a measure of prosocial tendencies for adolescents. *Journal of Early Adolescence, 23,* 107–134.

Carlson, E. A., Sroufe, L. A., & Egeland, B. (2004). The construction of experience: A longitudinal study of representation and behavior. *Child Development, 75,* 66–83.

Carlson, V., Cicchetti, D., Barnett, D., & Braunwald, K. (1989). Disorganized/disoriented attachment relationships in maltreated infants. *Developmental Psychology, 25,* 525–531.

Carnagey, N. C., Anderson, C. A., & Bushman, B. J. (2007). The effect of videogame violence on physiological desensitization to real-life violence. *Journal of Experimental Social Psychology, 43,* 489–496.

Carney, J. V., & Hazler, R. J. (2007, March). *An innovative research model integrating levels of biological markers, exposures to bullying, anxiety, and trauma.* Paper presented at the annual meeting of the American Counseling Association, Detroit, MI.

Carpendale, J., & Lewis, C. (2006). *How children develop social understanding.* Malden, MA: Blackwell.

Carpenter, L. P. (1999). The determinants of parenting in low-income African-American mothers. *Dissertation Abstracts International: Section B: The Sciences and Engineering, 60,* 2980.

Carson, J., & Parke, R. D. (1996). Reciprocal negative affect in parent-child interactions and children's peer competency. *Child Development, 67,* 2217–2226.

Carstensen, L. L., Gross, J., & Fung, H. (1997). The social context of emotional experience. In K. W. Schaie & M. P. Lawton (Eds.), *Annual Review of Gerontology and Geriatrics* (pp. 325–352). New York: Springer.

Carstensen, L. L., Pasupathi, M., Mayr, U., & Nesselroade, J. R. (2000). Emotional experience in everyday life across the adult life span. *Journal of Personality and Social Psychology, 79,* 644–655.

Carter, C. S. (2005). Biological perspectives on social attachment and bonding. In C. S. Carter, L. Ahnert, K. E. Grossmann, S. B. Hardy, M. E. Lamb, S. W. Porges, & N. Sachser (Eds.), *Attachment and bonding: A new synthesis* (pp. 85–100). Cambridge, MA: MIT Press.

Carter, C. S., Freeman, J. H., & Stanton, M. E. (1995). Neonatal medial prefrontal lesions and recovery of spatial delayed alternation in the rat: Effects of delay interval. *Developmental Psychobiology, 28,* 269–279.

Carter, C. S., & Keverne, E. B. (2002). The neurobiology of social affiliation and pair bonding. In D. Pfaff, A. P.

Arnold, A. M. Etgen, S. E. Fahrbach, & R. T. Rubin (Eds.), *Hormones, brain, and behavior* (pp. 299–337). San Diego, CA: Academic Press.

Carter, E. J., & Pelphrey, K. A. (2008). Friend or foe? Brain systems involved in the perception of dynamic signals of menacing and friendly social approaches. *Social Neuroscience. 3*, 151–163.

Carver, K., Joyner, K., & Udry, J. R. (2003). National estimates of adolescent romantic relationships. In P. Florsheim (Ed.), *Adolescent romantic relations and sexual behavior: Theory, research, and practical implications* (pp. 23–56). Mahwah, NJ: Erlbaum.

Carver, P. R., Egan, S. K., & Perry, D. G. (2004). Children who question their heterosexuality. *Developmental Psychology, 40*, 43–53.

Case, R., Hayward, S., Lewis, M., & Hurst, P. (1988). Toward a neo-Piagetian theory of cognitive and emotional development. *Developmental Review, 8*, 1–51.

Casey, B. J. (2001). Disruption of inhibitory control in developmental disorders: A mechanistic model of implicated frontostriatal circuitry. In J. McClelland & R. Siegler (Eds.), *Mechanisms of cognitive development* (pp. 327–349). Mahwah, NJ: Erlbaum.

Cashwell, T. H., Skinner, C. H., & Smith, E. S. (2001). Increasing second-grade students' reports of peers' prosocial behaviors via direct instruction, group reinforcement, and progress feedback: A replication and extension. *Education and Treatment of Children, 24*, 161–175.

Casiglia, A. C., Lo Coco, A., & Zapplulla, C. (1998). Aspects of social reputation and peer relationships in Italian children: A cross-cultural perspective. *Developmental Psychology, 34*, 723–730.

Caspi, A., Elder, G. H., & Bem, D. J. (1987). Moving against the world: Life-course patterns of explosive children. *Developmental Psychology, 23*, 308–313.

Caspi, A., Elder, G. H., & Bem, D. J. (1988). Moving away from the world: Life-course patterns of shy children. *Developmental Psychology, 24*, 824–831.

Caspi, A., Harrington, H., Milne, B., Amell, J. W., Theodore, R. F., Moffitt, T. E. (2003). Children's behavioral styles at age 3 are linked to their adult personality traits at age 26. *Journal of Personality, 71*, 495–513.

Caspi, A., McClay, J., Moffitt, T. E., Mill, J., Martin, J., Craig, I. W., Taylor, A., & Poulton, R. (2002). Role of genotype in the cycle of violence in maltreated children. *Science, 297*, 851–854.

Caspi, A., & Shiner, R. L. (2006). Personality development. In W. Damon, & R. M. Lerner (Series Eds.), & N. Eisenberg (Vol. Ed.), *Handbook of child psychology: Vol. 3. Social, emotional, and personality development* (6th ed., pp. 300–365). Hoboken, NJ: Wiley.

Caspi, A., & Silva, P. A. (1995). Temperamental qualities at age three predict personality traits in young adulthood: Longitudinal evidence from a birth cohort. *Child Development, 66*, 486–498.

Caspi, A., Sugden, K., Moffitt, T. E., Taylor, A., Craig, I. W., Harrington, H., . . . Poulton, R. (2003). Influence of life stress on depression: Moderation by a polymorphism in the 5-HTT gene. *Science, 301*, 386–389.

Cassidy, J. (1988). Child-mother attachment and the self in six-year-olds. *Child Development, 59*, 121–135.

Cassidy, J. (2008). The nature of the child's ties. In J. Cassidy & P. R. Shaver (Eds.), *Handbook of attachment: Theory, research, and clinical applications* (2nd ed., pp. 3–22). New York: Guilford Press.

Cassidy, J., & Berlin, L. J. (1994). The insecure/ambivalent pattern of attachment: Theory and research. *Child Development, 65*, 971–991.

Cassidy, J., & Marvin, R. S. (1992). Attachment organization in preschool children: Procedures and coding manual. Unpublished manuscript, MacArthur Group on Attachment, Seattle, WA.

Cassidy, K. W., Fineberg, D. S., Brown, K., & Perkins, A. (2005). Theory of mind may be contagious, but you don't catch it from your twin. *Child Development, 76*, 97–106.

Castelli, F., Frith, C., Happe, F., & Frith, U. (2002). Autism, Asperger syndrome and brain mechanisms for the attribution of mental states to animated shapes. *Brain, 125*, 1839–1849.

Cates, D. S., Shontz, F. C., Fowler, S., Vavak, C. R., Dell'Oliver, C., & Yoshinoby, L. (1996). The effects of time pressure on social cognitive problem solving by aggressive and nonaggressive boys. *Child Study Journal, 26*, 163–190.

CBS News. (2000, December 22). *Americans convicted in German murders*. Retrieved from: http://www.cbsnews.com/stories/2000/12/01/world/main253905.shtml

CBS News. (2006, November 21). *Percentage of unmarried moms hits new high*. Retrieved from: http://www.cbsnews.com/stories/2006/11/21/national/main2204387.shtml

CBS News Poll. (2009, May 10). Poll: *Majority of moms feel appreciated*. Retrieved from: http://www.cbsnews.com/stories/2009/05/08/opinion/polls/main5002075.shtml

Ceci, S. J., & Bruck, M. (1995). *Jeopardy in the courtroom: A scientific analysis of children's testimony*. Washington, DC: American Psychological Association.

Celizic, M. (March. 6, 2009). Her teen committed suicide over 'sexting': Cynthia Logan's daughter was taunted about photo she sent to boyfriend. *Today Show*, MSNBC News. Retrieved from: http://today.msnbc.msn.com/id/29546030/

Center for Media and Public Affairs. (1999). Merchandizing mayhem: Violence in popular entertainment 1998–1999. *Media Monitor, 13* (4). Retrieved from: http://www.cmpa.com/files/media_monitor/99sepoct.pdf

Center on Addiction and Substance Abuse. (CASA). (2007). *The importance of family dinners III*. New York: Columbia University.

Centers for Disease Control and Prevention. (CDC). (2007, September 8). *Morbidity and morality*. Weekly Report. Atlanta, GA: CDC.

Centers for Disease Control and Prevention. (CDC). (2009). *Suicide rates: Facts at a glance*. Centers for Disease Control and Prevention National Center for Injury Prevention and Control. Retrieved from: www.cdc.gov/violenceprevention

Cervantes, C. A., & Callanan, M. (1998). Labels and explanations in mother-child emotion talk: Age and gender differentiation. *Developmental Psychology, 34*, 88–98.

Chaimongkol, N. N., & Flick, L. H. (2006). Maternal sensitivity and attachment security in Thailand: Cross-cultural validation of western measures. *Journal of Nursing Measurement, 14*, 5–17.

Chalk, F., & Jonassohn, K. (1990). *The history and sociology of genocide: Analyses and case studies*. New Haven, CT: Yale University Press.

Chamberlain, P., Leve, L. D., & DeGarmo, D. S. (2007). Multidimensional treatment foster care for girls in the juvenile justice system: 2-year follow-up of a randomized clinical trial. *Journal of Consulting and Clinical Psychology, 75*, 187–193.

Chambers, R. A., Taylor, J. R., & Potenza, M. N. (2003). Developmental neurocircuitry of motivation in adolescence: A critical period of addiction vulnerability. *American Journal of Psychiatry, 160*, 1041–1052.

Chandler, M. J., Greenspan, S., & Barenboim, C. (1973). Judgments of intentionality in response to videotaped and verbally presented moral dilemmas: The medium is the message. *Child Development, 44*, 315–320.

Chandler, M. J., Lalonde, C. E., Sokol, B. W., & Hallett, D. (2003). Personal persistence, identity development, and suicide. *Monographs of the Society for Research on Child Development, 68* (Serial No. 273).

Chandra, A., Martino, S., Collins, R., Elliott, M., Berry, S., Kanouse, D., & Miu, A. (2008). Does watching sex on television predict teen pregnancy? Findings from a national longitudinal survey of youth. *Pediatrics, 122*, 1047–1054.

Chang, F.-M., Kidd, J. R., Kivak, K. J., Pakstis, A. J., & Kidd, K. K. (1996). The world-wide distribution of allele frequencies at the human dopamine D4 receptor locus. *Human Genetics, 98*, 91–101.

Chang, L. (2003). Variable effects of children's aggression, social withdrawal and prosocial leadership as functions of teachers' beliefs and behaviors. *Child Development, 74*, 535–548.

Chao, R. K., & Tseng, V. (2002). Asian-American parents. In M. H. Bornstein (Ed.), *Handbook of parenting: Vol. 4. Social conditions and applied parenting* (2nd ed., pp. 59–93). Mahwah, NJ: Erlbaum.

Chapman, E., Baron-Cohen, S., Auyeung, B., Knickmeyer, R., Taylor, K., & Hackett, G. (2006). Fetal testosterone and empathy: Evidence from the Empathy Quotient (EQ) and the "Reading the Mind in the Eyes" test. *Social Neuroscience, 1*, 135–148.

Charles, S. T., & Carstensen, L. L. (2007). Emotion regulation and aging. In J. J. Gross (Ed.), *Handbook of emotion regulation* (pp. 307–327). New York: Guilford Press.

Charles, S. T., & Carstensen, L. L. (2008). Unpleasant situations elicit different emotional responses in younger and older adults. *Psychology & Aging, 23*, 495–504.

Charles, S. T., Mathers, M., & Carstensen, L. L. (2003). Aging and emotional memory: The forgettable nature of negative images for older adults. *Journal of Experimental Psychology, 132*, 310–324.

Charlesworth, R., & Hartup, W. W. (1967). Positive social reinforcement in the nursery school peer group. *Child Development, 38*, 993–1002.

Chase-Lansdale, P. L., Moffitt, R. A., Lohman, B. J., Cherlin, A. J., Coley, R. L., Pittman, L. D., Roff, J., & Votruba-Drzal, E. (2003). Mothers' transitions from welfare to work and the well-being of preschoolers and adolescents. *Science, 299*, 1548–1552.

Chavous, T. M., Hilkene Bernat, D., Schmeelk-Cone, K., Caldwell, C. H., Kohn-Wood, L., & Zimmerman, M. A. (2003). Racial identity and academic attainment among African American adolescents. *Child Development, 74*, 1076–1090.

Cheah, C. S. L., & Chirkov, V. (2008). Parents' personal and cultural beliefs regarding young children: A cross-cultural study of aboriginal and Euro-Canadian mothers. *Journal of Cross-Cultural Psychology, 39*, 402–423.

Chen, I. (2009, June). Brain cells for socializing: Does an obscure nerve cell help explain what gorillas, elephants, whales—and people—have in common? *Smithsonian Magazine*. Retrieved from: http://www.smithsonianmag.com/science-nature/The-Social-Brain.html?c = y&page = 2

Chen, S., Boucher, H. C., & Tapias, M. P. (2006). The relational self revealed: Conceptualization and implications for interpersonal life. *Psychological Bulletin, 132*, 151–179.

Chen, X. (2000). Growing up in a collectivist culture: Socialization and socioemotional development in Chinese children. In A. L. Comunian & U. P. Gielen (Eds.), *Human development in cross-culture perspective* (pp. 331–353). Padua, Italy: Cedam.

Chen, X., Cen, G., Li, D., & He, Y. (2005). Social functioning and adjustment in Chinese children: The imprint of historical time. *Child Development, 76*, 182–195.

Chen, X., Chang, L., & He, Y. (2003). The peer group as context: Mediating and moderating effects on relations between academic achievement and social functioning in Chinese children. *Child Development, 74*, 710–727.

Chen, X., Chen, H., Li, D., & Wang, L. (2009). Early childhood behavioral inhibition and social and school adjustment in Chinese children: A five-year longitudinal study. *Child Development, 80*, 1692–1704.

Chen, X., DeSouza, A., Chen, H., & Wang, L. (2006). Reticent behavior and experiences in peer interactions in Canadian and Chinese children. *Developmental Psychology, 42,* 656–665.

Chen, X., & French, D. C. (2008). Children's social competence in cultural context. *Annual Review of Psychology, 59,* 591–616.

Chen, X., He, Y., & Li, D. (2004). Self-perceptions of social competence and self-worth in Chinese children: Relations with social and school performance. *Social Development, 13,* 570–589.

Chen, X., & Rubin, K. H. (1994). Family conditions, parental acceptance, and social competence and aggression in Chinese children. *Social Development, 3,* 269–290.

Chen, X., Rubin, K. H., & Sun, Y. (1992). Social reputation and peer relationships in Chinese and Canadian children: A cross-cultural study. *Child Development, 63,* 1336–1343.

Chen, X., & Tse, H. C-H. (2008). Social functioning and adjustment in Canadian-born children with Chinese and European backgrounds. *Developmental Psychology, 44,* 1184–1189.

Chen, X., & Wang, Z. (2006, July). *Social and cultural changes and the development of social functioning.* Paper presented at the biennial meeting of the International Society for the Study of Behavioral Development, Melbourne, Australia.

Chen, X., Wang, L., & Wang, Z. (2009). Shyness-sensitivity and social, school, and psychological adjustment in rural migrant and urban children in China. *Child Development, 80,* 1499–1513.

Cheng, T. C. (2007). Impact of work requirements on the psychological well-being of TANF recipients. *Health & Social Work, 32,* 41–48.

Cheng, Y., Tzeng, O. J., Decety, J., & Hsieh, J. C. (2006). Gender differences in the human mirror system: A magnetoencephalography study. *NeuroReport, 17,* 1115–1119.

Cherlin, A. J. (Ed.)(1996). *The changing American family and public policy.* Washington DC: Urban Institute.

Cherlin, A. J., & Furstenberg, F. F. (1994). Stepfamilies in the United States: A reconsideration. *Annual Review of Sociology, 20,* 359–381.

Cherney, I. D., & London, K. (2006). Gender-linked differences in toys, television shows, computer games, and outdoor activities of 5- to 13-year-old children. *Sex Roles, 54,* 717–726.

Chess, S., & Thomas, A. (1986). *Temperament in clinical practice.* New York: Guilford Press.

Child Trends. (2005). *Facts at a glance, Publication 2005–02.* Washington, DC: Child Trends.

Child Trends. (2007). *Facts at a glance, Publication 2007–12.* Washington, DC: Child Trends.

Child Trends. (2008). *Facts at a glance, Publication 2008–29.* Washington, DC: Child Trends.

Child Welfare Information Gateway. (2006). *Long-term consequences of child abuse and neglect: Fact sheet.* Retrieved from: http://www.childwelfare.gov/pubs/factsheets/long_term_consequences.cfm

Children Now. (1998). *A different world: Children's perceptions of race and class in the media.* Oakland, CA: Children Now.

Children Now. (2004). *Fall colors 2003-04: Prime time diversity report. The Asian and Latino populations in the U.S. are more than twice those found on prime-time TV.* Retrieved from: www.childrennow.org

Children's Defense Fund. (2004). *The state of America's children: 2004.* Washington, DC: Children's Defense Fund.

Children's Rights. (2008). *Facts about abuse and neglect.* Retrieved from: http://www.childrensrights.org/issues-resources/child-abuse-and-neglect/facts-about-abuse-and-neglect/

Chin, J. C. (2007, March). *Taiwanese children's perspectives on coping with negative emotions.* Paper presented at the biennial meeting of the Society for Research in Child Development, Boston.

Chun, K. M., Organista, P. B., & Marin, G. (Eds.)(2003). *Acculturation: Advances in theory, measurement, and applied research.* Washington, DC: American Psychological Association.

Cicchetti, D., Rogosch, F. A., Gunnar, M. R., & Toth, S. L. (2010). The differential impacts of early physical and sexual abuse and internalizing problems on daytime cortisol rhythm in school-aged children. *Child Development, 81,* 252–269.

Cicchetti, D., & Toth, S. L. (2006). Developmental psychopathology and preventive intervention. In W. Damon & R. M. Lerner (Series Eds.), & K. A. Renninger & I. E. Sigel (Vol. Eds.), *Handbook of child psychology: Vol. 4. Child psychology and practice* (6th ed., pp. 497–547). Hoboken, NJ: Wiley.

Cillessen, A. H. N., & Mayeux, L. (2004). Sociometric status and peer group behavior: Previous findings and current directions. In J. B. Kupersmidt & K. A. Dodge (Eds.), *Children's peer relations* (pp. 3–20). Washington, DC: American Psychological Association.

Cillissen, A. H. N., & Rose, A. J. (2005). Understanding popularity in the peer system. *Current Directions in Psychological Science, 14,* 102–105.

Clark, E. V. (1983). Meanings and concepts. In P. H. Mussen (Series Ed.), & J. H. Flavell & E. M. Markman (Vol. Eds.), *Handbook of child psychology: Vol. 3. Cognitive development* (4th ed., pp. 787–840). New York: Wiley.

Clark, K. E., & Ladd, G. W. (2000). Connectedness and autonomy support in parent-child relationships: Links to children's socioemotional orientation and peer relationships. *Developmental Psychology, 36,* 485–498.

Clark, L. A., Kochanska, G., & Ready, R. (2000). Mothers' personality and its interaction with child temperament as predictors of parenting behavior. *Journal of Personality and Social Psychology, 79,* 274–285.

Clarke, G., Hops, H., Lewinsohn, P. M., & Andrews, J. (1992). Cognitive-behavioral group treatment of adolescent depression: Prediction of outcome. *Behavior Therapy*, *23*, 341–354.

Clarke-Stewart, K. A. (1989). Infant day care: Maligned or malignant? *American Psychologist*, *44*, 266–273.

Clarke-Stewart, K. A., & Allhusen, V. D. (2002). Nonparental caregiving. In M. H. Bornstein (Ed.), *Handbook of parenting: Vol. 3. Being and becoming a parent* (2nd ed., pp. 215–252). Mahwah, NJ: Erlbaum.

Clarke-Stewart, A., & Allhusen, V. D. (2005). *What we know about childcare*. Cambridge, MA: Harvard University Press.

Clarke-Stewart, A., & Brentano, C. (2005). *Divorce lessons: Real-life stories and what you can learn from them*. Charleston, SC: BookSurge Publishing.

Clarke-Stewart, A., & Brentano, C. (2006). *Divorce: Causes and consequences*. New Haven, CT: Yale University Press.

Clarke-Stewart, K. A., Goossens, F. A., & Allhusen, V. D. (2001). Measuring infant-mother attachment: Is the Strange Situation enough? *Social Development*, *10*, 143–169.

Clarke-Stewart, K. A., & Hayward, C. (1996). Advantages of father custody and contact for the psychological well-being of school-age children. *Journal of Applied Developmental Psychology*, *17*, 239–270.

Clarke-Stewart, K. A., Malloy, L. C., & Allhusen, V. D. (2004). Verbal ability, self-control, and close relationships with parents protect children against misleading suggestions. *Applied Cognitive Psychology*, *18*, 1037–1058.

Clarke-Stewart, K. A., Vandell, D. L., McCartney, K., Owen, M. T., & Booth, C. (2000). Effects of parental separation and divorce on very young children. *Journal of Family Psychology*, *14*, 304–326.

Clearfield, M. W., & Nelson, N. M. (2006). Sex differences in mothers' speech and play behavior with 6-, 9-, and 14-month-old infants. *Sex Roles*, *54*, 127–137.

Cloninger, C. R., Sigvardsson, S., Bohman, M., & van Knoring, A. L. (1982). Predisposition to petty criminality in Swedish adoptees: II. Cross-fostering analyses of gene-environmental interactions. *Archives of General Psychiatry*, *39*, 1242–1247.

Closson, L. M. (2009). Status and gender differences in early adolescents' descriptions of popularity. *Social Development*, *18*, 412–426.

Coalition to Stop the Use of Child Soldiers. (2008). *Child soldiers global report*. Retrieved from: http://www.childsoldiersglobalreport.org/

Coan, J. A. (2008). Toward a neuroscience of attachment. In J. Cassidy & P. R. Shaver (Eds.), *Handbook of attachment: Theory, research, and clinical applications* (2nd ed., pp. 241–265). New York: Guilford Press.

Coan, J. A., Allen, J. J. B., & McKnight, P. E. (2006). A capability model of individual differences in frontal EEG asymmetry. *Biological Psychology*, *72*, 198–207.

Coan, J. A., Schaefer, H. S., & Davidson, R. J. (2005). Marital adjustment and interpersonal styles moderate the effects of spouse and stranger hand holding on activation of neural systems underlying response to threat. *Psychophysiology*, *42*, S44.

Coats, A. H., & Blanchard-Fields, F. (2008). Emotion regulation in interpersonal problems: The role of cognitive-emotional complexity, emotion regulation goals, and expressivity. *Psychology & Aging*, *23*, 39–51.

Cochran, L., Feng, H., Cartledge, G., & Hamilton, S. (1993). The effects of cross-age tutoring on the academic achievement, social behaviors, and self-perceptions of low-achieving African-American males with behavioral disorders. *Behavioral Disorders*, *18*, 292–302.

Cohen, D. A., Farley, T. A., Taylor, S. N., Martin, D. H., & Schuster, M. A. (2002). When and where do youths have sex? The potential role of adult supervision *Pediatrics*, *110*, 1–6.

Cohen-Bendahan, C. C., Buitelaar, J. K., van Goozen, S. H. M., & Cohen-Kettenis, P. T. (2004). Prenatal exposure to testosterone and functional cerebral lateralization: A study in same sex and opposite sex twin girls. *Psychoneuroendocrinology*, *29*, 911–916.

Cohen-Kettenis, P. T., Delemarre-van de Waal, H. A., & Gooren, L. J. G. (2008). The treatment of adolescent transsexuals: Changing insights. *Journal of Sexual Medicine*, *5*, 1892–1897.

Coie, J. D., (2004). Negative social experience and antisocial behavior. In J. B. Kupersmidt & K. A. Dodge (Eds.), *Children's peer relations* (pp. 243–267). Washington, DC: American Psychological Association.

Coie, J. D., & Dodge, K. A. (1983). Continuities and changes in children's social status: A five-year longitudinal study. *Merrill-Palmer Quarterly*, *29*, 261–282.

Coie, J. D., & Dodge, K. A. (1998). Aggression and antisocial behavior. In W. Damon (Series Ed.), & N. Eisenberg (Vol. Ed.), *Handbook of child psychology: Vol. 3. Social, emotional, and personal development* (5th ed., pp. 779–862). New York: Wiley.

Coie, J. D., Dodge, K. A., & Kupersmidt, J. (1990). Peer group behavior and social status. In S. R. Asher & J. D. Coie (Eds.), *Peer rejection in childhood* (pp. 17–59). New York: Cambridge University Press.

Colby, A., & Kohlberg, L. (1987). *The measurement of moral judgment* (Vols. 1–2). New York: Cambridge University Press.

Colby, A., Kohlberg, L., Gibbs, J., & Lieberman, M. (1983). A longitudinal study of moral judgment. *Monographs of* the Society for Research in Child Development, *48* (Serial No. 200).

Colder, C. R., Lochman, J. E., & Wells, K. C. (1997). The moderating effects of children's fear and activity level on relations between parenting practices and childhood symptomology. *Journal of Abnormal Child Psychology, 25,* 251–263.

Cole, C. F., Arafat, C., Tidhar, C., Tafesh, W. Z., Fox, N. A., Killen, M., . . . Yung, F. (2003). The educational impact of Rechov Sumsum/Shara'a Simsim: A Sesame Street television series to promote respect and understanding among children living in Israel, the West Bank and Gaza. *International Journal of Behavioral Development, 27,* 409–422.

Cole, H. A., & Griffiths, M. D. (2007). Social interactions in massively multiplayer online role-playing gamers. *CyberPsychology & Behavior, 10,* 575–583.

Cole, P. M., Bruschi, C. J., & Tamang, B. L. (2002). Cultural differences in children's emotional reactions to difficult situations. *Child Development, 73,* 983–996.

Cole, P. M., Luby, J., & Sullivan, M. W. (2008). Emotions and the development of childhood depression: Bridging the gap. *Child Development Perspectives, 2,* 141–148.

Cole, P. M., Martin, S. E., & Dennis, T. A. (2004). Emotion regulation as a scientific construct: Methodological challenges and directions for child development research. *Child Development, 75,* 317–333.

Cole, P. M., & Tamang, B. L. (1998). Nepali children's ideas about emotional displays in hypothetical situations. *Developmental Psychology, 34,* 640–646.

Cole, P. M., & Tan, P. Z. (2007). Emotion socialization from a cultural perspective. In J. E. Grusec & P. Hastings (Eds.), *Handbook of socialization* (pp. 516–542). New York: Guilford Press.

Cole, S. A., Wehrmann, K. C., Dewar, G., & Swinford, L. (2005). Crisis nurseries: Important services in a system of care for families and children. *Children and Youth Services Review, 27,* 995–1010.

Coleman, L., Clancy, P.E., & Yates, J. (Eds.) (1999). *Has a child been molested? The disturbing facts about current methods of investigating.* Berkeley, CA: Berkeley Creek Productions.

Coley, R. L., & Chase-Lansdale, P. L. (1998). Stability and change in paternal involvement among African-American fathers. *Journal of Family Psychology, 13,* 416–435.

Coley, R. L., Lohman, B. J., Votruba-Drzal, E., Pittman, L. D., & Chase-Lansdale, P. L. (2007). Maternal functioning, time, and money: The world of work and welfare. *Children and Youth Services Review, 29,* 721–741.

Colin, V. L. (1996). *Human attachment.* New York: McGraw-Hill.

Collignon, F. E., Men, M., & Tan S. (2001). Finding ways in: Community-based perspectives on Southeast Asian family involvement with schools in a New England state. *Journal of Education for Students Placed at Risk, 6,* 27–44.

Collins, R. L., Elliott, M. N., Berry, S. H., Kanouse, D. E., Kunkel, D., Hunter, S. B., & Miu, A. (2004). Watching sex on television predicts adolescent initiation of sexual behavior. *Pediatrics, 114,* 1047–1054.

Collins, W. A. (1983). Interpretation and inference in children's television viewing. In J. Bryant & D. R. Anderson (Eds.), *Children's understanding of television: Research on attention and comprehension.* Academic Press, New York.

Collins, W. A. (2003). More than myth: The developmental significance of romantic relationships during adolescence. *Journal of Research on Adolescence, 13,* 1–24.

Collins, W. A. (2010). Historical perspectives on contemporary research in social development. In P. K. Smith & C. H. Hart (Eds.), *Wiley-Blackwell handbook of childhood social development* (2nd ed.). Oxford, UK: Wiley-Blackwell.

Collins, W. A., Maccoby, E. E., Steinberg, L., Hetherington, E. M., & Bornstein, M. H. (2000). Contemporary research on parenting: The case for nature and nurture. *American Psychologist, 55,* 218–232.

Collins, W. A., & Madsen, S. D. (2006). Close relationships in adolescence and early adulthood. In D. Perlman & A. Vangelisti (Eds.), *Handbook of personal relationships* (pp. 191–209). New York: Cambridge University Press.

Collins, W. A., & Repinski, D. J. (2001). Parents and adolescents as transformers of relationships: Dyadic adaptation to developmental change. In J. R. M. Gerris (Ed.), *Dynamics of parenting* (pp. 429–444). Leuven, Belgium: Garant.

Collins, W. A., Sobol, B. L., & Westby, S. (1981). Effects of adult commentary on children's comprehension and inferences about a televised aggressive portrayal. *Child Development, 52,* 158–163.

Collins, W. A., & Sroufe, L. A. (1999). Capacity for intimate relationships: A developmental construction. In W. Furman, B. B. Brown, & C. Feiring (Eds.), *The development of romantic relationships during adolescence* (pp. 125–147). New York: Cambridge University Press.

Collins, W. A., & van Dulmen, M. H. M. (2006). The course of true love(s): Origins and pathways in the development of romantic relationships. In A. C. Crouter & A. Booth (Eds.), *Romance and sex in adolescence and emerging adulthood: Risks and opportunities* (pp. 63–86). Mahwah, NJ: Erlbaum.

Collins, W. A., Welsh, D. P., & Furman, W. (2009). Adolescent romantic relationships. *Annual Review of Psychology, 60,* 631–652.

Collins-Standley, T., Gan, S., Yu, H. J., & Zillmann, D. (1996). Choice of romantic, violent, and scary fairy-tale books by preschool girls and boys. *Child Study Journal, 26,* 279–301.

Coltrane, S. (1996). *Family man: Fatherhood, housework, and gender equity*. New York: Oxford University Press.

Coltrane, S. (1998). *Gender and families*. Thousand Oaks, CA: Pine Forge Press.

Coltrane, S., & Adams, M. (2008). *Gender and families* (2nd ed.). Lanham, MD: Rowman & Littlefield.

Coltrane, S., & Collins, R. (2001). *Sociology of marriage and the family* (5th ed.). Belmont, CA: Wadsworth.

Colwell, M. J., & Hart, S. (2006). Emotion framing: Does it relate to children's emotion knowledge and social behavior? *Early Child Development & Care, 17*, 591–603.

Comings, D. E., Gade-Andavolu, R., Gonzalez, N., Wu, S., Muhleman, D., Blake, H., . . . MacMurray, J. P. (2000). A multivariate analysis of 59 candidate genes in personality traits: The temperament and character inventory. *Clinical Genetics, 58*, 375–385.

Comstock, G., & Scharrer, E. (2006). Media and pop culture. In W. Damon & R. M. Lerner (Series Eds.), & K. A. Renninger & I. Sigel (Vol. Eds.), *Handbook of child psychology: Vol. 4. Child psychology in practice* (6th ed., pp. 817–863). Hoboken, NJ: Wiley.

Conduct Problems Prevention Research Group. (2004). The Fast Track experiment: Translating the developmental model into a prevention design. In J. B. Kupersmidt & K. A. Dodge (Eds.), *Children's peer relations: From development to intervention* (pp. 181–208). Washington, DC: American Psychological Association.

Conger, R. D., & Conger, K. J. (1996). Sibling relationships. In R. L. Simons and Associates (Eds.), *Understanding differences between divorced and intact families* (pp. 104–124). Thousand Oaks, CA: Sage.

Conger, R. D., Cui, M., Bryant, C. M., & Elder, G. H. (2000). Competence in early adult romantic relationships: A developmental perspective on family influences. *Journal of Personality and Social Psychology, 79*, 224–237.

Conger, R. D., & Elder, G. H. (Eds.) (1994). *Families in troubled times: Adapting to change in rural America*. New York: Aldine.

Connellan, J., Baron-Cohen, S., Wheelwright, S., Batki, A., & Ahluwalia, J. (2000). Sex differences in human neonatal social perception. *Infant Behavior and Development, 23*, 113–118.

Connolly, J. A., Craig, W., Goldberg, A., & Pepler, D. (2004). Mixed-gender groups, dating, and romantic relationships in early adolescence. *Journal of Research on Adolescence, 14*, 185–207.

Connolly, J. A., Furman, W., & Konarski, R. (2000). The role of peers in the emergence of heterosexual romantic relationships in adolescence. *Child Development, 71*, 1395–1408.

Connolly, J. A., & Goldberg, A. (1999). Romantic relationships in adolescence: The role of friends and peers in their emergence and development. In W. Furman, B. B. Brown, & C. Feiring (Eds.), *The development of romantic relationships in adolescence* (pp. 266–290). New York: Cambridge University Press.

Connolly, K. J., & Smith, P. K. (1978). Experimental studies of the preschool environment. *International Journal of Early Childhood, 10*, 86–95.

Conrad, K. M., Flay, B. R., & Hill, D. (1992). Why children start smoking cigarettes: Predictors of onset. *British Journal of Addiction, 87*, 1711–1721.

Contreras, J. M., Kerns, K., Weimer, B. L., Gentzler, A. L., & Tomich, P. L. (2000). Emotional regulation as a mediator of association between mother-child attachment and peer relationships in middle childhood. *Journal of Family Psychology, 14*, 111–124.

Coogan, P. A., & Chen, C. P. (2007). Career development and counseling for women: Connecting theories to practice. *Counselling Psychology Quarterly, 20*, 191–204.

Cooksey, E. C., Menaghan, E. G., & Jekielek, S. M. (1997). Life course effects of work and family circumstances on children. *Social Forces, 76*, 637–667.

Cooney, T. M., Pedersen, F. A., Indelicato, S., Palkovitz, R. (1993). Timing of fatherhood: Is "on-time" optimal? *Journal of Marriage and Family, 55*, 205–215.

Cooper, C. R., Brown, J., Azmitia, M., & Chavira, G. (2005). Including Latino immigrant families, schools, and community programs as research partners on the good path of life—El buen camino de la vida. In T. Weisner (Ed.), *Discovering successful pathways in children's development: Mixed methods in the study of childhood and family life* (pp. 359–422). Chicago: University of Chicago Press.

Cooper, H. M. (2009). *Research synthesis and meta-analysis: A step by step approach* (4th ed.). Thousand Oaks, CA: Sage.

Cooper, R. P., & Aslin, R. N. (1990). Preference for infant-directed speech in the first month after birth. *Child Development, 61*, 1584–1595.

Coopersmith, S. (1967). *The antecedents of self-esteem*. Palo Alto, CA: Consulting Psychologists Press.

Coplan, R. J., Prakash, K., O'Neil, K., & Armer, M. (2004). Do you "want" to play? Distinguishing between conflicted shyness and social disinterest in early childhood. *Developmental Psychology, 40*, 244–258.

Corapci, F. (2008). The role of child temperament on Head Start preschoolers' social competence in the context of cumulative risk. *Journal of Applied Developmental Psychology, 29*, 1–16.

Cornell, A. H., & Frick, P. J. (2007). The moderating effects of parenting styles in the association between behavioral inhibition and parent-reported guilt and empathy in preschool children. *Journal of Clinical Child & Adolescent Psychology, 36*, 305–318.

Correll, S. J., & Benard, S. (2005, August). *Getting a job: Is there a motherhood penalty?* Paper presented at the annual meeting of the American Sociological Association, Philadelphia.

Retrieved from: http://www.news.cornell.edu/stories/Aug05/soc.mothers.dea.html

Corter, C., & Fleming, A. S. (2002). Psychobiology of maternal behavior in human beings. In M. H. Bornstein (Ed.), *Handbook of parenting: Vol. 2. Biology and ecology of parenting* (2nd ed. pp. 141–182). Mahwah, NJ: Erlbaum.

Cosgrove, J. M., & Patterson, C. J. (1977). Plans and the development of listener skills. *Developmental Psychology, 13,* 557–564.

Cost, Quality, and Child Outcomes Study Team. (1995). *Cost, quality, and child outcomes in child care centers.* Denver, CO: Economics Department, University of Colorado at Denver.

Cote, S. M., Vaillancourt, T., Barker, E. D., Nagin, D., & Tremblay, R. E. (2007). The joint development of physical and indirect aggression: Predictors of continuity and change during childhood. *Development and Psychopathology, 19,* 37–55.

Coughenour, J. C. (1995). Separate and unequal: Women in the federal criminal justice system. *Federal Sentencing Reporter, 8,* 142–144.

Courchesne, E. (2004). Brain development in autism: Early overgrowth followed by premature arrest of growth. *Mental Retardation and Developmental Disabilities Research Reviews, 10,* 106–111.

Cowan, C. P., & Cowan, P. A. (2000). *When partners become parents: The big life change for couples.* Mahwah, NJ: Erlbaum.

Cowan, C. P., Cowan, P. A., & Heming, G. (2005). Two variations of a preventive intervention for couples: Effects on parents and children during a transition to school. In P. A. Cowan, C. P. Cowan, J. C. Ablow, V. K. Johnson, & J. R. Measelle (Eds.), *The family context of parenting in children's adaptation to elementary school* (pp. 277–315). Mahwah, NJ: Erlbaum.

Cowan, P. A., & Cowan, C. P. (2002). What an intervention design reveals about how parents affect their children's academic achievement and behavior problems. In J. Borkowski, S. L. Ramey, & M. Bristol-Power (Eds.), *Parenting and the child's world* (pp. 75–98). Mahwah, NJ: Erlbaum.

Cowan, P. A., & Cowan, C. P. (2010). How working with couples fosters children's development: From prevention science to public policy. In M. Schulz, M. K. Pruett, P. Kerig, & R. D. Parke (Eds.), *Strengthening couple relationships for optimal child development* (pp. 211–228). Washington, DC: American Psychological Association.

Cowan, P. A., Cowan, C. P., Ablow, J. C., Johnson, V. K., & Measelle, J. R. (Eds.)(2005). *The family context of parenting in children's adaptation to elementary school.* Mahwah, NJ: Erlbaum.

Cowan, P. A., Cowan, C. P., Schulz, M., & Heming, G. (1994). Prebirth to preschool family factors predicting children's adaptation to kindergarten. In R. Parke & S. Kellam (Eds.), *Advances in family research: Vol. 4. Exploring family relationships with other social context* (pp. 75–114). Hillsdale, NJ: Erlbaum.

Cox, M. J., & Paley, B. (2003). Understanding families as systems. *Current Directions in Psychological Science, 12,* 193–196.

Coyne, S. M., Nelson, D. A., & Underwood, M. (2010). Aggression in children. In P. K. Smith & C. H. Hart (Eds.), *Wiley-Blackwell handbook of childhood social development* (2nd ed.). Oxford, UK: Wiley-Blackwell.

Coyne, S. M., & Whitehead, E. (2008). Indirect aggression in animated Disney films. *Journal of Communication, 58,* 382–395.

Craig, W., & Pepler, D. J. (1997). Observations of bullying and victimization in the schoolyard. *Canadian Journal of School Psychology, 13,* 41–57.

Craig, W. M., Vitaro, F., Gagnon, C., & Tremblay, R. E. (2002). The road to gang membership: Characteristics of male gang and nongang members from ages 10 to 14. *Social Development, 11,* 53–68.

Crain-Thoreson, C., & Dale, P. S. (1992). Do early talkers become early readers? Linguistic precocity, preschool language and emergent literacy. *Developmental Psychology, 28,* 421–429.

Cramer, P. (2004). Identity change in adulthood: The contribution of defense mechanisms and life experiences. *Journal of Research in Personality, 38,* 280–316.

Crane, D. A., & Tisak, M. S. (1995). Mixed-domain events: The influence of moral and conventional components on the development of social reasoning. *Early Education & Development, 6,* 169–180.

Crick, N. R. (1997). Engagement in gender normative versus nonnormative forms of aggression: Links to social-psychological adjustment. *Developmental Psychology, 33,* 610–617.

Crick, N. R., & Bigbee, M. A. (1998). Relational and overt forms of peer victimization: A multi-informant approach. *Journal of Consulting and Clinical Psychology, 66,* 337–347.

Crick, N. R., Casas, J. F., & Ku, H. (1999). Relational and physical forms of peer victimization in preschool. *Developmental Psychology, 35,* 376–385.

Crick, N. R., Casas, J. F., & Mosher, M. (1997). Relational and overt aggression in preschool. *Developmental Psychology, 33,* 579–588.

Crick, N. R., & Dodge, K. A. (1994). A review and reformulation of social information-processing mechanisms in children's social adjustment. *Psychological Bulletin, 115,* 74–101.

Crick, N. R., & Grotpeter, J. K. (1995). Relational aggression, gender, and social-psychological adjustment. *Child Development, 66,* 710–722.

Crick, N. R., & Ladd, G. W. (1993). Children's perceptions of their peer experiences: Attributions, loneliness, social anxiety, and social avoidance. *Developmental Psychology, 29,* 244–254.

Crick, N. R., & Nelson, D. A. (2002). Relational and physical victimization within friendships: Nobody told me there'd be friends like these. *Journal of Abnormal Child Psychology*, *30*, 599–607.

Crick, N. R., Ostrov, J. M., Appleyard, K., Jansen, E. A., & Casas, J. F. (2004). Relational aggression in early childhood: "You can't come to my birthday party unless." In M. Puttalaz & K. L. Bierman (Eds.), *Aggression, antisocial behavior, and violence among girls* (pp. 71–89). New York: Guilford Press.

Crick, N. R., Ostrov, J. M., Burr, J. E., Cullerton-Sen, C., Jansen-Yeh, E., & Ralston, P. (2006). A longitudinal study of relational and physical aggression in preschool. *Journal of Applied Developmental Psychology*, *27*, 254–268.

Crick, N. R., Ostrov, J. M., & Kawabata, Y. (2007). Relational aggression and gender: An overview. In D. Flannery, I. Waldman, & A. Valsonyi (Eds.), *Cambridge handbook of violent behavior and aggression* (pp. 245–259). New York: Cambridge University Press.

Crick, N. R., & Werner, N. E. (1998). Response decision processes in relational and overt aggression. *Child Development*, *69*, 1630–1639.

Crijnen, A. A., Achenbach, T. M., & Verhulst, F. C. (1997). Comparisons of problems reported by parents of children in 12 countries: Total problems, externalizing, and internalizing. *Journal of the American Academy of Child and Adolescent Psychiatry*, *36*, 1269–1277.

Crockenberg, S. B. (1981). Infant irritability, mother responsiveness and social support influences on the security of infant-mother attachment. *Child Development*, *52*, 857–865.

Crockenberg, S., & Langrock, A. M. (2001). The role of specific emotions in children's responses to interparental conflict: A test of the model. *Journal of Family Psychology*, *15*, 163–182.

Crockenberg, S., & Litman, C. (1990). Autonomy as competence in 2-year-olds: Maternal correlates of child defiance, compliance, and self-assertion. *Developmental Psychology*, *26*, 961–971.

Crosnoe, R., Johnson, M. K., & Elder, G. H. (2004). School size and the interpersonal side of education: An examination of race/ethnicity and organizational context. *Social Science Quarterly*, *85*, 1259–1274.

Cross, D., & Paris, S. (1988). Developmental and instructional analyses of children's metacognition and reading comprehension. *Journal of Educational Psychology*, *80*, 131–142.

Crouch, M., & Manderson, L. (1995). The social life of bonding theory. *Social Science & Medicine*, *41*, 837–844.

Crouter, A. C., & Bumpus, M. F. (2001). Linking parents' work stress to children's and adolescents' psychological adjustment. *Current Directions in Psychological Science*, *10*, 156–159.

Crouter, A. C., Helms-Erikson, H., Updegraff, K., & McHale, S. M. (1999). Conditions underlying parents' knowledge about children's daily lives in middle childhood: Between- and within-family comparisons. *Child Development*, *70*, 246–259.

Crouter, A. C., Whiteman, S. D., McHale, S. M., & Osgood, D. W. (2007). Development of gender attitude traditionality across middle childhood and adolescence. *Child Development*, *78*, 911–926.

Crowell, J. A., & Treboux, D. (1995). A review of adult attachment measures: Implications for theory and research. *Social Development*, *4*, 294–327.

Crowley, K., Callahan, M. A., Tennenbaum, H. R., & Allen, E. (2001). Parents explain more often to boys than to girls during shared scientific thinking. *Psychological Science*, *12*, 258–261.

Crowson, H. M., & DeBacker, T. K. (2008). Political identification and the defining issues test: Reevaluating an old hypothesis. *Journal of Social Psychology*, *148*, 43–60.

Cryer, D., & Burchinal, M. (1997). Parents as child care consumers. *Early Childhood Research Quarterly*, *12*, 35–58.

Crystal, D. (2007). *How language works: How babies babble, words change meaning, and languages live or die.* New York: Avery Publishing Group.

CTIA. (2009). *Teenagers: A Generation Unplugged. A National Survey by CTIA–The Wireless Association® and Harris Interactive.* Retrieved from: http://www.ctia.org/advocacy/research/index.cfm/AID/11483

Cui, M., & Conger, R. D. (2008). Parenting behavior as mediator and moderator of the association between marital problems and adolescent maladjustment. *Journal of Research on Adolescence*, *18*, 261–284.

Cullen, D. (2009). *Columbine.* Boston, MA: Twelve Publishing.

Cummings, E. M. (1980). Caregiver stability and day care. *Developmental Psychology*, *16*, 31–37.

Cummings, E. M., & Davies, P. (2010). Emotional regulation and marital conflict. In P. K. Smith & C. H. Hart (Eds.), *Wiley-Blackwell handbook of childhood social development* (2nd ed.). Oxford, UK: Wiley-Blackwell.

Cummings, E. M., Davies, P. T., & Campbell, S. B. (2000). *Developmental psychopathology and family process.* New York: Guilford Press.

Cummings, E. M., Faircloth, W. B., Mitchell, P. M., Cummings, J. S., & Schermerhorn, A. C. (2008). Evaluating a brief prevention program for improving marital conflict in community families. *Journal of Family Psychology*, *22*, 193–202.

Cummings, E. M., Goeke-Morey, M. C., & Graham, M. A. (2002). Interparental relations as a dimension of parenting. In J. Borkowski, S. L. Ramey, & M. Bristol-Power (Eds.), *Parenting and the child's world: Influences on academic, intellectual, and social-emotional development* (pp. 251–264). Mahwah, NJ: Erlbaum.

Cummings, E. M., Iannotti, R. J., & Zahn-Waxler, C. (1985). *Patterns of attachment* in two- and three-year-olds in normal families and families with parental depression. *Child Development, 56*, 884–893.

Cummings, E. M., Keller, P. S., & Davies, P. T. (2005). Towards a family process model of maternal and paternal depressive symptoms: Exploring multiple relations with child and family functions. *Journal of Child Psychology and Psychiatry, 46*, 479–489.

Cummings, E. M., & Merrilees, C. E. (2010). Identifying the dynamic processes underlying links between marital conflict and child adjustment. In M. Schultz, M. K. Pruett, P. Kerig, & R. D. Parke (Eds.), *Strengthening couple relationships for optimal child development* (pp. 27–40). Washington, DC: American Psychological Association.

Cummings, E. M., Schermerhorn, A. C., Davies, P. T., Goeke-Morey, M. C., & Cummings, J. S. (2006). Interparental discord and child adjustment: Prospective investigations of emotional security as an explanatory mechanism. *Child Development, 77*, 132–152.

Cummings, E. M., Simpson, K. S., & Wilson, A. (1993). Children's responses to interadult anger as a function of information about resolution. *Developmental Psychology, 29*, 978–985.

Cumsille, P., Darling, N., Flaherty, B. P., & Martinez, M. L. (2006). Chilean adolescents' beliefs about the legitimacy of parental authority: Individual and age-related differences. *International Journal of Behavioral Development, 30*, 97–106.

Cunningham, W., Johnson, M., Raye, C., Gatenby, J., Gore, J., & Banaji, M. (2004). Separable neural components in the processing of Black and White faces. *Psychological Science, 15*, 806–813.

Curtner-Smith, M., Smith, P. K., & Porter, M. (2010). Family-level intervention with bullies and victims. In E. Vernberg & B. Biggs (Eds.), *Preventing and treating bullying and victimization* (pp. 75–106). New York: Oxford University Press.

Cutting, A. L., & Dunn, J. (2002). The cost of understanding other people: Social cognition predicts young children's sensitivity to criticism. *Journal of Child Psychology and Psychiatry, 43*, 849–860.

Dale, P. S. (1976). *Language development: Structure and function* (2nd ed.). New York: Holt.

Daly, M., & Wilson, M. I. (1996). Violence against stepchildren. *Current Directions in Psychological Science, 5*, 77–81.

Damon, W., & Hart, D. (1986). Stability and change in children's self-understanding. *Social Cognition, 4*, 102–118.

Daniels, H., Cole, M., & Wertsch, J. (Eds.)(2007). *Cambridge companion to Vygotsky.* New York: Cambridge University Press,

Daniels, P., & Weingarten, K. (1988). The fatherhood click: The timing of parenthood in men's lives. In P. Bronstein & C. P. Cowan (Eds.), *Fatherhood today: Men's changing role in the family* (pp. 36–52). New York: Wiley.

Dannemiller, J. L., & Stephens, B. R. (1988). A critical test of infant pattern perception models. *Child Development, 59*, 210–216.

Dansereau, D. F. (1987). Transfer from cooperative to individual studying. *Journal of Reading, 30*, 614–619.

Dapretto, M. (2006). Understanding emotions in others: Mirror neuron dysfunction in children with autism spectrum disorders. *Nature Neuroscience, 9*, 28–30

D'Argembeau, A., Ruby, P., Collette, F., Degueldre, C., Balteau, E., Luxen, A., Maquet, P., & Salmon. E. (2007). Distinct regions of the medial prefrontal cortex are associated with self-referential processing and perspective taking. *Journal of Cognitive Neuroscience, 19*, 935–944.

Darroch, J. E., Singh, S., & Frost, J. J. (2001). Differences in teenage pregnancy rates among five developed countries: The roles of sexual activity and contraceptive use. *Family Planning Perspectives, 33*, 6.

Darvill, D., & Cheyne, J. A. (1981, April). *Sequential analysis of response to aggression: Age and sex effects.* Paper presented at the biennial meeting of the Society for Research in Child Development, Boston.

Darwin, C. (1872). *The expression of emotions in animals and man.* London: John Murray.

Datnow, A. (2002) (Ed). *Gender in policy and practice: Perspectives on single sex and co-educational schooling.* New York: Palmer Press.

D'Augelli, A. R. (2006). Developmental and contextual factors and mental health among lesbians, gay, and bisexual youths. In A. Omoto & H. Kurtzman (Eds.), *Sexual orientation and mental health: Examining identity and development in lesbian, gay, and bisexual people* (pp. 37–53). Washington, DC: American Psychological Association.

David, C. F., & Kistner, J. A. (2000). Do positive self-perceptions have a "dark side?" Examination of the link between perceptual bias and aggression. *Journal of Abnormal Child Psychology, 28*, 327–337.

David, K. M., & Murphy, B. C. (2007). Interparental conflict and preschoolers' peer relations: The moderating roles of temperament and gender. *Social Development, 16*, 1–23.

Davidson, E. S., Yasuna, A., & Tower, A. (1979). The effects of television cartoons on sex role stereotyping in young girls. *Child Development, 50*, 597–600.

Davidson, R. J. (1993) The neuropsychology of emotion and affective style. In M. Lewis & J. M. Haviland (Eds.), *Handbook of emotions* (pp. 143–154). New York: Guilford Press.

Davidson, R. J. (1994). Temperament, affective style, and frontal lobe asymmetry. In G. Dawson & K. W. Fischer (Eds.), *Human behavior and the developing brain* (pp. 518–536). New York: Guilford Press.

Davies, P. T., & Cummings, E. M. (2006). Interparental discord, family process, and developmental psychopathology. In

D. Cicchetti & D. Cohen (Eds.), *Developmental Psychopathology: Vol. 3. Risk, Disorder, and Adaptation* (2nd ed., pp. 86–128). New York: Wiley.

Davies, P. T., Sturge-Apple, M. L., Cicchetti, D., & Cummings, E. M. (2007). The role of child adrenocortical functioning on pathways between interparental conflict and child maladjustment. *Developmental Psychology, 43*, 918–930.

Davies, P. T., Sturge-Apple, M. L., Winter, M. A., Farrell, D., & Cummings, E. M. (2006). Adaptational development in contexts of interparental conflict over time. *Child Development, 77*, 218–233.

Davila, J. A., Steinberg, S. J. A., Kachadourian, L. B., Cobb, R. C., & Fincham, F. B. (2004). Romantic involvement and depressive symptoms in early and late adolescence: The role of a preoccupied relational style. *Personal Relationships, 11*, 161–178.

Davis, M. H., Luce, C., & Kraus, S. J. (1994). The heritability of characteristics associated with dispositional empathy. *Journal of Personality, 62*, 369–391.

Davis, S. (1990). Chemical dependency in women: A description of its effects and outcome on adequate parenting. *Journal of Substance Abuse Treatment, 1*, 225–232.

Davis, S. C., Leman, P. J., & Barrett, M. (2007). Children's implicit and explicit ethnic group attitudes, ethnic group identification, and self-esteem. *International Journal of Behavioral Development, 31*, 514–525.

Dawson, G. (1994). Development of emotional expression and regulation in infancy. In G. Dawson & K. W. Fischer (Eds.), *Human behavior and the developing brain* (pp. 346–379). New York: Guilford Press.

Dawson, G., Ashman, S. B., Hessl, D., Spieker, S., Frey, K., Panagiotides, H., & Embry, L. (2001). Autonomic and brain electrical activity in securely- and insecurely-attached infants of depressed mothers. *Infant Behavior and Development, 24*, 135–149.

Dawson, G., Meltzoff, A. N., Osterling, J., & Rinaldi, J. (1998). Neuropsychological correlates of early symptoms of autism. *Child Development, 19*, 1276–1285.

Dawson, G., Panagiotides, H., Klinger, L. G., & Spieker, S. (1997). Infants of depressed and nondepressed mothers exhibit differences in frontal brain electrical activity during the expression of negative emotions. *Developmental Psychology, 33*, 650–656.

Dawson, G., & Sterling, L. (2008). Autism spectrum disorders. In M. Haith & J. Benson (Eds.), *Encyclopedia of infant and early childhood development* (pp. 137–143). Oxford, UK: Elsevier.

Dawson-Tunik, T. L., Commons, M., Wilson, M., & Fischer, K. W. (2005). The shape of development. *European Journal of Developmental Psychology, 2*, 163–195.

Dayan, J., Doyle, A.-B., & Markiewicz, D. (2001). Social support networks and self-esteem of idiocentric and allocentric children and adolescents. *Journal of Social and Personal Relationships, 18*, 767–784.

Dearing, R. L., Stuewig, J., & Tangney, J. P. (2005). On the importance of distinguishing shame from guilt: Relations to problematic alcohol and drug use. *Addictive Behaviors, 30*, 1392–1404.

Deater-Deckard, K. (2000). Parenting and child behavioral adjustment in early childhood: A quantitative genetic approach to studying family processes. *Child Development, 71*, 468–484.

Deater-Deckard, K. (2001). Annotation: Recent research examining the role of peer relationships in the development of psychopathology. *Journal of Child Psychology and Psychiatry, 42*, 565–579.

Deater-Deckard, K., & Dodge, K. A. (1997). Externalizing behavior problems and discipline revisited: Nonlinear effects and variation by culture, context, and gender. *Psychological Inquiry, 8*, 161–175.

Deater-Deckard, K., Dodge, K. A., Bates, J. E., & Pettit, G. S. (1996). Physical punishment among African American and European American mothers: Links to children's externalizing behaviors. *Developmental Psychology, 32*, 1065–1072.

Deater-Deckard, K., Lansford, J. E., Dodge, K. A., Pettit, G. S., & Bates, J. E. (2003). The development of attitudes about physical punishment: An 8-year longitudinal study. *Journal of Family Psychology, 17*, 351–360.

Deater-Deckard, K., Pike, A., Petrill, S. A., Cutting, A. L., Hughes, C., & O'Connor, T. G. (2001). Nonshared environmental processes in social-emotional development: An observational study of identical twin differences in the preschool period. *Developmental Science, 4*, F1–F6.

DeBerry, K. M., Scarr, S., & Weinberg, R. (1996). Family racial socialization and ecological competence: Longitudinal assessments of African-American transracial adoptees. *Child Development, 67*, 2375–2399.

De Boysson-Bardies, B., Vihman, M., Roug-Hellichius, L., Durand, C., Landberg, I., & Arao, F. (1992). Material evidence of infant selection from target language: A cross-linguistic study. In C. A. Ferguson, L. Menn, & C. Stoel-Gammon (Eds.), *Phonological development* (pp. 369–391). Timonium, MD: York Press.

De Caroli, M. E., & Sagone, E. (2007). Toys, sociocognitive traits, and occupations: Italian children's endorsement of gender stereotypes. *Psychological Reports, 100*, 1298–1311.

DeCasper, A. J., & Spence, M. (1986). Newborns prefer a familiar story over an unfamiliar one. *Infant Behavior and Development, 9*, 133–150.

Decety, J., & Chaminade, T. (2003). Neural correlates of feeling sympathy. *Neuropsychologia, 41*, 127–138.

Decety, J., & Jackson, P. L. (2004). The functional architecture of human empathy. *Behavioral and Cognitive Neuroscience Reviews, 3*, 71–100.

Decety, J., Michalska, K. J., & Akitsuki, Y. (2008). Who caused the pain? An fMRI investigation of empathy and intentionality in children. *Neuropsychologia, 46*, 2607–2614.

de Chateau, P. (1980). Early post-partum contact and later attitudes. *International Journal of Behavioral Development, 3,* 273–286.

DeGarmo, D. (2010). Coercive and prosocial fathering, antisocial personality, and growth in children's post-divorce noncompliance. *Child Development, 81,* 503–516.

Degner, J., Wentur, D., Gniewosz, B., & Noack, P. (2009). *Implicit prejudice in eighth-graders.* Unpublished manuscript, Friedrich Schiller University, Jena, Germany.

de Guzman, M. R. T., & Carlo, G. (2004). Family, peer, and acculturative correlates of prosocial development among Latino youth in Nebraska. *Great Plains Research, 14,* 185–202.

Dehaene-Lambertz, G., Dehaene, S., & Hertz-Pannier, L. (2002). Functional neuroimaging of speech perception in infants. *Science, 298,* 20113–2015.

Delgado, C. E. F., Messinger, D. S., & Yale, M. E. (2002). Infant responses to direction of parental gaze: A comparison of two still-face conditions. *Infant Behavior and Development, 25,* 311–318.

Del Giudice, M., & Colle, L. (2007). Differences between children and adults in the recognition of enjoyment smiles. *Developmental Psychology, 43,* 796–803.

DeLisi, R., & McGillicuddy-DeLisi, A. V. (2002). Sex differences in mathematical abilities and achievement. In A. V. McGillicuddy & R. DeLisi (Eds.), *Biology, society and behavior: The development of sex differences in cognition* (pp. 155–182). Westport, CT: Ablex.

DeLoache, J., & Gottlieb, A. (Eds.)(2000). *A world of babies: Imagined childcare guides for seven societies.* New York: Cambridge University Press.

DeLoache, J. S., Simcock, G., & Macari, S. (2007). Planes, trains, automobiles—and tea sets: Extremely intense interests in very young children. *Developmental Psychology, 43,* 1579–1586.

Demo, D. H., Allen, K. R., & Fine, M. A. (Eds.). (2000). *Handbook of family diversity.* New York: Oxford University Press.

Denham, S. A. (1998). *Emotional development in young children.* New York: Guilford Press.

Denham, S. A., Bassett, H. H., & Wyatt, T. (2007). The socialization of emotional competence. In J. E. Grusec, & P. Hastings (Eds.), *Handbook of socialization* (pp. 516–542). New York: Guilford Press.

Denham, S. A., & Burton, R. (2003). *Social and emotional prevention and intervention programming for preschoolers.* Amsterdam: Kluwer-Plenum.

Denham, S. A., & Couchoud, E. A. (1991). Social-emotional predictors of preschoolers' responses to adult negative emotion. *Journal of Child Psychology and Psychiatry, 32,* 595–608.

Denham, S. A., & Holt, R. W. (1993). Preschoolers' likability as cause or consequence of their social behavior. *Developmental Psychology, 29,* 271–275.

Denham, S. A., Renwick-DeBardi, S., & Hewes, S. (1994). Emotional communication between mothers and preschoolers: Relations with emotional competence. *Merrill-Palmer Quarterly, 40,* 488–508.

Denham, S. A., Warren, H., von Salisch, M., Benga, O., Chin, J.-C., & Geangu, E. (2010). Emotions and social development in childhood. In P. K. Smith & C. H. Hart (Eds.), *Wiley-Blackwell handbook of childhood social development* (2nd ed.). Oxford, UK: Wiley-Blackwell.

Dennis, W. (1940). Does culture appreciably affect patterns of infant behavior? *Journal of Social Psychology, 12,* 305–317.

De Pauw, S. S. W., Mervielde, I., & Van Leeuwen, K. G. (2009). How are traits related to problem behavior in preschoolers? Similarities and contrasts between temperament and personality. *Journal of Abnormal Child Psychology, 37,* 309–325.

de Pillis, E., Kernochan, R., Meilich, O., Prosser, E., & Whiting, V. (2008). Are managerial gender stereotypes universal? The case of Hawaii. *Cross Cultural Management, 15,* 94–102.

de Quervain, D. J.-F., Fischbacher, U., Treyer, V., Schellhammer, M., Schnyder, U., Buck, A., & Fehr, E. (2004). The neural basis of altruistic punishment. *Science, 305,* 1254–1258.

DeRosier, M., & Kupersmidt, J. B. (1991). Costa Rican children's perceptions of their social networks. *Developmental Psychology, 27,* 656–662.

Deschesnes, M., Finès, P., & Demers, S. (2006). Are tattooing and body piercing indicators of risk-taking behaviours among high school students? *Journal of Adolescence, 29,* 379–393.

de Silva, D. G. H. (2007). Children needing protection: Experience from South Asia. *Archives of Disease in Childhood, 92,* 931–934.

Dettling, A. C., Parker, S. W., Lane, A., Sebanc, A., & Gunnar, M. R. (2000). Quality of care and temperament determine changes in cortisol concentration over the day for young children in childcare. *Psychoneuroendocrinology, 25,* 819–836.

De Wolff, M., & van IJzendoorn, M. H. (1997). Sensitivity and attachment: A meta-analysis on parental antecedents of infant attachment. *Child Development, 60,* 571–591.

Diamond, A. (2002). Normal development of prefrontal cortex from birth to young adulthood: Cognitive functions, anatomy, and biochemistry. In D. T. Stuss & R. T. Knight (Eds.), *Principles of frontal lobe function* (pp. 466–503). New York: Oxford University Press.

Dick, D. M., Purcell, S., Viken, R., Kaprio, J., Pulkkinen, L., & Rose, R. (2007). Parental monitoring moderates the importance of genetic and environmental influences on adolescent smoking. *Journal of Abnormal Psychology, 116,* 213–218.

Dickson, K. L., Walker, H., & Fogel, A. (1997). The relationship between smile type and play type during parent-infant play. *Developmental Psychology, 33,* 925–933.

Diekman, A. B., & Murnen, S. K. (2004). Learning to be little women and little men: The inequitable gender equality of nonsexist children's literature. *Sex Roles, 50,* 373–385.

Diener, E. (2000). Subjective well-being: The science of happiness and a proposal for a national index. *American Psychologist, 55,* 34–43.

Di Martino, A., Ross, K., Uddin, L. Q., Sklar, A. B., Castellanos, F. X., & Milham, M. P. (2009). Functional brain correlates of social and nonsocial processes in autism spectrum disorders: An activation likelihood estimation meta-analysis. *Biological Psychiatry, 65,* 63–74.

Dinstein, I., Thomas, C., Behrmann, M., & Heeger, D. J. (2008). A mirror up to nature. *Current Biology, 18,* R13–8.

Dionne, G., Boivin, M., Tremblay, R., Laplante, D., & Perusse, D. (2003). Physical aggression and expressive vocabulary in 19-month-old twins. *Developmental Psychology, 39,* 261–273.

DiPietro, J. (1981). Rough and tumble play: A function of gender. *Developmental Psychology, 17,* 50–58.

Dishion, T., & Bullock, B. M. (2002). Parenting and adolescent problem behavior: An ecological analysis of the nurturance hypothesis. In J. Borkowski, S. L. Ramey, & M. Bristol-Power (Eds.), *Parenting and the child's world* (pp. 231–249). Mahwah, NJ: Erlbaum.

Dishion, T. J., & Dodge, K. A. (2006). Deviant peer contagion within interventions and programs: An ecological framework for understanding influence mechanisms. In K. A. Dodge, T. J. Dishion, & J. E. Lansford (Eds.), *Deviant peer influences in programs for youth* (pp. 3–13). New York: Guilford.

Dishion, T. J., & Kavanagh, K. (2000). A multilevel approach to family-centered prevention in schools: Process and outcome. *Addictive Behaviors, 25,* 899–911.

Dishion, T. J., Nelson, S. E., & Yasui, M. (2005). Predicting early adolescent gang involvement from middle school adaptation. *Journal of Clinical Child and Adolescent Psychology, 34,* 62–73.

Dishion, T. J., & Patterson, G. R. (2006). The development and ecology of antisocial behavior. In D. Cicchetti & D. Cohen (Eds.), *Developmental psychopathology: Vol. 3. Risk, disorder, and adaptation* (pp. 503–541). Hoboken, NJ: Wiley.

Dishion, T. J., Poulin, F., & Burraston, B. (2001). Peer group dynamics associated with iatrogenic effects in group interventions with high-risk young adolescents. *New Directions for Child and Adolescent Development, 91,* 79–92.

Dittrichova, J. (1969). The development of premature infants. In R. J. Robinson (Ed.), *Brain and early development* (pp. 193–200). London: Academic Press.

Diversity on Television. (2002, Summer). *Media now: A children now newsletter,* 1–5.

Dixon, C., Charles, M. A., & Craddock, A. A. (1998). The impact of experiences of parental divorce and parental conflict on young Australian men and women. *Journal of Family Studies, 4,* 21–34.

Dixon, H. G., Scully, M. L., Wakefield, M. A., White, V. M., & Crawford, D. A. (2007). The effects of television advertisements for junk food versus nutritious food on children's food attitudes and preferences. *Social Science & Medicine, 65,* 1311–1323.

Dodge, K. A. (1986). A social information processing model of social competence in children. In M. Perlmutter (Ed.), *Minnesota Symposium on Child Psychology: Vol. 18. Cognitive perspectives on children's social and behavioral development:* (pp. 77–125). Hillsdale, NJ: Erlbaum.

Dodge, K. A. (2008). Framing public policy and prevention of chronic violence in American youths. *American Psychologist, 63,* 573–590.

Dodge, K. A., Coie, J. D., & Lynam, D. (2006). Aggression and antisocial behavior in youth. In W. Damon & R. L. Lerner (Series Eds.), & N. Eisenberg (Vol. Ed.), *Handbook of child psychology: Vol. 3. Social, emotional, and personality development* (6th ed., pp. 719–788). Hoboken, NJ: Wiley.

Dodge, K. A., Dishion, T. J., & Lansford, J. E. (2006). *Deviant peer influences in programs for youth: Problems and solutions.* New York: Guilford Press.

Dodge, K. A., Lansford, J. E., Burks, V. S., Bates, J. E., Pettit, G. S., Fontaine, R., & Price, J. M. (2003). Peer rejection and social information-processing factors in the development of aggressive behavior problems in children. *Child Development, 74,* 374–393.

Dodge, K. A., McLoyd, V. C., & Lansford, J. E. (2005). The cultural context of disciplining children. In V. C. McLoyd, N. E. Hill, & K. A. Dodge (Eds.), *African American family life* (pp. 245–263). New York: Guilford Press.

Dodge, K. A., & Pettit, G. S. (2003). A biopsychosocial model of the development of chronic conduct problems in adolescence. *Developmental Psychology, 39,* 349–371.

Dodge, K. A., Pettit, G. S., McClaskey, C. L., & Brown, M. M. (1987). Social competence in children. *Monographs of the Society for Research in Child Development, 51* (Serial No. 213).

Dodson, T. A., & Borders, L. D. (2006). Men in traditional and nontraditional careers: Gender role attitudes, gender role conflict, and job satisfaction. *Career Development Quarterly, 54,* 283–296.

Doherty, W. J., & Needle, R. H. (1991). Psychological adjustment and substance use among adolescents before and after a parental divorce. *Child Development, 62,* 328–337.

Domitrovich, C. E., Cortes, R. C., & Greenberg, M. T. (2007). Improving young children's social and emotional competence: A randomized trial of the preschool "PATHS" curriculum. *Journal of Primary Prevention, 28,* 67–91.

Donahue, E. H., Haskins, R., & Nightingale, M. (2008). Using the media to promote adolescent well-being. *The Future of Children, 18*, 7.

Dondi, M., Simion, F., & Caltran, G. (1999). Can newborns discriminate between their own cry and the cry of another newborn infant? *Developmental Psychology, 35*, 418–426.

Donnellan, M. B., Trzesniewski, K. H., Robins, R. W., Moffit, T. E., & Caspi, A. (2005). Low self-esteem is related to aggression, antisocial behavior, and delinquency. *Psychological Science, 16*, 328–335.

Donnelly, M., & Straus, M. (Eds.) (2005). *Corporal punishment of children in theoretical perspective.* New Haven, CT: Yale University Press.

Dornbusch, S. M., Ritter, P. L., Leiderman, P. H., Roberts, D. F., & Fraleigh, M. J. (1987). The relation of parenting style to adolescent school performance. *Child Development, 58*, 1244–1257.

Doucet, S., Soussignan, R., Sagot, P., & Schaal, B. (2007). The "smellscape" of mother's breast: Effects of odor making and selective unmasking on neonatal arousal, oral, and visual responses. *Developmental Psychobiology, 49*, 129–138.

Douglas, W. (2003). *Television families.* Mahwah, NJ: Erlbaum.

Dozier, M., Stoval, K. C., Albus, K. E., & Bates, B. (2001). Attachment for infants in foster care: The role of caregiver state of mind. *Child Development, 72*, 1467–1477.

Drabman, R. S., & Thomas, M. H. (1976). Does watching violence on television cause apathy? *Pediatrics, 52*, 329–331.

Dressel, P. L., Barnhill, S. K., Chambers, A., Gardner, C., Harris, R., & Jones, B. (1992). *Three generations at risk: A model intergenerational program for families of imprisoned mothers.* Atlanta, GA: Aid to Imprisoned Mothers, Inc.

Drevets, W. C., & Raichle, M. E. (1998). Reciprocal suppression of regional cerebral blood flow during emotional versus higher cognitive processes: Implications for interactions between emotion and cognition. *Cognition & Emotion, 12*, 353–385.

Drew, C. J., Hardman, M. L., & Logan, D. R. (1996). *Mental retardation: A life cycle approach* (6th ed.). New York: Macmillan.

Driesen, N. R., & Raz, N. (1995). The influence of sex, age, and handedness on corpus callosum morphology: A meta-analysis. *Psychobiology, 23*, 240–247.

Dube, E. M., Savin-Williams, R. C., & Diamond, L. M. (2001). Intimacy development, gender, and ethnicity among sexual minority youth. In A. R. D'Augelli & C. Patterson (Eds.), *Lesbian, gay, and bisexual identities among youth: Psychological perspectives* (pp. 129–182). New York: Oxford University Press.

DuBois, D. L., & Rhodes, J. E. (2006). Youth mentoring: Bridging science with practice. *Journal of Community Psychology, 34*, 547–565.

Dubow, E. F., Huesmann, L. R., & Greenwood, D. (2007). Media and youth socialization. In J. E. Grusec & P. D. Hastings (Eds.), *Handbook of socialization* (pp. 404–430). New York: Guilford Press.

Duchenne, G. (1862). *Mecanisme de la physiologie humaine.* Paris: J. B. Baillière.

Duggan, A., Fuddy, L., Burrell, L., Higman, S. M., McFarlane, E., Windham, A., & Sia, C. (2004). Randomized trial of a statewide home visiting program to prevent child abuse: Impact in reducing parental risk factors. *Child Abuse & Neglect, 28*, 623–643.

Duncan, G. J. (2005). Welfare reform and child well-being. In G. Elder & K. W. Schaie (Eds.), *Historical influences on lives and aging* (pp. 286–298). New York: Springer.

Duncan, G. J., & Brooks-Gunn, J. (Eds.)(1997). *Consequences of growing up poor.* New York: Russell Sage Foundation.

Duncan, G. J., & Brooks-Gunn, J. (2000). Family parenting, welfare reform and child development. *Child Development, 71*, 188–195.

Duncan, G. J., Young, W. J., Brooks-Gunn, J., & Smith, J. R. (1998). How much does childhood poverty affect life choices of children? *American Sociological Reviews, 63*, 406–423.

Dunham, P., Dunham, F., Tran, S., & Akhtar, N. (1991). The nonreciprocating robot: Effects on verbal discourse, social play, and social referencing at two years of age. *Child Development, 62*, 1489–1502.

Dunifon, R., Kalil, A., & Danziger, S. K. (2003). Maternal work behavior under welfare reform: How does the transition from welfare to work affect child development? *Children and Youth Services Review, 25*, 55–82.

Dunn, J. (1988). *The beginnings of social understanding.* Cambridge, MA: Harvard University Press.

Dunn, J. (1989). Siblings and the development of social understanding in early childhood. In P. G. Zukow (Ed.), *Sibling interaction across cultures* (pp. 106–116). New York: Springer-Verlag.

Dunn, J. (1993). *Young children's close relationships: Beyond attachment.* Thousand Oaks, CA: Sage.

Dunn, J. (2002). Sibling relationships. In P. K. Smith & C. H. Hart (Eds.), *Blackwell handbook of childhood social development* (pp. 223–237). Oxford, UK: Blackwell.

Dunn, J. (2004). *Children's friendships: The beginnings of intimacy.* Oxford, UK: Blackwell.

Dunn, J. (2005). Commentary: Siblings in their families [Special Issue]. *Journal of Family Psychology, 19*, 654–657.

Dunn, J. (2006a). Grandparents, grandchildren, and family change in contemporary Britain. In A. Clarke-Stewart &

J. Dunn (Eds.), *Families count* (pp. 299–318). New York: Cambridge University Press.

Dunn, J. (2006b). Moral development in early childhood, and social interaction in the family. In M. Killen & J. G. Smetana (Eds.), *Handbook of moral development* (pp. 331–350). Mahwah, NJ: Erlbaum.

Dunn, J., Bretherton, I., & Munn, P. (1987). Conversations about feeling states between mothers and their young children. *Developmental Psychology, 23*, 132–139.

Dunn, J., Brown, J. R., & Maguire, M. (1995). The development of children's moral sensibility: Individual differences and emotional understanding. *Developmental Psychology, 31*, 649–659.

Dunn, J., Brown, J., & Beardsall, L. (1991). Family talk about feeling states and children's later understanding of others' emotions. *Developmental Psychology, 27*, 448–455.

Dunn, J., Brown, J., Slomkowski, C., Tesla, C., & Youngblade, L. (1991). Young children's understanding of other people's feelings and beliefs: Individual differences and their antecedents. *Child Development, 62*, 1352–1366.

Dunn, J., Cheng, H., O'Connor, T. G., & Bridges, L. (2004). Children's perspectives on their relationships with their non-resident fathers: Influences, outcomes and implications. *Journal of Child Psychology and Psychiatry, 45*, 553–566.

Dunn, J., Cutting, A. L., & Demetriou, H. (2000). Moral sensibility, understanding others, and children's friendship interactions in the preschool period. *British Journal of Developmental Psychology, 18*, 159–177.

Dunn, J., Cutting, A., & Fisher, N. (2002). Old friends, new friends: Predictors of children's perspective on their friends at school. *Child Development, 73*, 621–635.

Dunn, J., & Davies, L. (2000). Sibling relationships and interpersonal conflict. In J. Grych & F. F. Fincham (Eds.), *Interparental conflict and child development* (pp. 273–290). New York: Cambridge University Press.

Dunn, J., & Hughes, C. (1998). Young children's understanding of emotions within close relationships. *Cognition and Emotion, 12*, 171–190.

Dunn, J., & Hughes, C. (2001). "I got some swords and you're dead!": Violent fantasy, antisocial behavior, friendship, and moral sensibility in young children. *Child Development, 72*, 491–505.

Dunn, J., & Kendrick, C. (1982). The speech of two- and three-year-olds to infant siblings: "Baby talk" and the context of communication. *Journal of Child Language, 9*, 579–595.

Dunn, J., & Munn, P. (1987). Development of justification in disputes with mother and sibling. *Developmental Psychology, 23*, 791–798.

Dunn, J., & Plomin, R. (1991). Why are siblings so different? The significance of differences in sibling experiences within the family. *Family Process, 30*, 271–283.

Dunsmore, J. C., & Karn, M. A. (2004). The influence of peer relationships and maternal socialization on kindergartners' developing emotion knowledge. *Early Education & Development, 15*, 39–56.

Duran, R., Duran, J., Perry-Romero, D., & Sanchez, E. (2001). Latino immigrant parents and children learning and publishing together in an after-school setting. *Journal of Education for Students Placed at Risk, 6*, 95–113.

Dusek, J. B. (1991). *Adolescent development and behavior* (2nd ed.). Englewood Cliffs, NJ: Prentice-Hall.

Dweck, C. (2001). Caution—Praise can be dangerous. In K. L. Frieberg (Ed.), *Human development* (9th ed., pp. 105–109). Guilford, CT: Dushkin/McGraw-Hill.

Dweck, C. (2006). *Mindset: The new psychology of success*. New York: Random House.

Dweck, C. S. (2008). Brainology: Transforming students' motivation to learn. *Independent School Magazine*. Retrieved from: http://www.nais.org/publications/ismagazinearticle.cfm?itemnumber = 150509&snItemNumber = 145956

Eagly, A. H. (1996). Differences between women and men: Their magnitude, practical importance, and political meaning. *American Psychologist, 51*, 158–159.

East, P. L. (1996). The younger sisters of childrearing adolescents: Their attitudes, expectations, and behaviors. *Child Development, 67*, 953–963.

East, P. L., & Jacobson, J. L. (2001). The younger siblings of teenage mothers: A follow-up of their pregnancy risk. *Developmental Psychology, 37*, 254–264.

East, P. L., & Khoo, S. T. (2005). Longitudinal pathways linking family factors and sibling relationship qualities to adolescent substance use and sexual risk behaviors. *Journal of Family Psychology, 19*, 571–580.

East, P. L., & Rook, K. S. (1992). Compensatory patterns of support among children's peer relationships: A test using school friends, nonschool friends, and siblings. *Developmental Psychology, 28*, 163–172.

Eccles, J. S. (2007). Families, schools, and developing achievement-related motivations and engagement. In J. E. Grusec & P. D. Hastings (Eds.), *Handbook of socialization* (pp. 665–691). New York: Guilford Press.

Eccles, J. S., Freedman-Doan, C., Frome, P., Jacobs, J., & Yoon, K. S. (2000). Gender socialization in the family: A longitudinal approach. In T. Ecker & H. Trautner (Eds.), *The developmental social psychology of gender* (pp. 333–365). Mahwah, NJ: Erlbaum.

Eccles, J., & Gootman, J. A. (Eds.) (2002). *Community programs to promote youth development*. Washington, DC: National Academy Press.

Eccles, J. S., Jacobs, J., Harold, R., Yoon, K. S., Abreton, A., & Freedman-Doan, C. (1993). Parents and gender-role socialization during the middle childhood and adolescent years. In S. Oskamp & M. Costanzo (Eds.), *Gender issues in contemporary society* (pp. 59–83). Thousand Oaks, CA: Sage.

Eccles, J. S., & Roeser, R. W. (2003). Schools as developmental contexts. In G. Adams & D. Beizonsky (Eds.), *Blackwell handbook of adolescence* (pp. 129–148). Malden, MA: Blackwell.

Eccles, J. S., Wigfield, A., & Schiefele, U. (1998). Motivation to succeed. In W. Damon (Series Ed.), & N. Eisenberg (Vol. Ed.), *Handbook of child psychology: Vol. 3. Social, emotional, and personal development* (5th ed., pp. 1017–1095). New York: Wiley.

Eckerman, C. O. (1993). Imitation and toddlers' achievement of coordinated action with others. In J. Nadel & L. Camaioni (Eds.), *New perspectives in early communicative development* (pp. 116–156). New York: Routledge.

Eckerman, C. O., Whatley, J. L., & Kutz, S. L. (1975). Growth of social play with peers during the second year of life. *Developmental Psychology, 11*, 42–49.

Eddy, J. M., Whaley, R. B., & Chamberlain, P. (2004). The prevention of violent behavior by chronic and serious male juvenile offenders: A 2-year follow-up of a randomized clinical trial. *Journal of Emotional and Behavioral Disorders, 12*, 2–8.

Edwards, A., & Lutzker, J. R. (2008). Iterations of the SafeCare model: An evidence-based child maltreatment prevention program. *Behavior Modification, 32*, 736–756.

Edwards, A., Shipman, K., & Brown, A. (2005). The socialization of emotional understanding: A comparison of neglectful and nonneglectful mother and their children. *Child Maltreatment, 10*, 293–304.

Edwards, C. P. (2000). Children's play in cross-cultural perspective: A new look at the six-cultures study. *Cross-Cultural Research: The Journal of Comparative Social Science.* [Special Issue in honor of Ruth H. Monroe]. Part 1, *34*, 318–338.

Edwards, C. P., & Whiting, B. B. (1993). "Mother, older sibling, and me": The overlapping roles of caregivers and companions in the social world of two- and three-year-olds in Ngeca, Kenya. In K. MacDonald (Ed.), *Parent-child play: Descriptions and implications* (pp. 305–329). Albany: State University of New York Press.

Egan, S. K., & Perry, D. G. (2001). Gender identity: A multidimensional analysis with implications for psychosocial adjustment. *Developmental Psychology, 37*, 451–463.

Egeland, B., Jacobvitz, D., & Sroufe, L. A. (1988). Breaking the cycle of abuse. *Child Development, 59*, 1080–1088.

Eggermont, S. (2005). Young adolescents' perception of peer sexual behaviors: The role of television viewing. *Child: Care, Health, and Development, 31*, 459–468.

Eiduson, B. T., Kornfein, M., Zimmerman, I. L., & Weisner, T. S. (1988). Comparative socialization practices in traditional and alternative families. In G. Handel (Ed.), *Childhood socialization* (pp. 73–101). Hawthorne, NY: Aldine de Gruyter.

Eisenberg, M. E., Neumark-Sztainer, D., Fulkerson, J. A., & Story, M. (2008). Family meals and substance use: Is there a long-term protective association. *Journal of Adolescent Health, 43*, 151–156.

Eisenberg, M. E., Olson, R. E., Neumark-Sztainer, D., Story, M., & Bearinger, L. H. (2004). Correlations between family meals and psychosocial well-being among adolescents. *Archives of Pediatrics & Adolescent Medicine, 158*, 792–796.

Eisenberg, N. (2000). Emotion, regulation, and moral development. *Annual Review of Psychology, 51*, 665–697.

Eisenberg, N., Cumberland, A., Guthrie, I. K., Murphy, B. C., & Shepard, S. A. (2005). Age changes in prosocial responding and moral reasoning in adolescence and early adulthood. *Journal of Research on Adolescence, 15*, 235–260.

Eisenberg, N., & Fabes, R. A. (1994). Mothers' reactions to children's negative emotions: Relations to children's temperament and anger behavior. *Merrill Palmer Quarterly, 40*, 138–156.

Eisenberg, N., Fabes, R. A., Bustamante, D., Mathy, R. M., Miller, P. A., & Lindholm, E. (1988). Differentiation of vicariously induced emotional reactions in children. *Developmental Psychology, 24*, 237–246.

Eisenberg, N., Fabes, R. A., Carlo, G., Speer, A. L., Switzer, G., Karbon, M., & Troyer, D. (1993). The relations of empathy-related emotions and maternal practices to children's comforting behavior. *Journal of Experimental Child Psychology, 55*, 131–150.

Eisenberg, N., Fabes, R. A., Miller, P. A., Shell, C., Shea, R., & May-Plumlee, T. (1990). Preschoolers' vicarious emotional responding and their situational and dispositional prosocial behavior. *Merrill-Palmer Quarterly, 36*, 507–529.

Eisenberg, N., Fabes, R. A., & Murphy, B. C. (1996). Parents' reactions to children's negative emotions: Relations to children's social competence and comforting behavior. *Child Development, 67*, 2227–2247.

Eisenberg, N., Fabes, R. A., Nyman, M., Bernzweig, J., & Pinuelas, A. (1994). The relations of emotionality and regulation to children's anger-related reactions. *Child Development, 65*, 109–128.

Eisenberg, N., Fabes, R. A., & Spinrad, T. (2006). Prosocial development. In W. Damon & R. M. Lerner (Series Eds.), & N. Eisenberg (Vol. Ed.), *Handbook of child psychology: Vol. 3. Social, emotional, and personality development* (6th ed., pp. 646–718). Hoboken, NJ: Wiley.

Eisenberg, N., Gershoff, E. T., Fabes, R. A., Shepard, S. A., Cumberland, A. J., Losoya, S. H., . . . Murphy, B. C. (2001). Mother's emotional expressivity and children's behavior problems and social competence: Mediation through children's regulation. *Developmental Psychology, 37*, 475–490.

Eisenberg, N., Guthrie, I. K., Murphy, B. C., Cumberland, A., & Carlo, G. (1999). Consistency and development of prosocial dispositions. *Child Development, 70*, 1370–1372.

Eisenberg, N., Lennon, R., & Roth, K. (1983). Prosocial development: A longitudinal study. *Developmental Psychology, 19*, 846–855.

Eisenberg, N., Losoya, S., & Spinrad, T. (2003). Affective and prosocial responding. In R. J. Davidson, K. R. Scherer, & H. H. Goldsmith (Eds.), *Handbook of affective sciences* (pp. 787–803). New York: Oxford University Press.

Eisenberg, N., Murray, E., & Hite, T. (1982). Children's reasoning regarding sex-typed toy choices. *Child Development, 49,* 500–504.

Eisenberg, N., Sallquist, J., French, D. C., Purwano, U., Suryanti, T. A., & Pidada, S. (2009). The relations of majority-minority group status and having an other-religion friend to Indonesian youths' socioemotional functioning. *Developmental Psychology, 45,* 248–259.

Eisenberg, N., Spinrad, T. L., Fabes, R. A., Reiser, M., Cumberland, A., Shepard, S. A., . . . Thompson, M. (2004). The relations of effortful control and impulsivity to children's resiliency and adjustment. *Child Development, 75,* 25–46.

Eisenberg, N., Zhou, Q., & Koller, S. (2001). Brazilian adolescents' prosocial moral judgments and behavior: Relations to sympathy, perspective taking, gender-role orientation, and demographic characteristics. *Child Development, 72,* 518–534.

Eisenberg-Berg, N., & Hand, M. (1979). The relationship of preschoolers' reasoning about prosocial moral conflicts to prosocial behavior. *Child Development, 50,* 356–363.

Eisenberger, N. I., Gable, S. L., & Lieberman, M. D. (2007). Functional magnetic resonance imaging responses to differences in real-world social experience. *Emotion, 7,* 745–754.

Eisenberger, N. I., & Lieberman, M. D. (2004). Why rejection hurts: A common neural alarm system for physical and social pain. *Trends in Cognitive Sciences, 8,* 294–300.

Eisenberger, N. I., Lieberman, M. D., & Williams, K. D. (2003). Does rejection hurt? An fMRI study of social exclusion. *Science, 302,* 290–292.

Ekman, P. (1972). Universals and cultural differences in facial expressions of emotion. In J. Cole (Ed.), *Nebraska Symposium on Motivation, 1971* (pp. 207–283). Lincoln: University of Nebraska Press, 1972.

Ekman, P. (1992). An argument for basic emotions. *Cognition & Emotion, 6,* 169–200.

Ekman, P. (1994). Strong evidence for universals in facial expression: A reply to Russell's mistaken critique. *Psychological Bulletin, 115,* 268–287.

Ekman, P. (2003). *Emotions revealed.* New York: Times Books.

Ekman, P. (2004). What we become emotional about. In A. S. R. Manstead, N. Frijda, & A. Fischer (Eds.), *Feelings & emotions: The Amsterdam symposium. Studies in emotion and social interaction* (pp. 119–135). New York: Cambridge University Press.

Ekman, P., Davidson, R., & Friesen, W. V. (1990). The Duchenne smile: Emotional expression and brain physiology. *Journal of Personality and Social Behavior, 58,* 342–353.

Ekman, P., & Friesen, W. V. (1982). Felt, false, and miserable smiles. *Journal of Nonverbal Behavior, 6,* 238–258.

Ekman, P., Friesen, W. V., O'Sullivan, M., Chan, A., Diacoyanni-Tarlatzia, I., Heider, K., . . . Tzavaras, A. (1987). Universals and cultural differences in the judgments of facial expressions of emotion. *Journal of Personality and Social Psychology, 52,* 712–717.

Elder, G. H. (1974). *Children of the Great Depression: Social change in life experiences.* Chicago: University of Chicago Press.

Elder, G. H. (1984). Families, kin, and the life course: A sociological perspective. In R. D. Parke (Ed.), *Advances in child development research: The family* (pp. 80–136). Chicago: University of Chicago Press.

Elder, G. H. (1998). The life course as developmental theory. *Child Development, 69,* 1–12.

Elder, G. H., & Conger, R. D. (2000). *Children of the land.* Chicago: University of Chicago Press.

Elder, G. H., & Shanahan, M. J. (2006). The life course and human development. In W. Damon & R. M. Lerner (Series Eds.), & R. M. Lerner (Vol. Ed.), *Handbook of child psychology: Vol. 1. Theoretical models of human development* (6th ed., pp. 665–715). Hoboken, NJ: Wiley.

Eley, T. C., Lichtenstein, P., & Stevenson, J. (1999). Sex differences in the etiology of aggressive and nonaggressive antisocial behavior: Results from two twin studies. *Child Development, 70,* 155–168.

Elfenbein, H. A., & Ambady, N. (2002). On the universality and cultural specificity of emotion recognition: A meta-analysis. *Psychological Bulletin, 128,* 203–235.

Elkins, V. H. (1978). *The rights of the pregnant parent.* Camberwell, VC, AU: Visa.

Elliott, D. S., Menard, S., Rankin, B., Elliott, A., Wilson, W. J., & Huizinga, D. (2006). *Good kids from bad neighborhoods: Successful development in social context.* New York: Cambridge University Press.

Elliott, R., & Leonard, C. (2004). Peer pressure and poverty: Exploring fashion brands and consumption symbolism among children of the 'British poor'. *Journal of Consumer Behaviour, 3,* 347–359.

Ellis, B. J., Bates, J. E., Dodge, K. A., Fergusson, D. M., Horwood, L. J., Pettit, G. S., & Woodward, L. (2003). Does father absence place daughters at special risk for early sexual activity and teenage pregnancy? *Child Development, 74,* 801–821.

Ellis, S., Rogoff, B., & Cromer, C. (1981). Age segregation in children's social interactions. *Developmental Psychology, 17,* 399–407.

Ellis, W. E., & Zarbatany, L. (2007). Explaining friendship formation and friendship stability: The role of children's and friends' aggression and victimization. *Merrill-Palmer Quarterly, 53,* 79–104.

El Nokali, N., Bachman, H. J., & Votruba-Drzal, E. (2010). Parent involvement and children's academic and social development in elementary school. *Child Development, 81*

Else-Quest, N. M., Hyde, J. S., Goldsmith, H. H., & Van Hulle, C. A. (2006). Gender differences in temperament: A meta-analysis. *Psychological Bulletin, 132*, 33–72.

Eluvathingal, T. J., Chugani, H. T., Behen, M. E., Juhasz, C., Muzik, O., Maqbool, M., . . . Makki, M. (2006). Abnormal brain connectivity in children after early severe socioemotional deprivation: A diffusion tensor imaging study. *Pediatrics, 117*, 2093–2100.

Embry, D. D., Flannery, D. J., Vazsonyi, A. T., Powell, K. E. & Atha, H. (1996). PeaceBuilders: A theoretically driven, school-based model for early violence prevention. *American Journal of Preventive Medicine, 12* (Suppl.), 91–100.

Embry, L., & Dawson, G. (2002). Disruptions in parenting related to maternal depression: Influences on children's behavioral and psychobiological development. In J. G. Borkowski, S. Ramey, & M. Bristol-Power (Eds.), *Parenting and the child's world* (pp. 203–213). Mahwah, NJ: Erlbaum.

Emde, R. N., & Buchsbaum, H. K. (1990). "Didn't you hear my mommy?" Autonomy with connectedness in moral self-emergence. In D. Cicchetti, & M. Beeghly (Eds.), *The self in transition: Infancy to childhood* (pp. 35–60). Chicago: University of Chicago Press.

Emde, R. N., Gaensbauer, T. J., & Harmon, R. J. (1976). Emotional expression in infancy: A biobehavioral study. *Psychological Issues, 10* (37).

Emde, R.N., Oppenheim, D., & Wolf, D. P. (Eds.)(2003). *Revealing the inner worlds of young children: The MacArthur Story Stem Battery and parent-child narratives.* New York: Oxford University Press.

Emslie, G. J., Rush, A. J., Weinberg, W. A., Kowatch, R. A., Hughes, C. W., Carmody, T., & Rintelmann, J. R. (1997). A double-blind, randomized, placebo-controlled trial of fluoxitine in children and adolescents with depression. *Archives of General Psychiatry, 54*, 1031–1037.

Ensor, R., & Hughes, C. (2008). Content or connectedness? Mother-child talk and early social understanding. *Child Development, 79*, 201–216.

Entertainment Software Association. (2009). *Industry Facts.* Retrieved from: http://www.theesa.com/facts/index.asp

Epstein, J. L. (2001). *School, family, and community partnerships: Preparing educators and improving schools.* Boulder, CO: Westview Press.

Epstein, L. H., & Sanders, M. G. (2002). Family, school, and community partnerships. In M. H. Bornstein (Ed.), *Handbook of parenting: Vol. 5. Practical issues in parenting* (2nd ed., pp. 407–438). Mahwah, NJ: Erlbaum.

Erdley, C. A., & Asher, S. R. (1998). Linkages between children's beliefs about the legitimacy of aggression and their behavior. *Social Development, 7*, 321–339.

Erdley, C. A., Cain, K. M., Loomis, C. C., Dumas-Hines, F., & Dweck, C. S. (1997). Relations among children's social goals, implicit personality theories, and responses to social failure. *Developmental Psychology, 33*, 263–272.

Erickson, P. E. (2000). Federal child abuse and child neglect policy in the United States since 1974: A review and critique. *Criminal Justice Review, 25*, 1–77.

Erikson, E. H. (1950). *Childhood and society.* New York: W. W. Norton & Company.

Erikson, E. H. (1959/1980). *Identity and the life cycle.* New York: W. W. Norton.

Ervin-Tripp, S. (1979). Children's verbal turn taking. In E. Ochs & B. Schieffelin (Eds.), *Developmental pragmatics* (pp. 391–414). New York: Academic Press.

Eslinger, P. J. (1998). Neurological and neuropsychological bases of empathy. *European Neurology, 39*, 193–199.

Espelage, D. L., Bosworth, K., & Simon, T. R. (2000). Examining the social context of bullying behaviors in early adolescence. *Journal of Counseling & Development, 78*, 326–333.

Etaugh, C., & Liss, M. B. (1992). Home, school, and playroom: Training grounds for adult gender roles. *Sex Roles, 26*, 129–147.

Evans, D. E., & Rothbart, M. K. (2007). Development of a model for adult temperament. *Journal of Research in Personality, 41*, 868–888.

Evans, D. E., & Rothbart, M. K. (2009). A two-factor model of temperament. *Personality and Individual Differences, 47*, 565–570.

Evans, O., & Steptoe, A. (2002). The contribution of gender-role orientation, work factors and home stressors to psychological well-being and sickness absence in male- and female-dominated occupational groups. *Social Science & Medicine, 54*, 481–492.

Everette, A., Fleming, D., Higgins, T., Tu, K., Bardi, M., Kinsley, C. H., & Lambert, K. G. (2007, June). Paternal experience enhances behavioral and neurobiological responsivity associated with affiliative and nurturing responses. Presentation at the International Behavioral Neuroscience Society, Rio de Janeiro, Brazil.

Fabes, R. A., & Eisenberg, N. (1996). *An examination of age and sex differences in prosocial behavior and empathy.* Unpublished data, Arizona State University.

Fabes, R. A., Eisenberg, N., Smith, M. C., & Murphy, B. (1996). Getting angry at peers: Associations with liking of the provocateur. *Child Development, 67*, 942–956.

Fabes, R. A., Martin, C. L., & Hanish, L. D. (2002, October). *The role of sex segregation in young children's prosocial behavior and disposition.* Paper presented at the Groningen Conference on Prosocial Dispositions and Solidarity, Groningen, The Netherlands.

Fabes, R. A., Martin, C. L., & Hanish, L. D. (2003). Young children's play qualities in same-, other-, and mixed-peer groups. *Child Development, 74,* 921–932.

Fabricius, W. V., Braver, S. L., Diaz, P., & Schenck, C. (2010). Custody and parenting time: Links to family relationships and well-being after divorce. In M. E. Lamb (Ed.), *The role of the father in child development* (5th ed., pp. 201–240). Hoboken, NJ: Wiley.

Fadiga, L., Fogassi, L., Pavesi, G., & Rizzolatti, G. (1995). Motor facilitation during action observation: A magnetic stimulation study. *Journal of Neurophysiology, 73,* 2608–2611.

Fadjukoff, P., Kokko, K., & Pulkkinen, L. (2007). Implications of timing of entering adulthood for identity achievement. *Journal of Adolescent Research, 22,* 504–530.

Fadjukoff, P., Pulkkinen, L., Kokko, K. (2005). Identity processes in adulthood: Diverging domains. *Identity, 5,* 1–20.

Fagot, B. I. (1985a). Beyond the reinforcement principle: Another step toward understanding sex role development. *Developmental Psychology, 21,* 1097–1104.

Fagot, B. I. (1985b). Changes in thinking about early sex role development. *Developmental Review, 5,* 83–98.

Fagot, B. I., & Leinbach, M. D. (1987). Socialization of sex roles within the family. In D. B. Carter (Ed.), *Current conceptions of sex roles and sex typing: Theory and research* (pp. 89–100). New York: Praeger.

Fagot, B. I., & Leinbach, M. D. (1989). The young child's gender schema: Environmental input, internal organization. *Child Development, 60,* 663–672.

Fagot, B. I., & Leinbach, M. D. (1992). Gender-role development in young children: From discrimination to labeling. *Developmental Review, 13,* 205–224.

Fahey, R. (2005). ESA study reveals "well-rounded lifestyle" of adult gamers. Retrieved from: http://www.gamesindustry.biz/articles/esa-study-reveals-well-rounded-lifestyle-of-adult-gamers

Falbo, T., & Polit, D. F. (1986). Quantitative review of the only child literature: Research evidence and theory development. *Psychological Bulletin, 100,* 176–189.

Falck-Ytter, T., Gredebäck, G., & von Hofsten, C. (2006). Infants predict other people's action goals. *Nature Neuroscience, 9,* 878–879.

Farrington, D. P. (1993). Motivations for conduct disorder and delinquency. *Development & Psychopathology, 5,* 225–241.

Farrington, D. P. (1995). The challenge of teenage antisocial behavior. In M. Rutter (Ed.), *Psychosocial disturbances in young people: Challenges for prevention* (pp. 83–130). New York: Cambridge University Press.

Farroni, T., Johnson, M. H., Menon, E., Zulian, L., Faraguna, D., & Csibra, G. (2005). Newborns' preference for face-relevant stimuli: Effects of contrast polarity. *Proceedings of the National Academy of Science, 102,* 17245–17250.

Farroni, T., Massaccesi, S., & Simion, F. (2002). La direzione dello sguardo di un'altra persona puo dirigere l'attenzione del neonato? [Can the direction of the gaze of another person shift the attention of a neonate?]. *Giornale Italiano di Psicologia, 29,* 857–864.

Farver, J. M., Kim, Y. K., & Lee, Y. (1995). Cultural differences in Korean- and Anglo-American preschoolers' social interaction and play behaviors. *Child Development, 66,* 1088–1099.

Farver, J. M., & Shin, Y. L. (1997). Social pretend play in Korean- and Anglo-American preschoolers. *Child Development, 60,* 544–556.

Farver, J. M., Xu, Y., Eppe, S., Fernandez, A., & Schwartz, D. (2005). Community violence, family conflict, and preschoolers' socioemotional functioning. *Developmental Psychology, 41,* 160–170.

Fearon, R. M. P., van IJzendoorn, M. H., Fonagy, P., Bakermans-Kranenburg, M. J., Schuengel, C., & Bokhorst, C. L. (2006). In search of shared and nonshared environmental factors in security of attachment: A behavior-genetic study of the association between sensitivity and attachment security. *Developmental Psychology, 42,* 1026–1040.

Featherman, D. L., Spenner, K. I., & Tsunematsu, N. (1988). Class and the socialization of children: Constancy, change, or irrelevance? In E. M. Hetherington, R. M. Lerner, & M. Perlmutter (Eds.), *Child development in life-span perspective* (pp. 67–90). Hillsdale, NJ: Erlbaum.

Feerick, M. M., Knutson, J. F., Trickett, P. K., & Flanzer, S. (2006). *Child abuse and neglect: Definitions, classifications, and a framework for research.* Baltimore: Brookes.

Fein, G. G. (1989). Mind, meaning and affect: Proposals for a theory of pretense. *Developmental Review, 9,* 345–363.

Feinberg, M., & Hetherington, M. E. (2001). Differential parenting as within-family variable. *Journal of Family Psychology, 15,* 22–37.

Feinman, S., & Lewis, M. (1983). Social referencing at ten months: A second-order effect on infants' responses to strangers. *Child Development, 54,* 878–887.

Feiring, C., & Lewis, M. (1987). The ecology of some middle class families at dinner. *International Journal of Behavioral Development, 10,* 377–390.

Feldman, R. (2006). From biological rhythms to social rhythms: Physiological precursors of mother-infant synchrony. *Developmental Psychology, 42,* 175–188.

Felner, R. D., Jackson, A. W., Kasak, D., Mulhall, P., Brand, S., & Flowers, N. (1997). The impact of middle school reform for the middle years: Longitudinal study of a network engaged in Turning Points-based comprehensive school transformation. *Phi Delta Kappan, 78,* 528–532 and 551–556.

Feng, D., Giarrusso, R., Bengtson, V. L., & Frye, N. (1999). Intergenerational transmission of marital quality and marital instability. *Journal of Marriage and Family, 61,* 451–463.

Feng, X., Shaw, D. S., Kovacs, M., Lane, T., O'Rourke, F. E., & Alarcon, J. (2008). Emotion regulation in preschoolers: The roles of behavioral inhibition, maternal affective behavior, and maternal depression. *Journal of Child Psychology and Psychiatry, 49,* 132–141.

Fenson, L., Dale, P. S., Reznick, J. S., Bates, E., Thal, D. J., & Pethick, S. J. (1994). Variability in early communicative development. *Monographs of the Society for Research in Child Development, 59* (Serial No. 242).

Ferguson, T. J., Stegge, H., Miller, E. R., & Olsen, M. E. (1999). Guilt, shame, and symptoms in children. *Developmental Psychology, 35,* 347–357.

Fergusson, D. M., Woodward, L. J., & Horwood, J. (1998). Maternal smoking during pregnancy and psychiatric adjustments in late adolescence. *Archives of General Psychiatry, 55,* 721–727.

Fernald, A. (1992). Meaningful melodies in mothers' speech to infants. In H. Papousek, U. Jurgens, & M. Papousek (Eds.), *Nonverbal vocal communication* (pp. 262–282). Cambridge, UK: Cambridge University Press.

Fernald, A., & Mazzie, C. (1991). Prosody and focus in speech to infants and adults. *Developmental Psychology, 27,* 209–221.

Fernald, A., & Morikawa, H. (1993). Common themes and cultural variations in Japanese and American mothers' speech to infants. *Child Development, 64,* 636–637.

Ferrari, P. F., Palanza, P., Parmigiani, S., de Almeida, R. M. M., & Miczek, K. A. (2005). Serotonin and aggressive behavior in rodents and nonhuman primates: Predispositions and plasticity. *European Journal of Pharmacology, 526,* 259–273.

Ferris, C. F., Kulkarni, P., Sullivan, Jr., J. M., Harder, J. A., Messenger, T. L., & Febo, M. (2005). Pup suckling is more rewarding than cocaine: Evidence from functional magnetic resonance imaging and three-dimensional computational analysis. *Journal of Neuroscience, 25,* 149–172.

Feyerick, D., & Steffen, S. (April 8, 2009). 'Sexting' lands teen on sex offender list. *American Morning,* CNN News. Retrieved from: http://www.cnn.com/2009/CRIME/04/07/sexting.busts/index.html

Field, T. M. (1990). *Infancy.* Cambridge, MA: Harvard University Press.

Field, T. M. (2001a). Massage therapy facilitates weight gain in preterm infants. *Current Directions in Psychological Science, 10,* 51–54.

Field, T. M. (2001b). *Touch.* Cambridge, MA: MIT Press.

Fiese, B. H. (1990). Playful relationships: A contextual analysis of mother-toddler interaction and symbolic play. *Child Development, 61,* 1648–1656.

Fiese, B. H. (2006). *Family routines and rituals.* New Haven, CT: Yale University Press.

Fiese, B. H., & Bickham, N. L. (2004). Pin-curling-grandpa's hair in the comfy chair: Parents' stories of growing up and potential links to socialization in the preschool years. In M. W. Pratt & B. H. Fiese (Eds.), *Families, stories, and the life course* (pp. 259–278). Mahwah, NJ: Erlbaum.

Fiese, B. H., Foley, K. P., & Spagnola, M. (2006). Routine and ritual elements in family mealtimes: Contexts for child well-being and family identity. *New Directions for Child and Adolescent Development, 111,* 67–90.

Fiese, B. H., & Schwartz, M. (2008). Reclaiming the family table: Mealtimes and child health and wellbeing. *Society for Research in Child Development Social Policy Report, 22.*

Fiese, B. H., Tomcho, T. J., Douglas, M., Josephs, K., Poltrock, S., & Baker, T. (2002). A review of 50 years of research on naturally occurring family routines and rituals: A cause of celebration? *Journal of Family Psychology, 16,* 381–390.

Fight Crime: Invest in Kids. (2006). *1 of 3 Teens & 1 of 6 preteens are victims of cyber bullying.* Retrieved from: http://www.fightcrime.org/state/pennsylvania/news/1–3-teens–1–6-preteens-are-victims-cyber-bullying

Figlio, D. N. (2007). Boys named Sue: Disruptive children and their peers. *Education, Finance, and Policy, 2,* 376–394.

Finkelhor, D. (2007). Prevention of sexual abuse through educational programs directed toward children. *Pediatrics, 120,* 640–645.

Finkelhor, D., Mitchell, K. J., & Wolak, J. (2000). *Online victimization: A report on the nation's youth* (6-00-020). Alexandria, VA: National Center for Missing and Exploited Children.

Finkelstein, J. W., Susman, E. J., Chinchilli, V. M., Kinselman, S. J., D'Arcangelo, M. R., Schwab, J., . . . Kulin, H. E. (1997). Estrogen or testosterone increases self-reported aggressive behaviors in hypogonadal adolescents. *Journal of Clinical Endocrinology and Metabolism, 82,* 2433–2438.

Finkelstein, N. W. (1982). Aggression: Is it stimulated by day care? *Young Children, 37,* 3–12.

Finn, J. D., & Pannozzo, G. M. (2004). Classroom organization and student behavior in kindergarten. *Journal of Educational Research, 98,* 79–82.

Finn, J. D., Pannozzo, G. M., & Achilles, C. M. (2003). The "why's" of class size: Student behavior in small classes. *Review of Educational Research, 73,* 321–368.

Finnegan, R. A., Hodges, E. V. E., & Perry, D. G. (1998). Victimization by peers: Associations with children's reports of mother–child interaction. *Journal of Personality and Social Psychology, 75,* 1076–1086.

Finnie, V., & Russell, A. (1988). Preschool children's social status and their mothers' behavior and knowledge in the supervisory role. *Developmental Psychology, 24,* 789–801.

Fischer, A., Hacien-Bey, S., Le Deist, F., De Saint, B., & Cavazzana-Colvo, M. (2001). Gene therapy of severe combined immunodeficiencies. In A. Mackiewicz, M. Kurpisz, & J. Zeromski (Eds.), *Progress in basic and clinical immunology* (pp. 199–204). New York: Springer.

Fischer, K. W., & Bidell, T. R. (2006). Dynamic development of action and thought. In R. M., Lerner & W. Damon (Eds.), *Handbook of child psychology: Vol. 1. Theoretical models of human development* (6th ed., pp. 313–399). Hoboken, NJ: Wiley.

Fish, M. (2004). Attachment in infancy and preschool in low socioeconomic status rural Appalachian children: Stability and change and relations to preschool and kindergarten competence. *Development & Psychopathology, 16*, 293–312.

Fisher, C. B. (2008). *Decoding the ethics code: A practical guide for psychologists* (2nd ed.). Thousand Oaks, CA: Sage.

Fisher-Thompson, D. (1990). Adult gender typing of children's toys. *Sex Roles, 23*, 291–303.

Fisher-Thompson, D., Sausa, A. D., & Wright, T. F (1995). Toy selection for children: Personality and toy request influences. *Sex Roles, 33*, 239–255.

Fite, J. E., Goodnight, J. A., Bates, J. E., Dodge, K. A., & Pettit, G. S. (2008). Adolescent aggression and social cognition in the context of personality: Impulsivity as a moderator of predictions from social information processing. *Aggressive Behavior, 34*, 511–520.

Fivaz-Depeursinge, E., & Corboz-Warner, A. (1999). *The primary triangle: A developmental systems view of fathers, mothers, and infants.* New York: Basic Books.

Fivush, R. (2007). Maternal reminiscing style and children's developing understanding of self and emotion. *Clinical Social Work Journal, 35*, 37–46.

Flannery, D. J, Vazsonyi, A. T., Liau, A. K., Guo, S., Powell, K. E., Atha, H., . . . Embry, D. (2003). Initial behavior outcomes for the PeaceBuilders universal school-based violence prevention program. *Developmental Psychology, 39*, 292–308.

Flavell, J. H. (1997). Cognitive development: Children's knowledge about the mind. *Annual Review of Psychology, 50*, 21–45.

Flavell, J. H., Flavell, E. R., Green, F. L., & Korfmacher, J. E. (1990). Do young children think of television images as pictures or real objects? *Journal of Broadcasting & Electronic Media, 34*, 399–419.

Flavell, J. H., Miller, P. H., & Miller, S. A. (2002). *Cognitive Development* (4th ed.). Upper Saddle River, NJ: Prentice Hall.

Fleming, A. S., Corter, C., Stallings, J., & Steiner, M. (2002). Testosterone and prolactin are associated with emotional responses to infant cries in new fathers. *Hormones and Behavior, 42*, 399–413.

Fletcher, A. C., Darling, N. E., Steinberg, L., & Dornbusch, S. (1995). The company they keep: Relation of adolescents' adjustment and behavior to their friends' perceptions of authoritative parenting in the social network. *Developmental Psychology, 31*, 300–310.

Fogassi, L., Ferrari, P. F., Gesierich, B., Rozzi, S., Chersi, F., & Rizzolatti, G. (2005). Parietal lobe: From action organization to intention understanding. *Science, 308*, 662–667.

Fogel, A. (1993). *Developing through relationships: Origins of communication, self, and culture.* Chicago: University of Chicago Press.

Fogel, A., Hsu, H., Shapiro, A. F., Nelson-Goens, G. C., & Secrist, C. (2006). Effects of normal and perturbed play on the duration and amplitude of different types of infant smiles. *Developmental Psychology, 42*, 459–473.

Folb, K. L. (2000). "Don't touch that dial!" TV as a – what? positive influence. *SIECUS Report, 28*, 16–18.

Foley, D. L., Eaves, L. J., Wormley, B., Silberg, J., Maes, H., Kuhn, J., & Riley, B. (2004). Childhood adversity, monamine oxidase A genotype and risk for conduct disorder. *Archives of General Psychiatry, 61*, 738–744.

Fonagy, P., Steele, H., & Steele, M. (1991). Maternal representations of attachment during pregnancy predict organization of infant-mother attachment at one year of age. *Child Development, 62*, 891–905.

Fontaine, R. G., Burks, V. S., & Dodge, K. A. (2002). Response decision processes and externalizing behavior problems in adolescents. *Development & Psychopathology, 14*, 107–122.

Foote, R. C., & Holmes-Lonergan, H. A. (2003). Sibling conflict and theory of mind. *British Journal of Developmental Psychology, 21*, 45–58.

Forman, D. R., Aksan, N., & Kochanska, G. (2004). Toddlers' responsive imitation predicts preschool-age conscience. *Psychological Science, 15*, 699–704.

Foster, E. M., Jones, D., & Conduct Problems Prevention Research Group. (2006). Can a costly intervention be cost effective? An analysis of violence prevention. *Archives of General Psychiatry, 63*, 1284–1291.

Fox, N. A. (1991). If it's not left, it's right: Electroencephalograph asymmetry and the development of emotion. *American Psychologist, 46*, 863–872.

Fox, N. A., & Calkins, S. (2003). The development of self-control of emotions: Intrinsic and external influences. *Motivation and Emotion, 27*, 7–26.

Fox, N. A., Calkins, S. D., & Bell, M. A. (1994). Neural plasticity and development in the first two years of life: Evidence from cognitive and socioemotional domains. *Development and Psychopathology, 6*, 677–696.

Fox, N. A., & Davidson, R. J. (1988). Patterns of brain electrical activity during facial signs of emotion in 10-month-old infants. *Developmental Psychology, 24*, 230–236.

Fox, N. A., Henderson, H. A., Rubin, K. H., & Calkins, S. D. (2001). Continuity and discontinuity of behavioral inhibition and exuberance: Psychophysiological and behavioral influences across the first four years of life. *Child Development, 72*, 1–21.

Fox, S. E., Levitt, P., & Nelson, C. A. (2010). How the timing and quality of early experiences influence the development of brain architecture. *Child Development, 81*, 28–40.

Fraley, R. C. (2002). Attachment stability from infancy to adulthood: Meta-analysis and dynamic modeling of developmental mechanisms. *Personality & Social Psychology Review, 6,* 123.

Fraley, R. C. (2004). *How to conduct behavioral research over the Internet.* New York: Guilford Press.

Fraley, R. C., & Spieker, S. J. (2003). Are infant attachment patterns continuously or categorically distributed? A taxometric analysis of Strange Situation behavior. *Developmental Psychology, 39,* 387–404.

Frank, R. H. (2001). Cooperation through emotional commitment. In R. M. Nesse (Ed.), *Evolution and the capacity for commitment* (Vol. 3, pp. 57–76). New York: Russell Sage Foundation.

Freedman, D. G. (1974). *Human infancy: An evolutionary perspective.* Hillsdale, NJ: Erlbaum.

Freitag, C. M. (2007). The genetics of autistic disorders and its clinical relevance: A review of the literature. *Molecular Psychiatry, 12,* 2–22.

French, D. C. (1990). Heterogeneity of peer rejected girls. *Child Development, 61,* 2028–2031.

French, D. C., Bae, A., Pidada, S., & Lee, O. (2006). Friendships of Indonesian, South Korean, and U.S. college students. *Personal Relationships, 13,* 69–81.

French, D. C., Pidada, S., Denoma, J., McDonald, K., & Lawton, A. (2005). Reported peer conflicts of children in the United States and Indonesia. *Social Development, 14,* 458–472.

French, S., Seidman, E., Allen, L., & Aber, J. (2006). The development of ethnic identity during adolescence. *Developmental Psychology, 42,* 1–10.

Freud, S. (1905). *Three essays on the theory of sexuality.* London: Hogarth Press.

Freud, S. (1910). The origin and development of psychoanalysis. *American Journal of Psychology, 2,* 181–218.

Frey, K. S., Hirschstein, M. K., Edstrom, L. V., & Snell, J. L. (2009). Observed reductions in school bullying, nonbullying aggression, and destructive bystander behavior: A longitudinal evaluation. *Journal of Educational Psychology, 101,* 466–481.

Frey, K. S., Hirschstein, M. K., Snell, J. L., Edstrom, L. V., MacKenzie, E. P., & Broderick, C. J. (2005). Reducing playground bullying and supporting beliefs: An experimental trial of the Steps to Respect program. *Developmental Psychology, 41,* 479–491.

Frey, K. S., & Ruble, D. N. (1992). Gender constancy and the "cost" of sex-typed behavior: A test of the conflict hypothesis. *Developmental Psychology, 28,* 714–721.

Frick, P. J., Cornell, A. H., Barry, C. T., Bodin, S. D., & Dane, H. E. (2003). Callous-unemotional traits and conduct problems in the prediction of conduct problem severity, aggression, and self-report of delinquency. *Journal of Abnormal Child Psychology, 31,* 457–470.

Frick, P. J., & Ellis, M. L. (1999). Callous-unemotional traits and subtypes of conduct disorder. *Clinical Child & Family Psychology Review, 2,* 149–168.

Frick, P. J., & Morris, A. S. (2004). Temperament and developmental pathways to conduct problems. *Journal of Clinical Child & Adolescent Psychology, 33,* 55–68.

Friedman, H. S. (2008). The multiple linkages of personality and disease. *Brain, Behavior, and Immunity, 22,* 68–675.

Friedman, H. S., Tucker, J. S., Schwartz, J. E., Tomlinson-Keasey, C., Martin, L. R., Wingard, D. L., & Criqui, M. H. (1995). Psychosocial and behavioral predictors of longevity: The aging and death of the "termites." *American Psychologist, 50,* 69–78.

Friedrich, L. K., & Stein, A. H. (1973). Aggressive and prosocial television programs and the natural behavior of preschool children. *Monographs of the Society for Research in Child Development, 38* (Serial No. 151).

Frodi, A. M., & Lamb, M. E. (1980). Child abusers' responses to infant smiles and cries. *Child Development, 51,* 238–241.

Frodi, A. M., Lamb, M. E., Leavitt, L. A., Donovan, W. L., Neff, C., & Sherry, D. (1978). Fathers' and mothers' responses to the faces and cries of normal and premature infants. *Developmental Psychology, 14,* 490–498.

Frosch, C. A., Mangelsdorf, S., & McHale, J. L. (2000). Marital behavior and the security of preschool-parent attachment relationships. *Journal of Family Psychology, 14,* 1438–1449.

Fry, R. (2008). *Latino settlement in the new century.* Washington, DC: Pew Hispanic Center.

Fu, G., Xu, F., Cameron, C. A., Heyman, G., & Lee, K. (2007). Cross-cultural differences in children's choices, categorizations, and evaluations of truths and lies. *Developmental Psychology, 43,* 278–293.

Fujioka, K. (2008, July). *Emotional competence in Japanese preschoolers: Gender differences and age differences.* Paper presented at the biennial meeting of the International Society for the Study of Behavioral Development, Würzburg, Germany.

Fukushima, H., & Hiraki, K. (2006). Perceiving an opponent's loss: Gender-related differences in the medial-frontal negativity. *Social Cognitive and Affective Neuroscience, 1,* 149–157.

Fuligni, A. J., & Tseng, V. (1999). Family obligation and the academic motivation of adolescents from immigrant and American born families. In T. Urban (Ed.), *Advances in motivation and achievement* (Vol. 11, pp. 159–183). Stamford, CT: JAI Press.

Fung, H. (2010). Cultural psychological perspectives on social development in childhood. In P. K. Smith & C. H. Hart (Eds.), *Wiley-Blackwell handbook of childhood social development* (2nd ed.). Oxford, UK: Wiley-Blackwell.

Funk, J. B., & Buchman, D. D. (1996). Children's perceptions of gender differences in social approval for playing electronic games. *Sex Roles, 35,* 219–232.

Furman, W. (2002). The emerging field of adolescent romantic relationships. *Current Directions in Psychological Science, 11,* 177–180.

Furman, W., Rahe, D. F., & Hartup, W. W. (1979). Rehabilitation of socially withdrawn preschool children through mixed-age and same-age socialization. *Child Development, 50,* 915–922.

Furman, W., & Shomaker, L. B. (2008). Patterns of interaction in adolescent romantic relationships: Distinct features and links to other close relationships. *Journal of Adolescence, 31,* 771–788.

Furman, W., Simon, V. A., Shaffer, L., & Bouchey, H. A. (2002). Adolescents' working models and styles for relationships with parents, friends, and romantic partners. *Child Development, 73,* 241–255

Furstenberg, F. F., Brooks-Gunn, J., & Chase-Lansdale, L. (1989). Teenaged pregnancy and child bearing. *American Psychologist, 44,* 313–320.

Furstenberg, F. F., Brooks-Gunn, J., & Morgan, P. (1987). *Adolescent mothers in late life.* New York: Cambridge University Press.

Furstenberg, F. F., & Harris, K. M. (1993). When and why fathers matter: Impacts of father involvement on children of adolescent mothers. In R. I. Lerman & T. J. Ooms (Eds.), *Young unwed fathers* (pp. 117–138). Philadelphia: Temple University Press.

Gabel, K., & Girard, K. (1995). Long term care nurseries in prisons: A descriptive study. In K. Gabel, & D. Johnston (Eds.), *Children of incarcerated parents* (pp. 237–254). New York: Lexington Books.

Gaines, L., & Esserman, J. (1981). A quantitative study of young children's comprehension of television programs and commercials. In J. Esserman (Ed.), *Television advertising and children: Issues, research, and findings* (pp. 96–105). New York: Child Research Service.

Galen, B. R., & Underwood, M. K. (1997). A developmental investigation of social aggression among children. *Developmental Psychology, 33,* 589–600.

Galinsky, E., Howes, C., & Kontos, S. (1995). *The family child care training study.* New York: Families and Work Institute.

Garbarino, J. (1982). Sociocultural risk: Dangers to competence. In C. Kopp & J. Krakow (Eds.), *Child development in a social context* (pp. 630–685). Reading, MA: Addison-Wesley.

Garbarino, J., & Kostelny, K. (2002). Parenting and public policy. In M. H. Bornstein (Ed.), *Handbook of parenting: Vol. 3. Being and becoming a parent* (2nd ed., pp. 419–436). Mahwah, NJ: Erlbaum.

Garbarino, J., & Sherman, D. (1980). High-risk neighborhoods and high-risk families: The human ecology of child maltreatment. *Child Development, 51,* 188–198.

Garber, J., & Martin, N. C. (2002). Negative cognitions in offspring of depressed parents: Mechanisms of risk. In S. H. Goodman & I. N. Gotlib (Eds.), *Children of depressed parents* (pp. 121–154). Washington, DC: American Psychological Association.

Garcia, L., Hart, D., & Johnson-Ray, R. (1997). What do children and adolescents think about themselves? A developmental account of self-concept. In S. Hala (Ed.), *The development of social cognition. Studies in developmental psychology* (pp. 365–394). Hove, England: Psychology Press.

Garcia, M. M., Shaw, D. S., Winslow, E. B., & Yaggi, K. E. (2000). Destructive sibling conflict and the development of conduct problems in young boys. *Developmental Psychology, 36,* 44–53.

Garcia Coll, C., Akiba, D., Palacios, N., Bailey, B., Silver, R., DiMartino, L., & Chin, C. (2002). Parental involvement in children's education: Lessons from three immigrant groups. *Parenting: Science and Practice, 2,* 303–324.

Garner, P. W. (2006). Prediction of prosocial and emotional competence from maternal behavior in African American preschoolers. *Cultural Diversity and Ethnic Minority Psychology, 12,* 179–198.

Garner, P. W., Jones, D. C., & Palmer, D. J. (1994). Social cognitive correlates of preschool children's sibling caregiving behavior. *Developmental Psychology, 30,* 905–911.

Garner, P. W., & Power, T. G. (1996). Preschoolers' emotional control in the disappointment paradigm and its relation to temperament, emotional knowledge and family expressiveness. *Child Development, 67,* 1406–1429.

Garrett, A. S., Menon, V., Mackenzie, K., & Reiss, A. (2004). Here's looking at you kid: Neural systems underlying face and gaze processing in fragile X syndrome. *Archives of General Psychiatry, 61,* 281–288.

Gatti, U., Tremblay, R. E., Vitaro, F., & McDuff, P. (2005). Youth gangs, delinquency and drug use: A test of the selection, facilitation, and enhancement hypotheses. *Journal of Child Psychology and Psychiatry, 46,* 1178–1190.

Gauvain, M. (2001a). Cultural tools, social interaction, and the development of thinking. *Human Development, 44,* 126–143.

Gauvain, M. (2001b). *The sociocultural context of cognitive development.* New York: Guilford Press.

Gazelle, H., & Ladd, G. W. (2002). Interventions for children victimized by peers. In P. A. Schewe (Ed.), *Preventing violence in relationships: Interventions across the life span* (pp. 55–78). Washington, DC: American Psychological Association.

Gazelle, H., & Ladd, G. W. (2003). Anxious solitude and peer exclusion: A diathesis-stress model of internalizing trajectories in childhood. *Child Development, 74,* 257–278.

Gazelle, H., & Rudolph, K. D. (2004). Moving toward and away from the world: Social approach and avoidance trajectories in anxious solitary youth. *Child Development, 75,* 829–849.

Gazzola, V., & Keysers, C. (2009). The observation and execution of actions share motor and somatosensory voxels in all tested subjects: Single-subject analyses of unsmoothed fMRI data. *Cerebral Cortex, 19,* 1239–1255.

Ge, X., Conger, R. D., & Elder, G. H. (2001). Pubertal transition, stressful life events, and the emergence of gender differences in adolescent depressive symptoms. *Developmental Psychology, 37,* 404–417.

Geary, D. C. (1998). *Male, female: The evolution of human sex differences.* Washington, DC: American Psychological Association.

Geary, D. C. (2006). Coevolution of paternal investment and cuckoldry in humans. In T. K. Shackelford & S. Platek (Eds.), *Female infidelity and paternal uncertainty* (pp. 14–34). New York: Cambridge University Press.

Geary, D. C., & Bjorklund, D. F. (2000). Evolutionary developmental psychology. *Child Development, 71,* 57–65.

Gelfand, D. M., & Drew, C. J. (2003). *Understanding child behavior disorders* (4th ed.). Belmont, CA: Wadsworth.

Gennetian, L. A., & Miller, C. (2002). Children and welfare reform: A view from an experimental welfare program in Minnesota. *Child Development, 73,* 601–620.

Gentile, D. A., Lynch, P. J., Linden, J. R., & Walsh, D. A. (2004). The effects of violent game habits on adolescent hostility, aggressive behaviors and school performance. *Journal of Adolescence, 27,* 5–22.

Georgiou, S. N. (2008). Bullying and victimization at school: The role of mothers. *British Journal of Educational Psychology, 78,* 109–125.

Gerbner, G., Gross, L., Morgan, M., & Signorielli, N. (1994). Growing up with television: The cultivation perspective. In J. Bryant, & D. Zillmann (Eds.), *Media effects: Advances in theory and research* (pp. 17–41). Hillsdale, NJ: Erlbaum.

Gerbner, G., Gross, L., Signorielli, N., & Morgan, M. (1980). Aging with television: Images on television drama and conceptions of social reality. *Journal of Communication, 30,* 37–47.

Gerbner, G., Morgan, M., & Signorielli, N. (1994). Analysis of "mean world" syndrome and prospects for cultural change. *Television Violence Profile, No 16.* Philadelphia: University of Pennsylvania.

Gerhold, M., Laucht, M., Texdorf, C., Schmidt, M. H., & Esser, G. (2002). Early mother-infant interaction as a precursor to childhood social withdrawal. *Child Psychiatry & Human Development, 32,* 277–293.

Gerris, J. R. M., Dekovic, M., Janssens, J. M. A. M. (1997). The relationship between social class and childrearing behaviors: Parents' perspective taking and value orientations. *Journal of Marriage and Family, 59,* 834–847.

Gerrits, M. H., Goudena, P. P., & van Aken, M. A. G. (2005). Child-parent and child-peer interaction: Observational similarities and differences at age seven. *Infant and Child Development, 14,* 229–241.

Gershoff, E. T. (2002). Corporal punishment by parents and associated child behaviors and experiences: A meta-analytic and theoretical review. *Psychological Bulletin, 128,* 539–579.

Gershoff, E. T., Aber, J. L., & Raver, C. C. (2005). Child poverty in the United States: An evidence based conceptual framework for programs and policies. In R. M. Lerner, F. Jacobs, & D. Wertlieb (Eds.), *Applied developmental science* (pp. 269–324). Thousand Oaks, CA: Sage.

Gershoff, E. T., & Bitensky, S. H. (2007). The case against corporal punishment of children: Converging evidence from social science research and international human rights law and implications for U.S. public policy. *Psychology, Public Policy, and Law, 13,* 231–272.

Gershoff, E. T., Grogan-Kaylor, A., Lansford, J. E., Chang, L., Zelli, A., Deater-Deckard, K. & Dodge, K. A. (2010). Parent discipline practices in an international sample: Associations with child behaviors and moderation by perceived normativeness. *Child Development, 81,* 487–502.

Gesell, A. L. (1928). *Infancy and human growth.* New York: Macmillan.

Gewirtz, J. L. (1967). The course of infant smiling in four child-rearing environments in Israel. In B. M. Foss (Ed.), *Determinants of infant behavior* (Vol. 3, pp. 105–248). London: Methuen.

Gewirtz, J. L. (1969). Mechanisms of social learning: Some roles of stimulation and behavior in early human development. In D. A. Goslin (Ed.), *Handbook of socialization theory and research* (pp. 121–162). Chicago: Rand McNally.

Gibbs, J. C. (2010). *Moral development and reality: Beyond the theories of Kohlberg and Hoffman.* Boston: Pearson Allyn & Bacon.

Gibbs, J. C., Basinger, K. S., Grime, R. L., & Snarey, J. R. (2007). Moral judgment development across cultures: Revisiting Kohlberg's universality claims. *Developmental Review, 27,* 443–500.

Gibbs, J. C., Potter, G. B., & Goldstein, A. P. (1995). *The EQUIP program: Teaching youth to think and act responsibly through a peer helping approach.* Champaign, IL: Research Press.

Gibbs, J. T. (1989). Black American adolescents. In J. T. Gibbs & L. N. Huang (Eds.), *Children of color* (pp. 179–223). San Francisco: Jossey-Bass.

Gibbs, N., & Roche, T. (1999, December). The Columbine tapes. *Time Magazine.* Retrieved from: www.time.com/time/magazine/article/0,9171,992873-13,00.html

Gibson, E. J., & Walk, R. D. (1960). The "visual cliff." *Scientific American, 202,* 64.

Gibson, F. L., Ungerer, J. A., Tennant, C. C., & Saunders, D. M. (2000). Parental adjustment and attitudes to parenting after in vitro fertilization. *Fertility and Sterility, 73,* 565–574.

Gifford-Smith, M. E., & Rabiner, D. L. (2004). Social information processing and children's social adjustment. In

J. Kupersmidt & K. A. Dodge (Eds.), *Children's peer relations: From development to intervention to policy: A festschrift to honor John D. Coie* (pp. 61–79). Washington, DC: American Psychological Association.

Giles, J. W., & Heyman, G. D. (2004). When to cry over spilled milk: Young children's use of category information to guide inferences about ambiguous behavior. *Journal of Cognition and Development, 5,* 359–382.

Gilissen, R., Bakermans-Kranenburg, M. J., van IJzendoorn, M. H., & van der Veen, R. (2008). Parent-child relationship, temperament, and physiological reactions to fear-inducing film clips: Further evidence for differential susceptibility. *Journal of Experimental Child Psychology, 99,* 182–195.

Gillham, J. E., Reivich, K. J., Jaycox, L. H., & Seligman, M. E. (1995). Prevention of depressive symptoms in schoolchildren: Two-year follow-up. *Psychological Science, 6,* 343–351.

Gilligan, C. (1982). *In a different voice.* Cambridge, MA: Harvard University Press.

Gilligan, C. (1993). Woman's place in man's life cycle. In A. Dobrin (Ed.), *Being good and doing right: Readings in moral development* (pp. 37–54). Lanham, MD: University Press of America.

Gilliom, M., Shaw, D. S., Beck, J. E., Schonber, M. A., & Lukon, J. L. (2002). Anger regulation in disadvantaged preschool boys: Strategies, antecedents, and the development of self-control. *Developmental Psychology, 38,* 222–235.

Ginsburg, H. J., Pollman, V. A., & Wauson, M. S. (1977). An ethological analysis of nonverbal inhibitors of aggressive behavior in male elementary school children. *Developmental Psychology, 13,* 417–418.

Giordano, P. C., Cernkovich, S. A., & Holland, D. D. (2003). Changes in friendship relations over the life course: Implications for desistance from crime. *Criminology, 41,* 401–436.

Gleason, T. R., Gower, A. L., Hohmann, L. M., & Gleason, T. C. (2005). Temperament and friendship in preschool-aged children. *International Journal of Behavioral Development, 29,* 336–344.

Global Initiative to End All Corporal Punishment of Children. (2009). Ending legalised violence against children. *Global Report 2008.* Retrieved from: http://www.endcorporalpunishment.org/pages/pdfs/reports/GlobalReport2008.pdf

Glucksberg, S., Krauss, R., & Higgins, E. T. (1975). The development of referential communication skills. In F. D. Horowitz (Ed.), *Review of child development research* (Vol. 4, pp. 305–345). Chicago: University of Chicago Press.

Goddard, R. D., LoGerfo, L., & Hoy, W. K. (2004). High school accountability: The role of perceived collective efficacy. *Educational Policy, 18,* 403–425.

Goeke-Morey, M. C., Cummings, E. M., Harold, G. T., & Shelton, K. H. (2003). Categories and continua of destructive and constructive marital conflict tactics from the perspective of U.S. and Welsh children. *Journal of Family Psychology, 17,* 327–338.

Goetz, G., & Myers-Walls, J. A. (2006). *Children's age-related fears.* West Lafayette, IN: Parent-Provider Partnerships at Purdue University Extension.

Goetz, T. E., & Dweck, C. S. (1980). Learned helplessness in social situations. *Journal of Personality Social Psychology, 39,* 246–255.

Goldbaum, S., Craig, W. M., Pepler, D., & Connolly, J. (2003). Developmental trajectories of victimization: Identifying risk and protective factors. *Journal of Applied School Psychology, 19,* 59–68.

Goldberg, W. A., Clarke-Stewart, K. A., Rice, J. A., & Dellis, E. (2002). Emotional energy as an explanatory construct for fathers' engagement with their infants. *Parenting: Science and Practice, 2,* 379–408.

Goldman, J., Salus, M. K., Wolcott, D., & Kennedy, K. Y. (2003). *A coordinated response to child abuse and neglect: The foundation for practice.* Washington, DC: U.S. Department of Health and Human Services.

Goldman-Rakic, P. (1997). Space and time in the mental universe. *Nature, 386,* 559–560.

Goldsmith, H. H. (1983). Genetic influences on personality from infancy to adulthood. *Child Development, 54,* 331–355.

Goldsmith, H. H., Aksan, N., Essex, M., Smider, N. A., & Vandell, D. L. (2001). Temperament and socioemotional adjustment to kindergarten: A multi-informant perspective. In T. D. Wachs & G. A. Kohnstamm (Eds.), *Temperament in context* (pp. 103–138). Mahwah, NJ: Erlbaum.

Goldstein, J. M., Seidman, L. J., Horton, N. J., Makris, N., Kennedy, D. N., Caviness, V. S., . . . Tsuang, M. T. (2001). Normal sexual dimorphism of the adult human brain assessed by in vivo magnetic resonance imaging. *Cerebral Cortex, 11,* 490–497.

Golinkoff, R. M. (1983). The preverbal negotiation of failed messages: Insights into the transition period. In R. M. Golinkoff (Ed.), *The transition from prelinguistic to linguistic communication* (pp. 57–78). Hillsdale, NJ: Erlbaum.

Golinkoff, R. M. (1986). "I beg your pardon?": The preverbal negotiation of failed messages. *Journal of Child Language, 13,* 455–476.

Golinkoff, R. M., & Hirsh-Pasek, K. (1999). *How babies talk.* New York: Penguin Group.

Golombok, S. (2000). *Parenting: What really counts?* New York: Routledge.

Golombok, S. (2006). New family forms. In A. Clarke-Stewart & J. Dunn (Eds.), *Families count: Effects on child and adolescent development* (pp. 273–298). New York: Cambridge University Press.

Golombok, S., MacCallum, F., & Goodman, E. (2001). The 'test tube' generation: Parent-child relationships and the psychological well-being of IVF children at adolescence. *Child Development, 72,* 599–608.

Golombok, S., MacCallum, F., Goodman, E., & Rutter, M. (2002). Families with children conceived by DI: A follow-up at age 12. *Child Development, 73,* 952–968.

Golombok, S., Murray, C., Jadva, V., MacCallum, F., & Lycett, E. (2004). Families created through surrogacy arrangements: Parent-child relationships in the first year of life. *Developmental Psychology, 40,* 400–411.

Golombok, S., Rust, J., Zervoulis, K., Croudace, T., Golding, J., & Hines, M. (2008). Developmental trajectories of sex-typed behavior in boys and girls: A longitudinal general population study of children aged 2.5–8 years. *Child Development, 79,* 1583–1593.

Goncu, A. (1993). Development of intersubjectivity in social pretend play. *Human Development, 36,* 185–198.

Gonzales, N. A., Cauce, A. M., & Mason, C. A. (1996). Interobserver agreement in the assessment of parental behavior and parent-adolescent conflict: African-American mothers, daughters, and independent observers. *Child Development, 67,* 1483–1498.

Gonzalez, Y. S., Moreno, D. S., & Schneider, B. H. (2004). Friendship expectations of early adolescents in Cuba and Canada. *Journal of Cross-Cultural Psychology, 35,* 436–445.

Goodman, G. S., & Melinder, A. (2007). Child witness research and forensic interview of young children: A review. *Legal & Criminological Psychology, 12,* 1–19.

Goodman, S. H., & Gotlib, I. N. (Eds.) (2002). *Children of depressed parents.* Washington, DC: American Psychological Association.

Goodvin, R., Meyer, S., Thompson, R. A., & Hayes, R. (2008). Self-understanding in early childhood: Associations with child attachment security and maternal negative affect. *Attachment & Human Development, 10,* 433–450.

Gorn, G. J., & Goldberg, M. E. (1982). Behavioral evidence of the effects of televised food messages on children. *Journal of Consumer Research, 9,* 200–205.

Gornick, J. C., & Meyers, M. K. (2003). *Families that work: Policies for reconciling parenthood and employment.* New York: Russell Sage Foundation.

Gosselin, P., Perron, M., Legault, M., & Campanella, P. (2002). Children's and adults' knowledge of the distinction between enjoyment and non-enjoyment smiles. *Journal of Nonverbal Behavior, 26,* 83–108.

Gotlib, I. H., Joormann, J., Minor, K. L., & Cooney, R. E. (2006). Cognitive and biological functioning in children at risk for depression. In T. Canli (Ed.), *Biology of personality and individual differences* (pp. 353–382). New York: Guilford Press.

Gottesman, I. I. (1963). Genetic aspects of intelligent behavior. In N. Ellis (Ed.), *Handbook of mental deficiency: Psychological theory and research* (pp. 79–96). New York: McGraw-Hill.

Gottesman, I. I., & Goldsmith, H. H. (1994). Developmental psychopathology of antisocial behavior: Inserting genes into its ontogenesis and epigenesis. In C. A. Nelson (Ed.), *Threats to optimal development: Integrating biological, psychological, and social risk factors* (pp. 69–104). Hillsdale, NJ: Erlbaum.

Gottfried, A. E., Gottfried, A. W., & Bathurst, K. (2002). Maternal and dual-earner employment status and parenting. In M. H. Bornstein (Ed.), *Handbook of parenting: Vol. 2. Biology and ecology of parenting* (2nd ed., pp. 207–230). Mahwah, NJ: Erlbaum.

Gottfried, A. W., Gottfried, A. E., & Guerin, D. W. (2006). The Fullerton Longitudinal Study: A long-term investigation of intellectual and motivational giftedness. *Journal for the Education of the Gifted, 29,* 430–450.

Gottlieb, A. (2000). Luring your child into this life: A Beng path for child care. In J. DeLoache & A. Gottlieb (Eds.), *A world of babies: Imagined childcare guides for seven societies.* (pp. 55–90). New York: Cambridge University Press.

Gottlieb, G. (1991). Experiential canalization of behavioral development theory. *Developmental Psychology, 27,* 4–13.

Gottlieb, G. (1992). *Individual development and evolution: The genesis of novel behavior.* New York: Oxford University Press.

Gottlieb, G., & Lickliter, R. (2004). The various roles of animal models in understanding human development. *Social Development, 13,* 311–325.

Gottman, J. M. (1983). How children become friends. *Monographs of the Society for Research in Child Development, 48* (Serial No. 201).

Gottman, J. M. (1986). The world of coordinated play: Same and cross-sex friendship in young children. In J. M. Gottman & J. G. Parker (Eds.), *The conversations of friends* (pp. 139–191). New York: Cambridge University Press.

Gottman, J. M. (1999). *The marriage clinic.* New York: W. W. Norton.

Gottman, J. M., & DeClaire, J. (1997). *Raising an emotionally intelligent child: The heart of parenting.* New York: Simon & Schuster.

Gottman, J. M., & Gottman, J. S. (2008). Gottman method couple therapy. In A. S. Gurmna (Ed.), *Clinical handbook of couple therapy* (pp. 138–166). New York: Guilford Press.

Gottman, J. M., Gottman, J. S., & DeClaire, J. (2007). *10 lessons to transform your marriage.* New York: Crown Publishing.

Gottman, J. M., Guralnick, M. J., Wilson, B., Swanson, C. C., & Murray, J. D. (1997). What should be the focus of emotion regulation in children? A nonlinear dynamic mathematical model of children's peer interaction in groups. *Development and Psychopathology, 9,* 421–452.

Gottman, J. M., Katz, L., & Hooven, C. (1996). *Meta-emotion.* Mahwah, NJ: Erlbaum.

Gottman, J. M., & Mettetal, G. (1986). Speculations on social and affective development: Friendship and acquaintanceship through adolescence. In J. M. Gottman & J. G. Parker

(Eds.), *The conversations of friends* (pp. 192–237). New York: Cambridge University Press.

Gottman, J. M., & Parker, J. G. (Eds.) (1986). *The conversations of friends*. New York: Cambridge University Press.

Gould, E., Reeves, A. J., Graziano, M. S., & Gross, C. G. (1999). Neurogenesis in the neocortex of adult primates. *Science, 286*, 548–555.

Graham, S., Doubleday, C., & Guarino, P. A. (1984). The development of relations between perceived controllability and the emotions of pity, anger and guilt. *Child Development, 55*, 561–565.

Grant, T. R. (2001). The family that eats together stays together. Cited in Larson, R. W., Branscomb, K. R., & Wiley A. R. (2006). Forms and functions of family mealtimes. *New Directions for Child and Adolescent Development, 111*, 1–15.

Graue, M. E., & Walsh, D. J. (1998). *Studying children in context*. Thousand Oaks, CA: Sage.

Gray, P., Yang, C. J., & Pope, H. G. (2006). Fathers have lower salivary testosterone levels than married men and married non-fathers in Beijing, China. *Proceedings of the Royal Society: B, 273*, 333–339.

Graziano, P. A., Keane, S. P., & Calkins, S. D. (2007). Cardiac vagal regulation and early peer status. *Child Development, 78*, 264–278.

Green, K. E., Groves, M. M., & Tegano, D. W. (2004). Parenting practices that limit transitional object use: An illustration. *Early Child Development and Care, 174*, 427–436.

Greenberg, B. S., & Mastro, D. E. (2008). Children, race, ethnicity and media. In S. L. Calvert & B. J. Wilson (Eds.), *The handbook of children, media, and development* (pp. 74–97). Malden, MA: Blackwell.

Greenberg, B. S., Fazal, S., & Wober, M. (1986). *Children's views on advertising*. London: Independent Broadcasting Authority.

Greenberg, M. (1999). Attachment and psychopathology in childhood. In J. Cassidy & P. R. Shaver (Eds.), *Handbook of attachment: Theory, research, and clinical applications* (pp. 449–456). New York: Guilford Press.

Greenberger, E., O'Neil, R., & Nagel, S. K. (1994). Linking workplace and homeplace: Relations between the nature of adults' work and their parenting behaviors. *Developmental Psychology, 30*, 990–1002.

Greene, J. D., Sommerville, R. B., Nystrom, L. E., Darley, J. M., & Cohen, J. D. (2001). An fMRI investigation of emotional engagement in moral judgment. *Science, 293*, 2105–2108.

Greene, M., Way, N., & Pahl, K. (2006). Trajectories of perceived adult and peer discrimination among Black, Latino, and Asian American adolescents: Patterns and psychological correlates. *Developmental Psychology, 42*, 218–278.

Greenfield, P. M. (2004). Inadvertent exposure to pornography on the Internet: Implications of peer-to-peer file sharing networks for child development and families. *Journal of Applied Developmental Psychology, 25*, 741–750.

Greenfield, P. M., Gross, E. E., Subrahmanyam, K., Suzuki, L. K., & Tynes, B. (2006). Teens on the Internet: Interpersonal connection, identity, and information. In R. Kraut, M. Brynin, & S. Kiesler (Eds.), *Computers, phones, and the Internet: Domesticating information technology* (pp. 185–200). New York: Oxford University Press.

Greenfield, P. M., Quiroz, B., & Raeff, C. (2000). Cross-cultural conflict and harmony in the social construction of the child. *New Directions for Child and Adolescent Development, 87*, 93–108.

Greenfield, P. M., Suzuki, L. K., & Rothstein-Fisch, C. (2006). Cultural pathways through human development. In K. A. Renninger, I. E. Sigel, W. Damon, & R. M. Lerner (Eds.), *Handbook of child psychology: Vol. 4. Child psychology in practice* (6th ed., pp. 655–699). Hoboken, NJ: Wiley.

Greenough, W., & Black, J. E. (1999). Experience, neural plasticity, and psychological development. In N. A. Fox, L. A. Leavitt, & J. G. Warhol (Eds.), *The role of early experience in infant development* (pp. 29–40). Newark, NJ: Johnson & Johnson Pediatric Institute.

Gregory A. C., Ball, H. A., & Button, T. M. M. (2010). Behavioural genetics. In P. K. Smith & C. H. Hart (Eds.), *Wiley-Blackwell handbook of childhood social development* (2nd ed.). Oxford, UK: Wiley-Blackwell.

Grello, C. M., Welsh, D. P., Harper, M. S., & Dickson, J. W. (2003). Dating and sexual relationship trajectories and adolescent functioning. *Adolescent and Family Health, 3*, 103–112.

Griffin, P. B., & Griffin, M. B. (1992). Fathers and childcare among the Cagayan Agta. In B. Hewlett (Ed.), *Father-child relations: Cultural and biosocial contexts* (pp. 297–320). New York: Aldine de Gruyther.

Griffiths, M. D., Davies, M. N. O., & Chappell, D. (2004). Demographic factors and playing variables in online computer gaming. *CyberPsychology & Behavior, 7*, 479–487.

Grigorenko, E. L. (2002). In search of the genetic engram of personality. In D. Cervone & W. Mischel (Eds.), *Advances in personality science* (pp. 29–82). New York: Guilford Press.

Grills, A., & Ollendick, T. (2002). Peer victimization, global self-worth, and anxiety in middle school children. *Journal of Clinical Child & Adolescent Psychology, 311*, 59–68.

Grimes, C. L., Klein, T. P., & Putallaz, M. (2004). Parents' relationships with their parents and peers: Influences on children's social development. In J. B. Kupersmidt & K. A. Dodge (Eds.), *Children's peer relations: From development to intervention* (pp. 141–158). Washington, DC: American Psychological Association.

Grimm-Thomas, K., & Perry-Jenkins, M. (1994). All in a day's work: Job experiences, self-esteem, and fathering in working-class families. *Family Relations, 43*, 174–181.

Groenendyk, A. E., & Volling, B. L. (2007). Coparenting and early conscience development in the family. *Journal of Genetic Psychology, 169*, 201–224.

Grolnick, W. S. (2003). *The psychology of parental control: How well-meant parenting backfires.* Mahwah, NJ: Erlbaum.

Gross, E. F. (2004). Adolescent Internet use: What we expect, what teens report. *Journal of Applied Developmental Psychology, 25,* 633–649.

Gross, R. T., Spiker, D., & Haynes, C. W. (Eds.) (1997). Helping low-birthweight, premature infants. *The Infant Health and Development Program.* Stanford, CA: Stanford University Press.

Grossman, F. K., Pollack, W. S., & Golding, E. (1988). Fathers and children: Predicting the quality and quantity of fathering. *Developmental Psychology, 24,* 82–91.

Grossmann, K., & Fremmer-Bombik, E. (1994, June). *Father's attachment representations and the quality of their interactions with their children in infancy and early childhood.* Poster presented at the biennial meeting of the International Society for the Study of Behavioral Development, Amsterdam.

Grossmann, K., Grossmann, K. E., Kindler, H., & Zimmermann, P. (2008). A wider view of attachment and exploration: The influence of mothers and fathers on the development of psychological security from infancy to young adulthood. In J. Cassidy & P. R. Shaver (Eds.), *Handbook of attachment: Theory, research, and clinical applications* (2nd ed., pp. 857–879). New York: Guilford Press.

Grossmann, K. E., Grossmann, K., Winter, M., & Zimmerman, P. (2002). Attachment relationships and appraisal of partnership: From early experience of sensitive support to later relationship representation. In L. Pulkkinen & A. Caspi (Eds.), *Paths to successful development: Personality in the life course* (pp. 73–105). New York: Cambridge University Press.

Grossmann, T., & Johnson, M. H. (2007). The development of the social brain in human infancy. *European Journal of Neuroscience, 25,* 909–919.

Grotevant, H. D. (2007). Openness in adoption: Re-thinking "family" in the United States. In M. C. Inhorn (Ed.), *Reproductive disruptions: Gender, technology, and biopolitics in the new millennium* (pp. 122–143). New York: Berghahn Books.

Grotevant, H. D., & McRoy, R. G. (1998). *Openness in adoption: Connecting families of birth and adoption.* Thousand Oaks, CA: Sage.

Grusec, J. E. (1973). Effects of co-observer evaluations on imitation: A developmental study. *Developmental Psychology, 8,* 141.

Grusec, J. E. (1992). Social learning theory and developmental psychology: The legacies of Robert Sears and Albert Bandura. *Developmental Psychology, 28,* 776–786.

Grusec, J. E., & Davidov, M. (2010). Integrating different perspectives on socialization theory and research: A domain-specific approach. *Child Development, 81,* 687–709.

Grusec, J. E., Dix, T., & Mills, R. (1982). The effects of type, severity, and victim of children's transgressions on maternal discipline. *Canadian Journal of Behavioural Science, 14,* 276–289.

Grusec, J. E., & Goodnow, J. J. (1994). Summing up and looking to the future. *Developmental Psychology, 30,* 29–31.

Grusec, J. E., Hastings, P., & Almas, A. (2010). Prosocial behaviour. In P. K. Smith & C. H. Hart (Eds.), *Wiley-Blackwell handbook of childhood social development* (2nd ed.). Oxford, UK: Wiley-Blackwell.

Grusec, J. E., & Ungerer, J. (2003). Effective socialization as problem solving and the role of parenting cognitions. In L. Kuczynski (Ed.), *Handbook of dynamics in parent-child relations* (pp. 211–228). Thousand Oaks, CA: Sage.

Grych, J. H., & Cardoza-Fernandes, S. (2001). Understanding the impact of interparental conflict on children: The role of social cognitive processes. In J. H. Grych, & F. D. Fincham (Eds.), *Interpersonal conflict and child development: Theory, research, and applications* (pp. 157–187). New York: Cambridge University Press.

Grych, J., & Fincham, F. F. (Eds.) (2001). *Interparental conflict and child development: Theory, research, and applications.* New York: Cambridge University Press.

Grych, J. H., & Fincham, F. D. (1990). Marital conflict and child adjustment: A cognitive-contextual framework. *Psychological Bulletin, 108,* 267–290.

Guastella, A. J., Mitchell, P. B., & Dadds, M. R. (2008). Oxytocin increases gaze to the eye region of human faces. *Biological Psychiatry, 63,* 3–5.

Guéguen, N. (2002). The effects of a joke on tipping when it is delivered at the same time as the bill. *Journal of Applied Social Psychology, 32,* 1955–1963.

Guerra, N. G., Eron, L. D., Huesmann, L. R., Tolan, P. H., & Van Acker, R. (1997). A cognitive-ecological approach to the prevention and mitigation of violence and aggression in inner-city youth. In D. P. Fry & K. Bjorkqvist (Eds.), *Cultural variation in conflict resolution: Alternatives to violence* (pp. 199–213). Mahwah, NJ: Erlbaum.

Guerra, N. G., Huesmann, L. R., Tolan, P. H., Van Acker, R., & Eron, L. D. (1995). *Correlates of environmental risk for aggression among inner-city children: Implications for preventive interventions.* Unpublished manuscript, University of Illinois at Chicago.

Guerra, N. G., Nucci, L., Huesmann, L. R. (1994). Moral cognition and childhood aggression. In L. R. Huesmann (Ed.), *Aggressive behavior: Current perspectives* (pp. 13–33). New York: Plenum Press.

Guerra, N. G., & Smith, E. P. (Eds.) (2006). *Preventing youth violence in a multicultural society.* Washington, DC: American Psychological Association.

Guidubaldi, J., Perry, J. D., & Nastasi, B. K. (1987). Growing up in a divorced family: Initial and long-term perspectives on children's adjustment. *Applied Social Psychology Annual, 7,* 202–237.

Gunji, A., Inagaki, M., Inoue, Y., Takeshima, Y., & Kaga, M. (2009). Event-related potentials of self-face recognition in children with pervasive developmental disorders. *Brain & Development, 31,* 139–147.

Gunnar, M. (1994). Psychoendocrine studies of temperament and stress in early childhood: Expanding current models. In J. Bates & T. Wachs (Eds.), *Temperament: Individual differences at the interface of biology and behavior*. New York: American Psychological Association.

Gunnar, M. R. (2000). Early adversity and the development of stress reactivity and regulation. In C. A. Nelson (Ed.), *Minnesota Symposia on Child Psychology: Vol. 31. The effects of early adversity on neurobehavioral development* (pp. 163–200). Mahwah, NJ: Erlbaum.

Gunnar, M. R. (2006). Social regulation of stress in early child development. In K. McCartney & D. Phillips (Eds.), *Blackwell handbook of early childhood development* (pp. 106–125). Malden, MA: Blackwell.

Gunnar, M. R., Kryzer, E., Van Ryzin, M. J., & Phillips, D. J. (2010). The rise in cortisol in family daycare: Associations with aspects of care quality, child behavior, and child sex. *Child Development, 81*, 851–869.

Gunnar, M. R., Sebanc, A. M., Tout, K., Donzella, B., & van Dulmen, M. M. H. (2003). Peer rejection, temperament, and cortisol activity in preschoolers. *Developmental Psychology, 43*, 346–358.

Gunnar, M. R., & Talge, N. M. (2007). Neuroendocrine measures in developmental research. In L. A. Schmidt & S. J. Segalowitz (Eds.), *Developmental psychophysiology: Theory, systems, and methods* (pp. 343–366). Cambridge, UK: Cambridge University Press.

Gupta, A. R., & State, M. W. (2007). Recent advances in the genetics of autism. *Biological Psychiatry, 61*, 429–437.

Gur, R. C., Gunning-Dixon, F., Bilker, W. B., & Gur, R. E. (2002). Sex differences in temporo-limbic and frontal brain volumes of healthy adults. *Cerebral Cortex, 12*, 998–1003.

Hadfield, L., Edwards, R., & Mauthner, M. (2006). Brothers and sisters: A source of support for children in school? *Education 3–13, 34*, 65–72.

Hadjikhani, N., Joseph, R. M., Snyder, J., & Tager-Flusberg, H. (2006). Anatomical differences in the mirror neuron system and social cognition network in autism. *Cerebral Cortex, 16*, 1276–1282.

Hahn, C.-S., & DiPietro, J. A. (2001). In vitro fertilization and the family: Quality of parenting, family functioning, and child psychological adjustment. *Developmental Psychology, 37*, 37–48.

Haidt, J. (2001). The emotional dog and its rational tail: A social intuitionist approach to moral judgment. *Psychological Review, 108*, 814–834.

Haight, W. L., & Miller, P. J. (1993). *Pretending at home: Early development in sociocultural context*. Albany: State University of New York Press.

Hair, E. C., Moore, K. A., Garrett, S. B., Ling, T., & Cleveland, K. (2008). The continued importance of quality parent–adolescent relationships during late adolescence, *Journal of Research on Adolescence, 18*, 187–200.

Haith, M. M., Bergman, T., & Moore, M. J. (1977). *Eye contact and face scanning in early infancy*. Unpublished manuscript, University of Denver.

Halberstadt, A. G., Denham, S. A., & Dunsmore, J. C. (2001). Affective social competence. *Social Development, 10*, 79–119.

Hales, D. J., Lozoff, B., Sosa, R., & Kennell, J. H. (1977). Defining the limits of the maternal sensitive period. *Developmental Medicine & Child Neurology, 19*, 454–461.

Hall, G. S. (1904). *Adolescence: Its psychology and its relations to physiology, anthropology, sociology, sex, crime, religion, and education*. New York: Appleton.

Halperin, J. M., Kalmar, J. H., Schulz, K. P., Marks, D. J., Vanshdeep, S., & Newcorn, J. H. (2006). Elevated childhood serotonergic function protects against adolescent aggression in disruptive boys. *Journal of the American Academy of Child and Adolescent Psychiatry, 45*, 833–40.

Halpern, D. F. (2000). *Sex differences in cognitive abilities* (3rd ed.). Mahwah, NJ: Erlbaum.

Halpern, D. F., Benbow, C. P., Geary, D. C., Gur, R. C., Hyde, J. S., & Gernsbacher, M. A. (2007). The science of sex differences in science and mathematics. *Psychological Science in the Public Interest, 8*, 1–51.

Halverson, C. F., & Deal, J. E. (2001). Temperamental changes, parenting and the family context. In T. D. Wachs & G. A. Kohnstamm (Eds.), *Temperament in context* (pp. 61–80). Mahwah, NJ: Erlbaum.

Hamann, S. (2005). Sex differences in the responses of the human amygdala. *Neuroscientist, 11*, 288–293.

Hammen, C. (2002). Context of stress in families with depressed parents. In S. H. Goodman & I. Gotlib (Eds.), *Children of depressed parents* (pp. 175–202). Washington, DC: American Psychological Association.

Hammen, C. (2005). Stress and depression. *Annual Review of Clinical Psychology, 1*, 293–319.

Hammen, C. (2009). Children of depressed parents. In I. H. Gotlib & C. L. Hammen (Eds.), *Handbook of depression* (2nd ed., pp. 275–297). New York: Guilford Press.

Hampson, S. E., Goldberg, L. R., Vogt, T. M., & Dubanoski, J. P. (2006). Forty years on: Teachers' assessments of children's personality traits predict self-reported health behaviors and outcomes at midlife. *Health Psychology, 25*, 57–64.

Han, W.-J. (2005). Maternal nonstandard work schedules and child cognitive outcomes. *Child Development, 76*, 137–154.

Han, W.-J., Waldfogel, J., & Brooks-Gunn, J. (2001). The effects of early maternal employment on later cognitive and behavioral outcomes. *Journal of Marriage and Family, 63*, 336–354.

Hane, A. A., Cheah, C., Rubin, K. H., & Fox, N. A. (2008). The role of maternal behavior in the relation between shyness and social reticence in early childhood and social withdrawal in middle childhood. *Social Development, 17*, 795–811.

Hanish, L. D., & Guerra, N. G. (2004). Aggressive victims, passive victims, and bullies: Developmental continuity or developmental change. *Merrill-Palmer Quarterly Review, 50*, 17–38.

Hansen, M., Bower, C., Milne, E., de Klerk, N., & Kurinczuk, J. J. (2005). Assisted reproductive technologies and the risk of birth defects—A systematic review. *Human Reproduction, 20*, 328–338.

Hanson, T. L. (1999). Does parent conflict explain why divorce is negatively associated with child welfare? *Social Forces, 72*, 1283–1316.

Harbaugh, B. T., Mayr, U., & Burghart, D. (2007). Neural responses to taxation and voluntary giving reveal motives for charitable donations. *Science, 316*, 1622–1625.

Harden, K. P., Lynch, S. K., Turkheimer, E., Emery, R. E., D'Onofrio, B. M., Slutske, W. S., . . . Martin, N. G. (2007). A behavior genetic investigation of adolescent motherhood and offspring mental health problems. *Journal of Abnormal Psychology, 116*, 667–683.

Harker, L., & Keltner, D. (2001). Expressions of positive emotion in women's college yearbook pictures and their relationship to personality and life outcomes across adulthood. *Journal of Personality and Social Psychology, 80*, 112–124.

Harkness, S., & Super, C. M. (2002). Culture and parenting. In M. H. Bornstein (Ed.), *Handbook of parenting: Vol. 2. Biology and ecology of parenting* (2nd ed., pp. 253–280). Mahwah, NJ: Erlbaum.

Harlow, H. F. (1964). Early social deprivation and later behavior in the monkey. In A. Abrams, H. H. Gurner, & J. E. P. Tomal (Eds.), *Unfinished tasks in the behavioral sciences* (pp. 154–173). Baltimore: Williams & Wilkins.

Harlow, H. F., & Suomi, S. J. (1971). Social recovery by isolation reared monkeys. *Proceedings of the National Academy of Sciences USA, 68*, 1534–1538.

Harlow, H. F., & Zimmerman, R. R. (1959). Affectional responses in the infant monkey. *Science, 130*, 421–432.

Harper, M. S., Dickson, J. W., & Welsh, D. P. (2006). Self-silencing and rejection sensitivity in adolescent romantic relationships. *Journal of Youth & Adolescence, 35*, 459–467.

Harper, M. S., & Welsh, D. P. (2007). Keeping quiet: Self-silencing and its association with relational and individual functioning among adolescent romantic couples. *Journal of Social & Personal Relationships, 24*, 99–116.

Harris, J. (1995). Where is the child's environment? A group socialization theory of development. *Psychological Review, 102*, 458–489.

Harris, P. L. (1989). *Children and emotion*. New York: Blackwell.

Harris, P. L. (2006). Social cognition. In W. Damon & R. M. Lerner (Series Eds.), & D. Kuhn & R. Siegler (Vol. Eds.), *Handbook of child psychology: Vol. 2. Cognition, perception, and language* (6th ed., pp. 811–858). Hoboken, NJ: Wiley.

Harris, P. L., Olthof, T., Meerum Terwogt, M., & Hardman, C. E. (1987). Children's knowledge of the situations that provide emotions. *International Journal of Behavioral Development, 10*, 319–343.

Harris-Britt, A., Valerie, C. R., Kurtz-Costes, B., & Rowley, S. J. (2007). Perceived racial discrimination and self-esteem in African American youth: Racial socialization as a protective factor. *Journal of Research on Adolescence, 17*, 669–682.

Harrison, A. O., Wilson, M. N., Pine, C. J., Chan, S. O., & Buriel, R. (1990). Family ecologies of ethnic minority children. *Child Development, 61*, 347–362.

Harrison, L. J., & Ungerer, J. A. (2002). Maternal employment and infant-mother attachment security at 12 months postpartum. *Developmental Psychology, 38*, 758–773.

Harrist, A. W., Pettit, G. S., Dodge, K. A., & Bates, J. E. (1994). Dyadic synchrony in mother-child interaction: Relation with children's subsequent kindergarten adjustment. [Special Issue: *Family processes and child and adolescent development*]. *Family Relations, 43*, 417–424.

Harsha, K. (2009, January). *Is your child "sexting"?* WCAX-TV. Retrieved from: http://www.wcax.com/Global/story.asp?S=9612361&nav=menu183_2.

Hart, B., & Risley, T. R. (1995). *Meaningful differences in the everyday experience of young American children*. Baltimore: Brookes.

Hart, C. H., Yang, C., Nelson, D. A., Jin, S., Bazarskaya, N., & Nelson, L. (1998). Peer contact patterns, parenting practices, and preschoolers' social competence in China, Russia, and the United States. In P. Slee & K. Rigby (Eds.), *Peer relations amongst children: Current issues and future directions* (pp. 3–30). London: Routledge.

Hart, D., & Fegley, S. (1995). Prosocial behavior and caring in adolescence: Relations to self-understanding and social judgment. *Child Development, 66*, 1346–1359.

Hart, S., Field, T., DelValle, C., & Letourneau, M. (1998). Infants protest their mothers attending to an infant-size doll. *Social Development, 7*, 54–61.

Harter, S. (1982). The Perceived Competence Scale for Children. *Child Development, 53*, 87–97.

Harter, S. (1999). *The construction of the self: A developmental perspective*. New York: Guilford Press.

Harter, S. (2006). The self. In W. Damon & R. M. Lerner (Series Eds.), & N. Eisenberg (Vol. Ed.), *Handbook of child psychology: Vol. 3. Social, emotional, and personality development* (6th ed., pp. 505–570). Hoboken, NJ: Wiley.

Harter, S., & Buddin, B. J. (1987). Children's understanding of the simultaneity of two emotions: A five-stage developmental acquisition sequence. *Developmental Psychology, 23*, 388–399.

Hartl, D. L., & Jones, E. W. (2005). *Essential genetics* (4th ed.). London: Jones and Bartlett.

Hartmann, D. P., & Pelzel, K. E. (2005). Design, measurement, and analysis in developmental research. In M. H. Bornstein & M. Lamb (Eds.), *Developmental science: An advanced textbook* (5th ed., pp. 103–186). Mahwah, NJ: Erlbaum.

Hartup, W. W. (1996). The company they keep: Friendships and their developmental significance. *Child Development, 67*, 1–13.

Hartup, W. W., & Abecassis, M. (2002). Friends and enemies. In P. K. Smith & C. H. Hart (Eds.), *Blackwell handbook of childhood social development* (pp. 285–306). Malden, MA: Blackwell.

Hartup, W. W., Laursen, B., Stewart, M. I., & Eastenson, A. (1988). Conflict and the friendship relations of young children. *Child Development, 59*, 1590–1600.

Harvey, E. (1999). Short-term and long-term effects of early parental employment on children of the National Longitudinal Survey of Youth. *Developmental Psychology, 35*, 445–459.

Harwood, R. L., Miller, J. G., & Irizarry, N. L. (1995). *Culture and attachment: Perceptions of the child in context.* New York: Guilford Press.

Hasebe, Y., Nucci, L., & Nucci, M. S. (2004). Parental control of the personal domain and adolescent symptoms of psychopathology: A cross-national study in the United States and Japan. *Child Development, 75*, 815–828.

Hastings, P. D., Rubin, K., & De-Rose, L. (2005). Links among gender, inhibition, and parental socialization in the development of prosocial behavior. *Merrill-Palmer Quarterly, 51*, 501–527.

Hastings, P. D., Utendale, W. T., & Sullivan, C. (2007). The socialization of prosocial behavior. In J. Grusec & P. Hastings (Eds.), *The handbook of socialization* (pp. 638–664). New York: Guilford Press.

Hastings, P. D., Zahn-Waxler, C., & McShane, K. E. (2005). We are, by nature, moral creatures: The biology of concern for others. In M. Killen & J. G. Smetana (Eds.), *Handbook of moral development* (pp. 483–516). New York: Erlbaum.

Hatchett, S. J., & Jackson, J. S. (1993). African American extended kin systems: An assessment. In H. P. McAdoo (Ed.), *Family ethnicity: Strength in diversity* (pp. 90–108). Thousand Oaks, CA: Sage.

Hauser, D. (2004). *Five years of abstinence-only-until-marriage education: Assessing the impact.* Washington, DC: Advocates for Youth.

Havinghurst, R. F., & Neugarten, B. L. (1955). *American Indian and white children.* Chicago: University of Chicago Press.

Hawkins, J. D., Catalano, R. F., Kosterman, R., Abbott, R., & Hill, K. G. (1999). Preventing adolescent health-risk behaviours by strengthening protection during childhood. *Archives of Paediatrics and Adolescent Medicine, 153*, 226–234.

Hawley, P. H. (1999). The ontogenesis of social dominance: A strategy-based evolutionary perspective. *Developmental Review, 19*, 97–132.

Hawley, P. H. (2002). Social dominance and prosocial and coercive strategies of resource control in preschoolers. *International Journal of Behavioral Development, 26*, 167–176.

Hawley, P. H. (2003a). Prosocial and coercive configurations of resource control in early adolescence: A case for the well-adapted Machiavellian. *Merrill-Palmer Quarterly, 49*, 279–309.

Hawley, P. H. (2003b). Strategies of control, aggression, and morality in preschoolers: An evolutionary perspective. *Journal of Experimental Child Psychology, 85*, 213–235.

Hawley, P. H. (2007). Social dominance in childhood and adolescence. In P. H. Hawley, T. D. Little, & P. Rodkin (Eds.), *Aggression and adaptation: The bright side to bad behavior* (pp. 1–27). Mahwah, NJ: Erlbaum.

Hawley, P. H., & Little, T. D. (1999). On winning some and losing some: A social relations approach to social dominance in toddlers. *Merrill-Palmer Quarterly, 45*, 188–214.

Hawley, P. H., Little, T. D., & P. Rodkin (Eds.) (2007). *Aggression and adaptation: The bright side to bad behavior.* Hillsdale, NJ: Erlbaum.

Hay, D. F. (1994). Prosocial development. *Journal of Child Psychology and Psychiatry, 35*, 29–71.

Hay, D. F., Castle, J., & Davies, L. (2000). Toddlers' use of force against familiar peers: A precursor of serious aggression? *Child Development, 71*, 457–467.

Hay, D. F., & Ross, H. S. (1982). The social nature of early conflict. *Child Development, 53*, 105–113.

Hayden, L., Turulli, D., & Hymel, S. (1988, May). *Children talk about loneliness.* Paper presented at the biennial meeting of the University of Waterloo Conference on Child Development, Waterloo, Ontario, Canada.

Hazan, C., & Shaver, P. R. (1987). Romantic love conceptualized as an attachment process. *Journal of Personality and Social Psychology, 52*, 511–524.

Hazan, C., & Shaver, P. R. (1990). Love and work: An attachment-theoretical perspective. *Journal of Personality and Social Psychology, 59*, 270–280.

Heath, S. B. (1983). *Ways with words.* Cambridge, UK: Cambridge University Press.

Heaven, P. C. L., Ciarrochi, J., & Vialle, W. (2008). Self-nominated peer crowds, school achievement, and psychological adjustment in adolescents: Longitudinal analysis. *Personality and Individual Differences, 44*, 977–988.

Heekeren, H. R., Wartenburger, I., Schmidt, H., Schwintowski, H.-P., & Villringer, A. (2003). An fMRI study of simple ethical decision-making. *NeuroReport, 14*, 1215–1219.

Heintz-Knowles, K. E. (2001). Balancing acts: Work-family issues on prime-time TV. In J. Bryant & J. A. Bryant (Eds.), *Television and the American family* (2nd ed., pp. 177–206). Mahwah, NJ: Erlbaum.

Heinz, A., Braus, D. F., Smolka, M. N., Wrase, J., Puls, I., Hermann, D., . . . Büchel, C. (2005). Amygdala-prefrontal coupling depends on a genetic variation of the serotonin transporter. *Nature Neuroscience, 8*, 20–21.

Helwig, C. C. (1998). Children's conceptions of fair government and freedom of speech. *Child Development, 69*, 518–531.

Helwig, C. C. (2003). Culture and the construction of concepts of personal autonomy and democratic decision making.

In J. E. Jacobs & P. A. Klaczynski (Eds.), *The development of judgment and decision making in children and adolescents* (pp. 181–212). Mahwah, NJ: Erlbaum.

Helwig, C. C. (2006). Rights, civil liberties, and democracy across cultures. In M. Killen & J. G. Smetana (Eds.), *Handbook of moral development* (pp. 185–210). Mahwah, NJ: Erlbaum.

Helwig, C. C., Arnold, M. L., Tan, D., & Boyd, D. (2003). Chinese adolescents' reasoning about democratic and authority-based decision making in peer, family, and school contexts. *Child Development, 74,* 783–800.

Helwig, C. C., Arnold, M. L., Tan, D., & Boyd, D. (2007). Mainland Chinese and Canadian adolescents' judgments and reasoning about the fairness of democratic and other forms of government. *Cognitive Development, 22,* 96–109.

Helwig, C. C., & Turiel, E. (2010). Children's social and moral reasoning. In P. K. Smith & C. H. Hart (Eds.), *Wiley-Blackwell handbook of childhood social development* (2nd ed.). Oxford, UK: Wiley-Blackwell.

Helwig, C. C., Zelazo, P. D., & Wilson, M. (2001). Children's judgments of psychological harm in normal and noncanonical situations. *Child Development, 72,* 66–81.

Hembree, S. E., & Vandell, D. (2000). *Reciprocity in rejection: The mutual role of antipathy and children's adjustment.* Unpublished manuscript, University of Wisconsin, Madison.

Hendrick, J., & Stange, T. (1991). Do actions speak louder than words? An effect of the functional use of language on dominant sex role behavior in boys and girls. *Early Childhood Research Quarterly, 6,* 565–576.

Henggeler, S. W., Edwards, J. J., Cohen, R., & Summerville, M. B. (1991). Predicting changes in children's popularity: The role of family relations. *Journal of Applied Developmental Psychology, 12,* 205–218.

Henggeler, S. W., Schoenwald, S. K., Borduin, C. M., Rowland, M. D., & Cunningham, P. B. (2009). *Multisystemic therapy for antisocial behavior in children and adolescents* (2nd ed.). New York: Guilford Press.

Henker, B., & Whalen, C. K. (1999). The child with attention deficit/hyperactivity disorder in school and peer settings. In H. C. Quay & A. E. Hogan (Eds.). *Handbook of disruptive behavior disorders* (157–178). New York: Plenum Press.

Herbert, J., & Martinez, M. (2001). Brain mechanisms in aggressive behavior. In J. Hill & B. Maughan (Eds.), *Conduct disorders in childhood and adolescence* (pp. 67–102). Cambridge, UK: Cambridge University Press.

Herrenkohl, T. I., Hill, K. G., Chung, I-J., Guo, J., Abbott, R. D., & Hawkins, J. D. (2003). Protective factors against serious violent behavior in adolescence: A prospective study of aggressive children. *Social Work Research, 27,* 179–191.

Herrenkohl, T. I., Tajima, E. A., Whitney, S. D., & Huang, B. (2005). Protection against antisocial behavior in children exposed to physically abusive discipline. *Journal of Adolescent Health, 36,* 457–465.

Herrera, N. C., Zajonc, R. B., Wieczorkowska, G., & Cichomski, B. (2003). Beliefs about birth rank and their reflection in reality. *Journal of Personality and Social Psychology, 85,* 142–150.

Herrold, K., & O'Donnell, K. (2008). Parent and Family Involvement in Education, 2006–07 School Year. From the National Household Education Surveys Program of 2007 (NCES 2008-050). Washington, DC: National Center for Education Statistics, Institute of Education Sciences, U.S. Department of Education.

Hespos, S. J., & Spelke, E. S. (2004). Conceptual precursors to language. *Nature, 430,* 453–456.

Hess, C. R., Papas, M. A., & Black, M. M. (2002). Resilience among African American adolescent mothers: Predictors of positive parenting in early infancy. *Journal of Pediatric Psychology, 27,* 619–629.

Hesse, E. (2008). The Adult Attachment Interview: Protocol, method of analysis, and empirical studies. In J. Cassidy & P. R. Shaver (Eds.), *Handbook of attachment: Theory, research, and clinical applications* (2nd ed., pp. 552–598). New York: Guilford Press.

Hetherington, E. M. (1965). A developmental study of the effects of sex of the dominant parent on sex-role preference, identification, and imitation in children. *Journal of Personality and Social Psychology, 2,* 188–194.

Hetherington, E. M. (1972). Effects of father absence on personality development in adolescent daughters. *Developmental Psychology, 7,* 313–326.

Hetherington, E. M. (1989). Coping with family transitions: Winners, losers and survivors. *Child Development, 60,* 1–14.

Hetherington, E. M. (1991). Families, lies and videotapes. *Journal of Adolescent Research, 1,* 323–348.

Hetherington, E. M. (1998). Relevant issues in developmental science: Introduction to the special issue. *American Psychologist, 53,* 167–184.

Hetherington, E. M. (2006). The influence of conflict, marital problem solving, and parenting on children's adjustment in non-divorced, divorced, and remarried families. In A. Clarke-Stewart & J. Dunn (Eds.), *Families count* (pp. 203–237). New York: Cambridge University Press.

Hetherington, E. M., Bridges, M., & Insabella, G. M. (1998). Five perspectives on the association between divorce and remarriage and children's adjustment. *American Psychologist, 53,* 167–184.

Hetherington, E. M., & Clingempeel, W. G. (1992). Coping with marital transitions: A family systems perspective. *Monographs of the Society for Research in Child Development, 57* (Serial No. 227).

Hetherington, E. M., & Jodl, K. M. (1994). Stepfamilies as settings for child development. In A Booth & J. Dunn (Eds.), *Stepfamilies: Who benefits? Who does not?* (pp. 55–79). Hillsdale, NJ: Erlbaum.

Hetherington, E. M., & Kelly, J. (2002). *For better or for worse.* New York: Norton.

Hetherington, E. M., & Stanley-Hagan, M. (2002). Parenting in divorced, single-parent, and stepfamilies. In M. H. Bornstein (Ed.), *Handbook of parenting: Vol. 3. Being and becoming a parent* (2nd ed., pp. 287–316). Mahwah, NJ: Erlbaum.

Hewlett, B. S. (2004). *Fathers in forager, farmer, and pastoral cultures.* Hoboken, NJ: Wiley.

Heyman, G. D. (2008). Children's critical thinking when learning from others. *Current Directions in Psychological Science, 17*, 344–347.

Heyman, G. D., Fu, G., & Lee, K. (2007). Evaluating claims people make about themselves: The development of skepticism. *Child Development, 78*, 367–375.

Heyman, G. D., & Gelman, S. A. (1999). The use of trait labels in making psychological inferences. *Child Development, 70*, 604–619.

Heyman, G. D., & Giles, J. W. (2006). Gender and psychological essentialism. *Enfance, 58*, 293–310.

Heyman, G. D., & Legare, C. H. (2005). Children's evaluation of sources of information about traits. *Developmental Psychology, 41*, 636–647.

Higgins, T., Everette, A., Fleming, D., Christon, L., Kinsley, C. H., & Lambert, K. G. (2007, June). Maternal experience enhances neurobiological and behavioral responses in an attention set-shifting paradigm. Presentation at the International Behavioral Neuroscience Society, Rio de Janeiro, Brazil.

Hill, D. B., Rozanski, C., Carfagnini, J., & Willoughby, B. (2007). Gender identity disorders in childhood and adolescence: A critical inquiry. *International Journal of Sexual Health, 19*, 57–75.

Hill, N. E. (2010). Culturally-based worldviews, family processes, and family-school interactions. In S. Christenson & A. Reschly (Eds.), *Handbook on school-family partnerships for promoting student competence* (pp. 101–128). New York: Routledge.

Hill, N. E., & Bromell, L. (2008). *Ethnic and SES differences in the corroboration of teachers' and parents' reports of child behavior across early elementary school.* Unpublished manuscript, Durham, NC.

Hill, N. E., Bush, K. R., & Roosa, M. W. (2003). Parenting and family socialization strategies and children's mental health: Low-income, Mexican-American and Euro-American mothers and children. *Child Development, 74*, 189–204.

Hill, N. E., & Tyson, D. F. (2009). Parental involvement in middle school: A meta-analytic assessment of the strategies that promote achievement. *Developmental Psychology, 45*, 740–763.

Hill, S. A., & Sprague, J. (1999). Parenting in Black and White families. *Gender and Society, 13*, 480–502.

Hinde, R. A. (1997). *Relationships: A dialectical perspective.* London: Routledge.

Hinduja, S., & Patchin, J. (2007). Offline consequences of online victimization: School violence and delinquency. *Journal of School Violence, 6*, 89–112.

Hinduja, S., & Patchin, J. W. (2009). *Bullying beyond the schoolyard: Preventing and responding to cyberbullying.* Thousand Oaks, CA: Corwin Press

Hines, M. (2004). *Brain gender.* New York: Oxford University Press.

Hines, M. (2009). Gonadal hormones and sexual differentiation of human brain and behavior. In D. W. Pfaff, A. P. Arnold, A. M. Etgen, S. E. Fahrback, & R. T. Rubin (Eds.), *Hormones, brain & behavior: Vol. 4. Development of hormone-dependent neuronal systems, sexual differentation* (2nd ed., pp. 1869–1909). New York: Academic Press.

Hines, S. (2006). What's the difference? Bringing particularity to queer studies of transgender. *Journal of Gender Studies, 15*, 49–66.

Hinshaw, S. P., Owens, E. B., Wells, K. C., Kraemer, H. C., Abikoff, H. B., Arnold, L. E., . . . Wigal, T. (2000). Family processes and treatment outcome in the MTA: Negative/ineffective parenting practices in relation to multimodal treatment. *Journal of Abnormal Child Psychology, 28*, 555–568.

Hirschfeld, L. A. (1996). *Race in the making: Cognition, culture, and the child's construction of human kinds.* Cambridge, MA: MIT Press.

Hirschfeld, L. A. (2008). Children's developing conceptions of race. In S. M. Quintana & C. McKown (Eds.), *Handbook of race, racism, and the developing child* (pp. 37–54). Hoboken, NJ: Wiley.

Hiscock, M., Israelian, M., Inch, R., Jacek, C., & Hiscock-Kalil, C. (1995). Is there a sex difference in human laterality? II. An exhaustive survey of visual laterality studies from six neuropsychology journals. *Journal of Clinical & Experimental Neuropsychology, 17*, 590–610.

Hobara, M. (2003). Prevalence of transitional objects in young children in Tokyo and New York. *Infant Mental Health Journal, 24*, 174–191.

Hodges, E. V. E., Boivin, M., Vitaro, F., & Bukowski, W. M. (1999). The power of friendship: Protection against an escalating cycle of peer victimization. *Developmental Psychology, 35*, 94–101.

Hodges, E. V. E., Malone, M. J., & Perry, D. G. (1997). Individual risk and social risk as interacting determinants of victimization in the peer group. *Developmental Psychology, 33*, 1032–1039.

Hodges, E. V. E., & Perry, D. G. (1999). Personal and interpersonal antecedents and consequences of victimization by peers. *Journal of Personality and Social Psychology, 76*, 677–685.

Hoff, E. (2006). How social contexts support and shape language development. *Developmental Review, 26*, 55–88.

Hoff, E., Laursen, B., & Tardif, T. (2002). Socioeconomic status and parenting. In M. H. Bornstein (Ed.), *Handbook of parenting: Vol. 2. Biology and ecology of parenting* (2nd ed., pp. 231–252). Mahwah, NJ: Erlbaum.

Hoff, E., & Naigles, L. (2002). How children use input to acquire a lexicon. *Child Development, 73*, 418–433.

Hofferth, S. L., & Sandberg, J. F. (2001). How American children spend their time. *Journal of Marriage and Family, 63*, 295–308.

Hoff-Ginsberg, E. & Tardif, T. (1995). Socioeconomic status and parenting. In M. H. Bornstein (Ed.), *Handbook of parenting: Vol. 2. Biology and ecology of parenting* (2nd ed, pp. 161–188). Mahwah, NJ: Erlbaum.

Hoffman, C., Crnic, K., & Baker, J. K. (2006). Maternal depression and parenting: Implications for children's emergent emotion regulation and behavioral functioning. *Parenting: Science and Practice, 6*, 271–295.

Hoffman, L. W. (2000). Maternal employment: Effects of social context. In R. D. Taylor & M. C. Wang (Eds.), *Resilience across contexts: Family, work, culture and community* (pp. 147–176). Mahwah, NJ: Erlbaum.

Hoffman, L. W., & Youngblade, L. M. (1999). *Mothers at work: Effects on children's well-being*. New York: Cambridge University Press.

Hoffman, M. L. (1981). Is altruism part of human nature? *Journal of Personality and Social Psychology, 40*, 121–137.

Hoffman, M. L. (1984). Empathy, its limitations, and its role in a comprehensive moral theory. In W. M. Kurtines & J. L. Gewirtz (Eds.), *Morality, moral behavior and moral development* (pp. 283–302). New York: Wiley.

Hoffman, M. L. (2000). *Empathy and moral development: Implications for caring and justice*. Cambridge, UK: Cambridge University Press.

Hogan, D., & Msall, M. E. (2002). Family structure and resources and the parenting of children with disabilities and functional limitations. In J. G. Borkowski, S. L. Ramey, & M. Bristol-Power (Eds.), *Parenting and the child's world* (pp. 311–328). Mahwah, NJ: Erlbaum.

Hogan, M. J. (2001). Parents and other adults: Models and monitors of healthy media habits. In D. G. Singer & J. L. Singer (Eds.), *Handbook of children and the media* (pp. 663–680). Thousand Oaks, CA: Sage.

Hoglund, W. L. G., Lalone, C. E., & Leadbeater, B. J. (2008). Social-cognitive competence, peer rejection and neglect, and behavioral and emotional problems in middle childhood. *Social Development, 17*, 528–553.

Holcombe, E., Peterson, K., & Manlove, J. (2009). Ten reasons to *still* keep the focus on teen childbearing. *Child Trends Research Brief, 2009–10*. Retrieved from: www.childtrends.org

Holden, G. W. (2002). Perspectives on the effects of corporal punishment: Comment on Gershoff (2002). *Psychological Bulletin, 128*, 590–595.

Holden, G. W. (2009). *Parenting: A dynamic perspective*. Thousand Oaks, CA: Sage.

Hollich, G. J., Hirsh-Pasek, K., & Golinkoff, R. M. (2000). Breaking the language barrier: An emergentist coalition model for the origins of word learning. *Monographs of the Society for Research in Child Development, 65* (Serial No. 262).

Hollon, S. D., & Dimidjian, S. (2009). Cognitive and behavioral treatment of depression. In I. H. Gotlib & C. L. Hammen (Eds.), *Handbook of depression* (2nd ed., pp. 586–603). New York: Guilford Press.

Hollos, M., Leis, P. E., & Turiel, E. (1986). Social reasoning in Ijo children and adolescents in Nigerian communities. *Journal of Cross-Cultural Psychology, 17*, 352–374.

Holmberg, M. C. (1980). The development of social interchange patterns from 12 to 42 months. *Child Development, 51*, 448–456.

Holton, J. K., & Harding, K. (2007). Healthy Families America: Ruminations on implementing a home visitation program to prevent child maltreatment. *Journal of Prevention & Intervention in the Community, 34*, 13–38.

Hops, H. (1996). Intergenerational transmission of depressive-symptoms: Gender and developmental considerations. In C. Mundt, M. Goldstein, K. Hahlweg, & P. Fiedler (Eds.), *Proceedings of the symposium of interpersonal factors in the origin and course of affective disorders* (pp. 113–129). London: Royal College of Psychiatrists.

Horn, S. S. (2003). Adolescents' reasoning about exclusion from social groups. *Developmental Psychology, 39*, 71–84.

Horn, S. S. (2007). Adolescents' acceptance of same-sex peers based on sexual orientation and gender expression. *Journal of Youth and Adolescence, 36*, 363–371.

Horowitz, S. M., Klerman, T. V., Kuo, H. S., & Jekal, J. F. (1991). School age mothers: Predictors of long term educational and economic outcomes. *Pediatrics, 87*, 862–867.

Hosoda, M., & Stone, D. L. (2000). Current gender stereotypes and their evaluative content. *Perceptual and Motor Skills, 90*, 1283–1294.

Houlette, M. A., Gaertner, S. L., Johnson, K. M., Banker, B. S., Rick, B. M., & Dovidio, J. F. (2004). Developing a more inclusive social identity: An elementary school intervention. *Journal of Social Issues, 60*, 35–55.

Howard, S. (1998). Unbalanced minds? Children's thinking about television. In S. Howard (Ed.), *Wired-up: Young people and the electronic media* (pp. 57–76). London: UCL Press.

Howe, N., Brody, M., & Recchia, H. (2006). Effects of task difficulty on sibling teaching in middle childhood. *Infant & Child Development, 15*, 455–470.

Howe, N., Rinaldi, C. M., Jennings, M., & Petrakos, H. (2002). "No! The lambs can stay out because they got cozies": Constructive and destructive sibling conflict, pretend play, and social understanding. *Child Development, 73*, 1460–1473.

Howe, N., & Ross, H. S. (1990). Socialization, perspective taking and the sibling relationship. *Developmental Psychology, 26,* 160–165.

Howe, T. R., & Parke, R. D. (2001). Friendship quality and sociometric status: Between-group differences and links to loneliness in severely abused and nonabused children. *Child Abuse and Neglect, 25,* 585–606.

Howell, J. C., & Egley, A., Jr. (2005). Moving risk factors into developmental theories of gang membership. *Youth Violence and Juvenile Justice, 3,* 334–354.

Howell, S., & Willis, R. (Eds.)(1989). *Societies at peace: Anthropological perspectives.* New York: Routledge.

Howes, C. (1987). Social competence with peers in young children. Developmental sequences. *Developmental Review, 7,* 252–272.

Howes, C. (1996). The earliest friendships. In W. M. Bukowski, A. F. Newcomb, & W. W. Hartup (Eds.), *The company they keep: Friendship in childhood and adolescence* (pp. 66–86). New York: Cambridge University Press.

Howes, C. (2000). Social-emotional classroom climate in child care, child-teacher relationships and children's second grade peer relations. *Social Development, 9,* 191–204.

Howes, C., Galinsky, E., Shinn, M., Gulcur, L., Clements, M., Sibley, A., Abbott-Shim, M., & McCarthy, J. (1996). *The Florida Child Care Quality Improvement Study.* New York: Families and Work Institute.

Howes, C., Hamilton, C. E., & Matheson, C. C. (1994). Children's relationships with peers: Differential associations with aspects of the teacher-child relationship. *Child Development, 65,* 253–263.

Howes, C., & Lee, L. (2006). *Peer relations in young children.* New York: Psychology Press.

Howes, C., Sanders, K., & Lee, L. (2008). Entering a new peer group in ethnically and linguistically diverse childcare classrooms. *Social Development, 17,* 922–940.

Howes, C., Smith, E., & Galinsky, E. (1995). *The Florida Child Care Quality Improvement Study.* New York: Families and Work Institute.

Howes, C., & Spieker, S. (2008). Attachment relationships in the context of multiple caregivers. In J. Cassidy & P. Shaver (Eds.), *Handbook of attachment: Theory, research, and clinical applications* (2nd ed., pp. 317–332). New York: Guilford Press.

Hsu, H-C., Fogel, A., & Messinger, D. S. (2001). Infant non-distress vocalization during mother-infant face-to-face interaction: Factors associated with quantitative and qualitative differences. *Infant Behavior and Development, 24,* 107–128.

Hudley, C., & Graham, S. (1993). An attributional intervention to reduce peer-directed aggression among African-American boys. *Child Development, 64,* 124–138.

Hudley, C., & Taylor, A. (2006). What is cultural competence and how can it be incorporated into preventive interventions? In N. G. Guerra & E. P. Smith (Eds.), *Preventing youth violence in a multicultural society* (pp. 249–270). Washington, DC: American Psychological Association.

Huesmann, L. R., Eron, L. D., Lefkowitz, M. M., & Walder, L. O. (1984). The stability of aggression over time and generations. *Developmental Psychology, 20,* 1120–1134.

Huesmann, L. R., & Guerra, N. G. (1997). Children's normative beliefs about aggression and aggressive behavior. *Journal of Personality and Social Psychology, 72,* 408–419.

Huesmann, L. R., Moise-Titus, J., Podolski, C., & Eron, L. D. (2003). Longitudinal relations between children's exposure to TV violence and their aggression and violent behavior in young adulthood: 1977–1992. *Developmental Psychology, 39,* 201–221.

Huesmann, L. R., & Taylor, L. D. (2006a). Developmental contexts in middle childhood: Bridges to adolescence and adulthood. In A. C. Huston & M. N. Ripke (Eds.), *Middle childhood: Contexts of development* (pp. 303–326). Cambridge, UK: Cambridge University Press.

Huesmann, L. R., & Taylor, L. D. (2006b). The role of media violence in violent behavior. *Annual Review of Public Health, 27,* 393–415.

Hughes, D., & Chen, L. (1997). When and what parents tell children about race: An examination of race-related socialization among African American families. *Applied Developmental Science, 1,* 200–214.

Hughes, D., & Chen, L. (1999). The nature of parents' race-related communications to children: A developmental perspective. In L. Balter & C. S. Tamis-LeMonda (Eds.), *Child psychology: A handbook of contemporary issues* (pp. 467–490). Philadelphia: Psychology Press/Taylor Francis.

Hughes, J. N., & Kwok, O. (2006). Classroom engagement mediates the effect of teacher-student support on elementary students' peer acceptance: A prospective analysis. *Journal of School Psychology, 43,* 465–480.

Hull, C. L. (1943). *Principles of behavior: An introduction to behavior theory.* New York: Appleton-Century.

Huntemann, N., & Morgan, M. (2001). Mass media and identity development. In D. Singer & J. Singer (Eds.), *Handbook of children and the media* (pp. 309–322). Thousand Oaks, CA: Sage.

Hurst, S., & Laird, J. (2006). Understanding American Indian youth violence and prevention. In N. G. Guerra & E. P. Smith (Eds.), *Preventing youth violence in a multicultural society* (pp. 149–168). Washington, DC: American Psychological Association.

Huston, A. C. (2008). From research to policy and back. *Child Development, 79,* 1–12.

Huston, A. C., Bickham, D. S., Lee, J. H., & Wright, J. C. (2007). From attention to comprehension: How children watch and learn from television. In N. Pecora, J. Murray, & E. A. Wartella (Eds.), *Children and television: Fifty years of research* (pp. 41–64). Mahwah, NJ: Erlbaum.

Huston, A. C., & Rosencrantz Aronson, S. (2005). Mothers' time with infant and time in employment as predictors of mother-child relationships and children's early development. *Child Development, 76,* 467–482.

Huston, A. C., & Wright, J. C. (1998). Mass media and children's development. In W. Damon (Series Ed.), & I. E. Sigel & K. A. Renninger (Vol. Eds.), *Handbook of child psychology: Vol. 4. Child psychology in practice* (5th ed., pp. 999–1058). New York: Wiley.

Huttenlocher, J. (1974). The origins of language comprehension. In R. L. Solso (Ed.), *Theories in cognitive psychology* (pp. 331–368). Hillsdale, NJ: Erlbaum.

Huttenlocher, J., Haight, W., Bryk, A., Seltzer, M., & Lyons, T. (1991). Early vocabulary growth: Relation to language impact and gender. *Developmental Psychology, 27,* 236–248.

Huttenlocher, J., Smiley, P., & Charney, R. (1987). Emergence of action categories in the child: Evidence from verb meanings. *Psychological Review, 90,* 72–93.

Huttenlocher, P. R. (1994). Synaptogenesis, synapse elimination, and neural plasticity in human cerebral cortex. In C. A. Nelson (Ed.), *Minnesota Symposia on Child Psychology: Vol. 27. Threats to optimal development* (pp. 35–54). Hillsdale, NJ: Erlbaum.

Huttenlocher, P. R., & Dabholkar, A. J. (1997). Regional differences in synaptogenesis in the human cerebral cortex. *Journal of Comparative Neurology, 387,* 167–178.

Hwang, P. (1987). The changing role of Swedish fathers. In M. E. Lamb (Ed.), *The father's role: Cross-cultural perspectives* (pp. 115–138). Hillsdale, NJ: Erlbaum.

Hyde, J. S. (2005). The gender similarities hypothesis. *American Psychologist, 60,* 581–592.

Hyde, J. S., Krajnik, M., & Skuldt-Neiderberger, K. (1991). Androgyny across the life span: A replication and longitudinal follow-up. *Developmental Psychology, 27,* 516–519.

Hymel, S. (1986). Interpretations of peer behavior: Affective bias in childhood and adolescence. *Child Development, 57,* 431–445.

Hymel, S., Closson, L. M., Caravita, S. C. S., & Vaillancourt, T. (2010). Social status among peers: From sociometric attraction to peer acceptance to perceived popularity. In P. K. Smith & C. H. Hart (Eds.), *Wiley-Blackwell handbook of childhood social development* (2nd ed.). Oxford, UK: Wiley-Blackwell.

Hymel, S., Vaillancourt, T., McDougall, P., & Renshaw, P. (2002). Acceptance and rejection by the peer group. In P. K. Smith, & C. H. Hart (Eds.), *Blackwell handbook of childhood social development* (pp. 265–284). London: Blackwell.

Hymel, S., Wagner, E., & Butler, L. (1990). Reputational bias: View from the peer group. In S. R. Asher & J. D. Coie (Eds.), *Peer rejection in childhood* (pp. 156–188). New York: Cambridge University Press.

Hymowitz, K. (2008). Quoted in S. Smith, *Grow up: Gamers over 20 are labeled "child-men."* Retrieved from: http://www.monstersandcritics.com/gaming/xbox360/news/article_1389095.php/Grow_up_Gamers_over_20_are_labelled_Child-men

Iacoboni, M., & Dapretto, M. (2006). The mirror neuron system and the consequences of its dysfunction. *Nature Reviews Neuroscience, 7,* 942–951.

Iacoboni, M., Molnar-Szakacs I., Gallese V., Buccino G., Mazziotta J. C., & Rizzolatti, G. (2005). Grasping the intentions of others with one's own mirror neuron system. *PLoS Biol3*(3), e79.

Iacoboni, M., Woods, R. P., Brass, M., Bekkering, H., Mazziotta, J. C., & Rizzolatti, G. (1999). Cortical mechanisms of human imitation. *Science, 286,* 2526–2528.

Ialongo, N., Poduska, J., Werthamer, L. & Kellam. S. (2001). The distal impact of two first-grade preventive interventions on conduct problems and disorder in early adolescence. *Journal of Emotional and Behavioral Disorders, 9,* 146–160.

Iervolino, A. C., Hines, M., Golombok, S. E., Rust, J., & Plomin, R. (2005). Genetic and environmental influences on sex-typed behavior during the preschool years. *Child Development, 76,* 826–840.

Inoff-Germain, G., Arnold, G. S., Nottleman, E. D., Susman, E. J., Cutler, G. B., & Chrousos, G. P. (1988). Relations between hormone levels and observational measures of aggressive behavior of young adolescents in family interactions. *Developmental Psychology, 24,* 129–139.

Institute of Medicine. (2004). *Ethical conduct of clinical research involving children.* Washington, DC: National Academic Press.

Irizarry, K. J., & Galbraith, S. J. (2004). Complex disorders reloaded: Causality, action, reaction, cause, and effect. *Molecular Psychiatry, 9,* 431–432.

Irvine, A. B., Biglan, A., Smolkowski, K., Metzler, C. W., & Ary, D. V. (1999). The effectiveness of a parenting skills program for parents of middle school students in small communities. *Journal of Consulting and Clinical Psychology, 67,* 811–825.

Irwin, A. R., & Gross, A. M. (1995). Cognitive tempo, violent video games, and aggressive behavior in young boys. *Journal of Family Violence, 10,* 337–350.

Irwin, E. C. (1985). Puppets in therapy: An assessment procedure. *American Journal of Psychotherapy, 39,* 389–400.

Isaacowitz, D. M., Wadlinger, H. A., Goren, D., & Wilson, H. R. (2006). Is there an age related positivity effect in visual attention? A comparison of two methodologies. *Emotion, 6,* 511–516.

Isabella, R. (1993). Origins of attachment: Maternal interactive behavior across the first year. *Child Development, 64,* 605–621.

Ishikawa, F., & Hay, D. F. (2006). Triadic interaction among newly acquainted 2-year-olds. *Social Development, 15,* 145–168.

Isley, S. L., O'Neil, R., Clatfelter, D., & Parke, R. D. (1999). Parent and child expressed affect and children's social competence: Modeling direct and indirect pathways. *Developmental Psychology, 35,* 547–560.

Isley, S., O'Neil, R., & Parke, R. D. (1996). The relation of parental affect and control behaviors to children's classroom acceptance: A concurrent and predictive analysis. *Early Education & Development, 7,* 7–23.

Izard, C. E. (1994). Innate and universal facial expressions: Evidence from developmental and cross-cultural research. *Psychological Bulletin, 115,* 288–299.

Izard, C. E., & Dougherty, L. M. (1982). Two complementary systems for measuring facial expressions in infants and children. In C. E. Izard (Ed.), *Measuring emotions in infants and children* (pp. 97–126). New York: Cambridge University Press.

Izard, C. E., Fantauzzo, C. A., Castle, J. M., Haynes, O. M., & Slomine, B. S. (1995). *The morphological stability and social validity of infants' facial expressions.* Unpublished manuscript, University of Delaware.

Izard, C. E., Hembree, E., Dougherty, L. M., & Spizzirri, C. C. (1983). Changes in facial expressions of 2- to 19-month-old infants following acute pain. *Developmental Psychology, 19,* 418–426.

Izard, C. E., Hembree, E., & Huebner, R. (1987). Infants' emotional expressions to acute pain: Developmental changes and stability of individual differences. *Developmental Psychology, 23,* 105–113.

Izard, C. E., King, K. A., Trentacosta, C. J., Morgan, J. K., Laurenceau, J.-P., Krauthamer-Ewing, E. S., & Finlon, K. J. (2008). Accelerating development of emotion competence in Head Start children: Effects on adaptive and maladaptive behavior. *Development & Psychopathology, 20,* 369–397.

Jabbi, M., Swart, M., & Keysers, C. (2007). Empathy for positive and negative emotions in the gustatory cortex. *NeuroImage, 34,* 1744–1753.

Jaccard, J., Blanton, H., & Dodge, T. (2005). Peer influences on risk behavior: An analysis of the effects of a close friend. *Developmental Psychology, 41,* 135–147.

Jacobsen, T., & Hofmann, V. (1997). Children's attachment representations: Longitudinal relations to school behavior and academic competency in middle childhood and adolescence. *Developmental Psychology, 33,* 703–710.

Jaffe, J., Beebe, B., Feldstein, S., Crown, C. L., & Jasnow, M. D. (2001). Rhythms of dialogue in infancy. *Monographs of the Society for Research in Child Development, 66* (Serial No. 265).

Jaffee, S. R., Caspi, A., Moffit, T. E., Dodge, K. A., Rutter, M., & Taylor, A. (2005). Nature x nature: Genetic vulnerabilities interact with physical maltreatment to promote conduct problems. *Developmental Psychopathology, 17,* 67–84.

Jaffee, S. R., Caspi, A., Moffit, T. E., Polo-Thomas, M., Price, T. S., & Taylor, A. (2004). The limits of child effects: Evidence for genetically mediated child effects on corporate punishment but not physical maltreatment. *Developmental Psychology, 40,* 1047–1058.

Jaffee, S., & Hyde, J. (2000). Gender differences in moral orientation: A meta-analysis. *Psychological Bulletin, 126,* 703–726.

Jellinek, M. B., & Snyder, J. B. (1998). Depression and suicide in children and adolescents. *Pediatric Review, 19,* 255–264.

Jhally, S. (1995). *Dreamworlds 2: Desire/sex/power in music video*[Video].Northhampton, UK: Media Education Foundation.

Jia, Y., Way, N., Ling, G., Yoshikawa, H., Chen, X., Ke, X., & Lu, Z. (2009). The influence of student perceptions of school climate on socio-emotional and academic adjustment: A comparison of Chinese and American adolescents. *Child Development, 80,* 1514–1530.

Johnson, J. G., Cohen, P., Smailes, E. M., Kasen, S., & Brook, J. S. (2002). Television viewing and aggressive behavior during adolescence and adulthood. *Science, 295,* 2468–2471.

Johnson, M., Beebe, I., Mortimer, J., & Snyder, M. (1998). Volunteerism in adolescence: A process perspective. *Journal of Research on Adolescence, 8,* 309–330.

Johnson, M. H. (1998). The neural basis of cognitive development. In W. Damon (Series Ed.), & D. Kuhn & R. S. Siegler (Vol. Eds.), *Handbook of child psychology: Vol. 2. Cognition, perception and language* (5th ed., pp. 1–49). New York: Wiley.

Johnson, M. H. (2000). Functional brain development in infants: Effects of an interactive specialization network. *Child Development, 71,* 75–81.

Johnson, M. H., Griffin, R., Csibra, G., Halit, H., Farroni, T., De Haan, M., . . . Richards, J. (2005). The emergence of the social brain network: Evidence from typical and atypical development. *Development and Psychopathology* [Special Issue]. *Integrating Cognitive and Affective Neuroscience and Developmental Psychopathology, 17,* 509–619.

Johnson, M. H., Grossmann, T., & Kadosh, K. C. (2009). Mapping functional brain development: Building a social brain through interactive specialization. *Developmental Psychology, 45,* 151–159.

Johnson, S. M., & Bolstad, O. (1973). Methodological issues in naturalistic observation: Some problems and solutions for field research. In L. A. Hamerlynck, L. C. Handy, & E. J. Marsh (Eds.), *Behavior change: Methodology concepts and practice* (pp. 5–17). Champaign, IL: Research Press.

Johnson, W., Emde, R. N., Pannabecker, B., Stenberg, C., & Davis, M. (1982). Maternal perception of infant emotion from birth through 18 months. *Infant Behavior and Development, 5,* 313–322.

Johnston, D. (1995). Parent-child visits in jails. *Children's Environments, 12*, 25–38.

Johnston, J., & Ettema, J. S. (1982). *Positive images: Breaking stereotypes with children's television*. Beverly Hills, CA: Sage.

Jones, D. J., Foster, S., Forehand, G., & O'Connell, C. (2005). Neighborhood violence and psychosocial adjustment in low-income urban African American children: Physical symptoms as a marker of child adjustment. *Journal of Child and Family Studies, 14*, 237–249.

Joussemet, M., Vitaro, F., Barker, E. D., Cote, S., Nagin, D. S., Zoccolillo, M., & Tremblay, R. E. (2008). Controlling parenting and physical aggression during elementary school. *Child Development, 79*, 411–425.

Joyner, K., & Udry, J. R. (2000). You don't bring me anything but down: Adolescent romance and depression. *Journal of Health and Social Behavior, 41*, 369–391.

Judge, T. A., & Livington, B. A. (2008). Is the gap more than gender? A longitudinal analysis of gender, gender role orientation, and earnings. *Journal of Applied Psychology, 93*, 994–1012.

Judy, B., & Nelson, E. S. (2000). Relations between parents, peers, morality, and theft in an adolescent sample. *High School Journal, 83*, 31–42.

Jusczyk, P. W., Friederici, A. D., Wessels, J., Svenkerud, V. Y., & Jusczyk, A. M. (1993). Infants' sensitivity to the sound patterns of native language words. *Journal of Memory and Language, 32*, 402–420.

Just, M. A., Cherkassky, V. L., Keller, T. A., Kana, R. K., & Minshew, N. J. (2007). Functional and anatomical cortical underconnectivity in autism: Evidence from an fMRI study of an executive function task and corpus callosum morphometry. *Cerebral Cortex, 17*, 951–961.

Juvonen, J., Graham, S., & Schuster, M. A. (2003). Bullying among young adolescents: The strong, the weak, and the troubled. *Pediatrics, 112*, 1231–1237.

Juvonen, J., Nishina, A., & Graham, S. (2006). Ethnic diversity and perceptions of safety in urban middle schools. *Psychological Science, 17*, 393–400.

Kagan, J. (1994). *Galen's prophecy*. New York: Basic Books.

Kagan, J. (1998). Biology and the child. In W. Damon (Series Ed.), & N. Eisenberg (Vol. Ed.), *Handbook of child psychology: Vol. 3. Social, emotional, and personal development* (5th ed., pp. 177–235). New York: Wiley.

Kagan, J., & Fox, N. A. (2006). Biology, culture, and temperamental biases. In W. Damon & R. M. Lerner (Series Eds.), & N. Eisenberg (Vol. Ed.), *Handbook of child psychology: Vol. 3. Social, emotional, and personality development* (6th ed., pp. 167–225). Hoboken, NJ: Wiley.

Kagan, J., Kearsley, R. B., & Zelazo, P. R. (1978). *Infancy: Its place in human development*. Cambridge, MA: Harvard University Press.

Kagan, J., & Moss, H. A. (1962). *Birth to maturity: A study in psychological development*. New York: Wiley.

Kagan, J., & Snidman, N. (2004). *The long shadow of temperament*. Cambridge, MA: Harvard University Press.

Kagan, J., Snidman, N., Kahn, V., & Towsley, S. (2007). The preservation of two infant temperaments into adolescence. *Monographs of the Society for Research in Child Development, 72* (Serial No. 287).

Kahen, V., Katz, L. F. & Gottman, J. M. (1994). Linkages between parent-child interaction and conversations of friends. *Social Development, 3*, 238–254.

Kaiser Family Foundation. (2001). *Parents and the V-Chip Survey*. Menlo Park, CA: Kaiser Family Foundation.

Kaiser Family Foundation. (2003). *National Survey of Adolescents and Young Adults: Sexual Health Knowledge, Attitudes and Experiences*. Publication 3218. Retrieved from: http://www.kff.org/youthhivstds/3218-index.cfm

Kaiser Family Foundation. (2005). *US teen sexual activity*. Menlo Park, CA: Kaiser Family Foundation.

Kaler, S. R., & Kopp, C. B. (1990). Compliance and comprehension in very young toddlers. *Child Development, 61*, 1997–2003.

Kalil, A., & Ziol-Guest, K. M. (2005). Single mothers' employment dynamics and adolescent well-being. *Child Development, 76*, 196–211.

Kamibeppu, K., & Sugiura, H. (2005). Impact of the mobile phone on junior high-school students' friendships in the Tokyo metropolitan area. *CyberPsychology & Behavior, 8*, 121–130.

Kandel, E. R., Schwartz, J. H., & Jessell, T. M. (2000). *Principles of neuroscience* (4th ed.). New York: McGraw-Hill.

Kanner, L. (1943). Autistic disturbances of affective contact. *Nervous Child, 2*, 217–250.

Kanwisher, N., & Yovel, G. (2006). The fusiform face area: A cortical region specialized for the perception of faces. *Philosophical Transactions of the Royal Society of London: Biological Section, 361*, 2109–2128.

Kaplan, M. S., & Sasser, J. E. (1996). Women behind bars: Trends and policy issues. *Journal of Sociology and Social Welfare, 23*, 43–56.

Kass, J. (2000, October 3). Witnesses tell of Columbine bullying. *Rocky Mountain News*. Retrieved from: http://Denver.rockymountainnews.com/shooting/1003col4.shtml

Kass, L. (2002). *Life, liberty, and the defense of dignity*. San Francisco: Encounter Books.

Katz, L. F., & Gottman, J. M. (1993). Patterns of marital conflict predict children's internalizing and externalizing behaviors. *Developmental Psychology, 29*, 940–950.

Katz, L. F., & Gottman, J. M. (1996). Spillover effects of marital conflict: In search of parenting and co-parenting mechanisms. In J. P. McHale & P. A. Cowan (Eds.),

Understanding how family-level dynamics affect children's development: Studies of two-parent families (pp. 57–76). San Francisco: Jossey-Bass.

Katz, L. F., & Gottman, J. M. (1997). Buffering children from marital conflict and dissolution. *Journal of Clinical Child Psychology, 26,* 157–171.

Katz, L. F., Hessler, D. M., & Annest, A. (2007). Domestic violence, emotional competence, and child adjustment. *Social Development, 16,* 513–538.

Katz, L. F., Kramer, L., & Gottman, J. M. (1992). Conflict and emotions in marital, sibling, and peer relationships. In C. U. Shantz & W. W. Hartup (Eds.), *Conflict in child and adolescent development* (pp. 122–149). Cambridge, UK: Cambridge University Press.

Katz, P. A. (2003). Racists or tolerant multiculturalists? How do they begin? *American Psychologist, 58,* 897–909.

Kazdin, A. (2000). *Psychotherapy for children and adolescents: Directions for research and practice.* New York: Oxford University Press.

Kazdin, A. E. (2003). Problem solving skills training and parent management training for conduct disorder. In A. E. Kazdin & J. R. Weisz (Eds.), *Evidence-based psychotherapies for children and adolescents* (pp. 241–262). New York: Guilford Press.

Kebir, O., Tabbane, K., Sengupta, S., & Joober, R. (2009). Candidate genes and neuropsychological phenotypes in children with ADHD: Review of association studies. *Journal of Psychiatry and Neuroscience, 34,* 88–101.

Kee, D. W., Gregory-Domingue, A, Rice, K., & Tone, K. (2005). A release from proactive interference analysis of gender schema encoding for occupations in adults and children. *Learning & Individual Differences, 15,* 203–211.

Keenan, K., Loeber, R., Zhang, Q., Stouthamer-Loeber, M., & Van Kammen, W. B. (1995). The influence of deviant peers on the development of boys' disruptive and delinquent behavior: A temporal analysis. *Development and Psychopathology, 7,* 715–726.

Keil, F. (2006). Cognitive science and cognitive development. In W. Damon & R. M. Lerner (Series Eds.), & D. Kuhn & R. Siegler (Vol. Eds.), *Handbook of child psychology: Vol. 2. Cognition, perception, and language* (6th ed., pp. 609–635). Hoboken, NJ: Wiley.

Keiley, M. K., Howe, T. R., Dodge, K. A., Bates, J. E., & Pettit, G. S. (2001). The timing of child physical maltreatment: A cross-domain growth analysis of impact on adolescent externalizing and internalizing problems. *Development and Psychopathology, 13,* 891–912.

Kellas, J. K. (2005). Family ties: Communicating identity through jointly told family stories. *Communication Monographs, 72,* 365–389.

Keller, M. (2004). A cross–cultural perspective on friendship research. *Newsletter of the International Society for the Study of Behavioral Development, 28,* 10–14.

Kelley, M. L., Power, T. G., & Wimbush, D. D. (1992). Determinants of disciplinary practices in low-income Black mothers. *Child Development, 63,* 573–582.

Kelley, M. L., Sanchez-Hucles, J., & Walker, R. R. (1993). Correlates of disciplinary practices in working- to middle-class African-American mothers. *Merrill-Palmer Quarterly, 39,* 252–264.

Kellman, P. J., & Arterberry, M. E. (2006). Infant visual perception. In W. Damon & R. M. Lerner (Series Eds.), & D. Kuhn & R. Siegler (Vol. Eds.), *Handbook of child psychology: Vol. 2. Cognition, perception, and language* (6th ed., pp. 109–160). Hoboken, NJ: Wiley.

Kelly, B. M., Schwartz, D., Gorman, A. H., & Nakamoto, J. (2008). Violent victimization in the community and children's subsequent peer rejection: The mediating role of emotion dysregulation. *Journal of Abnormal Child Psychology, 36,* 175–185.

Kelly, D., Quinn, P., Slater, A., Lee, K., Gibson, A., Smith M., . . . Pascalis, O. (2005). Three-month-olds, but not newborns, prefer own-race faces. *Developmental Science, 8,* F31–F36.

Kennedy, D. E. & Kramer, L. (2008). Improving emotional regulation and sibling relationship quality: The More Fun with Sisters and Brothers Program. *Family Relations, 57,* 567–578.

Kennell, J. H., Jerauld, R., Wolfe, H., Chester, D., Kreger, N. C., McAlpine, W., . . . Klaus, M. H. (1974). Maternal behavior one year after early and extended post-partum contact. *Developmental Medicine & Child Neurology, 16,* 172–179.

Kenny, M. C., Capri, V., Thakkar-Kolar, R. R., Ryan, E. E., & Runyon, M. K. (2008). Child sexual abuse: From prevention to self-protection. *Child Abuse Review, 17,* 36–54.

Kern, M. L., & Friedman, H. S. (2008). Do conscientious individuals live longer? A quantitative review. *Health Psychology, 27,* 505–512.

Kerns, K. A. (2008). Attachment in middle childhood. In J. Cassidy & P. R. Shaver (Eds.), *Handbook of attachment: Theory, research, and clinical applications* (2nd ed., pp. 366–382). New York: Guilford Press.

Kerr, M. (2001). Culture as a context for temperament: Suggestions from the life courses of shy Swedes and Americans. In T. D. Wachs & G. A. Kohnstamm (Eds.), *Temperament in context* (pp. 139–152). Mahwah, NJ: Erlbaum.

Kerr, M., & Stattin, H. (2000). What parents know, how they know it, and several forms of adolescent adjustment: Further support for a reinterpretation of monitoring. *Developmental Psychology, 36,* 366–380.

Kesler, S. R. (2007). Turner syndrome. *Child and Adolescent Psychiatry: Clinics of North America, 16,* 709–722.

Keysers, C., & Gazzola, V. (2006). Towards a unifying neural theory of social cognition. *Progress in Brain Research, 156,* 379–401.

Khatri, P., Kupersmidt, J., & Patterson, C. (1994, April). *Aggression and peer victimization as predictors of self-report of behavioral and emotional adjustment.* Poster presented at the biennial meeting of the Conference in Human Development, Pittsburgh, PA.

Khoury-Kassabri, M., Benbenishty, R., Astor, R. A., & Ziera, A. (2004). The contributions of community, family, and school variables to student victimization. *American Journal of Community Psychology, 34,* 187–204.

Kids Are Waiting. (2008). *Time for reform: Investing in prevention, keeping children safe at home.* Philadelphia, PA: Pew Charitable Trusts.

Kiernan, K, E. (2001). Non-marital childbearing: A European perspective. In L. Wu, & B. Wolfe (Eds.), *Out of wedlock: Causes and consequences of nonmarital fertility* (pp. 77–108). New York: Russell Sage Foundation.

Kiernan, K. E., & Smith, K. (2003). Unmarried parenthood: New insights from the Millennium Cohort Study. *Population Trends, 114,* 23–33.

Killen, M. (1990). Children's evaluations of morality in the context of peer, teacher-child, and familial relations. *Journal of Genetic Psychology, 151,* 395–410.

Killen, M., Breton, S., Ferguson, H., & Handler, K. (1994). Preschoolers' evaluations of teacher methods of intervention in social transgressions. *Merrill-Palmer Quarterly, 40,* 399–415.

Killen, M., Lee-Kim, J., McGlothlin, H., & Stangor, C. (2002). How children and adolescents evaluate gender and racial exclusion. *Monographs of the Society for Research in Child Development, 67* (Serial No. 271).

Killen, M., Margie, N. G., & Sinno, S. (2006). Morality in the context of intergroup relationships. In M. Killen & J. Smetana (Eds.), *Handbook of moral development* (pp. 155–184). Mahwah, NJ: Erlbaum.

Killen, M., Park, Y., Lee-Kim, J., & Shin, Y. (2005). Evaluations of children's gender stereotypic activities by Korean parents and nonparental adults residing in the United States. *Parenting: Science & Practice, 5,* 57–89.

Killen, M., & Stangor, C. (2001). Children's social reasoning about inclusion and exclusion in gender and race peer group contexts. *Child Development, 72,* 174–186.

Killen, M., & Sueyoshi, L. (1995). Conflict resolution in Japanese social interactions. *Early Education & Development, 6,* 317–334.

Kilner, J. M., Neal, A., Weiskopf, N., Friston, K. J., & Frith, C. D. (2009). Evidence of mirror neurons in human inferior frontal gyrus. *Journal of Neuroscience, 29,* 10153–10159.

Kim, H., Somerville, L. H., Johnstone, T., Alexander, A. L., & Whalen, P. J. (2003). Inverse amygdala and medial prefrontal cortex responses to surprised faces. *NeuroReport, 14,* 2317–2322.

Kim, J., & Cicchetti, D. (2010). Longitudinal pathways linking child maltreatment, emotion regulation, peer relations, and psychopathology. *Journal of Child Psychology and Psychiatry,*

Kim, J.-Y., McHale, S. M., Crouter, A. C., & Osgood, D. W. (2007). Longitudinal linkages between sibling relationships and adjustment from middle childhood through adolescence. *Developmental Psychology, 43,* 960–973.

Kim, K. J., Conger, R. D., Lorenz, F. O., & Elder, G. H., Jr. (2001). Parent-adolescent reciprocity in negative affect and its relation to early adult social development. *Developmental Psychology, 37,* 775–790.

Kimball, M. M. (1986). Television and sex role attitudes. In T. M. Williams (Ed.), *The impact of television: A natural experiment in three communities* (pp. 265–301). Orlando, FL: Academic Press.

Kim-Cohen, J., Caspi, A., Taylor, A., Williams, B., Newcombe, R., & Craig, I. W. (2006). MAOA, maltreatment, and gene-environment interaction predicting children's mental health: New evidence and a meta-analysis. *Molecular Psychiatry, 11,* 903–913.

Kindermann, T. A., McCollam, T. L., & Gibson, E., Jr. (1995). Peer networks and students' classroom engagement during childhood and adolescence. In K. Wentzel & J. Juvonen (Eds.), *Social motivation: Understanding children's school adjustment* (pp. 279–312). New York: Cambridge University Press.

King, J. A., Blair, R. J. R., Mitchell, D. G. V., Dolan, R. J., & Burgess, N. (2006). Doing the right thing: A common neural circuit for appropriate violent or compassionate behavior. *NeuroImage, 30,* 1069–1076.

Kinsley, C. H., & Lambert, K. G. (2006). The maternal brain. *Scientific American, 294,* 72–79.

Kinsley, C. H., & Lambert, K. G. (2008). Reproduction-induced neuroplasticity: Natural behavioural and neuronal alterations associated with the production and care of offspring. *Journal of Neuroendocrinology, 20,* 515–525.

Kinsley, C. H., Trainer, R., Stafisso-Sandoz, G., Quadros, P., Marcus, L. K., Hearon, C., . . . Lambert, K. G. (2006). Motherhood and the hormones of pregnancy modify concentrations of hippocampal neuronal dendritic spines. *Hormones and behavior, 49,* 131–142.

Kinzler, K. D., Dupoux, E., Spelke, E. S. (2007). The native language of social cognition. *Proceedings of the National Academy of Science, 104,* 12577–12580.

Kirby, D. B. (2008). The impact of abstinence and comprehensive sex and STD/HIV education programs on adolescent sexual behavior. *Sexuality Research and Social Policy: Journal of NSRC, 5,* 18–27.

Kirby, J. D. (2002). The influence of parental separation on smoking initiation in adolescents. *Journal of Health and Social Behavior, 43,* 56–71.

Kirkorian, H. L., Pempek, T. A., Murphy, L. A., Schmidt, M. E., & Anderson, D. R. (2009). The impact of background television on parent-child interaction. *Child Development, 80*, 1350–1359.

Kiselica, M. S. (2008). *When boys become parents: Adolescent fatherhood in America*. Newark, NJ: Rutgers University Press.

Kisilevsky, B. S., & Muir, D. W. (1991). Human fetal and subsequent newborn responses to sound and vibration. *Infant Behavior and Development, 14*, 1–26.

Kisker, E. E., Hofferth, S. L., Phillips, D. A., & Farquhar, E. (1991). *A profile of child care settings: Early education and care in 1990*. Report prepared for the U.S. Department of Education, Contract No. LC88090001.

Kitamura, C., & Burnham, D. (2003). Pitch and communicative intent in mother's speech: Adjustments for age and sex in the first year. *Infancy, 4*, 85–110.

Kitzinger, S. (1979). *Birth at home*. New York: Oxford University Press.

Kiuru, M., & Crystal, R. G. (2008). Progress and prospects: Gene therapy for performance and appearance enhancement. *Gene Therapy, 15*, 329–337.

Klaczynski, P. A. (2005). Metacognition and cognitive variability: A dual process model of decision-making and its development. In J. E. Jacobs & P. A. Klaczynski (Eds.), *The development of judgment and decision making in children and adolescents* (pp. 39–76). Mahwah, NJ: Erlbaum.

Klahr, D., & MacWhinney, B. (1998). Information processing. In W. Damon (Series Ed.), & D. Kuhn & R. Siegler (Vol. Eds.), *Handbook of child psychology: Vol. 2. Cognition, perception and language* (5th ed., pp. 631–678). New York: Wiley.

Klaus, M., & Kennell, J. (1976). *Maternal-infant bonding*. St. Louis: Mosby.

Kliegel, M., Jager, T., & Phillips, L. H. (2007). Emotional development across adulthood: Differential age-related emotional reactivity and emotion regulation in a negative mood induction procedure. *International Journal of Aging & Human Development, 64*, 217–244.

Kliewer, W., Cunningham, J. N., Diehl, R., Parrish, K. A., Walker, J. M., Atiyeh, C., . . . Mejia, R. (2004). Violence exposure and adjustment in inner-city youth: Child and caregiver emotion regulation skill, caregiver-child relationship quality, and neighborhood cohesion as protective factors. *Journal of Clinical Child and Adolescent Psychology, 33*, 477–487.

Klima, T., & Repetti, R. L. (2008). Children's peer relations and their psychological adjustment: Differences between close friendships and the larger peer group. *Merrill-Palmer Quarterly, 54*, 151–178.

Kling, K. C., Hyde, J. S., Showers, C. J., & Busell, B. N. (1999). Gender differences in self-esteem: A meta-analysis. *Psychological Bulletin, 125*, 470–500.

Klomek, A. B., Sourander, A., Kumpulainen, K., Piha, J., Tamminen, T., Moilanen, I., . . . Gould, M. S. (2008). Childhood bullying as a risk for later depression and suicidal ideation among Finnish males. *Journal of Affective Disorders, 109*, 47–55.

Klomek, A. B., Sourander, A., Niemelä, S., Kumpulainen, K., Piha, J., Tamminen, T., . . . Gould, M. (2009). Childhood bullying behaviors as a risk for suicide attempts and completed suicides: A population-based birth cohort study. *Journal of the American Academy of Child & Adolescent Psychiatry, 48*, 254–261.

Knafo, A., Israel, S., Darvasi, A., Bachner-Melman, R., Uzefovsky, F., . . . & Ebstein, R. P. (2008). Individual differences in allocation of funds in the dictator game associated with length of the arginine vasopressin 1a receptor RS3 promoter region and correlation between RS3 length and hippocampal mRNA, *Genes Brain Behavior, 7*, 266–275.

Knafo, A., & Plomin, R. (2006). Prosocial behavior from early to middle childhood: Genetic and environmental influences. *Developmental Psychology, 42*, 771–786.

Knight, G. P., Johnson, L. G., Carlo, G., & Eisenberg, N. (1994). A multiplicative model of the dispositional antecedents of a prosocial behavior: Predicting more of the people more of the time. *Journal of Personality & Social Psychology, 66*, 178–183.

Knight, G. P., Nelson, W., Kagan, S., & Gumbiner, J. (1982). Cooperative-competitive social orientation and school achievement among Anglo-American and Mexican-American children. *Contemporary Educational Psychology, 7*, 97–106.

Knobloch, S., Callison, C., Chen, L., Fritzsche, A., & Zillmann, D. (2005). Children's sex-stereotyped self-socialization through selective exposure to entertainment: Cross-cultural experiments in Germany, China, and the United States. *Journal of Communication, 55*, 122–138.

Knoester, C., Haynie, D. L, & Stephens, C. M. (2006). Parenting practices and adolescents' friendship networks. *Journal of Marriage and Family, 68*, 1247–1260.

Knox, G. W. (2006). Findings from the K–12 Survey Project: A special report of the NGCRC on gang problems in schools. *Journal of Gang Research, 14*, 1–52. Retrieved from: http://www.ngcrc.com/

Kobak, R., & Cole, H. (1994). Attachment and meta-monitoring: Implications for adolescent autonomy and psychopathology. In D. Cicchetti & S. L. Toth (Eds.), *Rochester Symposium on Developmental Psychology: Vol. 5. Disorders and dysfunctions of the self.* (pp. 267–297). Rochester, NY: University of Rochester Press.

Kobayashi, T., & Ikeda, K. (2007). The effect of mobile phone e-mailing in socialization in adolescents: Focusing on the homogeneity and heterogeneity of personal networks and tolerance. *Japanese Journal of Social Psychology, 23*, 82–94.

Kochanska, G. (1993). Toward a synthesis of parental social-ization and child temperament in early development of conscience. *Child Development, 64,* 325–347.

Kochanska, G. (1995). Children's temperament, mother's discipline, and security of attachment: Multiple pathways to emerging internalization. *Child Development, 66,* 597–615.

Kochanska, G. (1997). Multiple pathways to conscience for children with different temperaments: From toddlerhood to age 5. *Developmental Psychology, 33,* 228–240.

Kochanska, G. (2002). Committed compliance, moral self and internalization: A mediational model. *Developmental Psychology, 38,* 339–351.

Kochanska, G., & Aksan, N. (2006). Children's conscience and self-regulation. *Journal of Personality, 74,* 1587–1617.

Kochanska, G., & Aksan, N. (2007). Conscience in childhood: Past, present, and future. In G. W. Ladd (Ed.), *Appraising the human developmental sciences: Essays in honor of Merrill-Palmer Quarterly* (pp. 238–249). Detroit, MI: Wayne State University Press.

Kochanska, G., Aksan, N., & Joy, M. E. (2007). Children's fearfulness as a moderator of parenting in early socializa-tion: Two longitudinal studies. *Developmental Psychology, 43,* 222–237.

Kochanska, G., Aksan, N., Prisco, T. R., & Adams, E. E. (2008). Mother-child and father-child mutually responsive orien-tation in the first two years and children's outcomes at pre-school age: Mechanisms of influence. *Child Development, 79,* 30–44.

Kochanska, G., Coy, K. C., & Murray, K. T. (2001). The devel-opment of self-regulation in the first four years of life. *Child Development, 72,* 1091–1111.

Kochanska, G., DeVet, K., Goldman, M., Murray, K. T., & Putnam, S. P. (1994). Maternal reports of conscience development and temperament in young children. *Child Development, 65,* 852–868.

Kochanska, G., Gross, J. N., Lin, M-H., & Nichols, K. E. (2002). Guilt in young children: Development, determinants, and relations with a broader system of standards. *Developmental Psychology, 73,* 461–482.

Kochanska, G., & Knaack, A. (2003). Effortful control as a personality characteristic of young children: Antecedents, correlates, and consequences. *Journal of Personality, 71,* 1087–1112.

Kochanska, G., & Murray, K. T. (2000). Mother-child mutu-ally responsive orientation and conscience development: From toddler to early school age. *Child Development, 71,* 417–431.

Kochanska, G., Murray, K., & Coy, K. C. (1997). Inhibitory control as a contributor to conscience in childhood: From toddler to early school age. *Developmental Psychology, 68,* 263–277.

Kochanska, G., & Thompson, R. A. (1997). The emer-gence and development of conscience in toddlerhood and early childhood. In J. E. Grusec, & L. Kuczynski (Ed.), *Parenting and children's internalization of values: A handbook of contemporary theory* (pp. 53–77). Hoboken, NJ: Wiley.

Kochenderfer, B. J., & Ladd, G. W. (1996). Peer victimization: Manifestations and relations to school adjustment. *Journal of School Psychology, 34,* 267–283.

Kochenderfer-Ladd, B. (2003). Identification of aggressive and asocial victims and the stability of their peer victimization. *Merrill-Palmer Quarterly Review, 49,* 401–425.

Kochenderfer-Ladd, B., & Wardrop, J. (2001). Chronicity and instability in children's peer victimization experiences as predictors of loneliness and social satisfaction trajectories. *Child Development, 72,* 134–151.

Koenig, J., Barry, R. A., & Kochanska, G. (in press). Rearing difficult children: Parent's personality and children's prone-ness to anger as predictors of future parenting. *Parenting: Science and Practice.*

Kohlberg, L. (1966). A cognitive-developmental analysis of children's sex-role concepts and attitudes. In E. E. Maccoby (Ed.), *The development of sex differences* (pp. 82–173). Stanford, CA: Stanford University Press.

Kohlberg, L. (1969). *Stages in the development of moral thought and action.* New York: Holt.

Kohlberg, L. (1985). *The psychology of moral development.* San Francisco: Harper & Row.

Kohlberg, L., & Candee, D. (1984). The relationship of moral judgment to moral action. In W. M. Kurtines & J. L. Gewirtz (Eds.), *Morality, moral behavior and moral devel-opment* (pp. 52–73). New York: Wiley.

Kohn, A. (1993). *Punished by rewards: The trouble with gold stars, incentive plans, A's, praise, and other bribes.* Boston: Houghton Mifflin.

Kohn, M. (1977). *Class and conformity: A study of values.* Chicago: University of Chicago Press.

Kokko, K., & Pulkkinen, L. (2000). Aggression in childhood and long-term unemployment in adulthood: A cycle of maladaptation and some protective factors. *Developmental Psychology, 36,* 463–472.

Kolb, B., Gorny, G., Li, Y., Samaha, A., & Robinson, T. E. (2003). Amphetamine or cocaine limits the ability of later experience to promote structural plasticity in the neo-cortex and nucleus accumbens. *Proceedings of the National Academy of Sciences, 100,* 10523–10528.

Kopelman, S., Rosette, A. S., & Thompson, L. (2006). The three faces of Eve: Strategic displays of positive, nega-tive, and neutral emotions in negotiations. *Organizational Behavior & Human Decision Processes, 99,* 81–101.

Kopp, C. B. (1982). The antecedents of self-regulation. *Developmental Psychology, 18,* 199–214.

Kopp, C. B. (1991). Young children's progression to self-regulation. In M. Bullock (Ed.), *The development of intentional action: Cognitive, motivational, and interactive processes* (pp. 38–54). Basel, Switzerland: Karger.

Kopp, C. B. (2002). Commentary: The co-development of attention and emotional regulation. *Infancy, 3,* 199–208.

Koppe, N. B., Cano, R. M., Heyman, S. B., & Kimmel, H. (2003, November). Single gender programs: Do they make a difference? *ASEE Frontiers in Education Conference,* Boulder, CO.

Koren-Karie, N., Oppenheim, D., Dolev, S., Sher, E., & Etzion-Carassco, A. (2002). Mother's insightfulness regarding their infants' internal experience: Relations with maternal sensitivity and infant attachment. *Developmental Psychology, 38,* 534–542.

Korner, A. (1974). The effect of the infant's state, level of arousal, sex and ontogenic stage on the caregiver. In M. Lewis & L. Rosenblum (Eds.), *The effect of the infant on its caregiver* (pp. 187–214). New York: Wiley.

Kosfeld, M., Heinrichs, M., Zak, P. J., Fischbacher, U., & Fehr, E. (2005). Oxytocin increases trust in humans. *Nature, 435,* 673–676.

Koskinen, O., Sauvola, A., Valonen, P., Hakko, H., Marjo-Riitta, J., & Räsänen, P. (2001). Increased risk of violent recidivism among adult males is related to single-parent family during childhood: The Northern Finland 1966 Birth Cohort Study. *Journal of Forensic Psychiatry, 12,* 539–548.

Kouno, A., & Johnson, C. F. (1995). Child abuse and neglect in Japan: Coin-operated-locker babies. *Child Abuse & Neglect, 19,* 25–31.

Kovacs, D. M., Parker, J. G., & Hoffman, L. W. (1996). Behavioral, affective and social correlates of involvement in cross-sex friendship in elementary school. *Child Development, 67,* 2269–2286.

Kovacs, M., Joormann, J., & Gotlib, I. H. (2008). Emotional (dy)regulation and links to depressive disorders. *Child Development Perspectives, 2,* 149–155.

Kowal, A., & Kramer, L. (1997). Children's understanding of differential parental treatment. *Child Development, 60,* 113–126.

Kramer, L., & Gottman, J. M. (1992). Becoming a sibling—with a little help from my friends. *Developmental Psychology, 28,* 685–699.

Kramer, L., & Kowal, A. K. (2005). Sibling relationship quality from birth to adolescence: The enduring contributions of friends. *Journal of Family Psychology, 19,* 503–511.

Kramer, L., & Ramsburg, D. (2002). Advice given to parents on welcoming a second child: A critical review. *Family Relations, 51,* 2–14.

Kraut, R., Kiesler, S., Boneva, B., Cummings, J., Helgeson, V., & Crawford, A. (2002). Internet paradox revisited. *Journal of Social Issues, 58,* 49–74.

Kraut, R., Patterson, M., Lundmark, V., Kiesler, S., Mukopadhyay, T., & Scherlis, W. (1998). Internet paradox: A social technology that reduces social involvement and psychological well-being. *American Psychologist, 53,* 1017–1031.

Krebs, D. L., & Denton, K. (2005). Toward a more pragmatic approach to morality: A critical evaluation of Kohlberg's model. *Psychological Review, 112,* 629–649.

Krebs, D. L., Denton, K., & Wark, G. (1997). The forms and functions of real-life moral decision-making. *Journal of Moral Education, 26,* 131–145.

Kreider, R. M. (2003). *Adopted children and stepchildren: 2000.* Washington DC: U. S. Census Bureau.

Kreider, R. M., & Fields, J. M. (2001). *Current population reports.* Washington, DC: US Census Bureau.

Kress, J. S., & Elias, M. J. (2006). School based social and emotional learning programs. In W. Damon & R. Lerner (Series Eds.), & K. A. Renninger & I. E. Sigel (Vol. Eds.), *Handbook of child psychology: Vol. 4. Child psychology in practice* (6th ed., pp. 592–652). Hoboken, NJ: Wiley.

Krettenauer, T., & Eichler, D. (2006). Adolescents' self-attributed moral emotions following a moral transgression: Relations with delinquency, confidence in moral judgment and age. *British Journal of Developmental Psychology, 24,* 489–506.

Kroger, J. (2004). *Identity in adolescence: The balance between self and other* (3rd ed.). New York: Routledge.

Kruegera, F., Barbeya, A. K., & Grafman, J. (2009). The medial prefrontal cortex mediates social event knowledge. *Trends in Cognitive Sciences, 13,* 103–109.

Kruesi, M. J., Hibbs, E. D., Zahn, T. P., & Keysor, C. S. (1992). A 2-year prospective follow-up study of children and adolescents with disruptive behavior disorders: Prediction by cerebrospinal fluid 5-hydroxyindoleacetic acid, homovanillic acid and autonomic measures? *Archives of General Psychiatry, 49,* 429–435.

Krugman, R. D., & Leventhal, J. M. (2005). Confronting child abuse and neglect and overcoming gaze aversion: The unmet challenge of centuries of medical practice. *Child Abuse & Neglect, 29,* 307–309.

Ku, L., Sonnenstein, F., & Pleck, J. (1993). Neighborhood, family, and work: Influences on the premarital behaviors of adolescent males. *Social Forces, 72,* 479–503.

Kuczynski, L. (2003). Beyond bidirectionality: Bilateral conceptual frameworks for understanding dynamics in parent-child relations. In L. Kuczynski (Ed.), *Handbook of dynamics in parent-child relations* (pp. 1–24). Thousand Oaks, CA: Sage.

Kuczynski, L., & Parkin, C. M. (2007). Agency and bidirectionality in socialization. In J. E. Grusec & P. Hastings (Eds.), *Handbook of socialization* (pp. 259–283). New York: Guilford Press.

Kuhn, D. (2006). Do cognitive changes accompany developments in the adolescent brain? *Perspectives on Psychological Science, 1*, 59–67.

Kuklinksi, M. R., & Weinstein, R. S. (2001). Classroom and developmental differences in a path model of teacher expectancy effects. *Child Development, 72*, 1554–1578.

Kumru, A. & Edwards C. P. (2003, April). *Gender and adolescent prosocial behavior with the Turkish family*. Poster presented at the biennial meeting of the Society for Research in Child Development, Tampa, FL.

Kunkel, D. (2001). Children and television advertising. In D. Singer & J. Singer (Eds.), *Handbook of children and the media* (pp. 375–393). Thousand Oaks, CA: Sage.

Kunkel, D., Eyal, K., Biely, E., Cope-Farrar, K., Donnerstein, E., & Frandrich, R. (2003). *Sex on TV 3: A biennial report to the Kaiser Family Foundation*. Menlo Park, CA: Kaiser Family Foundation.

Kunkel, D., Farinola, W. J. M., Cope, K. M., Donnerstein, E., Biely, E., Zwarun, L., & Rollin, E. (2001). Assessing the validity of v-chip rating judgments: The labeling of high-risk programs. In B. S. Greenberg (Ed.), *The alphabet soup of television program ratings* (pp. 51–68). Cresskill, NJ: Hampton Press.

Kurtz-Costes, B., McCall, R., & Schneider, W. (1997). Implications from developmental cross-cultural research for the study of acculturation in Western civilizations. In J. Tudge, M. J. Shanahan, & J. Valsiner (Eds.), *Comparisons in human development* (pp. 162–192). New York: Cambridge, University Press.

Kyratzis, A., & Marx, T. (2001). Preschoolers' communicative competence: Register shift in the marking of power in different contexts of friendship group talk. *First Language, 21*, 387–429.

La Barbera, J. D., Izard, C. E., Vietze, P., & Parisi, S. A. (1976). Four- and six-month-old infants' visual responses to joy, anger, and neutral expressions. *Child Development, 47*, 535–538.

LaBounty, J., Wellman, H. M., Olson, S., Lagattuta, K., & Liu, D. (2008). Mothers' and fathers' use of internal state talk with their young children. *Social Development, 17*, 757–775.

Ladd, G. W. (1981). Effectiveness of a social learning method for enhancing children's social interaction and peer acceptance. *Child Development, 52*, 171–178.

Ladd, G. W. (2005). *Children's peer relationships and social competence: A century of progress*. New Haven, CT: Yale University Press.

Ladd, G. W. (2006). Peer rejection, aggressive or withdrawn behavior, and psychological maladjustment from ages 5 to 12: An examination of four predictive models. *Child Development, 77*, 822–846.

Ladd, G. W., Birch, S. H., & Buhs, E. S. (1999). Children's social and scholastic lives in kindergarten: Related spheres of influence? *Child Development, 70*, 1373–1400.

Ladd, G. W., & Emerson, E. S. (1984). Shared knowledge of children's friendships. *Developmental Psychology, 20*, 932–940.

Ladd, G. W., & Golter, B. S. (1988). Parents' management of preschoolers' peer relations: Is it related to children's social competence? *Developmental Psychology, 24*, 109–117.

Ladd, G. W., Herald-Brown, S. L., & Reiser, M. (2008). Does chronic classroom peer rejection predict the development of children's classroom participation during the grade school years? *Child Development, 79*, 1001–1015.

Ladd, G. W., & Pettit, G. S. (2002). Parents and children's peer relationships. In M. H. Bornstein (Ed.), *Handbook of parenting: Vol. 4. Social conditions and applied parenting* (2nd ed., pp. 377–409). Mahwah, NJ: Erlbaum.

Ladd, G. W., Profilet, S. M., & Hart, C. H. (1992). Parents' management of children's peer relations: Facilitating and supervising children's activities in the peer culture. In R. D. Parke & G. W. Ladd (Eds.), *Family-peer relationships* (pp. 215–253). Hillsdale, NJ: Erlbaum.

Ladd, G. W., & Troop-Gordon, W. (2003). The role of chronic peer difficulties in the development of children's psychological adjustment problems. *Child Development, 74*, 1344–1367.

LaFontana, K., & Cillessen, A. H. N. (1999). Children's interpersonal perceptions as a function of sociometric and peer-perceived popularity. *Journal of Genetic Psychology, 160*, 225–242.

LaFrance, M., Hecht, M. A., & Levy Paluck, E. (2003). The contingent smile: A meta-analysis of sex differences in smiling. *Psychological Bulletin, 129*, 305–334.

LaFreniere, P. J. (2000). *Emotional development: A biosocial perspective*. Belmont, CA: Wadsworth.

Lagattuta, K. H. (2007). Thinking about the future because of the past: Young children's knowledge about the causes of worry and preventative decisions. *Child Development, 78*, 1492–1509.

La Greca, A. M., & Harrison, H. M. (2005). Adolescent peer relations, friendships, and romantic relationships: Do they predict social anxiety and depression? *Journal of Clinical Child & Adolescent Psychology, 34*, 49–61.

La Greca, A. M., & Prinstein, M. J. (1999). Peer group. In W. K. Silverman, & T. H. Ollendick (Eds.), *Developmental issues in the clinical treatment of children* (pp. 171–198). Needham Heights, MA: Allyn & Bacon.

Laible, D. J., & Thompson, R. A. (1998). Attachment and emotional understanding in preschool children. *Developmental Psychology, 34*, 1038–1045.

Laird, R. D., Pettit, G. S., Bates, J. E., & Dodge, K. A. (2003). Parents' monitoring-relevant knowledge and adolescents' delinquent behavior: Evidence of correlated developmental changes and reciprocal influences. *Child Development, 74*, 752–768.

Laird, R. D., Pettit, G. S., Dodge, K. A., & Bates, J. E. (2003). Change in parents' monitoring knowledge: Links with parenting, relationships quality, adolescent beliefs and antisocial behavior. *Social Development, 12*, 401–419.

Lakatos, K., Nemoda, Z., Birkas, E., Ronai, Z., Kovacs, E., Ney, K., . . . Gervai, J. (2003). Association of D4 dopamine receptor gene and serotonin transporter promoter polymorphisms with infants' response to novelty. *Molecular Psychiatry, 8*, 90–97.

Lamb, M. E. (1976). Interactions between eight-month-old children and their fathers and mothers. In M. E. Lamb (Ed.), *The role of the father in child development* (pp. 393–417). New York: Wiley.

Lamb, M. E. (Ed.) (1987). *The father's role: Cross-cultural perspectives*. New York: Wiley.

Lamb, M. E. (Ed.) (2004). *The role of the father in child development* (4th ed.). New York: Wiley.

Lamb, M. E., & Ahnert, L. (2006). Childcare and youth programs. In W. Damon & R. L. Lerner (Series Eds.), & K. A. Renninger & I. E. Sigel (Vol. Eds.). *Handbook of child psychology: Vol. 4. Child psychology in practice* (6th ed., pp. 950–1016). Hoboken, NJ: Wiley.

Lamb, M. E., Easterbrooks, M. A., & Holden, G. W. (1980). Reinforcement and punishment among preschoolers: Characteristics, effects, and correlates. *Child Development, 51*, 1230–1236.

Lamb, M. E., & Hwang, P. (1982). Maternal attachment and mother-infant bonding: A critical review. In M. E. Lamb & A. L. Brown (Eds.), *Advances in developmental psychology* (Vol. 2, pp. 1–39). Hillsdale, NJ: Erlbaum.

Lamb, M. E., Suomi, S. J., & Stephenson, G. R. (1979). *Social interaction analysis: Methodological issues*. Madison: University of Wisconsin Press.

Lamb, S., & Zakhireh, B. (1997). Toddlers' attention to the distress of peers in a day care setting. *Early Education & Development, 8*, 105–118.

Lambert, K. G., & Kinsley, C. H. (2009). The neuroeconomics of motherhood: The costs and benefits of maternal investment. In R. S. Bridges (Ed.), *The neurobiology of the parental brain* (pp. 481–492). San Diego: Academic Press.

Lamborn, S. D., Mounts, N. S., Steinberg, L., & Dornbusch, S. M. (1991). Patterns of competence and adjustment among adolescents from authoritative, authoritarian, indulgent, and neglectful families. *Child Development, 62*, 1049–1065.

Landers, A. (February 24 and April 8, 1969). Syndicated column, *Ask Ann Landers*.

Langlois, J. H. (1986). From the eye of the beholder to behavior reality: Development of social behaviors and social relations as a function of physical attractiveness. In C. P. Herman, M. P. Zanna, & E. T. Higgins (Eds.), *Physical appearance, stigma, and social behavior* (Vol. 3, pp. 23–51). Hillsdale, NJ: Erlbaum.

Langlois, J. H., & Downs, C. A. (1980). Mothers, fathers and peers as socialization agents of sex-typed play behaviors in young children. *Child Development, 51*, 1237–1247.

Langlois, J. H., Kahakanis, L., Rubenstein, A. J., Larson, A., Hallam, N., & Smoot, M. (2000). Maxims or myths of beauty: A meta-analytic and theoretical review. *Psychological Bulletin, 126*, 390–423.

Langlois, J. H., & Stephan, C. (1981). Beauty and the beast: The role of physical attractiveness in the development of peer relations and social behavior. In S. S. Brehm, S. H. Kassin, & F. X. Gibbons (Eds.), *Developmental social psychology* (pp. 152–168). New York: Oxford University Press.

Lansford, J. E., Chang, L., Dodge, K. A., Malone, P. S., Oburu, P., Palmerus, K., . . . Quinn, N. (2005). Cultural normativeness as a moderator of the link between physical discipline and children's adjustment: A comparison of China, India, Italy, Kenya, Philippines, and Thailand. *Child Development, 76*, 1234–1246.

Lansford, J. E., & Dodge, K. A. (2008). Cultural norms for adult corporal punishment of children and societal rates of endorsement and use of violence. *Parenting: Science and Practice, 8*, 257–270.

Lansford, J. E., Dodge, K. A., Petit, G. S., Bates, J. E., Crozier, J., & Kaplow, J. (2002). A 12-year prospective study of the long-term effects of early child physical maltreatment on psychological, behavioral, and academic problems in adolescence. *Archives of Pediatrics & Adolescent Medicine, 156*, 824–830.

Lansford, J. E., & Parker, J. G. (1999). Children's interactions in triads: Behavioral profiles and effects of gender and patterns of friendships among members. *Developmental Psychology, 35*, 80–93.

Lareau, A. (2003). *Unequal childhoods: Class, race, and family life*. Berkeley: University of California Press.

Larose, S., Bernier, A., Tarabulsy, G. M. (2005). Attachment state of mind, learning dispositions, and academic performance during the college transition. *Developmental Psychology, 41*, 281–289.

Larsen, J. T., To, Y. M., & Fireman, G. (2007). Children's understanding and experience of mixed emotions. *Psychological Science, 18*, 186–191.

Larson, R. W. (2000). Toward a psychology of positive youth development. *American Psychologist, 55*, 170–183.

Larson, R. W., & Brown, J. R. (2007). Emotional development in adolescence: What can be learned from a high school theater program? *Child Development, 78*, 1083–1099.

Larson, R. W., & Richards, M. H. (1994). *Divergent realities: The emotional lives of mothers, fathers and adolescents*. New York: Basic Books.

Larson, R. W., & Sheeber, L. (2008). The daily emotional experience of adolescents. In N. Allen & L. Sheeber (Eds.), *Adolescent emotional development and the emergence of depressive disorders* (pp. 11–32). New York: Cambridge University Press.

Larson, R. W., & Verma, S. (1999). How children and adolescents around the world spend time: Work, play, and developmental opportunities. *Psychological Bulletin, 125*, 701–736.

Larzelere, R. E., & Kuhn, B. R. (2005). Comparing child outcomes of physical punishment and alternative disciplinary tactics: A meta-analysis. *Clinical Child and Family Psychology Review, 8*, 1–37.

Laursen, B., Bukowski, W. M., Aunola, K., & Nurmi, J-E. (2007). Friendship moderates prospective associations between social isolation and adjustment problems in young children. *Child Development, 78*, 1395–1404.

Laursen, B., Hartup, W. W., & Koplas, A. L. (1996). Towards understanding peer conflict. *Merrill-Palmer Quarterly, 42*, 76–102.

Laursen, B., & Jensen-Campbell, L. A. (1999). The nature and functions of social exchange in adolescent romantic relationships. In W. Furman, B. Brown, & C. Feiring (Eds.), *The development of romantic relationships in adolescence: Cambridge studies in social and emotional development* (pp. 50–74). New York: Cambridge University Press.

Laursen, B., & Williams, V. A. (1997). Perceptions of interdependence and closeness in family and peer relationships among adolescents with and without romantic partners. In S. Shulman & W. A. Collins (Eds.), *Romantic relationships in adolescence: Developmental perspectives* (pp. 3–20). San Francisco: Jossey-Bass.

Lawry, J., Upitis, R., Klawe, M., Anderson, A., Inkpen, K., Ndunda, M., . . . Sedighian, K. (1995). Exploring common conceptions about boys and electronic games. *Journal of Computers in Mathematics and Science Teaching, 14*, 439–459.

Lawton, M. P. (2001). Emotion in later life. *Current Directions in Psychological Science, 10*, 120–123.

Lawton, M. P., Kleban, M. H., & Dean, J. (1993). Affect and age: Cross-sectional comparisons of structure and prevalence. *Psychology & Aging, 8*, 165–175.

Le, H-N. (2000). Never leave your little one alone: Raising an Ifaluk child. In J. DeLoache & A. Gottlieb (Eds.), *A world of babies: Imagined childcare guides for seven societies* (pp. 199–220). New York: Cambridge University Press.

Leadbeater, B. J., Banister, E. M., Ellis, W. E., & Yeung, R. (2008). Victimization and relational aggression in adolescent romantic relationships: The influence of parental and peer behaviors, and individual adjustment. *Journal of Youth & Adolescence, 37*, 359–372.

Leadbeater, B. J., & Hoglund, W. L. G. (2009). The effects of peer victimization and physical aggression on changes in internalizing from first to third grade. *Child Development, 80*, 843–859.

Leadbeater, B. J., & Way, N. (2001). *Growing up fast*. Mahwah, NJ: Erlbaum.

Leaper, C. (1994). *Childhood gender segregation: Causes and consequences*. San Francisco: Jossey-Bass.

Leaper, C. (2002). Parenting girls and boys. In M. H. Bornstein (Ed.), *Handbook of parenting: Vol. 1. Children and parenting* (2nd ed., pp. 189–226). Mahwah, NJ: Erlbaum.

Leaper, C., Anderson, K. J., & Sanders, P. (1998). Moderators of gender effects on parents' talk to their children: A meta-analysis. *Developmental Psychology, 34*, 3–27.

Leaper, C., & Friedman, C. K. (2007). The socialization of gender. In J. Grusec & P. Hastings (Eds.), *Handbook of socialization* (pp. 561–587). New York: Guilford Press.

Leclerc, C. M., & Kensinger, E. A. (2008). Age-related differences in medial prefrontal activation in response to emotional images. *Cognitive, Affective, & Behavioral Neuroscience, 8*, 153–164.

LeDoux, J. (2000). Emotion circuits in the brain. *Annual Review of Neuroscience, 23*, 155–184.

LeDoux, J. (2002). *Synaptic self: How our brains become who we are*. New York: Viking Press.

Lee, J. H., & Huston, A. C. (2003). Educational televisual media effects. In E. L. Palmer & B. M. Young (Eds.), *The faces of televisual media: Teaching, violence, selling to children* (2nd ed., pp. 83–106). Mahwah, NJ: Erlbaum.

Lee, K.-H., Baillargeon, R. H., Vermunt, J. K., Wu, H.-X., & Tremblay, R. E. (2007). Age differences in the prevalence of physical aggression among 5–11-year-old Canadian boys and girls. *Aggressive Behavior, 33*, 26–37.

Lee, M. L., & Yang, G. S. (1998). Endurance in Chinese people: Conceptual analysis and empirical study. *Indigenous Psychological Studies, 10*, 3–68.

Lee, V., & Bryk, A. (1986). Effects of single-sex secondary schools on student achievement and attitudes. *Journal of Educational Psychology, 78*, 381–395.

Lee, V. E., & Burkam, D. T. (2003). Dropping out of high school: The role of school organization and structure. *American Educational Research Journal, 40*, 353–393.

Leeb, R. T., & Rejskind, F. G. (2004). Here's looking at you, kid! A longitudinal study of perceived gender differences in mutual gaze behavior in young infants. *Sex Roles, 50*, 1–5.

Legerstee, M. (1997). Contingency effects of people and objects on subsequent cognitive functioning in three-month-old infants. *Social Development, 6*, 307–321.

Leinbach, M. D., & Fagot, B. I. (1992). *Gender-schematic processing in infancy: Categorical habituation to male and female faces.* Unpublished manuscript. University of Oregon, Eugene.

Lemerise, E. A., & Arsenio, W. F. (2000). An integrated model of emotion processes and cognition in social information processing. *Child Development, 71,* 107–118.

Lengua, L. J. (2002). The contribution of emotionality and self-regulation to the understanding of children's response to multiple risk. *Child Development, 73,* 144–161.

Lengua, L. J., & Kovacs, E. A. (2005). Bidirectional associates between temperament and parenting and the prediction of adjustment problems in middle childhood. *Journal of Applied Developmental Psychology, 26,* 21–38.

Lenneberg, E. H., Rebelsky, F. G., & Nichols, I. A. (1965). The vocalizations of infants born to deaf and hearing parents. *Human Development, 8,* 23–37.

Lepper, M. R. (1985). Microcomputers in education: Motivation and social issues. *American Psychologist, 40,* 1–18.

Lepper, M. R., & Gurtner, J. (1989). Children and computers: Approaching the twenty-first century. *American Psychologist, 44,* 170–178.

Lepper, M. R., & Henderlong, J. (2000). Turning "play" into "work" and "work" into "play": 25 years of research in intrinsic versus extrinsic motivation. In C. Sansome & J. M. Harackiewicz (Eds.), *Intrinsic and extrinsic motivation: The search for optimal motivation and performance* (pp. 252–307). New York: Academic Press.

Lerman, R. L., & Ooms, T. J. (1993). *Young unwed fathers.* Philadelphia: Temple University Press.

Lerner, R. M. (2002). *Concepts and theories of human development* (3rd ed.). Mahwah, NJ: Erlbaum.

Leve, L. D., & Fagot, B. I. (1997). Gender-role socialization and discipline processes in one- and two-parent families. *Sex Roles, 36,* 1–21.

Leve, L. D., Kerr, D. C. R., Shaw, D., Ge, X., Neiderhiser, J. M., Scaramella, L. V., ... Reiss, D. (2010). Infant pathways to externalizing behavior: Evidence of genotype x environment interaction. *Child Development, 81,* 340–356.

Leventhal, T., & Brooks-Gunn, J. (2000). The neighborhoods they live in: The effects of neighborhood residence on child and adolescent outcomes. *Psychological Bulletin, 126,* 309–337.

Leventhal, T., & Brooks-Gunn, J. (2003). Moving on up: Neighborhood effects on children and families. In M. H. Bornstein & R. H. Bradley (Eds.), *Socioeconomic status, parenting, and child development* (pp. 209–230). Mahwah, NJ: Erlbaum.

Levine, L. J. (1995). Young children's understanding of the causes of anger and sadness. *Child Development, 66,* 697–709.

Levitt, M. J., Weber, R. A., & Clark, M. C. (1986). Social network relationships as sources of maternal support and well-being. *Developmental Psychology, 22,* 310–316.

Levy, G. D. (1994). High and low gender schematic children's release from proactive interference. *Sex Roles, 30,* 93–108.

Levy, G. D., Taylor, M. G., & Gelman, S. A. (1995). Traditional and evaluative aspects of flexibility in gender roles, social conventions, moral rules, and physical laws. *Child Development, 66,* 515–531.

Lewinsohn, P. M., & Rohde, P. (1993). The cognitive-behavioral treatment of depression in adolescents: Research and suggestions. *The Clinical Psychologist, 46,* 177–183.

Lewis, M. (1991). Ways of knowing: Objective self awareness or consciousness. *Developmental Review, 11,* 231–243.

Lewis, M. (1992). *Shame: The exposed self.* New York: Free Press.

Lewis, M. (1998). Emotional competence and development. In D. Pushkar, W. M. Bukowski, A. E. Schwartzman, D. M. Stack, & D. R. White (Eds.), *Improving competence across the lifespan* (pp. 27–36). New York: Plenum Press.

Lewis, M. (1999). Contextualism and the issue of continuity: Does infancy matter? *Infant Behavior and Development, 22,* 431–444.

Lewis, M. (2000). Self-conscious emotions: Embarrassment, pride, shame, and guilt. In M. Lewis & J. Haviland (Eds.), *Handbook of emotions* (2nd ed., pp. 623–636). New York: Guilford Press.

Lewis, M. (2001). Origins of the self-conscious child. In W. R. Cozier & L. E. Alden (Eds.), *International handbook of social anxiety: Concepts, research and interventions relating to the self and shyness* (pp. 101–118). New York: Wiley.

Lewis, M. (2007). *The rise of consciousness and the development of emotional life.* New York: Guilford Press.

Lewis, M., Alessandri, S., & Sullivan, M. W. (1992). Differences in shame and pride as a function of children's gender and task difficulty. *Child Development, 63,* 630–638.

Lewis, M., Feiring, C., & Rosenthal, S. (2000). Attachment over time. *Child Development, 71,* 707–720.

Lewis, M., & Michaelson, L. (1985). *Children's emotions and moods.* New York: Plenum Press.

Lewis, M., & Ramsay, D. S. (2002). Cortisol response to embarrassment and shame. *Child Development, 73,* 1034–1045.

Leyens, J.-P., Camino, L., Parke, R. D., & Berkowitz, L. (1975). Effects of movie violence on aggression in a field setting as a function of group dominance and cohesion. *Journal of Personality and Social Psychology, 32,* 346–360.

Li, X., Stanton, B., Pack, R., Harris, C., Cottrell, L., & Burns, J. (2002). Risk and protective factors associated with gang involvement among urban African American adolescents. *Youth & Society, 34,* 172–194.

Liben, L. S., & Bigler, R. S. (2002). The developmental course of gender differentiation. *Monographs of the Society for Research in Child Development, 67* (Serial No. 269).

Lickliter, R., & Honeycutt, H. (2003). Developmental dynamics: Toward a biologically plausible evolutionary psychology. *Psychological Bulletin, 129,* 819–835.

Lieb, R., Wittchen, H. U., Hofler, M., Fuetsch, M., Stein, M. B., & Merikangas, K. R. (2000). Parental psychopathology, parenting styles, and the risk of social phobia in offspring: A prospective-longitudinal community study. *Archives of General Psychiatry, 57,* 859–866.

Liebert, R. M., & Baron, R. A. (1972). Some immediate effects of televised violence on children's behavior. *Developmental Psychology, 6,* 469–475.

Lieven, E. V. M. (1994). Crosslinguistic and cross cultural aspects of language addressed to children. In C. Gallaway & B. J. Richards (Eds.), *Input and interaction in language acquisition* (pp. 74–106). Cambridge, UK: Cambridge University Press.

Liker, J. K., & Elder, G. H. (1983). Economic hardship and marital relations in the 1930s. *American Sociological Review, 48,* 343–359.

Lillard, A. S. (1998). Ethnopsychologies: Cultural variations in theory of mind. *Psychological Bulletin, 123,* 3–33.

Lillard, A. S. (2006). The socialization of theory of mind: Cultural and social class differences in behavior explanation. In A. Antonietti, O. Liverta-Simpio, & A. Marchetti (Eds.), *Theory of mind and language in developmental contexts* (pp. 65–76). New York: Springer.

Lin, A. J., & Santelli, J. S. (2008). The accuracy of condom information in the three selected abstinence-only education curricula. *Sexuality Research & Social Policy, 5,* 56–70.

Lindell, A. K., & Lumb, J. A. G. (2008). Priming vs. rhyming: Orthographic and phonological representations in the left and right hemispheres. *Brain & Cognition, 68,* 193–203.

Linder, J. R., & Gentile, D. A. (2009). Is the television rating system valid? Indirect, verbal, and physical aggression in programs viewed by fifth grade girls and associations with behavior. *Journal of Applied Developmental Psychology, 30,* 286–297.

Lindhout, I. E., Markus, M. T., Hoogendijk, T. H. G., & Boer, F. (2009). Temperament and parental child-rearing style: Unique contributions to clinical anxiety disorder in childhood. *European Child & Adolescent Psychiatry, 18,* 439–446.

Lindsey, E. W., Caldera, Y. M., & Tankersley, L. (2009). Marital conflict and the quality of young children's peer play behavior: The mediating and moderating role of parent child emotional reciprocity and attachment security. *Journal of Family Psychology, 23,* 130–145.

Lines, P. M. (2000a). Homeschooling comes of age. *The Public Interest, 140,* 74–85.

Lines, P. M. (2000b). When homeschoolers go to school: A partnership between families and schools. *Peabody Journal of Education, 75,* 159–186.

Linney, J. A., & Seidman, E. (1989). The future of schooling. *American Psychologist, 44,* 336–340.

Linnoila, V. M., & Virkkunen, M. (1992). Aggression, suicidality, and serotonin. *Journal of Clinical Psychiatry, 53,* 46–51.

Lipman, E. L., Boyle, M. H., Dooley, M. D., & Offord, D. R. (2002). Child well-being in single-mother families. *Journal of the American Academy of Child & Adolescent Psychiatry, 41,* 75–82.

Liu, D., Sabbagh, M. A., Gehring, W. J., & Wellman, H. M. (2009). Neural correlates of children's theory of mind development. *Child Development, 80,* 318–326.

Livesley, W. J., & Bromley, D. B. (1973). *Person perception in childhood and adolescence.* London: Wiley.

Lobel, T. E., Gruber, R., Govrin, N., & Mashraki-Pedhatzur, S. (2001). Children's gender-related inferences and judgments: A cross cultural study. *Developmental Psychology, 37,* 839–846.

Lochman, J. E., & Wells, K. C. (2004). The coping power program for preadolescent aggressive boys and their parents: Outcome effects at the 1-year follow-up. *Journal of Consulting & Clinical Psychology, 72,* 571–578.

Lock, A. (2004). Preverbal communication. In G. Bremner & A. Fogel (Eds.), *Handbook of infant development* (pp. 379–403). London: Blackwell.

Lockhart, K. L., Chang, B., & Story, T. (2002). Young children's beliefs about the stability of traits: Protective optimism? *Child Development, 73,* 1408–1430.

Loehlin, J. C., Willerman, L., & Horn, J. M. (1988). Human behavior genetics. In M. R. Rosenzweig & L. W. Porter (Eds.), *Annual Review of Psychology* (Vol. 39, pp. 101–133). Palo Alto, CA: Annual Reviews.

Logan, T. K., Walker, R., Horvath, L. S. & Leukefeld, C. (2003). Divorce, custody, and spousal violence: A random sample of circuit court docket records. *Journal of Family Violence, 18,* 269–279.

Lollis, S. P., Ross, H. S., & Tate, E. (1992). Parents' regulation of children's peer interactions: Direct influences. In R. D. Parke & G. W. Ladd (Eds.), *Family–peer relationships: Modes of linkage* (pp. 255–281). Hillsdale, NJ: Erlbaum.

Long, J. L., & Chen, G.-M. (2007). The impact of Internet usage on adolescent self-identity development. *China Media Research, 3,* 99–109.

Longley, R. (2005). Many U.S. jobs have become less male-dominated. BLS statistics show changing face of American workplace. Retrieved from: http://usgovinfo.about.com/od/censusandstatistics/a/menwomenjobs.htm

Lorberbaum, J. P., Newman, J. D., Dubno, J. R., Horwitz, A. R., Nahas, Z., Teneback, C. C., . . . George, M. S. (1999). The feasibility of using fMRI to study mothers responding to infant cries. *Depression and Anxiety, 10,* 99–104.

Lord, H., & Mahoney, J. L. (2007). Neighborhood crime and self care: Risks for aggression and lower academic performance. *Developmental Psychology, 43,* 1321–1333.

Lorenz, K. (1952). *King Solomon's ring*. New York: Crowell.

Losh, M., & Capps, L. (2006). Understanding of emotional experience in autism: Insights from the personal accounts of high functioning children with autism. *Developmental Psychology, 42*, 809–818.

Lounds, J. J., Borkowski, J. G., Whitman, T. L., Maxwell, S. E., & Weed, K. (2005). Adolescent parenting and attachment during infancy and early childhood. *Parenting: Science & Practice, 5*, 91–117.

Love, J. A., & Buriel, R. (2007). Language brokering, autonomy, parent-child bonding, biculturalism, and depression: A study of Mexican American adolescents from immigrant families. *Hispanic Journal of Behavioral Sciences, 29*, 472–491.

Love, J. M., Kisker, E. E., Ross, C., Raikes, H., Constantine, J., Boller, K., . . . Vogel, C. (2005). The effectiveness of early Head Start for 3-year-old children and their parents: Lessons from policy and programs. *Developmental Psychology, 41*, 885–901.

Lucas-Thompson, R., & Clarke-Stewart, K. A. (2007). Forecasting friendship: How marital quality, maternal mood, and attachment security are linked to children's peer relationships. *Journal of Applied Developmental Psychology, 28*, 499–514.

Ludwig, J., & Phillips, D. A. (2007). *The benefits and costs of Head Start*. National Poverty Center Working Paper Series. Retrieved from: http://www.npc.umich.edu/publications/working_papers/

Luecke-Aleksa, D., Anderson, D. R., Collins, P. A., & Schmitt, K. L. (1995). Gender constancy and television viewing. *Developmental Psychology, 31*, 773–780.

Luntz, B. K., & Widom, C. S. (1994). Antisocial personality disorders in abused and neglected children grown up. *American Journal of Psychiatry, 151*, 670–674.

Luthar, S. S. (2003). The culture of affluence: Psychological costs of material wealth. *Child Development, 74*, 1581–1593.

Luthar, S. S., & Brown, P. J. (2007). Maximizing resilience through diverse levels of inquiry: Prevailing paradigms, possibilities, and priorities for the future. *Development and Psychopathology, 19*, 931–955.

Luthar, S. S., Cicchetti, D., & Becker, B. (2000). The construct of resilience: A critical evaluation and guidelines for future work. *Child Development, 71*, 543–562.

Luyckx, K., Soenens, B., Vansteenkiste, M., Goossens, B., & Berzonsky, M. (2007). Parental psychological control and dimensions of identity formation in emerging adulthood. *Journal of Family Psychology, 21*, 546–550.

Lykken, D. T. (1995). *The antisocial personalities*. Hillsdale, NJ: Erlbaum.

Lyman, D. R., Caspi, A., Moffitt, T. E., Wikstrom, P. O., Loeber, R., & Novak, S. P. (2000). The interaction between impulsivity and neighborhood context on offending: The effects of impulsivity are stronger in poorer neighborhoods. *Journal of Abnormal Psychology, 109*, 563–574.

Lynch, S. M., Turkheimer, E., D'Onofrio, B. M., Mendle, J., Emery, R. E., Slutske, W. S., & Martin, N. G. (2006). A genetically informed study of the association between harsh punishment and offspring behavioral problems. *Journal of Family Psychology, 20*, 190–198.

Lynn, M. (2004). Black-White differences in tipping of various service providers. *Journal of Applied Social Psychology, 34*, 2261–2271.

Lyons-Ruth, K. (1996). Attachment relationships among children with aggressive behavior problems: The role of disorganized early attachment patterns. *Journal of Consulting & Clinical Psychology, 64*, 64–73.

Lyons-Ruth, K., & Jacobvitz, T. (2008). Attachment disorganization. In J. Cassidy & P. Shaver (Eds.), *Handbook of attachment: Theory, research, and clinical applications* (2nd ed., pp. 666–697). New York: Guilford Press.

Lytton, H. (1980). *Parent-child interaction: The socialization processes observed in twin and singleton families*. New York: Plenum.

Lytton, H., & Romney, D. M. (1991). Parents' differential socialization of boys and girls: A meta-analysis. *Psychological Bulletin, 109*, 267–296.

MacBeth, T. M. (1996). Indirect effects of television: Creativity, persistence, school achievement, and participation in other activities. In T. M. MacBeth (Ed.), *Tuning in to young viewers: Social science perspectives on television* (pp. 149–219). Thousand Oaks, CA: Sage.

Maccoby, E. E. (1990). Gender and relationships: A developmental account. *American Psychologist, 45*, 513–520.

Maccoby, E. E. (1998). *The two sexes*. Cambridge, MA: Harvard University Press.

Maccoby, E. E. (2002). Gender and group process: A developmental perspective. *Current Directions in Psychological Science, 11*, 53–58.

Maccoby, E. E., & Jacklin, C. N. (1974). *The psychology of sex differences*. Stanford: Stanford University Press.

Maccoby, E. E., & Martin, J. A. (1983). Socialization in the context of the family: Parent-child interaction. In P. H. Mussen (Series Ed.), & E. M. Hetherington (Vol. Ed.), *Handbook of child psychology: Vol. 4. Socialization, personality, and social development* (pp. 1–102). New York: Wiley.

MacDonald, K. (1993). Parent-child play: An evolutionary perspective. In K. MacDonald (Ed.), *Parent-child play: Descriptions and implications* (pp. 113–143). Albany: State University of New York Press.

MacIver, D. J., Young, E. M., & Washburn, B. (2002). Instructional practices and motivation during middle school (with special attention to science). In A. Wigfield & J. Eccles (Eds.), *The development of achievement motivation* (pp. 333–351). San Diego, CA: Academic Press.

MacKinnon, D. P., & Dwyer, J. H. (2003). Major data analysis issues in drug prevention research. In Z. Sloboda & W. J. Bukoski (Eds.), *Handbook for drug abuse prevention: Theory, science, and practice* (pp. 541–556). New York: Springer.

MacKinnon, D. P., Fairchild, A. J., & Fritz, M. S. (2007). Mediation analysis. *Annual Review of Psychology, 58,* 593–614.

MacMillan, H. L., Wathen, C. N., Barlow, J., Fergusson, D. M., Leventhal, J. M., & Taussig, H. N. (2009). Interventions to prevent child maltreatment and associated impairment. *The Lancet, 373,* 250–266.

Mahoney, J. L. (2000). School extracurricular activity participation as a moderator in the development of antisocial patterns. *Child Development, 71,* 502–516.

Mahoney, J. L., Parente, M. E., & Lord, H. (2007). After-school program engagement: Developmental consequences and links to program quality and content. *The Elementary School Journal, 107,* 385–404.

Mahoney, J. L., Vandell, D. L., Simpkins, S., & Zarrett, N. (2009). Adolescent out-of-school activities. In R. M. Lerner & L. Steinberg (Eds.), *Handbook of adolescent psychology: Vol. 2. Contextual influences on adolescent development* (3rd ed., pp. 228–269). Hoboken, NJ: Wiley.

Main, M. (1973). *Exploration, play and level of cognitive functioning as related to child-mother attachment.* Unpublished doctoral dissertation. Johns Hopkins University, Baltimore.

Main, M., & Cassidy, J. (1988). Categories of response to reunion with the parent at age 6: Predictable from infant attachment classification and stable over a 1-month period. *Developmental Psychology, 24,* 415–426.

Main, M., & George, C. (1985). Responses of abused and disadvantaged toddlers to distress in agemates: A study in the daycare setting. *Developmental Psychology, 21,* 407–412.

Main, M., & Hesse, E. (1990). Parents' unresolved traumatic experiences are related to infant disorganized attachment status: Is frightened and/or frightening parental behavior the linking mechanism? In M. T. Greenberg, D. Cicchetti, & E. M. Cummings (Eds.), *Attachment in the preschool years: Theory, research, and intervention* (pp. 161–182). Chicago: University of Chicago Press.

Main, M., Kaplan, N., & Cassidy, J. (1985). Security in infancy, childhood, and adulthood: A move to the level of representation. *Monographs of the Society for Research in Child Development, 50* (Serial No. 209), 66–104.

Main, M., & Weston, D. (1981). The quality of the toddler's relationship to mother and father: Related to conflict behavior and readiness to establish new relationships. *Child Development, 52,* 932–940.

Malatesta, C. Z. (1982). The expression and regulation of emotion: A lifespan perspective. In T. Field & A. Fogel (Eds.), *Emotion and early interaction* (pp. 1–24). Hillsdale, NJ: Erlbaum.

Malatesta, C. Z., Culver, C., Tesman, J., & Shepard, B. (1989). The development of emotional expression during the first two years of life: Normative trends and patterns of individual differences. *Monographs of the Society for Research in Child Development, 54* (Serial No. 219).

Malcolm, K. T., Jensen-Campbell, L. A., Rex-Lear, M., & Waldrip, A. M. (2006). Divided we fall: Children's friendships and peer victimization. *Journal of Social and Personal Relationships, 23,* 721–740.

Mallick, S. K., & McCandless, B. R. (1966). A study of catharsis of aggression. *Journal of Personality and Social Psychology, 4,* 591–596.

Mallon, G. P., & DeCrescenzo, T. (2006). Transgender children and youth: A child welfare practice perspective. *Child Welfare Journal, 85,* 215–241.

Mandara, J., Gaylord-Harden, N. K., Richards, M. H., & Ragsdale, B. L. (2009). The effects of changes in ethnic identity and self-esteem on changes in African American adolescents' mental health. *Child Development, 80,* 1660–1675.

Mandell, S. (2000). Child abuse prevention at report card time. *Journal of Community Psychology, 28,* 687–690.

Mangelsdorf, S. C., Shapiro, J. R., & Marzolf, D. (1995). Developmental and temperamental differences in emotion regulation in infancy. *Child Development, 66,* 1817–1828.

Mangelsdorf, S. C., Watkins, S., & Lehn, L. (1991, April). *The role of control in the infant's appraisal of strangers.* Paper presented at the biennial meeting of the Society for Research in Child Development, Seattle, WA.

Manlove, J., Franzetta, K., & Moore, K. A. (2006). Adolescent sexual relationships, contraceptive consistency, and pregnancy prevention approaches. In A. C. Crouter & A. Booth (Eds.), *Romance and sex in adolescence and emerging adulthood: Risks and opportunities* (pp. 181–212). Mahwah, NJ: Erlbaum.

Manlove, J., Logan, C., Moore, K. A., & Ikramullah, E. (2008). Pathways from family religiosity to adolescent sexual activity and contraceptive use. *Perspectives on Sexual and Reproductive Health, 40,* 105–117.

Manly, J. T., Cicchetti, D., & Barnett, D. (1994). The impact of subtype, frequency, chronicity and severity of child maltreatment on social competence and behavior problems. *Development and Psychopathology, 6,* 121–143.

Manning, W. O., & Smock, P. J. (1999). New families and nonresidential father-child visitation. *Social Forces, 78,* 87–116.

Marcia, J. E. (1966). Development and validation of ego-identity status. *Journal of Personality and Social Psychology, 3,* 551–558.

Marcia, J. E. (1993). The relational roots of identity. In J. Kroger (Ed.), *Discussions on ego identity* (pp. 101–120). Hillsdale, NJ: Erlbaum.

Marcon, R. A., & Freeman, G. (1996). Linking gender-related toy preferences to social structure: Changes in children's letters to Santa since 1978. *Journal of Psychological Practice, 2*, 1–10.

Mares, M., & Woodard, E. H. (2001). Prosocial effects on children's interactions. In D. G. Singer & J. Singer (Eds.), *Handbook of children and the media* (pp. 183–203). Thousand Oaks, CA: Sage.

Mares, M., & Woodard, E. H. (2005). Positive effects of television on children's social interactions: A meta-analysis. *Media Psychology, 7*, 301–322.

Mark, G. Y., Revilla, L. A., Tsutsumoto, T., & Mayeda, D. T. (2006). Youth violence prevention among Asian American and Pacific Islander youth. In N. G. Guerra & E. P. Smith (Eds.), *Preventing youth violence in a multicultural society* (pp. 129–148). Washington, DC: American Psychological Association.

Markham, R., & Wang, L. (1996). Recognition of emotion by Chinese and Australian children. *Journal of Cross-Cultural Psychology, 27*, 616–643.

Markman, E. M. (1977). Realizing that you don't understand: A preliminary investigation. *Child Development, 48*, 986–992.

Marsh, H. W., Gerlach, E., Trautwein, U., Ludtke, O., & Brettschneider, W.-D. (2007). Longitudinal study of preadolescent sport self-concept and performance: Reciprocal effects and causal ordering. *Child Development, 78*, 1640–1656.

Martin, C. L. (1993). Theories of sex typing: Moving toward multiple perspectives. *Monographs of the Society for Research in Child Development, 58* (Serial No. 232), 75–85.

Martin, C. L., Eisenbud, L., & Rose, H. (1995). Children's gender-based reasoning about toys. *Child Development, 52*, 1119–1134.

Martin, C. L., & Fabes, R. (2001). The stability and consequences of young children's same-sex peer interactions. *Developmental Psychology, 37*, 431–446.

Martin, C. L., & Halverson, C. F. (1983). The effects of sex-typing schemas on young children's memory. *Child Development, 54*, 563–574.

Martin, C. L., & Little, J. K. (1990). The relation of gender understanding to children's sex-typed preferences and gender stereotypes. *Child Development, 61*, 1427–1439.

Martin, C. L., & Ruble, D. N. (2004). Children's search for gender cues. *Current Directions in Psychological Science, 13*, 67–70.

Martin, C. L., & Ruble, D. N. (2010). Patterns of gender development. *Annual Review of Psychology, 61*, 353–381.

Martin, C. L., Ruble, D. N., & Szkrybalo, J. (2002). Cognitive theories of early gender development. *Psychological Bulletin, 128*, 903–933.

Martin, J. L., & Ross, H. S. (2005). Sibling aggression: Sex differences and parents' reactions. *International Journal of Behavioral Development, 29*, 129–138.

Martin, L. R., Friedman, H. S., Clark, K. M., & Tucker, J. S. (2005). Longevity following the experience of parental divorce. *Social Science & Medicine, 61*, 2177–2189.

Martin, L. R., Friedman, H. S., Tucker, J. S., Tomlinson-Keasey, C., Criqui, M. H. & Schwartz, J. E. (2002). A life course perspective on childhood cheerfulness and its relation to mortality risk. *Personality and Social Psychology Bulletin, 28*, 1155–1165.

Martinez, P., & Richters, J. E. (1993). The NIMH community violence project: II. Children's distress symptoms associated with violence exposure. *Psychiatry: Interpersonal and Biological Processes, 56*, 22–35.

Mash, E. J., Johnston, C., & Kovitz, K. (1983). A comparison of the mother-child interactions of physically abused and non-abused children during play and task situations. *Journal of Clinical Child Psychology, 12*, 337–346.

Masse, N., &.Barnett, W. S. (2002). A benefit-cost analysis of the Abecedarian Early Childhood Intervention. In H. Levin & P. McEwan (Eds.), *Cost effectiveness and educational policy* (pp. 157–176). Larchmont, NY: Eye on Education.

Masten, A. S. (2006). Developmental psychopathology: Pathways to the future. *International Journal of Behavioral Development, 30*, 47–54.

Masten, A. S., & Obradovi, J. (2006). Competence and resilience in development. *Annals of the New York Academy of Sciences, 1094*, 13–27.

Masuda, T., Ellsworth, P. C., Mesquita, B., Leu, J., Tanida, S., & Van de Veerdonk, E. (2008). Placing the face in context: Cultural differences in the perception of facial emotion. *Journal of Personality & Social Psychology, 94*, 365–381.

Matas, L., Arend, R., & Sroufe, L. A. (1978). Continuity of adaptation in the second year: The relationship between quality of attachment and later competence. *Child Development, 49*, 547–556.

Mather, M., Canli, T., English, T., Whitfield, S., Wais, P., Ochsner, K., . . . Carstensen, L.L. (2004). Amygdala responses to emotionally valenced stimuli in older and younger adults. *Psychological Science, 15*, 259–263.

Mather, M., & Carstensen, L. L. (2003). Aging and attentional biases for emotional faces. *Psychological Science, 14*, 409–415.

Mather, M., & Carstensen, L. L. (2005). Aging and motivated cognition: The positivity effect in attention and memory. *Trends in Cognitive Sciences, 9*, 496–502.

Mathur, R., & Berndt, T. J. (2006). Relations of friends' activities to friendship quality. *Journal of Early Adolescence, 26*, 365–388.

Matson, J. L., & Taras, M. (1989). A 20 year review of punishment and alternative methods to treat problem behaviors of developmentally delayed persons. *Research in Developmental Disabilities, 10,* 85–104.

Matsumoto, D., Yoo, S. H., & Fontaine, J. (2008). Mapping expressive differences around the world. *Journal of Cross-Cultural Psychology, 39,* 55–74.

Matthews, A. E. (2008). Children and obesity: A pan-European project examining the role of food marketing. *European Journal of Public Health, 18,* 7–11.

Maughan, A., Cicchetti, D., Toth, S. L., & Rogosch, F. A. (2007). Early occurring maternal depression and maternal negativity in predicting young children's emotional regulation and socioemotional functioning. *Journal of Abnormal Child Psychology, 35,* 685–703.

Maurer, D., & Salapatek, P. (1976). Developmental changes in scanning of faces by young infants. *Child Development, 47,* 523–527.

Maxwell, J. A. (1992). Understanding and validity in qualitative research. *Harvard Educational Review, 62,* 279–300.

Mayeux, L., Sandstrom, M. J., & Cillessen, A. H. N. (2008.). Is being popular a risky proposition? *Journal of Research on Adolescence, 18,* 49–74.

Mayeux, L., Underwood, M. K., & Risser, S. D. (2007). Perspectives on the ethics of sociometric research with children: How children, peers, and teachers help to inform the debate. *Merrill-Palmer Quarterly, 53,* 53–78.

Maynard, A. E. (2004). Cultures of teaching in childhood: Formal schooling and Maya sibling teaching at home. *Cognitive Development, 19,* 517–535.

Mazur, E., Wolchik, S. A., Virdin, L., Sandler, I. N., & West, S. G. (1999). Cognitive moderators of children's adjustment to stressful divorce events: The role of negative cognitive errors and positive illusions. *Child Development, 70,* 231–245.

Mbwana, K., & Moore, K. A. (2008). Parental involvement in middle childhood: Can it protect children from harmful TV viewing habits and behavior? *Child Trends Fact Sheet, Publication 2008–28.* Washington, DC: Child Trends.

McCabe, K. M. (1997). Sex differences in the long term effects of divorce on children: Depression and heterosexual relationship difficulties in the young adult years. *Journal of Divorce & Remarriage, 27,* 123–135.

McCall, R., Beach, S. R., & Lan, S. (2000). The nature and correlates of underachievement among elementary school children in Hong Kong. *Child Development, 71,* 785–801.

McCaul, K. D., Gladue, B. A., & Joppa, M. (1992). Winning, losing, mood, and testosterone. *Hormones and Behavior, 26,* 486–504.

McCloskey, L. A., & Stuewig, J. (2001). The quality of peer relationships among children exposed to family violence. *Developmental Psychopathology, 13,* 83–86.

McClure, E. B. (2000). A meta-analytic review of sex differences in facial expression processing and their development in infants, children, and adolescents. *Psychological Bulletin, 126,* 424–453.

McCormick, M. C., Brooks-Gunn, J., Buka, S. L., Goldman, J., Yu, J., Salganik, M., . . . Casey, P. (2006). Early intervention in low birth weight premature infants: Results at 18 years of age for the infant health and development program. *Journal of Pediatrics, 117,* 771–780.

McDevitt, T. M., & Ormrod, J. E. (2007). *Child development and education* (3rd ed.). Upper Saddle River, NJ: Pearson/Merrill Prentice Hall.

McDowell, D. J., & Parke, R. D. (2000). Differential knowledge of display rules for positive and negative emotions: Influences from parents influences on peers. *Social Development, 9,* 415–432.

McDowell, D. J., & Parke, R. D. (2005). Parental control and affect as predictors of children's display rule use and social competence with peers. *Social Development, 14,* 440–457.

McDowell, D. J., & Parke, R. D. (2009). Parental correlates of children's peer relations: An empirical test of a tripartite model. *Developmental Psychology, 45,* 224–235.

McDowell, D., Parke, R. D., & Spitzer, S. (2002). Parent and child cognitive representations of social situations and children's social competence. *Social Development, 11,* 469–486.

McElwain, N. L., Booth-LaForce, C., Lansford, J. E., Wu, X., & Dyer, W. J. (2008). A process model of attachment-friend linkages: Hostile attribution biases, language ability, and mother-child affective mutuality as intervening mechanisms. *Child Development, 79,* 1891–1906.

McElwain, N. L., Halberstadt, A. G., & Volling, B. L. (2007). Mother- and father-reported reactions to children's negative emotions: Relations to young children's emotional understanding and friendship quality. *Child Development, 78,* 1407–1425.

McElwain, N. L., & Volling, B. L. (2005). Preschool children's interactions with friends and older siblings: Relationship specificity and joint contributions to problem behavior. *Journal of Family Psychology, 19,* 486–496.

McGue, M., Sharma, A., & Benson, P. (1996). Parent and sibling influences on adolescent alcohol use and misuse: Evidence from a US adoption cohort. *Journal of Studies on Alcohol, 57,* 8–18.

McGuire, S. (2001). Nonshared environment research: What is it and where is it going? *Marriage and Family Review, 33,* 31–56.

McHale, J. P. (2010). The construct of co-parenting: Evolution of a key family paradigm. In M. Schultz, M. K. Pruett, P. Kerig, & R. D. Parke (Eds.), *Strengthening couple relationships for optimal child development* (pp. 77–94). Washington, DC: American Psychological Association.

McHale, J. P., Laurette, A., Talbot, J., & Pouquette, C. (2002). Retrospect and prospect in the psychological study of coparenting and family group process. In J. P. McHale & W. Grolnick (Eds.), *Retrospect and prospect in the psychological study of families* (pp. 127–165). Mahwah, NJ: Erlbaum.

McHale, S. M., Crouter, A. C., & Whiteman, S. D. (2003). Family contexts of gender development in childhood and adolescence. *Social Development, 12*, 125–148.

McHale, S. M., Shanahan, L., Updegraff, K. A., Crouter, A. C., & Booth, A. (2004). Developmental and individual differences in girls' sex-typed activities in middle childhood and adolescence. *Child Development, 75*, 1575–1593.

McHale, S. M., Updegraff, K. A., Helms-Erikson, H., & Crouter, A. C. (2001). Sibling influences on gender development in middle childhood and early adolescence: A longitudinal study. *Developmental Psychology, 37*, 115–125.

McKee, L., Roland, E., Coffelt, N., Olson, A. L., Forehand, R., Massari, C., . . . Zens, M. S. (2007). Harsh discipline and child problem behaviors: The roles of positive parenting and gender. *Journal of Family Violence, 22*, 187–196.

McKenna, K. Y. A, & Bargh, J. A. (2000). Plan 9 from cyberspace: The implications of the Internet for personality and social psychology. *Personality and Social Psychology Review, 4*, 57–75.

McKenna, K. Y. A., Green, A. S., & Gleason, M. E. J. (2002). Relationship formation on the Internet: What's the big attraction? *Journal of Social Issues, 58*, 9–31.

McKinney, K. (2003). OJJDP's tribal youth initiatives. *Juvenile Justice Bulletin*. Washington, DC: U.S. Department of Justice, Office of Juvenile Justice and Delinquency Prevention. Retrieved from: http://www.ncjrs.gov/pdffiles1/ojjdp/193763.pdf

McKown, C., & Strambler, M. J. (2009). Developmental antecedents and social and academic consequences of stereotype consciousness in middle childhood. *Child Development, 80*, 1643–1659.

McKown, C., & Weinstein, R. S. (2003). The development and consequences of stereotype consciousness in middle childhood. *Child Development, 74*, 498–515.

McLanahan, S. S. (1999). Father absence and the welfare of children. In E. M. Hetherington (Ed.), *Coping with divorce, single parenting, and remarriage* (pp. 117–145). Mahwah, NJ: Erlbaum

McLaughlin, A. E., Campbell, F. C., Pungello, E. P., & Skinner, M. (2007). Depressive symptoms in young adults: The influences of the early home environment and early educational childcare. *Child Development, 78*, 746–756.

McLean, A. (2003). *The motivated school*. London: Paul Chapman.

McLellan, J. A., & Youniss, J. (2003). Two systems of youth service: Determinants of voluntary and required youth community service. *Journal of Youth and Adolescence, 32*, 47–58.

McLoyd, V. C., Aikens, N. L., & Burton, L. M. (2006). Childhood poverty, policy, and practice. In W. Damon & R. Lerner (Series Eds.), K. A. Renninger & I. E. Sigel (Vol. Eds.), *Handbook of child psychology: Vol. 4. Child psychology in practice* (6th ed., pp. 750–775). Hoboken, NJ: Wiley.

McLoyd, V. C., Cauce, A. M., Takeuchi, D., & Wilson, L. (2000). Marital processes and parental socialization in families of color: A decade review of research. *Journal of Marriage and Family, 62*, 1070–1093.

McLoyd, V. C., & Ceballo, R. (1998). Conceptualizing and assessing economic context: Issues in the study of race and child development. In V. C. McLoyd & L. Steinberg (Eds.), *Studying minority adolescents: Conceptual, methodological, and theoretical issues* (pp. 251–278). Mahwah, NJ: Erlbaum.

McLoyd, V. C., Harper, C. I., & Copeland, N. L. (2001). Ethnic minority status, interparental conflict and child adjustment. In J. Grych & F. D. Fincham (Eds.), *Interparental conflict and child development* (pp. 98–125). New York: Cambridge University Press.

McWayne, C., Hampton, V., Fantuzzo, J., Cohen, H. L., & Sekino, Y. (2004). A multivariate examination of parent involvement and the social and academic competencies or urban kindergarten children. *Psychology in the Schools, 41*, 363–377.

Mead, M. (1928). *Coming of age in Samoa*. New York: William Morrow.

Meadows, S. O., Land, K. C., & Lamb, V. L. (2005). Assessing *Gilligan vs. Sommers*: Gender-specific trends in child and youth well-being in the United States, 1985–2001. *Social Indicators Research, 70*, 1–52.

Meaney, M. J. (2010). Epigenetics and the biological definition of gene x environment interactions. *Child Development, 81*, 41–79.

Mednick, S. A., & Christiansen, K. O. (1977). *Biosocial bases of criminal behavior*. New York: Gardner Press.

Medrich, E. A. (1981). *The serious business of growing up: A study of children's lives outside the school*. Berkeley: University of California Press.

Meehan, B. J., Hughes, J. N., & Cavell, T. A. (2003). Teacher-student relationships as compensatory resources for aggressive children. *Child Development, 74*, 1145–1157.

Meeus, W., van de Schoot, R., Keijsers, L., Schwartz, S. J., & Branje, S. (2010). On the progression and stability of adolescent identity formation: A five-wave longitudinal study in early-to-middle and middle-to-late adolescence. *Child Development, 81*,

Mehler, J., Jusczyk, P., Lambertz, G., Halsted, N., Bertoncini, J., & Amieltison, C. (1988). A precursor of language acquisition in young infants. *Cognition, 29*, 143–178.

Meins, E., Fernyhough, C., Wainwright, R., Gupta, M. D., Fradley, E., & Tuckey, M. (2002). Maternal mind-mindedness and attachment security as predictors of theory of mind understanding. *Child Development, 73,* 1715–1726.

Mellanby, J., Martin, M., & O'Doherty, J. (2000). The 'gender gap' in final examination results at Oxford University. *British Journal of Psychology, 91,* 377–390.

Melson, G. F. (2003). Child development and the human-companion animal bond. *The American Behavioral Scientist, 47,* 31.

Mendle, J., Turkheimer, E., & Emery, R. E. (2007). Detrimental psychological outcomes associated with early pubertal timing in adolescent girls. *Developmental Review, 27,* 151–171.

Mennella, J. A., & Beauchamp, G. K. (1996). The early development of human flavor preferences. In E. D. Capaldi (Ed.), *Why we eat what we eat: The psychology of eating* (pp. 83–112). Washington, DC: American Psychologist Association.

Menon, M., Tobin, D. D., Corby, B. C., Menon, M., Hodges, E. V. E., & Perry, D. G. (2007). The developmental costs of high self-esteem for antisocial children. *Child Development, 78,* 1627–1639.

Mervis, C. B., & Klein-Tasman, B. P. (2000). Williams syndrome: Cognition, personality, and adaptive behavior. *Mental Retardation and Developmental Disabilities Research Review, 6,* 148–158.

Messinger, D. S., & Fogel, A. (2007). The interactive development of social smiling. In R. V. Kail (Ed.), *Advances in child development and behavior* (Vol. 35, pp. 327–366). San Diego, CA: Elsevier Academic Press.

Messinger, D. S., Fogel, A., & Dickson, K. L. (1999). What's in a smile? *Developmental Psychology, 35,* 701–708.

Messinger, D. S., Fogel, A., & Dickson, K. L. (2001). All smiles are positive but some smiles are more positive than others. *Developmental Psychology, 37,* 642–653.

Metropolitan Area Child Study Research Group. (2002). A cognitive-ecological approach to preventing aggression in urban settings: Initial outcomes for high-risk children. *Journal of Consulting and Clinical Psychology, 70,* 179–194.

Metz, E., McLellan, J., & Youniss, J. (2003). Types of voluntary service and adolescents' civic development. *Journal of Adolescent Research, 18,* 188–203.

Meyerowitz, J. (2002). *How sex changed: A history of transsexuality in the United States.* Cambridge, MA: Harvard University Press.

Meyers, B. (1984). Mother-infant bonding: The status of this critical period hypothesis. *Developmental Review, 4,* 240–274.

Mikulincer, M., Florian, V., Cowan, P. A., & Cowan, C. P. (2002). Attachment security in couple relationships: A systematic model and its implications for family dynamics. *Family Process, 41,* 405–434.

Milgram, S. (1974). *Obedience to authority: An experimental view.* London: Tavistock.

Miller, C. F., Lurye, L. E., Zosuls, K. M., & Ruble, D. N. (2009). Accessibility of gender stereotype domains: Developmental and gender differences in children. *Sex Roles, 60,* 870–881.

Miller, C. L., Miceli, P. J., Whitman, T. L., & Borkowski, J. G. (1996). Cognitive readiness to parent and intellectual-emotional development in children of adolescent mothers. *Developmental Psychology, 32,* 533–541.

Miller, D. B. (1999). Racial socialization and racial identity: Can they promote resiliency for African American adolescents? *Adolescence, 34,* 493–501.

Miller, J. G. (1987). Cultural influences on the development of conceptual differentiation in person description. *British Journal of Developmental Psychology, 5,* 309–319.

Miller, J. G., & Bersoff, D. M. (1992). Culture and moral judgment: How are conflicts between justice and interpersonal responsibilities resolved? *Journal of Personality and Social Psychology, 62,* 541–554.

Miller, P. H. (2002). *Theories of developmental psychology* (4th ed.). New York: Worth.

Miller, P. H., & Scholnick, E. K. (Eds.)(2000). *Toward a feminist developmental psychology.* New York: Routledge.

Miller, S. A. (2007). *Developmental research methods.* Thousand Oaks, CA: Sage.

Mills-Koonce, W. R., Ganepy, J.-L., Propper, C., Sutton, K., Calkins, S., Moore, G., & Cox, M. (2007). Infant and parent factors associated with early maternal sensitivity: A caregiver-attachment systems approach. *Infant Behavior and Development, 30,* 114–126.

Milner, D. (1983). *Children and race.* Beverly Hills, CA: Sage.

Minagawa-Kawai, Y., Matsuoka, S., Dan, I., Naoi, N., Nakamura, K., & Kojima, S. (2009). Prefrontal activation associated with social attachment: Facial-emotion recognition in mothers and infants. *Cerebral Cortex, 19,* 284–292.

Miner, J. L., & Clarke-Stewart, K. A. (2008). Trajectories of externalizing behavior from age 2 to age 9: Relations with gender, temperament, ethnicity, parenting, and rater. *Developmental Psychology, 44,* 771–786.

Minneapolis Star Tribune (November 14, 2008). How do preschoolers learn better? Follow the turtle. Retrieved from: http://www.startribune.com/nation/34497164.html?elr=KArksLc kD8EQDUoaEyqyP4O:DW3ckUiD3aPc:_Yyc:aUUF

Minuchin, P., & Shapiro, E. K. (1983). The school as a context for social development. In P. H. Mussen (Series Ed.), & E. M. Hetherington (Ed.), *Handbook of child psychology: Vol. 4. Socialization, personality, and social development* (4th ed., pp. 197–274). New York: Wiley.

Mirowsky, J. (2002). Parenthood and health: The pivotal and optimal age at first birth. *Social Forces, 81,* 315–149.

Mischel, L., Bernstein, J., & Schmitt, J. (1999). *The state of working America: 1998–1999.* Ithaca, NY: ILR Press.

Mischel, W., & Ayduk, O. (2004). Willpower in a cognitive-affective processing system: The dynamics of delay of gratification. In R. F. Baumeister & K. D. Vohs (Eds.), *Handbook of self-regulation: Research, theory, and applications* (pp. 99–129). New York: Guilford Press.

Mischel, W., Shoda, Y., & Peake, P. K. (1988). The nature of adolescent competencies predicted by preschool delay of gratification. *Journal of Personality & Social Psychology, 54,* 687–696.

Mitchell, K. J., Finkelhor, D., & Wolak, J. (2001). Risk factors for and impact of online sexual solicitation of youth. *Journal of the American Medical Association, 285,* 3011–3014.

Mitchell, K. J., Finkelhor, D., & Wolak, J. (2003). The exposure of youth to unwanted sexual material on the Internet: A national survey of risk, impact, and prevention. *Youth and Society, 34,* 330–359.

Mitchell, S. (2000). Jack and the giant school. *The New Rules, 2,* Summer, 1–10. Retrieved from: http://www.newrules.org/equity/article/jack-and-giant-school; http://www.newrules.org/journal/nrsum00schools.htm

Mitsis, E. M., Halperin, J. M., & Newcorn, J. H. (2000). Serotonin and aggression in children. *Current Psychiatry Reports, 2,* 95–101.

Miyazaki, M., & Hiraki, K. (2006). Delayed intermodal contingency affects young children's recognition of their current self. *Child Development, 77,* 736–750.

Mize, J., & Ladd, G. W. (1990). Toward the development of successful social skills for preschool children. In S. R. Asher & J. D. Coie (Eds.), *Peer rejection in childhood* (pp. 338–364). New York: Cambridge University Press.

Modell, J., & Elder, G. H. (2002). Children develop in history: So what's new? In W. W. Hartup & R. A. Weinberg (Eds.), *Minnesota Symposia on Child Psychology: Vol. 32. Child psychology in retrospect and prospect: In celebration of the 75th anniversary of the Institute of Child Development* (pp. 173–205). Mahwah, NJ: Erlbaum.

Moeller, T. G. (2001). *Youth aggression and violence.* Mahwah, NJ: Erlbaum.

Moffitt, T. E. (2002). Teen-aged mothers in contemporary Britain. *Journal of Child Psychology and Psychiatry, 43,* 727–742.

Moffitt, T. E. (2006). Life-course-persistent versus adolescence-limited antisocial behavior. In D. Cicchetti, & D. J. Cohen (Eds.), *Developmental psychopathology: Vol. 3. Risk, disorder, and adaptation* (2nd ed., pp. 570–598). Hoboken, NJ: Wiley.

Moffitt, T. E., & Caspi, A. (2001). Childhood predictors differentiate life-course persistent and adolescence-limited antisocial pathways among males and females. *Development and Psychopathology, 13,* 135–151.

Moffitt, T. E., & Caspi, A. (2007). Evidence from behavioral genetics for environmental contributions to antisocial conduct. In J. Grusec & P. Hastings (Eds.), *Handbook of socialization* (pp. 96–123). New York: Guilford Press.

Moffitt, T. E., Caspi, A., & Fawcett, P. (1997). Whole blood serotonin and family background relate to male violence. In A. Raine, P. A. Brennan, D. P. Farrington, & S. A. Mednick (Eds.), *Biosocial bases of violence* (pp. 321–340). New York: Plenum Press.

Moffitt, T. E., Caspi, A., & Rutter, M. (2006). Measured gene-environment interactions in psychopathology: Concepts, research strategies and implications for research intervention and public understanding of genetics. *Perspectives on Psychological Science, 1,* 5–27.

Moffitt, T. E., Caspi, A., Rutter, M., & Silva, P. A. (2001). *Sex differences in antisocial behaviour: Conduct disorder, delinquency, and violence in the Dunedin Longitudinal Study.* Cambridge, UK: Cambridge University Press.

Moncloa, F., Johns, M., Gong, E. J., Russell, S., Lee, F., & West, E. (2003). Best practices in teen pregnancy prevention practitioner handbook. *Journal of Extension, 41,* 2. Retrieved from: www.joe.org.

Mondloch, C. J., Lewis, T. L., Budreau, D. R., Maurer, D., Dannemiller, J. D., Stephens, B. R., & Kleiner, K. A. (1999). Face perception during early infancy. *Psychological Science, 10,* 419–422.

Money, J. (1987). Human sexology and psychoneuroendocrinology. In D. Crews (Ed.), *Psychobiology of reproductive behavior: An evolutionary perspective* (pp. 323–344). Englewood Cliffs, NJ: Prentice-Hall.

Money, J., & Ehrhardt, A. A. (1972). *Man and woman, boy and girl: Differentiation and dimorphism of gender identity from conception to maturity.* Baltimore: Johns Hopkins University Press.

Monk, C. S., Klein, R. G., Telzer, E. H., Schroth, F. A., Mannuzza, S., Moulton, J. L., . . . Ernst, M. (2008). Amygdala and nucleus accumbens activation to emotional facial expressions in children and adolescents at risk for major depression. *American Journal of Psychiatry, 165,* 90–98.

Montague, D. P. F., & Walker-Andrews, A. S. (2002). Mothers, fathers, and infants: The role of person familiarity and parental involvement in infants' perception of emotion expressions. *Child Development, 75,* 1339–1352.

Moore, D., & Florsheim, P. (2001). Interpersonal processes and psychopathology among expectant and nonexpectant adolescent couples. *Journal of Consulting & Clinical Psychology, 69,* 101–113.

Moore, K. A. (2009). Teen births: Examining the recent increase. *Child Trends Research Brief.* Retrieved from: http://www.childtrends.org/Files/Child_Trends_2009_03_13_FS_TeenBirthRate.pdf

Moore, K. A., Redd, Z., Burkhauser, M., Mbwana, K., & Collins, A. (2009). Children in poverty: Trends, consequences, and policy options. *Child Trends Research Brief, Publication #2009–11.* Retrieved from: www.childtrends.org.

Moore, M. R., & Brooks-Gunn, J. (2002). Adolescent parenthood. In M. H. Bornstein (Ed.), *Handbook of parenting: Vol. 3.*

Being and becoming a parent (2nd ed., pp. 173–214). Mahwah, NJ: Erlbaum.

Moore, R. (1986). Research on sociability. *The Parent Educator and Family Report, 4,* 1.

Morelli, G., & Tronick, E. Z. (1992). Male care among Efe foragers and Lese farmers. In B. Hewlett (Ed.), *Father-child relations: Cultural and biosocial contexts* (pp. 231–262). New York: Aldine de Gruyther.

Morgan, B. L. (1998). A three-generational study of tomboy behavior. *Sex Roles, 39,* 787–858.

Morgan, G.A., & Ricciuti, H. (1969). Infants' responses to strangers during the first year. In B. M. Foss (Ed.), *Determinants of infant behavior* (Vol. 4, pp. 253–272). London: Methuen.

Morgan, M., & Rothschild, N. (1983). Impact of the new television technology: Cable, TV, peers and sex-role cultivation in the electronic environment. *Youth and Society, 15,* 33–50.

Moroz, K., & Jones, K. (2002). The effects of Positive Peer Reporting on children's social involvement. *School Psychology Review, 31,* 235–245.

Morris, A. S., Silk, J. S., Steinberg, L., Myers, S. S., & Robinson, L. R. (2007). The role of the family context in the development of emotion regulation. *Social Development, 16,* 361–388.

Morris, A. S., Silk, J. S., Steinberg, L., Sessa, F. M., Avenevoli, S., & Essex, M. J. (2002). Temperamental vulnerability and negative parenting as interacting predictors of child adjustment. *Journal of Marriage and Family, 64,* 461–471.

Morris, J. S., Friston, K. J., Buchel, C., Frith, C. D., Young, A. W., Calder, A. J., & Dolan, R. J. (1998). A neuromodulatory role for the human amygdala in processing emotional facial expressions. *Brain, 121,* 47–57.

Morris, P. A. (2002). The effects of welfare reform policies on children. *Social Policy Report, 16,* 4–19.

Morris, P. A., Gennetian, L. A., & Duncan, G. J. (2005). Effects on welfare and employment policies on young children: New findings on policy experiments conducted in the early 1990's. *Social Policy Report, 19* (2).

Morrison, D. R., & Cherlin, A. J. (1995). The divorce process and young children's well-being: A prospective analysis. *Journal of Marriage and Family, 57,* 800–812.

Morrongiello, B. A., & Hogg, K. (2004). Mothers' reactions to children misbehaving in ways that can lead to injury: Implications for gender differences in children's risk taking and injuries. *Sex Roles, 50,* 103–118.

Morrongiello, B. A., Midgett, C., & Stanton, K. (2000). Gender biases in children's appraisals of injury risk and other children's risk-taking behaviors. [Special Issue: *Sex and -gender development*]. *Journal of Experimental Child Psychology, 77,* 317–336.

Moshman, D. (2005). *Adolescent psychological development: Rationality, morality, and identity* (2nd ed.). New York: Psychology Press.

Moss, E., Cyr, C., Bureau, J-F., Tarabulsy, G. M., & Dubois-Comtois, K. (2005). Stability of attachment during the preschool period. *Developmental Psychology, 41,* 773–783.

Moss, E., Smolla, N., Cyr, C., Dubois-Comtois, K., Mazzarello, T., & Berthiaume, C. (2006). Attachment and behavior problems in middle childhood as reported by adult and child informants. *Development & Psychopathology, 18,* 425–444.

Mott, F. L., Kowaleski-Jones, L., & Mehaghan, E. G. (1997). Paternal absence and child behavior: Does a child's gender make a difference? *Journal of Marriage and Family, 59,* 103–118.

Mounts, N. S. (2000). Parental management of adolescent peer relationships: What are its effects on friend selection? In K. A. Kerns, J. M. Contreras, & A. M. Neal-Barnett (Eds.), *Family and peers: Linking two social worlds* (pp. 169–193). Westport, CT: Praeger Publishers

Mrug, S., Hoza, B., Gerdes, A. C., Hinshaw, S., Arnold, L. E., Hechtman, L., & Pelham, W. E. (2009). Discriminating between children with ADHD and classmates using peer variables. *Journal of Attention Disorders, 12,* 372–380.

Mueller, E. (1989). Toddlers' peer relations: Shared meaning and semantics. In W. Damon (Ed.), *Child development today and tomorrow.* San Francisco: Jossey-Bass.

Mueller, E., & Brenner, J. (1977). The origins of social skills and interaction among playgroup toddlers. *Child Development, 48,* 854–861.

Mueller, E., & Lucas, T. A. (1975). A developmental analysis of peer interaction among toddlers. In M. Lewis & L. A. Rosenblum (Eds.), *Friendship and peer relations* (pp. 223–257). New York: Wiley.

Mumme, D. L., Fernald, A., & Herrera, C. (1996). Infants' responses to facial and vocal emotional signals in a social referencing paradigm. *Child Development, 67,* 3219–3237.

Mumola, C. (2000). *Incarcerated parents and their children.* Washington, DC: U.S. Department of Justice.

Munroe, R. H., Shimmin, H. S., & Munroe, R. L. (1984). Gender understanding and sex role preferences in four cultures. *Developmental Psychology, 20,* 673–682.

Muntean, A., & Roth, M. (2001). Romania. In B. M. Schwartz-Kenney, M. McCauley, & M. A. Epstein (Eds.), *Child abuse: A global view* (pp. 175–193). Westport, CT: Greenwood.

Muris, P., Bos, A. E. R., Mayer, B., Verkade, R., Thewissen, V., & Dell'Avvento, V. (2009). Relations among behavioral inhibition, big five personality factors, and anxiety disorder symptoms in non-clinical children. *Personality & Individual Differences, 46,* 525–529.

Muris, P., Vermeer, E., & Horselenberg, R. (2008). Cognitive development and the interpretation of anxiety-related physical symptoms in 4–13-year-old non-clinical children. *Journal of Behavior Therapy & Experimental Psychology, 39,* 73–86.

Murphy, F. C., Nimmo-Smith, I., & Lawrence, A. D. (2003). Functional neuroanatomy of emotions: A meta-analysis. *Cognitive, Affective, & Behavioral Neuroscience, 3,* 207–233.

Murphy-Cowan, T., & Stringer, M. (1999). Physical punishment and the parenting cycle: A survey of Northern Irish parents. *Journal of Community & Applied Social Psychology, 9,* 61–71.

Murray, J. P., Liotta, M., Ingmundson, P. T., Mayberg, H. S., Pu, Y., Zamarripa, F., . . . Fox, P. T. (2006). Children's brain activations while viewing televised violence revealed by fMRI. *Media Psychology, 8,* 25–37.

Murray, T. A. (1996). *The worth of a child.* Berkeley: University of California Press.

Mutz, D. C., Roberts, D. F., & Van Vuuren, D. P. (1993). Reconsidering the displacement hypothesis: Television's influence on children's time use. *Communication Research, 20,* 51–75.

Muzzatti, B., & Agnoli, F. (2007). Gender and mathematics: Attitudes and stereotype threat susceptibility in Italian children. *Developmental Psychology, 43,* 747–759.

Nabi, R. L., & Clark, S. (2008). Exploring the limits of social cognitive theory: Why negatively reinforced behaviors on TV may be modeled anyway. *Journal of Communication, 58,* 407–427.

Nachmias, M., Gunnar, M., Mangelsdorf, S., Parritz, R. H., & Buss, K. (1996). Behavioral inhibition and stress reactivity: The moderating role of attachment security. *Child Development, 67,* 508–522.

Nagin, D., & Tremblay, R. E. (1999). Trajectories of boys' physical aggression, opposition, and hyperactivity on the path to physically violent and nonviolent juvenile delinquency. *Child Development, 70,* 1181–1196.

Nangle, D. W., Erdley, C. A., Newman, J. E., Mason, C. A., & Carpenter, E. M. (2003). Popularity, friendship, quantity, and friendship quality: Inter-active influences on children loneliness and depression. *Journal of Clinical Child and Adolescent Psychology, 32,* 546–555.

Nansel, T. R., Overpeck, M., Pilla, R. S., Ruan, W. J., Simons-Morton, B., & Scheidt, P. (2001). Bullying behaviors among U.S. youth. *Journal of the American Medical Association, 285,* 2094–2100.

Narumoto, J., Okada, T., Sadato, N., Fukui, K., & Yonekura, Y. (2001). Attention to emotion modulates fMRI activity in human right superior temporal sulcus. *Cognitive Brain Research, 12,* 225–231.

Nash, J. M. (1997, February 3). Fertile minds. *Time,* pp. 49–62.

Nathanson, A. L., & Cantor, J. (2000). Reducing the aggression-promoting effect of violent cartoons by increasing fictional investment with the victim: A study of active mediation. *Journal of Broadcasting and Electronic Media, 44,* 125–142.

National Campaign to Prevent Teenage and Unplanned Pregnancy, The. (2009). *Relationship Redux: Tips and Scripts for Talking to Your Kids about Relationships.* Retrieved from: http://www.thenationalcampaign.org/resources/pdf/pubs/Relationship_Redux.pdf

National Institute of Mental Health. (2007). Autism spectrum disorders (pervasive developmental disorders). Retrieved from: http://www.nimh.nih.gov/publicat/nimhautism-spectrum.pdf

National Institutes of Health. (2002). *The National Human Genome Research Institute Website.* Retrieved from: http://www.nhgri.nih.gov/

National Research Council, Division of Behavioral and Social Sciences and Education. (2007). *Evidence for use: Improving the quality and utility of social science research. A proposal.* Washington, DC: National Research Council.

Neff, K. D. (2001). Judgments of personal autonomy and interpersonal responsibility in the context of Indian spousal relationships: An examination of young people's reasoning in Mysore, India. *British Journal of Developmental Psychology, 19,* 233–257.

Neiderhiser, J. M., Reiss, D., Pedersen, N., Lichtenstein, P., Spotts, E. L., Hansson, K., Cederblad, M., & Elthammer, O. (2004). Genetic and environmental influences on mothering of adolescents: A comparison of two samples. *Developmental Psychology, 40,* 335–351.

Nelson, C. A. (1999). Change and continuity in neurobehavioral development: Lessons from the study of neurobiology and neural plasticity. *Infant Behavior and Development, 22,* 415–429.

Nelson, C. A., & Bosquet, M. (2000). Neurobiology of fetal and infant development: Implications for infant mental health. In C. Zeanah (Ed.), *Handbook of infant mental health* (pp. 37–59). New York: Guilford Press.

Nelson, C. A., Thomas, K. M., & de Haan, M. (2006). Neural bases of cognitive development. In W. Damon & R. M. Lerner (Series Eds.), & D. Kuhn & R. S. Siegler (Vol. Eds.), *Handbook of child psychology: Vol. 2. Cognition, perception, and language* (6th ed., pp. 3–57). Hoboken, NJ: Wiley.

Nelson, C. A., Zeanah, C. H., & Fox, N. A. (2007). *The effects of early deprivation on brain-behavioral development: The Bucharest early intervention project.* New York: Oxford University Press.

Nelson, D. A., Robinson, C. C., & Hart, C. H. (2005). Relational and physical aggression of preschool-age children: Peer status linkages across informants. *Early Education & Development, 16,* 115–139.

Nelson, G., Laurendeau, M-C., & Chamberland, C. (2001). A review of programs to promote family wellness and prevent the maltreatment of children. *Canadian Journal of Behavioural Science, 33,* 1–13.

Nelson, K. (2007). *Young minds in social worlds: Experience, meaning, and memory.* Cambridge, MA: Harvard University Press.

Nelson, S. E., & Dishion, T. J. (2004). From boys to men: Predicting adult adaptation from middle childhood sociometric status. *Development & Psychopathology, 16,* 441–459.

Nesdale, D., & Lambert, A. (2008). Effects of experimentally induced peer-group rejection on children's risk-taking behaviour. *European Journal of Developmental Psychology, 5,* 19–38.

Nesse, R. M. (2001). *Evolution and the capacity for commitment.* New York: Russell Sage Foundation.

Neville, B., & Parke, R. D. (1997). Waiting for paternity: Interpersonal and contextual implications of the timing of fatherhood. *Sex Roles, 37,* 45–59.

Neville, H. J., & Bruer, J. T. (2001). Language processing: How experience affects brain organization. In D. B. Bailey, J. T. Bruer, F. J. Simons, & J. W. Lichtman (Eds.), *Critical thinking about critical periods* (pp. 151–172). Baltimore: Broker.

New, R. S., & Benigni, L. (1987). Italian fathers and infants: Cultural constraints on paternal behavior. In M. E. Lamb (Ed.), *The father's role: Cross-cultural perspectives* (pp. 139–167). Hillsdale, NJ: Erlbaum.

Newcomb, A. F., Bukowski, W. M., & Pattee, L. (1993). Children's peer relations: A meta-analytic review of popular, rejected, neglected, controversial, and average sociometric status. *Psychological Bulletin, 113,* 99–128.

Newcomer, S., & Udry, J. R. (1987). Parental marital status effects on adolescent sexual behavior. *Journal of Marriage and Family, 48,* 235–240.

Newhouse, P., Newhouse, C., & Astur, R. S. (2007). Sex differences in visual-spatial learning using a virtual water maze in pre-pubertal children. *Behavioural Brain Research, 183,* 1–7.

New York Times (June 17, 1895). The work that women do. Retrieved from: http://query.nytimes.com/mem/archive-free/pdf?_r=2&res=9500EEDA103AE533A25754C1A96 09C94649ED7CF

NICHD Early Child Care Research Network. (1997a). Familial factors associated with the characteristics of non-maternal care for infants. *Journal of Marriage and Family, 59,* 389–408.

NICHD Early Child Care Research Network. (1997b). The effects of infant child care on infant-mother attachment security: Results of the NICHD Study of Early Child Care. *Child Development, 60,* 860–879.

NICHD Early Child Care Research Network (1998). Relations between family predictors and child outcomes: Are they weaker for children in child care? *Developmental Psychology, 34,* 1119–1128.

NICHD Early Child Care Research Network. (1999). Chronicity of maternal depressive symptoms, maternal sensitivity, and child functioning at 36 months. *Developmental Psychology, 35,* 1297–1310.

NICHD Early Child Care Research Network. (2000). Factors associated with fathers' caregiving activities and sensitivity with young children. *Journal of Family Psychology, 14,* 200–219.

NICHD Early Child Care Research Network. (2001). Before Head Start: Income and ethnicity, family characteristics, child care experiences and child development. *Early Education & Development, 12,* 545–576.

NICHD Early Child Care Research Network. (2002). Early child care and children's development prior to school entry: Results from the NICHD Study of Early Child Care. *American Educational Research Journal, 39,* 133–164.

NICHD Early Child Care Research Network. (2003a). Does amount of time spent in child care predict socioemotional adjustment during the transition to kindergarten? *Child Development, 74,* 976–1005.

NICHD Early Child Care Research Network. (2003b). Does quality of child care affect child outcomes at age 4½? *Developmental Psychology, 39,* 451–469.

NICHD Early Child Care Research Network. (2004a). Are child developmental outcomes related to before/after school care arrangements? *Child Development, 75,* 280–295.

NICHD Early Child Care Research Network. (2004b). Trajectories of physical aggression from toddlerhood to middle childhood: Predictors, correlates, and outcomes. *Monographs of the Society for Research in Child Development, 69* (Serial No. 278).

NICHD Early Child Care Research Network. (2005). *Child care and child development: Results from the NICHD Study of Early Child Care and Youth Development.* New York: Guilford Press.

NICHD Early Child Care Research Network. (2006). Infant-mother attachment classification: Risk and protection in relation to changing maternal caregiving quality. *Developmental Psychology, 42,* 38–58.

NICHD Early Child Care Research Network. (2009). Family-peer linkages: The mediational role of attentional processes. *Social Development, 18,* 875–895.

Nielsen, M., Suddendorf, T., & Dissanayake, C. (2006). Imitation and self-recognition in autism: In search of an explanation. In S. J. Rogers, & J. H. G. Williams (Eds.), *Imitation and the social mind: Autism and typical development* (pp. 138–156). New York: Guilford Press.

Nigg, J. T., & Goldsmith, H. H. (1994). Genetics of personality disorders: Perspectives from personality and psychopathology research. *Psychological Bulletin, 115,* 346–380.

Nikken, P., & Peeters, A. L. (1988). Children's perceptions of televised reality. *Journal of Broadcasting & Electronic Media, 32,* 441–452.

Nopoulos, P., Flaum, M., O'Leary, D., & Andreasen, N. C. (2000). Sexual dimorphism in the human brain: Evaluation of tissue volume, tissue composition and surface anatomy using magnetic resonance imaging. *Psychiatry Research: Neuroimaging, 98*, 1–13.

Norlander, T., Erixon, A., & Archer, T. (2000). Psychological androgyny and creativity: Dynamics of gender roles and personality traits. *Social Behavior and Personality, 28*, 423–435.

Norrick, N. R. (1997). Twice-told tales: Collaborative narration of familiar stories. *Language in Society, 26*, 199–220.

Nucci, L., Camino, C., & Sapiro, C. M. (1996). Social class effects on northeastern Brazilian children's conceptions of areas of personal choice and social regulation. *Child Development, 67*, 1223–1242.

Nucci, L., Guerra, N., & Lee, J. (1991). Adolescent judgments of the personal, prudential, and normative aspects of drug usage. *Developmental Psychology, 27*, 841–848.

Nucci, L., & Turiel, E. (1993). God's word, religious rules, and their relation to Christian and Jewish children's concepts of morality. *Child Development, 64*, 1475–1491.

Nucci, L., & Weber, E. K. (1995). Social interactions in the home and the development of young children's conceptions of the personal. *Child Development, 66*, 1438–1452.

Nucci, L. P. (1984). Evaluating teachers as social agents: Students' ratings of domain appropriate and domain inappropriate teacher responses to transgressions. *American Educational Research Journal, 21*, 367–378.

Nucci, L. P. (1996). Morality and the personal sphere of action. In E. Reed, E. Turiel, & T. Brown (Eds.), *Values and knowledge* (pp. 41–60). Hillsdale, NJ: Erlbaum.

Nucci, L. P. (2002). The development of moral reasoning. In U. Goswami (Ed.), *Blackwell handbook of childhood cognitive development* (pp. 303–325). Malden, MA: Blackwell.

Nunner-Winkler, G. (2007). Development of moral motivation from childhood to early adulthood. *Journal of Moral Education, 36*, 399–414.

Oakhill, J., Garnham, A., & Reynolds, D. (2005). Immediate activation of stereotypical gender information. *Memory & Cognition, 33*, 972–983.

Oberlander, S. E., Black, M. M., & Starr, R. H. (2007). African American adolescent mothers and grandmothers: A multigenerational approach to parenting. *American Journal of Community Psychology, 39*, 37–46.

Oberman, L. M., Hubbard, E. M., McCleery, J. P., Altschuler, E. L., Ramachandran, V. S., & Pineda, J. A. (2005). EEG evidence for mirror neuron dysfunction in autism spectral disorders. *Cognitive Brain Research, 24*, 190–198.

O'Brien, M., Huston, A. C., & Risley, T. (1983). Sex-typed play of toddlers in a day care center. *Journal of Applied Developmental Psychology, 4*, 1–9.

Ocampo, K. A., Knight, G. P., & Bernal, M. E. (1997). The development of cognitive abilities and social identities in children: The case of ethnic identity. *International Journal of Behavioral Development, 21*, 479–500.

O'Connell, P., Pepler, D., & Craig, W. (1999). Peer involvement in bullying: Insights and challenges for intervention. *Journal of Adolescence, 22*, 437–452.

O'Connor, T. G., Deater-Deckard, K., Fulker, D., Rutter, M., & Plomin, R. (1998). Genotype-environment correlations in late childhood and early adolescence: Antisocial behavioral problems and coercive parenting. *Developmental Psychology, 34*, 970–981.

Oden, S., & Asher, S. R. (1977). Coaching children in social skills for friendship making. *Child Development, 48*, 495–506.

Ogbu, J. U. (2003). *Black American students in an affluent suburb.* Mahwah, NJ: Erlbaum.

Office of Juvenile Justice and Delinquency Prevention. (1999). Violence after School. *Juvenile Justice Bulletin: 1999 National Report Series.* Washington, DC: U.S. Department of Justice. Retrieved from: http://www.ncjrs.gov/pdf-files1/ojjdp/178992.pdf

Oh, W., Rubin, K. H., Bowker, J. C., Booth-LaForce, C. L., Rose-Krasnor, L., & Laursen, B. (2008). Trajectories of social withdrawal from middle childhood to early adolescence. *Journal of Abnormal Child Psychology, 36*, 553–566.

Ojanen, T., & Perry, D. G. (2007). Relational schemas and the developing self: Perceptions of mother and of self as joint predictors of early adolescents' self-esteem. *Developmental Psychology, 43*, 1474–1483.

Okagaki, L., & Bingham, G. E. (2005). Parents' social cognitions and their parenting behaviors. In T. Luster & L. Okagaki (Eds.), *Parenting: An ecological perspective* (2nd ed., pp. 3–33). Mahwah, NJ: Erlbaum Associates.

Olds, D. L., Eckenrode, J., Henderson, C. R., Kitzman, H., Powers, J., Cole, R., . . . Luckey, D. (1997). Long-term effects of home visitation on maternal life course and child abuse and neglect: Fifteen-year follow-up of a randomized trial. *Journal of the American Medical Association, 27*, 637–643.

Olds, D. L., Robinson, J., O'Brien, R., Luckey, D. W., Pettit, L. M., Henderson, C. R., . . . Talmi, A. (2002). Home visiting by nurses and by paraprofessionals: A randomized controlled trial. *Pediatrics, 110*, 486–496.

O'Neil, R., Parke, R. D., & McDowell, D. J. (2001). Objective and subjective features of children's neighborhoods: Relations to parental regulatory strategies and children's social competence. *Journal of Applied Developmental Psychology, 21*, 135–155.

Ollendick, T. H., & King, N. J. (1998). Empirically supported treatments for children with phobic and anxiety disorders: Current status. *Journal of Clinical Child Psychology, 22*, 156–167.

Olweus, D. (1979). Stability of aggressive reaction patterns in males: A review. *Psychological Bulletin, 86*, 852–875.

Olweus, D. (1993). *Bullying and school: What we know and what we can do.* Oxford, UK: Blackwell.

Olweus, D. (1997). Bully/victim problems in school: Facts and intervention. *European Journal of Psychology of Education, 12,* 495–510.

Olweus, D. (1999). Bullying in Norway. In P. K. Smith, Y. Morita, J. Junger-Tas, D. Olweus, R. Catalano, & P. Slee (Eds.), *The nature of school bullying: A cross-national perspective* (pp. 28–48). New York: Routledge.

Olweus, D. (2001). Peer harassment: A critical analysis and some important issues. In J. Juvonen & S. Graham (Eds.), *Peer harassment in school: The plight of the vulnerable and victimized* (pp. 3–20). New York: Guilford Press.

Olweus, D. (2004). The Olweus Bullying Prevention Programme: Design and implementation issues and a new national initiative in Norway. In P. K. Smith, D. Pepler, & K. Rigby (Eds.), *Bullying in schools: How successful can interventions be?* (pp. 13–36). New York: Cambridge University Press.

Olweus, D., Mattson, A., Schalling, D., & Low, H. (1988). Circulating testosterone levels and aggression in adolescent males: A causal analysis. *Psychosomatic Medicine, 50,* 261–272.

Onishi, K. H., & Baillargeon, R. (2005). Do 15-month-old infants understand false beliefs? *Science, 308,* 255–258.

Ontai, L. L., & Thompson, R. A. (2002). Patterns of attachment and maternal discourse effects on children's emotion understanding from 3 to 5 years of age. *Social Development, 11,* 433–450.

Onyango, P. P. M., & Kattambo, V. W. M. (2001). Kenya. In B. M. Schwartz-Kenney, M. McCauley, & M. A. Epstein (Eds.), *Child abuse: A global view* (pp. 117–130). Westport, CT: Greenwood.

Orfield, G., & Gordon, N. (2001). *Schools more separate: Consequences of a decade of resegregation.* Retrieved from: http://www.law.harvard.edu/civilrights/publications/schoolsseparate.pdf

Organisation for Economic Co-operation and Development (OECD). (2008). *Social expenditure database 1980–2005, OECD Family database.* Retrieved from: www.oecd.org/els/social/family/database

Orlick, T., Zhou, Q., & Partington, J. (1990). Co-operation and conflict within Chinese and Canadian kindergarten settings. *Canadian Journal and Behavioural Science, 22,* 20–25.

Ormel, J., Oldehinkel, A. J., Ferdinand, R. F., Hartman, C. A., De Winter, A. F., Veenstra, R., . . . Verhulst, F. C. (2005). Internalizing and externalizing problems in adolescence: General and dimension-specific effects of familial loadings and preadolescent temperament traits. *Psychological Medicine, 35,* 1825–1835.

Osofsky, J. D., Rovaris, M., Hammer, J. H., Dickson, A., Freeman, N., & Aucoin, K. (2004). Working with police to help children exposed to violence. *Journal of Community Psychology, 32,* 593–606.

Osterman, K. F. (2000). Students' needs for belonging in the school community. *Review of Educational Research, 70,* 323–367.

Osterman, K. F., Bjorkqvist, K., Lagerspetz, K. M., Kaukiainen, A., Huesmann, L. R., & Fraczek, A. (1994). Peer and self-estimated aggression and victimization in 8-year-old children from five ethnic groups. *Aggressive Behavior, 20,* 411–428.

Ostrov, J. M. (2006). Deception and subtypes of aggression during early childhood. *Journal of Experimental Child Psychology, 93,* 322–336.

Ostrov, J. M., & Crick, N. R. (2007). Forms and functions of aggression during early childhood: A short-term longitudinal study. *School Psychology Review, 66,* 22–43.

Oyserman, D., Coon, H. M., & Kemmelmeier, M. (2002). Rethinking individualism and collectivism: Evaluation of theoretical assumptions and meta-analysis. *Psychological Bulletin, 128,* 3–72.

Ozer, E. J. (2005). The impact of violence on urban adolescents: Longitudinal effects of perceived school connection and family support. *Journal of Adolescent Research, 20,* 167–192.

Padilla-Walker, L. M., & Carlo, G. (2006). Adolescent perceptions of appropriate parental reactions in moral and conventional social domains. *Social Development, 15,* 480–500.

Pahl, K., & Way, N. (2006). Longitudinal trajectories of ethnic identity among urban Black and Latino adolescents. *Child Development, 77,* 1403–1415.

Paik, H., & Comstock, G. (1994). The effects of television violence on antisocial behavior: A meta analysis. *Communication Research, 21,* 516–546.

Palacios, N., Gutmannova, K., & Chase-Lansdale, P. L. (2008). Immigrant differences in early reading achievement: Evidence from the ECLS-K. *Developmental Psychology, 44,* 1381–1395.

Panksepp, J. & Panksepp, J. A. (2000). The seven sins of evolutionary psychology. *Evolution and Cognition, 6,* 108–131.

Park, J. H., Essex, M. J., Zahn-Waxler, C., Armstrong, J. M., Klein, M. H., & Goldsmith, H. H. (2005). Relational and physical aggression in middle childhood: Early child and family risk factors. *Early Education & Development, 16,* 233–256.

Parke, R. D. (1974). Rules, roles, and resistance to deviation: Recent advances in punishment, discipline, and self-control. In A. D. Pick (Ed.), *Minnesota Symposia on Child Psychology* (Vol. 8, pp. 111–143). Minneapolis: University of Minnesota Press.

Parke, R. D. (1977). Punishment in children: Effects, side-effects and alternative strategies. In H. Hom & P. Robinson (Eds.), *Psychological processes in early education* (pp. 71–97). New York: Academic Press.

Parke, R. D. (1996). *Fatherhood*. Cambridge, MA: Harvard University Press.

Parke, R. D. (2002). Fatherhood. In M. H. Bornstein (Ed.), *Handbook of parenting: Vol. 3. Being and becoming a parent* (2nd ed., pp. 27–74). Mahwah, NJ: Erlbaum.

Parke, R. D., & Buriel, R. (2006). Socialization in the family: Ethnic and ecological perspectives. In W. Damon & R. M. Lerner (Series Eds.), & N. Eisenberg (Vol. Ed.), *Handbook of child psychology: Vol. 3. Social, emotional and personality development* (6th ed., pp. 429–504). Hoboken, NJ: Wiley.

Parke, R. D., & Clarke-Stewart, K. A. (2003a). Developmental psychology. In I. B. Weiner (Ed. in Chief), & D. K. Freedheim (Vol. Ed.), *Handbook of psychology: Vol. 1. History of psychology* (pp. 205–221). Hoboken, NJ: Wiley

Parke, R. D., & Clarke-Stewart, K. A. (2003b). Effects of parental incarceration on children: Perspectives, promises, and policies. In J. Travis & M. Waul (Eds.), *Prisoners once removed: The impact of incarceration and reentry on children, families, and communities* (pp. 189–232). Washington, DC: Urban Institute Press.

Parke, R. D., Coltrane, S., Bothwick-Duffy, S., Powers, J., Adams, M., Fabricius, W., . . . Saenz, D. (2003). Assessing father involvement in Mexican-American families. In R. Day & M. E. Lamb (Eds.), *Conceptualizing and measuring father involvement* (pp. 15–33). Mahwah, NJ: Erlbaum.

Parke, R. D., Coltrane, S., Duffy, S., Buriel, R., Dennis, J., Powers, J., . . . Widaman, K. F. (2004). Economic stress, parenting and child adjustment in Mexican-American and European-American families. *Child Development, 75,* 1632–1656.

Parke, R. D., Lio, S., Schofield, T., Tuthill, L., Vega, E., & Coltrane, S. (2010). Neighborhood environments: A multi-measure, multi-level approach. In L. C. Mayes & M. Lewis (Eds.), *The environment of human development: A handbook of theory and measurement.* New York: Cambridge University Press.

Parke, R. D., McDowell, D. J., Cladis, M., & Leidy, M. S. (2006). Family and peer relationships: The role of emotion regulatory processes. In D. K. Snyder, J. Simpson, & J. N. Hughes (Eds.), *Emotion regulation in couples and families: Pathways to dysfunction and health* (pp. 143–162). Washington, DC: American Psychological Association.

Parke, R. D., & Neville, B. (1995). Late-timed fatherhood: Determinants and consequences for children and families. In J. L. Shapiro, M. J. Diamond, & M. Greenberg (Eds.), *Becoming a father: Contemporary, social, developmental, and clinical perspectives* (pp. 104–116). New York: Springer.

Parke, R. D., & O'Leary, S. E. (1976). Father-mother-infant interaction in the newborn period: Some findings, some observations, and some unresolved issues. In K. Riegel & J. Meacham (Eds.), *The developing individual in a changing world* (Vol. 2, pp. 653–663). The Hague: Mouton.

Parke, R. D., & O'Neil, R. (2000). The influence of significant others on learning about relationships: From family to friends. In R. S. L. Mills & S. Duck (Eds.), *The developmental psychology of personal relationships* (pp. 15–47). New York: Wiley.

Parker, J. G., & Asher, S. R. (1987). Peer acceptance and later personal adjustment: Are low-accepted children at risk? *Psychological Bulletin, 102,* 357–389.

Parker, J. G., & Asher, S. R. (1993). Friendship and friendship quality in middle childhood: Links with peer group acceptance and feelings of loneliness and social dissatisfaction. *Developmental Psychology, 29,* 611–621.

Parker, J. G., & Gottman, J. M. (1989). Social and emotional development in a relational context: Friendship interaction from early childhood to adolescence. In T. J. Berndt & G. W. Ladd (Eds.), *Peer relationships in child development* (pp. 95–132). New York: Wiley.

Parker, J. G., & Seal, J. (1996). Forming, losing, renewing and replacing friendships: Applying temporal parameters to the assessment of children's friendship experiences. *Child Development, 67,* 2248–2268.

Parkhurst, J. T., & Asher, S. R. (1992). Peer rejection in middle school: Subgroup differences in behavior, loneliness and interpersonal concerns. *Developmental Psychology, 28,* 231–241.

Parks, M. R., & Roberts, L. D. (1998). "Making MOOsic": The development of personal relationships on-line and a comparison to their off-line counterparts. *Journal of Social and Personal Relationships, 15,* 517–537.

Parten, M. (1932). Social play among pre-school children. *Journal of Abnormal and Social Psychology, 28,* 231–241.

Partnership for Children News. (2006, February). Zippy heads for Shanghai. Retrieved from: www.partnershipforchildren.org.uk

Partnership for Children News. (2008, December). Beijing programme helps China's single children. Retrieved from: www.partnershipforchildren.org.uk/china–2

Passman, R. H. (1998). Security objects. In J. Kagan (Ed.), *Gale encyclopedia of childhood and adolescents.* Detroit: Gale Research.

Pasterski, V. L., Geffner, M. E., Brain, C., Hindmarsh, P., Brook, C., & Hines, M. (2005). Prenatal hormones and postnatal socialization by parents as determinants of male-typical toy play in girls with congenital adrenal hyperplasia. *Child Development, 76,* 264–278.

Pasterski, V. L., Geffner, M. E., Brain, C., Hindmarsh, P., Brook, C., & Hines, M. (2007). Increased aggression and activity level in 3- to 11-year-old girls with congenital adrenal hyperplasia (CAH). *Hormones and Behavior, 52,* 368–374.

Pasterski, V. L., Golombok, S., & Hines, M. (2010). Sex differences in social development. In P. K. Smith & C. H. Hart (Eds.), *Wiley-Blackwell handbook of childhood social development* (2nd ed.). Oxford, UK: Wiley-Blackwell.

Patriarca, A., Di Giuseppe, G., Albano, L., Marinelli, P., & Angelillo, I. F. (2009). Use of television, videogames, and computer among children and adolescents in Italy. BMC Public Health, 9:139 doi:10.1186/1471–2458–9–139. Retrieved from: http://www.biomedcentral.com/content/pdf/1471–2458–9–139.pdf

Patterson, C. J. (1995). Families of the lesbian baby boom: Parents' division of labor and children's adjustment. *Developmental Psychology, 31,* 115–123.

Patterson, C. J. (2004). Gay fathers. In M. E. Lamb (Ed.), *The role of the father in child development* (pp. 397–416). New York: Wiley.

Patterson, C. J. (2006). Children of lesbian and gay parents. *Current Directions in Psychological Science, 15,* 241–244.

Patterson, C. J., & Hastings, P. D. (2007). Socialization in the context of family diversity. In J. Grusec & P. D. Hastings (Eds.), *Handbook of socialization* (pp. 328–351). New York: Guilford Press.

Patterson, C. J., & Kister, M. C. (1981). Development of listener skills for referential communication. In W. P. Dickerson (Eds.), *Children's oral communication skills* (pp. 143–166). New York: Academic Press.

Patterson, G. R. (1982). *Coercive family process.* Eugene, OR: Castalia Press.

Patterson, G. R. (1993). Orderly change in a stable world: The antisocial trait as a chimera. *Journal of Consulting and Clinical Psychology, 61,* 911–919.

Patterson, G. R. (1996). Some characteristics of a developmental theory for early-onset delinquency. In M. F. Lenzenweger & J. J. Haugaard (Eds.), *Frontiers of developmental psychopathology* (pp. 81–124). New York: Oxford University Press.

Patterson, G. R. (2002). The early development of coercive family processes. In J. B. Reid, G. R. Patterson, & J. Snyder (Eds.), *Antisocial behavior in children and adolescents* (pp. 25–44). Washington, DC: American Psychological Association.

Patterson, G. R., & Bank, L. (1989). Some amplifying mechanisms for pathologic processes in families. In M. Gunnar & E. Thelen (Eds.), *Minnesota Symposium on Child Psychology: Vol. 22. Systems and development* (pp. 167–209). Hillsdale, NJ: Erlbaum.

Patterson, G. R., & Capaldi, D. M. (1991). Antisocial parents: Unskilled and vulnerable. In P. A. Cowan & E. M. Hetherington (Eds.), *Family transitions* (pp. 195–218). Hillsdale, NJ: Erlbaum.

Patterson, G. R., DeBarshyshe, B., & Ramsey, R. (1989). A developmental perspective on antisocial behavior. *American Psychologist, 44,* 329–335.

Patterson, G. R., Littman, R. A., & Bricker, W. (1967). Assertive behavior in children: A step toward a theory of aggression. *Monographs of the Society for Research in Child Development, 32* (Serial No. 5).

Patterson, G. R., Reid, J. B., & Eddy, J. M. (2002). A brief history of the Oregon model. In J. B. Reid, G. R. Patterson, & J. Snyder (Eds.), *Antisocial behavior in children and adolescents: A developmental analysis and model for intervention* (pp. 3–20). Washington, DC: American Psychological Association.

Patterson, G. R., & Stouthamer-Loeber, M. (1984). The correlation of family management practices and delinquency. *Child Development, 55,* 1299–1307.

Paulussen-Hoogeboom, M. C., Stams, G. J. J. M., Hermanns, J. M. A., Peetsma, T. T. D., & van den Wittenboer, G. L. H. (2008). Parenting style as mediator between children's negative emotionality and problematic behavior in early childhood. *Journal of Genetic Psychology, 169,* 209–226.

Pavlov, I. P. (1927). Conditioned reflexes: An investigation of the physiological activity of the cerebral cortex. Retrieved from: http://psychclassics.yorku.ca/Pavlov/lecture10.htm

Peake, P. K., Hebl, M., Ahrens, C., Lepper, M., & Mischel, W. (2001). *Early adult correlates of preschool delay of gratification and obedience to authority.* Unpublished manuscript, Columbia University, New York.

Pearce, M. J., Boergers, J., & Prinstein, M. J. (2002). Adolescent obesity, overt and relational peer victimization, and romantic relationships. *Obesity Research, 10,* 386–393.

Pearson, J. L., Hunter, A. G., Ensminger, M. E., & Kellam, S. G. (1990). Black grandmothers in multigenerational households: Diversity in family structure and parenting involvement in the Woodlawn community. *Child Development, 61,* 434–442.

Pedersen, F. A., Zaslow, M. J., Cain, R. L., & Anderson, B. J. (1980, April). *Cesarean birth: The importance of a family perspective.* Paper presented at the biennial conference of the International Society on Infant Studies, New Haven, CT.

Pedersen, S., Vitaro, F., Barker, E., & Borge, A. (2007). The timing of middle-childhood peer rejection and friendship: Linking early behavior to early-adolescent adjustment. *Child Development, 78,* 1037–1051.

Peets, K., Hodges, E., Kikas, E., & Salmivalli, C. (2007). Hostile attributions and behavioral strategies in children: Does relationship matter? *Developmental Psychology, 43,* 889–900.

Pegg, J. E., Werker, J. F., & McLeod, P. J. (1992). Preference for infant-directed over adult-directed speech: Evidence from 7-week-old infants. *Infant Behavior and Development, 15*, 325–345.

Peisner-Feinberg, E. S., Burchinal, M. R., Clifford, R. M., Culkin, M. L., Howes, C., Kagan, S. L., & Yazejian, N. (2001). The relation of preschool child-care quality to children's cognitive and social developmental trajectories through second grade. *Child Development, 72*, 1534–1553.

Peláez-Nogueras, M., Field, T. M., Hossain, Z., & Pickens, J. (1996). Depressed mothers' touching increases infants' positive affect and attention in still-face interaction. *Child Development, 67*, 1780–1792.

Pellegrini, A. D., Long, J. D., Roseth, C. J., Bohn, C. M., & van Ryzin, M. (2007). A short-term longitudinal study of preschoolers' (*Homo sapiens*) sex segregation: The role of physical activity, sex, and time. *Journal of Comparative Psychology, 121*, 282–289.

Pelphrey, K. A., & Carter, E. J. (2008). Charting the typical and atypical development of the social brain. [Special Issue: *Imaging brain systems in normality and psychopathology*]. *Development and Psychopathology, 20*, 1081–1102.

Pena, D. C. (2000). Parent involvement: Influencing factors and implications. *Journal of Educational Research, 94*, 42–54.

Pena, E. (2007). Lost in translation: Methodological considerations in cross-cultural research. *Child Development, 78*, 1255–1264.

Pepler, D. J., Craig, W. M., & Roberts, W. L. (1998). Observation of aggressive and nonaggressive children on the school playground. *Merrill-Palmer Quarterly, 44*, 55–76.

Pepler, D. J., Corter, C., & Abramovitch, R. (1982). Social relations among children. Comparisons of siblings and peer interaction. In K. Rubin & H. S. Ross (Eds.), *Peer relationships and social skills in childhood* (pp. 209–227). New York: Springer-Verlag.

Pepler, D. J., Jiang, D., Craig, W., & Connolly, J. (2008). Developmental trajectories of bullying and associated factors. *Child Development, 79*, 325–338.

Pepler, D. J., Madsen, K. C., Webster, C., & Levine, K. S. (Eds.) (2005). *The development and treatment of girlhood aggression.* Mahwah, NJ: Erlbaum.

Perlman, S. B., Camras, L. A., & Pelphrey, K. (2008). Physiology and functioning: Parents' vagal tone, emotion socialization, and children's emotion knowledge. *Journal of Experimental Child Psychology, 100*, 308–315.

Perlman, S. B., Kalish, C. W., & Pollak, S. D. (2008). The role of maltreatment experience in children's understanding of the antecedents of emotion. *Cognition & Emotion, 22*, 651–670.

Perls, T. T., & Fretts, R. C. (2001). The evolution of menopause and human life span. *Annals of Human Biology, 28*, 237–245.

Perner, J., Ruffman, T., & Leekam, S. R. (1994). Theory of mind is contagious: You can catch it from your sibs. *Child Development, 65*, 1228–1238.

Perper, K., & Manlove, J. (2009). Estimated percentage of females who will become teen mothers: Differences across states. *Child Trends Research Brief.* Retrieved from: http://www.childtrends.org/Files//Child_Trends–2009_03_19_RB_PercentTeenMothers.pdf

Perry, B. D. (1997). Incubated in terror: Neurodevelopmental factors in the "cycle of violence." In J. D. Osofsky (Ed.), *Children in a violent society* (pp. 124–149). New York: Guilford Press.

Perry, D. G., Hodges, E. V., & Egan, S. (2001). Determinants of chronic victimization by peers: A review and new model of family influence. In J. Juvonen & S. Graham (Eds.), *Peer harassment in school: The plight of the vulnerable and victimized* (pp. 73–104). New York: Guilford Press.

Perry, D. G., Perry, L. C., & Weiss, R. J. (1989). Sex differences in the consequences children anticipate for aggression. *Developmental Psychology, 25*, 312–320.

Perry, D. G., Williard, J. C., & Perry, L. C. (1990). Peers' perceptions of the consequences that victimized children provide aggressors. *Child Development, 61*, 1310–1325.

Perry, W. C. (1996). Gender based education: Why it works at the middle school level. *NASSP Bulletin, 80*, 32–35.

Perry-Jenkins, M., Repetti, R., & Crouter, A. C. (2000). Work and family in the 1990s. *Journal of Marriage and Family, 62*, 981–998.

Persson, G. E. B. (2005). Young children's prosocial and aggressive behaviors and their experiences of being targeted for similar behaviors by peers. *Social Development, 14*, 206–228.

Peter, J., & Valkenberg, P. M. (2006). Adolescents' exposure to sexually explicit material on the Internet. *Communication Research, 33*, 178–204.

Peterson, J. L., & Zill, N. (1986). Marital disruption, parent-child relationships and behavior problems in children. *Journal of Marriage and Family, 48*, 295–307.

Pettigrew, T. F. (2004). Justice deferred: A half century after *Brown vs. Board of Education. American Psychologist, 59*, 521–529.

Pettigrew, T. F., & Tropp, L. (2006). A meta-analytic test of intergroup contact theory. *Journal of Personality and Social Psychology, 90*, 751–783.

Pettit, G. S., Bakshi, A., Dodge, K. A., & Coie, J. D. (1990). The emergence of social dominance in young boys' play groups: Developmental differences and behavioral correlates. *Developmental Psychology, 26*, 1017–1025.

Pettit, G. S., Laird, R. D., Dodge, K. A., Bates, J. E., & Criss, M. N. (2001). Antecedents and behavior problem outcomes of parental monitoring and psychological control in early adolescence. *Child Development, 72*, 583–598.

Pettit, G. S., & Mize, J. (1993). Substance and style: Understanding the ways in which parents teach children about social relationships. In S. Duck (Ed.), *Understanding relationships processes: Vol. 2. Learning about relationships* (pp. 118–151). Thousand Oaks, CA: Sage.

Pew Internet. (2009). *Survey data collected by the Pew Internet & American Life Project*. Retrieved from: http://www.pewinternet.org/Reports/2009/14—Teens-and-Mobile-Phones-Data-Memo.aspx

Pew Research Center. (2006). *A barometer of modern morals. Sex, drugs, and the 1040*. Retrieved from: http://pewresearch.org/pubs/307/a-barometer-of-modern-morals

Phillips, D. A., Voran, M., Kisker, E., Howes, C., & Whitebook, M. (1994). Child care for children in poverty: Opportunity or inequity? *Child Development, 65*, 472–492.

Phillips, L. H., Henry, J. D., Hosie, J. A., & Milne, A. B. (2006). Age, anger regulation, and well-being. *Aging & Mental Health, 10*, 250–256.

Phillips, S. U. (2001). Participant structures and communicative competence: Warm Springs children in community and classroom. In A. Duranti (Ed.), *Linguistic anthropology: A reader* (pp. 302–318). Malden, MA: Blackwell.

Phinney, J. S. (1989). Stages of ethnic identity development in minority group adolescents. *Journal of Early Adolescence, 9*, 34–49.

Phinney, J. S. (1992). The multigroup ethnic identity measure: A new scale for use with diverse groups. *Journal of Adolescent Research, 7*, 156–176.

Phinney, J. S. (2000). Ethnic and racial identity: Ethnic identity. In A. E. Kazdin (Ed.), *Encyclopedia of psychology* (Vol. 3, pp. 254–259). New York: Oxford University Press.

Phinney, J. S., Ferguson, D. L., & Tate, J. D. (1997). Intergroup attitudes among ethnic minority adolescents: A causal model. *Child Development, 60*, 955–969.

Phinney, J. S., Jacoby, B., & Silva, C. (2007). Positive intergroup attitudes: The role of ethnic identity. *International Journal of Behavioral Development, 31*, 478–490.

Phinney, J. S., & Rosenthal, D. (1992). Ethnic identity in adolescence: Process, context, and outcome. In G. Adams, T. Gullotta, & R. Montemayer (Eds.), *Adolescent identity formation* (pp. 145–172). Thousand Oaks, CA: Sage.

Phipps, M. G., Blume, J. D., & DeMonner, S. M. (2002). Young maternal age associated with increased risk of postneonatal death. *Obstetrics & Gynecology, 100*, 481–486.

Piaget, J. (1928). *The child's conception of the world*. London: Routledge and Kegan Paul.

Piaget, J. (1932). *The moral judgment of the child*. New York: Harcourt, Brace.

Pianta, R. C. (1999). *Enhancing relationships between children and teachers*. Washington, DC: American Psychological Association.

Pianta, R. C., Belsky, J., Houts, R., Morrison, F., & the NICHD Early Child Care Research Network. (2007). Opportunities to learn in America's elementary classrooms. *Science, 315*, 1795–1796.

Pianta, R. C., Steinberg, M. S., & Rollins, K. B. (1995). The first two years of school: Teacher-child relationships and deflections in children's classroom adjustment. *Development and Psychopathology, 7*, 295–312.

Pike, A., Manke, B., Reiss, D., & Plomin, R. (2001). A genetic analysis of differential experiences of adolescent siblings across three years. *Social Development, 9*, 96–114.

Pine, K. J., & Nash, A. (2002). Dear Santa: The effects of television advertising on young children. *International Journal of Behavioral Development, 26*, 529–539.

Pine, K. J., & Nash, A. (2003). Barbie or Betty? Preschool children's preference for branded products and evidence for gender-linked differences. *Journal of Developmental & Behavioral Pediatrics, 24*, 219–224.

Pine, K. J., Wilson, P., & Nash, A. (2007). The relationship between television advertising, children's viewing, and their requests to Father Christmas. *Journal of Developmental & Behavioral Pediatrics, 28*, 456–461.

Pinker, S. (2009, January 11). My genome, my self. *New York Times Magazine*, pp. 24–31, 46, 50.

Piper, W. (1930). *The little engine that could*. New York: Platt & Munk.

Pizarro, D. A., & Bloom, P. (2003). The intelligence of the moral intuitions: A comment on Haidt (2001). *Psychological Review, 110*, 193–196.

Pleck, J. H. (2004). Two dimensions of fatherhood: A history of the good dad-bad dad complex. In M. E. Lamb (Ed.), *The role of the father in child development* (4th ed., pp. 32–57). Hoboken, NJ: Wiley.

Pleck, J. H. (2010). Paternal involvement: Revised conceptualization and theoretical linkages with child outcomes. In M. E. Lamb (Ed.), *The role of the father in child development* (5th ed., pp. 58–93). Hoboken, NJ: Wiley.

Pleck, J. H., & Masciadrelli, B. P. (2004). Paternal involvement by U.S. residential fathers: Levels, sources, and consequences. In M. E. Lamb (Ed.), *The role of the father in child development* (4th ed., pp. 222–271). Hoboken, NJ: Wiley.

Plomin, R. (1990). *Nature and nurture: An introduction to human behavioral genetics*. Pacific Grove, CA: Brooks/Cole.

Plomin, R. (1995). Genetics and children's experiences in the family. *Journal of Child Psychology and Psychiatry, 36*, 33–68.

Plomin, R., & Daniels, D. (1987). Why are children in the same family so different from one another? *The Behavioral and Brain Sciences, 10*, 1–16.

Plomin, R., & Davis, O. S. P. (2009). The future of genetics in psychology and psychiatry: Microarrays, genome-wide association, and non-coding RNA. *Journal of Child Psychology and Psychiatry, 50*, 63–71.

Plomin, R., DeFries, J. C., Craig, I. W., & McGuffin, P. (2002). *Behavior genetics in the postgenomic era*. Washington, DC: American Psychological Association.

Plomin, R., DeFries, J. C., McClearn, G. E., & McGuffin, P. (2001). *Behavioral genetics* (4th ed.). New York: Worth.

Plomin, R., McClearn, G. E., Pedersen, N. L., Nesselroade, J. R., & Bergeman, C. S. (1988). Genetic influence on childhood family environment perceived retrospectively from the last half of the life span. *Developmental Psychology, 24*, 738–745.

Plomin, R., & Rutter, M. (1998). Child development, molecular genetics and what to do with genes once they are found. *Child Development, 69*, 1223–1242.

Pluess, M., & Belsky, J. (2009). Differential susceptibility to rearing experience: The case of childcare. *Journal of Child Psychology and Psychiatry, 50*, 396–404.

Poehlmann, J. (2005). Representations of attachment relationships in children of incarcerated mothers. *Child Development, 76*, 679–696.

Polce-Lynch, M., Myers, B. J., Kliewer, W., & Kilmartin, C. (2001). Adolescent self-esteem and gender: Exploring relations to sexual harassment, body image, media influence, and emotional expression. *Journal of Youth & Adolescence, 30*, 225–244.

Pollak, S. D., Nelson, C. A., Schlaak, M. F., Roeber, B. J., Wewerka, S. S., Wilk, K. L., Frenn, K. A., Loman, M. M., & Gunnar, M. R. (2010). Neurodevelopmental effects of early deprivation in postinstitutionalized children. *Child Development, 8*, 212–223.

Pollak, S. D., & Sinha, P. (2002). Effects of early experience on children's recognition of facial displays of emotion. *Developmental Psychology, 38*, 784–791.

Pollak, S. D., & Tolley-Schell, S. A. (2003). Selective attention to facial emotion in physically abused children. *Journal of Abnormal Psychology, 112*, 323–38.

Pomerantz, E. M., Altermatt, E. R., & Saxon, J. L. (2002). Making the grade but feeling distressed: Gender differences in academic performance and internal distress. *Journal of Educational Psychology, 94*, 396–404.

Pomerantz, E. M., & Ruble, D. N. (1998). A multidimensional perspective of control: Implications for the development of sex differences in self-evaluation and depression. In J. Heckhausen & C. Dweck (Eds.), *Motivation and self-regulation across the life span* (pp. 159–184). New York: Cambridge University Press.

Pomerleau, A., Bolduc, D., Malcuit, G., & Cossette, L. (1990). Pink or blue: Environmental gender stereotypes in the first two years of life. *Sex Roles, 22*, 359–367.

Pomery, E. A., Gibbons, F. X., Gerrard, M., Cleveland, M. J., Brody, G. H., & Wills, T. A. (2005). Families and risk: Prospective analyses of familial and social influences on adolescent substance use. *Journal of Family Psychology, 19*, 560–570.

Pons, F., Harris, P. L., & de Rosnay, M. (2004). Emotion comprehension between 3 and 11 years: Developmental periods and hierarchical organization. *European Journal of Developmental Psychology, 1*, 127–152.

Poresky, R. H., & Hendrix, C. (1989, April). *Companion animal bonding, children's home environments, and young children's social development*. Paper presented at the biennial meeting of the Society for Research in Child Development, Kansas City, MO.

Porter, R. H., Makin, J. W., Davis, L. B., & Christensen, K. M. (1992). Breast-fed infants respond to olfactory cues from their own mother and unfamiliar lactating females. *Infant Behavior and Development, 15*, 85–93.

Porter, R. H., & Winberg, J. (1999). Unique salience of maternal breast odors for newborn infants. *Neuroscience and Biobehavioral Reviews, 23*, 439–449.

Portes, A., & Rumbaut, R. G. (2001). *Legacies: The story of the immigrant second generation*. Berkeley, CA: University of California Press.

Portes, P. R., Dunham, R. M., & Williams, S. (1986). Assessing child-rearing style in ecological settings: Its relation to culture, social class, early age intervention and scholastic achievement. *Adolescence, 21*, 723–735.

Portwood, S. G. (2006). What we know—and don't know—about preventing child maltreatment. *Journal of Aggression, Maltreatment, & Trauma, 12*, 55–80.

Posada, G., Gao, Y., Wu, F., Posada, R., Tascon, M., Schelmerich, A., ...Synnevaag, B. (1995). The secure-base phenomenon across cultures: Children's behavior, mothers' preferences, and experts' concepts. In E. Waters, B. E. Vaughn, G. Posada, & K. Kondo-Ikemura (Eds.), *Caregiving, cultural, and cognitive perspectives on secure-base behavior and working models: New growing points of attachment theory and research. Monographs of the Society for Research in Child Development, 60* (Serial No. 244), 27–48.

Posada, G., Jacobs, A., Richmond, M. K., Carbonell, O. A., Alzate, G., Bustamante, M. R., & Quiceno, J. (2002). Maternal caregiving and infant security in two cultures. *Developmental Psychology, 38*, 67–78.

Posner, M. I., & Rothbart, M. K. (2007). *Educating the human brain*. Washington, DC: American Psychological Association.

Posner, M. I., Rothbart, M. K., & Sheese, B. E. (2007). Attention genes. *Developmental Science, 10*, 24–29.

Postlethwait, J. H., & Hopson, J. L. (1995). *The nature of life* (3rd ed.). New York: McGraw-Hill.

Postmes, T., & Spears, R. (1998). Deindividuation and antinormative behavior: A meta-analysis. *Psychological Bulletin, 123*, 238–259.

Postmes, T., Spears, R., & Lea, M. (1998). Breaching or building social boundaries? SIDE-effects of computer-mediated communication. *Communication Research, 25*, 689–715.

Poulin, F., Dishion, T., & Haas, E. (1999). The peer influences paradox: Friendship quality and deviancy training within male adolescents. *Merrill-Palmer Quarterly, 45*, 42–61.

Povinelli, D. J., Landau, K. R., & Perilloux, H. K. (1996). Self-recognition in young children using delayed versus live feedback: Evidence of a developmental asynchrony. *Child Development, 67*, 1540–1554.

Power, T. G. (2000). *Play and exploration in children and animals.* Mahwah, NJ: Erlbaum.

Powlishta, K. K., Serbin, L. A., Doyle, A.-B., & White, D. R. (1994). Gender, ethnic, and body type biases: The generality of prejudice in childhood. *Developmental Psychology, 30*, 526–536.

Pöyhönen, V., & Salmivalli, C. (2008). New directions in research and practice addressing bullying: Focus on defending behavior. In D. Pepler & W. Craig (Eds.), *An international perspective on understanding and addressing bullying. PREVNet Publication Series, 1*, 26–43.

Prakash, K., & Coplan, R. J. (2007). Socioemotional characteristics and school adjustment of socially withdrawn children in India. *International Journal of Behavioral Development, 31*, 123–132.

Pratt, M. W., & Fiese, B. H. (Eds.) (2004). *Family stories and the life course.* Mahwah, NJ: Erlbaum.

Pratt, M. W., Hunsberger, B., Prancer, S. M., & Alisat, S. (2003). A longitudinal analysis of personal values socialization: Correlates of a moral self-ideal in late adolescence. *Social Development, 12*, 563–585.

Pratt, M. W., Skoe, E. E., & Arnold, M. L. (2004). Care reasoning development and family socialisation patterns in later adolescence: A longitudinal analysis. *International Journal of Behavioral Development, 28*, 139–147.

Prentice, D. A., & Carranza, E. (2002). What women should be, shouldn't be, are allowed to be, and don't have to be: The contents of prescriptive gender stereotypes. *Psychology of Women Quarterly, 26*, 269–281.

Preston, S. D., & de Waal, F. B. M. (2002). Empathy: Its ultimate and proximate bases. *Behavioral and Brain Sciences, 25*, 1–72.

Priess, H. A., Lindberg, S. M., & Hyde, J. S. (2009). Adolescent gender-intensification identity and mental health: Gender intensification revisited. *Child Development, 80*, 1531–1544.

Princiotta, D., & Bielick, S. (2006). *Homeschooling in the United States 2003: Statistical Analysis Report* (No. NCES2006-042). Washington, DC: U.S. Department of Education.

Prinstein, M. J., & Cillessen, A. H. N. (2003). Forms and functions of adolescent peer aggression associated with high levels of peer status. *Merrill-Palmer Quarterly, 49*, 310–342.

Pryor, J. (Ed.) (2008). *The international handbook of stepfamilies: Policy and practice in legal, research, and clinical environments.* Hoboken, NJ: Wiley.

Puma, M., Bell, S., Cook, R., Heid, C., & Lopez, M. (2005). *Head Start Impact Study: First year findings.* Washington, DC: U.S. Department of Health and Human Services, Administration for Children and Families.

Purcell, P., & Stewart, L. (1990). Dick and Jane in 1989. *Sex Roles, 22*, 177–185.

Putallaz, M. (1987). Maternal behavior and children's sociometric status. *Child Development, 58*, 324–340.

Putallaz, M., & Gottman, J. M. (1981). An interactional model of children's entry into peer groups. *Child Development, 52*, 986–994.

Putallaz, M., Grimes, C. L., Foster, K. J., Kupersmidt, J. B., Coie, J. D., & Dearing, K. (2007). Overt and relational aggression and victimization: Multiple perspectives within the school setting. *Journal of School Psychology, 45*, 523–547.

Putallaz, M., & Heflin, A. H. (1990). Parent-child interaction. In S. R. Asher & J. D. Coie (Eds.), *Peer rejection in childhood* (pp. 189–216). New York: Cambridge University Press.

Putnam, S. P., Sanson, A. V., & Rothbart, M. K. (2002). Child temperament and parenting. In M. H. Bornstein (Ed.), *Handbook of parenting: Vol. 1. Children and parenting* (2nd ed., pp. 255–278). Mahwah, NJ: Erlbaum.

Quintana, S. (2008). Racial perspective taking ability: Developmental, theoretical, and empirical trends. In S. M. Quintana & C. McKown (Eds.), *Handbook of race, racism, and the developing child* (pp. 16–36). Hoboken, NJ: Wiley.

Quintana, S. M. (2010). Ethnicity, race, and children's social development. In P. K. Smith & C. H. Hart (Eds.), *Wiley-Blackwell handbook of childhood social development* (2nd ed.). Oxford, UK: Wiley-Blackwell.

Raag, T. (1999). Influences of social expectations of gender, gender stereotypes, and situational constraints on children's toy choices. *Sex Roles, 41*, 809–831.

Raag, T., & Rackliff, C. L. (1998). Preschoolers' awareness of social expectations of gender: Relationships to toy choices. *Sex Roles, 38*, 685–700.

Raaijmakers, Q. A. W., Engels, R. C. M. E., & Van Hoof, A. (2005). Delinquency and moral reasoning in adolescence and young adulthood. *International Journal of Behavioral Development, 29*, 247–258.

Rabiner, D., Lenhart, L., & Lochman, J. E. (1990). Automatic versus reflective social problem-solving in relation to sociometric status. *Developmental Psychology, 26*, 1010–1016.

Radke-Yarrow, M., & Klimer-Dougan, B. (2002). Parental depression and offspring disorders: A developmental perspective. In S. H. Goodman & I. Gotlib (Eds.), *Children of depressed parents* (pp. 155–173). Washington, DC: American Psychological Association.

Radke-Yarrow, M., & Zahn-Waxler, C. (1983). Roots, motives and patterns in children's prosocial behavior. In J. Reykowski, T. Karylowski, D. Bar-Tal, & E. Staub (Eds.), *Origins and maintenance of prosocial behaviors* (pp. 81–99). New York: Plenum Press.

Raeff, C., Greenfield, P.M., & Quiroz, B. (2000). Conceptualizing interpersonal relationships in the cultural contexts of individualism and collectivism. *New Directions for Child and Adolescent Development, 87*, 59–74.

Raffaelli, M., & Crockett, L. J. (2003). Sexual risk taking in adolescence: The role of self-regulation and attraction to risk. *Developmental Psychology, 39*, 1036–1046.

Ragozin, A. S., Basham, R. B., Crnic, K. A., Greenberg, M. T., & Robinson, N. M. (1982). Effects of maternal age on parenting role. *Developmental Psychology, 18*, 627–634.

Rah, Y., & Parke, R. D. (2008). Pathways between parent-child interactions and peer acceptance: The role of children's social information processing. *Social Development, 17*, 341–357.

Raikes, H. A. (1993). Relationship duration in infant care: Time with a high-ability teacher and infant-teacher attachment. *Early Childhood Research Quarterly, 8*, 309–325.

Raikes, H. A., & Thompson, R. A. (2005). Links between risk and attachment security: Models of influence. *Journal of Applied Developmental Psychology, 26*, 440–455.

Raikes, H. A., & Thompson, R. A. (2008). Attachment security and parenting quality predict children's problem-solving, attributions, and loneliness with peers. *Attachment & Human Development, 10*, 319–344.

Raine, A. (2002). Biosocial studies of antisocial and violent behavior in children and adults: A review. *Journal of Abnormal Child Psychology, 30*, 311–326.

Raine, A. (2008). From genes to brain to antisocial behavior. *Current Directions in Psychological Science, 17*, 323–328.

Raine, A., Brennan, P., & Mednick, S. A. (1994). Birth complications combined with early maternal rejection at age 1 year predispose to violent crime at age 18 years. *Archives of General Psychiatry, 51*, 984–988.

Raine, A., Brennan, P., & Mednick, S. A. (1997). Interaction between birth complications and early maternal rejection in predisposing individuals to adult violence: Specificity to serious, early-onset violence. *American Journal of Psychiatry, 154*, 1265–1271.

Raine, A., Reynolds, C., Venables, P. H., Mednick, S. A., & Farrington, D. P. (1998). Fearlessness, stimulation-seeking and large body size at age 3 years as early predispositions to childhood aggression at age 11 years. *Archives of General Psychiatry, 55*, 745–751.

Ramey, C. T., Campbell, F. A., & Blair, C. (1998). Enhancing the life course for high-risk children: Results from the Abecedarian Project. In J. Crane (Ed.), *Social programs that work* (pp. 163–183). New York: Russell Sage Foundation.

Ramey, C. T., Dorval, B., & Baker-Ward, L. (1983). Group day care and socially disadvantaged families: Effects on the child and the family. *Advances in Early Education & Day Care, 3*, 69–106.

Ramey, S. L., & Ramey, C. T. (1992). Early educational intervention with disadvantaged children–to what effect? *Applied and Preventive Psychology, 1*, 131–140.

Ramirez, M. (1983). *Psychology of the Americas: Mestizo perspectives on personality and mental health*. New York: Pergamon Press.

Ramos-McKay, J. M., Comas-Diaz, L., & Rivera, L. A. (1988). Puerto Ricans. In L. Comas-Diaz & E. E. H. Griffith (Eds.), *Clinical guidelines in cross-cultural mental health* (pp. 204–232). New York: Wiley.

Rapee, R. (1997). Potential role of child rearing practices in the development of anxiety and depression. *Clinical Psychology Review, 17*, 47–67.

Rasanen, P., Hakko, H., Isohanni, M., Hodgins, S., Jarvelin, M. R., & Tiihonen, J. (1999). Maternal smoking during pregnancy and risk of criminal behavior among adult male offspring in the northern Finland 1996 birth cohort. *American Journal of Psychiatry, 156*, 857–862.

Raval, V. V., Martini, T. S., & Raval, P. H. (2007). "Would others think it is okay to express my feelings?" Regulation of anger, sadness, and physical pain in Gujarati children in India. *Social Development, 16*, 79–105.

Ray, B. D. (2003). *Home educated and now adults: Their communities and civic involvement, views about homeschooling and other traits*. Salem, OR: National Home Educational Research Institute.

Raymore, L. A., Barber, B. L., Eccles, J. S., & Gobdey, G. C. (1999). Leisure behavior pattern stability during the transition from adolescence to young adulthood. *Journal of Youth & Adolescence, 28*, 79–103.

Recchia, H. E., & Howe, N. (2009). Associations between social understanding, sibling relationship quality, and siblings' conflict strategies and outcomes. *Child Development, 80*, 1564–1578.

Recchia, H. E., Howe, N., & Alexander S. (2009). "You didn't teach me, you showed me": Variations in sibling teaching strategies in early and middle childhood. *Merrill-Palmer Quarterly, 55*, 55–78.

Reddy, R., Rhodes, J. E., & Mulhall, P. (2003). The influence of teacher support on student adjustment in the middle school years: A latent growth curve study. *Development and Psychopathology, 15*, 119–138.

Reid, J. B., Patterson, G. R., & Snyder, J. J. (Eds.) (2002). *Antisocial behavior in children and adolescents: A developmental analysis and model for intervention*. Washington, DC: American Psychological Association.

Reiner, W. G., & Gearhart, J. P. (2004). Discordant sexual identity in some genetic males with cloacal exstrophy assigned to female sex at birth. *The New England Journal of Medicine, 350*, 333–341.

Reinius, B., Saetre P., Leonard J. A., Blekhman R., Merino-Martinez R., Gilad, Y., & Jazin, E. (2008). An evolutionarily conserved sexual signature in the primate brain. *PLoS Genetics* 4(6): e1000100. doi:10.1371/journal. pgen.1000100.

Reiss, A., & Hall, S. S. (2007). Fragile X syndrome: Assessment and treatment implications. *Child and Adolescent Psychiatry Clinics of North America, 16*, 663–675.

Reiss, D. (2005). The interplay between genotypes and family relationships: Retaining concepts of development and prevention. *Current Directions in Psychological Science, 14*, 139–143.

Reiss, D., Neiderhiser, J. M., Hetherington, E. M., & Plomin, R. (2000). *The relationship code: Deciphering genetic and social influences on adolescent development.* Cambridge, MA: Harvard University Press.

Renninger, K. A. (1998). Developmental psychology and instruction: Issues from and for practice. In W. Damon, I. E. Sigel, & K. A. Renninger (Eds.), *Handbook of child psychology: Vol. 4. Child psychology in practice* (5th ed., pp. 211–274). New York: Wiley.

Repetti, R. (1989). Effects of daily workload on subsequent behavior during marital interaction: The roles of withdrawal and spouse support. *Journal of Personality and Social Psychology, 57*, 651–659.

Repetti, R. (1996). Short-term and long-term linking job stressors to father child interaction. *Social Development, 1*, 1–15.

Repetti, R., & Wood, J. (1997). The effects of stress and work on mothers' interactions with preschoolers. *Journal of Family Psychology, 1*, 90–108.

Rest, J. R., Narvaez, D., & Thoma, S. J. (2000). *Postconventional moral thinking: A neoKohlbergian approach.* Mahwah, NJ: Erlbaum.

RESULTS. (2008). *Head Start.* Retrieved from: http://www.results.org/issues/head_start/

Revelle, G. L., Wellman, H. M., & Karabenick, J. D. (1985). Comprehension monitoring in preschool children. *Child Development, 56*, 654–663.

Reynolds, A. J., & Temple, J. A. (1998). Extended early childhood intervention and school achievement: Age thirteen findings from the Chicago Longitudinal Study. *Child Development, 69*, 231–246.

Rhee, S. H., & Waldman, I. D. (2002). Genetic and environmental influences on antisocial behavior: A meta-analysis of twin and adoption studies. *Psychological Bulletin, 128*, 490–529.

Rheingold, H. L. (1982). Little children's participation in the work of adults, a nascent prosocial behavior. *Child Development, 53*, 114–125.

Rheingold, H. L., & Cook, K. V. (1975). The content of boys' and girls' rooms as an index of parent behavior. *Child Development, 46*, 459–463.

Rheingold, H. L., & Eckerman, C. (1970). The infant separates himself from his mother. *Science, 168*, 78–83.

Rheingold, H. L., & Eckerman, C. O. (1973). The fear of strangers hypothesis: A critical review. In H. Reese (Ed.), *Advances in child development and behavior* (Vol. 8, pp. 185–222). New York: Academic Press.

Rheingold, H. L., Hay, D. F., & West, M. J. (1976). Sharing in the second year of life. *Child Development, 47*, 1148–1158.

Rhodes, J., & DuBois, D. (2006). Understanding and facilitating the youth mentoring movement. *Social Policy Report, 20*, 3–19.

Rhodes, J., & Fredricksen, K. (2004). The role of teacher relationships in the lives of children and adolescents. *New Directions for Youth Development, 103*, 243–261.

Rhodes, J. E., Grossman, J. B., & Resch, N. R. (2000). Agents of change: Pathways through which mentoring relationships influence adolescents' academic adjustment. *Child Development, 71*, 1662–1671.

Ribak, R. (2009). Remote control, umbilical cord and beyond: The mobile phone as a transitional object. *British Journal of Developmental Psychology* [Special Issue]. *Young People and the Media, 27*, 183–196.

Richards, M. H., Crowe, P. A., Larson, R., & Swarr, A. (1998). Developmental patterns and gender differences in the experience of peer companionship during adolescence. *Child Development, 69*, 154–163.

Richmond, M. K., Stocker, C. M., & Rienks, S. L. (2005). Longitudinal associations between sibling relationship quality, parental differential treatment, and children's adjustment. *Journal of Family Psychology, 19*, 550–559.

Rideout, V. J., Foehr, U. G., Roberts, D. F., & Brodie, M. (1999). *Executive summary: Kids & media @ the millennium.* Menlo Park, CA: Kaiser Family Foundation.

Rideout, V., Roberts, D. F., & Foehr, U. G. (2005). *Generation M: Media in the lives of 8–18 year olds.* Retrieved from: http://d.scribd.com/docs/24lsurq12ylde9ic1vmi.pdf

Riese, M. L. (1990). Genetic influences on neonatal temperament. *Acta Genet Med Gemellol, 39*, 207–213.

Rigby, E., Ryan, R. M., & Brooks-Gunn, J. (2007). Child care quality in different policy contexts. *Journal of Policy Analysis and Management, 26*, 887–907.

Rigby, K. (2001). *Stop the bullying: A handbook for schools.* Melbourne: Australian Council for Educational Research.

Rigby, K., & Johnson, B. (2006). Expressed readiness of Australian schoolchildren to act as bystanders in support of children who are being bullied. *Educational Psychology, 26*, 425–440.

Ritchey, P. N., & Fishbein, H. D. (2001). The lack of an association between adolescent friends' prejudices and stereotypes. *Merrill-Palmer Quarterly, 47*, 188–206.

Ritzer, G. (2007). *The McDonaldization of society.* Thousand Oaks, CA: Pine Forge Press.

Rivers, I., Poteat, V. P., & Noret, N. (2008). Victimization, social support, and psychosocial functioning among children of same-sex and opposite-sex couples. *Developmental Psychology, 44,* 127–134.

Rizzo, M. (2003). Why do children join gangs? *Journal of Gang Research, 11,* 65–75.

Robarchek, C. A., & Robarchek, C. J. (1998). Reciprocities and realities: World views, peacefulness, and violence among Semai and Waorani. *Aggressive Behavior, 24,* 123–133.

Robbins, L. (1963). The accuracy of parental recall of aspects of child development and of child-rearing practices. *Journal of Abnormal and Social Psychology, 66,* 261–270.

Roberts, B., Walton, K., & Viechtbauer, W. (2006). Patterns of mean-level change in personality traits across the life-course: A meta-analysis of longitudinal studies. *Psychological Bulletin, 132,* 1–25.

Roberts, D. F., & Foehr, U. G. (2004). *Kids and media in America.* New York: Cambridge University Press.

Roberts, D. F., Foehr, U. G., Rideout, V. J., & Brodie, M. (1999). *Kids and media at the new millennium: A comprehensive national analysis of children's media use.* Menlo Park, CA: Kaiser Family Foundation.

Roberts, W., & Strayer, J. (1996). Empathy, emotional expressiveness and prosocial behavior. *Child Development, 67,* 449–470.

Roberts, W. L. (1999). The socialization of emotional expression: Relations with prosocial behaviour and competence in five samples. *Canadian Journal of Behavioural Science, 31,* 72–85.

Robertson, B. (February 23, 2010). George Clooney: 10 things you need to know about the Oscar-nominated actor. *Mirror.* Retrieved from: http://www.mirror.co.uk/tv-entertainment/oscars/nominees/2010/02/23/george-clooney-10-things-you-need-to-know-about-the-oscar-nominated-actor-115875-22064238/

Robertson, D., Snarey, J., Ousley, O., Bowman, D., Harenski, K., & Kilts, C. (2007). The neural processing of moral sensitivity to issues of justice and care: An fMRI study. *Neuropsychologia, 45,* 755–766.

Robertson, G. (2007). *Pirate movies no big deal say most Americans.* Retrieved from: http://www.downloadsquad.com/2007/01/25/pirate-movies-no-big-deal-say-most-americans/

Robinson, B. (1988). *Teenage fathers.* Lexington, MA: Lexington Books.

Robinson, J. L., Kagan, J., Reznick, J. S., & Corley, R. (1992). The heritability of inhibited and uninhibited behavior. A twin study. *Developmental Psychology, 28,* 1030–1037.

Rodgers, B., Power, C., & Hope, S. (1997). Parental divorce and adult psychological distress: Evidence from a national cohort: A research note. *Journal of Child Psychology and Psychiatry, 38,* 867–872.

Rodkin, P. C., & Berger, C. (2008). Who bullies whom? Social status asymmetries by victim gender. *International Journal of Behavioral Development, 32,* 473–485.

Rodkin, P. C., Farmer, T. W., Pearl, R., & Van Acker, R. (2000). Heterogeneity of popular boys: Antisocial and prosocial configurations. *Developmental Psychology, 30,* 14–24.

Rodkin, P. C., & Hodges, E. V. E. (2003). Bullies and victims in the peer ecology: Four questions for psychological and school professionals. *School Psychology Review, 32,* 384–401.

Rodkin, P. C., & Roisman, G. I. (2010). Antecedents and correlates of the popular-aggressive phenomenon in elementary school. *Child Development, 81,* 837–850.

Roeser, R. W., Eccles, J. S., & Sameroff, A. J. (2000). School as a context of early adolescents' academic and social-emotional development: A summary of research findings. *Elementary School Journal, 100,* 443–471.

Rogoff, B. (1998). Cognition as a collaborative process. In D. Kuhn & R. Siegler (Eds.), & W. Damon (Series Ed.), *Handbook of child psychology: Vol. 2. Cognition, perception and language* (5th ed., pp. 679–744). New York: Wiley.

Rogoff, B. (2003). *The cultural nature of human development.* New York: Oxford University Press.

Rohe, W., & Patterson, A. H. (1975). The effects of varied levels of resources and density on behavior in a day care center. In D. H. Carson (Ed.), *Man-Environment Interactions* (pp. 161–171). New York: Halsted Press.

Rohner, R. P., Bourque, S. L., & Elordi, C. A. (1996). Children's perspectives of corporal punishment, caretaker acceptance, and psychological adjustment in a poor, biracial, southern community. *Journal of Marriage and Family, 58,* 842–852.

Roisman, G., Collins, W. A., Sroufe, L. A., & Egeland, B. (2005). Predictors of young adults' representations of and behavior in their current romantic relationships: Prospective tests of the prototype hypothesis. *Attachment & Human Development, 7,* 105–121.

Roisman, G. I., Masten, A. S., Coatsworth, J. D., & Tellegen, A. (2004). Salient and emerging development tasks in the transition to adulthood. *Child Development, 75,* 123–133.

Roisman, G. I., Padron, E., Sroufe, L. A., & Egeland, B. (2002). Earned-secure attachment states in retrospect and prospect. *Child Development, 73,* 1204–1219.

Ronka, A., Kinnunen, U., & Pulkkinen, L. (2001). Continuity in problems of social functioning in adulthood: A cumulative perspective. *Journal of Adult Development, 8,* 161–171.

Roopnarine, J. (2004). African American and African Caribbean fathers: Level, quality and meaning of involvement. In M. E. Lamb (Ed.), *The role of the father in child development* (4th ed., pp. 58–97). Hoboken, NJ: Wiley.

Roopnarine, J. L., Fouts, H. N., Lamb, M. E., & Lewis-Elligan, T. Y. (2005). Mothers' and fathers' behaviors toward their 3- to 4-month-old infants in lower, middle class, and upper socioeconomic African-American families. *Developmental Psychology, 41*, 723–732.

Rose, A. J. (2002). Co-numeration in the friendships of girls and boys. *Child Development, 73*, 1830–1843.

Rose, A. J., Carlson, W., & Waller, E. (2007). Predictive associations of co-rumination with friendship and emotional adjustment: Considering the socioemotional trade offs of co-numeration. *Developmental Psychology, 43*, 1019–1031.

Rose, A. J., & Rudolph, K. D. (2006). A review of sex differences in peer relationship processes: Potential trade-offs for the emotional and behavioral development of girls and boys. *Psychological Bulletin, 132*, 98–131.

Rose, S. A., Jankowski, J. J., & Feldman, J. F. (2002). Speed of processing and face recognition at 7 and 12 months. *Infancy, 3*, 435–455.

Rosenbaum, J. E. (2009). Patient teenagers? A comparison of the sexual behavior of virginity pledgers and matched nonpledgers. *Pediatrics, 123*, 110–120.

Rosenblum, G. D., & Lewis, M. (1999). The relations among body image, physical attractiveness, and body mass in adolescence. *Child Development, 70*, 50–64.

Rosenkoetter, L. I., Rosenkoetter, S., Ozretich, R. A., & Acock, A. C. (2004). Mitigating the harmful effects of violent television. *Applied Developmental Psychology, 25*, 25–47.

Rosenstein, D., & Oster, H. (1988). Differential facial response to four basic tastes in newborns. *Child Development, 59*, 1555–1568.

Rosenthal, R. (2002). Covert communication in classrooms, clinics, courtrooms, and cubicles. *American Psychologist, 57*, 839–849.

Rosenthal, R. (2006). Applying psychological research on interpersonal expectations and covert communications in classrooms, clinics, corporations, and courtrooms. In S. I. Donaldson, D. E. Berger, & K. Pezdek (Eds.), *Applied psychology: New frontiers and rewarding careers* (pp. 107–118). Mahwah, NJ: Erlbaum.

Rosenthal, R., & DiMatteo, M. R. (2001). Meta-analysis: Recent developments in quantitative methods for literature reviews. *Annual Review of Psychology, 52*, 59–82.

Rosenthal, R., & Jacobson, L. (1968). *Pygmalion in the classroom: Teacher expectation and pupil's intellectual development.* New York: Holt, Rinehart, & Winston.

Rosenzweig, M. R. (2003). Effects of differential experience on brain and behavior. *Developmental Neuropsychology, 24*, 523–540.

Rosenzweig, M. R., Leiman, A. S., & Breedlove, S. M. (1996). *Biological psychology.* Sunderland, MA: Sinauer.

Rosin, H. (2008, November). A boy's life. *The Atlantic.* Retrieved from http://www.theatlantic.com/doc/200811/transgender-children/5

Ross, H. S., & Conant, C. L. (1992). The social structure of early conflict: Interactions, relationships, and alliances. In C. U. Shantz & W. W. Hartup (Eds.), *Conflict in child and adolescent development* (pp. 153–185). Cambridge, UK: Cambridge University Press.

Ross, H. S., Conant, C., Cheyne, J. A., & Alevizos, E. (1992). Relationships and alliances in the social interactions of kibbutz toddlers. *Social Development, 1*, 1–17.

Rothbart, M. K. (1981). Measurement of temperament in infancy. *Child Development, 52*, 569–578.

Rothbart, M. K. (2007). Temperament, development, and personality. *Current Directions in Psychological Science, 16*, 207–212.

Rothbart, M. K., Ahadi, S. A., & Evans, D. E. (2000). Temperament and personality: Origins and outcomes. *Journal of Personality and Social Psychology, 78*, 122–135.

Rothbart, M. K., Ahadi, S. A., & Hershey, K. L. (1994). Temperament and social behavior in childhood. *Merrill-Palmer Quarterly, 40*, 21–39.

Rothbart, M. K., & Bates, J. (2006). Temperament. In W. Damon & R. Lerner (Series Eds.), & N. Eisenberg (Vol. Ed.), *Handbook of child psychology: Vol. 3. Social, emotional, and personality development* (6th ed., pp. 99–166). Hoboken, NJ: Wiley.

Rothbart, M. K., & Derryberry, D. (1981). Development of individual differences in temperament. In M. E. Lamb, & A. L. Brown (Eds.), *Advances in developmental psychology* (Vol. 1, pp. 37–86). Hillsdale, NJ: Erlbaum.

Rothbart, M. K., & Posner, M. I. (2006). Temperament, attention, and developmental psychopathology. In D. Cicchetti, & D. J. Cohen (Eds.), *Developmental psychopathology: Vol. 2. Developmental neuroscience* (2nd ed., pp. 465–501). Hoboken, NJ: Wiley.

Rothbart, M. K., Sheese, B. E., & Posner, M. I. (2008). Executive attention and effortful control: Linking temperament, brain networks, and genes. *Child Development Perspectives, 1*, 2–7.

Rothbaum, F., Pott, M., Azuma, H., Miyake, K., & Weisz, J. (2000). The development of close relationships in Japan and the United States: Paths of symbiotic harmony and generative tension. *Child Development, 71*, 1121–1142.

Rothbaum, F., Rosen, K., Ujiie, T., & Uchida, N. (2002). Family systems theory, attachment theory, and culture. *Family Process, 41*, 328–350.

Rothbaum, F., Weisz, J., Pott, M., Miyake, K., & Morelli, G. (2000). Attachment and culture: Security in the United States and Japan. *American Psychologist, 35*, 1093–1104.

Rotherman-Borus, M. J., & Langabeer, K. A. (2001). Developmental trajectories of gay, lesbian, & bisexual youths. In A. R. D'Augelli & C. Patterson (Eds.), *Lesbian, gay, and bisexual identities among youth: Psychological perspectives* (pp. 97–128). New York: Oxford University Press.

Rotherman-Borus, M. J., Piacentini, J., Cantwell, C., Belin, T. R., & Song, J. (2000). The 18-month impact of an emergency room intervention for adolescent female suicide attemptees. *Journal of Consulting and Clinical Psychology, 68,* 1081–1093.

Rovee-Collier, C. K. (1987). Learning and memory in infants. In J. D. Osofsky (Ed.), *Handbook of infant development* (pp. 98–148). New York: Wiley.

Roy, K., & Burton, L. M. (2007). Mothering through recruitment: Kinscription of non-residential fathers and father figures in low-income families. *Family Relations, 56,* 24–39.

Rubin, J. Z., Provenzano, F. J., & Luria, A. (1974). The eye of the beholder: Parents' views on sex of newborns. *American Journal of Orthopsychiatry, 43,* 720–731.

Rubin, K. H., Bukowski, W. M., & Parker, J. G. (2006). Peer interactions, relationships, and groups. In W. Damon & R. M. Lerner (Series Eds.), & N. Eisenberg (Vol. Ed.), *Handbook of child psychology: Vol. 3. Social, emotional, and personality development* (6th ed., pp. 571–645). Hoboken, NJ: Wiley.

Rubin, K. H., Burgess, K. M., & Hastings, P. D. (2002). Stability and social-behavioral consequences of toddlers' inhibited temperament and parenting behaviors. *Child Development, 73,* 483–495.

Rubin, K. H., Cheah, C. S. L., & Fox, N. (2001). Emotion regulation, parenting and display of social reticence in preschoolers. *Early Education & Development, 12,* 97–115.

Rubin, K. H., Coplan, R. J., & Bowker, J. C. (2009). Social withdrawal in childhood. *Annual Review of Psychology, 60,* 141–172.

Rubin, K. H., Wojslawowicz, J. C., Rose-Krasnor, L., Booth-LaForce, C., & Burgess, K. B. (2006). The best friendships of shy/withdrawn children: Prevalence, stability, and relationship quality. *Journal of Abnormal Child Psychology, 34,* 143–157.

Rubin, Z. (1980). *Children's friendships.* Cambridge, MA: Harvard University Press.

Ruble, D. N., Martin, C., & Berenbaum, S. (2006). Gender development. In W. Damon & R. M. Lerner (Series Eds.), & N. Eisenberg (Vol. Ed.), *Handbook of child psychology: Vol. 3. Social, emotional, and personality development* (6th ed, pp. 858–932). Hoboken, NJ: Wiley.

Ruby, P., & Decity, J. (2001). Effect of subjective perspective taking during simulation of action: A PET investigation of agony. *Nature and Neuroscience, 4,* 546–550.

Rudolph, K. D., Lambert, S. F., Clark, A. G., & Kurlakowsky, K. D. (2001). Negotiating the transition to middle school: The role of self-regulatory processes. *Child Development, 72,* 929–946.

Ruffman, T., Slade, L., & Crowe, E. (2002). The relation between children's and mothers' mental state language and theory-of-mind understanding. *Child Development, 73,* 734–751.

Rump, K. M., Giovannelli, J. L., Minshew, N. J., & Strauss, M. S. (2009). The development of emotion recognition in individuals with autism. *Child Development, 80,* 1434–1447.

Rushton, J. P., Fulker, D. W., Neale, M. C., Nias, D. K. B., & Eysenck, H. J. (1986). Altruism and aggression: The heritability of individual differences. *Journal of Personality and Social Psychology, 50,* 1192–1198.

Russell, A., & Finnie, V. (1990). Preschool children's social status and maternal instructions to assist group entry. *Developmental Psychology, 26,* 603–611.

Russell, A., Russell, G., & Midwinter, D. (1991). Observer effects on mothers and fathers: Self-reported influence during a home observation. *Merrill-Palmer Quarterly, 38,* 263–283.

Rust, J., Golombok, S., Hines, M., Johnston, K., Golding, J., & ALSPAC Study Team. (2000). The role of brothers and sisters in the gender development of preschool children. *Journal of Experimental Child Psychology, 77,* 292–303.

Rutter, M. (1989). Pathways from childhood to adult life. *Journal of Child Psychology and Psychiatry, 30,* 23–51.

Rutter, M. (1992). Nature, nurture and psychopathology. In B. Tizard & V. Varma (Eds.), *Vulnerability and resilience in human development* (pp. 21–38). London: Jessica Kingsley.

Rutter, M. (2002a). Family influences on behavior and development: Challenges for the future. In J. McHale & W. S. Grolnick (Eds.), *Retrospect and prospect in the psychological study of families* (pp. 321–351). Mahwah, NJ: Erlbaum.

Rutter, M. (2002b). Nature, nurture, and development: From evangelism through science toward policy and practice. *Child Development, 73,* 1–21.

Rutter, M. (2006a). *Genes and behavior.* New York: Blackwell.

Rutter, M. (2006b). The psychological effects of early institutional rearing. In P. Marshall & N. Fox (Eds.), *The development of social engagement: Neurobiological perspectives* (pp. 355–391). New York: Oxford University Press.

Rutter, M. (2007, September). *Autism research: Lessons from the past and prospects for the future.* Presentation at the New York University Child Study Center.

Rutter, M., Giller, H., & Hagell, A. (1998). *Antisocial behavior by young people.* Cambridge, UK: Cambridge University Press.

Rutter, M., Kreppner, J., O'Conner, T., & the English & Romanian Adoptees (ERA) Study Team. (2001). Risk and resilience following profound early global privation. *British Journal of Psychiatry, 179,* 97–103.

Rutter, M., Pickles, A., Murray, R., & Eaves, L. (2001). Testing hypotheses on specific environmental causal effects on behavior. *Psychological Bulletin, 127,* 291–324.

Ryan, A. M. (2001). The peer group as a context for the development of young adolescent motivation and achievement. *Child Development, 72,* 4, 1135–1150.

Rymer, R. (1994). *Genie: A scientific tragedy*. New York: Harper Perennial.

Saarni, C. (1999). *The development of emotional competence*. New York: Guilford Press.

Saarni, C. (2007). The development of emotional competence: Pathways to helping children become emotionally intelligent. In R. Bar-On, J. G. Maree, & M. J. Elias (Eds.), *Educating people to be emotionally intelligent* (pp. 15–36). New York: Praeger.

Saarni, C., Campos, J. J., Camras, L., & Witherington, D. (2006). Emotional development. In W. Damon & R. M. Lerner (Series Eds.), & N. Eisenberg (Vol. Ed.). *Handbook of child psychology: Vol. 3. Social, emotional, and personality development* (6th ed., pp. 226–299). Hoboken, NJ: Wiley.

Sabbagh, M. A., Xu, F., Carlson, S. M., Moses, L. J., & Lee, K. (2006). The development of executive functioning and theory of mind: A comparison of Chinese and U.S. preschoolers. *Psychological Science*, *17*, 74–81.

Saffran, J. R., Werker, J., & Werner, L. A. (2006). The infant's auditory world. In W. Damon & R. M. Lerner (Series Eds.), & D. Kuhn & R. Siegler (Vol. Eds.), *Handbook of child psychology: Vol. 2. Cognition, perception & language* (6th ed., pp. 58–108). Hoboken, NJ: Wiley.

Sagi, A., Lamb, M. E., Lewkowicz, K. S., Shoham, R., Dvir, R., & Estes, D. (1985). Security of infant-mother, father, and metapelet attachments among Kibbutz-reared Israeli children. *Monographs of the Society for Research in Child Development*, *50* (Serial No. 209), 257–275.

Sagi, A., van IJzendoorn, M. H., Aviezer, O., Donnell, F., & Mayseless, O. (1994). Sleeping out of home in a kibbutz community arrangement: It makes a difference for infant-mother attachment. *Child Development*, *65*, 992–1004.

Sakuma, M., Endo, T., & Muto, T. (2000). The development of self-understanding in preschoolers and elementary school children: Analysis of self-descriptions and self-evaluations. *Japanese Journal of Developmental Psychology*, *11*, 176–187.

Salmivalli, C., & Voeten, M. (2004). Connections between attitudes, group norms, and behaviors associated with bullying in schools. *International Journal of Behavioral Development*, *28*, 246–258.

Salmivalli, C., Peets, K., & Hodges, E. V. E. (2010). Bullying. In P. K. Smith & C. H. Hart (Eds.), *Wiley-Blackwell handbook of childhood social development* (2nd ed.). Oxford, UK: Wiley-Blackwell.

Sameroff, A. J. (1994). Developmental systems and family functioning. In R. D. Parke & S. G. Kellam (Eds.), *Exploring family relationships with other social contexts* (pp. 199–214). Hillsdale, NJ: Erlbaum.

Sameroff, A. J. (2009). The transactional model. In A. J. Sameroff (Ed.), *The transactional model of development: How children and contexts shape each other* (pp. 3–22). Washington, DC: American Psychological Association.

Sameroff, A. J. (2010). A unified theory of development: A dialectic integration of nature and nurture. *Child Development*, *8*, 6–22.

Sampaio, R., & Truwit, C. (2001). Myelination in the developing human brain. In C. Nelson & M. Luciana (Eds.), *Handbook of developmental cognitive neuroscience* (pp. 35–44). Cambridge, MA: MIT Press.

Sampson, R. J., & Laub, J. H. (1994). Urban poverty and the family context of delinquency: A new look at structure and process in a classic study. *Child Development*, *65*, 523–540.

Sampson, R. J., & Laub, J. H. (2003). Life-course desisters? Trajectories of crime among delinquent boys followed to age 70. *Criminology*, *41*, 555–592.

Sanders, L. D., Weber-Fox, C. M., & Neville, H. J. (2007). Varying degrees of plasticity in different subsystems of language. In J. R. Pomerantz & M. Crair (Eds.), *Topics in integrative neuroscience: From cells to cognition* (pp. 125–153). New York: Cambridge University Press.

Sanders, M. G., Epstein, J. L., & Connors-Tadros, L. C. (1999). *Family partnerships with high schools: The parents' perspective*. Baltimore: Center for Research on the Education of Students Placed at Risk, Johns Hopkins University.

Sanderson, J. A., & Siegal, M. (1991). *Loneliness in young children*. Unpublished manuscript. University of Queensland, Brisbane, Australia.

Sanders Thompson, V. L. (1994). Socialization to race and its relationship to racial identification among African Americans. *Journal of Black Psychology*, *20*, 175–188.

Sandstrom, M. J. (2007). A link between mothers' disciplinary strategies and children's relational aggression. *British Journal of Developmental Psychology*, *25*, 399–407.

Sandstrom, M. J., & Coie, J. D. (1999). A developmental perspective on peer rejection: Mechanisms of stability and change. *Child Development*, *70*, 955–966.

Sanson, A., Hemphill, S. A., Yagmurlu, B., & McClowry, S. (2010). Temperament and social development. In P. K. Smith & C. H. Hart (Eds.), *Wiley-Blackwell handbook of childhood social development* (2nd ed.). Oxford, UK: Wiley-Blackwell.

Santelli, J. S., Lindberg, L. D., Finer, L. B., & Singh, S. (2007). Explaining recent declines in adolescent pregnancy in the United States: The contribution of abstinence and improved contraceptive use. *American Journal of Public Health*, *97*, 150–156.

Santucci, A. K., Silk, J. S., Shaw, D. S., Gentzler, A., Fox, N. A., & Kovacs, M. (2008). Vagal tone and temperament as predictors of emotion regulation strategies in young children. *Developmental Psychobiology*, *50*, 205–216.

Sarkisian, N., Gerena, M., & Gerstel, N. (2007). Extended family integration among Euro and Mexican Americans: Ethnicity, gender, and class. *Journal of Marriage and Family*, *69*, 40–54.

Saroglou, V., & Galand, P. (2004). Identities, values, and religion: A study among Muslim, other immigrant, and native Belgian young adults after the 9/11 attacks. *Identity, 4,* 97–132.

Savin-Williams, R. C. (1987). *Adolescence: An ethological perspective.* New York: Springer-Verlag.

Savin-Williams, R. C. (1998). *". . . and then I became gay." Young men's stories.* New York: Routledge.

Savin-Williams, R. C., & Cohen, K. M. (2004). Homoerotic development during childhood and adolescence. *Child and Adolescent Psychiatric Clinics, 13,* 529–549.

Savin-Williams, R. C., & Ream, G. (2003). Sex variations in the disclosure to parents of same-sex attractions. *Journal of Family Psychology, 17,* 429–438.

Sawhill, I. (2002, January). Abstaining from sex. *Blueprint Magazine.* Retrieved from: http://www.dlc.org/ndol_ci.cfm?kaid = 114&subid = 144&contentid = 250088

Sax, L. (2005). *Why gender matters: What parents and teachers need to know about the emerging science of sex differences.* New York: Doubleday.

Sayfan, L., & Lagattuta, K. H. (2009). Scaring the monster away: What children know about managing fears of real and imaginary creatures. *Child Development, 80,* 1756–1774.

Scaramella, L. V., & Conger, R. D. (2003). Intergenerational continuity of hostile parenting and its consequences: The moderating influence of children's negative emotional reactivity. *Social Development, 12,* 420–439.

Scarr, S. (1996). How people make their own environments: Implications for parents and policy makers. *Psychology, Public Policy and Law, 2,* 204–228.

Scarr, S., & McCartney, K. (1983). How people make their own environments: A theory of genotype environment effects. *Child Development, 54,* 424–435.

Scarr, S., & Weinberg, R. A. (1983). The Minnesota adoption studies: Genetic differences and malleability. *Child Development, 54,* 260–267.

Schaffer, H. R. (1996). *Social development.* Cambridge, MA: Blackwell.

Schaffer, H. R. (2000). The early experience assumption: Past, present, and future. *International Journal of Behavioral Development, 24,* 5–14.

Schaffer, H. R., & Emerson, P. E. (1964). The development of social attachments in infancy. *Monographs of the Society for Research in Child Development, 29* (Serial No. 94).

Schell, K. (1996). *Family-peer linkages: Adolescence and high risk behaviour.* Unpublished doctoral dissertation, University of Guelph, Guelph, Ontario, Canada.

Schermerhorn, A. C., & Cummings, E. M. (2008). Transactional family dynamics: A new framework for conceptualizing family influence processes. In R. Kail (Ed.), *Advances in Child Development and Behavior* (Vol. 36, pp. 187–250). San Diego: Academic Press

Schermerhorn, A. C., Cummings, E. M., DeCarlo, C. A., & Davies, P. T. (2007). Children's influence in the marital relationship. *Journal of Family Psychology, 21,* 259–269.

Schieve, L. A., Rasmussen, S. A., & Reefhuis, J. (2005). Risk of birth defects among children conceived with assisted reproductive technology: Providing an epidemiologic context to the data. *Fertility and Sterility, 84,* 1320–1324.

Schilt, K., & Wiswall, M. (2008). Before and after: Gender transitions, human capital, and workplace experiences. *Journal of Economic Analysis & Policy, 8*(1). Retrieved from: http://www.bepress.com/bejeap/vol8/iss1/art39/

Schlossman, S., & Cairns, R. B. (1993). Problem girls: Observations on past and present. In G. H. Elder, J. Modell, & R. D. Parke (Eds.), *Children in time and place* (pp. 110–130). New York: Cambridge University Press.

Schmitt, K. L., Dayanim, S., & Matthias, S. (2008). The effects of online homepage construction as an expression of social development. *Developmental Psychology, 44,* 496–506.

Schmidt, M. E., Pempek, T. A., Kirkorian, H. L., Lund, A. F., & Anderson, D. R. (2008). The effects of background television on the toy play behaviors of very young children. *Child Development, 79,* 1137–1151.

Schneider, B. H. (2000). *Friends and enemies: Peer relations in childhood.* London: Arnold.

Schneider, B. H., Atkinson, L., & Tardif, C. (2001). Child-parent attachment and children's peer relations: A quantitative review. *Developmental Psychology, 37,* 86–100.

Schneider, B. H., Smith, A., Poisson, S. E., & Kwan, A. B. (1997). Cultural dimensions of children's peer relations. In S. Duck (Ed.), *Handbook of personal relationships* (2nd ed., pp. 121–146). New York: Wiley.

Schofield, J. W., & Eurich-Fulcer, R. (2001). When and how school desegregation improves intergroup relations. In R. Brown & S. L. Gaertner (Eds.), *Blackwell handbook of social psychology: Intergroup processes* (pp. 475–494). Malden, MA: Blackwell.

Schoppe-Sullivan, S. J., Diener, M. L., Mangelsdorf, S. C., Brown, G. L., McHale, J. L., & Frosch, C. A. (2006). Attachment and sensitivity in family context: The roles of parent and infant gender. *Infant and Child Development, 15,* 367–385.

Schoppe-Sullivan, S. J., Weldon, A. H., Cook, J. C., Davis, E. F., & Buckley, C. K. (2009). Coparenting behavior moderates longitudinal relations between effortful control and preschool children's externalizing behavior. *Journal of Child Psychology and Psychiatry, 50,* 698–706.

Schreiber, N., Bellah, L. D., Martinez, Y., McLaurin, K. A., Strok, R., Garven, S., & Wood, J. M. (2006). Suggestive interviewing in the McMartin Preschool and Kelly Michaels daycare abuse cases: A case study. *Social Influence, 1,* 16–47.

Schulenburg, C. (2006), *Dying to entertain: Violence on prime time broadcast television 1998-2006.* Parents Television Council.

Retrieved from: www.parentstv.org/ptc/publications/reports/violencestudy/exsummary.asp

Schulte-Rüther, M., Markowitsch, H. J., Fink, G. R., & Piefke, M. (2007). Mirror neuron and theory of mind mechanisms involved in face-to-face interactions. *Journal of Cognitive Neuroscience, 19*, 1354–1372.

Schulte-Rüther, M., Markowitsch, H. J., Shah, N. J., Fink, G. R., & Piefke, M. (2008). Gender differences in brain networks supporting empathy. *NeuroImage, 42*, 393–403.

Schultz, R. M., & Williams, C. J. (2002). The science of art. *Science, 296*, 2188–2190.

Schulz, M. S., Cowan, C. P., & Cowan, P. A. (2006). Promoting healthy beginnings: A randomized controlled trial of a preventive intervention to preserve marital quality during the transition to parenthood. *Journal of Consulting and Clinical Psychology, 74*, 20–31.

Schulz, M. S., Cowan, P. A., Cowan, C. P., & Brennan, R. T. (2004). Coming home upset: Gender, marital satisfaction and the daily spillover of workday experience into couple interactions. *Journal of Family Psychology, 18*, 250–263.

Schumacker, R. E., & Lomax, R. G. (2004). *A beginner's guide to structural equation modeling* (2nd ed.). Mahwah, NJ: Erlbaum.

Schumm, W. R., McCollum, E. E., Bugaighis, M. A., Jurich, A. P., Bollman, S. R., & Reitz, J. (1988). Differences between Anglo and Mexican American family members on satisfaction with family life. *Hispanic Journal of Behavioral Sciences, 10*, 39–53.

Schwartz, A., & Bugental, D. B. (2004). *Infant habituation to repeated stress as an interactive function of child temperament and maternal depression*. Unpublished paper, University of California, Santa Barbara.

Schwartz, D., Dodge, K., Pettit, G., & Bates, J. (1997). The early socialization of aggressive victims of bullying. *Child Development, 60*, 665–675.

Schwartz, D., Gorman, A. H., Duong, M. T., & Nakamoto, J. (2008). Peer relationships and academic achievement as interacting predictors of depressive symptoms during middle childhood. *Journal of Abnormal Psychology, 117*, 289–299.

Schwartz, D., Proctor, L. J., & Chien, D. H. (2001). The aggressive victim of bullying: Emotional and behavioral disregulation as a pathway to victimization by peers. In J. Juvonen & S. Graham (Eds.), *Peer harassment in school: The plight of the vulnerable and victimized* (pp. 147–174). New York: Guilford Press.

Schwartz, S. J. (2001). The evolution of Eriksonian and neo-Eriksonian identity research: A review and integration. *Identity, 1*, 7–58.

Schweinhart, L. J., Montie, J., Xiang, Z., Barnett, W. S., Belfield, C. R., & Nores, M. (2005). *Lifetime effects: The HighScope Perry Preschool study through age 40.* Ypsilanti, MI: HighScope Press.

Scott, S. (2005). Do parenting programmes for severe child antisocial behaviour work over the longer term, and for whom? One-year follow-up of a multi-centre controlled trial. *Behavioural and Cognitive Psychotherapy, 33*, 403–421.

Sears, R. R., Maccoby, E. E., & Levin, H. (1957). *Patterns of child rearing.* Evanston, IL: Row Peterson.

Seay, B., Alexander, B. K., & Harlow, H. F. (1964). Maternal behavior of socially deprived Rhesus monkeys. *Journal of Abnormal and Social Psychology, 69*, 345–354.

Sebanc, A. M. (2003). The friendship features of preschool children: Links with prosocial behavior and aggression. *Social Development, 12*, 249–268.

Sedikides, C., & Brewer, M. (2001). *Individual self, relational self, collective self.* Philadelphia: Psychology Press.

Seem, S. R., & Clark, M. D. (2006). Healthy women, healthy men, and healthy adults: An evaluation of gender role of stereotypes in the twenty-first century. *Sex Roles, 55*, 247–258.

Segal, U. A. (1995). Child abuse by the middle class? A study of professionals in India. *Child Abuse and Neglect, 19*, 213–227.

Segal, U. A. (2001). India. In B. M. Schwartz-Kenney, M. McCauley, & M. Epstein (Eds.), *Child abuse: A global view* (pp. 51–65). Westport, CT: Greenwood.

Seidman, E., & French, S. E. (1997). Normative school transitions among urban adolescents: When, where, and how to intervene. In H. J. Walberg, O. Reyes, & R. P. Weissberg (Eds.), *Children and youth: Interdisciplinary perspectives: Vol. 7. Issues in children's and families' lives* (pp. 166–189). Thousand Oaks, CA: Sage.

Seiffge-Krenke, I., & Lang. J. (2002, March). *Forming and maintaining romantic relations from early adolescence to young adulthood: Evidence of a developmental sequence.* Paper presented at the biennial meeting for Social Research on Adolescence, New Orleans, LA.

Seiter, J. S. (2007). Ingratiation and gratuity: The effect of complimenting customers on tipping behavior in restaurants. *Journal of Applied Social Psychology, 37*, 478–485.

Seitz, V. (1990). Intervention programs for impoverished children: A comparison of educational and family support models. *Annals of Child Development, 7*, 73–103.

Self-Brown, S., Rheingold, A. A., Campbell, C., & de Arellano, M. A. (2008). A media campaign prevention program for child sexual abuse: Community members' perspectives. *Journal of Interpersonal Violence, 23*, 728–743.

Seligman, M. E. P. (1974). Depression and learned helplessness. In R. J. Friedman & M. M. Katz (Eds.), *The psychology of depression: Contemporary theory and research* (pp. 83–113). Washington, DC: Winston-Wiley.

Seligman, M. E. P. (2002). *Authentic happiness: Using the new positive psychology to realize your potential for lasting fulfillment.* New York: Simon & Schuster.

Selman, R. L. (1980). *The growth of interpersonal understanding.* New York: Academic Press.

Selman, R. L. (2003). *The promotion of social awareness.* New York: Russell Sage Foundation.

Selman, R. L., & Byrne, D. F. (1974). A structural-developmental analysis of levels of role taking in middle childhood. *Child Development, 45,* 803–806.

Selman, R. L., & Jacquette, D. (1978). Stability and oscillation in interpersonal awareness: A clinical-developmental analysis. In C. B. Keasey (Ed.), *The 25th Nebraska Symposium on Motivation* (pp. 250–304). Lincoln: University of Nebraska Press.

Semel, E., & Rosner, S. R. (2003). *Understanding Williams syndrome: Behavioral patterns and interventions.* Mahwah, NJ: Erlbaum.

Serbin, L. A., Poulin-Dubois, D., & Eichstedt, J. A. (2002). Infants' response to gender-inconsistent events. *Infancy, 3,* 531–542.

Serbin, L. A., Poulin-Dubois, D., Colburne, K. A., Sen, M. G., & Eichstedt, J. A. (2001). Gender stereotyping in infancy: Visual preferences for and knowledge of gender-stereotyped toys in the second year. *International Journal of Behavioral Development, 25,* 7–15.

Serbin, L. A., Powlishta, K. K., & Gulko, J. (1993). The development of sex typing in middle childhood. *Monographs of the Society for Research in Child Development, 58* (Serial No. 232), 5–74.

Serketich, W. J., & Dumas, J. E. (1996). The effectiveness of behavioral parent training to modify antisocial behavior in children: A meta-analysis. *Behavior Therapy, 27,* 171–186.

Serpell, J. A. (1996). Why do people love their pets? *Evolution and Human Behavior, 18,* 237–259.

Servin, A., Nordenstrom, A., Larsson, A., & Bohlin, G. (2003). Prenatal androgens and gender-typed behavior: A study of girls with mild and severe forms of congenital adrenal hyperplasia. *Developmental Psychology, 39,* 440–450.

Shakin, M., Shakin, D., & Stern-Glanz, S. H. (1985). Infant clothing: Sex labeling for strangers. *Sex Roles, 12,* 955–963.

Sharabany, R. (2006). The cultural context of children and adolescents: Peer relationships and intimate friendships among Arab and Jewish children in Israel. In X. Chen, D. C. French, & B. H. Schneider (Eds.), *Peer relationships in cultural context* (pp. 452–478). New York: Cambridge University Press.

Shatz, M. (1994). Theory of mind and the development of socio-linguistic intelligence in early childhood. In C. Lewis & P. Mitchell (Eds.), *Children's early understanding of mind: Origins and development* (pp. 311–329). Hillsdale, NJ: Erlbaum.

Shaw, D. S., Gilliom, M., Ingoldsby, E. M., & Nagin, D. S. (2003). Trajectories leading to school-age conduct problems. *Developmental Psychology, 39,* 189–200.

Shaw, D. S., Keenan, K., Owens, E. B., Winslow, E. B., Hood, N., & Garcia, M. (1995, April). *Developmental precursors of externalizing behavior among two samples of low-income families: Ages 3 to 5.* Paper presented at biennial meeting of the Society for Research in Child Development, Indianapolis, IN.

Shaw, D. S., & Winslow, E. B. (1997). Precursors and correlates of antisocial behavior from infancy to preschool. In D. M. Stoff, J. Breiling, & J. D. Maser (Eds.)*Handbook of antisocial behavior* (pp. 148–158). Hoboken, NJ: Wiley.

Shaw, I. (2008). *Social skills and homeschooling: Myths and facts.* Retrieved from: http://familyeducation. com/homeschooling/human relations/56224. html

Shaywitz, B. A., Shaywitz, S. E., Pugh, K. R., & Constable, R. T. (1995). Sex differences in the functional organization of the brain for language. *Nature, 373,* 607–609.

Shea, D. L., Lubinski, D., & Benbow, C. P. (2001). Importance of assessing spatial ability in intellectually talented young adolescents: A 20-year longitudinal study. *Journal of Educational Psychology, 93,* 604–614.

Shek, D. T. L. (2001). Chinese adolescents and their parents' views on a happy family: Implications for family therapy. *Family Therapy, 28,* 73–104.

Sherif, M. (1966). *Group conflict and cooperation.* London: Routledge & Kegan Paul.

Sherman, M. H. (1990). Family narratives: Internal representations of family relationships and affective themes. *Infant Mental Health Journal, 11,* 253–258.

Shields, A., Ryan, R. M., & Cicchetti, D. (2001). Narrative representations of caregivers and emotional dysregulation as predictors of maltreated children's rejection by peers. *Developmental Psychology, 37,* 321–337.

Shipman, K. L., Schneider, R., Fitzgerald, M. M., Sims, C., Swisher, L., & Edwards, A. (2007). Maternal emotion socialization in maltreating and non-maltreating families: Implications for children's emotion regulation. *Social Development, 16,* 268–285.

Shoda, Y., Mischel, W., & Peake, P. K. (1990). Predicting adolescent cognitive and self-regulatory competencies from preschool delay of gratification: Identifying diagnostic conditions. *Developmental Psychology, 26,* 978–986.

Shonkoff, J. P., Lippitt, J. A., & Cavanaugh, D. A. (2000). Early childhood policy: Implications for infant mental health. In C. H. Zeanah, (Ed.), *Handbook of infant mental health* (2nd ed., pp. 503–518). New York: Guilford Press.

Shonkoff, J. P., & Phillips, D. (Eds.) (2000). *From neurons to neighborhoods.* Washington, DC: National Academy Press.

Shrum, W., & Cheek, N. H. (1987). Social structure during the school years: Onset of the degrouping process. *American Sociological Review, 52,* 218–223.

Shulman, S., & Klein, M. M. (1993). Distinctive role of the father in adolescent separation-individuation. In

S. Shulman & A. W. Collins (Eds.), *Father-adolescent relationships* (pp. 41–57). San Francisco: Jossey-Bass.

Shure, M. B., & Spivack, G. (1980). Interpersonal problem solving as a mediator of behavioral adjustment in preschool and kindergarten children. *Journal of Applied Developmental Psychology, l*, 29–44.

Shweder, R. A., Much, N. C., Mahapatra, M., & Park, L. (1997). The "big three" of morality (autonomy, community, divinity) and the "big three" explanations of suffering. In A. M. Brandt & P. Rozin (Eds.), *Morality and health* (pp. 119–169). Florence, KY: Taylor & Frances/Routledge.

Shyers, L. (1992). *Comparison of social adjustment between home and traditionally schooled children*. Unpublished doctoral dissertation. University of Florida.

Siegler, R. S. (2000). The rebirth of children's learning. *Child Development, 71*, 26–36.

Siegler, R. S., & Alibali, M. W. (2005). *Children's thinking* (4th ed.). Upper Saddle River, NJ: Prentice Hall.

Signorella, M. L., Bigler, R. S., & Liben, L. S. (1993). Developmental differences in children's gender schemata about others: A meta-analytic review. *Developmental Review, 13*, 147–183.

Signorielli, N., & Morgan, M. (2001). Television and the family: The cultivation perspective. In J. Bryant & J. A. Bryant (Eds.), *Television and the American family* (2nd ed., pp. 333–351). Mahwah, NJ: Erlbaum.

Silberg, J. L., Rutter, M., & Eaves, L. J. (2001). Genetic and environmental influences on the temporal association between early anxiety and later depression in girls. *Biological Psychology, 49*, 1040–1049.

Silvern, D. (1995). Making friends is a primary goal. *San Diego Tribune*, May 2, B1–B3.

Silverstein, L. (2002). Fathers and families. In J. McHale & W. Grolnick (Eds.), *Retrospect and prospect in the psychological study of families* (pp. 35–64). Mahwah, NJ: Erlbaum.

Simmons, R. G., Burgeson, R., Carlson-Ford, S., & Blyth, D. A. (1987). The impact of cumulative change in early adolescence. *Child Development, 58*, 1220–1234.

Simmons, T., & O'Connell, M. (2003). *Married-couple and unmarried-partner households: 2000*. Washington, DC: U. S. Census Bureau.

Simon, R. J., & Landis, J. (1991). *The crimes women commit, the punishments they receive*. Lexington, MA: Lexington Books.

Simon, S. (May 22, 1999). Brooks Brown and Pam Glasner, students at Columbine High School, talk about their school, the shootings and how their lives have changed. *NPR Weekend Edition*. Retrieved from: http://www.highbeam.com/doc/1P1-71222906.html

Simons, R. L., Johnson, C., Beaman, J., Conger, R. D., & Whitbeck, L. B. (1996). Parents and peer group as mediators of the effect of community structure on adolescent problem behavior. *American Journal of Community Psychology, 24*, 145–171.

Simons, R. L., Lin, K. H., Gordon, L. C., Conger, R. D., & Lorenz, F. O. (1999). Explaining the high incidence of adjustment problems among children of divorce compared with those in two parent families. *Journal of Marriage and Family, 61*, 1020–1033.

Simpkins, S. D., Fredericks, J. A., Davis-Kearn, & Eccles, J. S. (2006). Healthy habits, healthy minds: The influence of activity involvement in middle childhood. In A. C. Huston & M. N. Ripke (Eds.), *Developmental contexts in middle childhood* (pp. 283–302). New York: Cambridge University Press.

Simpkins, S. D., & Parke, R. D. (2001). The relations between parental friendships and children's friendships: Self-report and observational analysis. *Child Development, 72*, 569–582.

Simpson, J. A., Collins, W. A., Tran, S., & Haydon, K. C. (2007). Attachment and the experience and expression of emotions in romantic relationships: A developmental perspective. *Journal of Personality & Social Psychology, 92*, 355–367.

Sinclair, S., Dunn, E., & Lowery, B. S. (2005). The relationship between parental racial attitudes and children's implicit prejudice. *Journal of Experimental Social Psychology, 41*, 283–289.

Singer, D. G., & Singer, J. L. (Eds.) (2001). *Handbook of children and the media*. Thousand Oaks, CA: Sage.

Singer, E., & Doornenbal, J. (2006). Learning morality in peer conflict: A study of school children's narratives about being betrayed by a friend. *Childhood: A Global Journal of Child Research, 13*, 225–245.

Singer, J. L., & Singer, D. G. (1981). *Television, imagination & aggression: A study of preschoolers*. Hillsdale, NJ: Erlbaum.

Singer, J. L., Singer, D. G. Desmond R., Hirsch, B., & Nikol, A. (1988). Family meditation and children's cognition, aggressive, and comprehension of television: A longitudinal study. *Journal of Applied Developmental Psychology, 9*, 329–347.

Singer, T., Seymour, B., O'Doherty, J., Kaube, H., Dolan, R. J., & Frith, C. D. (2004). Empathy for pain involves the affective but not sensory components of pain. *Science, 303*, 1157–1162.

Sirotnak, A. P. (2008). *Child Abuse & Neglect: Psychosocial Dwarfism: Multimedia*. Retrieved from: http://emedicine.medscape.com/article/913843-overview

Skinner, B. F. (1953). *Science and human behavior*. New York: Macmillan.

Slaby, R. G., & Frey, K. S. (1975). Development of gender constancy and selective attention to same-sex models. *Child Development, 46*, 849–856.

Slade, E. P., & Wissow, L. S. (2004). Spanking in early childhood and later behavior problems: A prospective study of infants and toddlers. *Pediatrics, 113,* 1321–1330.

Slater, A. M., Bremner, G., Johnson, S. P., Sherwood, P., Hayes, R., & Brown, E. (2000). Newborn preferences for attractive faces: The role of internal and external facial features. *Infancy, 1,* 265–274.

Slavin, R. E. (1996). Research on cooperative learning and achievement: What we know, what we need to know. *Contemporary Educational Psychology, 21,* 43–69.

Slavin, R. E. (2005). Evidence-based reform in education: Promise and pitfalls. *Mid-Western Educational Researcher, 18,* 8–13.

Slavin, R. E., & Cooper, R. (1999). Improving intergroup relations: Lessons learned from cooperative learning programs. *Journal of Social Issues, 55,* 647–663.

Slomkowski, C., Rende, R., Conger, K. J., Simons, R. L., & Conger, R. D. (2001). Sisters, brothers, and delinquency: Evaluating social influence during early and middle adolescence. *Child Development, 72,* 271–283.

Smetana, J. G. (1981). Reasoning in the personal and moral domains: Adolescent and young adult women's decision-making regarding abortion. *Journal of Applied Developmental Psychology, 2,* 211–226.

Smetana, J. G. (1983). Social-cognitive development: Domain distinctions and coordinations. *Developmental Review, 3,* 131–147.

Smetana, J. G. (1984). Toddlers' social interactions regarding moral and conventional transgressions. *Child Development, 55,* 1767–1776.

Smetana, J. G. (1988). Concepts of self and social convention: Adolescents' and parents' reasoning about hypothetical and actual family conflicts. In M. R. Gunnar & W. A. Collins (Eds.), *Minnesota Symposia on Child Psychology: Vol. 21. Development during the transition to adolescence* (pp. 79–122). Hillsdale, NJ: Erlbaum.

Smetana, J. G. (1989). Adolescents' and parents' reasoning about actual family conflict. *Child Development, 60,* 1052–1067.

Smetana, J. G. (1995). Morality in context: Abstractions, ambiguities, and applications. In R. Vasta (Ed.), *Annals of child development* (Vol. 10, pp. 83–130). London: Jessica Kingsley.

Smetana, J. G. (1997). Parenting and the development of social knowledge reconceptualized: A social domain analysis. In J. E. Grusec & L. Kuczynski (Eds.), *Parenting and children's internalization of values* (pp. 162–192). New York: Wiley.

Smetana, J. G. (2002). Culture, autonomy, and personal jurisdiction in adolescent-parent relationships. In H. W. Reese & R. V. Kail (Eds.), *Advances in child development and behavior* (Vol. 29, pp. 51–87). New York: Academic Press.

Smetana, J. G. (2006). Social domain theory: Consistencies and variations in children's moral and social judgments. In M. Killen & J. G. Smetana (Eds.), *Handbook of moral development* (pp. 119–154). Mahwah, NJ: Erlbaum.

Smetana, J. G., & Braeges, J. L. (1990). The development of toddlers' moral and conventional judgments. *Merrill-Palmer Quarterly, 36,* 329–346.

Smetana, J. G., Campione-Barr, N., & Daddis, C. (2004). Longitudinal development of family decision making: Defining healthy behavioral autonomy for middle-class African American adolescents. *Child Development, 75,* 1418–1434.

Smetana, J. G., & Letourneau, K. J. (1984). Development of gender constancy and children's sex-typed free play behavior. *Developmental Psychology, 20,* 691–696.

Smith, J., & Ross, H. (2007). Training parents to mediate sibling disputes affects children's negotiations and conflict understanding. *Child Development, 78,* 790–805.

Smith, P. K., & Drew, L. M. (2002). Grandparenthood. In M. H. Bornstein (Ed.), *Handbook of parenting: Vol. 3. Being and becoming a parent* (2nd ed., pp. 141–172). Mahwah, NJ: Erlbaum.

Smith, S. (2008, January). *Grow up: Gamers over 20 are labeled 'Child-men.' XBox 360 News.* Retrieved from: http://www.monstersandcritics.com/gaming/xbox360/news/article_1389095.php/Grow_up_Gamers_over_20_are_labelled_Child-men

Smollar, J., & Youniss, J. (1982). Social development through friendship. In K. H. Rubin & H. S. Ross (Eds.), *Peer relationships and social skills in childhood* (pp. 279–298). New York: Springer-Verlag.

Smyke, A. T., Zeanah, C. H., Fox, N. A., Nelson, C. A., & Guthrie, D. (2010). Placement in foster care enhances quality of attachment among young institutionalized children. *Child Development, 81,* 212–223.

Snarey, J. R. (1993). *How fathers care for the next generation: A four-decade study.* Cambridge, MA: Harvard University Press.

Snarey, J. R. (1994). Cross-cultural universality of social-moral development: A critical review of Kohlbergian research. In B. Puka (Ed.), *New research in moral development* (pp. 268–298). New York: Garland.

Snarey, J. R., & Bell, D. (2003). Distinguishing structural and functional models of human development: A response to "What transits in an identity status transition?" *Identity, 3,* 221–230.

Snarey, J., & Hooker, C. (2006). Lawrence Kohlberg. In E. M. Dowling & W. G. Scarlett (Eds.), *Encyclopedia of spiritual and religious development* (pp. 251–255). Thousand Oaks, CA: Sage.

Snell, T. I. (1994). *Special report: Women in prison.* Washington, DC: U.S. Department of Justice Statistics.

Snyder, H. N., & Sickmund, M. (2006). Juvenile offenders and victims. *2006 National Report.* Washington, DC:

U.S. Department of Justice, Office of Juvenile Justice and Delinquency Prevention.

Snyder, J., Reid, J., & Patterson, G. (2003). A social learning model of child and adolescent antisocial behavior. In B. B. Lahey, T. E. Moffit, & A. Caspi (Eds.), *Causes of conduct disorder and juvenile delinquency* (pp. 27–48). New York: Guilford Press.

Snyder, J., Schrepferman, L., McEachern, A., Barner, S., Johnson, K., & Provines, J. (2008). Peer deviancy training and peer coercion: Dual processes associated with early-onset conduct problems. *Child Development, 79*, 252–268.

Sober, E., & Wilson, D.S. (1998). *Unto others: The evolution and psychology of unselfish behavior.* Cambridge, MA.:Harvard University Press.

Society for Research on Child Development, Committee on Ethical Conduct in Child Development Research. (2007). *Society for Research on Child Development Ethical Standards for Research with Children.* Ann Arbor, MI: Society for Research in Child Development.

Solomon, J., & George, C. (1999). The development of attachment in separated and divorced families: Effects of over-night visitations, parent and couple variables. *Attachment & Human Development, 1*, 2–33.

Solomon, J., & George, C. (2008). The measurement of attachment security and related constructs in infancy and early childhood. In J. Cassidy & P. R. Shaver (Eds.), *Handbook of attachment: Theory, research, and clinical applications* (2nd ed., pp. 287–318). New York: Guilford Press.

Solomon, S. E., Rothbaum, E. D., & Balsam, K. F. (2004). Pioneers in partnership: Lesbian and gay male couples in civil unions and married heterosexual siblings. *Journal of Family Psychology, 18*, 275–286.

Solomon, Z. (1988). The effect of combat-related post-traumatic stress disorder on the family. *Psychiatry: Journal for the Study of Interpersonal Processes, 51*, 323–329.

Sommer, I. E., Aleman, A., Somers, M., Boks, M. P., & Kahn, R. S. (2008). Sex differences in handedness, asymmetry of the Planum Temporale and functional language lateralization. *Brain Research, 1206*, 76–88.

Sommer, I. E. C., Aleman, A., Bouma, A., & Kahn, R. S. (2004). Do women really have more bilateral language representation than men? A meta-analysis of functional imaging studies. *Brain: A Journal of Neurology, 127*, 1845–1852.

Song, M., Smetana, J. G., & Kim, S. Y. (1987). Korean children's conceptions of moral and conventional transgressions. *Developmental Psychology, 23*, 577–582.

Sorber, A. V. (2001). The role of peer socialization in the development of emotion display rules: Effects of age, gender, and emotion. *Dissertation Abstracts International: Section B: The Sciences and Engineering, 62*, 1119.

Sowell, E. R., Peterson, B. S., Thompson, P. M., Welcome, S. E., Henkenius, A. L., & Toga, A. W. (2003). Mapping cortical change across the human life span. *Nature Neuroscience, 6*, 309–315.

Spangler, G., & Grossmann, K. E. (1993). Biobehavioral organization in securely and insecurely attached infants. *Child Development, 64*, 1439–1450.

Spence, J., & Buckner, C. (2000). Instrumental and expressive traits, trait stereotypes, and sexist attitudes. *Psychology of Women Quarterly, 24*, 44–62.

Spencer, M. B. (2006). Phenomenology and ecological systems theory. In W. Damon & R. Lerner (Series Eds.) & D. Kuhn & R. Siegler (Vol. Eds.), *Handbook of child psychology: Vol. 1. Theoretical models of human development* (6th ed., pp. 829–893). Hoboken, NJ: Wiley.

Spencer, M. B., Cross, W. E., Harpalani, V., & Goss, T. N. (2003). Historical and developmental perspectives on Black academic achievement: Debunking the "acting White" myth and posing new directions for research. In C. C. Yeakey (Ed.), *Surmounting all odds: Education, opportunity, and society in the new millennium* (pp. 273–304). Greenwich, CT: Information Age Publishers.

Spencer, M. B., Noll, E., Stoltzfus, J., & Harpalani, V. (2001). Identity and school adjustment: Revisiting the "acting White" assumption. *Educational Psychologist, 36*, 21–30.

Spergel, I. A., Ross, R. E., Curry, G. D., & Chance, R. (1989). *Youth gangs: Problem and response.* Washington, DC: U.S. Department of Justice, Office of Juvenile Justice and Delinquency Prevention.

Spiker, D., & Ricks, M. (1984). Visual self-recognition in autistic children: Developmental variations. *Child Development, 55*, 214–225.

Sponsel, L. E., & Gregor, T. (Eds.)(1994). *The anthropology of peace and nonviolence.* Boulder, CO: Lynne Rienner.

Springer, S. P., & Deutsch, G. (1993). *Left brain, right brain.* New York: Freeman.

Sroufe, L. A. (1996). *Emotional development: The organization of emotional life in the early years.* New York: Cambridge University Press.

Sroufe, L. A. (2002). Attachment and development: A prospective longitudinal study from birth to adulthood. *Attachment & Human Development, 7*, 349–367.

Sroufe, L. A., Egeland, B., Carlson, E. A., & Collins, W. A. (2005). *The development of the person: The Minnesota study of risk and adaptation from birth to adulthood.* New York: Guilford Press.

Sroufe, L. A., Waters, E., & Matas, L. (1974). Contextual determinants of infant affectional response. In M. Lewis & L. Rosenblum (Eds.), *Origins of fear* (pp. 49–72). New York: Wiley.

Sroufe, L. A., & Wunsch, J. P. (1972). The development of laughter in the first year of life. *Child Development, 43*, 1326–1344.

Stams, G. J. M., Brugman, D., Dekovic, M., van Rosmalan, L., van der Laan, P., & Gibbs, J. C. (2006). The moral judgment of juvenile delinquents: A meta-analysis. *Journal of Abnormal Child Psychology, 34,* 697–713.

Stams, G. J. M., Dekovic, M., Brugman, D., Rutten, E. A., Van den Wittenboer, G. L. H., Tavecchio, L. W. C., . . . Van Schijndel, M. (2008). The relationship of punishment- and victim-based moral orientation to prosocial, externalizing, and norm trespassing behaviour in delinquent and non-delinquent adolescents: A validation study of the Moral Orientation Measure. *Journal of Experimental Criminology, 4,* 41–60.

Stams, G. J. M., Juffer, F., & van IJzendoorn, M. H. (2002). Maternal sensitivity, infant attachment and temperament in early childhood predict adjustment in middle childhood: The case of adopted children and their biologically unrelated parents. *Developmental Psychology, 38,* 806–821.

Statistics and Cell Phones. (2008, August). Retrieved from: http://www.articlesbase.com/computersarticles/statistics-and-cell-phones–538109.html#

Stein, J. A., & Newcomb, M. D. (1999). Adult outcomes of adolescent conventional and agentic orientations: A 10-year longitudinal study. *Journal of Early Adolescence, 19,* 39–65.

Steinberg, L. (1986). Latchkey children and susceptibility to peer pressure: An ecological analysis. *Developmental Psychology, 22,* 433–439.

Steinberg, L. (2007). Risk taking in adolescence: New perspectives from brain and behavior science. *Current Directions in Psychological Science, 16,* 55–59.

Steinberg, L., & Cauffman, E. (2001). Adolescents in adult court: A developmental perspective on the transfer of juveniles to criminal court. *SRCD Social Policy Report, 15,* 1–13.

Steinberg, L., Dornbusch, S. M., & Brown, B. B. (1992). Ethnic differences in adolescent achievement: An ecological perspective. *American Psychologist, 47,* 723–729.

Steinberg, L., Grisso, T., Woolard, J., Cauffman, E., Scott, E., Graham, S., . . . Schwartz, R. (2003). Juveniles' competence to stand trial as adults. *SRCD Social Policy Report, 17,* 1–15.

Steinberg, L., Mounts, N. S., Lamborn, S. D., & Dornbusch, S. M. (1991). Authoritative parenting and adolescent adjustment across varied ecological niches. *Journal of Research on Adolescence, 1,* 19–36.

Steinberg, L., & Scott, E. S. (2003). Less guilty by reason of adolescence. *American Psychologist, 58,* 1009–1018.

Steinberg, L. D., Catalano, R., & Dooley, D. (1981). Economic antecedents of child abuse and neglect. *Child Development, 52,* 975–985.

Steiner, J. E. (1979). Human facial expression in response to taste and smell stimulation. In H. W. Reese & L. P. Lipsitt (Eds.), *Advances in child development and behavior* (Vol. 13, pp. 257–295). New York: Academic Press.

Stenberg, C., & Campos, J. (1989). *The development of anger expressions during infancy.* Unpublished manuscript, University of Denver, CO.

Stenberg, C., Campos, J., & Emde, R. N. (1983). The facial expression of anger in seven-month-old infants. *Child Development, 54,* 178–184.

Stephan, K. E., Marshall, J. C., Friston, K. J., Rowe, J. B., Ritzl, A., Zilles, K., & Fink, G. R. (2003). Lateralized cognitive processes and lateralized task control in the human brain. *Science, 301,* 384–386.

Stern, D. N. (1974). Mother and infant at play: The dyadic interaction involving facial, vocal, and gaze behaviors. In M. Lewis, & L. A. Rosenblum (Eds.), *The effect of the infant on its caregiver.* New York: Wiley-Interscience.

Stern, M., & Karraker, K. H. (1989). Sex stereotyping of infants: A review of gender labeling studies. *Sex Roles, 20,* 501–522.

Stern, S. T. (2007). *Instant identity: Adolescent girls and the world of instant messaging.* New York: Peter Lang.

Stevahn, L., Johnson, D. W., Johnson, R. T., Oberle, K., & Wahl, L. (2000). Effects of conflict resolution training integrated into a kindergarten curriculum. *Child Development, 71,* 772–784.

Stevenson, H. C. (1994). Racial socialization in African American families: The art of balancing intolerance and survival. *The Family Journal: Counseling and Therapy for Couples and Families, 2,* 190–198.

Stevenson, M. R., & Black, K. N. (1988). Paternal absence and sex-role development: A meta-analysis. *Child Development, 59,* 793–814.

Stifter, C. A., & Fox, N. A. (1987). Preschool children's ability to identify and label emotions. *Journal of Nonverbal Behavior, 11,* 43–54.

Stiles, J. (2000). Spatial cognitive development following prenatal or perinatal focal brain injury. In H. S. Levin & J. Grafman (Eds.), *Cerebral reorganization of function after brain damage* (pp. 207–217). New York: Oxford University Press.

Stipek, D. J., Feiler, R., Beyler, P., Ryan, R., Milburn, S., & Salmon, S. (1998). Good beginnings: What difference does the program make in preparing young children for school? *Journal of Applied Developmental Psychology, 19,* 41–66.

Stipek, D. J., Feiler, R., Daniels, D., & Milburn, S. (1995). Effects of different instructional approaches on young children's achievement and motivation. *Child Development, 66,* 209–223.

Stipek, D. J., Recchia, S., & McClintic, S. (1992). Self-evaluation in young children. *Monographs of the Society for Research in Child Development, 57* (Serial No. 226).

Stocker, C. M., & Richmond, M. K. (2007). Longitudinal associations between hostility in adolescents' family relationships and friendships and hostility in their romantic relationships. *Journal of Family Psychology, 21,* 490–497.

Stocker, C. M., & Youngblade, L. (1999). Marital conflict and parental hostility: Links with children's sibling and peer relationships. *Journal of Family Psychology, 13,* 598–609.

Stolley, K. S. (1993). Statistics on adoption in the United States. *The Future of Children, 3,* 26–42.

Stoneman, Z., Brody, G., & MacKinnon, C. E. (1986). Same sex and cross-sex siblings: Activity choices, roles, behavior, and gender stereotypes. *Sex Roles, 15,* 495–511.

Storey, A. E., Walsh, C. J., Quinton, R. L., & Wynne-Edwards, K. E. (2000). Hormonal correlates of paternal responsiveness in new and expectant fathers. *Evolution and Human Behavior, 21,* 79–95.

Story, L. B., & Repetti, R. (2006). Daily occupational stressors and marital behavior. *Journal of Family Psychology, 20,* 690–700.

Stouthamer-Loeber, M., Wei, E., Loeber, R., & Masten, A. S. (2004). Desistance from persistent serious delinquency in the transition to adulthood. *Development and Psychopathology, 16,* 897–918.

Strasburger, V. C., & Wilson, B. J. (2002). *Children, adolescents, and the media.* Thousand Oaks, CA: Sage.

Straughan, R. (1986). Why act on Kohlberg's moral judgments? (or how to reach stage 6 and remain a bastard). In S. Modgil & C. Modgil (Eds.), *Lawrence Kohlberg: Consensus and controversy* (pp. 149–157). Philadelphia: Falmer Press.

Straus, M. A. (2001). *Beating the devil out of them: Corporal punishment in American families and its effects on children.* New Brunswick, NJ: Transaction.

Straus, M. A. (2005). *The primordial violence: Corporal punishment by parents, cognitive development, and crime.* Walnut Creek, CA: Alta Mira Press.

Straus, M. A., & Donnelly, D. A. (1994). *Beating the devil out of them: Corporal punishment in American families.* New York: Lexington Books.

Straus, M. A., & Stewart, J. H. (1999). Corporal punishment by American parents: National data on prevalence, chronicity, severity, and duration, in relation to child and family characteristics. *Clinical Child and Family Psychology Review, 2,* 55–70.

Strayer, J., & Roberts, W. (2004). Children's anger, emotional expressiveness, and empathy: Relations with parents' empathy, emotional expressiveness, and parenting practices. *Social Development, 13,* 229–254.

Streri, A., Lhote, M., & Dutilleul, S. (2000). Haptic perception in newborns. *Developmental Science, 3,* 319–327.

Streri, A., & Pecheux, M. (1986). Tactual habituation and discrimination of form in infancy: A comparison with vision. *Child Development, 57,* 100–104.

Stright, A. D., Gallagher, K. C., & Kelley, K. (2008). Infant temperament moderates relations between maternal parenting in early childhood and children's adjustment in first grade. *Child Development, 79,* 186–200.

Struck, S. (2007). *The video game generation grows up: How video game playing adults balance family and fun.* Retrieved from: http://www.associatedcontent.com/article/462219/the_video_game_generation_grows_up.html?cat = 19

Stuewig, J., & McCloskey, L. A. (2005). The relation of child maltreatment to shame and guilt among adolescents: Psychological routes to depression and delinquency. *Child Maltreatment, 10,* 324–336.

Sturge-Apple, M. L., Davies, P. T., & Cummings, E. M. (2010). Typologies of family functioning and children's adjustment during the early school years. *Child Development, 81*

Sturge-Apple, M. L., Davies, P. T., Winter, M. A., Cummings, E. M., & Schermerhorn, A. C. (2008). Interparental conflict and children's school adjustment: The mediating role of emotional security in direct and indirect pathways. *Developmental Psychology, 44,* 1678–1690.

Subrahmanyam, K., & Greenfield, P. M. (1999). Computer games for girls: What makes them play? In J. Cassell, & H. Jenkins (Eds.), From Barbie to mortal combat: Gender and computer games (pp. 46–71). Cambridge, MA: MIT Press.

Subrahmanyam, K., & Greenfield, P. M. (2008). Media technology and adolescence: Identity, interpersonal connection and well being. *Future of Children, 18,* 119–146.

Subrahmanyam, K., Greenfield, P. M., & Tynes, B. (2004). Constructing sexuality and identity on an online teen chat room. *Journal of Applied Developmental Psychology, 25,* 651–666.

Subrahmanyam, K., Kraut, R. E., Greenfield, P. M., & Gross, E. F. (2001). New forms of electronic media: The impact of interactive games and Internet on cognition, socialization, and behavior. In D. Singer & J. Singer (Eds.), *Handbook of children and the media* (pp. 73–99). Thousand Oaks, CA: Sage.

Subrahmanyam, K., Smahel, D., & Greenfield, P. M. (2006). Connecting developmental processes to the internet: Identity presentation and sexual exploration in online teen chatrooms. *Developmental Psychology, 42,* 395–406.

Sullivan, C. J. (2006). Early adolescent delinquency: Assessing the role of childhood problems, family environment, and peer pressure. *Youth Violence & Juvenile Justice, 4,* 291–313.

Sullivan, M. L. (1993). Culture and class as determinants of out of wedlock childbearing and poverty during late adolescence. *Journal of Research in Adolescence, 3,* 295–317.

Sullivan, M. W., Bennett, D. S., Carpenter, K., & Lewis, M. (2008). Emotion knowledge in young neglected children. *Child Maltreatment, 13,* 301–306.

Sulloway, F. J. (1995). Birth order and evolutionary psychology: A meta-analytic overview. *Psychological Inquiry, 6,* 75–80.

Suomi, S. J. (2003). Gene-environment interactions and the neurobiology of social conflict. *Annals of the New York Academy of Sciences, 1008,* 132–139.

Suomi, S. J. (2008). Attachment in rhesus monkeys. In J. Cassidy & P. R. Shaver (Eds.), *Handbook of attachment: Theory, research, and clinical applications* (2nd ed., pp. 173–191). New York: Guilford Press.

Suomi, S. J., & Harlow, H. F. (1972). Social rehabilitation of isolate-reared monkeys. *Developmental Psychology, 6,* 487–496.

Susman-Stillman, A., Kalkoske, M., Egeland, B., & Waldman, I. (1996). Infant temperament and maternal sensitivity as predictors of attachment security. *Infant Behavior and Development, 19,* 33–47.

Sutherland, L. (1983). Post-marital depression: A medical or cultural problem? *New Parent, 5,* 12.

Sylva, K., Melhuish, E., Sammons, P., Siraj-Blatchford, I., Taggart, B., & Elliot, K. (2003). *The effective provision of pre-school education (EPPE) project: Findings from the pre-school period.* Department for Education and Skills, Institute of Education, University of London.

Tager-Flusberg, H. (2007). Evaluating the theory-of-mind hypothesis of autism. *Current Directions in Psychological Science, 16,* 311–315.

Takeshita, C., & Takeshita, I. (2002). *Hui Malama O Ke Kai: Impact survey results, June 2003.* Waimanalo, HI: Hui Malama O Ke Kai.

Tamis-LeMonda, C. S., Cristofaro, T. N., Rodriguez, E. T., & Bornstein, M. H. (2006). Early language development: Social influences in the first years of life. In L. Balter & C. S. Tamis-LeMonda (Eds.), *Child psychology: A handbook of contemporary issues* (2nd ed., pp. 79–108). New York: Psychology Press.

Tangney, J. P., & Dearing, R. L. (2002). *Shame and guilt.* New York: Guilford Press.

Tangney, J. P., Stuewig, J., & Mashek, D. J. (2007). Moral emotions and moral behavior. *Annual Review of Psychology, 58,* 345–372.

Tangney, J. P., Wanger, P. E., Hill-Barlow, D., Marschall, D. E., & Gramzow, R. (1996). Relation to shame and guilt to constructive versus destructive responses to anger across the lifespan. *Journal of Personality and Social Psychology, 70,* 797–809.

Tarabulsy, G. M., Bernier, A., Provost, M. A., Maranda, J., Larose, S., Moss, E., Larose, M., & Tessier, R. (2005). Another look inside the gap: Ecological contributions to the transmission of attachment in a sample of adolescent mother-infant dyads. *Developmental Psychology, 41,* 212–224.

Tarabulsy, G. M., Pascuzzo, K., Moss, E., St. Laurent, D., Bernier, A., Cyr, C., & Dubois-Comtois, K. (2008). Attachment-based intervention for maltreating families. *American Journal of Orthopsychiatry, 78,* 322–332.

Taumoepeau, M., & Ruffman, T. (2006). Mother and infant talk about mental states relates to desire language and emotion understanding. *Child Development, 77,* 465–481.

Taumoepeau, M., & Ruffman, T. (2008). Stepping stones to others' minds: Maternal talk relates to child mental state language and emotion understanding at 15, 24, and 33 months. *Child Development, 79,* 284–302.

Taylor, I. S., Addison, O. W., & Henggeler, S. W. (2004). *Multisystemic therapy and neighborhood partnerships: Reducing adolescent violence and substance abuse.* New York: Guilford Press.

Taylor, J. (1986). *Self-concept in home schooling children.* Ann Arbor, MI: University Microfilms International.

Taylor, T. J., Peterson, D., Esbensen, F., & Freng, A. (2007). Gang membership as a risk factor for adolescent violent victimization. *Journal of Research in Crime and Delinquency, 44,* 351–380.

Teichman, Y. (2001). The development of Israeli children's images of Jews and Arabs and their expression in human figure drawings. *Developmental Psychology, 37,* 749–761.

Tenenbaum, H. R., Alfieri, L., Brooks, P. J., & Dunne, G. (2008). The effects of explanatory conversations on children's emotion understanding. *British Journal of Developmental Psychology, 26,* 249–263.

Tenenbaum, H. R., & Leaper, C. (2002). Are parents' gender schemas related to their children's gender-related cognitions? A meta-analysis. *Developmental Psychology, 38,* 615–630.

Tenenbaum, H. R., & Leaper, C. (2003). Parent-child conversations about science: The socialization of gender inequalities. *Developmental Psychology, 39,* 34–47.

Tenenbaum, H. R., & Ruck, M. D. (2007). Are teachers' expectations different for racial minority than for European American students? A meta-analysis. *Journal of Educational Psychology, 99,* 253–273.

Tenenbaum, H. R., Visscher, P., Pons, F., & Harris, P. L. (2004). Emotional understanding in Quechua children from an agro-pastoralist village. *International Journal of Behavioral Development, 28,* 471–478.

Teti, D. M. (2002). Retrospect and prospect in the psychological study of sibling relationships. In J. McHale & W. Grolnick (Eds.), *Retrospect and prospect in the psychological study of families* (pp. 193–224). Hillsdale, NJ: Erlbaum.

Tharp, R. G. (1989). Psychocultural variables and constants: Effects on teaching and learning in schools. *American Psychologist, 44,* 349–359.

Tharp, R. G., & Gallimore, R. (1988). *Rousing minds to life: Teaching, learning, and schooling in social context.* Cambridge, UK: Cambridge University Press.

Théoret, H., & Pascual-Leone. A. (2002). Language acquisition: Do as you hear. *Current Biology, 12,* R736–R737.

Thevenin, D. M., Eilers, R. E., Oller, D. K., & LaVoie, L. (1985). Where's the drift in babbling drift? A cross-linguistic study. *Applied Psycholinguistics, 6,* 3–15.

Thijs, J., & Verkuyten, M. (2008). Peer victimization and academic achievement in a multiethnic sample: The role of perceived academic self-efficacy. *Journal of Educational Psychology, 100,* 754–764.

Thomaes, S., Reijntjes, A., de Castro, B. O., Bushman, B. J., Poorthuis, A., & Telch, M. J. (2010). I like me if you like me: On the interpersonal modulation and regulation of preadolescents' self-esteem. *Child Development, 81*

Thomas, A., & Chess, S. (1986). The New York Longitudinal Study: From infancy to early adult life. In R. Plomin & J. Dunn (Eds.), *The study of temperament: Changes, continuities and challenges* (pp. 39–52). Hillsdale, NJ: Erlbaum.

Thomas, A., Chess, S., & Birch, H.G. (1968). *Temperament and behavior disorders in children.* New York: New York University Press

Thompson, I. (2000). Human gene therapy: Harsh lessons, high hopes. *FDA Consumer, 34,* 19–24.

Thompson, R. A. (1989). Causal attributions and children's emotional understanding. In C. Saarni & P. L. Harris (Eds.), *Children's understanding of emotions* (pp. 117–150). New York: Cambridge University Press.

Thompson, R. A. (1990). Vulnerability in research: A developmental perspective on research risk. *Child Development, 61,* 1–16.

Thompson, R. A. (2006). The development of the person: Social understanding, relationships, self, conscience. In W. Damon & R. M. Lerner (Series Eds.), & N. Eisenberg (Vol. Ed.), *Handbook of child psychology: Vol. 3. Social, emotional, and personality development* (6th ed., pp. 24–98). Hoboken, NJ: Wiley.

Thompson, R. A. (2008). Early attachment and later development: Familiar questions, new answers. In J. Cassidy & P. R. Shaver (Eds.), *Handbook of attachment: Theory, research, and clinical applications* (2nd ed., pp. 348–365). New York: Guilford Press.

Thompson, R. A., Lamb, M. E., & Estes, D. (1982). Stability of infant-mother attachment and its relationship to changing life circumstances in an unselected middle-class sample. *Child Development, 53,* 144–148.

Thompson, R. A., & Meyer, S. (2007). The socialization of emotion regulation in the family. In J. Gross (Ed.), *Handbook of emotion regulation* (pp. 249–268). New York: Guilford Press.

Thompson, R. A., Meyer, S., & McGinley, M. (2006). Understanding values in relationships: The development of conscience. In M. Killen & J. G. Smetana (Eds.), *Handbook of moral development* (pp. 267–297). Mahwah, NJ: Erlbaum.

Thompson, W. C., Clarke-Stewart, K. A., & Lepore, S. J. (1997). What did the janitor do? Suggestive interviewing and the accuracy of children's accounts. *Law & Human Behavior, 21,* 405–426.

Thornberry, T. P., Krohn, M. D., Lizotte, A. J., Smith, C. A., & Tobin, K. (2003). *Gangs and delinquency in developmental perspective.* Cambridge, UK: Cambridge University Press.

Thorne, B. (1986). Girls and boys together . . . but mostly apart: Gender arrangements in elementary schools. In W. W. Hartup & Z. Rubin (Eds.), *Relations and relationships* (pp. 167–184). Hillsdale, NJ: Erlbaum.

Thurber, C. A., & Weisz, J. R. (1997). "You can try or you can just give up": The impact of perceived control and coping style on childhood homesickness. *Developmental Psychology, 33,* 508–517.

Tibbetts, S. G. (1997). Shame and rational choice in offending decisions. *Criminal Justice & Behavior, 24,* 234–255.

Tinbergen, N. (1951). *The study of instinct.* Oxford, UK: Clarendon Press.

Tisak, M. S., & Turiel, E. (1984). Children's conceptions of moral and prudential rules. *Child Development, 55,* 1030–1039.

Toeplitz, Z., Matczak, A., Piotrowska, A., & Zygier, A. (1995). *Impact of keeping pets at home upon the social development of children.* Paper presented at the International Conference on Human-Animal Interactions, Animals, Health, and Quality of Life, Geneva, Switzerland.

Tolan, P. H., Gorman-Smith, D., & Henry, D. B. (2003). The developmental ecology of urban males' youth violence. *Developmental Psychology, 39,* 274–291.

Tolson, T. F., & Wilson, M. N. (1990). The impact of two- and three-generational Black family structure on perceived family climate. *Child Development, 61,* 416–428.

Tomasello, M. (1999). *The cultural origins of human cognition.* Cambridge, MA: Harvard University Press.

Tomasello, M. (2006). Acquiring metalinguistic constructions. In W. Damon & R. M. Lerner (Series Eds.), & D. Kuhn & R. Siegler (Vol. Eds.), *Handbook of child psychology: Vol. 2. Cognition, perception, and language* (6th ed., pp. 255–298). Hoboken, NJ: Wiley.

Tomasello, M. (2008). *Origins of human communication.* Cambridge, MA: MIT Press.

Tomasello, M., Carpenter, M., Call, J., Behne, T., & Moll, H. (2005). Understanding and sharing intentions: The origins of cultural cognition. *Behavioral and Brain Sciences, 28,* 675–735.

Tomasello, M., & Rakoczy, H. (2003). What makes human cognition unique? From individual to shared to collective intentionality. *Mind and Language, 18,* 121–147.

Tomizawa, K., Iga, N., Lu, Y.-F., Moriwaki, A., Matsushita, M., Li, S.-T., Miyamoto, O., Itano, T., & Matsui, H. (2003). Oxytocin improves long-lasting spatial memory during motherhood through MAP kinase cascade. *Nature Neuroscience, 6,* 384–390.

Towers, H., Spotts, E., & Reiss, D. (2003). Unraveling the complexity of genetic and environmental influences on family. In F. Walsh (Ed.), *Normal family processes* (3rd ed., pp. 608–631). New York: Guilford Press.

Tracy, J. L., Robins, R. W., & Tangney, J. P. (Eds.)(2007). *The self-conscious emotions: Theory and research.* New York: Guilford Press.

Tremblay, R. E., Hartup, W. W., & Archer, J. (Eds.)(2005). *Developmental origins of aggression.* New York: Guilford Press.

Tremblay, R. E., Pihl, R. O., Vitaro, R., & Dobkin, P. L. (1994). Predicting early onset of male antisocial behavior from preschool behavior. *Archives of General Psychiatry, 51,* 732–739.

Tremblay, R. E., Schall, B., Boulerice, B., Arsonault, L., Soussignan, R. G., & Paquette, D. (1998). Testosterone, physical aggression, and dominance and physical development in adolescence. *International Journal of Behavioral Development, 22,* 753–777.

Trenholm, C., Devaney, B., Fortson, K., Quay, L., Wheeler, J., & Clark, M. (2007). *Impacts of four Title V, Section 510 Abstinence Education Programs Final Repor.* Princeton, NJ: Mathematica Policy Research.

Trentacosta, C. J., & Shaw, D. S. (2008). Maternal predictors of rejecting parenting and early adolescent antisocial behavior. *Journal of Abnormal Child Psychology, 36,* 247–259.

Trickett, P. K., & Putnam, F. W. (1998). The developmental impact of sexual abuse. In P. Trickett & C. Schellenbach (Eds.), *Violence against children in the family and the community* (pp. 39–56). Washington, DC: APA Books.

Triebenbacher, S. L. (1998). Pets as transitional objects: Their role in children's emotional development. *Psychological Reports, 82,* 191–200.

Tronick, E. (1989). Emotions and emotional communication in infants. *American Psychologist, 44,* 12–119.

Tronick, E., & Cohn, J. (1989). Infant-mother face-to-face interaction: Age and gender differences in coordination and the occurrence of miscoordination. *Child Development, 60,* 85–92.

Tronick, E. Z., Messinger, D. S., Weinberg, M. K., Lester, B. M., LaGasse, L., Seifer, R., . . . Liu J. (2005). Cocaine exposure is associated with subtle compromises of infants' and mothers' social-emotional behavior and dyadic features of their interaction in the face still face paradigm. *Developmental Psychology, 41,* 711–722.

Tronick, E. Z., Morelli, G. A., & Ivey, P. K. (1992). The Efe forager infant and toddler's pattern of social relationships: Multiple and simultaneous. *Developmental Psychology, 28,* 568–577.

True, M. M., Pisani, L., & Oumar, F. (2001). Infant-mother attachment among the Dogan of Mali. *Child Development, 72,* 1451–1466.

Trumbull, E., Rothstein-Fisch, C., & Hernandez, E. (2003). Parent involvement in school: According to whose values? *School Community Journal, 13,* 45–72.

Tsao, D. Y., Freiwald, W. A., Tootell, R. B. H., & Livingstone, M. S. (2006). A cortical region consisting entirely of face-selective cells. *Science, 311,* 670–674.

Tschann, J. M., Johnston, J. R., Kline, M., Wallerstein, J. S. (1990). Conflict, loss, change, and parent-child relationships: Predicting children's adjustment during divorce. *Journal of Divorce, 13,* 1–22.

Tschann, J. M., Kaiser, P., Chesney, M. A., Alkon, A., & Boyce, W. T. (1996). Resilience and vulnerability among preschool children: Family functioning, temperament and behavior problems. *Journal of the American Academy of Child and Adolescent Psychiatry, 35,* 184–192.

Turati, C. (2004). Why faces are not special to newborns: An alternative account of the face preference. *Current Directions in Psychological Science, 13,* 5–8.

Turiel, E. (1983). *The development of social knowledge: Morality and convention.* New York: Cambridge University Press.

Turiel, E. (2002). *The culture of morality.* New York: Cambridge University Press.

Turiel, E. (2005). Resistance and subversion in everyday life. In L. Nucci (Ed.), *Conflict, contradiction, and contrarian elements in moral development and education* (pp. 3–20). Mahwah, NJ: Erlbaum.

Turiel, E. (2006). The development of morality. In W. Damon & R. M. Lerner (Series Eds.), & N. Eisenberg (Vol. Ed.), *Handbook of child psychology: Vol. 3. Social, emotional, and personality development* (6th ed., pp. 789–857). Hoboken, NJ: Wiley.

Turiel, E., & Wainryb, C. (1998). Concepts of freedoms and rights in a traditional, hierarchically organized society. *British Journal of Developmental Psychology, 16,* 375–395.

Turiel, E., & Wainryb, C. (2000). Social life in cultures: Judgments, conflict, and subversion. *Child Development, 71,* 250–256.

Turkheimer, E. (2000). Three laws of behavior genetics and what they mean. *Current Directions in Psychological Science, 9,* 160–164.

Turner, P. J., & Gervai, J. (1995). A multidimensional study of gender typing in preschool children and their parents: Personality, attitudes, preferences, behavior and cultural differences. *Developmental Psychology, 31*, 759–772.

Turner-Bowker, D. M. (1996). Gender stereotyped description in children's picture books: Does "Curious Jane" exist in literature? *Sex Roles, 35*, 461–488.

Twenge, J. M. (1997). Attitudes toward women, 1970–1995: A meta-analysis. *Psychology of Women Quarterly, 21*, 35–51.

Twenge, J. M., Campbell, W. K., & Foster, C. A. (2003). Parenthood and marital satisfaction: A meta-analytic review. *Journal of Marriage and Family, 65*, 574–583.

Tynes, B., Giang, M., & Thompson, G. (2008). Ethnic identity, intergroup contact, and outgroup orientation among diverse groups of adolescents on the Internet. *CyberPsychology and Behavior, 11*, 459–465.

Tynes, B., Reynolds, L., & Greenfield, P. M. (2004). Adolescence, race and ethnicity on the Internet: A comparison of discourse in monitored and unmonitored chat rooms. *Journal of Applied Developmental Psychology, 25*, 667–684.

TYRA'S SEX SURVEY SHOCKS (November 14, 2008). *New York Post.* Retrieved from: http://www.nypost.com/p/entertainment/tv/item_aQdaGhDyjjGULQ1gtnSffL

U.S. Bureau of Labor Statistics. (1998). *Occupational outlook handbook: Child care workers.* Washington, DC: U.S. Bureau of Labor Statistics.

U.S. Bureau of Labor Statistics (2007). *Current Population Survey.* Washington, DC: U.S. Bureau of Labor Statistics.

U.S. Bureau of Labor Statistics. (2009). *Labor force participation of mothers with infants in 2008.* Retrieved from: http://www.bls.gov/opub/ted/2009/may/wk4/art04.htm

U.S. Department of Energy. (2002). *Human genome news.* Washington, DC: U.S. Government Printing Office.

U.S. Department of Health and Human Services. Administration on Children, Youth, and Families (2008). *Child maltreatment 2006.* Washington, DC: U.S. Government Printing Office.

Umana-Taylor, A. J., Yazedjian, A., & Bamaca-Gomez, M. (2004). Developing the ethnic identity scale using Eriksonian and social identity perspectives. *Identity, 4*, 9–38.

Underwood, M. K. (2003). *Social aggression among girls.* New York: Guilford Press.

Underwood, M. K. (2004). Gender and peer relations. In J. Kupersmidt & K. A. Dodge (Eds.), *Children's peer relations* (pp. 21–36). Washington, DC: American Psychological Association.

Underwood, M. K., Galen, B. R., & Paquette, J. A. (2001). Top ten methodological challenges for understanding gender and aggression: Why can't we all just get along? *Social Development, 10*, 248–267.

Underwood, M. K., Schockner, A. E., & Hurley, J. C. (2001). Children's responses to same- and other-gender peers: An experimental investigation with 8-, 10-, and 12-year-olds. *Developmental Psychology, 37*, 362–372.

Updegraff, K. A., McHale, S. M., & Crouter, A. C. (1996). Gender roles in marriage: What do they mean for girls' and boys' school achievement? *Journal of Youth and Adolescence, 25*, 73–88.

Urban Institute. (2000). *Child care patterns of school-age children with employed mothers.* Washington, DC: Author.

Urban Institute. (2002). *Primary Child Care Arrangements of Employed Parents: Findings from the 1999 National Survey of America's Families.* Washington, DC: Author. Retrieved from: http://www.urban.org/publications/310487.html

Us Magazine (August 20, 2009). Octo-mom Nadya Suleman: "I Screwed Up My Kids' Lives." Retrieved from: http://www.usmagazine.com/celebritynews/news/octo-mom-nadya-suleman-i-screwed-up-my-kids-lives-2009208

Vaillancourt, T., Brendgen, M., Boivin, M., & Tremblay, R. (2003). Longitudinal confirmatory factor analysis of indirect and physical aggression: Evidence of two factors over time? *Child Development, 74*, 1628–1638.

Vaillancourt, T., Hymel, S., & McDougall, P. (2003). Bullying is power: Implications for school-based intervention strategies. *Journal of Applied School Psychology, 19*, 157–176.

Vairami, M., & Vorria, P. (2007). Interparental conflict and (pre)adolescents' peer relationships. *Hellenic Journal of Psychology, 4*, 257–280.

Valdes, G. (1996). *Con respeto: Bridging the distances between culturally diverse families and schools—An ethnographic portrait.* New York: Teachers College Press.

Valentine, J. C., DuBois, D. L., & Cooper, H. (2004). The relation between self-beliefs and academic achievement: A meta-analytic review. *Educational Psychologist, 39*, 111–133.

Valenzuela, M. (1997). Maternal sensitivity in a developing society: The context of urban poverty and infant chronic under nutrition. *Developmental Psychology, 33*, 845–855.

Valian, V. (1986). Syntactic categories in the speech of young children. *Developmental Psychology, 22*, 562–579.

Valiente, C., & Eisenberg, N. (2006). Parenting and children's adjustment: The role of children's emotional regulating. In D. K. Snyder, J. A. Simpson, & J. N. Hughes (Eds.), *Emotion regulation in couples and families* (pp. 123–142). Washington, DC: American Psychological Association.

Valiente, C., Eisenberg, N., Smith, C. L., Reiser, M., Fabes, R. A., Losoya, S. . . . Murphy, B. C. (2003). The relations of effortful control and reactive control to children's externalizing problems: A longitudinal assessment. *Journal of Personality, 71*, 1171–1196.

Valkenburg, P. M. (2004). *Children's responses to the screen.* Mahwah, NJ: Erlbaum.

Valkenburg, P. M., & Peter, J. (2008). Adolescents' identity experiments on the Internet: Consequences for social competence and self-concept unity. *Communication Research, 35,* 208–231.

Van de Gaer, E., Pustjens, H., Van Damme, J., & DeMunter, A. (2004). Effects of single-sex versus co-educational classes and schools on gender differences in progress in language and mathematics achievement. *British Journal of Sociology of Education, 25,* 307–322.

Vandell, D. L., Belsky, J., Burchinal, M., Steinberg, L., Vandergrift, N., & the NICHD Early Child Care Research Network. (2010). Do effects of early child care extend to age 15 years? *Child Development, 81,* 737–756.

Vandell, D. L., Pierce, K. M., & Dadisman, K. (2005). Out-of-school settings as a developmental context for children and youth. In R. V. Kail (Ed.), *Advances in child development and behavior* (Vol. 33, pp. 43–77). New York: Academic Press.

Vandell, D. L., Shernoff, D. J., Pierce, K. M., Bolt, D. M., Dadisman, K., & Brown, B. B. (2005). Activities, engagement, and emotion in after-school programs and elsewhere. *New Directions for Youth Development, 105,* 121–129. San Francisco: Jossey-Bass.

Vandell, D. L., Shumow, L., & Posner, J. (2005). After-school programs for low-income children: Differences in program quality. In J. L. Mahoney, R. W. Larson, & J. S. Eccles (Eds.), *Organized activities as contexts of development: Extracurricular activities, after-school and community programs* (pp. 437–456). Mahwah, NJ: Erlbaum.

van den Boom, D. C. (1994). The influence of temperament and mothering on attachment and exploration: An experimental manipulation of sensitive responsiveness among lower-class mothers with irritable infants. *Child Development, 65,* 1457–1477.

Van Den Oord, E. J. C. G., Verhulst, F. C., & Boomsma, D. I. (1996). A genetic study of maternal and paternal ratings of problem behaviors in 3-year-old twins. *Journal of Abnormal Psychology, 105,* 349–357.

van der Mark, I. L., van IJzendoorn, M. H., & Bakermans-Kranenburg, M. J. (2002). Development of empathy in girls during the second year of life: Associations with parenting, attachment, and temperament. *Social Development, 11,* 451–468.

Van Egeren, L. A., Barratt, M. S., & Roach, M. (2001). Mother-infant responsiveness: Timing, mutual regulation, and interactional context. *Developmental Psychology, 37,* 684–697.

Van Hecke, A. V., Mundy, P. C., Acra, C. F., Block, J. J., Delgado, C. E. F., Parlade, M. V., . . . Pomares, Y. B. (2007). Infant joint attention, temperament, and social competence in preschool children. *Child Development, 78,* 53–69.

Van Houtte, M. (2005). Global self-esteem in technical/vocational versus general secondary school tracks: A matter of gender? *Sex Roles, 53,* 753–761.

van IJzendoorn, M. H. (1995). Adult attachment representations, parental responsiveness, and infant attachment: A meta-analysis on the predictive validity of the Adult Attachment Interview. *Psychological Bulletin, 117,* 387–403.

van IJzendoorn, M. H., & De Wolff, M. (1997). In search of the absent father: Meta-analyses of infant-father attachment. *Child Development, 60,* 604–609.

van IJzendoorn, M. H., Sagi, A., & Lamberman, M. W. E. (1992). The multiple caretaker paradox: Data from Holland and Israel. In R. C. Pianta (Ed.), *Beyond the parent: The role of other adults in children's lives* (pp. 5–24). San Francisco: Jossey-Bass.

van IJzendoorn, M. H., & Sagi-Schwartz, A. (2008). Cross-cultural patterns of attachment: Universal and contextual dimensions. In J. Cassidy & P. R. Shaver (Eds.), *Handbook of attachment: Theory, research, and clinical applications* (2nd ed., pp. 880–905). New York: Guilford Press.

van IJzendoorn, M. H., Vereijken, C. M. J. L., Bakermans-Kranenburg, M. J., & Riksen-Walraven, J. M. (2004). Assessing attachment security with the attachment Q sort: Meta-analytic evidence for the validity of the observer AQS. *Child Development, 75,* 1188–1213.

van Lier, P. A. C., Muthen, B. O., van der Sar, R. M., & Crijnen, A. A. M. (2004). Preventing disruptive behavior in elementary school children: Impact of a universal classroom-based intervention. *Journal of Consulting and Clinical Psychology, 72,* 467–478.

Vaughn, B. E., Bost, K. K., & van IJzendoorn, M. H. (2008). Attachment and temperament: Additive and interactive influences on behavior, affect, and cognition during infancy and childhood. In J. Cassidy & P. R. Shaver (Eds.), *Handbook of attachment: Theory, research, and clinical applications* (2nd ed., pp. 192–216). New York: Guilford Press.

Vaughn, B. E., Kopp, C. B., & Krakow, J. B. (1984). The emergence and consolidation of self-control from eighteen to thirty months of age: Normative trends and individual differences. *Child Development, 55,* 990–1004.

Vaughn, B. E., Vollenweider, M., Bost, K. K., Azria-Evans, M. R., & Snider, J. B. (2003). Negative interactions and social competence for preschool children in two samples: Reconsidering the interpretation of aggressive behavior for young children. *Merrill-Palmer Quarterly, 49,* 245–278.

Veenstra, R., Lindenberg, S., Munniksma, A., Dijkstra, J. K. (2010). The complex relation between bullying, victimization, acceptance, and rejection: Giving special attention to status, affection, and sex differences. *Child Development, 81,* 480–486.

Veenstra, R., Lindenberg, S., Zijlstra, B. J. H., DeWinter, A. F., Verhulst, F. C., & Ormel, J. (2007). The dyadic nature of bullying and victimization: Testing a dual-perspective theory. *Child Development, 78*, 1843–1854.

Vega, E., Parke, R. D., Coltrane, S., & Duffy, S. (2005, May). The role of parent and student perceptions in the educational achievement of language minority students: A qualitative approach. Paper presented at the University of California Linguistic Minority Research Institute Annual Conference, San Francisco.

Videon, T. M., & Manning, C. K. (2003). Influences on adolescent eating patterns: The importance of family meals. *Journal of Adolescent Health, 32*, 365–373.

Vierikko, E., Pulkkinen, L., & Rose, R. J. (2006). Genetic and environmental factors in girls' and boys' socioemotional behavior. In L. Pulkkinen, J. Kaprio, & R. J. Rose (Eds.), *Socioemotional development and health from adolescence to adulthood*. (pp. 176–196). New York: Cambridge University Press.

Vieth, V. I. (2006). Unto the third generation: A call to end child abuse in the United States within 120 years. *Journal of Aggression, Maltreatment, & Trauma, 12*, 5–54.

Villarruel, F. A., Walker, N. E., Minifiee, P., Riveravázquez, O., Peterson, S., & Perry, K. (2002). *¿Dónde está la justicia? A call to action on behalf of Latino and Latina Youth in the U.S. Justice System.* Washington, DC: Building Blocks for Youth.

Virkkunen, M., Kallio, E., Rawlings, R., Tokola, R., Poland, R. E., Guidotti, A. . . . Linnoila, M. (1994). Personality profiles and state aggressiveness in Finnish alcoholic, violent offenders, fire setters, and healthy volunteers. *Archives of General Psychiatry, 51*, 28–33.

Vitaglione, G. D., & Barnett, M. A. (2003). Assessing a new dimension of empathy: Empathetic anger as a predictor of helping and punishing desires. *Motivation & Emotion, 27*, 301–324.

Vitale, A. (2001). Implications of being gender dysphoric: A developmental review. *Gender & Psychoanalysis, 6*, 121–141.

Voices of Youth Newsletter. October 2007. No. 28, p.2. Retrieved from: http://www.unicef.org/voy/media/news_2007-10.doc

Volkmar, F. R., State, M., & Klin, A. (2009). Autism and autism spectrum disorders: Diagnostic issues for the coming decade. *Journal of Child Psychology and Psychiatry, 50*, 108–115.

Volling, B. L. (2005). The transition to siblinghood: A developmental ecological systems perspective and directions for future research. *Journal of Family Psychology, 19*, 542–549.

Volling, B. L., McElwain, N. L., & Miller, A. L. (2002). Emotion regulation in context: The jealousy complex between young siblings and its relations with child and family characteristics. *Child Development, 73*, 581–600.

von Salisch, M. (2000). The emotional side of sharing, social support, and conflict negotiation between siblings and between friends. In R. Mills, & S. Duck (Eds.), *Developmental psychology of personal relationship* (pp. 49–70). Chichester, UK: Wiley.

von Salisch, M. (2008). Themes in the development of emotion regulation in childhood and adolescence and a transactional model. In M. Vandekerckhove, C. von Scheve, S. Ismer, S. Jung, & S. Kronast, (Eds.), *Regulating emotions: Social necessity and biological inheritance* (pp. 146–167). Malden, MA: Blackwell.

Vybiral, Z., Smahel, D., & Divinova, R. (2004). Growing up on a virtual reality–Adolescents and the Internet. In P. Mares (Ed.), *Society, reproduction, and contemporary challenges*. Brno: Barrister & Principal.

Wachs, T. D., & Kohnstamm, G. A. (Eds.) (2001). *Temperament in context*. Mahwah, NJ: Erlbaum.

Waddington, C. H. (1962). *New patterns in genetics and development*. New York: Columbia University Press.

Waddington, C. H. (1966). *Principles of development and differentiation*. New York: Macmillan.

Wahler, R. G. (1967). Infant social attachments: A reinforcement theory interpretation and investigation. *Child Development, 38*, 1079–1088.

Wainright, J. L., & Patterson, C. J. (2008). Peer relations among adolescents with female same-sex parents. *Developmental Psychology, 44*, 117–126.

Wainryb, C. (2006). Moral development in culture: Diversity, tolerance, and justice. In M. Killen & J. Smetana (Eds.), *Handbook of moral development* (pp. 211–240). Mahwah, NJ: Erlbaum.

Wainryb, C., & Pasupathi, M. (2008). Developing moral agency in the midst of violence: Children, political conflict, and values. In I. A. Karawan, W. McCormack, & S. E. Reynolds (Eds.), *Values and violence: Intangible aspects of terrorism* (pp. 169–188). New York: Springer.

Wainryb, C., Shaw, L. A., Laupa, M., & Smith, K. R. (2001). Children's, adolescents', and young adults' thinking about different types of disagreements. *Developmental Psychology, 37*, 373–386.

Wakschlag, L. S., Chase-Lansdale, P. L., Brooks-Gunn, J. (1996). Not just "Ghosts in the Nursery": Contemporary intergenerational relationships and parenting in young African-American families. *Child Development, 67*, 2131–2147.

Walden, T. (1991). Infant social referencing. In J. Garber & K. Dodge (Eds.), *The development of emotional regulation and dysregulation* (pp. 69–88). New York: Cambridge University Press.

Waldinger, R. J., Vaillant, G. E., & Orav, E. J. (2007). Childhood sibling relationships as a predictor of major depression in adulthood: A 30-year prospective study. *American Journal of Psychiatry, 164*, 949–954.

Walker, L. J. (2004). Gus in the gap: Bridging the judgment-action gap in moral functioning. In D. K. Lapsley & D. Narvaez (Eds.), *Moral development, self, and identity* (pp. 1–20). Mahwah, NJ: Erlbaum.

Walker, L. J. (2006). Gender & morality. In M. Killen & J. G. Smetana (Eds.), *Handbook of moral development* (pp. 93–118). Mahwah, NJ: Erlbaum.

Walker, L. J., deVries, B., & Trevethan, J. D. (1987). Moral stages and moral orientations in real-life and hypothetical dilemmas. *Child Development, 58*, 842–858.

Walker, L. J., Gustafson, P., & Hennig, K. H. (2001). The consolidation/transition model in moral reasoning development. *Developmental Psychology, 37*, 187–197.

Walker, L. J., Hennig, K. H., & Krettenauer, T. (2000). Parent and peer contexts for children's moral reasoning development. *Child Development, 71*, 1033–1048.

Walker, L. J., & Taylor, J. H. (1991). Family interactions and the development of moral reasoning. *Child Development, 62*, 264–283.

Walker, T. R., & Ehrenberg, M. F. (1998). An exploratory study of young persons' attachment styles and perceived reasons for parental divorce. *Journal of Adolescent Research, 13*, 320–342.

Waller, B. M., & Dunbar, R. I. M. (2005). Differential behaviour effects of silent bared teeth display and relaxed open mouth display in chimpanzees. *Ethology, 111*, 129–142.

Walsh, S. P., White, K. M., & Young, R. M. (2008). Overconnected? A qualitative exploration of the relationship between Australian youth and their mobile phones. *Journal of Adolescence, 31*, 77–92.

Walters, G. C., & Grusec, J. E. (1977). *Punishment.* San Francisco: Freeman.

Walton, G. E., Bower, N. J. A., & Bower, T. G. R. (1992). Recognition of familiar faces by newborns. *Infant Behavior and Development, 15*, 265–269.

Wang, A. T., Lee, S. S., Sigman, M., & Dapretto, M. (2006). Neural basis of irony comprehension in children with autism: The role of prosody and context. *Brain: A Journal of Neurology, 129*, 932–943.

Wang, C.-T., & Holton, J. (2007). *Total estimated cost of child abuse and neglect in the United States.* Chicago: Prevent Child Abuse America.

Wang, Q. (2001). Cultural effects on adults' earliest childhood recollection and self-description: Implications for the relation between memory and the self. *Journal of Personality and Social Psychology, 81*, 220–233.

Wang, Q. (2003). Emotion situation knowledge in American and Chinese preschool children and adults. *Cognition & Emotion, 17, 5*, 725–746.

Wang, Q. (2004a). Cultural context of parent-child reminiscing. In M. W. Pratt & B. H. Fiese (Eds.), *Family stories and the life course* (pp. 279–302). Mahwah, NJ: Erlbaum.

Wang, Q. (2004b). The emergence of cultural self-constructs: Autobiographical memory and self-description in European American and Chinese children. *Developmental Psychology, 40*, 3–15.

Wang, Q., & Fivush, R. (2005). Mother-child conversations of emotionally salient events: Exploring the functions of emotional reminiscing in European-American and Chinese families. *Social Development, 14*, 473–495.

Wang, Q., & Ross, M. (2007). Culture and memory. In H. Kitayama & D. Cohen (Eds.), *Handbook of cultural psychology* (pp. 645–667). New York: Guilford Publications.

Wang, Y., Matthews, V. P., Kalnin, A. J., Mosier, K. M., Dunn, D. W., Saykin, A. J., & Kronenberger, W. G. (2009). Short term exposure to a violent video game induces changes in frontolimbic circuitry in adolescents. *Brain Imaging and Behavior, 3*, 38–50.

Wang, Z.-H., & Liu, J.-X. (2007). Impacts of sex, gender role on undergraduates' gender belief. *Chinese Journal of Clinical Psychology, 15*, 381–382.

Ward, L. M. (2003). Understanding the role of entertainment media in the sexual socialization of American youth: A review of empirical research. *Developmental Review, 23*, 347–388.

Ward, L. M., & Friedman, K. (2006). Using TV as a guide: Associations between television viewing and adolescents' sexual attitudes and behavior. *Journal of Research on Adolescence, 16*, 133–156.

Wark, G. R., & Krebs, D. L. (1996). Gender and dilemma differences in real-life moral judgment. *Developmental Psychology, 32*, 220–230.

Wartella, E. A., Vandewater, E. A., & Rideout, V. J. (2005). Electronic media use in the lives of infants, toddlers, and preschoolers. *American Behavioral Scientist, 48*, 501–504.

Wartella, J., Amory, E., Macbeth, A. H., McNamara, I., Stevens, I., Lambert, K. G., & Kinsley, C. H. (2003). Single or multiple reproductive experiences attenuate neurobehavioral stress and fear responses in the female rat. *Physiology and Behavior, 92*, 373–381.

Watamura, S. E., Donzella, B., Alwin, J., & Gunnar, M. R. (2003). Morning to afternoon increases in cortisol concentration for infants and toddlers at child care: Age differences and behavioral correlates. *Child Development, 74*, 1006–1020.

Waterman, A. S. (1999). *The development of personality, self, and ego in adolescence.* New York: Routledge.

Waters, E. (1987). *Attachment Q-set (Version 3).* Retrieved from: http://www.psychology.sunysb.edu/attachment/measures/content/aqs_items.pdf

Waters, E. (1995). The Attachment Q-Set (Version 3.0). In E. Waters, B. Vaughn, G. Posada, & K. Kondo-Ikemura (Eds.), *Caregiving, cultural, and cognitive perspectives on secure-base phenomena and working models: New growing points of attachment* theory and research. *Monographs of the Society for Research in Child Development, 60* (Serial No. 244), 133–145.

Waters, E., Merrick, S., Treboux, D., Crowell, J., & Albersheim, L. (2000). Attachment security in infancy and early childhood: A twenty-year longitudinal study. *Child Development, 71,* 684–689.

Watson, C. M., Quatman, T., Edler, E. (2002). Career aspirations of adolescent girls: Effects of achievement level, grade, and single-sex school environment. *Sex Roles, 46,* 323–335.

Watson, J. B. (1913). Image and affection in behavior. *Journal of Philosophy, Psychology, and Cognition, 10,* 421–428.

Watson, J. B. (1926). What the nursery has to say about instincts. In C. Murcheson (Ed.), *Psychologies of 1925* (pp. 1–35). Worcester, MA: Clark University Press.

Watson, J. B. (1928). *Psychological care of infant and child.* New York: Norton.

Watson-Gegeo, K. A., & Gegeo, D. W. (1986). Calling-out and repeating routines in Kwara'ae children's language socialization. In B. B. Schieffelin & E. Ochs (Eds.), *Language socialization across cultures* (pp. 17–50). Mahwah, NJ: Erlbaum.

Webb, T., Jenkins, L., Browne, N., Afifi, A. A., & Kraus, J. (2007). Violent entertainment pitched to adolescents: An analysis of PG–13 films. *Pediatrics, 119,* e1219–e1229 DOI: 10.1542/peds.2006–1319. Retrieved from: http://www.pediatrics.org/cgi/content/full/119/6/e1219

Weber, E. K. (1999). Children's personal prerogative in home and school contexts. *Early Education & Development, 10,* 499–515.

Weber, R., Ritterfield, U., & Mathiak, K. (2006). Does playing violent video games induce aggression? Empirical evidence of a functional magnetic resonance imaging study. *Media Psychology, 8,* 39–60.

Webster-Stratton, C. (1998). Preventing conduct problems in Head Start children: Strengthening parenting competencies. *Journal of Consulting & Clinical Psychology, 66,* 715–730.

Web Wise Kids. (2009). Retrieved from: http://www.webwisekids.org/index.asp?page=parents; http://www.webwisekids.org/index.asp?page=teens

Weinberg, M. K., & Tronick, E. Z. (1994). Beyond the face: An empirical study of infant affective configurations of facial, vocal, gestural, and regulatory behaviors. *Child Development, 65,* 1503–1515.

Weinberg, M. K., & Tronick, E. Z. (1998). *Infant and caregiver engagement phases system.* Boston: Harvard Medical School.

Weinraub, M., & Lewis, M. (1977). The determinants of children's responses to separation. *Monographs of the Society for Research in Child Development, 42* (Serial No. 172).

Weisgram, E. S., Bigler, R.S., & Liben, L. S. (2010). Gender, values, and occupational interests among children, adolescents, and adults. *Child Development, 81*

Weisner, T. S. (2008). African Childhood. In R. A. Shweder, T. R. Bidell, A. C. Dailey, S. D. Dixon, P. J. Miller, & J. Modell (Eds.), *The Chicago companion to the child.* Chicago: University of Chicago Press.

Weisner, T. S., & Wilson-Mitchell, J. E. (1990). Nonconventional family lifestyles and multischematic sex typing in six year olds. *Child Development, 61,* 1915–1933.

Weissman, M. M., Warner, V., Wickramatne, P. J., & Kandel, D. B. (1999). Maternal smoking during pregnancy and psychopathology in offspring followed to adulthood. *Journal of American Academy of Child and Adolescent Psychiatry, 38,* 892–899.

Wellman, H. M., & Lempers, J. D. (1977). The naturalistic communicative abilities of two-year-olds. *Child Development, 48,* 1052–1057.

Wells, A. S. (1995). Reexamining social science research on school desegregation: Long- versus short-term effects. *Teachers College Report, 96,* 691–706.

Wentzel, K. R., Barry, C. M., & Caldwell, K. A. (2004). Friendships in middle school: Influences on motivation and school adjustment. *Journal of Educational Psychology, 96,* 195–203.

Werker, J. F., Pegg, J. E., & McLeod, P. J. (1994). A cross-language investigation of infant preference for infant-directed communication. *Infant Behavior and Development, 17,* 323–333.

Werner, N. E., & Hill, L. G. (2010). Individual and peer group normative beliefs about relational aggression. *Child Development, 81,*

Wessells, M. G. (2006). *Child soldiers: From violence to protection.* Boston: Harvard University Press.

Weyer, M., & Sandler, I. N. (1998). Stress and coping as predictors of children's divorce-related ruminations. *Journal of Clinical Child Psychology, 27,* 78–86.

Whitebook, M. C., Howes, C., & Phillips, D. A. (1990). *Who cares? Child care teachers and the quality of care in America.* Oakland, CA: National Child Care Staffing Study.

Whiting, B., & Edwards, C. (1988). *Children of different worlds. The formation of social behavior.* Cambridge, MA: Harvard University Press.

Whiting, B. B., & Whiting, J. W. M. (1975). *Children of six cultures: A psychocultural analysis.* Cambridge, MA: Harvard University Press.

Whitlock, J. L., Powers, J. L., & Eckenrode, J. (2006). The virtual cutting edge: The Internet and adolescent self-injury. *Developmental Psychology, 42,* 407–417.

Whitman, T. L., Borkowski, J. G., Keogh, D. A., & Weed, K. (2001). *Interwoven lives: Adolescent mothers and their children.* Mahwah, NJ: Erlbaum.

Wicker, B., Fonlupt, P., Hubert, B., Tardif, C., Gepner, B., & Deruelle, C. (2008). Abnormal cerebral effective connectivity during explicit emotional processing in adults with autism spectrum disorder. *Social Cognitive and Affective Neuroscience, 3,* 135–143.

Widom, C. S. (1989). The cycle of violence. *Science, 244,* 160–166.

Wigfield, A., Eccles, J. S., Schiefele, U., Roeser, R. W., & Davis-Kean, P. (2006). Development of achievement motivation. In W. Damon & R. Lerner (Series Eds.), & N. Eisenberg (Vol. Ed.), *Handbook of child psychology: Vol. 3. Social, emotional, and personality development* (6th ed., pp. 933–1062). Hoboken, NJ: Wiley.

Williams, C. L., & Pleil, K. E. (2008). Toy story: Why do monkey and human males prefer trucks. *Hormones & Behavior, 54,* 355–358.

Williams, E., Radin, N., & Allegro, T. (1992). Sex role attitudes of adolescents reared primarily by their fathers: An 11-year follow-up. *Merrill-Palmer Quarterly, 38,* 457–476.

Williams, J. E., & Best, D. L. (1990). *Measuring sex stereotypes: A multinational study* (2nd ed.). Thousand Oaks, CA: Sage.

Williams, K., & Guerra, N. (2007). Prevalence and predictors of Internet bullying. *Journal of Adolescent Health, 41,* S14–S21.

Williams, T. M. (Ed.)(1986). *The impact of television: A natural experiment in three communities.* Orlando, FL: Academic Press.

Williams, T. M., & Handford, A. C. (1986). Television and other leisure activities. In T. M. Williams (Ed.), *The impact of television: A natural experiment in three communities* (pp. 143–213). Orlando, FL: Academic Press.

Wilson, A. E., Smith, M. D., & Ross, H. S. (2003). The nature and effects of young children's lies. *Social Development, 12,* 21–45.

Wilson, B. J., & Weiss, A. J. (1993). The effects of sibling coviewing on preschooler's reactions to a suspenseful movie scene. *Communication Research, 20,* 214–248.

Wimmer, H., & Perner, J. (1983). Beliefs about beliefs: Representation and constraining function of wrong beliefs in young children's understanding of deception. *Cognition, 13,* 103–128.

Winkielman, P., & Harmon-Jones, E. (2006). *Social neuroscience.* New York: Oxford University Press.

Wismer Fries, A. B., & Pollak, S. D. (2004). Emotion understanding in postinstitutionalized Eastern European children. *Development and Psychopathology, 16,* 355–369.

Wismer Fries, A. B., Shirtcliff, E. A., & Pollak, S. D. (2008). Neuroendocrine dysregulation following early social deprivation in children. *Developmental Psychobiology, 50,* 588–599.

Wismer Fries, A. B., Ziegler, T. E., Kurian, J. R., Jacoris, S., & Pollak, S. D. (2005). Early experience in humans is associated with changes in neuropeptides critical for regulating social behavior. *Proceedings of the National Academy of Sciences, 102,* 17237–17240.

Wolak, J., Mitchell, K. J., & Finkelhor, D. (2002). Close online close relationships in a national sample of adolescents. *Adolescence, 37,* 441–455.

Wolak, J., Mitchell, K. J., & Finkelhor, D. (2006). *Online victimization of youth: 5 years later.* Alexandria, VA: National Center for Missing & Exploited Children.

Wolchik, S. A., Tein, J. Y., Sandler, I. N., & Doyle, K. (2002). Fear of abandonment as a mediator between divorce stressors and mother-child relationship quality and children's adjustment problems. *Journal of Abnormal Child Psychology, 30,* 401–418.

Wolchik, S. A., Wilcox, K. L., Tein, J.-Y., & Sandler, I. N. (2000). Maternal acceptance and consistency of discipline as buffers of divorce stressors on children's psychological adjustment problems. *Journal of Abnormal Child Psychology, 28,* 87–102.

Wolff, P. H. (1987). *The development of behavioral states and the expression of emotions in early infancy: New proposals for investigation.* Chicago: University of Chicago Press.

Woltman, A. G. (1972). Puppetry as a tool in child psychotherapy. *International Journal of Child Psychiatry, 1,* 84–96.

Wong, C. A., Eccles, J. S., & Sameroff, A. (2003). The influence of ethnic discrimination and ethnic identification on African American adolescents' school and socioemotional adjustment. *Journal of Personality, 71,* 1197–1232.

Wood, J. J., McLeod, B. D., Sigman, M., Hwang, W. C., & Chu, B. C. (2003). Parenting and childhood anxiety: Theory, empirical findings, and future directions. *Journal of Child Psychology and Psychiatry, 44,* 134–151.

Wood, W., & Eagly, A. H. (2000). Once again, the origins of sex differences. *American Psychologist, 55,* 1062–1063.

Wood, W., & Eagly, A. H. (2002). A cross-cultural analysis of the behavior of women and men: Implications for the origins of sex differences. *Psychological Bulletin, 128,* 699–727.

Woodard, E. H. (2000). *Media in the home 2000: The fifth annual survey of parents and children.* Philadelphia: The Annenberg Public Policy Center of the University of Pennsylvania.

Woodward, A. L. (2003). Infants' developing understanding of the link between looker and object. *Developmental Science, 6,* 297–311.

Woodward, A. L., & Guajardo, J. J. (2002). Infants' understanding of the point gesture as an object-directed action. *Cognitive Development, 17,* 1061–1084.

World Bank(2006). *World development indicators 2006.* Washington, DC: World Bank.

World Health Organization. (1999). *World health statistics annual.* Geneva: World Health Organization.

Wren, B. (2002). 'I can accept my child is transsexual but if I ever see him in a dress I'll hit him': Dilemmas in parenting a transgendered adolescent. *Clinical Child Psychology & Psychiatry, 7*, 377–397.

Wright, J. C., Huston, A. C., Murphy, K. C., St. Peters, M., Pinon, M., Scantlin, R., & Kotler, J. (2001). The relations of early television viewing to school readiness and vocabulary of children from low-income families: The Early Window Project. *Child Development, 72*, 1347–1366.

Wright, J. C., Huston, A. C., Reitz, A. L., & Piemyat, S. (1994). Young children's perceptions of television reality: Determinants and developmental differences. *Developmental Psychology, 30*, 229–239.

Wright, J. C., Huston, A. C., Vandewater, E. A., Bickham, D. S., Scantlin, R. M., Kotler, J. A., . . . Finkelstein, J. (2001). American children's use of electronic media in 1997: A national survey. *Journal of Applied Developmental Psychology, 22*, 31–47.

www.nursefamilypartnership.org. Retrieved from: http://www.nursefamilypartnership.org/assets/PDF/Fact-sheets/NFP_Snapshot_Oct_09.

Wyatt, E. (2008). *Disappearing diversity on TV, with young exceptions.* Retrieved from: www.newyorktimes.com.

Wyrobek, A. J., Eskenazi, B., Young, S., Arnheim, N., Tiemann-Boege, I., Jabs, E. W., . . . Evenson, D. (2006). Advancing age has differential effects on DNA damage, chromatin integrity, gene mutations, and aneuploidies in sperm. *Proceedings of the National Academy of Sciences, USA, 103*, 9601–9606.

Xie, H., Cairns, B. D., & Cairns, R. B. (2005). The development of aggressive behavior among girls: Measurement issues, social functions, and differential trajectories. In D. J. Pepler, K. C. Madsen, C. Webster, & K. S. Levene (Eds.), *The development and treatment of girlhood aggression* (pp. 105–136). Mahwah, NJ: Erlbaum.

Xie, Y. L., Boucher, S. M., Hutchin, B. C., & Cairns, B. D. (2006). What makes a girl (or a boy) popular (or unpopular)? African American children's perceptions and developmental differences. *Developmental Psychology 42*, 599–612.

Xu, F., Bao, X., Fu, G., Talwar, V., & Lee, K. (2010). Lying and truth-telling in children: From concept to action. *Child Development, 81*, 581–596.

Xu, I., & Corno, L. (1998). Case studies of families doing third-grade homework. *Teachers College Record, 100*, 402–436.

Yale, M. E., Messinger, D. S., Cobo-Lewis, A. B., & Delgado, C. F. (2003). The temporal coordination of early infant communication. *Developmental Psychology, 39*, 815–824.

Yamasue, H., Kuwabara, H., Kawakubo, Y., & Kasai, K. (2009). Oxytocin, sexually dimorphic features of the social brain, and autism. *Psychiatry & Clinical Neurosciences, 63*, 129–140.

Yan, Z., & Greenfield, P. M. (2006). Children, adolescents, and the Internet: A new field of inquiry in developmental psychology. *Developmental Psychology, 42*, 391–394.

Yang, C. Y., Decety, J., Lee, S., Chen, G., & Cheng, Y. (2009). Gender differences in the Mu rhythm during empathy for pain: An electroencephalographic study. *Brain Research, 1251*, 176–184.

Yang, D. (2001). Anxiety of middle school students: The role of teacher-student relationship and peer relationship. *Chinese Mental Health Journal, 15*, 78–80.

Yau, J., & Smetana, J. (2003). Adolescent-parent conflict in Hong Kong and Shenzhen: A comparison of youth in two cultural contexts. *International Journal of Behavioral Development, 27*, 201–211.

Ybarra, M. L. (2004). Linkages between depressive symptomatology and Internet harassment among young regular Internet users. *CyberPsychology & Behavior, 7*, 247–257.

Ybarra, M. L., & Mitchell, K. J. (2004a). Online aggressor/targets, aggressors, and targets: A comparison of associated youth characteristics. *Journal of Child Psychology and Psychiatry, 45*, 1308–1316.

Ybarra, M. L., & Mitchell, K. J. (2004b). Youth engaging in online harassment: Associations with caregiver–child relationships, Internet use, and personal characteristics. *Journal of Adolescence, 27*, 319–336.

Ybarra, M. L., & Mitchell, K. J. (2007). Prevalence and frequency of Internet harassment instigation: Implications for adolescent health. *Journal of Adolescent Health, 41*, 189–195.

Yeung, W. J., Sandberg, J. F., Davis-Kean, P. E., & Hofferth, S. L. (2001). Children's time with fathers in infant families. *Journal of Marriage and Family, 63*, 136–154.

Yip, T., & Fuligni, A. J. (2002). Daily variation in ethnic identity, ethnic behaviors, and psychological well-being among American adolescents of Chinese descent. *Child Development, 73*, 1557–1572.

Yip, T., Seaton, E. K., & Sellers, R. M. (2010). Interracial and intraracial contact, school-level diversity, and change in racial identity status among African American adolescents. *Child Development, 81*

Young, S. K., Fox, N. A., & Zahn-Waxler, C. (1999). The relations between temperament and empathy in two-year-olds. *Developmental Psychology, 35*, 1189–1197.

Young, W. C., Goy, R. W., & Phoenix, C. H. (1967). Hormones and sexual behavior. *Science, 143*, 212–218.

Young-Eisendrath, P. (2008). *The self-esteem trap: Raising confident and compassionate kids in an age of self-importance.* Little, Brown.

Youniss, J. (1980). *Parents and peers in social development.* Chicago: University of Chicago Press.

Yuill, N., & Pearson, A. (1998). The development of bases for trait attribution: Children's understanding of traits as causal mechanisms based on desire. *Developmental Psychology, 34,* 574–586.

Zaff, J. F., Moore, K. A., Papillo, A. R., & Williams, S. (2003). Implications of extracurricular activity participation during adolescence on positive outcomes. *Journal of Adolescent Research, 18,* 599–630.

Zahn-Waxler, C. (2000). The development of empathy, quiet and internalization of distress: Implications for gender differences in internalizing and externalizing problems. In R. Davidson (Ed.), *Wisconsin Symposium on Emotion*: Vol. 1. *Anxiety, depression, and emotion* (pp. 222–235). New York: Oxford University Press.

Zahn-Waxler, C., Cole, P. M., Welsh, J. D., & Fox N. A. (1995). Psychophysiological correlates of empathy and prosocial behaviors in preschool children with problem behaviors. *Development and Psychopathology, 7,* 27–48.

Zahn-Waxler, C., Friedman, R. J., Cole, P. M., Mizuta, I., & Hiruma, N. (1996). Japanese and United States preschool children's responses to conflict and distress. *Child Development, 67,* 2462–2477.

Zahn-Waxler, C., Klimes-Dougan, B., & Kendizora, K. T. (1998). The study of emotion socialization: Conceptual, methodological, and developmental considerations. *Psychological Inquiry, 9,* 313–316.

Zahn-Waxler, C., & Kochanska, G. (1990). The origins of guilt. In R. A. Dientsbier (Series Ed.), & R. A. Thompson (Vol. Ed.), *The 36th Annual Nebraska Symposium on Motivation* (Vol. 36, pp. 183–257). Lincoln: University of Nebraska Press.

Zahn-Waxler, C., & Radke-Yarrow, M. (1982). The development of altruism: Alternative research strategies. In N. Eisenberg (Ed.), *The development of prosocial behavior* (pp. 109–137). New York: Academic Press.

Zahn-Waxler, C., Radke-Yarrow, M., & King, R. A. (1979). Child rearing and children's prosocial initiations toward victims of distress. *Child Development, 50,* 319–330.

Zahn-Waxler, C., Schiro, K., Robinson, J. L., Emde, R. N., & Schmitz, S. (2001). Empathy and prosocial patterns in young MZ and DZ twins: Development and genetic and environmental influences. In R. N. Emde & J. K. Hewitt (Eds.), *Infancy to early childhood* (pp. 141–162). New York: Oxford University Press.

Zajonc, R. B., & Mullally, P. R. (1997). Birth order: Reconciling conflicting effects. *American Psychologist, 52,* 685–699.

Zani, B. (1993). Dating and interpersonal relationships in adolescence. In S. Jackson & H. Rodriguez-Tome (Eds.), *Adolescence and its social worlds* (pp. 95–119). Hillsdale, NJ: Erlbaum.

Zarbatany, L., McDougall, P., & Hymel, S. (2000). Gender-differentiated experience in the peer culture: Links to intimacy in preadolescence. *Social Development, 9,* 62–69.

Zaslow, M., Jekielek, S., Gallagher, M. (2005). Work-family mismatch through a child developmental lens. In S. M. Bianchi, L. M. Casper, & B. R., King (Eds.), *Work, family, health, and well-being* (pp. 259–278). Mahwah, NJ: Erlbaum.

Zeanah, C. H., Smyke, A. T., Koga, S. F., Carlson, E., & the Bucharest Early Intervention Project Care Group. (2005). Attachment in institutionalized and community children in Romania. *Child Development, 76,* 1015–1028.

Zehr, J. L., Maestripieri. D., & Wallen, K. (1998). Estradiol increases female sexual initiation independent of male responsiveness in rhesus monkeys. *Hormones and Behavior, 33,* 95–103.

Zelazo, P. D., Helwig, C. C., & Lau, A. (1996). Intention, act, and outcome in behavioral prediction and moral judgment. *Child Development, 67,* 2478–2492.

Zeller, M. H., Reiter-Purtill, J., & Ramey, C. (2008). Negative peer perceptions of obese children in the classroom environment. *Obesity, 16,* 755–62.

Zellman, G. I., & Johansen, A. S. (1998). *Examining the implementation and outcomes of the Military Child Care Act of 1998.* Santa Monica, CA: RAND National Defense Research Institute.

Zevalkink, J. (1997). *Attachment in Indonesia: The mother-child relationship in context.* Ph.D. dissertation, University of Nijmegen, The Netherlands.

Zhou, Q., Eisenberg, N., Losoya, S. H., Fabes, R. A., Reiser, M., Guthrie, I. K., Murphy, B. C., Cumberland, A. J., & Shepard, S. A. (2002). The relations of parental warmth and positive expressiveness to children's empathy-related responding and social functioning: A longitudinal study. *Child Development, 73,* 893–915.

Zigler, E. F., & Hall, N. W. (2000). *Child development and social policy.* New York: McGraw-Hill.

Zill, N. (1986). *Happy, healthy and insecure.* New York: Cambridge University Press.

Zill, N., Morrison, D. R., & Coiro, M. (1993). Long-term effects of parental divorce on parent-child relationships, adjustment, and achievement in young adulthood. *Journal of Family Psychology, 7,* 91–103.

Zimmer-Gembeck, M. J., Siebenbruner, J., & Collins, W. A. (2001). Diverse aspects of dating: Associations with psychosocial functioning from early to middle adolescence. *Journal of Adolescence, 24,* 313–336.

Zimmer-Gembeck, M. J., Siebenbruner, J., & Collins, W. A. (2004). A prospective study of intraindividual and peer influences on adolescents' heterosexual romantic and sexual behavior. *Archives of Sexual Behavior, 33,* 381–394.

Zimmerman, F. J., Christakis, D. A., & Meltzoff, A. N. (2007). Television and DVD/video viewing in children younger than 2 years. *Archives of Pediatric & Adolescent Medicine, 16,* 473–9.

Zimring, F. E. (1998). *American youth violence*. New York: Oxford University Press.

Zollo, P. (1999). *Wise up to teens: Insights into marketing and advertising to teenagers* (2nd ed.). Ithaca, NY: New Strategist Publications.

Zosuls, K. M., Ruble, D. N., Tamis-LeMonda, C. S., Shrout, P. E., Bornstein, M. H., & Greulich, F. K. (2009). The acquisition of gender labels in infancy: Implications for sex-typed play. *Developmental Psychology, 45*, 688–701.

Zukow-Goldring, P. (2002). Sibling caregiving. In M. H. Bornstein (Ed.), *Handbook of parenting: Vol. 3. Being and becoming a parent* (2nd ed., pp. 177–208). Mahwah, NJ: Erlbaum.

Zuzanek, J. (2000). The effects of time use and time pressure on child-parent relationships. *Health Canada Research Report*. Waterloo, Ontario, Canada: Otium Publishing.

Author Index

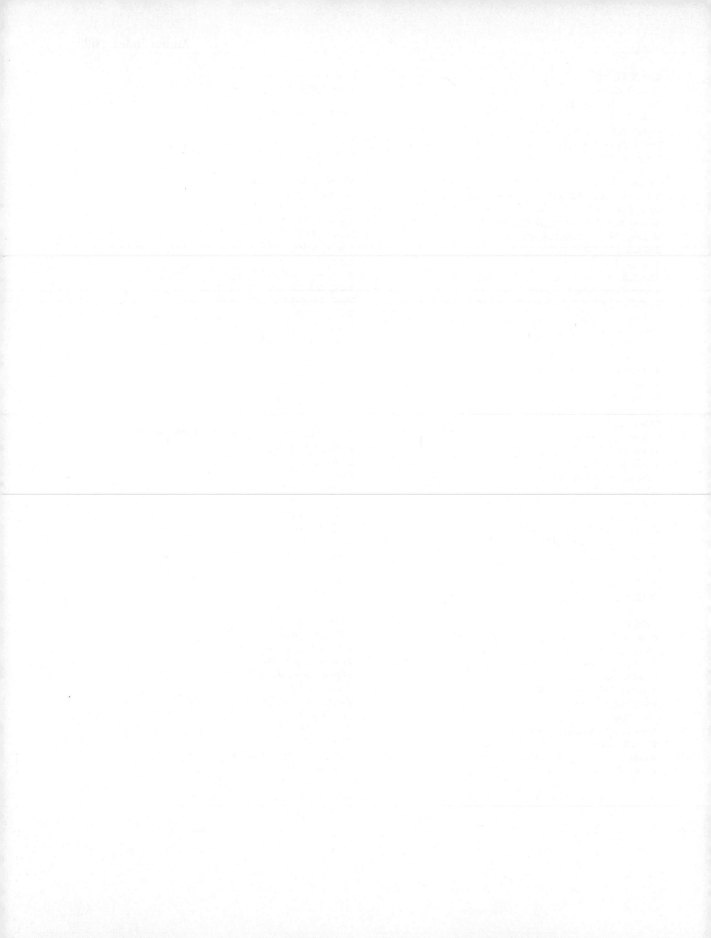

Subject Index

Note: Page numbers with f indicate figures; those with t indicate tables.

ABAB experiment, 45
Abstinence education, 446–48, 447f
Accommodation, 22, 231
Active gene-environment association, 92
Adaptive behaviors, preparedness for social interaction and, 77–78
Adolescents standing trial as adults, 380–81
Adoption, 237–38
Adoption and Safe Families Act (ASFA), 457
Adoption studies, 86–87, 92, 401, 404
Adult Attachment Interview (AAI), 128–29, 128t, 133
Affect Knowledge Test, 163
African American children
  aggressive behavior of, 396–97, 407
  drug use and, 94
  early childhood education for children in poverty and, 436
  ethnic identity and, 188–91
  parent-child interactions and, 58
  physical appearance and peer status and, 263
  prejudice against, 199
  preverbal communication and, 202
  racial integration in schools and, 302–3
  smiling rates of, 147
  suicide rates among, 169
  teacher-student relationships of, 296
  violence in, preventing, 423
Age cohort, 31, 48, 49, 70
Aggression, 393–425. *See also* Bullying
  abusive parents and, 405
  brain and, 403–4
  child soldiers and, 408–9
  coercion model of, 405–6
  combined biological and social influences on, 410–12, 412f
  cultural determinants of, 407–8
  developmental changes in, 396–97, 397t
  environmental triggers of, 412, 413f
  gender differences in, 397–99
  genetics and, 401, 402f, 412, 413f
  hormonal reasons for, 404
  indirect aggression, 394, 395t, 415
  individual differences in, stability of, 400–401
  neighbor influences on, 407
  neurological basis of, 403–4
  parents' as providers of opportunities for, 406
  parents' influence on, 404–5
  peer influences on, 406–7
  prenatal conditions and, 404
  sociocognitive factors in development of, 413–15
  temperament and, 403
  types of, 394–95, 395t
  violence in electronic media and, 409–10
Aggression, control of, 419–23
  by catharsis (letting off steam), 419
  by cognitive modification strategies, 420
  multifaceted approach to, 421–23

  parents as agents for, 420
  schools as venue for intervention, 420–21
Aggressive-rejected children, 259
Alleles, 90, 97
Alpert, Phillip, 319
Altruistic behavior, 382–90, 383t. *See also* Prosocial behavior
American Academy of Pediatrics, 303
American family, changing, 234–45
  adoption, 237–38
  divorce, 239–45
  gay and lesbian parents, 238
  parenting after thirty, 236–37
  parenting alone, 238–39
  remarriage, 245
  reproductive technologies, new, 237
  working mothers and, 235–36
  working stress and children's adjustment, 236
Amygdala, 78, 83–84, 84t, 335
Analysis of variance (ANOVA), 66
Androgynous, 352–53
Anger, 152
Anger recognition, 156
Anterior cingulate cortex (ACC), 83, 84t
Anterior insula (AI), 83, 84t
Anxious-ambivalent attachment, 119
Approach-avoidance behavior, 126
Asian American children, 100, 179, 189, 191
Asperger's syndrome, 425
Assimilation, 22
Assisted reproductive technique, 97
Associative play, 252, 253t
Attachment, 109–40
  to caregiver, 124–26
  consequences of (*See* Attachment, consequences of)
  cultural differences in, 122–23
  defined, 110
  development of, 114–17, 115t
  to father, 117, 123–24
  to grandparents, 117
  hormones necessary for secure attachment, 126–27
  infant characteristics and, 131
  infants' attachment development, parents' role in, 123–30
  in the making phase, 115t
  maternal bonding and, 113–14
  to mother, 116, 123
  mothers in prison and, 130–31
  to objects, 117
  in older children, 132–33
  parent's input into (*See* Attachment, parents' input into)
  representation, 127–29
  to siblings, 117
  stability of, 131–33
  theories of, 110–13
  types (*See* Attachment types)